DOMAIN NAME ARBITRATION

Domain Name Arbitration

Trademarks, Domain Names, and Cybersquatting

A Practical Guide to the Uniform Domain Name Dispute Resolution Policy

Gerald M. Levine

Foreword by
The Hon. Neil A. Brown QC

Second Edition
(Revised and Expanded)

legal corner press

Domain Name Arbitration

Cover design and art direction by Stephanie Tevonian
Design implementation by Alex Grover

Printed in the United States

ISBN (Paperback) 978-0-9915829-4-5
ISBN (epub) 978-0-9915829-5-2
ISBN (mobi) 978-0-9915829-6-9

Legal Corner Press, LLC
800 2nd Avenue, 3rd Fl (Suite 300)
New York, NY 10017
E-mail: inquiries@legalcornerpress.com

ACKNOWLEDGMENTS

The author aside, there are two groups of essential contributors that made this book possible. The first are the panelists whose collective wisdom forms the substance of the developing jurisprudence I have attempted to describe. The second is the team that assisted me in bringing the book to publication. Without either, there would have been no book. Over the past nineteen years the panelists have developed a new body of law that makes the Uniform Domain Name Dispute Resolution Policy the forum of choice for adjudicating claims of cybersquatting. This is a remarkable achievement. The publishing team members are Stephanie Tevonian, Alex Grover, and Melissa Rosati. I cannot thank them enough. No acknowledgment would be complete without a special thanks to my wife and law partner Sheila J. Levine for taking on the daunting task of reading the entire manuscript again (as she had done with the First Edition), to its vast improvement. How I have described the jurisprudence, analyzed the evidentiary requirements, interpreted its direction, and deliberated on the tensions between trademark owners and domain name holders is entirely my responsibility.

CONTENTS

2 | Contract Obligations

3 | The Scope of the UDRP

4 | Complainant's Burden of Proof

8 | Before, During, and After UDRP Proceedings

| Appendices

FOREWORD TO THE SECOND EDITION

It is sometimes said that second editions of books are simply additions to the first editions and nothing more. This cannot be said of the second edition of Gerald Levine's *Domain Name Arbitration* in which the author continues to develop his view of an evolving jurisprudence of domain names. Between 2015, when the first edition was published and the present year, there have been several thousand new decisions under the Uniform Domain Name Dispute Resolution Policy (UDRP). But it is not just that there are more decisions available to illustrate positions taken on various issues, as the author is interested in how they reinforce and strengthen the concept of trends reported in the First Edition.

It is in this way that the second edition goes much further than becoming an expanded version of the first edition. Indeed, you do not have to go far into the author's Preface to the second edition to see that he has developed a philosophy around the UDRP, discerned "a system of law" equated with the development of the common law and the reasoned decisions of judges. He says there has emerged a body of "Panel-made law [resting] on published, reasoned decisions."

In its Overview of Panel Views on Selected UDRP Questions, now in its third edition the World Intellectual Property Organization (WIPO) has expressed the view that "[t]he UDRP does not operate on a strict doctrine of precedent." While this is the official view, the practice in some decisions might be said to be different. The more you delve into the text of *Domain Name Arbitration*, the more apparent it becomes that the tension between precedent and consensus fudges the reality of the decision-making process.

In the Preface to this second edition, the author describes it in this way:

> "Although WIPO makes the point that Panels do not have to follow precedent, it is customary to invoke and rare not to cite supporting authority, because, as WIPO reports in the Overview, 'panels consider it desirable that their decisions are consistent with prior panel decisions dealing with similar fact situations.' Precedent is highly valued because deviation destabilizes parties' expectations. The key is predictability. The aim of both consensus and precedent is to assure consistency."

It can be seen, therefore, that the second edition advances the case for a precedential approach and that this stimulus to the debate is a valuable contribution to our understanding of the process. Having said this, it is equally clear that the tension between consensus and precedent is a highly contentious issue. Panellists are not strictly bound by precedent, but most would give high regard to the value of consensus in decision-making.

Notwithstanding these tensions (and I speak from having decided more than a thousand UDRP decisions) the real value in the UDRP process is that there has been a high level of consistency in decision-making, which leads to predictability and hence enables prospective parties to UDRP proceedings to assess their rights and liabilities with more accuracy than if the thousands of decisions were simply regarded as a wilderness of single instances. Thus, the author's ability to detect and articulate themes and consensus views in decisions, which he does with eloquence and persuasion throughout the work, is of great value.

At the same time, it is to be hoped that the UDRP process, being essentially a process of arbitration, does not become over-legalistic and rigid because of the increasing emphasis being placed on prior decisions, elevating them to the level of "authority". WIPO may say that panels do not have to follow "precedent", but some prior decisions, picking up on the value of earlier decisions have gone as far as saying that "...[w]hen such a consensus has developed, it is incumbent upon panels to follow the consensus (or the majority view) to promote consistency among UDRP decisions." (***Symark International, Inc. v. Gary McCurty***, D2005-0235 (WIPO June 15, 2005), citing ***Fresh Intellectual Properties, Inc. v. 800Network.com***, D2005-0061 (WIPO March 21, 2005). In fact, in one of the cases I participated in and which illustrates the tension, the three-member Panel acknowledged that "[w]hilst previous decisions under the Policy do not have the status of precedent, similar cases are generally decided similarly." ***Compañía Logística de Hidrocarburos CLH S.A. v. Privacy Administrator, Anonymize, Inc. / Sam Dennis, Investments.org Inc.***, D2018-0793 (WIPO June 13, 2018).

It may come as a surprise to some registrants of domain names to find that they have subjected themselves by contract to a mandatory arbitration process where it is "incumbent" on those sitting in judgement on them to "follow" prior decisions implementing certain interpretations of the UDRP, when they have not so agreed to any such form of adjudication and in particular have not agreed to be bound by interpretations reached after they have registered their domain names. Trademark owners may be equally surprised that their path to a remedy depends upon concrete proof of cybersquatting, not merely having a mark and asserting a claim.

However, despite the undoubted value of prior decisions, it should not be forgotten that panellists are bound by the UDRP and the Rules made under the UDRP which requires a panel to make its decision in accordance with "the Policy, these Rules and any rules and principles of law that it deems applicable." (Rule 15 (a)). Indeed, there must be great value for parties to know that their cause will be decided by a panellist operating in a flexible system who is not bound by rigid legalities and one where it is not "incumbent" on him or her to take a pre-determined view on any issue.

None, of this, of course, means that panellists should ignore previous decisions. They should consider them and take them into account in reaching a decision. I have found something of value and interest in every decision I have read and have no doubt that I will continue to do so. That being so, it must be said that the second edition is an extremely valuable contribution for its commentary on the jurisprudence. It is extensive, it highlights the essence of each decision cited without any wordiness, it analyses how decisions fit in with the trend of other decisions and the new light that many of them throw on the wording and application of the UDRP. I use and cite this work and will continue to do so.

The Hon Neil A. Brown QC
Melbourne
19 January 2019

FOREWORD TO THE FIRST EDITION

The Uniform Domain Name Dispute Resolution Policy (the UDRP) was devised to achieve several objectives.

First and foremost, the objective was to provide a dispute resolution process as an alternative to court proceedings to resolve disputes concerning Internet domain names more quickly and efficiently; and, in particular, to determine whether the registration of a disputed domain name was abusive or improper in one way or another, conduct that is popularly known as cybersquatting. The regular structure of courts and law would normally be thought to be adequate for achieving this purpose, but it was felt that a different process was needed to address several specific needs of the domain name system, not least of which was the cost and difficulty of engaging in litigation against parties in different national jurisdictions. Had the resolution of disputes about domain names been left to the courts, and the different national laws usually applied to claims of infringement of trademark rights, the process would inevitably have been bogged down in never-ending arguments about the appropriate forum, choice of laws, procedure and the enforcement of any judgment that might be obtained.

It was rightly felt that it would simply be too cumbersome to have the regular courts and the law applied in them as the main means of solving domain name disputes. Naturally, there would still be a right to sue in the courts as a fallback procedure and even today, on occasion, parties turn to the courts to resolve domain name disputes, using the traditional causes of action like trademark infringement, passing off, breach of contract or breach of national statutes on false and misleading activities or other untoward conduct. But for the main and principal way of resolving these disputes, it was rightly felt that a separate forum was needed in which a specially tailored process could be applied to the unique nature of domain names themselves. The UDRP is that process and has been so since its inception at the end of 1999.

In turn, it was clear that the UDRP had to be fashioned to meet the unique needs of the domain name system. Thus, a particular need was to provide a system that was international in character, given that the person or company that registered a domain name could well be in a different country from that of the person or company making the complaint, a situation that has often turned out, although not always, to be the case.

If the process had been left to the courts, an immense problem would have arisen, namely in which country and which courts should an action be brought: the country of the party that registered the domain name or the party that claimed its rights were infringed? Following hot on the heels of that question came another one: what law should be applied to the dispute, the law of the state where the domain name was registered, the law of California where the Internet Corporation for Assigned Names and Numbers (ICANN) is based, or the law of the place of the claimant or perhaps somewhere else? And then still another question: who would be the defendant, the party in whose name the domain name was registered, a party using it or someone else, perhaps a nominal defendant?

Other questions came thick and fast: how would you find the defendant, given that some might have taken on assumed names and false addresses, as has sometimes turned out to be the case. Then, how would the proposed defendant be served with the claim? Moreover, what sort of service of documents would be required, personal or some form of substituted service? Then: what would be determined in the proceedings, that the claimant had the only claim to the domain name, a better claim, or an equal claim to the defendant and how would you express that claim? Moreover, what sort of procedure would be followed, what remedies would be available and how would any order or judgement be enforced? It was to such issues that those who drew up the UDRP turned their attention. Above all, they wanted the UDRP to be quick and efficient; it had to be reasonably cheap and reasonably straightforward, not too complicated in the law and, probably most important of all, the process had to end in a result that could be enforced.

The UDRP therefore had to be fashioned to meet those needs and I think it is reasonably safe to say that it has largely done so. The issue of identifying the defendant or respondent was resolved by deeming it to be the person in whose name the domain name was registered. There would be no real problem of service of the claim because the provider of arbitration services would simply send the Complaint to the address provided by the person registering the domain name and if it turned out that the address was nonexistent or fanciful, so be it; the proceeding still went ahead. Simple rules provided for the contents of the claim and any response to it that might be submitted and what information had to be included in both. Time limits for the major steps in the proceeding were included in the rules and they have largely--although not always--been complied with.

The cost of the proceedings was kept under control by imposing a fixed fee for filing a Complaint, so an aggrieved party may bring a claim under the UDRP by spending no more than the filing fee, although it could also retain its own lawyers if it wanted to. The issues to be determined in the proceeding were also set out in a reasonably straightforward manner, requiring the complainant to prove the three essential limbs set out in paragraph 4 of the Policy. When it came to the all-important requirement of execution and enforcement of orders for the transfer or cancellation of a domain name, this was provided for by the requirement that the order be sent to the registrar on whose books the domain name is registered and the registrar be required to put the order into effect and, if the order so requires, transfer the registration of the domain name to the successful complainant under pain of incurring the wrath of ICANN by breaching the agreement that allows it to operate as a registrar of domain names.

So, the UDRP was an ingenious solution that arose to combat a particular problem connected with the invention of the Internet that promptly became the proceeding of choice for trademark owners alleging abusive registration of domain names and the main instrument for recovering them. It was a practical alternative to litigation in the courts and became recognised as a dispute resolution scheme that provided for the unique features of the Internet naming system. It is not perfect and it raises several unanswered questions of substance and procedure.

But what I have described above is only the start of the UDRP story. The very efficacy of the UDRP and its concern for speed and economy of time and money gave rise to significant gaps. For instance, the UDRP requires a complainant to have a trademark before it has standing to bring the complaint; but does this mean a registered trademark or is a common law trademark sufficient?

And a trademark where? If the parties are two U.S. companies engaged in trench warfare as they compete for a valuable domain name, is it enough for the complainant to show that it has a trademark registered in Tunisia or the European Community, but not in the U.S.?

When the UDRP requires a complainant to prove that the respondent does not have a right or legitimate interest in the domain name, does that not require it to prove a negative, an impossible task and, if so, how can it get around that requirement?

What is meant by the broad expression "bad faith"? Can bad faith be retrospective, that is, dated back to the time the domain name was registered because of the respondent's bad faith conduct since then, although it may have registered the domain name in good faith? Do equitable remedies and principles apply to UDRP proceedings? For instance, can a respondent rely on laches or estoppel? What has to be proved to obtain a finding of reverse domain name hijacking against an oppressive complainant?

These questions are unanswered in the UDRP itself, but the answers were waiting to be discovered in its language. And discovered they have been in the thousands of decisions written since 2000 by panellists, as UDRP arbitrators are called, some of them expressing different views of the law before unifying into consensus on many of the core principles. In total, this great number of decisions make up a large body of learning that helps the UDRP function better by encouraging consistency and acts as a guide and reference for parties and their legal advisers to discern how similar fact situations might be decided in the future.

In other words, the bare bones of the Policy and its Rules will take you part of the way in understanding how it operates, but only part of the way. That is where *Domain Name Arbitration* comes in to perform its valuable role. It provides an in-depth examination of the evidentiary requirements of the Policy and its Rules and how panellists have construed and applied them in adjudicating parties' rights to continue holding or forfeiting disputed domain names. The author points out that the UDRP is a forum of limited jurisdiction; it is not a trademark court even though infringement is the underlying basis for the claim of abusive registration. He makes it clear that success in capturing or defending a domain name depends in large measure on the parties attending to the evidentiary demands of the Policy. If the registration is found to be abusive, the trademark owner has an option of remedies that in effect cause the respondent to forfeit its registration of the domain name. But, if the trademark owner fails to prove its case, then the registration remains with the domain name registrant.

Domain Name Arbitration is valuable too in providing a penetrating examination of all aspects of the UDRP, profusely illustrated with decided cases. The author has uncovered answers to a variety of questions that arise from the text of the UDRP as well as presenting useful analogies to many complex factual situations that might come along in the future and valuable insights into the philosophy of the UDRP and the view taken by panellists of the most contentious issues that continue to be debated. Having such a practical guide, therefore, is of immense value.

Readers will find the author's approach extremely forthright. He begins by first laying out the philosophy and origins of the UDRP and how it differs from other dispute resolution policies; its *sui generis* jurisprudence; its scope and core principles; the parties' evidentiary burdens; complainants' relatively low bar for proving standing; the concept of the *prima facie* case that respondent lacks rights or legitimate interests in the disputed domain name and the shifting of the burden of production to rebut that contention; complainants' higher bar for proving bad faith, which results from the conjunctive requirement; the all-important Rules made to support the UDRP; court proceedings before and after a UDRP case; and the hundred and one other subsidiary questions that arise.

Domain Name Arbitration puts flesh on the bones by illustrating how the jurisprudence crafted by panellists makes the UDRP a living and working dispute resolution regime. It should certainly be on the desk, or on the computer, of every activist in the domain name world, every practitioner and everyone else that works in the field. I already use it in my practice and find it an essential source of knowledge and opinion in this new and exciting field. I highly recommend it. It promises to be the *Grey's Anatomy* of domain name arbitration.

The Hon Neil A. Brown QC
Melbourne
28 February 2015

PREFACE TO THE SECOND EDITION

What will be described in the following pages are the assorted sprockets, wheels, joints, screws, and levers of a "bottom up" jurisprudence, meaning it is law created by Panels construing a set of minimalist directives (the text of the Uniform Domain Name Dispute Resolution Policy (UDRP)), rather than "top down" decrees from legislators. It has grown into a jurisprudence in a way very much like the development of common law, which is judge made law; here, it is Panel made law.

Conceptually, a jurisprudence is a storehouse of accrued knowledge available alike to decision-makers and the wider community for whose benefit it is created. Although the UDRP was crafted as a rights protection mechanism for trademark owners, and only they have standing to challenge domain name registrations, the wider community includes those named in the bottom half of the caption whose registrations are being challenged. Regardless whether parties are asserting or defending rights they want the assurance of being engaged in a stable and reliable process of law that is at once consistent and predictable.

It is particularly striking with UDRP jurisprudence that without any legislative planning and possibly with unexpected consequences panelists have facilitated the development of an entirely new commercial market, one based on acquiring, holding, monetizing, and reselling domain names. The emergence of this "secondary market" is not the subject of the treatise and I mention it only in passing because the tension created by competition for strings of characters that mark owners believe are infringing and investors believe are lawful is palpably present in UDRP disputes; not in all disputes, but in approximately 10% of claims that are genuinely disputable. For 90% of claims, respondents have no defensible rights to their choices of domain names and generally default in appearance. It is also important to note that only an infinitesimal fraction of domain names held by investors for sale in the secondary market are ever the subject of complaints filed for relief under the UDRP.

Striking too is that the UDRP is even-handed, even though it was designed as a special forum for mark owners to challenge registrations of domain name they believe infringe their statutory rights. But the UDRP is not a silver-platter favoring their claims of cybersquatting. Decisions are made on the merits of the case. To prevail, mark owners must prove that registrants both registered and are using (or have used) the domain name in bad faith. This is easier for well-known and famous marks that are inherently distinctive; harder, sometimes impossible, for marks fashioned from dictionary words, alone or combined to form common phrases, or composed of descriptive terms that only qualify for trademark status by having acquired distinctiveness.

There are three kinds of UDRP disputes: those that are out-and-out cybersquatting, those that are genuinely contested, and those that are flat-out overreaching by trademark owners.

The first group comprises plain vanilla disputes; sometimes incorporating the marks with legacy TLDs (<paypal.com>) or new gTLD extensions (<mckinsey.careers> and <legogames.online>; sometimes typosquatting (<rnerial.com>; the "rn" looks like an "m"), <virginmiedia.com>, and <wiikipedia.org>); other times combining dominant terms of marks with a qualifier (<pleinphilipp-shop.com> and <legostarwars2015.com>).

Respondents in the first group have no defensible right to the domain names and invariably default in appearance. Their acquisitions are essentially opportunistic and mischievous and clearly in breach of their registration warranties and representations. This group comprises by far the largest number of defaults, between 85% and 90% of the 4,000 plus complaints annually.

The second group are complainants with registered marks with priority over respondents or who allege unregistered marks predating registration of contested domain names. A small number of complaints in this group include claims against participants actively buying and selling in the new market (<goodr.com> a non-dictionary word found infringing of the coined term GOODR). However, even with priority complainants can lose for any one of three reasons: they either 1) had no reputation in the marketplace when the domain name was registered (<lawyersservice.com>), 2) are located in different markets or countries from respondents who can plausibly deny knowledge of the marks (<loading.com>), or 3) the trademarks consist of generic or descriptive terms capable of being used independent of any reference to or association with complainant's trademark (<circus.com>).

The third group consists of complainants who have registered marks postdating the registration of contested domain names. Complainants in this group have no actionable claims or remedy under the UDRP. Their complaints are essentially abusive of the administrative process and deserving of sanctions for reverse domain name hijacking. Occasionally, they carry their grievances to U.S. federal court, but here too there is no actionable statutory claim under the Anticybersquatting Consumer Protection Act (ACPA) and they risk exposing themselves to damages up to $100,000 per domain name and possibly attorney's fees.

About this Second Edition, I have rewritten many of the sections; and where I have not added I have tweaked and refined my thoughts about the jurisprudence to make the principles, factors, and concepts of the law more accessible. I have also included an expansive Index, a revised version of the one that first appeared in the Supplement and Update (January 2017). All of this is useful, I think, for preparing parties, representatives, and practitioners for the substantive and procedural challenges they will experience in asserting and defending claims of cybersquatting in the UDRP forum.

Gerald M. Levine
New York, April 2019

PREFACE TO THE FIRST EDITION

Domain Name Arbitration is principally devoted to explaining the process, jurisprudence, and demands of the Uniform Domain Name Dispute Resolution Policy, popularly referred to by its acronym, UDRP. The regime was implemented by the Internet Corporation for Assigned Names and Numbers (ICANN) in 1999 following a two-year study by the World Intellectual Property Organization (WIPO). As Neil Brown points out in his Foreword, "the UDRP was an ingenious solution that arose to combat a particular problem connected with the invention of the Internet that promptly became the proceeding of choice for trademark owners alleging abusive registration of domain names and the main instrument for recovering them."

The UDRP is unusual when compared with typical ADR regimes in several respects. There is no discovery and no in-person hearing. The proceeding is paper-only and conducted entirely online. Also, the UDRP is a nonexclusive alternative, and not a substitute for an action in a court of law. While the initial decision to commence a UDRP proceeding rests with the complainant, the respondent has the right (although it is rarely exercised) to remove the dispute to a court of law before it is heard. At the conclusion of the proceeding the aggrieved party is expressly permitted to challenge the award in a *de novo* legal action, which is also an unusual feature since arbitration awards are generally final and binding.

In the United States the other forum to which the UDRP is the alternative and the court to which a party goes either to challenge an award or for direct suit is a United States district court in an action under the Anticybersquatting Consumer Protection Act (ACPA). While the two regimes share a family resemblance they are profoundly different in essentials. For both, the ultimate remedy in a cybersquatting claim is either a mandatory injunction against the domain name holder or a finding in its favor, but the ACPA authorizes a judgment for damages topped with reasonable attorney's fees to the prevailing party and the UDRP does not.

However important these immediate similarities and differences are, there is one further difference that is likely to be overlooked by general practitioners and uninitiated parties, which is that the regimes are constructed on different liability models: the UDRP is a conjunctive "and" model; the ACPA is a disjunctive "either/or" model. "Intent" is the key element in both, but under the UDRP a trademark owner cannot succeed on its complaint unless it proves the domain name holder both registered the domain name in bad faith and is using it in bad faith. This view has been challenged, but the consensus is firm that bad faith use alone is insufficient to warrant forfeiture of the domain name. Under the "either/or" model of the ACPA "bad faith intent" can be found if the registrant either "registers, traffics in, or uses a domain name" in a proscribed manner.

Four other points should be highlighted: first, the Policy is designed only for a limited class of persons, namely trademark owners without regard to the national jurisdictions in which their trademarks were acquired; second, the Policy is not designed to adjudicate who has the better right to a disputed domain name; it is concerned with a different question, namely whether the registration infringes another's right of exclusivity to a particular symbol in commerce; third, the Policy is effectively limited to trademarks whose existence predates domain name registration—this comes about because it is impossible for the registrant/respondent to have acted intentionally in bad faith (that is, with knowledge of another's rights) when at the time of registration of the domain name there is no existing trademark; and fourth, the Policy is not available to complainants who may be injured by choices of domain names but whose names are not otherwise eligible for trademark protection, which (in the U.S.) includes prospective marks either not currently in commerce, pending registration or accepted on the Supplemental Register and (in all jurisdictions) personal names unless they have acquired distinctiveness.

An appellate court has remarked that the UDRP proceeding is "adjudication lite" because of "its streamlined nature and its loose rules regarding applicable law."[1] But to give the Policy its due, "lite" is not a flaw. Parties undercut their arguments by ignoring the substantive requirements that determine the outcome of a claim. It is not sufficient for parties to assert a right (or, for respondent, a defense) unsupported by factual evidence that validates their positions. The evidentiary demands for both parties are substantial: for complainants whose trademarks are on the lower end of protectability, as well as for respondents whose choices correspond with trademarks ascendant on the classification scale. Whether asserting or defending claims of cybersquatting, parties should know what to expect and what is expected of them. Parties who understand the expectations of a UDRP proceeding will fare better than those who ignore them.

Gerald M. Levine
New York, March 2015

---

* *Barcelona.com, Inc. v. Excelentisimo Ayuntamiento De Barcelona*, 330 F.3d 617, 624 (4th Cir. 2003).

DOMAIN NAME ARBITRATION

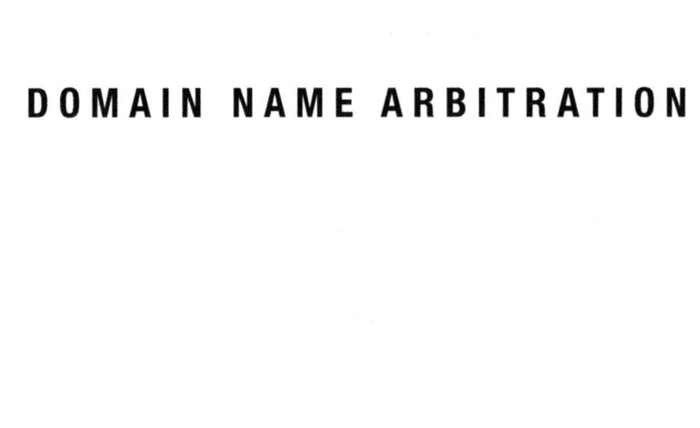

A Note on the Footnotes

UDRP decisions are shown in ***bold italics***.

Court decisions are shown in *italics*.

Supplement to

Domain Name Arbitration is available on

http://www.legalcornerpress.com/dna-supplement/

Hot links to UDRP documents are available on

http://www.legalcornerpress.com/links

1 Overview of the Procedure for the Administrative Proceedings

1.01 FOUNDATION OF THE UNIFORM DOMAIN NAME DISPUTE RESOLUTION POLICY 1.01

1.01-A Creating Legal Processes to Counter Cybersquatting on Trademarks 1.01.-A

1.01-A.1 Conflict In Cyberspace 1.01-A.1

Every new invention is followed by unanticipated consequences. The test for the Internet came in the form of parties gaming the system by registering domain names identical or confusingly similar to trademarks. At the beginning of the Internet's transformation from its academic origins in the United States, there was no single, supranational forum for resolving disputes of alleged infringement of statutory rights and no jurisprudence. The earliest cases filed in United States federal courts invoked trademark law. At first, it was a matter of claims searching for the right theoretical basis. Two defendants stand out in particular for registering domain names that framed the early parameters of cybersquatting: Toeppen and Zuccarini.[1]

The first tentative steps to formulate rules governing parties' rights and remedies began in the mid-1990s. It ended with the implementation of a specialized forum conceptualized by the World Intellectual Property Organization (WIPO) for the Internet Corporation for Assigned Names and Numbers (ICANN)[2] which implemented the Uniform Domain Name Dispute Resolution Policy (UDRP) in October 1999; in the same year the U.S. Congress enacted the Anticybersquatting Consumer Protection Act as a new section of the Trademark Act of 1946 (as amended).

Cybersquatting is an actionable wrong. The question in any claim of unlawful conduct is defining what makes it so. Zuccarini believed he had "just as much right to own the Domain Names [with typographic variations of the mark] as the person who owns the correct spelling of [the mark]."[3] Other registrants believed

---

[1] *Intermatic Inc. v. Toeppen*, 947 F. Supp. 1227 (N.D. Ill. 1996) (The court characterized the defendant as a "spoiler" who prevented the trademark holder from doing business on the Internet under its trademark name unless it paid the Respondent's fee); *Panavision International v. Toeppen*, 141 F.3d 1316, 46 U.S.P.Q. 2d 1511 (9th Cir. 1998) ("Toeppen's 'intention to arbitrage the 'intermatic.com' domain name constitutes a commercial use"); *Shields v. Zuccarini*, 254 F.3d 476 (3rd Cir. 2001) ("We are aware of no authority providing that a defendant's 'fair use' of a distinctive or famous mark only after the filing of a complaint alleging infringement can absolve that defendant of liability for his earlier unlawful activities. Indeed, were there such authority we think it would be contrary to the orderly enforcement of the trademark and copyright laws.")

[2] ICANN is "an internationally organized, non-profit corporation [formed in 1998] that has responsibility for Internet Protocol (IP) address space allocation, protocol identifier assignment, generic (gTLD) and country code (ccTLD) Top-Level Domain name system management, and root server system management functions." See The Management of Internet Names and Addresses: Intellectual Property Issues, Final Report of the World Intellectual Property Organization Internet Domain Name Process (April 30, 1999), hereinafter referred to as the WIPO Final Report.

that adding generic terms to marks distinguished their domain names sufficiently to overcome claims of abusive registration. This may work with marks composed of generic elements or random letters but less so for those well known or famous. There are clearly gradations of strength and weakness that have to be parsed to establish the metes and bounds of parties' rights.[4]

This is precisely what UDRP Panels have achieved in creating the jurisprudence described in the following chapters.

The question that must be answered is, who, as between mark owners and domain name registrants, is entitled to contested strings of alpha and numeric characters corresponding to marks? Before the Internet this question could not even be framed; it could only be asked once it became apparent that domain names had economic potential separate and apart from the value of trademarks. Before the creation of a navigational protocol of electronic addresses for the Internet,[5] the sole competition for strings of alpha and numeric characters employable as marks was limited to different businesses vying to use the same or similar strings for their own products and services. National registries solved this competition by allowing businesses in different channels of commerce to register the same strings, but prohibiting competitors in the same industries or trades from using identical or confusingly similar marks as likely (at best) to create confusion and (at worst) consumer deception.

The Internet disrupted this historical paradigm by creating a global marketplace unregulated by national laws[6] in which the prevailing certainties for countering misappropriation of marks no longer applied. This had consequences to mark owners' historically privileged position by introducing a new class of competitor for

---

[3] ***Dow Jones & Company, Inc. and Dow Jones LP v. John Zuccarini***, D20000578 (WIPO September 10, 2000) ("It is plain that [in registering the domain names] Zuccarini [was] taking advantage of the tendency of Internet users to misspell."

[4] The metaphor is appropriate because domain names have been analogized to real property. U.S. federal courts have equated cybersquatting as "the Internet version of a land grab." See *Virtual Works, Inc. v. Volkswagen of Am., Inc.*, 238 F.3d 264, 267 (4th Cir. 2001); *Kremen v. Cohen*, 337 F.3d 1024, 1030 (9th Cir. 2003) ("Registering a domain name is like staking a claim to a plot of land at the title office.") Later cases have cooled on the real property metaphor in favor of intangible personal property, a concept that has also been endorsed by other common law courts in the United Kingdom, Canada, and India.

ICANN keeps the metaphor alive by labeling one of the periods for purchasing domain names in new gTLDs spaces introduced in 2013 as "Landrush." (The .com, . net, .org, and .biz generation of TLDs are known as "legacy" gTLDs). During Landrush period domain names can be acquired by any eligible interested person on a first-to-register basis, subject to preexisting rights. Landrush follows "Sunrise" which is reserved for trademark owners.

[5] Statutory definitions found in the U.S. Trademark Act of 1946, as Amended (the "Lanham Act"), 15 U.S.C. §1127: "The term 'domain name' means any alphanumeric designation which is registered with of assigned by any domain name registrar, domain name registry, or other domain name registration authority as part of an electronic address on the Internet."

[6] WIPO Final Report Paragraph 40: "[domain name] registration[s] give[ ] rise to a global presence."

"alphanumeric" character strings having distinct values separate from the values of marks in the commercial marketplace even though they could conceivably be identical or confusingly similar to prior registered or unregistered marks, thus raising concerns about registrants' intentions. Time and cost factors became increasingly relevant. Constraints and remedies that were designed to prevent infringement in actual marketplaces were unsuitable to combat cybersquatting.

The root cause of cyber conflict lies with the different functions names play in the actual and virtual spheres. Both Internet addresses and marks are composed of strings of lexical characters that to mark owners and domain name registrants are highly desirable for different reasons. Each party is capable of crossing the line into abusive conduct.[7] In order for the Internet to be workable, computer scientists transformed the impossible to remember strings of 1s and 0s into memorable "human friendly forms."[8] The solving of one problem introduced another.

The need for human friendly forms is no less true of names in their commercial role as identifiers of source, but unlike domain names marks have the capacity to combine two roles, as Internet addresses and designations of origin. Because addresses in virtual space have values separate and distinct from values attributed to marks, their registrations and uses sometimes lead to disputes with mark owners, which, as a byproduct, aggravates competing interests.

Both mark owners and investors prize memorable strings of lexical and numeric characters, but prize them for different reasons. For mark owners, they are identifiers of source primarily but also condensed forms of communication in conveying information about products and services beyond the purely denotative meaning of the words, letters, or numbers of their composition; for registrants they are noninfringing assets that can be monetized or inventoried for future sales.

While it is less of an issue in actual marketplaces, trademarks and service marks vary in strength[9] and where they lie on the continuum between weak and strong has consequences to the outcome of conflicts between mark owners and registrants. For marks composed of common words and descriptive terms, it could be said that when they function as electronic addresses they cease to function as marks. This is because distinctiveness acquired in actual marketplaces is not necessarily transferred to addresses in the virtual marketplace. If these domain names draw visitors it is likely it will be for some reason other than association with marks. The opposite is true for well-known and famous marks. Approximately eighty-five to ninety percent

---

[7] Registrants who acquire their domain names prior to an owner's first use of its mark in commerce cannot be cybersquatters because bad faith registration implies knowledge of the existence of a mark. It would therefore be an abuse to allege cybersquatting if the mark postdates the domain name. The issue is discussed further in "Reverse Domain Name Hijacking" (Sec. 7.11). .

[8] WIPO Final Report, Paragraph 22.

[9] The terms trademark and service mark "includes any words, name, symbol, or device, or any combination thereof."

of cybersquatting involves domain names in which a mark's connotative message is conveyed in the address. So powerful are such marks to attract visitors that opportunists seek to mine them as potential sources of income.

The question that naturally arises in situations of conflicting rights is whether domain name registrants' choices of character strings were intended to target particular marks, or lawful even though identical or confusingly similar to them? The answer lies in marshaling and deconstructing the facts relating to a complainant's reputation when the domain name was registered, respondent's knowledge of the trademark, its historical and current use of the domain name, and the plausibility of its registering a domain name for its semantic value. For some domain names, it is inconceivable they could be used without infringing third-party rights.

It will become clear in the following pages and from the descriptive analysis of the jurisprudence developed from the tens of thousands of reasoned decisions filed in UDRP cases that owners of marks and domain names have competing rights when it comes to certain lexical strings, and even though domain names may be identical or confusingly similar to marks, that by itself is not unlawful. It will also become clear in describing the jurisprudence for resolving disputes between mark owners and domain name registrants that has developed since UDRP was implemented that where the proof supports infringement, mark owners have rights paramount to registrants' contract rights. It has been the universal policy of governments for centuries to protect the integrity of marks from being used opportunistically and fraudulently for gain at the expense of mark owners and consumers.

This first chapter will examine the UDRP from a bird's-eye view as a means of introducing the issues parties typically encounter in asserting and defending their rights. The chapters that follow will then home in on the procedural and substantive details that inform the jurisprudence. Readers should keep in mind the nature of the underlying tensions between the two principal constituencies jostling to protect rights to words and phrases that to each have value essential to its business. While rights holders are privileged by having statutory protection it is insufficient in itself to override the rights of others who by happenstance have registered domain names identical or confusingly similar to existing marks. As the strength of a mark weakens owing to its dictionary word or descriptive composition, its distinctiveness dissolves to its primitive nature which is the language of everyday use, to be protected if it can at all only by evidence of abusive registration.

1.01-A.2 1.01-A.2 Infringement in Cyberspace

The term "cybersquatting" describes the act of squatting on virtual property in cyberspace reserved for trademark owners. It is a species of economic tort against trademark owners and deceit against the consuming public. The squatting part of the portmanteau "cyber-squatting" is drawn from real property law, where "squatter" is defined as "one who settles on land without a right or title." A cybersquatter is one who settles on a piece of Internet property, a location in cyberspace (an I[nternet] P[rotocol] address) that it has no right or title to occupy. That address (whether identical or confusingly similar to a complainant's mark) is off limits unless the registration is lawful. Trademark owners have statutory rights to exclusive use of their signs and symbols to identify themselves, promote their goods or services, and prevent others from appropriating them in both actual and virtual marketplaces.

What we recognize today as self-evident about the World Wide Web with its mixture of opportunity and opportunism was beyond the horizon in the mid-1980s when it began its transformation from the earlier non-commercial system developed by computer scientists in the late 1960's. In its commercial form, the Internet invites anyone, anywhere in the world, without oversight or restriction, to register domain names and launch them into cyberspace for anyone, anywhere in the world to access. There are no gatekeepers at the acquisition stage to demand justification for a registrant's choice of domain name. Therein lies the seed of infringement.

As the Internet evolved into a borderless commercial marketplace, businesses, manufacturers, trades, service providers, individuals, and domain investors began acting on its business potential. From a trickle before ICANN's formation in 1998 (approximately 2 million domain names) to a steadily increasing volume of acquisitions by 2000 (approximately 10 million domain names) cyberspace had the feel of prospecting in newly found land. Today there are over 348 million top level domain names. In addition to trademark owners extending their market range, registrants included businesses in every conceivable niche as well as investors acquiring domain names as assets—for monetizing, selling, financing, trading and (for the prescient) warehousing for future exploitation.[10] It also included opportunists registering domain names infringing on the secured rights of third parties, which aroused intellectual property owners and the business community generally to demand remedial measures to counter the perceived threat to their economic interests.

Cybersquatting concerns abusive registration of domain names at the second level.[11] The closer second level domains resemble trademarks the more likely

---

[10] The oft repeated complaint that a respondent's earlier in time registration relative to trademark acquisition is abusive because the only purpose to the website is to "produce advertising revenues by attracting consumers at the expense of legitimate businesses with similar or corresponding names is not a violation of the Policy." Discussed further in "Earlier Registered Domain Names; Subsequently Acquired Trademarks" (Sec. 5.01-F2).

[11] Going from right to left of the electronic address, the two or three letter extension is known as the Top Level Domain (TLD); and because the TLDs are generic they are called gTLDs). Dot com, dot org, dot net and dot edu are examples of gTLDs. They are also known as legacy TLDs to distinguish them from new TLDs (.auto, .career, .club, .dentist, .lawyer, .loan, .management, .nyc, .photography, .shop, .xyz, and so on for over a thousand extensions) that ICANN began to approve in 2013.

To the immediate left of the dot is the Second Level Domain, which consists of a string of characters that can spell out words, phrases, names, acronyms, or even be arbitrary letters without dictionary or cultural meaning. To the left of the Second Level Domain is the acronymic prefix

Internet users will be confused and possibly deceived into believing the resolving websites are associated with the trademark owner. Opportunism and confusion are a cybersquatter's stock in trade. It was apparent that in the absence of legal mechanisms sufficiently robust to deal with abusive registration of domain names the illegitimate would overwhelm the legitimate.

Well-known and famous trademarks stand out actually and virtually for their "magnetism"[12] in attracting consumers who identify the signs and symbols as sources of goods and services. That same magnetism that attracts consumers also attracts the clans of domain name registrants who squat, phish, whale, snatch, spoof, and scam trademark owners and consumers alike. For convenience, all of these enterprising netizens are bundled into an inclusive phylum as cybersquatters. Traditionally, trademark owners looked to courts for relief, but in the nonterritorial virtual space of the Internet this became a challenging legal and economic problem.[13]

1.01-A.3

1.01-A.3 Crafting Remedial Measures

By the mid-1990s business leaders, intellectual property owners and trademark representatives had grown increasingly alarmed about the conduct of some domain name registrants taking advantage of the ease of registering domain names. They were reacting to the emergence of a new tort that had some of the characteristics of trademark infringement but for which there was no tailored remedy. This concern quickly grew in intensity.[14] There was a rising demand for a more efficient legal mechanism for challenging opportunists taking advantage of statutory rights as an

"www" for the World Wide Web; and to the far left is the hypertext transfer protocol (http), which is the foundation of data communication for the Wide Web. 99.9% of cybersquatting claims involve legacy domain names with the overwhelming number in the dot com space. See further discussion in "Sunrise and Other Rights Protection Mechanisms."See also *Statistical Analysis of DNS Abuse in gTLDs Final Report* (August 18, 2017).

[12] Cf: *Mishawaka Rubber & Woolen Mfg., Co. v. S.S. Kresge Co.*, 316 U.S. 203 (1942) ("If another poaches upon the commercial magnetism of the symbol [the trademark owner] has created, the owner can obtain legal redress.")

[13] WIPO Final Report, *supra.*, Paragraph 2(v) reads: "The Internet is multi-jurisdictional. Users can access it from any place on earth. Because of packetswitching technology, information may travel through various countries or jurisdictions in order to reach its destination. It is a global medium transposed on the historical system of separate physical jurisdictions."

[14] A stab at providing a simpler procedure for alleged cybersquatting had been implemented in 1995 by the then sole registry/registrar of domain names in the .com, .net, .org and .edu spaces, Network Solutions Inc. (NSI). NSI was acquired by Verisign, Inc. in 2000 which spun off the registrar business in 2003 while maintaining the registry business. NSI's dispute resolution policy was heavily criticized by both mark owners and domain name holders. Its shortcomings are described in Carl Oppedahl, *Analysis and Suggestions Regarding NSI Domain Name Trademark Dispute Policy*, Vol. 7, Issue 1, Article 7 (1996); Steven A. McAuley, *The Federal Government Giveth and Taketh Away: How NSI's*

alternative to enduring the costs and delays of civil litigation in remote and possibly inhospitable jurisdictions.

Once the alarm sounded, deliberations to craft extraterritorial remedial measures and (in the U.S.) legislation were extraordinarily swift. In June 1998, the National Telecommunications and Information Administration (NTIA), an agency within the U.S. Department of Commerce, issued a Statement of Policy in which it stated that it had become clear that there was a "need to change" the government's approach to the Internet.[15] "Conflicts between trademark holders and domain name holders [said the NTIA] . . . [were] becoming more common . . . [while] [m]echanisms for resolving these conflicts [were] expensive and cumbersome."

From the White Paper, the baton then passed to the World Intellectual Property Organization (WIPO). It was generally agreed that cybersquatting had to be suppressed[16] and that purposeful confusion and injurious conduct justified the establishment of a special purpose forum for trademark owners without regard to their territorial location or dependence on local law. Commencing in July 1998, WIPO began an extensive international process of consultations with the aim of making recommendations to ICANN[17] for a rights protection mechanism for trademarks.[18] The experience of cybersquatting was particularly felt by owners

Domain Name Dispute Policy (Revision 02) Usurps a Domain Name Owner's Fifth Amendment Procedural Due Process, 15 J. Marshall J. Computer & Info. L. 547 (1997).

15 Statement of Policy on the Management of Internet Names and Addresses, U.S. Department of Commerce, National Telecommunications and Information Administration (June 5, 1998) (White Paper). The Policy is available on the Internet at http://www.ntia.doc.gov/federalregisternotice/1998/statementpolicymanagementinternetnamesandaddressesere.

16 WIPO Final Report at paragraph 168: "We are persuaded by the wisdom of proceeding firmly but cautiously and of tackling, at the first stage, problems which all agree require a solution. It was a striking fact that in all the 17 consultation meetings held throughout the world in the course of the WIPO Process, all participants agreed that 'cybersquatting' was wrong. It is in the interests of all, including the efficiency of economic relations, the avoidance of consumer confusion, the protection of consumers against fraud, the credibility of the domain name system and the protection of intellectual property rights, that the practice of deliberate abusive registrations of domain names be suppressed."

17 Until September 29, 2009 ICANN operated as a quasi-administrative agency under a Memorandum of Understanding with the U.S. Department of Commerce. This relationship changed with the signing of The Affirmation of Commitments effective September 30, 2009. An explanation of the Affirmation and the text is available at <http://www.icann.org/en/announcements/announcement 30sep09en.htm>. The National Telecommunications and Information Administration (NTIA) announced on March 14, 2014 that the U.S. Government will let the MOU expire. However, according to its spokesman the "announcement in no way diminishes our commitment to preserving the Internet as an engine for economic growth and innovation." The U.S. Government is not abandoning its oversight commitment to the Internet. See http://www.ntia.doc.gov/blog/2014/promoting internetgrowth and innovationthroughmultistakeholderinternetgovernance. The MOU expired on September 20, 2016.

of well-known and famous marks. Persons suspected of cybersquatting were condemned as "predators" and "parasites," although there were already entrepreneurs sensing an opportunity for a future market in domain names as well as good faith registrants that were neither.

WIPO issued an interim report in December 1998 and a final report in April 1999.[19] It emphasized the following points: "[d]isputes have now become numerous, while mechanisms for their settlement, outside of litigation, are neither satisfactory nor sufficiently available"[20]; trademark owners were "incurring significant expenditures to protect and enforce their rights in relation to domain names"[21]; and the sheer number of instances precluded "many trademark owners from filing multiple suits in one or more national courts."[22] The reference to national courts underscores the multiplicity of jurisdictions involved and the hurdles to obtaining relief against extraterritorial parties. ICANN implemented the UDRP a mere sixteen months after NTIA's Statement of Policy, October 1999. It was (and is) transformative in offering a forum liberated from national jurisdictions that matches the "simple, fast and relatively inexpensive process for the registration of domain names"[23] with an equally simple, fast and relatively inexpensive process for challenging domain name choices.[24] As conceived, Panels appointed to hear and decide disputes were expected to create a functioning jurisprudence sensitive to parties' rights as that may appear from the record and established by proof.[25] Equally important, the UDRP

---

18 ICANN is "an internationally organized, non-profit corporation [formed in 1998] that has responsibility for Internet Protocol (IP) address space allocation, protocol identifier assignment, generic (gTLD) and country code (ccTLD) Top-Level Domain name system management, and root server system management functions." ["Background Points" posted by ICANN on its web site at <icann.org/general/background.htm>.] Its mission "is to coordinate, at the overall level, the global Internet's systems of unique identifiers, and in particular to ensure the stable and secure operation of the Internet's unique identifier systems."

19 See WIPO Final Report. In the course of the domain name process WIPO held "seventeen consultation meetings in 15 different cities throughout the world and received written submissions from 334 governments, intergovernmental organizations, professional associations, corporations and individuals" (Background)

20 WIPO Final Report at paragraph 130. A contractual remedy was available through Network Solutions, Inc. See *Dorer v Arel*, 60 F. Supp. 2d 558 (E.D. Va 1999).

21 *Id.* at paragraph 131.

22 *Id.* Paragraph 132(i) reads: "The global presence may give rise to alleged infringements in several jurisdictions, with the consequence that several different national courts may assert jurisdiction, or that several independent actions must be brought because separate intellectual property titles in different jurisdictions are concerned."

23 WIPO Final Report paragraph 48.

24 The Policy does not grant monetary awards for cybersquatting. The remedy is a mandatory-like injunction cancelling or transferring the disputed domain name to complainant. Abusive conduct by complainants is sanctionable by a declaration of reverse domain name hijacking, but without monetary damages. Discussed further in Reverse Domain Name Hijacking. ICANN implemented

is *sui generis* as an arbitration in that it provides for an automatic execution of the demanded remedy without having to apply to a court of competent jurisdiction for confirmation of the award.

Contemporaneously with the WIPO process the U.S. Congress began working on a bill for suppressing cybersquatting. During hearings the Senate acknowledged WIPO's Interim Report of December 1998 that "[f]amous and well-known marks have been the special target of a variety of predatory and parasitical practices on the Internet."[26] The domestic response came in the form of amendments to the Trademark Act of 1946 (amendments, coincidentally, that were also enacted in 1999) that included new sections for injunctive and legal remedies against cybersquatting and (as a necessary balance against overreaching by trademark owners) for adjudicating false claims of cybersquatting.[27]

Taken together these provisions constitute the Anticybersquatting Consumer Protection Act (ACPA).[28] In its enactment report the U.S. Senate stated that "[r]egardless of what is being sold the result of online brand names abuse, as with other forms of trademark violations, is the erosion of consumer confidence in brand name identifiers and in electronic commerce generally."[29] Both the UDRP and the ACPA condemn cybersquatting and both protect trademarks, but their orientations are different and as a result so are the evidentiary demands.

Statutory cybersquatting is defined by its nesting in the Lanham Act and thus by association is a form of trademark infringement, although less demanding in

---

a complementary procedure in June 2013, the Uniform Rapid Suspension System (URS) for New gTLDs that began coming to market in 2013. Discussed further in Prospective Sunrises.

[25] WIPO Final Report, 150(5): "[I]t is desirable that the use of the administrative procedure should lead to the construction of a body of consistent principles that may provide guidance for the future . . . [with the proviso that] the determinations of the procedure should not have (and cannot have) the effect of binding precedent in national courts. It would be up to the courts of each country to determine what weight they wish to attach to determinations made under the procedure."

[26] Senate Hearing Report, 106-687: "WIPO, in addition to identifying cybersquatting as a global problem, recognized in its interim report on the domain name process that, indeed, '[f]amous and well-known marks have been the special target of a variety of predatory and parasitical practices on the Internet.'"

[27] 15 U.S.C. § 1114(2)(D). The Senate in its hearing report stated that the "purpose of the bill is to protect consumers and American businesses, to promote the growth of online commerce, and to provide clarity in the law for trademark owners by prohibiting the bad-faith and abusive registration of distinctive marks as Internet domain names with the intent to profit from the goodwill associated with such marks—a practice commonly referred to as cybersquatting," Id.,"I. Purpose" Senate Hearing Report.

[28] · 15 U.S.C. § 1125(d)(1)(A)(i) and (ii). The Act provides statutory remedies against anyone who, with "a bad faith intent to profit from that mark ... [either] registers, traffics in, or uses a domain name ... that ... in the case of a mark that is distinctive at the time of registration of the domain name, is identical or confusingly similar to that mark."

[29] Senate Hearing Report 106-140 on the enactment of the ACPA (August 5, 1999).

satisfying the required proof of infringement. However, the two regimes are both procedurally and substantively different, not only in the expected ways in which arbitration differs from litigation but also in its different model of liability. The UDRP demands proof that respondent both registered *and* is using the domain name in bad faith—the "conjunctive model". The ACPA is an "either/or" model: proof of liability is established if the domain name holder either "registers, traffics in, or uses a domain name" in bad faith—the "disjunctive model."[30]

In some respects, the UDRP can be seen as friendlier to domain name holders because of the heightened evidentiary demands on the trademark owner; while the ACPA can be seen as friendlier to trademark owners because the disjunctive model expands the basis for finding bad faith, although it also exposes the trademark owner to statutory damages for reverse domain name hijacking should it overreach its rights, a point illustrated further in Chapter 8. However, parties should not underestimate the risks or be overconfident in achieving the rewards in committing themselves to the ACPA.

1.01-A.4

1.01-A.4 Trademarks and the Value of Their Reputations

Of all the "netizens" on the Internet (as occupants in cyberspace have been called[31]) domain names that also function as trademarks are in the minority. The overwhelming majority of netizens consist of a diverse range of registrants that includes domain investors,[32] non-trademark (trade name) businesses, individuals, assorted goods/service providers, and others attracted to the cyber marketplace for whatever gives them pleasure or may be rewarding. Any one of these registrants may be challenged for cybersquatting if their choices are identical or confusingly similar to marks predating the registrations of the domain names, but whether their registrations are unlawful is a matter of proof.

Ideally, domain names and trademarks occupy different strata on the Internet. If they come into conflict it would be for two reasons: first, when registrants seek an economic advantage by purposely incorporating marks as domain names that violate owners' rights; and second, when registrants acquire domain names for lawful

---

[30] In contrast to the UDRP, the ACPA provides for damages and reasonable attorney fees to the prevailing party, 15 U.S.C. § 1117(a) and statutory damages, § 1117(d).

[31] Registrants are "netizens" ***Tata Sons Ltd v. mmt admin / Oktatabyebye.com***, D20090646 (WIPO August 11, 2009) (TATA and <oktatabyebye.com>, transferred).

[32] Where they have not been taken by brands, domain investors have registered every word in general and specialized dictionaries as well as a substantial volume of letters in arbitrary arrangements. According to Verisign's statistics "99% of all registrar searches today [2016] result in a 'domain taken' page.... [O]ut of approximately two billion requests it receives each month to register a .com name, fewer than three million—less than one percent—actually are registered." *Verisign, Inc. v. Xyz. Com LLC*, 848 F.3d 292 (4th Cir., 2017).

use. There is no *per se* rule that domain names identical or confusingly similar to marks are for that reason alone unlawful.

By definition all domain names by whom or for whatever reason acquired and maintained point or have the potential of pointing to destinations in cyberspace, but only trademarks have marketplace reputations preexisting domain registrations. However, for reasons that will become clear in the following sections and chapters, statutory protection goes only so far; it does not create in mark owners a "better right" over innocent and lawful registrations.[33] No better illustration of this are failed attempts by owners of newly acquired marks complaining that earlier registered domain names are cybersquatters. This is an impossibility under both the UDRP and the ACPA. There is, however, a hierarchy of rights. Where mark owners have actionable claims and there is provable evidence of cybersquatting, their statutory rights are paramount over contract rights regardless the length of time domain names have been held. Laches as an equitable defense has largely been rejected although as discussed in Sec. 5.01-E Paragraph 4(c)(i) of the Policy offers a safe harbor if before notice the respondent can affirmatively demonstrate it used the "domain name in connection with a bona fide offering of goods or services."

Owners of weak marks with less or no particular consumer recognition for the goods or services they offer, or whose marks can as readily be used by others without infringing any rights, or whose marks are recognized in one country or region but not in another must work harder to persuade triers of fact that registrants had them "in mind" when registering accused domain names. The first dispute was submitted to WIPO (in its provider role) in December 1999, which the Panel decided on default of the registrant responding to the complaint the following January. Its decision established a common law construction of the Policy that became the consensus view that the Policy requires complainant to prove respondent both registered the domain name in bad faith and was using it in bad faith.[34] The conjunctive requirement distinguishes the UDRP from the statutory regime discussed below and other dispute resolution policies governing country code TLDs summarized in Appendix C.

---

[33] WIPO Final Report, Paragraph 34: "[T]he goal of this WIPO Process is not to create new rights of intellectual property, nor to accord greater protection to intellectual property in cyberspace than that which exists elsewhere. Rather, the goal is to give proper and adequate expression to the existing, multilaterally agreed standards of intellectual property protection in the context of the new, multijurisdictional and vitally important medium of the Internet...."

[34] The panelist subsequently recanted his conclusion in favor of the "unitary concept" that justifies forfeiture of the domain name despite registration in good faith. Discussed further in "Justifying Forfeiture Despite Good Faith Registration" (Sec. 4.03-A.4.b)

1.01-B

1.01-B Domain Names and Trademarks Draw from a Common Linguistic and Cultural Heritage

1.01-B.1

1.01-B.1 Vulnerability of Trademarks to Cybersquatters

The WIPO Final Report identified a number of weaknesses at the interface of the Domain Name and Intellectual Property Systems that enabled registrants intent on doing so to take advantage of "trademarks and other recognized rights of identity as they had existed in the world before the arrival of the Internet."[35] The power to lodge some form of condensed communication in the minds of visitors and consumers depends on the selection and arrangement of characters. Potential confusion lies in the fact that domain names having risen in status from mere functional elements of the Internet to intangible property can be seen as near equivalents of trademarks, not in any statutory sense but in terms of each party's possessory or statutory rights.

Paradoxically, the ascribed weaknesses are also the strengths of the Internet if regarded from the vantage point of developing its commercial potential, which has included the rise of a secondary market for domain names. The technology responsible for transforming the underlying computer vocabulary of 0s and 1s into the lexical and numeric language of everyday use can be said to have created unanticipated consequences for trademark owners in the form of competition for domain names composed of generic and descriptive terms, thus the urgent need by the mid-1990s for rights protection mechanisms to remedy violations of statutory rights.

Because second level domains and trademarks are composed of the same lexical material the argument in contested disputes generally invites the question whether registrants acquired the domain names for their trademark values or the values of their semantic meaning. The answer is complicated because marks composed of common lexical terms (albeit transformed into distinctive signs of identification) can lose their association with the goods/services that distinguish them in their native habitats, the actual local, regional, national, or international marketplaces in which they operate. To ordinary consumers, domain names may not appear to be marks at all.

Nevertheless, regardless of their lexical similarity, trademarks and domain names remain functionally different even though as domain names they perform the same function on the Internet. The difference lies in the fact that marks are condensed forms of expressive communication and domain names are merely addresses on the Internet.

---

[35] WIPO Final Report at paragraph 22: "One consistent thread in the fabric of discussions and consultations concerning the management of the DNS [Domain Name System] has been the interface between domain names as addresses on the Internet and intellectual property or, more specifically, trademarks and other recognized rights of identity as they had existed in the world before the arrival of the Internet."

As such they are "much like a postal address in the real world.", but they are "more than an address."[36] They are unique in that "only one entity can be registered as a domain throughout the world."[37] This is not true of trademarks. Theoretically, trademarks may be owned by multiple parties whose rights are limited by the categories of goods or services to which the marks relate and the geographic boundaries of their territorial protections. Even where there is precise identity of a mark used by two parties "there may be no consumer confusion, and thus no trademark infringement, if the alleged infringer is in a different geographic area or in a wholly different industry."[38]

These orderly differentiations that are carefully regulated by national trademark registries can become chaotic in cyberspace, where complainants are frequently disputing microscopic differences as minimal as additions or subtractions of single letters. Trademark owners have a preclusive right to the domain name corresponding to their marks only if they can prove respondents have no right or legitimate interest and registered and are using the disputed domain in bad faith.

Both domain name holders and trademark owners are interested in traffic, but for different reasons. Light or heavy Internet traffic is an indicator of value. For domain name holders the goal *is* traffic; they are in the business of monetizing their holdings. So, for example, XYZ and aurally indistinguishable variations thereof (assuming XYZ is a well-known trademark of ABC)—such as putting an "E" in front of the "X", a "wh" before "y", and an "EE" after "Z" to match sounds with spellings, <exwhyzee.com>—are desirable for their ability to attract Internet users already familiar with the trademark in their daily lives. However, these lexical variations are also a form of cybersquatting, known as typosquatting. For ABC Corp.

---

[36] WIPO Final Report, at paragraph 10: "[W]hereas telephone and facsimile numbers consist of an anonymous string of numbers without any other significance, the domain name, because of its purpose of being easy to remember and to identify, often carries an additional significance which is connected with the name or mark of a business or its product or services." See *Panavision International v. Toeppen*, 141 F.3d 1316, 46 U.S.P.Q. 2d 1511 (9th Cir. 1998), ruling against the domain name registrant on the theory of dilution. A domain name is more than an address: "It marks the location of the site within cyberspace, much like a postal address in the real world, but it may also indicate to users some information as to the content of the site, and, in instances of well-known trade names or trademarks, may provide information as to the origin of the contents of the site."

[37] ***Cimcities, LLC v. John Zuccarini D/B/A Cupcake Patrol***, D2001-0491 (WIPO May 31, 2001) (ACCESS ATLANTA and <accesatlanta.com> [typosquatting]). See *Satyam Infoway Ltd. vs Sifynet Solutions Pvt. Ltd.*, AIR 2004 SC 3540, 2004 (3) AWC 2366 SC (Supreme Ct of India, 6 May, 2004): "A domain name is easy to remember and use, and is chosen as an instrument of commercial enterprise not only because it facilitates the ability of consumers to navigate the Internet to find websites they are looking for, but also at the same time, serves to identify and distinguish the business itself, or its goods or services, and to specify its corresponding online Internet location."

[38] *Brookfield Communications, Inc. v. West Coast Entertainment Corp.*, 174 F.3d 1026, 1054 (9th Cir. 1999). See ***ACE Limited v. WebMagic Ventures, LLC***, FA0802001143448 (Forum April 8, 2008) (ACE [Complainant claims a common law trademark] and <ace.com>, but Respondent has a

the goal is the more traditional one of offering and selling its goods and services to consumers from an online store through its <xyz.com> domain name. In the meantime, the registrant of <exwhyzee.com> is either syphoning off Internet visitors or benefiting from the goodwill associated with the XYZ brand.

1.01-B.2

1.01-B.2 Cyber Adjudication

Whether owners have actionable claims for abusive registration of domain names incorporating their trademarks depends in part on two principal factors, namely their lexical choices (common words that others can use without infringing another's rights) and priority (that is, the relative timing of domain name acquisition and first use of the mark in commerce). Regardless of timing, the UDRP does not prohibit registrants from trafficking in domain names; and it is not unlawful to register domain names identical or confusingly similar to trademarks or service marks. However, for marks postdating the domain name, while complainants have standing they have no actionable claim, thus no remedy. Under the ACPA they would not have standing either, but they could (depending on the factual circumstances) have an actionable claim for trademark infringement.

While domain names registered earlier than corresponding marks are invulnerable to forfeiture it does not follow that those registered later are infringing. This is particularly true of generic and descriptive terms employed denotatively by high-volume registrants and domain investors.[39] If the second level string contains generic or descriptive terms the assessment turns on a mark owner's lexical choice together with other factors that prove or rebut bad faith registration. The issue here is not priority but the reputation of the mark at the time of the registration of the domain name.

The legitimacy of a domain name registered after a mark's first use in commence depends on proof that respondent had the mark "in mind"; that the mark was the intended target. Domain names that resemble trademarks can easily be mistaken for them, but suspicion of cybersquatting turns to certainty when domain names mimic inherently distinctive marks or resolve to websites that take advantage of marks by displaying goods or services competitive with those of complainant. The process requires complainants to prove their claims but also compels respondents to defend their choices of domain names in a mandatory cyber adjudication limited to a narrow class of cases of "abusive registration."[40] The UDRP is nonexclusive so

---

registered trademark with the USPTO. "To strip Respondent of its right to use the at issue mark in a domain name the Panel would have to effectively invalidate Respondent's registered trademark.")

[39] Discussed further in "Contractual Basis for the UDRP" (Sec. 2.01).

[40] ICANN Second Staff Report on Implementation Documents for the Uniform Dispute Resolution Policy, Paragraph 4.1(c): "Except in cases involving 'abusive registrations' made with bad faith intent to profit commercially from others' trademarks (e.g., cybersquatting and cyberpiracy), the adopted

that if either party is dissatisfied with the result of the arbitration it can institute an action in a court of competent jurisdiction.[41]

The key to compelling a registrant to arbitrate a complainant's challenge lies in registrant's agreement with the registrar upon acquisition of the domain name. As discussed more fully in Chapter 2, registration agreements contain language dictated by ICANN that if challenged the domain name holder shall submit to adjudication under the UDRP "without prejudice to other potentially applicable jurisdictions."[42] A complainant is equally bound to the jurisdictional requirements of the UDRP by invoking its remedial procedures. There are defenses but no monetary counterclaims.

As an arbitral regime, the UDRP differs from commercial arbitrations in three respects. First, the administrative proceeding is decided entirely on paper submissions; there is no discovery, no person to person confrontation, and no live testimony. Second, the UDRP is a public rather than a private ADR. The names of the parties, the nature of the claims, the conduct of the respondents and findings of exoneration or condemnation are fully disclosed in reasoned decisions publicly available on provider databases. With private ADRs nothing substantive is intended to leak into the public sector. The seal is broken only if the parties disclose the details of their dispute in moving to confirm or vacate the award.

The third difference (which is mentioned above) is that by its own characterization the UDRP is a nonexclusive regime. Respondents before submission to a Panel and either party after an award may proceed to litigate the question as to whether the registration of the domain name was lawful. Under U.S. trademark law, the issue of lawful registration is tried *de novo*, without reference to the earlier proceeding. A UDRP decision, it has been said, is entitled to no deference.[43]

---

policy leaves the resolution of disputes to the courts (or arbitrators where agreed by the parties) and calls for registrars not to disturb a registration until those courts decide."

This policy statement was incorporated into the UDRP at paragraph 5: "All other disputes between you and any party other than us regarding your domain name registration that are not brought pursuant to the mandatory administrative proceeding provisions of Paragraph 4 shall be resolved between you and such other party through any court, arbitration or other proceeding that may be available." The term "abusive registration" subsumes "malicious registration."

[41] This has to be qualified because while the Policy is ostensibly nonexclusive the right to challenge an award depends upon whether the court has subject matter jurisdiction. The ACPA expressly provides for subject matter jurisdiction but the UK High Court has declared that it does not have subject matter jurisdiction. See United Kingdom (Sec. 8.01-B.3.b). Canadian courts have subject matter jurisdiction. See *Black v. Molson Canada* (2002), 60 O.R. (3d) 457 (Ont. S.C.J.) and *Boaden Catering Limited v. Real Food for Real Kinds Inc.*, 2016 CarswellOnt 10560, 2016 ONSC 4098, 268 A.C.W.S. (3d) 688, aff'd 2017 CarswellOnt 4247, 2017 ONCA 248.

[42] Discussed further in "Contractual Basis for the UDRP" (Sec. 2.01).

[43] Discussed further in Paragraph 4(k) of the Policy (Sec. 8.01-A).

1.02 1.02 LEGISLATING DECEPTIVE PRACTICES

1.02-A 1.02-A Defining Proscribed Conduct

1.02-A.1 1.02-A.1 The Concept of Abusive Registration

In the actual marketplace businesses attract consumers and maintain loyalties by establishing differences. It begins with choices of names protected by law either examined and registered by national registries or long and continued (but unregistered) use in commerce. In the virtual marketplace the strategy for parties intending to take advantage of the goodwill and reputation of trademarks is to erase differences by adding or subtracting fragments of speech—a letter (<xgoogle.com>, <goooglee.com>, <agogle.com>), word (<googlejobs.com>, <gooooglemaps.com>), phrase (<googlegameroom.com>, <goog-ad-development.com>), or functional element (<googler.co>). The ability to do this is assisted by the absence of gatekeepers.[44] Whether differences are established or domain name choices are abusive is defined solely by the terms of the Policy.[45]

In popular terms conduct that violates protected rights is known as "cybersquatting" (or "cyberpiracy" as the key noun phrase in the ACPA), but WIPO chose a different name for the prescribed conduct: "abusive registration."[46] It did so because of "the elastic meaning of cybersquatting in popular terminology" and because "the term has different meanings to different people." Abusive registration was thought to have "a more precise meaning."[47] However, because "abusive registration" is higher on the taxonomic scale than "cybersquatting" it is arguably more inclusive.

A case can be made that instead of being more precise the term "abusive registration" opened up opportunities to include by construction other acts as distinct species of abusive conduct within the scope of the Policy.[48] If this is the case,

---

[44] No gatekeeping in the legacy TLD spaces. See Berhad v. Godaddy.Com, Inc., 737 F.3d 546 (9th Cir., 2013) ("When actionable cybersquatting occurs, mark holders have sufficient remedies under the ACPA without turning to contributory liability.") There is some degree of gatekeeping of new TLDs. See further discussion on the tension among different stakeholders in "Sunrise and Other Rights Protection Mechanisms" (Sec. 2.03-A).

[45] WIPO Final Report at paragraph 135(ii). ICANN explicitly incorporated this and another limitation—that it is "not applicable to disputes between parties with competing rights acting in good faith" (135 [i])—into the UDRP. The limitations are repeated in paragraphs 153 and 166.

[46] *Id.*, paragraph 170.

[47] *Id.*

[48] An example of this stretching is "opportunistic bad faith." The dissent in ***Ha'aretz Daily Newspaper Ltd. v. United Websites, Ltd.***, D2002-0272 (WIPO August 21, 2002) stated that "[a]s for 'opportunistic bad faith,' I must make it clear that I reject the validity of that poorly-conceived bad faith precedent." Discussed further in "Opportunistic Bad Faith" (Sec. 6.01-C.1).

As regards new gTLDs, see Donuts Inc's statement of "Acceptable Use and Anti-Abuse Policy." Abusive use of a domain name is described as an illegal, disruptive, malicious, or fraudulent action.

cybersquatting is a narrower, and abusive registration a wider and more inclusive concept.[49] A complainant is entitled to relief if it presents a persuasive record of bad faith in the wider sense implicit in "abusive registration." This can include intentional, even malicious acts injurious to complainant and consumers alike that do not necessarily fit any of the bad faith circumstances and are criminal in nature.

Invoking the UDRP empowers a Panel to assess the merits of a complainant/trademark owner's claim that respondent's registration of a particular domain name infringes its right to exclusive use of a term in commerce.[50] The core issue is respondent's alleged appropriation of a term that evokes complainant's identity which it is using or holding for an unlawful purpose. However, whether a complainant has an actionable claim depends on a number of factors that are more fully detailed in the pages and chapters that follow.

When registrants purchase domain names they represent and warrant in their registration agreements that they "will not infringe the legal rights of a third party." To infringe upon or otherwise violate another's right presupposes that the term incorporated in the domain name is of such a quality or strength that any consumer seeing it would immediately associate it with complainant, but experience teaches that trademarks are not equally ranked or memorable.

On the continuum from weakness to strength, the more generic the term — qualifying as a mark for its acquired distinctiveness — the less recognition the mark will have, thus a narrower scope of protection for an owner's exclusivity rights; while marks on the suggestive, arbitrary and fanciful end of the continuum — those that qualify as inherently distinctive — will enjoy greater protection for their owners' exclusive rights. There can be drawn from this a guide that reflects the actual experience of UDRP claims, namely that owners of marks on the weak end of the continuum rarely succeed and those on the strong end rarely lose.

The Policy includes a substantial list of abusive conduct. Donut Inc is a registry for numerous new gTLDs. Its Policy is available at http://www.donuts.co/policies/acceptable-use/.

[49] See for example, ***Delta Air Transport NV (trading as SN Brussels Airlines) v. Theodule De Souza***, D2003-0372 (WIPO August 5, 2003) (<brusselsairliner. com>) where the Panel determined that the requirement for bad faith was satisfied where Respondent had "abused the system." Abusive conduct has been stretched to include unfounded representations of fraud by complainants. See ***Comercializadora de Lacteos y Derivados, S.A. de C.V. v. Apple Inc.***, D2017-1351 (WIPO October 23, 2017) (<lala.com>. "The majority of the Panel considers that rashly accusing anybody of bad faith is an abuse of the system.") Scope of the Policy is discussed further in Chapter Three and was also the subject of a letter from the Forum to Members of the Implementation Recommendation Team formed by ICANN dated May 6, 2009: "Complainants have pushed, and Panelists have taken the opportunity, over time, to broaden the scope of the UDRP, but it started out as a mechanism only for clear cut cases of cybersquatting."

[50] WIPO Final Report, paragraph 166. The touchstone of a traditional trademark infringement analysis is whether one person's use of another's mark "is likely to cause confusion, or to cause

That a trademark has a present reputation is not probative of respondent's knowledge of it when it registered the domain name. The longer the time intervening between an alleged abusive registration and commencement of an administrative proceeding the greater the demand for proof that complainant had a sufficient reputation in the marketplace when the domain name was registered. Complainant cannot make a case without proof that whatever reputation it may have had in the past respondent was aware of it, but respondent's rebuttal burden (should it appear and argue its right or legitimate interest) is heavier as the mark ascends the scale.

In practice, the qualifying requirement of complainant having a trademark or service mark in which it has a right (Paragraph 4(a)(i) of the Policy) is not inelastic. The definition of "mark" includes unregistered signs and can be stretched further to include trade names[51] but not personality rights (also known as publicity rights), statutory and regulatory rights created to protect geographic indicators as designations of origin,[52] or personal names.[53]

1.02-A.2

1.02-A.2 Protecting Existing Trademarks from Predators and Parasites

Initially the intellectual property community was slow to recognize the vulnerabilities of trademarks, and since there was no international mechanism for resolving disputes the vacuum drew "predators and parasites"[54] into this new space. ICANN's arbitral regime is a response to such opportunism,[55] but its narrow jurisdiction

---

mistake, or to deceive." 15 U.S.C. §1125(a)(1). Registration of a domain name without more does not constitute service mark or trademark infringement. *Brookfield Commc'ns, Inc. v. W. Coast Entm't Corp.*, 174 F.3d 1036, 1052 (9th Cir. 1999).

[51] For example, the WIPO Final Report declares that complainants have no actionable claim for trade name infringement, Paragraph 167, but the Second Report explains that "[w]here a trade name is used in widespread markets, it . . . often . . . satisfies the conditions for protection as an unregistered trademark so as to qualify, in appropriate circumstances, for protection against bad faith, deliberate misuse under the UDRP" (WIPO Second Report, Paragraph 318(ii). Discussed further in "Trade Names Brought Within the Policy's Scope" (Sec. 4.01-E.3.b).

[52] Although there are existing international norms that prohibit false and deceptive indications of geographical source on goods "those norms were confined to the use of terms on goods" rather than source of goods. The Policy has not been revised and "geographical indications, as such, remain outside the scope of the Policy." ***Comité Interprofessionnel du vin de Champagne v. Steven Vickers***, DCO2011-0026 (WIPO June 21, 2011).

[53] Discussed further in" Personal Names" (Sec. 5.03-B.2).

[54] WIPO Final Report, Executive Summary (vii), paragraphs 23, 176, 246, 262 and section subtitled "Predatory and Parasitical Practices" that introduces paragraphs 318 et seq.

[55] The main concern of the Policy is "curb[ing] the abusive registration of domain names in circumstances where the registrant is seeking to profit from and exploit the trademark of another." ***Match.com, LP v. Bill Zag and NWLAWS.ORG***, D2004-0230 (WIPO June 2, 2004), but in this particular case the trademark is the dictionary word "match." "Respondent has registered nine domain

is effectively limited to trademarks whose existence predates domain name registration.[56] It does not protect owners whose trademarks come into existence after registration of the domain name or applicants for trademark registration unless they are able to demonstrate infringement of common law rights antedating domain name registration.[57] A complainant demonstrates standing under the UDRP when in its complaint it alleges and proves that respondent has incorporated in its domain name in whole (identical) or varied or combined with the dominant part with other lexical elements (confusingly similar) of a mark in which complainant has rights.

However, it will become clear in the following pages that owners of registered trademarks acquired after domain name registration, although they have standing,- cannot succeed under the UDRP because (whether or not the registrant has rights or legitimate interests and however infringing the use may be) respondent cannot be shown to have registered the domain name in bad faith.

Actionable conduct encompasses a variety of practices, from passive holding of domain names corresponding to trademarks to a variety of squatting and piratical actions that directly injure trademark owners by taking advantage of their commercial reputations and deceiving consumers as to the identity of the party sponsoring the website. Breaches of contract and fiduciary duty, tortious interference and passing off, misappropriation and conversion are not in themselves the legal basis for relief, but any one of them combined with other acts can be a factor in assessing bad faith.[58] Except in four instances that are presumptively abusive registrations there is no *per se* violation. The four are distribution of malware (fraud and conversion),[59]

---

names which contain the descriptive term and common English word 'match' in combination with other common English words or numbers in the generic Top Level Domain (gTLD) .com. This Respondent is entitled to do. By registering the service mark MATCH.COM, Complainant cannot thereby preclude anyone else from ever registering the common term 'match' in combination with other common words in the .com gTLD."

[56] A complainant whose trademark postdates the registration of a domain name but owns the trademark when it serves its complaint has standing despite the impossibility of proving a UDRP infringement. Discussed further in "Knowledge and Targeting Are Prerequisites to Finding Bad Faith Registration" (Sec. 4.02-C).

[57] "Common law" also includes an exception to the rule of a preexisting right. Discussed further in "Acting on Media Coverage and Insider Information" (Sec. 6.01-C.1.b) and "Opportunistic Bad Faith" (Sec. 6.01-C.1).

[58] Discussed further in Chapter 3.

[59] Evidence of malware infection is relevant in the Panel's determination of bad faith under paragraph 4(a)(iii) of the Policy. See ***Humble Bundle, Inc. v. Domain Admin, Whois Privacy Corp.***, D2016-0914 (WIPO June 21, 2016) (<humble-bundle.net>. "[Spreading malware] implies abusive conduct of a particularly serious nature . . . that goes well beyond the activities of the typical cybersquatter"); ***Euroview Enterprises LLC v. Jinsu Kim***, D2016-1124 (WIPO September 12, 2016) (<euroview.com>).

fraudulent transfer (conversion), "spoofing and phishing" (larceny), and pointing or threatening to point domain names to pornography (extortion).[60]

The right trademark owners seek to vindicate, however, can be no greater than that to which the law entitles them.[61] Trademark law confers no legal right to a domain name corresponding to a trademark *unless the choice violates the Policy*.[62] There is nothing in the WIPO Final Report or the Policy that outlaws registering common words, generic terms, descriptive phrases and/or number and letter combinations that someone sometime in the future will want as a perfect fit to its newly acquired trademark. The first party to register a domain name without intention to take advantage of the complainant's reputation has committed no actionable wrong.[63]

---

[60] This is not meant to suggest that operating a pornographic website is a per se violation of a complainant's rights. Lawful registration, ***Knud Jepsen A/S v. Rick Schwartz, Virtual Dates Inc.***, D2017-0679 (WIPO June 20, 2017) (<queen.com>) ("Where a domain name registrant tries to obtain financial gain by registering and using a non-generic domain name in which it has no rights or legitimate interests, the offering of adult content may be evidence of bad faith use, However, as the Disputed Domain Name [in this case, 'queen'] has a dictionary meaning, those cases do not apply." Abusive conduct, ***Little Acorns Fostering Ltd. v. W P, The Cloud Corp / Al Perkins***, D2017-1776 (WIPO October 18, 2017) (<littleacornfostering.com>. "[I]t is unfortunate that the business practices of Mr. Perkins appear to have carried on for the most part unchecked for many years, notwithstanding the multiple findings made against him in UDRP proceedings and the brazen nature of his conduct.")

[61] Thus, trademark rights that postdate domain name registration cannot be infringed since cybersquatting is an intentional act upon an existing mark. See WIPO Final Report at paragraph 34: It was not "the goal of this WIPO Process ... to create new rights of intellectual property, nor to accord greater protection to intellectual property in cyberspace than that which exists elsewhere. Rather, the goal is to give proper and adequate expression to the existing, multilaterally agreed standards of intellectual property protection in the context of the new, multijurisdictional and vitally important medium of the Internet and the DNS that is responsible for directing traffic on the Internet. The WIPO Process seeks to find procedures that will avoid the unwitting diminution or frustration of agreed policies and rules for intellectual property protection."

[62] ***David Tobin v. ZeitGeist Corp.***, FA1112001421947 (Forum February 13, 2012) ("Before applying to register the trademark, Complainant discovered in 2007 that the corresponding Domain Name [<audiojack.com>] was taken. After contacting the former owner, Complainant awaited the expiry of the Domain Name registration and then found that it had been acquired by Respondent, a company that buys domains for the sole purpose of inflating the cost and selling to the highest bidder." Complaint dismissed against current Respondent). See also ***Wirecard AG v. Telepathy Inc., Development Services***, D2015-0703 (WIPO June 22, 2015) (<boon.com>. 1) No fraud in counter-offering to sell domain names for substantial sums; 2) No condemnation of domain name holders for maximizing their profits on domain names acquired many years prior to complainant's trademark rights; 3) No illegitimacy in being a "professional domain grabber."

[63] A distinction must clearly be made between domain investors and developers (referred to as "domainers") and cybersquatters. Domainers (as with Respondent in Wirecard, *supra.*) are engaged in lawful economic transactions. Decisions too numerous to cite but see ***Solon AG v. eXpensive-Domains.com Project***, D2008-0881 (WIPO August 1, 2008) ("Complainant evidently takes the view that domain name dealers are cybersquatters, because they acquire domain names without any

If a legal rule were applied prohibiting speculation in domain names it would inhibit commercial activity at too prohibitive a cost to freedom of the marketplace.[64] Rather, what is prohibited is speculating in domain names with knowledge of another's rights.[65] First generation registrants with priority are favored under the UDRP while transferees and successors are answerable for their choices from the dates the new registrations are recorded in their names.

1.02-B Varieties of Predators and Parasites 1.02-B

1.02-B.1 Tension between Domain Name and Intellectual Property Systems 1.02-B.1

The Internet's frictionless operation depends on the interoperability of two very different systems. In its Final Report WIPO identified a tension between the domain name and intellectual property systems, but the tension is better described by the colliding of interests. The tension rises, first of all, from the different functions of the systems aggravated by the possibility of conflict in their uses. In the words of the Final Report, the tension is "exacerbated by a number of predatory and parasitical practices that have been adopted by some to exploit the lack of connection between the purposes for which the DNS was designed and those for which intellectual [property rights] protection exists."[66]

Conflict rises as soon as registrants acquire domain name composed of words that by happenstance mimic marks with or without intention to infringe third-party rights. No sure inference can be drawn solely from the act of registration. Domain names acquired for their semantic value do not by virtue of being identical

---

intention of making any genuine active use of them and for no reason other than to sell them [ ] at a profit. . . . That is not the definition of a cybersquatter envisaged by the Policy.")

64 The dissent in ***The American Automobile Association, Inc. v. QTK Internet c/o James M. van Johns***, FA1261364 (Nat. Arb. Forum, July 25, 2009) (<aaa.net>) opined that speculative registrations of dictionary and/or letter combinations with the intention of reselling them at a profit "[o]nce someone wants to acquire the domain name . . . were intended to be prohibited by the policy. . . ." As the Panel in ***Solon*** states, no such intention is expressed in the foundation documents or in case law and the jurisprudence does not support that view.

65 ***Allocation Network GmbH v. Steve Gregory***, D2000-0016 (WIPO March 24, 2000): "The difficulty lies in the fact that the domain name allocation.com, although descriptive or generic in relation to certain services or goods, may be a valid trademark for others. This difficulty is [com]pounded by the fact that, while 'Allocation' may be considered a common word in English speaking countries, this may not be the case in other countries, such as Germany.

Therefore, although the registration and offering for sale of allocation.com as a domain name may constitute a legitimate interest of Respondent in the domain name, this is different if it were shown that allocation.com has been chosen with the intent to profit from or otherwise abuse Complainant's trademark rights."

66 WIPO Final Report at paragraph 23 and 172. WIPO also recognized there were innocent and good faith registrants. See Sec. 1.02-C. These labels represented the bookends, but it was well understood,

or confusingly similar to marks lose their generic character which is their principal attraction, but when words and combinations transcend their generic origins their semantic value diminishes, mostly (but not always) to the point where they only have trademark value.

The practices WIPO identifies include but are not limited to conduct expressly proscribed in the Final Report and the UDRP. Trademarks and service marks are terse and powerful forms of communication about source and quality of owners' goods or services. Their value to owners and cybersquatters alike lies in consumers' recognition and responsiveness to associations inherent in the signs.

The WIPO Final Report[67] identifies two types of "predatory and parasitical practices": 1) "the deliberate, bad faith registration as domain names of well-known and other trademarks in the hope of being able to sell the domain names to the owners of those marks"; and, 2) registering domain names "simply to take unfair advantage of the reputation attached to those marks." The range includes conduct that constitutes unfair competition and evokes familiar tests under national laws.[68] In his testimony to the U.S. House of Representatives on July 28, 1999, Francis Gurry, then legal counsel of WIPO (currently Director General) stated, "[t]he most egregious manifestation of this problem is the exploitation in bad faith of the ease and simplicity of obtaining a domain name registration in order to register, as a domain name, the trademark of another person *with a view to extracting a premium from the owner of the mark"*[69] (emphasis added).

---

and the development of the jurisprudence bears this out, factual circumstances supporting or undercutting complainants' claims of cybersquatting are more complex than these two extremes.

67 *Id.*

68 WIPO Final Report at paragraph 175 reads: "The case law which has developed in the application of national laws for the protection of trademarks and service marks and for protection against unfair competition also supports the prohibition of the predatory and parasitical practices that would be caught under the definition of abusive registration given above."

69 Mr. Gurry's statement focuses principally on the first type of predatory practice, "extracting a premium from the owner of the mark." That practice changed over time from direct extraction to indirect by exploiting the value of the trademark, frequently under the owner's radar that in some cases can go undetected for years. A copy of Mr. Gurry's full testimony can be found at http://www.wipo.int/amc/en/processes/process1/testimony/. Compare Senate Report No. 106-140 (1999) (Anticybersquatting Consumer Protection Act): "Congress finds the following:
(1) The registration, trafficking in, or use of a domain name that is identical to, confusingly similar to, or dilutive of a trademark or service mark of another that is distinctive at the time of registration of the domain name, without regard to the goods or services of the parties, with the bad-faith intent to profit from the goodwill of another's mark (commonly referred to as 'cyberpiracy' and 'cybersquatting')—
(A) results in consumer fraud and public confusion as to the true source or sponsorship of goods and services;
(B) impairs electronic commerce, which is important to interstate commerce and the United States economy;

1.02-B.2 Four Varieties of "Predatory/Parasitical Practices" 1.02-B.2

ICANN refined the two types of predatory/parasitical practices into four varieties of opportunists about which more will be discussed later in the pages that follow. The four[70] are: 1) extortionists [paragraph 4(b)(i)], 2) expropriators [paragraph 4(b)(ii)], 3) competitors who engage in foul play [paragraph 4(b)(iii)], and 4) impersonators [paragraph 4(b)(iv)]. Their common denominator is targeting complainant's trademark with the intent of profiting from it, although the first three are distinguished by focusing on registration. In contrast impersonators target mark owners through their use of the domain name. Even if the stated motive is not to injure complainant the consequence of the registrant sitting in complainant's space is complainant's economic loss and registrant's financial gain.

The first category includes respondents who register and hold domain names hostage for ransom (extortion),[71] which one Panel has labeled a cybersquatter's "most offensive act."[72] Panels in early UDRP decisions distinguished between offers to sell domain names acquired for that purpose and responding to inquiries to purchase by putative complainants, which is not an offensive act.[73] However, extortionate conduct by holding the domain name for ransom has diminished significantly for

---

(C) deprives legitimate trademark owners of substantial revenues and consumer goodwill; and
(D) places unreasonable, intolerable, and overwhelming burdens on trademark owners in protecting their valuable trademarks."

The Senate Report defines cybersquatters as those who:
[1] "register well-known brand names as Internet domain names in order to extract payment from the rightful owners of the marks;" [2] "register well-known marks as domain names and warehouse those marks with the hope of selling them to the highest bidder;" [3] "register well-known marks to prey on consumer confusion by misusing the domain name to divert customers from the mark owner's site to the cybersquatter's own site;" and [4] "target distinctive marks to defraud consumers, including to engage in counterfeiting activities," *Id.* at 5-6.

[70] The list of nonexclusive circumstances is introduced by Paragraph 4(b): "For the purposes of Paragraph 4(a)(iii), the following circumstances, in particular but without limitation, if found by the Panel to be present, shall be evidence of the registration and use of a domain name in bad faith."

[71] ***The Pep Boys Manny, Moe and Jack of California v. ecommerce today, Ltd.***, AF0145 (e-Resolution May 3, 2000): "the panel concludes that the Respondent's actions in registering the present domain name amount to nothing less than an attempt to register and hold the present name 'hostage' in pursuit of a sufficiently large ransom from its rightful user." See also ***Commonwealth Hotels Inc. v. CCD Internet***, AF-00771 (eResolution April 9, 2001) (<commonwealthhotels.com>. "The language of *Policy* paragraph 4(a) should be interpreted in a purposive manner consistent with the Policy's remedial nature and objective – to prevent the extortionate behaviour known as 'cybersquatting.'")

[72] ***Freddy Addu v. Frank Fusible***, D2004-0682 (WIPO October 27, 2004) in which the Panel found that Respondent attempted to cash in on athlete's success in the guise of a fan club: "The most offensive act of a cybersquatter is to hold another's mark for ransom."

[73] There are two exceptions to the application of paragraph 4(b)(i) ["selling, renting, or otherwise transferring"]: where 1) respondent has rights to or legitimate interests in the domain name at issue, ***Avnet, Inc. v. Aviation Network, Inc.***, D2000-0046 (WIPO March 24, 2000); and 2) respondent

a combination of reasons. Respondents have learned that ransoming as a business model is not as lucrative as other models. As a result, they have migrated away from overtly demanding payment to release domain names. If a respondent found to be holding a domain name as hostage also makes active use of it to attract visitors the holding also violates paragraph 4(b)(iv) of the Policy.[74]

In contrast to extortionists, expropriators, competitors, and impersonators siphon customers from trademark owners to feed on the reputation and goodwill of the trademarks they mimic. While abusive registration by competitors occurs, conduct of expropriators and impersonators tends to predominate proceedings under the UDRP.[75] Monetizing domain names has become common, sales and auctions from inventory are routine, and portals for advertising and search services have created new sources of revenue. None of these business models is necessarily illegitimate and could very well be lawful.

Condemnation rests on the respondent's purpose in registering a particular domain name, not the business model. It is abusive to appropriate trademarks, whether in whole or in part or by varying their lexical elements by adding terms or omitting letters (known as typosquatting) for the purpose of capturing complainant's goodwill for commercial gain often "with little or no attention to third-party intellectual property rights."[76]

---

is making a counter-offer in response to complainant's inquiry to purchase the domain name, ***SOUTHBank v. Media Street***, D2001-0294 (WIPO April 11, 2001).

[74] See cases decided under the ACPA. U.S. courts have identified two "quintessential example[s]" of bad faith: 1) "purchas[ing] a domain name very similar to the trademark and then offer[ing] to sell the name to the trademark owner at an extortionate price; and 2) where a defendant] intend[s] to profit by diverting customers from the website of the trademark owner to the defendant's own website, where those consumers would purchase the defendant's products or services instead of the trademark owner's," *Utah Lighthouse Ministry v. Found. for Apologetic Info. & Research*, 527 F.3d 1045, 1058 (10th Cir. 2008), citing decisions from different circuits but parody a complete defense to bad faith registration or bad faith use.

[75] Article 10bis of the Paris Convention which is quoted in the WIPO Final Report establishes an obligation to provide protection against unfair competition. The Article reads in relevant part:
(1) The countries of the [Paris]Union are bound to assure to nationals of such countries effective protection against unfair competition.
(2) Any act of competition contrary to honest practices in industrial or commercial matters constitutes an act of unfair competition.
(3) The following in particular shall be prohibited:
  1. all acts of such a nature as to create confusion by any means whatever with the establishment, the goods, or the industrial or commercial activities, of a competitor;
  2. false allegations in the course of trade of such a nature as to discredit the establishment, the goods, or the industrial or commercial activities, of a competitor;

The United States is one of 169 country subscribers to the Paris Convention.

[76] ***HBC Finance Corporation v. Clear Blue Sky Inc. and Domain Manager***, D2007-0062 (WIPO June 4, 2007). However, the UDRP forum is not a trademark court (Sec. 3.01).

Proof of intention to violate a complainant's trademark rights is satisfied by a combination of direct and circumstantial evidence and inferences derived therefrom,[77] including choice of characters for the second level domain; timing of the trademark and domain name acquisitions; geographic nearness or remoteness; responding to or ignoring cease-and desist notices; the nature and location of the respondent's business; the respondent's relationship if any with complainant;[78] and the historical and current content of the website.[79] Because the UDRP is a submission-only proceeding nothing should be taken for granted or proof omitted; speculation about the respondent's intention is not evidence however sincerely expressed and believed.[80]

1.02-C Innocent and Good Faith Registration 1.02-C

While the Policy is crafted primarily to protect trademark owners from predators and parasites, it is applied in a balanced way to protect respondents from overreaching trademark owners for their lawful domain name choices. It is not intended to suppress legitimate competition,[81] restrain commerce,[82] or impair protected Constitutional or statutory rights.[83] The "behavior of innocent or good faith

---

[77] The rules of the Policy allow for inferences to be drawn from evidence both apparent and hidden. See Rule 14(b). Since intent like other states of mind is rarely susceptible of direct proof and is ordinarily inferred from the facts, it puts a premium on the record. It is necessary to draw inferences from the submitted facts because "matters involving a respondent's motive, intent, purpose and other subjective factors determinative under Paragraphs 4(a)(ii) and 4(a)(iii) will not always be susceptible of direct proof. . . ," ***Brooke Bollea, a.k.a Brooke Hogan v. Robert McGowan***, D2004-0383 (WIPO June 29, 2004). To be valid, however, inferences must rest on established facts, "Creating a Proper Foundation" (Sec. 7.09-A.1).

[78] Representative cases: ***Bootie Brewing Company v. Deanna D. Ward and Grabebootie Inc.***, D2003-0185 (WIPO May 22, 2002); ***Grace From Fire, LLC v. ConnectDomain.com Worldwide domains, Inc***, D2010-0143 (WIPO March 9, 2010) (<jackjackass.com>, Hosting agreement, no safe harbor for past due account).

[79] Discussed further in "Researching the Past. Historical Screenshots from the Wayback Machine" (Sec. 7.05-A-3.b). The Wayback Machine can be found on the Internet at http://www.archive.org/index.php.

[80] Contentions of abusive registration by complainant no less than assurances of good faith registration by respondent are equally worthless without proof. Of many losing complainants see ***Jireh Industries Ltd. v. DVLPMNT MARKETING, INC. / Domain Administrator***, FA1703001719671 (Forum April 14, 2017) (<jireh.com>) ("Such assertions alone, without facts to support a claim of common law rights, are insufficient to satisfy the requirements of the Policy.") Discussed further in "Prosecuting a UDRP Complaint and Defending Rights or Legitimate Interests in Disputed Domain Name" (Sec. 7.04-A).

[81] ***Wisconsin Emergency Medical Technicians Association, Inc. DBA Wisconsin Emergency Medical Services Association, Inc***. (WEMSA) v. Marsha Everts, EMS Professionals, Inc., D2018-2841 (WIPO February 7, 2019) (<emsprofessionals.net>. "The mere use by Respondent of EMS PROFESSIONALS as a name on a sales catalog related to Respondent's legitimate business does not establish, without more, that Respondent lacks legitimate interests in using the name EMS

domain name registrants is not to be considered abusive."[84] The prescient (if not intended) consequence of this doctrine is a cyber marketplace of competing interests for strings of characters by parties who in every other respect are not competitors.[85]

In its implementation report, ICANN did not explicitly detail what constitutes unlawful registrations, but the WIPO Final Report offers two examples of innocent behavior[86]: small businesses that are able to show "through business plans, correspondence, reports, or other forms of evidence, that [they] had a bona fide intention to use the [domain] name[s] in good faith"; and "Domain name registrations

---

PROFESSIONALS for the completely different purpose of selling products online, nationwide, to emergency medical providers, first responders and law enforcement professionals."

[82] See as one early example ***Allocation***, *supra*. ("As the commercial value of such domain names has increased, brokers . . . have seized the opportunity to sell such domain names to the highest bidder. In principle, such a practice may constitute use of the domain name in connection with a bona fide offering of goods or services (i.e. the sale of the domain name itself.") See also WIPO Final Report at paragraph 34: "the goal is to give proper and adequate expression to the existing, multilaterally agreed standards of intellectual property protection in the context of the new, multijurisdictional and vitally important medium of the Internet and the DNS that is responsible for directing traffic on the Internet."

[83] 15 U.S.C. § 1125(3): "The following shall not be actionable as dilution by blurring or dilution by tarnishment under this subsection: (A) Any fair use, including a nominative or descriptive fair use, or facilitation of such fair use, of a famous mark by another person…." Included in fair use is (ii) "parodying, criticizing, or commenting upon the famous mark owner or the goods or services of the famous mark owner..."

[84] WIPO Final Report at paragraph 172: "The cumulative conditions of the first paragraph of the definition make it clear that the behavior of innocent or good faith domain name registrants is not to be considered abusive." See for example ***J. R. Andorin, Inc. d/b/a Natural Wellness v. Natural Wellness Centers Of America Inc.***, FA1107001399143 (Forum September 13, 2011) (<naturalwellness.com>, Denied. "Respondent has been incorporated in the State of California since July 31, 2000 under the name NATURAL WELLNESS CENTERS OF AMERICA INC., has been doing business continuously under this name, and has operated an online shop under the domain name in dispute.")

[85] See *Dorer v. Arel*, 60 F. Supp. 2d 558 (E.D. Va 1999) ("Some domain names . . . are valuable assets as domain names irrespective of any goodwill which might be attached to them. . . . Indeed, there is a lucrative market for certain generic or clever domain names that do not violate a trademark or other right or interest, but are otherwise extremely valuable to Internet entrepreneurs.")

[86] *Id.*, paragraph 172, last sentence. The WIPO Final Report recommended that a respondent to the arbitral proceedings should have the opportunity of proving its right or legitimate interest in the disputed domain name which is embodied in paragraph 4(c) of the Policy: "Any of the following circumstances [that is, the circumstances set forth in 4(c)(iiii)], in particular but without limitation, if found by the Panel to be proved based on its evaluation of all evidence presented, shall demonstrate your rights or legitimate interests to the domain name for purposes of Paragraph 4(a)(ii)." Demonstration of right or legitimate interest in the domain name ends the proceedings in the respondent's favor. The proof requirements for rebutting complainant's *prima facie* case that respondent lacks rights or legitimate interests are discussed further in Chapter Five. Discussed further in "Rival Trademarks in Foreign Jurisdictions" (Sec. 4.02-A.1.c).

that are justified by legitimate free speech rights or by legitimate non-commercial considerations would likewise not be considered to be abusive." A third kind of dispute which ICANN describes as being in "[g]ood faith" involves "disputes between competing rights holders or other competing legitimate interests over whether two names were misleadingly similar."[87]

As developed in the jurisprudence, innocent and good faith registrations extend to circumstances that both predate and postdate complainants' trademark rights. When registrations predate, complainants have no actionable claim under the UDRP because they cannot satisfy the "registration in bad faith" element.[88] When they postdate, the question of cybersquatting must be answered by examining parties' lexical choices[89] or unauthorized but lawful use of marks, such as for nominative fair use[90] or its equivalent under UDRP jurisprudence. The Policy attempts to strike a balance. It is "concerned . . . with defining the boundary between unfair and unjustified appropriation of another's intellectual creations or business identifiers."[91] Whether a respondent crosses the boundary and its conduct is assessed to be abusive is a matter of proof and not of assertion.[92] This stricture is equally true for respondents alleging lawful registration.

At the heart of cybersquatting challenges are deliberate targeting of marks, unfair business practices, and deception. While all presumptions are rebuttable, the stronger the mark the more probable abusive registration; the weaker the mark the heavier the burden of proving bad faith. Registrations of domain names are not abusive merely

---

[87] These innocent and good faith circumstances are those set forth as affirmative defenses in Paragraph 4(c)(i-iii) of the UDRP.

[88] See "Earlier Registered Domain Names; Subsequently Acquired Trademarks" (Sec. 5.01-F.2).

[89] Discussed further in "Dictionary Words and Descriptive Phrases" (Sec. 5.01-D.1). Also use of foreign words as evidence of lawful registration. See ***Target Brands, Inc. v. Quinv S.A. / Korchia Thibault***, FA1205001442068 (Forum June 12, 2012) (TARGET and <taget.com>) (Complaint denied. "Respondent asserts that the word 'taget' has several meanings, most of which are associated with 'touch' (Latin) and in Swedish, the word means 'touched', 'moved' or 'affected.' Respondent claims that Google translates the term to 'time,' also in Swedish and in Danish the word has a variety of meanings including foggy (as in meteorology), taken, and when combined as a phrase to form 'strengt taget' translates to 'strictly speaking.'"

[90] ***Mind Candy Ltd v. Gamers Guides L.L.C***, D2010-0995 (WIPO August 12, 2010) (MOSHI MONSTERS and <moshi-cheates.com>, "The use of the images may have breached Complainant's copyright but that, per se, is irrelevant to the question of whether or not Respondent has a right or legitimate interest in the domain name." See further in Nominative Fair Use.

[91] WIPO Final Report at paragraph 13. Unlike trademark law which prevents competitors from using the same mark as one with priority, respondents in the same industry as complainants using dictionary words or common expressions as their commercial signs (absent proof of direct and knowing competition) can coexist even though respondent would be unable to get a trademark. See ***Anyclean Premium Limited v. Jethro Denahy, Any-Clean***, D2017-0581 (WIPO April 28, 2017) (ANY CLEAN and <any-clean.com>).

[92] Discussed further in "Rule 10(d)" (Sec. 7.05).

because they happen to be identical or confusingly similar to a trademark. Something more is required, such as taking advantage of a party's mark for commercial gain, which requires proof that respondent had complainant's mark "in mind" when it registered the domain name. There can be no violation of a right without knowledge of a mark's existence,[93] or proof the domain name was registered with the intention of capitalizing on the mark.[94]

When complainants do not persuade, it is not because they lack rights; it is because in the balancing of rights, complainants either do not have sufficient evidence that their marks transcend generic values, or respondents have persuasive arguments and proof that their registrations are lawful.[95]

The issue of abusive registration is reached in two stages: whether the respondent has any right or legitimate interest in using or passively holding the domain name (paragraph 4(a)(ii) of the Policy); and, if it does not whether the registration and use are in bad faith (paragraph 4(a)(iii)). The conjunctive phrasing is a holdover from the WIPO Final Report. The "purpose" for the registration must have been unlawful.[96] Two of the four paragraph 4(b) examples of bad faith incorporate the word "purpose" (paragraphs 4(b)(i) and 4(b)(iii)); registering the domain name for an "unlawful purpose" is implicit in the other two. Relative timing of domain name registration and trademark acquisition and content of the website are critical factors in deducing "purpose" in all four examples of bad faith.

The "mere fact that the previously registered disputed domain name prevents complainant from reflecting its subsequently registered trademark in a corresponding domain name does not [indeed, could not!] give rise to any inference that this was the Respondent's purpose in registering the disputed domain name."[97] Complainants may contend that "domain name dealers are cybersquatters because

---

[93] Some panelists accept the view that it is unfair for a domain name holder to withhold an inactive domain name registered prior to complainant's acquisition of its mark. This view has not gained traction, but its expression undermines predictability, further discussed below in "Consistency and Predictability" (Sec. 1.05). See ***Benoit Thiercelin v. Medicalexpo.com***, CAC 100235 (ADR.eu May 23, 2011) and ***Coffee Bean Direct LLC v. Claude Pope***, CAC 100654 (ADR.eu November 12, 2013) which rejects the view. Further discussed in "Renewal: Not Equivalent to New Registration" (Sec. 4.03-B.1).

[94] ***Sven Mark Sawatzki v. WHOIS PRIVACY PROTECTION SERVICE, INC.***, CAC 101337 (ADR.eu January 3, 2017) (<lunchmail.com>) (Domain name abandoned by earlier registrant and immediately registered by Respondent for its own account.)

[95] ***Darryl Davis Seminars, Inc. v. Privacydotlink Customer 656889 / Domain Admin, Abstract Holdings International Ltd.***, D2018-2238 (WIPO January 21, 2019) (<poweragent.com>. "[T]he Respondent has satisfied the Panel that it registered the disputed domain name for its inherent value as a domain name incorporating a common descriptive term, as part of its business as an investor in such domain names."

[96] Policy, paragraph 2. "Your Representations. ***(c) you are not registering the domain name for an unlawful purpose."

they acquire domain names without any intention of making any genuine active use of them and for no reason other than to sell them at a profit,"[98] but that "is not the definition of a cybersquatter envisaged by the Policy."[99] Although large scale domain dealing carries a risk of heightened duties of diligence in defense of challenged registrations,[100] it is not of itself an unlawful activity or "a vice at which the Policy is directed."[101] Rather, the vice is directed at registering and using domain names chosen intentionally to take advantage of a complainant's reputation as embodied by its trademark. "[M]uch turns on the Respondent's motivation for having selected the . . . Domain Name."[102]

1.03 ARCHITECTURE OF THE UDRP 1.03

1.03-A The 3-Part Structure 1.03-A

Complainant initiates an administrative proceeding by filing a complaint and annexes (which must include proof of trademark rights) with an ICANN certified Provider.[103] This package is unlike pleadings in a court of competent jurisdiction in that it performs a dual function in both giving notice of a claim and moving for relief; in this respect the submission more resembles a motion for summary

---

[97] ***Eclipse International N.V. v. Luma, Inc.***, D2009-0380 (WIPO May 22, 2009) (<luma.com>). See also ***ClearBank Limited v. Privacydotlink Customer 2450865 / Kwangpyo Kim, Mediablue Inc.***, D2018-2481 (WIPO January 15, 2019) (<clearbank.com>. "The website contained no links to Complainant but Complainant put its business name into the search field in order to fabricate evidence of a link to its business.".

[98] ***Solon AG v. eXpensiveDomains.com Project***, D2008-0881 (WIPO August 1, 2008) (<solon.net>).

[99] *Id.*

[100] Discussed further in "Enhanced Investigative Responsibilities for High-Volume Registrants" (Sec. 6.03-B).

[101] *Id.*, ***Solon AG.***

[102] ***Which? Limited v. Michael KAddo and Which? Media Group***, D2012-2210 (WIPO December 19, 2012).

[103] Rule 3(b)(xv) requires annexation of the jurisdiction document. ICANN announced on November 17, 2014 the implementation of amended rules for the UDRP, effective July 31, 2015. The updates include:

1. "Lock" and "pendency" are now defined terms in the UDRP Rules;
2. UDRP complainants no longer have to transmit a copy of the complaint to the respondent (rule 3(b)(xii));
3. Rule 4(b) requires registrars to lock the disputed domain name(s) within two (2) business days of receiving a UDRP complaint from a UDRP provider;
4. Rule 4(e) provides that when a UDRP provider informs the registrar that the UDRP proceeding has been withdrawn or dismissed, the registrar must remove the lock within one (1) business day of receiving notice;
5. Rule 5(b) provides that respondents may request an additional four (4) calendar days to respond to a complaint and UDRP providers will automatically grant the extension, if requested;

judgment, thus its drafting and content demand a greater level of attention than a litigation complaint.[104] After reviewing the complaint for compliance (which includes submitting it to the registrar for registrant verification and for locking the domain name[105]) the provider forwards it to the respondent[106] with notice that it has 20 days to respond. If the complaint is not compliant, if it names a privacy/proxy rather than beneficial owner of the domain name and the latter is disclosed by the registrar in the verification process as customarily happens, complainant is given the opportunity to cure by filing an amended complaint.[107]

The architecture of the UDRP is based on a simple three-part structure. Complainant must prove it has standing to maintain the proceedings (paragraph 4(a)(i)); that respondent lacks rights or legitimate interests in the disputed domain

---

6. Rule 16(a) provides that registrars must notify the parties, the provider and ICANN of the date for implementation of the decision within three (3) business days of receiving the decision from the provider;
7. Rule 17 outlines a new procedure to be used in cases that are settled between parties outside the UDRP case.

There are currently six Providers for UDRP: WIPO located in Geneva, Switzerland; the Forum, located in the United States; The Czech Arbitration Court Arbitration Center for Internet Disputes, located in Prague, Czechoslavkia; The Asian Dispute Resolution Centre, with offices in Hong Kong, Beijing, Seoul and Kuala Lumpur; and The Arab Center for Domain Name Dispute Resolution, located in Amman, Jordan; and the Canadian International Internet Resolution Centre.

[104] Litigation pleadings essentially provide notice of claims rather than ultimate proof that claims have merit. UDRP complaints on the other hand are not simply notices of claims but must carry proof the domain names were registered in bad faith and are being used in bad faith, thus for anything less than that the complaints will be dismissed. Whereas litigation pleadings can survive a motion to dismiss without proof, UDRP complaints cannot hence numerous decisions finding insufficiency of proof in dismissing complaints.

[105] Locking simply prevents domain names from being transferred to other registrars. The UDRP has no procedure for instantly silencing offensive websites. They will remain available for the pendency of the claim. To silence a website, the trademark owner would have to file a complaint in a court of competent jurisdiction for a preliminary injunction to take down the website.

[106] Rule 4(a) of the Rules of the Policy reads: "[If the complaint is in] compliance [the Provider] shall forward the complaint, including any annexes, electronically to the Respondent and shall send Written Notice of the complaint (together with the explanatory cover sheet prescribed by the Provider's Supplemental Rules) to the Respondent." See ***Mrs. Eva Padberg v. Eurobox Ltd.***, D2007-1886 (WIPO March 10, 2008) in which the Panel noted that "what is important here is that proceedings are brought in respect of the Domain Name and that the procedures are then followed to ensure that the person or persons who are reasonably identifiable as having an interest in that name are properly notified." Compare *in rem* jurisdiction under the ACPA for adjudicating rights to the domain name where *in personam* jurisdiction cannot be obtained. 15 U.S.C. §1125(d)(2)(A)(i) and (ii).

[107] See as a representative example ***BlankPage AG v. Waleed Altywaijri***, D2012-2189 (WIPO November 11, 2012) (<keetab.com>) in which Provider pointed out deficiencies Complainant failed to cure in its amended complaint. Where the domain name holder as listed on the Whois directory

name (paragraph 4(a)(ii)); and that respondent registered and is using the domain name in bad faith (paragraph 4(a)(iii)).

Paragraph 4(b) provides four broadly worded, nonexclusive circumstances that support a finding of bad faith. Paragraph 4(c) provides a trio of nonexclusive circumstances that support a respondent's right or legitimate interest.[108] Complainant has the overall burden of proving its case.[109]

The first and second limbs of complainant's burden, respectively paragraphs 4(a)(i) and (ii) of the Policy, can be satisfied on an either/or basis: 1) the domain name is either identical or confusingly similar to a trademark in which complainant has a right [paragraph 4(a)(i)]; and 2) respondent either has a right or legitimate interest in the disputed domain name or it does not [paragraph 4(a)(ii)].

Paragraph 4(a)(ii) is a fulcrum for both parties. It is not presumed respondent lacks rights or legitimate interests in the domain name. To satisfy its burden complainant must, first, make a *prima facie* showing that respondent lacks rights or legitimate interests in the domain name. If complainant succeeds the burden shifts to respondent to rebut the *prima facie* case. If respondent demonstrates it has a right or legitimate interest in the domain name it will prevail, as complainant will have failed to prove an essential element in its case. But if respondent fails to rebut the *prima facie* case, complainant has prevailed on that issue and then, but only then, will the Panel proceed to examine the question of bad faith. Complainant satisfies the third requirement by proving respondent both registered and is using the domain name in bad faith [paragraph 4(a)(iii)].[110]

Unlike the procedure in a court of competent jurisdiction, a respondent's default in appearance is not an admission of any material allegation of the complaint. Complainant's burden is independent of respondent's appearance.[111] It must prove each element to support cancellation or transfer of a domain name[112] "via

---

is a proxy for the beneficial owner of the domain name the Provider typically invites complainant to file an amendment to its complaint. Discussed further in "Use and Abuse of Proxy and Privacy Services" (Sec. 2.04). Also review the impact of the General Data Protection Regulation Sec. 2.05-B.

108 The burdens of persuasion and production are discussed further in "Prosecuting a UDRP Complaint and Defending Rights or Legitimate Interests in Disputed Domain Name" (Sec. 7.04-A).

109 If it prevails it has a choice of remedies, either cancellation or transfer of the registration to its account. Cancellation simply returns a domain name to the public domain after its registration expires, thereby permitting any entity including a prior respondent-registrant to then register the name.

110 "One of [complainant's] arguments, that the failure to provide a response results in a default judgment (as would occur in civil litigation in the United States or Canada), is mistaken as a matter of Policy precedent. Failure to respond in a Policy proceeding does not of itself constitute an admission of any pleaded matter or result in the Policy equivalent of the default judgment," ***DNA (Housemarks) Limited v. Tucows.com Co.***, D2009-0367 (WIPO May 5, 2009).

111 Discussed further in "Conflicting Rights Favor Respondent" (Sec. 4.02-A.1.b).

112 Discussed further in "No Record, No Case" (Sec. 7.04-B).

competent evidence, not by conjecture or innuendo."[113] Ultimately, a complainant prevails on its claim only if it is able to prove respondent both registered and is using the disputed domain name in bad faith.[114]

1.03-B

1.03-B Complainant's Burden to Prove Its Case

A trademark owner has standing to commence a UDRP proceeding if the alleged offending domain name is identical or confusingly similar to an existing registered or unregistered trademark regardless of its temporal or geographical acquisition, although the timing of acquisition relative to date of domain name registration factors into the issue of bad faith. However, trademark ownership alone carries with it no presumption of right to the corresponding domain name. Paragraph 4(a)(i) sets a low bar for a trademark right. The "requirement can be satisfied by proof that complainant is the owner or licensee of a registered mark anywhere in the world—not just in the country of the Respondent's residence."[115] A certificate of registration or license agreement suffices as proof. However, unless the mark has priority, complainant could have standing but no actionable claim for cybersquatting.[116]

The bar is significantly higher for unregistered trademarks. A complainant alleging common law protection or its equivalent in civil law jurisdictions must offer documentary evidence that it had the claimed right prior to domain name registration; otherwise it lacks standing.[117] Complainant's failure to offer evidence within its custody and control justifies a negative inference of the right it alleges it had at the earlier time.[118] If complainant fails to prove any registered or unregistered right, the second level domain (SLD) is neither identical nor confusingly similar

---

[113] ***AOL LLC v. Joe DiMarco.***, FA0907001275978 (Forum September 9, 2009).

[114] Compare ACPA's disjunctive model. UDRP's conjunctive model is friendlier to respondents than the ACPA. The ACPA is satisfied by proof that respondent either "registers, traffics in, or uses a domain name" in bad faith, 15 U.S.C. 1125(d)(1)(A) (ii).

[115] That complainant's trademark registration is in a different country than respondent's residence is not a complete defense, particularly with strong marks. ***WalMart Stores, Inc. v. Stork***, D2000-0628 (WIPO August, 2000) (Complainant has rights to the name when the mark is registered in a country even if the complainant has never traded in that country); ***Advanced Magazine Publishers Inc. v. Computer Dazhong***, D2003-0668 (WIPO December 12, 2003); ***WilliamsSonoma, Inc. v. Fees***, FA 937704 (Forum April 5, 2007) (It is irrelevant whether the complainant has registered its trademark in the country of the respondent's residence).

[116] Cybersquatting presupposes knowledge of the mark and an intention to take advantage of it. Neither knowledge nor intention can be inferred if the mark postdates the registration of the domain name.

[117] Discussed further in "Distinctiveness of Unregistered Trademark Not Presumed" (Sec. 4.01-B.2.a)

[118] Registration of a mark by a complainant is typically presumptive evidence that the complainant has trademark or service mark rights, but unless a State examines marks for distinctiveness they

to the trademark, or there is insufficient proof under common law principles, the complaint must be dismissed.

Paragraph 4(a)(ii) sets a medium bar. Complainant's burden is said to be "relatively light."[119] This is because "such information [of definitive proof] is known to and within the control of the respondent."[120] Panelists early established a shifting burden rule. Complainant is required to make a *prima facie* case that respondent lacks rights or legitimate interests in the domain name, which if successful shifts the burden to respondent to produce evidence to the contrary.[121] The procedure is not prescribed in the Policy or Rules, but is a well-established principle of the law of evidence that gives to each party the opportunity to present its case and rebut its adversary's.[122]

Where there is uncertainty between conflicting allegations, insufficiency of evidence is a basis for a finding against the party with the burden of proof or production.[123] If respondent remains silent and the *prima facie* case establishes respondent lacks rights or legitimate interests it is conclusive against it on that issue,[124] "It is generally agreed that "[t]he absence of good faith [that is, failing to rebut complainant's assertions and proof] does not constitute bad faith,"[125] and although lacking rights or legitimate interests without more is not evidence of bad faith, it remains a factor in determining abusive registration. Proof of bad faith is an independent and successive inquiry. To the extent that facts are verified, so much the better, and more likely to persuade.

---

are not accorded the customary presumption. ***Fred T. Elsberry, Jr. v. Mechanic's Responds News Publication***, D2012-1295 (WIPO July 31, 2012). Presumption is discussed further in "Principal Register: Presumption of Validity" (Sec. 4.01-A.3.b).

119 ***Educational Testing Service v. Netkorea Co.***, D2000-0087 (WIPO April, 2000).

120 The "light" standard is explained by the relative difficulty of marshaling evidence "uniquely within [the respondent's] . . . knowledge and control," ***G.D. Searle v. Martin Mktg.***, FA 118277 (Forum Oct. 1, 2002).

121 The "prima facie" approach ameliorating complainant's burden under paragraph 4(a)(ii) by shifting to a respondent the burden of demonstrating that it has rights or legitimate interests under paragraph 4(c)(i-iii) entered the UDRP vocabulary tentatively in April 2000 in two cases by the same panelist [D2000-0096 and 0120]. It took several more months to solidify as a rule in the decision process [D2000-0252, 0270, 0374, 0624].

122 ***Intocast AG v. Lee Daeyoon***, D2000-1467 (WIPO January 17, 2001) ("Many legal systems . . . rely on the principle negativa non sunt probanda. If a rule contains a negative element it is generally understood to be sufficient that the complainant, by asserting that the negative element is not given, provides prima facie evidence for this negative fact. The burden of proof then shifts to the respondent to rebut the complainant's assertion.")

123 ***Percy Miller dba Boutit, Inc./Soldier University, Inc.v. Divine Mafa dba The New No Limit Records, Inc.***, FA0207000114771 (Forum September 19, 2002).

124 ***Western Research 3000, Inc. v. NEP Products, Inc.***, D2004-0755 (WIPO November 5, 2004)

125 ***Enrique Bernat F., SA v. Marrodan***, D2000-0966 (WIPO October 4, 2000) ("There is no obligation whatsoever on the Respondent to prove good faith, and in any event it is equally important

1.03-C 1.03-C Respondent's Rebuttal Burden

The burden shift demands respondent produce evidence that its registration of the domain name was lawful, by rebutting complainant's claim that it lacks rights or legitimate interests in the domain name. The rebuttal burden pairs paragraph 4(a)(ii) with paragraph 4(c) and its three subdivisions (the safe harbor defenses discussed more fully in Chapter 5). These comprise three nonexclusive circumstances of lawful registration of the domain name [paragraph 4(c)(i-iii)]:

> i. [B]efore any notice to you of the dispute, your use of, or demonstrable preparations to use, the domain name or a name corresponding to the domain name in connection with a bona fide offering of goods or services.
> ii. [Y]ou (as an individual, business, or other organization) have been commonly known by the domain name, even if you have acquired no trademark or service mark rights.
> iii. [Y]ou are making a legitimate noncommercial or fair use of the domain name, without intent for commercial gain to misleadingly divert consumers or to tarnish the trademark or service mark at issue.

Subparagraphs 4(c)(i) and (iii) are use based defenses. Subparagraph (c)(i) looks at past legitimate activity ("before any notice") and present legitimate use ("you are making"), while subparagraph (c)(iii) looks at uses that are noncommercial or fair (commentary and criticism come under this head). Non-use is inconsistent with either, although factual circumstances may justify a reprieve.[126] Monetizing web sites qualify as bona fide offerings under paragraph 4(c)(i) but they cannot qualify under (c)(iii) (or any unenumerated circumstances).

Proof (regardless of its source[127]) that a respondent has rights or legitimate interests in the domain name rebuts complainant's assertion and concludes the proceedings in respondent's favor. Respondent's failure to offer evidence within its

---

to note that the absence of good faith does not constitute bad faith. The two concepts are not related in such a direct fashion.")

[126] See for example, ***Apple Computer, Inc. v. DomainHouse.com, Inc.***, D2000-0341 (WIPO July 5, 2000) ("a delay in using a domain name for a legitimate noncommercial or fair use purpose in response to a cease and desist demand might be justified," although not justified in this particular case); same Panel found no justification in ***Helen Fielding v. Anthony Corbert aka Anthony Corbett***, D2000-1000 (WIPO May 28, 2000) but went slightly further in recognizing the possibility: "there are contexts in which the registrant of a domain name should not be expected to make immediate use of that name, including for legitimate noncommercial or fair use purposes." In ***Pfizer Inc v. Van Robichaux***, D2003-0399 (WIPO July 16, 2003) (LIPITOR and <lipitor info.com> same Panel found justification).

[127] The reason for this qualification is that complainant's submission may contain evidence that the respondent has rights or legitimate interests, where for example complainant includes screenshots that support good faith use of a domain name composed of common words or descriptive phrases. Discussed further in "Researching the Past: Historical Screenshots from The Wayback Machine" (Sec. 7.04-A.3.ii).

control justifies a negative inference of its right or legitimate interest under Rule 14 of the Rules of the Policy but is not otherwise determinative that its registration was abusive, which complainant must independently prove.

1.03-D Complainant's Burden to Prove Bad Faith in the Conjunctive 1.03-D

Domain names may be identical or confusingly similar to trademarks; and respondents may lack rights or legitimate interests yet retain their domain names on insufficient proof of bad faith registration and bad faith use. This results because the UDRP is a "conjunctive" regime. It is an "and" model rather than an "or" model. This distinguishes it from the ACPA and country code dispute resolution policies separately administered by self-regulated authorities in a number of countries[128].

In order to prevail complainant must prove respondent both registered the disputed domain name in bad faith and is using it in bad faith.[129] Under "disjunctive" regimes respondent may forfeit the domain name if it either registered *or* is found to be using it in bad faith. The UDRP, however, sets a higher bar. Proof of bad faith is an independent and successive inquiry to rights or legitimate interests. It is not an abusive registration to hold a domain name identical or confusingly similar to complainant's trademark which was lawfully registered.[130]

In the same way that paragraph 4(a)(ii) is paired with paragraph 4(c) and its subdivisions for the purpose of assessing the evidence that respondent has or has not a right or legitimate interest, paragraph 4(a)(iii) is paired with paragraph 4(b) and its subdivisions. Subparagraphs 4(b)(i) through (iv) provide in counterpoint to 4(c)(i) through (iii) four nonexclusive "circumstances" of bad faith. By their terms, the circumstances are expressly not intended to cover the universe of possibilities.[131] They are:

> i. [C]ircumstances indicating that you have registered or you have acquired the domain name primarily for the purpose of selling, renting, or otherwise transferring the domain name registration to complainant who is the owner of the trademark or service mark or to a competitor of that Complainant, for valuable consideration in excess of your documented out-of-pocket costs directly related to the domain name.

---

[128] See Appendix C for summary of country code Dispute Resolution Policies.

[129] "The consensus view is that there must be bad faith both at the time of registration and subsequently," ***Mile, Inc. v. Michael Burg***, D2010-2011 (WIPO February 7, 2011) (<lionsden.com>).

[130] ***Modefine S.A. v. A.R. Mani***, D2001-0537 (WIPO July 20, 2001) (ARMANI and <armani.com> spelling out Respondent's name for personal use. It is improper to import into the "test for legitimate interest an element of confusion or bad faith.")

[131] ***Home Interiors & Gifts, Inc. v. Home Interiors***, D2000-0010 (WIPO Mar. 7, 2000) ("[J]ust because Respondent's conduct does not fall within the 'particular' circumstances set out in [paragraph 4(b) of the Policy], does not mean that the domain names at issue were not registered in and are not being used in bad faith.")

ii. [Y]ou have registered the domain name in order to prevent the owner of the trademark or service mark from reflecting the mark in a corresponding domain name, provided that you have engaged in a pattern of such conduct.
iii. [Y]ou have registered the domain name primarily for the purpose of disrupting the business of a competitor.
iv. [B]y using the domain name, you have intentionally attempted to attract, for commercial gain, Internet users to your web site or other on-line location, by creating a likelihood of confusion with complainant's mark as to the source, sponsorship, affiliation, or endorsement of your web site or location or of a product or service on your web site or location.

If any of these circumstances is found "to be present . . . [it] shall be evidence of the registration and use of a domain name in bad faith."[132] Paragraphs (i), (ii), and (iii) refer to registration, while subparagraph (iv) refers to use. Some evidence is not conclusive evidence, but the offer must be sufficiently concrete to be able to draw reasonable inferences of respondent's intentions.

The reason for the caution is that the UDRP does not condemn selling domain names to the highest bidder, preventing trademark owners from reflecting their marks in corresponding domain names, competing in the open market with the trademark owner, or creating a likelihood of confusion *unless from the outset it is coupled with the intention to take advantage of complainant and its trademark.* It is complainant's burden to prove its case, not respondent's to disprove the claim.

If the circumstances do not support bad faith the complaint must be dismissed. Thus, where complainant's trademark did not exist before the registration of the domain name or did exist but respondent creditably claims it had no knowledge of the trademark and is using the second level domain in its semantic sense, then inferentially the registration could not have been made in bad faith. Indeed, by initiating a proceeding under these circumstances complainant exposes itself to a finding of reverse domain name hijacking, a concept that is discussed further in Chapter 7 at section 7.11.

---

[132] Paragraph 4(b) of the Policy. See ***Trade Me Limited v. Vertical Axis Inc***, D2009-0093 (WIPO April 7, 2009) (<trademe.com>. "What makes paragraph 4(b) important in so many cases is that subparagraph 4(b)(iv) addresses only current use by a respondent yet, where non bona fide current use is proven, that conduct is deemed to be evidence of bad faith use and bad faith registration. Absent evidence of good faith registration, this deemed evidence can be pivotal to many cases.")

1.04 JURISPRUDENCE OF THE UDRP 1.04

1.04-A Emergence and Consolidation of Domain Name Jurisprudence 1.04-A

1.04-A.1 Minimalist Policy and Rules 1.04-A.1

It is particularly appropriate in considering domain name law to keep in mind that it did not spring fully formed upon ICANN's implementation of the UDRP. ICANN took from the WIPO Final Report a framework for the arbitral regime which it transformed into sets of "minimalist" (ICANN's word) prescriptions as the Policy and Rules, anticipating as did WIPO that decision making under the proposed arbitral regime "should lead to the construction of a body of consistent principles that may provide guidance for the future."[133]

That prospect of "guidance for the future" which is the ultimate goal of all lawful process is precisely what has come about. That the UDRP is only lightly prescriptive and in other parts open-ended encourages Panels to engage with its language. They began immediately interpreting and construing the separate elements of the limbs for a foundational jurisprudence which has grown and consolidated in such a way as to have achieved an independent existence from the Policy and Rules. In essence, the jurisprudence has superseded the basic text by encrusting it with interpretation and construction. What this means is that a simple reading of the Policy and Rules will not by itself enlighten a party about the law or its evidentiary demands; they or their representatives must have a working knowledge of the jurisprudence." When complainants do not they will be reprimanded and likely sanctioned.

This development of a jurisprudence resulted from a convergence of a number of factors, but four in particular: language in the WIPO consensus that insists on the conjunctive model for the regime ("and" rather than "or"); a concept ICANN adopted from the Final Report empowering panelists to apply "any rules and principles of law [they] deem[ ] applicable"[134] (the invitation opened space for panelists to respond to a wide range of factual circumstances and legal issues[135]); the commodification of

---

133 · WIPO Final Report, paragraph 149(v). Paragraph 4(j) of the Policy mandates that "All decisions under this Policy will be published in full over the Internet . . . ." Each provider maintains its own database of decisions. A consolidated database is available at <www.udrpsearch.com>.

134 Paragraph 15(a) of the Rules of the Policy reads "[the] Panel shall decide a complaint on the basis of the statements and documents submitted and in accordance with the Policy, these Rules and any rules and principles of law that it deems applicable." The Final Report recommended that "in applying the definition of abusive registration, the panel of decision-makers shall, to the extent necessary, apply the law or rules of law that it determines to be appropriate in view of all the circumstances of the case." Paragraph 177(ii).

135 The Ur-Rules are set forth in Annex V to the WIPO Final Report. Article 31 states only that "[t]he Panel shall determine the Complaint in accordance with the Policy."

dictionary words (alone or combined), random letters that could be acronyms, and common expressions, in essence privatizing them (which fueled the emergence and consolidation of a secondary market for the buying and selling of domain names; and a cadre of neutral panelists trained in the law and determined to apply the rules of evidence evenly.

A "body of consistent principles" began emerging quickly as Panels grappled with the difficult task of balancing rights and insisting on complainants proving their claims.[136] As discussed in the next section, WIPO declares in its Overview and Panels pay lip service to the proposition that "previous decisions are not binding" while at the same time "striving for consistency in the application of the Policy" which essentially means acknowledging authority which the WIPO Overview encourages even though it prefers using the term consensus rather than precedent.

Not unexpectedly, the direction of the jurisprudence has provoked protest from both sides of the caption, that it either goes too far in protecting mark owners or not far enough in protecting domain name investors operating within the secondary market. This raises the issue of Panel bias. It has been pointed out that providers' rosters of neutrals are principally drawn from the ranks of attorneys representing trademark owners. This gives rise to a concern that panelists whose interests are aligned with trademark clients may (in close cases) favor complainants. In response to the concern providers' managers respond that rosters are best filled by panelists who have rich backgrounds in intellectual property, are knowledgeable in trademark and business law, and experienced in weighing evidence. Providers rely of their neutrals' professionalism to decline appointments for perceived conflicts of interest. Some instances of overt bias have been noted; unconscious bias is less easy to identify but some decisions are suspect and others have been dealt with in ACPA actions.

It can be offered as a general proposition that a jurisprudence is an antidote to bias. There is, in fact, a substantial body of law, not merely "a wilderness of single instances" (as Neil Brown puts it in his Foreword to this book), that establishes the metes and bounds of parties' rights. Claims are decided according to legal standards capable of producing a high level of consistency. While questionable decisions can certainly be cited—panelists either misapplying the standards or attempting to create new law---they have failed to corrupt or redirect the jurisprudence to the point where it can be said that it favors one party over the other.

Complaints succeed if their proof supports their contentions; respondents succeed if they either prove their affirmative defenses or (as a matter of law and facts) there can be no finding of bad faith. As is usual in the development of a jurisprudence,

---

136 Rule 10(b) of the Rules of the UDRP provides that each party have "a fair opportunity to present its case."

core principles are examined and refined by later Panels for use as raw material in formulating or adapting principles for application to novel matrices of fact.

1.04-A.2 Sources of UDRP Law 1.04-A.2

In crafting their decisions panelists draw inspiration from a variety of sources including the Final and Second WIPO reports—the "closest equivalent to a legislative history for the Policy"[137]—national trademark and unfair competition laws, legal decisions, common law principles and scholarly writings, and earlier UDRP decisions. All have strongly influenced the creation a non-legislated jurisprudence of cybersquatting. The process resembles the development judge-made law in common law jurisdictions by advancing the jurisprudence through deliberative conversations and reasoned decisions that alembic-like refine the principles that control and the factors panelists' apply in their decision making.

The result has been a gradual buildup of precedent[138] and adherence to consensus.[139] Judicial decisions have long been recognized as a source of law; no less it is with UDRP decisions. Looking back to early decisions it can be seen that panelists quickly established the Policy's core principles and the factorial tools for assessing lawful and unlawful registrations. From the start respondent defaults significantly outnumbered appearances. The first docketed case in 1999 established as a core principle that complainant could not prevail absent proof that respondent both registered and was using the domain name in bad faith.[140] It affirmed the UDRP is *sui generis* as a conjunctive as opposed to the disjunctive model the U.S. Congress created for the ACPA.

---

137 ***Broadcom Corporation v. Michael Becker***, FA0108000098819 (Forum October 21, 2001).

138 ***'NPick Enterprises, Inc. v. Domains by Proxy, LLC, DomainsByProxy.com / Woman to Woman Healthcare / Just Us Women Health Center f/k/a Woman to Woman Health Center***, D2012-1555 (WIPO September 22, 2012) ("[t]he Policy has been in force for more than a decade and the thousands of cases decided under it now constitute a workable body of (to use a legal term) precedent. In my opinion any complainant, and even more so any professional representative of a complainant, should be at least minimally versed in the Policy, the Rules, their scope, and their limits. It is no excuse that a party or its representative is unfamiliar with clear Policy precedent, much less the clear language of the Policy and the Rules themselves . . . .")

139 WIPO publishes a "restatement" of domain name law on its website under the title The WIPO Overview of WIPO Panel Views on Selected UDRP Questions. It released 3.0 in May 2017. Unless otherwise noted, citations will be to the Third Edition and referred to as the Jurisprudential Overview 3.0." At Paragraph 4.1 the Overview states the consensus view that "[t]he UDRP does not operate on a strict doctrine of precedent." In actuality, Panels invariably invoke precedent in their opinions for the reasons noted in the Overview, that it "ensures that the UDRP system operates in a fair, effective and predictable manner for all parties, while responding to the continuing evolution of the domain name system." There is no publication comparable to the Overview by the Forum, formerly known as the National Arbitration Forum.

140 ***World Wrestling Federation Entertainment, Inc. v. Michael Bosman***, D1999-0001 (WIPO January 14, 2000) construing paragraph 4(a)(iii) of the Policy. However, the Panel later recanted

The first three cases were uncontested (fourth case terminated before decision). Respondents appeared in the fifth and sixth cases (0005 and 0006 of 2000). They denied the material allegations and prevailed on their affirmative defenses. The decisions established that respondents had legitimate interests in domain names registered prior to complainants acquiring marks (0005); and acquiescently registered and used for selling complainants' goods (0006). Both respondents could be described as operating small businesses (investor and distributor).

Other decisions defined the metes and bounds of good and bad faith for actively used or passively held domain names (0003). Still others defined good and bad faith use of domain names composed of dictionary words (0016) or phrases descriptive of products or services offered by respondent (0096). Of the first 100 cases filed with WIPO in 2000 that went to decision complainants prevailed in 85 of them. That percentage has fluctuated over the years between eighty-five and ninety-two percent with Panels striving to distinguish actionable conduct and the associated factors for good and bad faith registration and use. In so doing, an argument can be made that in creatively shaping the jurisprudence panelists broadened it beyond the scope of the Policy as originally conceived.[141]

Three examples will put this observation into perspective. First, under paragraph 4(a)(i) of the Policy complainants are not denied standing for lack of trademark registration. The term "trademark" is defined broadly to include indicators of source whether registered or unregistered. Second, under paragraph 4(a)(ii) the burden shifts to respondent to rebut complainant's *prima facie* case that respondent lacks any right or legitimate interest in the disputed domain name.

While defaulting respondents are rarely found to have any right or legitimate interest (assuming complainants prevail on their *prima facie* proof), they do not automatically forfeit domain names for that reason alone.[142] This brings up the

---

this view and in his dissent in ***Guru Denim Inc. v. Ibrahim Ali Ibrahim abu-Harb***, D2013-1324 (WIPO September 27, 2013) explained that: "It would be much easier for this panelist to maintain that his original decision [approving the binary concept] was correct, and not recant. But in view of the evidence [of the correctness of the unitary view], I am unable to do so." This tussle over binary vs. unitary is an example of the deliberative conversations mentioned above. Nevertheless, the consensus of opinion remains in favor of the binary concept. The underlying case law and assertive rejection of the unitary view is discussed further in "Justifying Forfeiture Despite Good Faith Registration" (Sec. 4.03-A.4.b).

141 The perceived broadening of the Policy is not to every panelist's liking. The dissenting panelist in ***Ha'aretz Daily Newspaper Ltd. v. United Websites, Ltd.***, D2002-0272 (WIPO August 21, 2002) stated that the majority has "decided to treat the UDRP as a kind of eminent domain, which gives important trademark holders the right to take others' property *regardless of whether registrants have actually contravened the Policy*" (emphasis added).

142 "It is possible for a respondent to be infringing the trademark rights of a complainant, yet be found not to have acted in bad faith," ***Ni Insan Kaynaklari Personel ve Danismanlik Limited Sti v. Timothy Michael Bright***, D2009-0315 (WIPO May 7, 2009). Respondent can be found to be using

third example: a loosening of the Policy's scope. Two developments illustrate this shift of view. First, an acceptance of nominative fair use as a defense either under paragraph 4(c)(iii) of the Policy—commercial, but fair use—or a non-enumerated circumstance.[143] Second, privity relationships between parties known to one another (partners, former employees, and counter parties to contracts—vendors, designers, etc.—that were initially regarded as outside the scope because the claims were ostensibly for breaches of contract or fiduciary duty were brought within.[144] There have also been some attempts to expand the scope that have failed to gain acceptance, of which the most notable example is an attempt to construe paragraph 4(a)(iii) as allowing bad faith disjunctively if the wrongful conduct is found under 4(b)(iv) of the Policy.[145]

In enumerating a few examples of decisions that led to a broadening of scope it is not intended to suggest they encompass all. As one panelist put it, "the [e]volution of panel thinking in response to new developments in the domain name system is no doubt something, which should be encouraged,"[146] although in the particular case from which this quotation is taken the Panel also stated that not all new constructions of the Policy offer "attractive answers."[147] It is possible that a respondent's choice of a domain name—identical or confusingly similar to a trademark though it may be—is legitimized by the timing of its registration. The Policy cannot be used "to prevent uses [or upset ownership of domain names] that ICANN deemed to be legitimate, including the use of domain names in connection with the bona fide offering of goods and services."[148]

1.04-B Construing Basic Principles 1.04-B

1.04-B.1 Deliberative Conversations 1.04-B.1

As suggested above UDRP jurisprudence has developed incrementally in the common law tradition. It is Panel-made law incubated by deliberative conversations among actors in the administrative proceedings and rests on published, reasoned

---

the domain name in bad faith but to have registered it lawfully. Discussed further in "Good Faith Not Vitiated by Change of Use" (Sec. 4.03-A.4.a).

143 Paragraph 4(c)(iii) reads "legitimate noncommercial *or* fair use" (emphasis added). Nominative fair use is discussed further in "Non-Authorized But Lawful Use of Trademarks" (Sec. 5.01-C.2). Although the "fair use" element of Paragraph 4(c)(iii) is more generally associated with free speech it has a wider reach.

144 Discussed further in "Disputes Within the Scope of the Policy" (Sec. 3.03).

145 Discussed further in "Justifying Forfeiture Despite Good Faith Registration" (Sec. 4.03-A.4.b).

146 ***Torus Insurance Holdings Limited v. Torus Computer Resources***, D2009-1455 (WIPO January 10, 2010).

147 This was said in the context of a new construction of the Policy proposed in 2009 for determining whether bad faith use alone is sufficient to find bad faith registration. The issue is discussed further in "Justifying Forfeiture Despite Good Faith Registration" (Sec. 4.03-A.4.b).

decisions. Precedent is respected even as the jurisprudence accommodates some diversity of views. This accommodation comes about because there is no formal appellate authority built into the UDRP to dictate harmony, although the absence of authority is compensated by the right under paragraph 4(k) of the Policy to challenge truly aberrational (or thought to be) awards in courts of competent jurisdiction as already noted and discussed further in Chapter 8.

The developmental process in shaping the jurisprudence is illustrated in the construction of the "rights" element in paragraph 4(a)(i) of the Policy. Initially, this posed a temporal question: does the complainant have standing to maintain a proceeding where its asserted right postdates registration of the domain name? Although not the dispositive issue in the below cited case and offered as dictum, the Presiding panelist thought it important to set forth the Panel's disparate views:[149]

> Whilst the Panel agree that this issue is not necessary to its Decision, given its view on complainant's failure to satisfy the third element of paragraph 4(a) of the Policy, they disagree as to when trademark rights must exist for the requirements of paragraph 4 (a)(i) of the Policy. The Presiding Panelist and Panelist Chrocziel believe that such trademark rights must be in existence at the time the domain name is registered, i.e. here March 6, 2000. Panelist Creel believes that such trademark rights need only exist at the time of the Complaint.

A consensus quickly formed rejecting the view of the Presiding Panelist. To have standing, a trademark right need only exist at the time of the complaint. While a right acquired after domain name registration does not negate standing it will be impossible for complainant to prove registration in bad faith, leading to an anomaly earlier noted that complainant can have standing but no actionable claim.[150]

In another case, the majority granted Complainant's request for transfer of a dictionary word trademark on the theory that Respondent was "a speculator who

---

[148] Complainant in ***The American Automobile Association, Inc. v. QTK Internet c/o James M. van Johns***, FA0905001261364 (Forum July 25, 2009) (<aaa.net>) contended that "pay per click advertising site[s] cannot give rise to a legitimate claim to a domain name" but Panels have declined the invitation "to find [them] per se illegitimate." Whether advertising is a bona fide offering of goods or services turns on whether respondent is piggybacking on complainant's mark by offering advertisements that confuse Internet users for commercial gain. Discussed further under Paragraph 4(c)(i) of the Policy.

[149] ***Firstgate Internet A.G. v. David Soung***, D2000-1311 (WIPO January 29, 2001).

[150] Complainants whose rights postdate registration of domain names have no actionable claim even though they have standing. See WIPO Final Report paragraph 80. "***The availability of the date of registration is useful as a means of protecting the interests of both the domain name holder and any third party that considers its rights to have been violated. For example, the date of the registration of a domain name may indicate that the domain name holder has established use of a name before any corresponding use or registration of that name as a trademark by a third party." Discussed further in "Timing of Trademark Acquisition Not a Factor in Determining Standing" (Sec. 4.01-F).

registers domain names in the hopes that others will seek to buy or license the domain names from it."[151] That view, however, failed to persuade other panelists and has not prevailed. Speculation is not condemned under the Policy unless there is proof of abusive registration.[152]

It is now accepted that dictionary words chosen without intention to take advantage of trademarks, consistent with their semantic meanings or capable of having other associations than with a mark owner, are not violations of owners' rights. The majority's decision in ***Crew*** to transfer <crew.com> on the theory that speculation favored Complainant failed to gain traction.[153] Panelists in later decisions agreed with the dissent in concluding that speculation is not grounds for forfeiture. Dictionary words used as domain names can create their own associations unrelated to owners' marks. "In my judgment," (the dissent said)

> the majority's decision prohibits conduct which was not intended to be regulated by the ICANN Policy. This creates a dangerous and unauthorized situation whereby the registration and use of common generic words as domains can be prevented by trademark owners wishing to own their generic trademarks in gross. I cannot and will not agree to any such decision, which is fundamentally wrong.

It can be argued that acceptance of the majority opinion would have cut off the oxygen needed for a healthy Internet marketplace. The developing consensus took the position that "the acquisition and offering for sale of domain names and/or using them to provide links to other sites may well (provided it is not directed at trademark misuse in breach of the Policy) be a legitimate business."[154] Absent

---

[151] ***J. Crew International, Inc. v. crew.com***, D2000-0054 (WIPO April 20, 2000) (<crew.com>); ***Hearst Communications, Inc. and Hearst Magazines Property, Inc. v. David Spencer d/b/a Spencer Associates, and Mail.com, Inc.***, FA0093763 (Forum April 13, 2000).

[152] See (for example) ***Whispering Smith Limited v. Domain Administrator, Tfourh, LLC***, D2016-1175 (WIPO September 27, 2016) (<bravesoul.com>. "Respondent was engaged in legitimate speculation and the Complainant can only fault itself for not contacting the Respondent prior to adopting its brand.") Speculating on an anticipated event and right was found acceptable in ***Union des associations europeennes de football (UEFA) v. Chris Hallam***, D2001-0717 (WIPO July 10, 2001) (<uefa2004.com>) but subsequently rejected by other panelists. Compare, ***MADRID 2012, S.A. v. Scott Martin-MadridMan Websites***, D2003-0598 (WIPO October 8, 2003). Commenting on ***UEFA***, the Panel in ***Pacific 10 Conference v. Kevin Lee***, D2011-0200 (WIPO May 17, 2011) noted that "[l]ater panels are not bound by the decisions of earlier panels . . . [where they] consider[ ] that the approach set out [in later cases] more accurately reflects the purpose and intent of this requirement under the Policy."

[153] The majority view in ***Crew*** is reawakened in a line of cases stemming from ***Octogen Pharmacal Company, Inc. v. Domains By Proxy, Inc. / Rich Sanders and Octogen e Solutions***, D2009-0786 (WIPO August 19, 2009). Discussed further in "Justifying Forfeiture Despite Good Faith Registration" (Sec. 4.03-A.4.b).

[154] ***Pantaloon Retail India Limited v. RareNames, WebReg***, D2010-0587 (WIPO June 21, 2010). "Whether [the consensus in holding that a respondent in the domain name business] is justified may

evidence that respondent in registering a generic term intended to profit from its value as a trademark, the registration cannot be considered abusive. The term "crew" is no more exclusively associated with the clothier of that name than is "noble" with Barnes & Noble booksellers.[155]

Not all decisions, however, contribute equally to the development of domain name jurisprudence. In a significant number of disputes respondents have no defense to bad faith and rarely appear. Submissions in undefended cases in which complainant has marshaled sufficient proof contribute less because they lack "the advantage of a sustained argument that [brings] out the real issues for decision."[156] Contested cases and cases in which complainants fail to marshal sufficient evidence or the claims are rebutted[157] offer the most insight and contribute the most in reinforcing the evolving principles because of the sustained arguments.

Taken as a whole and despite differences of view on some legal principles, panelists have developed a body of law that for the most part inarguably delivers sound judgment on claims of abusive registration. In the words of one panelist "[t]he Policy has been in force for more than a decade and the thousands of cases decided under it now constitute a workable body of (to use a legal term) precedent."[158] The sum of all this precedent (even if not fully documented) is gathered in the previously mentioned Jurisprudential Overview 3.0.

1.04-B.2

1.04-B.2 Core Precedential Principles

Precedent (or "consensus" as WIPO terms it since there is no "strict doctrine of binding precedent") is generally thought of as having become established by a higher authority from a chorus of conflicting views from lower courts, but where there is no appellate authority (as there is not with the UDRP) core principles have to be discovered through deliberative conversations until accepted by consensus or recognized as precedent. This is not to suggest that domain name jurisprudence

---

be a matter for debate, but in the opinion of the Panel there is a strong body of precedent which, though not binding, is strongly persuasive."

155 ***Barnesandnoble.com, LLC v. Rosenblum, FA*** 1089020 (Forum November 15, 2007). See also, ***National Grid Electricity Transmission Plc, NGrid Intellectual Property Limited v. Re Tron Technologies***, D2013-0925 (WIPO July 11, 2013) (NATIONAL GRID and <my gridpower.com and <mygridstore.com>. The domain names "incorporate only the 'grid' element of the Complainant's trademarks. . . . The term 'grid' (on its own) is a generic, non distinctive term, which is not associated exclusively with the Complainant's business.")

156 ***Churchill Insurance Co. Ltd. v. Churchhill Financial Services, Ltd.***, FA0906001270466 (Forum September 1, 2009) (three member Panel denying complaint).

157 Complaints are dismissed or denied in approximately 9% of cases for one of three reasons: complainants have no actionable claim; respondents have rights or legitimate interests; or complainants fail to prove conjunctive bad faith.

158 ***Credit Europe Bank N.V. v. Peter Yu***, D2010-0737 (WIPO July 14, 2010).

is spun out of whole cloth. It has legal heritage conceptually related to trademark law, which is evident in its protective purpose; but there is an important difference: cybersquatting is a lower included tort under trademark law, which means there are different standards of proof, hence different sets of evidentiary demands that separate cybersquatting from trademark infringement.

The WIPO Final Report envisioned that panelists would draw on "case law which has developed in the application of national laws for the protection of trademarks and service marks and for protection against unfair competition."[159] These cases "support[] the prohibition of the predatory and parasitical practices that would be caught under the definition of abusive registration . . . ."[160] At the same time, panelists have to keep in mind they are not applying the law of any particular jurisdiction. Core precedential principles were established quickly, some within the first months of the new arbitral regime, leaving refinement to later Panels. Other principles have developed over time, with Panels building on earlier, tentative formulations until announcing a construction of the Policy later endorsed by a consensus of panelists.

The first principle (it can be called this since it was announced in the first decision) is that complainants must plead and prove that respondent both registered and is using the domain name in bad faith.[161] Other principles include a) the Policy recognizes registered and unregistered trademark rights[162]; b) no trademark rights for pending applications or supplemental register[163]; c) complainant succeeds in proving respondent lacks rights or legitimate interests in the disputed domain name by offering an unrebutted *prima facie* case[164]; d) "an offer to sell cannot be held to

---

159 WIPO Final Report at paragraph 175. The recommendation is reflected in Rule 15(a) of the Policy, discussed in Chapter 7 (Sec. 7.10).

160 *Id.*

161 ***World Wrestling Federation Entertainment, Inc. v. Michael Bosman***, D1999-0001 (WIPO January 14, 2000) construing paragraph 4(a)(iii) of the Policy. The Panel subsequently renounced its construction and advocated a retroactive bad faith construction that had been soundly and roundly rejected. See dissent in ***Guru Denim Inc. v. Ibrahim Ali Ibrahim abu-Harb***, D2013-1324 (WIPO September 27, 2013) in which the Panel swerved from his original view: "It would be much easier for this panelist to maintain that his original decision [approving the binary concept] was correct, and not recant. But in view of the evidence [of the correctness of the unitary view], I am unable to do so." This tussle over binary vs. unitary is an example of the deliberative conversations mentioned above. Nevertheless, the consensus remains in favor of the binary concept. Discussed further in "Justifying Forfeiture Despite Good Faith Registration" (Sec. 4.03-A.4.b).

162 ***The British Broadcasting Corporation v. Jaime Renteria***, D2000-0050 (WIPO March 23, 2000) construing paragraph 4(a)(i) of the Policy. Discussed further in "Qualifying for a Trademark Right" (Sec. 4.01-A-3). Common law trademarks and the equivalent in civil law jurisdictions are granted standing to maintain a UDRP proceeding. See ***S.N.C. Jesta Fontainebleau v. Po Ser***, D2009-1394 (WIPO November 21, 2009).

163 ***Aspen Grove, Inc. v. Aspen Grove***, D2001-0798 (WIPO October 17, 2001). Discussed further in "No Right Accrues to Pending Application for Trademark" (Sec. 4.01-A-3.c).

constitute evidence of bad faith use if the offer was solicited by the Complainant"[165]; e) some use of marks without permission is lawful[166]; f) "use in bad faith" is not limited to active websites; passive use may qualify[167]; g) renewal of registration after a mark's emergence or bad faith use is not actionable[168]; h) to have an actionable claim, marks must predate the registration of domain names[169]; i) respondents are responsible for the content of their websites; and j) in determining whether a domain name has been registered in bad faith, the Panel may look at the "totality of circumstances."[170] In regard to reverse domain name hijacking it is inexcusable for a party or its representative to be ignorant of the clear language of the Policy and Rules and Policy precedent,[171] but a weak claim that has a sound basis is insufficient to establish abuse of the administrative proceeding.[172]

1.04-C 1.04-C The Role of Local Law

1.04-C.1 1.04-C.1 Creating a Supra-National Jurisprudence

Rule 15(a) of the Rules of the Policy authorizes panelists to decide disputes on the basis of "any rules and principles of law that it deems applicable."[173] This is not an invitation to apply any particular national law and none is officially centric in

---

[164] This approach construing paragraph 4(a)(ii) of the Policy entered the UDRP vocabulary tentatively in April 2000 in two decisions by the same panelist [***EAuto, Inc. v. Available Domain- Names. com, d/b/a Intellectual Assets.com, Inc.***, D2000-0120 (WIPO April 13, 2000) and ***EAuto, L.L.C. v. EAuto Parts***, D2000-0096 (WIPO April 9, 2000)].

[165] ***HPE DESIGN LLC v. NetIncome Ventures Inc.***, FA1209001461370 (Forum October 20, 2012) (<hennessey.com>. "[S]uch a situation provides no evidence to indicate that the Respondent registered the disputed domain name with the intent to sell it to the Complainant or one of its competitors.")

[166] ***Oki Data Americas, Inc. v. ASD, Inc***, D2001-0903 (WIPO November 6, 2001) construing paragraph 4(c)(i) of the Policy. The Panel formulated a four-part test, which is discussed further in "Non-Authorized But Lawful Use of Trademarks" (Sec. 5.01-C.2).

[167] ***Telstra Corporation Limited v. Nuclear Marshmallows***, D2000-0003 (WIPO February 18, 2000) construing paragraph 4(a)(iii) of the Policy formulated the "inconceivability principle." Discussed further in "Inactive or Passive Use" (Sec. 5.01-B.2).

[168] ***Crystallize, Inc. v. James Eixenberger***, D2000-0528 (WIPO October 13, 2000) (<crystallize. com>).

[169] ***Whispering Smith Limited v. Domain Administrator, Tfourh, LLC***, D2016-1175 (WIPO September 27, 2016) (<bravesoul.com>). Discussed further in "Earlier Registered Domain Names; Subsequently Acquired Trademarks" (Sec. 5.01-F.2).

[170] ***Twentieth Century Fox Film Corp. v. Risser***, FA 93761 (Forum May 18, 2000) construing paragraph 4(b) of the Policy. Discussed further in "Defining the Burden" (Sec. 6.01-A.1.a).

[171] ***Credit Europe Bank N. V. v. Peter Yu***, D2010-0737 (WIPO July 14, 2010) (Concurring opinion: "The Policy has been in force for more than a decade and the thousands of cases decided under it now constitute a workable body of (to use a legal term) precedent.")

[172] Discussed further in "Reverse Domain Name Hijacking" (Sec. 7.10-A).

adjudicating parties' rights under the UDRP. The Policy is "a set of rules that operates within its own unique context."[174] Nevertheless, case law and statutes from common law jurisdictions have been significant contributors to the jurisprudence.[175] For example, certain offensive arguments, misleading Internet users under the "Initial Interest Confusion" theory; and certain defensive arguments, permissible use under the "Nominative Fair Use" theory are drawn from U.S. trademark law. Protected speech issues are frequently decided by reference to U.S. Constitutional law, but application of constructive notice has been rejected as antithetical to UDRP principles; knowledge of complainant's trademark and targeting it for commercial gain are the twin factors in determining abusive registration.

Although other examples of conflicting views can be mentioned, for the most part panelists have created a harmonized, supra-national jurisprudence of domain names built on normative international standards.[176] Issues "should not be decided on the basis of national law if the relevant provision does not import or refer to national law."[177] Rather (continues the Panel), they "should be determined by engaging in a legal analysis that incorporates recognition of normative principles of international law."

The enterprise of Panels developing an inventory of core principles in response to the contingencies of fact before them was well under way within months of the Policy's introduction. This is emphasized strongly by one panelist who stated that "[a]lthough entitled to consider principles of law deemed applicable, [he found] it

---

173 The Rule reads in full: "Panel shall decide a complaint on the basis of the statements and documents submitted and in accordance with the Policy, these Rules and any rules and principles of law that it deems applicable." An argument can be made for a strong common law presence in UDRP jurisprudence reflecting the fact that an overwhelming number of cases are decided in English.

174 ***Diet Center Worldwide, Inc. v. Jason Akatiff***, D2012-1609 (WIPO October 5, 2012).

175 English is the dominant language of the UDRP. Dubiously perhaps, but on some issues (personalized e-mail addresses for example) panelists look to U.S. law. See ***F. Hoffmann La Roche AG v. Domain Admin Tucows.com Co.***, D2006-1488 (WIPO February 27, 2007) (Complaint denied for <roche.org>. Dissent: "[B]ad faith is not solely a question of intent. It is an objective standard of fairness rather than the evidence of a subjective willingness to commit an act of piracy. If objectively, the Respondent trades on the reputation of the trademark right owner, it may be acting in bad faith even though some precedents might have turned out to be favorable to its practice.") The dissent's argument is revisited in ***Marker Völkl (International) GmbH v. Tucows.com Co.***, D2012-1461 (WIPO November 14, 2012) where the Panel questioned the application of Avery Dennison to non-U.S. parties. "The decision in Avery Dennison was . . . made based on interpretation of the US Federal Trademark Dilution Act. However, in this case, the Complainant is a Swiss entity and the Respondent a Canadian entity."

176 There are instances of panelists applying national law to disputes in which parties are domiciled in the same jurisdiction. An example of this is allowing laches as an affirmative defense, which has only been applied where the parties are either domiciled in the United States or the complainant's residence. Discussed further in "Sleeping on One's Rights" (Sec. 5.01-E).

177 ***Coast Hotels Ltd. v. Bill Lewis and UNITE HERE***, D2009-1295 (WIPO November 23, 2009).

unnecessary to do so in any depth [because the] jurisprudence which is being rapidly developed by a wide variety of Panelists worldwide under the ICANN Policy provides a fruitful source of precedent."[178] In referring to national law the WIPO Final Report offers a single example of its application to parties governed by the same national law[179]:

> [I]f the parties to a procedure were resident in one country, the domain name was registered through a registrar in that country and the evidence of the bad faith registration and use of the domain name related to activity in the same country, it would be appropriate for the decision-maker to refer to the law of the country concerned in applying the definition.

Even accepting this invitation panelists still make a point of emphasizing that their assessment is based on the Policy's criteria not local law.[180] In ruling for complainant in the case cited in the footnote, the Panel explained that it was legitimate to look at, even though it was unnecessary to rely on local law:

> Since respondent is domiciled in the United Kingdom, and any legal action would have to be taken against him in that country, the Panel considers principles of law set out in decisions of Courts in the United Kingdom. I do so in deference to the legal submissions in the Response. It is not strictly necessary to do so, because *I find that complainant succeeds in terms of the Policy.* However, I believe that the case law in the United Kingdom supports the view I have taken. (Emphasis added).

Even panelists who may consider local law "would most likely agree that where neither of the parties are based in the United States and the dispute would most likely be litigated in another jurisdiction (in this case Germany) there is simply no justification for importing a United States trade mark law doctrine."[181]

In general, panelists early determined not to import local law equity defenses into the jurisprudence except those explicit or discoverable through construction of paragraphs 4(c)(i-iii) of the Policy. They have consistently rejected the application of local laws that would bar untimely proceedings as well as other available equity defenses, opting instead for a pragmatic case by case approach in balancing parties' rights. If passage of time favors respondent it is not because of laches. The consensus is that "the equitable defense of laches does not properly apply to this Policy proceeding."[182] If there is sufficient proof of abusive registration lapse of time is not a

---

[178] ***3636275 Canada, dba eResolution v. eResolution.com***, D2000-0110 (WIPO April 10, 2000). The Panel also noted that "Courts in the United States have come to similar conclusions about those who act in a manner similar to respondent who endeavor to sell domain names to trademark owners for a profit."

[179] Paragraph 176.

[180] ***Which? Limited v. James Halliday.***, D2000-0019 (WIPO March 27, 2000).

[181] ***ENX (European Network Exchange) Association v. Ahven Tolunay***, D2009-1218 (WIPO October 28, 2009).

factor. However, lapse of time can become a factor when it is impossible because of it to prove bad faith registration[183]

The "sole lodestar for a Panel must be the Policy . . . WIPO decisions have steadfastly maintained that the laws of any particular country do not apply to the dispute."[184] When Panels have applied local law it is to parties resident in the same country, subject to the same jurisprudence.[185] Thus, it has been held appropriate where the parties are "domiciled in the United States and United States courts have recent experience with similar disputes . . . the Sole Panelist shall look to rules and principles of law set out in decisions of the courts of the United States."[186] The rationale is that conforming decisions under the Policy to the relevant national law "help[s] ensure consistent application of the law and discourage[s] unnecessary litigation."[187]

---

[182] ***Tom Cruise v. Network Operations Center / Alberta Hot Rods***, D2006-0560 (WIPO July 5, 2006). Neither do other equitable defenses "often available in trademark infringement litigation, such as . . . non enforcement, or abandonment . . . although they may bear upon the panel's determination of the [second and third] . . . requirements of paragraph 4(a)," ***Asbach GmbH v. Econsult Ltd., d.b.a. Asbach Communities and Whois Privacy Services***, D2012-1225 (WIPO August 7, 2012).

[183] Discussed further in "Sleeping on One's Rights" (Sec. 5.01-E). Waiting has consequences that can defeat the trademark owner. See ***Board of Trustees of the University of Arkansas v. FanMail.com***, LLC, D2009-1139 (WIPO November 2, 2009) in which the majority noted that "it is not unreasonable to consider laches as falling within Rule 15(a) given that, in many if not most jurisdictions in the United States and in countries such as the United Kingdom and Australia, the formerly sharp line between law and equity has been blurred if not effaced by the amalgamation of law and equity."

[184] Panel in ***Edmunds.com, Inc. v. Ult. Search Inc.***, D2001-1319 (WIPO February 1, 2002) (U.S. Complainant, Chinese Respondent). See ***McMullan Bros Limited, Maxol Limited and Maxol Direct Limited Maxol Lubricants Limited, Maxol Oil Limited Maxol Direct (NI) Limited v. Web Names Ltd.***, D2004-0078 (WIPO April 16, 2004) (Both parties, Northern Ireland. The Panel rejected the invitation to apply Northern Ireland statute of limitations as "inherently unattractive.")

[185] In ***Coast Hotels Ltd. v. Bill Lewis and UNITE HERE.***, D2009-1295 (WIPO November 23, 2009) the Panel concluded that the relevant provision—paragraph 4(c)(iii) of the Policy, which provides noncommercial and fair use defenses to a claim for abusive registration—did "import or refer to national law."

[186] ***KeyCorp and City of Seattle v. i-designsolutions.com, Inc***, D2005-0104 (WIPO April 14, 2005) citing ***Autosales Incorporated v. Don Terrill***, D2001-1341 (WIPO February 24, 2002) (typosquatting), that cites ***Tribeca Film Center, Inc. v. Brusasco-Mackenzie***, D2000-1772 (WIPO April 10, 2001) that cites ***EAuto, L.L.C. v. Triple S. Auto Parts d/b/a Kung Fu Yea Enterprises, Inc.***, D2000-0047 (WIPO March 24, 2000).

[187] ***Xtraplus Corporation v. Flawless Computers***, D2007-0070 (WIPO March 9, 2007). See also ***XM Satellite Radio v. Michael Bakker***, FA0612000861120 (Forum February 27, 2007) in which the three member Panel denied the complaint, but the Regional Court in Cologne ruled that "In court proceedings under Paragraph 4(k) UDRP the national court shall only apply the relevant national law (e.g. trademark or unfair competition law). Whether the requirements stipulated by Paragraph

1.04-C.2

1.04-C.2 Local Law versus Conflict of Laws

It has been suggested that Panels should apply a conflict of laws analysis in determining applicable law.[188] The Policy already requires complainants as a condition for maintaining an administrative proceeding to submit to the jurisdiction of the courts in one of two locations, the "mutual jurisdiction" referred to in ***Sermo*** in the below footnote, in the event either party challenges the UDRP award under Paragraph 4(k).[189] Since "there is some question about the laws that may apply, then a Panel should also consider the location of mutual jurisdiction, and the conflict of laws principles that would be applied by courts in that jurisdiction."[190]

However, application of a conflict of laws analysis has not persuaded panelists who subscribe to UDRP jurisprudence as the "sole lodestar." They find the ***Sermo*** formulation unnecessary. The Panel in a later case stated that it was "skeptical that either the analysis or the solution offered in ***Sermo*** to the local law problem is wholly convincing."[191] Although the suggestion for a conflict of laws analysis has not won converts, there are occasional decisions that recognize its appropriateness. In one case, the Panel applied U.S. law to resolve an issue of common law rights "because not every country recognizes common law rights, and the relevant law of each jurisdiction has its own nuances."[192]

4(a) UDRP (on which the NAF Panel had based its decision) are satisfied or not is considered irrelevant." (Case no. 33 O 45/08, 16 June 2009, translation adr.eu.)

[188] Suggestion made by the dissent to look to the location of mutual jurisdiction in ***Richard Starkey v. Mr. Bradley***, FA0612000874575 (Forum February 12, 2007) (U.K. Complainant; U.S. Respondent involving a respondent's right to use the disputed domain name for a fan club) (Complaint granted over dissent). The dissenting Panel in ***Richard Starkey*** was appointed sole panelist in ***Sermo, Inc. v. CatalystMD, LLC***, D2008-0647 (WIPO July 2, 2008) (Complaint denied. "[T]here is some question about the laws that may apply . . . since [the mutual jurisdiction] . . . is the jurisdiction in which the courts may be asked to consider the parties' respective rights if a challenge is filed under Paragraph 4(k) of the rules.")

[189] The jurisdiction is mutual because the respondent in acquiring the domain name has through the registration agreement also submitted to the same jurisdiction. See 2013 Registrar Accreditation Agreement (RAA) at Paragraph 3.7.7.10 (Either: "(1) of the Registered Name Holder's domicile and (2) where Registrar is located.") Likewise Paragraph 1 of the Rules of the Policy. The term "mutual jurisdiction" is defined as "a court jurisdiction at the location of either (a) the principal office of the Registrar . . . or (b) the domain-name holder's address as shown for the registration of the domain name in Registrar's Whois directory at the time complaint is submitted to the Provider."

Rule 3(b)(xiii) of the Rules of the Policy provides that the "Complainant will submit, with respect to any challenges to a decision in the administrative proceeding canceling or transferring the domain name, to the jurisdiction of the courts in at least one specified Mutual Jurisdiction."

[190] *Id.*, Dissent ***Richard Starkey*** and Panel in ***Sermo***.

[191] ***Aubert France SA v. Tucows.com Co***, D2008-1986 (WIPO March 17, 2009) ("The Policy is of international scope and the framers required it to be capable of practical application by a panelist that might be drawn from any jurisdiction (and more often than not a panelist who would not be drawn from the jurisdiction of either of the parties to a dispute.")

1.05 CONSISTENCY AND PREDICTABILITY 1.05

1.05-A Fair Resolution Based on the Facts and the Law 1.05-A

The Policy mandates that "[i]n all cases, the Panel shall ensure that the Parties are treated with equality and that each Party is given a fair opportunity to present its case."[193] This incorporates language from the WIPO Final Report on procedural fairness.[194] There are expectations of the Provider,[195] the parties,[196] and the appointed neutral.[197] The Policy provides that "[a] Panel shall decide a complaint on the basis of the statements and documents submitted and in accordance with the Policy, these Rules and any rules and principles of law that it deems applicable."[198] Although WIPO makes the point that Panels do not have to follow precedent,[199] it is customary to invoke and rare not to cite supporting authority, because, as WIPO reports in the Overview, "panels consider it desirable that their decisions are consistent with prior panel decisions dealing with similar fact situations."[200] Precedent is

---

[192] ***Kaizen Applications, LLC v. Private Whois Service***, FA1005001324496 (Forum July 8, 2010) (U.S. Complainant; Canadian Respondent). See also ***Coast Hotels Ltd. v. Bill Lewis and UNITE HERE.***, D2009-1295 (WIPO November 23, 2009).

[193] Paragraph 10(b) of the Rules of the Policy.

[194] Paragraph 180: "***Thus, procedural rules will deal typically with the documentation that the parties are expected to produce, the time limits within which they must produce it, who the decision maker will be and how he or she will be appointed, what remedies may be granted by the decision maker and who will supervise the administration of the procedures."

[195] Rules of the Policy, paragraph 2. See for example: ***CafePress.com v. Michael Fragomele***, FA0502000428848 (Forum April 27, 2005) ("[D]ue process requirements dictate that complainant's objections must be adequately communicated to respondent both in an appropriate manner and with sufficient content to properly place respondent on notice of its objectionable conduct.")

[196] A complainant's failure to create a factual record and respondent's silence have negative consequences, although it should be noted that in arbitration default is not an admission but a denial of liability. Strategic withholding of evidence by complainant and silence of respondent are discussed further in "No Record, No Case" (Sec. 7.05-B) and "Consequences of Default" (Sec. 7.03-B).

[197] ***CBS Broadcasting Inc. v. VanityMail Services Inc.***, D2000-0379 (WIPO July 3, 2000) (Complaint denied: "The function of the Panel is to do justice between the parties."); ***Choice Hotels International, Inc. v. AnnaValdieri***, FA0607000758830 (Forum August 23, 2006) (Complaint granted: "The Panel finds that it is permissible to consider prior decisions of UDRP panels in the determination of a dispute even when such decisions are neither recognized nor cited by either party, even when the content of such decisions may cast an unfavorable light upon one of the parties and when the content of such prior decisions assist the Panel in the proper resolution of the proceedings at hand. The Panel considers prior domain name dispute decisions as 'principles of law' under Rule 15 which may be considered by a Panel.")

[198] Rule 15(a) of the Rules of the Policy.

[199] Jurisprudential Overview 3.0, Paragraph 4.1 ("[t]he UDRP does not [officially] operate on a strict doctrine of precedent").

highly valued because deviation destabilizes parties' expectations. The key is predictability. The aim of both consensus and precedent is to ensure consistency.

A general view formed early in the jurisprudence is that the UDRP should not be a roulette wheel. It "should consist of more than, '[i]t depends [on] what panelist you draw.'"[201] The goal (as stated in many UDRP decisions) is achieved through "a strong body of precedent" which "is strongly persuasive" even if not binding.[202] Nevertheless on some issues—most notably, what speech qualifies for protection (there are differing views),[203] and occasionally the scope of the Policy,[204] bad faith measured from renewal of registration,[205] and declaration of reverse domain name hijacking[206]—it truly does depend on "what panelist you draw."

Many of the core principles of UDRP jurisprudence were quickly identified and cogently laid out in early decisions. Where there were uncertainties of construction Panels sought (and continue) to build on and refine the work of their colleagues. There are also decisions setting forth or proposing constructions and legal standards that fail to ripen to consensus, which have either been abandoned as dead ends or rejected in later decisions.[207] In one case in which Respondent cited

---

200 *Id.* "However, panels consider it desirable that their decisions are consistent with prior panel decisions dealing with similar fact situations. This ensures that the UDRP system operates in a fair, effective and predictable manner for all parties."

201 ***Time Inc. v. Chip Cooper***, D2000-1342 (WIPO February 13, 2001) (<lifemagazine.com>).

202 ***Pantaloon Retail India Limited v. RareNames, WebReg***, D2010-0587 (WIPO June 21, 2010). "Whether [the consensus in holding that a respondent in the domain name business] is justified may be a matter for debate, but in the opinion of the Panel there is a strong body of precedent which, though not binding, is strongly persuasive."

203 184. Jurisprudential Overview 3.0, Paragraph 2.6.1. ***Yellowstone Mountain Club LLC v. Offshore Limited D and PCI.***, D2013-0097 (WIPO April 12, 2013) ("It might be said that Respondent must transfer two of the disputed domain names simply as a result of having the bad luck to draw two panelists who adhere to a variant of the 'View 1' approach [to the issue of fair use and free speech issues].") Discussed further in "Ambivalence of Application" (Sec. 5.04-A.2).

204 Discussed further in "Disputes Within the Scope of the Policy" (Sec. 3.03).

205 ***Eastman Sporto Group LLC v. Jim and Kenny***, D2009-1688 (WIPO March 1, 2010); ***Big 5 Corp. v. EyeAim.com / Roy Fang***, FA1308001513704 (Forum October 11, 2013) ("Respondent's Paragraph 2 of the Policy representation and warranty given in January 7, 2012 [when the registration for the domain name was renewed] was knowingly false since: i) Respondent intentionally changed his use of the disputed domain name; ii) The new use is unrelated to Respondent's earlier business and trademark registration; iii) The new use is the display of pay per click links which are basically there to profit from consumers' confusion between the disputed domain name and Complainant's trademarks; iv) The new use occurred prior to the renewal held to be a registration for purposes of paragraph 4(a)(iii) and; v) There has been no legitimate use since renewal.") Discussed further in "Renewal of Registration" (Sec. 4.03-A.3.c).

206 There is a split among panelists as to whether reverse domain name hijacking must be requested or an obligation on the part of the Panel to declare it. Jurisprudential Overview 3.0 reports a consensus in favor of panelists making that decision whether or not requested. Discussed further in Sec. 7.11.

cases to the effect that "the existence of a mark as to the date of registration is a rigid prerequisite for a finding of bad faith registration," the Panel responded that "these were both cases in early days of the existence of the Policy. Things have moved on from then . . . [and] the position now is somewhat more nuanced."[208]

The majority in ***Time*** stated that it "believes potential users of the UDRP are entitled to some degree of predictability."[209] That is, if "a principle enunciated in a decision is well-reasoned and repeatedly adopted by other panels, the majority believes that absent compelling reasons, which require a determination otherwise, that the rule established should be respected." Also, "users of the internet are better served through panel decisions that promote consistency and predictability."[210] This is assured by the Policy's openness in requiring public accessibility to all decisions. Databases are the sources of authority that should guard against a result that "depends [on] what panelist you draw.'"[211]

After ***Time*** the twin themes of consistency and predictability were further pursued and refined in ***Nikon***[212] and ***Howard Jarvis***.[213] The ***Nikon*** Panel held that "[n]ot only do such decisions frequently have persuasive weight and authority, but also, they reflect a consensus that is worthy of some deference." This is because "such a consensus helps to ensure consistency among UDRP decisions, a critical component of any system of justice." Ignoring past decisions would be fatal because "the expected result in any given case would be random based on the identity of the panelists, which would undermine the credibility of the entire UDRP process." The underlying rationale is that "[p]arties in UDRP proceedings are entitled to know that, where the facts of two

---

207 Other legal theories rejected: The majority in ***AgStar Financial Services, ACA v. Ashantiplc Ltd.***, FA1405001557154 (Forum July 1, 2014) dismissed the complaint but the dissent would have decreed transfer of the domain name on the theory that Respondent's use of a privacy service "gives rise to a rebuttable presumption of bad faith registration and use."

208 ***Igor Lognikov v. Web Ventures, Nerdec, Inc. and Charles Edmunds***, D2009-1684 (WIPO January 29, 2010).

209 ***Time***, *supra*. There is less predictability where panelists are split on the legal standards as they are, for example, concerning protection of domain names used for noncommercial fair use and free speech [paragraph 4(c)(iii) of the Policy].

210 ***Chanel, Inc. v. LaPorte Holdings***, D2005-0487 (WIPO July 5, 2005): "The Panel accepts this consensus view."

211 The dissent in ***Time*** believed that complainant had failed to prove that respondent had registered and was using the domain name in bad faith because <lifemagazine.com> did not resolve to an active website. The issue of passive holding had in fact already been tackled a year earlier in the most cited case in the UDRP canon, ***Telstra Corporation Limited v. Nuclear Marshmallows***, D2000-0003 (WIPO February 18, 2000). The Panel construed the term "use" to include passive holding when it is "not possible to conceive of any plausible actual or contemplated active use of the domain name by respondent that would not be illegitimate."

212 ***Nikon, Inc. v. Technilab. Inc.***, D2000-1774 (WIPO February 26, 2001).

213 ***Howard Jarvis Taxpayers Association v. Paul McCauley.***, D2004-0014 (WIPO April 22, 2004).

cases are materially indistinguishable, the complaints and responses will be evaluated in a consistent manner regardless of the identity of the panelist; this goal is undermined when different panels can be expected to rule differently on the same types of facts."[214] A precedential holding should be followed despite reluctance.[215]

WIPO's digital treatise and overview of domain name jurisprudence, already noted in earlier pages, has a twofold purpose. First, it assists parties in understanding the process when preparing their submissions; second, it assists panelists in preparing decisions.[216] Although the Jurisprudential Overview instructs the reader that the Policy does not operate on a "strict doctrine of precedent," it nevertheless encourages a disciplined adherence to consensus views. This was made clear in ***Symark International***[217] in which the Panel noted that the Overview "reflect[s] a studied and considered summary of consensus positions culled from the decisions of numerous panels during the first five years of administration of the UDRP." Accordingly, "[w]hen such a consensus has developed, it is incumbent upon panels to follow the consensus (or the majority view) to promote consistency among UDRP decisions."

1.05-B 1.05-B Inconsistency in Applying the Law: Different Cases and Panels

Emerson famously said that "[a] foolish consistency is the hobgoblin of little minds."[218] In law, however, inconsistency undermines predictability and subverts trust in the jurisprudence. In earlier versions of the WIPO Overview (now termed "Jurisprudential Overview") WIPO expressly acknowledged "diversity of view" rather than inconsistency. While there is not a strict equation between "diversity of view" and inconsistency both affect predictability. There have been disagreements of legal principles and interpretation of facts. Inconsistency can take three

---

[214] ***Howard Jarvis***, *supra*. Nevertheless, there are panelists who follow neither precedent nor the Jurisprudential Overview even where the domain name is shown to have been registered years before complainant acquires its trademark and there is no transfer of ownership. For example, the Panel in ***Jordan Sparks d/b/a Open Dental Software v. Jee Young Ko***, FA0906001266265 (Forum August 5, 2009) found for complainant on the twin grounds that respondent was not using the domain name and was willing to sell it at a price. A similar aberrational view was expressed by the dissent in ***The American Automobile Association, Inc. v. QTK Internet c/o James M. van Johns***, FA1261364 (Nat. Arb. Forum, July 25, 2009). See Jurisprudential Overview 3.0, Paragraph 1.1.3.

[215] The Panel in ***PAA Laboratories GmbH v. Printing Arts America***, D2004-0338 (WIPO July 13, 2004) explained that it "wishe[d] to clarify that its decision under this element is based on the need for consistency and comity in domain name dispute 'jurisprudence.'"

[216] In addition to the Jurisprudential Overview WIPO has an online Index to UDRP Panel Decisions at <http://www.wipo.int/amc/en/domains/search/legalindex.jsp?lang=en>.

[217] ***Symark International, Inc. v. Gary McCurty***, D2005-0235 (WIPO June 15, 2005), citing ***Fresh Intellectual Properties, Inc. v. 800Network.com***, D2005-0061 (WIPO March 21, 2005).

[218] Ralph Waldo Emerson, "Self-Reliance."

forms: diversity of view which WIPO acknowledges as a feature of the process in the Overview; different assessments of facts and applicable law; and manifest disregard of the law. While there is not a strict equation between "diversity of view" and inconsistency all three affect predictability, but inconsistency can be pernicious.

Inconsistencies occur in decision making for a number of reasons. Sometimes they stem from an insufficiency of evidence for which the parties themselves can be faulted; at other times they stem from a flawed analysis of the facts. Trial courts (if the analogy is accepted) do not get it right all the time either, but there is appellate review to correct errors and mistakes of judgment.

The closest to appellate review of a UDRP decision is a subsequent action in a court of competent jurisdiction, which in the United States (as previously noted) would be in a district court under the Anticybersquatting Consumer Protection Act. The most troublesome UDRP inconsistencies have shown up in split decisions where either the majority or dissent is at odds with precedent[219]; where the same complainant in two proceedings before different Panels receives contrary results[220]; where the same issue is treated differently by two different Panels,[221] or where Panels file decisions inconsistent with consensus and precedent or simply get it wrong.[222]

---

[219] Disagreement within the Panel. See ***J. Crew International, Inc. v. crew.com***, D2000-0054 (WIPO April 20, 2000) discussed above in "Construing Basic Principles" (Sec. 1.04-B). Also, ***Time Inc.***, *supra*. Split decision in 3-Member Panel in ***easyGroup Limited v. Easy Group Holdings Limited***, D2014-2128 (WIPO February 19, 2015). The majority dismissed the complaint and declared Complainant abused the proceedings. The dissent disagreed entirely, arguing renewal as grounds for finding bad faith: "If the registration of a domain name and its use is actionable at least in the jurisdiction of the registrant then the representation cannot be made and the renewal of the registration is at best an inaccuracy and at worse an untruth. In either case, it is registration and use in bad faith."

[220] ***SPECS GmbH v. SPECS Scientific Instruments, Inc. d/b/a SPECS Technologies Corporation***, D2009-0308 (WIPO April 27, 2009) (Complaint granted) and ***SPECS Surface Nano Analysis GmbH v. Rickmer Kose / Domain Name Administrator, PrivacyProtect.org***, D2010-1173 (WIPO September 24, 2010) (<specsus.com>; Complaint denied). In the first case, "it appears that the then respondent registered the disputed domain names under a distribution arrangement which was subsequently terminated by the Complainant. . . . In particular, the then panel found that there was sufficient evidence to support an inference that the then respondent registered the domain name in dispute primarily for the purpose of disrupting the business of a competitor, which constitutes bad faith under paragraph 4(b)(iii) of the Policy."

In the second case, the Panel "[did] not consider that there [was] sufficient evidence . . . to support an inference of bad faith at the time of registration of the disputed domain name. The Complainant's evidence is primarily directed toward establishing bad faith from the Respondent's subsequent conduct, particularly after the date of the termination of the Respondent as its sales agent. While this evidence goes towards the issue of bad faith use, there is little evidence in the Complaint that would support a finding of bad faith at the time of registration."

See also ***NSK LTD. v. Li shuo***, FA1701001712449 (Forum February 16, 2017) (<skfnsk.com>) (Denied standing); ***NSK LTD. v. DINA MCINTIRE***, FA1701001712452 (Forum February 21, 2017) (nsk-fag-skf-ntn.com>) (Awarded domain name to Complainant).

Diversity of view that produces inconsistency but is an accepted part of the jurisprudence is codified in the Jurisprudential Overview. The most prominent diversity of view occurs with domain names used for commentary and criticism.[223] Some panelists adhere to the view that it is abusive to register a domain name identical or confusingly similar to a mark regardless of content; others, that content is the test of abusive registration.[224] There are other anomalies that will be pointed out in the following pages. One of them is whether renewal of registration following bad faith use violates registrant's representation in purchasing a domain name that it "will not infringe upon or otherwise violate the rights of any third party." Although no inference of bad faith registration should be drawn from subsequent bad faith use, yet some panelists find the inference acceptable. In other cases, panelists simply come to different conclusions in their assessments of factually similar circumstances, which is why it is imperative for parties to clearly state the facts they believe controlling with sufficient evidence to persuade the Panel in their favor.

The Panel in ***Morgan Stanley***[225] ("Morgan Stanley 1") found that the Respondent's use of <morganstanleyplatinum> was fair because it was making use of complainant's mark in a "non-trademark manner," that is, "only for illustration of purported negligence and ineptitude in the seminars [the Respondent] conducts." The Panel supported its view ostensibly on the authority of ***U.S. of Am. Dep't of***

---

[221] Domain names turned over to website vendors for ongoing maintenance with opposite results: ***Michael's Bakery Products, LLC v. SD Onsite***, FA1305001499075 (Forum June 21, 2013) (Respondent default. Complaint denied); and ***Alaska Health Fair, Inc. v. Chris Jacobson***, FA130500 1500868 (Forum June 24, 2013) (Respondent appeared. Complaint granted).

[222] The Panel in ***NSK LTD. v. Li shuo***, supra. explained that Complainant lacked standing and gave as its reason that Complainant "alleges no nexus between it and the owner of the [SKF] mark. As such, Complainant essentially has standing to bring this claim regarding the NSK mark but not the SKF mark." The decision is a departure from a line of earlier cases decided by WIPO appointees and relies on a single case that cites no authority for rejecting standing where the mark owner of the other mark is absent. ***NIKE, Inc. and Nike Innovate, C.V. v. Mattia Lumini and Yykk Snc.*** FA1606001679233 (Forum July 15, 2016) (<nikegoogle.com>). See line of decisions from WIPO appointees such as ***Kabbage, Inc. v. Oneandone Private Registration 1, 1&1 Internet Inc. – www.1.and1.com/oert Hanssen, Ridiculous File Sharing***, D2015-1507 (WIPO November 20, 2015) (<kabbage4amazon.com>). For getting it wrong, see challenged awards in Appendix B.

[223] Fair use and free speech defenses under paragraph 4(c)((iii) are discussed further in "Appropriating Complainant's Trademark for Noncommercial or Fair Use and Free Speech" (Sec. 6.04-A).

[224] It is unusual to get decisions filed on the same day involving the same respondent, one expressing the restrictive view and the other the protective one. See ***Vince Andrich v. AnonymousSpeech AnonymousSpeech***, FA1109001406333 (Forum October 26, 2011) (<vinceandrich.net>, transferred); and, ***Dr. A. Scott Connelly v. AnonymousSpeech AnonymousSpeech***, FA1109001406376 (Forum October 26, 2011) (<ascottconnelly.com>, complaint denied). In ***Spokane Civic Theatre v. James Ryan***, FA1109001409107 (Forum November 1, 2011), a three member Panel, the majority held in favor of the Respondent's right to free speech, while the dissent held abusive registration.

[225] ***Morgan Stanley v. Michael Woods***, FA0512000604103 (Forum January 16, 2006) (U.S. parties).

the Navy,[226] which stands for the proposition that when a "non-trademark use is made, that does not depend for its value on the existence of the trademark, it is then appropriate to use the trademark as another's domain."[227] However, when the same Respondent subsequently registered another confusingly similar domain name to the MORGAN STANLEY mark in the name of his cat, "Morgan Stanley 2, the Meow case",[228] the new panelist was firm in rejecting the principle of fair use in such a circumstance: "This use cannot be considered legitimate, because there is no reason actually to register such domain names in order to discuss such failures to register."

Houghton Mifflin Company commenced two separate proceedings that were assigned to two different panelists. The cases were decided one day apart. Respondents defaulted in both cases, but the complaint was dismissed in the first and the domain name ordered transferred in the second. In the first decision the Panel did not apply the evidentiary rule of shifting the burden of production to Respondent to explain why he registered the HOUGHTON mark, and in the second case the Panel applied the evidentiary rule.[229]

The point about inconsistency is further illustrated in two sets of cases, one involving complainant Jason Claiborne decided on the same day[230] and Drugstore.com.[231] In the first set of cases both Respondents defaulted. In the first decision, the Panel denied transfer on two grounds: 1) Complainant's registration of the trademark postdated registration of the domain name; and, 2) improbability that Respondent could have known of Complainant's trademark, although there was

---

[226] ***U.S. of Am. Dep't of the Navy NAVSEA v. NAVYWEB***, FA 105977 (Forum May 21, 2002).

[227] The proposition is more suitably applied to domain names composed of terms used for their generic value. See "Attracting Internet Traffic" (Sec. 5.01-D).

[228] ***Morgan Stanley v. Meow***, FA0604000671304 (Forum May 22, 2006) (U.S. parties) (<mymorganstanleyplatinum>). Respondents cannot absolve themselves of bad faith by alleging the domain name is the name of their pet guinea pig—***YUM! Brands Inc. and KFC Corporation v. Ether Graphics a/k/a Andrew Gruner***, 212651 (Forum January 2, 2004) (<colonelsanders.com>) —or dog—***Pier Giorgio Andretta v. Corrado Giubertoni***, D2016-2496 (WIPO February 2017) (<giordana.com>). Respondent successful in ***Finter Bank Zurich v. Gianluca Olivieri***, D2000-0091 (WIPO March 23, 2000) (<finter>) because he submitted vaccination certificates as evidence that the name of his household dog was "Finter."

See also "Nicknames, False Names, and Stage Names" (Sec. 5.03-B3).

[229] ***Houghton Mifflin Company v. Unasi Management Inc.***, FA0504000469107 (Forum June 16, 2005) (Complaint denied); ***Houghton Mifflin Company v. LaPorte Holdings c/o Admin.***, FA0504000469115 (Forum June 17, 2005) (Transferred).

[230] ***Jason Claiborne v. StreamlineNet***, FA0508000535350 (Forum September 30, 2005) (<jase.net>) and ***Jason Claiborne v. Naylor Networks***, FA0508000535347 (Forum September 30, 2005) (<jase.com>).

[231] ***Drugstore.com, Inc. v. Nurhul Chee/ Robert Murry***, D2008-0230 (WIPO May 9, 2008) (<drugstoretm.com>, Complaint denied over dissent); ***Drugstore.com, Inc. v. Kevin Andrews***, D2008-0231 (WIPO May 9, 2008) (<mydrugstore1.com>, Transferred over dissent).

indication that the present respondent was a successor registrant.[232] In the second decision the Panel granted transfer on the grounds that passive holding of the domain name constituted abusive registration. It found that complainant also held a Nevada trademark that predated registration of the domain name.

The majority in ***Drugstore 2*** noted about ***Drugstore 1*** that the different results "may in part simply reflect a differing assessment of facts and likely motive given the examined record in each case, rather than any underlying divergence of opinion as to applicable principles under the Policy." The dissent in ***Drugstore 1***, however, was adamant that the majority was wrong in its analysis. The majority "ignore[d] the objective criteria of paragraphs 4(b)(i)(iv) and substitute[d] their subjective determination or personal motivations that a claimed mark is generic or is weak as descriptive, then proceed[ed] to find a lack of bad faith and deny relief to complainant."

Some inconsistency can be explained by examining parties' submissions. Indeed, similarity of factual circumstances may be misleading in condemning particular decisions. The 3-member Panel in ***Public Storage*** explained that "complete uniformity is, in practice, unattainable owing, in part, to different perspectives held by different panels and differing interpretations of the facts, the evidence presented and governing law taken by those panels."[233] While prior decisions at "first blush . . . may seem inconsistent [they] may very well, under more discerning scrutiny, appear quite consistent in view of subtle, but key factual differences which were not previously appreciated by the reader."[234]

In one case there may be sufficient proof to support or rebut abusive registration and in another case the record is insufficient for the Panel to form an opinion. Other Panels genuinely disagree as to certain core principles, for example (to take two sharp differences) whether 1) the representation and warranty against infringement of third party rights is a continuing duty that is not confined to the purchasing date of the domain name; and 2) the First Amendment of the U.S. Constitution or normative views of free speech generally regarded around the world protect domain name choices or expressions on the website (discussed further in 5.04-A.2).

---

[232] Bad faith for a successor registrant is measured from the date of its registration of the domain name without reference to the timing of its predecessor's registration. Discussed further in "Second and Subsequent Generations of Holders" (Sec. 4.03-B.2.a).

[233] ***Public Storage v. Deer Valley Mini Storage***, D2012-1149 (WIPO August 21, 2012) involving a refiled complaint bringing to the Panel's attention another case in which Public Storage prevailed, ***Public Storage v. Southwest Self Storage Advisors / Jeff Cain***, D2011-1396 (WIPO October 4, 2011). The decision in 1396 is inconsistent with ***Public Storage v. Deer Valley Mini & RV Storage and Deer Valley Mini Storage***, D2011-1397 (WIPO October 17, 2011).

[234] *Id.*, D2012-1149.

2 Contract Obligations

2.01 CONTRACTUAL BASIS FOR THE UDRP 2.01

2.01-A Conditions for Registering Domain Name 2.01-A

Domain name registrations come with conditions dictated by the Internet Corporation for Assigned Names and Numbers (ICANN). The conditions (described more fully below) are nonnegotiable. Among the conditions, registrants must "submit to a mandatory administrative proceeding in the event that a third party" challenges their choices of domain names.[1] The UDRP is one of the several parts of a structured order designed by ICANN in which each plays a critical role in maintaining the functionality, security, and integrity of the Internet. The UDRP's part is providing complainants an injunction-like remedy against abusive, malicious, and unjustified registrations of domain names infringing their statutory rights.

Every actor in the domain name system is subject to duties and obligations spelled out in bilateral contracts: registries and registrars with ICANN; domain name registrants with registrars; and trademark owners with ICANN certified providers by agreeing to a "mutual jurisdiction" (discussed below) when they file their complaints. Only certified registrars under contract with ICANN are authorized to provide registration services for domain names.[2] Significantly, registrars do not act as gatekeepers and have no liability to trademark owners for registering and hosting infringing domain names.[3]

To close the circle, registrants must agree to terms ICANN dictates to registrars in the Registrar Accreditation Agreement ("RAA").[4] If a registrant's choice of domain name is challenged "the Registered Name Holder shall submit [to adjudication under the UDRP], without prejudice to other potentially applicable jurisdictions, to the [mutual] jurisdiction of the courts (1) of the Registered Name Holder's domicile and (2) where Registrar is located."[5] Also, "[t]he Registered Name Holder shall agree that

---

[1] Uniform Domain Name Dispute Resolution Policy, Paragraph 4(a) (UDRP): "You [Registrant] are required to submit to a mandatory administrative proceeding in the event that a third party (a 'complainant' asserts" a claim of abusive registration.

[2] Registrars for country code TLDs contact with self-administering authorities in each country.

[3] 15 U.S.C. §1114(D)(iii) ("A domain name registrar, a domain name registry, or other domain name registration authority shall not be liable for damages under this section for the registration or maintenance of a domain name for another absent a showing of bad faith intent to profit from such registration or maintenance of the domain name.") See *Petroliam Nasional Berhad (Petronas) v. Godaddy.com, Inc.*, 737 F.3d 546 (9th Cir. 2013) (No cause of action for contributory cybersquatting, notwithstanding "the availability of such remedies under traditional trademark liability.")

[4] The latest version of the RAA dated June 27, 2013 is available at <http://www.icann.org/en/resources/registrars/raa/approved-with-specs-27jun13en.pdf>. It superseded the version of May 21, 2009, http://www.icann.org/en/about/agreements/registrars. The RAA also requires disclosure of certain personal information to be publicly available for inspection on the record. Discussed further in "The Whois Directory" (Sec. 2.05).

its registration of the Registered Name shall be subject to suspension, cancellation, or transfer pursuant to any ICANN adopted specification or policy."[6]

Unlike typical ADR regimes in which the parties contract to resolve their disputes by arbitration, there is no bilateral agreement between a mark owner and a domain name registrant it accuses of infringing its rights. The assent to be bound by an arbitral decision is a nonnegotiable feature of the registration agreement.[7] By assenting to be bound, the registrant authorizes its registrar to cancel, transfer or otherwise make changes to domain name registrations upon "our receipt of an order from a court or arbitral tribunal, in each case of competent jurisdiction, requiring such action; and/or . . . our receipt of a decision of an Administrative Panel requiring such action in any administrative proceeding to which you were a party and which was conducted under this Policy or a later version of this Policy adopted by ICANN."[8] Argument that the UDRP did not apply because the domain name was registered prior to its implementation failed to impress Panels. Challenges to ICANN's power to compel a registrant to answer for its choice of domain name and to order the registration canceled or transferred to complainant for abusive registration were definitively rejected as a jurisdictional defense.[9]

The separate bilateral contracts among ICANN, registries and registrars, and registrars and domain name registrants create a closed universe. A trademark owner has no contractual relationship with any of these parties, but when initiating

---

[5] RAA, 3.3.7.10. The submission by registrant to jurisdiction parallels complainant's submission under Rule (b)(xiii) of the Policy. See WIPO Final Report, paragraphs 141-146. "Mutual Jurisdiction" is defined in Rule 1 of the Rules of the Policy as either respondent's domicile or registrar's location.

[6] RAA, 3.7.7.11. "The Registered Name Holder shall agree that its registration of the Registered Name shall be subject to suspension, cancellation, or transfer pursuant to any ICANN adopted specification or policy, or pursuant to any registrar or registry procedure not inconsistent with an ICANN adopted specification or policy . . . for the resolution of disputes concerning the Registered Name." The Rules for the UDRP provide "Except in the case of deliberate wrongdoing neither the Provider nor a Panelist shall be liable to a Party for any act of omissions in connection with any administrative proceeding under these Rules" (Rule 20 Exclusion of Liability). The suspension remedy is not available for UDRP complainants; it became available to complainants challenging registrations of domain names with new gTLD extensions under the Uniform Rapid Suspension System (URS).

[7] Network Solutions Service Agreement, Version 9.27 provides "You acknowledge and agree that your rights to any domain name registered or renewed by Network Solutions on your behalf or otherwise used in conjunction with the Services are not being granted by Network Solutions but are subject to the rules and regulations of ICANN, the related registry and applicable law. As such, in addition to this Agreement, you agree to also abide by any and all terms and conditions promulgated by ICANN, as amended from time to time, which are hereby incorporated and made a part of this Agreement by reference, for all domain name registrations or renewals, including but not limited to, the Uniform Domain Name Dispute Resolution Policy."

[8] Paragraphs 3(b) and 3(c) of the Policy. The RAA provision (quoted in footnote 6) also includes the word "suspension." This applies to a sub-set of the UDRP, the Uniform Rapid Suspension

a proceeding against a domain name holder it must signify which mutual jurisdiction it agrees to be subject to in the event that an award in its favor is challenged. Respondent has three options upon receipt of a complaint: to answer; to default; or to commence an action in a court of competent jurisdiction.[10]

Registrants who are not trademark owners have contractual rights to hold their domain names for stipulated periods that can be indefinitely renewed pursuant to the terms of their registration agreements. They own their domain names only in the sense that while the registration agreements are in force registrants can treat domain names as assets to monetize, license, hold, or sell, as long as they were lawful when registered and are not being used in bad faith.[11] However, domain names can be lost without recourse to recovery if not renewed.[12] Renewals are regarded as continuations of the original registrations, the measuring date for determining bad faith registration.[13]

System (URS) discussed further below in Section 2.03-A initiated as an additional rights protection mechanism together with the Trademark Clearinghouse in 2013.

9 ***Beiersdorf AG v. Web4comm Srl Romania***, DRO2005-0002 (WIPO June 15, 2005); ***OSRAM GmbH, v. web4COMM SRL Romania***, DRO2005-0004 (WIPO October 5, 2005) (Romanian Respondents); ***Deutsche Telekom AG v. Oded Zucker***, D2004-0749 (WIPO November 18, 2004) (Israeli Respondent); ***Société des Bains de Mer v. Michael Ditursi***, D2005-1343 (WIPO February 28, 2006) (U.S Respondent). As the Panel points out in ***Television Broadcasts Limited v. Shen, Ying-Wei/The Vacation Bacchic Studio, Perfect Privacy, LLC.***, HK-1400665 (ADNDRC December 11, 2014) Respondent's agreement with the registrar provides that it is bound by any revision or change in the terms of the registration agreement which it acknowledges each renewal of registration.

10 The first sentence of paragraph 4(k) of the Policy provides that the "mandatory administrative proceeding requirements set forth in Paragraph 4 shall not prevent either you or complainant from submitting the dispute to a court of competent jurisdiction for independent resolution before such mandatory administrative proceeding is commenced or after such proceeding is concluded. . . ."

11 Domain names are either intangible property or contracts to provide Internet services. See "Distinguishing Owning and Holding" (Sec. 4.02-A.1.a.i).

12 The reverse is true of trademark owners. Purchasers of lapsed domain names may have to answer for their registrations. See "Right of Trademark Owner to Recapture Domain Name After Lapse of Registration" (Sec. 4.01-G).

13 Some Panels have seized on the theory that renewal may support abusive registration if respondent is using the domain name in bad faith. See "Renewal of Registration" (Sec. 4.03-A.4.c). Federal law under the ACPA takes a different approach. If bad faith use occurs at any point postdating the existence of a trademark, the domain name is liable to be forfeited. See *DSPT International v. Nahum,* 624 F.3d 1213 (9th Cir. 2010) (www.eq-Italy.com); *Newport News Holdings Corporation v. Virtual City Vision,* Incorporated, d/b/a Van James Bond Tran, 650 F3d 423 (4th Cir. 2011) (<newport-news.com>)

2.01-B

2.01-B What "Mandatory" Means

Paragraph 4 of the Policy describes the arbitral procedure as a "mandatory administrative proceeding."[14] The term "mandatory administrative proceeding" refers to the respondent's contractual agreement to have the claim of abusive registration submitted to an impartial arbitrator to determine its merits. "It is these Rules with which all applicants for the registration of domain names agree to be bound."[15] The term "mandatory" should not be misunderstood to mean that respondents are compelled to appear. In fact, in the vast majority of cases they default, most likely because the claims of abusive registration cannot be defended.[16] The term "mandatory" is used in the sense that respondents are "obliged by virtue of the [registration] agreement to recognize the validity of a proceeding initiated by a third-party claimant."[17] Due process dictates that respondent be given notice of the complaint and an opportunity to be heard, but it is the disposition of the domain name that is in issue. The proceeding is *in personam* only in the sense that respondent has a right to participate and defend, but if it chooses not to appear the proceeding is effectively *in rem*.[18]

---

[14] "This Paragraph sets forth the type of disputes for which you are required to submit to a mandatory administrative proceeding. These proceedings will be conducted before one of the administrative dispute resolution service providers listed at www.icann.org/udrp/approved-providers.htm (each, a 'Provider')." There is no intra-UDRP procedure for reviewing errors of law. The remedy under the UDRP against an overreaching trademark owner is a declaration sanctioning a complainant for abusing the Policy. Discussed further in "Complaint Filed in Bad Faith" (Sec. 7.11).

[15] ***Cimcities, LLC v. John Zuccarini D/B/A Cupcake Patrol***, D2001-0491 (WIPO May 31, 2001). Respondent is also bound by its representations and warranties to the Registrar, ***Carolina Herrera, Ltd. v. Alberto Rincon Garcia***, D2002-0806 (WIPO October 16, 2002).

[16] WIPO prepared an informative overview of the UDRP and its role in a paper dated August 2011 "for the purpose of informing discussion at the September 2011 INTA Conference on Trademarks and the Internet on the issue of whether it would be wise to review and make changes to the UDRP, at least at this time." It stated that over 35,000 cases had been processed by ICANN Providers of which the two most productive are WIPO and the Forum, previously known as National Arbitration Forum. The "transfer rate" is slightly lower for WIPO (86.1%) than the Forum (87.8%). WIPO decides approximately 52% of cases and the Forum approximately 45%. Appearing respondents prevail in about 30% of the cases with single member panels and 56.7% with three member Panels. Defaulting respondents (approximately 80% in 2011) lose 93% of the time decided by single-member Panels and 83.8% decided by three member Panels. That 16% of defaulting respondents before three member Panels retain their disputed domain names is a tribute to panelists' careful assessment of the record, but is also the result of the conjunctive model of the UDRP.

[17] *Storey v. Cello Holdings, L.L.C.*, 347 F.3d 370, 381 (2nd Cir. 2003). See also WIPO Final Report at paragraph 170. "[Mandatory is used] in the sense that each domain name applicant would, in the domain name registration agreement, be required to submit to the procedure if a claim was initiated against it by a third party."

[18] ***Two Way NV/SA v. Moniker Privacy Services, LLC / [4079779]: Domain Administrator***, D2012-2413 (WIPO June 7, 2013) ('yu.com'. "[A]lthough a UDRP action is nominally brought against the

UDRP's forfeiture granting power, which is akin to a mandatory injunction, is a powerful tool carried out administratively by the registrar on receipt of an order from the provider. The process begins with the initiation of a UDRP proceeding by filing and serving a complaint. Filing triggers a series of administrative acts by the provider and the registrar with whom the disputed domain name has been registered. The provider is required to review the complaint for compliance and request the registrar to confirm that the party named in a complaint is the registrant of record and is bound by the domain name registration agreement to submit the dispute to arbitration. Commencing a proceeding is discussed further in Sec. 7.01.

The registrar is required under the terms of the RAA to respond to a provider's request promptly.[19] A typical statement in WIPO decisions confirms that the registrar has disclosed the registrant and contact information and that "the Center has formally notified the Respondent of the Complaint and the [date for responding to it]." In Forum decisions the formulaic statement reads that the registrar has "verified that Respondent is bound by the registration agreement." It also advises Respondeent of "the deadline for a response[20] On due process grounds this assures that the proper party has been notified of a claim and will be properly served via e-mail with the complaint at the disclosed address. Respondent having given its (in) voluntary assent in acquiring the domain name thus becomes an unwilling even if (statistically) absent participant to the UDRP proceeding. Alternatively, respondent at its election may "before or during the proceeding" commence a plenary action in a court of competent jurisdiction which in the U.S. would be a legal proceeding under the Anticybersquatting Consumer Protection Act (ACPA) for a declaratory

---

domain name registrant, in practice it is brought against the domain name—i.e. effectively it is an action *in rem*, not *in personam*.")

The "mutual jurisdiction" clause is not a submission to personal jurisdiction. See *Marchex Sales, Inc. v. Tecnologia Bancaria*, S.A. 14cv1306 (E.D. Va. Alexandria Division May 21, 2015) in which the domain name holder challenged a UDRP award in an in rem proceeding. The Court held that "the agreement is limited to a challenge of a decision to the transfer of the domain name.... The language is specific; it involves only a challenge to a panel's decision to transfer a domain name [and cannot be enlarged to include damages and attorney's fees]."

19 Tardiness has been officially condemned by WIPO in a letter dated April 16, 2008 calling ICANN's attention to "certain registrar related practices . . . having a potentially adverse effect on the function of the ICANN mandated Uniform Domain Name Dispute Resolution Policy." Some of the practices identified by WIPO are inconsistent with and others are in violation of the RAA. A copy of the letter is available at <http://www.wipo.int/export/sites/www/amc/en/docs/icann160408.pdf>. A number of Panels have discussed registrar breaches of the RAA. In ***The Saul Zaentz Company d/b/a Tolkein Enterprises v. Eurobox Ltd. / "The Saul Zaentz Company"***, D2008-0156 (WIPO May 20, 2008), the registrar permitted a change in registrant identity after the complaint was filed. The Panel stated that it "suggests that respondent has sought to frustrate these proceedings." It also suggests collusion between the wayward registrar and the registrant.

20 The GDPR discussed further below does not change this obligation.

judgment that its registration was not unlawful, that it is not a cybersquatter, and is entitled to reasionable attorney's and damages.[21]

After notice of a decision determining the right to the disputed domain name either party may challenge the order canceling, transferring, or denying the complaint in a court of competent jurisdiction, but for respondent to enjoy the benefit of an automatic stay under paragraph 4(k) of the Policy it must commence an action within ten days of the issuance of the decision canceling or transferring the domain name, either in the mutual jurisdiction stipulated by complainant[22]; or, in a jurisdiction available to respondent "under normally applicable law."[23]

2.02 2.02 REGISTRANT'S RESPONSIBILITY FOR DETERMINING WHETHER DOMAIN NAME INFRINGES THIRD PARTY RIGHTS

A person is free to choose any string of letters,[24] words and phrases,[25] numbers[26] or combinations of words and numbers[27] for its domain name as long as it does not infringe the legal rights of any third party. The RAA provides

---

[21] Discussed further in Chapter 8. ICANN has anticipated a situation in which the registration expires during the course of the proceedings. The Registrar Accreditation Agreement 3.7.5.7 which is known as the Expired Domains Deletion Policy provides that "In the event that a domain which is the subject of a UDRP dispute is deleted or expires during the course of the dispute, the complainant in the UDRP dispute will have the option to renew or restore the name under the same commercial terms as the registrant. If the complainant renews or restores the name, the name will be placed in Registrar HOLD and Registrar LOCK status, the WHOIS contact information for the registrant will be removed, and the WHOIS entry will indicate that the name is subject to dispute. If the complaint is terminated, or the UDRP dispute finds against the complainant, the name will be deleted within 45 days. The registrant retains the right under the existing redemption grace period provisions to recover the name at any time during the Redemption Grace Period, and retains the right to renew the name before it is deleted." *See* ***Michael Aiduss LLC v. UDRP Compliance / UDRP Pending Renewal***, FA1403001549535 (Forum May 6, 2014).

[22] Staying transfer of a domain name is discussed further in "Paragraph 4(k) of the Policy" (Sec. 8.01). Second sentence of paragraph 4(k) reads: "***If an Administrative Panel decides that your domain name registration should be canceled or transferred, we will wait ten (10) business days (as observed in the location of our principal office) after we are informed by the applicable Provider of the Administrative Panel's decision before implementing that decision. We will then implement the decision unless we have received from you during that ten (10) business day period official documentation (such as a copy of a complaint, file-stamped by the clerk of the court) that you have commenced a lawsuit against complainant in a jurisdiction to which complainant has submitted under." Failure to act timely does not preclude a later filing but the stay will have expired.

"Mutual jurisdiction" is further discussed in "Plenary Adjudication After an Adverse Decision" (Sec. 8.01-B).

[23] WIPO Final Report, para. 142: "[A]n agreement to submit to jurisdiction in a domain registration agreement should be without prejudice to the possibility of establishing jurisdiction under normally applicable law and should not exclude that possibility."

[24] Discussed further in "Random Letters and Acronymic Trademarks" (Sec. 4.01-C).

> The Registered Name Holder shall represent that, to the best of the Registered Name Holder's knowledge and belief, neither the registration of the Registered Name nor the manner in which it is directly or indirectly used infringes the legal rights of any third party. (3.7.7.9)

The typical Registration Agreement requires the registrant to "agree to be bound by our current Dispute Resolution Policy" (which is the UDRP).[28]

Both the registration agreement and Paragraph 2 of the Policy ("Your Representations") extract representations from registrants about their purpose in registering domain names. The phrasing found in a typical registration agreement is similar to Paragraph 2 but not identical, which can be seen by comparing them. The Network Solutions subparagraphs (i) and (vi) and Paragraph 2(b) are similar in concept,[29] but Paragraph 2 goes further with subparagraphs (c) and (d) by defining the legal standards for lawful registration.

Not only are "(a) the statements that you made in your Registration Agreement ... complete and accurate; [and] (b) to your knowledge, the registration of the domain name will not infringe upon or otherwise violate the rights of any third party" but more explicitly "(c) you are not registering the domain name for an

---

25 Strings do not have to reproduce grammatically correct speech any more than do trademarks. For example, the trademark and Complainant's domain name in ***Pet Holdings Inc. v. Vladimir Prudnikov***, D2009-1003 (WIPO September 21, 2009) is I CAN HAS CHEEZBURGER <icanhascheezburger.com>; the disputed domain name—in this case confusingly similar—is <icanhashotdog.com> (Complaint granted).

26 ***Mäurer + Wirtz GmbH & Co. KG v. Lajos Kiss, Delux Befektetes***, D2007-1696 (WIPO February 5, 2008) (<711.org>); ***Maurer + Wirtz GmbH & Co. KG v. ROMFAB c/o Alf Temme***, FA0902001246453 (Forum March 31, 2009) (<711.us>) (Complaint granted).

27 ***GR8 Industries B.V v. Graffito / Active8 Partnership***, D2005-1341 (WIPO March 24, 2006) (<gr8.com>) (Default; Complaint denied).

28 According to the WIPO Final Report (Para. 108), ICANN's formulation in the Registrar Accreditation Policy is slightly different and "superior" to the one contained in the WIPO Interim Report in that it "requires a representation from the domain name applicant that extends beyond the intellectual property rights of third parties. It requires the applicant to represent that, to the best of its knowledge and belief, neither the registration nor the manner in which it is directly or indirectly used infringes the legal rights of a third party."

29 See Network Solutions Service Agreement version 9.33:

> "11. REPRESENTATIONS AND WARRANTIES. You agree and warrant that: (i) neither your registration nor use of the any of the Network Solutions services nor the manner in which you intend to use such Network Solutions Services will directly or indirectly infringe the legal rights of a third party, (ii) you have all requisite power and authority to execute this Agreement and to perform your obligations hereunder, (iii) you have selected the necessary security option(s) for your domain name registration record, (iv) you are of legal age to enter into this Agreement (or you are at least 13 years of age and have your parents' permission to apply for services hereunder); and (vi) [sic] you agree to comply with all applicable laws and regulations."

unlawful purpose; and (d) you will not knowingly use the domain name in violation of any applicable laws or regulations".[30]

Paragraph 2 concludes with the statement: "It is your responsibility to determine whether your domain name registration infringes or violates someone else's rights." The reason for underscoring registrant's responsibility is that domain names are not vetted upon acquisition. Registrars are not gatekeepers.[31] The consequences are spelled out in the registration agreement, namely that "if your use of our domain name registration services is challenged by a third party, you will be subject to the provisions specified in our dispute policy in effect at the time of the dispute."[32]

There is no contractual agreement between registrant and ICANN. Notes prefacing the Policy state that "3. The policy is between the registrar (or other registration authority in the case of a country-code top-level-domain) and its customer (the domain name holder or registrant). Thus, the policy uses 'we' and 'our' to refer to the registrar and it uses 'you' and 'your' to refer to the domain-name holder."[33]

The WIPO Final Report contemplated a light duty of investigation insofar as researching trademark databases,[34] but for registrants in domain businesses the

---

[30] The phrasing of the paragraph 2 representations is at the core of an alternative construction of the Policy advanced by some panelists starting in 2009. The alternative construction is discussed further in "Justifying Forfeiture Despite Good Faith Registration" (Sec. 4.03-A.4.b).

[31] In 2013, ICANN implemented a new set of rights protection mechanisms to the UDRP, one of which mandated claims warnings to registrants at the point of acquisition to discourage them from completing their registrations of domain names identical or confusingly similar to marks. See below "Sunrise and Beyond" (Sec. 2.03-A).

[32] *Id.* Network Solutions.

> "7. Domain Name Disputes Brought by Third Parties. You agree that, if your use of our domain name registration services is challenged by a third party, you will be subject to the provisions specified in our dispute policy in effect at the time of the dispute. For the adjudication of any disputes brought by a third party against you concerning or arising from your use of a domain name registered with us or your use of our domain name registration services, you (but not Network Solutions) agree to submit to subject matter jurisdiction, personal jurisdiction and venue of the United States District Court for the Eastern District of Virginia, Alexandria Division and the courts of your domicile."

[33] Paragraph 2 of the Policy is an added layer of representation of lawful registration. As noted above, some Panels have construed this to mean the representation is not limited to the purchase date of the domain name. Discussed further in "Justifying Forfeiture Despite Good Faith Registration" (Sec. 4.03-A.4.b).

[34] WIPO Final Report paragraph 103: "The WIPO Interim Report recommended that the performance of a prior search for potentially conflicting trademarks should not be a condition for obtaining a domain name registration. Almost unanimously, commentators agreed with this recommendation, whether searches were to be required to be carried out by the registration authorities or by the domain name applicants themselves. Particularly in an international context, the requirement of searches prior to the registration of a domain name was generally considered to be unrealistic and conducive to unnecessary delays in the registration process."

burden can be markedly heavier particularly if they have acquired portfolios that include domain names that currently postdate trademarks.[35] In the policy discussions underlying the WIPO Report it was considered unrealistic and conducive to unnecessary delays in the registration process, but there was also ambivalence about what is required of a registrant. Some investigation is necessary even if it stops short of researching national trademark databases. This appears to be anticipated two paragraphs later in the WIPO Report, in which the requirement is qualified to suggest that the applicant is not free to do nothing.[36]

The constraints suggested in Paragraph 105 were subsequently built into ICANN's contracts with registrars and registrars' contracts with registrants, and further reaffirmed in Paragraph 2 of the Policy. The Policy does not state that a registrant may register a domain name as long as it is available.[37] It conditions the registration on the representation that the domain name "will not infringe upon or otherwise violate the rights of any third party." This language underpins the argument that respondent has a continuing obligation not to violate the rights of any third party, which (as discussed below) is played out in decisions arguing for a unitary rather than a binary construction of the Policy.

Even though the responsibility falls short of researching trademark databases— "it is clear from the travaux preparatoires of the Policy that mere failure to conduct a trademark search does not constitute bad faith"[38]—it is equally clear that respondent is required to undertake some degree of due diligence, particularly for those strings of words that are arguably inherently distinctive. The phrases "to

---

Paragraph 105 reads: "It is not recommended that domain name registrations be made conditional upon a prior search of potentially conflicting trademarks, but it is recommended that the domain name application contain appropriate language encouraging the applicant to undertake voluntarily such a search."

35 There is a line of cases in which high-volume registrants are held to a higher level of investigation, thereby creating a dual standard. Discussed further in "Enhanced Investigative Responsibilities for High-Volume Registrants" (Sec. 6.03-B). This concept is not fully accepted by all panelists and has come under attack, "It seems at a minimum inconsistent to require a registrant registering multiple domain names to perform some kind of trademark search in order to establish good faith registration, while a registrant registering only one or two domain names is not required to do any search whatsoever," ***City Views Limited v. Moniker Privacy Services / Zander, Jeduyu, ALGEBRAL VE***, D-2009-0643 (WIPO July 3, 2009). The enhanced investigative standard is more likely to affect domain companies that purchase portfolios of domain names from original registrants who acquired them in good faith. This follows because as successors they may be holding domain names that postdate trademarks that did not exist when the domain names were originally registered. See "Transfer/Subsequent Holders=New Registration" (Sec. 4.03-B.2).

36 WIPO Final Report paragraph 105, *supra*.

37 ***Meloche Monnex Inc., and The Toronto-Dominion Bank v. Konstantin Vydria***, D2004-1045 (WIPO February 22, 2005).

38 ***FormLinc Information v. Credit Suisse Grp.***, FA 96750 (Forum April 18, 2001).

your knowledge" and "not registering the domain name for an unlawful purpose" presuppose that the registrant has assured itself that "the registration of the domain name will not infringe upon or otherwise violate rights of any third party." However, complainant must prove that respondent acted with knowledge and intention to "infringe or otherwise violate" its rights.

The diligence requirement is heightened and denial increasingly implausible as trademarks rise from the lesser or unknown to the well-known and famous.[39] In a case involving a ".biz" suffix,[40] the Panel stated that "[i]f the warranty to the Registrar is to be regarded as anything other than reckless (i.e. made without caring whether it be true or false) then a registrant should take some reasonable steps to satisfy him/herself that the warranty is true." However, this is a hard rule to apply to domain names that are generic as addresses (even though distinctive as marks) but plausibly acquired for their semantic rather than trademark values. .

In choosing a domain name, registrants are doubly bound by their representations and warranties in the domain registration agreement and Paragraph 2 of the Policy. Breach of these provisions has been construed to refer solely to the respondent's knowledge at the time of registration of the domain name and not to its subsequent bad faith use (if such occurs). That is, respondent represents and warrants its good faith in registering the domain name at the specific moment that it made its purchase. The representation and warranty does not extend to renewals of registration.[41]

However, there is a counter construction of the Policy already alluded to as the binary/unitary debate that the respondent's representations and warranties have continuing applicability, and that any future violation supports a finding of retroactive registration in bad faith.[42] This construction effectively reads a continuing promise into the original act of registration, with the result that any subsequent breach supports abusive registration regardless of registrant's motivation for acquiring the domain name. A variant of this construction reads the representation and warranty into renewals of the registration. In contrast, the precedential reading under the UDRP is that abusive registration is not proved by showing subsequent bad faith use. That issue is more likely to arise under the ACPA which applies

---

[39] ***Bold Limited v. Toni Georgiev / Outsourcing International Ltd***, FA1709001749693 (Forum November 3, 2017) (<myresumenow.com>. "The Panel recognizes that it is easy for a respondent to say that it had no knowledge of a complainant's business or trade name when it registered its domain name. The plausibility of such denial, however, diminishes as the fame or notoriety of the complainant increases.")

[40] ***MGM Mirage & the Primadonna Company, LLC v. Young Joon Choi***, DBIZ2001-00036 (WIPO February 14, 2002) (<primadonna.biz>).

[41] Discussed further in "Renewal of Registration vs. Registration by Transfer" (Sec. 4.03-B).

[42] The dueling constructions of the Policy are discussed further in "Justifying Forfeiture Despite Good Faith Registration" (Sec.4.03-A.4.b).

an either/or measure for proving cybersquatting—"registers, traffics in, *or* uses a domain name [in bad faith]" (emphasis added).

2.03 SUNRISE AND OTHER RIGHTS PROTECTION MECHANISMS 2.03

2.03-A Sunrise and Beyond 2.03-A

Commencing in 2012 ICANN began a formal process of reviewing, approving, and delegating hundreds of new gTLDs—dictionary words, professions, industries, hobbies, countries, regions, cities, and more—to supplement the familiar first-generation abbreviation suffixes (dot com, dot org, dot info, dot edu, etc) ("legacy" gTLDs). This brought into existence an entrepreneural generation of registries competing for the right to operate and market the new gTLDs under terms and conditions that are sometimes more demanding on registrants in terms of warranties and favorable to trademark owners than the base requirements set forth in the RAA.[43]

The process began by allowing trademark owners to object to proposed strings—"legal rights objections" (LROs)—to determine whether they were likely to infringe their existing legal rights.[44] It ended with successful registries marketing new gTLDs through registrars in successive periods: "Sunrise", followed by the connotatively rich "Landrush",[45] and ending with "General Availability" (at market prices).

Even as this process of approving new gTLDs was underway WIPO expressed concerns (widely shared by its intellectual property constituency) that "[t]he unprecedented expansion of the Internet domain name space . . . is likely to disrupt existing strategies for trademark protection on the web."[46] As a counter measure to expected cybersquatting opportunities ICANN implemented four additional rights

---

[43] Donuts, Inc., for example, offers a program under which brand owners are enabled to block third parties from registering domain names that only partially match their brands including misspellings, across all of the new gTLDs that it controls. This right is not limited to the sunrise period.

[44] There were very few successful LROs. The one that stands out is ***The DirecTV Group Inc. v. Dish DBS Corporation***, LRO2013 0005 (WIPO July 29, 2013) in which the Panel unanimously found that "[o]n the record before it [proof that the parties are direct competitors] . . . Respondent likely chose the <.direct> string for the sole purpose of disrupting the business of Objector." The Panel gave the following example of a possible abusive domain name, <television.direct>. LRO decisions are fully reported on the WIPO website.

[45] During "Landrush" any interested eligible persons may register domain names on a first-come-first-served basis even if the registrations are ultimately ruled infringing.

[46] WIPO Release dated March 17, 2014 is available at http://www.wipo.int/pressroom/en/articles/2014/article_0003.html. The Trademark Clearinghouse further discussed below allows brand owners to submit their trademark details for entry into a centralized database and enables the rights holder, after verification, to participate in the sunrise program and Trademark Claims service across all eligible new gTLDs. As with the UDRP, "Protections afforded to trademark registrations do not

protection mechanisms for trademark owners (RPMs): Trademark Clearinghouse (a registry-like service that verifies marks and their uses) (TMCH), Sunrise (a 90-day period during which owners whose trademarks have been verified by the TMCH may preregister names that are the same or similar to their trademarks), and Trademark Claims Notices (a TMCH warning service to registrants of possible infringements intended to discourage them from completing purchases of domain names identical or confusingly similar to marks);[47] The final piece is a new arbitral procedure, the Uniform Rapid Suspension System (URS). The URS is not intended for legacy gTLDs, and for new gTLDs, it applies only for that class of dispute colloquially referred to as a "slam dunk."[48] In terms of numbers the URS has not been overly utilized for reasons discussed further below principally having to do with the remedy which is limited to suspension for the duration of the registration, although

---

extend to applications for registrations, marks within any opposition period or registered marks that were the subject of successful invalidation, cancellation or rectification proceedings." Trademark owners wishing to track the Sunrise and Trademark Claim periods can do so for these new TLDs by going to ICANN's tracking website.

[47] The TMCH performs a kind of vetting for new gTLDs by giving notice to registrants in the act of registering domain names that they may be infringing but the TMCH has no power to prevent the registrations. It is described in a circular dated January 11, 2012 "allows brand owners to submit their trademark data into one centralized database, prior to and during the launch of new TLDs [the so-called Sunrise periods]." Further information is available at the TMCH website, http://trademark-clearing-house.com/ and ICAAN, https://www.icann.org/en/system/files/files/outreach-tmch-19sep13-en.pdf. See, ***Virgin Enterprises Limited v. Michelle Meads, Virgin Yachts***, D2016-2162 (WIPO March 13, 2017) ("Among other services, the TMCH provides warning notices to potential domain name registrants when they attempt to register a domain name that matches a trademark registered with the TMCH. If, after receiving and accepting the warning notice, the domain name registrant continues to register the domain name, the trademark holder with a corresponding mark in the TMCH receives a notification of the domain name registration, so they can take any appropriate action if they so choose. On June 20, 2016, the Complainant received a notification from the TMCH regarding the registration of the disputed domain name <virgin.yachts>").

[48] ICANN implemented the URS in June 2013. It describes the URS as "complement[ing] the existing (UDRP) by offering a lower-cost, faster path to relief for rights holders experiencing the most clear-cut cases of infringement." URS Procedure and Rules March 2013. The following other registries have adopted the URS: .cat, .jobs, .mobi, .pro, .pw, .travel, and .xxx. ICANN has proposed lifting price controls on .info, .org. .asia, biz, and extending the URS which has met with vigorous opposition. The standards for success are higher than the UDRP. Complainants must prove that the "registered domain name(s) is/are identical or confusingly similar to a word mark: (i) for which the Complainant holds a valid national or regional registration and that is in current use [thus no common law basis]; or (ii) that has been validated through court proceedings; or (iii) that is specifically protected by a statute or treaty in effect at the time the URS complaint is filed" [*Id.*] Three URS features particularly to be noted: 1) "the burden of proof shall be clear and convincing evidence" (URS Procedure 8.2)—as it is with the CEDRP above for the .xxx suffix; 2) the remedy is suspension of the domain name for the balance of the registration period (URS Procedure 10.2, 10-4); and 3) there is an appeal procedure (URS Procedure 12). URS Procedure, Rules, and Technical

suspension if employed as a substitute for injunctive relief can be a valuable tool for rapidly shutting down infringing websites.

These RPMs have largely eased WIPO's concerns but they have not alleviated tensions between mark owners and investors wishing to acquire domain names in character strings mark owners claim would be infringing but the investor led constituency claims could be used without infringing third-party rights.[49] That tension comes about as a result of competition among cyber stakeholders. It concerns (to use another real estate metaphor[50]) the metes and bounds of each constituency's rights.

During the Sunrise period mark owners have preemptive rights to register their marks if they hold "a valid national or regional registration ... that is in current use" and registered with the TMCH.[51] As between the UDRP and URS, though, the striking difference is that the URS is not available to complainants of unregistered marks with priority of use. This privilege of preemption is not without controversy because (the argument goes) it grants mark owners a right they otherwise would not have under trademark law, namely the ability to prevent others from registering domain names incorporating the same strings of characters that could have noninfringing uses and would not be unlawful. Tied into this controversy is the further question as to whether TMCH notices to registrants for a period following Sunrise discourage registrations that would otherwise be lawful.[52]

The URS and UDRP are similar in that both are crafted to protect owners from infringing use of their marks incorporated in domain names, but the jurisdiction of the URS is limited to claims in which the alleged second level domains have new gTLD extensions. They are also similar in that they are structured along the same lines (a three-part architecture) and employ identical language in itemizing

---

Requirements can be accessed from http://newgtlds.icann.org/en/applicants/urs. As with the UDRP, the domain name is locked but continues to resolve to the offending website pending determination of the claim. However, the turn around time to an award can be as little as twenty days.

49 All words that are not coined start off as generic terms, either as dictionary words or combined in phrases or expressions common in the community. Unless they are particularly distinctive others can use them without infringing on another's intellectual property rights.

50 In a 2007 news release Steve Forbes stated that "Internet traffic and domains [he said] are the prime real estate of the 21st century." The text can be found in <circleid.com> at http://www.circleid.com/posts/792113_steve_forbes_domain_name_economics/.

51 URS Procedure 1.2.6.1. Validation by the TMCH which includes proof of use complies with the standing requirement. Trademark owners wishing to track the Sunrise and Trademark Claim periods can do so for these new TLDs by going to ICANN's tracking website http://newgtlds.icann.org/en/program-status/ sunrise-claims-periods.

52 Scholar's Letter to ICANN GNSO RPM Working Group dated March 17, 2017 available at https://www.eff.org/document/trademark-scholars-letter-icann-gnso-rpm-working-group. EFF White Paper dated July 27, 2017 Which Internet Registries Offer the Best Protection For Domain Name Owners? The White Paper is available at https://www.eff.org/files/2017/07/28/domain_registry_whitepaper.pdf . It states that "[u]nfortunately, the Trademark Clearinghouse admits many

the evidentiary demands complainants must satisfy to prevail and the defenses available to respondents to avoid forfeiture. However, these similarities are superficial as opposed to the differences.

There are three principal differences between the UDRP and the URS: evidentiary demands, remedies, and appeal.[53] A trademark owner satisfies its burden of proof under the UDRP by a preponderance of the evidence standard, whereas the URS requires the more demanding clear and convincing standard (URS Procedure, Art. 8.2). Under the UDRP a successful trademark owner has the choice of having the domain name registration cancelled or transferred into its own name. Under the URS there is no choice. On proof of infringement the domain name is suspended for the duration of the registration (URS Procedure, Art. 10.2). Either party has the right to an administrative appeal: "Appellant shall have a limited right to introduce new admissible evidence that is material to the Determination. . . provided the evidence clearly pre-dates the filing of the Complaint" (URS Rules 19(b)).

A partial list of approved dictionary word gTLDs that have already been implicated in URS proceedings since 2014 including: .bike, .blue, .club, .clothing, .digital, .email, .expert, .guru, .gallery, .social, .space, .store, .technology, .ventures, and .vip of which a very high percentage are suspended and very few decisions are appealed.[54] Some trademark owners prefer to commence a UDRP rather than a URS

---

questionable entries into its database, with the result that legitimate domain registrants are prevented from registering domains during the sunrise period, or are needlessly frightened away from doing so during the subsequent Claims period."

53 Differences specific to each requirement include:

First limb: URS Complainants must have registered rights, and those rights must be for "word" marks. See URS Procedure 1.2.6.1: "The registered domain name(s) is/are identical or confusingly similar to a word mark: (i) for which the Complainant holds a *valid national or regional registration and that is in current use*" (emphasis added). In contrast, Panels have construed the UDRP to include unregistered marks if there is persuasive evidence of use in commerce predating the registration of the domain name. Examiners do not inherit this construction and have no authority to consider extending the jurisdiction.

Second limb: If respondents are passively holding domain names that could conceivably be lawful—such as <whitecastle.space> but not <dior.clothing>—the complaint must be dismissed because it cannot be said (until there is clear and convincing evidence) that Respondent lacks legitimate rights or interests. In contrast, UDRP Complainants succeed on this limb by making a *prima facie* showing that Respondents lack rights or legitimate interests.

Third limb: If Complainant succeeds under the second limb it has to overcome the consensus (to surmount the higher bar of clear and convincing proof) that passive holding of domain names not particularly associated with it or its goods or services is not probative of bad faith registration. Under UDRP's lower standard of proof, bad faith use can be probative of bad faith registration absent rebuttal based on the persuasive lack of knowledge (parties located in different national jurisdictions, for example, or marks composed of such common elements it is not improbable registrants lacked knowledge), or good faith under the first-come, first-served doctrine.

54 Early URS decisions include ***International Business Machines Corporation v. Denis Antipov***, FA1402001542313 (Forum February 12, 2014) (<ibm.guru> and ibm.ventures>). Registrars of

proceeding because the UDRP remedy gives them greater control in removing the domain name from cyberspace entirely[55]. Under the URS the domain name is "limited to suspension … for the balance of the registration" (URS Rule 14A) at which point it returns to the pool of available names and possible new infringements.[56]

2.03-B No Prejudice for Failure to Take Advantage of the Sunrise Period 2.03-B

Trademark owners do not have to take advantage of the Sunrise period, but failure makes them vulnerable to opportunistic registrations in and after Sunset. Precedential decisions involving the .mobi and .tel suffixes[57] (discussed here) and the .xxx suffix (discussed separately below) indicate the consequences for owners of

---

gTLDs and ccTLDs may opt into the URS, see ***Facebook Inc. v. Radoslav***, FA130800 1515825 (Forum September 27, 2013) (<facebok.pw>. Dot pw is the suffix for Palau). Complainants are not precluded from applying the UDRP in a URS proceeding. URS, Art. 13: "The URS Determination shall not preclude any other remedies available to the appellant, such as UDRP (if appellant is the Complainant), or other remedies as may be available in a court of competent jurisdiction."

[55] Examples of UDRP rather than URS include, ***Louis Poulsen Lighting A/S v. Spear Lighting, Amru Al-Kadhi***, D2014-0623 (WIPO June 10, 2014) (<louispoulsen.lighting>; ***Ancestry.com Operations, Inc. v. Kerry Shahan***, FA1405001560028 (Forum July 6, 2014) (<ancestry.pro>).

[56] It could be argued that shutting down websites effectively grants Complainant the equivalent of a preliminary injunction. See URS Procedure 10.2: "[If the determination is made in favor of Complainant] the Registry Operator shall suspend the domain name, which shall remain suspended for the balance of the registration period, and would not resolve to the original web site." URS Procedure 10.2: "[If the determination is made in favor of Complainant] the Registry Operator shall suspend the domain name, which shall remain suspended for the balance of the registration period, and would not resolve to the original web site." See URS cases involving 1) phishing, spoofing [***Virgin Enterprises Limited v. WhoisGuard, Inc.***, FA1709001748703 (Forum September 28, 2017) (<virginpulse.life>], and 2) selling counterfeit goods [***W.L. Gore & Associates Inc v. WhoisGuard, Inc. et al.***, FA1711001758178 (Forum December 6, 2017) (<goretexgiyim.world>. "[T]he impression created by ... Registrant's website is [that it is] an original online shop of the Complainant with even more convenient prices but offering counterfeit products"); ***Eli Lilly and Company v. Shaternik et al.***, FA170500 1731038D (Forum June 1, 2017) (Offering counterfeit products on dozens of websites).

[57] ***C. Bechstein Pianofortefabrik AG v. Melvin Besbrode, Besbrode Pianos Leeds***, D2008-1528 (WIPO December 4, 2008) (<bechstein.mobi> i); ***Adidas AG v. Zhifang Wu***, D2007-0032 (WIPO March 21, 2007) (<adidas.mobi>); and ***Mansueto Ventures, LLC v. Jonathan Witte***, D2006-1479 (WIPO January 19, 2007) (<inc.mobi>); ***Omron Corporation v. Yuri A Ivanov***, D2011-1071 (WIPO September 2, 2011) (<omron.tel>, Transferred. "Respondent . . . contends that the Complainant must prove that the Respondent has no rights or legitimate interests in respect of the disputed domain name.") See also a URS decision, ***GFPI S.A. v. Michael Meyer et al.***, FA1702001716444F (Forum February 21, 2017) (<tagheuer.digital>. (<tagheuer.digital>. Initially denied; reversed and suspended on appeal FA1702001716444A (Forum March 22, 2017). "The Respondent claimed that the disputed domain name was available for purchase in the commercial market once the sunrise period expired. The Panel disagrees. The Sunrise period provides a priority for trademark owners to register their marks as domain names.... However, trademark rights are not released or waived as a

well-known and famous marks of not taking advantage of Sunrise periods are principally time and expense of prosecuting registrants for abusive registration in post-Sunrise proceedings.

While there is no prejudice in waiting where the marks are well known,[58] it could affect the less well known and marks composed of generic elements.[59] If there can be said to be a formulaic (but unpersuasive) argument to avoid forfeiture of abusively registered domain names it is that complainant is equitably barred from maintaining a proceeding for failure to act timely in securing its Sunrise rights.

In ***Adidas***, respondent stated that it offered the domain name for sale "only after the priority or sunrise period for registration" had expired, implying thereby that by failing to register in every gTLD complainant has nothing to complain about. In Respondent's view he was the aggrieved party: "[C]omplainant should take the responsibility of securing the different domain names incorporating the ADIDAS mark and not attempt to seize them from others like respondent who has legitimately registered the domain name." However, this is "not the law":

> [N]either Respondent's compliance with the '.mobi' sunrise procedures nor Complainant's failure to apply for [a domain name], in and of itself, confers upon Respondent a right to use Complainant's mark in that domain name for a business that competes with Complainant's. . . . [E]ven success in a Sunrise Challenge does not insulate a '.mobi' domain name from a subsequent attack under the Policy.

---

result of the passage of the Sunrise period or for that matter any other period relating to the registration of domain names."

[58] See for example ***SEGA Games Co., Ltd. v. Amman Sabet***, D2016-2060 (WIPO November 24, 2016) (<sega.games>) ("Whether or not the Complainant failed to register the disputed domain name during the relevant "sunrise" period, the mere registration of the disputed domain name by the Respondent (by whatever method) does not vest him with rights or legitimate interests in respect of the disputed domain name.") Similar judgments have been reached with country codes. In Albania, an opportunist beat Coca-Cola to registration for <coca-cola.al>. Tirana District Court rejected Coca-Cola's claim. On appeal to the Tirana Court of Appeal, judgment reversed and registration cancelled (November 2011). The Court held that a trademark owner does not lose its right to a corresponding domain name. Reported by Gjergji Gjika, Drakopoulos Law Firm, http://www.drakopoulos-law.com/mediaupload/ pdf_ip/IAM_coca_cola.pdf.

[59] ***Bloomberg Finance L.P. v. zhang guo jie***, FA1703001721683 (Forum March 31, 2017) (<Bloomberg.site>. A URS proceeding: "The Complaint is . . . devoid of any allegations or proof of facts tending to show, even *prima facie*, either that Respondent has no right to or legitimate interest in the <bloomberg.site> domain name, or that the domain name was registered and is being used by Respondent in faith.") Complaint then commenced a UDRP with the same result, ***Bloomberg Finance L.P. v. zhang guo jie***, FA1704001727926 (Forum June 8, 2017) ("[E]ven taking account of the public use which has been made of the trademark, it is a common family name . . . which might remain open to use in good faith by any number of traders. . . . This is not a case of an invented word with no connotation other than the goods or services of a single trader where it is difficult to perceive of any good faith use. Absent any use or other telling indicia, an inference of likely bad faith use could here only rest on supposition.

The fact that "complainant did not avail itself of the 'sunrise' procedure for .mobi names [is irrelevant]. That failure is no obstacle to complainant exercising its rights under the UDRP."[60] Respondents have made similar arguments for the .xxx gTLD that have been similarly rejected.

2.03-C Canceling Domain Names in the xxx gTLD Space 2.03-C

The .xxx gTLD became generally available on December 6, 2011.[61] If a proceeding for abusive registration is commenced under the CEDRP the domain name is "locked against transfers between registrants and/or registrars."[62] Complainant is not precluded from presenting its complaint in "concurrent administrative proceedings"[63] so that "[i]f a domain name in the .XXX gTLD is subject to a UDRP proceeding, the factors set forth in the CEDRP may be alleged in such proceeding as applicable terms of legitimate rights or registration and use under the UDRP."[64]

To carry its burden in a CEDRP proceeding a qualified complainant must show "by clear and convincing evidence that the domain name in the .XXX TLD has been improperly registered or used under one or more of the circumstances in this section."[65] Correspondingly, respondent must prove that it is a member of the sponsored community for which the TLD space was created.[66] The Policy continues:

> Any claim premised on non-use or improper use of a registered domain name in the .XXX TLD under this CEDRP shall be evaluated in light of practical circumstances relative to the length of time the domain name has been registered by its registrant and the adequacy thereof for engaging in preparation for eligible use of the domain name.

The CEDRP differs from the UDRP in at least one fundamental way, namely that

> "Non-commercial commentary or criticism" of a specific person or business entity targeted by a registered domain name in the .XXX TLD will not be deemed a legitimate use.

---

60 ***Mansueto Ventures, supra. The Panel in Yahoo! Inc. v. David Blanco***, FA0908001280452 (Forum October 14, 2009) reached a similar result for ".tel" in <yahoo.tel>.

61 As well as being subject to the UDRP, the .xxx gTLD is also subject to the Charter Eligibility Dispute Resolution Policy (CEDRP) which became effective as of September 1, 2011.

62 Paragraph 5 of the CEDRP.

63 Paragraph 8 of the CEDRP.

64 *Id.* See ***McKool Smith, P.C. v. Chelsea Davis***, FA1311001529145 (Forum December 30, 2013) (<mckoolsmith.xxx>. Law firm and former employee).

65 Under the CEDRP the sole remedy is cancellation, paragraph 3 of the Policy and 5(e) of Forum Rules.

66 See, for example, ***HEB Grocery Company, L.P. v. Eric Gonzales***, FA1112001421851 (Forum February 7, 2012) (<heb.xxx>).

Reference to a "specific person" introduces a new protective shield for individuals.[67] The reference appears both in the Policy and the Rules promulgated by the Forum. The Rules read

> Complainant means the single person or entity claiming to have rights in the domain name in the .XXX TLD, or multiple persons or entities who have a sufficient nexus who can each claim to have rights to the domain name listed in the complaint (emphasis added).

While trademark ownership continues to be the rule, there is reason to believe that by employing the phrase "single person" as a distinct class the standard for unregistered trademark rights is intended to include protection of personal names. Membership in the sponsored community is a sine qua non as explained in the cited case:

> Absent any industry connection or involvement, Respondent cannot be a member of the relevant "sponsored community" and is ineligible to register any domain name on the .XXX registry.

If not a member of the sponsored community, and ineligible to register an .xxx TLD, respondent lacks rights or legitimate interests and this in turn supports a finding of abusive registration:

> While on the one hand Respondent submits that the name RICHARD BRANSON is not unique or unusual, Respondent nevertheless registered the domain because of Complainant's notoriety. Respondent should have recognized that his registration and control of <richardbranson.xxx> would serve to vex or embarrass Complainant. Registering and holding a .XXX domain name identical to Complainant's mark without having any rights or interests therein is evidence of bad faith registration and use under Policy §4(a)(iii).

The Panel explained that "Respondent's defiance of the applicable .XXX gTLD registration eligibility requirements . . . [was] an additional independent ground demonstrating bad faith."

2.04 2.04 USE AND ABUSE OF PROXY AND PRIVACY SERVICES

2.04-A 2.04-A Legitimate Use of Proxy and Privacy Services[68]

Privacy (also referred to as "shield") and proxy services are described in a 2007 case as a relatively recent phenomenon.[69] Registrars developed the shield services in reaction to ICANN's requirement that registrants disclose their identity and

[67] ***Richard Branson v. Sean Truman***, FA1201001423689 (Forum February 14, 2012) (<richardbranson.xxx>). Compare with decisions discussed below in "Personal Names" (Sec. 4.01-E.1).

[68] The General Data Protection Regulation (GDPR) discussed further below in the Whois Directory makes it unnecessary for natural persons to continue using these services since their contact information will be hidden after May 25, 2018. The services will still have value for juristic persons since

contact information for inclusion on a public database, the Whois Directory, and in response to a demand among the community of registrants concerned about exposure to spam or worse.[70] Using a shield or proxy registration service is not evidence of bad faith and may be consistent with good faith.[71]

The consensus view of shield and proxy registration services is that they are "not in and of [themselves] an indication of bad faith . . . [but] the manner in which such service[s] [are] used can in certain circumstances constitute a factor indicating bad faith."[72] While the services may "aid cybersquatters by facilitating delays, cyberflight . . . and hiding from mark owners"[73] the practice is accorded only the weight it deserves, which is generally minimal unless there are other facts such as concealing true identity and false contact information that together support bad faith.[74]

No bad faith can be imputed to registrants for simply purchasing services, and there are good reasons for not doing so. Three reasons have been offered: 1) ease of account management and renewal of registration (especially where the registrant has registered a portfolio of domain names); 2) avoidance of identity theft; and 3)

---

the GDPR does not protect them from having their contact information disclosed in the Whois Directory.

[69] ***Divex Limited v. ZJ, Sam Chang and Tim NG.***, D2007-0861 (WIPO September 27, 2007) (complaint denied). The current Registrar Accreditation Agreement at Section 3.14 (2013) and the Specification on Privacy and Proxy Registrations (2016) address the respective responsibilities of registrars and services. The earlier Accreditation Agreements 2001 and 2009 did not address the issue and the Privacy and Proxy Accreditation Program referred to in Section 3.14 is (as of December 2016) yet to be implemented. However, pending the implementation registrars and services are governed by the Specification. The United States Department of Commerce ruled in February 2005 that "proxy or anonymous" registration services are not permitted for the ".us" country code. The requirement was challenged and rejected. See footnote 93 below in "The Whois Directory" (Sec. 2.05).

[70] The worst is spamming, spoofing, phishing, and distribution of malware discussed further in "Spoofing and Phishing" (6.01-C.2.c).

[71] See WIPO Overview 2.0, Paragraph 3.9:

> Consensus view: Although use of a privacy or proxy registration service is not in and of itself an indication of bad faith, the manner in which such service is used can in certain circumstances constitute a factor indicating bad faith. For example, registrant use of a privacy service in combination with provision of incomplete contact information to such service or a continued concealment of the 'true' or 'underlying' registrant (possibly including that registrant's actual date of acquisition) upon the institution of a UDRP proceeding may be evidence of bad faith.

[72] *Id.*, WIPO Overview 2.0: The "common practice ... to which reputable registrars offering such services appear to subscribe. . . [is to] disclose the details of the underlying registrant to the Center during UDRP proceedings in response to the Center 's verification request." The Jurisprudential Overview revises the language slightly, Paragraph 3.6.

[73] *Id.*

[74] ***H & M Hennes & Mauritz AB v. Whois Privacy Protection Service, Inc. / Dvl Den***, D2016-2474 (WIPO January 31, 2017) ("In connection with this finding, it also carries weight in the eyes of the

evasion of spam. Their use also gives respondent "the ability to maintain the confidentiality of a registration strategy, such as the registration of numerous domain names related to a specific industry (such as travel, or goods and services available in specific geographic areas.")[75]

A further reason for giving less weight to a respondent's use of proxy and privacy services is that the beneficial registrant is generally unmasked prior to the provider submitting the complaint and annexes to the Panel,[76] which averts concern they are being used to obstruct or subvert the proceedings. Even if the beneficial owner is not unmasked, there is a diminished likelihood of its appearing, and while "Foul intent" must still be proved[77] Panels are apt to examine the factual circumstances carefully.[78] Accordingly, no conclusive inference is drawn from the use of privacy or proxy services. They have "never been given primacy in [themselves] as a circumstance amounting to bad faith, in the absence of some further element of fraud or deception."[79]

Panel that Respondent not only made use of a WhoIs privacy shield apparently in an attempt to conceal his true identity, but also provided false WhoIs contact information, since the delivery of the notification of the Complaint sent to Respondent via DHL on November 16, 2016 failed due to an apparent invalid postal address.")

[75] ***iFranchise Group v. Jay Bean / MDNH, Inc. / Moniker Privacy Services [2658]***, D2007-1435 (WIPO December 18, 2007).

[76] Complainants typically name the registrant identified in the Whois directory as of the date the complaint is filed. If the named registrant is a privacy service the Provider typically invites the complainant to amend its complaint. ***WSFS Financial Corporation v. Private Registrations Aktien Gesellschaft 2***, D2012-0033 (WIPO March 5, 2012). Discussed further in "Use and Abuse of Proxy and Privacy Services" (Sec. 2.04).

[77] ***CyBerCorp Holdings, Inc. v. Jay Allman***, FA 0403000244090 (Forum May 14, 2004). Registrants' responsibilities are typically spelled out in respective registrar services' agreements. The personal and contact information maintained by the services will be produced upon request "to resolve any and all third party claims, whether threatened or made, arising out of Your use of IDP Domain, or take any other action which Backend Service Provider deems necessary" (from Name.com ID Protection Service Agreement, sec. 5). The action deemed necessary is to disclose the beneficial holder and its contact information when requested in connection with a UDRP proceeding.

[78] The Panel in ***The Jennifer Lopez Foundation v. Jeremiah Tieman, Jennifer Lopez Net, Jennifer Lopez, Vaca Systems LLC***, D2009-0057 (WIPO March 24, 2009) (<jenniferlopez.net> and <jenniferlopez.org>) found foul intent when respondent resorted to a privacy service after Complainant filed its complaint. These manipulations are "strongly evocative of cyberflight, and appear to have been calculated to obstruct or delay this proceeding under the Policy." See also ***Teva Pharmaceutical Industries Ltd. v. Teva Pharm***, CAC 101326 (ADR.eu December 5, 2016). Respondent (who did not appear) registered <tevapharmscareers.com> using a privacy service but it provided false information about its name and address, namely it registered under the name of "TEVA PHARM". The Panel concluded it did this "on purpose": "It shows that the Respondent [identified as 'Susan Fowler'] intended to appear as being the Complainant when sending emails to third parties."

[79] ***Integrated Payment systems, Inc. v. Integratedpaymentsystems.com c/o Whois Identity Shield***, D2006-1214 (WIPO November 12, 2006).

It is not the Policy's aim to interfere with respondents' business decisions to shield personal information, but to find "a proper balance between privacy, on the one hand, and the need for accountability and cybersquatting prevention, on the other hand."[80]

2.04-B Abusive Use of Proxy and Privacy Services 2.04-B

The path to consensus began with the less nuanced view that "by operating through a Whois Agent, respondent took deliberate steps to hide its true identity so as to make impossible for third parties any direct communication with it, which behavior has been found to constitute evidence of bad faith within the meaning of the Policy."[81] The more nuanced view is that employing a privacy or proxy service is a factor among others.[82] Hiding the name of the beneficial holder of the domain name is not on a par with any of the bad faith circumstances listed in paragraph 4(b) of the Policy.[83] While in theory privacy and proxy services are not intended to facilitate evasion of process by registrants, there are instances in which they have been found to frustrate a trademark owner's claim of abusive registration.[84] A critical issue is whether respondent has a right not to disclose his or her identity in registering the domain name for use as anonymous speech.[85] As a general rule, evidence of bad faith is strengthened when coupled with false and misleading contact information,[86] found to be spamming, spoofing, and phishing[87] or hidden beneath another layer of protection.[88]

---

[80] ***Ustream.TV, Inc. v. Vertical Axis, Inc***, D2008-0598 (WIPO July 29, 2008).

[81] ***Countrywide Financial Corporation, Inc. and Countrywide Home Loans, Inc. v. Marc Bohleren***, D2005-0248 (WIPO June 9, 2005), citing ***Consitex S.A., Lanificio Ermenegildo Zegna & Figli S.p.A., Hermenegildo Zegna Corporation v. LionHeart securities Corp.***, D2003-0285 (WIPO May 15, 2003).

[82] ***iFranchise Group, supra.; Charter Communications, Inc. v. CK Ventures Inc. / Charterbusiness.com***, D2010-0228 (WIPO June 25, 2010).

[83] ***Two Way NV/SA v. Moniker Privacy Services, LLC / [4079779]: Domain Administrator***, D2012-2413 (WIPO June 7, 2013) (<yu.com>. "[It is not] something that is regarded by itself as of such significance that it can constitute bad faith and result in the transfer of a domain name.")

[84] ***Fifth Third Bancorp v. Secure Whois Information Service***, D2006-0696 (WIPO September 14, 2006) ("[A] feature shared with many cybersquatting cases involv[es] fictitious registrant data."); ***TDS Telecommunications Corporation v. Registrant*** [20758] ***Nevis Domains and Registrant [117460] Moniker Privacy Services***, D2006-1620 (WIPO March 7, 2007).

[85] The Panel in ***Retail Royalty Company and AE. Direct Co LLC v. AK***, FA140900 1580871 (Forum October 31, 2014) (Complaint granted) held it was "unusual ... for a registrant of a domain name who has taken advantage of the anonymity granted by a privacy shield, to remain anonymous after the shield has been lifted. One has to ask why the Respondent would want to continue to hide his/her/its identity if the Respondent's intention was to provide an objective review of the pluses and minuses of the Complainant's credit card offering. Any dispassionate reviewer, one would have thought, had little to fear."

Use of privacy shields by high-volume registrants has been criticized by panelists who question their "need" to protect [their] identit[ies] except to frustrate the purposes of the Policy or make it difficult for a brand owner to protect [its] trademark[] against infringement, dilution and cybersquatting."[89] The concern is that "the privacy shield may also allow registrants to transfer domain name registrations amongst themselves without any public record that there has been a transfer, thus allowing them to evade enforcement of legitimate third party rights or to obstruct proceedings commenced under the Policy." The Panel in this last cited case continued that use of a privacy shield can be "treated as evidence of bad faith . . . when serial registrants use privacy shields to mask each registrant's actual date of registration."

According to the Panel in ***Ustream*** "[s]uch use defies the Policy's overriding objectives to preserve accountability for unlawful acts on the Internet and to curb the abusive registration of domain names and cybersquatting." Anonymity is particularly troublesome where respondent is a commercial venture competing with complainant.[90] It is legitimate to ask why "a commercial business with over 10,000 domain names requires the benefit of a privacy shield."[91] The Panel continued, "Our view that such a practice inhibits and can be used to thwart the achievement of swift outcomes under the UDRP is another reason to exercise our discretion in favour of complainant by admitting the Supplementary Submission."

---

86 ***Dr. Ing. h.c. F. Porsche AG v. Domains by Proxy, Inc. and Vladimir Putinov***, D2004-0311 (WIPO July 1, 2004) (finding bad faith on the part of the proxy service provider as well as by the real party in interest); ***Fifth Third Bancorp***, *supra*. ("Given the covert nature of the registration—disclosing neither the name of the service provider nor of the real party in interest . . . the inference of bad faith is strengthened.")

87 ***Teva Pharmaceutical Industries Ltd. v. Teva Pharm***, CAC 101326 (ADR.eu December 5, 2016) ("[U]sing a false name spoofing Complainant's name . . . as a first and last name to register the disputed domain name, and using Complainant's address in the U.S. headquarters as its residential address is additional evidence of bad faith registration and use.") See "Spoofing and Phishing" (Sec. 6.01-C.2.c).

88 The Panel notes in ***WSFS Financial***, *supra*, that "for this practice to operate at all, it requires a registrar to control the privacy service in question and/or to have access to accurate underlying registrant data." However, the procedure "can be defeated if behind the registrar 's service there is merely recorded the name of another third party privacy service (the so called 'Russian doll' scenario). Further, there appears to be no legitimate justification for such 'Russian doll' registrations. Indeed, panels have concluded that a Russian doll registration is evidence of bad faith."

89 See ***Sermo, Inc. v. CatalystMD, LLC***, D2008-0647 (WIPO July 2, 2008) and ***Ustream.TV, Inc. v. Vertical Axis, Inc.***, D2008-0598 (WIPO July 29, 2008). The criticism parallels the view that high-volume registrants have an enhanced investigative duty.

90 ***Bank of America Corporation v. [Registrant]***, FA0809001226147 (Forum November 7, 2008) (Domain transferred).

91 ***Trade Me Limited v. Vertical Axis Inc.***, D2009-0093 (WIPO April 7, 2009).

Panel views of privacy blocks have moderated over the years once it was established they could be pierced to disclose the beneficial owner of the accused domain name who can be joined in the proceeding with the proxy.

2.05 THE WHOIS DIRECTORY 2.05

2.05-A As Conceived 2.05-A

ICANN committed itself in agreements with the U.S. Department of Commerce[92] to preserve a publicly accessible record of domain name registrants.[93] With the cutting of the umbilical cord in September 2016, this commitment is satisfied through agreements with accredited registrars under the RAA, which requires registrars to collect and provide free public access to information about the domain name registrant "sufficient to contact a responsible party for a particular gTLD domain name who can resolve, or reliably pass on data to a party who can resolve, issues related to the configuration of the records associated with the domain name within a DNS name server."[94]

However, the model of the Whois directory described in this section has been narrowed by two developments, namely 1) registrars offering proxy and privacy services dating from 2005, and 2) a privacy regulation adopted by the European Union effective May 25, 2018, the General Data Protection Regulation (GDPR).[95] While the default of the Whois directory as originally conceived is to collect and

---

92 Before ICANN became independent of the U.S. government there had been periodic Memoranda of Understanding including the September 30, 2009 Affirmation of Commitments with the U.S. Department of Commerce. See Chapter 1, Footnote 17.

93 Paragraph 9.3.1 of the Affirmation reads: "ICANN additionally commits to enforcing its existing policy relating to WHOIS, subject to applicable laws. Such existing policy requires that ICANN implement measures to maintain timely, unrestricted and public access to accurate and complete WHOIS information, including registrant, technical, billing, and administrative contact information." The National Telecommunications and Information Administration (NTIA) was challenged on the privacy issue in an action entitled *Peterson v. NTIA*, 478 F.3d 626 (E.D. VA 2006). Plaintiff had argued that disclosures he was required to make violated his First Amendment Rights to speak anonymously.

94 Generic Names Supporting Organization (GNSO) Counsel, April 12, 2006. In a Final Report dated October 31, 2013 the GNSO voted unanimously to recommend a change to the Whois service requirements. ICANN adopted the Final Report on February 7, 2014. Beginning in 2014, registrars under the 2013 RAA will be required to publish WHOIS data that includes registrar abuse contacts. Nevertheless, there is an ongoing debate within the ICANN community concerning publication of personal data in the Whois directory—a requirement under the RAA—that affects registrars operating in countries that have strict data protection laws. For some countries, complying with the RAA is tantamount to disobeying the law.

95 The GDPR is intended to protect all EU citizens and residents from privacy and data breaches but given the internationalism of registrars the regulation effectively has application beyond EU borders. Since registrars operating in the EU must comply with the GDPR they cannot comply with

make available registrant's contact information (thereby allowing proxy and privacy services to flourish by blocking it), the default of the GDPR is to protect personal contact information for registrants who are natural persons although they can agree to having their contact information disclosed.[96] The GDPR does not affect the collection of data, only access to it. The GDPR is discussed in the next section.

The GDPR notwithstanding, once a UDRP proceeding is initiated registrars have a contractual obligation to identify beneficial holders when they receive notice from a provider that a complaint has been filed alleging abusive registration.[97] This disclosure requirement was extended in 2016 to include requests for disclosure of customer contact information before commencement of any action or administrative proceedings,[98] although this is likely to be a casualty of the GDPR and may lead to an increase in the number of UDRP filings as a means of obtaining that information.[99]

---

the RAA. See Temporary Specification for gTLD Registration Data, adopted by ICANN Board on May 17, 2018, effective May 25, 2018 which was "aimed to ensure the continued availability of the WHOIS system to the greatest extent possible while maintaining the security and stability of the Internet's system of unique identifiers."

96 The GDPR does not apply to juristic persons; natural persons can opt out (GDPR Art. 6 para. 1lit.a). See further in footnote 112.

97 Temporary Specification, *supra*, Appendix E: "1.1. "Registrar Requirement: The Registrar MUST provide the UDRP provider with the full Registration Data for each of the specified domain names, upon the UDRP provider notifying the Registrar of the existence of a complaint, or participate in another mechanism to provide the full Registration Data to the Provider as specified by ICANN.
1.2. Complainant's complaint will not be deemed defective for failure to provide the name of the Respondent (Registered Name Holder) and all other relevant contact information required by Section 3 o the UDRP Rules if such contact information of the Respondent is not available in registration data publicly available in RDDS or not otherwise known to Complainant. In such an event, Complainant may file a 'Doe' complaint and the Provider shall provide the relevant contact details of the Registered Name Holder after being presented with a 'Doe' complaint."

98 Final Report on the & Proxy Services Accreditation Issues dated January 21, 2016. The Final Report states that "Disclosure [of the registrant's true Whois details] cannot be refused solely for lack of any of the following: (i) a court order; (ii) a subpoena; (iii) a pending civil action; or (iv) a UDRP or URS proceeding; nor can refusal to disclose be solely based on the fact that the Request is founded on alleged intellectual property infringement in content on a website associated with the domain name." However, in making a submission to require disclosure "Requester and the rights holder agrees to submit, without prejudice to other potentially applicable jurisdictions, to the jurisdiction of the courts (1) where it is incorporated (or of its home address, if an individual), AND (2) where the Provider specifies on its request form, solely for disputes arising from alleged improper disclosures caused by knowingly false statements made by the Requester, or from Requester's and/or rights holder's knowing misuse of information disclosed to it in response to its request.

99 See WIPO Center informal Q&A concerning the European Union's (EU) General Data Protection Regulation (GDPR) as it relates to the Uniform Domain Name Resolution Policy (UDRP) at http://www.wipo.int/amc/en/domains/gdpr/.

In appropriate circumstances, incorrect and misleading contact information on the Whois directory may be conclusive evidence of deception, but merely alleging respondent's failure to provide or correct contact information is not by itself sufficient to prove bad faith.[100] Negligence in failing to maintain contact information in the Whois directory and inattention to the required disclosures (as opposed to deception by providing fictitious information, discussed further below) are not by themselves evidence of bad faith. Complainant must prove that respondent intended to evade service, hide its true identity and obstruct arbitral proceedings.

As presently written, the RAA requires the registrar to provide a "free public query-based access to up-to-date . . . data concerning all active Registered Names sponsored by Registrar for each TLD in which it is accredited."[101] This includes displaying the following information (except as permissibly shielded by a privacy service and now redacted by directive of the GDPR until released by the Provider upon its receiving notice of a complaint): 1) The identity of the Registered Name; 2) The names of the primary name server and secondary name server(s) for the Registered Name; 3) The identity of the Registrant (which may be provided through Registrar's website); 4) The original creation date of the registration; 5) The expiration date of the registration; 6) The name and postal address of the Registered Name Holder; 7) The name, postal address, e-mail address, voice telephone number, and (where available) fax number of the technical contact for the Registered Name; and 8) The name, postal address, e-mail address, voice telephone number, and (where available) fax number of the administrative contact for the Registered Name. e-mail address, voice telephone number, and (where available) fax number of the administrative contact for the Registered Name.[102]

The typical registration agreement requires that the contact information be kept current:

> ACCURATE INFORMATION. You agree to: (1) provide certain true, current, complete and accurate information about you as required by the application process; and (2) maintain and update according to our modification

[100] ***Greenvelope, LLC v. Virtual Services Corporation***, D2017-0006 (WIPO February 25, 2017) (<greenenvelope.com>. "Even assuming this is true, this conduct, without any evidence of targeting of a trademark, does not alone amount to bad faith registration in this case for purposes of the Policy. A review of UDRP cases reveals that providing false registration information is sometimes considered as one of several elements, which on a cumulative basis (e.g., in combination with the targeting of a complainant's trademark), can result in a finding of bad faith registration.")

[101] Article 3.3.1 provides that "At its expense, Registrar shall provide an interactive web page and a port 43 Whois service providing free public query-based access to up-to-date (i.e., updated at least daily) data concerning all active Registered Names sponsored by Registrar for each TLD in which it is accredited."

[102] RAA Section 3.3.1. See also See ICANN, Registrar Advisory Concerning Whois Data Accuracy, May 10, 2002, available at <http://www.icann.org/en/announcements/advisory-10may02.htm>.

> procedures the information you provided to us when purchasing our services as needed to keep it current, complete and accurate. We rely on this information to send you important information and notices regarding your account and our services.[103]

While negligence may be excusable, providing false and misleading contact information to the registrar is a violation of the Policy and constitutes a breach of the "Representations and Warranties" clause of the Registration Agreement and Paragraph 2 of the Policy.[104] In ***Royal Bank of Scotland***[105] the Panel found that the registrant had created a fictitious address and name. The escalation of false or misleading contact information tends to support drawing a negative inference,[106] although there must be sufficient evidence to infer that respondent either has a "foul intent," ***CyBerCorp Holdings***,[107] or it has no affirmative defense to abusive registration.[108] Resting on false or misleading contact information is not specifically enumerated in the Policy, but is critical in assessing intent. In contrast, the Anticybersquatting Consumer Protection Act (ACPA) explicitly lists "material and misleading false contact information" as factors to consider in determining bad faith registration.[109]

Respondents have tried a number of ploys to avoid discovery of their identities, but all of them underscore respondent's pretense to legitimacy rather than acting as a defense to it. A Whois Directory listing respondent as having the same

---

[103] Network Solutions Service Agreement version 9.27, paragraph 4. See also Go Daddy Domain Name Registration Agreement:

4. You agree to notify Go Daddy within five (5) business days when any of the information you provided as part of the application and/or registration process changes. It is your responsibility to keep this information in a current and accurate status. Failure by you, for whatever reason, to provide Go Daddy with accurate and reliable information on an initial and continual basis, shall be considered to be a material breach of this Agreement. Failure by you, for whatever reason, to respond within five (5) business days to any inquiries made by Go Daddy to determine the validity of information provided by you, shall also be considered to be a material breach of this Agreement.

[104] ***Wachovia Corporation v. Peter Carrington***, D2002-0775 (WIPO October 2, 2002).

[105] ***Royal Bank of Scotland Group v. Stealth Commerce v. a.k.a. Telmex Management Services, Inc.***, D2002-0155 (WIPO April 24, 2002).

[106] ***Yahoo!, Inc. v. Eitan Zviely et al.***, D2000-0273 (WIPO June 14, 2000 (registrations under phony names).

[107] ***CyBerCorp Holdings, Inc. v. Jay Allman***, FA 0403000244090 (Forum May 14, 2004).

[108] ***ECCO Sko A/S v. Protected Domain Services – Customer ID: NCR-2448048 / jizhiteam***, D2010-1113 (WIPO September 3, 2010) ("An applicant for registration of a domain name has a duty to act honestly."

[109] The importance of the data is also reflected in the Anticybersquatting Consumer Protection Act, which provides that a court may consider a variety of factors, including "(VII) the person's provision of material and misleading false contact information when applying for the registration of the domain name, the person's intentional failure to maintain accurate contact information, or the person's prior conduct indicating a pattern of such conduct."

name as complainant, for example, fails because it is an inherent contradiction. The Panel in ***Ogden Publications***[110] held that a respondent representing itself to be complainant for registration purposes is guilty of bad faith in the registration and use of the disputed domain name.

If the respondent's purpose is avoidance of service to delay the proceedings it will be disappointed. Proceedings continue with or without respondent on a schedule dictated by the Policy. If the place of service does not happen to be the Respondent's address as advised to the Registrar, then Respondent has only itself to blame in that circumstance. Nevertheless, while it is possible for the beneficial holder to remain anonymous,[111] concealing its true identity carries a strong negative inference that the respondent's intention for registering the disputed domain name was to take advantage of complainant's trademark.[112]

2.05-B Impact of the GDPR 2.05-B

The GDPR opens with a statement of its core principle: "The protection of natural persons in relation to the processing of personal data is a fundamental right." Although it is ostensibly effective only in the EU it essentially affects databases internationally, including the Whois directory by effectively causing registrars to redact personal contact information of natural persons unless they expressly permit it to be publicly accessible.[113] The initial reaction to its implementation in the U.S. was an "unmitigated victory for the spammers and scammers that plague consumers and businesses."[114] The Assistant Secretary of Commerce stated that the U.S. government was working with the European Data Protection Board and other groups to address it.

While the GDPR does not place restrictions on collecting data, it prohibits disclosing and using it without permission of the persons whose data it is. As previously noted it does not apply to juristic persons who, if they want privacy, will

110 ***Ogden Publications, Inc. v. MOTHEARTHNEWS.COM c/o Whois IDentity Shield/OGDEN PUBLICATIONS INC., Administrator, Domain***, D2007-1373(WIPO November 26, 2007). Misidentification is discussed further in Faux Registrant.

111 ***Bank of America***, *supra*. Whatever the status of the(Whois directory, no changes may be made after a lock has been placed on the registration pursuant to Rule 4(b) of the UDRP Rules. See discussion in ***National Cable Satellite Corporation, d/b/a C-SPAN vs. Michael Mann / Omar Rivero***, FA1707001741966 (Forum September 20, 2017) ("Any modification(s) of the Respondent's data following the two (2) business day period may be addressed by the Panel in its decision [meaning that it cannot be changed by the registrar even if it is incorrect].")

112 ***Richard Rowe v. Namespro.ca PrivateWHOIS***, D2016-2451 (WIPO March 5, 2017)(Respondent effectively prevented the Panel from assessing the truth Respondent's statements).

113 Investors who are natural persons will almost certainly want to have their data viewable if registrars offer that service.

have to preserve it by subscribing to proxy and privacy services but the redaction of information has an inimical effect on a range of lawful reasons for having access to it.

There are conflicting legitimate interests in collecting and disclosing personal contact information. The GDPR does not question ICANN's purposes for collectiving the data, but it makes third-party rights subordinate to personal privacy.[115] The sudden darkening of the database confronts ICANN and those who need access to it with the conundrum of unlocking the information for lawful purposes while preserving personal privacy. Although the effective date of the GDPR was known well in advance it seemed to take ICANN by surprise and unprepared for protecting the openness of the Whois directory as originally conceived under the Affirmation of Commitments with the U.S. Department of Commerce. This resulted in a flurry of activity by ICANN including a law suit and appeals in Germany[116] and publications of proposed solutions and follow-ups to deal with the new conditions.[117]

For UDRP complainants, there are three consequences to a redacted Whois directory, first they will have to commence proceedings in the dark as to respondents'

---

[114] Remarks of David J. Redl, Assistant Secretary of Commerce for Communications and Information IGF-USA 2018, Washington, D.C. July 27, 2018.

[115] See Milton Mueller, *Whois Reform Grinds forward*, Posted September 28, 2018 (Internet Governance Project, Georgia Tech—School of Public Policy). Mr. Mueller posits two competing caucuses in the third party group: contracted parties who supply domains – and individual rights advocates in the noncommercial stakeholders group; and intellectual property, government and law enforcement interests, and commercial cybersecurity services. However, public availability of contact information does not align with ICANN's "purposes" for data collection. Whatever ICANN's purposes are in performing its mission it is not for the Whois directory to function as a database analogous to a trademark database.

[116] ICANN commenced an action against EPAG Domain Services, a German registrar owned by Tucows on the effective date of the GDPR in the 10th Civil Chamber of the Regional Court of Bonn dealing with the collection of information (May 30, 2018, English translation available at https://www.icann.org/en/system/files/files/litigation-icann-v-epag-request-court-order-prelim-injunction-redacted-30may18-en.pdf): "the person wishing to register will also be able to voluntarily provide their consent to the collection and storage of corresponding personal data in the future (Art. 6 para. 1 lit. a) GDPR and para. 7.2.2 of the RAA) -- but he was not forced to do so even before." Affirmed on appeal (August 1, 2018).

[117] See Temporary Specification for gTLD Registration Data, adopted by ICANN Board on May 17, 2018, effective May 25, 2018: "Consistent with ICANN's stated objective to comply with the GDPR, while maintaining the existing WHOIS system to the greatest extent possible, the Temporary Specification maintains robust collection of Registration Data (including Registrant, Administrative, and Technical contact information), but restricts most Personal Data to layered/tiered access. Users with a legitimate and proportionate purpose for accessing the non-public Personal Data will be able to request such access through Registrars and Registry Operators. Users will also maintain the ability to contact the Registrant or Administrative and Technical contacts through an anonymized email or web form." On June 18, ICANN published a high level frame-work for a Unified Access Model for Continued Access to the full WHOIS data and on August 20, 2018 ICANN issued a Draft Framework for a Possible Unified Access Model for Continued Access to full WHOIS Data–for Discussion: "The

rights or legitimate interests (which had they known in advance would have influenced their decision whether to sue); second, it will affect the ability to consolidate claims against multiple domain names; and third there will be a short delay in having their claims submitted to Panels for determination. The Temporary Specification which in some form will become a consensus policy expressly binds registries and registrars to disclose the "full Registration Data for each of the specified domain names [to the provider], upon the UDRP provider notifying the Registrar of the existence of a complaint, or participate in another mechanism to provide the full Registration Data to the Provider as specified by ICANN." Providers have indicated they will accept "Doe" complaints, which means the bottom half of the caption will have to be amended upon receipt of contact and beneficial owner information from the registrar, as is presently the case where registrations are in names other than the beneficial owner (proxy or privacy service).

To accommodate other third party interests in accessing the unredacted Whois directory, the terms under which beneficial ownership and contact information will be available depends on what arrangements are ultimately agreed upon for permitting access to content information.[118] For the protection of other kinds of fundamental rights and to enforce the law, ICANN contemplates the WhoIs will be succeeded by a Registration Directory Access Protocol (RDAP) that will have to be crafted to provide tiered access to contact information for law enforcement, security, investors, escrow agents, and academic research as well as some degree of access for rights holders (actual or potential claimants) prior to their commencing UDRP proceedings.

---

model described in this paper incorporates the concept of defining eligible user groups to attempt to strike a balance between potential third party users who may request access to non-public WHOIS data on a regular basis where additional safeguards and process may be required or warranted, versus those who may request non-public WHOIS data on a more limited or one-off basis.").

ICANN contemplates the WhoIs will be succeeded by the Registration Directory Access Protocol (RDAP) which is still in the Working Group stage but once approved and implemented it will provide for a method for gaining access to or disclosure of collected information. A letter to ICANN from Mr. Redl dated April 4, 2019 pressuring ICANN to "achieve substantial progress" in finding a solution by November 2019) speaks to the difficulty of the issue.

118 The European Data Protection Board has endorsed the concept of "a Whois model which will enable legitimate uses by relevant stakeholders" (Statement dated May 27, 2018 available at https://edpb.europa.eu/news/news/2018/european-data-protection-board-endorsed-statement-wp29-icannwhois_en). In the First Semiannual Report on NTIA'S ICANN Activities (FY2018) available at https://www.ntia.doc.gov/files/ntia/publications/first_semiannual_report_on_ntias_icann_activities.pd, NTIA noted that it supports "ICANN taking action to keep the WHOIS service working, but has made clear ... that while the Temporary Specification is necessary, it is not sufficient, as it does not clearly articular how WHOIS users are to be allowed access to this data in a predictable fashion." Further, "NTIA is also pursuing avenues for specifically addressing the development and implementation of a unified access mechanism to permit access to non-public WHOIS information rather than solely through an undefined requirement for registries and registrars to provide 'reasonable access.'"

3

The Scope of the UDRP

3.01 THE UDRP IS NOT A TRADEMARK COURT 3.01

There are predators in both the actual and cyber marketplaces and different remedies depending on the nature of the alleged unlawful acts. The UDRP is a special purpose arbitral regime designed for trademark owners to challenge domain name registrants allegedly infringing their rights to exclusive use of their trademarks on the Internet. It is not a trademark court.[1] Cybersquatting concerns infringement of a different kind; it is a lesser included tort of trademark infringement, and although the UDRP forum is not a trademark court *as such* in some ways it is since it empowers (assuming the right alignment of facts) to divest registrants of domain names that infringe a complainant's trademark rights.

When registering domain names registrants "shall represent that, to the best of [their] knowledge and belief, neither the registration of the Registered Name nor the manner in which it is directly or indirectly used *infringes* the legal rights of any third party" (emphasis added).[2] In contrast, trademark infringement is an unlawful appropriation of a mark for the intended purpose of causing economic injury to its owner (by enjoying benefits at the owner's expense) and deceiving consumers as to the likelihood of an association with the mark owner.

Under the UDRP the question is whether an objective observer directly comparing mark and domain name would find the domain name identical or confusingly similar to the trademark, not whether the domain name causes confusion as to source. If the domain name is identical or confusingly similar to the mark, complainant has satisfied the jurisdictional requirement. Complainant does not have to prove trademark infringement, only that the domain name was registered and is being used in bad faith. This gives rise to an anomaly that a complainant may fail to

---

[1] Representative case: ***Cameron & Company, Inc. v. Patrick Dudley***, FA1811001818217 (Forum December 26, 2018) (<cameronmatch.com>. "The complaint raises the issue of abusive registration vs. trademark infringement. 'CAMERON' being a common personal name, the Panel finds that Respondent may indeed have a right to register and use the <cameronmatch.com> domain name.... [But] [c]ases involving disputes regarding trademark rights and usage, trademark infringement, unfair competition, deceptive trade practices and related U.S. law issues are beyond the scope of the Panel's limited jurisdiction under the Policy. " ***Ascension Health Alliance v. Prateek Sinha, Ascension Healthcare Inc.***, D2018-2775 (WIPO January 25, 2019) (<ascensionhealthcare.com>. "The website to which the disputed domain name resolves app ears to offer bona fide healthcare-related services. Indeed, Complainant contends that Respondent provides healthcare management services that are 'very similar, if not identical' to those offered by Complainant, but Complainant does not contend that Respondent is offering counterfeit or deceptive services.... Although Complainant may have the starting ingredients of an ordinary, trademark infringement case against Respondent, the Complainant has not demonstrated to the satisfaction of the Panel that Respondent is not making a bona fide offering of services. The UDRP is not appropriate to resolve such ordinary trademark infringement claims, which would be better resolved by a court of competent jurisdiction."

[2] Registrar Accreditation Agreement, 3.7.7.9.

prove abusive registration of a domain name under the UDRP that would (with the proper alignment of facts) otherwise be condemned under trademark law.[3] Neither marks postdating the registration of identical or confusingly similar domain names nor proof of bad faith use alone will satisfy complainant's burden of proof.

Although both the Anticybersquatting Consumer Protection Act (ACPA) and UDRP condemn cybersquatting the regimes differ in striking ways. The principal distinction that has already been alluded to is the UDRP is designed as a conjunctive and the ACPA as a disjunctive model. In addition, the UDRP is asymmetrical, meaning that only the complainant has a substantive remedy, a mandatory-like injunction, while under the ACPA the parties are treated equally in having injunctive[4] and monetary remedies.[5] The ICANN Panel has no authority to assess damages, which is the exclusive jurisdiction of a court of competent jurisdiction.[6]

An infringement claim ripens when a trademark owner perceives a violation of its right. Upon initiation of a UDRP proceeding (or before if respondent has

---

[3] ***Ni Insan Kaynaklari Personel ve Danismanlik Limited Sti v. Timothy Michael Bright***, D2009-0315 (WIPO May 7, 2009) ("An administrative proceeding under the Policy is not a proceeding in 'equity' in which a panel seeks to generally determine whether one party or another has acted more or less fairly toward the other, thereafter fashioning a 'just' remedy. A proceeding under the Policy is not an assessment of civil trademark infringement. It is possible for a respondent to be infringing the trademark rights of a complainant, yet be found not to have acted in bad faith." See also ***Disney Enters. Inc. v. Meyers***, FA 697818 (Forum June 26, 2006) (<disneyparks.com>) (Respondent questioned the validity of Complainant's DISNEY mark. The Panel held that "recognition of [equitable remedies] . . . requires the Panel to make a legal determination regarding the continuing validity of Complainant's DISNEY mark. Such action is beyond the scope of the UDRP proceeding and if Respondent desires such an outcome it should avail itself of the proper judicial proceedings by which such a result might be accomplished.")

[4] *Lemond v. Stinchfield*, Civil No. 17-2071 (D. Minn., 2017) (Preliminary injunction granting removal of all content from websites, cease using the domain names, selling or assigning the domain names, and enjoining further registrations incorporating plaintiff's mark. Case settled).

[5] The ACPA grants statutory damages to the prevailing party discretionary with the court up to one hundred thousand dollars ($100,000) plus reasonable attorney's fees for either party's misjudgment of its rights. Discussed further in "Submitting Dispute to a Court of Competent Adjudication" (Sec. 8.01-A).

[6] In a federal action complainant may be entitled to "damage control costs" which is a different remedy than damages. When Respondent in ***Lisa Migliore Black, Migliore and Associates LLC v. Kentuckiana Reporters***, D2012-1588 (WIPO September 20, 2012) refused to turn over infringing domain names in compliance with a cease-and-desist letter complainant commenced an administrative proceeding that concluded with a finding of abusive registration. Miglior then commenced a federal action for, among other relief, "damage control costs." The court in *Migliore & Associates, LLC and Lisa Migliore Black v. Kentuckiana Reporters*, LLC, 3:13-cv-315 (D.C. Western D of Kentucky at Louisville Feb. 19, 2015) denied defendant's motion for summary judgment dismissing the complaint. It explained that "Lanham Act plaintiffs can sometimes recover for damage control without showing actual confusion or actual damages [citing *Balance Dynamics Corp. v. Schmitt Industries, Inc.*, 204 F. 3d 683, 689-90 (6th Cir. 2000)]." It continued: "Damage control costs are what they

received a cease-and-desist notice and wishes to take the initiative) a respondent may challenge the claim by removing the dispute to a court of competent jurisdiction, but if the dispute continues under the UDRP the Panel's jurisdiction is limited to determining whether a respondent's registration and use of the disputed domain name (or inactively holding it without proof of any conceivable non-infringing use) is consistent with its representation and warranty in acquiring it.[7] Only if the Panel concludes that the respondent registered and is using the disputed domain name in bad faith can it grant complainant the relief requested in the complaint.[8]

However, if respondent is found to have registered the domain name without intent to take advantage of a complainant's mark, but subsequently begins using it in bad faith the Policy does not authorize canceling the respondent's registration or ordering the domain name transferred to complainant. Lawful registration (even if bad faith use commences at some subsequent time) prevents complainant from proving its conjunctive case under the Policy.[9] Subsequent use in bad faith raises issues of trademark infringement and (in the U.S.) statutory cybersquatting under the ACPA. Hence the formulaic conclusion in many UDRP cases that dismissing the complaint is "not to be construed as a finding that there is no likelihood of confusion between the parties' respective uses of [the trademark],"[10] suggesting trademark infringement. Rather, "[g]iven the nature of this dispute, it is properly resolved . . . in a forum of competent jurisdiction."[11]

---

sound like: they are costs plaintiffs must incur to protect themselves from nefarious acts of their competitors. '[L]ike an injunction, damage control is undertaken precisely to prevent such things as lost sales, lost profits, and lost goodwill.'" Id. at 691. Jury trial, complaint dismissed.

[7] It has been noted above in "Registrant's Responsibility for Determining Whether Domain Name Infringes Third Party Rights" that the representations and warranties provision of the registration agreement uses the word "infringes," while paragraph 2 of the Policy uses "violates." "Infringement" and "violation" are parallel terms. They refer to proscribed conduct which may also when examined by a court of competent jurisdiction constitute infringement or dilution in a trademark sense. The conduct that warrants cancellation or transfer of the domain name is discussed more fully in Paragraphs 4(b) and 4(b)(i) through (iv) in Chapter 5.

[8] Most complainants elect transfer, probably because cancelled domain names return to the pool while transfer may have some strategic benefits.

[9] However, there may be a basis for forfeiture under the Lanham Act. See *DSPT International v. Nahum*, 624 F.3d 1213 (9th Cir. 2010). The Court held that "[e]ven if a domain name was put up innocently and used properly for years, a person is liable under 15 U.S.C. §1125(d) if he subsequently uses the domain name with a bad faith intent to profit from the protected mark by holding the domain name for ransom." Also, *Newport News Holdings Corporation v. Virtual City Vision, Incorporated, d/b/a Van James Bond Tran*, 650 F3d 423 (4th Cir. 2011) (Registered in good faith; subsequent use in bad faith.)

[10] ***Credit Management Solutions, Inc. v. Collex Resource Management***, D2000-0029 (WIPO May 17, 2000) ("We merely conclude that Complainant is not entitled to relief on the record presented under the standards applicable to this proceeding.")

[11] ***Meredith Corp. vs. CityHome, Inc.***, D2000-0223 (WIPO May 18, 2000).

The apparent anomaly that a respondent may maintain its registration yet be infringing a statutory right strengthens the distinction between domain name and trademark law. The limited authority under the Policy extends no further than deciding which party is entitled to the disputed domain name *at the time of the proceeding*. Respondents with legitimate rights or interests include businesses monetizing their domain name assets, resellers of domain names, legitimate businesses with unregistered marks or known by their trade names, and individuals and businesses using domain names as email addresses.[12] There is an open ended range of possibilities.[13] Not all domain names alleged to violate complainant's rights constitute cybersquatting. Only those registrations are cancelled or transferred that are warranted by the proof, but if a complainant believes the Panel has wrongly decided the facts or a respondent that an award forfeiting the domain name is unwarranted then neither is barred by *res judicata* from pursuing statutory remedies in a court of competent jurisdiction.[14]

---

[12] ***Advanced Personnel Systems, Inc., v. Domain Admin / Mighty Products, Inc.*** FA1804001780243 (Forum May 25, 2018) (<smartsearch.com>. "Respondent has been utilizing the disputed domain name as a parking page for PPC advertising links. None of the links appear to be related to Complainant, its trademark or its business. Instead, the links seem to reflect descriptive matters that one might search for on the Internet, such as 'games' and 'movies.' Because these links are sufficiently related to a website that offers 'smart' 'search' on the Internet, and because none of the links are related to Complainant or its personnel staffing program, the Panel finds that Complainant has failed to establish that Respondent lacks rights or legitimate interests in the disputed domain name"); ***Rolyn Companies Inc. v. Mediablue Inc.***, D2018-0072 (WIPO April 4, 2018) (<rolyn.com>. "The fact that the Respondent buys three or four-letter domain names as a part of its business does not, of itself, create rights or a legitimate interest in a domain name corresponding with the trademark of another," the Panel was unanimous in denying the complaint because Complainant had the same opportunity to acquire the domain name and, rare though it is, there are other businesses with that name); ***Informa Business Information, Inc. v. Privacydotlink Customer 640040 / Domain Manager, Web D.G. Ltd.***, D2017-1756 (WIPO December 11, 2017) (<pinksheet.com>. "Inflated" price for domain name not grounds for forfeiting it to Complainant: "As in any market for commodities, domain name brok[er]ing is about matching supply with demand; in the absence of any indicia of bad faith, there is nothing wrong per se with what the Complainant characterises as an 'excessive offer...'"). Discussed further in "Not All Offers to Sell Violate the Policy" (Sec. 5.01-D.3).

[13] ICANN Second Staff Report on Implementation Documents for the Uniform Dispute Resolution Policy (October 25, 1999), paragraph 4.1 (c): "only cases of abusive registrations are intended to be subject to the streamlined administrative dispute resolution procedure.... [P]arties hav[ing] long-standing trademark rights in the name when it was registered as a domain name—[are relegated] to the courts."

[14] Para. 4(k) discussed further in "Plenary Adjudication After an Adverse Decision" (Sec. 8.01-B).

3.02 DISPUTES OUTSIDE THE SCOPE OF THE POLICY 3.02

3.02-A Policy Not Applicable to Disputes Between Parties with Competing Rights Acting in Good Faith 3.02-A

The WIPO Final Report states that the "scope of the procedure is limited so that *it is available only in respect of deliberate, bad faith, abusive, domain name registrations* . . . and is not applicable to disputes between parties with competing rights acting in good faith"[15] (emphasis added). The string of qualifiers—"deliberate," "bad faith" and "abusive"—suggests that the WIPO consensus did not intend to pin down actionable conduct to a formula for mechanical application.[16] Panelists have respected this in their decisions. It is they who are called upon to establish the boundaries. The UDRP forum is available to trademark owners to resolve disputes of abusive registration, but not for commercial disputes in which domain names are merely incidental to other claims or for claims of trademark infringement.

As formulated, the Policy's scope is limited to "'abusive registrations' made with bad faith intent to profit commercially from others' trademarks."[17] The ICANN Report continues that "the adopted policy leaves the resolution of disputes to the courts (or arbitrators where agreed by the parties) and calls for registrars not to disturb a registration until those courts decide."[18] Where there is no intent "to profit commercially from others' trademarks" there can be no bad faith. Claims for breaches of contract and fiduciary duty that require the Panel to delve into the parties' legal relations are generally outside the scope of the Policy.

Panels initially struggled to pin down the boundary as though there could be a metes and bounds answer, but the demarcation can be elusive.[19] The line separating disputes within from those outside the scope of the Policy is a matter of judgment,

---

[15] The WIPO Final Report at paragraph 135(i).

[16] So too with the Anticybersquatting Consumer Protection Act. See *Storey v. Cello Holdings, L.L.C.*, 347 F.3d 370, 385 (2d Cir. 2003) ("Congress intended the cybersquatting statute to make rights to a domain name registration contingent on ongoing conduct rather than to make them fixed at the time of registration.")

[17] *Id.*, ICANN Second Staff Report.

[18] *Id.*, "The adopted policy establishes a streamlined, inexpensive administrative dispute resolution procedure intended only for the relatively narrow class of cases of 'abusive registrations.' Thus, the fact that the policy's administrative dispute resolution procedure does not extend to cases where a registered domain name is subject to a legitimate dispute (and may ultimately be found to violate the challenger's trademark) is a feature of the policy, not a flaw. The policy relegates all 'legitimate' disputes—such as those where both disputants had longstanding trademark rights in the name when it was registered as a domain name—to the courts."

[19] ***Luvilon Indus. NV v. Top Serve Tennis Pty Ltd.***, DAU2005-0004 (WIPO September 6, 2005) ("[The Policy's purpose is to] combat abusive domain name registrations and not to provide a prescriptive code for resolving more complex trade mark disputes"; ***Courtney Love v. Brooke Barnett,*** FA0703000944826 (Forum May 14, 2007) "A dispute, such as the present one, between parties who

dependent on factual circumstances.[20] Nominally,[21] "only cases of abusive registration are intended to be subject to the streamlined administrative dispute-resolution procedure."[22] Sometimes the line separating cybersquatting and trademark infringement is not so certain but is seen to reside in that area of the continuum where one leaves off and the other begins. Where this happens what is within and outside jurisdiction is in the eyes of the beholder. Some panelists will accept what others decline.

As a general rule the Policy cannot be invoked for disputes involving contract interpretation,[23] actionable tortious and felonious conduct, and statutory claims *in which the domain name is viewed as only tangential to the dispute.*[24] Thus, business disputes in which the domain name is inseparable from "much larger, complex disputes between the parties, involving alleged breaches of contract, breaches of fiduciary duty, and tortious conduct" are more likely to be categorized as "legitimate disputes" that are outside the scope of the Policy.[25] ICANN instances a single example of a "legitimate dispute" which is introduced with the phrase "such as"—"such

---

each have at least a prima facie case for rights in the disputed domain names is outside the scope of the Policy"); T***he American Association of the Order of St. Lazarus, Inc. v. Howard Browne / Order of St Lazarus***, D2014-0738 (WIPO June 23, 2014) ("Whether Respondent's use and registration violates the parties' 2006 Agreement is not for this Panel to decide, although for reasons stated above, it appears that the Agreement did not directly address the disputed domain name."

[20] *Courtney Love, supra.* ("I write separately because I agree with the outcome of the majority opinion, but not with its reasoning. I would not find that this dispute lies beyond the scope of the UDRP–it does not–but that Complainant wholly fails to meet her burden of proof on each of the three required elements.")

[21] Panelists have incrementally stretched the scope of the Policy to include cases of abusive conduct not specifically targeting complainants but using them to target consumers. Discussed further below in, "Disputes Within the Scope of the Policy" (Sec. 3.03).

[22] ICANN Second Staff, *supra.*

[23] Two kinds of disputes arise with distribution agreements, namely they either provide for a divorce contingency and specifically address the issue of domain names; or they fail to specify post termination rights to domain names lawfully registered to perform services under the agreement. If contracts fail to specify the parties' intentions, the matter does not belong in UDRP. ***Private Media Group v. Anton Enterprises Inc. d/b/a Private USA***, D2002-0692 (WIPO September 10, 2002) (Contractual dispute about the interpretation of the Distribution Agreement)); ***Innovative Marketing and Distribution, Inc d/b/a Engel Coolers v. Michael Harrington***, FA1606001678152 (Forum July 5, 2016) (<buyengelcoolers.com>). For distribution agreement properly terminated see ***MasterCraft Boat Company, LLC v. Debbie Hayes***, FA1610001696484 (Forum November 23, 2016) (<mastercraftaz.com>) (If a distribution agreement is properly drafted for domain name use to cease upon termination, then continuing use will be a violation of the Policy. Here, without authorization Respondent renewed the registration for the domain name.)

[24] It is not outside the scope when the claim is relevant to the dispute, as discussed below in "Within the Scope of the Policy" (Sec. 3.03). When copyright infringement is offered as conduct supporting bad faith it is within the scope of the Policy because it demonstrates intention to capitalize on complainant's reputation. If the claim were copyright or trademark infringement is would be outside the scope of the Policy.

as those where both disputants had longstanding trademark rights in the name when it was registered as a domain name are subject to national law."[26]

Rival trademarks in different jurisdictions or business entities incorporated in jurisdictions in which complainants have no presence,[27] are only the most obvious example but business disputes are equally important. The Policy does not usually apply and should not be used to "shoehorn what is essentially a business dispute between former partners."[28] The Policy "simply does not grant such authority to panels to resolve disputes that hinge on contractual provisions, breaches of fiduciary relationships, fraud, and the like."[29]

However, in practice factual circumstances determine abusive registration. For example, claims against former employees are likely to survive dismissal despite breach of fiduciary duty, because the controlling factor is not the breach but appropriation of the employer's intellectual property. Conversely, claims are likely to be dismissed where the employer has authorized the registration of the disputed domain name to be held in the employee's name.

3.02-B Factual Circumstances Outside the Scope of the Policy 3.02-B

It is generally agreed that disputes that involve the "ownership of the business and its assets,"[30] or "distill[ ] down . . . to just one dispositive issue [that does] not implicate cybersquatting at all,"[31] or "hinge mostly on a business or civil dispute between the parties,"[32] or involve disputes between family members arguing over inheritance issues,[33] or ownership of a domain name after breakup of a business

---

[25] ***Jason Crouch and Virginia McNeill v. Clement Stein***, D2005-1201 (WIPO January 31, 2006), citing ***Clinomics Biosciences, Inc. v. Simplicity Software, Inc.***, D2001-0823 (WIPO August 28, 2001).

[26] ICANN Second Staff Report at paragraph 4.1(c).

[27] ***Bloomberg Finance L.P. v. Lankanspace.com / Nimo Perera,*** FA1902001828409 (Forum February 28, 2019) (<bloombergspl.com>. Business incorporated in Sri Lanka. "Ownership of a corporate entity whose name bears on the disputed domain name can demonstrate rights or legitimate interests in a domain name.")

[28] ***The Thread.com, LLC v. Jeffrey S. Poploff,*** D2000-1470 (WIPO January 5, 2001) ("Respondent asserts that he has legitimate rights in the domain name because he is a founder of Complainant.")

[29] ***Thump Records, Inc. v. WebPros***, FA0503000446911 (Forum May 11, 2005). While civil and criminal law theories of liability cannot be the legal bases for UDRP relief they may be factors in determining violation. See below "Disputes Within the Scope of the Policy" (Sec. 3.03).

[30] Partners: ***ITMetrixx, Inc. v. Kuzma Productions***, D2001-0668 (WIPO August 2, 2001). Shareholders: ***Careflight Australia Limited v. Domain Admin, Privacy Protection Service INC d/b/a PrivacyProtect.org / CareFlight Australia Limited,*** D2016-1624 (WIPO December 5, 2016).

[31] ***The Estate of Marlon Brando v. WhisGuard c/o WhoisGuard Protected,*** FA0506000503817 (Forum August 29, 2005).

[32] ***Courtney Love***, *supra.*

venture[34] are better left to courts of competent jurisdiction. Questions of trademark infringement, dilution, and invalidity are "clearly not within the purview of any ICANN proceeding and are best left for court adjudication."[35] The more practical course for parties with competing rights is to present their argument to a court of competent jurisdiction.[36]

Also outside the scope of the Policy are disputes based on allegations that respondent engages in tortiously or unlawfully using a domain name that is neither identical nor confusingly similar to complainant's trademark.[37] In Yahoo! the Panel found that Respondent "facilitate[d] the distribution [of spam]." Nevertheless, the Panel denied the complaint because the "differences between the mark and domain name [<yprog.com>] are simply too many and too profound" even though Respondent was using the domain name to harm complainant and consumers:

> At the same time, we are constrained to observe that Complainant appears to be using this proceeding to attempt to achieve through the processes of the Policy an end best accomplished in another forum under the law of trademark infringement, unfair competition or the like.

Similarly, the Policy cannot be invoked to enforce a court order relating to a domain name because "the court presumably maintains a continuing jurisdiction to enforce its judgment."[38] The same barrier does not exist where the court has denied an application for an order staying domain name arbitration.[39] This would be analogous in a civil action to the court granting an application to compel arbitration.

---

33 ***Correct Craft, Inc. v. SouthEast Correct Craft***, FA0810001231091 (Forum December 15, 2008).

34 ***Superior Gold Group, Inc. v. Team Hollywood GlobalNetworks c/o Kevin Finn***, FA0904001256919 (Forum May 21, 2009).

35 ***Register.com, Inc. v. Wolfgang Reile a/k/a RWG Internet and Marketing Rightway Gate Inc., 101 Internet Service, Internet Service, Rightway Gate Inc., RWG Marketing Rightway Gate Inc., NA, 101register.net, webpageregister.org, 101register.org, webpageregister.net***, FA0311000208576 (Forum January 27, 2004) (the disputed domain names were <register.net> and <register.org>).

36 ***First Franklin Financial Corporation and National City Corporation v. The Franklin Savings and Loan Company***, D2005-0762 (WIPO September 27, 2005). If the matter is already before a court of competent jurisdiction, the Panel may terminate the proceeding. Discussed further in "Terminating Proceeding: Respondent's Request" (Sec. 7-12).

37 ***Yahoo! Inc. v Bill Skipton d/b/a Cowboy Clothing***, FA0510000575666 (Forum November 23, 2005) (YAHOO! and <yprog.com>).

38 ***Mattel, Inc. v. Barbie of Cleveland a/k/a Barbie Beeler***, FA0403000248741 (Forum May 12, 2004) (Complainant obtained a default judgment in the District Court for the Southern District of New York but the registrar located in Australia refused to enforce the judgment).

39 ***Sonido, Inc. v. MU21C.COM Inc.***, D2006-0685 (WIPO September 6, 2006) (Court sitting in New York denied Respondent's application to stay arbitration: "The purposes of the Policy would be frustrated if any complaint were dismissed merely because a respondent had filed a case in national court claiming some sort of right to the disputed domain name.")

3.03 DISPUTES WITHIN THE SCOPE OF THE POLICY 3.03

3.03-A Willingness to Consider Ancillary Legal Principles and Issues 3.03-A

While the scope of the UDRP appears clear, that it is intended "only for the relatively narrow class of cases of 'abusive registrations,'"[40] in practice there is a shifting boundary that depends equally on the factual circumstances as relationships of the parties. Ostensibly similar but distinguishable circumstances can fall on either side of the outside/within scope of the Policy.[41] It is insufficient to allege a grievance and offer evidence on a theory outside the scope of the Policy.[42]

Thus, while evidence of intellectual property infringement to prove a statutory liability may state a claim in a court of competent jurisdiction it will be outside the scope of the Policy. Similarly with claims for breach of contract in which parties assert claims without specific reference to domain names.[43] The Panel in ***Railroad Earth*** pointed out that a "provision regarding intellectual property rights does not perforce encompass domain names; a domain name is not in itself an intellectual property right, as it can be used for many purposes unrelated to intellectual property." How parties construct their arguments and their choices of language and proofs can be significant factors in accepting or rejecting claims and defenses. Evidence marshaled to prove business disputes or a statutory violations fail to prove cybersquatting unless they are tailored to demonstrate violations of the Policy.

In determining scope Panels recognize that "some disputes routinely and oftentimes of necessity require Panels to consider broad ancillary legal principles

---

40 ICANN Second Staff Report, Paragraph 4.1(c).

41 ***Vassilios Pantazopoulos v. Anthony Paolillo***, FA1310001522817 (Forum December 2, 2013) ("The Panel agrees that the scope of the Policy is limited; however, the Panel believes that it should act if it can do so within the scope of the Policy, notwithstanding that the facts as alleged might also give rise to claims of copyright infringement and/or unfair competition.") See also ***Anchor Drilling Fluids USA, Inc. v. anchordf, anchor drills***, D2012-0383 (WIPO April 12, 2002) ("The evidence demonstrates that the disputed domain name was used for a website which was plainly intended to mimic the Complainant's genuine website, but with changes made so that emails would be diverted to the Respondent, with obvious deceptive intent. There was clearly potential for diversion of, and significant damage to, the Complainant's business. The Respondent was operating a website using the Complainant's name and mark, for unauthorized and abusive purposes, which could certainly have included facilitating spamming, phishing and related fraudulent activities.")

42 Registered with permission but parties subsequently falling out is within the scope of the Policy. See ***Quadrific Media Private Limited v. Rajat Agarwal***, D2017-1050 (WIPO August 31, 2017) ("[T]here is no need for the Panel to consider any subsequent dispute that arose between the Parties or who owns the intellectual property rights in the Disputed Domain Name. What is important to consider is the Respondent's intention at the time he registered the Disputed Domain Name, and it is clear that the Respondent acted in good faith by registering the Disputed Domain Name.")

43 ***Railroad Earth, LLC v. Brian Ross and Ross Artist Management, Inc.***, D2017-0039 (WIPO February 20, 2017) (<railroad Earth.com).

and issues that lie outside the sharp confines of the Policy."[44] Disputes can be within the scope of the Policy even where the factual circumstances are sharply disputed[45] or complainant alleges as a component of the claim breaches of contract and fiduciary duty,[46] conversion and fraud,[47] statutory violations,[48] or even criminal acts.[49] That a respondent has come into possession of the domain name fraudulently and is using it in violation of a trademark owner's rights is circumstantial evidence of abusive registration.[50] Fraudulent schemes run the gamut from seeking personal information from customers to spoofing brand owners.

All these schemes are within the scope of the Policy whether they target mark owners, consumers, or the public at large.[51] Unexplained conduct adds weight to

---

44 ***Rudy Rojas v. Gary Davis***, D2004-1081 (WIPO April 18, 2005) ('nativestyles.net'), but in this particular case the Panel found that both "parties are using [the] Policy proceeding to gain a tactical or psychological advantage in a broader business dispute between them" and for that reason concluded that the case lay "outside the Panel's core jurisdiction."

45 Discussed further below in "Complexity Not Reason for Abdicating Making a Decision Under the UDRP" (Sec. 3.03-B).

46 ***Arma Partners LLP v. Me, Victor Basta***, D2009-0894 (WIPO August 26, 2009) ("[W]hat may have originally appeared as a good faith registration . . . can no longer be so regarded. Previous panels have recognized, and this Panel does also, that what may appear to have been a good faith registration initially may be 'coloured' by the subsequent conduct of a respondent in for example breaching the specific terms of a contractual undertaking.")

Breach of contract is illustrated in those disputes in which respondents agree but fail to return domain names upon expiration of their agencies or distributorships. However, the issue is not straightforward because there may be circumstances that warrant denial of the complaint. Discussed further in "Rights to Domain Name After Termination of Contract" (Sec. 6.01-E).

47 Hacking (conversion) and phishing (fraud and larceny) are within the scope of the Policy. See ***Bjorn Kassoe Andersen v. Direction International***, D2007-0605 (WIPO June 27, 2007) (<direction.com>. Hijacking); ***ITX sarl, and Ziad M. Mugraby v. Tom Steiner***, FA0809001222737 (Forum October 24, 2008) (<beirut.com>. Hijacking) (The dispute is no more "outside the scope of the Policy . . . than the claim that the domain name was registered in bad faith and the counter claim of domain name hijacking . . . are inappropriate for determination on a civil standard by an administrative panel.")

48 Dilution: ***Yoga Works, Inc. v. Arpita, FA*** 155461 (Forum June 17, 2003) (<shantiyogaworks.com>).

49 Discussed further in "Spoofing and Phishing" (Sec. 6.01-C.2.c).

50 ***Channel Tunnel Group Ltd. v. Powell***, D2000-0038 (WIPO March 17, 2000) ("[J]ust because Respondent's conduct does not fall within the 'particular' circumstances set out in [Paragraph 4(b)] of the Policy, is not conclusive that the domain name in issue was registered in and is being used in bad faith.") In the context of fraudulent transfer the term "registered" simply means respondent is the registered holder of the domain name. In words or substance the respondent is held to have acted with abusive intent. Discussed further in "Fraudulent Transfer of Domain Names" (Sec. 6.01-C.2.b).

51 ***Accenture Global Services Limited v. Patel Holdings***, D2016-0367 (WIPO April 29, 2016) (<accenturejobs.com>. "The Complainant reported a fraudulent scheme worked out using the email

respondent's lack of rights or legitimate interests under the second limb of the Policy, and bad faith registration and use under the third.[52] Provable misconduct that establishes an intent to take advantage of a complainant's reputation or consumers' trustfulness is a key to bad faith, regardless of whether the respondent acquired the domain name directly from a registrar, through a hacker, or was itself the hacker.[53]

Where the parties "have submitted materials sufficient for [the Panel] to form a clear opinion of what transpired between [them] and how the UDRP could in fact decide where to place the disputed domain names" there is no reason to dismiss the complaint.[54] Some Panels have determined that under the appropriate circumstances they can even question the legitimacy of the trademark.[55] There are, moreover, a variety of factual circumstances on the cusp that are also properly within the scope of the Policy. The dispute in ***Giles Thomas v. UKMuscle Nutrition***[56] raised the issue of self-help in the context of the dissolution of a business relationship. Complainant owned the domain name, which Respondents caused to be transferred. The Panel stated

> By no stretch of the imagination can this transfer of the First Domain Name be regarded as anything other than abusive. Even if respondent genuinely believed that it was, as is asserted in the Response, the legal owner of the Domain Name, this was not the proper way of going about it. Respondent was effectively taking the law into its own hands.

Similar results are reported against respondents who take control of domain names as hostage for unpaid invoices.[57]

'recruiting@accenturejobs.com'. In this scheme, the Respondent contacted individuals via LinkedIn, offering career opportunities in Accenture and requesting their current cv. Following this, the individual received an email offering to interview him/her upon the payment of GBP 468. This email was sent from an individual posing as Accenture's current Chief Leadership & Human Resources officer.")

52 ***Advance Magazine Publishers Inc., Les Publications Conde Nast S.A. v. HostMonster.com INC / Stephen Lee***, D2010-1355 (WIPO October 18, 2010) (Selling counterfeit or fake designer products.)

53 ***EZQUEST, INC. v. BAORUI, FA*** 1445631 (Forum July 3, 2012) (Complainant argues Respondent is attempting to unlawfully extract money from Complainant and/or steal identity and banking information.)

54 ***Bell Helmets, Inc. v. 4X Development***, FA0602000651064 (Forum April 11, 2006) (Respondent appeared and prevailed.)

55 Discussed further in "Priority as a Legally Enforceable Interest" (Sec. 4.02-A.1.a).

56 D2008-0824 (WIPO August 19, 2008). See also ***Automobile Atlanta, Inc. v. Treadway Solutions***, FA0910001292305 (Forum December 18, 2009) ("[W]hatever the motives, there is no excuse for [inactivating domain names or retaliating for perceived slights] . . . both are clear evidence of bad faith.")

57 ***Alaska Health Fair, Inc. v. Chris Jacobson***, FA1305001500868 (Forum June 24, 2013) ("Based upon the screenshot of the website resolving from the Domain Name, it is clear that Respondent

3.03-B 3.03-B Complexity Not Reason for Abdicating Making a Decision Under the UDRP

Complexity of factual circumstances is not in itself a reason for abdicating making a decision. A concurring opinion in one case expressed some hesitation with that proposition but joined with the majority in finding that "just because the record is complex does not mean that the Panel should decline to review it."[58] This view has generally been adopted. Each panelist in another early case had his and her own view about the Policy's mandate.[59] One member took issue with the majority's holding of bad faith, but nevertheless supported the view: "a panel should not decline to reach a conclusion simply because there are hotly disputed facts . . . . We are however restricted by the record and the limited jurisdiction given to us under the Policy." Panels should try to resolve disputes of fact. If "allegations [of fraud] and conversion were always to put a complaint outside of the scope of the Policy, the Policy would be ineffective."[60]

Nevertheless, there are respondents who deliberately create complexity in support of an argument that the "case is unsuitable for determination by the Panel . . . because of the parties competing views of the circumstances of the case."[61] The question is whether the conflicting facts are irresolvable without recourse to the forensic toolkit ordinarily available in a court of competent jurisdiction. The problem is highlighted "[w]hen the parties differ markedly with respect to the basic facts" and the Panel is unable to "determine which presentation of the facts is more

---

holds the Domain Name as security for the payment of his invoice; that is his only basis for refusing to return it to Complainant now, and it was an important, if not the primary reason, for his registering the Domain Name in himself in the first place"); ***Athena Infonomics India Private Limited v. Registration Private, Domains By Proxy, LLC / Renji Mathew***, D2017-1779 (WIPO November 1, 2017) ("Respondent's admitted conduct supports a strong inference that Respondent registered the Disputed Domain Name in his own name in order to control the ultimate disposition of the Disputed Domain Name.")

[58] ***Bootie Brewing Company v. Deanna D. Ward and Grabebootie Inc.***, D2003-0185 (WIPO May 28, 2003).

[59] ***Dean Hill Systems Ltd. v. Gregory Santana d/b/a Invicta***, D2002-0404 (WIPO September 20, 2002).

[60] ***ITX sarl, and Ziad M. Mugraby v. Tom Steiner***, FA0809001222737 (Forum October 24, 2008) (<beirut.com>) (domain name hijacking). However, compare ***William Mushi v. Great Thinkers***, FA0805001183235 (Forum June 23, 2008) ("The UDRP does not cover disputes concerning conversion of a disputed domain name where the registration information was freely given to Respondent.")

[61] ***Edward G. Linskey Jr. v. Brian Valentine***, D2006-0706 (WIPO September 18, 2006) (In a concurring opinion joined by his colleagues, one of the members stated "I fear that Respondent's success in this proceeding may encourage other cybersquatters or their counsel to attempt to 'complicate' Policy proceedings with far fetched or apparently outright fraudulent contentions or evidence,

credible."[62] To some extent uncertainty may be resolved by the Panel requesting further statements or documents from either of the parties.[63]

Complexity involving issues that (for example) "range far beyond forgery of the purchase agreement and invoice and banking instruction"—in which the Panel cannot reasonably rule on entitlement to the domain name—puts a case outside the scope of the Policy.[64] In the cited case there was also a question as to "the very existence of the principal." The Panel concluded that the Respondent's contentions (even if far-fetched and fraudulent) were too factually complicated to be resolved on papers alone.

In these cases, jurisdiction depends on parsing factual circumstances to determine whether "the domain names are [separable or] inseparable from the larger, complex disputes between the parties."[65] In the cited case the parties were respectively Mexican and U.S. citizens in which complainant alleged it lost the domain name to a fraudulent scheme. The factual circumstances are complex, with each party disputing the allegations of the other—the kind of case that raises questions of credibility better suited to plenary review and not amenable to determination without adversarial confrontation and discovery.

3.03-C Disputes Between Formerly Related Parties 3.03-C

3.03-C.1 Business Disputes 3.03-C.1

UDRP complaints are mostly against strangers, in which questions of rights or legitimate interests in disputed domain names are unencumbered by contractual relationships. A smaller class of cases involves disputes between formerly related parties bound by contract. This smaller class is itself divided into genuine business disputes and disputes dominated by domain name issues. Genuine business disputes belong in a court of competent jurisdiction.[66] Although Panels have held that the UDRP cannot be used to settle part of a dispute between parties known to each

---

then claim that these 'complications' raise issues that cannot and were not intended to be resolved in Policy proceedings.")

62 ***Courtney Love***, *supra.*

63 One of the tools available to the Panel is issuance of a procedural order pursuant to Rule 12 of the Rules of the Policy. Rule 12, which is exercised cautiously, is discussed further in "Procedural Orders" (Sec. 7.07-A).

64 ***Eric Haddad Koenig v. All Ltd, Selena Kovalski***, D2008-0322 (WIPO June 17, 2008).

65 ***Eric Haddad***, *supra.*

66 ICANN Second Staff Report, Paragraph 4.1(c), dated October 24, 1999. Numerous decisions. See as examples ***Transact Network Limited v. MobiStub LLC***, FA0808001221820 (Forum October 27, 2008) (Alleged breach of fiduciary duty, not cybersquatting); ***Grace From Fire, LLC v. ConnectDomain.com Worldwidedomains, Inc***, D2010-0143 (WIPO March 9, 2010) (<jackjackass.com>, Hosting agreement).

other,[67] it has also been observed that "[j]ust as cybersquatting can occur between strangers, so can it occur between business partners."[68]

First year Panels (2000) initially viewed an employee's or business partner's refusal to transfer a domain name as outside the scope of the policy.[69] A discernible shift of view began to occur in second–year decisions as Panels increasingly focused on respondent's conduct[70] rather than the parties' relationship.[71] Disputes may belong in a UDRP proceeding even if the theories presented in the complaint can also be classified as breaches of contract or fiduciary duty. Proof of violation may be established by breaches of contract and fiduciary duty, but it is respondent's acts with respect to the domain name that constitute the actionable claim and support an order of cancellation or transfer.[72]

The ***Thread*** Panel concluded that the UDRP was not the proper forum for business disputes because attempting "to shoehorn what is essentially a business dispute between former partners into a proceeding to adjudicate cybersquatting is, at its core, misguided, if not a misuse of the Policy . . . . It cannot be used to

---

[67] ***Vail Valley Partnership d/b/a Vail Valley Chamber & Tourism Bureau f/k/a Vail Valley Tourism & Convention Bureau v. ecomshare c/o Office Manager***, FA0803001163682 (Forum May 7, 2008) and ***Interactive Study Systems Inc. v. BFQ***, D2008-0205 (WIPO April 2, 2008) both involved parties known to each other and (mis)using the UDRP to settle one part of their dispute. ***Vail Valley Partnership*** (both Colorado residents) and ***Interactive Study Systems*** (Florida and Texas) intersect in their businesses and principally involve contract and fiduciary disputes to which the domain names are "ancillary to and inseparable."

[68] ***Bootie Brewing***, *supra*.

[69] ***Latent Technology Group, Inc. v. Bryan Fitchie***, FA0007000095285 (Forum September 1, 2000) (defended, "[D]ispute concerning employee's registration of domain name in his own name and subsequent refusal to transfer it to employer raises issues of breach of contract and breach of fiduciary duty that are more appropriately decided in court, not before a UDRP panel."); ***The Thread.com, LLC v. Jeffrey S. Poploff***, D2000-1470 (WIPO January 5, 2001) (defended). It is noteworthy that the presiding panelist in ***Bootie***, *supra*, had been the sole panelist in ***The Thread***. In ***The Thread*** he had carved out business disputes from the scope of the Policy while in ***Bootie*** he was in the majority that held the dispute fell within its scope.

[70] ***Bootie Brewing***, *supra*. (Split decision, six domain names transferred; three retained by respondent. The Panel "notes that this is an atypical UDRP case. Unlike many cases that concern traditional allegations of cybersquatting, this case instead concerns a business dispute between two parties who started with the best of intentions, but regrettably found their relationship in tatters. As is the norm in such business disputes, the facts are hotly contested, which creates a challenge for the trier of fact given the expedited nature of these proceedings and the limited record presented to the Panel.")

[71] ***Condotels International, Inc. v. Surfside Rental Management, Inc. d/b/a Condotels***, FA0105000097127 (Forum June 5, 2001) (Complaint denied, Franchisee appeared and defended). See ***Grace From Fire, LLC v. ConnectDomain.com Worldwidedomains, Inc***, D2010-0143 (WIPO March 9, 2010) (Complaint granted. Hosting agreement does not support appropriating domain name for past due account.)

[72] Numerous decisions. See as a representative example ***Cricket Technologies, LLC v. Martin a/k/a Cricket Technologies LLC***, FA 311353 (Forum September 27, 2004).

litigate all disputes involving domain names." Nevertheless, the Panel also made it clear—expressing a moral rather than a legal judgment—that "it strains credibility for Respondent to argue that he is holding the Domain Name for any purpose other than as 'leverage' in his negotiations with Complainant."[73] Similar reasoning can be found in other cases contemporary with ***The Thread***[74] and continues to have vitality.[75]

The database of decisions includes cases in which panelists have retained jurisdiction of abusive conduct that could in a court of competent jurisdiction be actionable for breaches of contract and fiduciary duty and tortious interference by former partners, employees, independent contractors, agents and consultants. Registering a domain name solely to prevent complainant from using it in its own business supports bad faith regardless of whether it resolves to an active website.[76] Use or non-use is irrelevant if the domain name impermissibly incorporates the trademark.[77] In ***Arma Partners***[78] a former partner refused to relinquish the domain names even though he had deeded them to the partnership at its formation. The Panel held:

> Although the 'armaparners.com' domain name may appear to have been originally registered in good faith by the Respondent, it is in this Panel's view clear from the contractual commitments to which he became party by the LLP Deed and the contemporaneous Deed of Transfer that ownership of that domain name was transferred to complainant's predecessor and that respondent as a Member of complainant agreed to devolution of that ownership to complainant.

---

[73] *Id.* ***The Thread.com***. Leveraging is a core example of cybersquatting, Paragraph 4(b)(i) of the Policy. The contractually related respondent violates the Policy even if the benefit sought is not money, but (for example) angling for employment or another benefit. See *DSPT Int'l v. Nahum*, 624 F.3d 1213, 1219 (9th Cir. 2010) ("As for whether use to get leverage in a business dispute can establish a violation, the statutory factors for 'bad faith intent' establish that it can.")

[74] ***Latent,*** *supra.*

[75] ***William Mushi v. Great Thinkers***, FA0805001183235 (Forum June 23, 2008).

[76] This does not apply to registrations lawfully acquired either under the UDRP or ACPA. See *Southern Grouts & Mortars, Inc. V. 3M Company*, 575 F.3d 1235 (11th Cir. July 23, 2009) (For the proposition that domain names not vulnerable to forfeiture for holding them inactive if acquired lawfully). For UDRP see "Redirecting, Liquidating, and Passively Holding" (Sec. 5.01-B.1.a).

[77] ***William Hill Org. Ltd. v. Fulfillment Mgmt. Servs. Ltd.***, D2000-0826 (WIPO September 17, 2000) (Respondent acknowledged that it "has not and will not use the disputed domain name, whether in good faith, bad faith or at all . . .. There is an automatic registration period for the purchase of a domain name. Once this has expired, anyone is free to purchase the domain name and respondent will not be renewing its interest. Any amount payable would be to the registration company and not to the respondent.") See also ***Savino Del Bene Inc. v. Gennari***, D2000-1133 (WIPO December 12, 2000).

[78] ***Arma Partners LLP v. Me, Victor Basta***, D2009-0894 (WIPO August 26, 2009).

Apparent good faith (this Panel continues) "may be 'coloured' by the subsequent conduct of a respondent by for example breaching the specific terms of a contractual undertaking."[79]

The list of complaints held to be within the scope of the Policy includes: 1) former officer and director of Complainant who allegedly paid for registration of domain name out of his own pocket[80]; 2) former employee continuing jewelry business under a different name, allegedly honoring warranties from past sales[81]; 3) termination of license[82]; 4) "unlawful termination" of employment[83]; and 5) independent contractors.[84] Meritorious arguments include fair use of the domain name for criticism or commentary.[85] As a general rule, however, business disputes between parties that involve assessing multiple issues and complex facts beyond holding domain names lie outside the scope of the Policy.[86] Legitimate trademark disputes,[87] contract issues that cannot be interpreted without an understanding of their contexts,[88] and unclear business or personal relationships[89] properly belong in a court of competent jurisdiction.[90]

---

[79] Retaining jurisdiction to rule on these kinds of contract issues can be traced back to some of the earliest cases in the canon.

[80] ***Simple Abilities Inc. v. Jeff Hoogveld and Adaptivies Abilities Inc.***, D2006-0143 (WIPO June 4, 2006) (registered for the benefit of Complainant).

[81] ***Glenn Hugh, Inc. v. The Sporn Company, Inc.***, FA0507000515478 (Forum August 29, 2005) ("[I]n the Panel's view, [the history of the parties' relationship] does not rise to the level of a legitimate trademark dispute that would preclude resolution under the Policy.")

[82] ***Gary Ensz v. Tax Express Incorporated***, FA0510000583079 (Forum January 4, 2006) (<gotax-express.com>. "The Panel disagrees [with Respondent] and recognizes the dispute as one of domain name ownership that is within the scope of the Policy.")

[83] ***Al Dostor Journal for Press, Publications, Advertisement and Circulation v. Moniker Privacy Services/ Hany Albeshry (MONIKER3747617)***, D2011-2230 (WIPO March 2, 2012) (Terminated employee re-registered domain name in his own name.)

[84] ***All Packaging Mach. Supplies, Corp. v. Crystal Flex Packaging Corp.***, D2002-0383 (WIPO July 17, 2002) (U.S. parties, <allpackagingmachinery.com>. A "phrase may be descriptive, [but] it is entitled to protection as a mark based on 20 years of use.")

[85] ***Spokane Civic Theatre v. James Ryan***, FA1109001409107 (Forum November 1, 2011) (Safe harbor under paragraph 4(c)(iii) of the Policy, fair use of the domain name for criticism and commentary.)

[86] "[T]he present case appears to hinge mostly on a business or civil dispute between the parties," ***Courtney Love***, FA 944826 (Nat. Arb. Forum May 14, 2007).

[87] ***Abbott Labs. v. Patel***, FA 740337 (Forum August 15, 2006) (assertions of trademark infringement are "entirely misplaced and totally inappropriate for resolution" in a domain name dispute); ***Stevenson Indus., Inc. v. CPAP PRO Online***, FA 105778 (Forum April 25, 2002) ("If the existence of [rights or legitimate interests] turns on resolution of a legitimate trademark dispute, then Respondent must prevail, because such disputes are beyond the scope of this proceeding.")

[88] ***Telbio Credit Union, Inc. v. Braden McParlin***, D2007-1224 (WIPO October 27, 2007) ("There is no dispute that Respondent was Complainant's employee at the time the disputed domain names

In assessing the merits of disputes between parties known to each other it is irrelevant that trademarks are on the lower end of the classification scale. Reputation assumes greater importance where (as is generally the case) parties are strangers, since in those circumstances there can be plausible ignorance. Since Respondent in ***All Packaging*** had been an independent contractor of the Complainant when it registered the disputed domain deniable of knowledge would be implausible.

3.03-C.2 Employer/Employee Disputes 3.03-C.2

An actionable claim for abusive registration against a former employee rests on the proposition that the employee has no right or legitimate interest in the domain name whether it was registered during or after employment. This does not extend to registrations of domain names with complainant's permission. They will remain with respondent under the conjunctive rule of 4(a)(iii) of the Policy.[91]

However, domain names registered during employment belong to the employer regardless in whose names they were registered. An employee charged with the responsibility for his employer's intellectual property assets can have no independent right or legitimate interest in domain names he registers in his own name,[92] except where he may have acquired a right prior to his current employment.[93]

---

were registered. The Panel finds that Respondent was not authorized to register or use any of the domain names under his own name.")

89 ***Brantley Gilbert v. Jason Chastain***, FA1107001397800 (Forum August 22. 2011) ("Complainant . . . states that it leased the disputed domain name from Respondent for its own purposes and to be used to promote and market Complainant's music career . . . . This implicitly indicates that Complainant and Respondent may have different interpretations of true ownership of the disputed domain name and the nature of their contractual relationship.")

90 Business disputes are likely also not to be found cybersquatting under the ACPA. See *Ar2, LLC d/b/a Liv Institute v. Rudnick, 14-80809-civ*, 15 (S.D.FL, August 7, 2014) ("At bottom, this case is a business dispute between partners which has morphed into an acrimonious divorce. Notwithstanding any other claims Plaintiff might assert against Defendant related to his retention of the domain names, this case does not involve the type of cybersquatting that the ACPA was intended to redress.")

91 ***Macado's Inc. v. C. B. Henderson***, FA0804001180994 (Nat. Arb. Forum June 17, 2008).

92 ***The Marigny Corporation v. Discount Coffee.com, Inc.***, D2001-0354 (WIPO May 17, 2001) (former employee of licensee); ***Sonic Crest Cadillac, LLC v. Hayes***, FA 212652 (Forum January 14, 2002) ("Respondent registered the disputed Domain Names on behalf of and with instruction from Complainant, but registered them in the name of Respondent's entity . . . Respondent's registration of the Domain Names for any other entity than Complainant is evidence of a bad faith."); ***Science, Engineering and Technology Associates Corporation v. John Freeman***, FA0601000637300 (Forum March 14, 2006) (defended, former chief financial officer registered domain name without employer's knowledge, transferred.) Other early cases, but undefended, include ***Top Driver, Inc. v. Benefits Benefits,*** D2002-0972 (WIPO January 7, 2003); ***Cricket Techno-logies, LLC v. Martin a/k/a Cricket Technologies LLC***, FA 311353 (Forum September 27, 2004) (Former employee registered the domain name in the name of the employer but listed himself as the "administrative contract." As a result Complainant needed a UDRP order to transfer the domain name); ***Champion***

A similar conclusion was drawn in ***Top Driver***.[94] The Panel found that the registrant "surreptitiously and without permission altered the registrant, contact information, Registrar and hosting server associated with the Domain Name . . . [with the] result . . . that complainant no longer has control over the domain name associated with its trademark." While the Panel did not find that the Respondent's conduct constituted, in Complainant's words, a "breach of fiduciary duty and misappropriation of company property" it did find that respondent registered and was using the domain name in bad faith.[95]

Registration of a domain name by a former employee with knowledge of "complainant's initiative to rebrand the company" is bad faith even though it predates the registration of the mark.[96] Denial of corrupt intention when registering the domain name—"[t]here was never any mention of the company changing names to the domain name in question nor was there any mention of a trademark"[97]—is not a safe harbor defense if the evidence establishes there was.[98] "An employee or former employee is not a licensee and thus has no authorization to use a company's trademark or a confusingly similar variation thereof without permission."[99] His or her refusal to transfer the domain name upon request or termination of employment may support an inference that he had an ulterior motive in registering the domain

---

Innovations, Ltd. v. Udo Dussling (45FHH), D2005-1094 (WIPO December 16, 2005) (Former employee, without employer's knowledge).

[93] ***ITMetrixx, Inc. v. Kuzma Productions***, D2001-0668 (WIPO August 2, 2001) (<itmetrixx.com>).

[94] Sole panelist in ***The Thread***, *supra.*

[95] This is an illustration of the principle that conduct is the key to bad faith. Discussed further in "Disputes Within the Scope of the Policy" (Sec. 3.03). See ***T 2 d.o.o. v Matev Turk***, CAC 100656 (ADR.eu October 30, 2013) for a variant on the issue of bad faith where the bad faith use was a failure to transfer the domain name to Complainant: "Respondent's failure to transfer the Domain Name into the Complainant's name since its acquisition over 8 years ago is a clear indication of the Respondent's ongoing bad faith.")

[96] ***Distinct Holdings, Inc., d/b/a Diversified v. Robert Schweitzer***, FA1706001737080 (Forum July 27, 2017) ("The Panel recognizes that the registered trademarks of Complainant for DIVERSIFIED were not registered until May 23, 2017 and that the domain names were registered prior to that date namely on August 20, 2016. However, Complainant clearly had common law trademark rights in DIVERSIFIED from at least December 2015, rights that had been well established at the time Respondent was employed there and of course prior to the domain names being registered.")

[97] *Id.*

[98] See *Atigeo LLC v. Offshore Ltd.*, No. 2:13 cv 01694 JLR, 2014 WL 239096 (W.D. Wash. Jan. 22, 2014) (slip op.) (Complaint states a claim under the ACPA. "Specifically, Plaintiffs allege that (1) Defendants threatened Plaintiffs with retaliation, (2) Defendants created a website containing false and defamatory statements about Atigeo, (3) Defendants used certain meta tags to lure members of the public searching for the legitimate Atigeo website to atigeo.co, etc.")

[99] ***Ruby's Diner, Inc. v. Joseph W. Popow***, D2001-0868 (WIPO August 29, 2001). See also ***Octogen Pharmacal Company, Inc. v. Domains By Proxy, Inc. / Rich Sanders and Octogen e Solutions***, D2009-0786 (WIPO August 19, 2009) ("Respondent registered the domain name at issue under his

name in his own rather than his employer's name.[100] Abusive registration is presumed, and conclusive absent exonerating evidence.

3.03-C.3 Vendor/Agent Disputes

3.03-C.3

Vendor/Agent disputes generally rest on unanticipated circumstances or claims of unfulfilled obligations. As with former employees, partners and corporate officers, vendors and agents are connected through contract but have a separate status. That separate status can give rise to two distinct kinds of disputes: 1) agents retained to purchase and provide services for domain names who register them in their own rather than their principals' names and refuse to turn them over when their employment terminates[101]; and 2) agents claiming liens for unpaid services who hold the domain names for ransom. Complainants of the first kind may be more "sympathetic"[102] but in the absence of contractual terms if the registration was authorized it could not have been in bad faith. The second kind of dispute may also involve an authorized registration but holding the domain name may be actionable for abusive conduct that is within the scope of the Policy.

Vendors/agents' claims to rights or legitimate interests in domain names may be justified on proof of a contractual relationship and assertion of a lien, but "[a]ny such claim must be carefully reviewed by the panel in order to ensure that it is underpinned by at least a prima facie basis and is not merely pled as a device to circumvent the aims of the Policy."[103] Justifying conduct offered as a defense is within the scope of the Policy and assessed on the merits as previously discussed.[104]

---

own name in connection with the business of Complainant in full contemplation of Complainant's assertion of rights in the OCTOGEN mark. The subsequent use of the domain name has been principally in connection with Complainant's business.")

[100] Respondents do not forfeit domain name registered with complainant's permission under the conjunctive rule of 4(a)(iii) of the Policy, ***Macado's Inc. v. C. B. Henderson***, FA0804001180994 (Forum June 17, 2008).

[101] ***Indoor Air Technologies, Inc. v. Casey Janke / My Tech Company LLC / Privacy Administrator / Anonymize, Inc.***, FA1701001714547 (Forum March 14, 2017) (<iatcorpusa.com>, <indoorair technologies.net>, and <iatcorpusa.net>. The Panel found the dispute outside the scope of the Policy: "Both parties agreed ... that Complainant engaged with Respondent to make use of Respondent's IT services in developing and promoting Complainant's business.")

[102] ***Kimmel Scrap Iron & Metal Co. v. Michael Bader, P-1 Enterprises***, D2016-1148 (WIPO August 8, 2016) (<kimmelscrap.com>) ("The Panel is sympathetic to the Complainant's plight; it is not the first company to realize that its agent has kept control of a domain name when their relationship ended. These problems can be avoided with appropriate contract provisions and supervision, and they may be amenable to legal remedies, but often not in a UDRP proceeding.")

[103] ***Lescottstewart Limited v. Saeed Izadifar***, D2012-1998 (WIPO December 4, 2012) ("With some reluctance, in light of its skepticism expressed above, the Panel accepts that these factors constitute a prima facie basis for the Respondent's claim to a lien in this specific case"), citing ***Clinomics Biosciences, Inc. v. Simplicity Software, Inc.***, D2001-0823 (WIPO August 28, 2001) ("The claims

A finding that a complaint is outside the scope because there may be a genuine contractual issue involved does not for that reason imply a respondent's good faith; only that complainant is unable to prove bad faith registration. This results from the nature of the contractual relationship, which imposes on complainant a heavier burden of proving entitlement to relief.[105] Complaints with disputed (triable) issues resist resolution in a UDRP proceeding.

While Panels *may* recognize that properly documented and supported claims *could* give rise to a legitimate interest in the disputed domain name[106] they have generally refrained from drawing ultimate conclusions.[107] The rationale for distinguishing one set of vendors/agents from another is embedded in domain name jurisprudence: complaints in cases with disputed facts should be "decided by traditional means, as they turn on questions of law beyond the Policy."[108]

Panels that accept the proposition that a respondent may have a legitimate interest for unpaid services and deny the complaint are ruling in essence that the dispute is within the scope of the Policy. It can be argued, however, that in denying the complaint they are accepting respondent's defense of a right or legitimate interest in

---

of the parties here turn on whether or not there is a genuine dispute over Respondent's contractual or legal right to retain the domain name as security for payment.")

104 ***Map Supply, Inc. v. On-line Colour Graphics***, FA 96332 (Forum February 6, 2001) (An alleged unpaid services defense. However, the Panel did not believe there was a legitimate dispute over a lien: "The Respondent has failed to persuade me that there is any chance that the law would permit it, without the consent of the client, to take control of a domain name, and then retain control as a security against payment for web design work"); ***Nova Banka v. Iris***, D2003-0366 (WIPO June 30, 2003) (Respondent registered domain name to keep control because the domain name was its "one and only protection" for recovering on unpaid invoices. Panel ordered the domain name transferred to Complainant); ***Grace From Fire, LLC v. ConnectDomain.com Worldwidedomains, Inc***, D2010-0143 (WIPO March 9, 2010) (<jackjackass.com>) (Self-enforcement supports finding of bad faith.) See also ***Pitchtime, Inc. v. Constantine Zamiesov (a/k/a Kostiantyn Zamiesov, a/k/a Konstantine Zamiesov), Cruxlab, Inc.*** D2019-0511 (WIPO April 25, 2019) (<pitchtime.com> and others. "Respondent used the disputed domain names as a lever to secure payment from Complainant of monies allegedly owed.")

105 ***Dish Network LLC v. Digital Satellite Connections LLC,*** FA1306001504221 (Forum August 16, 2013) (UDRP denied; summary judgment granted under the Trademark Act).

106 ***Amy's Orchids v. EIC***, D2009-0466 (WIPO June 8, 2009) (Complaint dismissed. "The Panel finds the dicta of Map Supply v. On-line Colour Graphics, FA0096332 persuasive: 'The Respondent['s] argument does raise the interesting question whether an unpaid web designer once given control over a domain name by the client can retain it as a security for payment. In my view, this may be so. The law may recognize some sort of lien or charge against a domain name. To assert such a claim is to assert a legitimate interest." But it nevertheless falls outside the scope of the UDRP.

107 ***Airbak Tech, LLC v. Blazon Marketing, Inc.***, D2012-1000 (WIPO August 15, 2012) ("Notwithstanding this recognition . . . a genuine dispute over a respondent's contractual or legal right to retain the domain name in dispute as security for payment would require further evidence and an evaluation of the commercial law of liens.")

108 ***Family Watchdog LLC v. Lester Schweiss***, D2008-0183 (WIPO April 23, 2008).

the domain name. This view is inconsistent with consensus. Respondents may have an alleged money claim for services performed but this is not a basis for denying a UDRP complaint.[109] Tbere are two reasons for this, namely UDRP resolves only those forms of predatory conduct that are clearly evident from the record; and secondly, unpaid fee claims raise triable issues of fact outside the Panel's jurisdiction to hear and decide.

---

[109] There are no reported federal actions under 15 U.S.C. §1125(d), but there is a case under Sec. 8131. See *Salle v. Meadows*, 6:07-cv-1089-Orl-31 (M.D. FL, August 6, 2007) (Defendant admitted that he purchased the domain name and attempted to sell it to the plaintiff for $9,500, but justified his conduct on the grounds that plaintiff was indebted to him in that amount. Holding: "cyber extortion is not a permissible way of recovering a debt.")

4 Complainant's Burden of Proof

4.01 SUBJECT MATTER JURISDICTION AND STANDING—PARAGRAPH 4(a)(i) OF THE POLICY 4.01

4.01-A Threshold for Jurisdiction 4.01-A

4.01-A.1 Standing to Maintain an Administrative Proceeding 4.01-A.1

4.01-A.1.a *Trademark or Service Mark in Which Complainant Has Rights* *4.01-A.1.a*

Complainants have standing to maintain a claim of cybersquatting only if they have trademarks or service marks in which they have a right. Of rights, those registered unquestionably succeed even if they postdate the registration of the domain names, although complainants of postdated marks most likely will have no actionable claim. Unregistered marks only succeed if they demonstrate secondary meaning predating registration of the domain names. Anticipated rights such as applications awaiting approval by trademark registries are not deemed to qualify. This also includes marks registered on the Supplemental Register in the U.S. Unregistered rights may include trade names and personal names if they are found to be functioning as trademarks.[1]

The elements for proving standing are set out in paragraph 4(a)(i) of the Policy.[2] Domain names must either be "identical" or "confusingly similar" to complainants' marks. If they are similar but not confusing they fail to satisfy the requirement. The second element completes the sentence. Complainant must demonstrate it "has rights" that are infringed by the domain name. Rights are irrefutable for registered trademarks because they are officially documented but for unregistered marks proving rights is a challenge, as discussed separately below.[3]

The "rights" complainants have to establish spring from trademark ownership which is not limited to signs formally registered by trademark authorities. It can be established by proving use in commerce earlier than registration of the accused domain name. Early Panels explained that the Policy "does not distinguish between registered and unregistered trademarks and service marks in the context of abusive registration of domain names."[4] Complainant achieves standing by proving it has a trademark. It does not have to prove a right to the domain name. That is

---

[1] Trademarks are classified on a scale in which the lower the classification—generally dictionary words and descriptive phrases—the greater the burden of proving respondent's knowledge and infringement. The higher the classification— suggestive, arbitrary or fanciful terms—the greater their protection against unauthorized use of complainants' marks. See *Two Pesos, Inc. v. Taco Cabana, Inc.*, 505 U.S. 763, 768 (1992) ("Marks are often classified in categories of generally increasing distinctiveness ....") See also "Trade Names Brought Within Policy's Scope" (Sec. 4.01-D.3.b).

[2] The first limb of the Policy reads: "the disputed domain name is identical or confusingly similar to a trademark or service mark in which the complainant has rights."

[3] Discussed further in "Unregistered Marks, Recognition in the Marketplace and Proof of Secondary Meaning" (Sec. 4.01-B). See ***Bangz, Inc. v. Afrodite Pelardis***, FA1302001486688 (Forum April 24, 2013).

respondent's burden in rebutting complainant's proof in the second and third limbs of the Policy.[5] Complainant's sole task under paragraph 4(a)(i) of the Policy is to persuade the Panel that it satisfies the threshold requirement. Where complainant lacks standing to maintain the administrative proceeding because of failure to prove an unregistered mark, or complainant has only a pending trademark application, or the domain name is neither identical nor confusingly similar, the complaint must be dismissed for lack of standing.[6]

There are four possible factual patterns: 1) complainant has both a registered right postdating registration of the domain name and proof of unregistered right predating the domain name; 2) complainant satisfies its standing requirement by having a registered mark, however lacks proof to support the second and third requirements; 3) complainant establishes that it has an unregistered right; and 4) complainant makes a naked claim but lacks sufficient proof to establish an unregistered right (3 and 4 are discussed further in "Unregistered Marks" (Sec. 4.01-B).

In the case of unregistered marks doubt is resolved in favor of complainant only if the proof supports its allegation that the mark existed prior to the registration of the domain name.[7] In the case of registered marks it is irrelevant when they were acquired as long as they were used in commerce prior to the commencement of the administrative proceedings.[8] It is irrelevant, also, that the trademark is weak or strong, or little or well-known. The sole issue is whether the complainant has rights in the mark at the commencement of the proceedings.

A finding that a trademark owner has standing simply recognizes that it satisfies the threshold requirement—that is, it gets to "first base."[9] Because complainants control the evidence of their rights under the first limb of the Policy, their success

---

[4] ***The British Broadcasting Corporation v. Jaime Renteria***, D2000-0050 (WIPO March 23, 2000).

[5] The argument that a complainant must have rights in the domain name "turns this element of the Policy on its head. Complainant does not have the burden to show rights in the infringing domain name, only rights in the mark. . . ." ***Scripps Networks, LLC v. Chief Architect, Inc.***, D2009-0633 (WIPO June 29, 2009). Rather, it is the respondent's burden to prove it has a right or legitimate interest in a domain name that is identical or confusingly similar to a complainant's trademark.

[6] ***Intermark Media, Inc. v. Wang Logic Corp.***, FA0212000139660 (Forum February 19, 2003) (no enforceable interest under paragraph 4(a)(i) of the Policy, therefore no standing). See also ***FIBO Consulting, LTD v. MohammadReza FakhrMoghaddam***, FA1708001744548 (Forum September 15, 2017).

[7] Registration is not a necessary precondition for a trademark right, although without a registration the burden of proving a right is heavier because the right must have existed prior to registration of the domain name. Discussed further in "Unregistered Marks, Recognition in the Marketplace and Proof of Secondary Meaning" (Sec. 4.01-B) and "Supplemental Register" (Sec. 4.01-B.2.c).

[8] Relative timing of domain name purchase and trademark acquisition is a factor in determining bad faith registration. See Jurisprudential Overview, Paragraph 1.2. A party can have standing but no actionable claim. Discussed further in "Timing of Trademark Acquisition Not a Factor in Determining Standing" (Sec. 4.01-E).

is expected for that limb, but having a right is not a prediction of the merits of their claims. It merely allows complainant to proceed with proof that respondent lacks "rights or legitimate interests" in the domain name [paragraph 4(a)(ii)] followed, if successful on the second limb, with proof of abusive registration on the third [paragraph 4(a)(iii)].

Confusion is basic to cybersquatting. The concept appears twice in the UDRP; once in paragraph 4(a)(i) in the adjectival phrase "confusing similarity"; and once in paragraph 4(b)(iv) in the phrase "likelihood of confusion." Each phrase demands a different level of assessment, as it does of proof. The first phrase relates to standing; the second to infringement.[10] In making the initial assessment panelists act as "objective bystander[s]"[11], while with the ultimate assessment they are not bystanders but triers of fact applying legal standards to the facts of the case. An objective bystander is one who simply compares; the strings look alike (transposing letters or adding words) or aurally alike ("eco" and "eko").

That complainant establishes standing neither enlarges its right to the disputed domain name nor diminishes respondent's right or legitimate interest in it.[12] Success is based on proof that the disputed domain name is "identical or confusingly similar to a trademark in which [complainant] has rights." If complainant is an assignee or licensee it must demonstrate its right by offering evidence of the chain of title that connects it to the last known mark owner.[13]

---

[9] ***RapidShare AG, Christian Schmid v. N/A Maxim Tvortsov***, D2010-0696 (WIPO June 22, 2010) (RAPIDSHARE and <rapidbay.net>. Complainant failed the first limb). As complainant proceeds from limb to limb the evidentiary demands correspondingly increase. Discussed further in Chapters 5 and 6.

[10] One of the differences between the Uniform Domain Name Dispute Resolution Policy and the Anticybersquatting Consumer Protection Act is the burden for establishing standing to maintain an administrative proceeding or commence an action. Under the UDRP a trademark owner can proceed if its mark is in existence prior to filing the complaint *even though its trademark postdates registration of the domain name.* This is a panel made rule that has solidified into precedent. In contrast, the ACPA requires plaintiffs to show they have registered or unregistered marks predating the registration of the domain name. This is a statutory *not* a judge made requirement. The "identical or confusingly similar" is the same as the UDRP but "the mark [has to be] distinctive [or famous] at the time of registration of the domain name." If a trademark owner has any actionable claim at all for a postdated mark it would have to rest on another legal theory than cybersquatting.

[11] ***Open Society Institute v. Gil Citro***, FA1007001333304 (Forum August 24, 2010) (a view expressed by the dissent).

[12] A respondent with a predated domain name may prevail even if it lacks rights or legitimate interests under paragraph 4(a)(ii) (lack of rights or legitimate interests). Success in proving the first and second limbs does not support abusive registration under paragraph 4(a)(iii) of the Policy. Discussed further in "Complainant's Acquisition of Trademark Right" (Sec. 4.01-E.1).

[13] Proof of assignment: ***Remithome Corp v. Pupalla***, FA 1124302 (Forum February 21, 2008). No proof of assignment: ***Commercial Vehicle Group, Inc. v. Worldwide Media, Inc.***, FA1309001518310

The standard of proof for "this limb of the Policy is relatively low."[14] When a complainant proves there is "enough goodwill and reputation in and to a name and sufficient association of the same with the [complainant], no matter how strong or weak those trademark and service mark rights may be" it is sufficient to satisfy the first limb of the Policy.[15] The low bar applies to marks registered in any jurisdiction, but the bar is raised for unregistered marks for which the proof demands are significantly higher.

Ordinarily, a complainant proves ownership of a trademark by offering a certificate of registration from a national registry. Attaching documentation to the complaint is easier than having to prove a reputation with an historical reach prior to the registration of the domain name (discussed below). Unregistered marks are accepted or rejected upon proof or absence of secondary meaning.[16] In neither case is succeeding on the standing element dispositive of either rights or legitimate interests in a domain name (paragraph 4(a)(ii)[17]) or bad faith registration and use (paragraph 4(a)(iii) of the Policy). The successive requirements are separate and cumulative.[18]

The term "complainant" can embrace a single person or entity or more than one or others having a sufficient nexus to the owner of the right or having a vested interest in it, for example a license.[19] It does not matter that the trademark was

---

(Forum October 18. 2013) ("The Complainant's name is Commercial Vehicle Group, Inc., located at 7800 Walton Parkway, New Albany, OH 43054. However, in the evidence, the ROADMARK mark was assigned to Commercial Vehicle Systems, Inc. located at 171 Great Oak Drive Canton NC/USA 28716. Moreover, according to the Complainant's evidence, Commercial Vehicle Systems, Inc. changed its name to Sprague Devices, Inc. in May 2005. Sprague Devices, Inc. is the last registered owner of the ROADWATCH trademark. Therefore, Commercial Vehicle Group Inc. does not appear anywhere in the evidence.")

14 ***Asset Marketing Systems, LLC v. Silver Lining***, D2005-0560 (WIPO July 22, 2005).

15 ***Action Sports Videos v. Jeff Reynolds***, D2001-1239 (WIPO December 13, 2001).

16 Discussed further in "Proving Unregistered Trademark Rights" (Sec. 4.01-B.2).

17 ***Societe des Produits Nestle S.A. v. Pro Fiducia Treuhand AG***, D2001-0916 (WIPO October 12, 2001) ("Although failure to make bona fide use of a domain name has been cited in some cases as a factor to consider in determining bad faith, lack of bona fide use on its own is insufficient to establish bad faith.") Discussed further in "Proving a *Prima Facie* Case" (Sec. 4.02-B)

18 See ***Modefine S.A. v. A.R. Mani***, D2001-0537 (WIPO July 20, 2001) in which the Panel notes that Complainant's submission "seems to be predicated on the fact that by [registering a domain name composed of his initials and last name] . . . respondent is likely to cause confusion with complainant's mark" and emphasizes that such a theory "wrongly imports into the test for legitimate interest an element of confusion or bad faith."

19 ***Kimmel Center, Inc. v. Tech Support, Trade Out Investments Ltd.***, D2011-0293 (WIPO April 22, 2011). Rule 3(b)(xv) of the Rules of the Policy provides that "the complaint shall include documentary or other evidence, including a copy of . . . any trademark or service mark registration upon which the complaint relies. . . ." Failure to attach copy of trademark registration can be fatal. See ***Eric Levy v. Joseph Ahmadi***, D2014-1369 (WIPO October 2, 2014) ("Complainant holds rights in a mark containing the words YOURNEIGHBORHOOD LOVE WHERE YOU LIVE. . . .

acquired later than the registration of the domain name. Timing of the respective rights is an issue for the second and third limbs of the Policy.[20]

Rights in a trademark exist without regard to its strength or weakness, which is also an issue for the second and third limbs. A trademark owner may maintain a UDRP proceeding even if it is clear (to everyone but itself) that it cannot succeed on the merits because of the timing of its right.[21] Similarly, where the domain name dispute is secondary to other issues outside the scope of the Policy the trademark owner may have standing, but no actionable claim in a UDRP proceeding.[22] This applies also to claims involving post domain paths,[23] subdomains,[24] or third level domains which are outside the scope of the Policy absent an agreement to the contrary.[25]

Throughout the Complaint, Complainant refers solely to the YOURNEIGHBORHOOD component of this mark, and makes no mention of the other words. Nor did Complainant attach a copy of the USPTO registration as an annex to the Complaint, which would have been common practice. This omission is important, because it obscures the fact that the registration specifically disclaims any right in the text YOURNEIGHBORHOOD apart from the mark as shown. The Panel suspects legerdemain on the part of Complainant. Not only was this important information omitted from the Complaint, but Complainant actually asserted in the pleadings that 'the Domain Name completely incorporates Complainants' [sic] Mark.' The manifest falsity of that statement persuades the Panel that Complainant was trying to pull a fast one.")

20 WIPO Overview 2.0, Paragraphs 1.4 and Overview 3.0 Paragraph 1.1.3.

21 This issue most frequently arises in situations in which the domain name is registered prior to complainant acquiring a trademark right. For an example of extreme "bad faith" in maintaining a UDRP proceeding, see ***ELK Accesories Pty Ltd. v. Parnaz Farahani / Elk.com***, D2012-0455 (WIPO May 14, 2012) ("[E]ven if the Panel were to find confusing similarity, any interest the Complainant acquired in the trademark ELK . . . must have been after it incorporated in 2008, which is 13 years after the Respondent registered the Disputed Domain Name in 1995 and 15 years after the Complainant's trademark registrations issued in 2010.") Discussed further in "Timing of Trademark Acquisition Not a Factor in Determining Standing" (Sec. 4.01-E). The sole penalty for commencing and maintaining a proceeding based on meritless arguments is a finding against complainant of reverse domain name hijacking (Sec. 7.11-A). The ***Elk*** Complainant was found to have abused the Policy by initiating the proceeding in bad faith.

22 Discussed further in "Defining Proscribed Conduct" (Sec. 1.02-A). However, the existence of complex facts should not for that reason alone justify abdicating making a decision under the UDRP. Discussed further in "Complexity Not Reason for Abdicating Making a Decision" (Sec. 3.03-B).

23 ***Romantic Tours, Inc. v. Whois Privacy Protection Service, Inc.***, FA1003001316557 (Forum April 28, 2010) ("[The] UDRP does not offer relief for infringements via use of registered trademarks in post domains. . . . [T]he proceedings under the UDRP may be applied only to domain names." The same conclusion has been reached for claims under the ACPA. See *Interactive Prod. v. A2z Mobile Off. Solution*, 326 F.3d 687, 698 (6th Cir. 2003) ("Because post domain paths do not typically signify source, it is unlikely that the presence of another's trademark in a post domain path of a URL would ever violate trademark law."); *Goforit Entertainment LLC v. Digimedia.com LP*, 750 F. Supp.2d 712 (N.D. Tex. October 25, 2010): "Because third level domains—whether specifically designated or using Wildcard DNS—are not 'registered with or assigned by any domain name registrar,' a straightforward reading of the text shows that GEL cannot recover under the ACPA for defendants' use of Wildcard DNS in a third level domain."

4.01-A.1.b

4.01-A.1.b *Existing Trademarks*

As paragraph 4(a)(i) has come to be construed the mark in which complainant has a right is one that exists at the time complainant commences the administrative proceeding, *whether or not the right precedes or postdates the registration of the domain name.*[26] If complainant fails to carry the burden of proving it has a trademark right the complaint must be dismissed.[27] "Existing" comprehends both "potentially extant" and "extant."

Trademarks are potentially extant (next section) when opportunists with advanced knowledge of complainants' business or corporate intentions register domain names in anticipation of complainants' trademark applications.[28] "Extant" refers to an existing mark. It does not include "intent to use" applications pending for publication or registration, but it can include common law marks where the first use in commerce precedes domain registration. If complainant either has no trademark or if it does but the domain name is not identical or confusingly similar it has no standing to complain.[29]

---

[24] ***Comfort Window Co., Inc. v. AL SADEQOUN LIL TASWEEQ LLC***, FA1206001447758 (Forum July 25, 2012) ("The UDRP rules do not apply to subdomain names. In order for the UDRP Policy to apply, there must be evidence that these subdomains are registered with a registrar.")

[25] See ***Yahoo! Inc. v. YAHOO.COM / YAHOO! INC.***, FA1311001532273 (Forum January10, 2014) (Preliminary issue, third-level domain 'ymail.com.co', but "the registry administrating the '.co' top level domain, has agreed to the application of the UDRP to its third level domain names, such as the '.com.co' domain names, the Panel finds that the UDRP is applicable to this dispute.")

[26] ***Smart Design LLC v. Carolyn Hughes***, D2000-0993 (WIPO October 18, 2000) ("While the Panel is aware that certain previous Panels have taken the view that in these circumstances the Complaint must fail at the first hurdle, this Panel does not take that view. In this Panel's view the test under paragraph 4(a)(i) of the Policy, which makes no mention of 'exclusive rights' is or ought to be a relatively easy test for a Complainant to satisfy, its purpose simply being to ensure that the Complainant has a bona fide basis for making the Complaint in the first place.")

The consensus reported in the Jurisprudential Overview 3.0. Paragraph 3.8 is that "where a respondent registers a domain name before the complainant's trademark rights accrue, panels will not normally find bad faith on the part of the respondent. (This would not however impact a panel's assessment of a complainant's standing under the first UDRP element.)." However, some Panels bypass the issue, as in ***Credit Europe Bank N.V. v. Peter Yu***, D2010-0737 (WIPO July 14, 2010) ("Typically, a Panel considers each of the three requirements under paragraph 4(a) of the Policy in turn. Because paragraph 4(a)'s requirements are conjunctive, however, no matter what the findings under the first and second sub-paragraphs, the Complainant must fail under the requirement to demonstrate that the disputed domain name has been both registered and used in bad faith.")

The Anticybersquatting Consumer Protection Act takes a different approach. It requires the plaintiff to prove distinctiveness of its trademark "at the time of registration of the domain name," 15 U.S.C. §1125(d)(1)(A)(ii).

[27] Discussed further in "Complainant's Acquisition of Trademark Right" (Sec. 4.01-E.1).

[28] Discussed further in "Potentially Existing Trademarks" (Sec. 4.01-A.1.c).

[29] Discussed further in "Similar, But Not Confusingly Similar" (Sec. 4.01-A.2.c).

4.01-A.1.c *Potentially Existing Trademarks* 4.01-A.1.c

There is one departure from the rule that requires the complainant to have an existing trademark. It is "well established" (notes one Panel) "that a high profile announcement of a new corporate name can generate goodwill in that name . . . and [is] recognised as sufficient for the purposes of the first element of the UDRP."[30] This principle is reported in the Jurisprudential Overview. "In certain situations, when respondent is clearly aware of complainant, and it is clear that the aim of the registration was to take advantage of the confusion between the domain name and any potential complainant rights, bad faith can be found."[31]

The "potentiality" principle was initially applied to domain names combining trademarks of merger partners. This is made clear in a later sentence in the same paragraph of the WIPO Overview: "This often occurs after a merger between two companies, before the new trademark rights can arise." All the early cases cited in the WIPO Overview were of this type. For example, MONSANTO and PHARMACIA[32]; or MAERSK and SEA-LAND.[33] However, the final clause of the WIPO Overview recognizes extension of the principle to include circumstances in which "respondent is aware of complainant's potential rights, and registers the domain name to take advantage of any rights that may arise from complainant's enterprises."[34]

Media coverage of complainant and its activities in or around the time respondent registered the domain name provides insight into its motivation for choosing it. Although complainants of lesser known trademarks and marks unknown outside their regional market have a heightened burden, the marks are equally protected if the evidence of media coverage is persuasive that respondent had the complainant in mind.[35]

---

30 ***The Old Course Limited v. Patrick Woods***, D2010-0682 (WIPO June 6, 2010).

31 Jurisprudential Overview 3.0, Paragraph 3.8.2.

32 ***Pharmacia & Upjohn AB v. Monsantopharmacia.com Inc.***, D2000-0446 (WIPO August 1, 2000).

33 ***A.P. Møller v. Web Society***, D2000-0135 (WIPO April 15, 2000) (<maersksealand.com> and 'maersk-sealand.com').

34 Opportunistic registrations generally involve paragraph 4(b)(i) of the Policy, that the domain name was acquired primarily for the purpose of exchanging it "for valuable consideration in excess of your documented out of pocket costs directly related to the domain name." See ***Body Accounting, Inc. v. Affinity Domains, Energy First***, D2009-1419 (WIPO December 11, 2009). However, offering to sell a domain name acquired in good faith "in excess of your documented out-of-pocket costs" is not unlawful. Discussed further in "Not All Offers to Sell Violate the Policy" (Sec. 6.02-B).

35 Application of the potentiality principle is discussed further in "Opportunistic Bad Faith" (Sec. 6.01-C.1) and "Acting on Media Coverage and Insider Information" (Sec. 6.01-C.1.b).

4.01-A.2 4.01-A.2 Comparing Domain Name and Trademark Side by Side

4.01-A.2.a 4.01-A.2.a *Identical and Confusingly Similar*

The term "identical" carries its ordinary dictionary definition that the lexical parts of the second level domain and trademark essentially correspond.[36] "Confusingly similar" is a matter of assessing the degree of similarity and its potential to confuse the Internet user.[37] Confusing similarity is not to be equated with the trademark concept of "likelihood of confusion" (phrasing found in paragraph 4(b)(iv) of the Policy.)[38] The use of the word "confusing" or "confusion" (in their two appearances) are not intended to imply the same evidentiary requirements mark owners would be expected to prove for trademark infringement.

A domain name identical to a trademark is confusing on its face, while similarity that is not confusing is not actionable. Whether similarity is sufficiently confusing to qualify as confusingly similar requires a deft calibration. Is <brooklynbeer.com> confusingly similar to BROOKLYN BREWERY? A three-member Panel concluded it was because it had the "same connotation and commercial impression."[39] Second level domains composed of English transliterations of foreign

---

[36] Some panelists have used the term "virtually identical" when there is a minor variation, but the phrase is simply another way of saying "confusingly similar." ***The Stanley Works and Stanley Logistics, Inc v. Cam Creek. Co., Inc***, D2000-0113 (WIPO April 13, 2000) (<stanleybostitch.com> combining two trademarks). Compare, *In re Sears, Roebuck and Co.*, 2 USPQ2d 1312, 1314 (TTAB 1987) (CROSSOVER and CROSS OVER held "legally identical in sound and appearance"); *Harvey Hubbell, Incorporated v. Red Rope Industries, Inc.*, 191 USPQ 119, 123 (TTAB 1976) (DATALOK and DATA. LOK held "legally identical").

[37] The use of a precisely similar name is not required for a finding of trademark infringement under Sections 32 and 43(a) of the Lanham Act. "A name which is 'confusingly similar' or a 'colorable imitation' of the trademark is sufficient," *Advance Magazine Publishers Inc. v. Vogue International*, 123 F. Supp. 2d 790 (D.N.J. 2000) (<teenvogue.com>, <teenvogue.net> and <vogue international.com>), citing *Fisons Horticulture, Inc. v. Vigoro Industries, Inc.*, 30 F.3d 466, 477 (3d Cir. 1994). "Marks are confusingly similar if ordinary consumers are likely to conclude that they share a 'common source, affiliation, connection or sponsorship.'" *Jews for Jesus v. Brodsky*, 993 F. Supp. 282, 296 (D.N.J. 1998).

[38] Confusion in the trademark sense found in such phrases as: "lead to confusion," "compound the confusion," "likely to cause confusion," "confusion to consumers," "create the confusion described in the Policy," etc. is not relevant for the jurisdictional analysis. Under the UDRP such allegations of fact are reserved for consideration under paragraphs 4(a)(ii) and 4(a)(iii). See ***OVB Vermögensberatung AG v. Michele Dinoia and SZK.com***, D2009-0307 (WIPO May 6, 2009) (<ovb.com>).

[39] ***The Brooklyn Brewery Corporation v. Private Registration at Account Privacy/Jeffrey Matthews Ltd.***, D2015-1258 (WIPO October 29, 2015) ("Although Complainant does not own a mark for the terms 'Brooklyn' alone or for 'Brooklyn beer,' Complainant does own rights to the mark 'Brooklyn Brewery,' which has the same first term, as well as the same connotation and commercial impression, as the disputed domain name <brooklynbeer.com>") (However, complaint denied

words have been found to be confusingly similar "if a considerable part of the public understands the meaning of the translation."[40]

The terms "identical" and "confusingly similar to" refer to the lexical elements to the immediate left of the dot—also known as the second level domain ("SLD"). Whether a domain name is identical or confusingly similar to a trademark is simply a matter of making a side by side comparison with the domain name without regard to prefixes ("www" and "qualifier+SLD"), suffixes ("SLD+qualifier"), or top-level domain extensions.[41] A domain name is identical to the trademark when it is a character for character match.[42] It is confusingly similar when it varies the trademark in some indistinguishable way, such as making a phonetic substitution (ECOLAB and <ekolab.com>),[43] adding generic terms to the dominant part of a trademark[44] and misspelling,[45] reversing or transposing the order of letters[46] or words.[47]

---

because Respondent had priority, and hence could not possibly have registered the domain name in bad faith).

[40] ***Société pour l'Oeuvre et la Mémoire d'Antoine de Saint Exupéry B Succession Saint Exupéry B D'Agay v. Perlegos Properties***, D2005-1085 (WIPO January 2, 2006) ("Le Petit Prince" and <the little prince.com>); ***Al Arabiya News Channel FZ LLC v. ALCLICK***, D2013-0079 (WIPO March 29, 2013) ("Al Arabiya" in Arabic text and <alarabiya.com>).

[41] The alternative is to dismiss the complaint notwithstanding the domain name incorporates complainant's trademark where the similarity is not confusing. See below, "Similar, But Not Confusingly Similar" (Sec. 4.01-A.2.c). This latter procedure appears to make sense when the domain name that incorporates the trademark resolves to a website whose content is protected speech under paragraph 4(c)(iii) of the Policy. In ***Twentieth Century Fox Film Corporation v. DISH Network LLC***, FA1010001350483 (Forum November 22, 2010) (a decision made over dissent) respondent incorporated commercial, disputatious and sloganeering commentary in the disputed domain names [<foxshakedowndish.com>, <weofferedfoxafairdeal.com>, <foxrefused.com>, and <jointhefightagainstfox.com>].

[42] ***Oculus VR, LLC v. Ivan Smirnov***, FA 1625898 (Forum July 27, 2015) ("[T]he removal of spaces between words of a mark is irrelevant.")

[43] ***Ecolab USA Inc. v. Tomasz Kluz / Ekolab s.c. Tomasz I Aleksandra Kluz***, FA 1386906 (June 3, 2011).

[44] Example: ***Sun Microsystems, Inc. v. Cyber Business Holdings Ltd.***, D2007-1439 (WIPO January 11, 2008) (<javaroulette.com>, <javacraps.com>, <java21.com> and <javavegas.com>). Discussed further in "Forming a Domain Name by Incorporating Complainant's Trademark Plus an Additional Term" (Sec. 6.05-D).

[45] ***Magnum Piering, Inc. v The Mudjackers and Garwood S. Wilson, Sr.***, D2000-1525 (WIPO January 21, 2001) ("As numerous prior panels have held [the purposes of the Policy are satisfied] when a domain name wholly incorporates a complainant's registered mark.") One of the disputed domain names in Magnum Piering was identical and the other confusingly similar (<magnum piering.com> and <magnumpiers.com>). Dashes do not create a distinguishable name. Other representative cases include ***Amazon.com, Inc. v. DomainSource.com, Inc.***, FA0606000741767 (Forum August 17, 2006) (<amazoon.com> and <amqzon.com>).

[46] Discussed further in "Typosquatting" (Sec. 6.05-E.1).

Ordinarily, if there is no confusing similarity on a side by side comparison the complaint must be dismissed. However, Panels have justified looking ahead in the record to see whether facts offered in the second and third limbs warrant using them to determine complainant's standing. In ***Kames Capital PLC v. Tom Harrison / Kames Capital Plc Limited*** the Panel found that "it has some, although limited, discretion in determining whether or not to consider the content of the resolving webpage in making a Policy ¶ 4(a)(i) decision."[48] The "limited discretion" is most likely to be applied in cases involving fraudulent and malicious conduct, including spoofing and phishing.[49]

4.01-A.2.b 4.01-A.2.b *Test for Confusing Similarity*

4.01-A.2.b.i 4.01-A.2.b.i ***Functional Necessities***

The suffix to the right of the dot—whether three or four-letter legacy gTLDs (.com, .org, .edu, .info, etc.), new gTLDs that began coming online in 2013, or two-letter country codes—has no source indicating significance, but is merely a functional element in the Internet Protocol address. Ordinarily, panels disregard it in comparing the second-level domain with the trademark.[50]

This does not mean that in all instances the suffix is only a functional necessity; as explained below it can also be a lexical or morphological element that completes the second level string (identical or confusingly similar to a mark) and reinforces abusive registration (reading across the dot below at 4.01-A.2.b.iii). However, the weight of comparison rests with characters interior to the composition of the second level domain. These have included personal pronouns, articles, single letters or words that have been added to the trademark. Examples include prefixes [<x+sld.tld>, <e+sld.tld>, <www+sld.tld>, <my+sld.tld>] and suffixes [<sld+x.tld>, <sld+hotel.tld>, <sld+shop.tld>].

---

[47] ***The State of Florida, Department of the Lottery v. Valhalla Properties SA / Kattia Rodriguez Chacon***, D2012-0316 (WIPO April 3, 2012) (FLORIDA LOTTERY and <lotteryflorida.com> "[does not] alter the perceived meaning of the combination that results by placing the two words together.")

[48] FA1604001671583 (Forum May 20, 2016) (<kclfx.com>).

[49] Discussed further at "Spoofing and Phishing" (6.01-C.2.c). See ***Bridgewater Associates, LP v. Private Registration***, FA1511001650226 (Forum January 18, 2016) (Bridgewater 2) (BWATER and <bwater.site>) and (on re-filing of complaint, the Panel considered content in determining standing) ***Bridgewater Associates, LP v. Private Registration***, FA1509001637996 (Forum October 19, 2015) (Bridgewater 1) (BRIDGEWATER and <bwater.site>).

[50] ***The Forward Association, Inc., v. Enterprises Unlimited***, FA0008000095491 (Forum October 3, 2000) ("[Prefix www and gTLD suffix] are merely devices that every Internet site provider must use as part of its address.") See also, ***U.S. News & World Report, Inc. v. Zhongqi***, FA 917070 (Forum Apr. 9, 2007) ("Elimination of punctuation and the space between the words of Complainant's mark, as well as the addition of a gTLD does not sufficiently distinguish the disputed domain name from the mark pursuant to Policy paragraph 4(a)(i).")

Testing whether a second level domain is distinguishable from a trademark, and if it is not, whether it has an independent identity calls for an objective, though flexible analysis. Minor changes do not prevent a finding of confusing similarity of second level domain and trademark,[51] but neither does it compel a conclusion of bad faith for the reasons discussed in Chapter 6.

4.01-A.2.b.ii *Visual and Aural Comparison* *4.01-A.2.b.ii*

The concept of confusing similarity lies at the very heart of all cybersquatting disputes. It is central to assessing infringement under the Policy, but it is not to be confused with the classic test for trademark infringement. The "question is whether 'confusingly similar' means something different from 'likely to cause confusion.'"[52] The same Panel continued: "[a]t least one court has held that the phrase 'confusingly similar', at least in the context of the ACPA, implies a narrower test than is required to establish full-blown likelihood of confusion." The test is whether the name bears a similarity that may be confusing rather than confusion in the mind of a consumer as to the source of particular goods or services signified by a particular mark.[53] Source related confusion is a factor "properly [to] be addressed at other stages of the analysis (such as factors that bear on a registrant's legitimate interest or bad faith)."[54]

The "question of identity and confusing similarity is evaluated based solely on a comparison between a complainant's word mark and the [alpha or] numeric string constituting the domain name at issue."[55] At the threshold it is necessary only to consider "whether a domain name is similar enough in light of the purpose of the Policy to justify moving on to the other elements of a claim for cancellation or transfer of a domain name."[56] No consideration is given to "extraneous factors such as the types of goods or services on which the mark is used or the contents of

---

[51] Examples include: articles <**the**greenbrierresort.com>; nouns, "brand" and "catalog" <dell-**brand**.com> and <zippo**catalog**.com>; and place names <landrover**cambodia**.com>; pronouns <**my**homedepot accouont.com> (sic); adjectives **best**.com>; verbs <groupon-**share**.com>, <planfi-delity.com> (although "share" and "plan" could also be nouns) and <buynewportcigs.com>; adverbs <hermesby**immediately**jp.org> ("by" for "buy"); prepositions <coupons**for**enterprise.com> and <xenical-**without**-prescription.com>.

[52] ***Smoky Mountain Knife Works v. Carpenter***, AF 230ab (eResolution July 3, 2000).

[53] The Staff Manager's Issues Report on UDRP Review (August 1, 2003) posed the following question: "Should the policy be amended to provide guidance regarding the interpretation of "confusing similarity"? The proposition was that "Clarifying the definition of 'confusing similarity' would increase registrants' certainty and the predictability of decisions."

"The contra position was that "National (and local) trademark laws vary with respect to the definition of 'confusing similarity', so harmonization would not be feasible or within ICANN's scope." However, a definition has been arrived at by construction, rather than legislated by amendment to the UDRP.

[54] ***Magnum Piering***, *supra*.

[55] *Id.*

the website to which the domain name resolves."[57] The focus is solely on the "narrower test" comparing mark and domain name. "Rather than performing a detailed analysis of the totality of the circumstances in the relevant markets, a trier of fact need merely perform a phonetic or alphabetic comparison of the domain name and the trademark in question."[58] Sound, look, sense, and feel are prominent clues in making the assessment. This is evident by Panels adding "phonetic or alphabetic" comparison to "visual," "aural," and "conceptual" similarities to the test.[59]

The "touchstone in determining confusing similarity is whether the composition of the domain name has the potential to mislead unsuspecting users."[60] A string of characters that spell out a dictionary word or descriptive phrase or contains random letters that if isolated could conceivably be identical to a complainant's trademark does not support confusing similarity. The WIPO Overview (2.0) illustrates the point with <theatre.com>.[61] Although the domain name contains within it the dictionary word "heat" it is not confusingly similar to the trademark HEAT.[62]

---

[56] ***Nicole Kidman v. John Zuccarini, d/b/a Cupcake Party***, D2000-1415 (WIPO January 23, 2001). The Panel continued: "An independent basis for finding that a domain name is confusingly similar to a trademark is that, by virtue of the domain name itself, the domain name may confuse Internet users as to whether the site is associated or affiliated with, or sponsored by, the trademark holder."

[57] ***Verridian Plc v. Nadine Leech***, D2008-1539 (WIPO November 20, 2008).

[58] *Id.*

[59] Too many to cite, but representative cases include ***Expedia, Inc. v. hotels4cheap*** and ***Yosef Swird***, D2001-1221 (WIPO February 20, 2002) (<expediah.com>. Aural, visual, or conceptual similarity); ***Apple Inc. v. Contact Privacy Inc. / Grand Slam Co.***, D2012-0844 (WIPO June 4, 2012) ("Application of the confusing similarity test under the UDRP would typically involve a straightforward visual or aural comparison of the trademark with the alphanumeric string in the domain name[.]")

Although concerning "likelihood of confusion" rather than "confusing similarity" a number of Panels have cited ***Sabel v. Puma*** (General Court of the European Union, Case No. C-251/95) (One must take into account "...the visual, aural or conceptual similarity of the marks in question...based on the overall impression given by the marks, bearing in mind, in particular, their distinctive and dominant components."

[60] ***Telstra Corporation Limited v.Kids"m-a-i-l.com***, D2003-0169 (WIPO April 23, 2003). See also ***Arthur Guinness Son & Co. (Dublin) Limited v. Dejan Macesic***, D2000-1698 (WIPO January 25, 2001) ("The use to which the site is put has no bearing upon the issue whether the domain name is confusingly similar to the trademark, because by the time Internet users arrive at the Website, they have already been confused by the similarity between the domain name and the Complainant's mark into thinking they are on their way to the Complainant's Website.")

[61] WIPO Overview 2.0, Paragraph 1.2. ("[T]here must be a risk that Internet users may actually believe there to be a real connection between the domain name and the complainant and/or its goods and services.") WIPO does not reprise "theatre" in 3.0.

[62] As is not "Plein" in <peopleincasinos>, ***Philipp Plein v. Kimberly Webb***, D2014-0778 (WIPO July 30, 2014) ("It is not sufficient that the trademark is only visible when the viewer is told it is definitely there.")

However, as a general rule adding a generic, descriptive, or geographical term to a well-known mark is confusing because it builds on a distinctive name consumers have come to recognize as a source of goods or services.[63] If any part of the domain name plus modifier is identical to the trademark or to its dominant part, the domain name will be confusingly similar to it.[64] A dominant part of a compound word mark is a lexical unit that alone suffices to identify the whole.[65] However, for there to be confusing similarity where the domain name is an unregistered abbreviation of a mark, there must be a sufficient number of identical letters to suggest the whole. Thus, "fuj" and "chev" combined with generic elements "film" and "oil" are confusingly similar to FUJI and CHEVRON but "zim" is not of ZIMMERMAN.[66]

Nevertheless, the bar for determining whether similarity is confusing is low. The content of respondent's website at this stage is irrelevant to the analysis.[67] As a general rule if the SLD contains the trademark in whole or in dominant part it is confusingly similar to the trademark.[68] The guiding principle is "whether the

---

63 WIPO Overview 2.0, Paragraph 1.9; Overview 3.0, Paragraph 1.8. A different rule applies to domain names composed of generic, descriptive and geographic terms. See ***American Independence Funds Trust and Intrust Financial Corporation v. NestEgg Advisors, Inc.***, FA1007001333697 (Forum September 2, 2010) (NESTEGG FUND, NESTEGG CONSULTING and <nesteggadvisors.net>).

64 ***Sony Kabushiki Kaisha (also trading as Sony Corporation) v. Inja, Kil***, D2000-1409 (WIPO December 9, 2000) (<sonyacademy.com>, <dreamsony>); ***Bayerische Motoren Werke AG v. Kang M.***, D2011-1086 (WIPO August 19, 2011) (<shopbmw.com>). The dominant terms are respectively "sony" and "bmw."

65 "Although there is no mechanical test to select a dominant element of a compound word mark, consumers would be more likely to perceive a fanciful or arbitrary term, rather than a descriptive or generic term, as the source-indicating feature of the mark." Trademark Manual of Examining Procedure, 1207.01(b)(viii). Example: ***Barnesandnoble.com, LLC v. Rosenblum***, FA 1089020 (Forum November 15, 2007) ("There is no reason at all why a reader would assume that a domain name using, not the words of the trademark itself (BARNESANDNOBLE) or even the first element of the trademark (BARNES), but the least dominant part of it (NOBLE), was invoking the trademark.")

66 ***Fuji Photo Film U.S.A., Inc. v. Center for Ban on Drugs***, D2004-0970 (WIPO Feb. 25, 2005) (<fujifilm.com>), ***Chevron Intellectual Property LLC v. Linda Hearn***, FA 1409285 (FORUM Nov. 15, 2011) (chevoil.com>, ***Zimmermann Wear Pty Ltd v. Sam Dumond***, FA1808001802176 (Forum September 17, 2018) (<zimoutlet.com>. "Confusing similarity is particularly likely to be found where a mark is commonly referred to by its first syllable, and of course where the complainant also possesses trademark rights in the truncated form of the mark."

67 ***Fondation Le Corbusier v. Monsieur Bernard Weber, Madame Heidi Weber***, D2003-0251 (WIPO July 4, 2003) (The test is "confined to a comparison of the disputed domain name and the trademark alone, independent of the other marketing and use factors usually considered in trademark infringement or unfair competition cases.")

68 Similarly, spelling variations and word order—typosquatting as it has been labeled—presume confusing similarity, ***Reuters Ltd. v. Global Net 2000, Inc.***, D2000-0441 (WIPO July 13, 2000) (<ruters.com>) or functional additions as in <wwwreuters.com>. Contra: ***Hoffmann La Roche Inc. v. Mikhail Pavlishin***, D2010-0998 (WIPO December 3, 2010) [***Hoffman La Roche***(1)], in which

combination of terms used in a domain name has the potential to mislead unsuspecting users."[69] The assessment is supposed to be made without regard to the content of the respondent's website,[70] but looking ahead has also been justified. It could "provide a pointer as to how Internet users will perceive a domain name that in turn might inform the relevant comparison."[71]

4.01-A.2.b.iii

4.01-A.2.b.iii *When Top-Level Suffix Forms Part of the Infringed Trademark*

As explained above panelists generally disregard the top-level suffixes as functional necessities, but there could be instances where second levels and extensions combine to infringe a trademark. The WIPO Overview states that "[t]he applicable top-level suffix in the domain name (e.g., .com) would usually be disregarded under the confusing similarity test (as it is a technical requirement of registration), *except in certain cases where the applicable top-level suffix may itself form part of the relevant trademark*" [emphasis added].[72] Where in combination with the second level

---

the Panel states that she "does not agree with the approach" of a significant body of precedent reaching back to the beginning of UDRP because "it effectively transforms a general principle into a mechanistic rule severed from the general principle's underlying logic." She holds this view despite awareness "of a substantial line of cases in which panels appear to have effectively applied this principle [that is, incorporating in full the trademark] under the first element of the Policy as a per se rule." She continues: "Notably, one panel recently ruled that the domain name <buygenericaccutane.net> is confusingly similar to the mark ACCUTANE. ***Hoffmann La Roche Inc. v. Michail Sidorenko***, D2010-0581 (WIPO June 10, 2010) [***Hoffman La Roche*** (2)]." Inconsistency and its effect on predictability are discussed further in "Consistency and Predictability" (Sec. 1.05).

[69] ***Telstra Corporation Limited v. Kids @ m-a-i-l.com***, D2003-0169 (WIPO, April 23, 2003); ***The California Milk Processor Board of San Clemente v. Domains By Proxy, LLC / Del Polikretis***, D2012-2285 (WIPO February 13, 2013) (GOT MILK and <gotmilf.com>) ("[T]here must be a risk that it raises the risk level that Internet users may actually believe there to be a real connection between the domain name and the complainant and/or its goods and services.")

[70] Jurisprudential Overview, Paragraph 1.15 ("[I]s the content of a website associated with a domain name relevant in determining identity or confusing similarity?" The answer is that the location of the trademark, its date of registration (or first use) and the goods and/or services for which it is registered, are all irrelevant for the purpose of finding rights in a trademark under the first element of the UDRP. See ***A&F Trademark, Inc. and Abercrombie & Fitch Stores, Inc v. Justin Jorgenson***, D2001-0900 (WIPO September 19, 2001).

[71] ***RapidShare AG and Christian Schmid v. majeed randi***, D2010-1089 (WIPO September 2, 2010); ***Philip Morris Products S.A. v. Registration Private, Domains By Proxy, LLC / Tony Mak***, D2018-0602 (WIPO May 17, 2018) (<myheatshop.com>. "The Panel accepts the Complainant's assertion that website content can be considered in order to assess confusing similarity. Such content may support a finding of confusing similarity.... In the present case, the Respondent's website features the widespread use of the Complainant's IQOS mark, the use of the word "sticks" as a menu item corresponding to an element of the Complainant's HEATSTICKS mark and a large number of images bearing the Complainant's branding.")

[72] WIPO Overview 2.0, Paragraph 1.11; Jurisprudential Overview at 1.11.2.

domain the top level domain appears to take advantage of complainants' trademarks the dot is no barrier and can be ignored.[73]

The issue of reading across the dot is illustrated in several cases in the generation of gTLDs composed of abbreviations (.com, .net, .org, etc.) and country code suffixes, which are two letter strings (.au, .co, .do, .me, .uk, .us, etc., Australia, Colombia, Montenegro, United Kingdom and the United States). The two earliest cases involved dot tv (the country code suffix for Tuvalu).[74] The combination of second and top-level domains to support a claim of abusive registration is also showing up in disputes involving new gTLDs. There are two possibilities. The first incorporates the trademark in its entirety in the second level domain (CANYON) and the gTLD describes the product associated with the mark (canyon.bike>); the second possibility is that part of the trademark is incorporated in the second level and part in the TLD (NYCWEWORK and <nycwe.work>).[75]

The Panel in ***Koninklijke Philips Electronics*** pointed out that "[w]hilst it is recognized that the gtld, used for a domain name in combination with a mark of the Complainant, cannot be taken into consideration as an element which would exclude or diminish confusing similarity, in the present case the [country code] 'tv' even increases the confusing similarity, as users will generally not understand it as reference to Tuvalu." In ***Channel Television*** the Panel held there was confusing similarity, but on the penultimate requirement Complainant failed to demonstrate that Respondent lacked rights or legitimate interests in the domain name: "Respondent has made the plausible claim that it was legitimately engaging the secondary market for domain names in ignorance of the Complainant's business." Complainant in ***Koninklijke Philips Electronics*** proved both the second and third requirements based on Respondent's use of the domain name to divert visitors to adult oriented websites.

---

[73] Respondent in ***Raincat Online Services v. fluder***, CAC 101125 (ADReu February 1, 2016) (AD6MEDIA and <ad6.media>) argued that "[t]he ICANN rules only apply to what's left of the dot [, and that any other reading would be] an abuse of the administrative proceeding." The consensus holds otherwise; domain name transferred.

[74] ***Koninklijke Philips Electronics N.V. v. Alan Horswill***, DTV2002-0004 (WIPO July 30, 2002) (<buyaphilips.tv.> and <widescreenphilips.tv>); ***Channel Television Limited v. Legacy Fund LLC / Protected Domain Services Customer ID: R 3108040***, DTV2011-0008 (WIPO October 18, 2011) (CHANNEL TELEVISION and <channel.tv>). Reading across the dot may also be true for .glass in claims initiated by Google for registrations such as <gooogle.glass>.

[75] First possibility: ***Canyon Bicycles GmbH v. Domains By Proxy, LLC/ Rob van Eck***, D2014-0206 (WIPO March 14, 2014) where the trademark owner manufactures bicycles (<canyon.bike>); but in ***Delta Air Line, Inc. v. Chad Meyerson***, FA1509001636800 (Forum October 19, 2015) (DELTA and <delta.tours>) the Panel rejected Complainant's contention because the combination of trademark and TLD did not point to Complainant specifically as it did in ***Securian Financial Group, Inc. v. mes / enom***, FA1595614 (Forum January 16, 2015) (MINNESOTA LIFE and <minnesota.life>). Second possibility: ***WeWork Companies, Inc. v. Michael Chiriac, Various Concepts Inc.***, D2016-1817 (WIPO October 17, 2016) (<joinwe.work>, <weworkwe.live>).

In a "dot co" case that spelled out the trademark Complainant argued that the second level and suffix should be combined and the dot ignored.[76] Respondent countered that "the gTLD suffix should be ignored for comparison purposes, and that the overwhelming body of authority relies on analysing only the second level domain or their equivalent third level domain (where the gTLD is in two parts, such as 'co.uk' or 'com.au')." The Panel rejected this construction.

Although it is not usual Panels are not precluded from taking gTLDs into account. This is because "most of the analysis that takes place is at the second level. And that is because, simply, the TLD, being generic in nature, does not usually form part of the trademark to which a domain name is being compared. But that does not establish any kind of rule that precludes TLDs being taken into account." Contrary to Respondent's belief that taking TLDs into account is "a novel and improper approach" the Panel's reasoning has precedential support,[77] although it must be emphasized that this does not guarantee success in the second and third requirements. ***Tesco Stores*** and ***BookIt.com*** were able to prove abusive registration, while **project.me** got no further than "first base."[78]

4.01-A.2.b.iv 4.01-A.2.b.iv *Immaterial Changes*

Immaterial changes such as inserting or omitting hyphens, commas or other punctuation[79] and parts of speech such as articles,[80] pronouns,[81] adjectives, and adverbs are signifiers of confusion.[82]

---

[76] ***Tesco Stores Limited v. Mat Feakins***, DCO2013-0017 (WIPO October 4, 2013) (TESCO and <tes.co>).

[77] See ***project.me GmbH v. Alan Lin***, DME2009-0008 (WIPO November 11, 2009) (***<project.me>***. "This Panel considers that the appropriate approach in this case to determining identicalness or similarity of the disputed .me domain name with the Complainant's trademark is to not ignore the ccTLD identifier '.me'. The reality is that, unlike most ccTLD identifiers, the TLD identifier '.me' can be seen to have a meaning beyond being the International Standards Organization (ISO) two letter code for the country Montenegro—in particular, it has the additional meaning of being the common English objective pronoun for oneself"); ***BookIt.com, Inc. v. PrivacyProtect.org / ICS INC.***, D2013-0775 (WIPO June 26, 2013) ("[O]ne must ask whether the generic top level domain (gTLD) suffix '.com' can be claimed to be a part of the disputed domain name per se. As mentioned, Complainant has rights to the mark BOOKIT.COM, but not necessarily to the mark BOOKIT. The question is thus whether the Panel must take into account the generic TLD '.com' when considering the issue of identity or confusing similarity of the disputed domain name to Complainant's mark.")

[78] ***RapidShare AG, Christian Schmid v. N/A Maxim Tvortsov***, D2010-0696 (WIPO June 22, 2010).

[79] Representative: Respondent in ***InfoSpace.com, Inc. v. Tenenbaum Ofer***, D2000-0075 (WIPO April 27, 2000) inserted a hyphen to create <info-space.com>; ***Health Devices Corp. v. Aspen S T C***, FA 158254 (Forum July 1, 2003) (DOC JOHNSON and <docjohnsonsextoys.com>).

[80] ***Manhattan Center Studios, Inc. v. High pr Network***, FA1205001445131 (Forum June 20, 2012) (MANHATTAN CENTER and <themanhattancenter.com>), citing ***Marriott Int'l, Inc. v. Stealth***

They are relevant in assessing confusing similarity. Taking out a hyphen is no different from putting one in.[83] Neither creates a distinctive name different from the trademark. Complainant in ***Chernow Communications*** alleged that the domain name was identical to its trademark, which the dissent interpreted as an "elect[ion] not to pursue a claim of confusing similarity for strategic reasons. . . ." and would have dismissed the complaint for failure to state a claim. The dissent explained that "confusing similarity is not merely a lesser included version of identicality, and alleging one of these does not automatically allege the other."[84] The majority, however, saw the dissent's explanation as "elevat[ing] form over substance." If that were the criterion "it would be very easy in the future for a prospective cybersquatter, by inserting or deleting a hyphen" to avoid losing the domain name to complainant.[85] The general rule, which is consistent with United States court decisions under the Lanham Act, holds that the use or absence of punctuation marks does not alter the fact that a name is identical or confusingly similar to a mark.

4.01-A.2.c *Similar, But Not Confusingly Similar* 4.01-A.2.c

4.01-A.2.c.i ***Incorporating Part of Trademark*** 4.01-A.2.c.i

4.01-A.2.c.i.I ***Confusing to the Ordinary Internet User*** 4.01-A.2.c.i.I

The bar for confusingly similar is low, but not so low that complainant can satisfy its burden by simply asserting that the trademark and the domain name are phonetically/phonemicaly or lexically similar (sounds and words).[86] Three approaches have developed where the domain name is similar but not confusingly

---

Commerce, FA 109746 (Forum May 28, 2002) ("[T]he addition of the [article] 'the' to the beginning of the domain names fails to make them separate and distinct, as distinguishable from Complainant's marks.") However, no abusive registration where the dominant phrase is generic, absent knowledge of complainant and its mark, ***Fetish Factory, Inc. v. The Fetish Factory a/k/a Stanford Stuart a/k/a Pamela Hancock a/k/a Internetwork Partners***, FA0108000099610 (Forum November 8, 2001) (FETISH FACTORY and <thefetishfactory.com>); ***Fabricators & Manufacturers Association, International v. NameFind***, FA 1728625 (Forum June 1, 2017) (THE FABRICATOR and <fabricator.com>).

[81] Representative: ***PC2Call Limited v. Bernard Ferrie***, FA 0112000103181 (Forum February 21, 2002) (PC2CALL and <mypc2call.com>). However, in the case of pronouns a generic or descriptive trademark may be too weak to challenge the prefix as in ***Southwest Airlines Co. v. Cattitude a/k/a LJ Gehman***, D2005-0410 (WIPO June 12, 2005) (<mysouthwest.com>).

[82] Discussed further in "Forming a Domain Name by Incorporating Complainant's Trademark Plus an Additional Term" (Sec. 5.05-D).

[83] ***Chernow Communications, Inc. v. Jonathan D. Kimball***, D2000-0119 (WIPO May 18, 2000) (C-COM [the registered trademark] and <ccom.com> [the disputed domain name]).

[84] The dissent stated that he saw "no need to supplement the allegations that Complainant actually made with others that Complainant chose not to include, or to afford Complainant a second opportunity to allege what frankly is an obvious component of a prima facie case under the UDRP."

similar to complainant's trademark. The first approach terminates the proceedings forthwith on the theory that the complainant lacks standing to assert a claim.[87] The second approach takes a wait and see position.[88] The third approach accepts confusing similarity if there is proof of abusive registration.

With respect to the first approach, if complainant fails to prove the threshold element it should be conclusive regardless of the content of the website. The second approach gives complainant the benefit of the doubt, but makes evidentiary demands that if unsatisfied support denying the complaint.[89] The second approach is more pragmatic in considering the facts as a whole. The third approach described in WIPO Overview focuses on the "risk that Internet users may actually believe there [is] a real connection between the domain name and complainant and/or its

---

[85] *Id.*, ***Chernow Communications citing Shirmax Retail Ltd./Detaillants/Shirmax LTEE v. CES Marketing Group, Inc.***, AF0104 (eResolution March 20, 2000) (sometimes referred to as the "thyme.com case"). In the "thyme.com" case, "the Panel found that if it were determined that a domain name is identical to a mark, then such a determination would satisfy the first of the three prong test for bad faith under the Policy, and there is no need to show a likelihood of confusion. If the dissent's reasoning were to be adopted, a would-be cybersquatter could simply eliminate the hyphen in 'Hewlett-Packard' or insert a hyphen in 'Microsoft' and thereby avoid an automatic finding of bad faith under §4(a)(i) of the Policy. Such conduct should not be encouraged."

[86] ***SportSoft Golf, Inc. v. Sites to Behold Ltd.***, FA 94976, (Forum July 27, 2000) (GOLF SOCIETY OF THE US and <golfsociety.com>. Complainant's mark clearly referred to an entity or organization, whereas the domain name clearly referred to the generic nature of a society interested in golf or the general body or community of golfers.)

[87] Examples include: ***America Online, Inc. V. Johuathan Investments, Inc. & Aollnews.com***, D2001-0918 (WIPO September 14, 2001)(<fucknetscape.com>); the majority in ***Twentieth Century Fox Film Corporation v. DISH Network LLC***, FA1010001350483 (Forum November 22, 2010) voted to terminate the proceeding after concluding that <foxshakedowndish.com>, <weofferedfoxafairdeal.com>, <foxrefused.com>, and <jointhefightagainstfox.com> were not confusingly similar to complainant's trademark. These examples implicate a protected speech defense under paragraph 4(c)(iii) of the Policy. By their very nature declare they positions in opposition to complainant. See also ***The Dow Chemical Company and E. I. du Pont de Nemours and Company v. Jung Chang Seap***, D2016-0596 (WIPO July 13, 2016). For <duchemical.com> the Panel held that "DuPont's rights to DUPONT cannot be reasonably expanded to cover uses of DU alone, a term that can also be viewed as a simple French article. Further, there is no evidence that would suggest that DUPONT is commonly abbreviated or referred to as DU alone"; ***Fabricators & Manufacturers Association, International v. NameFind***, FA 1728625 (Forum June 1, 2017) (THE FABRICATOR and <fabricator.com>).

[88] The Panel in ***Morgan Stanley and Morgan Stanley Smith Barney Holdings LLC v. EnviroCitizen, LLC***, FA1008001342402 (Forum November 26, 2010) (<screwedbymorganstanley.com>) "elect[ed] to evaluate the remaining elements for the sake of completeness." ***Open Society***, *supra*. The Panel held that Respondent lacked rights or legitimate interests in the disputed domain name but "[c] onsidering all of the circumstances, the Panel determines that the evidence is insufficient to show that Respondent engaged in any conduct that would constitute bad faith registration and use.")

[89] ***Harry Winston Inc. and Harry Winston S.A. v. Jennifer Katherman***, D2008-1267 (WIPO October 18, 2008) (<hairywinston.com>, Complaint denied.); ***Covance, Inc. and Covance***

goods and services."[90] If there is no risk the complaint must be dismissed, but if there is risk demonstrated by content (not ordinarily the subject of the standing requirement) then the bar on similarity is lowered.[91]

The similarity between the allegedly infringing domain name and the allegedly targeted trademark must be confusing to the ordinary Internet user, not just the part but the whole. To employ a word separately that a complainant is using combined with another to form a trademark is not *a priori* a violation of a right. A useful statement of the rule is: "[w]here a complainant's mark consists of a combination of two common descriptive or generic words, and only one of those words has been used in the disputed domain name, satisfying the requirements of Paragraph 4(a)(i) can be a formidable task."[92] So, for example, "rapid" is not owned by RapidShare and "noble" is not owned by Barnes & Noble.[93] Freestanding, the words "rapid" and "noble" make no statement of association with companies in the Internet servicing or bookstore businesses.[94]

Laboratories Ltd. v. The Covance Campaign, D2004-0206 (WIPO April 30, 2004) (<covancecampaign.com>, Complaint denied.)

90 WIPO Overview 2.0, Paragraph 1.2. The concept continues in Jurisprudential 3.0 but with different language. Confusion has been found in sound and word similarities: GOULDS and "goods" in<itt-goodspumps.com> (where "itt" is the trade name, GOULDS the mark, and it manufactures pumps). Other confusing similarities are FILTECH and "phil-tech," INDEED and "endeed," and MAPCREST and "mapquest." Or substituting words for numbers, PHILLIPS 66 and "seventy six gas station." These registrations can also be analyzed as typosquatting. Rejected includes CALIFORNIA STATE BAR and "calsb," AMEGI BANK and "amogi," and SFORCE and "forces."

91 ***Kames Capital PLC v. Tom Harrison / Kames Capital Plc Limited***, FA1604001671583 (Forum May 20, 2016) ("Having regard to prior UDRP decisions the Panel finds that it has some, although limited, discretion in determining whether or not to consider the content of the resolving webpage in making a Policy ¶ 4(a)(i) decision. Having regard to all the circumstances of the instant case, including the evidence of the fraudulent activities for which the domain name has been used, the Panel finds that it may have regard to the contents of the website and having done so finds that the disputed domain name is confusingly similar to Complainant's trademark."

92 ***RapidShare AG and Christian Schmid v. Ilya, Ilya Efimov***, D2010-1105 (WIPO August 17, 2010). See also ***National Grid Electricity Transmission Plc, NGrid Intellectual Property Limited v. Re Tron Technologies***, D2013-0925 (WIPO July 11, 2013) (NATIONAL GRID and <mygridpower.com> and <mygridstore.com>. The domain names "incorporate only the 'grid' element of the Complainant's trade marks. . . . The term 'grid' (on its own) is a generic, non distinctive term, which is not associated exclusively with the Complainant's business.")

93 ***Barnesandnoble.com, LLC v. Rosenblum***, FA 1089020 (Forum November 15, 2007) (<noble.com>. The Panel held that "[m]erely to state the proposition [that 'noble.com' is confusingly similar to the trademark BARNESANDNOBLE.COM] shows that it has little to commend it. The test to be applied is whether an objective bystander, presented with both the wording of the domain name and the wording of the trademark would probably conclude that the 'noble' of the domain name was referring to the 'noble' of the trademark and hence to the trademark as a whole. The Panel finds that no reasonable bystander could reach that conclusion.")

Other examples include "PC" or "web" and "mall." Even though "mall" is the dominant word and is the "surname" in a family of marks (MACMALL and others), owners have no monopoly on detached words.[95] While the owner of PCMALL can prevent others from using registered combinations it has no claim to "mall" in other combinations: "mobile" and "mall" combined (<mobilemall.com>) stands on its own without confusion with PCMALL. The Panel in ***Softlayer Technologies*** (SOFTLAYER and <corporatelayer.com>) states what can usefully be taken as the general rule, namely that a trademark composed of dictionary words is never "great enough to trump all subsequently registered domains containing the word 'layer' in association with another word in the domain name."

In these examples, freestanding common words, alone or in new combinations, are capable of forming new associations. "Nudescape" is not "Netscape."[96] The owner of REVZILLA has no exclusive right to "zilla" derivative from "Godzilla, something extravagantly large, monstrous or immense."[97] Attaching a different prefix to a dictionary word can create a different impression. Similarly, singularizing and pluralizing words may create new domains distinctive in their own right.[98] Thus, although the

---

[94] In contrast, immaterial variances, such as adding, removing, reversing, substituting or transposing letters, do not form true words: "xgoogle", "sstatefarm," "statefarmm," "bankofamericana" are clearly composed to take advantage of the original.

[95] ***PCI Mall, Inc. v. Pygmy Computer Systems, Inc***, D2004-0437 (WIPO August 25, 2004) (<mobilemall.com>) ("the issue is whether Complainant has shown that Complainant's family of MALL based marks has achieved recognition among the purchasing public that the common characteristic of its marks—i.e., the 'mall' component—is indicative of the common origin of Complainant's goods.") See also ***SoftLayer Technologies, Inc. v. UltimatumHost.com / Rodrigo Martins***, FA1202001429575 (Forum March 22, 2012) (<corporatelayer.com>). This issue is discussed further in "Family of Marks" (Sec. 6.01-D.1.e).

[96] ***America Online Inc. v. Media Dial Communications***, D2001-0799 (WIPO August 8, 2001) ("The question has to be answered to some extent by asking whether the Respondent has the right to use the words 'nude' and 'scape' to describe its pornographic services. That is quite apart from whether the Complainant may have rights in these or similar words. It seems to the Panel that there is a reasonably good argument that the Respondent should have a right to use these common English words to describe its pornographic services. Otherwise, parts of the English language would soon be acquired and removed from common use by those wishing to name their businesses or describe their services."); ***Ecrush, Inc. v. Cox, Davis & Simpson, LLC***, D2004-0552 (WIPO Sept. 11, 2004) (ESPIN THE BOTTLE and <ispinthebottle.com>). See also ***Spark Networks USA, LLC v. Dennis Tesic***, FA1411839 (Forum Nov. 23, 2011) (CHRISTIAN MINGLE and <christianmingler.com>. Adding an "r" to "mingle" creates an understandable word distinguishable from the trademark and implying a different association.)

[97] ***RevZilla Motorsports LLC v. Tom D'Azevedo***, FA1304001496506 (Forum June 25, 2013) ('partzilla'. "The Panel believes it is not unreasonable to hold that there is no confusing similarity where, as in this case, the two names have a suffix in common ["Zilla"] and one moreover that is also a dictionary word, but no similarity between their prefixes ['Rev' and 'Part'].")

[98] No confusion: ***Sears Brands, LLC v. Domain Asset Holdings***, FA0912001298052 (Forum January 22, 2010) (NORTHWEST TERRITORY and <northwestterritories.com>) create distinctive names.

threshold requirement sets a low bar, small differences affect the way Internet users are likely to perceive associations between trademarks and domain names.

4.01-A.2.c.i.II *Assessing When Similarity Gives Rise to Confusion*

4.01-A.2.c.i.II

In assessing whether "similarity may give rise to confusion or false association, it is necessary to consider not only the degree of similarity of the terms in the literal sense but also the degree of distinctiveness of the mark given that, obviously, the greater the distinctiveness or originality of the registered mark, the greater the risk of confusion."[99] If there is no confusion in a trademark sense (because the words in the domain name are not equivalent to the words in the trademark, as illustrated in the case cited in the footnote) there can be no confusing similarity as that term has come to be construed. Similarity is confusing where the domain name can be mistaken for the mark, but the more common the word or phrase the less likely any Internet user would be confused into believing that the domain name is associated with the complainant.

Letters added to, exchanged with, substituted for, or subtracted from[100] the trademark are evidence of confusing similarity only where the names are "phonetically, visually [, aurally] or conceptually similar." In one-word trademarks composed of common abbreviations, "eco" (for "ecological") and "lab" (for "laboratory") in ECOLAB, substituting "k" for the "c" to create 'ekolab' is not distinguishable from the trademark.[101] The various changes, additions and subtractions violate complainant's rights if visitors mistakenly believe that the domain name is associated with or belongs to a mark owner, but not otherwise. A second level domain that spells out an everyday word or phrase may be identical or confusingly similar to a trademark but if it is used to attract Internet visitors to a website offering goods or services consistent with its dictionary meaning it is unlikely to be an abusive registration.

While substituting letters similar or closely related in sound favors complainant as noted above with ECOLAB and <ekolab.com>,[102] substituting a letter that may suggest typosquatting (as it did in that particular case) is not necessarily infringing in other cases. Not all similarity is confusing even if aurally homonymous: "PROXIFIER" and <proxyfire.com>[103] and "77" and <seventyseven.com>.[104] The

---

[99] ***Todito.com, S.A. de C.V. v. Affordable Webhosting, Inc.***, D2004-0688 (WIPO October 11, 2004) (TODITO.COM and <todomail.com>).

[100] ***CEC Entertainment, Inc. v. Peppler***, FA104208 (Forum March 21, 2002) (CHUCK E. CHEESE and <chuckcheese.com>. Omitting "E" not distinguishable from mark).

[101] ***Ecolab USA Inc. v. Tomasz Kluz / Ekolab s.c. Tomasz I Aleksandra Kluz***, FA 1386906 (June 3, 2011). These kinds of minimal changes are discussed further in "Typosquatting" (Sec. 5.05-E.1).

[102] ***Korn/Ferry International v. The Careermosaic Cornperry, Inc***, FA0508000538465 (Forum October 7, 2005) (KORN FERRY and <cornperry.com> and <ecornperry.com>).

analysis that leads to these findings is adopted from U.S. case law, which holds that "[s]imilarity of marks or lack thereof are context-specific concepts. In the Internet context, consumers are aware that domain names for different Web sites are quite often similar, because of the need for language economy, and that very small differences matter."[105]

There are also trademarks composed of generic terms disclaimed by applicants at the time of trademark application to satisfy legal requirements or whose registration has been permitted subject to disclaimer and proof of continuous use.[106] Similarity is not confusing when the violations are based on the disclaimed elements. The general rule is that "when descriptive or generic words are disclaimed in a registration on the Principal Register, the legal effect is that the registration does not evidence any trademark rights in the disclaimed words; rather, those words are protected only when used with the mark as a whole."[107]

There can be no confusing similarity where "the mark and name create readily distinguishable commercial impressions."[108] The Panel in the case cited below concluded it is a matter of a weak mark in a crowded field (THE MEDICINE SHOPPE and <canadamedicineshop>). In urging the threshold assessment in its favor "a complainant cannot rely on alleged deceptive content on a respondent's website to obtain a finding that a domain name is confusingly similar to complainant's mark when it is not in itself confusingly similar."[109] The content of the website is irrelevant if complainant fails to prove that the domain name is identical or confusingly similar to its trademark,[110] although "understandably, [some Panels are] drawn to the view that an overwhelming showing of lack of legitimate interest (factor two) or of bad faith (factor three) should reduce the need for a showing of

---

[103] ***UpsideOut. v. Lin Han***, D2009-388 (WIPO July 7, 2009) (Panel declined to reach the issue of rights or legitimate interests based on her conclusion that complainant had failed to prove bad faith registration or bad faith use.)

[104] ***Retail Royalty Company, and AEO Management Co. v. Modern Empire Internet Ltd.***, FA1103001378458 (Forum April 21, 2011).

[105] *Id.*, citing *Entrepreneur Media, Inc. v. Smith*, 279 F.3d 1135, 1147 (9th Cir. 2002).

[106] Disclaimer of words within a design is discussed further in "Design-Plus-Word Trademarks," (Sec. 4.01-A.3.e). No confusion: ***Tire Discounters, Inc. v. TireDiscounter.com***, FA0604000679485 (Forum June 14, 2006) (TIRE DISCOUNTERS and <tirediscounter.com>. Stylized trademark for which the owner disclaimed the words "tire discounters." Descriptive of the goods offered.)

[107] ***Advance News Service Inc. v. Vertical Axis, Inc. / Religionnewsservice.com***, D2008-1475 (WIPO December 11, 2008).

[108] ***Pinnacle Intellectual Property v. World Wide Exports***, D2005-1211 (WIPO February 17, 2006). Similarly, "Home Exchange" and <homeexchange.com>, *supra*.

[109] ***General Electric Company v. Edison Electric Corp. a/k/a Edison Electric Corp. General Energy, Edison GE, Edison-GE and EEEGE.COM***, D2006-0334 (WIPO December 16, 2009) ("In reality, so far as <eege.com> is concerned, the Complainant's cause for complaint is not the domain name, but the content of the Respondent's website, a matter not covered by the Policy.")

factor one [confusing similarity]."[111] This view makes less sense, however, when the lexical parts "eliminate the possibility of confusion."[112]

One panelist has proposed that the similarity must be confusing to an "objective bystander."[113] In that case the dissent rejected <opensociety.org> as being confusingly similar to OPEN SOCIETY INSTITUTE. Because the adjectival phrase "open society" is able to stand alone the domain name cannot (the dissent insisted) be confusingly similar to complainant's trademark that is distinctive only when anchored to its noun, "Institute." Whether the domain name is "confusingly similar" or simply similar to the trademark but not confusing to a fictional "objective bystander" focuses on differences in the composition of the string of letters, words, phrases, or numbers. There is a fuzziness in distinguishing the confusingly similar from the similar but not confusing. If a clinical distinction is to be made Panels generally give complainant the benefit of the doubt and focus their attention on the second and third limbs.

4.01-A.2.c.ii *Distinguishable Commercial Impression*

4.01-A.2.c.ii

The same analysis discussed above has also been applied to domain names composed of phrases formed by combining ordinary words. Combinations that may be similar to trademarks (actually, phonetically, or aurally) cannot by reason of their cultural currency be monopolized to the exclusion of other users.[114] Respondents who vary the language to create distinctive phrases similar to complainant's trademark may be acting in good faith even if they target the same market of users. Respondent who registered: 1) <tillpaydayloan.com> does not infringe CASH 'TIL PAYDAY and CASH 'TIL PAYDAY LOANS[115]; 2) <hot18to30.com> does not infringe CLUB 1830[116]; and 3) <firstlookimaging.com> does not infringe FIRSTLOOK SONOGRAM.[117] There are many ways to convey a competing message without infringing a third party's rights. Complainant in ***First Look*** complained about the

---

[110] Examples include ***Citigroup, Inc. v. Allman***, FA 1066738 (Forum October 16, 2007) adding "rip-off" (<primericaisarip-off.com>) and the ***Royal Bank of Scotland Group plc v. natwestfraud.com***, D2001-0212 (WIPO June 18, 2001) adding "fraud" (<natwestfraud.com>).

[111] ***Medimmune***, *supra.*

[112] ***Morgan Stanley and Morgan Stanley Smith Barney Holdings LLC v. EnviroCitizen, LLC***, FA1008001342402 (Forum November 26, 2010) (<screwedbymorganstanley.com>).

[113] ***Open Society Institute v. Gil Citro***, FA1007001333304 (Forum August 24, 2010).

[114] ***Halo Innovations, Inc. v. Name Administration Inc. (BVI)***, FA1009001344653 (Forum November 3, 2010) (<sleepsack.com>): the "domain name is comprised entirely of common terms that have many meanings and that the registration and use of a domain name comprising such common terms is not necessarily done in bad faith."

[115] ***Dollar Fin. Group, Inc. v. Oakridge***, FA94977 (Forum July 17, 2000).

[116] ***Thomas Cook Holdings Ltd. v. Aydin***, D2000-0676 (WIPO September 11, 2000).

[117] ***First Look Sonogram, Inc. v. Computer Care***, FA0710001092259 (Forum December 10, 2007).

Respondent's use of "first look" in <firstlookimaging>, but the term "imaging" has a far broader meaning than complainant's term "sonogram."[118]

As a general rule if the domain name incorporates the trademark in its entirety the similarity is likely to be confusing, but if the incorporation is coupled with another term that identifies a wholly different business or a specialty within a niche the similarity is likely to dissolve.[119] Similarly, if the mark is composed of two words that indivisibly identify the source and the domain name comprises one of them there may be similarity of part but not of the whole.[120]

In many of the claims for confusing similarity complainants fail to recognize the limited reach of their lexical choices and the transformative effect of substituted or additional words. In one case, Complainant alleged that the Respondent's <flipandgrowrich.com> infringed its trademark, THINK AND GROW RICH.[121] However, sharing three quarters of the phrase—"and grow rich"—is not enough. In ***Napoleon Hill*** the Panel explained that "[h]aving 'flip' instead of 'think' as the initial word changes the meaning of the phrase. The phrase 'think and grow rich' is general and does not suggest real estate transactions, while the phrase 'flip and get rich' suggests 'flipping' real estate to get rich." The similarity is of no account because the substituted wording creates a distinctive association.

While it is possible for accused domain names to incorporate nondescript trademarks without infringing third party rights, as for example when the SLD creates a distinctive separate impression[122] or distinctive trademarks are incorporated for nominative fair use,[123] common affixes alone cannot justify an infringing domain name. Adding geographic identifiers,[124] incorporating the Internet identification letters in the SLD (SLDcom, SLDnet, etc.) and affixing common words do not create distinctive commercial impressions. Where the TRADEMARK is the dominant

---

118 *Id.*

119 ***B2BWorks, Inc. v. Venture Direct Worldwide, Inc.***, FA 97119 (Forum June 5, 2001) (B2BWORKS and <b2badworks.com>, <b2bmediaworks.com>, <b2badswork.com>, and <b2badwork.com>. The Panel held "Complainant did not have exclusive rights to use of the terms 'B2B' and 'Works' in association with other words, even with a registered trademark for B2BWORKS."

120 ***Barnesandnoble.com LLC v. John Frank Frank Rosenblum***, FA06030001089020 (Forum November 15, 2007) (BARNES AND NOBLE and <noble.com>); ***Fabricators & Manufacturers Association, International v. NameFind***, FA 1728625 (Forum June 1, 2017) (THE FABRICATOR and <fabricator.com>. "[T]he Panel agrees with Respondent's contentions that Complainant does not have any right to monopolize the dictionary word 'fabricator' alone because the mark is indivisible: neither the article 'the' nor the noun 'fabricator' is distinctive in its own right.")

121 ***Napoleon Hill Foundation v. pmweb***, FA0907001275894 (Forum September 28, 2009).

122 ***bet365 Group Limited v. Domains by Proxy, Inc.*** / Steve Prime, D2011-1242 (WIPO September 14, 2011) (<365bets365.com> [confusingly similar to BET 365] while <365casino365.com>, <365poker365.com>, and <365wager365.com> are similar but not confusing.)

123 ***Medimmune, Inc. v. Jason Tate***, D2006-0159 (WIPO April 14, 2006) (<synagisisbadforyou.com> and <synagisisnotsafe.com>.)

element, adding "cheaper" to LACOSTE[125] or "New York" to VOGUE[126]is no more than the well-known trademark with an affix. In contrast, affixes that dominate the term alleged to be a targeted trademark composed of dictionary words can be similar only to the extent of the common part.[127]

4.01-A.3 Qualifying for a Trademark Right 4.01-A.3

4.01-A.3.a *Trademark Registered in Any Country* *4.01-A.3.a*

A complainant has standing to prosecute a UDRP dispute regardless of the national jurisdiction in which it acquired its trademark, the strength of the trademark, the market in which it employs the trademark, or the parties' residencies in different countries.[128] Proof of trademark rights registered or unregistered in any country is sufficient for the purposes of paragraph 4(a)(i) of the Policy.[129] That the trademark is not registered or complainant has no presence in respondent's country of residence does not defeat its right to maintain a UDRP proceeding,[130] although they

---

[124] ***Red Bull GmbH v. Chai***, D2003-0709 (WIPO November 11, 2003) (<thairedbull.com>, short for Thailand); ***Sally Holdings, Inc. v. Pagelifter.com***, D2006-0266 (WIPO May 17, 2006) (<sallyguate.com>, where "guate" is short for Guatemala.)

[125] ***Lacoste Alligator S.A. v. Priscilla, Ranesha, Angel, Jane, Victor, Olivier, Carl, Darren, Angela, Jonathan, Michell, Oiu, Matthew, Pamela, Selima, Angela, John, Sally, Susanna***, D2010-0988 (WIPO August 11, 2010) (<cheaperlacoste.com>. "It is long established by past panel decisions that a domain name incorporating a trademark in its entirety with the addition of generic and non distinctive prefixes and/or suffixes is confusingly similar to the trademark.")

[126] ***Advance Magazine Publishers Inc. v. Vanilla Limited/ Domain Finance Ltd./Minakumari Periasany***, D2004-1068 (WIPO April 18, 2005)("VOGUE", adding New York to form <newyork vogue>.)

[127] ***Homeexchange.com, Inc. v. Frank Kelly, Intervac International***, D2011-2239 (WIPO February 15, 2012) (HOME EXCHANGE and <intervachomeexchange>, where "intervac"—the Respondent's name—dominates the descriptive phrase.)

[128] ***United Way of America v. Alex Zingaus***, FA 1036202 (Forum August 30, 2007) ("Panels have long recognized Complainant's registration of a mark with a trademark authority is sufficient to confer rights in the mark pursuant to [UDRP] Policy ¶ 4(a)(i)"); ***NYSE Group, Inc. v. Val Sklarov / BentleyTek / America 2030 Capital***, FA170900 1748855 (Forum October 23, 2017) (<nyseloan.com> + 20 other domains including <nyse-trader.com>. Registrant argued that "Complainant does not have rights in the NYSE mark throughout the world, specifically in Ukraine, where Respondent resides."

[129] ***Koninklijke KPN N.V. v. Telepathy Inc.***, D2001-0217 (WIPO May 7, 2001) (MONEY PLANET, TRAVEL PLANET and <moneyplanet.com> and <travelplanet.com>. The Policy does not require that the mark be registered in the country in which the Respondent operates; therefore it is sufficient that Complainant can demonstrate a mark in some jurisdiction). However, as ***Koninklijke*** also illustrates denial is warranted where Respondent registered the domain names prior to Complainant's trademark.

[130] In a case involving a U.S. trademark owner and a South Korean domain name holder in a South Korean court, the registrant insisted plaintiff was not a 'legitimate rights holder' according

may be factors in determining whether respondent registered the domain name in bad faith.[131] Geographical nearness or remoteness may be relevant for answering the question whether respondent had knowledge of complainant or its trademark for a finding under paragraph 4(a)(iii).[132] Standing is not affected by complainant failing to renew registration or abandoning its trademark in any jurisdiction,[133] although those too can be factors in assessing respondent's intentions and conduct.[134]

4.01-A.3.b

4.01-A.3.b *Principal Register: Presumption of Validity*[135]

A trademark registered on the Principal Register (United States) or certified by any national registry is presumptively valid and unassailably satisfies the threshold requirement for UDRP standing without regard to its timing in relation to

---

to Article 12 of the Internet Address Resource Act because the mark had no public recognition in South Korea. In rejecting registrant's argument, the South Korean court reviewed the totality of the circumstances, such as the public recognition of the mark in the United States, especially in connection with goods associated with the mark. In the final appeal, "the Supreme Court specifically stated that local public recognition of the subject mark was not required under Article 12 of the act, thereby issuing a noteworthy ruling that has clarified the ambiguities of past decisions." The case is reported at http://www.internationallawoffice.com/newsletters/ detail.aspx?g=aaf2f355-30e3-4bce-8b27-9d84b95a4ea3. See also, ***Rockefeller & Co. Inc. v. William Foo***, D2014-1886 (WIPO December 17, 2014) ("The Panel notes that the Complainant's trademarks have not been registered in Malaysia, the Respondent's country. However, the Panel also notes that the Policy does not require the trademarks of the Complainant to be protected in the Respondent's country.")

131 ***Renaissance Hotel Holdings, Inc. v. Renaissance Cochin***, FA 932344 (Forum April 23, 2007) (U.S. trademark, doing business in India. "In India, it has two registrations, neither of which predate Respondent's registration of the disputed domain name <renaissancecochin.com>"); ***Williams-Sonoma, Inc. v. Kurt Fees c/o K Fees***, FA07703000937704 (Forum April 25, 2007) (<potterybarn.org>. "[T]he Panel finds that under the Policy [] it is irrelevant whether COMPLAINANT registered the POTTERY BARN mark in the country of Respondent's residence.")

132 The physical location of the parties as a factor in determining the respondent's knowledge of complainant or its trademark is not relevant to a finding under paragraph 4(a)(i) of the Policy. Discussed further in "Nearness and Remoteness in Proving Knowledge and Intention" (Sec. 4.02-C.3).

133 In ***Asia Pacific Breweries Limited v. Chris Kwan***, D2003-0920 (WIPO January 20, 2004). Respondent contended that Complainant had lost or abandoned trademark rights in the United States and Canada, but this would not affect Complainant's common law rights. See also ***Jeffrey Kaplan v. Societe des Produits Nestle S.A.***, FA1606001680748 (Forum July 28, 2016) (<chipwich.com>. Complainant specializes in registering abandoned trademarks; but Respondent has trademarks for CHIPWICH in other countries.)

134 However, complainant will not have standing to maintain the administrative proceeding where evidence shows abandonment supported by USPTO cancellation of trademark and re-branding. ***j2 Cloud Services, Inc. v. Jack Miller***, FA1501001598217 (Forum February 6, 2015).

135 Under U.S. law "A certificate of registration of a mark upon the principal register ... shall be prima facie evidence of the validity of the registered mark and of the registration of the mark, of the owner's ownership of the mark, and of the owner's exclusive right to the registered mark in commerce," Trademark Act of 1946, §1057(b).

respondent's registration of the domain name. Once a trademark office "has made a determination that a mark is registrable, by so issuing a registration . . . an ICANN panel is not empowered to nor should it disturb that determination."[136] However, presumption and validity aside the concept of exclusive right is contextual and not absolute.

The result is different where the mark is registered by a local agency, rather than a national registry.[137] In that event "no such deference is due because State registrations, which are usually granted automatically or only after a cursory review for exact matches on the State's trademark registry, are unexamined and thus are not deserving of any presumption of validity."[138] For the same reason unexamined registrations of business or trade names are also denied common law trademark rights[139] unless they are found to function as trademarks.[140] In that event they are not precluded from establishing standing by proving unregistered rights.[141]

Not only does trademark registration bestow a presumption of validity, it also carries the presumption that the mark is distinctive; or in the case of dictionary words or descriptive terms that they have acquired distinctiveness by their market presence and recognition.[142] "Any claim that the registration should not have been granted or should be revoked falls to be decided by the Courts of the relevant

---

136 ***U.S. Office of Pers. Mgmt. v. MS Tech. Inc.***, FA 198898 (Forum December 9, 2003).

137 There is no presumption for marks registered on the Supplemental Register (4.01-B.2.c), but this does not prevent complainant proving unregistered rights established by use in commerce (4.01-B.1).

138 ***Town of Easton Connecticut v. Lightning PC Inc.***, FA0808001220202 (Forum October 12, 2008) (<eastonct.org>). Similarly, unexamined business registrations and trade names (Sec. 4.01-D.3.b). Although the Panel in ***OCOM IP BV, Fiberring B.V. v. Dialogic Srl***, D2014-1314 (WIPO October 8, 2014) dismissed the complaint on other grounds it noted Respondent's claim that the Benelux Trademark Office issued a registration for the trademark that predated domain name registration at a time when Office did not subject applications to any substantive review.

139 The reasoning is equally applicable to respondents. See ***President and Fellows of Harvard College v. Yousuf Shakeel and Shakeel Ahmad***, D2013-1816 (WIPO December 20, 2013) (<harvardcasestudies.com>. "If the mere registration of a business name (as opposed to an examined trade mark) was sufficient to show rights or legitimate interests it would be possible for a professional cybersquatter to defeat any UDRP case merely by obtaining an unexamined business name registration upon the commencement of a claim against it.").

140 Discussed further in "Trade Names as Such Outside Policy's Scope" (Sec. 4.01-D.3.a).

141 Compare ***Mark C. Spicher v. Frogi Design, s.r.o. / The Artwork Factory, s.r.o.***, D2015-0606 (WIPO June 3, 2015) with ***Missouri Lottery Commission v. SED Domain Services / Common Law***, D2014-0118 (WIPO March 7, 2014). In ***Missouri Lottery*** Complainant "demonstrated longstanding and very substantial use and promotion of the MISSOURI LOTTERY trademark to the extent that the Panel is satisfied that it has established a reputation such as to confer common law rights in that trademark for purposes of the Policy." In ***Spicher***, Complainant offered no evidence of commercial activity at the time that Respondent registered the domain name.

142 ***Janus Int'l Holding Co. v. Rademacher***, D2002-0201 (WIPO March 5, 2002) (<janus.info>).

country."[143] Panelists have no authority to disregard valid trademark registrations that have been subject to examination and opposition.[144]

Should respondent wish to challenge a trademark office's determination of a complainant's registered mark, there are "appropriate administrative and/or judicial avenues available [for that purpose] such as by filing an action in the USPTO to cancel that registration or alternatively instituting federal litigation."[145] In ***Sound Unseen*** respondent did neither, and not having done so

> this Panel will simply defer, as it must, to the USPTO's determination implicit in its having granted corresponding registrations, i.e., that each of Complainant's federally registered APPLE BOTTOMS Marks has acquired sufficient distinctiveness and hence is not merely descriptive or generic, and thus qualifies for federal trademark protection and enjoys all the rights afforded thereby.

Respondent in another case argued that complainant had abandoned its mark by "improper'" use, or that such "improper" use stripped Complainant of its recourse to the Policy.[146] The Panel disagreed. It held that respondent's argument failed "for two fundamental reasons":

> First, a panel's sustaining a finding of abandonment, no less than denying on any other grounds rights in a mark that a national authority has duly registered, would be tantamount to setting aside the official act of a government authority. A panel in a limited administrative proceeding under the Policy lacks both the jurisdiction to make such a finding and the means of obtaining and evaluating evidence advanced to support such a claim.
>
> Second, Respondent's evidence falls far short of establishing abandonment or any use that is unlawful, tortious, or otherwise 'improper.'

Where a respondent has followed the agency route and abandoned rather than exhausted a cancellation proceeding it is thereafter precluded from arguing that the "TTAB's finding do[es] not equal . . . a final determination on the issue of genericness."[147]

The principle that Panels defer to the registering authority is not a constraint on their finding respondents' identical or confusingly similar choices in good faith.

---

[143] ***Hola S. A. v. Idealab***, D2002-0089 (WIPO March 27, 2002).

[144] ***The Cyberbingo Corporation v. 207 Media Inc.*** D2005-0714 (WIPO October 4, 2005) (Canadian parties).

[145] ***Sound Unseen, Ltd.; Apple Bottoms, LLC; and Cornell Haynes p/k/a "Nelly" v. Patrick Vanderhorst***, D2005-0636 (WIPO August 18, 2005).

[146] ***Julie & Jason, Inc. d/b/a The Mah Jongg Maven v. Faye Scher d/b/a Where the Winds Blow***, D2005-0073 (WIPO March 6, 2005).

[147] ***Robert Bosch Corporation v. Derek Atkin***, FA0801001139093 (Forum March 17, 2008) (<hydroboost.com>).

It merely affirms the proposition that common words and descriptive phrases circulating in a party's linguistic community are conditionally available as domain names. That respondents' choices may have become distinctive in a trademark sense is not a dispositive factor. Trademarks on the lower end of the classification scale earn protection against use by others only on proof that it is they in particular that respondent had in mind and is targeting.[148] So, for example, a descriptive mark may have qualified for registation on the principal register,[149] but words alone or combined do not relinquish their generic character because they have been adopted as marks. They could support respondent's defense that it nevertheless has an equal right that legitimizes its interest in the domain name.[150]

4.01-A.3.c *No Right Accrues to Pending Application for Trademark* 4.01-A.3.c

As a general rule no right accrues to pending applications for trademark registration absent evidence of prior commercial use.[151] While presumption of validity is conferred upon trademarks subsisting and registered on the Principal Register (in the United States),[152] application "for a mark [as opposed to issuance of registration] is not *per se* sufficient to establish rights in a trademark for the purposes of the UDRP."[153] The "broad consensus under the Policy is that a trademark application

---

148 Representative Example: ***Men's Wearhouse, Inc. v. Wick***, FA 117861 (Forum September 16, 2002) (THE SUIT WAREHOUSE <suitwarehouse.com>); ***Rockwell Automation v. zheqiang***, FA1811001818237 (Forum December 16, 2018) (<factorytalk.com> "Especially given that the Disputed Domain Name is composed solely of two common words in combination, absent direct proof that the generic Disputed Domain Name was registered solely for the purpose of profiting from Complainant's trademark rights, there can be no finding of bad faith registration and use." Discussed further in "Common Words, Common Phrases" (Sec. 5.01-D.1.c).

149 15 U.S.C. §1052 (f): "The Director may accept as prima facie evidence that the mark has become distinctive, as used on or in connection with the applicant's goods in commerce, proof of substantially exclusive and continuous use thereof as a mark by the application in commerce for the five years before the date on which the claim of distinctiveness is made."

150 ***Discount Embroidery Supply v. AllStitch LLC***, FA1007001336136 (Forum September 6, 2010) (<discountembroiderysupplies.com>); ***Wes Madan / United Oil Heat, Inc., d/b/a OrderMyOil.com v. michael Meehan***, FA1701001715122 (Forum March 9, 2017) (ORDER YOUR OIL and <ordermyoil.com>. "[T]he fact that the disputed domain name is a descriptive phrase of the provided services by the resolving website, rebuts any allegation of bad faith.")

151 The distinction between an "intent to use mark" (ITU) and an already in commerce mark not previously registered is discussed below. Also, there is an exception to the general rule. Complainants whose activities have received intense media coverage prior to the registration of the domain name are acknowledged to qualify for a right before application or issuance of a certificate of trademark registration. Discussed further in "Acting on Media Coverage and Insider Information" (Sec. 5.01-C.1.b).

152 ***Aspen Grove, Inc. v. Aspen Grove***, D2001-0798 (WIPO October 17, 2001) ("Certainly, under the Policy, while Panels have been willing to recognize that proof of a valid and subsisting trademark

alone is not sufficient to establish rights in a mark,"[154] but once the registration issues protection dates back to the filing date of the application.[155]

Whether an alleged trademark qualifies as a right under the UDRP depends on the basis for the trademark application, as discussed below. As a matter of law, trademark applications that postdate registrations of domain names without proof of common law rights or earlier use are equivalent to "intent to use" applications because these trademarks are admittedly not in commerce. "In use" trademark applications fare better because the first use in commerce is always earlier than the filing date, which allows for argument of an unregistered right preceding the registration of the domain name.

4.01-A.3.d

4.01-A.3.d *Applying for Trademark Registration*

4.01-A.3.d.i

4.01-A.3.d.i *"Intent to Use" Application*

Under U.S. law applicants may reserve a trademark or service mark by filing an "intent to use" application (ITU); or, if the applicant already has a presence in the marketplace it may file a use-based application. ITU is discussed here and the use-based application below. A certificate of registration satisfies the threshold requirement while a mere application to register a trademark confers no rights. As further enlarged upon in "Unregistered Marks, Recognition in the Marketplace and Proof of Secondary Meaning" (Sec. 4.01-B) rights accrue only where complainant offers persuasive evidence that it owns an unregistered trademark. On its face an ITU application implicitly informs the world that applicant's entry into the marketplace is prospective.[156] This does not preclude the possibility as indicated in the cited cases that complainant may have entered the marketplace and accrued a right in the interim between filing and registration of the trademark. Because an ITU application is prospective the applicant is not asked for a date of first use in commerce. The fact that the Trademark Office has advanced an applied for trademark to publication after issuance of a Notice of Allowance (NOA) does not create a right.

---

registration is prima facie evidence of trademark rights, no such presumption arises from a pending application to register a mark.")

153 ***Wave Indus., Inc. v. Angler Supply***, FA 304784 (Forum September 20, 2004) (U.S. parties); ***Amsec Enterprises, L.C. v. Sharon McCall***, D2001-0083 (WIPO April 3, 2001) (U.S. parties).

154 ***PRGRS, Inc. v. Pak***, D2002-0077 (WIPO April 24, 2002).

155 ***Planetary Soc'y v. Rosillo***, D2001-1228 (WIPO February 12, 2002).

156 ***Planetary***, *supra*. See also ***NAOP LLC v. Name Administration Inc. (BVI)***, FA0808001220825 (Forum October 7, 2008), citing ***Xoft Inc. v. Name Administration Inc. (BVI)***, FA1154179 (Forum April 25, 2008). Complainants filed intent to use trademark applications prior to the time that the domain name was registered. The Panels ruled that "the date of registration does not relate back to the date that the application was filed unless there is clear evidence of use in commerce sufficient to create a secondary meaning in the mark."

"The NOA is not a registration, but indicates that the mark will be allowed to register after an acceptable Statement of Use (SOU) is filed."[157] A pending ITU application in which an SOU has been filed at best indicates a marketplace presence and at worst is an admission there was no common law right predating the domain name registration. To successfully assert an unregistered right demands incontestable proof that "complainant either established, in the UDRP proceeding, that the mark had acquired a secondary meaning through its use sufficient to support common law rights in the unregistered mark"[158] or complainant at least made "uncontested allegations of use in conjunction with the USPTO's issuance of the corresponding Notice of Allowance."[159] This proof is precisely what complainants are generally unable to offer until the applied for trademarks have advanced to registration.

Complainant's burden on "intent to use" applications is illustrated in the ***Martha Stewart*** case.[160] Complainant filed an "intent to use" application to register EVERYDAY FOOD, which the USPTO refused to register as descriptive. The company then acquiesced in the mark's registration on the Supplemental Register. Within months of complainant's ITU application respondent registered <everyday-food.com> and <everydayfood.com>. Complainant argued that an "intent to use" application *ought to be* treated as notice of its prior right to the trademark as would a subsequent trademark registration for the same term in the same Class(es):

> Since respondent is located within the U.S., he has notice of Complainant's prior rights to its EVERYDAY FOOD mark. The fact of (a) the prior pending intent to use application combined with (b) the fact that a search of the USPTO records prior to the date of the registration of the Offending Domains would have revealed Complainant's claim to rights and (c) the fact of the nature of the use of the Offending Domains to promote competing goods and services via a payperclick interface which makes direct reference to Complainant and its MARTHA STEWART and EVERYDAY FOOD magazine marks all support a finding of bad faith registration.

---

[157] See the USPTO's website at http://www.uspto.gov/trademarks/process/tm_sec1btimeline.jsp.

[158] ***Mercury Radio Arts, Inc. and Glenn Beck v. Isaac Eiland Hall***, D2009-1182 (WIPO October 29, 2009); ***Abraxis BioScience, LLC v. Les Rubin***, D2008-0066 (WIPO March 13, 2008). See also ***Yahoo! Inc. v. Ashy***, D2000-0241 (WIPO June 14, 2000) (<yahooventures.com> in which Respondent sought to create a right by filing an ITU application).

[159] ***Elementage LLC v. Chris Hayes***, D2008-0059 (WIPO March 5, 2008) ("The Panel finds that [Complainant's] . . . uncontested allegations of use in conjunction with the USPTO's issuance of the corresponding Notice of Allowance just clears the hurdle required under the Policy, and is therefore, sufficient for purposes of this proceeding to establish the existence of common law trademark rights in the ELEMENTAGE mark." No appearance by Respondent).

[160] ***Martha Stewart Living Omnimedia, Inc. v. Joe Perez***, FA0904001259275 (Forum June 24, 2009). See also ***Neal & Massy Holdings Limited v. Gregory Ricks***, FA1403001549327 (Forum April 12, 2014) ("In filing the ITU application Complainant thereby admits that it has not yet used the MASSY mark in commerce, but instead intends to use the mark at some point in the future.")

The argument is eloquent but Panels have rejected the concept of constructive notice.[161] While it is undoubtedly correct procedurally that the USPTO will reject subsequent trademark applications for confusingly similar terms to those already under consideration (depending on the conjunction of goods or services) the same principle is not applied in determining bad faith.

Until a trademark applicant is successful in proving distinctiveness—establishing entitlement to have the trademark registered on the Principal Register—it is vulnerable to interlopers taking advantage of attractive common words and phrases such as "everyday food." It is not (as Complainant's counsel argues in ***Martha Stewart***) "a straightforward case that offers the Panel a stark choice between applying the plain language of the Policy or creating a safe haven for U.S. based cybersquatters to poach domain names based upon Intent to Use trademark applications."[162] The Policy does not protect proto-trademarks and there is no "stark choice." The principle for which Martha Stewart argues is not actionable under the UDRP. Complainant's argument is essentially for a change of policy to enlarge the Policy's jurisdiction to prohibit poaching from "intent to use" applications. Since Martha Stewart did not have a protectable right at the time respondent registered the domain names it could not satisfy the threshold requirement.[163]

4.01-A.3.d.ii

4.01-A.3.d.ii *Use-Based Application*

A pending use-based application presupposes that upon its filing the applicant has an already established presence in the marketplace indicated by its representations of "first use" and "first use in commerce" dates. The complainant is better positioned than an ITU applicant (discussed further above) because it claims to have a current presence in the marketplace. This is because the representation of "first use in commerce" is probative of a common law right that supports standing if the date is earlier than the registration of the domain name. A successful argument rests on a two-part demonstration: date of commencement of marketplace presence and historical reputation. Proof of the first is not conclusive of the second. If complainant's

---

161 Jurisprudential Overview 3.0, Paragraph 3.8.2 indicates a new "exception to the general proposition described above in 3.8.1 [concerning] certain limited circumstances where the facts of the case establish that the respondent's intent in registering the domain name was to unfairly capitalize on the complainant's nascent (typically as yet unregistered) trademark rights, panels have been prepared to find that the respondent has acted in bad faith." It states that "]s]uch scenarios include registration of a domain name: "(iv) following the complainant's filing of a trademark application." See ***Aveva Group Plc. v. Edward Kim***, D2015-2349 (WIPO March 2, 2015) but there is no authority that indicates a shift of view or emerging consensus. The addition of a fourth scenario is a case of the tail wagging the dog.

162 ***Martha Stewart***, *supra.*

163 The principle that an application for a trademark is insufficient to pass the threshold test has an exception that is explained more fully in "Acting on Media Coverage and Insider Information"

proof validates the first representation it must still prove it had a reputation when respondent registered the domain name. It must do this for two reasons: to secure standing to maintain the proceeding and in anticipation of respondent's rebuttal denying knowledge of the yet to be registered trademark.

Indeed, because assertions are merely that and not proof of truth, priority of use depends on complainant demonstrating that its trademark was actually used in commerce earlier in time than registration of the domain name. "[C]laimed dates of first use are meaningless without supporting evidence."[164] Under U.S. trademark law, "[t]he allegation in an application for registration, or in a registration, of a date of first use is not evidence on behalf of the applicant or registrant; a date of first use must be established by competent evidence."[165] There is no "evidentiary presumption in favor of trademark registrant."[166] In consequence, if complainant has represented a date of first use in commerce later than the domain name registration it constitutes an admission against interest. The admission cannot be undone.[167]

Where the critical date is first use and respondent has priority complainants are hoisted by their contradictory representations in complaint and trademark applications.[168] Although priority is not an essential element for standing it is essential for proving bad faith. Thus, while complainants may have standing to maintain the administrative proceeding they have no actionable claim for cybersquatting. This conundrum is eliminated under the ACPA because the statute limits standing to owners whose marks are "distinctive [or famous] at the time of registration of the

---

(Sec. 6.01-C.1.b). Complainants whose activities have received intense media coverage prior to the registration of the domain name are acknowledged to qualify for a right before formally applying for the trademark. The ***Martha Stewart*** record (insofar as reported in the decision) is silent on media coverage, so complainant was not eligible to take advantage of the exception.

164 ***eSnipe, Inc. v. Modern Empire Internet, Ltd.***, D2009-0719 (WIPO August 5, 2009).

165 Rules of Practice in Trademark Cases, 37 C.F.R. §2.122(b)(2), "Matters in Evidence." See also ***Kay Hill, Ltd. v. Texas International Property Associates NA NA***, FA0805001190984 (Forum July 9, 2008). A representation of first use in a trademark application is not necessarily accepted as presumptive proof of a right without corroborating evidence.

166 ***Hidden Values***, *supra.*

167 ***Greenline Financial Technologies, Inc. v. Griffin IT Media, Inc. a/k/a Tim Griffin***, FA0605000701179 (Forum June 28, 2006).

168 ***inExile Entertainment, Inc. v. Telecom Tech Corp.***, D2009-0655 (WIPO July 3, 2009) (<superstacker2.com>. "Complainant does not appear to have claimed any 'first use' date in its subsequent trademark application"); ***DealerX v. Gurri Kahlon, ROiQ.com***, D2017-0488 (WIPO May 4, 2017) (<roiq.com>) ("Complainant alleges that it has used the ROIQ mark in interstate commerce since 2007, but provides no factual support for this claim. Instead, it contradicts the claim by submitting the only evidence relating to Complainant's use – the U.S. Registration for the ROIQ trademark – which claims first use in commerce on November 2013." Respondent acquired the domain name in 2009. Award vacated under the Lanham Act on default. *Dealerx v. Kahlon*, 2:17-cv-1444 (E.D. Cal., 2017) ("[While] the facts [Page 10] do not support a finding of bad faith in relation to defendant's

domain name."[169] In a UDRP proceeding, establishing an earlier right affirms only that complainant has standing to present its case. A later right disqualifies complainant from maintaining an administrative proceeding.

Absent evidence to the contrary, complainant's exclusive right of use relates back to the application date[170] or earlier only if the proof supports acquired distinctivenesspreceding the domain name registration.[171] Accordingly, where the critical date is the date complainant filed its application respondent's argument that it registered the domain name before approval of the trademark registration is unpersuasive, since the effective date for a use-based trademark registration is the date of its application.[172] A respondent's good faith in registering the domain name after the trademark has come into existence demands explanation, but even a finding that it lacks a right or legitimate interest in it will not support a forfeiture of the domain name absent proof of registration in bad faith. On these facts complainant may have standing, but no actionable claim under the Policy.

4.01-A.3.e 4.01-A.3.e *Design-Plus-Word Trademarks*

4.01-A.3.e.i 4.01-A.3.e.i ***Rights to Lexical Elements in Design Trademark***

Design-plus-word trademarks are registrable as combinations of figurative and lexical element(s), but the right attaches to the whole, not the lexical part, unless the isolated or dominant part is itself capable of being registered as a trademark. This follows because design elements are incapable of representation in a domain name.[173] It has been noted that confusing similarity "can be difficult [to assess]

---

initial acquisition of the 'roiq] domain name ... [however,] defendant did demonstrate bad faith upon learning of plaintiff's mark and attempting to improperly extract profit from plaintiff. Plaintiff has demonstrated defendant's bad faith attempt to profit by submission of an e-mail chain between plaintiff and defendant showing defendant attempting to extract a high price from the plaintiff for purchase of the domain name.")

[169] 15 U.S.C. §1125(d) (1)(A)(ii)(I) and (II). This statutory requirement of priority was fatal, for example, in *New World Solutions, Inc. v. Namemedia Inc.*, 11-cv-2763 (SDNY December 15, 2015) where plaintiff's application for trademark registration stated that its first use of the mark in commerce occurred later than the registration of the domain name. See also *Philbrick v. Enom*, 593 F.Supp.2d 352, 375 (D. New Hampshire, 2009) ("Because the plaintiffs' mark is not distinctive (or famous) [before the domain name registration], it is simply not entitled to protection under the ACPA.")

[170] ***Thompson v. Zimmer***, FA 190625 (Forum October 27, 2003); ***Coppertown Drive-Thru Systems, LLC v. R. Snowden***, FA0605000715089 (Forum July 17, 2006).

[171] Discussed further in "General Rule: Common Law Rights" (Sec. 4.01-D.1.b.i).

[172] ***Kemosabe Entertainment, LLC v. Mike Nazzaro***, D2012-1893 (WIPO November 19, 2012) ("Complainant has failed to get out of the starting gate.")

[173] See Jurisprudential Overview 3.0, Paragraph 1.10: "To the extent that design (or figurative/stylized) elements would be incapable of representation in domain names, these elements are largely disregarded for purposes of assessing identity or confusing similarity under the first element. Such

where a complainant relies on a figurative mark comprising a logo and a descriptive . . . expression."[174]

The procedure for assessing whether domain names are identical or confusingly similar to a mark is limited to the lexical element of the design. In the cited case the Panel rejected Complainant's contention it owned the word "Paris" (the sole word in the logo): "[the question of confusing similarity] can be difficult where a complainant relies on a figurative mark comprising a logo and a descriptive or geographical expression." In ***Palace Sports & Entertainment*** the Panel rejected Complainant's claim to "Palace" because the lexical element was "The Palace of Auburn Hills."[175] The Panel found that "the additional words in Complainant's mark—[the] 'the' and 'of Auburn Hills'—serve to differentiate it from the Domain Name in appearance, pronunciation, and connotation, and is therefore not convinced of the likelihood of Internet user confusion in this case." The Complainant had no trademark registration for "Palace" standing alone.

Non-registrable terms fall into a category that cannot acquire trademark status, although they may be "relevant to the decision in certain circumstances such as where, for example, they form an especially prominent or distinctive part of the trademark overall."[176] This is usually taken to refer to the dominant part of the figurative element that standing alone may be registrable as a trademark. Registrability is pursued further below but it will become obvious that dictionary words—as with the case of geographical terms—are either not registrable or (even if distinctive in a trademark sense) too weak to sustain a claim of cybersquatting.

Where the dominant part of the lexical element is registrable as a trademark the Panel is likely to find the domain name identical or confusingly similar, sufficient for standing but other factors such as the commonness of the word claimed to be protected may argue against bad faith registration, as in ***Ambit Holdings***.[177] AMBIT ENERGY is a registered trademark. The disputed domain name is <ambit.com>. Although the parties are located in the same geographic area "there is a world of separation between the distribution of electrical energy, on the one hand, and the provision of investment services, on the other hand." While the Panel accepted the domain name as confusingly similar based on a comparison with the dominant element, it denied the complaint because "ambit" disconnected from "energy" loses

---

design elements may be taken into account in limited circumstances e.g., when the domain name comprises a spelled-out form of the relevant design element."

174 ***Ville de Paris v. Salient Properties LLC***, D2009-1279 (WIPO December 3, 2009).

175 ***Palace Sports & Entertainment LLC v. Palace Enterprises, NV***, D2013-0559 (WIPO June19, 2013).

176 Jurisprudential Overview 3.0, *supra*.

177 ***Ambit Holdings, L.L.C. v. Josh Koppang***, FA1302001485245 (Forum April 20, 2013) ("From the record in this proceeding, Respondent had a valid, good faith intention, when launching his investment algorithm services, to conduct that business without causing injury to the Complainant.")

its association with the company. The consuming public knows the company by the joined words. Separated, the word "ambit" creates its own association.

4.01-A.3.e.ii

4.01-A.3.e.ii *Assessing Confusing Similarity*

Panels assess confusing similarity between domain names and trademarks comprising a combination design and word mark in different ways, but there are "certain commonalities" regardless of whether the word mark element is disclaimed.[178] These include: "the overall impression given by the mark, taking into account as appropriate the strength of the word mark element which is being directly compared with the domain name and considering the relevant prominence of the word mark element in the context of the overall impression given by the trademark." Two illustrations will assist in understanding the analysis, ***Cap Gemini*** and ***Packet Clearing House*** referred to in the footnotes below. In ***Cap Gemini*** the stylized design included the word "Capgemini" in bold letters above the phrase "Consulting Technology Outsourcing." The Panel held that "'Capgemini' is without question the dominant part of the stylized mark both visually and semantically."[179]

The second design, in contrast, shows a three letter acronym sitting above Complainant's name and trademark, PACKET CLEARING HOUSE.[180] The Panel concluded that in "view[ing the design trademark] in its entirety" it

> must be understood as comprising a mark in which the elements PCH and PACKET CLEARING HOUSE are read together. The mark as a whole makes it clear that PCH serves as an acronym standing for "Packet Clearing House". In a real sense, the words qualify the acronym, and serve as an important context in evaluating whether an impugned domain name can be viewed as identical or confusingly similar. Plainly put complainant's registered mark is PCH PACKET CLEARING HOUSE not PCH.

Complainant offered no evidence "to support a finding that the letters PCH are distinctive of its business." Protection for common words, including acronyms, that

---

[178] ***Limited Liability Company Infomedia v. c/o Office Mail processing center / Whois privacy services, provided by DomainProtect LLC / 1) Eurofirm Ltd. 2) Ethno Share PO, Domain Manager***, D2010-1239 (WIPO October 27, 2010) (<ethno.com>. "While ['ethno'] is a prominent element in the combined trademark, in this Panel's view the word . . . is no more prominent than the propeller like device element, which the Panel notes does not conjure up any particular association with the common meaning of the term 'ethno' as defined above.")

[179] ***Cap Gemini v. Anant Goel***, D2011-1310 (WIPO September 23, 2011) ("The disputed domain name [<capgeminiconsulting.com>] incorporates the mark CAPGEMINI along with the word 'consulting' which, although descriptive, is one of the elements of one of Complainant's marks and corresponds to one of the services provided by Complainant, thus increasing the confusing similarity.")

[180] ***Packet Clearing House, Inc. v. Howard Lee***, D2005-0828 (WIPO September 28, 2005).

are not the registered trademark depend entirely on their having separately achieved secondary meaning. This is as equally true of "Palace" and "ethno" as it is of "PCH."

4.01-A.3.e.iii *Disclaiming Lexical Elements*

4.01-A.3.e.iii

The USPTO explains that some words and designs in a mark are not registrable because they are needed by other persons/businesses to be able to describe their goods, services, and/or business. While a disclaimer does not physically remove the unregistrable portion from the applied-for mark or affect the appearance of it or the way in which it is used the disclaimer announces to the world that the disclaimed words are freely available for other businesses to use in marketing non-competing goods or services.[181]

Where the figurative + word elements together qualify for trademark registration but the words alone are not distinctive complainant cannot prove violation of paragraph 4(a)(i) of the Policy unless the evidence supports targeting.[182] "Once the disclaimed words have been discounted, it would be difficult to see anything left in the trademark with which there can be said to be confusing similarity."[183] "[R]ather, those words are protected only when used with the mark as a whole."[184]

A similar finding was made in ***High Class Distributions*** where Complainant had disclaimed "high class." The disclaimer "would generally be regarded as incapable of distinguishing [the term] by reason of descriptiveness."[185] A similar conclusion was

---

181 See Jurisprudential Overview 3.0, Paragraph 1.2.3: "[I]f the similar elements of the domain name are made up exclusively of disclaimed terms, trademark rights under the Policy may not be found unless the complainant can show sufficient secondary meaning in the disclaimed terms." ***Minibar North America Inc. v. Ian Musk & GEMS Global Electronic Minibar Systems AS***, D2005-0035 (WIPO March 2, 2005); ***Fine Tubes Limited v. Tobias Kirch, J. & J. Ethen, Ethen Rohre GmbH***, D2012-2211 (WIPO January 30, 2013) (Complainant failed to disclose that the OHIM rejected "its application to register 'Fine Tubes' ... and the implicit rejection of its application (based on Complainant's withdrawal) by the UK IPO. While 'Fine Tubes' may be the dominant part of its registered trademark, it does not have rights in 'Fine Tubes' standing alone ... [and] Complainant is left without enforceable trademark rights.")

182 ***Goway Travel Limited v. Tourism Australia***, D2006-0344 (WIPO June 6, 2006) (<downunder.travel>. "[T]he registration protects only the specific design mark shown, and does not give rise to any prima facie evidence that Complainant has trademark rights in the word 'downunder,' standing alone.")

183 ***Minibar North America***, *supra*.

184 "The purpose of a disclaimer is to permit the registration of a mark that is registrable as a whole but contains matter that would not be registrable standing alone, without creating a false impression of the extent of the registrant's right with respect to certain elements in the mark." (USPTO Glossary). See ***Advance News Service, Inc. v. Vertical Axis, Inc./ Religionnewsservice.com***, D2008-1475 (WIPO December 11, 2008).

185 ***High Class Distributions S.r.l v. OnpneEntertainment Services***, D2000-0100 (WIPO May 4, 2000). Similarly with ***Ideation Unlimited, Inc. v. Dan Myers***, D2008-1441 (WIPO November 12,

reached by a three-member Panel in ***Airborne Systems*** in which complainant was found to have disclaimed "Airborne Systems."[186] The dominant part of the design were the letters "AS." The three-member Panel (taking into account the disclaimer) held that those letters were the dominant element and dismissed the complaint.

That commercial actors receive statutory protection for lexical or numeric strings of characters is not intended to restrict their use by others if the same strings are equally capable of conveying information or creating associations unrelated to those protected as marks. In "Deutsche Post" it would be "highly artificial to contend that this is a trademark for the word 'Post' when it clearly is far more than that."[187] The "far more than that" is the image of a horn, which in the overall design is the dominant element of the design. Whether or not any part of the text is disclaimed and regardless of the dominant feature if the text is generic the trademark owner would not be entitled "to prevent use of those words by others in commerce accurately and descriptively in accordance with their primary meaning in the English language."[188] However, if respondent's choice combines the dominant term in juxtaposition with a generic qualifier that refers or circles back to the complainant's business the registration is abusive, <qnx-phone.com> where the addition of "phone" is determinitive.

The dominant term in the design created by Caesars Entertainment which features a line drawing of the Eiffel Tower are the words "Paris Las Vegas."[189]

2008) (<prescriptioncosmetics.com> in which Complainant disclaimed Respondent's choice of phrase.)

[186] ***Airborne Systems North America and Airborne Systems Group, Ltd. v. Virtual Point, Inc***, D2008-1669 (WIPO March 6, 2009), citing, ***MAHA Maschinenbau Haldenwang GmbH & Co. KG v. Deepak Rajani***, D2000-1816 (WIPO March 2, 2001).

[187] ***Deutsche Post AG v. NJDomains***, D2006-0001 (WIPO March 1, 2006) ("The pictorial representation of the horn is such a prominent and dominating part of the trademark that the result is a logo of the horn as well as the word 'Post'. It is highly artificial to contend that this is a trademark for the word 'Post' when it clearly is far more than that.")

The same issue is revisited in a Legal Rights Objection by the United States Postal Service to an anticipated new gTLD, .mail. See ***United States Postal Service v. Amazon EU S.à.r.l***, LRO 2013-0044 (WIPO July 18, 2013) (The objector argued that in the United States "consumers will expect the .mail gTLD to originate from the United States Postal Service.")

[188] ***Porto Chico Stores, Inc. v. Otavio Jambon***, D2000-1270 (WIPO November 15, 2000) (LOVELY GIRL and <lovelygirls.com>. "Even if the respondent had constructive knowledge of the complainant's registered trademark rights, the use by the respondent of the disputed domain name so as accurately to describe the content of the pictures it offers negates any presumption of an intent to deceive the public or to derive benefit from the complainant's mark.") Other representative design-plus word cases: ***QC Holdings, Inc. v. NetIncome Ventures Inc.***, FA1208001459705 (Forum October 4, 2012) (<quikcash.com>); ***Marco Aurich v. Johannes Kuehrer, World4You Webservice***, D2012-1147 (WIPO July 24, 2012) (<domainhosting.com>); ***DataServ, L.L.C. v. Name Administration Inc. (BVI)***, D2012-1538 (WIPO September 27, 2012) (<dataserve.com>).

Complainant disclaimed "Paris." Respondent incorporated the whole of the trademark, PARIS LAS VEGAS, with a noun addition, "casino." However, the addition is a term associated with Complainant's business, which supports a finding that Respondent was motivated by Complainant's reputation in the gaming industry. The Panel held: "[I]f the Respondent had no intention of benefitting from opportunistically exploiting any of those marks—let alone to the detriment of the Complainant, then why did it register a name that so resembles those marks? The Panel can think of no credible reason. Moreover, since the Respondent failed to file a response, the Panel simply infers that no such reason exists."[190] There was no such circling back to the Complainant or evidence of targeting for <quickcash.com>, <domainhosting.com>, and <dataserv.com> cited in earlier footnotes.

The decision that there is a violation of the Policy does not rest on the weakness of the mark or that any part of it has been disclaimed. Rather, the decision rests on the use of the domain name, which together with other circumstantial evidence supports the conclusion that respondent either did or did not register the domain name for its value as a trademark.[191]

4.01-A.3.e.iv *Persuasive Evidence of Secondary Meaning*

4.01-A.3.e.iv

In cases where the lexical elements of the designs are generic expressions and not inherently distinctive it would be rare for a complainant to make a case for infringement absent persuasive evidence of abusive conduct by respondent to take advantage of complainant's reputation in the marketplace. Complainants succeed where the lexical element is distinctive—that is, it has been granted registration—or the respondent competes with complainant. The second circumstance is illustrated in two RUGGEDCOM cases[192] in which the Respondent had actual knowledge of complainant and competed with it, but rested its case on the theory that "rugged"

---

189 ***Caesars Entertainment, Inc. v. Nova Internet Inc.***, D2005-0411 (WIPO June 22, 2005).

190 *Id.*

191 ***Christian Medical & Dental Associations v. David Mayer, KAT Communications***, D2016- 1670 (WIPO October 11, 2016) ("Complainant registered GLOBAL HEALTH OUTREACH as a design plus words mark, and the USPTO required the Complainant to disclaim the word element 'Global Health Outreach' apart from the mark as shown. Presumably the USPTO considered the word element to be descriptive. However, given the Complainant's continuous use of the mark since 1998, the Panel is persuaded that the word mark GLOBAL HEALTH OUTREACH has acquired distinctiveness." ***Major Wire Industries Limited v. DigitalOne AG***, D2015-0284 (WIPO May 2, 2015) (<major.com>. "Complainant has demonstrated common law rights in its MAJOR trademark, despite the disclaimers in its registered marks ... [but] the Panel finds that Respondent was reasonably entitled to acquire the Domain Name containing the ordinary English word 'major' on a 'first come first served' basis).

192 In ***RUGGEDCOM, Inc. v. James Krachenfels***, D2009-0130 (WIPO April 7, 2009) (<ruggedrouter>) and ***RUGGEDCOM, Inc. v. James Krachenfels***, D2009-0119 (WIPO March 31, 2009) (<ruggedswitch>) complainant rested its right on a Canadian design trademark registration

in "router" and "switch" were generic and descriptive of the products they sold. Although Respondent's assertion was supported by the USPTO's refusal to register RUGGEDROUTER and RUGGEDSWITCH on the Principal Register both terms had been accepted for registration under Canadian law. The Panel concluded that the Respondent's motivation was clear

> ***by the date of registration of the Domain Name the respondent was well aware of the use by complainant of the term "RuggedSwitch" for its products. They both operated in the same or similar industries and complainant had at that point already commenced two sets of domain name proceedings against LANStore. . . .
>
> Ultimately, the Panel has reached the conclusion that on the balance of probabilities respondent registered the Domain Name because of associations between the term "ruggedswitch" and complainant, and with the intent of diverting users looking for information on complainant to the web page operating from the Domain Name.

Where the term is an acronym set in a stylized mark complainant may satisfy its burden of proof by demonstrating a common law right to the expansion of the acronym that is both distinctive (as "airborne systems" is not) and acquired prior to the registration of the domain name (as with SBD—not distinctive and "Savino Del Bene," which is).[193]

Trademark owners of figurative trademarks acquired after domain name registration are in no better position than trademark owners generally: they may have standing if the domain name is identical or confusingly similar to a dominant element in the design that is not disclaimed, but no actionable claim under the UDRP unless, taking "rugged switch" as an example, respondent is shown to be a competitor.

---

that included the term RUGGED, which is dominant, and "switch" which it disclaimed. ***RUGGED.COM*** is distinguished from cases like ***Martha Stewart***, *supra*, in that complainant had a Canadian trademark, albeit on the Supplemental Register in the United States. It is also distinguished in that the Respondent was in competition with Complainant and regarded the lexical element as distinctive. The dissent in ***RUGGEDCOM, Inc. v. James Krachenfels***, D2009-0130 (WIPO April 7, 2009) (<ruggedrouter>) who dissented also in the second dispute between the same parties, ***RUGGEDCOM, Inc. v. James Krachenfels***, D2009-0119 (WIPO March 31, 2009) (<ruggedswitch>) would have dismissed the complaints (as she stated more fully in <ruggedswitch>) because "[d]esign mark rights exist only in combination with the design" and since a "domain name contains no design element . . . it would seem that Respondent violated no trademark rights when it registered the Domain Name."

193 ***Savino Del Bene Inc. v. Graziano Innocenti Gennari***, D2000-1133 (WIPO December 12, 2000) (Complainant owned an Italian trademark "SBD" in a stylized three-dimensional box at the time of the UDRP proceeding but no registered trademark in SAVINO DEL BENE. Proof supported common law trademark in the spelled-out name and evidence of abusive registration.)

4.01-B Unregistered Marks, Recognition in the Marketplace and Proof of Secondary Meaning 4.01-B

4.01-B.1 Unregistered Trademark Rights Protected 4.01-B.1

Paragraph 4(a)(i) of the Policy is silent on whether the right complainant is seeking to protect must be registered, but panelists quickly construed the Policy to include unregistered marks.[194] This construction is supported by the WIPO Final Report[195] and is the consensus view.[196] However, it comes with a proviso to have standing, namely complainant must prove the mark predated registration of the challenged domain name and achieved secondary meaning in the marketplace before that time.[197]

For unregistered trademarks (common law, 1b applications in the U.S, supplemental register in the U.S., and state as opposed to registrations in national

---

[194] ***The British Broadcasting Corporation v. Jaime Renteria***, D2000-0050 (WIPO March 23, 2000); ***SeekAmerica Networks Inc. v. Masood***, D2000-0131 (WIPO April 13, 2000) ("[The Policy] does not distinguish between registered and unregistered trademarks and service marks in the context of abusive registration of domain names.") Under U.S. trademark law registration of generic or descriptive marks on the Principal Register requires the registrant to prove that it has made "substantially exclusive and continuous use [of a designation] as a mark . . . in commerce for the five years before the claim of distinctiveness is made," Section 2(f) of the Trademark Act, 15 U.S.C.§1052(f).

Passing off of unregistered trademarks is actionable regardless of the jurisdiction. See Jurisprudential Overview, Paragraph 1.3 : "[F]or a number of reasons, including the global nature of the Internet and Domain Name System, the fact that secondary meaning may only exist in a particular geographical area or market niche does not preclude the complainant from establishing trademark rights (and as a result, standing) under the UDRP" and ***Aston Merrygold v. Martyn O'Brien***, D2014-1462 (WIPO October 7, 2014).

[195] Paragraphs 149-150. It also conforms with U.S. law. 15 U.S.C. §1125(a) (Lanham Act) §43 reads in pertinent part: "Any person who, on or in connection with any goods or services, or any container for goods, uses in commerce any word, term, name, symbol, or device, or any combination thereof...which (A) is likely to cause confusion, or to cause mistake, or to deceive as to the affiliation, connection, or association of such person with another person shall be liable in a civil action by any person who believes that he or she is or is likely to be damaged by such act."

[196] Jurisprudential Overview 3.0, Paragraph 1.3: "Also noting the availability of trademark-like protection under certain national legal doctrines (e.g., unfair competition or passing-off) and considerations of parity, where acquired distinctiveness/secondary meaning is demonstrated in a particular UDRP case, unregistered rights have been found to support standing to proceed with a UDRP case including where the complainant is based in a civil law jurisdiction." See ***Beijing Qunar Information Technology Co., Ltd. v. Whois Privacy Protection Service, Inc./ Shanghai shebai industrial co., ltd***, D2013-1174 (WIPO September 12, 2013) ("There remains . . . an apparent conflict between Chinese trade mark law, which . . . does not usually recognise unregistered trade marks per se, and the Policy. In this regard, however, the Panel notes it has a wide discretion regarding the rules and principles of law it deems applicable.")

[197] See *Int'l Bancorp, LLC v. Société des Bains de Mer et du Cercle des Étrangers à Monaco*, 329 F.3d 359 (4th Cir., 2003) (Respondent in five UDRPs, D2000-1323, D2000-1326,D2000-1327,

registries) complainants must prove their rights, which means a presence in the marketplace predating the challenged domain names.[198] A complainant earns standing by proving its unregistered mark has acquired distinctiveness; that is, the words, names, symbols, or devices comprising it are recognized by the consuming public as sources of goods or services unrelated to their denotative meanings.[199]

In assessing whether complainant's sign has acquired the distinctiveness necessary to qualify as a mark, Panels approach the issue of proof of unregistered trademark rights "in a slightly more relaxed manner than does the USPTO [or comparable registries in other jurisdictions] when it requires proof of secondary meaning."[200] "Slightly more relaxed," however, is not satisfied by merely asserting priority of use or consumer recognition without establishing the truth of the assertion.

The principle of accepting unregistered trademarks as actionable rights quickly found expression in many early decisions and is securely lodged in the jurisprudence of domain names. "The procedure should allow all relevant rights and interests of the parties to be considered and ensure procedural fairness for all concerned parties."[201] The typical representation and warranty provision of domain name registration agreements refers to "legal rights of a third party"[202], or more explicitly that "the registration of the domain name will not infringe upon or otherwise violate the rights of any third party."[203] Nothing in any of these provisions suggests that "[l]egal rights in a trade mark . . . require that the trade mark must be registered."[204]

D2000-1328, and D2000-1315 (WIPO 2000) (Mark registered in Monaco, no U.S. registration: "[T]he Lanham Act extends protection to marks that meet the statutory requirements for being 'used in commerce,' provided they also enjoy secondary meaning." Defendant satisfied that requirement).

198 The language in the Anticybersquatting Consumer Protection Act is more explicit and clearer than the UDRP in that it requires the mark to be "distinctive at the time of the registration of the domain name."

199 If there were only denotation and no secondary meaning the composition of letters or words would be unregistrable as a trademark. Too numerous to cite, but the formula rejecting a right is illustrated in ***Kip Cashmore v. URLPro***, D2004-1023 (WIPO March 14, 2005) (<usacashservice.com>. "Complainant has not presented any credible evidence establishing acquired distinctiveness.") Trade names are denotative and not protectable as trademarks although they may qualify as marks if they function as indicators of source. See ***New Jersey Lawyers Service, LLC v. Guaranteed Subpoena Service, Inc.***, FA160900169565 (Forum November 10, 2016) (<lawyers service.com>) ("[E]vidence of use of a trade name is insufficient to prove that Complainant has Common Law rights on a trademark and that such trademark has acquired secondary meaning through the use of a trade name. Previous panels have held that usage as a trade name does not serve to establish common law rights in a mark.")

200 ***NJRentAScooter v. AM Business Solutions LLC***, FA0909001284557 (Forum November 4, 2009). If this is true about the "relaxed manner" it is because for the UDRP the issue is standing to maintain the proceeding, rather than Complainant's right to the domain name; whereas acceptance by the USPTO leads to registration of the mark. A mark composed of generic or descriptive elements may pass the 4(a)(i) test but not be eligible for the Principal Register.

201 WIPO Report Paragraph 150 (ii).

However, unregistered marks stand on a different footing from those registered. Their owners cannot claim for them any presumption of validity or distinctiveness.[205] Owners of registered marks succeed in proving their trademark rights by simply submitting copies of their registration certificates—which "is *prima facie* evidence of [the trademark's] validity,"[206] and also "creates a rebuttable presumption that the mark is inherently distinctive."[207] That is not the case with claimed unregistered marks. Although they are no less marks if they qualify, they are not distinctive until they are proved to have secondary meaning; that the mark is in fact a trademark.[208]

So, for example, it would be difficult to imagine "how the public would come to identify" a mark composed of a geographic location alone or combined with a dictionary word,[209] or, two common words combined to form a descriptive or common phrase.[210] Unregistered marks must be capable of distinguishing one merchant's goods/services from the goods/services of another.[211] This is possible when an owner uses its mark in such a way that its primary significance in the minds of prospective consumers is not the product/service itself, but the association of the product/service with a single source.[212]

---

202 Network Solutions Service Agreement Version 9.27: "You represent that, to the best of your knowledge and belief, neither the registration of the domain name nor the manner in which it is directly or indirectly used infringes the legal rights of a third party."

203 Discussed further in "Registrant's Responsibility for Determining Whether Domain Name Infringes Third Party Rights" (Sec. 2.02).

204 ***Jeanette Winterson v. Mark Hogarth***, D2000-0235 (WIPO May 22, 2000).

205 ***County Bookshops Limited v. Guy Loveday***, D2000-0655 (WIPO September 22, 2000) ("As the mark [<countybookshops.com>] is unregistered . . . there can be no . . . presumption of entitlement to rights under English law and the onus is on the Complainant to provide convincing evidence that it should be entitled to such rights.")

206 ***NetApp, Inc. v. July Linett c/o Jolly Co.***, FA0812001238829 (Forum February 5, 2009).

207 ***Janus International Holding Co. v. Scott Rademacher***, D2002-0201 (WIPO March 5, 2002). Under U.S. law continuous use of a mark "for five consecutive years subsequent to the date [of its] registration and is still in use in commerce, shall be incontestable." 15 U.S.C. §1065.

208 ***British Heart Foundation v. Harold A Meyer III***, AF0957 (eResolution November 13, 2001): "Thus, complainant must produce evidence proving that, prior to the filing of the Complaint, it has provided goods or services under the unregistered mark and had thereby acquired a reputation such that members of the public would associate those goods or services with complainant and not with others not authorized by complainant to use the mark. That is to say, complainant must prove that, prior to filing the Complaint, it had acquired a right in the unregistered mark such as would enable it to bring a legal action against a third person using the mark without its consent." See below, complainant's burden under the UDRP is less than demanded under international trademark regimes only in degree. The more distinctive the mark the less the proof and vice versa.

209 ***Keystone Publishing, Inc. v. UtahBrides.com***, D2004-0725 (WIPO November 17, 2004) (<utah-wedding.com>, "Respondent tellingly points out, numerous other websites with highly similar or nearly identical names . . . [are] contemporaneously offering similar wedding services in the State of Utah. [Response Exhibit B lists <utahweddings.info>, <weddingsutah.com>, <utahweddings.net>

4.01-B.2 4.01-B.2 Proving Unregistered Trademark Rights

4.01-B.2.a 4.01-B.2.a *Distinctiveness of Unregistered Trademark Not Presumed*

The test of entitlement to the challenged domain name is priority of use in the marketplace. Complainant must prove respondent registered the disputed domain name with the intention of capitalizing on complainant's goodwill and reputation, which in turn requires proof of reputation *at the time respondent purchased the domain name.* Both U.S. courts and ICANN Panels insist that proof of secondary meaning "includes evidence as to (1) the length and continuity of a mark's use, (2) sales, advertising, and promotional activities, (3) expenditures relating to promotion and marketing, (4) unsolicited media coverage, and (5) sales or admission figures."[213] Since these facts are within a complainant's knowledge and control, to withhold proof (to be silent or evasive) supports an adverse inference.

The trademark in the case cited in the last footnote was granted registration only under Section 2(f) of the Trademark Act based on acquired distinctiveness.[214] This "indicates only that the mark had acquired distinctiveness in the public mind as an indicator of source by the time of the USPTO's registration of the mark in January 2009; it does not involve a determination that the Complainant's mark, at the time of the Respondent's registration of the disputed domain names, had

---

and many others]") Complainant in ***Museum of Science and Industry v. Sam Wilkinson***, FA080600 1211341 (Forum August 12, 2008) (<msichicago.com>) failed to persuade Panel that it had an unregistered mark for "msi" based on its domain name, <msichicago.org>.

[210] ***Pet Warehouse v. Pets.Com, Inc.***, D2000-0105 (WIPO April 13, 2000) (<petwarehouse.com>. "The Panel does not accept Complainant's suggestion that 'Pet Warehouse' is a suggestive mark, such that Complainant should not be required to prove secondary meaning. No imagination is required to associate the term with a retail establishment selling pet supplies.")

[211] 15 U.S.C. §1125 (Section 43 of the Lanham Act).

[212] However, a generic domain name which can equally be claimed by multiple businesses that respondent is using without offense to any particular complainant cannot be infringing by simply corresponding to a complainant's mark. See for example ***OVB Vermögensberatung AG v. Michele Dinoia and SZK.com***, D2009-0307 (WIPO May 6, 2009) (<ovb.com>. Respondent used the domain name for "a portal site containing advertising links for knives and cutlery." The target was not complainant but a trademark owner in the cutlery business.)

[213] ***San Diego Hydroponics & Organics v. Innovative Growing Solutions, Inc.***, D2009-1545 (March 3, 2010), citing *First Brands Corp. v. Fred Meyer, Inc.*, 809 F.2d 1378, 1383 (9th Cir. 1987). Other Panels have cited *Paco Sport, Ltd. v. Paco Rabanne Parfums*, 86 F.Supp. 2d 305, 313 (S.D.N.Y. 2000) and *Centaur Communications, Ltd. v. A/S/M Communications, Inc.*, 830 F.2d 1217, 1222 (2d. Cir. 1987). See also ***S.N.C. Jesta Fontainebleau v. Po Ser***, D2009-1394 (WIPO November 21, 2009) (Discussing the common law theories of passing off and deception); ***Marquette Golf Club v. Al Perkins***, FA1706001738263 (Forum July 27, 2017) (<marquettegolfclub.com>. Marquette Golf Club made "intense efforts to advertise and promote its golf club"); ***Biofert Manufacturing Inc. v. Muhammad Adnan / Biofert manufacturing***, FA171000 1753132 (Forum November 27, 2017)

acquired secondary meaning sufficient for the public to recognize it as a symbol distinguishing the Complainant's goods and services from those of others."[215]

The evidentiary demands for proof of secondary meaning must be answered by the mark's market penetration at the time the domain name was registered. Solicited media coverage is not such evidence[216]; nor is an earlier registration of a domain name.[217] Although a mark whose distinctiveness is "acquired" is no less distinctive in a statutory sense it lacks the quality of a mark that is inherently distinctive. For a mark on the lower end of the classification scale the greater complainant's burden "to present compelling evidence of secondary meaning," while the "more obvious the viability of a complainant's claim" the lesser the burden.[218] At a minimum, to establish secondary meaning complainant must show that the public identifies the source of the product rather than the product itself.[219] Complainant succeeds if it presents credible evidence of distinctiveness and fails if it does not. The manner and amount of advertising employed to promote a mark may support secondary meaning, but "conclusory statements presented in the body of the Complaint" fall short of meeting complainant's burden.[220]

(<biofert.com>. Complainant supported its claim for common law rights by submitting evidence of "substantial sales and extensive advertising and promoting [through which it has] become very well-known [ ] as identifying fertilizers and supplements for agricultural use originating from, sponsored by, or associated with Complainant.").

214 15 U.S.C. §1052(f): "The Director may accept as prima facie evidence that the mark has become distinctive . . . [upon] proof of substantially exclusive and continuous use thereof as a mark by the applicant in commerce for the five years before the date on which the claim of distinctiveness is made."

215 *Id.* ***San Diego Hydroponics & Organics v. Innovative Growing Solutions.***

216 ***Katch, LLC v. Thomas Korula / Mahayta***, FA1508001633953 (Forum October 3, 2015) ("[A]lthough several business outlets carried the news of the change of name of Complainant "the Panel is not convinced that the reports in the business media outlets relied on were unsolicited, as they appear to be services that carry the press releases of companies who issue them, a useful service of course but not evidence that the market has come to associate the alleged mark with the goods and services of Complainant.")

217 ***Grant A. Wright v. Robert Thompson / w& w / Richard Lanham / No Company***, FA180900 1805540 (Forum November 5, 2018) ("A domain name registration alone establishes no protectable trademark rights.")

218 ***Jason Hachkowski v Lucas Barnes***, D2009-1800 (WIPO February 5, 2010) (<aidsdrugsonline.com>, "The more descriptive the term the more extensive must be the use to show that the mark has acquired secondary meaning to become distinctive of a particular company.") The evidentiary demand is encapsulated in Jurisprudential Overview 3.0, 1.3 *supra*: "In cases involving unregistered or common law marks that are comprised solely of descriptive terms which are not inherently distinctive, there is a greater onus on the complainant to present evidence of acquired distinctiveness/secondary meaning. [Other] panels have noted that the more obvious the viability of a complainant's claim to common law or unregistered trademark rights, the less onus there tends to be on that complainant to present the panel with extensive supporting evidence."

An unregistered trademark comprising a common generic word—"cream"—or descriptive phrase—"British meat"—offered by a complainant either unable to document its historical reputation or acquired after registration of the domain name falls short of the necessary proof.[221] The UDRP database is littered with decisions denying standing for undocumented rights, particularly for alleged marks used by others in industrial or service niches. While current reputation for an undocumented right is generally insufficient to establish standing, affirmative proof of respondent's knowledge of complainant prior to its registration of the domain name is generally conclusive of bad faith.

To succeed on the standing requirement, complainant must demonstrate that its mark achieved secondary meaning prior to domain name registration. As one Panel explained, "one would have expected to see sales figures, details of advertising and promotional expenditure, sample advertisements and promotional material to suggest that complainant has a reputation and goodwill associated with the name."[222] However, in that case Complainant produced none of these and simply made "a few very general unsupported statements as to the nature of [its] business."

---

[219] ***Florida Weimaraner Rescue, Inc. d/b/a Weimaraner Rescue of Florida v. weimaraner rescue of florida a/k/a Lauren R Simmons and TechKraft Inc. c/o Jim Horn***, FA1011001356030 (Forum December 28, 2010) ("The Panel finds that the principle [that for registration purposes secondary meaning is deemed to be established after five years of continuous and relatively exclusive use] . . . has no relevance to the determination of secondary meaning in a UDRP proceeding.") In ***Barnes Crossing Auto LLC v. Jonathon Hewitt, SEO Sport, LLC.***, D2017-1782 (WIPO December 5, 2017) (<bcauto.com>, <bcchevrolet.com>, <bchyundai.com>, and three more) Complainant relied on the combination of "bc" with manufacturers' marks as well as "bcauto" which is generic.)

[220] ***AOL LLC v. DiMarco***, FA 1275978 (Forum September 9, 2009) (Claim for unregistered AUTOBLOG and <autoblogreviews.com>. "While advertising amount and manner may suggest secondary meaning, evidence of the actual advertising amount and manner of advertising promoting the AUTOBLOG mark is not offered outside of the conclusory statements presented in the body of the Complaint." Respondent in ***CSP International Fashion Group S.p.a. v. NameFind LLC***, D2018-0163 (WIPO March 13, 2018) alleged common law rights for MYBOUTIQUE based on an earlier registered domain name: "The registration of a domain name does not by itself create a trademark." See *Tropic Ocean Airways, Inc. v. Floyd*, 14-12424 (11th Cir., 2014) (Direct action under the ACPA: "As for the argument the mark had acquired secondary meaning, the court found plaintiff's allegations to be insufficient. The complaint instead made conclusory allegations about secondary meaning that were insufficient to survive a motion to dismiss. The court held that plaintiff failed to allege the nature and extent of its advertising and promotion, and, more importantly, did not allege any facts about the extent to which the public identified the mark with plaintiff's services.")

[221] ***Cream Holdings Limited v. National Internet Source, Inc.***, D2001-0964 (WIPO September 28, 2001) (<cream.com>. "Complainant must establish that, prior to the registration of the disputed domain name, it had acquired through use of the word CREAM, trademark rights at common law.") See also ***EDREAMS, Inc. v Arise Company Ltd.***, D2006-0725 (WIPO July 24,2006) ("[h]aving considered [cited] authorities and the submissions of the parties, the Panel finds that complainant is unable to satisfy the test in paragraph 4(a)(i) of the Policy because it has no trademark rights which

Conclusory allegations of secondary meaning are insufficient to establish a right without proof of market presence,[223] which complainant is expected to establish by material evidence, not merely by assertion.[224] While sufficiency may be found in length of time coupled with evidence of presence in the marketplace,[225] three years without additional proof will not be persuasive.[226] The Complainant in ***Progressive Lighting*** not only "failed to produce any evidence relating to the extent of advertising, promotion, sales, or media coverage, but it has also neglected to reveal to the Panel the day on which it began using the LEE LIGHTING mark in commerce."[227]

While the relevant time for determining whether or not complainant has rights in a mark is the time that respondent registered the disputed domain name, it comes with a caveat. The Policy requires that complainant prove the earlier date.[228] A complainant's disclosure of first use in commerce on a trademark application (which as earlier noted is merely an unverified assertion) is not probative of secondary meaning. The principle of relation back applies only to the date of application, not to first use in commerce. For standing in a UDRP proceeding complainant must prove (not simply allege) the earlier date "in commerce."

This leads to an anomaly that although a declaration of continuous use of a descriptive mark for at least five years prior to the application may be sufficient for trademark registration it is not necessarily adequate to prevail under the UDRP.[229]

---

predate the date of creation of the disputed domain name [<edream.com>]"). However, unregistered, arguably distinctive marks are treated no differently than registered marks insofar as standing is concerned. See ***New Forests Asset Management Pty Limited v. Kerry Schorsch, Global Advertizing, LLC***, D2015-1415 (WIPO November 13, 2015) (<newforests.com>).

[222] ***The Monticello Group, Ltd. v. Teletravel, Inc.***, D2002-1157 (WIPO April 16, 2003); ***Digital Ceramic Systems Limited v. Baltea SRL***, D2012-1198 (WIPO July 24, 2012)("For cases . . . in which the trademark DIGITAL CERAMICS consists of descriptive words, the burden of proof is even higher.")

[223] Jurisprudential Overview 3.0: "[C]onclusory allegations of unregistered or common law rights, even if undisputed in the particular UDRP case, would not normally suffice to show secondary meaning."

[224] ***Operation Homefront v. Illinois Office of Lt. Governor***, D2007-1037 (WIPO October 1, 2007); ***Kay Hill, Ltd. v. Texas International Property Associates NA NA***, FA0805001190984 (Forum July 9, 2008).

[225] ***Tuxedos by Rose v. Nunez***, FA95248 (Forum October 11, 2006) (43 years).

[226] ***Hugo Daniel Barbaca Bejinha***, *supra*. Compare with ***Realmark Cape Harbor L.L.C. v. Lawrence S Lewis***, D2000-1435 (WIPO December 11, 2000), also three years, but complainant provided evidence of advertising expenditure and media recognition. However, see ***Bama Rags, Inc. v. Derrick James***, FA1311001529751 (Forum December 20, 3013) ("Here, the evidence submitted by Complainant shows that Complainant has done extensive marketing through social media outlets.")

[227] ***Progressive Lighting, Inc. DBA Lee Lighting, Inc. v. Manja Klimenko***, FA0502000424539 (April 8, 2005).

[228] ***NAOP LLC v. Name Administration Inc. (BVI)***, FA0808001220825 (Forum October 7, 2008), citing ***Xoft Inc. v. Name Administration Inc. (BVI)***, FA1154179 (Forum April 25, 2008).

In ***Xoft***, as in ***NAOP***, complainant had filed an intent to use trademark application prior to the time the domain name was registered. The Panels held:

> the date of registration does not relate back to the date that the application was filed unless there is clear evidence of use in commerce sufficient to create a secondary meaning in the mark" [NAOP].

No presumption attaches to marks on the lower end of the classification scale.[230] The secondary meaning must be earned and proved.

Being well-known or even having a household name does not excuse complainant from the burden of proving the distinctiveness of its unbranded, unregistered trademark, nor can it prevail on conjecture of the respondent's motivation. In an ***AOL*** dispute complainant alleged that <autoblogreviews.com> infringed its unregistered rights.[231] However, the Panel found AOL's proof deficient when measured by standards laid down by U.S. courts and prior UDRP Panels. "[I]t is Complainant's burden to not only plead, but also prove that its descriptive mark has acquired distinctiveness and thereby is a protectable trademark."[232] There is "no presumption in Complainant's favor. Complainant must prove the status of its mark via competent evidence, not by conjecture or innuendo."[233]

4.01-B.2.b 4.01-B.2.b *Unregistered Right Disproved By Admission*

It was earlier pointed out that while disclosure of first use in commerce on a trademark application may with additional proof strengthen complainant's allegations of priority and cybersquatting, a date subsequent to the registration of the domain name will be determinative against complainant as an admission against interest.[234] Complainant's burden is heavier where the Trademark Office has rejected its application for the Principal Register,[235] or if accepted as a design mark, complainant has disclaimed the textual component respondent has chosen as a domain

---

229 ***Discount Embroidery Supply v. AllStitch LLC***, FA1007001336136 (Forum September 6, 2010).

230 ***Dow Jones & Company, Inc. v. Idea Studios LLC dba Envent***, D2009-1033 (WIPO October 18, 2009) (<marketwatch.net>. Complaint denied).

231 ***AOL LLC v. Joe DiMarco***, FA0907001275978 (Forum September 9, 2009).

232 *Id.*

233 *Id.*

234 ***Javacool Software Development, L.L.C. v. Elbanhawy Investments***, FA0611000836772 (Forum January 2, 2007) ("Complainant had not yet used its SPYWAREGUARD Mark in commerce as of the date when the Respondent registered <spywareguard.com>. Therefore, although there are indications that Respondent has since used <spywareguard.com> in a bad faith manner, there is insufficient evidence to find that this Domain Name was registered in bad faith.")

235 ***Pet Warehouse v. Pets.Com, Inc.***, D2000-0105 (WIPO April 13, 2000) (<petwarehouse.com>) ("As a consequence [of the PTO rejecting Complainant's attempt to register PET WAREHOUSE] Complainant does not enjoy any presumption of secondary meaning for its claimed service mark, and shoulders the burden of establishing distinctiveness, assuming that the name is not generic.");

name.[236] Admissions by complainant on its trademark application and actions taken by the USPTO may be significant in establishing or discrediting first use in commerce and the protectability of the mark.

For example, complainant in ***Game X Change*** suffered two disabilities. It first abandoned its trademark; then in filing a new application it disclaimed the words GAME EXCHANGE "apart from the mark as shown."[237] The Panel held that the "disclaimer eliminated any special common law trademark rights Complainant may ever have had to 'GAME EXCHANGE' [and it] also eliminated any special common law trademark rights Complainant may ever have had to phonetic and telescoped equivalents such as 'GAME X CHANGE.'"[238]

In ***Bar Code*** the unfavorable evidence came from actions by the USPTO. The Panel stated that "[a]lthough Complainant might eventually overcome [the USPTO's] initial refusal with adequate evidence of secondary meaning in its proposed mark, the USPTO refusal is certainly material to this proceeding as evidence of the descriptive character of Complainant's proposed mark, and Complainant should have disclosed this refusal to the Panel."[239]

In equivocal situations—where the alleged trademark is composed of dictionary words or descriptive phrases[240] or there is proof that the term is used by others in different parts of the country[241]—complainant can succeed only on proof that respondent's registration intentionally targeted complainant's trademark. In more obvious situations—where the trademark is well-known—registration is said to be opportunistic. Opportunism, which is discussed further below in Section 6.01-C is a concept that describes appropriating well-known and famous trademarks that have significant goodwill and reputation in the marketplace.

---

also, ***1451 International Ltd. and Second Renaissance, LLC v. Steven Levine c/o Domain Systems, Inc.***, FA0510000583774 (Forum December 22, 2005) (abandoned trademark application).

236 "The purpose of a disclaimer is to permit the registration of a mark that is registrable as a whole but contains matter that would not be registrable standing alone, without creating a false impression of the extent of the registrant's right with respect to certain elements in the mark." (USPTO Glossary)

237 ***Game X Change, Inc. v. Modern Empire Internet Ltd. c/o Administrator***, FA080300 1155839 (Forum May 6, 2008) (<gamexchange.com>).

238 *Id.*, citing ***VideoCall Co. v. M Koenig***, FA 167922 (Forum Aug. 20, 2003).

239 ***Bar Code Disc. Warehouse, Inc. v. Barcodes, Inc.***, D2001-0405 (WIPO July 27, 2001).

240 Discussed further in "Unregistered Marks, Recognition in the Marketplace and Proof of Secondary Meaning" (Sec. 4.01-B) and "Common Words, Common Phrases" (Sec. 6.01-D.1.c).

241 ***Bangz, Inc. v. Afrodite Pelardis***, FA1302001486688 (Forum April 24, 2013) (<bangz.com>. Complainant itself brought multiple users to the Panel's attention. It alleged that it "does not possess the trademark rights to 'Bangz' because there are multiple 'Bangz' salons located in the Washington, DC area. However, Complainant, Bangz, Inc. has done business in New Jersey since 1994 under the 'Bangz' name and has continuously used this name since this time." One of many using the term is not good enough to prove abusive registration.).

The reason for the heightened burden is that trademarks gain reputation over time as complainants penetrate and extend their markets. Failure to establish the existence and reputation of an unregistered mark prior to the registration of the domain name supports a negative inference that it had any.[242] Alleged fear of future harm is irrelevant absent proof that respondent registered the domain name with complainant and its trademark in mind.[243]

4.01-B.2.c

4.01-B.2.c *Supplemental Register*

It has been explained above that owners of unregistered trademarks qualify for standing by proving rights acquired prior in time to registrations of domain names.[244] This does not require proof of registered marks, but it does require proof of sufficient market presence to pass the priority test.[245] Unsuccessful applicants for trademarks on the Principal Register who accept registration on the Supplemental Register are similarly placed. Such names signify lack of distinctiveness when accepted.[246] Their registrations "create[ ] a presumption that the mark[s] [are] merely a generic or descriptive term[s].[247] None of the usual presumptions are conferred on trademarks on the Supplemental Register such as "prima facie evidence of validity, ownership, and distinctiveness."[248]

---

[242] ***Transportes AEROMAR S.A. SE C.V. v. Aeromar, Inc.***, D2010-0098 (WIPO March 19, 2010) ("[I]n the absence of proof of reputation outside Mexico, at the time of domain name registration and the lack of international trademark rights, the Panel is not prepared to infer that the Respondent was aware of the Complainant's rights in the AEROMAR trademark at the time of registration of the subject domain name.") See also ***Rba Edipresse, S.L. v. Brendhan Hight / MDNH Inc.***, D2009-1580 (WIPO March 2, 2010) (Parties reside in different jurisdictions).

[243] Complainant in ***Paragon Micro, Inc. v. Julian Pretto***, D2010-0721 (WIPO July 1, 2010) argued that respondent "could 'at any time' begin using the disputed domain name in a manner that would disrupt its business and cause confusion as to the source of the parties' respective goods and services." Discussed further in "Earlier Registered Domain Names; Subsequently Acquired Trademarks" (Sec. 6.01-F.2).

[244] See Jurisprudential Overview 3.0, paragraph 1.3 and "Proving Unregistered Trademark Rights" (Sec. 4.01-B.2).

[245] ***Starpixel Marketing LLC d/b/a Vape Magazine v. Geoffrey Stonham***, D2016-0773 (WIPO June 23, 2016) ("Even though Complainant submitted more evidence of secondary meaning to the USPTO than it has submitted here, the USPTO examiner rejected the evidence as insufficient, whereupon Complainant amended its application to the Supplemental Register, which does not confer proprietary rights," citing 15 U.S.C. § 1094).

[246] Registration on the Supplemental Register means that registrant's mark is inherently a descriptive mark. 15 U.S.C. §1091. The mark may be capable of acquiring distinctiveness, which is what is meant by secondary meaning but it has to earn it in the marketplace.

[247] ***Virtual Dates, Inc. v. Xedoc Holding SA***, FA0503000433802 (Forum April 27, 2005) (<voyuer.com>).

[248] ***Advance News Service Inc. v. Vertical Axis, Inc. / Religionnewsservice.com***, D2008-1475 (WIPO December 11, 2008).

Trademarks refused registration on the Principal Register and accepted on the Supplemental Register are only capable of someday improving their status upon proof of acquired distinctiveness.[249] Under U.S. trademark law proof of "substantially exclusive and continuous use . . . as a mark . . . in commerce for the five years before the date on which the claim of distinctiveness is made" qualifies for registration on the Principal Register.[250]

Acquired distinctiveness rests on evidence that a term has become more than its primary generic or descriptive meaning. Transformation to secondary meaning (if at all) takes place over time. There can be no liability without showing respondent had knowledge of the mark before it registered the domain name. Without that proof registration on the Supplemental Register "provides complainant with no protectable rights" in the presumed mark.[251] Indeed, it is "evidence that there are no common law rights at the time of application."[252] For this reason, a complainant seeking to establish an exclusive right to a term "carries a heavy burden of proof for removing [it] from the public domain."[253]

Regardless whether complainant is currently on the Principal Register, it is not "particularly help[ed]" if at the time the domain name was registered it was on the Supplemental Register.[254] Nevertheless, there are instances in which a generic or descriptive term denied UDRP standing years earlier is later found to have matured to acquired distinctiveness. The Panel in ***Easygroup*** held that a dictionary word functioning as a mark—"easy" in this case—that achieves an international

---

[249] ***Cashmore v. URLPro***, D2004-1023 (WIPO March 14, 2005). Complainant owns US CASH SERVICE on the Supplemental Register; the PTO refused to register the mark on the Principal Register. Discussed further in "Unregistered Right Disproved by Admission" (Sec. 4.01-B.2.b).

[250] 15 U.S.C. §1052(f) (Section 2(f) of the Lanham Act): "The Director may accept as prima facie evidence that the mark has become distinctive, as used on or in connection with the applicant's goods in commerce, proof of substantially exclusive and continuous use thereof as a mark by the applicant in commerce for the five years before the date on which the claim of distinctiveness is made."

[251] Supplemental Register. ***CyberTrader, Inc. v. Bushell***, D2001-1019 (WIPO Octobrt 30, 2001). Other representative decisions include: ***Mario Rodriguez BBS Technologies, lnc. v. Guangzhou Tianji Technology Co. Ltd Pengfei Zhang***, D2009-0477 (WIPO June 11, 2009) (<continuousdataprotection.com>. The Panel found a "complete absence of proof of reputation, extensive use, acquired distinctiveness, or secondary meaning by complainant" in the descriptive phrase "continuous data protection" thus "not sufficient to support a finding of trademark rights owned by complainant.")

[252] ***Roberta Chiapetta dba Discount Hydroponics v. C.J. Morales***, D2002-1103 (WIPO January 20, 2003). However, a putative trademark can mature over time and become distinctive. See "Maturation of Trademark Reputation Over Time" (Sec. 4.01-E.2).

[253] ***Lodging Kit Company Inc. v. Natalie Soffer***, FA0909001283398 (Forum November 5, 2009) (<lodgingkits.com>).

[254] ***Wall Street.com, LLC v. Marcus Kocak / Internet Opportunity Entertainment (Sports) Limited, Sportingbet PLC.***, D2012-1193 (WIPO September 12, 2012) (<wallstreet.com>. "The evident weakness of the Complainant's UDRP claim is one of timing: the Disputed Domain Name came into the control of the Respondent's group in 2001, yet the Complainant's mark was not registered on the

reputation "puts complainant's claims on quite a different footing."[255] As with generic and descriptive terms generally that only secondarily function as marks it is not sufficient to prove a present right without establishing a reputation antedating respondent's purchase of the domain name.

4.01-B.3 4.01-B.3 Unregistered Rights Extended to Celebrities and Complainants in Civil Law Jurisdictions

Despite initial hesitations, recognition that owners of unregistered trademarks satisfied the standing requirement was quickly extended to celebrities[256] as well as complainants residing in civil law jurisdictions.[257] Standing for unregistered cultural personalities and celebrities is discussed further below. Whatever uncertainty there may initially have been has been decided by construction: complainants of unregistered marks in any jurisdiction that can satisfy the proof demands have standing to maintain an administrative proceeding.

As pointed out by a later Panel for complainants from civil law jurisdictions, "[g]iven the global nature of the domain name system and the international nature of much of the world's trading activity"[258] establishing a barrier against holders of unregistered marks from civil law jurisdictions would put them at a "disadvantage when compared to their counterparts from common law jurisdictions and those

---

Principal Register of the U.S. Patent and Trademark Office (USPTO) until 2005. Its registration on the Supplemental Register from September 2001 is not particularly helpful for the Complainant's UDRP case, since that register is used precisely for marks currently ineligible for registration on the Principal Register because, for example, they are descriptive or geographic and have not yet acquired distinctiveness.")

255 ***Easygroup IP Licensing Limited v. N. Hilton, Easycentre.com***, D2005-0935 (WIPO October 31, 2005) (<easycentre.com>).

256 ***Julia Fiona Roberts v. Russell Boyd***, D2000-0210 (WIPO May 29, 2000); ***Mick Jagger v. Denny Hammerton***, FA7000095261 (Forum September 11, 2000).

257 Jurisprudential Overview 3.0, Paragraph 1.3 ("Unregistered rights can arise even when complainant is based in a civil law jurisdiction.") See ***St Andrews Links Ltd v. Refresh Design***, D2009-0601 (WIPO June 22, 2009) in which the Panel noted that "not all jurisdictions recognise unregistered trade mark rights. Therefore if the Respondent's arguments were right it would lead to a situation that a complainant might fail in an allegation of bad faith registration simply because it conducts its activities in such a jurisdiction and the domain name in issue was registered prior to complainant having registered its rights. The Panel does not believe that the Policy operates in that way. So far as possible, the concept of bad faith should be interpreted in such a way that it has its own separate meaning under the Policy and is not dependent on the laws of the country in which complainant or respondent operates," Fn. 5. For a contra analysis see ***Antonio de Felipe v. Registerfly.com***, D2005-0969 (WIPO December 19, 2005) ("These rights derive from national laws and do not exist divorced from such laws. . . . No such nebulous international unregistered trademark right exists. However, on this occasion this is not fatal to the Complainant's case [because Complainant practices his art in a common law jurisdiction].")

258 ***S.N.C. Jesta Fontainebleau v. Po Ser***, D2009-1394 (WIPO November 21, 2009).

civil law jurisdictions, such as Germany, which make special statutory provision for unregistered trademark rights."[259]

4.01-B.4 Unregistrable and Generic Terms 4.01-B.4

The status of names alleged to be unregistered marks presuppose they qualify in all respects as marks except they are not registered. The analysis in the prior subsections concentrated on the burden of establishing qualification through proof of secondary meaning predating registration of the subject domain names. Complainants have no standing if their unregistered marks postdate the domain names.[260] Businesses may call themselves by any name, but only those names that function as marks and otherwise meet the statutory requirements are protectable against unlawful use by others.[261]

Where indicator of source is the defining attribute, words and phrases incapable of communicating anything more than their denotative meaning are unregistrable as generic terms. Many of these will be encountered in the next section and further discussed in Chapter 5, Section 5.01-D. Dictionary words, alone or combined to form common phrases—"City Utilities"[262] and "Totally Free Stuff,"[263] for example—are included in this category, although this is not to imply that words and phrases composed of common linguistic elements cannot acquire distinctiveness.[264]

---

[259] *Id.*, "The Panel takes the view that the Policy needs to be applied as uniformly as possible across the globe, particularly when dealing with a domain name in one of the gTLDs (which can be obtained and accessed around the world, irrespective of jurisdiction." See also ***MCP Holding Ltd. v. Linh Wang***, D2010-1999 (WIPO February 4, 2011) ("[U]nder highly specific circumstances, unregistered trademarks based in civil law jurisdictions may yet be protected under the Policy if narrowly defined requirements are fulfilled. In order to qualify for such protection, Complainant would have to show successfully that its name for example has become a distinctive identifier associated with its business or services.")

[260] ***Snap Inc. v. Tracy Grand, Primary Knowledge, Inc.***, D2017-0495 (WIPO June 2, 2017) (<geofilters.com>. "In the final analysis, the Complainant has failed to show that the consuming public has come to recognize 'Geofilter' as an indicator of the source of the product rather than the product itself.")

[261] ***County Bookshops Limited v. Guy Loveday***, D2000-0655 (WIPO September 22, 2000) (<countybookshops.com>. "[T]he Panelist considers that it would certainly require more than mere assertion to justify any claim to proprietary rights in such a descriptive mark.") Generic terms are words and phrases so inherently descriptive of a product or service or of an entire class of products or services as to be incapable of ever functioning as a mark.

[262] ***City Utilities of Springfield, Missouri, aka City Utilities v. Ed Davidson***, D2000-0407 (WIPO June 17, 2000). See also ***CSP International Fashion Group S.p.a. v. NameFind LLC***, 2018-0163 (WIPO March 13, 2018) (<myboutique.com>. A "boutique" is simply a store with a pronoun.

[263] ***Link Clicks Inc. d/b/a Ad Here and TOTALLYFREESTUFF.COM v. John Zuccarini d/b/a Cupcake Patrol***, D2000-1547 (WIPO January 12, 2001) (Rejected by USPTO).

[264] HOTEL BEDS registered USPTO and <hotelbeds.top> found to be using the website for phishing Complainant's customers ***Hotelbeds Spain, S.L.U. v. WhoisGuard Protected, WhoisGuard, Inc. / Macnoel Enterprise***, D2017-2304 (WIPO January 29, 2018).

However, alleging the status of a name as more than what it is —calling it an unregistered mark when it is either an unregistrable or generic term such as "Geo Filters" (an industrial term) or "Air Suspension Shop"[265] where the two-word qualifier has a specific commercial meaning—does not lift it to a higher class.

4.01-C 4.01-C Random Letters and Acronymic Trademarks

4.01-C.1 4.01-C.1 Legitimate Use by Many Third Parties

Domain names composed of few letters are "extremely prized," as potential signifiers, for their brand worthiness and for their economic value, and by investors recognizing their value in the secondary market to third parties that could legitimately lay claim to them.[266] Two, three and four letter strings have often been claimed as acronymic trademarks which respondents defend as strings of arbitrary letters. There are iconic acronyms that are not merely random strings of letters such IBM, HP, NBC and VW, but LV (a trademark owned by Louis Vuitton Malletier S.A.) could stand for Las Vegas or Latvia and other strings can be used by "unrelated third parties for goods and services seemingly different than those offered by Complainant."[267]

The greater the pool of businesses capable of claiming rights to the domain name the heavier complainant's burden to prove respondent intended it be the

---

[265] ***ABBT Netherlands B.V. v. Oliver Miessler, Miessler Automotive GmbH & Co KG***, D2015- 2378 (WIPO February 25, 2016) ("[C]ases involving claimed common law or unregistered trademarks that are comprised of descriptive or dictionary words, and therefore not inherently distinctive [impose] ... a greater onus on the complainant to present compelling evidence of secondary meaning or distinctiveness.")

[266] ***Kis v. Anything.com Ltd.***, D2000-0770 (WIPO November 20, 2000) (<kis.com>. Registration of 2 and 3 letter domain names found to be legitimate.) ***Valio Ltd. v. Telepathy, Inc.***, CAC 100558 (ADR.eu June 4, 2013) (<lgg.com>).

Two letter combination. ***Deutsch Welle v. Diamondware Capital Ltd***, D2000-1202 (WIPO January 2, 2001) (<dw.com>). Three letter combination. ***Trans Continental Records, Inc. v. Compana LLC***, D2002-0105 (WIPO April 30, 2002) (<lfo.com>. "[S]hort terms that may be appropriate for a vanity email business, or even for sale, is a legitimate business model"); ***USU AG v. DMP Enterprises***, D2009-0761 (WIPO August 17, 2009) (<usu.com>. "A 3 letter domain name is a valuable asset and the Respondent was quite at liberty to attempt to sell this asset especially in view of the Panel's finding of Respondent's use of the domain name in connection with its business").

[267] Letter strings are analyzed in ***General Nutrition Investment Company v. John Gates / The Web Group***, D2014-0982 (WIPO September 8, 2014) (Complainant argues that Respondent's registration of GNC infringes its right to exclusivity of those characters. However, "[a]lthough it is apparent to the Panel that the GNC Trademark has a long history of use and is well-known in numerous countries, it is also apparent to the Panel that the acronym 'GNC' also is used by numerous unrelated third parties for goods and services seemingly different than those offered by Complainant.") See also ***Electronic Arts Inc. v. Abstract Holdings Int'l LTD / Sheren Blackett***, FA 1415905 (FORUM January 4, 2012) ("The<ssx.com> domain name is comprised entirely of a common term that

target of the registration.[268] Unless a mark is present "in the jurisdiction where the Respondent is based [and proof of targeting conclusive it] will not support forfeiture."[269] Common words, random letters, and even acronymic trademarks are as likely as generic terms to be on the lower end of protectability, unless they have ascended the scale and achieved suggestive status or above.[270] Strings of letters meaningful to the trademark owner, for the domain name holder and consuming public may be no more than random letters,[271] and as such are owned by the first to register them.[272]

---

has many meanings apart from use in Complainant's SSX mark, including registration as a mark by other businesses and use of the term as a business name or acronym."); ***Advanced Analytical Technologies, Inc. v. Hare, Myles / URL Enterprises Ltd.***, FA161100 1701430 (Forum January 1, 2017) ("The disputed domain name <aati.com> is comprised entirely of a common acronym that has many meanings apart from the use of the AATI acronym alleged by Complainant"); ***Georg Mez AG v. Mez Kalra***, D2016-1932 (WIPO January 6, 2017) (<mez.com>. Respondent "has established that, as one might expect, the term 'MEZ' is in widespread use, particularly as an acronym and that the disputed domain name is part of a pattern of similar three-letter domain names owned by it.")

268 ***Banca Monte dei Paschi di Siena S.p.A v. Charles Kirkpatrick***, D2008-0260 (WIPO April 14, 2008) (<mps.mobi>: "The Panel acknowledges that MPS appears to be an extremely common 3-letter combination which can relate to a number of third parties other than complainant. MPS is also an acronym for a substantial number of things, including systems, societies, and syndromes"); ***BioDelivery Sciences International, Inc v HLK Enterprises, Inc. c/o Domain Admin***, FA 0804002275189 (Forum May19, 2008) (<bdsi.com>. "[B]ased on the fact that the disputed domain name and Complainant's mark contain only four letters that could stand for many things unrelated to Complainant's business, the Panel finds that Respondent's use of the disputed domain name as a portal website is a showing of rights or legitimate interests under Policy Paragraph 4(a)(ii).")

269 ***Enrique Salinas Pérez v. Buydomains.com, Inventory Management***, D2011-1950 (WIPO January 25, 2012) (<solanum.com>, a botanical, dictionary word. "While the Complainant has recently registered a trademark in [Respondent's] jurisdiction, this was not in force when the Respondent registered the disputed domain name.")

270 The Panel in ***Physik Instrumente GmbH. & Co. v. Stefan Kerner and Jeremy Kerner and Magic Moments Design Limited***, D2000-1001 (WIPO October 3, 2000) (<pi.com>) rejected Complainant's analogy of "pi" with the iconic status of "vw" and "ibm."

271 In ***CEAT Limited, CEAT Mahal, v. Vertical Axis Inc. / Whois Privacy Services Pty Ltd.***, D2011-1981 (WIPO February 20, 2012) (The majority advanced the proposition that "where the domain name is a trademark and has no dictionary meaning" it is impossible for it to be used in a non-trademark sense and awarded the domain name to Complainant on the theory of willful blindness. The dissent notes that "[i]t is clear from previous decisions that the first part of that statement is, with respect, not correct, as an acronym may give rise to a right or legitimate interest even if it is a trademark. Nor is it a requirement of the Policy or any relevant law that an acronym must have a dictionary meaning; many, if not most, acronyms would have no dictionary meaning, some have many meanings, some have whatever meaning the user gives to them and others have value simply because they are short, catchy and easy to remember." See also ***Clasen Quality Chocolate, Inc. v. Earthlink, Inc.***, D2017-0129 (WIPO March 1, 2017) (<cqc.com>).

272 Respondent in ***Rocky Mountain Health Maintenance Organization, Incorporated v. Domain Administrator / PortMedia***, FA1112001418881 (Forum January 27, 2012) specializes in 3- and

Even though random letters may have acquired distinctiveness sufficient for trademark registration they are not for that reason alone lifted on the classification scale. By happenstance a string of letters could be a trademark for complainant but simply random letters for respondent.[273] It has been pointed out that "[a]n abbreviation of a mark [or just as easily an acronym], and particularly an unregistered abbreviation [or acronym], does not necessarily itself become a mark protectable under the Policy."[274] Domains identical or confusingly similar to trademarks fall afoul of paragraph 4(a)(iii) only where complainant is able to establish that respondent chose the string of characters with its trademark in mind to take unfair advantage of its goodwill and reputation in the marketplace.

There are two exceptions to low protectability for random letters and acronymic trademarks: first, where the combinations are instantly recognizable as distinctive, well-known, or famous trademarks; second, where the domain name is composed of letters that spell out the mark plus a generic term in which the addition circles back to make reference to complainant's business.[275] Complainants who own acronymic trademarks with deep market penetration are more likely to prevail than complainants whose goods or services are offered in regional or niche markets geographically remote from respondent.[276] Unsurprisingly, the class that includes AMEX, BBC, BMW, GAP, HP, IBM, NFL[277], RBS, SONY, and VW is relatively small. It has been found not to include "daf,"[278] "lfo",[279] "cblc,"[280] "dnn"[281] and "tds,"[282] although

---

4-letter combinations. The Panel noted that the domain name in issue, <rmhp.com>, is not a true acronym for Complainant; it would have been "rmhpo." Discussed further in "'First-Come First-Served' Doctrine" (Sec. 5.01-F); ***NTI Cadcenter A/S v. Domain Admin, Ashantiplc Limited***, CAC 101591 (ADR.eu September 21, 2017) (""NTI' can be found on the web to mean many different things in world commerce.")

273 ***Aena, S.A., ENAIRE v. John Hamblin, All England Netball Association***, D2015-0996 (WIPO July 17, 2015) (AENA and acronym for "All England Netball Association").

274 ***This Old House Ventures, Inc. v. Telepathy, Inc.***, FA0602000651060 (Forum April 19, 2006) (THIS OLD HOUSE and <toh.com>). See also ***Hall & Wilcox Lawyers v. Mookstar Media Pty Ltd***, ACN 038 167 293, DAU2014-0040 (WIPO March 9, 2015) ("the evidence in the Complaint that the Complainant refers to itself as 'HW' is very modest and there is no evidence at all that anyone else refers to the Complainant as 'HW'. That is understandable as 'HW' is not distinctive by itself. Indeed, the Response includes evidence that there are some 26 registered or pending trade mark applications on the Australian Register of Trade Marks for, or based on, 'HW'. No doubt there are many other businesses and consumers who use, or could wish to use, the two letter combination without misrepresenting any association with the Complainant.")

275 An example is QNX + phone as in <qnx-phone.com>, ***QNX Software Systems Limited v. Jing Rung***, D2012-1597 (WIPO October 23, 2012). The trademark does not have to be instantly recognizable, but an added word that is referential to the trademark supports targeting. In QNX Software, Complainant is a subsidiary of RIM Limited (developer of the Blackberry smartphones and tablets), thus the suffix "phone" is meaningful for establishing bad faith registration.

276 ***Louis Vuitton Malletier S.A. v. Manifest Information Services c/o Manifest Hostmaster***, FA0609000796276 (Forum November 7, 2006) (<lv.com>).

the trademark owner of "4711"[283] has been more successful in claiming that domain names composed of those numerals infringe its exclusive rights.

A review of letter combinations finds few that are truly recognized nationally and internationally and in many cases the same letters could be claimed by parties unconnected with any particular complainant.[284] However, once the evidence shows that the website to which the domain name resolves targets a particular mark owner who is the complainant in the UDRP proceeding the respondent is called upon to explain its choice.[285]

The cases illustrate a variety of explanations for denying the complaint.[286] For example, Louis Vuitton (an internationally recognized brand) was unable to

---

277 ***National Football League Players Association, Inc. v. Cayman Trademark Trust d/b/a Trademark***, D2005-0234 (WIPO May 13, 2005) (U.S. Complainant; Cayman Islands Respondent, <nflp.com>. No trademark for the acronym NFL, but Complainant found to own an unregistered mark for it). Discussed further below.

278 ***Tenenhaus Philippe v. Telepathy, Inc***, 94355 (Forum May 17, 2000).

279 ***Trans Continental Records, Inc. v. Compana LLC***, D2002-0105 (WIPO April 30, 2002).

280 ***Bolsa de Valores de Sao Paulo S.A. BVSP v. Domainsource.com Inc.***, D2008-1362 (WIPO November 4, 2008).

281 ***Perpetual Motion Interactive Systems Inc. v. NameBubble LLC***, FA0806001212590 (Forum August 13, 2008).

282 ***Telephone and Data Systems, Inc. v. Protected Domain Services B Customer ID: NCR 813584 / Daniel Wang***, D2011-0435 (WIPO May 10, 2011).

283 ***Mäurer + Wirtz GmbH & Co. KG v. Lajos Kiss, Delux Befektetes***, D2007-1696 (WIPO February 5, 2008) (<711.org>); ***Maurer + Wirtz GmbH & Co. KG v. ROMFAB c/o Alf Temme***, FA0902001246453 (Forum March 31, 2009) (<711.us>).

284 UDRP Panels essentially adopted or found their way to a consensus that small number of letter domain names have independent value. Illustrative among early decisions is ***Trans Continental Records, Inc. v. Compana LLC***, D2002-0105 (WIPO April 30, 2002) (<lfo.com>. "[S]hort terms that may be appropriate for a vanity email business, or even for sale, is a legitimate business model"); middle decisions include ***USU AG v. DMP Enterprises***, D2009-0761 (WIPO August 17, 2009) (<usu.com>. "A 3-letter domain name is a valuable asset and the Respondent was quite at liberty to attempt to sell this asset especially in view of the Panel's finding of Respondent's use of the domain name in connection with its business"); later decisions include ***J.D.M. Software B.V. v. Robert Mauro, WDINCO***, D2017-1182 (WIPO August 23, 2017) (<jdm.com>. "In the present case, the disputed domain name consists of a three letter acronym, which the evidence shows has a very wide range of potential associations and is in fact in use by numerous business other than the Complainant."

285 See ***Archer-Daniels-Midland Company v. Shawn Downey***, D2015-0415 (WIPO May 4, 2015) (<adm.international>. The result is different where Complainant "had extensively protected its 3-letter mark through trademark registrations and, moreover, the panel found that the complainant's trademark had developed substantial goodwill and reputation such that it was a well-known mark, including in the United States where the respondent was located."

286 ***Hewlett Packard Development Company, L.P. and Hewlett Packard Company v. Rob Mikulec***, FA1106001392730 (Forum July 27, 2011) (using <hppre.com> for a commentary website. "[T]he

capture <lv.com> because despite its fame the evidence established that Respondent registered the domain name as a portal for businesses in Las Vegas.[287] Nevertheless, the use to which a domain name is put can ultimately determine whether its holder is liable under statutory law for trademark infringement.[288]

Unlike acronyms in the class that includes HP, trademarks well-known in one territory or jurisdiction may be unrecognized in another. The four-letter string "umuc" may be well-known in the State of Maryland, but excite no recognition in the U.K.[289] The Panel pointed out that

> The case is no different from the many WIPO cases where a trademark owner in Country A is unable to produce evidence from which a Panel can infer that a domain name registrant in Country B would or should have known of the fame of the mark.

It is not sufficient for a complainant's trademark to be known simply in a niche or regional market to be entitled to monopolize letters or numbers.[290] That is not the level of consumer recognition that equates to knowledge. The Panel in

---

Panel agrees with Respondent's contention that a website need not have content original to respondent in order to fall within paragraph 4 (c)(iii) of the Policy. News and commentary is news and commentary no matter the source.")

[287] ***Louis Vuitton Malletier S.A. v. Manifest Information Services c/o Manifest Hostmaster,*** FA0609000796276 (Forum November 7, 2006) (<lv.com>). See also ***Homer TLC, Inc. V. Andy Dorrani / HomeDept.com Inc.***, FA1202001429319 (Forum March 28, 2012) (Panel held there is no confusing similarity between HOME DEPOT and <homedept>. The addition of "dept," an abbreviation of "department," is not a simple misspelling of Complainant's mark, but a different identity. Complainant has no monopoly on the word "home.")

[288] See *Virtual Works, Inc. v. Volkswagen of Am., Inc.*, 238 F.3d 264, 269 (4th Cir. 2001) (Before the UDRP was implemented in 1999, disputes could be brought to the sole registrar of domain names at that time, Network Solutions, Inc. VW invoked the procedures under the Network Solutions process and Network Solutions locked the domain name <vw.net>. To unfreeze the domain name Virtual Works moved for declaratory judgment under the ACPA that its registration was legal. Judgment entered in favor of VW.)

[289] ***University of Maryland University College v. NUCOM Domain Brokers & Urban Music Underground Club***, D2002-0081 (WIPO April 29, 2002) (<umuc.com>). See, ***Hong Kong Trade Development Counsel v. Rocmary Media Group***, HK-1300549 (ADNDRC November 13, 2013) (<almc.com>). Discussed further in "The 'Primary Purpose' Test" (Sec. 6.02-A).

[290] This can apply even where complainant is well-known in its niche but not in the larger marketplace, as in NATURE (***Macmillan Publishers Limited, Macmillan Magazines Limited and HM Publishers Holdings Limited v. Telepathy, Inc***, D2002-0658 (WIPO September 27, 2002) and KIWI (***Kiwi European Holdings B.V. v. Future Media Architects, Inc.***, D2004-0848 (WIPO January 4, 2005). See also ***Rocky Mountain Health Maintenance Organization*** in which the Panel concluded that although "Complainant may think itself as being substantial, its activities do appear to be confined to a fairly small geographical area, and to a small section of a huge industry." The issue of distance is further discussed in "Nearness and Remoteness in Proving Knowledge and Intention" (Sec. 4.02-C.3).

another dispute noted that complainant's analogy of "PI" to "IBM" and "VW" is misplaced:[291]

> The 'IBM' and 'VW' letter trademarks are used by two of the world's largest industrial corporations and without doubt are 'well-known' within the meaning of Article 6bis of the Paris Convention. If 'PI' is known (or well-known) in Europe to identify Complainant, it is among a discrete group of persons who are familiar with sophisticated equipment used in technical production processes. Complainant has not submitted evidence sufficient to persuade the Panel that 'PI' is a well-known mark. It should also be noted that neither 'IBM' nor 'VW' is descriptive, while 'PI' is.

Where letters are clearly used as an abbreviation by a number of parties unconnected with complainant, absent evidence of targeting no party can claim rights superior to that of the domain name holders.[292] In rebuking Complainant in another case the Panel noted that a quick search on the Google search engine would have "shown that 'aro' is used by many different users . . . as an abbreviation."[293] These holdings are consistent with decisions by other Panels from the earliest decided cases.[294] The principle is captured in the following quotation: "[g]iven the brevity of the disputed domain name, the obscurity of the mark, the geographic locations of the parties, and the nature of the parties' activities, it would not be reasonable to infer that Respondent had actual knowledge of Complainant or its mark when it registered the disputed domain name."[295]

There are two factors critical to the outcomes in these disputes, namely complainants' lack of any special identification with particular strings of random letters

---

291 ***Physik Instrumente GmbH. & Co. v. Stefan Kerner and Jeremy Kerner and Magic Moments Design Limited***, D2000-1001 (WIPO October 3, 2000) (<pi.com>).

292 ***Koninklijke KPN N.V. v. Konstantinos Zournas***, D2008-0055 (WIPO April 12, 2008) (<kpn.info>) (The Panel found that the letters "'kpn' could stand for entities ranging from the Greek State-founded Youth Information Centre, to the Polish Conservative Party, a Catholic Church in Sweden, the IATA Code for an airport in the United States, a Music Academy, a Travel Company, a Finnish Company and an acronym for Kahn Process Networks.") The Panel in ***CTV Inc. v. Murat Yikilmaz***, FA0804001177671 (Forum June 10, 2008) denied the Complaint for <ctv.com> over dissent that argued that registering "a domain name without a prior Google search seems to me to be wilful blindness."

293 ***ARO v. Philip Price***, D2005-0498 (WIPO August 1, 2005) (<aro.com>) (Respondent defaulted).

294 ***VZ VermögensZentrum AG v. Anything.com***, D2000-0527 (WIPO August 22, 2000) (<vz.com>) and ***KCTS Television Inc. v. Get-on-the-Web Limited***, D2001-0154 (WIPO April 20, 2001) (<kcts.com>).

295 ***Hydrologic Services, Inc.. v. Name Delegation c/o Steven Sacks***, FA0605000707617 (Forum July 12, 2006) (<hysr.com>) (unanimous three member Panel). Cf.: ***The Lords Commissioners of Her Majesty's Treasury v. ITIL International***, D2005-0230 (WIPO May 10, 2005) in which the Panel ordered the transfer of <itil.com> but in that case respondent failed to file a response and the Panel credited complainant's evidence that its mark had achieved worldwide prominence in the industry in which respondent apparently functioned.

and words, and respondents' prior or contemporaneous rights to register letters and words common in the public domain. Domain names composed of random letters are valuable precisely because of their desirability to many parties even though by happenstance they may be identical or confusingly similar to complainants' marks. For domain names composed of common words parties in different (even though related) fields must live with the fact that "small differences matter."[296]

4.01-C.2

4.01-C.2 Disfavoring Respondent

The scale tips against respondent where complainant's evidence demonstrates targeting. The characters then take on an identity specific to complainant. If the domain name is passively held and the characters spell out well-known trademarks (which ordinarily supports lack of rights or legitimate interests), but there is no direct proof of targeting, Panels find bad faith where it is "[im]possible to conceive of any plausible actual or contemplated active use of the domain name by respondent that would not be illegitimate."[297] National recognition disfavors respondent when there is either common domicile[298]; or the parties are in the same region of the country[299]; or the content of its website evidences knowledge of complainant or its mark.[300] In ***National Football***, the Panel found that when complainant is equally well-known by its unregistered acronym and by its registered name

> there is no need to explore the legal intricacies of the relationship between registered marks and possible derivative protection to a Complainant's initials that are not contained in formal registrations when, as here, complainant can

---

296 See also "Common Words, Common Phrases" (Sec. 5.01-D.1.c).

297 Targeting is ordinarily deduced from website content, but if the domain name is being passively held the applicable principle is that formulated in ***Telstra Corporation Limited v. Nuclear Marshmallows***, D2000-0003 (WIPO February 18, 2000) construing paragraph 4(a)(iii) of the Policy. Discussed further in "Inactive or Passive Use" (Sec. 5.01-B.2).

Lufthansa was successful with <lh.com>, ***Deutsche Lufthansa AG v. Future Media Architects, Inc.***, FA0802001153492 (Forum April 17, 2008). The registration was ordered transferred over dissent. The principle that the "traditional analyses of the rights to or legitimate interests element" is superseded when the "business model involves the indiscriminate acquisition" of domain names, should be tested in a court proceeding. Within the stipulated period respondent filed a post-UDRP action under the ACPA in the district court for the Southern District of New York. See "Plenary Adjudication After an Adverse Decision" (Sec. 8.01-B).

298 ***Irish Institute of Purchasing and Materials Management v. Association for Purchasing and Supply, and Owen O'Neill***, D2001-0472 (WIPO May 30, 2001) (Irish parties; <iipmm.com>).

299 ***Freedom of Information Foundation of Texas v. Steve Lisson***, D2001-0256 (WIPO April 22, 2001) (<foift.com>, both parties are Texas residents).

300 ***National Football League Players Association, Inc. v. Cayman Trademark Trust d/b/a Trademark***, D2005-0234 (WIPO May 13, 2005) (U.S. Complainant; Cayman Islands Respondent, <nflp.com>).

and has submitted overwhelming proof that establishes its common law rights to its acronym.

Good or bad faith depends as much on the composition of the domain name (whether there are affixes to the second level domain or misspellings, for example) as it does on content. Thus, the Panel in ***Hewlett-Packard*** held that the "letters 'HP' . . . have acquired a famous and distinctive secondary meaning, even though one may research and find HP acronyms."[301] However, the proof in that case turned on the affix "web" to "hp," <hpweb.com>. Respondent's second level domain has no semantic value. Rather, the addition points to the conclusion that the domain name was registered for its trademark value, though indignantly denied by an appearing (in this case, Korean) respondent. Abusive registration is reinforced by calling attention—"web"—to the business products for which complainant is known.[302]

Unaccompanied strings of characters that may reasonably be associated with other parties than complainant reveal respondent's intention by choice of content. In a case involving the three-letter string "str" (for "Smith Travel Research"), the Panel noted that the acronym was "a very popular abbreviation and has been used by many businesses."[303] However, "[d]espite Respondent's protestations to the contrary . . . complainant and respondent both compete in the travel business." The Panel concluded that the "Respondent was clearly trying to associate its offerings with the goodwill of Complainant's well-known mark."[304]

4.01-C.3 Offers of Proof 4.01-C.3

Insufficiency of proof can bedevil both complainants and respondents. For complainants, their brands may be known but not by the acronyms in issue. For example, acronyms unregistered as trademarks but assigned as symbols by stock exchanges may qualify for common law protection under the Policy but are unlikely to be "widely known by those outside of its business or those not familiar with stock symbols on the New York Stock [or any other] Exchange."[305]

---

301 ***Hewlett-Packard Company v. Kim Yong Hwan***, FA0008000095358 (Forum September 7, 2000) (U.S. Complainant; Korean Respondent, <hpweb.com>. "Respondent is not a 'bad man,' but objective reality and a presumption of deception militates against him," citing *Interstellar Starship Services, Ltd. v. Epix, Inc.* 184 F.3d 1107, 1111 (9th Cir. 1999) where the court observed that "ISS became aware of the 'EPIX' trademark when it applied for its own registration of 'EPIX.' Adopting a designation with knowledge of its trademark status permits a presumption of intent to deceive.")

302 Further discussed in "Opportunistic Bad Faith" (Sec. 6.01-C.1).

303 ***Smith Travel Research, Inc. v. Victor An***, FA0904001259999 (Forum June 15, 2009). In fact, the USPTO database lists 95 alive and dead registrations that include the letters "str."

304 *Id.*

305 ***Equifax Inc. v. Future Media Architects Inc.***, FA0805001195133 (Nat Arb. Forum July 23, 2008) (<efx.com>).

The difficulty of marshaling proof for bad faith registration is illustrated in ***Reckitt Benckiser***.[306] Complainant has a worldwide marketing presence. Its trademark includes the letters RB which is also its stock symbol on the FTSE 100. The Panel found that although complainant had a protectable unregistered right in the RB mark it offered no evidence that it was known by the acronym when respondent registered <rb.net>. Its FTSE symbol, though apparently obtained before the registration of the domain name, did not become effective until many years later. Timing of the trademark and domain name registrations are clearly significant factors complainant has to address. In ***Reckitt Benckiser*** Complainant failed to offer evidence that answered the question, "How could respondent have known about its trademark at the time it registered the domain name?"

Respondents are unlikely to forfeit their choices absent proof of targeting, except in the case of pornography where the trademark is distinctive and well-known and there is evidence that pointing to offending websites (or threatening to) is tantamount to extortion.[307] Proof of bad faith registration must necessarily be stronger in quality and more persuasive as the trademark slides to the lower end of the classification scale with the concomitant increase in the number of potential users of the term.

As previously noted, absent proof that consumers associate a sign or symbol exclusively with complainant's goods or services, respondents are likely to avoid forfeiting the domain name. This is particularly true if the parties are in different geographic locations or the combination of letters is nondescript even though meaningful to the complainant.

However, a registrant does not gain legitimacy by adopting an acronym that mimics an inherently distinctive trademark, on the theory that the same letters work equally well with its own trade name.[308] Respondents in the cited case argued that "they adopted 'ets' because it was the natural acronym of their trade name "Educational Training Service," but they failed to present any evidence

---

306 ***Reckitt Benckiser Plc v. Eunsook Wi.***, D2009-0239 (WIPO May 20, 2009) (Complainant's name and trademark were the result of a merger. However, "this is not a typical merger case where a complainant establishes broad media coverage that is likely to have come to the attention of the respondent.") See "Acting on Media Coverage and Insider Information" (Sec. 6.01-C.1.b).

307 ***The National Deaf Children's Society and Ndcs Limited v. Nude Dames, Chat, Sex,*** D2002-0128 (WIPO April 19, 2002) (Complainant's acronym "NDCS" had acquired sufficient common law trademark protection to challenge the domain name registration of <ndcs.org>). See also, ***SIX Group AG v. Xedoc Holding SA***, D2012-1548 (WIPO October 11, 2012) (Involving the three letter string "six." Respondent redirects the domain name to <sexvideos.com>. "[T]here is extensive third party use of the term 'six', both as trade marks and as domain names, and that it cannot by any stretch of the imagination be considered famous or exclusively associated with the Complainant.") Discussed further in "Commercial Gain from Tarnishment" (Sec. 6.05-C).

308 ***Educational Testing Service v. Educational Training Services, Sonny Pitchumani, Randal Nelson and MLI Consulting, Inc.***, D2004-0324 (WIPO June 18, 2004).

demonstrating they had been commonly known as ETS prior to registration of the domain name.[309]

4.01-D A Question of Standing 4.01-D

4.01-D.1 Personal Names 4.01-D.1

4.01-D.1.a *Not Source Indicators* *4.01-D.1.a*

UDRP's limited jurisdiction extends to personal names only if they qualify as trademarks.[310] Some attempt has been made to justify widening the included class, as discussed below, but the argument in its favor has failed to persuade other panelists and the consensus remains undisturbed.[311] If the personal name is not in commerce as the source of goods or services the complainant has no remedy under the UDRP,[312] but may have recourse under statutory law.[313] Excluded are living persons with secure reputations engaged in the figurative scrum of their businesses or professions but whose names are not source indicators of goods or services in a trademark sense.

---

309 The "commonly known defense" under 4(c)(ii) of the Policy is further discussed below in "Commonly Known By The Domain Name" (Sec. 5.03).

310 The Lanham Act, 15 U.S.C. §1052(e)(4) provides that "No trademark by which the goods of the applicant may be distinguished from the goods of others shall be refused registration on the principal register on account of its nature *unless* it . . . [c]onsists of a mark which is primarily merely a surname" (emphasis added on "unless").

311 See Jurisprudential Overview 3.0, Paragraph 1.5.2: "Can a complainant show UDRP-relevant rights in a personal name?" Yes, "where a personal name is being used as a trademark-like identifier in trade or commerce, the complainant may be able to establish unregistered or common law rights in that name for purposes of standing to file a UDRP case where the name in question is used in commerce as a distinctive identifier of the complainant's goods or services."

312 Report of the Second WIPO Internet Domain Name Process, The Recognition of Rights and the Use of Names In the Internet Domain Name System, dated September 3, 2001 (the "WIPO Second Report"). The WIPO Second Report concludes that "the application of the UDRP to the protection of personal names [is authorized only] when they constitute trademarks," Paragraph 179. A couple of decisions filed before the publication of the Report found in Complainants' favor, ***Philip Berber v. Karl Flanagan and KP Enterprises***, D2000-0661 (WIPO August 8, 2000) and ***Steven Rattner v. BuyThisDomanName (John Pepin)***, D2000-0402 (WIPO July 3, 2000). That a complainant is in business operating under a name other than her personal name is not proof of common law trademark in her personal name. ***Karen Finerman v Ben Johnston / Bookclout***, FA1412001596768 (Forum February 12, 2015).

313 The Lanham Act provides a remedy for cyberpiracy of personal names that do not qualify for trademark protection, formerly codified at 15 U.S.C. §1129 (1)(A), now 15 U.S.C. §8131 (Cyberpiracy protections for individuals). Section 8131 provides that "Any person who registers a domain name that consists of the name of *another living person*, or a name substantially and confusingly similar thereto, *without that person's consent*, with the *specific intent to profit* from such name *by selling the domain name for financial gain* to that person or any third party, shall be liable in a civil action by such person (emphasis added). See statement by Senator Orren Hatch: "As with trademark

This rule applies however extraordinary the individual's contribution is to business, science, politics, the professions, and the Academy. [314] The WIPO Report recognizes that it may result in an "injustice" and is undoubtedly an unhappy limitation: "many sensitivities [will be] offended by the unauthorized registration of personal names as domain names" and the "result is that there are some perceived injustices."[315] Among the earliest UDRP decisions Panelists granted unregistered trademark status to notable personalities and celebrities in the fields of sports, entertainment, culture, and media whose names are branded by their contributions.[316] This list of protected persons extends to eponymous founders of businesses but not to non-marquee founders.[317] It does not include distinguished employees[318] or law partners.[319]

---

cybersquatting, cybersquatting of personal names poses similar threats to consumers and e-commerce in that it causes confusion as to the source or sponsorship of goods or services, including confusion as to the sponsorship or affiliation of websites bearing individuals' names. In addition, more and more people are being harmed by people who register other people[']s names and hold them out for sale for huge sums of money or use them for various nefarious purposes." 145 Cong. Rec. S14,986, S15,019 daily ed. Nov. 19, 1999).

In an unreported case from the Middle District of Florida, *Salle v. Meadows*, 6:07-cv-1089-Orl-31 (August 6, 2007), the defendant admitted that he purchased the domain name and attempted to sell it to the plaintiff for $9500, but claimed the plaintiff was indebted to him in that amount and he had no intent to profit when he registered the domain name, because he merely attempted to recover money that he was owed. The court rejected this defense: "cyber extortion is not a permissible way of recovering a debt" and ordered the domain name transferred. See also *Schmidheiny v. Weber*, 319 F.3d 581 (3d Cir. 2003) (granting the complaint); *Carl V. Bernardjcarl.com.*, 409 Fed.Appx. 628 (4th Cir. 2010) (dismissing the complaint on the grounds that defendant had no "specific intent to profit" from the domain registration, thus there was no violation of Section 8131); *Randazza v. Cox*, 920 F.Supp.2d 1151 (D. Nevada, 2013) (granting temporary injunction and ordering the domain names transferred to plaintiff).

California has a robust antipiracy statute at Cal. Bus. & Prof. Code §17525. New York has a similar but less robust statute at NY General Business Law §148.

314 ***Sir Peter Scott v. Dr. Howard Fredrics***, D2009-0276 (WIPO May 1, 2009) ("There is no evidence that the Complainant has commercially exploited his name in trade, for example as an author or broadcaster to a sufficient extent for it to constitute a 'brand'. It does not appear that the mark 'Sir Peter Scott' would be understood by a substantial segment of the public, when used in connection with services or business, as necessarily referring to the Complainant.")

315 Report of the Second WIPO Internet Domain Name Process, paragraph 199. Noncommercial and fair use of celebrity names is discussed in "Celebrity Names and Fan Sites" (Sec. 5.04-A.4). There is a secondary consequence when the person held and inadvertently lost the domain name because without a trademark there will be no actionable claim. See 4.01-G (Right of Trademark Owner to Recapture Domain Name After Lapse of Registration.)

316 See WIPO Overview 2.0, paragraph 1.6: "A trademark-equivalent basis has been found in the common law action of passing-off, which is generally intended to prevent the making of misrepresentations to the public in the context of trade, and which if established may provide grounds for reliance on a personal name for the purpose of the UDRP." Jurisprudential Overview 3.0, Paragraph 1.3 ("availability of trademark-like protection").

Complainants well-known in their professions have been rejected on the grounds that it is not they who are associated with the source of goods or services but the businesses they manage or in which they have controlling financial interests.[320] In ***Israel Harold Asper***, the panelist stated that it "would be helpful in these personal name cases . . . [to explain] what the nature of the commercial connection would be in complainant's use of the Domain Name in issue." In this case, complainant "has not shown on a preponderance of the evidence that he uses his personal name for the purpose of the merchandising or other commercial promotion of goods or services, or that he intended to do so."

Attempts have been made to work around the limitation by associating complainant with owners of well-known and famous trademarks, but that approach only highlights the institutions or businesses in which they are involved.[321] Complainant has to prove that his or her name has been used in commerce for "the purpose of merchandising or other commercial promotion of goods or services." A person who disclaims public life and whose "reputation has been established by the work [he does], not through self-publicity"[322] cannot prove a common law trademark right.[323]

---

[317] A number of decisions have diverged from the consensus on the issue of founders. They are collected and discussed in ***Thomas Pritzker, The Pritzker Organization, LLC v. Richard Brown***, D2009-0911 (WIPO October 12, 2009) and below in "Expanding the General Rule" (Sec. 4.01-D.1.b.ii).

[318] ***Jonathan Ive v. Harry Jones***, D2009-0301 (WIPO May 5, 2009).

[319] ***Gregg M. Mashberg v. Crystal Cox***, D2011-0677 (WIPO June 30, 2011), ***Allen Fagin v. Crystal Cox***, D2011-0678 (WIPO June 30, 2011), ***Joseph Leccese v. Crystal Cox***, D2011-0679 (WIPO June 30, 2011) ("The evidence in th[ese] case[s] falls short. The record[s] before the Panel[s] suggest[] that Complainant[s] [are] highly respected, prominent lawyer[s] who [are] partner[s] with a major law firm. There is insufficient evidence here that Complainant[s] market[] or provide[] services independently of the Proskauer law firm. Rather, it appears that the Proskauer firm is the platform on which Complainant[s] provide[] [their] legal services.")

[320] ***Israel Harold Asper v. Communication X Inc.***, D2001-0540 [WIPO June 11, 2001]) and "Ted Turner" (R.E. 'Ted' ***Turner and Ted Turner Film Properties, LLC v. Mazen Fahmi***, D2002-0251 (WIPO July 4, 2002) (<tedturner.com>. Although denied over a vigorous dissent: "The name 'Turner' has been used in the names of several media companies, in addition to its inclusion in the name of complainant Ted Turner Film Properties. The majority needs numerous pages of explanation to dispel the obvious and lose the forest for the trees.")

[321] ***Planned Parenthood Federation of America, Inc. and Gloria Feldt v. Chris Hoffman***, D2002-1073 (WIPO February 21, 2003) (complaint on behalf of Complainant's president, Complaint denied); ***David Pecker v. Mr. Ferris***, D2006-1514 (WIPO January 15, 2007) (businessman, Complaint denied).

[322] ***Jonathan Ive***, *supra*. Ive, who is renowned for his contributions to Apple Inc., stated that "I do not usually give interviews . . . I seek to avoid publicity. I'm a very private person." The evidence indicated that complainant had pending applications for trademarks of his name. The Panel stated that a "different result . . . could occur if or when complainant's Community Trade Marks are registered, or if for instance Apple Inc., takes different steps in relation to the branding and use of

Mere politicians are equally ill-served: "an individual politician's name, no matter how famous,[324] is outside the scope of the Policy since it is not connected with commercial exploitation as set out in the Second WIPO Report,"[325] although there have been anomalies.[326] On the other hand, political organizations enjoy trademark status under the trademark laws of the United States. Thus, political action committees are protected even though the politicians for whom they are formed are not.[327]

4.01-D.1.b

4.01-D.1.b *Source Indicators*

4.01-D.1.b.i

4.01-D.1.b.i ***General Rule: Common Law Rights***

Like businesses, individuals can satisfy the paragraph 4(a)(i) test for unregistered rights by demonstrating 1) their names are recognized by consumers as source indicators of goods or services; and 2) their marks preceded the domain name registration dates.[328] However, success in protecting a personal name that "has been used in trade or commerce" depends on the degree of fame or renown of the person.

Complainant's personal name. In such circumstances, complainant may be entitled to file another UDRP case."

[323] Similarly, ***The Reverend Dr. Jerry Falwell and The Liberty Alliance v. Gary Cohen, Profile.net and God.Info***, D2002-0184 (WIPO June 3, 2002) ("Complainant is careful to avoid any suggestion that he has exploited his name for 'materialistic' or 'commercial' purposes.")

[324] Former President Clinton was unsuccessful in ***William J. Clinton and The William J. Clinton Presidential Foundation v. Web of Deception***, FA0904001256123 (Forum June 1, 2009) (<williamclinton.com>, <williamjclinton.com> and <presidentbillclinton.com>).

[325] ***Kathleen Kennedy Townsend***, D2002-0030 (WIPO April 11, 2002) (Maryland politician); ***Peter Bober v. National Institute for Mortgage Education***, D2008-1668 (WIPO December 15, 2008) (Mayor of the City of Hollywood, Florida, and a lawyer; is the author of scholarly articles but not of commercially successful books); ***Fields for Senate v. Toddles Inc.***, D2006-1510 (WIPO March 14, 2007) (New York politician) (Complaint dismissed).

[326] Decided prior to the Report of the Second WIPO Internet Domain Name Process: ***Anne McLellan v. smartcanuk.com***, AF 303a and AF 303b (eResolution August 8, 2000) (Panel found for Complainant, a Canadian politician). Anomaly, post Report: ***Eliot Spitzer v. Eliot Spitzer***, FA0702000919828 (Forum March 30, 2007) (<eliotspitzer.com> and <eliotspitzer.org>. Spitzer is not associated as a source indicator of goods or services. However, according to the Panel complainant was entitled to the domain name "as Governor of New York and as a prominent public figure, establishing secondary meaning in the mark.")

[327] *National Rural Electric Cooperative Association v. National Agricultural Chemical Association*, 26 U.S.P.Q. 2d 1294 (D.C.D.C. 1992). Political organizations that adopt platforms and endorse candidates are also protected. See *United We Stand America Inc. v. United We Stand, America New York Inc.*, 44 U.S.P.Q. 2d 1351 (2d Cir. 1997). Both types of political entities act "in commerce" and have trademark rights in their names.

[328] WIPO Final Report. Paragraph 177 reads: "The status of the personal name as a potential asset may be secured through the registration of a trademark (or service mark). Most national laws, and the Agreement on Trade Related Aspects of Intellectual Property Rights (the TRIPS Agreement), explicitly recognize that personal names are eligible for registration as trademarks."

The greater his or her fame or renown the easier to satisfy the burden of proof. Concomitantly, the lower the fame or renown the higher the proof requirement. The Panel in ***Fox News Network*** stated the proposition in the following way[329]:

> As the degree of fame decreases from clearly identifiable celebrities with worldwide renown, to nationwide renown or to less well-known authors, actors or businessmen with limited renown in a specific field, the burden of proof on complainant increases and the need for clear and convincing evidence becomes paramount.

A wide range of personalities and celebrities have successfully challenged registrants' choices of domain names, although some panelists in early cases were cautious in recognizing unregistered trademarks for celebrities.[330] Nevertheless, there was a nascent consensus.[331] Common law (unregistered marks) have been granted to: film and stage stars,[332] television performers,[333] athletes,[334] columnists,[335] musicians,[336] fashion designers[337], fashion models,[338] and authors.[339] Length of time between registration of the domain name and a complainant's assertion of his or

---

329 ***Fox News Network, L.L.C. v. C&D International Ltd. and Whois Privacy Protection Service***, D2004-0108 (WIPO July 22, 2004) (Complaint granted for <tonysnow.com>. Tony Snow was a television personality who hosted the "Tony Snow Show" and news programs).

330 In ***Bruce Springsteen v. Jeff Burgar and Bruce Springsteen Club***, D2000-1532 (WIPO January 25, 2001) (complaint denied over a strong dissent) the majority gave Respondent the benefit of the doubt. However, the ***Springsteen*** decision was subsequently repudiated in ***Kevin Spacey v. Alberta Hot Rods***, FA0205000114437 (Forum August 1, 2002) in which one of the panelists also sat on the Springsteen Panel as the Presiding Panelist. He noted that Respondent in the earlier proceeding was given the "benefit of the doubt" at that time. See also ***Judy Larson v. Judy Larson Club***, FA0101000096488 (Forum March 13, 2001) (the Majority opinion in ***Springsteen*** is "soundly rejected.")

331 ***Moynahan v. Fantastic Sites, Inc.*** D2000-1083 (WIPO October 22, 2000) (Movie actress, born Kathryn Bridget Moynahan, adopted the public name "Bridget Moynahan" sometime in 1989).

332 ***Julia Fiona Roberts v. Russell Boyd***, D2000-0210 (WIPO May 29, 2000).

333 ***Larry King v. Alberta Hot Rods***, D2005-0570 (WIPO July 21, 2005).

334 ***Freddy Adu v. Frank Fushille***, D2004-0682 (WIPO October 27, 2004), ***Marino v. Video Images Prods***, D2000-0598 (WIPO August 2, 2000), ***ETW*** [Tiger Woods] ***Corp. v. Jim Mallamo d/b/a Kids Golf***, FA0302000145284 (Forum April 17, 2003), ***Maria Sharapova v. Whois Privacy Protection Service, Inc. c/o Whois Agent***, FA0601000621125 (Forum February 17, 2006).

335 ***Ann Coulter v. Mark Vadnais***, FA0212000137221 (Forum February 11, 2003).

336 ***Madonna Ciccone, p/k/a Madonna v. Dan Parisi and Madonna.com***, D2000-0847 (WIPO October. 12, 2000); ***Dr. Billy Taylor v. Phil Maher***, D2009-0154 (WIPO March 27, 2009).

337 ***Roland Mouret v. Domains by Proxy, Inc. and Sonia Liang***, D2009-1435 (WIPO December 10, 2009).

338 ***Ms. Esther Heesch v. esther heesch***, FA1306001505507 (Forum July 26, 2013).

339 ***Margaret Drabble v. Old Barn Studios Limited***, D2001-0209 (WIPO March 26, 2001); ***Julian Barnes v. Old Barn Studios Limited***, D2001-0121 (WIPO March 26, 2001); ***Dr. Michael Crichton v. In Stealth Mode***, D2002-0874 (WIPO November 25, 2002). This list of celebrities is by no means complete. See also "Celebrity Names and Fan Sites" (Sec. 5.04-A.4).

her right is not fatal. In some cases the interval is measured in years.[340] However, protection does not necessarily extend to performers who adopt common dictionary words as their stage names.[341] "Neither does celebrity status on its own provide a complainant with rights in a trademark or service mark."[342]

Merely having a famous name, such as a member of a wealthy family has been rejected as a basis for unregistered trademark rights.[343] In the case cited in the footnote the Panel stated that complainant "does not appear to have become well-known because she has written books." Rather, "[s]he was well-known before that, due in part to her membership of the well-known Rausing family." It does not "necessarily follow that every well-known person who writes a book (or any other kind of publication) obtains trademark rights in their name."

Critical to the determination is whether Birgit Rausing became well-known for her creative work or through her professional or social status: that is, whether it is her creative work for which she is known and recognized in the marketplace. Hillary Rodham Clinton, for example, succeeded on the basis of her worldwide recognition and as an author rather than as a *mere* politician. The "HILLARY CLINTON mark has become distinctive through Complainant's use and exposure of the mark in the marketplace and through use of the mark in connection with Complainant's political activities, including a successful Senate campaign,"[344] but her husband's complaint (as noted in an earlier footnote) as merely a politician and ex-President was denied.

4.01-D.1.b.ii

4.01-D.1.b.ii *Expanding the General Rule*

UDRP jurisprudence on surnames as unregistered trademarks for business leaders is not entirely consistent. The general rule is that acceptance of common law rights is limited to those whose names are directly associated with goods and services. A "mark comprising a personal name [is said to have] . . . acquired secondary meaning if a substantial segment of the public understands the designation, when used in connection with services or business, not as a personal name, but as referring

340 ***Ashley Judd v. Alberta Hot Rods, Jeff Burgar***, D2009-1099 (WIPO September 25, 2009) (domain name registered in 1996). Lapse of time versus laches is discussed further in "Laches vs. Lapse of Time" (Sec. 5.01-E.1).

341 ***Sumner p/k/a Sting v. Urvan***, D2000-0596 (WIPO July 24, 2000) (<sting.com>. "[T]he personal name in this case is also a common word in the English language, with a number of different meanings.")

342 ***Vanisha Mittal v. info@setrillonario.com***, D2010-0810 (WIPO August 8, 2010).

343 ***Birgit Rausing, AB Tetra Pak v. Darren Morgan***, D2008-0212 (WIPO April 5, 2008) (Of course "[a]ny already well-known person who writes a book trades on their name, to the extent [at least] that their pre-existing fame is likely to generate sales of their book.")

344 ***Hillary Rodham Clinton v. Michele Dinoia a/k/a SZK.com***, FA0502000414641 (Forum March 18, 2005) (<hillaryclinton.com>).

to a particular source or organization."[345] Eponymous founders qualify because their names are used in a trademark sense. All others fail because their names have no such association in consumers' minds.[346]

For some panelists, rejecting protection for business leaders has become less categorical. A divergent view dating from cases decided in 2005 takes the position that the rule should be extended to include those behind the scenes,[347] but that has failed to create any collegial interest and is likely a dead end. Non-eponymous but engaged leaders' names may (according to this view) qualify as trademarks, but to prevail complainant must offer a denser resume or a more compelling narrative of his or her association with the goods or services offered in the marketplace.[348]

Under this view leaders have been found to qualify for unregistered rights of their personal names on proof of their association with the businesses they own or manage. Thus, a Steven Rattner passes[349] but an Asper and Turner do not [350] even though the latter two (like Rattner) were the driving forces behind their numerous business enterprises. The Panel in ***Thomas Pritzker*** identifies ***Chung, Kotak Mahindra*** and ***Soin International***[351] as advocating a construction of the Policy that he regards as heretical.[352] These Panels have expanded the general rule to include persons significant in their businesses who are not themselves source indicators of goods or services.

---

345 ***Ahmanson Land Company v. Save Open Space and Electronic Imaging Systems***, D2000-0858 (WIPO December 4, 2000).

346 ***Falwell v. Cohn***, D2002-0184 (WIPO June 3, 2002).

347 The Panel in Thomas Pritzker, ***The Pritzker Organization, LLC v. Richard Brown***, D2009-0911 (WIPO October 12, 2009) sets forth a full and articulate review of the law.

348 ***Chung, Mong Koo and Hyundai Motor Company v. Individual***, D2005-1068 (WIPO December 21, 2005) (<chungmongku.com>) discussed further below, and ***Kotak Mahindra Bank Limited v. Richard Brown***, D2008-0243 (WIPO April 9, 2008) (<udaykotak.com>).

349 ***Steven Rattner v. BuyThisDomanName (John Pepin)***, D2000-0402 (WIPO July 3, 2000) (As previously noted, this case antedated the WIPO Second Report).

350 ***Israel Harold Asper v. Communication X Inc.***, D2001-0540 (WIPO June 11, 2001) and "Ted Turner" (***R.E. 'Ted' Turner and Ted Turner Film Properties, LLC v. Mazen Fahmi***, D2002-0251 (WIPO July 4, 2002).

351 ***Soin International LLC v. Michael W. Solley, PrivateRegContact Admin/TECH***, D2007-0094 (WIPO March 7, 2007).

352 Heretical, because on their face the WIPO Reports of 1999 (para. 167) and 2001 (para. 181 et. seq.) do not support such view. Paragraph 167 recommended that the Policy apply only to trademarks and service marks. The Second WIPO Report deals with the issue at greater length and reaches the same conclusion. Jurisprudential Overview, Paragraph 1.5.2 states that "Merely having a famous name (such as a businessperson or cultural leader who has not demonstrated use of their personal name in a trademark/source-identifying sense), or making broad unsupported assertions regarding the use of such name in trade or commerce, would not likely demonstrate unregistered or common law rights for purposes of standing to file a UDRP complaint."

In ***Chung*** the Panel stated that the problem "eventually . . . come[s] down to whether the evidence establishes [a] sufficient . . . nexus between the name itself and its use and association in trade and commerce" and provided the following guidelines to establish whether there was proof of such a nexus.[353] These include:

- the extent to which the commercial community identifies the individual with the company;
- the extent to which the individual is seen by relevant media and sections of the public as the alter ego and driving force behind the company;
- the extent of the personal ownership of the company by the individual;
- the degree of personal control that the individual exercises over the enterprise;
- the extent to which the individual is identified with any major achievements of the enterprise; and
- whether it can be said that the individual and/or the company has a demonstrable interest in protecting the individual's name for commercial use.

In other words, these non-eponymous leaders emerge from their narratives as having the same status as eponymous leaders except their companies do not adopt their leaders' names. The Panel in ***Thomas Pritzker*** rejects this construction entirely because it "creates a special exception for prominent business persons from the requirement that a personal name must be used as a trademark or service mark to be entitled to protection under the UDRP," which is inconsistent with "the majority view of panelists, and with paragraph 4(a)(i)."[354]

4.01-D.2

4.01-D.2 Geographic Terms as Domain Names

4.01-D.2.a

4.01-D.2.a *Purely Descriptive of Location*

Geographic identifiers purely descriptive of location are not registrable as trademarks[355] and are not protectable under the UDRP.[356] The Second WIPO Report states that this was a "difficult area" to consider. Not only were views expressed

---

[353] The Panel in ***Thomas Pritzker*** is critical of this approach: "Paragraph 4(a)(i) of the Policy requires complainant to prove that the domain name at issue is identical or confusingly similar to a trademark or service mark in which complainant has rights. It does not refer to a nexus between the personal name and its use in trade and commerce. It does not refer to the respondent's state of mind. It does not refer to the respondent's conduct. It does not refer to respondent at all.

It does say that complainant must prove that complainant has rights in a trademark or service mark and that the domain name at issue is confusingly similar or identical to that trademark or service mark."

[354] Unless ***Chung*** is a dead end the divergence of views is problematic in that the decision will depend on who is drawn as Panel. Complainants will hope for the ***Chung*** Panel; respondents for the ***Thomas Pritzker*** Panel, thus undermining predictability. See also ***The Key to Polo Enterprises. Corp. v. PrivacyProtect.org / Domain Admin.***, FA1112001420371 (Forum January 23, 2012). The consensus favors the Pritzker approach.

by participating stakeholders divided, but they were "ardently held." The Report's authors concluded that without complete harmonization of the law governing geographic indicators the attempt to legislate rights was "doomed to fail." They believed "[p]anels would be put in the awkward position of having to make decisions with insufficient guidance available to them, which would lead inevitably to the undesired creation of new law." Moreover, to legislate rights "would jeopardize the UDRPs long-term viability as an effective dispute resolution system":

> This risk is considered particularly acute in the area of geographical indications because there has been, for many years now, continuing intense debate internationally between governments on the subject matter.

This consideration "alone is a cause for reflection about the desirability of introducing a modification dealing with this area to a consensus-based dispute-resolution procedure that is functioning efficiently and cost effectively."[357] For these reasons geographical indications remain outside the scope of the Policy.[358]

The result is that regional and municipal complainants with rights that may be protected under local law lack standing under the UDRP. The mere fact that complainant exists at a geographical location included in the trademark is not a sufficient basis to capture a geographical domain name standing alone.[359] Thus, the Rouen Chamber of Commerce, which had a trademark that included the word "Rouen,"

---

[355] See 15 U.S.C. §1052(e) (Section 2(e) of the Lanham Act). ***Spherion Corp. v. Solomon***, FA 112454 (Forum July 22, 2002) ("[i]t has been held that in the United States a geographically descriptive name is to be treated as a generic term and does not by its registration with the United States Patent and Trademark Office become absolutely protectable" [finding for Respondent in <saratoga.biz>].)

French law protects geographic names for the ".fr" suffix. Decree 2007 162 of February 6 2007 on the regulation of the French domain name space provides:

> Unless otherwise permitted by the relevant local authority, the name of a local authority. . .can only be registered by this local authority. . .as a domain name under the country code top level domain. . . However, the above provision shall not prevent renewals of domain names registered before the Decree: by a company whose name is identical to the domain name and provided that a trade mark application in the same name has been filed prior to 1 January 2004.

David Taylor and Vincent Denoyelle, "<tignes.com> registrant is white as snow," International Law Office Blog, May 10, 2010.

[356] WIPO Second Report, Chapter 6, paragraphs 229 through 237. Paragraph 205: "While the misuse of geographical attributions may offend many feelings, only certain types of such misuse are sanctioned by the law."

[357] *Id.* In paragraph 243 WIPO "recommended that no modification be made to the UDRP, at this stage, to permit complaints to be made concerning the registration and use of domain names in violation of the prohibition against false indications of source or the rules relating to the protection of geographical indications."

[358] This is also true for designations of origin. See ***Comité Interprofessionnel du vin de Champagne v. Steven Vickers***, DCO2011-0026 (WIPO June 21, 2011) for Champagne, <champagne.co>; ***Consorzio del Prosciutto di Parma v Domain Name Clearing Company, LLC***, D2000-0629 (WIPO September 18, 2000) for "Parma ham."

was not entitled to capture <rouen.com> and <rouen.net> because it had no mark for "Rouen" standing alone.[360] "Unless the evidence demonstrates that the name of a geographical location is in fact performing the function of a trademark, such a name should not be considered a trademark for the purposes of the Uniform Policy."[361]

St. Moritz tried twice to wrest <stmoritz.com> from the domain name holder and the second time found itself on the wrong end of a finding of reverse domain name hijacking.[362] In another case by a Visitors Bureau, the Panel held that "[a] mark is primarily geographically descriptive if the primary significance of the term in the mind of the consumer is to indicate the geographic origin of the goods or services."[363] Similarly in ***Consejo de Promocin Turística de México***, where the successor to the Tourism Ministry of Mexico alleged it had a right to <mexico.com>.[364] The Panel denied the complaint because "there is no indication that Respondent has used the disputed domain name in a manner related to its trademark sense rather than its geographic sense." Seaports, airports, cities and municipalities have fared equally badly in their requests to have domain names reflecting their designations transferred to them.[365]

---

[359] A trademark such as JUMEIRAH BEACH HOTEL has no claim on <jumeira.com>, which is purely a geographic location, ***Jumeirah International LLC, Jumeirah Beach Resort LLC v. Vertical Axis, Inc, Domain Administrator / Jumeira.com***, D2009-0203 (WIPO May 21, 2009).

[360] ***Chambre de Commerce et d'Industrie de Rouen v. Marcel Stenzel***, D2001-0348 (WIPO June 18, 2001).

[361] ***Brisbane City Council v. Warren Bolton Consulting Pty Ltd.***, D2001-0047 (WIPO May 7, 2001).

[362] ***Kur- und Verkehrsverein St. Moritz v. Domain Finance Ltd.***, D2004-0158 (WIPO June 13, 2004) and ***Kur- und Verkehrsverein St. Moritz v. Domain Finance Ltd.***, D2000-0617 (WIPO August 17, 2000). In November 2008, St. Moritz filed a civil action before the court in Chur, Grison, Switzerland, claiming infringement not only of trademark rights, but also of personality rights in the name St. Moritz). The court held that because St. Moritz could rely on rights in the name St. Moritz, the content of the website accessible under the domain name stmoritz.com was irrelevant. In a judgment dated 4 May 2009, it ordered the transfer of the domain name to St. Moritz (more precisely claimant, which was the tourism authority of St. Moritz). (Reported on Class 46 by Mark Schweizer, August 26, 2009, https://www.marques.org/class46/).

[363] ***Greater Birmingham Convention and Visitors Bureau v. Acme Information Services***, FA0410000356351 (Forum December 29, 2004) (<birmingham.com>, citing U.S. law and Circuit case); ***Stadt Heidelberg v. Media Factory***, D2001-1500 (WIPO March 6, 2002) (denying transfer of <heidelberg.net> because complainant failed to show trademark rights in the city name of Heidelberg). SIMILARLY DECIDED: ***City of Salinas v. Baughn***, FA 97076 (Forum June 4, 2001) (<cityofsalinas.com>); ***City of Myrtle Beach v. Info. Ctrs., Inc.***, FA 103367 (Forum Mar. 8, 2002) (<myrtlebeach.com>); ***Junta de Andalucia Consejeria de Turismo, Comercio y Deporte, Turismo Andaluz, S.A. v. Andalucía.Com Limited***, D2006-0749 (WIPO October 13, 2006) (<andalucia.com>).

[364] ***Consejo de Promocin Turística de México, S.A. de C.V. v. Latin America Telecom Inc.***, D2004-0242 (WIPO July 19, 2004).

A distinction has been drawn between official and unofficial geographic locations. Whatever their origins, "Atlantic Station"[366] and "Deer Valley"[367] are official in having been recognized by the U.S. Post Office. The Panel in ***Deer Valley Resort Company*** held that "the term 'Deer Valley' [is] a commonly used geographic indicator that refers to a specific region of Park City, Utah," but since respondent was using it in a purely descriptive manner to market various properties (*i.e.*, condominiums, <deervalleycondos.us>) over the Internet, it was found to have a legitimate interest in the domain name. Trademarks composed of unofficial locations brought into existence by commercial enterprises are more likely to receive greater protection.[368] This is because they designate a brand which is singular to the trademark owner.

4.01-D.2.b *Geography as Source* 4.01-D.2.b

To the extent that a complainant's use of a geographic mark standing alone or joined with another word has acquired secondary meaning as a source of goods or services, it is entitled to protection,[369] although standing alone is a more difficult case against respondents using the designation in its ordinary sense.[370] The greater the market penetration of the trademark, the heavier the respondent's burden to support its contention that the domain name was registered for its *descriptive value*.

---

365 ***Port of Helsinki vs. Paragon International Projects Ltd.***, D2001-0002 (WIPO February 12, 2001) (refusing to transfer <portofhelsinki.com> because geographic indicators are not per se trademarks, and Complainant failed to show any registered or common law trademark rights.); ***BAA plc v. Bob Larkin***, D2004-0555 (WIPO November 11, 2004) (<gatwick.com>) the Panel rejected Complainant's contentions that as operator of Gatwick airport it had a protectable right to the name "Gatwick"—agreeing with respondent that it could legitimately use the domain name descriptively. ***Ville de Paris v. Whois Privacy Services/Comar Ltd.***, D2009-1255 (WIPO December 3, 2009) (<wifi-paris.com>, cannot claim exclusive right to a geographic term.)

BAA was successful in ***BAA plc, Aberdeen Airport Limited v. Mr. H. Hashimi***, D2004-0717 (WIPO October 21, 2004) (<aberdeenairport.com>) because the domain name included the term "airport," although this did not help Complainant in ***Manchester Airport plc v. Club Club Ltd***, D2000-0638 (WIPO August 22, 2000) (<manchesterairport.com>).

366 ***Atlantic Station, LLC v. Dargan Burns III***, FA0903001250592 (Forum April 26, 2009) ("On the one hand ATLANTIC STATION is a trademark; on the other it is a geographic place." The Panel held that adding a descriptor "condo" did not violate complainant's right even though it was in the real estate market and the parties competed for the same customers.)

367 ***Deer Valley Resort Company v. Intermountain Lodging***, FA0505000471429 (Forum June 21, 2005).

368 ***Big Canoe Company, LLC v. Daniel J. Elliot***, FA0609000799382 (Forum November 17, 2006) (<bigcanoerealestate.net>).

369 ***Kabushiki Kaisha Hitachi Seisakusho (Japan Corporation), d/b/a Hitachi, Ltd. v. Hilaire Shioura***, DWS2004-0002 (WIPO July 23, 2004) (<hitachi.ws>. "Hitachi" is a place name in Japan. Respondent argued that it intended to use the domain for its geographic meaning but offered no evidence to satisfy a paragraph 4(c)(i) defense); ***Intrawest Sandestin Company LLC v. Admin***

This is equally true for geographic terms employed as trademarks, as illustrated with the trademarks HITACHI and NEUSIEDLER. "Hitachi" is a geographical region of Japan but is also a trademark with an international reputation in the automobile industry. Respondent offered no evidence that prior to receiving notice it used or was making demonstrable preparation to use the domain name legitimately.

However, protection for a geographic trademark of any kind is no greater than that accorded to generic and descriptive terms. A complainant's adoption of a geographically descriptive term such as "Neusiedler" for its service mark "faces a greater risk that the combination of that term with another common term will in fact distinguish the new combination."[371] The use of geographic indicators alone for commercial purposes unrelated to complainant's trademark infringes no protectable right. Thus, "Neusiedler" as well as being complainant's trademark is also a lake in Europe.[372] The Panel explained that

> Geographic names cannot be monopolized by registering a trademark or company name. The use of geographic terms as such in domain names or otherwise by third parties is generally possible despite a trade-mark registration. . . .
>
> Although it may play a part in a panel's assessment of a decision, registering a domain name or a geographic term in a language other than that of the Registrant cannot be interpreted *per se* as an indication of bad faith. Holding otherwise would mean that a great number of English language registrations of domain names by non-English nationals, such as Germans and/or Austrians, would be contentious.

SUPERGA is a trademark, but it is also "a hill overlooking the city of Turin (Torino) and the site of an 18th Century basilica and royal tombs." The evidence supported Respondent's contention that it had acquired the domain name as part of a business plan to use geographic indicators descriptively.[373] This was also the result in a case previously cited in which the mark was composed of a geographic term plus the phrase "beach resort" while the domain name was solely the geographic term.[374]

Contact, FA0910001289075 (Forum December 7, 2009) (SANDESTIN and <sandestinweddings.com>. "Sandestin" is a golf club, not a geographic location.)

370 ***Neusiedler Aktiengesellschaft v. Kulkarni***, D2000-1769 (WIPO February 5, 2001) (<neusiedler.com>); ***Superga Trademark, S.A. v. Gilberto, Publinord S.r.l.***, D2008-1890 (WIPO February 24, 2009). See also ***Granarolo S.p.a. v. Dinoia***, FA649854 (Forum April 17, 2006) (GRANAROLO and <granarolo.com>. Respondent argued that because "Granarolo" is the name of a municipality, it could not have registered the domain name in bad faith. However, the name of the municipality is "Granarolo dell 'Emilia' not "Granarolo." Moreover, "[t]he Respondent could not have registered the domain name in good faith if it had to alter the content after the Complainant contacted the Respondent.")

371 ***Southwest Airlines Co. v. Cattitude a/k/a LJ Gehman***, D2005-0410 (WIPO June 12, 2005) (<mysouthwest.com>).

372 ***Neusiedler Aktiengesellschaft***, *supra*. (Complainant invited to refile if Respondent uses the domain name in the future in bad faith.)

A respondent has a legitimate interest in a domain name used for a business purpose demonstrably inconsistent with a complainant's allegation of original intention to take advantage of the trademark.[375]

Even if trademark owners in the "Neusiedler" and "Superga" class succeed on their *prima facie* case they can only prevail on the merits on proof that the domain names are being used in bad faith. This does not extend to complainants who create, develop and transform geographic locations into unincorporated communities. Their trademarks are protected against competitors marketing similar goods or services.[376] In the case cited in the footnote, the Panel found in favor of the Complainant-developer. The distinction between "Big Canoe" and "Deer Valley" (discussed above) is that "Deer Valley"

> was a[n already existing] geographic area that had been identified and referred to as such by the local populace for a number of years before Complainant's registration of the mark[], [in] this situation . . . complainant's use and registration of BIG CANOE predated the use of this term as the name of a geographical area by several years.

The geographic term in ***Big Canoe*** was less determinative than the added modifier "real estate"—<bigcanoerealestate.net>—in that it increased the likelihood of confusion since Complainant also provided real estate services.

A geographical indicator + another term as opposed to a geographical designation alone (without proof of targeting) is protectable. "La Quinta" alone falls into the Neusiedler class, but adding "inn" transforms it into a protectable mark. In ***La Quinta Worldwide*** the Panel found that[377]

> [the] fact that "La Quinta" is the name of a city has no consequence since LA QUINTA INN acquired secondary meaning through its use and registration with the USPTO.

Protectability of a trademark containing a geographic designation plus another term is also illustrated in decisions relating to cultural institutions, but there are anomalies.[378] If the domain name is "not the kind of expression the Panel would expect someone to simply pull out of the air"[379] respondent must explain its choice. Silence

---

[373] ***Superga Trademark***, *supra*.

[374] ***Jumeirah International***, *supra*. Complainant has no rights to a geographic name standing alone.

[375] ***Okruzhnost LLC v. WhoIs Privacy Protection Service, Inc./Six Media Ltd.***, D2014-0373 (WIPO June 2, 2014) ("The registration and use of the Disputed Domain Name and Website therefore appears consistent with the Respondent's preexisting business operations.")

[376] ***Big Canoe Company***, *supra*. Compare with ***Atlantic Station***, *supra*.

[377] ***La Quinta Worldwide, LLC v Fisk Enterprises c/o J Fisk***, FA0508000540243 (Forum September 25, 2005).

[378] ***New York City Ballet, Inc. v. Tucker Brown***, FA0806001210744 (Forum August 27, 2008) (<nycballet.net>. Successful in capturing domain name.) Cf. ***Scottish Ballet v. Duncan Macleod a/k/a***

allows for a negative inference. Complainant succeeded in capturing <melbourne-deck> for its trademark MELBOURNE OBSERVATION DECK on the grounds the domain name did not have the feel of being "pull[ed] out of the air." This is reinforced where the domain name is passively held.

4.01-D.3 4.01-D.3 Domain Names Mimicking Trade Names

4.01-D.3.a 4.01-D.3.a *Trade Names as Such Outside Policy's Scope*

Although "trade names [can] perform the same 'origin function' as trademarks, indicating the source or nature of the business entity they represent, and perform the same investment or advertising function," they do not (or at least do not formally) fall within the definition of being a "right" for the purposes of the administrative procedure.[380] However, as explained in the next section this does not mean complainants are categorically shut out of the UDRP for infringements of their trade names.[381]

Where complainants rely on their trade names for standing, "the Panel is not allowed to examine [their] contentions [as to the content of the website] in order to determine whether the requirement set out in paragraph 4 a (1) of the Policy has been met."[382] The reason for this is that the "Policy is specifically limited to trade mark rights."[383] The manner in which the domain name is being used is irrelevant if the Panel lacks jurisdiction. The Panel in ***Baltimore Gas and Electric Company*** noted that

---

DuncanSketch, FA0803001163688 (Forum May 20, 2008) (<scottish ballet.com>. Unsuccessful in capturing domain name.) The unconvincing difference is that Respondent in the second case identified himself as a collector of domain names having a "Scottish" theme who according to the Panel "plausibly" contended that he had no knowledge of the Scottish Ballet.

[379] ***St Martins Victoria Pty Ltd, Grollo Australia Pty Ltd v. Texas International Property Associates***, D2008-1464 (WIPO December 4, 2008) ("In the absence of any explanation from the Respondent for its choice of the Domain Name, the Panel finds as a fact that the Respondent was targeting the Complainants and their marks, and that the Respondent did so with a view to free riding on the Complainants' goodwill in their marks.")

[380] WIPO Final Report, paragraph 167: "[R]egistrations that violate trade names, geographical indications or personality rights would not be considered to fall within the definition of abusive registration **for the purposes of the administrative procedure**. (**Bold** in the original).

[381] Where trade names function as marks, complainants must prove targeted consumers recognize them as signifying goods or services from that source, that is proving their secondary meaning as equivalent to common law marks. See "Distinctiveness of Unregistered Trademark Not Presumed" (Sec. 4.01-B.2). The failure to satisfy the evidentiary demands are explained in ***Fitness People B.V. v. Jes Hvid Mikkelsen***, CAC 101587 (ADR.eu October 23, 2017) (<fitnesspeople.club>. There is a "dispute as to whether that company is engaging in trade at all.")

[382] ***SGS Société générale de surveillance S.A. v. Inspectorate,*** D2000-0025 (WIPO March 17, 2000) (<sgs.net> and <sgsgroup.net>).

[383] ***Baltimore Gas and Electric Company v. National Material Supply Co., LLC***, D2001-0315 (WIPO May 17, 2001) (<baltimoregasandelectric.com>).

Although personal names and trade names that serve as trademarks have been properly protected under the Policy, the Policy does not extend to protection of personal or trade names in which trademark rights have not been established.

Panels tend to determine the status of unregistered names by assessing their reception by the ordinary consumer. Generic and descriptive terms lacking anchors to specific providers of goods or services cannot be monopolized if use by others exploits their semantic meanings.[384]

4.01-D.3.b *Trade Names Brought Within Policy's Scope* 4.01-D.3.b

Notwithstanding the formal exclusion of trade names as rights qualifying for standing under the UDRP discussed in the WIPO Final Report, there is no categorical bar.[385] As already noted in the preceding section, the WIPO Second Report softens the Final Report's strictness by recognizing that trade names have a dual nature: "[t]o the extent that trade names serve an identifying function, like trademarks, there was support for their protection in the DNS, equivalent to that accorded to trademarks."[386] U.S. trademark law (although not the ACPA) carries this one step further for famous marks[387] while country code policies expressly give trademark status to trade names and business names.[388]

Given how panelists construe the Policy their assessment of trade names does not necessarily conclude the matter of whether they are not also trademarks. There is no absolute dividing line that in all instances can be said to separate one from

---

384 ***Diversified Mortgage, Inc. v. World Fin. Partners***, FA 118308 (Forum October 30, 2002) (DIVERSIFIED MORTAGE and <diversifiedmortgage>. "UDRP panels and decisions have almost universally denied protection to a trade name used as a domain name, which this Panel concludes it is bound under existing precedent to do here."); ***Mega Shoes, Inc. v. Ostrick***, FA 1362894 (February 1, 2011) (Combining "mega" and "shoes"); ***WorldClaim Global Claims Management v. Bishop, Atticus / Bishop***, FA1609001694577 (Forum November 7, 2016) ("world" and "claim". "One would need very compelling evidence to show that the combination of two descriptive words" supported a common law claim).

385 At the dawn of the Internet, Network Solutions, Inc.'s registration agreement included a warranty that the "use or registration of the domain name ... does not interfere with or infringe the rights of any third party in any jurisdiction with respect to trademark, service mark, trade name, company name or any other intellectual property right."

386 WIPO Second Report Paragraph 311; also Paragraph 318(ii): "[W]here a trade name is used in widespread markets, it is often also the subject of trademark protection, or satisfies the conditions for protection as an unregistered trademark so as to qualify, in appropriate circumstances, for protection against bad faith, deliberate misuse under the UDRP."

387 15 U.S.C. §1125(c): "[T]he owner of a famous mark that is distinctive, inherently or through acquired distinctiveness shall be entitled to an injunction against another person who . . . commences use of [that] mark or trade name in commerce." See *Panavision International v. Toeppen*, 141 F.3d 1316, 46 U.S.P.Q. 2d 1511 (9th Cir. 1998). A UDRP example would be ***Philip Morris USA Inc. v. Doug Nedwin/ SRSPlus Private Registration***, D2014-0339 (WIPO May 1, 2014) (<phillip-morris.com>).

the other. While trade names composed of generic terms or descriptive phrases that could be suitable for many kinds of businesses may fail to qualify as a right,[389] others composed of the same or stronger terms with the difference that they have achieved recognition in the marketplace have qualified on proof of secondary meaning.[390]

In order for complainant to bring itself within the jurisdiction of the Policy it must prove that its trade name is both its name for trade and (if unregistered) a common law trademark. The proof demands are not insignificant. Claiming trade names as unregistered marks is given the same heightened scrutiny as is necessary to make a case of standing for unregistered trademarks.[391] Registration of trade names with a governmental agency is not automatically sufficient to confer trademark rights.[392]

Secondary meaning "requires proffering supportive evidence or information that indicates relevant consumers identify [Complainant's] alleged . . . mark as representative of its services and identity."[393] The ***Savino Del Bene*** case discussed above in design-plus-word trademarks illustrates the point. So too does ***Baltimore Gas and Electric***, although in this case the trade name did not function as a trademark:

---

388 The WIPO Final Report notes at paragraph 320 that "[i]n the case of ccTLDs, we believe that much greater scope exists for allowing complaints under a dispute resolution procedure for abusive registrations of trade names. Within the ccTLD, the problem of diversity does not exist in the same way and there is greater scope for applying the relevant national implementation of protection of trade names." The Panel in ***Supre Pty Ltd v. Paul King***, DAU2004-0006 (WIPO December 22, 2004) for example explains that "unlike the Uniform Domain Name Dispute Resolution Policy, the .au Domain Name Dispute Resolution Policy prohibits identity or confusing similarity with a 'name' as well as with a trade or service mark. 'Name' is then defined to include a complainant's registered company name. So, in the present case, respondent has chosen a domain name, which is confusingly similar to complainant's company name." See also ***Cruisewinkel.nl B.V. v. Meier Gunter***, DNL2016-0025 (WIPO July 8, 2017) (<cruiswinkel.nl>) (Netherlands policy).

389 ***Neptune Orient Lines Limited v. cnwonder.com c/o Wu Guiqiang***, FA1002001310401 (Forum April 14, 2010) (<nol.com>. A common abbreviation).

390 ***Alain-Martin Pierret d/b/a Bordeaux West v. Sierra Technology Group, LLC***, FA0505000 472135 (Forum July 1, 2005) (<bordeauxwest.com>); Workers United Union v. Wesley Perkins, D2010-0738 (WIPO June 20, 2010) (<workersunitedunion.org>); Nu Mark LLC v. Bui, Long, D2013-1785 (WIPO December 22, 2013) ("Complainant's trade name 'Nu Mark' had become a distinctive identifier associated with its business and products on its website and thus demonstrated complainant's unregistered trademark rights".) The Panel in ***Mr. Alen Baibekov Booking Group SIA v. Mr. Daniel Chestnut***, CAC 101650 (ADR.eu October 13, 2017) suggests that domain names could also benefit from the protection afforded to unregistered trademarks on proof of secondary meaning. See Booking.com v. Matal, 1:16-cv-425 (E.D. Virginia 2017).

391 See "Unregistered Marks, Recognition in the Marketplace and Proof of Secondary Meaning" (Sec. 4.01-B).

392 ***Jay S. Cohen d/b/a Elite Cruises v. Smoking Domains, LLC***, FA0803001155799 (Forum May 7, 2008) (ELITE CRUISES registered Illinois and Pennsylvania). However, registration by a respondent may support its right or legitimate interest. ***Enduris LLC v. Washington Governmental Entity Pool c/o Alric Balka***, FA0901001245314 (Forum March 25, 2009). See also discussion at "Rival Trademarks in Foreign Jurisdictions" (Sec. 4.02-A.1.c).

> [T]he fact that [Complainant] has used the trade name for many years in itself is not sufficient. To serve as a trademark, the name must be used in a manner so that the public can come to recognize it as an indication of source. Since the name is descriptive, complainant must also show that the name has become distinctive as an indication of a single source, and is not simply viewed by the public as a description applicable to the goods or services from various sources.

A person claiming rights in a descriptive term must show that the term has acquired secondary meaning denoting its business. If complainant fails to present its proof and the record is otherwise bare, the omission allows for a negative inference against it and for support that the lexical string is available to the first to register.[394]

4.01-E Timing of Trademark Acquisition Not a Factor in Determining Standing 4.01-E

4.01-E.1 Complainant's Acquisition of Trademark Right 4.01-E.1

Formative UDRP decisions quickly established that a complainant has standing to maintain a proceedings if it demonstrates it "has rights" (present tense).[395] For the purpose of paragraph 4(a)(i) the term "has rights" is construed to mean that complainant has them at the time of filing the complaint rather than having had them (past tense) prior to the registration of the disputed domain name.[396] The qualification is necessary because it was initially uncertain whether trademarks that postdated the registration of the domain name complied with the rights requirement of paragraph 4(a)(i) of the Policy.[397] The right accrues for registered and unregistered marks, but with a proviso as to the latter, which is that for an unregistered mark complainant must prove a right preexisting domain name registration.[398]

---

393 ***Weatherford Int'l, Inc. v. Wells***, FA 153626 (Forum May 19, 2003); ***Golden Title Loans, LLC dba 745Cash v. roylee***, FA 1618801 (Forum June 23, 2015) ("Secondary meaning may be acquired through "continuous and ongoing use of a mark, holding of a domain name identical to the mark, or using the mark in commerce before a disputed domain name is created.")

394 ***Front Range Internet, Inc. v. Murphy***, FA 145231 (Forum Apr. 4, 2003) ("Front Range Internet"); ***Seaway Bolt & Specials Corp. v. Digital Income Inc.***, FA 114672 (Forum August 5, 2002) ("Seaway"); ***Glasgow Signs v. 1st Signs Limited trading as Sign A Rama***, D2010-0409 (WIPO May 4, 2010) ("Glasgow Signs").

395 In contrast, under the ACPA the mark has to be "distinctive at the time of registration of the domain name." 15 U.S.C. §1125(d)(1)(A). See *Philbrick v. Enom*, 593 F.Supp.2d 352, 375 (D. New Hampshire, 2009) ("Because the plaintiffs' mark is not distinctive (or famous) [before the domain name registration], it is simply not entitled to protection under the ACPA.")

396 Paragraphs 4(b)(i-iv) demand proof of past and present conduct; paragraphs 4(c)(i) and 4(c)(ii) demand proof of past use—or, in the case of "demonstrable preparations" proof that preparations are under way; and, paragraph 4(c)(iii) demands proof of past to present good faith use.

397 See ***Firstgate Internet A.G.v. David Soung***, D2000-1311 (WIPO January 29, 2001) ("Whilst the Panel agree that this issue is not necessary to its Decision, given its view on complainant's failure

While timing of registered marks is not an issue for standing,[399] it is a determinative factor in assessing bad faith under paragraph 4(a)(iii) of the Policy.[400] By consensus an earlier domain registration date does not affect a complainant's standing to maintain a proceeding, but passing the first test is likely to be illusory since having standing does not cure the deficiency of priority.[401] This leads to the conundrum that Panels may have jurisdiction but owners of later acquired trademarks have no actionable claim for cybersquatting, regardless whether the domain names correspond to their marks.[402]

---

to satisfy the third element of paragraph 4(a) of the Policy, they disagree as to when trademark rights must exist for the requirements of paragraph 4 (a)(i) of the Policy. The Presiding Panelist and Panelist Chrocziel believe that such trademark rights must be in existence at the time the domain name is registered, i.e. here March 6, 2000. Panelist Creel believes that such trademark rights need only exist at the time of the Complaint.")

By the end of 2001, the consensus had fixed on a trademark right at the time of the complaint. See ***Digital Vision, Ltd. v. Advanced Chemill Sys***, D2001-0827 (WIPO September 23, 2001) (<digital vision.com>). The Panel held that the "Complainant has provided the registration documents for its DIGITAL VISION marks, within the USA and the EU. Registration for these marks postdates the domain name registration; however, Paragraph 4(a)(i) does not require that the trade mark be registered prior to the domain name." See ***New York Times Company v. Name Administration Inc. (BVI)***, FA100900 1349045 (Forum November 17, 2010) (<dealbook.com>) and other cases discussed below. Nevertheless, some panelists are of the view that complainants lack standing if they fail on the second and third limbs of the Policy: ***NLY Scandinavia AB v. Alexander Tchousov, PS Pay Solutions UG***, D2018-0498 (WIPO May 8, 2018) (<nelly-model.com>. "Since all the requirements of paragraph 4(a) of the Policy must be met, the failure on the part of the Complainant to demonstrate one element of the Policy will result in failure of the Complaint in its entirety. Accordingly, in light of the Panel's below findings regarding the issue of registration and use in bad faith, it is unnecessary for the Panel to decide whether the disputed domain name is identical or confusingly similar to the Complainant's trademark or whether the Respondent has any rights or legitimate interests in the disputed domain name.")

398 See for example, ***Foundation Source Philanthropic Services, Inc. v. Arlene B Gibson/ Foundations That Make a Difference/Domain Discreet***, D2007-0875 (WIPO December 4, 2007).

399 Timing is the subject of WIPO Overview 2.0, Paragraph 1.4. It reads in part: "Registration of a domain name before a complainant acquires trademark rights in a name does not prevent a finding of identity or confusing similarity." As noted in "Potentially Existing Trademarks" [Sec. 4.01-A.1.c] a complainant does not have to have a trademark to have standing or for a finding of bad faith, as explained in Jurisprudential Overview 3.0, Paragraph 3.1.

400 For an exception to the rule see "Potentially Existing Trademarks" (Sec. 4.01-A.1.c)

401 The rationale for granting standing to a complainant whose rights postdate the registration of the domain name is explained by the possibility of there being one of two factual circumstances that could possibly defeat priority of domain name registration, namely 1) respondent registered the domain name in anticipation of complainant's associated marks for a specific business; and 2) the domain name was transferred to an unrelated party subsequent to the mark coming into existence. These factual circumstances are further developed in later sections.

402 See for example, ***Telaxis Communications Corp. v. William E. Minkle***, D2000-0005 (WIPO March 5, 2000) (<telaxis.com> and <telaxis.net) (Domain names acquired prior to Complainant

The consensus that Paragraph 4(a)(i) does not require that the trademark be registered prior to the domain name competes with a minority view, that it does.[403] A later acquired trademark is thought by some panelists to preclude jurisdiction because the Policy "necessarily implies that Complainant's rights predate Respondent's registration . . . of the domain name."[404] Some Panels have terminated their analysis upon finding that trademark rights accrued after the domain name registration,[405] explaining that since "the respondent's registration of the domain name . . . predated complainant's alleged rights complainant did not have standing to bring a claim under the UDRP."[406] The view continues to exercise a hold over some panelists; complaints are dismissed or denied where proof establishes that respondent either has priority of right or legitimate interest in the domain name or the timing of the registration is such that respondent could not possibly have registered the domain name in bad faith.[407]

The different approaches do not necessarily change the outcome of the proceeding. Even if complainant succeeds on the threshold requirement and proves respondent lacks rights or legitimate interests there can be no affirmative proof that the registration was made in bad faith.[408] A postdated right takes nothing away from a trademark owner but neither is it rewarded with a presumption that its registration takes precedence over respondent's right of possession. It is contrary to the intent of the Policy to allow a new trademark owner to succeed against a prior domain name

---

rebranding its business from Millitech Corporation (Complaint denied); ***Success Bank v. ZootGraphics c/o Ira Zoot***, FA0904001259918 (Forum June 29, 2009) (Rebranding without owning corresponding domain name).

403 ***Credit Europe Bank N.V. v. Peter Yu***, D2010-0737 (WIPO July 14, 2010) (Panel bypassed 4(a)(i) on the premise that "[b]ecause paragraph 4(a)'s requirements are conjunctive . . . no matter what the findings under the first and second sub paragraphs, the Complainant must fail under the requirement to demonstrate that the disputed domain name has been both registered and used in bad faith.")

404 ***Phoenix Mortgage Corp. v. Toggas***, D2001-0101 (WIPO March 30, 2001).

405 A minority view holds that "[t]his provision necessarily implies that Complainant's rights predate the registration of Registrant's domain name," ***Expert Computers Inc. v. Name Delegation c/o Domain Administrator***, FA0609000787937 (Forum October24, 2006), citing ***Intermark Media, Inc. v. Wang Logic Corp.***, FA0212000139660 (Forum February 19, 2003).

406 ***Razorbox, Inc. v. Skjodt***, FA 150795 (Forum May 9, 2003) (<razorbox.com>).

407 ***EDREAMS, Inc. v Arise Company Ltd.***, D2006-0725 (WIPO July 24,2006) ("[h]aving considered [cited] authorities and the submissions of the parties, the Panel finds that complainant is unable to satisfy the test in paragraph 4(a)(i) of the Policy because it has no trademark rights which predate the date of creation of the disputed domain name.")

408 The uncertainty of which approach is correct whether to deny or grant standing is illustrated in ***Ode v. Intership Ltd.***, D2001-0074 (WIPO May 1, 2001): "However, in case we are wrong on this issue [that is, skipping the threshold finding], we find that the Complaint fails to meet any of the requirements of paragraph 4b of the Policy."

registration on the grounds that its later acquired trademark gives it a better right to the domain name.[409]

4.01-E.2

4.01-E.2 Maturation of Brand Reputation Over Time

New businesses enter the market without reputation. They are usually one among many competing for attention. If at all, their reputations are earned over time. It has already been explained that the slighter a mark's reputation the greater the burden of proving actual knowledge of its existence. Two aspects of timing have emerged in cybersquatting disputes. The first (a fundamental element) is priority, that complainant's mark exists earlier in time than the registration of the domain name. The other turns priority upside down; respondent does not deny the mark predated the domain name but that at the time the domain name was registered the mark had no reputation such as to put the respondent on notice of its existence.[410]

The issue of reputation is addressed more specifically below in section 4.02-C.1.a. The greater complainant's reputation at the time of registration of the domain name (or lesser reputation but geographically close) the greater the likelihood respondent had knowledge of complainant and its mark. This and other evidence can point to abusive registration. Conversely, lack of market penetration or geographical separation is likely to undermine a complainant's contention that respondent registered the domain name to take advantage of its goodwill in the trademark.[411]

A trademark owner whose previous UDRP complaint was denied against unrelated respondents is not necessarily foreclosed in subsequent proceedings where its reputation has matured over time. This principle is illustrated in a number of proceedings initiated by Easygroup IP Licensing Limited. In the first case[412] the Panel held that it was "not persuaded that the announcements (or any preparatory

---

409 ***Well-Link Industry Co. Ltd. v. Jeff Park, Nexpert, Inc.***, D2017-0036 (WIPO March 1, 2017) (<welllink.com>. "Complainant argues that it has a more justifiable claim to the disputed domain name than Respondent because Complainant is conducting business under the trademark reflected in the second level domain of the disputed domain name." Complaint denied; domain name registration predated trademark).

410 ***CIA. Industrial H. Carlos Schneider v. WHOIS Privacy Service Pty Ltd. / Domain Admin, Ashantiplc Limited***, D2016-2167 (WIPO January 26, 2016) (<ciser.com>. "Respondent does not dispute that Complainant, as of the time the disputed domain name was acquired by Respondent, possessed regional rights in the CISER trademark in South America and Mexico in connection with screws and nuts. However, Respondent considers that Complainant's geographic expansion post-dates Respondent's acquisition of the disputed domain name.")

411 Evidence that proves reputation at the time of commencing the proceeding may be insufficient to prove bad faith. Reputation has to be proved proved as of the time of the registration of the domain name. ***Transportes AEROMAR S.A. SE C.V. v. Aeromar, Inc.***, D2010-0098 (WIPO March 19, 2010); and ***Rba Edipresse, S.L. v. Brendhan Hight / MDNH Inc.***, D2009-1580 (WIPO March 2, 2010).

412 ***EasyGroup (UK) Ltd v. Easymaterial.com Limited***, D2000-0711 (WIPO September 7, 2000).

work behind those announcements) give rise to any relevant rights. Even if they did, the Panel takes the view that no trader could monopolise the use of that word ['easy'] as part of a trading style or domain name without very impressive evidence of long and exclusive use. No such evidence was put before the Panel."[413]

However, adding passage of time and maturity to the factual mix changed the result for the Easygroup. A trademark composed of a common word that achieves an international reputation "puts complainant's claims on quite a different footing."[414] In the 2005 case for <easycentre.com>, the Panel rejected Respondent's argument that Complainant did not have rights to monopolize EASY:

> All the points made by the learned panelist are, with respect, apposite today. However, that decision was made in 2000 when complainant's "www.easy.com" website/portal was either still in contemplation or the early stages of use. In 2005, there has been almost five years of use, evidence of over 338,000 visitors each week to the website portal at "www.easy.com" and more than 58 million visitors to complainant's easy Internet cafés.

There was also evidence of targeting that supported both lack of rights or legitimate interests and abusive registration.

4.01-F Right of Trademark Owner to Recapture Domain Name After Lapse of Registration 4.01-F

4.01-F.1 Recapturing Domain Name 4.01-F.1

4.01-F.1.a *Complainants Do Not Lose Their Statutory Priority* *4.01-F.1.a*

Under U.S. trademark law cancellation for failure to renew registration does not foreclose a senior user from applying for a new registration or successfully opposing an intervening application for the lapsed registration. Common law rights are unaffected assuming continued use in commerce. Domain names are similar to trademarks in that holders can lose their registrations for failure to renew, with an important difference: loss by complainant is more consequential in that domain names have no statutory status, which means that a domain name inadvertently lost and not reclaimed within the period stipulated in the registration agreement, can be irretrievably lost.[415]

---

413 Similarly, in ***Easygroup (UK) Limited, Easyjet Airline Company Limited, Easyeverything Limited, Easy Rentacar (UK) Limited v. Rencross Technology Limited/Michael Kong***, D2000-0950 (WIPO October 11, 2000).

414 ***Easygroup IP Licensing Limited v. N. Hilton, Easycentre.com***, D2005-0935 (WIPO October 31, 2005). The result is different where Respondent proves a right (not just a legitimate interest) as with <easyhotel.ch>, ***EasyGroup IP Licensing Ltd v. Pascal de Vries***, DCH2005-0019 (WIPO December 2, 2005).

415 ICANN's Expired Domain Name Deletion Policy (ERRP) and its companion Expired Domain Name Deletion Policy (EDNDP) implemented in 2013 were intended to resolve inadvertent lapses

While complainants do not lose their statutory priority to respondents registering lapsed domain names their ability to reclaim domain names can be uncertain. It depends on the strength of the trademark,[416] the length of time elapsed,[417] and how respondent is using the domain name.[418] Owners of "strong" trademarks and demonstrable market presence[419] have a higher degree of security after inadvertent lapse or registrar error[420] than do owners of less distinctive trademarks on the lower end of the classification scale.

Although protected in theory, in practice a complainant's ability to reclaim a lapsed domain name incorporating a lesser known mark registered by a respondent

---

of registration. The new policies established mechanisms to alert registrants to impending expiration of their registrations, although no amount of safety features are foolproof. The ERRP provides in 2.1.1 that "Prior to the expiration of any gTLD registration, registrars must notify the registered name holder of the expiration at least two times. One of these notices must be sent approximately one-month prior to expiration and one must be sent approximately one week prior to expiration." The EDNDP incorporates a capsulated version of the ERRP in the Registrar Accreditation Agreement (RAA). The pertinent provision reads: "3.7.5 At the conclusion of the registration period, failure by or on behalf of the Registered Name Holder to consent that the registration be renewed within the time specified in a second notice or reminder shall, in the absence of extenuating circumstances, result in cancellation of the registration by the end of the auto-renew grace period."

[416] ***NYLSTAR S.A. v. Domain Administrator, Meryl Blog***, D2016-0561 (WIPO June 13, 2016) (<meryl.com> intentionally abandoned domain name and now wants to reclaim it, Respondent appeared) — while stronger marks and recent loss have succeeded — ***Dymocks Holdings Pty Ltd. v. Heng Zhong / Whois Agent, Whois Privacy Protection Service, Inc.***, D2016-0560 (WIPO May 18, 2016) (<dymocks.com> inadvertent loss; no appearance by Respondent); ***Enviro Tech International, Inc. v. Corp New Ventures Services***, FA1604001671545 (Forum May 17, 2016) (<ensolve.com> inadvertent loss; no appearance by Respondent).

[417] ***Telect, Inc. v. Arvind Reddy***, D2017-1270 (WIPO August 15, 2017) (Complainant took no action for over two years to reclaim <connectingthefuture.com>; complaint denied).

[418] ***FBomb Clothing c/o Joel Jordan v. Domainly.com***, FA0902001245522 (Forum March 16, 2009) ((Transferred) ("Since Respondent has allegedly not used the <fbomb.com> domain name for any reason other than to offer it for sale, the Panel concludes that Respondent registered the <fbomb.com> domain name primarily for the purpose of selling it."). See also ***Little Acorns Fostering Ltd. v. W P, The Cloud Corp / Al Perkins***, D2017-1776 (WIPO October 18, 2017) (<littleacornfostering.com>. "[I]t is unfortunate that the business practices of Mr. Perkins appear to have [been] carried on for the most part unchecked for many years [registering dropped domain names and extorting mark owners by threatening to point them to pornographic sites], notwithstanding the multiple findings made against him in UDRP proceedings and the brazen nature of his conduct.")

[419] ***Disney Enterprises, Inc. v. Intec Solutions OU***, FA1305001500886 (Forum July 3, 2013) (<disneymusicals.com>. Registered three months after lapse); ***Zevex, Inc. v. Isaac Goldstein***, FA1005001323005 (Forum June 15, 2010) (Respondent registered disputed domain name one day after Complainant's redemption period ended. "Zevex" has no meaning in the English language so could not be used in any dictionary sense. The Panel inferred bad faith registration from bad faith use in populating the website with links to the pharmaceutical industry and Complainant's competitors).

[420] ***Booz Allen Hamilton Inc. v. Human Works Inc.***, D2002-0656 (WIPO September 23, 2002) (Respondent acquired the domain name due to an administrative error by the domain name registrar

in a different geographical market can succeed only with proof of respondent's actual knowledge of and intent to take advantage of complainant.[421] This also applies to unregistered marks for which complainants offer no proof of acquired distinctiveness.[422] Lapse of registration for former holders without any trademark right is an irretrievable loss.[423] However, persons who own unregistered trademarks as artists, athletes, musicians, entertainers, and writers are in a favored position to capture abusive registrations of their names or recapture lapsed domain names depending on the extent of their fame.[424]

Panels have taken one of four positions when complainants fail inadvertently to re-register domain names: 1) favoring claimants whose domain names have been extensively used before lapse and have acted promptly[425]; 2) favoring the fanciful and arbitrary and perhaps the suggestive[426]; 3) disfavoring the generic and descriptive[427];

---

following an earlier proceeding, ***Booz-Allen & Hamilton, Inc. v. Servability Ltd.***, D2001-0243 (WIPO April 5, 2001), in which the Panel ruled that <booz.com> had been registered and used in bad faith.)

421 ***World Wide Commerce Corporation v. WebContents, Inc.***, FA0712001124467 (Forum February 13, 2008) ("Complainant's previous registration and use of the disputed domain name before the registration inadvertently lapsed coupled with Respondent's immediate registration and refusal to transfer further supports that Respondent's registration and use of the <worldwidecommerce.com> domain name was in bad faith pursuant to Policy paragraph 4(a)(iii).") Compare with ***Telect***, *supra*.

422 ***Canned Foods, Inc. v. Ult. Search Inc.***, FA0012000096320 (Forum February 13, 2001) (<groceryoutlet.com>. "Where the domain name is a generic term, it is difficult to conclude that there is a deliberate attempt to confuse. . . . There are dozens of other enterprises that use the term 'Grocery Outlet' therefore one cannot conclude that Complainant must necessarily be the special target.")

423 ***Ramsey Mankarious v. Stanley Pace***, D2015-1100 (WIPO August 11, 2015) (<mankarious>) (Held domain name for fifteen years but no trademark use of the name, thus no standing to maintain the UDRP proceeding); see ***Wagner v. Lindawagner.com***, 16-CV-53 (E.D. VA, Alexandria Division, August 15, 2016) for similar result under the Anticybersquatting Consumer Protection Act.

424 Unregistered rights of celebrities are discussed further in "Personal Names as Trademarks" (Sec. 4.01-E.1). *Garth Brooks v. Commbine.com, LLC*, FA0011000096097 (Forum January 2, 2001).

425 See ***Red Nacional De Los Ferrocarriles Espanoles v Ox90***, D2001-0981 (WIPO November 21, 2001). Respondent (admittedly a knowledgeable Internet analyst) registered the recently lapsed domain name <renfe.com>. The Panel held that "where there is an intentional registration of a domain name by one with obvious reason to believe that it might be the trademarked name of another, combined with an intentional or reckless failure to verify whether that is the case and without making even the most basic inquiry, constitutes registration of that domain name in bad faith." There was a vigorous dissent but the majority view for lapsed domain names (assuming the marks have established themselves in the marketplace) is the consensus opinion: "when the facts demonstrate clearly that someone else has been extensively using the Domain Name and that it has obvious value, at least some minimal investigation is required in order to dispel the logical inference that the Domain Name is someone else's trademark or at least another s well known business name."

426 ***Donna Karan Studio v. Raymond Donn***, D2001-0587 (WIPO June 27, 2001) (<dknyjeans.com>).

and 4) rejecting excuses altogether.[428] The fourth category, "finders keepers," has been criticized as a "quaint and classic saying" but this is "an oversimplification of the underlying law."[429] The decision in the cited case is itself open to criticism because the disputed domain name was the hackneyed phrase "worldwide commerce." However, the complainant's right is enhanced or undermined by the nature and relative strength of the mark in the context of "rights in the domain name" and "bad faith." Complainant is more likely to prevail, as did World Wide Commerce, if it has an established reputation earned over a lengthy period.

Tensions between trademark owners and new registrants are understandable, particularly where a new registrant is unaware of complainant or its trademark and is not in competition with it.[430] A domain name inadvertently allowed to lapse and then acquired by another company with the same name cannot be recovered.[431] Panels also take into account the parties' relative geographic locations. UDRP panels have declined except in the most egregious cases[432] to infer bad faith registration by respondents in a different country from where complainants or their registered marks have built their reputations.[433]

---

[427] ***Paper Denim & Cloth, LLC v. Pete Helvey***, FA1201001425020 (Forum March 5, 2012) (The domain name comprises three common dictionary words, "paper," "denim" and "cloth." Although Complainant demonstrated Respondent lacked rights or legitimate interests it "provided no evidence that its mark, although registered on the Principal Register of the USPTO, is sufficiently well known as to enable the inference to be drawn that Respondent must have had that mark in mind when he registered the Domain Name. Nor is there any other evidence from which the Panel can conclude that Respondent had Complainant or its trademark in mind when he registered the Domain Name.")

[428] ***Corbis Corporation v. Zest***, FA0107000098441 (Forum September 12, 2001) (Three member Panel: "There is an element of 'finders keepers, losers weepers' in this decision. We believe that is as it should be.")

[429] ***World Wide Commerce Corporation***, *supra.*

[430] ***CB Publishing, LLC v. Akway International Ltd c/o Hostmaster***, FA0702000926506 (Forum April 18, 2007) (Not competitors, and parties established in different countries).

[431] ***Berenson & Company, Inc. v. Berenson Corp. c/o Babij, Terry***, FA0909001283183 (Forum October 23, 2009).

[432] ***General Motors LLC v. Shenzhen Belding Golf Planning Co., ltd.***, D2009-1781(WIPO February 10, 2010) (<cadillacgolf.com>. Chinese Respondent targeted an English language audience).

[433] ***John Fairfax Publ'ns Pty Ltd v. Domain Names 4U***, D2000-1403 (WIPO December 13, 2000) (<financialreview.com>. Australia and United States); ***Craig Media, Inc. v. Kim Hyungho***, D2004-0091 (WIPO March 22, 2004) (<achannel.com>. Canada and South Korea. "Needless to say, if the Complainant had produced evidence to show that the Respondent had registered the Domain name with the Complainant in mind and/or was in the habit of adopting other people's trade marks for his domain names, the result would have been very different.")

4.01-F.1.b *Respondent's Conduct Not Condoned Where Domain Name Not Abandoned* 4.01-F.1.b

The reputation of the trademark is a significant factor in determining parties' respective rights. The fact that a domain name registration has expired and inadvertently lapsed "does not mean that respondent has any right to use the well-known trademark as its domain name when such use could cause confusion to consumers and damage to the owner of the trademark."[434] The "Policy does not condone such attempts to 'catch' a domain name after an unintentional failure to renew, when the registrant has no right or legitimate interest thereto and no intention of making a fair use of same."[435] Registering a long-held domain name following complainant's inadvertent lapse in renewing it without showing how it is intended to be used without infringing complainant's right will be sufficient to support a finding of abusive registration."[436] The Panel in ***World Wide Commerce*** (previously cited) held that a "finder takes as to all the world except the true owner, or the prior peaceable possessor."

This rule is particularly applied against respondents in the business of acquiring lapsed domain names composed of trademarks well known to the public and known to have significant Internet traffic. "Intentional registration of a domain name by one with obvious reason to believe that it might be the trademarked name of another, combined with an intentional or reckless failure to verify whether that is the case and without making even the most basic inquiry, constitutes registration of that domain name in bad faith."[437]

Inadvertently allowing a registration to expire "does not mean that any Registrant is permitted to swoop in and acquire the registration."[438] When respondents do "swoop in" they cannot establish their legitimacy by pleading they acquired

---

434 ***Donna Karan Studio***, *supra*.

435 ***Bronx Arts Ensemble, Inc. v. Vilma Morales, e:bOOm, S.A***, D2004-0493 (WIPO August 30, 2004).

436 This conclusion is drawn from two widely accepted theories of cybersquatting, enunciated respectively in ***Telstra Corporation Limited v. Nuclear Marshmallows***, D2000-0003 (WIPO February 18, 2000) (An inference will be drawn from respondent's choice of name when "it is not possible to conceive of any plausible actual or contemplated active use of the Domain Name by respondent that would not be illegitimate) and ***Veuve Clicquot Ponsardin, Maison Fondée en 1772 v. The Polygenix Group Co.***, D2000-0163 (WIPO May 1, 2000) (Opportunistic bad faith).

See also ***Danette Haworth v. Jack Leeds***, FA1591257 (Forum December 30, 2014) ("Because Complainant is an author of books for young readers, and Complainant's name is the entirety of the mark and of this domain name, it is clear that Respondent has something unfair in mind with holding onto this domain name. This Panel may trace Respondent's bad faith to the doctrine of opportunistic bad faith—namely, that Respondent capitalized on Complainant's failure to re-register its long held domain name in order to profit from Complainant's error.")

437 ***Red Nacional De Los Ferrocarriles Espanoles v Ox90***, D2001-0981 (WIPO November 21, 2001).

438 ***Tercent Inc. v. Lee Yi***, FA 139720 (Forum February 10, 2003).

the lapsed domain names for their intrinsic rather than their trademark values when the facts (which may include evidence of Internet traffic) support the opposite conclusion, that the domain names have a history of association with trademarks. It is understandable in these circumstances that complainants will initiate contact with respondents to reclaim or buy back their domain names at non-prohibitive prices.[439]

4.01-F.2 4.01-F.2 Uncertainty of Recapturing Lapsed Domain Name

4.01-F.2.a 4.01-F.2.a *No Presumption of Bad Faith*

Registrants of lapsed domain names are equally as likely to be innocent of abusive registration as opportunistic. The Policy does not condemn registrants who acquire domain names with knowledge of prior holders who appear to have knowingly abandoned their trademarks[440]; or, who acquire domain names after they are returned to the general pool who are not attempting to "use the name to compete with the mark holder or disrupt its business . . . whether the mark is a common law or a registered mark."[441] There is no presumption of bad faith. An owner is less likely to recover possession of the domain name where its trademark is based on a common word or descriptive phrase[442] or the trademark has been abandoned.[443] Acquiring recently lapsed domain names is not inconsistent with innocent motives. When a generic or descriptive domain name comes to market purchasers may genuinely have no way of knowing that it belonged to a trademark owner who

---

[439] Ordinarily, in non-lapse disputes which party first approaches the other could be a material factor in determining the legitimacy of a paragraph 4(b)(i) defense. See "Revenue Model Not Condemned" (6.01-A.2.a) and "Not All Offers to Sell Violate the Policy" (5.02-B). However, in inadvertent lapse disputes it is not material that complainants take the initiative in offering to repurchase their domain names; what is material is that "Respondent offered to sell the Disputed Domain Name" for a sum exceeding the cost of acquiring it. ***Flowserve Corporation v. Domain Admin / Ashantiplc Limited***, FA160500 1674825 (Forum July 12, 2016) ($100,000. The Majority held that at best Respondent was "'willfully blind' in failing to make … quick and simple enquiries to find out if SIHI belonged to third parties").

[440] ***Jeremy Same v. Richard Weston / dreamGEAR, LLC***, FA1311001531432 (Forum January 20, 2014).

[441] ***Diamond Trust Consultancy (UK) Limited v. Kim, James***, D2015-2051 (WIPO January 27, 2016) (<diamondtrust.com> acquired through auction) (The Panel's concluding phrase "whether the mark is 'strong' or 'weak'" is questionable as to "strong" since that factor demands respondent rebut complainant's proof).

[442] ***Mediaset S.p.A. v. Didier Madiba, Fenicius LLC***, D2011-1954 (WIPO February 4, 2012) (MEDIASET [trademark owned by an Italian television company] and <mediaset.com>). The domain name is composed of words generic in the English language. Complainant thereafter commenced a civil action in Rome and obtained judgment recovering the domain name.

[443] ***PFIP, LLC v. Blast Fitness Group, LLC / Thomas Moran***, FA1204001440897 (Forum June 3, 2012) (<blastfitness.com>).

inadvertently allowed it to lapse. Indeed, subsequent purchasers without knowledge of complainants' trademarks are by definition bona fide possessors.[444]

In this respect the principles are no different from those applied to registering generic and descriptive terms that by happenstance are identical or confusingly similar to a complainant's trademark. Recapture of domain names formerly owned by non-trademark owners is out of the question because a complainant without trademark rights has no standing.[445] Recapture by prior owners whose trademarks postdate the loss or abandonment of the domain name[446] or trademarks that make few ripples in the marketplace or are composed of generic terms may have standing but no actionable claim.[447]

With respect to abandoned (or seemingly abandoned) trademarks, where a respondent registers a domain name and establishes a business competitive with complainant's, proof that the complainant both abandoned the trademark and changed its business name[448] successfully establishes a legitimate interest under paragraph 4(c)(i) of the Policy. In such case complainant is in a position no different from a party that acquires a trademark subsequent to the registration of the same term as a domain name. Reregistration of an abandoned trademark gives a trademark owner no superior right to the corresponding domain name without proof of proscribed conduct.[449]

To overcome respondent's argument that it registered an abandoned domain name there must be some proof that the lapse of registration was unintentional. "Although complainant had previously registered the Domain Name . . . <midlandheart.co.uk>, it had allowed these registrations to lapse, and there is no evidence that respondent knew that complainant intended to reregister them."[450] A lengthy passage of time between the lapse and commencing a proceeding gives credence to

---

444 Although this is the consensus, some panelists have advanced a competing theory that respondents are nonetheless liable for infringement even if they registered the domain names in good faith: "what has changed is not the Respondent's use, but the emergence of the Complainant's new and powerful trademark . . . [which] raises the question of the obligations of the owners of domain names used to generate PPC revenue to the owners of new, emerging, trademarks." ***Camilla Australia Pty Ltd v. Domain Admin, Mrs Jello, LLC.***, D2015-1593 (WIPO November 30, 2015). However, in a subsequent ACPA action Camilla Australia (now defendant) stipulated to vacate the UDRP award in its entirety. *Mrs. Jello, LLC v. Camilla Australia Pty Ltd.* 15-cv-08753 (D. NJ 8/1/2016). The discontinuance should clarify the law as it ought to be applied in UDRP disputes. For a further discussion on retroactive bad faith go to Sec. 4.03-A.4.b.

445 ***Connie Campbell Bratcher v. Inspirational Poetry Quebec***, FA0902001249815 (Forum May 8, 2009) (<inspirationalpoetry.com>).

446 ***Forex Club International Limited v. INO.com, Inc.***, FA1003001316362 (Forum May 17, 2010).

447 ***GLB Serivicos Interativos S.A. v. Ultimate Search Inc.***, D2002-0189 (WIPO May 29, 2002) (<paparazzo.com>).

448 These were the facts in ***PFIP, LLC***, *supra*.

449 Discussed further at "Earlier Registered Domain Names; Subsequently Acquired Trademarks" (Sec. 5.01-F.2).

the argument that the domain name has been abandoned.[451] Fitting into "one of the preferred categories"[452] is an evidentiary hurdle, as complainant discovered in ***Promatic***.[453] Respondent pointed out that complainant did not have a trademark to which the domain name was identical or confusingly similar. It owned a design mark rather than a word mark registration. The case is instructive because it shows the Panel's close attention to the evidence—what was offered and what withheld. The Panel expressed concern that "the Complaint failed to describe complainant's trade marks accurately."

The principle that emerges from ***Promatic*** is that complainants have to do more than simply assert that a respondent has used an automated program to pick up its expired domain name. One of the questions much discussed among panelists after automated programs began scooping up domain names is whether respondents have "a duty to conduct a search to check that the domain name in issue is not a trade mark of a third party." The answer is "no," unless there is "evidence that the domain name was registered (whether automatically or otherwise) . . . .[because] of any goodwill or reputation that complainant has built up in the name."

4.01-F.2.b

4.01-F.2.b *Respondent's Conduct*

Decisions on lapsed registrations are governed by the same factors that apply to assessing the conduct of respondents generally. For example, if respondent is an adjudicated serial cybersquatter or is populating the website with hyperlinks to the complainant's competitors, it can be inferred that it has acted opportunistically.[454] However, "it is not in and of itself evidence of bad faith [for a respondent] to make use of software or services that identify, reserve, and register domain names that

---

450 ***Midland Heart Limited v. Uton Black***, D2009-0076 (WIPO March 30, 2009). Failing to take timely action against a cybersquatter is subject to a different set of rules than loss of domain name due to inadvertence. "Normally those who sleep on their rights do so at their peril," ***Official Pillowtex***, *supra*. Discussed further in "Sleeping on One's Rights" (Sec. 5.01-E).

451 ***Radio Italia S.p.A. v. Mdnh Inc, Brendhan Hight***, D2010-0329 (WIPO May 14, 2010). Complainant owned <radioitalia.com> until 2000. On the other hand, inadvertence is not fatal if the trademark owner acts reasonably quickly to remedy the oversight. ***ChemRite CoPac, Inc. v. Isaac Goldstein***, D2010-0279 (WIPO May 7, 2010).

452 ***World Wide Commerce***, *supra*.

453 ***Promatic International Limited v. Name Administration Inc.***, D2006-0673 (WIPO July 19, 2006) (<promatic.com>).

454 ***Aspen Holdings Inc. v. Christian P. Vandendorpe***, D2009-1160 (WIPO October 16, 2009) (As respondent registered <firstquote.net> only 5 days after complainant had first started using the term 1STQUOTE in commerce, had been involved in an earlier UDRP proceeding, and had not replied to complainant's contentions, the panel decided that these "factors when combined . . . are sufficient to tip the scales in complainant's favour on the balance of probabilities.")

have become available by reason of nonrenewal, transfer, or legitimate sale by their owners."[455]

Respondent in the case cited in the footnote appeared and argued that it had a legitimate interest in <carbonfootprint.org> as a generic term. The Panel held that

> In previous cases in which a panel ordered transfer of a domain name based upon a trafficker's duty to undertake a reasonable investigation and found bad faith, either the domain name at issue was distinctive (and not a common word or phrase) or respondent had been found frequently to have ignored others' trademark rights, as evidenced by losing domain names in previous Policy proceedings.

This finding is consistent with precedent in that it focuses on the strength of the trademark and the probability of its having been known to respondent when it registered the domain name. Not only is "carbon footprint" not distinctive, there was no evidence Respondent was of the class "found frequently to have ignored others' trademark rights."

4.02 RESPONDENT'S LACK OF RIGHTS OR LEGITIMATE INTERESTS—PARAGRAPH 4(a)(ii) OF THE POLICY 4.02

4.02-A Distinguishing Rights and Legitimate Interests 4.02-A

4.02-A.1 Right by Priority 4.02-A.1

4.02-A.1.a *Priority as a Legally Enforceable Interest* *4.02-A.1.a*

4.02-A.1.a.i ***Distinguishing "Owning" and "Holding"*** *4.02-A.1.a.i*

Domain names come into existence by contract rather than use in commerce. They can be said to be "owned" but are really "held" for renewable terms unless relinquished or lost. However, their legal status has evolved over time in judicial decisions from a contract for services to intangible personal property. The Ninth Circuit Court of Appeals in the U.S.,[456] the Court of Appeal Ontario, Canada,[457] and high courts in the U.K. and India have held that domain names are intangible

---

[455] ***Carbon Footprint Ltd v. Adrian Fuller***, D2007-0642 (WIPO July 26, 2007).

[456] *Kremen v. Cohen*, 337 F.3d 1024 (9th Cir. 2003) "[A] domain name is intangible property because it satisfies a three part test for the existence of a property right: it is an interest capable of precise definition; it is capable of exclusive possession or control; and it is capable of giving rise to a legitimate claim for exclusivity"; *Office Depot, Inc. v. Zuccarini*, 621 F.Supp.2d 773, 778 (N.D. Cal. 2007), aff'd 596 F.3d 696 (9th Cir. 2010) ("[D]omain name[s] [are] subject to receivership in the district of domain name registrar."); *GOPETS Ltd. v. Hise, Digital Overture, Inc.*, 657 F.3d 1024, 1032 (9th Cir. 2011) ("Nothing in the text or structure of the statute indicates that Congress intended that rights in domain names should be inalienable.")

[457] *Tucows.com Co. v. Lojas Renner, S.A.*, 106 O.R. (3d) 561, 211 ONCA 548 (Court of Appeal for Ontario, August 5, 2011), leave to appeal to the Supreme Court of Canada denied, 2012 CanLII 28261 (SCC).

property with all the rights that accrue to ownership.[458] *Office Depot* (9th Circuit) teaches that they are also garnishable property.[459] However, this is not the law in the Fourth Circuit.[460] The status of domain names under bankruptcy law in the United States is governed by state law, and if they are deemed property they must be scheduled together with a petitioner's other assets.[461]

---

[458] *O.G. Ltd. v. Allan* [2007] 1 A.C. 1 (H.L.), in which Lord Hoffmann for the majority observed at para. 101, "I have no difficulty with the proposition that a domain name may be intangible property, like a copyright or trademark." Similar conclusions about domain names as intangible personal property have been found in *Satyam Infoway Ltd. vs Sifynet Solutions Pvt. Ltd.*, AIR 2004 SC 3540, 2004 (3) AWC 2366 SC (Supreme Ct of India, 6 May, 2004) ("What is important for the purposes of the present appeal is the protection given to intellectual property in domain names. A prior registrant can protect its domain name against subsequent registrants. . . . The defences available to a complaint are . . . substantially similar to those available to an action for passing off under trademark law.")

Domain names as intangible property does not apply to dot uk. NominetUk, Terms and Conditions of Domain Name Registration, Effective from May 4, 2014 provides that "A domain name is not an item of property and has no 'owner'. It is an entry on our register database reflected by our name servers which we provide as part of this contract" (Para.10).

[459] The ACPA has made it unnecessary to apply for a writ to take possession of a domain name that is the subject of an action but garnishment is a possible tool for enforcing money judgments against defendants holding other domain names, as it did in ***Office Depot***. See ***Sprinkler Warehouse, Inc. v. Systematic Rain, Inc.***, A14-1121 (Minn.App. 2-2-2015). In Virginia, ***Network Solutions v. Umbro International, Inc.***, 529 S.E. 80, 86-87 (Va. 2000) held that domain names are not garnishable citing a federal ruling, ***Dorer v Arel***, 60 F. Supp. 2d 558 (E.D. Va 1999) that predates the ACPA.

In ***Dorer***, however, court found that garnishment of domain names was a "knotty issue" which fortunately "need not be resolved because there is a more readily available, practical solution to the problem to be found in [Network Solutions Inc.'s] policies." NCI's solution, cancellation or transfer of the domain name to trademark owner, is the remedy now available under the UDRP and the ACPA. California, Louisiana and Minnesota have ruled that domain names are garnishable assets, although for California note ***Palacio Del Mar Homeowners Ass'n, Inc. v. McMahon***, 174 Cal. App.4th 1386, 1391, 95 Cal.Rptr.3d 445 (2009) in which the Court held that "domain names do not constitute property subject to a turnover order because they cannot be taken into custody." The *Office Depot* court did not regard *Palacio Del Mar* as ruling that domain names are not garnishable because the court "based its holding on a reading of California Civil Procedure Code § 699.040, which provides that, with respect to a turnover order, property must be levied upon by taking it into custody. However, the court left open the question whether domain names constitute intangible property generally, and it cited Kremen with approval. Moreover, the 'taking it into custody' language in § 699.040 does not appear in § 708.620, which governs the appointment of receivers. We conclude that Kremen is still an accurate statement of California law, and that domain names are intangible property subject to a writ of execution."

[460] *Dorer, supra.* cited in *Network Solutions v. Umbro International, Inc.*, 529 S.E. 80, 86-87 (Va. 2000) ("[W]hatever contractual rights the judgment debtor has in the domain names at issue in this appeal, those rights do not exist separate and apart from NSI's services that make the domain names operational Internet addresses."); *Alexandria Surveys International, LLC. v. Alexandria Consulting Group, LLC*, 13 -CV-00891 (E.D. Virginia, Alexandria Div. November 7, 2013) ("[I]t is well-settled that the contours of the property interests assumed by the trustee are determined by state law.") For New

Issues of status that are fought over in courts of competent jurisdiction have no practical relevance in a UDRP proceeding. The only circumstance for which "holding" can be said to be less than "ownership" occurs where non-trademark owners inadvertently allow their registrations to lapse and irretrievably lose them to unrelated entities.[462] Otherwise, to hold rather than own domain names signifies no diminution of their value as evidenced by their role in the Internet economy and robustness of transactions in the secondary market.

A holder's interest when challenged under the Policy is characterized either as a "[legal] right" or a "legitimate interest." Having either is sufficient to defeat a claim of bad faith, but having neither is insufficient to prove abusive registration. Respondent's priority of registration generally disfavors complainant; but complainant's priority raises fact-laden issues in proving bad faith. Respondents who have legal rights can also be said to have legitimate interests, but those that only have a legitimate interest have no legal right. So, while it is appropriate for complainant to allege and panels to hold that a respondent that has neither rights nor legitimate interests lacks both, it is inaccurate to say that a respondent has both *rights **and** legitimate interests* if it has only legitimate interests. The reason for insisting on this distinction even though it is generally ignored is that rights and interests carry different possessory consequences, which is explained below.

4.02-A.1.a.ii *Establishing Right or Legitimate Interest* *4.02-A.1.a.ii*

Having a right or legitimate interest is assessed as of the time of the filing of the complaint, or any past time if the use to which the domain name is put has changed (as distinguished from bad faith which is assessed at the time the domain name was registered) (Burdens of proof and production are further considered in Sec. 5.01-A.1).

Of the three paragraph 4(c) defenses the first and third share a common element, namely proof of legitimate activity. Paragraph 4(c)(i) requires proof of continuous use "before notice" of infringement; or an intention manifested by "demonstrable preparations" (also "before notice") to use the disputed domain name for bona fide offerings of goods or services. Paragraph 4(c)(iii) demands proof the domain name is non-infringing by reason of its noncommercial or fair use of the domain name.

York see *Wornow v. Register.Com, Inc.*, 8 AD 3d 59, 59-60 (1st Dept. 2004) ("a domain name that is not trademarked or patented is not personal property, but rather a contract right that cannot exist separate and apart from the services performed by a registrar.")

461 *LARRY KOENIG & ASSOC., LLC Debtor Martin A. SCHOTT, Trustee for Larry Koenig & Assoc., LLC and Larry and Nydia Koenig v. Andrea Lynn MCLEAR, Larry Koenig & Assoc., LLC and Larry and Nydia Koenig, 2004* WL 3244582 (Bkrtcy. M.D. La.) If not disclosed petitioners risk losing unscheduled domain names in post-bankruptcy discharge proceedings to bidders for whom they have value.

462 A holder who has lost its domain name through lapse of registration is in a worse position than a trademark owner because it has no trademark and would have no actionable claim to recover the lost domain name unless it is able to establish common law rights to it.

Although it is possible for respondents to passively hold disputed domain names and prevail under paragraph 4(a)(ii) of the Policy, where for example a respondent is in the business of reselling domain names and not actively monetizing them, it would be difficult to establish rights or legitimate interests under 4(c)(iii) without having an active website.[463] This is not true for paragraph 4(c)(ii) for which the defense rests on being "commonly known" by the domain name. Respondents can have a right to the domain name even if passively held,[464] although the name by which respondent is commonly known is not proof that it has a right or legitimate interest in it.[465]

The disjunctive "or" underlines a distinction between "right" and "legitimate interest." In practice a present right to a domain name can be both a legal right *and* a legitimate interest or either one depending on the factual circumstances. As one Panel explains: "The intention was that, first, if the registrant had an actual legal right to the domain name, that would defeat the trademark owner's claim by itself. But, secondly, the Policy went further and added another criterion, that of legitimate interest."[466] Words chosen with care "have to be given some work to do or they serve no purpose." The Panel continues, "[t]he intention here was to cover cases where the registrant may not have a legal right, but where it nevertheless has a bona fide association or connection of some sort with the domain name, where for example . . . respondent has not registered the domain name for merely speculative reasons . . ."[467]

A "[legal] right" (as distinct and separate from a "legitimate interest") arises in one of two circumstances: either respondent is the senior user of the disputed term that independently qualifies as a trademark[468] or the domain name registration precedes trademark acquisition. To prevail complainant must prove that respondent has (present tense) either no right or no legitimate interest or lacks both. Except for a legal right to a domain name created by priority, a defense based on choice of

---

[463] Passive holding could give rise to negative inferences but even if it does it would not sufficient alone to establish bad faith registration. The issue is discussed further in "Drawing Inferences" (Sec. 7.09-A).

[464] Registrations renewed but not currently active: ***Angelica Fuentes Téllez v. Domains by Proxy, LLC / Angela Brink***, D2014-1860 (WIPO December 18, 2014); ***Microsonic Gesellschaft für Mikrotechnik und Ultra schalltechnik mbH v. Alex Rad***, D2014-1715 (December 1, 2014).

[465] ***Sebastian International, Inc. v. Sebastian Contracting Services, Inc.***, FA0711001106694 (Forum January 7, 2008) ("As the Respondent is dissolved, it cannot have any further rights or legitimate interests in the domain name." But there was no evidence of bad faith).

[466] ***International E-Z UP, Inc. v. PNH Enterprises, Inc.***, FA0609000808341 (Forum November 15, 2006).

[467] *Id.*, citing ***MAHA Maschinenbau Haldenwang GmbH & Co. KG v. Deepak Rajani***, D2000-1816 (WIPO March 2, 2001).

[468] See *Sunearth, Inc. and The Solaray Ccorporation v. Sun Earth Solar Power Co., Ltd.; NBSolar USA, Inc.* C 11 4991 (N.D. Calif. August 23, 2013).

common words or phrases and descriptive terms identical or confusingly similar to a mark for which complainant has precedence is merely a legitimate interest.

A respondent has no right to a domain name incorporating complainant's trademark unless 1) its legal right precedes or is concurrent with that of the trademark owner's[469]; 2) its registration precedes complainant's acquisition of a trademark—a right based on the first to register doctrine[470]; or 3) its use (or more specifically, its content) is curated for its semantic sense without reference to complainant or association with its mark.

With regard to the first point, a complainant is no more elevated by having a later acquired trademark than a respondent prejudiced by failing to renew its trademark registration if it had one.[471] With regard to the second point, the domain name registrant is secure while it remains the holder. Otherwise, a respondent's right by virtue of precedence or its choice of domain name is "transient" because while a prior registration of a a string of characters later coveted by a trademark owner is most likely a legal right or legitimate interest in the portfolio of an original registrant, in the portfolio of an assignee or transferee it may be neither a right nor a legitimate interest.[472] With regard to the third point, while subsequent bad faith use by the original holder likely refutes rights or legitimate interests it will not under the traditional construction of the Policy support registration in bad faith.[473]

While a domain name holder cannot create a right or legitimate interest by merely registering a domain name,[474] it can have an alienable asset comparable

---

469 The question of "right" is "whether the application is bona fide or merely a way of bolstering the respondent's domain name registration," ***BECA Inc. v. CanAm Health Source, Inc***, D2004-0298 (WIPO July 23, 2004) ("Whether an application is to be given the same status as a trademark for the purpose of paragraph 4(a)(i) of the Policy is a complex issue. . . . However, even if an application does not provide rights in a trademark for the purposes of paragraph 4(a)(i) of the Policy, it does not follow that it is not sufficient to found rights or legitimate interests in a name under paragraph 4(a)(ii). The tests are different.") In ***Ciccone, p/k/a Madonna v. Parisi and "Madonna.com"***, D2000-0847 (WIPO October 12, 2000) the Panel found that it was "merely a way of bolstering respondent's domain name registration." See further discussion below on this point.

470 A right by contract or acquiescence is discussed further in "Permissive Use of Trademarks" (Sec. 6.01-C.1).

471 ***MNM Media LLC v. leftlane.com***, FA0806001211465 (Forum August 12, 2008) ("the fact that the LEFTLANE.COM trademark registration was allowed to lapse has no bearing on continued use of the <leftlane.com> domain name in connection with the Respondent's business. Renewal of domain name registration is not an inquiry relevant for review by the Panel and that it is not considered to be bad faith under the UDRP.")

472 Discussed further in "Second and Subsequent Generations of Holders" (Sec. 4.03-B.2.a).

473 Some panelists hold that renewal is a new act of registration. Discussed further in "Justifying Forfeiture Despite Good Faith Registration" (Sec. 4.03-A.4.b). Panelists espousing the view that bad faith use followed by renewal of registration is conclusive against respondent include ***Benoit Thiercelin v. Medicalexpo.com, CAC*** 100235 (ADR.eu May 23, 2011) (<medicalexpo.com>) and ***Eastman Sporto Group LLC v. Jim and Kenny***, D2009-1688 (WIPO March 1, 2010) (<sporto.com>).

to ownership of other forms of property by being the first to register the domain name either because there was no existing trademark, or if there was it was plausibly unaware of another's alleged right.[475] The Policy does not condemn selling domain names that happen to correspond to trademarks.[476] They can be sold to the highest bidder without violating a third party's rights or raising an issue of bad faith under paragraph 4(b)(i) of the Policy. However, there is an economic consequence to holding as a "right" and holding as a "legitimate interest." A respondent with a legally enforceable *right* has an interest in a domain name different in value than that possessed by a respondent with a *legitimate interest.*

For the former, it is irrelevant that the domain name is identical or confusingly similar to complainant's trademark. Where there is parity of right with a registered or unregistered trademark owner the domain name holder holds an alienable asset. For respondents whose claims are based on legitimate interests value to an arm's length purchaser depends on being able to use the domain name without infringing third-party rights.[477] This is because successors in interest are regarded as new registrants who are answerable to claims of abusive registration without regard to their predecessors' good faith registrations. While bad faith use subsequent to good faith registration shields assignors/transferors, assignees/transferees who acquire domain names for the market value related to their prior use and continue that prior use are exposed to liability for abusive registration.[478]

4.02-A.1.b

4.02-A.1.b *Conflicting Rights Favor Respondent*

Three factual circumstances support respondent's right to a disputed domain name identical or confusingly similar to complainant's trademark: 1) respondent owns a registered trademark "legitimately acquired"[479] in a different national jurisdiction[480]; 2) one of the parties has a registered and the other an unregistered

---

474 ***Nokia Corporation v. Nokia Ringtones & Logos Hotline***, D2001-1101 (WIPO October 18, 2001) (<worldnokia.com>). Discussed further in "First-Come First-Served Doctrine" (Sec.5.01-F).

475 ***Webanywhere Ltd. v. Marchex Sales, LLC / Brendhan Hight***, FA1303001491617 (Forum May 13, 2013) (Complaint denied. "Complainant contacted Respondent, inquiring about purchasing the domain name, and was told the domain name is for sale for $30,000.")

476 *GOPETS Ltd., supra.* the "primary purpose rule" is discussed further in "Not All Offers to Sell Violate the Policy" (Sec. 6.02-B).

477 Discussed further in "Renewal of Registration vs. Registration by Transfer" (Sec. 4.03-B) and "Transfer/Subsequent Holders = New Registration" (Sec. 4.03-B.2).

478 Even though alienable, the existence of a later acquired trademark affects and most likely diminishes the value of the asset to a transferee.

479 This qualification is necessary to account for opportunistic trademark registrations in foreign jurisdiction illustrated in the line of cases stemming from ***Ciccone, p/k/a Madonna v. Parisi and "Madonna.com."***, D2000-0847 (WIPO October 12, 2000). The ***Ciccone*** case is discussed further below.

trademark[481]; and 3) irrespective of the timing of their acquisitions the trademark and domain name (whenever purchased) are equally suitable for the parties' commercial[482] or private needs.[483]

In ***PRL USA Holdings*** Complainant/owner of the well-known POLO trademark challenged Respondent's registration of <polomag.com>. Respondent adopted "polo" and holds an Australian trademark registration for a sports magazine. The Panel held that as the parties' businesses were different each was entitled to the trademark in its class. Where respondent has for years operated a business by the same name as another's trademark[484]; or, coexisted for years[485] its right to use the term for its Internet presence cannot be denied. The parties in ***American Information*** had equal rights to AINET or AiNET. However, respondent proved that it was the senior, albeit unregistered user of the mark.[486] In ***Kelly*** both parties had "homonymous trademark rights to the GAYDAR mark." In ***Canned Foods*** Respondent was

---

[480] ***PRL USA Holdings, Inc .v. Catherine Mary Witham***, D2002-0361 (WIPO July 29, 2002) (<polomag.com>). Coexistence of marks in different Classes is fundamental to trademark law.

[481] ***American Information Corporation d/b/a American Information Network v. American Infometrics, Inc.***, FA0105000097339 (Forum July 19, 2001) (<ainet.com>); ***Kelly v. Qsoft Consulting Ltd.***, D2003-0221 (WIPO April 30, 2003) (<mygaydar.com>). See also ***Can I Do Better Internet Corp. v. Blastapplications***, D2011-0055 (WIPO March 8, 2011) (Panel found that Complainant has common law right in CANIDOBETTER.COM, but Respondent has a USPTO registration for CANDOBETTER, which is identical to its second level domain. Complainant argued that Respondent's trademark registration is subject to cancellation by Complainant due to Complainant's prior use dates. However, the argument is outside the scope of the UDRP. Discussed further in "Principal Register: Presumption of Validity" (Sec. 4.01-A.3.b).

[482] ***EAuto, L.L.C. v. EAuto Parts***, D2000-0096 (WIPO April 9, 2000) (<eautoparts.com>. "The weakness of the EAUTO trademark makes it difficult for Complainant to argue that Respondent lacks a legitimate interest in the domain name eautoparts.com. That is because this domain name eautoparts.com is descriptive of a business that offers, through the Internet, information about or sales of automobile parts, and it is inappropriate to give Complainant a wide monopoly over all domain names, even descriptive ones, that incorporate the mark EAUTO"); ***Action Sports Videos v. Jeff Reynolds***, D2001-1239 (WIPO December 13, 2001) ("The Panel does not believe it is the function of the Policy to serve to disentangle the conflicting rights of parties to a mark once it is apparent both parties have colorable claims to a mark underlying a disputed domain name.")

[483] Example: ***Canned Foods, Inc. v. Ult. Search Inc.***, FA 96320 (Forum February 13, 2001) (claim for common law trademark in GROCERY OUTLET); ***Shoeby Franchise B.V. v. Shoebuy.com, Inc. / SHOEBUY.COM***, D2010-2142 (WIPO March 20, 2011) (Respondent "adopted a defensive domain name registration policy pursuant to which [it purchased] the Domain Name and many other variants of its primary domain name.") Discussed further in "Dictionary Words and Descriptive Phrases" (Sec. 6.01-D.1). See also "'First-Come First-Served' Doctrine" (Sec. 5.01-F).

[484] ***Nature's Way Products, LLC v. Symbiant***, D2013-2156 (WIPO February 13, 2014).

[485] ***Pacific Bearing Corp. v. Pacific International Bearing Sales Inc.***, FA0812001238265 (Forum January 28, 2009) (<pacificbearingsales.com>).

[486] This is consistent with U.S. law. Common law rights of a senior user are preserved by the Lanham Act, 15 U.S.C. §§1057(c)(1) and 1065.

found to be using the phrase "grocery outlet" descriptively, in the same manner as many other businesses, none of which infringed Complainant's rights.

4.02-A.1.c

4.02-A.1.c *Rival Trademarks in Foreign Jurisdictions*

4.02-A.1.c.i

4.02-A.1.c.i ***No "Right" Where Trademark Registration is to Bolster Domain Name Registration***

Proof that a respondent is "commonly known" is satisfied when its personal or commercial identity has a historical correspondence with the domain name. The paragraph 4(c)(ii) defense[487] is not satisfied by respondent adventitiously adopting a name or registering a trademark to frustrate a preexisting statutory right. However, respondent's right is bolstered if it can claim a mark in its own jurisdiction, "even if doing so results in a domain name that is identical or confusingly similar to another entity's trademark that has also been duly registered, but in another country."[488] By itself coexistence of trademarks does not support a claim for abusive registration of a domain name.[489]

Since the right to a disputed domain name is independent of a statutory claim—that is, respondent's right is not tied to its having a trademark or service mark—it would be unpersuasive to argue in the alternative that a respondent loses a right because it neither had or if it did have it lost a trademark for failure to file a declaration of continued use under applicable law. While never having a trademark or abandoning one is not fatal to respondent's right or legitimate interest in a domain name,[490] no credit is given to a respondent who registers a trademark in a foreign jurisdiction as a ploy for gaining a superior position over a trademark holder in another jurisdiction.[491] Trademark registration can be disregarded "if the overall circumstances demonstrate it was obtained primarily to circumvent the application of the UDRP."[492]

An attempt to gain such right illegitimately is illustrated in ***Ciccone***. Complainant owns an unregistered trademark in her stage name, "Madonna."

[487] Discussed further in "Commonly Known By The Domain Name" (Sec. 5.03).

[488] ***ZPower, Inc. (formerly known as Zinc Matrix Power, Inc.) v. Kissan Battery House c/o Mr. Sachin***, FA0903001254829 (Forum June 1, 2009).

[489] ***ACE Limited v. WebMagic Ventures, LLC***, FA0802001143448 (Forum April 8, 2000) ("Trademark infringement laws prevent consumer confusion by regulating the use of similar marks only on competing goods.")

[490] ***Stonz Wear, Inc. v. Framez l Wear***, D2011-1764 (WIPO December 8, 2011) ("The next question is whether the fact that . . . the Respondent's trade mark registration was cancelled for failure to file an affidavit of use in 2007. . . nullifies the defense for the purpose of the second element of the Policy. The Panel is of the view that it does not.")

[491] ***Ciccone, p/k/a Madonna v. Parisi and "Madonna.com,"*** D2000-0847 (WIPO October 12, 2000).

[492] ***win.rarGmbH v. Win Road Assistance Repairs Pvt. Ltd.***, D2015-0398 (WIPO June 2, 2015).

Respondent registered MADONNA in Tunisia subsequent to his registration of the domain name, <madonna.com>. Both parties were U.S. citizens; respondent was not a resident in Tunisia and admitted he had obtained the trademark registration to protect his interests in the domain name. The Panel held that it "would be a mistake to conclude that mere registration of a trademark creates a legitimate interest under the Policy. . . . To conclude otherwise would mean that a Respondent could rely on intentional infringement to demonstrate a legitimate interest, an interpretation that is obviously contrary to the intent of the Policy."[493] The Madonna principle distinguishes between illegitimate and legitimate rival trademarks where the proof undermines good faith and supports opportunism. It does not apply to rival trademarks that are clearly not opportunistic or where the Panel would have to choose to whom to give the benefit of the doubt.[494]

The disputed domain name in ***BECA*** consisted of two dictionary words, "medicine" and "assist." Although the "mere fact that a trademark has been applied for or obtained by a respondent is not an absolute bar to a complainant succeeding under the UDRP" respondent's rights or legitimate interests cannot easily be dismissed.[495] Unlike ***Madonna*** Respondent's applications in ***BECA*** for trademarks in Canada and the U.S. preceded its registration of the disputed domain name. Although the applications had not matured to registration the Panel held they constituted a "right" under paragraph 4(a)(ii) of the Policy.

The Panel in ***BECA*** built on ***Madonna*** by demanding more evidence to support Complainant's contention of registration in bad faith for the reason that if it were a question of benefit of the doubt the benefit would have to go to respondent[496]:

---

493 *Id.*, "[T]o establish cognizable rights, the overall circumstances should demonstrate that the registration was obtained in good faith for the purpose of making bona fide use of the mark in the jurisdiction where the mark is registered and not obtained merely to circumvent the application of the Policy." The rule has also been applied to domestic trademarks. ***Goldman, Sachs & Co. v. Lis Wevers c/o Goldman Advertising Services BV***, FA0610000812109 (Forum November 22, 2006) (<goldmansex.com>) ("When the evidence shows that respondent obtained a trademark 'to shield a domain name from an unfavorable UDRP result . . . a Panel should not be bound by an immutable rule that would, if followed blind[ly], work an inequity on one of the parties or pervert the objectives of the Policy.")

494 ***BECA Inc. v. CanAm Health Source, Inc***, D2004-0298 (WIPO July 23, 2004) (<medicineassist.com>. "[F]or a panel to form a view upon the outcome of an application [to a national registry] . . . involves trespassing upon issues best left to national courts and registries. If a panel is not willing to do this, the issue becomes one of to whom the Panel should give the benefit of the doubt. Given that the burden of proof is on the Complainant it should not be surprising if the benefit of the doubt falls in favour of registration in the case of rights and legitimate interests under paragraph 4(a)(ii). . ..")

495 Whether complainant or respondent, mere application for trademark does not qualify as a "right." Respondent: ***duPont Publishing, Inc. v. Simon S. McNally***, FA0212000137169 (Forum February 3, 2003). For complainant discussed further at "No Right Accrues to Pending Application for Trademark" (Sec. 4.01-A.3.c).

> (i) When considering the question of "rights or legitimate interests" under paragraph 4(a)(ii), a panel can, in an appropriate case, question the legitimacy of a trademark relied upon by a respondent. . . . In a case where, in the opinion of the panel, a trademark has not been sought or obtained for a legitimate or bona fide purpose, but merely in order to bolster a domain name registration, the trademark can be disregarded.
>
> (ii) The chronology of events is an important factor in determining whether the application is bona fide or merely a way of bolstering the respondent's domain name registration. A trademark application made subsequent to notice of a dispute or the domain name registration may indicate a lack of legitimate interest.
>
> (iii) The knowledge and intention of respondent at the time the disputed domain name is registered is highly relevant, but knowledge of complainant's rights does not, in itself, preclude respondent from having a right or legitimate interest in the domain name.
>
> (iv) The connection, or lack of it, between respondent and the jurisdiction in which it is seeking a trademark registration may indicate whether the trademark application or registration is 'legitimate'.

An inference of targeting complainant's trademark is more compelling when the rival trademark is registered after the domain name. It suggests respondent is attempting to improve its position in anticipation of a UDRP challenge.[497]

4.02-A.1.c.ii

4.02-A.1.c.ii *Legitimate Trademark Registrations*

Absent circumstances discussed above that support bad faith, where respondent owns a trademark accepted for certification by a national registry there is no challengeable claim under the Policy. In ***Angels Baseball***[498] (involving a dictionary word, "Angels," although it is also the name of a well-known baseball club) the Panel found that the "Respondent obtained the [trademark] registration before he received any notice of the dispute . . . [and] without any opposition from

---

[496] ***BECA**, supra.* ("Given that the burden of proof is on the Complainant it should not be surprising if the benefit of the doubt falls in favour of registration in the case of rights and legitimate interests under paragraph 4(a)(ii) and falls against registration in the case of rights in a trademark under paragraph 4(a)(i).") See also ***ISL Marketing AG, and the Union des Associations Européennes de Football v. The European Unique Resources Organisation 2000 B.V.***, D2000-0230 (WIPO July 5, 2000) in which Complainant had also commenced an action in a Paris Court which established that by reason of its trademark Respondent had a "right" to the domain name, thus defeating Complainant's demand in the UDRP proceedings.

[497] See, for example, ***The Automobile Association Limited, Automobile Association Developments Limited v. Fish4travel, Inc.***, D2009-0401 (WIPO May 15, 2009) (AA PARKING was registered on June 24, 2008, the domain name was registered on September 23, 2004).

[498] ***Angels Baseball, L.P. v. Lee Dongyeon***, FA 925418 (Forum May 14, 2007) (<angels.com>).

Complainant [which had trademark registrations in South Korea and would have been in a position to commence such a proceeding]."[499]

In ***Sun Studio Entertainment***[500] the Respondent, an independent U.K. record label created in 2005, in the business of marketing CDs and DVDs in Europe and other countries, registered the domain name <memphisrecordingservice.com> in 2004 and obtained an EU trademark in 2006. Complainant had actual knowledge of respondent's business and even offered some of its products for sale in its Memphis store. The Panel held 1) Respondent's ownership of an EU trademark registration for the MEMPHIS RECORDING SERVICE mark was not obtained merely to circumvent the Policy; and 2) Respondent registered its domain name and mark not to capitalize on complainant's mark but, rather, "on the history surrounding a recording studio in Memphis known as the 'Memphis Recording Service.'"

The question is not whether the rival trademark is validly registered—an issue outside the scope of the Policy—but respondent's intent and motive for acquiring a trademark that supports its registration of a domain name identical or confusingly similar to a preexisting trademark recognized in another country. There are cases in which complainant has business operations in the same foreign jurisdiction as respondent and its failure to oppose the rival trademark registration is a factor favoring respondent, as in ***Angels Baseball.***

In ***The Elizabeth Taylor Cosmetics Company***[501] the Chinese national Respondent registered a trademark in China for "ELIZAB TAYLOR" before registering <elizabtaylor.com>. Although skeptical of respondent's motivation the Panel nevertheless dismissed the complaint because complainant, which had opposed other Elizabeth Taylor applications, did not oppose ELIZAB TAYLOR, and the trademark registration preceded the domain name registration.[502] Where respondent owns a trademark accepted for certification by a national registry that has examined the trademark, the claim raises issues that should properly be addressed by a court of competent jurisdiction" and is therefore outside the scope of the Policy.[503]

---

499 *Id.*, "In absence of contrary evidence, the Panel finds that Respondent's trademark registration for ANGELS is a valid title under Korean law."

500 ***Sun Studio Entertainment, Inc. v. Memphis Recording Service***, FA0805001189842 (Forum June 19, 2008).

501 ***The Elizabeth Taylor Cosmetics Company v. Yong Huang***, D2009-0919 (WIPO September 7, 2009).

502 *Id.* "However the Panel wishes to highlight that the present decision is issued without prejudice to any future re-filed Complaint by complainant under the Policy in light of any materially relevant subsequent developments, such as any lapse or successful trade mark challenge to Digasun's Chinese trade mark registration 4409305, bearing in mind the considerations for allowing a re-filed Complaint."

503 ***Mubadala Trade Marks Holding Company, LLC, Al Yah Satellite Communications Company PrJSC, and Al Maisan Satellite Communications Company, LLC v. Emedia Development Ltd. and***

4.02-A.1.d

4.02-A.1.d *Concurrent Use of Common Lexical Strings*

U.S. trademark law recognizes with some qualification that two parties may be entitled to use similar, even identical lexical compositions where the concurrent user offers the public unrelated goods or services. It has been noted (in a trademark context, although equally applicable to the UDRP) that "the Lanham Act's tolerance for similarity between competing marks varies inversely with the fame of the prior mark."[504] That is, "[a]s a mark's fame increases, the Act's tolerance for similarities between competing marks falls." This principle is carried over into UDRP jurisprudence.

In and of itself a domain name identical or confusingly similar to a trademark is not remarkable. Owners whose trademarks consist of lexical compositions attractive to many users have limited protection, hence the allowance for "similarities between competing marks." Current multiple trademark registrations in different classes undercut a complainant's allegation that in registering the disputed domain name respondent is targeting its (rather than another's) trademark.[505] No bad faith is imputed for registering a domain name respondent uses to describe its offering of goods or services.[506] Where, without knowledge and in some instances with it,[507] a party operates in a different market[508] and offers goods or services in different channels of trade[509] or the same goods and services in a different market,[510] it has a legitimate interest (if not a right) in the domain name.[511]

Whois Privacy Services Pty Ltd., D2013-0570 (WIPO May 23, 2013) (YAHCLICK and YAHLIVE and <yahclick.com> and <yahlive.com>).

504 *Kenneth Parker Toys Inc .v. Rose Art Industries Inc.*, 963 F. 2d 350, 353 (Fed. Cir. 1992).

505 ***Meredith Corp. vs. CityHome, Inc.***, D2000-0223 (WIPO May 18, 2000) ("[T]here are at least seven United States trademark registrations for Country Home by others for diverse uses and 'hundreds' for common variations thereof, e.g., Home Country. Furthermore, Complainant's trademark registrations are in classes 16 and 31 for such things as printed materials, magazines and seed. On the other hand, Respondent's potential use in connection with real estate and mortgage services would be in International Classes 35 and 36.")

506 ***Kaleidoscope Imaging, Inc. v. V Entm't***, FA 203207 (Forum January 5, 2004) (<kaleidoscope.com>).

507 Discussed further in "Nominative Fair Use" (Sec. 6.01-D.3).

508 ***Streetwise Maps, Inc. v. Ryan Gibson***, D2010-0984 (WIPO August 6, 2010).

509 ***GDATA Software AG v. Geologic Data Systems***, D2010-0389 (WIPO May 10, 2010). Respondent uses Complainant's trademark <gdata.com> as a domain name and e-mail address, while complainant uses the sign as its mark.

510 ***Park 'N Fly Service Corporation v. Elias Tesfa***, FA1202001427761 (Forum March 15, 2012).

511 ***Lytro, Inc. v. Drift Alliance Pty Ltd***, DAU2014-0019 (WIPO July 29, 2014) ("[K]nowledge of the Complainant's trade mark alone may not amount to bad faith registration or use if the primary intent is to use the domain name for goods and services different to those of the trade mark owner, provided use of the domain name is non-confusing, non-competitive and without intent to divert

Factors to be considered in determining respondent's right or legitimate interest in the disputed domain name include the parties' respective locations and customer and market overlaps.[512] Setting aside the issue of nominative fair use, which implies knowledge of complainant and its trademark, or timing of domain name and trademark registrations, the proper assessment extends to determining whether the respondent is a competitor.

However, even if this is so a competitor is not *ipso facto* a cybersquatter because its domain name is identical or confusingly similar to complainant's trademark. Nor does it follow that because a respondent offers the same goods or services it should have had knowledge or been aware of complainant. Such a conclusion requires a threshold analysis of intrinsic and extrinsic evidence that includes "markets" and "channels of trade." A competitor is either a cybersquatter or innocent holder depending upon the factors set forth in paragraphs 4(c)(i) and 4(c)(ii) of the Policy.[513] It is not the Policy's role to stifle competition where the evidence supports respondent's claim to a right or legitimate interest in the domain name. Nevertheless, whereas geographical and linguistic separation may favor respondent, proximity strengthens complainant.[514]

4.02-A.2 Legitimate Interests 4.02-A.2

A "legitimate interest" is something less than a "[legal] right" and may be temporally limited.[515] It is conditional on continued legitimate use and, although not vulnerable to forfeiture in a UDRP proceeding, may be vulnerable under U.S. trademark law if the domain name subsequently infringes the complainant's trademark.[516] The domain name held as a legitimate interest can be sold, but the purchaser as a new registrant takes it with imputed knowledge of its predecessor's use,[517] with the

Internet users who are seeking out the Complainant," citing ***Kosciuszko Thredbo Pty Limited v ThredboNet Marketing Pty Limited*** [2014] FCAFC 87 (21 July 2014).

512 This is the conclusion in ***Streetwise Maps***, *supra*. "While Respondent does refer to maps on its website" (the Panel notes) it "does not offer to sell maps to the public or sell maps to the public on its website. Respondent offers its services to develop a system, not to sell products such as maps."

513 Passive use of a domain name makes respondent's contention of differentiating prospective use less plausible. See ***Omni Development, Inc. d/b/a The Omni Group v. Graffle, Inc.***, FA1104001385743 (Forum June 14, 2011). A respondent is not "commonly known as" the domain name or even by its alleged corporate name if it fails to also show that the domain and corporate name is connected to a bona fide offering of goods or services distinct from that offered by complainant.

514 Geographic distance, for example, makes more plausible respondent's denial of knowledge of complainant or its trademark. See ***Interbanking S.A. v. Alexander Lerman***, D2013-1884 (WIPO January 23, 2014) (<interbanking.com>). Discussed further in "Nearness and Remoteness in Proving Knowledge and Intention" (Sec. 4.02-C.3).

515 As by contract for example, a right granted by contract is not such a "right" as to triumph over the trademark owner, but akin to a "legitimate interest" that either terminates upon notice or expires with the contract. See "Rights to Domain Name After Termination of Permission" (Sec. 5.01-E).

consequence that if the purchaser continues a bad faith use it exposes itself to forfeiture by reason of its predecessor's prior infringing content.[518] A legitimate interest by the original registrant is an interest acquired over time that is legitimized by *bona fide* use of the domain name "before any notice [to the respondent] of a dispute" [Paragraph 4(c)(i) of the Policy].

As noted above, respondents cannot create legitimate interests by registering domain names. Nor can they create rights by estoppel, except as otherwise provided in 4(c)(i) of the Policy.[519] Rights or legitimately interests typically arise from the use of the domain name or the circumstances under which it was registered, whether authorized or through continued acquiescent use.[520] The first to register a domain name identical or confusingly similar to a trademark has a conditional legitimate interest, which may ripen into a legal right.[521]

However, if the facts establish that respondent is an insider to a merger and acquisition or learned of complainant's intentions from advance publicity, its opportunistic registration gives it neither a right nor legitimate interest. The present tense "has" for the 4(c) defenses is construed to mean that respondent has a legitimate interest "at the time this decision is being made."[522] The term "legitimate interest" "cover[s] cases where the registrant may not have a legal right, but where it nevertheless has a bona fide association or connection of some sort with the domain name."[523] Respondent cannot create for itself a right or legitimate interest on the theory that its use of the domain name benefits the trademark owner.[524]

---

516 Respondent kept <newportnews.com> in ***Newport News, Inc. v. Vcv Internet***, AF 0238 (eResolution July 18, 2000) and lost it in *Newport News Holdings Corporation v. Virtual City Vision, Incorporated, d/b/a Van James Bond Tran*, 650 F3d 423 (4th Cir. 2011).

517 ***United Parcel Service of America, Inc. v. Michael Robert***, D2008-0339 (WIPO April 29, 2008).

518 ***Daimler AG v. William Wood***, D2008-1712 (WIPO February 25, 2009).

519 In ***Stevland Morris a/k/a Stevie Wonder v. Unofficial Fan Club c/o Web Master***, FA0504000453986 (Forum June 22, 2005) respondent claimed that he had "acquired Common Law rights in the name <steviewonder.com> through his nine year use of it as a domain name." The Panel labeled this "a novel concept with very little merit." Discussed further in "Sleeping on One's Rights" (Sec. 6.01-E).

520 Discussed further in "Right or Legitimate Interest: Expressly, Impliedly, and Lawfully" (Sec. 6.01-C).

521 Discussed further in "First-Come-First Served" (Sec. 5.01-F).

522 ***International E-Z UP***, *supra*.

523 ***Id.*** citing ***MAHA Maschinenbau Haldenwang GmbH & Co. KG v. Deepak Rajani***, D2000-1816 (WIPO March 2, 2001) (<maha.com> "[R]espondent has not registered the domain name for merely speculative reasons"). The implication is that respondent with an expired dealership will not always have a legitimate interest, but its retention of the domain name "at the time this decision is being made" is governed by contract. In that event, respondent can be said to have a conditional legitimate interest.)

4.02-B Proving a *Prima Facie* Case 4.02-B

4.02-B.1 Lowering the Proof Bar 4.02-B.1

4.02-B.1.a *Respondent Controls the Facts to be Proved* *4.02-B.1.a*

The assignment of burdens in a UDRP proceeding is well established. It is for complainants to prove their case; not for respondents to disprove the complaint. In limbs one [4(a)(i) of the Policy] and three [4(a)(iii)] their task is to prove each element by a preponderance of the evidence. Paragraph 4(a)(ii) of the Policy requires a different approach. This is so because respondents control the facts of their rights or legitimate interests, and without the discovery tools available in a plenary action complainants would be at a disadvantage in establishing respondents have neither one or the other.

For this reason, panelists found it necessary to adjust the burden for the second limb by lowering the proof bar to a *prima facie* case that respondent lacks rights or legitimate interests in the domain name.[525] Complainant must proffer sufficient evidence to support the contention that respondent cannot establish the paragraph 4(c) safe harbor circumstances. The burden then shifts to respondent to rebut the *prima facie* case by contradictory or defensive evidence supporting the non-exclusive circumstances set forth in the subsections of the paragraph.

While it is not respondent's burden to prove a right or legitimate interest in the disputed domain name it will be conclusive against respondent if it fails to rebut a successful showing that it lacks either. This favors complainant if respondent defaults.[526] Where respondent appears and defends it carries a burden of producing evidence of sufficient quality to rebut complainant's evidence.[527] Complainant succeeds only if it both carries its lighter burden and respondent offers no defense or a defense without merit. The lighter burden for the paragraph 4(a)(ii) requirement recognizes complainants' disadvantage in marshaling evidence about respondents' motives except to the extent they can be inferred from use or non-use of the disputed domain names. Facts about respondents are peculiarly within their knowledge and control.[528]

---

524 A respondent's assertion that a domain name registered without complainant's permission is legitimate because it allegedly "benefits" complainant is based on a false premise that one who appropriates another's trademark has the power to "unilaterally determine whether [its] use . . . is appropriate or 'beneficial' to the mark owner," ***C. Crane Company Inc. Robbie Crossley***, D2009-0815 (WIPO August 10, 2009).

525 A *prima facie* case is one that "will suffice until contradicted and overcome by other evidence." *Black's Law Dictionary* (Revd Fourth Ed). For discussion on standard of proof see "Evidentiary Expectations" (Sec. 7.05-A.1.b).

526 Discussed further in "Consequences of Default" (Sec. 7.03-B).

527 Discussed further in "Qualifying for Safe Harbor" (Sec. 5.01-A). This is called a burden of production, or sometimes burden of persuasion.

The test is not whether complainant has "more of an interest than Respondent in the domain name" but whether respondent "has any right or legitimate interest in it at all."[529] The "correct approach" is for complainant to "put[] forward what he can in support" of his contention.[530] A *prima facie* case is made by alleging without contradiction two factual statements within complainant's personal knowledge: it has no relationship with respondent and did not authorize respondent to use its trademark; and three assertions based on such facts as may be marshaled or deduced: 1) respondent is not making any *bona fide* offering of goods or services [4(c)(i)] (e.g. current screenshots of the content of the website); 2) respondent is not commonly known by the domain name [4(c)(ii)][531] (e.g. screenshot of the Whois Directory); and 3) respondent is not using the website for legitimate noncommercial or fair use purposes [4(c)(iii)] (e.g., current and historical screenshots from the Internet Archive[532]). When properly alleged "the Respondent has a case to answer and that is where paragraph 4(c) comes in.[533] Otherwise, failure to make assertions or produce evidence may preclude a complainant's claim under this limb.[534]

Paragraph 4(a)(ii) of the Policy is framed in the present tense: "[Respondent] *lacks* any right or legitimate interest" in the disputed domain name. For this element of the Policy complainant succeeds subject to rebuttal that respondent lacks either a right or legitimate interest "at the time of the complaint," whether or not respondent may have had either in time past.[535] Respondent carries the rebuttal burden by

---

528 ***Julian Barnes v. Old Barn Studios Limited***, D 2001-0121 (WIPO March 26, 2001).

529 ***Choice Courier systems, Inc. v. William H. Kirkendale***, 2002-0483 (WIPO July 23, 2002).

530 ***Julian Barnes***, *supra*: "In the Panel's view the correct approach is as follows: the Complainant makes the allegation and puts forward what he can in support (e.g. he has rights to the name, the Respondent has no rights to the name of which he is aware, he has not given any permission to the Respondent.")

531 The typical formula is "[g]iven the WHOIS contact information for the disputed domain [name], one can infer that Respondent [] is not commonly known by the [trademark] in any derivation." ***Wells Fargo & Co. v. Onlyne Corp. Services11, Inc.***, FA 198969 (Forum Novenber 17, 2003). The registrant's obligation to maintain a current listing is discussed further in "The Whois Directory" (Sec. 2.05). Registrants are also known to fictionalize their identities, discussed further in "Faux Registrant" (Sec. 6.01-C.2.a).

532 Discussed further in "Researching the Past: Historical Screenshots from the Wayback Machine" (Sec. 7.05-A.3.b).

533 ***Julian Barnes***, supra.

534 Success by either party on this requirement is not so conclusive as to be *res judicata* against a challenge for trademark infringement or reverse domain name hijacking in a court of law. See for example, for Complainant: *Volvo Trademark Holding AB v. Volvospares*, 703 F.Supp.2d 563 (E.D. Va. Apr. 1, 2010) (Unreported), summary judgment in favor of plaintiff, formerly Complainant in ***Volvo Trademark Holding AB v. Volvospares / Keith White***, D2008-1860 (WIPO February 10, 2009). For Respondent: *Barcelona.com, Inc. v. Excelentisimo Ayuntamiento De Barcelona*, 330 F.3d 617, 626 (4th Cir. 2003), summary judgment in favor of plaintiff, formerly ***Respondent in Excelentisimo Ayuntamiento de Barcelona v. Barcelona.com Inc.*** D2000-0505 (WIPO August 7, 2000).

establishing one of the three affirmative defenses. The determination hinges either on the weakness of complainant's prima facie case or the merit of respondent's rebuttal.

The emphasis in paragraphs 4(c)(i) and (iii) is on use; in paragraph 4(c)(ii) on respondent's name. Registration plays a subsidiary role under 4(a)(ii) of the Policy because sustaining any one of the defenses disproves lack of rights or legitimate interests. Proof of any one of the defenses establishes it could not be otherwise. If it could not be otherwise it is irrelevant that respondent may not have any right or legitimate interest in the domain name. However, if respondent fails on rebuttal complainant must then prove the paragraph 4(a)(iii) requirement that respondent both registered *and* is using the domain name in bad faith.

4.02-B.1.b *Fulcrum for Both Parties* 4.02-B.1.b

Paragraph 4(a)(ii) of the Policy is a fulcrum for both complainant and respondent. If complainant either fails to present a *prima facie* case[536] or respondent is successful in rebutting complainant's allegations,[537] or the proof is too "finely balanced" to draw a conclusion,[538] the complaint must be denied.[539] In satisfying this burden complainant is assisted by respondent's default only to the extent there is no

---

535 ***A. Nattermann & Cie. GmbH and Sanofi aventis v. Watson Pharmaceuticals, Inc.***, D2010-0800 (WIPO August 31, 2010) ("The Panel considers that paragraph 4(a)(ii) of the UDRP refers to a right or legitimate interest existing at the time of the complaint. The present tense is used and the inclusion of this requirement would make no sense if it did not refer to the present. A registrant who did not have any right or legitimate interest at the date of registration may subsequently acquire a right or legitimate interest, for example by using the disputed domain name in connection with a bona fide offering of goods. Equally a registrant who had a right or legitimate interest may lose it, for example if the trademark owner legitimately withdraws its consent or the registrant ceases to distribute the trademark owner's goods or uses the domain name to promote rival products.")

536 Too numerous to cite. Example, ***Terminal Supply, Inc. v. HI-LINE Electric***, FA 746752 (Forum August 24, 2006) (<terminalsupply.com>. Registered as a design mark; Complainant disclaimed "Terminal Supply" and failed on all 3 requirements).

537 A respondent who registers a domain name after complainant's acquisition of a trademark right may have a right or legitimate interest in it if its proof satisfies paragraph 4(c) of the Policy. Discussed further in Chapter 5.

538 ***Intel Corporation v. Intelsitio Mexico, Jesús Guerrero Jiménez***, D2012-0718 (WIPO June 21, 2012)("The Panel is thus faced with a very finely balanced case. . . . The Panel reminds itself that according to the Policy, it is the Complainant who must prove each of the 3 necessary elements of the Policy on the balance of probabilities to the Panel's satisfaction, including that the Respondent has no rights or legitimate interests in the disputed domain name. In such a finely balanced case, where neither side is able to tip the balance in its favour, the Panel considers that the Complaint must fail on the basis that the Complainant has failed to carry its burden.")

539 Decisions too numerous to cite. An example, See ***Lockheed Martin Corp. V. Skunkworx Custom Cycle***, D2004-0824 (WIPO January 18, 2005). Complainant's inability to prove respondent lacks rights and legitimate interests or respondent's affirmative showing that it has either one or the other

evidence in the record to the contrary.[540] However, if complainant fails to make a *prima facie* case the absence of explanation is inconsequential. Only if complainant makes its *prima facie* case can it move forward with proof of bad faith registration and bad faith use under paragraph 4(a)(iii).[541] Rebuttal of the *prima facie* case is conclusive against complainant's claim.[542]

The low bar for complainant does not mean "no" bar. Complainant cannot succeed on its burden of proof by simply alleging that respondent lacks rights or legitimate interests.[543] It fails when it offers no evidence of "Respondent's use of the disputed domain name in a way that infringes upon [its] rights"[544]; fails to show how respondent is using the disputed domain name[545]; or fails to corroborate respondent's use or nonuse of the domain name.[546] Whether or not a respondent

---

is preemptive of abusive registration. The Respondent did not appear in ***Snapchat, Inc. v. Private Registrant / a Happy Dreamhost Customer***, FA1412001593519 (Forum January 12, 2015) but the Panel concluded from the website that the registration satisfied 4(c)(iii) of the Policy: "Respondent's web site allows use[r]s to see if their data was leaked as part of that security breach (taking the web site at face value)." See also ***Lockheed Martin Corp. v. Skunkworx Custom Cycle***, D2004-0824 (WIPO January 18, 2005) (finding that the issue of bad faith registration and use was moot once the panel found the respondent had rights or legitimate interests in the disputed domain name); ***Vanguard Group Inc. v. Investors Fast Track***, FA 863257 (Forum January 18, 2007) ("Because Respondent has rights and legitimate interests in the disputed domain name, his registration is not in bad faith.").

540 ***VeriSign Inc. v. VeneSign C.A.***, D2000-0303 (WIPO June 28, 2000). Discussed further in "Consequences of Default" (Sec. 7.03-B).

541 ***Clark Associates, Inc. v. Belize Domain WHOIS Service Lt***, FA1010001353058 (Forum December 6, 2010). The Panel "declines to find that Complainant made a prima facie showing" in that it failed to provide 1) any factual evidence regarding the allegedly infringing website; or 2) detailed descriptions of the offending website or screenshots of the website.

542 Discussed further in Chapter 5.

543 ***AWGI, LLC v. Cordelli Brian Scarlet / null***, FA180800 1801553 (Forum September 18, 2018) (<atlasglobalvanlines.com>. "Because Complainant has left this question unattended [whether Respondent has rights or legitimate interests], we cannot, on the record before us, conclude that Complainant has met its three-pronged obligations of proof." See also ***Johnson & Johnson v. Chad Wright, WebQuest.com, Inc.***, D2012-0010 (WIPO April 5, 2012) ("Complainant made a broad assertion that the burden of proof is on respondent. This is incorrect: respondent's burden is not to prove it has rights or legitimate interests but rebut the *prima facie* case that is does not.")

544 ***Nike, Inc. v. nikerotterdam***, FA0804001180664 (Forum August 19, 2008) (<nikerotterdam>) ("Complainant must bring evidence of Respondent's use of the disputed domain name in a way that infringes upon Complainant's rights." This case is not alone in illustrating a complainant's failure to provide evidence establishing that respondent lacks rights or legitimate interests. It is not sufficient to simply allege a fact without presenting corroborating evidence to establish the truth of that fact. See further discussion in "Admissibility, Relevance, Materiality, and Weight of the Evidence" (Sec. 7.05).

545 ***Claessens Prod. Consultants BV v. Claessens Int'l Ltd.***, FA 238656 (Forum April 23, 2004).

appears, if website content clearly demonstrates it is active in a completely different line of business, does not interfere with complainant, and is directed to a different class of consumers, registering a domain name confusingly similar to a trademark does not for that reason alone support lack of rights or legitimate interests and may well establish the opposite.[547] Lack of rights or legitimate interests is not conclusive of bad faith, which must be independently established.

4.02-B.2 Shifting the Burden to Respondent 4.02-B.2

The consensus solution for lightening complainant's burden rests on respondent's exclusive control of facts that would (if it had any to offer) support its defense.[548] Facts necessary to establish intention are "uniquely" within respondent's knowledge and control,[549] which makes it virtually impossible without discovery for complainant to marshal conclusive evidence of respondent's right or legitimate interest in the domain name.[550]

The procedure for shifting the burden to respondent under 4(a)(ii) of the Policy entered the UDRP vocabulary tentatively in April 2000 in two decisions by the same panelist.[551] It took only a few more months to harden as a rule in the decision process.[552] Under the shifting rule, complainant satisfies its minimal burden by asserting that respondent is not making a *bona fide* offering of goods or services, is not commonly known by the domain name, and is not making a noncommercial or fair use of it.[553]

---

546 ***Skyy Spirits LLC v. Stanislaw Krzenszczynski***, FA0808001220829 (Forum November 26, 2008) (Respondent did not appear. However, the fact that the Panel dismissed the complaint without prejudice implies that but for the specific deficiency noted complainant was entitled to its remedy.) See ***BlankPage AG v. Waleed Altywaijri***, D2012-2189 (WIPO November 11, 2012) (<keetab.com>) in which Provider pointed out deficiencies Complainant failed to cure in its amended complaint.

547 ***General Electric Company v. Estephens Productions***, D2009-1438 (WIPO December 17, 2009) (<geentertainment.com>, Respondent did not respond. Panel noted that "It is by no means obvious, as complainant asserts, that anyone choosing a company name and logo prominently featuring the letters 'GE' must be targeting the GE mark, no matter the nature of the business." The record indicated that the initials G.E. are for "General Entertainment" not "General Electric.")

548 ***Educational Testing Service v. Netkorea Co.,FabJob Inc. v. Compana LLC***, D2006-0610 (WIPO August 16, 2006) ("[S]uch information is known to and within the control of the respondent.")

549 ***G.D. Searle v. Martin Mktg.***, FA 118277 (Forum Oct. 1, 2002); ***Croatia Airlines d.d. v. Modern Empire Internet Ltd.***, D2003-0455 (WIPO August 21, 2003).

550 *Id.*, ***Croatia*** ("Since it is difficult to prove a negative . . . especially where the Respondent, rather than complainant, would be best placed to have specific knowledge of such rights or interests—and since Paragraph 4(c) describes how a Respondent can demonstrate rights and legitimate interests, a Complainant's burden of proof on this element is light.")

551 ***EAuto, Inc. v. Available Domain Names.com, d/b/a Intellectual Assets.com, Inc.***, D2000-0120 (WIPO April 13, 2000) and ***EAuto, L.L.C. v. EAuto Parts***, D2000-0096 (WIPO April 9, 2000).

552 D2000-0252, 0270, 0374, 0624.

The lighter burden is offset by paragraph 4(c) of the Policy, which "gives respondents ample opportunity to rebut any evidence tendered by complainants."[554] Assuming complainant makes a *prima facie* case, the narrow issue of rights or legitimate interests then falls to respondent to make its case, either through rebuttal (if it appears) or evidence present in the record (if it does not appear).[555] Where respondent prevails for either of these reasons the issue of bad faith does not have to be reached,[556] although many Panels prefer to round off their decisions with an analysis of the bad faith factors.[557]

Beyond the minimal proof for the *prima facie* case complainants have marshaled a variety of adventitious facts to support their allegations. These include deconstructing the website for historical evidence of its use through tools available on the Internet[558] to responses to cease-and-desist notices and other communications prior to or contemporaneous with the initiation of the proceedings.[559] However, respondent's failure to rebut establishes only that it lacks rights or legitimate interests in the domain name. Therefore, a *prima facie* case is tentative since complainant must still prove respondent registered and is using the domain name in bad faith.

---

553 ***Deutsche Telekom AG v. Britt Cordon***, D2004-0487 (WIPO September 13,2004) ("[O]nce a complainant establishes a prima facie case that none of the three circumstances establishing legitimate interests or rights applies, the burden of production on this factor shifts to the Respondent.")

554 Panels have rejected respondents' contentions that a prima facie case is inadequate in proving lack of rights or legitimate interests. See ***Tommy Bahama Group, Inc. v. Domains by Proxy, Inc. / Aware Marketing***, D2011-2127 (WIPO January 31, 2012) (represented by counsel, "Respondent aggressively denies it has the burden to prove it has established rights or legitimate interests in the 'tommybahama sucks.com' domain name. . . . [However], [t]his case ultimately turns on the quality of Respondent's [rebuttal] evidence.")

555 *Id.*, ***Educational Testing Service.***

556 ***Lockheed Martin Corp. v. Skunkworx Custom Cycle***, D2004-0824 (WIPO Jan. 18, 2005) (finding that the issue of bad faith registration and use was moot once the panel found the respondent had rights or legitimate interests in the disputed domain name).

557 Decisions too numerous to cite. One reason for extending the discussion into a bad faith analysis may be educational—that is, Panels are taking the opportunity to explain that even if the respondent lacked rights or legitimate interests complainant would have failed the bad faith requirement. In ***National Trust for Historic Preservation v. Barry Preston***, D2005-0424 (August 10, 2005) (HISTORIC HOTELS OF AMERICA and <historic hotels.com>, Panel explained that "while the Respondent clearly is using the disputed domain name to attract Internet users to the Respondent's website for commercial gain, the record as a whole is consistent with the Respondent's use of the domain name in its descriptive sense.") See also ***Upbeat, Inc. v. Scott Fabian***, D2006-0332 (WIPO May 15, 2006) ('UPBEAT and <upbeat.com>). Trademarks composed of common words and descriptive phrases are inherently vulnerable. Discussed further in "Common Words, Common Phrases" (Sec. 6.01-D.1.c).

558 A full catalogue of the tools can be found at http://www.domaintools.com.

559 Some panelists take the position that complainant has to furnish affirmative proof that respondent lacks rights or legitimate interests in the domain name. The position can lead to humorous

4.02-C Knowledge and Targeting Are Prerequisites to Finding Bad Faith Registration 4.02-C

4.02-C.1 Knowledge, Awareness, and Implausible Denial 4.02-C.1

4.02-C.1.a *Prerequisites of Knowledge* 4.02-C.1.a

Knowledge of a complainant's mark, if not directly evident or denied, can be inferred or rebutted from website content, strength of mark—established from its lexical composition (dictionary words and common phrases)—a mark's reputation and presence in registrant's market, and respective timing of a mark's use in commerce and registration of the domain name. Each factor is weighed in a matrix specific to the particular circumstances.[560]

While lack of infringing content is not conclusive of lawful registration in respondent's favor, it may be if complainant lacks proof of any other factor favoring its claim. Weak or lesser-known marks with no market presence in respondent's geographical location favor respondent while well-known marks and those with strong reputations favor complainant. To the same but opposite extent that complainants must prove knowledge, respondents must explain their choices for offsetting any suggestion that it had knowledge.

The less reputation a complainant had at the time of the registration (even though its reputation may have risen and be significant in the present) the greater the likelihood respondent's plausible denial of knowledge will prevail on the merits.[561] As trademarks composed of dictionary words or descriptive phrases descend the classification scale there is an increasing likelihood of registrants registering and using domain names corresponding to trademarks plausibly without knowledge of the marks. Unless there is evidence to the contrary such as reputation in respondent's geographical location it is difficult to persuade the Panel to find that respondent

---

results, ***Penguin Books Limited v. The Katz Family and Anthony Katz***, D2000-0204 (WIPO May 20, 2000) ("Respondent has produced evidence, which this Administrative Panel must accept in the absence of any rebuttal evidence from complainant, that Mr. Katz has for many years been known by the nickname 'Penguin.'")

560 ***Marden Group B.V. v. Tucows.com.co***, D2011-1061 (WIPO August 24, 2011) ("There are cases that suggest that what actually matters here is (a) whether at the time of registration of the domain name the relevant term embodied in the domain name was being (or about to be) used in a trade mark sense by the complainant and (b) whether the domain name was registered with knowledge of that use and with the intention of taking advantage of the reputation that had or would attach to that term by reason of that use." Discussed further in "Admissibility, Relevance, Materiality, and Weight of the Evidence" (Sec. 7.05).

561 See ***Record Connect, Inc. v. Chung Kit Lam / La-Fame Corporation***, FA1609001693876 (Forum November 3, 2016) (<recordconnect.com>) (Although Complainant has common law rights the Panel found that it was "unclear how far those rights date back.").

had complainant's trademark "in mind" in choosing a particular term. "In mind" proof—either direct or by inference—is a necessary step to finding bad faith.

UDRP disputes roughly divide into three groups: 1) complainants who own strong trademarks prior to domain name acquisition; 2) domain name holders who register their choices before a complainant owner's acquisition of a trademark; and 3) holders who register domain names earlier or contemporaneously with owners' acquisition of lesser known or weak marks. A complainant in the first group has a trademark with a secure historical reputation and is most likely to succeed in capturing a domain name that infringes its exclusive right; a complainant in group two can have had no reputation if it acquired its trademark after registration of the domain name[562]; and, in group three, both parties are put to their proof: complainant has to prove its historical reputation and respondent either has to explain its choice or show that the choice is evident from use.[563]

Success for either party in the third group rests on the strength of complainant's trademark—in its primary and extended markets—and respondent's use of the domain name. Challenged holders of domain names composed of generic terms (dictionary words, random letters, and descriptive phrases) who use names consistent with the meaning of the words, letters, and phrases without violation of complainant's rights are more likely to keep their registrations.[564] Even if complainant establishes respondent lacks rights or legitimate interests its reputation in the present is ultimately irrelevant for the reasons noted in the WIPO Overview quoted below. Unless there is a preponderance of evidence in complainant's favor respondent maintains its registration,[565] regardless whether it responds to the complaint.

4.02-C.1.b 4.02-C.1.b *Complainant's Reputation*

By far the largest number of cases on the UDRP docket are brought by complainants with trademarks whose current and historical reputations are sufficiently well established at the *time of the complaint* to be ripe for unauthorized exploitation.[566]

---

562 WIPO Overview, 2.0 Paragraph 1.4: "Consensus view: Registration of a domain name before a complainant acquires trademark rights in a name does not prevent a finding of identity or confusing similarity. The UDRP makes no specific reference to the date of which the owner of the trade or service mark acquired rights. *However it can be difficult to prove that the domain name was registered in bad faith as it is difficult to show that the domain name was registered with a future trademark in mind,*" (emphasis added).

563 See discussion in "Willful Blindness Standard" (Sec. 4.02-C-2).

564 Discussed further in "Common Words, Common Phrases" (Sec. 5.01-D.1.c) and "Random Letters and Acronymic Trademarks" (Sec. 4.01-C).

565 ***Est Marjinal Medikal Tanitim ve Iletisim Sanayi Ticaret Limited Sirketi v. Kerim Ture***, D2014-1137 (WIPO September 3, 2014) (<safamerve.com>. "The allegation of the Complainant in its Supplemental Filing stating that a third party who attended the meeting at which the "sefamerve" project was first discussed subsequently informed the Respondent of the idea seems to the Panel

As trademarks ascend the classification scale respondents are challenged to explain their choices of domain name. The reverse is true with owners of weak trademarks who are challenged to support their contentions of abusive registration. Trademarks on the weak end of the continuum are particularly vulnerable not only because complainant must prove it had a reputation at the time the domain name was registered, but also because weak marks are not especially (and others are equally capable of being) associated as a source of any one person's good or services.

A mark's placement on the classification scale is inversely proportionate to the evidentiary demand on a party. The stronger complainant's trademark and extensive its reputation the lighter its burden for proving bad faith and the correspondingly heavier respondent's to rebut knowledge and infringement of complainant's exclusive right to exclude others from using it.

A modicum of cases are brought by complainants whose reputations have grown over time but who had little or none when the domain name was registered.[567] Where a mark's reputation has grown over time so that any present denial by respondent of past knowledge may be plausible, complainant must demonstrate by evidence that more likely than not respondent was aware of the mark when it registered the domain name. However well-known or famous a complainant's trademark may be in the present is not probative of any past reputation.

Even if the domain name is identical to the trademark there can be no presumption in complainant's favor. At the very least a complainant has to show that "Respondent was (or was likely to have been) aware of the existence of complainant [when it registered the domain name]."[568] Lesser known trademarks on or below the cusp on the continuum gain no foothold by being owned by complainants of

---

not to go beyond a mere allegation. Even if the allegation of the Complainant is true, it needs to be proven to be the case on the preponderance of evidence and a UDRP administrative proceeding is an inappropriate forum for the determination of such complex matters of fact and law. These matters would be properly examined before a court where the parties and their evidence can be examined by a judge.")

566 For new gTLDs a TMCH Trademark Claims Notice has been found sufficient to support respondent's prior knowledge of third-party rights. See ***Citigroup Inc. v. dong huang / freedom***, FA1512001652703 (Forum January 7, 2016) (<citigroup.club>).

567 ***Reliance Telecom Limited v. Domains ByProxy.com and Sukhraj Randhawa***, D2013-1470 (WIPO October 8, 2013) (<reliancegroup.com>. "The failure to adduce any evidence of the reputation of the RELIANCE Mark at the time of registration would be less of an issue if the Domain Name was a coined word, such that there was no other logical reason for the Respondent to register the Domain Name.")

568 ***Rusconi Editore S.P.A. v. Bestinfo***, D2001-0656 (WIPO July 5, 2001); ***PayPal, Inc. v. Daniel Benel***, D2013-0621 (WIPO June 28, 2013) (<mypaypal.com>. "The Panel finds that in all likelihood Respondent knew of Complainant when he registered the disputed domain name, based on the facts that Complainant's business was increasing exponentially in size since the launch of its website

well-known brands.[569] The lesser known trademark must itself have a reputation in the marketplace separate from the trademark owner's.

4.02-C.1.c

4.02-C.1.c *Actual Knowledge Demonstrated or Inferred from the Record*

Under U.S. trademark law registration of a mark on the Principal Register is constructive notice of the registrant's claim of ownership.[570] The statutory rule eliminates lack of knowledge as a defense to trademark infringement. However, under the Policy, constructive notice is not evidence of knowledge. Rather, actual knowledge or knowledge inferred from the totality of facts is an essential element. There is no presumption of knowledge that because the trademark exists respondent knew about it. A Panel has to resolve whether in registering the domain name respondent intended to take advantage of the complainant's mark *at that time.* To allege that respondent "must have had knowledge" when it plausibly denies it is insufficient to establish knowledge as a fact.

Proof rests on facts either conclusive on their face or by persuasive inference. Knowledge means actual intelligence or awareness of complainant's trademark when respondent registered the domain name.[571] Plausible denial of knowledge is tantamount to lack of intent to target, but as plausibility moderates intent is inferred from the totality evidence.[572] This can include 1) passive holding of domain name that could not conceivably be used without infringing complainant's rights, 2) linking to competitors, 3) typosquatting, 4) pretending to be complainant, and 5) failing to explain coincidences of choice.

---

in October 1999 and that numerous national and international news stories had been published regarding that website prior to Respondent's registration of the disputed domain name.")

[569] ***Mastercard International Incorporated v. Wesley Wobles***, D2011-2311 (WIPO March 8, 2012) (<pricelessamsterdam.com>); ***Mastercard International Incorporated v. Education, Ersin Namli***, D2011-2312 (WIPO March 8, 2012) (<pricelessistanbul.com>). Complainant owns PRICELESS. See also ***AOL LLC v. Joe DiMarco***, FA0907001275978 (Forum September 9, 2009) where Complainant alleged that <autoblogreviews.com> infringed its unregistered rights, but the Panel concluded that "[I]t is Complainant's burden to not only plead, but also prove that its descriptive mark has acquired distinctiveness and thereby is a protectable trademark." Discussed further in "Common Words, Common Phrases" (Sec. 6.01-D.1.c).

[570] The Lanham Act, 15 U.S.C. §1072.

[571] Although registration of a domain name before a complainant acquires trademark rights does not prevent a finding of identity or confusing similarity with a mark subsequently acquired, it negates bad faith. WIPO Overview 2.0, Paragraph 3.1. A registrant could not have had any knowledge of a then nonexistent right.

[572] See ***Google Inc. v. Ahmed Humood***, FA1411001591796 (Forum January 7, 2015) (Inference of actual knowledge "based on the fame of Complainant's ... mark." Or, "notoriety," ***Webster Financial Corporation v. Carolina Rodrigues / Fundacion Comercio Electronico***, FA1811001816249 (Forum December 9, 2018) (<hsaabank.com>).

Unless in the unlikely event a respondent admits intent it must be inferred from circumstantial evidence, which can be a matrix of visual evidence from the website (as when it exhibits knowledge by linking to competitors or pretending to be complainant) and silences (by failing to explain coincidences of knowledge). "The essence of the complaint is an allegation of bad faith, bad faith targeted at complainant."[573] For this, "[k]nowledge is important since without knowledge . . . it will be difficult to show that a respondent has the necessary intent for bad faith."[574] Timing, geographic location, strength of the trademark[575] and content of the website[576] to which the domain name resolves are critical factors in determining respondent's knowledge and intent.

At one end of the knowledge spectrum is proof of respondent's actual intelligence of complainant and its trademark as demonstrated by the evidence. At the other end, it is knowledge inferred circumstantially from the timing of respondent's registration in relation to complainant's acquisition of its mark (as when the domain name is registered following publicity of complainant's plans, discussed in Sec. 6.01-C.1.b), geographic[577] or product proximity,[578] or the purpose of the website to which the domain name resolves (as when it lures visitors unsuspecting that the landing page has no association with the mark owner and is set up for spoofing or phishing). In many instances, the closer the parties in geographic proximity or niche the less plausible the denial[579]; the greater the commercial and geographic distance the more plausible denial becomes.[580] A state of mind less than actual knowledge

---

573 ***The Way International, Inc. v. Diamond Peters***, D2003-0264 (WIPO May 29, 2003) (THE WAY and the <thewayministry.org>. "If the existence of a trade mark registration was sufficient to give respondent knowledge, thousands of innocent domain name registrants would, in the view of the Panel, be brought into the frame quite wrongly.")

574 ***Aubert International SAS and Aubert France SA v. Tucows.com Co.***, D2008-1986 (WIPO March 17, 2009). Discussed further in "Enhanced Investigative Responsibilities for High-Volume Registrants" (Sec. 5.03-B). The "necessary intent for bad faith" was found in ***Aubert International.***

575 ***Zero Int'l Holding GmbH & Co KG v. Beyonet Servs.***, D2000-0161 (WIPO May 12, 2000) (<zero.com>. Generic terms are legitimately subject to registration as domain names on a 'first-come, first-served' basis.") Coined words do not have to prove their strength since they are one of a kind.

576 ***QlikTech International AB v. shenzhen kejianuoyouxiangongsi / liang wu***, FA1212001478158 (Forum February 7, 2013) (Actual knowledge is "evidenced by Respondent's numerous uses of Complainant's mark, including the use of Complainant's distinctive Q design logo.")

577 See ***Jupiters Limited v. Aaron Hall***, D2000-0574 (WIPO August 3, 2000) ("In the present case the fact that Complainant's name and trade mark is so well and widely known, coupled with the fact that Respondent's mailing address is in the same district as Complainant's business, makes it inevitable that Respondent registered the domain names in full knowledge of Complainant's rights and interests.")

578 ***Hoboken Publications, LLC v. Hoboken411.com, LLC***, FA1111001414530 (Forum January 13, 2012) (<hmag.com>). The parties "operat[e] in the same limited Hoboken geographical area and in the same general business as Complainant."

may be acceptable evidence of bad faith if the Panel concludes that denial of knowledge is implausible. Implausible denial is more likely found where the trademark in issue is particularly strong, well-known in respondent's domicile and heavily advertised or promoted in national or international markets.[581]

The burden of proving a violation of the Policy is lighter for suggestive, arbitrary and fanciful terms and heavier for generic and descriptive terms capable of non-infringing use by multiple parties[582] or used in non-trademark senses (whether or not for purposes unrelated and distant from complainant's goods or services).[583] If a complainant's mark is highly distinctive— a made-up term without any known meaning, for example[584]—and denial of knowledge is implausible the conclusion that an identical or confusingly similar domain name is infringing is unavoidable. The reverse follows from a mark composed of common elements even where the parties are engaged in similar businesses.

While competition alone is probative in determining whether respondent acted intentionally in registering the domain name to take advantage of the trademark[585] it does not exclude registration and use for some permissible purpose,[586]

---

579 ***Layby Services Australia Pty Ltd. v. Chrisco Hampers Australia Ltd.***, D2009-1066 (WIPO November 3, 2009) (HAMPER KING and <hamperking.com>) (Direct competitor who registered the disputed domain name one year after Complainant established its business.)

580 ***EURO DATA GmbH & Co. KG v. Excel Signs***, D2009-0465 (WIPO May 5, 2009) (Germany and U.S.A.) (<eurodata.com>); ***Javier Narvaez Segura, Grupo Loading Systems S.L. v. Domain Admin, Mrs. Jello***, LLC, D2016-1199 (WIPO August 31, 2016) (<loading.com>. Complainant Spanish, Respondent U.S.)

581 ***La Quinta Worldwide, L.L.C bv. Rudi Seiberlich***, D2011-0385 (WIPO April 11, 2011) (Complainant "is the registered proprietor of many trademarks for LA QUINTA and variants of that trademark both within the United States and internationally, including in Italy where respondent is domiciled.")

582 ***Take Two Interactive Software Inc. v. Name Administration Inc.***, D2010-0845 (WIPO August 6, 2010) (<bioshock.com>, "[Alleged trademark] is associated with fields other than computer games and consistent with the scientific fields conjured up by the constituent components of Domain Name.") See also ***HSM Argentina S.A. v. Vertical Axis, Inc***, D2007-0017 (WIPO May 1, 2007) in which the Panel pointed out that evidence of third party use of terms identical to the trademark "mitigates against a finding that respondent knew specifically of complainant or its mark when the disputed domain name was registered." This is particularly so where the terms "may have a number of potential associations, unconnected with complainant."

583 A trademark that equally describes businesses conducted by many other people is not a protectable term, unless the domain registration was intended to harm the complainant. Example: GROCERY OUTLET and <groceryoutlet.com> in ***Canned Foods, Inc. v. Ult. Search Inc.***, FA 96320 (Forum February 13, 2001). Discussed further in "Attracting Internet Traffic" (Sec. 5.01-D).

584 ***INVISTA North America S.a.r.l. v. Whois Privacy Service***, FA1502001607177 (Forum April 14, 2015) ("While constructive notice is generally regarded as insufficient to support a finding of bad faith, the Panel here concludes that Respondent had actual notice of Complainant's mark because of its fame which has been established by the evidence and the absence of any known meaning of TERATE other than as an identifier of Complainant's products.")

and is only grounds for forfeiture on proof of abusive registration. Similarly, having knowledge of complainant's trademark is not by itself conclusive of bad faith. There can be knowledge without any proscribed act, such as registering a domain name for nominative fair use.

Feigned ignorance has been found to be tantamount to knowledge.[587] However, while intent may be inferred[588] from the totality of evidence it cannot rest on supposition, which is entirely subjective.[589] The "mere existence of Complainant's trademark rights at the time Respondent registered the disputed domain name does not . . . create any presumption of knowledge."[590] This simply means that complainant satisfies its burden by offering sufficient evidence from which inference of actual knowledge can be drawn. Plausible denial of knowledge undermines contentions to the contrary and supports a finding in respondent's favor.

4.02-C.1.d *Website Content Probative of Knowledge*

4.02-C.1.d

Website content is probative of complainant's contentions under 4(a)(ii) as well as respondent's knowledge of its trademark under 4(a)(iii) of the Policy.[591] Linking to goods or services competitive with complainant is evidence of targeting even if not necessarily conclusive for marks on the lower end of the classification scale; but as marks ascend the scale the more certain respondent registered the domain name with complainant's trademark in mind.[592]

Knowledge has been found where respondents domiciled in different territorial jurisdictions than complainants design their websites in complainants' languages and populate them with links to complainants' competitors.[593] In such instances the

---

585 The exact phrasing in the Policy is "for the primary purpose of." It is an essential element in paragraphs 4(b)(i) and (iii) and implied in 4(b)(ii) (a "pattern of such conduct") and (iv) ("creating a likelihood of confusion").

586 A respondent may have knowledge and not have permission to incorporate a trademark in the disputed domain name, yet have acted in good faith. Further discussed in "Permissive Use of Trademark" (Sec. 5.01-C.1).

587 Discussed further in "Willful Blindness Standard" (Sec. 4.02-C.2).

588 Discussed further in "Drawing Inferences" (Sec. 7.09-A).

589 Paragraph 2 of the Policy reads that by "applying to register a domain name, or by asking us to maintain or renew a domain name registration, you hereby represent and warrant to us that . . . (b) *to your knowledge*, the registration of the domain name will not infringe upon or otherwise violate the rights of any third party" (emphasis added).

590 ***Salmi Oy v. PACWEBS***, D2009-0040 (WIPO February 4, 2009).

591 Discussed further in "Researching the Past: Historical Screenshots from the Wayback Machine" Sec. 7.04-A.3.b).

592 Discussed further in "Populating Web Pages: The 'Not Me' Defense" (Sec. 6.05-F).

593 ***ChemRite CoPac, Inc. v. Isaac Goldstein***, D2010-0279 (WIPO May 7, 2010) (Parties in the United States and Hong Kong). Respondent acquired <raceglaze.com> after complainant

website "speaks" for respondent and is conclusive even though respondent may be ignorant of complainant or its trademark. No such inference of knowledge can be drawn where a mark is not present in respondent's marketplace or the website is designed for a "language market far removed from the Complainant's market."[594]

Optimally, an inference of respondent's knowledge or awareness can be adduced from 1) the fame or obscurity of the trademark[595]; 2) the content of the website over time[596]; 3) the relationship of the parties [such as online membership in complainant's services[597]]; and 4) the parties' respective businesses and locations.[598] As to the first, the WIPO Final Report lists six non-exhaustive factors for determining whether a mark is well-known.[599] Under U.S. law, the term "famous marks" is defined as marks that are "widely recognized by the general consuming public as a designation of source of the goods or services of the mark's owner."[600] The probability of abusive registration increases exponentially with the rise in classification of the mark[601] and puts a heavier onus on respondent "to express himself . . . by responding

---

inadvertently allowed its registration to lapse. Although each word has a dictionary meaning the combination of "race" and "glaze" is meaningless apart from its referent. Respondent denied knowledge, but operated a website populated with competitive links.

594 ***A & H Sportswear Co., Inc. v. Hu Yanlin***, D2010-0476 (WIPO May 12, 2010) (<magicbra.com>. "In the overall circumstances that the Complainant has been unable to point to evidence of bad faith or use which is otherwise not legitimate and considering that the Respondent appears to be seeking to operate in a separate geographical and largely Chinese language market far removed from the Complainant's market . . . the Panel considers that the Complainant has not on the present record made out a prima facie case that the Respondent has no rights or legitimate interests in the Disputed Domain Name.")

595 ***Royal Crown Co. v. New York Broadcast Services, Inc.***, D2000-0315 (WIPO June 14, 2000) (<dietrite.com>) (the Panel found "it virtually inconceivable that Spider Web did not know of DIET RITE soft drinks"); ***Sony Kabushiki Kaisha v. Inja, Kil***, D2000-1409 (WIPO December 9, 2000) ("inconceivable that respondent could make any active use of the disputed domain names without creating a false impression of association with complainant.")

596 Information about the history of the disputed domain name retrieved from Archive.org.

597 ***Classmates Online Inc. v. Adam Drake and Lori Drake***, D2008-1642 (WIPO December 18, 2008).

598 ***Forex Club International Limited v. INO.com, Inc.***, FA1003001316362 (Forum May 17, 2010) (U.S. and Belgium).

599 WIPO Final Report, Paragraph 284.

600 The Trademark Dilution Revision Act of 2006 (TDRA). In determining whether a mark is famous, a court may consider all relevant factors, including (1) "the duration, extent, and geographic reach of advertising and publicity of the mark"; (2) "the amount, volume, and geographic extent of sales of goods or services offered under the mark"; (3) "the extent of actual recognition of the mark"; and (4) "whether the mark was registered . . . on the principal register," 15 U.S.C. §1125(c)(2)(A)(i-iv).

601 Famous marks have a higher level of protection in international intellectual property agreements (see e.g., Article 16(2) and (3) of the TRIPS Agreement).

to communications and/or indicating a good faith use of the domain name."[602] Obversely, the "less distinctive a mark (i.e., the more descriptive or generic are the word or words making up the mark), the greater the scrutiny required to sustain a complainant's assertion" that it was registrant's target.[603]

Complainants have argued of particular domain names that bad faith must follow where there could be no conceivable non-infringing use of the disputed domain name—a concept traceable to ***Telstra Corporation.***[604] However, the concept is limited to domain names passively held and can only be persuasive if the assertion is true.

The "difficulty with this argument" (in the words of one Panel expressing an observation that could be made by many) "is that respondent has put forward a plausible reason for his registration and use of the disputed domain name." Not only that, but the "evidence of the Respondent's website also supports his story. . . . The website otherwise does not suggest to the Panel that there is an ulterior motive behind it."[605] If the Panel can conceive of plausible actual or contemplated uses of the domain name then the registration is unlikely to have had complainant's mark as its target.[606] This contrasts with respondents in ***Telstra*** and other cases who offered no or implausible explanations for their choices of well-known trademarks.[607]

For trademarks composed of dictionary words, descriptive phrases or slang that may have been accepted for registration for their acquired distinctiveness,[608] a complainant's inability to prove knowledge coupled or not with a declaration

---

[602] ***Sanofi Aventis v. Davie Kearney***, D2006-0861 (WIPO August 21, 2006).

[603] ***Hugo Daniel Barbaca Bejinha v. Whois Guard Protected***, FA 836538 (Dec. 28, 2006), (citing ***One Creative Place, LLC v. Kevin Scott***, D2006-0518 (WIPO June 16, 2006)(<globalchip.org>).

[604] ***Telstra Corporation Limited v. Nuclear Marshmallows***, D2000-0003 (WIPO February 18, 2000). If a domain name may conceivably be used without infringing, complaint must be dismissed.

[605] ***Bulmers Limited and Wm. Magner Limited v. (FAST 12785240) magnersessions.com 1,500 GB Space and 15,000 Monthly Bandwidth, Bluehost.Corn INC/Jason LaValla***, D2010-1885 (WIPO January 17, 2010) (<magnasessions.com>); ***American Funds Distributors, Inc., and the Capital Group Companies, Inc. v. Eunice May***, D2011-0361 (WIPO April 25, 2011) (<americanfund.com>).

[606] ***PetMed Express, Inc. v. Brian Schiffman, Inc.***, D2012-0326 (WIPO April 4, 2012) (<petmedsnmor.com>, "the Complainant's 'petmeds' formative United States trademark registrations were obtained under Section 2(f) of the Lanham Act, an indication that the marks were descriptive of the essence of the Complainant's business and required secondary meaning for purposes of registration on the USPTO's principal register.")

[607] This principle extends to well-known albeit descriptive trademarks such as 1 800 MATTRES, AND LEAVE OFF THE LAST S THAT'S THE S FOR SAVINGS, ***Dial A Mattress Operating Corporation v. ICS***, D2000-1738 (WIPO January 31, 2001) (franchisee registered <800mattress.com>). Complainant operated under the fictitious name of "1 800 Mattress" in many cities in the United States. However, see *In re 1800Mattress.com IP, LLC*, 586 F.3d 1359 (Fed. Circ. 2009) affirming the refusal of the Trademark Office to register 1800MATTRESS.COM.

[608] ***CeWe Color AG & Co. OHG v. Shenbun Limited***, D2008-0810 (WIPO July 10, 2008) (<cewe.net>).

by respondent that it had none is more likely to result in denial of forfeiture. In ***CeWe Color*** complainant's trademark CEWE, which it believed was arbitrary (as it appears to be in German), was used as a "slang word in the Bahasa Indonesia language meaning 'girl or young woman.'" While a registrant of a single domain name may be credited with lack of knowledge of a mark unfamiliar in its marketplace, registrants of multiple domain names are held to a higher standard.[609]

4.02-C.1.e 4.02-C.1.e *Examples of Awareness*

Respondent may be unaware of complainant's trademark for a variety of reasons: 1) the mark is at the weak end of the spectrum—the more common word and descriptive phrase increase the likelihood respondent had other reasons for its choice; 2) the parties are geographically separated; 3) the parties offer different goods or services; and 4) respondent registered the disputed domain name prior to complainant's acquisition of its mark. Greater distances in content, space and time make the burden of proving awareness more difficult.

Denial of knowledge is less plausible and demands more explanation if respondent:

> 1) omits or transposes letters [typosquatting] which indicate actual knowledge of the trademark and is circumstantial evidence respondent had it in mind[610];
>
> 2) adds another term to the domain name before or after the incorporated mark that circles back to complainant or makes reference to its goods or services[611];
>
> 3) admits awareness in its pleading while denying bad faith registration[612];
>
> 4) reveals motive in pre-arbitration correspondence, such as offering the domain name for sale[613];

---

[609] ***Sprunk Jansen A/S v. Chesterton Holdings***, D2006-1080 (WIPO November 17, 2006) ("[E]ven if Respondent did not actually know of Complainant's mark, it cannot avoid a finding of bad faith by registering large numbers of domain names through the use of automated programs.") The issue is discussed further in "Enhanced Investigative Responsibilities for High-Volume Registrants" (Sec. 5.03-B).

[610] Representative examples include: ***Reuters Ltd. v. Global Net 2000, Inc.***, D2000-0441 (WIPO July 13, 2000) (<reters.com>, <ruters.com>, <reuers.com>); ***Homer TLC, Inc. v. Fundacion Private Whois / Domain Administrator***, FA1304001494705 (Forum May 28, 2013). <hhomedepot.com>, <homedepeot.com>, <homedepit.com>, <homedepor.com>, <homedepoth.com>, <homehepot.com>, <homepdepot.com>, <nomedepot.com>, and <thehomedepo.com>).

[611] ***Caesars Entertainment, Inc. v. Nova Internet Inc.***, D2005-0411 (WIPO June 22, 2005) (PARIS LAS VEGAS and <parislasvegascasino.com>).

[612] ***Julie & Jason, Inc. d/b/a The Mah Jongg Maven v. Faye Scher d/b/a Where the Winds Blow***, D2005-0073 (WIPO March 6, 2005); ***Paule Ka v. Paula Korenek***, D2003-0453 (WIPO July 24, 2003).

5) creates a website containing hyperlinks competitive to complainant's goods or services[614];

6) as a competitor acquires the disputed domain name to capture visitors intended for complainant[615];

7) imitates a complainant's website or impersonates a complainant for a criminal purpose[616];

8) registers the domain name and uses it to offer similar goods or services[617]; or

9) registers additional disputed domain names identical or similar to complainant's mark after having been served with cease-and-desist notices for earlier violations.[618]

---

613 ***Wal-Mart Stores, Inc. v. Long***, D2004-0816 (WIPO November 29, 2004); ***Martha Stewart Living Omnimedia. Inc. v. Josh Gorton***, D2005-1109 (WIPO December 13, 2005) ("It is telling that the Respondent, on the same day he registered the domain names, solicited complainant to purchase the domain names or else see them put up for public auction.")

614 ***Kabushiki Kaisha Square ENX dba Square ENX Co. Ltd. v. NOLDC, Inc.***, D2006-0630 (WIPO July 14, 2006) (Japanese Complainant; U.S. Respondent: "Respondent's website does not simply contain references to 'Valkyrie Profile' but also has a tab or 'button' labeled with the title of another of complainant's games, 'Star Ocean.'")

615 ***PartyGaming Plc v. WHOis Privacy Protection Service, Inc./Henao Berenice***, D2006-0508 (WIPO June 26, 2006); ***Pfizer, Inc. v. Suger***, D2002-0187 (WIPO April 24, 2002) (Panel found that because the link between Complainant's mark and the content advertised on Respondent's website was obvious, Respondent "must have known about complainant's mark when it registered the subject domain name.") See also ***Party Maniacs, Inc. v. Michael Kuklinski***, FA0904001258597 (Forum June 2, 2009). Discussed further below.

616 ***Capital One Fin. Corp. v. Howel***, FA 289304 (Forum August 11, 2004); Phishing or imitating the design and layout of complainant with or without a disclaimer, ***Business For Social Responsibility v. Dr. R.L. Bhatia, Center for Change Management***, D2007-1008 (WIPO September 5, 2007): "As to bad faith registration, the Panel believes that the Respondent, by the apparent nature of its business and by its substantial use of material from complainant's website and the nature of that material, must in the circumstances have been well aware of complainant's business and its marks at the time that it registered the disputed domain name." See also, ***Société Air France v. job recruitment***, D2008-1395 (WIPO October 29, 2008).

617 ***Canon Kabushiki Kaisha v. Price-Less Inkjet Cartridge Company***, D2000-0878 (WIPO September 21, 2000) (<canonink.com>, <canoninkjet.net>. The Panel held "Although the offering of replacement inkjet cartridges is a lawful and legitimate business, the use of these . . . disputed domain names as the initial contact points and web page banners deprives that business of the character of being bona fide, within the meaning of paragraph 4(c)(i) of the Policy.") See also ***Lubbock Radio Paging v. Venture Tele-Messaging***, FA 96102 (Forum December 23, 2000) (<lubbockradiopagingservice.com>).

618 ***Foot Locker Retail, Inc. v. Bruce Gibson***, FA0212000139693 (Forum February 4, 2003) (Complainant's rights in the "family of marks" prior to registration of the subsequent infringing domain names).

Decisions frequently turn on the answer to the question: Does the evidence support targeting of complainant's mark? The majority in ***E-Switch***[619] focused on a pattern of abusive registration in ordering transfer of the name, while the dissent emphasized the failure to prove targeting. In ***BzzAgent***[620] Respondent argued that "bzzing" was generic in the marketing industry and it was using the term descriptively, meaning "word of mouth." Its denials were implausible in light of evidence that its website copied content from complainant's website.

Similarly for implausibility, in ***Orange Glo***[621] Respondent's domain name had originally resolved to a website that offered goods competitive with Complainant's cleaning product. The Panel found that these "circumstances indicat[ed] that Respondent was aware [that is, could not plausibly deny knowledge] of Complainant's right in the OXICLEAN mark." Respondent was implicitly aware even if unacknowledged.[622]

4.02-C.1.f

4.02-C.1.f *No Imputed Knowledge*

The UDRP regime balances the rights of the parties. It does not presume respondent registered the domain name with knowledge of complainant or its mark. "Panels have mostly declined to introduce the U.S. concept of constructive (deemed) notice *per se* into the UDRP."[623] However, the Jurisprudential Overview also points out some Panels apply a "knew or should have known" standard where

---

[619] ***E Switch, Inc. v. VerticalAxis, Inc. c/o Domain Administrator***, FA0803001163985 (Forum May 7, 2008) (E-SWITCH and <eswitch.com>, transferred over dissent. U.S. based parties. "Complainant contends that following its cease and desist letter to Respondent, the content on the website was altered to display hyperlinks about 'witches' instead of the previous links regarding 'switches.'")

[620] ***BzzAgent, Inc. v. Bzzing, Inc., Diego Berdakin***, D2009-0295 (WIPO April 22, 2009) (<bzzing.com>, Complainant resides in California, Respondent in Massachusetts).

[621] ***Orange Glo Int'l v. Blume***, FA 118313 (Forum October 4, 2002) (No response. "Respondent is a competitor of Complainant, thereby operating in the identical industry and offering similar goods.")

[622] See below, "Willful Blindness Standard" (Sec. 4.02-C.2).

[623] Paragraph 2 of the Policy. See WIPO Overview 2.0, Paragraph 3.4 , which asks and answers the following question:

> "3.4 Can constructive notice form a basis for finding registration and/or use in bad faith?
> Most panels have declined to introduce the concept of constructive notice into the UDRP. However, where a complainant had a United States registered trademark and respondent was located in the United States, this concept has been used in a few cases to support a finding of registration and/or use in bad faith. In those cases, where complainant's trademark registration preceded the respondent's domain name registration, respondent was presumed to have notice of the trademark."

The Jurisprudential Overview places constructive notice in the "knew or should have known" section, paragraph 3.2.2: "In limited circumstances – notably where the parties are both located in the United States and the complainant has obtained a federal trademark registration pre-dating the relevant domain name registration – panels have been prepared to apply the concept of constructive notice. Application of this concept may depend in part on the complainant's reputation and the

the complainant's trademark "is shown to be well-known or in wide use on the Internet... [and] respondent's denial of knowledge is otherwise highly improbable."[624]

If imputed knowledge is recognized at all its application is limited to parties domiciled in the same jurisdiction,[625] although there too it is "notable that, even in those cases where the doctrine has been applied, there have been other circumstances indicating bad faith, including evidence that the relevant trade mark had been widely used beforehand both in [that jurisdiction] and elsewhere, and was well-known, quite apart from the fact of registration."[626]

The rationale for not applying the imputed knowledge doctrine is that "the essence of the complaint is an allegation of bad faith targeted at complainant,"[627] which requires proof that respondent actually knew or had reason to know of complainant's trademark. Further, "[i]f the registrant is unaware of the existence of the trademark owner, how can he sensibly be regarded as having any bad faith intentions directed at complainant?" The Panel in ***The Way International*** concluded that there was no place for the concept under the Policy because if

> the existence of a trade mark registration was sufficient to give respondent knowledge, thousands of innocent domain name registrants would, in the view of the Panel, be brought into the frame quite wrongly.

Later Panels have agreed with this view.[628] In ***Advanced Drivers***, the Panel stated:

---

strength or distinctiveness of its mark, or facts that corroborate an awareness of the complainant's mark."

[624] *Id.*, The issue is discussed further below in "Willful Blindness Standard" (Sec. 4.02-C.2).

[625] ***Super Fun Sports v. Superfun Hendrik Niefeld***, FA0207000117022 (Forum September 6, 2002) ("The constructive notice of the Canadian trademark registration is a teaser, but doesn't add any weight to Complainant's position, because it is inherently constructive notice to Canadians. It simply cannot be extraterritorially constructive notice to Germans who, so far as we know, have never been to Canada nor paid any attention to what is registered among trademark registers in the U.S., France or Britain, much less the industrially smaller and distant country of Canada. Even constructive notice has some bounds of practical reality and geographical extent of duty, and constructive notice does not come close in this case to reaching a German resident, a sole operator, in a different language, in a different industry or commercial activity, 5,000 or so miles away on a different continent, from the trademark registrant.") See discussion in "Creating a Supra-National Jurisprudence" (Sec. 1.04-C.1).

[626] ***Swimways Corporation v. Richard Nugent***, D2008-0786 (WIPO July12, 2008) (U.S. Complainant, U.K. Respondent) (<toypedo.com>), citing ***Ticketmaster Corporation v. Spider Web Design, Inc.***, D2000-1551 (WIPO February 4, 2001) (<tickmaster.org>).

[627] ***The Way International Inc. v. Diamond Peters***, D2003-0264 (WIPO May 29, 2003) (U.S. parties involving an unregistered mark).

[628] ***Asset Marketing Systems, LLC v. Silver Lining***, D2005-0560 (WIPO July 22, 2005); ***Advanced Drivers Education Products and Training, Inc v. MDNH, Inc. (Marchex)***, FA0509000567039 (Forum November 10, 2005).

> [I]f Complainant's position were adopted, it would essentially establish a per se rule of bad faith any time a domain name is identical or similar to a previously-registered trademark, since constructive notice could be found in every such case. Such a result would be inconsistent with both the letter and the spirit of the policy, which requires actual bad faith.

Even if imputed knowledge were applicable to U.S. based parties "it does not apply in this case where one of the parties is in the U.S. and the other in Sweden."[629]

While respondents have no duty to investigate and are not charged with imputed knowledge of another's trademark rights the same is not true of complainants. Trademark owners claiming cybersquatting by respondents with rights to their own trademarks have constructive notice of subsequently applied-for trademarks that may infringe their rights. It is because constructive notice applies to them that services exist to monitor new applications in national registries to alert owners to possible confusing trademarks so they can oppose them.[630]

4.02-C.2

4.02-C.2 Willful Blindness Standard

Cases involving domain names composed of common words or phrases that complainants have adopted as commercial signs tend to favor respondent. Plausible denial of knowledge is reinforced by non-infringing use and complainant's inability to demonstrate its reputation extended beyond its territorial market *at the time of domain name registration*. However, the result shifts in the opposite direction when the mark is well-known or famous; or, if less well-known, the respondent is in the same location as complainant and it would be implausible for it to deny knowledge.[631] The existence of trademarks with a reputation in the marketplace cannot simply be ignored because they are composed of common words or descriptive phrases. Failure to investigate or willful disregard of another's rights[632] may support a finding of abusive registration if denial is implausible.[633]

---

[629] ***Williams Electronics Games, Inc. v. Ventura Domains***, D2005-0822 (WIPO September 30, 2005) (<williamspinball.com>).

[630] ***Jobvertise, Inc. v. Oscar Moreno / Diversity Job Seekers, LLC.***, FA1507001629481 (Forum August 24, 2015) ("Complainant had the opportunity to oppose. Nonetheless, no opposition was filed against Respondent trademark registration"); similarly, ***Angels Baseball, L.P. v. Lee Dongyeon***, FA 925418 (Forum May 14, 2007).

[631] WIPO Overview 3.0, Paragraph 3.2.3. "[Referring to Paragraph 2 of the Policy, Panels have found that] respondents who (deliberately) fail to search and/or screen registrations against available online databases would be responsible for any resulting abusive registrations under the concept of willful blindness; depending on the facts and circumstances of a case, this concept has been applied irrespective of whether the registrant is a professional domainer." Paragraph 2 provides: "It is your responsibility to determine whether your domain name registration infringes or violates someone else's rights."

[632] Too many cases to cite. See for example, ***Avaya Inc. v. Holdcom***, FA0806001210545 (Forum August 9, 2008) (<magiconhold.com>, discussed earlier. Respondent was a competitor); ***Traditional***

There has been a discernible progression of view toward a willful blindness standard, particularly against respondents using automated software programs.[634] Ignorance is not an acceptable excuse for intentionally appropriating a trademark for commercial gain. In ***V&S Vin & Sprit***[635] the Panel noted that "'willful blindness' . . . is equivalent to intent under most jurisdictions."[636] Therefore, Respondent's attitude in failing to conduct basic research

> is the classical case of "dolus eventualis" or "willful blindness". . . . Respondent registered the Disputed Domain Name in spite of knowing that there was a risk that this could infringe on someone's trademark. The Panel will certainly not endorse such a conduct.

While there may be circumstances for invoking willful blindness Panels tend to calibrate its application carefully in weighing the evidence.[637] This is because there is no specific obligation for domain name registrants to search national registries for trademark registrations.[638]

However, willful blindness has been applied to professional traders and domain name aggregators, who are expected to have greater knowledge of the Internet marketplace. This means in practice they need persuasive explanations for their choices, which is an increasingly heavier burden as trademarks grow in strength. In ***AirTran Holdings***[639] the Panel concluded that "it is the duty of Respondent to undertake

---

Medicinals Inc. v. Worldwide Media Inc. c/o Domain Administrator, FA0902001247728 (Forum April 7, 2009) (<smooth move.com>), ***Dollar Bank, Federal Savings Bank v. Paul Stapleton, The New Media***, D2016-0518 (WIPO April 24, 2016) (<dollarbankers.com>) (held passively for sale and no explanation other than Respondent is in the business of selling domain names).

633 ***Tata Communications International Pte Ltd (f/k/a VSNL International Pte Ltd) v. Portmedia Inc. / TRUEROOTS.COM c/o Nameview Inc. Whois***, D2010-0217 (WIPO June 1, 2010).

634 See for example ***CEAT Limited, CEAT Mahal, v. Vertical Axis Inc. / Whois Privacy Services Pty Ltd.***, D2011-1981 (WIPO February 20, 2012). The issue is discussed further in "Enhanced Investigative Responsibilities for High-Volume Registrants" (Sec. 5.03-B).

635 ***V&S Vin & Sprit AB v. Ooar Supplies***, D2004-0962 (WIPO December 27, 2004).

636 See also *Safeco Insurance Company of America v. Burr*, 551 U.S. 47, 127 S. Ct. 2208 09 (2007) in which the Supreme Court of the United States held that "[w]here willfulness is a statutory condition of civil liability, we have generally taken it to cover not only knowing violations of a standard, but reckless ones as well[.]"

637 See ***S.P.C.M. SA v. Whois Privacy Services Pty Ltd / Vertical Axis Inc., Domain Administrator***, D2014-0327 (WIPO May 20, 2014) (3-member Panel refrains but implicitly criticizes the holding in ***CEAT Ltd***, *supra*. One member of the Panel was the dissent in that earlier case.)

638 WIPO Final Report paragraphs 103 and 105. Paragraph 105 reads: "It is not recommended that domain name registrations be made conditional upon a prior search of potentially conflicting trademarks, but it is recommended that the domain name application contain appropriate language encouraging the applicant to undertake voluntarily such a search."

639 ***AirTran Holdings Inc. v. Sinclare Vabalon, BHG***, D2008-1165 (WIPO October 8, 2008).

due diligence to ensure that the selection or choice of a domain name does not infringe the intellectual property rights of third parties." Consequently,

> in the absence of contrary evidence and satisfactory explanations from Respondent, the Panel finds that the term "airtran" in Complainant's AIRTRAN marks . . . is not one that domain name holders could legitimately adopt without giving rise to the inference that Respondent is creating an impression of an association with Complainant.

The Panel in ***Aspen Holdings*** (a dispute over the phrase "first quote") noted that it was unclear to him "how the Respondent could have formed a good faith belief that the disputed domain name's value derived from its generic or descriptive qualities when the Respondent has been unable to bring to the Panel's attention any evidence that 'firstquote' is a commonly recognized and used descriptive term in the field of insurance."[640] Respondent in that case described itself as being a "leading performance-based marketing agency specializing in search marketing" to which the Panel responded that it was "clearly a sophisticated user of the Internet and the domain name system."[641]

4.02-C.3 4.02-C.3 Nearness and Remoteness in Proving Knowledge and Intention

Although complainants are not limited territorially in asserting claims for abusive registration geographic distances, timing of domain name registration and mark acquisition, and identity or similarity of goods/services can be significant factors in assessing a respondent's knowledge of the trademark. Actual knowledge of the mark

---

[640] ***Aspen Holdings Inc. v. Rick Natsch, Potrero Media Corporation*** D2009-0776 (WIPO August 20, 2009) (<firstquote.org>. Other Panels have credited respondents' good faith belief in the legitimacy of their conduct as negating bad faith registration). See ***Snap on Incorporated v. Jeffrey Scotese***, D2013-0577 (WIPO May 9, 2013) ("Respondent points out that there are twenty resellers selling "Snap On socks" on eBay, all of which identify the socks using the SNAP ON mark. Respondent could have registered the Disputed Domain Name under the reasonable good faith belief that Complainant gave general tacit permission for this type of resale activity using its SNAP ON mark.")

The concept of good faith belief as a defense derives from the Anticybersquatting Consumer Protection Act, 15 U.S.C. §1125 (d)(1)(B)(ii): "bad faith shall not be found in any case in which the court determines that the person believed and had reasonable grounds to believe that the use of the domain name was a fair use or otherwise lawful." Under this model, a finding of "good faith belief" may exonerate a party from bad faith use but not bad faith registration. The defense is a mitigating factor in determining the issue of damages. This defense is either a mitigating factor in determining damages or, analogizing it to nominative fair use, constitutes a complete defense to cybersquatting. UDRP panelists have exonerated hobbyists under the analogous provision in paragraph 4(c)(iii). See ***Etihad Airways v. Whoisguard Protected, Whoisguard, Inc / Hamza Ali***, D2016-0615 (WIPO July 3, 2016) (<vetihadairways.com>) (for virtual airlines). Discussed further in "Qualifying for Safe Harbor" (Sec. 5.01-A).

[641] *Id.* ("Nothing in the language of [paragraph 2 of the Policy] . . . suggests that the obligations imposed thereunder should be limited solely to" registrants of bulk registrations of domain names.)

if not admitted or implausibly denied gains or loses credibility according to distances.[642] The principle underlying temporal distance, for example, denies respondent could have registered the domain name in bad faith if the trademark had not then come into existence. The greater the distance of all three factors combined the lower the probability of bad faith. Geographical distance by itself may not be unfavorable to respondent's claim that it lacked knowledge of complainant or its mark,[643] but temporal distance (acquiring the domain name prior to existence of the trademark) is conclusive against abusive registration.

The numerous proceedings by Western complainants against Asian respondents whose websites are in English and contain links to competitive good/services are more likely to favor complainant for the reasons previously mentioned. Geographical distance of non-English-speaking respondents whose websites are in complainant's language and populated with hyperlinks to competing goods or services supports an inference that respondents are seeking to capture complainant's visitors even if they have no knowledge of its trademark. Where this is not the case respondents are more likely to prevail where the distances support a more probable than not conclusion that their choices were unrelated to complainants or the reputations of their marks.

To prove its claim complainant must demonstrate that at the time the domain name was registered it already had a demonstrable reputation[644] that extended to the respondent's marketplace.[645] Geographically separated parties even in the same industry can plausibly have no knowledge of each other's existence.[646] While strong

---

642 ***Compagnie Financière Européenne de Literie (COFEL) v. LKN Media***, D2011-1611 (WIPO November 29, 2011) (France and United States, MARINOS and <merinosfurniture.com>, <merinosfurnitureware house.com> and <merinoshomefurnishings.com>).

643 ***Rueducommerce v. Chain Avocats***, 100866 (ADR.eu December 31, 2014) (<rdecommerce.com>. "It must not be forgotten that the Complainant focuses on the French market and has no presence or trade marks in the USA where the Respondent is based. Thus the Panel is convinced that the Respondent is being honest in stating that it had never heard of the Complainant when it registered the disputed Domain Name.")

644 ***eDreams, Inc. v. CK Ventures Inc.***, D2009-1508 (WIPO January 8, 2010) (EDREAMS and <edrams.com>): "Where the mark was not widely used at the date of the registration, it cannot be inferred that the registrant's intended use of a corresponding domain name would give rise to a serious risk of confusion or diversion of Internet users through such links, and hence that the registration was effected with a reckless disregard for this risk"; ***Indiamart Intermesh v. Portmedia Inc./Intermesh.com, D2009-1804 (WIPO March 15, 2010).*** "The rapid growth of Complainant's advertising supports the inference that nine years ago . . . the level of international advertising and scope of secondary association globally was fairly limited.")

645 ***QAS Systems Limited v. Hopewiser Limited***, D2001-0273 (WIPO April 29, 2001) (<quickaddress.net>, "This Panel is of the view that a complaint under the Policy cannot succeed in relation to bad faith unless, at the very least, complainant is able to prove that at the time of registration/acquisition of the Domain Name respondent had complainant in mind.")

646 ***Roco Modellspielwaren GmbH and Dipl. Wirt. Ing. (FH) Peter Maedgdefrau v. Plantraco Ltd.***, D2005-0112 (WIPO April 8, 2005) (<minitank.com>).

marks have an enduring reputation,[647] complainants with weaker marks must prove their earlier market presence. Trademarks that are not generally recognized outside their country of origin or their regional market have a descending level of protection.[648] At a minimum, complainant must prove that its trademark has a presence in respondent's place of residence.[649] If a trademark is distinctive, well-known or famous extraterritorially, respondent's registration of an identical or confusingly similar domain name cannot trump complainant's rights.[650] If the mark's range is territorially limited even if well-known in its niche complainant must demonstrate respondent registered the disputed domain name with knowledge of its mark.[651] A finding of fame (or something less than that but well-known) in one jurisdiction does not necessarily "extend to other jurisdictions in which it is not famous."[652]

Although marks in one jurisdiction may become known in another it is not assumed respondents had knowledge of them. As a rule, rights do not extend beyond the territories in which the mark's adopter sells its products, renders its

---

647 ***Those Characters From Cleveland Inc. v. User51235 (38so92lf@whoisprivacy.net)***, D2006-0950 (WIPO October 10, 2006) (<carebears.com>; Transferred, delay of 10 years); ***Tom Cruise v. Network Operations Center / Alberta Hot Rods***, D2006-0560 (WIPO July 5, 2006) (<tomcruise.com>; Transferred, delay of 10 years).

648 ***Banco Macro S.A. v. Affordable Webhosting Inc. Advertising***, D2010-1759 (WIPO December 11, 2010) ("While complainant asserts that this is what respondent had in mind when registering the Domain Name, what is there in the way of evidence before the Panel to support that assertion? Complainant relies solely upon the fame of its trade marks, but produces no evidence to show why respondent based in Oregon should have been aware of the existence of those marks, the use of which (on the evidence before the Panel) has been restricted to Argentina. Complainant places 'Banco Macro' in the same category as 'Coca Cola,' 'American Express' and 'McDonalds' but does not show any use of 'Banco Macro' outside Argentina.")

649 ***Starwood Hotels & Resorts Worldwide, Inc. v. Samjo CellTech.Ltd.***, FA0501000406512 (Forum March 9, 2005) (<starwoods.com>). Complaint denied because "Complainant has not proven that the STARWOOD mark was so famous in Korea at the time of Respondent's registration of the Domain Name in January 2000 that Respondent must have known of the mark and must have intended to register the Domain Name with a bad faith intent to profit from Complainant's trademark."

650 ***American Information Corporation d/b/a American Information Network v. American Infometrics, Inc.***, FA0105000097339 (Forum July 19, 2001).

651 ***Interbanking S.A. v. Alexander Lerman***, D2013-1884 (WIPO January 23, 2014) (<interbanking.com>. "The Panel recognizes that the Complainant has established a substantial reputation in Argentina, but at the time the disputed domain name was registered by the Respondent [a U.S. resident], the Complainant's business had only recently started, and was only operating in Argentina.")

652 ***Churchill Insurance Co. Ltd. v. Churchhill Financial Services, Ltd.***, FA0906001270466 (Forum September 1, 2009) (<churchhill.com>), citing ***KCTS Television Inc. v. Get on the Web Ltd***, D2001-0154 (WIPO April 20, 2001) in which the Panel refused to infer that the call letters of a "public television station operating in the U.S. Northwest and in British Columbia, Canada would or should be known to someone living in London, England."

services, establishes recognition of its mark, or draws its trade. Territorial penetration becomes an issue because the more local complainant's use of the alleged mark the more questionable its reputation in another jurisdiction.[653]

Unless the trademark has demonstrably traveled out of its jurisdiction there is no basis for discrediting a respondent's denial of knowledge. The Panel in ***University of Maryland University College*** explained there is no reason "a registrant in Scotland would know of the fame of complainant's mark at the date of registration."[654] Similarly in ***EURO DATA***[655] in which complainant alleged respondent "should have known" of its trademark, but Complainant resided in Germany and Respondent in the United States. Assertion alone without proof fails to explain "how exactly respondent should have known, in view of the Respondent's claim that the term 'eurodata' is not very distinctive, fanciful or arbitrary as such, is widely used by many others than Complainant and that respondent is unfamiliar with complainant and its trademarks."

As geographic and goods/services distances decrease and the trademark rises on the classification scale respondent must explain the coincidences. While geographic remoteness supports respondent's denial of knowledge of complainant's mark prior to registering the domain name its good faith is challenged by its use of the domain name. If the content of the website offers links that include complainant's competitors it is more likely the registration will be found abusive. It is insufficient for respondent simply to deny knowledge[656] as it is for complainant to assert that its geographic reach should have put respondent on actual notice of its trademark.[657]

---

653 ***Everphone GmbH v. Privacydotlink Customer 2772294 / Kwangpyo Kim, Mediablue Inc***, D2017-0698 (WIPO July 3, 2017) (<everphone.com>. "The Complainant, which only started trading in 2016, has provided virtually no evidence in support of its claim to have become widely known in Germany in a short period, still less internationally." Then concludes: "The Respondent, located in the Republic of Korea, cannot be expected to have become aware of Complainant's German trade mark application, simply on the basis of its publication on the website of the German Patent and Trade Mark Office"); ***Zeca S.p.A. v. Whois Privacy Protection Service, Inc. / Domain Vault LLC***, D2017-0158 (WIPO April 3, 2017) (<zeca.com>, generic personal name, geographic location in Portugal, has a musical association. Complainant located in Italy, Respondent in the U.S.)

654 ***University of Maryland University College v. NUCOM Domain Brokers & Urban Music Underground Club***, D2002-0081 (WIPO April 29, 2002) (<umuc.com>).

655 ***EURO DATA GmbH & Co. KG v. Excel Signs***, D2009-0465 (WIPO May 5, 2009) (<eurodata.com>).

656 ***Hoerbiger Holding AG v. Texas Internationa Property Associates***, D2007-0943 (WIPO October 19, 2007) (German Complainant and U.S. [Texas] Respondent).

657 In ***Churchill Insurance***, *supra*. the U.K. Complainant demanded transfer of <churchhill.com> on the theory that it was typosquatting, but Respondent claimed it was two dictionary words, "church" and "hill." Respondent residing in the Cayman Islands denied knowledge of Complainant. The Panel found that complainant submitted evidence only "of use, advertising, and promotion . . . [in] the United Kingdom"—but the personality invoked by trademark was that of Sir Winston Churchill, the wartime Prime Minister of Great Britain. It appeared from the evidence that "in

The greater complainant's presence in respondent's jurisdiction the less persuasive respondent's denial of knowledge.[658] The Panel in ***Expedia, Inc.*** held that "given the widespread use of complainant's EXPEDIA website" it was improbable that in registering <xpediatravel.com>, Respondent was unaware of the trademark since there is no aural difference between the mark and the domain name. Typosquatting (discussed further in Section 6.05-E.1) presumes knowledge. Consistent with this view are parties geographically near and in the same line of commerce regardless of the fame or obscurity of the trademark. This is illustrated in ***Party Maniacs***.[659] Not only were the parties in the same niche business in the same geographical location, but respondent was a former employee of complainant.

4.02-C.4

4.02-C.4 Targeting: Appropriating for Trademark Value

Targeting is the essence of a complaint.[660] Complainant proves bad faith by showing respondent had its trademark "in mind" when registering the disputed domain name and is using it to take advantage of complainant's goodwill and reputation in the cyber marketplace. It would be "inconsistent with existing trademark principles and with the limited language and scope of the Policy" to construe paragraph 4(b)(iv) "without a requirement of direct action by the Respondent."[661] Targeting presumes a mark distinctive at the time the domain name was registered.[662]

Examples of targeting include: populating the website with hyperlinks to competing goods and services[663]; mimicking the "look and feel" of complainant's website[664]; diverting the domain name to websites related and unrelated to

---

some jurisdictions the insurance services of Complainant are offered under the name of the parent company, The Royal Bank of Scotland, rather than that of complainant. It therefore seems highly artificial to suggest that when the name Churchill or 'churc[h]hill' is used, or when the reader thinks it is being used or evoked, it is complainant that springs to mind."

[658] ***Expedia, Inc. v. European Travel Network***, D2000-0137 (WIPO April 18, 2000).

[659] ***Party Maniacs, Inc. v. Michael Kuklinski***, FA0904001258597 (Forum June 2, 2009) (<thepartymaniacs.com>).

[660] ***Asset Mktg. Sys., LLC v. Silver Lining***, D2005-0560 (WIPO July 22, 2005); ***Terana, S.A. v. RareNames, WebReg***, D2007-0489 (WIPO June 7, 2007) ("[T]he essence of the Complaint is an allegation of bad faith . . . targeted at complainant.")

[661] ***First American Funds, Inc. v. Ult.Search, Inc.***, D2000-1840 (WIPO April 20, 2001) (<firstamerican.com>).

[662] See ***Google Inc. v. Blue Arctic LLC***, FA1206001447355 (Forum July 25, 2012) (<oogle.com>). Complaint denied because the name was registered before Google had established rights in its trademark.

[663] Theme park: ***Disney Enters., Inc. v. Noel***, FA 198805 (Forum November 11, 2003) (<euro-disney.com>).

[664] ***Consumer Opinion Corp. v. John Cross***, FA1012001362852 (Forum January 21, 2011) (PISSED CONSUMER and <thepissedoffconsumer.com>. Appeared; transferred. Respondent explained that

complainant's goods and services[665]; and pretending to be complainant or associated with it.[666] In this last cited case involving Google the Panel explained that the "Respondent's use of the disputed domain name to operate a search engine website that prominently displays Complainant's GOOGLE mark provides evidence that it registered the domain name primarily to disrupt Complainant's business."

However, targeting must be evident either from the markets served by the parties[667] or the content of the website,[668] whether or not displaying third party links to a complainant's competitors.[669] Operating a business unrelated to complainant's with an appropriate domain name composed of common words is sufficient to support a legitimate interest.[670] In such a circumstance, while complainant may be aggrieved by the use of a domain name identical or confusingly similar to its trademark it has no actionable claim.

In ***First American Funds*** referred to in an earlier footnote the majority explains that it would "[c]reate a tremendous scope of protection around existing owners of marks of common words and mundane expressions and prevent new entrants from using these words and terms even in entirely different fields from existing uses."[671] As already noted, where a number of parties claim a right to a shared term complainant has the burden of demonstrating that it was the one targeted by respondent.[672]

---

the reason for the "look and feel" was because in creating the website it used "a stock joomla template called 'JA Barite Red,' and that no changes were made by Respondent to the website's template. Respondent indicates that he chose the color red because it is a common color associated with anger or being 'pissed off.'")

665 ***Autodesk, Inc. v. A Kiansu***, D2013-0312 (WIPO March 27, 2013); ***Golden Bear Int'l, Inc. v. Kangdeock ho***, FA 190644 (Forum October 17, 2003).

666 ***Google Inc. v. Cencom Inc.***, FA0603000669284 (Forum May 8, 2006) (GOOGLE and <securitygoogle.com>).

667 *Id.*

668 ***Duke University v. David Hanley***, FA1609001692961 (Forum November 9, 2016) (<dukecareers.com>. Content of the resolvingwebsite creates "confusion by suggesting a connection between the website and Complainant through the display of Complainant's trademarks and mimicry of Complainant's use of such trademarks and the targeting of graduates of Complainant's university.)

669 ***ConsumerInfo.com, Inc. v. Netcorp Netcorp c/o Netcorp***, FA0909001283469 (Forum November 11, 2009) (1,017 variants of complainant's trademark).

670 ***Rising Star AG v. Moniker Privacy Services / Domain Administrator***, D2012-1246 (WIPO August 16, 2012) (<risingstar.com>. "For . . . subject matters [of Respondent's website], the term 'Rising Star' is a word that bears a positive connotation, meaning either a person, who succeeds in his or her job ('the rising star of the xyz company') or gives an outstanding performance in the entertainment sector, to which the links 'recordsong', 'karaoke' or 'casino' relate.")

671 The dissent rejected the majority's view that complainant had no priority over other entities, which had equal claims to the domain name: "[n]owhere in the Policy or the Uniform Rules is the Panel asked to consider in its analysis the number of parties who have registered a trademark identical or similar to that registered by complainant or who use business names similar to that of

In ***OVB Vermögensberatung*** Respondent used the domain name for "a portal site containing advertising links for knives and cutlery," which was a business unrelated to complainant's. Although "[e]vidence of the rights of third parties is not evidence of rights or legitimate interests of the Respondent"[673] a complainant who is one of a number of parties claiming to be harmed by respondent's registration must still prove that it was the intended target.[674] Since the target was not complainant but a trademark owner in the cutlery business, and since jurisdiction of the UDRP is "limited to disputes between the parties before it",[675] the complaint was denied. Similarly in ***Yeshiva University*** where the Panel explained that "[w]here respondent appears to have been targeting the Einstein College of Engineering [located in or near Tirunelveli, Tamil Nadu, India] and not complainant, there is no proper basis for an order directing the transfer of the Domain Name to complainant."[676]

As a general rule, it is more probable than not that domain names identical or confusingly similar to strong trademarks have been chosen for their value to capture visitors or divert Internet traffic to websites consumers would otherwise have no

---

Complainant, nor in what fields of commerce or in what geographic areas such trademark registrations are effective or in which such businesses are engaged."

672 ***Argenta Spaarbank NV v. Argenta, Mailadmin Ltd.***, D2009-0249 (WIPO June 8, 2009) ("The evidence in the case file suggests that Respondent has engaged in the speculative registration of domain names, including such that correspond to Community trademarks and to Community trademark applications of third parties." However, "[g]iven the Latin origin of the word, Complainant's ARGENTA trademark is not very distinctive for financial services and banking, and certain third parties also have trademark registrations containing the ARGENTA word element.")

673 ***Yakka Pty Ltd v. Mr. Paul Steinberg***, D2004-0502 (WIPO September 3, 2004). See also ***Versa Capital Management, LLC v. Roger Schmidt***, FA0903001250974 (Forum April 23, 2009). The USPTO database showed 471 "live" records for "versa" either standing alone or with another word. Although 'versa.com' may have been claimed by others, the Panel awarded the domain name to Complainant without a showing of targeting. In a previous UDRP proceeding Versa Capital had been admonished for commencing an abusive proceeding to capture <VersaCapital.com> from an original registrant prior to Complainant acquiring its trademark. See also "Timing of Trademark Acquisition Not a Factor in Determining Standing" (Sec. 4.01-E). The rights of first and second generation domain name registrants are discussed further in "Subsequent Bad Faith Use" (Sec. 4.03-A.4) and "Transfer/Subsequent Holders=New Registration" (Sec. 4.03-B.2).

674 Could not prove: ***OVB Vermögensberatung AG v. Michele Dinoia and SZK.com***, D2009-0307 (WIPO May 6, 2009); ***Yeshiva University v. SS Media, Joy Dhivakar S Singh***, D2010-1588 (WIPO November 24, 2010). Proved: ***St Andrews Links Ltd v. Peter Arnold / SC202991 Limited f/k/a St Andrews.com Ltd***, D2013-1711 (WIPO December 12, 2013) ("[W]hilst the Panel concludes that the Respondent has no legitimate interest in the name 'St Andrews' it may well be that there are other entities or organizations which could claim such an interest.")

675 *Id.* ***OVB Vermögensberatung***. In addition the "appreciable evidence" indicated that the three letter combination "ovb" is attractive "independent of any trademark value derived from complainant's use of the mark in relation to financial services."

676 ***Yeshiva University***: "There is no evidence that the Respondent registered the Domain Name with a view to selling it to the Complainant for a profit, and nor are there any sponsored links to

interest in visiting. The opposite is true for trademarks less well-known or composed of common words and descriptive phrases. Denial of knowledge is less plausible the greater the market penetration of complainant's trademark (even if not well-known) or where the market penetration is local or regional rather than national and the parties are engaged in the same business and operate in the same territory.[677]

4.02-D Lawful Business, *Mala Fide* Use of Domain Name 4.02-D

The term "legitimate interest" in paragraphs 4(a)(ii) and 4(c) of the Policy refers to a respondent being entitled to its choice of domain name, rather than the legality of the business it carries out on the resolving website. A business may be lawful but respondent's use of the domain name *mala fides.* Replacing inkjet cartridges is lawful but the "use of these . . . disputed domain names as the initial contact points and web page banners deprives that business of the character of being bona fide."[678] If legality of business were the standard, then "any cybersquatter that conducted a lawful business could always find refuge."[679] A respondent may very well have in mind a legitimate business in the future, but to rebut the assertion that it lacks rights or legitimate interests it must demonstrate that in registering the domain name it had no "exploitative intent" *when it made its choice.*[680]

It is *mala fides* to register and use a domain name identical or confusingly similar to a complainant's trademark that resolves to a website or redirects to another website that advertises or offers competing goods or services. It is presumptively bad faith for illegal transactions such as selling counterfeit versions of a complainant's products.[681] "It is by now well established that PPC parking pages built around a trademark (as contrasted with PPC pages built around a dictionary word and used

---

third party websites on the College website from which the Respondent might have been deriving pay per click revenue. The Domain Name simply resolves to a website (the College website) that appears to be operated by a real 'Einstein' college [of Engineering]."

677 ***Texas Wind Power Company v. Wind Works c/o Savvy Dog Design, LLC***, FA0903001252746 (Forum May 12, 2009) (<texaswindworks.com>).

678 ***Canon Kabushiki Kaisha v. Price Less Inkjet Cartridge Company***, D2000-0878 (WIPO September 21, 2000) (<canonink.com> and <canoninkjet.net>).

679 ***The New England Vein & Laser Center, P.C. v. Vein Centers for Excellence, Inc.***, D2005-1318 (WIPO February 22, 2006).

680 A geographic location is not registrable and the addition of a geographic location does not create a distinctive mark. ***Abu Dhabi Future Energy Company PJSC v. John Pepin***, D2008-1560 (WIPO December 22, 2008) (<masdarcity.com> and <masdarcity.net>); ***Sally Holdings, Inc. v. Pagelifter.com***, D2006-0266 (WIPO May 17, 2006) (The question is not the legitimacy of the business "but whether respondent has a legitimate right or interest in using the disputed domain name <sallyguate.com>"—where "guate" is short for Guatemala.)

681 Too numerous to cite. Representative decisions include ***Prada S.A. v. Domains For Life***, D2004-1019 (WIPO January 27, 2005); ***Affliction, Inc. v. Chinasupply***, FA 1223521 (Forum October 23, 2008); ***Victoria's Secret Stores Brand Management, Inc. v. Rafidah Ramly***, FA100400 1318154

only in connection with the generic or merely descriptive meaning of the word) do not constitute a *bona fide* offering of goods or services pursuant to paragraph 4(c)(i) of the Policy, nor do they constitute a legitimate non-commercial or fair use pursuant to paragraph 4(c)(iii)."[682]

By itself "[c]ontinuous use adverse to the interest of Complainant is not a basis from which Respondent can acquire rights in the domain name."[683] This explains why laches is not favored as a basis for denying a complaint. A paragraph 4(c) defense is credible if the website to which the domain name resolves offers *bona fide* goods or services, 4(c)(i), or is noncommercial or fair use, 4(c)(iii) of the Policy.[684] Either of these defenses has merit if there was no malicious or exploitative intent directed at complainant or its trademark when respondent registered the domain name. In such event "it would take an exceptional case" to order a domain name cancelled or forfeited to complainant.[685]

4.03

4.03 RESPONDENT HAS REGISTERED AND IS USING THE DOMAIN NAME IN BAD FAITH—PARAGRAPH 4(a)(iii) OF THE POLICY

4.03-A

4.03-A Bad Faith in the Conjunctive

4.03-A.1

4.03-A.1 Evidence of Bad Faith Registration

Paragraph 4(a)(ii) of the Policy discussed in the previous section addresses the question of respondent's right or legitimate interest in the disputed domain name. Respondent does not have to prove it has either, but if complainant either fails in

---

(Forum May 24, 2010); ***DKH Retail Limited t/a Laundry Athletics v. wangzhenhua***, D2012-1032 (WIPO August 1, 2012). But ***see Oakley, Inc. v. H intel***, FA1207001454892 (Forum August 21, 2012) for a stark distinction between abusive registration and trademark infringement. Panel denied complaint because it found that <myfakeoakleysunglasses.com> is not confusingly similar to OAKLEY: "While it would seem obvious there is trademark infringement that is not the test under the UDRP." See also "Opportunistic Bad Faith" (Sec. 6.01-C.1). Mark owners have also used the Uniform Rapid Suspension System (URS) to suspend the domain name from resolving to the website. See ***Eli Lilly and Company v. Shaternik et al.***, FA170500 1731038D (Forum June 1,2017) (Too many domain names to count used for counterfeit goods).

Under the ACPA, "any similarities or distinctions between the products themselves, i.e., whether or not the content of [domain name holder's] website might compete with [trademark owner's] product, are irrelevant." *Prime Publishers, Inc. v. American-Republican, Inc.*, 160 F. Supp. 2d 266, 279 (D.Conn 2001). See 15 U.S.C. §1125(d)(1)(A) (liability attaches under the ACPA "without regard to the goods or services of the parties.")

682 ***Ustream.TV, Inc. v. Vertical Axis, Inc***, D2008-0598 (WIPO July 29, 2008).

683 ***Avaya Inc. v. Holdcom***, FA0806001210545 (Forum August 9, 2008) (<magiconhold.com>, transferred. "Respondent acknowledges that it was aware of Complainant's claim of rights at the time of registration, [but] it nevertheless asserts that it believed that Complainant's mark was generic.")

684 ***LEGO Juris A/S v. Domain Administrator, Matthew Griffith***, D2011-1263 (WIPO October 1, 2011) (<legoworkshop.com>).

its *prima facie* case or respondent succeeds in rebutting complainant's assertions the finding is conclusive against complainant's claim of abusive registration. Whereas under 4(a)(ii) respondent has an either/or burden to prove right or legitimate interest, under 4(a)(iii) complainant prevails only on proof respondent both registered *and* is using the domain name in bad faith.[686]

While bad faith registration is harder to prove than bad faith use, for the reason that the latter is apparent and the former hidden and unlikely to be admitted, if there is proof of bad faith registration then bad faith use can be inferred but there can be inference of abusive registration the other way around. The consensus is that domain name registration earlier in time than trademark acquisition negates intent to take advantage of complainant's trademark,[687] but later in time is a factor among others, including trademark strength and reputation, composition of domain name and content of website. If respondent persuasively denies knowledge of a trademark on the weak end of the classification scale complainant will fail in proving bad faith registration even if the respondent lacks rights or legitimate interests in the domain name.[688]

It is not respondent's burden to disprove that it registered and is using the domain name in bad faith, but it has the opportunity to refute bad faith registration. Forfeiture is not warranted where respondent's proof (or evidence in the record if respondent defaults) shows that a generic or descriptive domain name is being used in keeping with its semantic value or registration preceded complainant's acquisition of

---

685 ***Velcro Industries B. V. and Velcro USA Inc. v. allinhosting.com/Andres Chavez***, D2008-0864 (WIPO July 28, 2008) (<velcroart.net>).

686 The UDRP conjunctive model is contrasted with the disjunctive models of country code policies and of the Anticybersquatting Consumer Protection Act. See H.R. Conf. Rep. 106-412: "The bill is carefully and narrowly tailored, however, to extend only to cases where the plaintiff can demonstrate the defendant . . . *used* the offending domain name with bad-faith intent to profit from the goodwill of a mark belonging to someone else" (emphasis added). Discussed further in "Plenary Adjudication After an Adverse Decision" (Sec. 8.01-B).

687 See WIPO Overview 2.0, Paragraph 3.1: "Can bad faith be found if the disputed domain name was registered before the trademark was registered or before unregistered trademark rights were acquired?" No, unless the respondent is gifted with clairvoyance. "Consensus view: Generally speaking, although a trademark can form a basis for a UDRP action under the first element irrespective of its date . . . when a domain name is registered by the respondent before the complainant's relied-upon trademark right is shown to have been first established (whether on a registered or unregistered basis), the registration of the domain name would not have been in bad faith because the registrant could not have contemplated the complainant's then non-existent right." The qualification to the consensus states that "In certain situations, when the respondent is clearly aware of the complainant, and it is clear that the aim of the registration was to take advantage of the confusion between the domain name and any potential complainant rights, bad faith can be found." WIPO Overview 3.0 does not explicitly repeat 3.1 but the consensus has not changed. Discussed further in "Acting on Media Coverage and Insider Information" (Sec. 6.01-C.1.b).

688 A minority of panelists argue for "Justifying Forfeiture Despite Good Faith Registration" (Sec. 4.03-A.4.b).

the mark. Respondent's failure under paragraph 4(a)(ii) to rebut complainant's *prima facie* showing does not foreclose success under paragraph 4(a)(iii) of the Policy.

Lack of rights or legitimate interests in the domain name by itself is insufficient to establish bad faith absent proof that respondent with knowledge of complainant's trademark 1) registered the domain name with the primary purpose of offering to sell it for profit, 2) is engaged in a pattern of conduct to deprive complainant of the ability to obtain domain names corresponding to its trademark,[689] 3) competes with complainant and is seeking to disrupt complainant's business, or 4) is using the domain name to divert Internet users to its own or other websites for commercial gain.[690] Respondent has "no obligation whatsoever . . . to prove good faith, and in any event it is equally important to note that the absence of good faith does not constitute bad faith. The two concepts are not related in such a direct fashion."[691]

When it comes to registration, respondent has a final opportunity to argue and prove that it did not act in bad faith, and although its silence is not proof of motivation that it did, it supports complainant's allegations in its favor.[692] The critical factors in assessing abusive registration are the timing of a complainant's acquisition of its mark relative to domain name registration, the mark's strength or weakness, the geographic/goods or services proximity of the parties, respondent's conduct and acts, and the manner in which the domain name is being used.

Separately or together when present these factors offer sufficient evidence of respondent's intent in acquiring and holding the domain name, either to take advantage of complainant's mark or for purposes unrelated to bad faith. If respondent's assertions are consistent with the provable facts the affirmative proof for abusive registration must be particularly strong to tip the scale in the opposite direction. Respondent in the described circumstances does not infringe any right by holding a domain name corresponding to a trademark.[693]

---

[689] "Pattern of conduct" is a phrase drawn from paragraph 4(b)(ii) of the Policy where it specifically relates to denying a complainant "from reflecting the mark in a corresponding domain name" but it can also be applied in disputes in which complainant's have inadvertently lost their registrations by missing the renewal deadlines. As a representative case, see ***Armor Building Solutions, LLC v. Al Perkins***, FA1708001745973 (Forum November 2, 2017) (<armorbuildingsolutions.com>. "The Panel agrees that the foregoing constitutes evidence that the instant dispute is merely a piece of a larger pattern of Respondent's pattern of bad faith domain name registration and usage under Policy ¶ 4(b)(ii).") See further in "Pattern of Conduct" (Sec. 6.03).

[690] ***Société des Produits Nestle S.A. v. Pro Fiducia Treuhand AG***, D2001-0916 (WIPO October 12, 2001).

[691] ***Enrique Bernat F., SA v. Marrodan***, D2000 0966 (WIPO October 4, 2000). Complainant's failure to prove registration and use in bad faith (emphasizing the conjunctive) only exonerates respondent of abusive registration under the Policy. It does not foreclose a trademark ruling that the registration or use (emphasizing the disjunction) is infringing complainant's statutory rights.

[692] Bad faith is discussed further in Chapter 6; good faith is discussed in Chapter 5.

4.03-A.2 Construction of the Phrase "Is Being Used" 4.03-A.2

Use in bad faith is the second of the two-element conjunctive requirement. ICANN made a subtle change to the recommendation in the WIPO Final Report.[694] For "is used in bad faith," which implies present use, it substituted "is being used," which Panels have construed as use at any time from registration.[695] Paragraph 4(a)(iii) reads "your domain name has been registered and is being used in bad faith." To satisfy its burden, complainant is required to plead and prove respondent both registered the domain name (past tense) and "*is*" using it in bad faith, even if respondent has discontinued that use.

When a proscribed use commenced, whether it is continuing, or when it stopped—is a critical factor in determining whether any inference can be drawn about respondent's intention in registering the domain name. Although the verb phrase "is being used" "does not refer to a particular point in time,"[696] the closer in time the two factors are united the more likely it supports abusive registration. This follows because subsequent bad faith use separated in time from lawful registration is not actionable under the UDRP. Non-use of a domain name without explanation favors complainant; temporal distance between registration and proscribed use favors respondent.[697]

---

693 See ***Qwest Commc'ns Int'l v. QC Publ'g Grp., Inc.***, FA 286032 (Forum July 23, 2004) (<qwestcorp.com>. "Respondent had as its sole motivation for registering the disputed domain name a legitimate interest in capturing otherwise lost business traffic caused by inadvertent misspellings of the company's name ('QuestCorp') among internet users."); ***Maria Guadalupe Arvizú Ramírez v. Jennifer DeGrave, Water Tec of Tucson***, D2013-1467 (WIPO October 9, 2013) (The Panel accepted "the concept of trademark owners defensively registering a variety of versions of domain names which may be extensions of their registered trademarks in order to protect them from being registered by third parties," citing ***Shoeby Franchise B.V. v. Shoebuy Inc. SHOEBUY.COM***, D2010-2142 (WIPO March 20, 2011).

694 Paragraph 171(1)(iii).

695 Factual examples of bad faith registration and use under paragraph 4(b)(i-iv) are discussed in Chapter 6.

696 ***Ingersoll-Rand Co. v. Frank Gully, d/b/a Advcomren***, D2000-0021 (WIPO March 29, 2000) ("The Panel believes that the term 'is being used' does not refer to a particular point in time (such as when the Complaint is filed or when the Panel begins deliberations), but refers to the period of time following registration of the domain name at issue." See also ***Howard B. Stevens, Inc., dba PC Professor v. The PC Professor***, D2001-1282 (WIPO December 21, 2001) (same Panel) ("If at any time following the registration the name is used in bad faith, the fact of bad faith use is established. Otherwise a party could stop and start such uses in order to avoid a finding and a transfer or cancellation of the party's registration"); ***Six Continents Hotels, Inc. v. Seweryn Nowak***, D2003-0022 (WIPO March 4, 2003).

697 The reason for this is that proscribed use alone is not conclusive of registration in bad faith. Discussed below in "Subsequent Bad Faith Use" (Sec. 4.03-A.4).

What weight to assign present bad faith use to prove registration in bad faith when the conduct is subsequent to good faith registration has energized a number of panelists to offer new constructions of respondent's representations (paragraph 2 of the Policy) and paragraph 4(a)(iii), more favorable to complainants. Although the consensus is firm that proof of use in bad faith alone is only some evidence of registration in bad faith, these panelists argue for a new consensus that present use in bad faith warrants a finding of abusive registration.

It is axiomatic that intention to acquire a domain name may be proved by the use to which the domain name is put, and bad faith use may be and frequently is the only evidence tending to show the purpose for which a domain name was registered.[698] However, while abusive registration may be conclusive where bad faith is contemporaneous or close to the registration it is only one among other factors pointing to abusive registration where the alleged bad faith act occurs subsequent to good faith registration.[699] Absent evidence of registration in bad faith, "[n]o amount of bad faith use will suffice to support transfer under the Policy."[700]

The consensus for the construction dubbed by one Panel[701] as the "traditional" approach was articulated within months of the inception of the UDRP.[702]

---

[698] ***Admiral Insurance Services Ltd. v. Mr. Adam Dicker***, D2005-0241 (WIPO June 4, 2005); ***Adidas AG and Adidas (Ireland) Limited v. Gabor Varga and Jozsef Petho***, DIE2006-0004 (WIPO January 18, 2007) (Changing the content of a website after service of a complaint undermines the defense of good faith and constitutes evidence from which an inference may be drawn of bad faith); ***PayPal, Inc. v. David Weiss / Paybyweb, Inc.***, FA1707001740061 (Forum August 17, 2017) (<paypals.com>. "[O]ne does not establish good faith merely by changing the content of a site in an attempt to make it non-infringing, especially after the receipt of a cease and desist letter.")

[699] In contrast, the Anticybersquatting Consumer Protection Act provides for either/or proof of bad faith: it applies against a registrant who either "registers, traffics in, or uses a domain name" protected as a mark, 15 U.S.C. §1125(d)(1)(A)(ii). Country code policies also adopted the either/or model. Although the "disjunctive approach to bad faith . . . has much to recommend it," ***Editions Milan v. Secureplus, Inc.***, D2010-0606 (WIPO June 10, 2010), it is "not importable into the UDRP."

[700] ***Free Bridge Auto Sales Inc. v. Larry Ross***, FA0903001250951 (Forum April 28, 2009). Country code policies for common law jurisdictions follow a different model: proof is sufficient that demonstrates bad faith registration or bad faith use. See Appendix C. Under a self-administered country code policy for all French domain names (.FR, .RE, .WF, .PM and .YT) offered by Système de Résolution de Litiges (SYRELI) and administered by the French Association for Cooperative Internet Naming (AFNIC) the applicant has to prove, in addition to his valid interest to act, that the contested domain name is:

- "liable to disrupt public order or morality, or the rights guaranteed by the French Constitution or French law; or
- liable to infringe intellectual property rights or personal rights, and that the owner has no legitimate interest and is acting in bad faith; or
- identical or related to that of the French Republic, of a local authority or group of local authorities, of an institution or a local or national public service, and that the owner has no legitimate interest and is acting in bad faith".

The Panel in ***Teradyne*** emphasized the conjunctive requirement under paragraph 4(a)(iii) of the Policy and was "not ready to extend the Policy to cover cases clearly intended to be outside its scope." Amendment of the Policy (said this Panel) is a task for ICANN. There is a complex relationship between the two bad faith elements. They are both intimately related and distinctly separate.[703] While bad faith use in the present may not support bad faith registration, contemporaneous bad faith use following registration indubitably does.[704] This is because temporal proximity of use to registration is more likely to demonstrate proscribed intent. Bad faith use can be found if the domain name is being used in violation of the Policy *at any time* after registration, but bad faith registration is different: there must be evidence of respondent intentionally targeting complainant to exploit the reputation and goodwill of its trademark.[705]

As a general rule the use of the domain name is considered first, except in those instances in which the domain name was registered prior to complainant acquiring its trademark.[706] In that event, the timing of acquisition is a significant factor weighing against abusive registration. In contrast, for domain names registered after the trademark the use to which the domain name is put and respondent's knowledge or awareness of complainant or its trademark either implicates[707] or exonerates[708] the respondent.

---

701 ***Eastman Sporto Group LLC v. Jim and Kenny***, D2009-1688 (WIPO March 1, 2010).

702 ***Teradyne, Inc. v. 4Tel Technology***, D2000-0026 (WIPO May 9, 2000).

703 The conjunctive requirement was particularly emphasized in the first decision reported under the UDRP, ***World Wrestling Federation Entertainment, Inc. v. Michael Bosman***, D1999-0001 (WIPO January 31, 2000) (Default; transferred).

704 ***Bass Hotels v. Rodgerall***, D2000-0568 (WIPO August 7, 2000) ("Moreover, the fact that the offending use of the website ceased sometime prior to the issuance of the Panel's decision, does not change the fact that the domain name at issue has been registered and is being used in bad faith, since the phrase 'is being used' has been interpreted to refer not to a particular point in time, but to any time during the period of time following registration of the domain name at issue.")

705 Discussed further in "Parking for Revenue" (Sec. 6.01-A.2) and "Populating Web Pages: the 'Not Me' Defense" (Sec. 6.05-F).

706 ***e Duction, Inc. v. John Zuccarini, d/b/a The Cupcake Party & Cupcake Movies***, D2000-1369 (WIPO February 5, 2001) (<eduction.com>), "Although bad faith use may, in appropriate cases, give rise to an inference of bad faith registration, such an inference cannot be made where . . . Complainant's mark was not yet in existence at the time of the domain name registration.")

707 ***Cisco Technology, Inc. v. Nicholas Strecha, E-Careers LTD***, D2010-0391 (WIPO May 7, 2010) (Transferred. Respondent offered IT training through <ciscouk.com> to help students understand and use Cisco technologies in competition with Cisco).

708 ***Dr. Ing. h.c. F. Porsche AG v. The Eight Black Group, Simon Chen and Denise Marble***, D2009-0989 (WIPO September 12, 2009) (<porscheexperience.com> and < porscheguides.com>. "If, as complainant accepts, the Respondents registered the Domain Names for the purpose of promoting Mr Chen's electronic book, it follows that the Respondents did not register [the domain names]

The reason for the order in which the elements are addressed is straightforward. Domain name registration postdating trademark acquisition may not be conclusive of registration in bad faith.[709] However, if the use to which respondent has put the domain name at any time infringed complainant's rights by displaying links to its competitors (or is itself a competitor, which implicates paragraph 4(b)(iii) of the Policy) the probability strengthens that from the date of registration respondent intended to mislead Internet users into believing it had an existing relationship with complainant, which is proscribed under paragraph 4(b)(iv).[710]

4.03-A.3 4.03-A.3 Content as a Factor in Determining Bad Faith Use

Content is either a "smoking gun" that confirms bad faith use[711] or evidence that respondent had another purpose "in mind" than taking advantage of complainant's trademark. Even if holding a domain name may be insufficient to prove a right or legitimate interest, it may be sufficient to avoid a finding of bad faith use. use, although using a domain name for a business that is legal does not rebut the claim of use in bad faith for a well-known or famous mark if it is likely to cause consumer confusion. Registering domain names composed of characters having different referents[712] and dictionary words used (or available to be used even if passively held) in their ordinary senses is not for those reasons alone violations of a complainant's trademark rights.[713]

No bad faith can be inferred from a domain name legitimately used in the past and presently parked,[714] although a domain name legitimately used in the past by a

---

primarily for the purpose of sale, even though the Respondents subsequently offered to sell them for a substantial price to complainant."

[709] ***William Hill Organisation Ltd. V. Lisa Jane Statton***, D2000-0827 (WIPO October 31, 2000): "[A finding that bad faith may have] existed after the date of registration . . . does not automatically lead to the conclusion that this intention existed at the time of registration."

[710] ***National Association of Realtors v. John Fothergill***, D2010-1284 (WIPO September 20, 2010); ***Pendragon PLC v. Mr. Patrick Meehan***, D2010-1297 (WIPO September 10, 2010).

[711] Displaying links to competitive goods or services, discussed further in Commercial Gain Through Hyperlinking. ***Am. Online, Inc. v. Miles***, FA 105890 (Forum May 31, 2002) ("Respondent is using the domain name at issue to resolve to a website at which Complainant's trademarks and logos are prominently displayed...").

[712] ***Louis Vuitton Malletier S.A. v. Manifest Information Services c/o Manifest Hostmaster***, FA060900 0796276 (Forum November 7, 2006) (<lv.com>, Denied. Respondent once used the website (presently inactive) as a portal for businesses in Las Vegas).

[713] ***Zero International Holding GmbH & Co. Kommanditgesellschaft v. Beyonet Services and Stephen Urich***, D2000-0161 (WIPO May 12, 2000) (<zero.com>, "[w]e do not accept that complainant's contention that registration of a domain name which is only to be used for [e-mail and file transfer operations] is in some way improper and constitutes bad faith.")

[714] ***Louis Vuitton Malletier S.A.***, *supra*. Inactive domain names are discussed further in "Inactive or Passive Use" (Sec. 5.01-B.2).

prior holder does not protect a successor holder.[715] A closer issue involves unrelated successors that acquire their domain names after non-renewal by prior registrants.[716] While a transferee's registration is tainted by its transferor's bad faith use, an unrelated successor registrant is not presumed tainted by any prior bad faith use. In that event abusive registration must be proved rather than presumed.[717]

4.03-A.4 Subsequent Bad Faith Use 4.03-A.4

4.03-A.4.a *Good Faith Not Vitiated by Change of Use* *4.03-A.4.a*

Panelists of the earliest decided cases held that the Policy required complainant to plead and prove respondent had infringing intent in registering the disputed domain name, manifested by immediate use. However, no inference of intent can be drawn from use separated in time from registration. The principle established, although not without dissent,[718] is that a domain name registered in good faith is not vitiated by a later change of use to bad faith[719] and is not grounds for forfeiture upon renewal of registration.[720] A "registration of a domain name that at inception did not reach but is found later to be used in bad faith does not fall foul of [paragraph]

---

[715] See ***Deutsche Lufthansa AG v. Whois Privacy Services Pty Ltd / Mediablue Inc, Kwangpyo Kim***, D2013-1844 (WIPO January 22, 2014) ("Complainant['s explanation] for its inaction [is because] . . . the previous owner of the disputed domain name did not use it in a way that interferes with the trademark rights of the Complainant.")

[716] Discussed further in "Transfer/Subsequent Holders=New Registration" (Sec. 4.03-B.2).

[717] ***A. D. Banker & Company v. Domain Invest***, D2010-1044 (WIPO September 30, 2010) contesting <adbankers.com>; decision by a three member Panel. Complainant is the owner of the trademark A.D. BANKER. Respondent contended that it was attracted to the domain name because it was composed of two letters, "ad," which is short for "advertising" and "bankers." There was insufficient proof of bad faith registration even though there was a transient period after acquisition of linking to Complainant's competitors. Discussed further in "Populating Pages: The "'Not Me' Defense" (Sec. 6.05-F).

[718] See "Justifying Forfeiture Despite Good Faith Registration" (Sec.4.03-A.4.b).

[719] ***Superiority, Inc. d/b/a Just Bulbs v. none/Mother boards.com***, D2003-0491 (WIPO October 9, 2003) (Complaint denied, later the subject of a refiling in 2013 when Respondent began using the domain name in bad faith, again denied, then a federal action under the ACPA resulting in an award to mark owner together with statutory damages and attorney's fees, *Bulbs 4 E. Side, Inc. v. Ricks*, (S.D. Tex., Houston Div. July 18, 2017). A change to non-infringing use after notice and filing of complaint, however, is treated differently. Discussed further in "Making Changes to the Website After Notice and Filing of Complaint" (Sec. 7.05-E).

[720] However, present infringing use coupled with good faith registration, while not actionable under the UDRP, may be actionable under the ACPA, or for trademark infringement under the Lanham Act. See *DSPT International v. Nahum*, 624 F.3d 1213 (9th Cir. 2010). The Court held that "[e]ven if a domain name was put up innocently and used properly for years, a person is liable under 15 U.S.C. §1125(d) if he subsequently uses the domain name with a bad faith intent to profit from the protected mark by holding the domain name for ransom." Also, *Newport News Holdings Corporation v. Virtual City Vision, Incorporated, d/b/a Van James Bond Tran*, 650 F3d 423 (4th Cir. 2011).

4(a)(iii)."[721] What is true for the original registrant, however, does not apply to the second and subsequent generations of transferee/assignee holders, who are accountable from their new registrations. For the original registrant, the emphasis is on the past rather than the present, while successors are assessed without advantage of their predecessors' good faith registrations. The issue is discussed further below.[722]

In ***Teradyne***, the Panel examined paragraphs 197 and 198 of the WIPO Final Report to reach the conclusion that while domain names may evolve over time to become infringing, the registrations are not for that reason retrospectively abusive:

> First of all, ¶197 itself contemplates not that the domain name will become an abusive registration, but rather that the domain name "may become infringing" (italics added). Second, the clarifying language in the following paragraph, ¶198, makes clear that the reference to "infringing" rather than "abusive" in ¶197 was intentional; and was not intended to create abusive registrations where none existed originally.

This construction applies even with "changed circumstances, the passage of years, or intervening events."[723] There are decisions suggesting that this principle may not cover all circumstances, but as a general rule a respondent's progressive encroachment of complainant's trademark is an issue for a court of law.[724] However, the progressive encroachment by a transferor will expose a transferee to liability if it continues the same use after its own registration.[725]

4.03-A.4.b 4.03-A.4.b *Justifying Forfeiture Despite Good Faith Registration*

4.03-A.4.b.i 4.03-A.4.b.i ***Misgivings About the Conjunctive Construction***

The Panel in the first decided case construed paragraph 4(a)(iii) of the Policy as requiring proof of both elements. It held that "It is clear from the legislative history that ICANN intended that the complainant must establish not only bad faith registration, but also bad faith use."[726] This construction quickly settled into the

---

[721] ***Weatherall Green & Smith v. Everymedia.com***, D2000-1528 (WIPO February 19, 2001), citing ***Teradyne, Inc. Teradyne, Inc. v. 4Tel Technology***, D2000-0026 (WIPO May 9, 2000). Respondent registered the domain name to reflect its own business name but subsequently sought to sell the name for profit when its business dissolved.

[722] Discussed further in "Second and Subsequent Generations of Holders" (Sec. 4.03-B.2.a).

[723] ***Substance Abuse Management, Inc. v. Screen Actors Modesl [sic] International, Inc. (SAMI),*** D2001-0782 (WIPO August 14, 2001) ("If a domain name was registered in good faith, it cannot, by changed circumstances, the passage of years, or intervening events, later be deemed to have been registered in bad faith.")

[724] A number of actions commenced under the Anticybersquatting Consumer Protection Act have considered subsequent bad faith use after good faith registration, and courts have ruled in favor of the mark owner. Two examples are noted in earlier footnotes. In ***Newport News, Inc. v. Vcv Internet***, AF 0238 (eResolution July 18, 2000), Respondent kept <newportnews.com> and in *Newport News*

consensus view discussed above. However, in a duo of cases decided in 2009 the first panelist expressed misgivings about his original construction and proposed an alternative approach.[727] He states that he has come to believe that in assessing conduct under paragraph 4(b)(iv) of the Policy forfeiture was justified even if respondent had registered the domain name in good faith. The Policy creators (he believed) never intended a result that allows registrants who have registered disputed domain names in good faith to take advantage of and prosper from complainants' emergent reputations. Although this alternative approach has been soundly rejected, it nevertheless continues to have adherents.[728]

In offering his revision the ***World Wrestling*** panelist together with a small number of others attracted to his reasoning discovered what they believed was the traditionalists' Achilles heel, that they "seem to have largely overlooked the language of the Policy regarding the respondent's representations and warranties." The unitary (or, sometimes referred to as the unified) concept rests on the proposition that for certain kinds of opportunism registrant should forfeit its registration for the disputed domain name.

There is a seductive logic to the concept. By broadening the Policy, it can be made to include instances of infringement excluded by the "and" requirement but this would defeat one of the founding principles of the jurisprudence, namely a balancing of rights.[729] A persuasive argument for rejecting the "unitary concept" (elaborated further below) is that it misinterprets ICANN's vision by aligning the

---

Holdings, supra. it was held to be a cybersquatter. See also discussion in "Mixing Innocent and Infringing Elements" (Sec. 6.01-F).

725 Discussed further in "Transfer/Subsequent Holders=New Registration" (Sec. 4.03-B.2).

726 ***World Wrestling Federation Entertainment, Inc. v. Michael Bosman***, D99-0001 (WIPO January 14, 2000).

727 ***City Views Limited v. Moniker Privacy Services / Xander, Jeduyu, ALGEBRALIVE***, D2009-0643 (WIPO July 3, 2009) (<mummygold.com>). The new construction was announced in this case, although the Panel denied the complaint. The same Panel later applied his new construction to grant the complaint in ***Octogen Pharmacal Company, Inc. v. Domains By Proxy, Inc. / Rich Sanders and Octogen e Solutions***, D2009-0786 (WIPO August 19, 2009). See also ***Alibaba Group Holding Limited v. Digital Domains MEPE***, HK-1100361 (ADNDRC July 26, 2011) (Complaint denied by majority over Mummygold/Octogen panelist dissent).

728 See for example ***Developmentex.com, Incorporated v. Manuel Schraner***, FA1710001755537 (Forum November 27, 2017) (<devex.org>. Domain name registered more than 4 years earlier than date of mark registration). The proposition has also migrated to renewal of registration as a measuring point for restarting the analysis of bad faith (Sec. 4.03-A.4.c).

729 ***Red Bull GmbH v. Roy Kenneth Nabben***, D2010-1358 (WIPO September 30, 2010) ("[A] registration originally made in good faith cannot turn into a registration in bad faith because the registrant subsequently uses it in bad faith," citing ***A. Nattermann & Cie. GmbH and Sanofi aventis v. Watson Pharmaceuticals, Inc.***, D2010-0800 (WIPO August 31, 2010) (over dissent); ***Mile, Inc. v. Michael Burg***, D2010-2011 (WIPO February 11, 2011); ***Randy A. Leslein v. Domain Hostmaster, Customer ID: 69323121876872, WhoIs Privacy Services Pty Ltd / Lisa Katz, Domain Protection***

UDRP with the "either/or" model of the Anticybersquatting Consumer Protection Act (ACPA) (Sec. 4.03-A.4.d).[730]

4.03-A.4.b.ii

4.03-A.4.b.ii *Challenging the Unitary Concept*

The "binary concept" according to the panelists who insist that subsequent bad faith use warrants unifying the paragraph 4(a)(iii) requirement is said to have gained strength from a misinterpretation of an admired early decision that formulated a bedrock principle for assessing a registrant's conduct in passive holding of a domain name confusingly similar to an inherently distinctive mark.[731] A domain name can be said to be used in bad faith even when it is inactive. A reconsideration of the consensus (the challengers argue) is therefore necessary to correct this misconstruction of the Policy.[732]

According to the challengers, a particularly egregious violation subsequent to apparent good faith registration justifies a finding of "retroactive bad faith [registration]."[733] To be accurate, the label "retroactive bad faith" is a misnomer because the *Mummygold/Octogen* analysis does not actually attribute bad faith to the registration.

LLC, D2017-1233 (WIPO August 14, 2017). The panelist responsible for the retrospective bad faith view offers a fuller analysis in dissent in ***Guru Denim Inc. v. Ibrahim Ali Ibrahim abu-Harb***, D2013-1324 (WIPO September 27, 2013). (Also see dissent in ***A. Nattermann*** for further elucidation on the unitary view where the same panelist points out that paragraph 4(a)(iii) reads: "your domain name has been registered and is being used in bad faith." It does not state that "your domain name has been registered [in bad faith] and is being used in bad faith." The absence of the bracketed phrase in that Panel's reasoning supports the unitary view.)

730 It can also be argued that if in the year 2000 the Panel had ruled as it did in 2009, it would likely have aborted the creation of a secondary market in domain names. The first principle provides the necessary security to investors that their registrations are lawful and they have marketable assets.

731 ***Telstra Corporation Limited v. Nuclear Marshmallows***, D2000-0003 (WIPO February 13, 2000) (Same panelist as in ***Octogen Pharmacal***).

732 The dissent in ***Alibaba***, *supra*. (same panelist as in ***Telstra*** and ***Octogen Pharmacal***) noted that common law courts "have overruled precedents in order to reach the correct result . . . [and if they can] [s]urely UDRP Panelists are even more free to determine that prior panel decisions, no matter how well intended, do not comport with the Policy."

733 ***Ville de Paris v. Jeff Walter***, D2009-1278 (WIPO November 19, 2009) (<parvi.org>. "In summary, it seems clear to this Panel that the intent and effect of the Policy is that the requirement of Paragraph 4(a)(iii) can, in certain circumstances, be met where respondent has used the domain name in bad faith even though it may have been acquired in good faith." While this position is endorsed under the ACPA there is no precedent that alleged bad faith use alone is actionable under the UDRP. The Respondent timely initiated an action under the ACPA; Ville de Paris failed to appear and judgment was entered on default declaring plaintiff's right to the domain name and awarding statutory damages, ***Walter v. Ville de Paris***, 4:2009cv03939 (S.D. Texas Houston Div. July 5, 2012). For fuller decisional analyses on this issue of use in bad faith under ACPA jurisprudence, See *DSPT International v. Nahum*, 624 F.3d 1213 (9th Cir. 2010) (www.eq-Italy.com); *Newport News Holdings Corporation v. Virtual City Vision, Incorporated, d/b/a Van James Bond Tran*, 650 F3d 423 (4th Cir. 2011) (<newportnews.com>).

Rather, it justifies forfeiture of the domain name for continuing, knowing violation of the trademark owner's rights after it has been put on notice of "the emergence of the Complainant's new and powerful trademark."[734]

According to this view, the unitary concept finds support in three provisions of the Policy: paragraphs 2 (representations and warranties that in acquiring the domain name registrant will not infringe third party rights[735]), 4(a)(iii) (requiring proof of "registration and use in bad faith" the meaning of which is said to be "far from unequivocal,"[736] in fact to be ambiguous,[737]) and 4(b)(iv) ("using" the domain name in bad faith, which is supported by the language of paragraph 4(b)—*shall be evidence of the registration and use* of a domain name in bad faith).

The registration agreements incorporate paragraph 2 without enlarging on the representations. Instead of simply representing that the registration "will not directly or indirectly infringe the legal rights of a third party," which is found in the typical registration agreement,[738] paragraph 2 contains two further representations regarding legality: (c) you are not registering the domain name for an unlawful purpose; and (d) you will not knowingly use the domain name in violation of any applicable laws or regulations. Subparagraph 2(d) is the linchpin of the unitary

---

734 ***Camilla Australia Pty Ltd v. Domain Admin, Mrs Jello, LLC***, D2015-1593 (WIPO November 30, 2015) ("The Respondent's argument therefore raises the question of the obligations of the owners of domain names used to generate PPC revenue to the owners of new, emerging, trademarks.") Award in Complainant's favor vacated by stipulation in subsequent challenge under the ACPA, ***Mrs. Jello, LLC v. Camilla Australia Pty Ltd.*** 15-cv-08753 (D. NJ 8/1/2016).

735 The consensus challengers find support for their view in Paragraph 2 of the Policy: "By applying to register a domain name, or *asking us to renew a domain name registration*, you hereby represent and warrant to us that . . . (d) you will not knowingly use the domain name in violation of any applicable laws or regulations. It is your responsibility to determine whether your domain name infringes or violates someone else's rights" (emphasis added).

736 ***Jappy GmbH v. Satoshi Shimoshita***, D2010-1001 (WIPO September 28, 2010) (The Panel explained that taking into account 1) paragraph 4(b), and 2) the purpose of the Policy (as explained in the Final Report of the WIPO Internet Domain Name Process, paragraph 168) the phrases "has been registered" and "is being used in bad faith" "can, in certain circumstances (of which paragraph 4(b)(iv) is one), be satisfied in the absence of registration in bad faith.")

737 Dissent in ***Guru Denim Inc. v. Ibrahim Ali Ibrahim Abu Harb***, D2013-1324 (WIPO September 27, 2013). The dissent was the same panelist who dissented in ***Nattermann***, *supra*.

738 See Network Solutions Service Agreement version 9.27:

"11. REPRESENTATIONS AND WARRANTIES. You agree and warrant that: (i) neither your registration nor use of the any of the Network Solutions services nor the manner in which you intend to use such Network Solutions Services will directly or indirectly infringe the legal rights of a third party, (ii) you have all requisite power and authority to execute this Agreement and to perform your obligations hereunder, (iii) you have selected the necessary security option(s) for your domain name registration record, (iv) you are of legal age to enter into this Agreement (or you are at least 13 years of age and have your parents' permission to apply for services hereunder); and (vi) you agree to comply with all applicable laws and regulations."

concept, but the question is whether the representation is meant to be a continuing duty. If it is, then domain name holders would be exposed to forfeiture at any time bad faith use subsequent to good faith registration can be demonstrated.

Under the "retroactive bad faith" view the duty to avoid infringing the legal rights of third parties is breached by subsequent bad faith use. It posits that paragraph 2 "is an integral part of the Policy, and it cannot be ignored."[739] It "imposes a duty on the part of the registrant to conduct an investigation at the time of registration, but also includes a representation and warranty . . . that it will not now or in the future use the domain name in violation of any laws or regulations."[740] It "clearly covers intellectual property rights and the laws protecting them, including . . . trademark."[741]

This duty (according to the retroactive bad faith panelists) "is not limited to the moment at which the registrant registers the domain name; rather, it extends to any use of the domain name in the future."[742] Commencement of bad faith use transforms that which was legitimate *when it occurred* into a breach of respondent's warranty, thereby justifying a finding of *male fide* registration regardless of respondent's knowledge when it executed the registration agreement. In effect, the "either/or" feature of the ACPA is forcibly imported into the UDRP as sufficient cause for forfeiture.

Paragraphs 4(a)(iii) and 4(b)(iv) enter into the "binary/unitary" argument because of the phrasing of their language. Paragraph 4(a)(iii) reads in pertinent part, "your domain name has been registered and is being used in bad faith." The retroactive bad faith panelists construe the positioning of "in bad faith" as meaning it applies only to "use" and not to "registration." The consensus reads the phrase "in bad faith" as qualifying both registration and use. The counter-argument is that this reading is logically and grammatically incorrect and insists it is not too late to set the UDRP in a new and proper direction.

Paragraph 4(b)(iv) differs from the other three 4(b) circumstances of bad faith in a significant way. Whereas the other 4(b) requirements begin or contain the phrase "you have registered", 4(b)(iv) begins with the phrase "by using the domain name" and does not use the word "registration" at all. This allows room to construe the 4(a)(iii) requirement as "unitary" as it applies to 4(b)(iv) of the Policy by arguing that bad faith registration is implicit in a finding of bad faith use regardless of a respondent's original intention in purchasing the domain name.

The primary question about the reach of paragraph 2, however, is whether it should be construed to mean that respondent has a continuing duty. To one panelist "[i]f paragraph 2 of the Policy can be brought into play to address the issue of bad faith, this Panel is concerned that the scope of the Policy will be extended far beyond

---

739 ***Octogen Pharmacal***, *supra.*

740 *Id.*

741 *Id.*

742 *Id.* See also dissent in ***A. Nattermann***, *supra.*

its original purpose."[743] To other Panels "reading 'registered' as a continuous act that can be abused at any time would appear to make it essentially synonymous with 'use' and deprive the conjunctive phrase of its full meaning."[744]

It is not that the *Mummygold/Octogen* construction is without merit, but in the words of one three-member Panel it is thirteen years too late: "If a consensus developed that a line of prior decisions had reached the wrong result, and if panels generally adopted a new approach on an issue, this Panel also would be open to considering whether a new approach was appropriate, both substantively under the Policy and in order to promote consistency."[745] The Panel's emphasis on consistency is a significant factor in its also arguing against changing current law which construes "'evidence of the registration and use of a domain name in bad faith' . . . merely [as] an evidentiary presumption which may be rebutted on a full consideration of all the circumstances of the case."[746]

However, the stronger argument against the retroactive bad faith view is that it forcibly imports an "either/or" feature into the UDRP as sufficient cause for forfeiture. To the extent that this privileges owners whose marks postdate the registration of the domain name it goes a step beyond the ACPA by awarding them domain names for what in essence would be trademark infringement, which is a remedy beyond the powers of UDRP Panels and should be outside the scope of the Policy.

4.03-A.4.b.iii *Claim of Good Faith Registration Not a Defense* *4.03-A.4.b.iii*

The "retroactive bad faith" analysis argues that "bad faith registration can be deemed to have occurred even without regard to the state of mind of the registrant at the time of registration."[747] It can be found despite the fact that the domain name may not *originally* have been registered by respondent in bad faith. Thus, even

---

[743] ***Camon S.p.A. v. Intelli Pet, LLC***, D2009-1716 (WIPO March 12, 2010).

[744] ***Mile***, *supra.*; ***Randy A. Leslein v. Domain Hostmaster, Customer ID: 69323121876872, WhoIs Privacy Services Pty Ltd / Lisa Katz, Domain Protection LLC***, D2017-1233 (WIPO August 14, 2017).

[745] For this reason, it "does not seem . . . to be an attractive answer," ***Torus Insurance Holdings Limited v. Torus Computer Resources***, D2009-1455 (WIPO January 10, 2010); ***Mile***, *supra.* ("The current Panel recognizes the value, in appropriate cases, of inferences of original intent based on subsequent conduct. But the Panel does not find a compelling Policy or legal basis for retroactively characterizing later abuses as bad faith in the 'registration' of a domain name.") See also ***Realty Mark, LLC v. Scott Rosenbaum (a/k/a "Scott Rose" and "Scott Rosen") / RealtyMark.com***, D2013-1694 (WIPO December 11, 2013) ("The Panel rejects the [unitary concept] view . . . of a small number of panelists that consider that bad faith use may suffice absent bad faith registration. The Panel considers that this view inappropriately disregards the significance of the conjunctive text of paragraphs 4(a)(iii) and 4(b) of the Policy (i.e. registered and used in bad faith"); ***Randy A. Leslein***, *supra.*

[746] ***Kids & Us English, S.L. v. Target Success.Com, Incorporated***, D2016-0356 (WIPO April 8, 2016) (<kidsandus.com>) responding to the argument that the traditional "approach can lead to outcomes which some WIPO panels have considered unjust." It would only be "unjust" if an owner

though a party may register or acquire a domain name in good faith, if it "uses the domain name in the future so as to call into question the party's compliance with the party's representations and warranties, this may be deemed to be retroactive bad faith registration."[748] According to one Panel "[t]here seems no reason in logic or in principle why the availability of redress [under the UDRP] should be limited to situations where bad faith is present at the time of acquisition of the domain name."[749]

Panelists who insist on the unitary concept argue that respondents *do* have a continuing duty to use their domain names according to their representations. To consensus panelists this view undermines the integrity of the UDRP by injecting into the jurisprudence a new theory of forfeiture.[750] The "fact that so many panelists have declined to apply the unitary concept "argues against an emerging consensus to overturn a long-established doctrine and provides yet another reason for this Panel to decline to adopt the Mummygold/Octogen reasoning."[751]

It is important for parties to know what to expect.[752] Overturning a fundamental jurisprudential construction would compromise and come at the expense of predictability and consistency.[753] Although the "retroactive bad faith" construction may be satisfying in "its practical effect in the small number of cases in which it has

---

of a later acquired mark were entitled to a domain name corresponding to its mark, but that is not the law and to assert it would give the mark owner more rights than the law grants.

747 *Id.*

748 ***Octogen***, *supra.* See also "Justifying Forfeiture Despite Good Faith Registration" (Sec.4.03.A-4.b) and "Renewal: Not Equivalent to New Registration" (Sec. 4.03-B.1)

749 ***Ville de Paris v. Jeff Walter***, D2009-1278 (WIPO November 19, 2009) (Complaint granted, but subsequent ACPA action resulted in default judgment in favor of domain name holder and ultimately a substantial damages award and attorney's fees, *Walter v. Ville de Paris*, 4:2009cv03939 (S.D. Texas Houston Div. July 5, 2012). The Panel in ***Zerospam Security Inc. v. Internet Retail Billing, Inc., Host Master***, D2009-1276 (WIPO December 18, 2009) is among a handful of other panelists who concur with the construction favored by the ***Ville de Paris*** panelist.

750 ***Torus Insurance Holdings***, *supra.* The Panel "doubts that the framers of the Policy could have intended that proof of bad faith use of the kind described at paragraph 4(b)(iv) of the Policy should always be deemed sufficient proof, on its own, that the disputed domain name has also been registered (possibly many years earlier) in bad faith. . . . [Rather, it] seems to this Panel that such evidence of bad faith use would need to be found to co exist with bad faith intent regarding the act of registration in order to satisfy the requirement of paragraph 4(a)(iii) of the Policy."

751 ***Validas, LLC v. SMVS Consultancy Private Limited***, D2009-1413 (WIPO January 29, 2010).

752 See for example, ***Jowissa Watch Ltd. v. Don Nichols***, D2011-0086 (WIPO March 31, 2011) (The Panel laments that "[i]t is unfortunate, in the face of such bad faith use that the Panel has arrived at the decision that the complaint should be denied. However, the Panel must render its decision within the confines of the Policy, which clearly requires that the Disputed Domain Name must be registered and used in bad faith.")

753 ***Developmentex.com, Incorporated v. Manuel Schraner***, FA1710001755537 (Forum November 27, 2017) (<devex.org>. Panel strayed from the principles of the UDRP jurisprudence by applying the alternative theories that are referred to above). Other examples include ***Big 5 Corp. v. EyeAim.***

been an issue . . . the only permissible way for this view to be achieved is for ICANN to amend the Policy . . . by changing 'and' into 'or.'"[754] Panels have expressed sympathy for complainants whose marks respondents have targeted but have followed precedent in denying complaints for failure to show bad faith registration.[755]

4.03-A.4.c *Renewal of Registration*

4.03-A.4.c

A variant of the *Mummygold/Octogen* construction discussed above insists that renewing registration of a domain name being used in bad faith is abusive regardless of original registration in good faith.[756] The circumstances justifying forfeiture rest on the proposition that renewal starts anew the assessment of bad faith in breach of

---

com / Roy Fang, FA1308001513704 (Forum October 11, 2013) (with dissent. <big5.com>. "[T]he Panel deems Respondent's 2012 renewal of the disputed domain name to be the date on which to measure whether the disputed domain name was registered and used in bad faith for purposes of paragraph 4(a)(iii).") See also ***Camilla Australia Pty Ltd v. Domain Admin, Mrs Jello, LLC.***, D2015-1593 (WIPO November 30, 2015) and *Mrs. Jello, LLC v. Camilla Australia Pty Ltd.* 15-cv-08753 (D. NJ 8/1/2016) (UDRP award vacated by stipulation, a result that should clarify the law as it ought to be applied in UDRP disputes.

[754] ***Validas***, *supra*. See also ***Mile, Inc. v. Michael Burg***, D2010-2011 (WIPO February 11, 2011) ("The current Panel recognizes the value, in appropriate cases, of inferences of original intent based on subsequent conduct. But the Panel does not find a compelling Policy or legal basis for retroactively characterizing later abuses as bad faith in the 'registration' of a domain name.")

[755] ***INDÚSTRIA E COMÉRCIO DE CONFECÇÕES DI MIRMAY LTDA v. Qingrui Chen***, D2013-1139 (WIPO August 22, 2013) ("[T]he Panel is mindful [in denying the complaint] . . . that the majority of UDRP panelists continue to adhere to a more literal interpretation of the third limb under paragraph 4(a) of the Policy.") See dissent in ***Guru Denim Inc. v. Ibrahim Ali Ibrahim Abu Harb***, D2013-1324 (WIPO September 27, 2013) ("In the present case, when the Respondent registered the disputed domain name, the trademark did not exist. Respondent was therefore entitled to continue using the domain name <truereligion.com> as he had been using it, or to use it for any purpose whatsoever, so long as he did not intentionally use it to profit from the goodwill associated with Complainant's later created trademark. However, as the Respondent candidly admitted, he is now using the disputed domain name to profit from the goodwill the Complainant created in the mark.") In ***Group One Holdings Pte Ltd v. Steven Hafto***, D2017-0183 (WIPO March 28, 2017) a three-member panel including the author of *Mummygold* unanimously rejected the reasoning of that case thereby essentially declaring the retroactive bad faith concept a dead end.

[756] Discussed further in "Renewal: Not Equivalent to New Registration" (Sec. 4.03-B.1). The Third and Ninth Circuit Courts of Appeal have construed the ACPA differently as noted by the three member Panel in ***Twitter, Inc. v. Geigo, Inc.***, D2011-1210 (WIPO November 2, 2011). The consensus view is set forth in the Jurisprudential Overview, Paragraph 3.9: "Where the respondent provides satisfactory evidence of an unbroken chain of possession, panels typically would not treat merely 'formal' changes or updates to registrant contact information as a new registration" and "[a]lso, irrespective of registrant representations undertaken further to UDRP paragraph 2, panels have found that the mere renewal of a domain name registration by the same registrant is insufficient to support a finding of registration in bad faith."

registrant's registration agreement and in violation of Paragraph 2 of the Policy.[757] It differs from "retroactive bad faith" in its timing.

In contrast to the ***Mummygold/Octogen*** construction which has been roundly rejected some panelists (citing ***Eastman Sporto***) have been willing to accept that bad faith use directed to later acquired trademarks rising in reputation commencing before and continuing after renewal of registration could be abusive.[758]

However, the settled law holds that renewal of registration that continues bad faith use does not justify a finding of bad faith registration. The Panel in ***PAA Laboratories*** is sympathetic to the concept that bad faith use followed by renewal constitutes abusive registration but elected ("reluctantly") to follow precedent: "[i]n making its finding, the Panel wishes to clarify that its decision under this element is based on the need for consistency and comity in domain name dispute 'jurisprudence.'"[759] In the ***PAA*** Panel's view "[t]he benefit of an original good faith registration should not be perpetual to the point where it can cloak successors in title and successors in 'possession' long after the original registration would have expired." But for "the persuasive force of the cited decisions, this Panel would have expressed the view that paragraph 2 of the Policy demonstrates that references to 'registration' in the Policy were probably intended to be references to registration or renewal of registration."

The Panel in ***Eastman Sporto*** emphasized that he "share[d] [***PAA*** Panel's] reservations," but instead of acquiescing rejected the traditional approach. He held that subsequent bad faith use "should be an act of a kind encompassed by paragraph 4(a)(iii)" and concluded that "[b]ased upon the record in this proceeding. . . [the] Panel deems Respondent's 2009 renewal of the disputed domain name to be the

---

757 ***Eastman Sporto Group LLC v. Jim and Kenny***, D2009-1688 (WIPO March 1, 2010).

The Panel formulated the following test that would justify forfeiture:

- Respondent intentionally changed its use of the disputed domain name.
- The new use is unrelated to Respondent's earlier business.
- The new use is textbook cybersquatting.
- The new use occurred prior to the renewal held to be a registration subject to for purposes of paragraph 4(a)(iii).
- There has been no legitimate use since renewal.

However, the Panel's theory that renewal is a new registration thus domain name holder's Paragraph 2 representations and warranties apply continues to have a hold on some panelists as evidenced by the strongly worded dissent in ***easyGroup Limited v. Easy Group Holdings Limited***, D2014-2128 (WIPO February 19, 2015), as well as a leaning in other cases further noted in the following footnotes.

758 ***Jody Kriss and East River Partners, LLC v. Felix Sater / Larissa Yudina***, FA1602001660728 (Forum March 22, 2016) (Domain names transferred following renewal of registration for continuing bad faith use after Complainant's trademark registration.)

759 ***PAA Laboratories GmbH v. Printing Arts America***, D2004-0338 (WIPO July 13, 2004).

date on which to measure whether the disputed domain name was registered and used in bad faith."

Forfeiture is justified when respondents intentionally change their uses of domain names to take advantage of complainants' marks. Some Panels have also justified this construction against respondents who openly compete with complainant (paragraph 4(b)(iii) of the Policy).[760] According to the ***Denver Newspaper*** Panel such "bad faith use is itself sufficient to establish 'registration and use in bad faith,' even in the absence of any allegations about Respondent's intent at the time of registration and whether Respondent had Complainant's trademark 'in mind' at the time it registered the domain name."

Renewal as the measurement date for registration in bad faith has been criticized by the Panel in ***BioClin*** as inconsistent with the "intention of the framers of the Policy."[761] If this approach were adopted it would be as significant a departure from established law as that proposed by the ***Octogen*** line of cases. Regardless how merited the forfeiture may be in theory, it violates precedent and the express language of the UDRP. Although constrained by the terms of the UDRP and precedent to rule in Respondent's favor, the Panel in ***BioClin*** nevertheless leaves no doubt of his view about the Respondent's *mala fide* conduct.[762] He is also clear that if there is to be an expansion of the UDRP it must come from ICANN and not from any new construction of the Policy.

In thinking through the problem the unitary view is attempting to address, it may be recalled that paragraphs (4)(b)(i-iii) refer to registration while 4(b)(iv) refers to use. If there is bad faith use under 4(b)(iv) an inference of registration in bad

---

760 ***Denver Newspaper Agency v. Jobing.com LLC***, FA0908001282148 (Forum October 16, 2009) (<denverpostjobs.com>).

761 ***BioClin B.V v. MG USA***, D2010-0046 (WIPO March 22, 2010). Panels in ***Squirrels LLC v. Giorgio Uzonian***, D2014-1434 (WIPO October 28, 2014) and ***Avenue 81, Inc. v. Karl Payne***, D2014-1825 (WIPO January 19, 2015) denied Complainants' relief but appeared to endorse the view expressed by the Panel in ***Eastman Group LLC v. Jim and Kenny***, D2009-1688 (WIPO March 1, 2010), namely that there may be circumstances justifying forfeiture of the domain name. In neither ***Squirrels*** nor ***Avenue 81*** did those "facts and circumstances" exist but the Panels nevertheless open the door to the possibility that renewal should be treated as a new registration that restarts respondent's warranty under Paragraph 2 where the bad faith use commences prior to renewal and continues after it. See ***VideoLink, Inc. v. Xantech Corporation***, FA1503001608735 (Forum May 12, 2015) and ***Playworld Systems, Inc. v. Domain Manager / Giant Distributors Inc.***, FA1504001613470 (Forum May 21, 2015). If this were to happen it could undermine the conjunctive requirement for forfeiture, a point made by the Panel in ***BioClin B.V v. MG USA***, D2010-0046 (WIPO March 22, 2010).

762 *Id.* "[R]egardless of the fact that complainant did not have a United States trademark registration until fairly recently, it looks as if respondent has deliberately made its products look very much like complainant's products. . . Add the near-identity between the Domain Name and complainant's mark, and complainant can hardly be blamed for taking the view that it had a strongly arguable case on the 'bad faith use' issue."

faith may be drawn from facts and circumstances surrounding respondent's purchase of the domain name.[763] However, if renewal is equated with registration then no respondent who has repurposed its domain name that arguably takes advantage of complainant's mark can escape forfeiture to a complainant of a newly acquired trademark. Such a result proposes a liability that is better adjudicated in a court of competent jurisdiction.[764]

While some panelists may see the ***Eastman Sporto*** view as a common sense development of the jurisprudence and not a departure from it[765] it nevertheless suffers the same infirmity for the reason expressed in ***Mile*** and other decisions cited in the footnotes that "reading 'registered' as a continuous act that can be abused at any time would appear to make it essentially synonymous with 'use.'" It would not only "deprive the conjunctive phrase of its full meaning" it would also declare unlawful domain names registered in good faith.

4.03-A.4.d

4.03-A.4.d *Inappropriate Alignment with the ACPA*

The "unitary concept" proposed a fundamental change of settled domain name law by removing a barrier that would otherwise have prevented complainant from a remedy under the UDRP against a respondent with a priority to the string of

[763] ***Baccarat SA v. Domains by Proxy, LLC, DomainsByProxy.com /VirtualClicks***, D2013-0305 (WIPO May 20, 2013) (Respondent argued that "baccarat" is a game, but the website included hyperlinks to crystals. The "presumption of bad faith [is] predicated on the basis that there is evidence before the Panel that the Respondent did intend to attract visitors to the associated website for commercial gain by creating confusion as to an association between the Respondent and Complainant, contrary to the fact.")

[764] That renewal of a domain name registered prior to the existence of a trademark could support a claim under the ACPA for cybersquatting spilled over into federal court in ***Office Space Solutions, Inc. v. Kneen***, 1:15-cv-04941 (SDNY) (Commenced June 24 and withdrawn with prejudice July 8, 2015 following argument on a motion for preliminary injunction in which the court rejected plaintiff's theory of liability).

[765] The Panel in ***Avenue 82, Inc. V. Karl Payne***, D2014-1825 (WIPO January 19, 2015) endorses *Eastman Sporto* by explaining that the view does not apply where the Respondent "had nothing to do with any changed circumstances after his initial registration of the disputed domain name." See also ***A'Gaci, L.L.C. v. Radio plus, spol. s r.o.***, D2014-2101 (March 10, 2014) ("This Panel does not share the view that a registrant who originally registered a domain name in good faith and retains ownership of it is necessarily free continuously and flagrantly to exploit the trademark of another person without fear of a Policy proceeding"); ***Adam Milstein v. Benjamin Doherty***, FA1511001647496 (Forum January 11, 2016) ("What is at issue here is the deliberate creating of a false impression by registering a domain name using the entirety of another person's name without permission and linking it to a website containing disparaging material about the person whose name has been used to create the domain name [and continuing that use after renewal of registration]"); in ***Saratoga Publishing LLC v. Rich Richbart / Saratoga Online Inc.***, FA1503001608704 (Forum April 27, 2015) the Panel found *Eastman Sporto* "persuasive", but he explained why in this particular case the analysis did not apply. Nevertheless, some panelists are beginning to use the renewal date for

characters. In one of the challenger panelist's dissents advocating "retroactive bad faith" he states that "[i]t would be much easier for [him] to maintain that his original decision was correct, and not recant. But in view of the evidence, I am unable to do so."[766] The counterpoint is that the analysis is "well meaning, but 'torturous.'"[767]

There are two powerful arguments against applying retrospective bad faith: first, it silently aligns the UDRP with the ACPA which effectively gives trademark owners a less expensive and faster forum to capture domain names registered in good faith and subsequently used (or allegedly so) in bad faith; and second, it introduces uncertainty by making winning or losing contingent on the panelist's adherence to or rejection of precedent.[768]

While there is "value, in appropriate cases, of inferences of original intent based on subsequent conduct"[769] in *inappropriate* cases it "subverts the conjunctive requirement of paragraph 4(a)(iii) of the Policy."[770] A respondent unlucky in the appointed panelist would not be able to escape forfeiture even if there were no proof that its domain name was registered in bad faith. In effect, the unitary concept is a shortcut that subverts the UDRP by transforming it into an administrative substitute for (in the U.S.) the ACPA and the Lanham Act.

Although the unitary concept has largely been rejected and is mostly expressed in dissents, sole panelists who adhere to that view have issued controversial decisions at odds with the consensus.[771] Several federal cases have already found that registration in good faith is not a defense to subsequent bad faith use. This would seem

---

measuring bad faith where respondent before renewal either holds the domain name inactive or commences bad faith use before and continues that use after renewal. See ***VideoLink, Inc. v. Xantech Corporation***, FA1503001608735 (Forum May 12, 2015) and ***Playworld Systems, Inc. v. Domain Manager / Giant Distributors Inc.***, FA1504001613470 (Forum May 21, 2015).

766 ***Guru Denim Inc. v. Ibrahim Ali Ibrahim Abu Harb***, *supra.*

767 ***Extreme Networks Limited, Extreme Drinks Limited v. Ex Drinks, LLC***, D2013-0197 (WIPO March 27, 2013) (Declined "to follow those well meaning but torturous decisions.")

768 ***Time Inc. v. Chip Cooper***, D2000-1342 (WIPO February 13, 2001) (<lifemagazine.com>).

769 ***Mile, Inc. v. Michael Burg***, D2010-2011 (WIPO February 11, 2011).

770 ***Extreme Networks***, *supra.*

771 ***Big 5 Corp.***, *supra*; ***Developmentex.com, Incorporated***, *supra.* Complainant in ***Milly LLC v. Domain Admin, Mrs. Jello, LLC***, D2014-0377 (WIPO May 25, 2014) (Respondent defaulted) requested the Panel consider various approaches under the third element considered in previous UDRP cases, such as retroactive bad faith or the unified concept approach. The Panel obliged although the result in both this case and ***Jappy GmbH v. Satoshi Shimoshita***, D2010-1001 (WIPO September 28, 2010) are contrary to precedent which holds that paragraph 4(a)(iii) is a unitary concept.

The ***Milly*** Panel concluded "[t]he fact Respondent may have registered the Disputed Domain Name prior to Complainant's acquisition of trademark rights does not *per se* preclude a finding of bad faith under the circumstances of this case for the purposes of paragraph 4(a)(iii)." The consensus view is that renewal of registration before or after trademark acquisition does not retrospectively

to acquit a Panel coming to the same conclusion, were it not for the fact that it is exceeding its power.[772]

The majority in ***Guru Denim*** (the case in which the first panelist in dissent announced his recantation of the "binary concept") observed that "if the drafters of the Policy had intended there to be no conjunctive requirement then they would have used different language, such as the term 'or', but they did not do so" and pointed out that "if the Complainant considers that its rights are being infringed then it should look to its remedies under relevant national laws." Guru Denim did just that by immediately filing a complaint in federal court for relief under the ACPA,[773] which it should have done in the first place. Even panelists who have acknowledged interest in considering the "unitary concept" argue that if the law were to be changed it would have to be done by ICANN amending the Policy.[774] However, there is no indication to date that ICANN has any enthusiasm to amend the UDRP.

4.03-A.5 4.03-A.5 Concealment and Falsification

4.03-A.5.a 4.03-A.5.a *Registration Information*

Concealing an owner's registration information by registering through privacy or proxy services is not *ipso facto* condemned as evidence of bad faith. Identity is generally disclosed by the Registrar or proxy service after notice of the complaint in response to an initial request for information from the Provider. The registration requirements and registrant's contractual representations and warranties in the registration agreement and Policy have already been noted. Registrant does not breach a covenant in concealing its identity, but concealment and false contact information coupled with other evidence may suggest an intention to deliberately delay or avoid application of the Policy.[775]

---

impair respondent's intention at the time it registered the domain name. Before trademark acquisition see ***Daredevil Brewing Company LLC v. Matthew O'Brien***, FA1503001608504 (Forum April 23 2015) (Renewal of registration of domain name registered prior to complainant's trademark right does not reset priority and "cannot justify the inference of Respondent's bad faith registration unless it is coupled with other circumstances.")

[772] ***DC Labs Inc. v. Stephen Gilfus***, FA1309001517659 (Forum November 13, 2013) (<ovation.com>) and *Gilfus v. DC Labs Inc.*, 13-cv-1462 (Middle District of FL, Jacksonville Div Nov. 27, 2013); ***Guru Denim Inc. v. Ibrahim Ali Ibrahim Abu Harb***, D2013-1324 (WIPO September 27, 2013) and *Guru Denim Inc. v. Ibrahim Ali Ibrahim Abu Harb*, 13 cv 12756 (D. Mass. 2013). Respondent in ***Big 5***, *supra*, did not commence an ACPA action.

[773] *Guru Denim*, *supra*.

[774] ***Validas, LLC v. SMVS Consultancy Private Limited***, D2009-1413 (WIPO January 29, 2010).

[775] ***Mäurer & Wirtz GmbH & Co. KG v. 4711 Society***, D2008-1022 (WIPO August 27, 2008) (Respondent styled itself "Phuket Internet Solutions Co. Ltd" with a false address). Privacy/proxy services and the Whois directory are discussed in Chapter 2 (Sections 2.04 and 2.05).

A representative sampling of identity and contact falsifications includes: hiding identity by not replying to demand or cease-and-desist letters from complainant and being unknown at the address listed as the administrative address in the Whois Directory[776]; providing false contact details[777]; continuing to hide true identity[778]; concealing true identity by operating under a name that is not a registered business name[779]; and failing to correct false contact details, all of which constitutes a breach of the registration agreement.[780]

4.03-A.5.b *Falsifying the Record*

4.03-A.5.b

Concealing facts in the Whois Directory and acting to impede the proceeding by cyberflight are two kinds of registrant misrepresentation. Complainant falsifications include resetting the time clock for first use in commerce to achieve priority and mischaracterizing the evidence as to duration of its rights.[781] In the case cited in the footnote complainant alleged first use of the trademark in commerce as 1979, to bring itself within the statutory presumption for incontestability, which the Panel found was "not corroborated by any compelling evidence of record." Respondent falsification includes pretense of concurrent rights in the trademark.[782]

In the cited case respondent pretended to have rights that it did not possess:

> The Panel cannot overlook the fact that in Respondent's attachment to the email with the Response, he added the "®" symbol to the TenClub term, thus attempting to create the false impression that he owned a registered trademark.

The Panel (noting that it did not read Dutch) requested translations of exhibits into English, the language of the proceeding. Only after respondent refused to submit full translations of its attachments into English did it appear that "no such trademark

---

776 ***Kabushiki Kaisha Bic Camera v. Netline Systems***, D2002-0817 (WIPO October 29, 2002).

777 ***Private Media Partners v. Martin Hallier***, D2007-0325 (WIPO April 26, 2007) ("it reinforces the conclusion that the domain name was registered and is being used in bad faith").

778 ***Pitcher Partners Licensing Pty Ltd v. N/A***, D2008-0989 (WIPO September 8, 2008).

779 ***Worldwide Pants Inc. v. VisionLink Communications Group, Inc.***, D2008-1796 (WIPO February 10, 2009).

780 Too numerous to cite, but examples are ***TPI Holdings, Inc. v. Elaine Noe***, D2009-0568 (WIPO June 24, 2009) (Failure to correct contact information constitutes a breach of the registration agreement); ***Dazzle Up, LLC v. Lam Hoang Phuc, Cheap Zone***, D2018-0386 (WIPO April 9, 2018) ("Respondent's 'Contact Us' link on the website at the disputed domain name lists an address in New York City as a physical address. The United States Postal Service has no record of this address, nor does the commercial mapping service Google Maps.") See also WIPO Overview 3.0, Paragraph 2.13.2.

781 ***Word of Faith International Christian Center v. Brendhan Hight c/o Mdnh Inc.***, FA0903001251581 (Forum May 1, 2009).

782 ***Pearl Jam, LLC. f/k/a Pearl Jam, A General Partnership v. J.S.E. Janssen a/k/a Stijn Enzo Holding BV***, FA0905001262659 (Forum July 1, 2009).

registration had ever been granted." Failure to provide translations allowed the Panel "to infer that such translations would not have been favorable to Respondent," referencing Paragraph 14(b) of the Rules ("If a Party, in the absence of exceptional circumstances, does not comply with any provision of, or requirement under, these Rules or any request from the Panel, the Panel shall draw such inferences therefrom as it considers appropriate.")[783]

4.03-B

4.03-B Renewal of Registration vs. Registration by Transfer

4.03-B.1

4.03-B.1 Renewal: Not Equivalent to New Registration

The consensus construction of the Policy is that renewal of registration represents a continuation of registration.[784] It does not a restart registrant's representation and warranty covenant that "to the best of [its] knowledge and belief, neither the registration of the Registered Name nor the manner in which it is directly or indirectly used infringes the legal rights of any third party."[785] This does not imply that respondents are necessarily exonerated from liability. Since there is no formal application of a statute of limitations or laches under UDRP jurisprudence complainants may prevail on claims for domain names registered many years earlier. although their claims of bad faith attenuate with passage of time and relative strength or weakness of the domain name (see "Sleeping on One's Rights" (Sec. 5.01-E).[786]

---

[783] In ***National Association of Competitive Soccer Clubs v. Bruce Binler***, D2009-0957 (September 7, 2009) the Panel criticized complainant for misstating its trademark rights by failing to disclose that the registration of US CLUB SOCCER was on the Supplemental Register.

[784] As noted earlier, the Third and Ninth Circuit Courts of Appeal have construed the ACPA differently. See, ***Twitter, Inc. v. Geigo, Inc.***, D2011-1210 (WIPO November 2, 2011) (three member Panel) ("A UDRP panel owes great deference to the national courts. Their rulings may well be part of 'applicable law' that a panel must consider (Rules, paragraph 15(a)), may become directly relevant in relation to mutual jurisdiction in the event of a court challenge (Policy, paragraph 4(k)), and are forged upon a record developed through full adversary proceedings. Nevertheless there are occasions when a [UDRP] panel may decline to follow a court's interpretation. The *Schmidheiny* case [*Schmidheiny v. Weber*, 319 F.3d 581 (3rd Cir. 2003)] cited but not followed by the Ninth Circuit and its reasoning [in *GOPETS Ltd. v. Hise, Digital Overture, Inc.*, 657 F.3d 1024 (9th Cir. 2011)] offer grounds for this Panel to follow the Third Circuit's holding. These two courts are co-equal; any difference in their rulings can only be resolved by the Supreme Court of the United States or superseding legislation. This Panel finds the Third Circuit's reasoning in *Schmidheiny* more convincing than the Ninth Circuit's in *GoPets*.")

[785] Registrar Accreditation Agreement at 3.7.7.9. See ***Spirit Airlines, Inc. v. Spirit Airlines Pty. Ltd.***, D2001-0748 (WIPO July 25, 2001) ("Renewal of a domain name registration . . . is no different from renewal of a trademark registration [as] it represents a continuation of the original registration. Were Complainant's argument to succeed, all 'innocent' registrants of domain names would be at risk of becoming branded 'cybersquatters.'") Contra, but isolated decision, ***Houlberg Development v. Adnet International***, FA0009000095698 (Forum October 27, 2000) ("Respondent had actual knowledge of Complainant's asserted rights in 'Retail Engine' as a trademark before it renewed the

While ordinarily a change of registration information could signal a new holder of the challenged domain name where there is "an unbroken chain of underlying ownership by a single person . . . a change in the recorded WhoIs details will not be considered a new registration for the purposes of the UDRP."[787] The critical date for determining whether a domain name has been registered in bad faith is the original date of registration.[788] The "maintenance or renewal in bad faith of a registration originally made in good faith does not suffice" for proof of abusive registration.[789]

As already noted in Section 4.03-A.4.c, this has led some Panels to revisit established views[790] and trademark owners to insist [791] that respondents who registered common words, descriptive phrases and random letters speculatively in the past, should be penalized for taking advantage of owners of later acquired trademarks. The conjunctive requirement (the argument goes) could be satisfied if

---

domain name."). Compare *Schmidheiny, supra.* ("We do not consider the 'creation date' of a domain name to control whether a registration is subject to the Anti-cybersquatting Act, and we believe that the plain meaning of the word 'registration' is not limited to 'creation registration.'")

U.S. federal court in GOPETS, *supra.* rejected the Third Circuit's reasoning—"[it] erred in assuming that Weber's initial registration was not covered by ACPA"—and noted that renewal is not a 'registration' within the meaning of §1125(d)(1): "Looking at ACPA in light of traditional property law, however, we conclude that Congress meant 'registration' to refer only to the initial registration," citing *Sporty's Farm L.L.C. v. Sportsman's Market, Inc.*, 202 F.3d 489, 496 97 (2d Cir. 2000). Liability for cybersquatting depends on the circumstances present at the time of the transferee's registration.

[786] For example, ***Airbnb, Inc. v. Norman King / Target Marketing Group***, FA1707001738345 (Forum July 27, 2017) (<air-bnb.org>. 10 years).

[787] ***Angelica Fuentes Téllez v. Domains by Proxy, LLC / Angela Brink***, D2014-1860 (WIPO December 18, 2014) (<angelisima.com>); ***Sheryl Sandberg Dave Goldberg Family Foundation v. WhoisGuard, Inc/Hecham Ghazal***, D2019-0213 (WIPO April 1, 2019) (<leanin.com>). Trademarks postdate original date of domain name registrations.

[788] In contrast, a transferee's legitimacy is based on its own conduct rather than original good faith registration of the domain name by the original registrant. Discussed in Sec. 4.03-B.2.

[789] ***Guildline Instruments Limited v. Anthony Anderson***, D2006-0157 (WIPO April 12, 2006). The result will be different for cases under the ACPA where the domain name is registered in good faith but transforms to infringing. See ***BMEzine.com, LLC. v. Gregory Ricks / Gee Whiz Domains Privacy Service***, D2008-0882 (WIPO August 21, 2008) (the Panel held that transfer to a new privacy service was a new registration and ordered <bme.com> transferred. In a subsequent ACPA action, the Court denied Ricks's motion for reverse domain name hijacking, *Ricks v. BMEzine.com LLC*, 727 F. Supp.2d 936 (D. Nevada 2010) (Motion for partial summary judgment denied, but good faith registration of domain name that postdates first use of trademark in commerce under U.S. law does not protect a registrant who subsequently uses the domain name in bad faith.)

[790] ***Ville de Paris v. Jeff Walter***, D2009-1278 (WIPO November 19, 2009) ("[I]n short, [it] give[s] a 'green light' to good faith domain name registrants to later abusively use their domain names, safe in the knowledge that any such bad faith use could not provide the basis for a successful action under the Policy.") Complaint granted, but subsequent ACPA action resulted in default judgment in favor of domain name holder and an award of damages, *Walter v. Ville de Paris*, 4:2009cv03939 (S.D. Texas

renewal of registration were interpreted to equal registration. However, this view which is a radical extension of liability has garnered few adherents and is not the law.

In ***PAA Laboratories***[792] for example (discussed above in connection with *Eastman Sporto*), in which the Panel bent a sympathetic ear—"[t]he abusive refreshing of the original registration" (it stated) "is an act which this Panel considers should be an act of a kind encompassed by paragraph 4(a)(iii) of the Policy"—but rejected endorsing the conclusion because the consensus is that "mere renewal does not amount to registration." According to the consensus respondent's right or legitimate interest in a disputed domain name depends on the timing of its acquisition and whether it was the original registrant,[793] a transferee,[794] or subsequent unrelated holder.

Whether or not respondent has a right or legitimate interest in a disputed domain name registered and initially used in good faith, its subsequent use or non-use of the domain name is insufficient for forfeiture.[795] Complainant in ***MediaTrac*** argued that Respondent has "continued to renew the domain in order to maintain control of it, yet serves no content on the site." Further (Complainant argued) "[t]his all points to the fact that Respondent maintained control to disrupt the business of Complainant and profit from Complainant's desire to use its federally trademarked name." Setting aside Complainant's misrepresentation of the facts--Respondent restricted use of the website to dealers who sign[ed] up for its program—it also mangles the law because renewal of registration is perfectly lawful; a right cannot be upset by a trademark owner's "desire to use its federally trademarked name."

MediaTrac is emblematic in that Respondent proved it had been "marketing and selling [its] computer program" before Complainant acquired its trademark. As a general rule respondents are not vulnerable to forfeiture of their domain names

---

Houston Div. July 5, 2012). An alternative reading of the Policy is discussed in "Justifying Forfeiture Despite Good Faith Registration" (Sec.4.03-A.4.b).

791 Discussed further in "Earlier Registered Domain Names; Subsequently Acquired Trademarks" (Sec. 5.01-F.2).

792 ***PAA Laboratories GmbH v. Printing Arts America***, D2004-0338 (WIPO July 13, 2004).

793 Discussed further in "Good Faith Not Vitiated by Change of Use" (Sec. 4.03-A.4.a).

794 ***Food Express, Inc. v. Nashville Boot Co.***, FA0611000852588 (Forum January 29, 2007) (Respondent argued that there was an identity between the present Respondent and a Respondent in a prior proceeding in which Complainant's request to transfer <foodexpress.com> was denied and for that reason the present proceeding was barred under the doctrine of *res judicata*. In rejecting the argument, the Panel held that "[i]t is clear . . . from the Rules and from the whole ICANN registration process that the process revolves around the person or party who is put forward as the holder of the domain name, which may not be the ultimate interest or entity that stands behind the holder. . . . Accordingly, the domain name holder may change from time to time and if a dispute arises, the only nominal party against whom the claim may be brought is the party who for the time being is registered by a Registrar as the holder of the domain name.")

795 ***MediaTrac, LLC v. eNet Buzz Inc.***, FA0908001281461 (Forum October 16, 2009) (<loyaltytrac.com>).

based solely on holding them inactive[796] or for renewing registrations that frustrate complainant's wish to secure for itself an asset owned by respondent. In some instances, as already pointed out with domain names used in bad faith that continue infringement after renewal the more likely remedy will be an action in a court of competent jurisdiction for trademark infringement rather than cybersquatting.

A complainant of a later acquired trademark has no superior right to an earlier registered domain name that continues to be held by the original registrant. However, subsequent holders of domain names are answerable for their choices from the dates of their own registrations.

4.03-B.2 Transfer/Subsequent Holders=New Registration 4.03-B.2

4.03-B.2.a *Second and Subsequent Generations of Holders* *4.03-B.2.a*

There is a thriving secondary market through auctions and direct sales to supply domain names to newly emerging businesses and also to investors speculating on their future values.[797] Second and subsequent generations of registrants in these assets are principally arms-length purchasers with no prior relationship with original registrants.[798] They are also differently circumstanced in taking possession of domain names after the existence of corresponding trademarks.[799] It is important to recognize, however, that although not previously vulnerable to forfeiture these domain names can then become challengeable to claims of bad faith either for continuing proscribed conduct or inactively holding potentially infringing domain names. Bad faith registration can be inferred from bad faith use.[800] Transfers between commonly controlled persons are discussed separately below.[801]

---

[796] A similar argument was made in *Southern Grouts & Mortars, Inc. v. 3M Company*, 575 F.3d 1235 (11th Cir. July 23, 2009). See below in "Transfer Between Commonly Controlled Persons" (Sec. 4.03-B.2.d). Asset sales of domain names are discussed further in "Not All Offers to Sell Violate the Policy" (Sec. 6.02-B).

As with all general rules, there are outlier panelists who take a different view. See ***Benoit Thiercelin v. Medicalexpo.com***, CAC 100235 (ADR.eu May 23, 2011) in which the Panel reasons against precedent and consensus that inactivity by itself supports conjunctive bad faith without regard to the fact that the domain name was registered prior to complainant's acquisition of its mark.

[797] ***True North Media, LLC and Good Universe Media, LLC v. 1soft Corporation, Greg Thorne***, D2012-1457 (WIPO September 28, 2012) (<gooduniverse.com>. "[S]peculating on the future commercial value of a domain name based on common words is simply a business risk, not an act in bad faith, unless the registrant has reason to know that a particular party has plans to use those words as a mark.")

[798] ***In Advanced Analytical Technologies, Inc. v. Hare, Myles/URL Enterprises Ltd.***, FA161100 1701430 (Forum January 1, 2017) (<aati.com>) the parties competed with each other (with many others) at an auction in which Respondent was the winning bidder. It then put the domain name up for sale within 24 hours. Complainant failed to prove rights to 'aati.'"

[799] In years past, names that would readily have been available from the public domain are now locked up. See *Verisign v. XYZ.com*, 848 F.3d 292, 121 U.S.P.Q.2d 1586 (4th Cir., 2017): "99% of

Acquiring a domain name previously held constitutes "a fresh act of registration . . . [and it is] that act . . . by the new registrant that must be examined for the requisite bad faith motivation."[802] A "fresh act" does not imply a predecessor's act is irrelevant to the successor's motivation for acquiring the domain name. The successor is entitled to no benefit from its predecessor's good faith registration if there is evidence that its predecessor subsequently used the domain name in bad faith.[803] While the successor infringes no rights if it continues a use consistent with the semantic value of the domain name[804] it does if it continues its predecessor's bad faith use or initiates its own.[805]

New holders are likely to have taken possession of disputed domain names under conditions factually different from original registrants.[806] However, if domain names are identical or confusingly similar to trademarks acquired after the original

---

all registrar searches today result in a 'domain taken' page....Verisign's own data shows that out of approximately two billion requests it receives each month to register a .com name, fewer than three million – less than one percent – actually are registered."

800 Challenged investors have been 1) high bidders at auctions; 2) arms-length and collusive transferees; 3) post-Sunrise registrants; 4) opportunistic registrants of lapsed domain names; and 5) registrants in good faith acquiring lapsed domain names either without knowledge of any trademarks or believing them to have been abandoned.

801 Sec.4.03-B.2.d.

802 ***Edward Nugee QC and the other members of Wilberforce Chambers v. Administrator System***, D2004-0780 (WIPO December 15, 2004). The Panel in ***Diet Center Worldwide, Inc. v. Jason Akatiff***, D2012-1609 (WIPO October 5, 2012) construed this to mean that "that the new registration [by an unrelated party] is tested under the terms of the Policy."

For construction under the ACPA see *Schmidheiny v. Weber*, 319 F.3d 581 (3d Cir. 2003) ("We hold that the word 'registration' includes a new contract at a different registrar and to a different registrant") and *GoPets*, *supra*: "We see no basis in ACPA to conclude that a right that belongs to an initial registrant of a currently registered domain name is lost when that name is transferred to another owner." The different results in *Schmidheiny* and *GoPets* are explained by the factual circumstances. In *GoPets* the transfer was to a related party.

803 ***Motorola, Inc. v. NewGate Internet, Inc.***, D2000-0079 (WIPO April 20, 2000) ("[R]espondent knew when it acquired, for consideration, the domain name from CFR that Motorola was requesting its transfer. . . This fact, together with the respondent's subsequent conduct, lead[s] the panel to infer that respondent already at that time had the intention of obtaining payments from Motorola in exchange for the transfer of the domain name.") For transfer to a related party see ***AB Svenska Spel v. Andrey Zacharov***, D2003-0527 (WIPO October 2, 2003) ("[T]he reason for Mr. Bråthén to transfer the Domain Name to the current holder was to avoid legal proceedings regarding the Domain Name in Sweden.")

804 For arm's length purchase see ***Mobile's Republic v. Kwangpyo Kim***, D2014-0089 (WIPO April 23, 2014 (<newsrepublic.com>. "[T]he disputed domain name was already in use [by the prior holder] for a similar website [providing hyperlinks to news websites] even before Complainant registered its trademark and launched its product.")

805 See ***Bank of Scotland Plc v. Shelley Robert, Diversity Network***, D2015-2310 (WIPO February 15, 2016) (<halifax.com>). Respondent paid $175,000 for the domain name, then "changed the

registration and complainant succeeds on its *prima facie* case respondent's burden to avoid forfeiture rests on the classification of the trademark and proof that the domain name was acquired for a legitimate purpose. If the original registrant acquired the disputed domain name on a first-come first-served basis the successor is invulnerable as long as it continues the same use or changes it to a use consistent with the semantic value of the domain name. However, it could be vulnerable to forfeiture if it fails or has made no demonstrable preparation to use the domain name for legitimate purposes.[807] These general observations aside registrants are not precluded from transferring registrations in-house, to related parties where the transfers are being made for legitimate business purposes.[808]

Challenge to a subsequent holder's acquisition of a domain name focuses on its motivation in acquiring the domain name, not that of its predecessor.[809] The original holder's motivation is irrelevant. Even if originally registered in good faith,

---

directory site content in a manner which was targeted to the Complainant's trade mark." Had the evidence shown that the domain name was acquired and used for its geographical association "this would have been sufficient to demonstrate the Respondent's rights and legitimate interests under the Policy." Respondent then compounded its problem by soliciting Complainant to lease or purchase the domain name.

806 ***Dixons Group Plc v. Abu Abdullah***, D2000-1406 (WIPO January 18, 2001) (DIXONS and <dixons online.com>. Respondent denied any relationship with original registrant, but was deemed to have acquired the domain names for the same purpose as prior holder: "It is . . . clear that the Complainant has a very widespread trading reputation, in particular within the United Kingdom. It is therefore difficult to believe that the Respondent, in taking his transfer of the disputed domain name was unaware of these facts and that such acquisition was therefore made in good faith.") The Respondent in ***A. D. Banker & Company v. Domain Invest***, D2010-1044 (WIPO September 30, 2010) escaped forfeiture by plausibly explaining that it had not had time to make content changes because it "take[s] several days . . . for these changes [the new use of the domain name] to be 'reflected in the various cached servers throughout the world.'" Discussed further in "Content as a Factor in Determining Bad Faith Use" (Sec. 4.03-A.3).

807 Subsequent holder's failure to demonstrate good faith can be conclusive against it. Complaint denied against original registrant, ***My Art v. Domain Discreet MyArt.com***, CAC 100281 (ADR.eu July 2011), but granted against successor, ***My Art v. Mark Mikullitz***, CAC 100751 (ADR.eu April 22, 2014). (Transferred on default. However, after Respondent woke up he commenced an ACPA action alleging he was the one and only holder of the domain name. Defendant capitulated upon receiving the complaint, made an offer of settlement to buy itself out of the lawsuit rather than contest the issue and be exposed to significant damages and attorney's fees for reverse domain name hijacking (*Mikullitz v. Mr. Art*, 14-cv-03276 (S.D.N.Y. July 15, 2014)).

808 See ***Información, Control y Planificación, S.A. v. JA Powell, BD Stansky, CA Morris Jt Tnts***, D2016-2005 (WIPO November 28, 2016) (<icp.com>) citing WIPO Overview 2.0 at paragraph 3.7: "Panels have tended to the view that formal changes in registration data are not necessarily deemed to constitute a new registration where evidence clearly establishes an unbroken chain of underlying ownership by a single entity or within a genuine conglomerate, and it is clear that any change in WhoIs registrant data is not being made to conceal an underlying owner's identity for the purpose of frustrating assessment of liability in relation to registration or use of the domain name."

the prior registration "does not cloak a subsequent purchaser of a domain name" if its use violates the Policy.[810] To believe otherwise is a fundamental misperception of the Policy and its objectives.

The Panel in ***HSBC Financial*** was unpersuaded that respondent's acquisition of the domain name "for the not insubstantial sum of $48,000 (USD)" was material in determining good faith. He noted that although the transferor

> has not been shown to have registered in bad faith, a fair inference can be drawn from the record that [the transferor] had begun, prior to the 2004 transfer to the Respondent, to use the domain in bad faith to intentionally attract internet users based on confusion with Complainant's trademark in violation of paragraph 4(b)(iv) of the Policy.

When a transferee acquires "a domain name that is being used in bad faith, the Panel may infer that [the] acquisition was motivated by an intent to continue the bad faith use."[811] Continuation of bad faith use by the subsequent holder is evidence of bad faith registration.

4.03-B.2.b

4.03-B.2.b *Examining Conduct: Retrospective*

Unrelated subsequent holders of domain names are regarded as new registrants answerable from the dates of their acquisitions.[812] The relevant date for assessing bad faith is when the current holder of the domain name acquired its interest, not the date of the original registration.[813] Even though the "Policy is only concerned with the actions and motives of registrants, not their predecessors,"[814] it is relevant to inquire whether there is any relationship between the original registrant and the present holder

---

809 ***Gaylord Entertainment Company v. Nevis Domains LLC.***, D2006-0523 (WIPO September 6, 2006) ("[W]here this Respondent sits the 'chain of Registrants' offers no protection. Manifestly, because of the manner in which the Domain Name was acquired and used, every person and entity up and down this chain can be found to have taken possession and, of necessity, registered the Domain Name with the same intent.").

810 ***HSBC Finance Corporation v. Clear Blue Sky Inc. and Domain Manager***, D2007-0062 (WIPO June 4, 2007) ('creditkeeper.com') ("The Respondent . . . fundamentally misperceives the Policy and its objectives in asserting that a previous registrant's good faith registration of a domain name immunizes one who subsequently acquires the domain name from further scrutiny.")

811 Transfer from a registrant who acquired the domain name and used it in good faith and apparently transferred it to evade a judgment does not exonerate a transferee who acquired it under suspicious circumstances. ***Axelion GmbH v. Eric H. Schunk***, D2008-1701 (WIPO December 18, 2008) (<axelion.com>).

812 The U.S. Court of Appeals for the Ninth Circuit construing the ACPA does not distinguish between related and unrelated transferees. "We see no basis in ACPA to conclude that a right that belongs to an initial registrant of a currently registered domain name is lost when that name is transferred to another owner." See *Airfx.com v. Airfx LLC*, CV 11-01064 (D.Ariz. October 20, 2011) ("GoPets did not distinguish between transfers of a domain name to related parties and other kinds of domain name transfers.") In the earlier administrative proceeding in ***GoPets Ltd. v. Edward Hise***,

of the domain name. Motivation of transferees is analyzed both retrospectively (their relationship with transferors) and prospectively (their use of the domain name); motivation of unrelated subsequent holders is assessed only prospectively.

The retrospective inquiry is appropriate to determine the existence or not of a relationship between predecessor and successor and the motivation for acquiring an already active domain name. In one case respondent acquired the disputed domain name from its managing director who had been in litigation with complainant prior to the transfer.[815] The Panel explained

> respondent had active knowledge of complainant's trademark rights when he acquired the Domain Name because the action against him before the German regional court was at least pending, if not decided. Therefore, the Panel finds that this acquisition (registration) occurred in bad faith.

The original registrant's conduct in registering the domain name is a factor,[816] as was its use (or in the case of ***Ideenhaus Kommunikationsagentur***, non-use) during the time of its holding.[817]

The transfer is scrutinized for evidence that it was made for legitimate purposes. The more recent the transfer without explanation the greater the probability of finding collusion. The Panel in ***Mutatis Mutandis***[818] held:

> When circumstances of a case tend to indicate that there is, on balance of probabilities, a likelihood of collusion or duplicity between the current registrant and its predecessor in title, such as in this case, it may become appropriate to take into account the behavior of the predecessor in title in the determination of bad faith by Respondent.

D2006-0636 (WIPO July 26, 2006) the Panel denied the complaint; in ***AirFX, LLC v. ATTNAIRFX.COM***, FA1104001384655 (Forum May 16, 2011) the Panel awarded <airfx.com> to Complainant. In both cases the domain name was registered before trademark acquisition.

See also "Registrant's Responsibility for Determining Whether Domain Name Infringes Third Party Rights" (Sec. 2.02) and "Enhanced Investigative Responsibilities for High-Volume Registrants" (Sec. 6.03-B).

813 ***BWR Resources Ltd. v. Waitomo Assoc. Ltd.***, D2000-0861 (WIPO October 4, 2000) ("The Panel accepts that 'registration' in the case of this Respondent refers to the date when it acquired the name from the person who first registered it.")

814 ***Ontos AG v. Ontos Institute, Antony Arcari***, D2006-0647 (WIPO July 9, 2006).

815 ***Ideenhaus Kommunikationsagentur GmbH v. Ideenhaus GmbH***, D2004-0016 (WIPO February 25, 2004).

816 ***DHL Operations B.V. v. Karel Salovsky***, D2006-0520 (WIPO June 22, 2006).

817 ***STX LLC v. Yu nae ho, Jinsu Kim***, D2006-0567 (WIPO August 14, 2006) (transferred over dissent).

818 ***Mutatis Mutandis Hebdomag Inc. v. Illuminaty Marketing***, D2001-0206 (WIPO April 17, 2001).

If "UDRP Panels could not impute conduct where appropriate between transacting registrants, then any prior registrant could very easily and successfully shield its names from transfer, and, by doing so, thwart the action of the Policy."[819]

If the relationship between the transferor and transferee is uncertain and unexplained, bad faith use by the original registrant will be imputed to his transferee. Retrospective analysis requires disclosure of the manner in which the domain name was transferred and the relationship if any between transferee and transferor. The Panel in ***United Parcel***[820] explains this reasoning:

> Under the circumstances, the bad faith underlying the original registration is properly imputed to the recipient of domain name in question. If this were not the case, unscrupulous parties could easily subvert the purpose and provisions of the Policy by transferring domain names to third persons in anticipation of a case being brought and have the third party nominally refrain from engaging in bad faith use while the case was pending thereby possibly avoiding a finding of bad faith registration and/or use.

The recognition of the trademark is equally determinative. Whether or not the domain name "was genuinely acquired on an arms-length basis" may be relevant for lesser known trademarks but is irrelevant for trademarks such as DSL and UNITED PARCEL. The Panel "would have little hesitation in concluding that Respondent was or should have been aware of Complainant's well-known mark at the time of acquisition of the Domain Name in question."[821] A transferee unrelated to a transferor who during its holding is alleged to have violated the Policy by offering to sell the domain name to complainant is not answerable for its predecessor's conduct.[822]

The Panel found in a case of a high-volume acquirer unrelated to the original registrant that it failed to explore "the possibility of third-party rights in any way before registering and using the disputed domain name."[823] Respondent argued that the previous registrant's good faith registration of a domain name immunizes the transferee from further scrutiny. According to the three-member Panel, this is a fundamental misperception:

> While a renewal is not considered equivalent to a "registration" in the context of the objectives of the Policy . . . the benefit of an original good faith registration should not be perpetual to the point where it can cloak successors in

---

819 ***National Collegiate Athletic Association v. Dusty Brown***, D2004-0491 (WIPO August 30, 2004).

820 ***United Parcel Service of America, Inc. v. Michael Robert***, D2008-0339 (WIPO April 29, 2008).

821 ***United Parcel***, *supra*.

822 ***Point Grey Research, Inc. v. Administrator Domain / Vertical Axis, Inc.***, FA1105001388025 (Forum June 30, 2011) ("Had Complainant believed that it had a legitimate UDRP claim it could have filed its Complaint in 2001 when the alleged offer to purchase was made.")

823 ***HSBC Finance Corporation v. Clear Blue Sky Inc. and Domain Manager***, D2007-0062 (WIPO June 4, 2007).

> title and successors in 'possession' long after the original registration would have expired.

The Panel held that although the transferor

> has not been shown to have registered in bad faith, a fair inference can be drawn from the record that [the transferor] had begun, prior to the 2004 transfer to the Respondent, to use the domain in bad faith to intentionally attract internet users based on confusion with Complainant's trademark in violation of paragraph 4(b)(iv) of the Policy.

Respondent's actions led to the inescapable conclusion that in acquiring

> a domain name that is being used in bad faith, the Panel may infer that that acquisition was motivated by an intent to continue the bad faith use. This is evidence of bad faith registration.

The Panel applied a retrospective lens to Respondent's acquisition based on the original registrant's bad faith use and a prospective lens on its continued use.

4.03-B.2.c *Examining the Record: Prospective*

4.03-B.2.c

A respondent unrelated to the original registrant is challenged to explain in rebuttal to complainant's *prima facie* case the basis for its right or legitimate interest in the disputed domain name, or if it has neither, its registration is not in bad faith. Since respondent is bound by its own representations it cannot "rest its claim of legitimacy on a continuation of the previous registrant's use of the domain name, in the absence of [its own] . . . good faith effort . . . to avoid registering and using a domain name corresponding to the trademark of another in violation of the Policy."[824]

While continuance of bad faith use by a related successor is *prima facie* proof of abusive registration, *bona fide* use by a new registrant is a complete defense.[825] In ***STX LLC*** the majority, focusing on meta-tags and content that attracted Internet users to a website containing links to complainant's competitors concluded that respondent acquired the domain name to continue its predecessor's bad faith use. Because there is no semantic meaning to the three-letter string standing alone the inference drawn from the continuation of bad faith use was that the value of the domain name was its association with the trademark owner.[826]

---

824 *Id.*, ***HSBC Finance.***

825 The Panel in ***Ontos AG*** held: "Clearly, if the Panel had been satisfied that the transaction was a sham transaction the Complaint would have succeeded either on the basis that respondent and the previous registrant are to be treated as one or that the motives of Respondent in acquiring the Domain Name were abusive."

826 *Id.* "Absent contrary evidence from the Respondent, this inference is fair, especially where the assignee pays a substantial sum for the acquisition. We note that the Respondent's affidavit does not deny knowledge of the contents of the Filing Date Webpage when he acquired rights to the disputed domain name. Respondent Yu may fairly be presumed, therefore, to have had knowledge of, not

Respondent in ***News Journal***[827] acquired <mytopia.com> contemporaneously with Complainant's alleged first use in commerce from a predecessor who purchased it many years prior to Complainant's service mark registration of MYTOPIA CAFÉ on the Principal Register. The question in such circumstances is "whether a registrant of a mark can use the relation back aspect of [15 U.S.C. §1057 (constructive notice to establish priority)] . . . to establish common law rights in the mark vis-à-vis a domain name whose registration and use predates the first use of the mark by some nine years, where the domain name at issue was transferred to Respondent after first use of complainant's mark, but before the issuance of the registration."

As applied to the factual circumstances present in ***News Journal*** and similar cases complainants have to show that their common law trademark rights antedate the registration of the domain names. In ***News Journal*** Complainant was unable to make the requisite showing:

> The original registrant transferred the domain name at issue to respondent on January 24, 2008. This is two days after Complainant filed its trademark application and some seven months before the registration issued. . . . However, as the transaction was brokered through Escrow.com, the offer to purchase had to have been made prior to Complainant's filing of its application for a service mark. Respondent paid in excess of USD 35,000 for the domain name at issue.

Also in ***News Journal*** there was no evidence that respondent's predecessor had used the domain name in bad faith—in fact it could not have done so since complainant's right had not yet come into existence during the predecessor's ownership—so that the totality of the evidence supported respondent's assertion that it acquired the domain name "for use in conjunction with [its] gaming web site."

4.03-B.2.d

4.03-B.2.d *Transfer Between Commonly Controlled Persons*

A successor in interest related to a predecessor that acquired and was using the disputed domain name in good faith[828] or by operation of law[829] inherits its predecessor's good faith registration and in most instances would be invulnerable

---

only the hockey and lacrosse product emphasis and links that appeared on the <stx.com> webpage, but also of the meta-tags that reveal use of the trademark STX ("stx lacrosse" and "stx field hockey") in the meta-tags."

[827] ***News Journal Corporation v. Amatzia Benartzi,*** D2008-1294 (WIPO October 16, 2008) (<mytopia.com>).

[828] ***FTR v. Synopsys Inc.***, D2010-1264 (WIPO October 7, 2010) (<lmc.com>): "Acquisition through merger of Logic Modeling Corporation (and therefore the disputed domain name) by respondent was for a legitimate business purpose. Therefore, there was no bad faith when respondent acquired its registration of the disputed domain name as part of this acquisition."

[829] ***Avomex, Inc. v. Barry Pierce / Tina D. Pierce Widow of Barry E. Pierce***, D2011-1253 (WIPO September 23, 2011) (descent from deceased husband); or from a brother as in ***Kitchens To Go,***

to forfeiture. "In the absence of some exceptional circumstance, there is no reason to conclude that transfers of domain names between commonly-controlled entities extinguishes pre-existing rights or legitimate interests in those domain names."[830] In ***Schweizerische Bundesbahnen*** the Panel drew a lesson from the ownership of trademarks. It held that "[b]usiness enterprises commonly assign and transfer trademarks among commonly controlled entities for a variety of reasons." There is no reason to treat domain names differently. Such a transferee not only succeeds to its predecessor's good faith registration, it holds the domain name as an asset to use or sell as it determines in its own best interests.[831]

Where the transfer does not "effect any material change in the beneficial ownership of the domain name" and its use "throughout [the] years has consistently promoted" the same goods "it is appropriate . . . to consider [as one and together] Respondents' and the prior, related registrants' rights and interests in the Disputed Domain Name."[832] However, a countervailing view holds that a transferee is not entitled to capitalize on a complainant's reputation in the marketplace on the theory that its related predecessor registered the domain name in good faith when at the time of registration no such trademark existed. The Panel in ***Certipost***[833] held that forfeiture was warranted where

> (i) There has been supervening bad faith of the disputed domain name by the original registrant; and

---

LLC v. KTG.COM, Whoisguard Protected / HUKU LLC, D2017-2241 (WIPO February 6, 2018) (<ktg.com>. "[T]he Panel does not accept the Complainant's submission that, on inheriting a large portfolio of domain names, this imposed on Mrs. Haggippavlou a duty of due diligence to search worldwide to see if any of them might infringe any third party rights, prior to registering them in her name."

830 ***Schweizerische Bundesbahnen SBB v. Gerrie Villon***, D2009-1426 (WIPO January 11, 2010) ("Complainant has presented no compelling legal grounds in the present case for distinguishing the treatment of assignment or transfer of domain names from the treatment typically accorded trademarks. In the absence of some exceptional circumstance, there is no reason to conclude that transfers of domain names between commonly controlled entities extinguishes pre existing rights or legitimate interests in those domain names.") Cf., *GoPets*, and *Airfx.com, supra.* discussed earlier.

831 *Id., Go Pets.* See also *Southern Grouts & Mortars, Inc. v. 3M Company*, 575 F.3d 1235 (11th Cir. 2009). 3M had come into possession of <diamondbrite.com> legally by acquiring the company that owned it years earlier. Its offense (as the plaintiff saw it) was not that it was using the domain name but was holding it inactive. Southern Grouts "accuse[d] 3M not of a design to sell a domain name for profit but of a refusal to sell one." The Court stated that "The Senate Report accompanying the Anticybersquatting Consumer Protection Act bolsters our understanding that a 'bad faith intent to profit' is the essence of the wrong that the Act seeks to combat . . . The report says nothing about those who [acquire a domain name in good faith and] hold onto [it through repeat renewals of registration] to prevent a competitor from using it."

832 ***Intellogy Solutions, LLC v. Craig Schmidt and IntelliGolf, Inc.***, D2009-1244 (WIPO November 24, 2009).

833 ***Certipost NV v. Virtual Point Inc.***, D2008-1183 (WIPO September 25, 2008).

(ii) The disputed domain name is transferred to another entity within the original registrant's business organization; and

(iii) That other entity acts in bad faith in acquiring the disputed domain name and in subsequently using it.

Where the facts support abusive registration, there is "no injustice . . . [in] giving the third-party trade mark owner who has been subjected to the bad faith use, an opportunity to invoke the Policy, which it would not otherwise have had (because it could not show that the original registration of the disputed domain name had been made in bad faith)."[834] If the transfer between commonly controlled persons is either questionable or unexplained Panels tend to favor complainant. They will not ignore transfers from one subsidiary to another within a conglomerate timed "coincidentally or otherwise with an event pertinent to the matters claimed to constitute bad faith."[835] To demonstrate good faith "[i]t should . . . be clear that any change in registrant data in the Whois is not being made to conceal an underlying owner's identity for the purpose of frustrating assessment of liability in relation to registration or use of the disputed domain name."[836]

Respondent in ***BMEzine.com***—found by the Panel to be "a seasoned domainer who has been the subject of many Policy proceedings"—failed the test because it had "made its latest transfer, from one privacy service to another, to conceal his identity as long as possible." Since "[t]his transfer occurred a few months after Complainant's filing its service mark application for BME, and Respondent's current use for a click through site began immediately thereafter" and since the "Respondent . . . offered no other reason for this or any other transfer," the natural inference was that the transfer was "something other than a pattern of mere renewals." In ***ehotel***, the Respondent "effectively abandoned his own prior use and actively sought to associate the Domain Name with complainant's business." Discontinuity of use and transfer point to opportunism, in which event the related successor will not be permitted to benefit from its predecessor's good faith registration.

4.03-C

4.03-C Acquiring and Disposing of Domain Names by Auction

Domain names acquired by public auction raise many of the same issues discussed earlier for dropped or lapsed domain names (Section 4.01-F). Although the public nature of the process can provide a layer of protection to the high bidder

834 *Id.*

835 ***BMEzine.com, LLC. v. Gregory Ricks / Gee Whiz Domains Privacy Service***, D2008-0882 (WIPO August 21, 2008) (footnotes 7 & 8. Footnote 8 reads: "A panel might ignore movement from one privacy service to another where a plausible explanation is provided and the evidence clearly establishes an unbroken chain of underlying ownership by a single entity or within a genuine conglomerate."); ***ehotel AG v. Network Technologies Polska Jasinski Lutoborski Sp.J.***, D2009-0785 (WIPO August 5, 2009).

as a bona fide purchaser for value there is no legal principle that "the acquisition of a domain name at a public auction necessarily means that the domain name is free from third party claims."[837] If there is any advantage to purchasing through a public auction it heavily favors dictionary words, common combinations, random letters,[838] and descriptive phrases.[839]

Respondent's knowledge (if not directly provable) has been inferred from a website's traffic history[840] and its content[841] as well as from the overall factual circumstances.[842] Where there is no proof of knowledge and no inference can be drawn, respondents may have no reason to question the legitimacy of their acquisitions. In one Respondent's view for <penthouse boutique.com> (and accepted by the Panel)[843]

> because it purchased the domain from the expired domain names auction, subject to the NSI rules on expired domains, and because it did so without

---

836 Jurisprudential Overview 3.0, Paragraph 3.7.

837 ***Deutsche Lufthansa AG v. Whois Privacy Services Pty Ltd / Mediablue Inc, Kwangpyo Kim***, D2013-1844 (WIPO January 22, 2014)(<flynet.com>. "The Panel is not aware of [any] legal principle.")

838 ***MSC Mediterranean Shipping Company Holding S.A. v. Registration Private / Sedo GmbH / Paul Kocher***, 2014-0694 (WIPO June 22, 2014) (<msc.com>. "[T]he evidence in the record does not demonstrate that the Complainant's trademark has been so extensively advertised and promoted to the public that the Respondent must have been aware of it. In this respect, it may be contrasted with the use and promotion of GM for General Motors' products in the USA.")

839 ***Mobile's Republic v. Kwangpyo Kim***, D2014-0089 (WIPO April 23, 2014) (newsrepublic.com>. "As Respondent points out, the disputed domain name was already in use for a similar website even before Complainant registered its trademark and launched its product. Having also registered a number of other domain names that include the word 'news,'" the Panel finds that Respondent has established, by a preponderance of the evidence, that it chose the disputed domain name as a dictionary or descriptive term – not because of its trademark value.")

840 ***Totem Core Ltd v. Zhao Li***, FA1609001693197 (Forum October21, 2016) (<idancer.com>. "The disputed domain name was acquired by means of an auction provided by a drop catch service, which means that Respondent knew or should have known of the existence of a previous owner of the disputed domain name when he applied for the drop catch service.... As explained before, the drop catch services are only offered in highly desirable domain names, due to their traffic, popularity or interest they have risen. If a domain names already has traffic, it is more valuable than a new domain name that has to be positioned in the market.")

841 ***Dollar Bank, Federal Savings Bank v. Paul Stapleton, The New Media Factory***, D2016-0518 (WIPO April 24, 2016) (<dollarbankers.com>. Offered for sale by auction as soon as acquired. Panel finds that "Respondent is seeking to take unfair financial advantage of goodwill associated with Complainant and its service marks.")

842 ***United Parcel Service of America Inc. v. Gary Selesko***, M&B Relocation and Referral, LLC, D2013-1555 (WIPO October 25, 2013) (<driveups.com>. "Respondent's argument that <driveups.com> does not necessarily have anything to do with UPS—but could instead relate to "drive-ups" as a slice of Americana from 'yesteryear'—is belied by the fact that Respondent contacted UPS and offered to sell the domain name to UPS within one month of acquiring the domain name.")

> actual or constructive knowledge of the prior ownership by Complainant of either the domain or a common law or registered trademark, it had every reasonable right to believe that it had the legitimate rights to register and use it for selling clothing, and no reason to believe it conflicted with Complainant nor any other entity or person.

The "situation would be different" if there were proof respondent "engaged in a clear effort to pass off as the Complainant, or engaged in the provision of services [similar to or in competition with Complainant]"[844] or respondent was "intentionally shielding its eyes from knowledge of the existence of a complainant's trademarks."[845]

However, as a general proposition respondents who acquire domain names by public auction for use in their own business operations (which can include investing in them for monetizing or reselling[846]) cannot be dispossessed absent affirmative proof of abusive registration.[847] In contrast, respondents who acquire domain names and continue prior registrants' bad faith uses will be found to have purchased them in bad faith and their domain names forfeited.[848]

Offering domain names for sale by public auction to the whole world (which includes complainants) is not evidence of bad faith absent proof they are associated solely with such complainants.[849] In ***Investone Retirement Specialists, Inc. v.***

---

[843] ***General Media Communications, Inc. v. Crazy Troll c/o CrazyTroll.com***, FA0602000 651676 (Forum May 26, 2006) (<penthouseboutique.com>. "Respondent relied on the NSI rules as giving it authority to use the domain purchased at the auction.")

[844] ***HomeAway.com, Inc. v. Name Administration Inc. (BVI)***, FA0909001283498 (Forum October 28, 2009) (<homeawayfromhome.com>. "The disputed domain was originally registered in 1999. It was purchased for $1,400 by Respondent in 2005 at a public auction held after the lapse of registration.")

[845] ***Mobile Communication Service, Inc. v. WebReg, RN***, D2005–1304 (WIPO February 24, 2006).

[846] Id. ***HomeAway.com; Joseph L. Carpenter V. Domain Administrator / Original Web Ventures Inc.***, FA1409001578228 (Forum September 30, 2014) (<myschool.com>).

[847] ***Everphone GmbH v. Privacydotlink Customer 2772294 / Kwangpyo Kim, Mediablue Inc.***, D2017-0698 (WIPO July 3, 2017) (<everphone.com>. "The Complainant further alleges that the Respondent's parking page at the disputed domain name included links to websites of the Complainant's 'direct competitors'. Even if that is true, the Complainant has not in any case satisfied the Panel that those links were based on trade mark rather than descriptive value. The difficulty for the Complainant is that the disputed domain name includes the word 'phone' and so, as the Respondent says, it is not surprising that the algorithm used on the page generated sponsored links for 'phone' – related businesses – potentially including the Complainant's competitors.")

[848] ***Accurist Watches Limited v. Whois Privacy Services Pty Limited / Dana Daste***, D2011-1328 (WIPO September 21, 2011) (Domain name purchased from an auction site. "[A]t the time the Complaint was filed, the disputed domain name reverted to a website which was effectively a 'parking site' which offered the disputed domain name for sale, provided links to a variety of third parties, including other watch makers and sellers, and provided links to third parties which featured pornographic material and content.")

Motohisa Ohno "[t]he Respondent admitted that his auction of the Domain Name was directed at the highest bid regardless of who might place it. However, the act of auctioning a domain name on a publicly available website to any willing purchaser does not always constitute a bad faith offer to sell the domain name."[850] It will constitute a bad faith offer if there is direct or circumstantial evidence of knowledge which includes website content that directly (in the body of the text) or indirectly (by hyperlinking) supports that conclusion.[851]

Where there is conflicting evidence as to the innocence of the purchaser for value the dispute must be dismissed as outside the scope of the Policy.[852] Where there is no conflicting evidence tainting respondents' acquisition by auction, Panels filter the evidence through the usual factors already discussed. In *ClearBank Limited v. Privacydotlink Customer 2450865 / Kwangpyo Kim, Mediablue Inc.*,[853] for example, Respondent had priority as Complainant's mark was not in existence prior to Respondent's acquiring <clearbank.com> at public auction following the expiration of the previous holder's registration. Even if that was not dispositive, the Panel found

---

849 ***Uovo Art LLC v. Mira Hold, Mira Holdings, Inc.***, D2016-0214 (WIPO April 18, 2016) (<uovo.com>. "The Respondent maintains that it seeks to acquire generic or descriptive domain names, and in particular short generic domain names that may attract a premium price when auctioned in the domain name secondary market." Complaint denied).

850 D2005-0643 (WIPO August 2, 2005) (<investone.com>. "It is clear that relief is predicated on the fact that the Respondent must be targeting the Complainant, directly or indirectly. The Policy does not contain any per se prohibition against trafficking in domain names"). See also ***Visual Gis Engineering S.L. v. Nitin Tripathi***, D2006-0079 (WIPO March 23, 2006) (<visualmap.com>. Complainant inadvertently failed to renew the Domain Name and Respondent purchased the Domain Name by paying $1,051 at an open auction held by SnapNames.com. The Panel points out that "Respondent has a legitimate interest in the Domain Name the Domain Name registration is a business asset of Respondent's and Respondent is free to offer to sell its legitimate business assets."

851 Discussed further in "Not All Offers to Sell Violate the Policy" (Sec. 5.01-D.3).

852 ***Andrew Prince v. Registrant [3197190]: Sven Echternach / Moniker Privacy Services (2579748)***, D2010-1661 (WIPO November 26, 2010) (<prince.com>. "This case ... concerns the question who is the rightful owner of the Domain Name. As the Complainant has put it, the purpose of his Complaint is to recover 'his stolen property'. The Respondent, on the other hand, takes the position that he purchased the Domain Name in a completely legitimate manner from an agent of its rightful owner. The Policy was not designed nor is it equipped to decide whether the Domain Name was taken without the Complainant's knowledge or consent, involving as it does legal issues outside the Policy and credibility of competing testimony that a Policy panel is incapable of resolving.")

853 Where there is no conflicting evidence tainting respondents' acquisition by auction, Panels filter the evidence through the usual factors already discussed. In ***ClearBank Limited v. Privacydotlink Customer 2450865 / Kwangpyo Kim, Mediablue Inc.***, for example, Respondent had priority as Complainant's mark was not in existence prior to Respondent's acquiring <clearbank.com> at public auction following the expiration of the previous holder's registration. Even if that was not dispositive, the Panel found that the "value the Respondent attaches to the Disputed Domain Name appears to be inspired by the dictionary meaning of the generic words in the Disputed Domain Name, and not by the identity of the parties that may be interested in acquiring the Disputed Domain Name."

that the "value the Respondent attaches to the Disputed Domain Name appears to be inspired by the dictionary meaning of the generic words in the Disputed Domain Name, and not by the identity of the parties that may be interested in acquiring the Disputed Domain Name."

5

Proving Rights or Legitimate Interests in the Disputed Domain Name 4(a)(ii) of the Policy

5.01 SAFE HARBOR— PARAGRAPH 4(C) OF THE POLICY 5.01

5.01-A Qualifying for Safe Harbor 5.01-A

5.01-A.1 "Any One of the Circumstances" 5.01-A.1

Paragraph 4(a)(ii) of the Policy is pivotal. Complainant may prevail on this second limb if it presents an unrebutted *prima facie* showing that respondent lacks rights or legitimate interests in the domain name, and only if it does can it proceed to the third requirement to prove conjunctive bad faith (paragraph 4(a)(iii)). It cannot succeed by alleging respondent has no statutory rights, is not operating a business with the domain name, or refuses to sell the domain name at a reasonable price. It succeeds by presenting evidence of sufficient strength for respondent to be called on to rebut complainant's *prima facie* case, discussed earlier in Section 4.02-B.

Rights and legitimate interests are defined solely by reference to paragraph 4(c) and its subparagraphs which constitute a nonexclusive menu of affirmative defenses. For respondent, successful rebuttal of complainant's *prima facie* case establishes its lawful registration of the domain name. However, failure to rebut complainant's claim is not conclusive of bad faith, which must still be proved.[1]

Paragraph 4(c) of the Policy provides that "any of the following circumstances [set forth in subparagraphs 4(c)(i-iii)], *in particular but without limitation*, if found by the Panel to be proved based on its evaluation of all evidence presented, shall demonstrate your rights or legitimate interests to the domain name for purposes of Paragraph 4(a)(ii)" (emphasis added). Two phrases stand out in this prologue: "in particular but without limitation" and "rights or legitimate interests." The first phrase recognizes the possibility of unenumerated circumstances; nominative fair use and acquiescence are examples (both discussed below). The second phrase is in the disjunctive (either/or), which means "rights" and "legitimate interests" are conceptually distinguishable, but because it is not easy to say what the distinction is Panels tend to merge them.[2] Both phrases inform the meaning of the enumerated circumstances and how they are intended to be understood.

The enumerated circumstances are:

> (i) [B]efore any notice to you of the dispute, your use of, or demonstrable preparations to use, the domain name or a name corresponding to the domain name in connection with a bona fide offering of goods or services.

---

[1] A respondent has two opportunities to counter complainant's demand for cancellation or transfer of a disputed domain name: 1) prove it has a right or legitimate interest in the domain name, which is discussed in this chapter; or 2) demonstrate that the domain name was not registered in bad faith – either because the timing of the registration or the choice of domain name – thereby rebutting complainant's paragraph 4(a)(iii) contentions, which is discussed in Chapter 4.

[2] See earlier discussion in "Establishing a Right or Legitimate Interest" (Sec. 4.02-A.1.a.ii).

(ii) [Y]ou (as an individual, business, or other organization) have been commonly known by the domain name, even if you have acquired no trademark or service mark rights.

(iii) [Y]ou are making a legitimate noncommercial or fair use of the domain name, without intent for commercial gain to misleadingly divert consumers or to tarnish the trademark or service mark at issue.

There is a parallel between the three sets of 4(c) and four sets of 4(b) circumstances in that both are nonexclusive, but there is also an important difference. Paragraph 4(a)(ii) to which 4(c) is attached makes no reference to any conjunctive requirement, as does 4(a)(iii) to which 4(b) is attached. Paragraphs 4(c)(i) and 4(c)(iii) are built around respondent's use of the domain name. Paragraph 4(c)(ii) focuses on proprietary rights or legitimate interests based on respondent's identity and the longevity of its name. Respondent's proof that it is and has been "commonly known" by the domain name alone satisfies its rebuttal burden.[3]

The three enumerated circumstances essentially comprise the possibilities for rebutting claimant's allegations.[4] Failure to satisfy any of them is not conclusive of

---

[3] ***Saltworks, Inc. v. Gary Pedersen, Salt Works***, D2013-0984 (WIPO July 15, 2013) ("Because Respondent has been commonly known by the disputed domain name, it is not necessary to determine whether Respondent has also made use of a name corresponding to the domain name for a bona fide offering of goods or services prior to notice of this dispute.")

[4] The analogous provisions in the ACPA are found at 15 U.S.C. §1125 (d)(1)(A)(I). The ACPA reads: "In determining whether a person has a bad faith intent ... a court *may* consider the following factors such as, but not limited to" (emphasis added) (Factors V through VIII are quoted in Sec. 6.01.A.1.a):

(I) the trademark or other intellectual property rights of the person, if any, in the domain name [**implicit in paragraph 4(c)(i) of the Policy**] ;

(II) the extent to which the domain name consists of the legal name of the person or a name that is otherwise commonly used to identify that person [**equivalent to paragraph 4(c)(ii) of the Policy**];

(III) the person's prior use, if any, of the domain name in connection with the bona fide offering of any goods or services [**equivalent to paragraph 4(c)(i) of the Policy**];

(IV) the person's bona fide noncommercial or fair use of the mark in a site accessible under the domain name [**equivalent to paragraph 4(c)(iii) of the Policy**];

[Factors V through VIII, the bad faith factors are identified in Chapter 5]

(IX) the extent to which the mark incorporated in the person's domain name registration is or is not distinctive and famous within the meaning of subsection (c)(1) of this section [**implicit in paragraphs 4(b) and 4(c) of the Policy**].

In addition to the above, the ACPA provides a catchall defense: "bad faith shall not be found in any case in which the court determines that the person believed and had reasonable grounds to believe that the use of the domain name was a fair use or otherwise lawful." 15 U.S.C. §1125 (d)(1)(B)(ii). A gloss on this "defense" is contained in H.R. Conf. Rep. 106-412: "The bill is carefully and narrowly tailored, however, to extend only to cases where the plaintiff can demonstrate the defendant ... *used* the offending domain name with bad-faith intent to profit from the goodwill of a mark belonging to someone else" (emphasis added). U.S. federal courts construe this safe harbor defense

bad faith, which, as previously noted, is a separate requirement. However, respondent's proof qualifying for safe harbor is conclusive against the complainant.[5]

If respondent demonstrates a right or legitimate interest the proceeding terminates in its favor. Such proof affirms registration was lawful and trumps complainant's mark regardless whether the domain name is identical or confusingly similar to it. If complainant succeeds on its *prima facie* case the Panel must then proceed to the next requirement under paragraph 4(a)(iii) of the Policy, discussed in Chapter 6.

5.01-A.2 Tense, A Key Factor 5.01-A.2

In assessing whether a respondent qualifies for safe harbor "it is necessary [not only] to consider the relationship between the Parties, their previous dealings and any knowledge that respondent may have of complainant's services"[6] but also the composition of the trademark—whether it is weak or strong—and its penetration in the marketplace. Taking 4(c)(i) and 4(c)(iii) first, a respondent proves its right or legitimate interest by using the domain name it acquired for an identifiable purpose. *Bona fide* use, whether offering goods or services under 4(c)(i) or noncommercial or fair use under 4(c)(iii) presupposes registration in good faith since it would be a *non sequitur* for it to be otherwise. Reselling domain names on the secondary market can qualify as a legitimate interest.

Timing of use, therefore, is a paramount factor, and proof that the use is legitimate is a full and complete defense to complainant's *prima facie* case.[7] To

---

"very sparingly and only in the most unusual cases." *Lahoti v. VeriCheck, Inc.*, 586 F.3d 1190 (9th Cir. 2009) (quoting *Audi AG v. D'Amato*, 469 F.3d 534, 549 (6th Cir. 2006). "Otherwise, the defense would 'undermine the rest of the statute' because '[a]ll but the most blatant cybersquatters will be able to put forth at least some lawful motives for their behavior.'" (Quoting *Virtual Works, Inc. v. Volkswagen of Am., Inc.*, 238 F. 3rd 264, 270 (4th Cir. 2001) (alterations in original).

[5] Safe harbor encompasses two distinct circumstances, namely 1) trademark owners' rights postdate the domain name in which case they have no actionable claim although they have standing; and 2) holders have rights or legitimate interests in the challenged domain names in which case they could not have registered them in bad faith. In the context of an action under the Anticybersquatting Consumer Protection Act, trademark owners would lack standing to maintain an action for the first of these two circumstances. See *Office Space Solutions, Inc. v. Kneen*, 1:15-cv-04941 (SDNY) (commenced June 24, 2015 and withdrawn with prejudice July 8 following argument on a motion for preliminary injunction in which the court rejected plaintiff's theory of liability). For the second of the two circumstances see Plan B discussion "Complaints Without Merit" (Sec. 7.11-B).

[6] ***Paul Plumadore, James Tindell, River Road Antiques, Ltd v. William Kilgore***, D2007-1922 (WIPO March 12, 2008).

[7] Regardless of whether respondent has rights or legitimate interests proof that it had "reasonable grounds to believe" that the use was fair may be a good and sufficient defense to bad faith use. The "reasonable grounds to believe" defense has been accepted by some UDRP Panels, not as a paragraph 4(c) right or legitimate interest defense but solely to defeat bad faith use. It appears to have been

succeed, respondents must establish "past" and "present" as opposed to "future" use of the disputed domain name. For paragraph 4(c)(i) respondent must demonstrate its "[present and past] use of" or "demonstrable [present] preparations to use" the domain name; for paragraph 4(c)(ii) respondent must demonstrate it has been "commonly known" by the domain name antecedent to the registration; and for paragraph 4(c)(iii) respondent must demonstrate that the manner in which the domain name is currently being used qualifies for "noncommercial or fair use." Any present *bona fide* use (or in the case of paragraph 4(c)(i) demonstrable preparations for future use) signifies good faith registration, whereas alleged future use unaccompanied by concrete evidence of what the use is to be is not a good defense under either 4(c)(i) or 4(c)(iii) of the Policy.[8]

Whatever the circumstances, the acts that legitimize a right or interest cannot occur after notice of the proceeding. The first defense, making a "*bona fide* offering of goods or services," expressly requires respondent to prove that its use or demonstrable preparations preceded notice of the dispute. Respondent "need only show a plausible non-infringing explanation for selecting the disputed domain name."[9] The second defense, being "commonly known by the domain name"[10] means that respondent was known by the domain name prior to registration, not as a result of registration. Implicit in the third defense is that respondent registered the domain name with the intention of operating a website that from its inception is noncommercial and fair use and is being used in a manner consistent with applicable Constitutional and statutory law.

The most frequently recognized non-enumerated defense (even where respondent is found to lack rights or legitimate interests in the disputed domain name) is a registration predating existence of the mark complainant alleges is being infringed. Other unenumerated defenses include nominative fair use if it is not folded into paragraph 4(c)(i) of the Policy with the "Oki Data" test, both discussed below, and "acquiescence."

---

first suggested in a dissent, ***MatchMaker Int'l Dev. Corp. v. Kaiser Dev. Corp.***, 146933 (Forum May 9, 2003). See ***Fireman's Fund Insurance Company v. Steve Schwartz***, FA1010001355350 (Forum December 15, 2010) ("There is no reason that the concept of domain name related 'bad faith' under federal law and under the UDRP should not be consistent"); ***Snap on Incorporated v. Jeffrey Scotese***, D2013-0577 (WIPO May 9, 2013). In both UDRP and ACPA registrant has the burden of proving that it had "reasonable grounds to believe." Used in a UDRP proceeding it undercuts complainant's attempt to prove bad faith use even if the registration is in bad faith, but if the dispute ever reaches federal court, it is not a good defense to proof of bad faith registration: "A defendant who acts even partially in bad faith in registering a domain name, however, is not entitled to benefit from the ACPA's safe harbor provision." *Virtual Works, Inc., supra.*

8 Discussed further in "Prior Use or Demonstrable Preparations to Use Before Notice" (Sec. 5.02).

9 ***Choice Courier Systems, Inc. v. William H. Kirkendale***, 2002-0483 (WIPO July 23, 2002).

10 The term "commonly known" means known prior to the registration of the domain name. Discussed further in "Commonly Known By The Domain Name" (Sec. 5.03).

5.01-B Rights and Legitimate Interests Are Dictated by Conduct 5.01-B

5.01-B.1 Active Website 5.01-B.1

Respondents acquire no rights or legitimate interests in domain names by merely registering them, but if they satisfy any of the circumstances set forth in paragraph 4(c) of the Policy, which may include monetizing their use or operating businesses acquiring and selling domain names, and they either have priority through registration or complainants lack any proof of pretextual conduct, they have unassailable rights or interests in them.

Whether respondents can establish rights or legitimate interests by affirmatively rebutting that it lacks either depends on a number of factors, such as the composition of domain names (whether of dictionary words or common phrases or uncommon combinations or rare words) and the content of the resolving website if used as a PPC platform (whether the hyperlinks reflect the semantic meanings of the domain names or in some way impinge on complainant's rights).

For two of the three affirmative defenses[11] it is respondent's conduct that defines its right or legitimate interest in the disputed domain name.[12] While inactive or passive use limits (but does not eliminate) respondent's defenses under paragraph 4(c) for the reasons discussed below, an active website is laden with information directly relevant to respondent's *bona fides* (whether or not it appears and answers the complaint[13]). Although websites are "the prevalent use"[14] e-mail,[15] FTP and hosting services are legitimate commercial uses: "[T]he lack of a formal web page does not detract from these real and viable commercial uses."[16]

---

[11] For Paragraph 4(c)(ii) it is the name by which respondent is "commonly known" prior to its registration of the domain name.

[12] ***Dynamic Language Center, Ltd v. LeAnn Hillman***, FA0901001242911 (Forum March 4, 2009) (Proprietor of a local business, Dynamic Language Services LLC registered in South Carolina, <dynamiclanguageservices.com>). Respondent argued that she chose the business name Dynamic Language Services, LLC because she offered language services and 'dynamic' described how she intended to conduct her business.

[13] Screenshots submitted by Complainant support a right by non-appearing Respondent in same business but different location, ***Park 'N Fly Service Corporation v. Elias Tesfa***, FA120200 1427761 (Forum March 15, 2012) (PARK 'N FLY and <ezparkfly>). Complainant cannot monopolize a descriptive phrase to the exclusion of non-competing parties.

[14] ***The Hong Kong and Shanghai Banking Corporation Limited v. Bill Lynn***, D2001-0915 (WIPO September 28, 2001).

[15] ***Nishan Systems, Inc. v Nishan Ltd***, D2003-0204 (WIPO January 5, 2003) (use of the domain name in connection with e-mail services is a legitimate use).

[16] ***Innotek, Inc. v. Sierra Innotek***, D2002-0072 (WIPO April 22, 2002); ***The Federal Tax Authority, LLC v. James Scanlon***, FA1108001402161 (Forum September 29, 2011) (Two other legitimate uses are "back end" for ecommerce transactions and blocking another from using the domain name).

Paragraph 4(c) explains that proof of any of the several defenses listed or otherwise[17] "shall demonstrate your rights or legitimate interests to the domain name for purposes of Paragraph 4(a)(ii)."[18] While the examples do not comprehend the universe of good faith the defenses are crafted to include most circumstances. The "common approach is for respondents to seek to bring themselves within one of the examples of paragraph 4(c) or put forward some other reason why they can fairly be said to have a relevant right or legitimate interest in respect of the domain name in question."[19] The applicable standard of proof is by a preponderance of the evidence.[20]

The three examples of good faith and any other circumstances that support a respondent's contention are temporally sensitive. It is not what a respondent will do (future tense) but what it has (past tense) or is doing (present tense) that satisfies its burden. Thus, paragraph 4(c)(i) of the Policy requires proof of respondent's historical conduct—"[your use] before any notice . . . of the dispute"—and present efforts—"demonstrable preparations" to use the domain name. In contrast, paragraph 4(c)(ii) requires proof that the name by which respondent is "commonly known" predates its acquisition of the domain name or there is a plausible explanation if that is not the case. Paragraph 4(c)(iii) of the Policy is oriented to both present and past: that is, respondent has not in the past and is not presently using the domain name for commercial gain.

Sanitizing the record after notice of infringement does not cure but supports complainant's contention that the domain name violates paragraph 4(b)(iv) of the Policy.[21] Where proof of use "before notice of the dispute" is required [4(c)(i)], proof of present use is insufficient[22]; where proof of present motivation is required [4(c)(iii)], assertions of what respondent intends to do in the future are insufficient.[23] "Commonly known" does not mean the name by which respondent adopts upon registering a domain name or adventitiously calls itself in the present.[24]

---

[17] For paragraph 4(b), Panels have crafted a non-enumerated circumstance which they call "totality of circumstances."

[18] The defenses parallel the subparagraphs of paragraph 4(b) discussed further in Chapter 6. Note that any one of the defenses demonstrates rights or legitimate interest only for the purposes of the Policy and is not an assessment of trademark infringement.

[19] ***Compagnie Generale des Matieres Nucleaires v. Greenpeace Int'l***, D2001-0376 (WIPO May 14, 2001).

[20] Discussed further in "Evidentiary Expectations" (Sec. 7.05-A.1.b).

[21] ***Sansum Clinic v. Sansumclinic.com / c/o Whois Identity Shield***, D2008-1008 (WIPO August 28, 2008).

[22] ***Hewlett Packard Development Company, L.P. v. Fredric Fransson***, DNU2013-0005 (WIPO December 23, 2013) ("The Panel notes that, at the time of the drafting of the decision, the disputed domain name is pointed to a web page providing links to third party sites hosting contents dedicated

5.01-B.2 Inactive or Passive Use 5.01-B.2

5.01-B.2.a *Inferring Bad Faith Registration from Passive Use* *5.01-B.2.a*

"Passive use" as a category of use distinct from legitimate inactivity entered the UDRP vocabulary in the third decided case.[25] While mere failure to maintain an active website does not automatically result in a finding of faith use, the stronger the mark the less credibility there is for good faith (such as claiming future use for example).[26] While it is not the deciding factor, passive holding is cumulative with other factors to support complainant's contention that respondent lacks rights or legitimate interests in the challenged domain name, and depending on the circumstances could also support abusive registration.

---

to higher education in Sweden. However, it appears that this change has been made by the Respondent only after the filing of the Complaint.")

[23] The same principle also applies to complainant. It may have a highly distinctive mark and reputation in the present but not necessarily any reputation at the time *respondent registered the domain name.*

[24] Respondent in ***Neiman Marcus Group, Inc. v. Neiman-Marcus***, FA 135048 (Forum January 13, 2003) called itself NEIMAN-MARCUS. The Panel in ***Alain-Martin Pierret d/b/a Bordeaux West v. Sierra Technology Group, LLC***, FA 0505000472135 (Forum July 1, 2005):

> Mere ownership of a domain name is not sufficient to show that a respondent has been 'commonly known by the domain name'; if it were, every domain name registrant automatically tomatically could claim protection under paragraph 4(c)(ii) of the Policy.

Discussed further in "What It Means to Be 'Commonly Known By The Domain Name'" (Sec. 5.03-A).

[25] ***Telstra Corporation Limited v. Nuclear Marshmallows***, D2000-0003 (WIPO February 18, 2000). The reasoning was quickly accepted by other Panels and represents the consensus. Early cases include ***Ingersoll Rand Co. v. Frank Gully, d/b/a Advcomren***, D2000-0021 (WIPO March 9, 2000); ***DCI S.A. v. Link Commercial Corp.***, D2000-1232 (WIPO December 7, 2000); ***Clerical Med. Inv. Group Ltd. v. Clericalmedical.com***, D2000-1228 (WIPO November 28, 2000); ***Distinct Holdings, Inc., d/b/a Diversified v. Robert Schweitzer***, FA1706001737080 (Forum July 27, 2017). Construing "use" to include acts that deprive mark owners from using domain names corresponding to their marks was foreshadowed by two U.S. cases, *Panavision International, L.P. v. Dennis Toeppen, et al.*, 141 F. 3d 1316 (9th Cir. 1998) and *Intermatic Inc. v. Toeppen*, 947 F. Supp. 1227 (N.D. Ill. 1996) ("Toeppen's intention to arbitrage the `intermatic.com' domain name constitutes a commercial use.")

[26] The ***Telstra*** test has specific reference to strong marks whose use in commerce predates the registration of the domain name. The stronger the mark the more likely complainant will prevail for the reasons explained in ***Telstra***. In ***NYSE Group, Inc. v. Val Sklarov / BentleyTek / America 2030 Capital***, FA170900 1748855 (Forum October 23, 2017) (<nyseloan.com> + 20 other domains including <nyse-trader.com> Respondent argued Complainant had no rights to the letters in Ukraine, but although marks are territorial rights, jurisdiction to protect marks is not). The *Telstra* principle has also been misapplied to find conjunctive bad faith for marks that are neither well-known nor famous. See, for example, ***T & P Holding Company, LLC v. Wendy Webbe and Ancient Holdings, LLC***, (Forum April 6,2018) (<youareok.com>. "Respondents who make no active use of

In ***Telstra Corporation*** the Panel drew a "fine distinction" in concluding that the concept of a domain name "'being used in bad faith' is not limited to positive action; inaction is within the concept." It explained that "[o]ccupying an entry in the DNS is 'use' . . . [because] it has a blocking function."[27] Acting in bad faith—a decision not to create a live website—can be evidence "amount[ing] to the domain name being used in bad faith," but the principle has no application where domain name registration precedes trademark acquisition or in the absence of proof respondent had complainant's mark in mind.

The proscribed conduct is said to be apparent when it is "not possible to conceive of any plausible actual or contemplated active use of the domain name by respondent that would not be illegitimate."[28] A dictionary word that has achieved prominence in the marketplace as a trademark registered as a domain name that could be either legitimate or not, is not necessarily legitimate if passively held and respondent offers neither excusable explanation nor demonstrable evidence of future use. The determination will turn on factors that cumulatively point to bad faith registration. "Aeried" for example could either be illegitimate if the added "d" is an intentional ploy (see Typosquatting, Section 6.05-E.1), or legitimate if the registration was without intent to capitalize on AERIE. To overcome the inference of typosquatting respondent would have to "actually show [an] intent to use [the domain name in a manner] that did not encroach on Complainant's protected commercial area."[29]

Since exonerating evidence is solely within respondent's control, failure to offer it undercuts any right or legitimate interest it may have alleged and ultimately supports a finding of abusive registration. Where respondent provides plausible evidence of actual use and complainant is aware of that use, complainant will itself be chargeable with abusive conduct.[30]

---

a domain name have been found to have registered and used said domain name in bad faith under Policy ¶ 4(a)(iii) [and so it is here]").

[27] ***Red Bull GmbH v. Manuel Sousa***, D2001-0584 (July 3, 2001).

[28] The dissent in ***Time Inc. v. Chip Cooper***, D2000-1342 (WIPO February 13, 2001) expressed a different view: "***Telstra*** is based on a conviction that the fame of the mark owner obliterates any possible legitimate use of the domain. This is simply not the law in the US, the jurisdiction where both parties [in ***Time***] reside." The dissent's view has not been accepted by other panelists and is antipathetic to UDRP's goal of balancing the party's rights. It should be noted, however, that ***Telstra*** does not hold that passive holding without more is equivalent to bad faith; there have to be other ingredients, one of which is the strength of the mark. Passive holding of weak marks carries little if any weight.

[29] ***Retail Royalty Company and AE Direct Co LLC v. Daniel Cormier***, FA1610001698852 (Forum November 23, 2016) ("The Panel does not agree with Respondent's contention here because Respondent has no use or planned use to support such a claim [that it has intentions for the domain name].")

As trademarks ascend the classification scale inferences bend in complainant's favor. The ***Telstra*** Panel formulated a five-point test to determine whether passive holding of a domain name identical or confusingly similar to the trademark was abusive:

> (i) Complainant's trademark has a strong reputation and is widely known, as evidenced by its substantial use,
>
> (ii) Respondent has provided no evidence whatsoever of any actual or contemplated good faith use by it of the Domain Name,
>
> (iii) Respondent has taken active steps to conceal its true identity, by operating under a name that is not a registered business name,
>
> (iv) Respondent has actively provided, and failed to correct, false contact details, in breach of its registration agreement, and
>
> (v) Taking into account all of the above, it is not possible to conceive of any plausible actual or contemplated active use of the Domain Name by respondent that would not be illegitimate, such as by being a passing off, an infringement of consumer protection legislation, or an infringement of complainant's rights under trademark law.

The first and fifth prongs of the test carry the greatest weight and are generally conclusive on the issue of abusive registration. This is logical, because where there is no conceivable use of a domain name that would not infringe complainant's rights, respondent cannot hide its motivation for registering the domain name.[31] It "makes no sense whatever to wait until [the Respondent] actually 'uses' the name, when inevitably . . . such use . . . will create the confusion described in the Policy."[32]

"Coming soon" announcements and long-term passive holding have also been found to constitute bad faith. One Panel[33] that made an independent visit to Respondent's website found that Respondent

> is confusing Web surfers or prospective customers of Cortefiel when it is promising them to 'come soon' while simultaneously not furnishing them

---

[30] See ***National Motor Club of America, Inc. v. Domain Names, Inc., Attn: NMC.COM c/o Network Solutions***, FA1103001381111 (Forum May 4, 2011) (<nmc.com>. Record contains no facts supporting an inference of bad faith for a string of letters that a number of businesses other than Complainant have registered trademarks). .")

[31] ***AlitaliaBLinee Aeree Italiane S.p.A v. Colour Digital***, D2000-1260 (WIPO November 23, 2000); ***Vodafone Group, Plc v. Phone Express***, D2004-0505 (WIPO August 31, 2004); ***Bronx Arts Ensemble, Inc. v. Vilma Morales, e:bOOm, S.A***, D2004-0493 (WIPO August 30, 2004) ("[I] t is difficult to conceive of any plausible actual or contemplated active use of the domain name by respondent that would not be infringing or tarnishing complainant's marks."); similarly, ***Hewlett-Packard Company v. Marcel Wieland***, FA0010000095852 (Forum November 20, 2000) (Panel held that any future use of the inactive website would result in consumer confusion).

[32] ***Phat Fashions v. Kruger***, FA 96193 (Forum December 29, 2000).

[33] ***Cortefiel S.A. v. Miguel Garcíia Quintas***, D2000-0140 WIPO April 24, 2000).

> with any indication that it has no relationship whatsoever to a Complainant's site or to Complainant's marks or activities, being the mark famous in the Spanish market.

Respondent's non-use of the disputed domain name for as little as two years and varying longer periods in other cases have led Panels to rule for complainant.[34] Marks composed of generic terms acquired prior to domain name registration are governed by a different set of considerations since as marks descend the classification scale the likelier the probability of non-infringing use.[35]

No right can be gained by adverse possession.[36] This applies *a fortiori* when non-use "coincides with a known, well-known or renowned trademark owned by someone else."[37] Or, as expressed by another Panel,[38]

> Other factors must be involved. An important element is that complainant's mark is sufficiently well-known such that a registrant might reasonably be inferred to have registered an identical or confusingly similar domain name in the expectation of taking advantage of the trademark holder.

Respondent's failure to respond, or if it appears but offers unpersuasive arguments for its choice, is tantamount to conclusive evidence of the second and third limbs of the Policy.

5.01-B.2.b 5.01-B.2.b *Non-Use No Evidence of Bad Faith Registration*

The Telstra test applies in limited circumstances after the Panel has determined that respondent lacks any right or legitimate interest in the domain name. Non-use is not a defense if any use would be infringing. However, non-use of an after-acquired domain name registered in good faith does not extinguish a right any more than long use after registration in bad faith creates one. While the test can apply to registrations predating existence of marks and may support complainants' prima facie cases it cannot support abusive registration since the domain name could not

---

[34] ***Internet Billing Co. Ltd. v. Fundu Technologies***, FA 95547 (Forum October 2, 2000) (<ibills.com>); ***Bayer Aktiengesellschaft v. Henrik Monssen***, D2003-0275 (WIPO May 30, 2003) (six months); ***The Cheesecake Factory Inc. and The Cheesecake Factory Assets Co., LLC v. Say Cheesecake***, D2005-0766 (WIPO September 12, 2005) (13 months); ***Decisioneering, Inc. v. PA Gordon***, FA 96668 (Forum March 31, 2000) (Panel found that non-use "during several years of registration, indicates a lack of legitimate interests.")

[35] Representative cases: ***Snap on Incorporated v. Jeffrey Scotese***, D2013-0577 (WIPO May 9, 2013) (<snaponsocks.com>); ***Microsystems Technology, Inc. d/b/a ANYDOC v. Matthew Lamb***, D2012-2193 (WIPO February 7, 2013) (<anydoc.com>).

[36] Discussed further in "Laches vs. Lapse of Time" (Sec. 5.01-E.1).

[37] ***LACER, S.A. v. Constanti Gomez Marzo***, D2001-0177 (WIPO March 29, 2001) (Occupying Complainant's space indicates bad faith in the sense of paragraph 4(b) of the Policy.)

[38] ***Barlow Lyde & Gilbert v. The Business Law Group***, D2005-0493 (WIPO June 24, 2005). A pejorative added to a trademark that resolves to a holding page fails to support the paragraph 4(c)

have been registered in bad faith.[39] One Panel noted that there "is nothing in the Policy that suggests a registrant may be divested of a domain name simply because he failed to use it actively online."[40]

There is no *per se* rule that inactivity of after-acquired domain names composed of common words and descriptive phrases violates third party rights. There is no affirmative obligation on a registrant to have a domain name resolve to an active website.[41] Targeting is inferred only where the possibilities of legitimate use of a disputed domain name identical or confusingly similar to a distinctive mark shrink to the vanishing point.[42] The Panel in one case noted that the "Complainant has provided no evidence that its mark is so well-known that any registration (without use) of a domain name cannot help but lead to the conclusion that respondent registered with *mala fides*."[43]

(iii) defense. Discussed further in "Adding Terms of Opposition to Pejorative Prefixes/Suffixes to Trademarks" (Sec. 5.04-B).

[39] ***Karma International, LLC v. David Malaxos***, FA1812001822198 (Forum February 15, 2019) ("Nowhere in the Policy is there a requirement that a respondent is under a positive obligation to use (or surrender an unused) domain name [or that] [f]ailure to use a domain name is ... per se evidence that its owner has no right or legitimate interest in [it]."

[40] ***National Football League v. Thomas Trainer***, D2006-1440 (WIPO December 29, 2006) (<nflnetwork.com>). This does not mean that holding a domain name passively justifies its registration. The Panel immediately qualified its statement by adding that "when a registrant, such as respondent here, obtains a domain name that is confusingly similar to a famous mark, with no apparent rights or legitimate interests in the name, and then fails to respond to infringement claims and a UDRP Complaint, an inference of bad faith is warranted." However, see ***Benoit Thiercelin v. Medicalexpo.com***, CAC 100235 (ADR.eu May 23, 2011) in which the Panel reasons against precedent and consensus that inactivity by itself supports conjunctive bad faith without regard to the fact the domain name was registered prior to complainant's acquisition of its mark. This view bears a resemblance to the argument advanced by panelists adhering to the "unitary concept." Discussed earlier in "Justifying Forfeiture Despite Good Faith Registration" (Sec. 4.03-A.4.b).

[41] ***Audi AG v. Stratofex***, D2012-1894 (WIPO November 7, 2012) (<audicity.com>).

[42] ***Hostess Brands, Inc. f/k/a Interstate Bakeries Corporation v. Domain Capital***, D2009-1357 (WIPO December 1, 2009) (<hostess.com>. "Although the Domain Name is identical to Complainant's well known trademark, Respondent is correct when it emphasizes that 'hostess' is also a common word subject to substantial third party use." Since there is no evidence of targeting the Panel could not "on the balance of the probabilities, adopt the inferences which Complainant urges"); ***Early Learning Centre Limited v. Kiansu Thoi***, D2005-0692 (WIPO August 12, 2005) (The domain name consisted of a simple descriptive string of words <earlylearningcentre.com> that could plausibly be used commercially for a different business than Complainant's.) Mothballing a domain name in which respondent has a right or legitimate interest is not grounds for forfeiture. ***Microsonic Gesellschaft für Mikrotechnik und Ultraschalltechnik mbH v. Alex Rad***, D2014- 1715 (WIPO December 1, 2014) ("[Complainant's case] is based on the fact that the business name registration was not renewed in November 2005 and that the disputed domain name is not currently used and does not appear to have been used since then.")

[43] ***AlbertoBCulver Company v. Pritpal Singh Channa***, D2002-0757 (WIPO October 7, 2002).

Inactivity is not cause for an actionable claim. The concept under trademark law of abandonment for non-use has no application to domain names passively held without explanation.[44] Respondents may hold domain names whether they use them or not for as long as they maintain their registrations. The sole qualification is complainant's right to refile a complaint if an activated domain name subsequently resolves to a website that infringes its rights.[45]

5.01-C

5.01-C Rights or Legitimate Interests: Expressly, Impliedly, and Lawfully

5.01-C.1

5.01-C.1 Permissive Use of Trademarks

Permissive use of trademarks incorporated into second level domains rests on consent, either expressly granted[46] or implied.[47] Non-authorized but lawful nominative use of trademarks is discussed below. Trademark owners "can readily protect [themselves from a finding of implied consent] by securing . . . clear written agreement[s]."[48] They prevail when they do so,[49] but not otherwise.[50] Where complainant's own actions created the circumstances from which respondent could

---

[44] ***Novatia LLC v. Matt Hite***, D2007-0728 (WIPO July 11, 2007).

[45] See for example, ***Gassan Diamonds B.V. v. Internet Dating.Com***, D2011-0774 (WIPO July 29, 2011). Refiling complaint discussed further in "Refiling a Complaint: New Facts or Fresh Evidence" (Sec. 7.02-B).

[46] ***R&M Italia SpA, Tycon Technoglass Srl v. EnQuip Technologies Group, Inc.***, D2007-1477 (WIPO December 7, 2007). Refusal to surrender domain names in breach of contract is discussed further in "Rights to Domain Name After Termination of Permission" (Sec. 6.01-E). Registering with permission is not converted to bad faith because the parties subsequently fall out. See ***Quadrific Media Private Limited v. Rajat Agarwal***, D2017-1050 (WIPO August 31, 2017) ("[T]here is no need for the Panel to consider any subsequent dispute that arose between the Parties or who owns the intellectual property rights in the Disputed Domain Name. What is important to consider is the Respondent's intention at the time he registered the Disputed Domain Name, and it is clear that the Respondent acted in good faith by registering the Disputed Domain Name.")

[47] ***Draw Tite Inc. v. Plattsburg Spring Inc.***, D2000-0017 (WIPO March 14, 2000) (<drawtite.com>): "Whether or not a formal license agreement exists, the evidence submitted to this Panel, coupled with Complainant's failure to take action against Respondent's website prior to July 1999, indicate Complainant's acquiescence to Respondent's use of the domain name."

[48] ***Red Bull GmbH v. Roy Kenneth Nabben***, D2010-1358 (WIPO September 30, 2010) (<trademark+geographic location.com>), citing ***A. Nattermann & Cie. GmbH and Sanofi aventis v. Watson Pharmaceuticals, Inc.***, D2010-0800 (WIPO August 31, 2010) (<ferrlecit.com>).

[49] ***Milwaukee Electric Tool Corporation v. Bay Verte Machinery, Inc. d/b/a The Power Tool Store***, D2002-0774 (WIPO October 22, 2002) ("Today, Respondent might be in breach of Complainant's terms of sale and Internet policy. Today, Respondent might not be able to register and use Complainant's mark in a domain name and make a bona fide offering of goods, because of an express breach of contract. The Panel is offering no opinion on those matters. Respondent's assertion of legitimate interests in the domain name is based on conduct occurring before Complainant adopted its terms and policy.") See also ***Herbalife International of America,*** *supra;* ***R&M Italia SpA***, supra.

reasonably conclude its conduct was permitted it would be difficult to find a violation of the Policy.[51] Consent by acquiescence rests on complainant's silence with knowledge of respondent's registration and use of the allegedly infringing domain name. While the burden lies with respondent to establish consent to the activity,[52] complainant carries the heavier burden to overcome respondent's affirmative showing it has a legitimate interest.[53]

In the cited case "it is common ground that the Domain Name was originally registered by the Respondent with the consent of the Complainant to enable the Respondent to market the Complainant's Red Bull product to consumers in Norway for the mutual benefit of both parties."[54] Whether complainant's withdrawal of permission is contractually justified raises a triable issue beyond the scope of the UDRP. Proof that complainant's representatives encouraged respondent to set up a website "and did so for over a year without [complainant's] objection" is tantamount to consent under UDRP jurisprudence.[55] It leaves the question to another forum to determine whether there is actual as well as apparent consent sufficient to escape a finding of trademark infringement.[56] However, for UDRP

---

50 ***Celebrity Signatures International, Inc. v. Hera's Incorporated Iris Linder***, D2002-0936 (WIPO December 16, 2002); ***Santa Monica Convention & Visitors Bureau v. WeAre LLC***, FA0902001247925 (Forum April 14, 2009).

51 ***Celebrity Signatures***, supra.("To a significant degree, Complainant's own actions created the circumstances in which Respondent could reasonably conclude that her conduct was permitted."); ***National Futures Association v. John L. Person***, D2005-0690 (WIPO August 15, 2005) ("The Parties agree that Complainant's policies do not authorize such use, but that is quite different than a stated prohibition. In the absence of a stated prohibition, it is again telling that Complainant reviewed and approved Respondent's advertising without objection. It is also significant that Complainant objected in 2004 to Respondent's use of testimonials on his website, but did not challenge the Domain Name until a year later.")

52 ***Igor Lognikov v. Web Ventures, Nerdec, Inc. and Charles Edmunds***, D2009-1684 (WIPO January 29, 2010) ("[respondent] bears the burden of proof that complainant consented to [the] activity.") See also ***Carlon Meter Co. v. Jerman***, D2002-0553 (WIPO July 30, 2002) (Respondent's right does not necessarily extend "to use the globally extensive domain name system by incorporating these trademarks in the Domain Names in a manner which links them to Respondent's web site.")

53 ***Red Bull GmbH***, supra.

54 Id.: Self-created difficulties are "a long way from the mischief which the UDRP was devised and adopted to address."

55 ***Verder B.V. v. Lou Mattaliano***, D2007-1687 (WIPO January 4, 2008), citing ***Celebrity Signatures International***, supra. For a variation on this theme see ***Britvic Soft Drinks Limited v. Chris Holland***, D2014-0211 (WIPO March 27, 2014) (Complainant encouraged Respondent to acquire domain names held by a third party, which it did, then initiated a complaint of abusive registration. Complaint denied).

56 ***Celebrity Signatures***, supra. The Panel pointed out that it recognized "the possibility that Respondent's current use after objection might be an infringement of Complainant's rights [under trademark law] and that Respondent may no longer be justified in believing its use is permitted

purposes longevity of use with knowledge while accepting benefits defeats a complainant's claim of abusive registration.[57]

The conjunctive rule for proving bad faith weighs heavily on trademark owners who enter into agreements without including provisions for conveying the domain name upon termination.[58] Where respondent registers a domain name with the express consent of complainant who later withdraws it,[59] or the contract is silent on conveyance of the domain name, continued use may be in bad faith but the claim fails because the registration was not abusive.[60] Complainant's burden is not satisfied by withdrawing permission prior to commencement of proceedings.

In ***Ivanko Barbell***[61] Complainant admitted it had authorized respondent to register <ivanko.com> to sell its goods but subsequently withdrew permission. Since the admission established respondent did not register the domain name in bad faith the complaint had to be dismissed for failure to prove its case. If respondent registered the domain name pursuant to a licensing agreement without complainant expressly reserving rights for its return upon expiration of the contract, respondent's continued use after termination of its business relationship is either arguably legitimate for the reason that the registration was in good faith (it could not arguably

---

after receiving Complainant's objections. Nevertheless, that possibility involves a dispute that is beyond the scope of this proceeding." See also ***Iberostar Hoteles Y Apartamentos, S.L. v. N/A, Yuri Smolyansky, Registrant Organization: N/A Registrant / Contact Privacy Inc.***, D2011-0952 (WIPO August 23, 2011) ("a decision which could have the effect of closing down or severely affecting the Respondent's business is better made by the judicial process.")

[57] ***Urbani Tartufi s.n.c. v. Urbani U.S.A.***, D2003-0090 (WIPO April 7, 2003) (<urbani.com>) (domain name registered "with the evident consent of Complainant at a time when Complainant and Respondent were in a business relationship.") The majority in ***A. Nattermann***, supra. points out in dictum that a "registrant who did not have any right or legitimate interest at the date of registration may subsequently acquire a right or legitimate interest, for example by using the disputed domain name in connection with a bona fide offering of goods. Equally a registrant who had a right or legitimate interest may lose it, for example if the trademark owner legitimately withdraws its consent or the registrant ceases to distribute the trademark owner's goods or uses the domain name to promote rival products."

[58] ***Green Tyre Company Plc. v. Shannon Group***, D2005-0877 (WIPO October 5, 2005) ("It is undisputed that the Complainant allowed the Respondent to register the Domain Name in order to promote the Complainant's products.") A different result may apply where complainant transfers its domain names to a service vendor to maintain its websites, which then refuses to return them. See ***Alaska Health Fair, Inc. v. Chris Jacobson***, FA1305001500868 (Forum June 24, 2013).

[59] ***A. Nattermann & Cie. GmbH and Sanofi aventis***, *supra*, D2010-0800 (WIPO August 31, 2010). Acquiring a right or legitimate interest is discussed further in "Rights or Legitimate Interests: Expressly, Impliedly, and Lawfully" (Sec. 5.01-C).

[60] ***Green Tyre Company***, supra.

[61] ***Ivanko Barbell Company v. Syclone Corporation c/o Adam Auerbach***, FA0805001191122 (Forum July 22, 2008).

have been otherwise[62] or because authorization refutes registration in bad faith) or is beyond the scope of the Policy.[63]

Even where the contract provides for conveyance, circumstances may dictate denial of the complaint. In one case, the Panel found that transfer would be economically harmful to a respondent who had registered the domain name with consent.[64] The Panelist in the cited case noted that respondent "is merely unwinding the detail that comes from having stock already acquired that it must dispose of. . .. [It] is not claiming a legitimate interest that comes from a right to resell Complainant's goods, *but a legitimate interest in maintaining its reputation and avoiding disruption*" (emphasis added).[65]

5.01-C.2 Non-Authorized But Lawful Use of Trademarks 5.01-C.2

5.01-C.2.a *Nominative Fair Use As Applied* *5.01-C.2.a*

Express or implied consent to use an owner's trademark presupposes a business relationship. However, parties may also establish legitimate interests in domain names that incorporate trademarks without consent. It was early pointed out[66] that nominative use of trademarks is an established principle of trademark law.[67] The

---

[62] ***The Prudential Insurance Company of America v. Sheri Jones***, FA0510000584625 (Forum December 19, 2005) (<prudentialmontana>); ***Miss Universe L.P., LLLP v. A Visual Group***, D2005-0738 (WIPO August 29, 2005).

[63] ***Urbani Tartufi s.n.c. v. Urbani U.S.A.***, D2003-0090 (WIPO April 7, 2003) (<urbani.com>); ***Greyson International, Inc. v. William Loncar***, D2003-0805 (WIPO, December 3, 2003); ***Danshar (1963) Ltd. v. Joey Gilbert/ Daisy Li***, D2011-2304 (WIPO March 11, 2012) (Complainant acquired the business for which Respondent without formal contract was an authorized distributor).

The Panel in ***Greyson International*** discerned another view (which it criticized) that would hold an authorized registration in bad faith on the fiction that had the later circumstances been contemplated by the parties at the time of the registration it would have been bad faith. The logic of this view is undercut by too many subjunctives. Two scenarios have been considered: "Respondent had an ulterior motive from the beginning in registering the domain names," ***Omnigraphics Capital (Pty) Ltd v. Fleximount, Guy Langevin***, D2004-0471 (WIPO August 17, 2004); and failure to transfer domain name breaches "the first condition [of the contract]," ***Exel Oyj v. KH Trading, Inc.***, D2004-0433 (WIPO August 9, 2004), even if it "appeared to have been a bona fide registration," ***R&M Italia***, supra. These views are filially related to another view discussed in "Justifying Forfeiture Despite Good Faith Registration" (Sec. 4.03-A.4.b). None of these views has gained traction.

[64] ***International E-Z UP, Inc. v. PNH Enterprises, Inc.***, FA0609000808341 (Forum November 15, 2006) ("Respondent is not claiming a legitimate interest that comes from a right to resell Complainant's goods, but a legitimate interest in maintaining its reputation and avoiding disruption.")

[65] The same Panel acknowledged: "Clearly this interest cannot last forever. . . . [But] [i]t seems contrary to common sense and all business practice to deny that these situations give rise to interests that are legitimate."

[66] ***Adaptive Molecular Technologies, Inc. v. Woodward***, D2000-0006 (February 28, 2000) (<militec.com>) ("While Respondent does not own MILITEC as a trademark, questions remain as to whether Complainant legally acquiesced in Respondent's registration and use of the domain, at least initially,

principle has been adopted by UDRP Panels under two theories: first, by associating it with "nominative fair use" as developed by case law in U.S. trademark cases; and second, creating an indigenous principle developed in UDRP cases, discussed below in "The Oki Data Test," where it appears as a safe harbor defense. Whichever theory is applied, a respondent's choice of a domain name incorporating a trademark for the purpose of identifying its business or the services it is offering to perform rather than competing with the owner does not require the owner's consent. The use is fair even though commercial.[68] The reverse would be true if the use of the words were

---

or whether Respondent's use is a nominative fair use. Acquiescence and fair use are principles of trademark law, each requiring full analysis of the underlying facts. These are issues for the courts.")

[67] ***Minnesota Mining and Manufacturing Company v. Mark Overbey***, D2001-0727 (WIPO October 15, 2001), citing *New Kids on the Block v. News Am. Publ'g, Inc.*, 971 F.2d 302, 308 (9th Cir. 1991). Nominative fair use has continuing validity in both UDRP proceedings and civil court actions. See *Playboy Enters. v. Welles*, 279 F.3d 796 (9th Cir. 2002); *Horphag Research v. Mario Pellegrini*, 328 F. 3d 1108 (9th Cir. 2003); *Century 21 Real Estate v. Lendingtree*, 425 F.3d 211 (3rd Cir., 2005); *Toyota Motor Sales USA Inc. v. Tabari*, 610 F.3d 1171(9th Cir. 2010); and *Int'l Info. Sys. Sec. Certification Consortium, Inc. v. Sec. Univ., LLC*, 823 F.3d 153 (2nd Cir. 2016).

The Third Circuit held that "we have today adopted a test for nominative fair use in which a court will pose three questions: (1) Is the use of the plaintiff's mark necessary to describe both plaintiff's product or service and defendant's product or service? (2) Is only so much of the plaintiff's mark used as is necessary to describe plaintiff's products or services? (3) Does the defendant's conduct or language reflect the true and accurate relationship between plaintiff's and defendant's products or services? If each of these questions can be answered in the affirmative, the use will be considered a fair one, regardless of whether likelihood of confusion exists."

In *Toyota*, the Court noted that the "nominative fair use doctrine allows such truthful use of a mark, even if the speaker fails to expressly disavow association with the trademark holder, so long as it's unlikely to cause confusion as to sponsorship or endorsement.... It is the wholesale prohibition of nominative use in domain names that would be unfair. It would be unfair to merchants seeking to communicate the nature of the service or product offered at their sites. And it would be unfair to consumers, who would be deprived of an increasingly important means of receiving such information."

In *Int'l Info*, the Court held that the "district court erred in applying solely the Ninth Circuit's test for nominative fair use, instead of applying our Court's Polaroid test." Further "[t]o this point, this Court has not adopted either the Ninth Circuit or the Third Circuit's rule on nominative fair use . . . [although] we 'have recognized that a defendant may lawfully use a plaintiff's trademark where doing so is necessary to describe the plaintiff's product and does not imply a false affiliation or endorsement by the plaintiff of the defendant,'" citing *Tiffany (NJ) Inc. v. eBay Inc.*, 600 F.3d 93, 102 (2d Cir. 2010).

The Third Circuit expressly labels nominative use an affirmative defense (defendant's burden), which the Second and Ninth Circuits reject in favor of placing the burden on plaintiff to prove likelihood of confusion. The Third Circuit fits more easily with the UDRP precisely because it focuses on respondents demonstrating rights or legitimate interests in the domain names, which means accused infringers can prevail without ever having to respond to the allegations that they registered and are using the domain names in bad faith. The Second and Ninth circuits would seem not to fit the UDRP currency because if literally followed Panels would have to assess the bad faith elements under paragraph 4(a)(iii) of the Policy. However, Panels only proceed to assessing likelihood of confusion

shown to be functioning as a trademark to identify the source of goods or services.[69] However, if the use is fair the Panel has completed its assessment in respondent's favor; in which event, the Panel does not proceed to examine the facts further for infringement under paragraph 4(b)(iv) of the Policy.[70]

UDRP Panels have essentially applied the legal standards developed by judges in U.S. federal courts,[71] which are: (1) the goods or services associated with the name must not be readily identifiable without use of the mark; (2) only so much of the mark may be used as is reasonably necessary to identify the goods or services; and (3) the user must do nothing that would, in conjunction with the mark, suggest sponsorship or endorsement by the trademark owner. Respondents succeed where their choices of domain name truthfully convey the name's promise. Offerings of goods or services properly identified and not competitive in the form of <trade-mark+-modifier> or <modifier+trademark> support a finding of registration in good faith.[72]

---

if complainants survive paragraph 4(a)(ii) which they will not do if respondents affirmatively prove nominative use.

[68] Paragraph 4(c)(iii) is expressed in an either/or construction: either "noncommercial" or "fair use." The full provision reads: "you are making a legitimate noncommercial or fair use of the domain name, without intent for commercial gain to misleadingly divert consumers or to tarnish the trade-mark or service mark at issue."

[69] ***Pepperdine University v. BDC Partners, Inc.***, D2006-1003 (WIPO September 25, 2006) (<pepperdineuniversitywaves.com> and <pepperdineuniversitywaves.net>. "Under a statutory analysis, the Panel finds that Respondent has fundamental problems trying to make a fair use defense. The Domain Names, which include only established trade and service marks belonging to Complainant, are not used only to describe Respondent's services. In fact, they do not appear to be used as descriptors at all. Rather, those Domain Names tend to look and function more like trademarks, as identifiers of the source or sponsorship of the websites to which they lead."

[70] It trumps paragraph 4(b)(iv), which reads: "by using the domain name, you have intentionally attempted to attract, for commercial gain, Internet users to your web site or other on line location, by creating a likelihood of confusion with complainant's mark as to the source, sponsorship, affiliation, or endorsement of your web site or location or of a product or service on your web site or location." See *Xtralis Technologies Limited v. Secusense BV*, DNL2014-0055 (WIPO February 26, 2015) ("The fact that the Complainant in its email of July 12, 2013 has stated that the use of the Trademark is not permitted without the express written consent of the Complainant, does not alter this. If the Respondent has a legitimate right or interest in the Domain Name, the Complainant cannot prohibit the use thereof under the Regulations.")

[71] For other UDRP decisions on this issue see WIPO Overview 3.0, Paragraph 2.8, "How do panels assess claims of nominative (fair) use by resellers or distributors?" The issue is whether resellers/distributors of trademarked goods or services can have rights or legitimate interests in a domain name which contains such trademark. The answer is that they can.

[72] ***Giddings & Lewis LLC v. McKean***, D2000-1150 (WIPO March 14, 2001) ("Complainant forthrightly acknowledges, 'used Fadal machine tools' or the colloquial equivalent, 'used Fadals,' accurately describe the line of products, which the Respondent has long been selling in a legitimate manner. Therefore, combining 'used' and 'Fadal' in a domain name is a fair, nominative use to describe the products that the registrant offers in its 'brick and mortar' and e commerce business ventures.")

While a line has been drawn for attorneys directing Internet users to their websites for the purpose of promoting lawsuits against complainants[73] or offering their services,[74] there are permissible circumstances. The Panel in ***CPA Global Limited*** agreed with Respondent that "Internet users in the United States are accustomed to seeing terms such as 'litigation' used in domain names in connection with business names or trademarks to provide information about class action lawsuits." This view has also been applied to attorney information about drug consequences.[75] For example, in ***Pfizer***,[76] Respondent, an attorney with a tort practice focusing on pharmaceuticals, registered <lipitorinfo.com> for the "purpose of providing information to the public concerning legal rights and treatment options should it ultimately be learned that 'lipitor' causes injuries to the consumer." In denying the complaint the ***Pfizer*** Panel noted that although incorporation of the trademark in the domain

---

See also ***Lutron Electronics Co., Inc. v. Welch Services Group Limited***, FA1103001377398 (Forum May 2, 2011) (<lutroninstaller.com>. "Respondent has a legitimate interest in the <lutroninstaller.com> domain name because it has been using the disputed domain name since 2007 to maintain a website offering a legitimate business fitting and installing Complainant's genuine products obtained through the commercial channels of Complainant"); ***Oxyhealth, LLC. v. Benjamin Galbraith***, FA1801001767229 (Forum February 22, 2018) (<oxyhealthused.com>. Complaint denied because Respondent uses the domain name in a strictly descriptive and informative manner, namely selling used equipment manufactured by Complainant).

73 Decisions are not consistent on the question of <trademark+lawsuit[litigation].com>. Complaint granted: ***Am. Int'l Group, Inc. v. Speyer***, FA 422815 (Forum April 7, 2005) (<aiglawsuit. com> and <aigfraud.com>); ***American International Group, Inc. v. Bruce Levin***, FA 591254 (Forum December 21, 2005); ***Ginn Real Estate Company LLC v. Hilton Wiener***, FA0806001211342 (Forum August 20, 2008) (<ginnlawsuit.com>). Complaint denied: ***KBR, Inc. v. Jeffrey L. Raizner / Jeffrey Raizner***, FA1110001413439 (Forum December 27, 2011) (<kbrlitigation.com>. "Nominative use is present where the respondent needs to use the mark to describe its goods or services, uses no more of the mark than necessary, and does not falsely suggest sponsorship or endorsement by the mark owner."); ***Cedars Sinai Medical Center v. Initiative Legal Group***, FA1207001455024 (Forum September 10, 2012) (<cedarssinaiunpaidwages.com>).

74 Although *Cedars-Sinai* refers to attorneys either marketing themselves (which is infringing) or providing information (which is not infringing) the proscription also extends to other professionals. See for example, ***Accuray Incorporated v. Sanjay Mongia / Nuero Network***, FA140900 1582340 (Forum November 3, 2014) (Respondent a surgeon alleged he had a right because "he is a 'Cyberknife Associate Consultant' and makes bona fide use of Complainant's equipment in carrying out [medical] operations." However, this does not support nominative fair use: "Respondent's website is clearly a marketing tool to promote his surgery services in addition to providing basic information about radio surgery technology to Internet users."

75 ***CPA Global Limited v. Perfect Privacy, LLC / Kobre and Kim LLP***, D2017-1964 (WIPO December 26, 2017) (<cpaglobal-litigation.com>. "The Respondent is using the Disputed Domain Name to provide information to the public about a legitimate lawsuit against the Complainant which the Respondent is conducting in relation to the Complainant's alleged overcharging practices.")

76 ***Pfizer Inc. v. Van Robichaux***, D2003-0399 (WIPO July 16, 2003) (U.S. parties) (The same panelist also decided ***Preston Gates and Ellis*** and ***Starwood Hotels***, supra.)

name raises an issue of initial interest confusion, that fact alone "cannot act as a *per se* preclusion" of nominative fair use. This result despite "commercial gain" because the purpose of the registration is not "to misleadingly divert consumers or to tarnish the trademark or service mark at issue."[77]

The Panel in another pharmaceutical dispute concluded that the plain meaning of adding "side effects" to the trademark "is much closer to 'the [product] may be dangerous or have risks associated with it' than to the kind of message that would be offered by its manufacturer."[78] It has been suggested that "[a] different result might obtain . . . in case[s] involving an industry that is heavily regulated, such as pharmaceutical products, or one involving a distributor whose contract has been terminated by its manufacturer prior to registration of the disputed domain name."[79] However, "fair use" trumps complainants even in heavily regulated industries, as is evident from decisions involving law firm use of pharmaceutical trademarks.[80]

5.01-C.2.b *The **Oki Data** Test* 5.01-C.2.b

Acceptance of a nominative fair use equivalent principle is traceable to a 2001 dispute involving a domain name that incorporated complainant's trademark plus a noun <trademark+parts>.[81] The Panel in ***Oki Data*** makes no reference to nominative fair use, but the "standards are functionally equivalent, and . . . shaped by the same underlying policy concerns."[82] The decision harmonizes a number of earlier

---

[77] The sole Panel in ***Pfizer Inc. v. Van Robichaux***, supra. dissented in ***Actelion Pharmaceuticals, Ltd v. Hackard & Holt***, D2007-0838 (WIPO September 7, 2007) (<tracleerinfo.com>), objecting to an order of transfer because it is preferable "to err on the side of fair use" where "the public has a compelling interest in information concerning products that have a substantial impact on public health, and the public has a strong interest in legal representation with respect to those products."

[78] ***N.V. Organon and Schering Plough Corporation v. Fields Law Firm and Stephen Fields***, FA0904001259266 (Forum June 16, 2009) (<nuvaringsideeffects.com>).

[79] ***General Motors LLC v. Flashcraft, Inc DBA Cad Company***, D2011-2117 (WIPO January 30, 2012) (Complaint denied for <cadillacperformance.com>.)

[80] ***Pfizer Inc.***, *supra*; ***N.V. Organon and Schering Plough Corporation, supra***; ***Amylin Pharmaceuticals, Inc. v. Watts Guerra Craft LLP.***, D2012-0486 (WIPO April 29, 2012) (BYETTA and <byetta-cancer.com>). Opposite result in ***Actelion Pharmaceuticals, Ltd v. Hackard & Holt***, D2007-0838 (WIPO September 7, 2007) (<tracleerinfo.com>) (transfer with dissent, the dissent coming from the ***Pfizer*** panelist).

[81] ***Oki Data Americas, Inc. v. ASD, Inc***, D2001-0903 (WIPO November 6, 2001) (<okidataparts.com>). ***Oki Data*** created certainty where before there had been none. The earliest decision to examine the issue, ***Adaptive Molecular Technologies, Inc. v. Priscilla Woodward & Charles R. Thorton, d/b/a Machines & More***, D2000-0006 (WIPO February 28, 2000) mentioned the trademark principle of nominative fair use, but concluded that the "key questions in this dispute fall outside the scope of the Policy." Nominative fair use has been applied only in UDRP cases in which the parties are U.S. residents.

views in establishing an unauthorized reseller's right to incorporate a complainant's trademark in its domain name.[83]

Respondent demonstrates a legitimate interest under paragraph 4(c)(i) of the Policy under the following circumstances:

> (1) [It] must actually be offering the goods or services at issue;[84]
>
> (2) [It] must use the site to sell only the trademarked goods; otherwise, it could be using the trademark to bait Internet users and then switch them to other goods;[85]
>
> (3) [Its] website must accurately disclose the registrant's relationship with the trademark owner; it may not, for example, falsely suggest that it is the trademark owner, or that the website is the official site, if, in fact, it is only one of many sales agents;[86]
>
> (4) [It] must not try to corner the market in all domain names, thus depriving the owner of reflecting its own mark in a domain name.[87]

---

[82] ***YETI Coolers, LLC v. Ryley Lyon / Ditec Solutions LLC***, FA1605001675141 (Forum July 11, 2016) (<yeti handles.net>, <yetihandle.net>, <yeticuphandles.com> and <yeticuphandle.com>).

[83] See ***Franke Technology and Trademark Ltd v. hakan gUlsoy***, CAC 101464 (ADR.eu May 11, 2017) (<franke-servisi.com>. In dismissing the complaint, Panel refers to ***Bayerische Motorenwerke AG (BMW) and BMW Nederland BV v. Ronald Karel Deenik***, C-63/97 (European Court of Justice, 3 December 1998) and ***Oki Data*** for the proposition that "no trade mark owner (in the EU) . . . has the right to monopolise the servicing or repair or resale (or previously sold) of its products . . . [where another is using the mark to] promote valid and honest competition." The Court in Bayerische Motorenwerke held that "Articles 5 to 7 of the [Trademark] directive do not entitle the proprietor of a trade mark to prohibit a third party from using the mark for the purpose of informing the public that he carries out the repair and maintenance of goods covered by that trade mark and put on the market under that mark by the proprietor or with his consent, or that he has specialised or is a specialist in the sale or the repair and maintenance of such goods, unless the mark is used in a way that may create the impression that there is a commercial connection between the other undertaking and the trade mark proprietor, and in particular that the reseller's business is affiliated to the trade mark proprietor's distribution network or that there is a special relationship between the two undertakings."

[84] ***World Wrestling Federation Entertainment, Inc. v. Ringside Collectibles***, D2000-1306 (WIPO January 24, 2001).

[85] ***Nikon, Inc. v. Technilab***, D2000-1774 (WIPO February 26, 2001); ***Kanao v. J.W. Roberts Co.***, CPR 0109 (July 25, 2001). In ***Experian Info. Solutions Inc. v Credit Research Inc.***, D2002-0095 (WIPO May 7, 2002) the Panel concluded that respondent failed at least the second of the four tests: "It is using domain names incorporating Complainant's marks in order to also sell the products of Complainant's competitors. Such a use cannot be considered bona fide, even if the 'triple merge' credit reports sold by Respondent also incorporate Complainant's products to some degree."

[86] ***Houghton Mifflin Co. v. The Weatherman, Inc.***, D2001-0211 (WIPO April 17, 2001); ***R.T. Quaife Engineering v. Luton***, D2000-1201 (WIPO November 14, 2000); ***Easy Heat, Inc. v. Shelter Prods.***, D2001-0344 (WIPO June 14, 2001).

[87] ***Magnum Piering, Inc. v. Mudjackers***, D2000-1525 (WIPO January 29, 2001).

The Panel held that a party not otherwise authorized to use a trademark may have a legitimate interest if its domain name is descriptive of respondent's business.[88] To come within this safe harbor by making a *bona fide* offering of goods or services an unauthorized reseller must satisfy each element of the test.[89] The formulation has been generally adopted and is the basis for the "consensus view."[90]

The WIPO Overview cites a minority view that rejects any use of a domain name that incorporates a trademark, but this view has lost vitality. It rests on the proposition that a "right to resell or distribute that trademark holder's products does not create a right to use a domain name that is identical, confusingly similar, or otherwise wholly incorporates the relevant trademark."[91] The rationale is that "even where a disputed domain name is used solely to promote and offer for sale genuine goods and services, the registrant is commercially benefitted through the use of the complainant mark's fame and name recognition, and the initial interest confusion created in the respondent's website."[92] Panels said to hold the minority view mostly reject respondent's legitimate interest in the domain name and are more likely to find abusive registration not because of the incorporated trademark but because respondents fail entirely the four-part test.

Under the *Oki Data* formulation, a respondent may permissibly register and use a domain name that is confusingly similar to complainant's trademark if it is "descriptive of the business conducted under the domain name."[93] Although no

---

88 The majority view favors respondent even where the domain name is identical to the trademark. See ***Marathon Enterprises, Inc. v. William I Bauer***, D2007-1036 (WIPO September 5, 2007) (<sabrett.net>. Authorized reseller/distributor. "Complainant remains at liberty to negotiate contractual restrictions with its distributors that would preclude resellers like Respondent from registering and using domain names that incorporate Complainant's SABRETT mark.")

89 The difference between cases in which respondents are arguing a right or legitimate interest based on acquiescence and decisions resting on the ***Oki Data*** principles is that in the former (although it may appear that respondents prevail) in actual fact complainants lose in the administrative proceeding because their conduct raises a triable issue of fact outside the scope of the Policy. In the latter cases respondents prevail because they are making a bona fide offer of goods or services.

90 WIPO Overview 3.0, Paragraph 2.8. The Overview (quoting ***Oki Data***) requires that "Respondent's website must accurately *and prominently* disclose[] the registrant's relationship with the trademark holder." Overview 2.0 classified this as the "consensus view." There are different outcomes where the encroachment on the trademark exceeds any right or legitimate interest.

91 Id.

92 ***Marathon Enterprises***, supra.

93 ***Volvo Trademark Holding AB v. Auto Shivuk***, D2005-0447 (WIPO June 8, 2005) [<volvo-auto-body-parts-online.com>] (Respondent defaulted; Relief denied), citing ***Oki Data***, supra. [<okidataparts.com>]. Relief was also denied in ***Volvo Trademark Holding AB v. Volvospares / Keith White***, D2008-1860 (WIPO February 10, 2009) involving <volvospares.com>, but in a subsequent ACPA action the court found in favor of the plaintiff and directed transfer of the disputed domain name, *Volvo Trademark Holding AB v. Volvospares.com*, 1:09 cv 01247 (E.D. Va. April 1, 2010).

express consent is required it presupposes the parties are engaged in entirely different enterprises and not competitors in the same market or targeting the same consumers[94] or taking advantage of the trademark.[95] The *Oki Data* test has been applied to a wide range of business enterprises not specifically limited to reselling and distributing goods (authorized or unauthorized) but extends to offering after-market parts and performing services and tests in connection with goods produced by trademark owners.

In ***Dr. Ing***[96] the Panel held that "the registration of [<porschebuy.com> as well as two other similar domain names for other makes of automobiles] . . . for which the domain names are descriptive, cannot be qualified per se as an abusive pattern of conduct." It concluded:

> Under the present facts if the Panel were to find in favour of complainant, the Panel can conceive of no case in which a party interested in the sale of certain used goods could ever register a domain name descriptive of, at least to a certain reasonable extent, that business.

Nominal use is sufficient to trump complainant in a UDRP proceeding. Claims of consumer deception properly belong in a court of law.[97]

The criterion is satisfied by use that distinguishes the goods or services offered on the domain name website from those of the trademark owner. A closer issue is presented in cases in which respondents offer testing services for a variety of brands, including complainants' goods, "but not the good themselves."[98] In the cited case the Panel held that while "application of [the *Oki Data* test] to this case is finely balanced" it is not fatal to respondent because "the Panel considers it likely that Internet users who find themselves directed to the Respondent's site may well be

---

[94] In ***Cisco Technology, Inc. v. Nicholas Strecha, E Careers LTD***, D2010-0391 (WIPO May 7, 2010) (<ciscouk.com>. "Respondent is not a reseller, and instead offers competing services. These are pivotal facts that defeat Respondent's claim to a legitimate interest and render the authority cited by Respondent inapplicable").

[95] ***Geoffrey, LLC v. Toys R.Russ and Days of '49***, D2011-0830 (WIPO August 8, 2011); ***as earDiamond Consortium, LLC d/b/a Diamond Doctor v. Brian Cummings***, FA160500 1675435 (Forum June 24, 2016); ***Zippo Manufacturing Company v. Perfect Privacy, LLC / Fred Martin***, D2015-0964 (WIPO August 12, 2015).

[96] ***Dr. Ing. h.c.F. Porsche AG v. Del Fabbro Laurent***, D2004-0481 (WIPO August 20, 2004) (<porschebuy.com>); ***General Motors LLC v. Flashcraft, Inc DBA Cad Company***, D2011-2117 (WIPO January 30, 2012) (<cadillacperformance.com>; "UDRP panels have consistently followed the Oki Data approach when dealing with unauthorized resellers in the automotive field.")

[97] ***Marvel Manufacturing Company Inc. v. Koba Internet Sales, LP*** D2008-0265 (WIPO May 5, 2008) (<marvelsawparts.com>) (Complaint denied). In a subsequently commenced ACPA action, Complainant alleged Respondent was offering inferior non-Marvel replacement parts (S.D. Texas, Houston Div. 2012).

[98] ***Alstom v. Industrial Tests, Inc.***, D2009-1702 (WIPO February 6, 2010) (Industrial testing. Split decision: allowed <alstomservice.com> but transferred <alstombreaker.com> and 10 others).

uninterested in the servicing of any brand of equipment except that which they already own. . . Indeed, the history and nature of the Respondent's business is made clear on the site." The test applies to a variety of goods and has also been extended to include consulting and other services.[99]

Respondent's defense "allows the use of a mark when it is reasonably necessary to facilitate free expression and the dissemination of information,"[100] but "the right . . . is not an unlimited one."[101] Any deviation from the ***Oki Data*** test has generally met with disapproval.[102] "The right to resell products does not create the right to use a mark more extensively than required to advertise and sell the product."[103] The use must be limited to that which is "reasonably necessary to identify Complainant's product" and no more.[104] The Panel in the cited case held that "Respondent's use of Complainant's trademark [ALLEN EDMONDS] as a domain name [<allenedmondsshoes.com>] is not reasonably necessary to allow resale of Complainant's products by Respondent. On the contrary, Respondent could use any domain name at all and still sell Complainant's products on its website." This suggests that adding generic terms to a trademark that connect the trademark to complainant's goods—"shoes" being what the complainant is known for in the marketplace—is an abusive registration.

---

99 Software consulting services, ***SAP AG v. UniSAP, Inc.***, D2009-0297 (WIPO April 28, 2009) (<unisap.com>); ***SAP AG v. SAP User List***, D2009-1285 (WIPO November 8, 2009) (<sapuserlist.com>). Vendor consulting services, ***Wal Mart Stores, Inc. v. Sergio Cabrera***, FA1008001344053 (Forum November 8, 2010) (<walmartvendor.com>). Packaged tours, ***National Association for Stock Car Auto Racing, Inc. v. Racing Connection / The Racin' Connection, Inc.***, D2007-1524 (WIPO January 28, 2008)(<nascartours.com>).

100 ***Preston Gates & Ellis, LLP v. defaultdata.com and Brian Wick***, D2001-1381 (February 13, 2002) (U.S. parties).

101 ***Starwood Hotels & Resorts Worldwide Inc. v. Franck Dossa***, D2008-1812 (WIPO January 27, 2009).

102 Compare two Caterpillar cases that illustrate this point, respectively ***Caterpillar Inc. v. Off Road Equipment Parts***, FA0008000095497 (Forum October 10, 2000) (<catparts.com>) in which the complaint was dismissed, and ***Caterpillar Inc. v. Ron Feimer***, FA0706001008998 (Forum July 28, 2007) (<aftermarketcat.com>), in which the disputed domain name was transferred because the record disclosed that respondent advertised third party parts competing with Caterpillar.

103 ***Motorola Inc. v. NewGate Internet, Inc.***, D2000-0079 (WIPO April 20, 2000) (<talkabout.com>).

104 ***Allen-Edmonds Shoe Corporation v. Takin' Care of Business***, D2002-0799 (WIPO October 10, 2002) (U.S. parties).

5.01-D 5.01-D Attracting Internet Traffic

5.01-D.1 5.01-D.1 Dictionary Words and Descriptive Phrases

5.01-D.1.a 5.01-D.1.a *Trademarks Not Equally Protected*

As noted earlier trademarks are protected on a sliding scale.[105] All words that are not coined start off as generic terms. Dictionary words, alone or combined, modified by other parts of speech, descriptive phrases, and strings of letters or numbers that have the capability of functioning as marks also retain in parallel their common meanings. Except where words alone or combined have become so indelibly associated with a single source, are they taken out of the public domain; but where they can be used by others without offending third party rights, they are free to the first to register them as domain names. These same terms, however, that are at once common and distictive, may qualify if they are shown to have acquired distinctiveness to a point that denial of bad faith can be seen as willful blindness to complainant's rights.[106]

As a rule of thumb, generic terms are not registrable as marks until they perceivably cross a threshold to descriptive and higher classifications. Even then, if terms are capable of multiple associations and there is no evidence of trespassing on complainant's rights, registrations of domain name identical or confusingly similar to marks will not violate the UDRP.[107] But where website content or other proof

---

[105] Trademarks are "typically classified into one of five categories, which are (in order from weakest to strongest): generic, descriptive, suggestive, arbitrary, or fanciful," ***Buy Owner International, Inc. v. John Frank***, D2002-0407 (WIPO July 23, 2002). In determining the strength of a mark, U.S. courts focus on two factors: (1) the mark's inherent distinctiveness and (2) its acquired distinctiveness in the marketplace. *Time, Inc. v. Petersen Publ'g Co.*, 173 F.3d 113, 118 (2d Cir. 1999).

A trademark on the lower end of the scale can be accepted for registration on the Principal Register under Section 2(f) of the Lanham Act (15 U.SC. 1052(f)), which provides that a mark becomes distinctive upon "proof of substantially exclusive and continuous use thereof as a mark by the applicant in commerce for the five years before the date on which the claim of distinctiveness is made."

[106] In a small number of cases involving weak marks in which mark owners prevailed in the UDRP, respondent challenges in federal court under the ACPA have restored the domain names, either by stipulation (with attorney's fees and damages) or by judgment (also with attorney's fees and damages). See ***Autobuses de Oriente ADO, S.A. de C.V. v. Private Registration / Francois Carrillo***, D2017-1661 (WIPO February 1, 2018) (<ado.com>) in which a three-member Panel applied questionable theories of liability such as the Respondent's position as a professional domainer, the amount demanded for the domain name, or willful blindness unsupported by the facts. Settled on the Record. Other cases cited in Appendix B (Settlements). Where dictionary-word and short-letter strings of domain names have been lawfully forfeited (<indeed.one> and <hike.app> are examples) it is generally for abusive conduct affirmatively established, such as using domain names maliciously, as much against complainants as against consumers.

[107] ***Darryl Davis Seminars, Inc. v. Privacydotlink Customer 656889 / Domain Admin, Abstract Holdings International Ltd.***, D2018-2238 (WIPO January 21, 2019) (<poweragent.com>.

supports the specific association created by complaint's mark then the registration is infringing even if actual knowledge of complainant or the mark is denied.[108]

While dictionary words, descriptive phrases, and acronyms that qualify as marks are distinctive in a statutory sense, rights holders' ability to prevent others from using them for noninfringing purposes is limited. The more generic the choice of terms the greater their capacity for attracting multiple associations. It follows that multiplicity weakens the argument for infringement.[109] As marks ascend the classification scale multiplicity dissolves to a single association, the complainant's mark, thereby strengthening the argument for infringement.

Actionable claims for registering dictionary words alone (except where they have ascended the classification scale to the well-known and famous) demand a greater quantum of proof simply because marks and domain names can coexist without infringement where each uses the terms for different ends, but when combined with other words can become distinctive both colloquially and in a trademark sense—"by achieving a sufficient level of secondary meaning in the relevant community"[110]—hence more protectable ("steel" and "case" and "wonder" and "forest" are examples as long as the combination transcends what are generally regarded as

---

"Respondent has satisfied the Panel that it registered the disputed domain name for its inherent value as a domain name incorporating a common descriptive term, as part of its business as an investor in such domain names.

108 Paragraph 1.3 of WIPO Overview 3.0 states that "In cases involving unregistered or common law marks that are comprised solely of descriptive terms which are not inherently distinctive, there is a greater onus on the complainant to present evidence of acquired distinctiveness/secondary meaning." This also applies to foreign words with distinctive meanings in other languages. See ***Graftex Prodcom SRL and Graffitti - 94 R.B.I. Prodcom S.R.L. v. Piazza Affari srl, Michele Dinoia***, D2017-0148 (WIPO March 22, 2017) (<bigotti.com>. "Respondent is Italian; 'bigotti' ('bigot' in English) is a dictionary word.... It is readily apparent that a dictionary word in one language may function as a protectable trademark in another language, and examples of this are legion.") In *KP Permanent Make Up, Inc. v. Lasting Impression I, Inc.*, 543 U.S. 111, 122 (2004) the U.S. Supreme Court held that "If any confusion results, that is a risk the plaintiff accepted when it decided to identify its product with a mark that uses a well known descriptive phrase."

109 See *Entrepreneur Media, Inc. v. Smith*, 279 F.3d 1135, 1147 (9th Cir. 2002) ("Similarity of marks or lack thereof are context-specific concepts. In the Internet context, consumers are aware that domain names for different Web sites are quite often similar, because of the need for language economy, and that very small differences matter." The Court concludes with the following caution: "Although EMI has the exclusive right to use the trademark 'ENTREPRENEUR' to identify the products described in its registration, trademark law does not allow EMI to appropriate the word 'entrepreneur' for its exclusive use. The descriptive nature and common, necessary uses of the word 'entrepreneur' require that courts exercise caution in extending the scope of protection to which the mark is entitled.")

110 *Mil Mar Shoe v. Shonac*, 75 F. 3d 1153, 1161 and n.15 (7th Cir. 1996) ("[I]t is possible for two generic terms taken together to achieve trademark or service mark status by achieving a sufficient level of secondary meaning in the relevant community. However, the burden on the party making

common expressions such as "pet" and "warehouse," bright" and "sign," or (in the federal action referred to in the footnote) "warehouse" and "shoes.")

While applications for "intent to use" trademarks and trademarks on the Supplemental Register with no market history do not automatically confer rights under the UDRP, complainants with accrued rights are not foreclosed from establishing common law rights antedating registration of the domain names. If complainant claims an unregistered mark or one registered on the Supplemental Register, it will be expected to offer persuasive evidence of secondary meaning.[111] The reason for the heavier burden rests on the proposition that generic terms commonly employed and chosen as trademarks can have independent, non-infringing uses and multiple associations.[112]

Nothing stated above precludes the possibility of dictionary words (virgin, apple, easy, and target are examples) eclipsing their common meanings, but it also cannot exclude others from using the words for unrelated associations.[113] This follows because in choosing dictionary words[114] or descriptive phrases[115] complainants must accept the fact that the scope of protection of their marks is limited to the description within their Classes. If actionable at all claims succeed or fail on the factual circumstances of priority, relative locations of the parties, respondent's acquisition

---

a claim to distinctiveness or secondary meaning in such a case is high because of the disinclination of the courts to take words of ordinary meaning out of common usage.") UDRP examples include ***BrightSign LLC v. Administrator, Domain / Vertical Axis, Inc.***, FA1103001379395 (Forum May 4, 2011) (<brightsign.com>. "[T]he more descriptive a mark, the more difficult becomes Complainant's burden of proof to establish registration and use with Complainant's mark as a target.")

[111] The question is whether complainant's mark "had acquired secondary meaning [at the time the domain name was registered] sufficient for the public to recognize it as a symbol distinguishing complainant's goods and services from those of others," ***San Diego Hydroponics & Organics v. Innovative Growing Solutions, Inc.***, D2009-1545 (March 3, 2010).

[112] ***PetsMed Express Inc. v. JLB a/k/a Joseph Brinton***, D2009-0179 (WIPO April 6, 2009) ("The Policy was not intended to permit a party who elects to register or use a common or descriptive term as a trademark to bar others from using the common term in a domain name, unless it is clear that the use involved is seeking to capitalize on the goodwill created by the trademark owner.")

[113] Virgin Enterprises Limited v. Domain Administrator, D2013-1678 (WIPO December 2, 2013) (<virgincare.com>).

[114] Representative cases: ***Mills & Associates, LLC v. Center for Internal Change Inc.***, FA0903001251337 (Forum May 4, 2009) (<onlinediscprofile.com> and <onlinediscprofiles.com>); ***Quester Group, Inc. v. DI S.A.***, D2010-1950 (WIPO February 14, 2011) (ULTIMATE GUITAR and <ultimateguitars.com>) ("The descriptive use of common dictionary words to link to sites that deal in the described goods may not avoid capitalizing on a similar trade mark using the same words. However, that is an exposure that owners of descriptive marks must accept when they select their brands using common product names.")

[115] ***First American Funds, Inc. v. Ult.Search, Inc.***, D2000-1840 (WIPO April 20, 2001) (<firstamerican.com>); ***Combined Insurance Group Ltd v. Xedoc Holding SA c/o domain admin.***, FA0905001261545 (Forum June 26, 2009) (<cheapautoinsurance.com>).

history, the manner in which dictionary words and phrases are being used,[116] and other indicia that may establish an infringing purpose.[117] A complainant may argue that a registration infringes its mark because the domain name is identical or confusingly similar to it, but unless the mark is well-known and there is proof of targeting it has no remedy against others using the same terms for their own businesses[118] or for purposes unrelated to complainant's.[119]

While the law allows no single party to monopolize words common to all (as noted in the U.S. federal law decision in the *Entrepreneur* case cited in an earlier footnote),[120] a mark owner with priority over a domain name registrant is not without remedy against an infringer using protected combinations of common words for their trademark value.[121] This possible UDRP remedy comes with the proviso that while consumers in local or regional markets may recognize complainant's sign, consumers in other locations and national territories may not.[122] It is for this reason

---

[116] ***Easton Corp Pty Ltd v. Privacydotlink Customer 951873/DNS Admin, Best Web Limited***, D2016-1975 (WIPO November 12, 2016) (<hottie.com>) (These factors apply "unless the Panel were persuaded that the Respondent's principle reason for acquiring the DomainName was in fact to exploit the Complainant's trademark.")

[117] ***Amazon Technologies, Inc. v. Robert Nichols***, FA1609001693499 (Forum October 20, 2016) (<amazoncarsandtrucks.com> and <amazonvehicles.com>. Under the right circumstances, here the inclusion of a well-known, even famous mark, "Panels have considered exorbitant offers to sell disputed domain names as a further indication of a lack of a *bona fide* purpose.")

[118] ***ARN Industries, Inc. d/b/a Halco Lighting Technologies v. CFM Holdings Limited (on behalf of Just Raw Pte Ltd)***, D2011-1094 (WIPO September 6, 2011) (<cfm-proled.com>, where Complainant, a U.S. company, owns PROLED). Respondent (citizen of Singapore) alleged that it "adopt[ed] . . . the name . . . [because] the word 'proled' is used commonly and generally in the LED industry to mean LED products of a 'professional' standard.") A Google search produced total results of 1.2 million users of the term.

[119] ***Advanced Drivers Education Products & Training, Inc. v. MDNH, Inc.***, FA 567039 (Forum November 10, 2005) (Respondent proved that it had a right or legitimate interest in <teensmart.com> because it was not using it in the trademark sense, but as "a descriptor of the site's intended content or theme [i.e. <teen's mart> not TEEN SMART]." See also ***Novartis AG v. Name Administration Inc. (BVI)***, FA1403001548210 (Forum April 24, 2014) (<clearcare.com>. "Respondent's use of the domain name for purposes of an unrelated hyperlink directory cannot rightfully constitute [infringement].")

[120] ***Zero International Holding v. Beyonet Services.***, D2000-0161 (WIPO May 12, 2000) (<zero.com>. "Common words and descriptive terms are legitimately subject to registration as domain names on a 'first come, first served' basis.")

[121] ***Fifth Third Bancorp v. Statistical Research Consulting***, D2012-1801 (WIPO December 8, 2012) ("Curious" and "bank" as in <curiousbank.com>).

[122] In ***ecarecenter, O.D., P.A. v. Eye Care Associates, ODPA***, FA1107001398961 (Forum August 30, 2011) (Respondent added the plural "s" to the domain name, <eyecarecenters.com> and EYE CARE CENTER. Both parties are in the eye care business).

that geographical distances must be taken into account in weighing parties' rights to a domain name.

As trademarks descend on the scale of protectability owners have less cause for actionable complaint and are more likely to overreach their exclusive rights. If it were otherwise—if common words and descriptive phrases were taken out of the public domain—complainants would have the ability to lock up a community's cultural and linguistic heritage. Registering domain names composed from common stock is abusive only if complainants prove respondents had their trademarks in mind *in particular*.[123] Merely being identical or confusingly similar to a complainant's trademark is not such proof; nor is the burden satisfied by a *prima facie* showing that respondent lacks rights or legitimate interests in the domain name.

If the proof falls short of bad faith, the confusing similarity may be noted but is inconsequential. Terms once unique may "over time [have] acquired currency across a wide spectrum of business activity."[124] To take "qwest" as an example, in a proceeding by the owner of QWEST the Panel determined that the "mark [is] limited to its application to the telecommunications industry." The decision is further rationalized by a "routine search of the Internet [that] reveals . . . instances, of which the Panel takes the equivalent of judicial notice, ranging from a charter yacht to a hotel to a line of recreational vehicles."

Ordinarily, registration and use of dictionary words singly or combined to form descriptive phrases are available to the first to register, on the principle that no person can monopolize common words (or phonetic variations, as noted with "qwest") and ordinary phrases (as in "eye care centers" challenged by the owner of EYE CARE CENTER as noted in an earlier footnote).[125] Where respondent uses an allegedly infringing term fairly and in good faith to describe respondent's goods or services, there is no legal basis for ordering the domain name canceled or transferred.[126]

---

[123] ***OVB Vermögensberatung AG v. Michele Dinoia and SZK.com***, D2009-0307 (WIPO May 6, 2009) (<ovb.com>. Respondent used the domain name for "a portal site containing advertising links for knives and cutlery." The target was not complainant but a trademark owner in the cutlery business.)

[124] ***Qwest Commc'ns Int'l v. QC Publ'g Grp., Inc.***, FA 286032 (Forum July 23, 2004) (<qwestcorp.com>. "Respondent, incorporated in the state of Texas and based in Dallas, Texas, has been doing business as QuestCorp Publishing Group, Inc. since March of 2000. . . Respondent had as its sole motivation for registering the disputed domain name a legitimate interest in capturing otherwise lost business traffic caused by inadvertent misspellings of the company's name ('QuestCorp') among Internet users. Consistent with this motivation, Respondent has also registered the domain name <guestcorp.com>.")

[125] The WIPO Overview 3.0, Paragraph 2.10.1 lists as factors to be considered in determining a respondent's legitimate interest 1) status and fame of the mark, 2) whether respondent has registered other generic names, and 3) what the domain name is used for.

If not used to take advantage of another's rights, employing linguistic elements common to a community of speakers for commercial gain, even with knowledge of complainant's trademark, can be a legitimate enterprise.[127] Unless there is "intent to capitalize on complainant's trademark interest, complainant does not have an exclusive right over a domain name that is a common generic term."[128]

The underlying theory in these cases is that parties who employ generic terms as trademarks or service marks cannot use the UDRP to bar others from using them separately or in combination with other common words as long as a respondent is not targeting complainant or its mark.[129] A domain name composed of a geographic location combined with a descriptive word, <location+wedding.com>, cannot qualify as a trademark.[130] Combined words may qualify and complainants succeed in registering a mark but only if the combination is capable of distinctive associations that may be evidenced by context and use.

Trademark monopoly does not extend to preventing others from creating associations through words and phrases as their own signs to the consuming public. In the words of one Panel, "[i]t is precisely because generic words are incapable of distinguishing one provider from another that trademark protection is denied them."[131] However, registering a domain name in the belief that complainant's trademark is generic does not absolve respondent,[132] although it may be some evidence that respondent reasonably believed "that the use of the domain name was a fair use or otherwise lawful."[133]

---

126 Such a defense is consistent with U.S. trademark law. Lanham Act, §33(b), 15 U.S.C. §1115(b)(4) (1976).

127 ***McMullen Argus Publishing Inc. v. Moniker Privacy Services/Jay Bean, MDNH, Inc.***, D2007-0676 (WIPO July 24, 2007) (<europeancar.com>).

128 ***Ultrafem Inc. v. Royal***, FA 97682 (Forum Aug. 2, 2001) (<instead.com>); See ***CITGO Petroleum Corporation v. Matthew S. Tercsak***, D2003-0003 (WIPO February 28, 2003) (<mystic.com>; domain name is confusingly similar to Complainant's mark but Respondent operates a *bona fide* business from that address).

129 ***Asphalt Research Tech., Inc. v. Anything.com***, D2000-0967 (WIPO Oct. 2, 2000) (<ezstreet.com>, "Respondent has a legitimate interest to use a trademark or domain name in which many persons hold an exclusive right in relation to different goods and services providing the goods or services are sufficiently far apart from the goods and services of others so as to distinguish the goods or services of Respondent.")

130 ***Kennedy Enterprises, Inc. v. John Neetz, individually and trading as Bigtime Limited***, FA0906001266923 (Forum August 3, 2009).

131 ***Canned Foods, Inc. v. Ult. Search Inc.***, FA 96320 (Forum February 13, 2001) (<grocery outlet.com>).

132 ***Avaya Inc. v. Holdcom***, FA0806001210545 (Forum August 9, 2008).

133 15 U.S.C. §1125 (d)(1)(B)(ii), H.R. Conf. Rep. 106-412: "The bill is carefully and narrowly tailored, however, to extend only to cases where the plaintiff can demonstrate the defendant . . . *used*

5.01-D.1.b

5.01-D.1.b *Distinctive Value of Domain Names*

Common and easily memorable words, combinations, phrases, and random letters that could also be acronyms (discussed earlier in Sec. 4.01-C) are no less attractive to domain investors than to merchants, manufacturers, institutions, and industries. Their attractiveness rests on the potential of their having shifting associations depending on their purpose and use. Used suggestively or fancifully they function as indicators to distinguish one person's goods or services from others but their trademark value is ended when registrants use them in other suggivestive or semantic ways. The UDRP does not condemn and there is no legal basis for cancelling or transferring domain names composed of generic terms whose meanings are commonly understood absent a finding they have been registered purposely to capitalize on the goodwill association with the mark.[134]

However, the fact that a term is common is not a license to use it where it has become a distinctive identifier of another's goods or services.[135] While "a respondent may have a right to register and use a domain name to attract Internet traffic based on the appeal of a commonly-used descriptive phrase, even where the domain name is confusingly similar to the registered mark of complainant" it does not have the right to sit in complainant's space if Internet users are attracted to the website because of the value of the trademark.[136]

One Panel offered "apple" as an example.[137] Should the word "apple" be used in <apple.com> with respect to a website offering fruit, namely apples, the registrant may have a legitimate interest in the name. However, "given the reputation of [the

---

the offending domain name with bad-faith intent to profit from the goodwill of a mark belonging to someone else" (emphasis added).

134 ***Aurelon B.V. v. AbdulBasit Makrani***, D2017-1679 (WIPO October 30, 2017) (<printfactory.com>. "The PPC links on the website associated with the Disputed Domain Name appear to be genuinely related to the dictionary meaning of the words comprising the Disputed Domain Name.") ***CIA. Industrial H. Carlos Schneider v. WHOIS Privacy Service Pty Ltd. / Domain Admin, Ashantiplc Limited***, D2016-2167 (WIPO January 26, 2016) (<ciser.com>. Complainant had regional rights in South America and Mexico but its geographic expansion post-dated Respondent's acquisition of the disputed domain name); ***Dr. Muscle v. Michael Krell,*** FA1903001833036 (Forum April 19, 2019) (<drmuscle.com>. Respondent did not take "any any steps to meet his obligations under Paragraph 2" but neither did Complainant prove abusive registration).

135 ***Advance Magazine Publishers Inc. v. Vanilla Limited/ Domain Finance Ltd./ Minakumari Periasany***, D2004-1068 (WIPO April 18, 2005)("VOGUE," adding geographic qualifiers to form among others <newyorkvogue>); ***Staples, Inc., Staples The Office Superstore, Inc., Staples Contract & Commercial, Inc. v. Staple.com***, D2003-1028 (WIPO May 17, 2004) (STAPLE, omitting the plural but evidence of past relationship through an affiliate program).

136 ***Aspen Holdings Inc. v. Rick Natsch, Potrero Media Corporation***, D2009-0776, fn. 6. (WIPO August 20, 2009).

137 ***Nat'l Ass'n of Prof'l Baseball Leagues v. Zuccarini***, D2002-1011 (WIPO January 21, 2003).

'apple' mark] then the intentional registration and use of the misspelled word or words (for example <appple.com>) clearly manifests an intent to capitalize on the mark and constitutes bad faith under the Policy."[138] Such use has been found to yield an inference of actual knowledge that impugns respondent's good faith.

While potential use by many entities of common words and descriptive strings may be an argument in favor of a respondent's good faith the test is whether respondent targeted complainant's trademark in particular. That is determined inferentially either from the resolving website's content or the parties' geographic or product/service proximity. If links or content have no obvious connection to the semantic value of the domain name and the domain name is registered after the acquisition of the trademark the scale tips in complainant's favor,[139] but not otherwise.[140] Viewed in this light distinctiveness is a fluid concept solidified by reputation.

Panels have consistently rejected the view often expressed by respondents that common words are always fair game for domain names irrespective of their use as trademarks.[141] Whether a registration is legitimate ultimately depends on respondent's intent. Registration of domain names composed of common names and descriptive phrases which precedes a complainant's trademark acquisition is *ipso facto* lawful.[142] However, mark acquisition which predates domain name registration[143] puts in issue respondent's knowledge of complainant's trademark, its purpose for registering the domain name, and the use to which the domain name is put.

5.01-D.1.c *Common Words, Common Phrases* 5.01-D.1.c

Based on the principles discussed above, complainants with trademarks on the lower end of the classification scale are vulnerable to non-infringing use by others.[144] Trademarks composed of common words and descriptive phrases are protected against infringement but not against others using the same terms legitimately. Common words alone or in combination with other common words, acronyms,

---

[138] Id.

[139] Discussed further in "Tortious Conduct That Supports Bad Faith" (Sec. 6.01).

[140] ***British Sky Broadcasting Group Plc. and British Sky Broadcasting Limited v. Global Access***, D2009-0817 (WIPO August 26, 2009) (<skytravel.com>).

[141] ***eLegalsupply.com, LLC v. Azeras LLC***, FA1204001438796 (Forum May 22, 2012) ("had the Respondent established that it was selling or otherwise dealing in legal supplies, the Panel might have decided differently.")

[142] See Jurisprudential Overview 3.0, Paragraph 3.8.1.

[143] Postdated registrations also implicate successor holders of domain names. Discussed earlier in "Transfer/Subsequent Holders =New Registration" (Sec. 4.03-B.2).

[144] This can include trademarks that have lost their distinctiveness to genericide. See ***Shop Vac Corporation v. Md Oliul Alam / Quick Rank***, FA1611001701026 (Forum December 10, 2016) (SHOP VAC and <bestshopvac.net>) ("[I]t appears on the material before the Panel that the word

and descriptive phrases can acquire distinctiveness on proof of secondary meaning, but if these terms are also generic their distinctiveness is diluted, thus available for registration and use by others.

So, for example, common words used in their ordinary senses and "registered because of their attraction as dictionary words, and not for their value as trademarks" do not contravene the Policy.[145] This is similarly true for strings of letters that to mark owners may be acronyms but to investors are arbitrary letters. In many instances domain names are "so generic or descriptive that the objective bystander could not responsibly conclude that [they were] evoking the trademark."[146]

A domain name may be similar to a complainant's trademark, but if it is composed of common words or, as illustrated in the footnoted case, a fictional character,[147] or an acronym conceivably equally referable to many other businesses,[148] consumer recognition or association with any specific source is diluted at best[149] and nonexistent at worst (particularly where the parties are separated by geographic and

---

'vac' is commonly used in the industry as an abbreviation for 'vacuum' and that the expressions 'shop vac' and 'best shop vac' are in common use with respect to vacuum cleaners other than those of Complainant.") GOOGLE not genericized, *Elliott v. Google, Inc.*, 860 F. 3d 1151 (9th Cir.2017).

[145] ***The Landmark Group v. Digimedia L.P.***, FA 285459 (Forum August 6, 2004) (LANDMARKS and <landmarks.com>). As with random letters and acronymic trademarks there are two factors critical to the outcomes in these disputes, namely complainants' lack of any special identification with particular strings of random letters and words, and respondents' prior or contemporaneous rights to register letters and words common in the public domain. See Sec. 6.01.C.

[146] ***Skycam, Inc. v. Administrator, Domain / Vertical Axis, Inc.***, FA1102001372311 (Forum April 29, 2011) (<skycam.com>. The majority denied the complaint, with concurring and dissenting opinions). Cf., *Advertise.com, Inc. v. AOL Advertising, Inc.*, 616 F.3d 974 (9th Cir. 2010), citing *Filipino Yellow Page, Inc. v. Asian Journal Publications*, 198 F. 3d 1143, 1147 (9th Cir. 1999) applying the "familiar 'who-are-you / what-are-you' test . . . [T]he (generic) name . . . answers the question 'what are you?'"

[147] The trademark in ***Betty Bossi Verlag AG v. SinoSwiss Co., Ltd.***, D2010-2264 (WIPO February 22, 2011) was (as the Panel points out) "a fictional character—a cook—whose name was invented in the 1950s and first used in a cooking magazine in 1972." Further, "[t]he available evidence shows that the Respondent has been using the disputed domain name for 11 years in connection with its apparently legitimate business of offering career enhancement for women. It obtained registered trademarks in Thailand, the country where it is located." Swiss Complainant; Thai Respondent.

[148] In ***Electronic Arts Inc. v. Abstract Holdings International LTD / Sherene Blackett***, FA1111001415905 (Forum January 4, 2012), the Panel found that "[t]he domain name, **<ssx.com>**, is comprised of common or generic letters. Complainant clearly does not have an exclusive monopoly on the term." This is because the "number of other persons or entities holding identical if non-competing marks and the number of other users with rights in the name are clear evidence of the limited ownership claims of the Complainant."

[149] ***Canned Foods***, supra., for the phrase <groceryoutlet.com>, which is used by many businesses; also ***Park 'N Fly Service Corporation v. Elias Tesfa***, FA1202001427761 (Forum March 15, 2012) for the phrase <ezparkfly.com>.

cultural distances). In these instances, complainant must offer affirmative evidence of real substance to support taking the domain name away from the respondent.[150]

On one side of the divide are common words and descriptive phrases available on a first-come first-served basis. Use of foreign terms as trademarks even highly recognized by consumers or parties engaged in specialized fields in one national jurisdiction may be no more than generic or descriptive terms in the borrowing language.[151] The issue in these cases is not the validity of the trademark but respondent's knowledge and the manner in which it is using the domain name.[152] The burden on complainant increases in proportion to the distance and culture separating the parties. Conversely, less distance and shared culture increase the evidentiary pressure on respondent to explain its choice and justify the registration.[153]

To take an example: "prudential" is a dictionary word first, then a sign or symbol combining two different states of mind—that is, being "prudential" by acquiring insurance and having an insurance company that is prudential in its handling of its assets[154]—but no right is infringed by using the word denotatively to express the projected quality of the good.

Combinations of common words and phrases are closer to the divide. A finding of "genericness [and no knowledge of complainant or its trademark], if established, will defeat a claim of trademark rights, even in a mark which is the subject of an incontestable registration."[155] The Panel in ***Rollerblade*** found that

---

150 See for example, ***Tractor Supply Co. of Texas, LP, and Tractor Supply Company v. Above.com Domain Privacy / Transure Enterprise Ltd.*** D2011-0487 (WIPO May 16, 2011) and earlier ***Tractor Supply Company v. Forum LLC***, D2006-1320 (WIPO December 15, 2006). The combination of words "tractor" and "supply" and "company" can be used by others in the business of supplying tractors—that is, the string is not "distinctive when applied to the sale and supply of tractors"—but where the proof demonstrates respondent is not in that business and its website contains links to complainant's competitors then the registration is abusive. Where there is no such proof of bad faith use, the domain name must stay with the respondent. Illustrations include ***National Trust for Historic Preservation v. Barry Preston***, D2005-0424 (August 10, 2005) and ***McMullen Argus Publishing Inc. v. Moniker Privacy Services/Jay Bean, MDNH, Inc.***, D2007-0676 (WIPO July 24, 2007), which involved the phrases "historic hotels" and "European car."

151 ***Spielwarenmesse eG v. Name Administration Inc. (BVI)***, D2013-0744 (WIPO July 11, 2013) (<spielwarenmesse.com>. "[T]he German Federal Patent Court only granted protection to the mark SPIELWARENMESSE [toy fair in English] as it considered it as having acquired distinctiveness in Germany and only in relation to specialists in the field of trade and manufacture of toys.")

152 ***Pernod Ricard v. Tucows.com Co.***, D2008-0789 (WIPO August 21, 2008) (The "surname/domain name in question (Ricard) [is] a very famous trademark in France and abroad.")

153 Id. Respondent is a resident of the French-speaking part of Canada.

154 ***Prudential Insurance Co. of America v. Quick Net Communications***, FA 146242 (Forum March 27, 2003) (<prudentialmotors.com>).

155 ***Rollerblade, Inc. v. CBNO and Redican***, D2000-0427 (WIPO August 24, 2000) (ROLLER BLADE and <rollerblading.com>). Cf. ***Diet Center Worldwide, Inc. v. Jason Akatiff***, D2012-1609

> the evidence appears to support Respondent's claim that it is merely seeking to trade on the popularity of a term used generically by many people for a popular sport. . . [This] appears to be a case where the public created a generic term derived from Complainant's mark, and Respondent has used that term in a manner consistent with common public use.

In many instances the difference between good and bad faith depends on the reputation of the trademark at the time of registration of the domain name, the use to which the domain name is put, respondent's explanation for its choice, and the quality of its proof.[156] Even if trademarks are registered as with LANDMARKS or incontestable as with ROLLERBLADE owners have no superior rights to corresponding domain names where respondents' demonstrable purposes are to use the strings of letters or words for their semantic values.

If the range of goods or services described by an applicant and accepted by the trademark office were determinative in preventing others from using words in "common public use," a registration would have the effect of giving complainant control of the cultural vocabulary. Complainant in a clutch of cases[157] owned a registration for PRICELESS for the following services:

> Financial services, namely, providing credit card, debit card [charge card and stored value smart card services, prepaid telephone calling card services, cash disbursement,] and transaction authorization and settlement services.

It claimed that the geographic additions "Amsterdam" and "Istanbul" infringed its right. The Panel was not persuaded:

> Although hotel reservations, restaurant coupons, and tours may be among the millions of things that might be obtained through use of Complainant's trademarked products and services, the Panel finds that the Complaint in this proceeding has not established that the PRICELESS family of marks is associated in the trademark sense with "hotel reservations, restaurant coupons, and tours."

Complainant quickly plugged the loophole by obtaining a trademark for PRICELESS NEW YORK.

(WIPO October 5, 2012) (DIET CENTER and <dietcenters.com>), citing *Park N' Fly v. Dollar Park and Fly*, 469 U.S. 189 (1985) for the proposition that a mark that is incontestable may not be challenged on grounds that it is merely descriptive.

[156] The Panel in ***Diet Center Worldwide*** also points out that "the trademark DIET CENTER has been registered at the USPTO for more than 25 years. . . Respondent was required to overcome a presumption of validity and to prove genericness with substantial evidence. It provided little evidence to support its position." There is an undercurrent view that high-volume purchasers and users of domain names are more accountable for their choices. Discussed further in "Enhanced Investigative Responsibilities for High-Volume Registrants" (Sec. 6.03-B).

[157] ***Mastercard International Incorporated v. Wesley Wobles***, D2011-2311 (WIPO March 8, 2012) (<pricelessamsterdam.com>); ***Mastercard International Incorporated v. Education, Ersin Namli***, D2011-2312 (WIPO March 8, 2012) (<pricelessistanbul.com>); ***Mastercard International***

5.01-D.1.d *Combinations and Compounds*

5.01-D.1.d

Common words combined into phrases have the power to transcend their origins and convey distinctive associations. However, to assert that a combination of words is protected (complainant) or unprotected (respondent) is so "potentially significant" that the burden of proof "falls on the asserting party."[158] "First" and "quote" combined in <firstquote.org> is confusingly similar to complainant's trademark 1ST QUOTE. The argument that because "each individual word in the mark is unprotectable . . . therefore the overall mark is unprotectable is at odds with the anti-dissection principle of trademark law."[159]

Nevertheless, common words retain their meanings. "First" and "quote" combined form a common phrase. In the second ***Aspen Holdings*** case, "Respondent . . . gave well founded reasons why he was unaware of any known corporations operating under the brand name 'first quote' when acquiring the disputed domain name, and, moreover, brought evidence to the Panel's attention that numerous insurance companies are advertising under the term 'first quote.'" There must be some evidence demonstrating that the public associates the allegedly infringed mark exclusively with the complainant.

Mere belief[160] that a registered phrase—MAGIC ON HOLD, for example—can be registered as a domain name because of its alleged descriptiveness does not absolve a respondent where complainant uses it as a mark for its business.[161] "Party" and "maniacs" are both dictionary words but distinctive when combined into PARTY MANIACS. When registered by a competitor the domain name

---

Incorporated v. PlayRage, D2011-2309 and D2011-2310 (Consolidated WIPO March 30, 2012) (<pricelesslondon.com>, <pricelessparis.com>, <pricelessnewyork.com>, <pricelesslosangeles.com> and <pricelessmexico.com>).

[158] Complainants asserting letters are protected: ***Aspen Holdings Inc. v. Rick Natsch, Potrero Media Corporation***, D2009-0776 (WIPO August 20, 2009) (Footnote 6. 1ST QUOTE and <first quote.org> transferred). Compare: ***Aspen Holdings, Inc. v. Isaac Goldstein***, D2010-0576 (WIPO June 3, 2010) (the Panel denied the complaint on proof that respondent has rights or legitimate interests in the domain name (<firstquote.com>. "From the point of view of this Panel, however, the present Respondent (other than the respondent[s] in [other] such case[s]) gave well founded reasons why he was unaware of any known corporations operating under the brand name 'first quote' when acquiring the disputed domain name, and, moreover, brought evidence to the Panel's attention that numerous insurance companies are advertising under the term 'first quote.'")

Respondents claiming letters are unprotected: ***The Restored Church of God v. Alexa Properties***, LLC, D2013-0320 (WIPO March 21, 2013) (<rn.com>. Alleged common law right based on the title of its magazine, "The Real Truth Magazine.") (Complaint denied.)

[159] ***David Hall Rare Coins v. Tex. Int'l Prop. Assocs***, FA 915206 (Forum April 9, 2007).

[160] The ACPA uses a catchall category: "bad faith shall not be found in any case in which the court determines that the person believed and had reasonable grounds to believe that the use of the domain name was a fair use or otherwise lawful." 15 U.S.C. §1125 (d)(1)(B)(ii). The Panel in ***Avaya Inc. v. Holdcom***, FA0806001210545 (Forum August 9, 2008) concluded that respondent had no

was judged by the Panel to have been registered "with the intention of disrupting Complainant's business."[162] The burden for establishing exclusive rights in these cases is lighter when the mark in issue is arbitrary or fanciful, somewhat heavier if suggestive and significantly heavier for the generic or descriptive.[163] "As to both registration and use, the generic nature of the disputed domain name itself rebuts any allegation by Complainant that Respondent registered or used the disputed domain name in bad faith."[164] For a complainant to prevail, the evidence must clearly establish that the use involved is seeking to capitalize on its reputation and goodwill.[165]

The heavier burden is based on the principle that the "Policy was not intended to permit a party who elects to register as a trademark or service mark a common word to bar all others from using the common word in combination with other common words."[166] There is no basis in the Policy "for articulating a general principle that a respondent with apparently clean hands must conduct a trademark search before registering a domain name comprised of dictionary words, in order to avoid an inference of bad faith."[167] The onus is on complainant to prove an intentional act, which is typically done deductively by examining respondent's conduct and the contents of its website.[168]

A rule of thumb test in weighing good faith for common words or generic phrases is 1) a declaration by a person with personal knowledge that respondent was unaware of complainant's mark when it registered the domain name; 2) evidence

---

reasonable grounds to believe that the registered trademark was a generic phrase since it competed with complainant in the same market and registered <magiconhold.com>. In ***Banca Monte dei Paschi di Siena S.p.A v. Charles Kirkpatrick***, D2008-0260 (WIPO April 14, 2008) Respondent believed that in registering <mps.mobi> no one company could claim exclusive rights in MPS because it stood for so many things. From its own searches of the term "MPS," the Panel found the Respondent's view reasonable.

161 Id., ***Avaya.***

162 Infringement: ***Party Maniacs, Inc. v. Michael Kuklinski***, FA0904001258597 (Forum June 2, 2009).

163 FORM-MAIL in ***Matthew Wright, Matt's Script Archive, Inc. v. Klemen Stirn***, D2005-0036 (WIPO March 15, 2005); LAWFINDER in ***Lawfinders Associates, Inc. v. Ultimate Search***, D2004-0163 (WIPO May 28, 2004); and COLLEGE SOURCE in ***Career Guidance Foundation v. Ultimate Search***, D2003-0323 (WIPO July 21, 2003).

164 ***Vitello v. Castello***, FA 159460 (Forum July 1, 2003) (<caution.com>).

165 Lacks proof of infringement: ***British Sky Broadcasting Group Plc. and British Sky Broadcasting Limited v. GlobalAccess***, D2009-0817 (WIPO August 26, 2009) (<skytravel.com>); ***Match.com, LP v. Bill Zag and NWLAWS.ORG***, D2004-0230 (WIPO June 2, 2004) (<match.com>).

166 ***Match.com***, supra.

167 ***Nursefinders, Inc. v. Vertical Axis, Inc / NURSEFINDER.COM c/o Whois IDentity Shield***, D2007-0417 (WIPO July 5, 2007) (U.S. Complainant; Canadian Respondent). Respondent has contractual responsibilities, discussed earlier in "Registrant's Responsibility for Determining Whether Domain Name Infringes Third Party Rights" (Sec. 2.02).

of historical use of the term to describe goods or services offered by the respondent; and 3) respondent's present use of the disputed domain name in connection with goods or services of the kind to which the word or phrase descriptively refers.

5.01-D.1.e *Family of Marks*

5.01-D.1.e

Trademarks that share a common characteristic or dominant element can receive protection as one of a family of marks. A number of U.S. federal cases have explained that possessing several marks with a common suffix, prefix or syllable can give rise to a protected "family" of marks. The common element is the family "surname,"[169] which is indicative of a common origin of the goods.[170] The "Mc" of "McDonald's" has been found to be a common element,[171] as has the "R Us" mark.[172] However, as with trademarks generally, some are strong and others weak. The same rules apply to "surnames" as to any other choice. Common word trademarks owned by a major brand complainant are no more protected from others using identical or confusingly similar words in their ordinary senses than if they were owned by parties without market stature.[173] As complainant's choice of trademark descends the scale, the less protectable it becomes.[174]

An addition to a mark that is equally dominant, "mobile" for example, combined with "Mall," creates a new distinctive name <mobile-mall.com>. The trademark owner of PC MALL does not have a monopoly on the word "mall." In

---

168 "A panel must often infer the respondent's state of mind based on the totality of circumstances," ***Cupa Materiales S.A. v. Stonepanel.com c/o Whois Identity Shield/Vertical Axis, Inc.***, D2009-0216 (WIPO April 29, 2009).

169 "The classic example is Eastman Kodak Company's family of KODA marks including KODACOLOR and KODACHROME," *Spraying Systems Company v. Delavan, Incorporated*, 975 F.2d 387 (7th Cir. 1992). (AIRJET, FOAMJET, CONEJET and QUICKJET).

170 *Victoria's Secret Stores Brand Management, Inc. v. SHC*, 07 Civ. 580 (S.D.N.Y. 2009) (the unresolved question is whether SEXY functions as a "surname." The court in *Spraying Systems* noted that ("some authorities have . . . stated that descriptive terms cannot constitute the common element in a family of marks. . . . The problem is that application of the doctrine requires a showing that the family feature or 'surname' is distinctive enough to trigger recognition 'in and of itself'. . . . But the family feature here is descriptive [-JET] . . . .").

171 *J & J Snack Foods Corp. v. McDonald's Corp.*, 932 F.2d 1460, 1463 (Fed.Cir.1991), in which the court found McDonald's family of "Mc" marks infringed by a competitor's "McPretzel."

172 ***Geoffrey, LLC v. The R Us Group, Mohiuddin, Tops***, D2011-0612 (WIPO July 25, 2011) (<bestcreditcardsrus.info>, <carinsurancequoterus.info>, <cheaptermlifeinsuranceratesrus.info>, <childrensbedroomfurniturerus.com>, <dentalinsuranceplansrus.com>, <digitalproductsrus.com>, <healthinsurancerus.info>, <injuryattorneyrus.info>, <insurancerus.info>, <makingmoneyonlinerus.com>, and <wholelifeinsurancerus.info>).

173 Discussed earlier in "Common Words, Common Phrases" (Sec. 5.01-D.1.c).

174 ***PCI Mall, Inc. v. Pygmy Computer Systems, Inc***, D2004-0437 (WIPO August 25, 2004) (<mobile-mall.com>).

contrast, "Veterinary manual" added to MERCK does not create a new distinctive name because that phrase is associated with the trademark owner.[175] The more well-known the "surname" the less respondent's credibility in explaining its choice. A weak surname is not transformed by association with a complainant's strong trademark.[176] Protectability increases or decreases depending on whether the mark is generic or descriptive,[177] suggestive,[178] arbitrary,[179] or fanciful.[180]

5.01-D.2

5.01-D.2 Descriptive Terms and Expressions Common in Everyday Life or in Industry and the Professions

The right trademark law grants does not prohibit others from using terms "fairly and in good faith only to describe the goods or services of such party, or their geographic origin."[181] The United States Supreme Court has held that there is "no indication that the [Lanham Act] was meant to deprive commercial speakers of the ordinary utility of descriptive words."[182] These principles are equally true for the UDRP. Dictionary words, specialized terms, compounds, common expressions, descriptive phrases, and random letters favor the first to register them for their semantic values.

---

[175] ***Merck Sharp & Dohme Corp. v. Janice Liburd***, D2011-0278 (WIPO April 18, 2011) where MERCK is well-known. The added words are subordinate to the dominant element: <merckspeakersservices.com> and <mercksveterinarymanual.com>.

[176] See ***Mastercard International*** cases, supra, in which Complainant claims PRICELESS is one of a family of trademarks, but it is as much a dictionary word as "mall."

[177] *Spraying Systems*, supra.

[178] ***General Nutrition Investment Company v. Jack Button***, FA1108001403047 (Forum September 12, 2011) for GNC where respondent registered <gncsuplementos.com> and <gncvitaminas.com>.

[179] The R US mark, ***Geoffrey, LLC*** supra, was successful against a variety of domain names including <bestcreditcardsrus.info>, <carinsurancequoterus.info>, <cheaptermlifeinsuranceratesrus.info>, <childrensbedroomfurniturerus.com>. However, compare an earlier dispute, ***Geoffrey, Inc. v. NOT THE USUAL***, D2006-0882 (WIPO October 18, 2006) in which the Panel denied Complainant's complaint for <pensrus.com>: "[N]ot a cybersquatter, but has a well-established business."

[180] ***The Wellcome Foundation Limited, BW USA, Inc., SmithKline Beecham Corporation d/b/a GlaxoSmithKline v. Michale Kelly***, D2004-0265 (WIPO May 24, 2004) (WELLBUTRIN family of marks) (Default; Transferred); ***Citigroup Inc. v. Ian Templeton***, D2002-0231 (WIPO April 29, 2002) (CITI family of marks) (Respondent appeared; Transferred); ***Delta Air Lines, Inc. v. Stonybrook Investments, Ltd.***, D2000-1686 (WIPO January 22, 2001) (DELTA family of marks) (Default; Transferred); ***Fleetboston Financial Corporation v. JFK Holdings, Inc.***, D2000-1352 (WIPO January 11, 2001) (<fleetbank.com>, Complainant owned both FLEET and FLEETBANK marks, among other FLEET family marks) (Default; Transferred).

[181] Lanham Act, §33(b)(4), 15 U.S.C. §1115(b)(4) (1976): "use of the name, term, or device charged to be an infringement is a use . . . which is descriptive of and used fairly and in good faith only to describe the goods or services of such party, or their geographic origin."

Where the mark is "a highly descriptive term, a party seeking to establish exclusive rights carries a heavy burden of proof in removing the term from the public domain."[183] Only if the evidence demonstrates that respondent registered and is using the domain name to exploit the trademark value of the term will it be forfeited to complainant, but absent targeting the complaint must be denied (whether or not respondent lacks rights or legitimate interests).[184] This outcome is premised on the binary requirement that complainant prove both registration and use in bad faith and that any uncertainty as to either favors respondent.

As a general rule descriptive terms extend to common linguistic constructions across the marketplace. Thus, it "is legitimate to build a service mark out of the highly suggestive and diluted mark [such as] 'Gold Line' for products or services not the same as or closely related to those covered by any existing registrations."[185] Trademarks composed of neologisms common in an industry are vulnerable,[186] although owners are likely to get more protection in a court of law.[187] Similarly with scientific terms employed to call attention to the content of the website, such as <rorschachonline.com>.[188]

In ***eSnipe***[189] the confusing similarity involved the expression "snipe." Wikipedia defines sniping in reference to auctions as "the process of watching a timed online auction (such as on eBay), and placing a winning bid at the last possible moment (often seconds before the end of the auction), giving the other bidders no time to outbid the sniper." Complainant owns SNIPE IT!; respondent registered <snipeit.com> prior to registration of the trademark. Even if the timing were

---

182 · *KP Permanent Make Up, Inc. v. Lasting Impression I, Inc.*, 543 U.S. 111, 122 (2004) (noting also "the undesirability of allowing anyone to obtain a complete monopoly on use of a descriptive term simply by grabbing it first.")

183 ***Snowboards-for-sale.com, Inc. v. Name Administration Inc.***, D2002-1167 (WIPO February 19, 2003) (<snowboardsforsale.com>).

184 ***Robert Chestnutt v. Jennifer Tumminelli***, D2000-1758 (WIPO February 2, 2001) (<racegirl.com>, "[R]ights to a descriptive term such as racegirl are limited to the class of goods for which the mark was issued.")

185 ***Goldline International, Inc. v. Gold Line***, D2000-1151 (WIPO January 8, 2001).

186 ***Super Krete International, Inc. v. Concrete Solutions, Inc.***, D2008-1333 (WIPO October 14, 2008). The Panel held that Respondent had a right or legitimate interest in <supercrete.com> despite the parties being competitors in the same industry.

187 In a subsequent ACPA action, the district court in *Super-Krete Int'l v. Sadleir*, 712 F.Supp.2d 1023 (C.D. Cal. 2010) granted plaintiff a preliminary injunction to prevent defendant's sale or transfer of the domain before the court decided the merits of plaintiff's claims.

188 ***Hogrefe AG v. Ney Limonge***, D2008-1206 (WIPO October 3, 2008) (Complaint denied). Complainant was the registered owner of RORSCHACH. Respondent, a clinical psychologist, registered the disputed domain name to distribute "an interactive online computer program used in the administration of the Rorschach inkblot test."

189 In ***eSnipe, Inc. v. Modern Empire Internet, Ltd.***, D2009-0719 (WIPO August 5, 2009).

otherwise, given the established meaning of snipe it "leaves open the strong possibility that entities in different parts of the world might quite likely come up with the same or similar snipe-related names independently of one another."

Although domain names formed of compound words identical or confusingly similar to a trademark become suspect when the website to which the domain name resolves includes links to complainant's website or to competitors, there is no prohibition against registering a domain name that plainly describes respondent's business, even if confusion results.[190]

5.01-D.3

5.01-D.3 Not All Offers to Sell Violate the Policy

The commodification of domain names cannot be disassociated from the commercial flowering of the Internet, and is an inseparable element of the cyber marketplace. Panelists quickly established parameters that distinguished unlawful conduct under paragraph 4(b)(i) from *bona fide* use under paragraph 4(c)(i) of the Policy. There is nothing inherently illegitimate about inventorying attractive domain names for the purpose of future sales, monetizing them for present revenue, and ultimately offering them for sale or leasing. The business of selling domain names does not contravene the Policy unless there is proof of bad faith conduct[191]: "[I]t is not a function of the Policy to interfere in people's bargains."[192]

Panels routinely explain there is no legal basis for cancelling or transferring registrations away from original holders with rights or legitimate interests in domain names. No inference can be drawn of bad faith for offering to sell what one owns,[193] although as explained in Section 6.03-B Panels routinely qualify this broad statement in disputes with domain resellers who are charged with enhanced investigative responsibilities when it comes to acquiring domain names.

---

[190] ***Austin Area Birthing Center, Inc. v. CentreVida Birth and Wellness Center c/o Faith Beltz and Family Centered Midwifery c/o June Lamphier***, FA0911001295573 (Forum January 20, 2010), AUSTIN AREA BIRTHING CENTER and <austinbirthcenter.com>.

[191] The Policy is violated only if respondent acquired the disputed domain name "primarily" for the interdicted purposes enumerated in paragraph 4(b) (i-iv) of the Policy. Discussed further in "The Primary Purpose Test" (Sec. 6.02-B.2). ***Hopscotch v. Perfect Privacy LLC/Joseph William Lee***, D2015-1844 (WIPO January 16, 2016) ("[T]he practice will not constitute bad faith unless the registrant knew of and was intentionally targeting a complainant's trademark rights at that time"); ***Informa Business Information, Inc. v. Privacydotlink Customer 640040 / Domain Manager, Web D.G. Ltd.***, D2017-1756 (WIPO December 11, 2017) (<pinksheet.com>. "Inflated" price for domain name not grounds for forfeiting it to Complainant: "As in any market for commodities, domain name broking is about matching supply with demand; in the absence of any indicia of bad faith, there is nothing wrong per se with what the Complainant characterises as an 'excessive offer.'")

[192] ***CSP International Fashion Group S.p.A. v. Domain Administrator, NameFind LLC***, D2018-0163 (WIPO March 13, 2018) (<myboutique.com>. "Trading in domain names happens in a marketplace. Prices are struck between buyer and seller and it is not a function of the Policy to interfere in people's bargains.")

However, "the fact that domain name registrants may legitimately and in good faith sell domain names does not imply a right in such registrants to sell domain names that are identical or confusingly similar to trademark or service marks of others without their consent."[194] While it is not probative of bad faith that a respondent is in the business of buying and selling domain names, neither is it a defense to a claim of bad faith. Domain names resolving to websites that pretend to be complainants or use them for their trademark value will be found abusive. In ***Dollar Bank, Federal Savings Bank v. Paul Stapleton, The New Media Factory***[195] the Panel noted:

> Respondent wishes to claim legitimate business interests as a buyer and seller of domain names, yet at the same [time] appears to rely on a lack of knowledge regarding how to determine whether a third party has service mark rights.

While <dollarbankers.com> could conceivably be used legitimately, here it is used "solely in connection with a GoDaddy Auction offering it for sale."

As the marketplace for domain names has matured, so too has an understanding of how parties' actions support or rebut bad faith. In considering whether offers to sell domain names corresponding to trademarks are proof of cybersquatting, panelists look for answers to the following questions: 1) who has priority of right?; 2) is the trademark strong or weak?; 3) is there proof respondent had knowledge of the trademark?[196]; 4) is respondent engaged in a deliberate business practice of registering domain names knowing them to be abusive?; 5) is respondent using the domain name in its semantic sense or holding it passively for sale as a name that would be of interest to many types of businesses?; and 6) does respondent have a history of cybersquatting?

If a weak mark predates the registration the determination turns on its reputation at that time. If the registrant has priority and the registration violates no exception to liability, it should make no difference that the registrant is offering to sell the domain name to the world, which includes the mark owner.[197] No bad faith can be inferred from an exorbitant sales offer.[198] However, if the mark owner claims

---

[193] Transferees are differently placed as discussed further in "Transfer/Subsequent Holders=New Registration."

[194] ***CBS Broadcasting, Inc. v. Gaddoor Saidi***, D2000-0243 (WIPO June 2, 2000).

[195] D2016-0518 (WIPO April 24, 2016) (Bad faith by inference, rather than proof Sec. 7.09).

[196] ***Kosmos SAS v. Domain Hostmaster - Customer ID: 48322848242624 / Domain Admin, Ashantiplc Limited***, D2015-2198 (WIPO February 19, 2016) (<kosmos.com>) ("The possibility that the Respondent, or a third party, may have opportunistically registered the Disputed Domain Name after noticing the Complainant's searches has not escaped the Panel's attention.... In view of this and taking into account that 'kosmos' is dictionary word, the Panel is prepared to accept the Respondent's statement that it did not have any knowledge of the Complainant prior to 2014, when the Complainant offered to purchase the Disputed Domain Name."

priority, it makes all the difference who initiates contact in offering the domain name for sale.[199]

It is not per se unlawful to own a supermarket of domain names for sale in the secondary market; or to offer domain names corresponding to trademarks, even to owners and their competitors as long as registrants acquired the domain names for legitimate purposes. In ***Mark Overbye*** the Panel found that "Respondent's offer to sell the disputed domain name to Complainant is not relevant as Respondent was first approached by Complainant to sell the disputed domain name."[200] Who approaches whom can be a significant factor in weighing bad and good faith.[201]

Because weak marks have less protection, who approaches whom is likely to be a material factor in determining bad faith, and when that party is the respondent it becomes a window to its intentions.[202] In both cases cited in the footnote, Respondents registered generic and descriptive words that were nevertheless also

---

[197] ***Complainant in Hippie Tours LLC v. Mansour Elseify and Crystal Elseify***, D2014-1975 (WIPO January 2, 2015) (<hippie.com>) alleged it engaged in negotiations with Respondents to purchase the Domain Name but Respondents repeatedly increased the purchase price and then improperly frustrated the transaction and withheld the Domain Name. However, holding domain name inactive for the purposes of reselling it is not a violation of the Policy where the domain name "pre-dates registration of Complainant's trademark by at least 5 years, and where the Domain Name is comprised of descriptive terms . . . [and] as described above, Respondents have established a legitimate equitable seniority interest in the Domain Name."

[198] ***Centroamerica Comercial, Sociedad Anonima de Capital Variable (CAMCO) v. Michael Mann***, D2016-1709 (WIPO October 3, 2016) (<dollarcity.com>. "While the mere registration of such a domain name will not generally give rise to rights or legitimate interests in the name, the Panel finds that the offer of the disputed domain name for sale in accordance with the Respondent's general business activities does give rise to a legitimate interest in this case (paragraph 4(c)(i) of the Policy). Furthermore, as there is no targeting of the Complainant's trademark, the price sought by the Respondent is not of relevance.")

[199] Typical cases include ***Mark Overbye v. Maurice Blank, Gekko.com B.V.***, D2016-0362 (WIPO April 15, 2016) (<gekko.com>) in which the Panel found that "Respondent's offer to sell the disputed domain name to Complainant is not relevant as Respondent was first approached by Complainant to sell the disputed domain name"; ***Egton Medical Information Systems Limited v. Eric Strikowski / Health Axis Group LLC, Shilen Patel***, D2014-0384 (WIPO May 28, 2014)(three member Panel) in which the Respondent responded to Complainant after it "had made several approaches asking to acquire the name without at any stage suggesting it had rights entitling it to acquire the name, or to prevent the Respondents using it." However, who approaches whom is not material in inadvertent lapse disputes. See discussion in "Respondent's Conduct Not Condoned Where Domain Name Not Abandoned" (Sec. 4.01-F.1.b).

[200] *Supra.*

[201] ***Bank of Scotland Plc v. Shelley Robert, Diversity Network***, D2015-2310 (WIPO February 15, 2016) (<halifax.com>. "The correspondence shows that it was the Respondent who made the approach to the Complainant, which was entirely unsolicited, and that the Respondent continually pushed for an answer from the Complainant and its representative in a high pressure style, neither of whom gave the Respondent any encouragement whatsoever for that behaviour.")

marks predating the registrations of the domain names. By soliciting sales from the mark owners, Respondents exposed themselves to liability under the UDRP and the domain names were ordered transferred. When complainant initiates the offer "[it] expressly disclaimed any legal rights over the disputed domain name."[203]

The issue is not the *bona fides* of the business model but respondent's motivation for its choice of domain name and the use to which it is put.[204] Respondent in ***Fifty Plus Media*** offered evidence from a Google search that there were more than sixty existing worldwide trademarks for the term 50Plus. The Panel in ***Primal Quest*** explained that

> The sale of domain names comprised of common terms, without some indicia of bad faith, is neither unlawful nor evidence of cybersquatting; it is only when domain names are registered for resale with knowledge that the names consist of another's trademark that the conduct fairly may be characterized as cybersquatting.

In ***Amazon Technologies***, the Panel explained that where marks are well-known "Panels have considered exorbitant offers to sell disputed domain names as a further indication of a lack of a *bona fide* purpose."[205]

However, where respondents acquire domain names composed of dictionary words or random letters without any evidence of trading on complainant's reputation Commentary Timing of a Party's Right they have a legitimate interest, and every right to sell them as they would any other asset: "it is a very common business practice."[206] The consensus view is that "the mere pricing of the Domain Name at a very high level cannot in itself indicate bad faith at the time of registration."[207] A

---

[202] ***Dollar Bank, Federal Savings Bank v. Paul Stapleton, The New Media Factory***, D2016-0518 (WIPO April 24, 2016) (DOLLAR BANK and <dollarbankers.com>. "Respondent has used the disputed domain name solely in connection with a GoDaddy Auction offering it for sale.").

[203] ***Corporacion Empresarial Altra S.L. v. Development Services, Telepathy, Inc.***, D2017-0178 (WIPO May 15, 2017) (<airzone.com>. The Panel denied the complaint but rejected sanctioning Complainant. Respondent thereupon commenced an action under the ACPA for reverse domain name damages and defendant settled by stipulating to pay plaintiff $40,000 dollars. See also ***Beautiful People Magazine, Inc. v. Domain Manager / PeopleNetwork ApS / Kofod Nicolai / People Network Aps / Nicolai Kofod / People Network***, FA1502001606976 (Forum May 4, 2015) (<beautifulpeople.com>. Respondent had priority; Complainant, now plaintiff commenced an ACPA, dismissed with attorney's fees to defendant, *Joshua Domond and Harold Hunter, Jr v. PeopleNetwork APS d/b/a Beautifulpeople.Com, Beautiful People, LLC, Greg Hodge, and Genevieve Maylam*, 16-24026-civ (S.D. FL. Miami Div. 11/9/17).

[204] ***Fifty Plus Media Corp. v. Digital Income, Inc.***, FA 94924 (Forum July 17, 2000) (in which respondent was an Internet business dealing in selling or leasing descriptive/generic domain names, 50+ MORGAN HALL and <50plus.com>); ***Primal Quest, LLC v. Gabriel Salas***, D2005-1083 (WIPO December 15, 2005).

[205] ***Amazon Technologies, Inc. v. Robert Nichols***, FA1609001693499 (Forum October 20, 2016) (<amazoncars andtrucks.com> and <amazonvehicles.com>. Under the right circumstances, here the

"totally excessive and unreasonable demand" (not an infrequent complaint) is not evidence of bad faith.

The same rules do not apply to successors who acquire domain names after a complainant's first use of its mark in commerce. They may run afoul of the Policy and not be immunized by their predecessors' good faith registrations if they either continue using the domain names in bad faith or their uses violate their representations that their registrations are lawful.[208]

5.01-E 5.01-E Sleeping on One's Rights

5.01-E.1 5.01-E.1 Laches vs. Lapse of Time

There is no time bar for claims under the UDRP and no formal laches defense, but lapse of time nevertheless has consequences. The no time bar principle initially found expression in the WIPO Final Report which states that "a time bar to the bringing of claims in respect of domain names (for example, a bar on claims where the domain name registration has been unchallenged for a designated period of years) should not be introduced."[209] The "should not be introduced" is then expressly endorsed: "*It is not recommended that claims under the administrative procedure be subject to a time limitation*" (Italics in original).[210]

---

inclusion of a well-known mark, "Panels have considered exorbitant offers to sell disputed domain names as a further indication of a lack of a *bona fide* purpose.")

[206] Domain names appreciate in value to the extent of demand, and where there is demand it is likely that the respondent's offering price will be in excess of its direct out-of-pocket costs for the domain name, but grossness is in the eyes of the suitor. See for example, ***Barlow Lyde & Gilbert v. The Business Law Group***, D2005-0493 (WIPO June 24, 2005) (<blg.com>) ("Standing alone, there is nothing wrong with offering to sell a domain name at a high price. It is a very common business practice"); ***X6D Limited v. Telepathy, Inc.***, D2010-1519 (WIPO November 16, 2010) in which Complainant contends that the disputed domain name, <xpand.com> has been used in bad faith because respondent indicates on its website that it "is likely to ignore offers below USD 40,000 for a domain name"; ***Bible Study Fellowship v. BSF.ORG / Vertical Axis Inc.***, D2010-1338 (WIPO November 29, 2010) in which respondent is offering <bsf.org> for sale through the website "www.domainbrokers.com" for the minimum price of USD 10,000.

[207] ***Camper, S.L. v. Detlev Kasten***, D2005-0056 (WIPO March 3, 2005).

[208] Discussed further "Transfer/Subsequent Holder=New Registration" (Sec. 4.03-B.2).

[209] WIPO Final Report paragraphs 197-199. Paragraph 199: "It is not recommended that claims under the administrative procedure be subject to a time limitation." However, delay in commencing a proceeding has consequences. Under U.S. trademark law the limitations period for laches starts when the plaintiff knew or should have known about its potential cause of action and distinguishes between inapplicability of a laches defense if the action is commenced within a limitations period and presumption of laches if outside of it. See *Jarrow Formulas, Inc. v. Nutrition Now, Inc.* 304 F.3d 829, 838 (9th Cir. 2002); *Internet Specialties West Inc. v. Milon-Digiorgio Enterprises, Inc.*, 559 F.3d 985 (9th Cir. 2009).

[210] *Id.*, paragraph 199.

While the recommendation for no time limitation did not achieve written recognition in the Policy, Panels quickly enshrined the concept in their decisions by specifically declining to adopt equitable defenses for the UDRP.[211] This was not intended to defeat respondents' rights to long-held domain names lawfully registered.[212] The Policy itself in Paragraph 4(c)(i) enshrines a principle that is a near companion to laches,[213] namely that respondent can accrue rights or legitimate interest if "before any notice to you of the dispute" you (respondent) are using "the domain name in connection with a bona fide offering of goods or services."[214] Lapse of time under these circumstances has the effect of legitimizing the registration and negating the effect of laches.

For this reason, the absence of a formal laches defense is of no consequence. In tracking the history of the UDRP it can be seen that panelists in the earliest cases quickly developed an approach that takes into account the totality of

---

[211] ***Edmunds.com, Inc. v. Ult. Search Inc.***, D2001-1319 (WIPO February 1, 2002) ("[There is] no room for general equitable doctrines under the Policy such as would be possessed by Courts in common law jurisdictions.") Other Panels too numerous to cite have held that there is no limitations period in the Policy. Even if laches were to be considered, it would require clean hands of the party asserting it. ***Univision Comm'cns Inc. v. Norte***, FA 1000079 (Forum August 16, 2007). See *Hermes Int'l v. Lederer de Paris Fifth Ave, Inc.*, 219 F. 3d (2nd Cir. 1981) ("It is well established that 'laches is not a defense against injunctive relief when the defendant intended the infringement.'") Even if laches were to be considered, it would require clean hands of the party asserting it. ***Univision Comm'cns Inc. v. Norte***, FA 1000079 (Forum August 16, 2007).

[212] For laches to apply under U.S. trademark law the defendant must show (1) "that the plaintiff had knowledge"—actual or constructive—"of the defendant's use of an allegedly infringing mark"; (2) "that the plaintiff inexcusably delayed in taking action with respect to the defendant's use"; and (3) "that the defendant would be prejudiced by allowing the plaintiff to assert its rights at this time." *Chattanoga Mfg., Inc. v. Nike, Inc.*, 301 F.3rd 789, 792-793 (7th Cir. 2002). Determining parties' rights "requires a qualitative examination of the parties' words and conduct and an equitable evaluation of the length of the delay and the degree of prejudice to the defendant if the trademark owner's rights are enforced," which "generally requires a factual record." *Hyson USA, Inc. v. Hyson 2U, Ltd.*, 821 F.3d 935, 941 (7th Cir. 2016). However, making a "qualitative examination" presupposes domain name registrants build a record, but in many cases they default and their silence condemns them.

[213] See for example *Internet Specialties West, Inc. v. Milon-Digiorgio Enterprises, Inc.*, 2009 U.S. App. Lexis 5454, 15 (9th Cir. 2009) in which the Court held that laches is a viable defense to a claim for trademark infringement under the Lanham Act if "during the plaintiff's delay in bringing suit, the infringer developed an identity as a business based on the mark."

[214] Paragraph 4(c)(i) of the Policy acts as a laches surrogate. Denying complaint where there is no evidence of any act of infringing conduct. See for example ***Novartis AG v. Name Administration Inc.*** (BVI), FA1403001548210 (Forum April 24, 2014) (<clearcare.com>. "[U]nrelated hyperlink directory cannot rightfully constitute a Policy ¶ 4(b)(iii) bad faith disruption of Complainant's business.") Under U.S. law, see *Internet Specialties West, Inc. v. Milon-Digiorgio Enterprises, Inc.*, 2009 U.S. App. Lexis 5454, 15 (9th Cir. 2009) in which the Court held that laches is a viable defense to a claim for trademark infringement under the Lanham Act if "during the plaintiff's delay in bringing suit, the infringer developed an identity as a business based on the mark."

circumstances.[215] Complainants benefit only to the extent they are not time barred but in all other respects they must still satisfy the burdens of Paragraphs 4(a)(ii)[216] and 4(a)(iii)[217] of the Policy. In practice, Panels view negatively parties' failure to either offer evidence or respond to the length of delay, the strength of the mark, the different markets in which complainant operates, and the geographical distance separating the parties.[218]

Whether or not a respondent alleges laches—it could default and still prevail[219]—the longer the passage of time the greater complainant's burden for establishing the merits of its claim of cybersquatting.[220] This is so, in part, because memory is unreliable and documentary evidence disappears if not preserved.[221] It gives rise, in the words of one Panel as "to some doubt whether Complainant believed Respondent had been guilty of bad faith in registering and using the

---

[215] ***Bosco Prod., Inc. v. Bosco email Servs.***, FA 94828 (Forum June 29, 2000) (<bosco.com> for "vanity e-mail" service. "Without determining if the passage of considerable time would alone bar Complainant from relief in this proceeding, the Panel notes that Complainant does not explain why it has waited nearly four years to try and resolve [the domain name dispute].") Laches expressly applied in ***Laminex, Inc. v. Yan Smith***, FA1211001470990 (Forum January 7, 2013); but not in ***Javier Zetter Casillas v. Domain Hostmaster/Vertical Axis Inc.***, D2014-0400 (WIPO June 6, 2014) in which Complainant waited over eight years from the date the Respondent purchased the disputed domain name [<bigbang.com>] to file a Complaint. "The Panel finds the long delay unexplained and detrimental since it makes it harder to ascertain the motives of the parties so long ago"; ***Dealhunter A/S v. Richard Chiang***, D2014-0766 (WIPO July 17, 2014) ("Opinions have differed on the applicability of laches or delay in UDRP proceedings. This Panel's view is that delay in filing a complaint is not an automatic bar to a complaint, but nor can it be ignored, for all the facts must be taken into account in all proceedings and a decision made in the light of all the circumstances of the individual case.")

[216] ***The Hebrew University of Jerusalem v. Alberta Hot Rods***, D2002-0616 (WIPO October 7, 2002) (<alberteinstein.com>, complaint denied; Panel found Respondent had a legitimate interest).

[217] ***The Sinclair Group Nevada, LLC v. behnam tabrizi***, FA1606001679802 (Forum August 3, 2016) (<rapidtransformation.com>. 7 years).

[218] Delay: ***Weeds, Inc. v. Registration Private, Domains By Proxy, LLC / Innovation HQ, Inc***, D2017-1517 (WIPO November 23, 2017) (W WEEDS INC. and WEEDS and <weeds.com>. First use in commerce claimed for 1966; domain name registration, 2001). Disputants in different jurisdictions: ***Kitchn Norge AS v. Abdulbasit Makrani***, D2016-1189 (WIPO August 12, 2016) (<kitchn.com>. Norway/Sweden and Pakistan).

[219] ***Uline, Inc. v. Hulmiho Ukolen***, D2016-0065 (WIPO March 13, 2016) (<uline.net>) (Respondent also defaulted).

[220] A representative example is ***National Gardening Association, Inc. v. CK Ventures Inc.***, FA0911001294457 (Forum February 16, 2010) (<gardeningwithkids.com>). See also ***Uline***, *supra*.

[221] ***Original Buff, S.A. v. Buff Blog***, D2012-1578 (WIPO October 29, 2012) (<buff.com>, Complaint denied. "Finally, there is the unexplained delay in the commencement of these Administrative Proceedings. The Respondent puts it at 15 years but even if the proper period is that during which the Respondent was the holder of the disputed domain name–from January 2007–there is still a lapse of time of more than 5 years during which the Complainant took no action. On the evidence, there

domain name."[222] Length of time and descriptiveness of mark (in the cited case as representative of consensus view, <visionworkseyecare.org>) also undercuts complainant's claim that respondent registered the domain name with the intention of capitalizing on it.

However, the ledger also has its other side. As fatal as delay may be to complainants it will not protect respondents who register unlawful and infringing domain names regardless of how much time has passed[223] While in many instances they reach safe harbor precisely because of the consequences of delay, they too have burdens that unsatisfied undermine any claim of good faith.[224] Failure to explain their registrations (particularly of domain names passively held clearly referring to complainant[225]) can be equally fatal to their continuing to hold the domain names.

Notwithstanding the consensus on the inapplicability of laches, some Panels have come to believe the "no limitations" principle is "unsound." In a 2010 decision, a three-member Panel held that laches "should be expressly recognized as a valid defense in any domain dispute where the facts so warrant."[226] It concluded that there was no "sound basis for ignoring the potential defense." While not

---

is a compelling argument that during that time the Complainant was quite aware of the third party ownership of the disputed domain name.") A finding in complainant's favor under paragraph 4(a)(ii) is not determinative of bad faith. Discussed further in "Lowering the Proof Bar" (Sec. 4.02-B.1).

[222] ***ECCA Enterprises, Inc. v. Eyefinity***, FA0905001261978 (Forum July 1, 2009); ***Vanguard Trademark Holdings USA LLC v. Nett Corp.***, FA1262162 (Forum July 26, 2009) (NATIONAL CAR RENTAL and <nationalrentacar>, 9 years. A concurring opinion by the sole Panel in ***ECCA Enterprises*** agreed that domain name was not confusingly similar to trademark.)

[223] Unlawful registrations will be cancelled or transferred regardless the length respondents have held them. ***Coles Pen Company Limited v. Cole, Samantha / Coles of London***, FA1702001717458 (Forum March 30, 2017) (<penheaven.com>. 8 years) (Prior employee redirecting domain name to "promote affiliate links and bolster Respondent's business which sells writing instruments online in an attempt to confuse Internet users for commercial gain.") See also ***The Board of Regents of The University of Texas System v. LLC Perfect Privacy***, FA1708001745104 (Forum September 18, 2017) (<theuniversityoftexas.com>. Fifteen and half years).

[224] ***Commonwealth Bank of Australia v. Registration Private, Domains By Proxy, LLC / Ravindra Patel, gbe***, D2017-0807 (WIPO July 6, 2017) (<bankwest.com>) (Held inactively 20 years, Transferred) ("Given that the Respondent is represented the Panel is left concluding that this silence on such critical issues is not simply inadvertent but represents a deliberate decision.")

[225] ***David Duchovny v. Alberta Hot Rods c/o Jeff Burgar***, FA1706001734414 (Forum July 4, 2017) (21 years. "Although no one would claim that the DAVID DUCHOVNY mark, in 1996, was as famous as GOOGLE is today, given the demonstrated notoriety of David Duchovny in 1996 and the totality of the circumstances, the Panel finds that Respondent had actual knowledge of Complainant's mark prior to the registration of the disputed domain name.")

[226] ***The New York Times Company v. Name Administration Inc. (BVI)***, FA1009001349045 (Forum November 17, 2010) (<dealbook.com>. "Prior decisions rejecting the applicability of the doctrine due to the failure of its express recognition in the UDRP Policies appear to be an unsound basis for ignoring the potential defense." Defense allowed [six years]). Acknowledged in WIPO Overview,

immediately endorsed by other Panels, and by no means universally accepted, the defense "has gained a foothold,"[227] sufficient to be "seriously regarded" if properly raised and argued.[228] Conversely, respondents cannot acquire rights or legitimate interests by passively holding domain names[229] or from "[c]ontinuous use adverse to the interest of Complainant."[230]

5.01-E.2

5.01-E.2 The Paragraph 4(c)(i) Defense

The specific antidote to complainants sleeping on their rights is expressly set forth in Paragraph 4(c)(i) of the Policy; that is, if in the long interval before complainant wakes up a respondent accrues rights in the domain name, the complaint must be denied. It will be noticed that the 4(c)(i) defense incorporates a key element of laches, namely detrimental reliance, so that while laches is ostensibly rejected it is nevertheless present without specifically naming it.[231]

---

supra: http://www.wipo.int/amc/en/domains/search/overview/index.html#410 concluding sentence reads: "A small number of panels have also begun to acknowledge the possible applicability, in appropriate and limited circumstances, of a defense of laches under the UDRP where the facts so warrant. The three member Panel in ***Harvard Lampoon, Inc. v. Reflex Publishing Inc.***, D2011-0716 (WIPO July 26, 2011) noted that although it has not applied the defense of laches it "has taken Complainant's inaction [13 years] into account in deciding certain of the issues above."

Applying laches: ***Novak v. Marchex Sales, Inc./Hight***, FA 1418478 (Forum March 1, 2012) (Panel found that where the trademark holder was "sophisticated, had been in business for a substantial period of time and had registered several trademarks and domain names, but then failed to pursue an alleged domain name infringer without excuse or explanation while the alleged domain name infringer built a business, laches should apply.") Recognizing laches, but unnecessary to apply: ***Instrumentation Northwest, Inc. v. INW.COM c/o Telepathy, Inc.***, D2012-0454 (WIPO June 1, 2012) ("The Panel also declines to rule on Respondent's laches defense here, since it is unnecessary to do so in view of the Panel's other rulings. Having said that, a majority of the Panel would have been prepared to apply the laches defense here, given the fact that Complainant sat on its perceived rights for many years–indeed, 15 years if one goes back to the original registration of the Domain Name.")

[227] ***Mars, Incorporated v. Ben Chen***, FA1109001405770 (Forum October 17, 2011); ***Avaya Inc. v. Moayyad Hamad***, FA1207001456063 (Forum September 14, 2012) (AVAYA and <ayava.us>. "Because the Complainant was a tech leader in the relevant marketplace yet did nothing for an extended period of time in regards to Respondent's business, either because of Respondent's small size, or the difference between Respondent's domain name and Complainant's mark, the facts that give rise to a laches defense further support Respondent's rights and legitimate interests in the disputed domain name.") Other cases are collated in ***Laminex, Inc. v. Yan Smith***, FA1211001470990 (Forum January 13, 2013).

[228] ***American Studies Center d/b/a Radio America v. Jet Stream Enterprises Limited c/o Jet Stream***, FA1307001511405 (Forum August 26, 2013) (15 years Respondent did not appear. Panel noted: "This case has proceeded and has been decided as a default matter. Had the Respondent filed a Response and pled laches in defense, the Panel would have seriously regarded that assertion.")

[229] The failure to rebut complainant's *prima facie* case, however, is not conclusive on the issue of bad faith. Discussed further in "Inactive or Passive Use" (Sec. 5.01-B.2).

[230] ***Avaya Inc. v. Holdcom***, FA0806001210545 (Forum August 9, 2008) (<magiconhold>).

The consequences of delay are built into the paragraph 4(c)(i) defense (which balances law and equity). It provides that "before notice [respondent] has use[d] or [has made] demonstrable preparations to use the domain name . . . in connection with a bona fide offering of goods or services." Length of time favors noncompeting respondents for domain names on the lower end of the classification scale where there is proof the domain name is being used for purposes consistent with respondent's business and unrelated to complainant's.[232]

Respondent's rights or legitimate interests are assessed by analyzing the factual circumstances existing between the time the domain name is registered and notice of the dispute. Delay in commencing a proceeding interacts with such other factors as the relative strength of the trademark, geographical locations of the parties, and complainant's reputation when respondent registered the domain name. While an excusable delay (i.e., one that can be satisfactorily explained) is not a bar to capturing the disputed domain name,[233] an inexcusable delay favors respondent.[234] Inexcusable delay is indefensible, not on account of the bar of laches but as a factor in determining bad faith registration.

Respondents prevail when they have either developed an identity as a business based on the mark or have demonstrated that their planning for such business is sufficiently advanced to rebut complainant's *prima facie* proof that it lacks rights or legitimate interests. In such cases a complainant's delay in exercising its legal right cannot overcome respondent's acquired right in the disputed domain name.[235] A domain name holder can defeat a trademark owner where the latter has failed

---

[231] Paragraph 4(a)(iii) also plays a role because the passage of time is a black hole; all evidence is lost if not maintained, so that even if respondent is found to lack rights or legitimate interests, if complainant cannot marshal evidence of bad faith registration the domain name must remain with respondent.

[232] ***C. Brewer and Sons Ltd. v. Vertical Axis, Inc.***, D2009-1759 (WIPO April 11, 2010) (WALL PAPER DIRECT and <wallpaperdirect.com>, 8 years); ***Vanguard Trademark Holdings USA LLC v. Nett Corp.***, FA0905001262162 (Forum July 26, 2009) (NATIONAL CAR RENTAL and <nationalrentacar.com>, 9 years).

[233] ***Arizona Board of Regents on behalf of the University of Arizona v. DNS, Admin, Nevis Domains / Gee Whiz Domains Privacy Service***, D2008-1543 (WIPO December 9, 2008) (9 years). The domain name <arizonawildcats.com> was registered in 1999 and the proceeding was commenced in October 2008. The Panel noted that at "all relevant times, the domain name has led to a site displaying advertising from which web-users may "click through" to various sites, including, for example, NFL and NBA sports sites," a clear violation under paragraph 4(b)(iv) of the Policy.

[234] 10 years: ***Tony Novak v. Marchex Sales, Inc / Brendhan Hight***, FA1112001418478 (Forum March 1, 2012) (FREEDOM BENEFITS, unregistered when registration lapsed in 2002 and still unregistered in 2012); 8 years, ***Jogos Atividades de Internet Ltda. v. Bennie Eeftink – Spil Games Intangibles B.V.***, D2012-0399 (WIPO April 13, 2012).

[235] The result is that while the doctrine of laches is not expressly recognized as a defense in UDRP proceedings it is applied silently. See ***Square Peg Interactive Inc. v. Naim Interactive Inc.***, FA 209572

to act for a lengthy period of time and offers no proof of targeting, coupled with a plausible explanation for registering the domain name, regardless of the lexical composition.[236]

There is consensus that "Complainant's delay in seeking relief is relevant to a determination of whether Respondent has been able to build up legitimate rights in the Domain Name in the interim, and whether it is using the Domain name in bad faith."[237] Delay demands explanation. Insufficiency or absence of proof supports a negative inference as noted in ***Square Peg Interactive***:

> [If] a trademark owner accuses another party of infringement but then fails to pursue the matter diligently, it may in some cases be concluded that the trademark owner has abandoned its claim and the accused infringer may be able to build up trademark rights.

Even if the bar of laches is not explicitly applied (in fact denied as a defense) it is nevertheless silently present. Various factors are considered: passage of time—"Respondent has been using the disputed domain names in relation to its online CD sales business [for] over 3 years before the Complaint was filed"[238] or as little as two years.[239] The class of goods or services in relation to complainant's is also a consideration. Where respondent has developed a business around the domain name before notice of a dispute and without evidence of targeting, its holding will not be disturbed.

(Forum December 29, 2003) ("Although laches by itself is not a defense to a complaint brought under the Policy, Complainant's delay in seeking relief is relevant to a determination of whether Respondent has been able to build up legitimate rights in the Domain Name in the interim, and whether it is using the Domain name in bad faith."); ***Meat & Livestock Comm'n v. Pearce***, D2003-0645 (WIPO October 27, 2003) ("Although laches is not a defence in itself under the Policy, the absence of any complaint over a long period of time in which domain names are in active use can suggest that such use does not give rise to a serious problem.")

236 Representative cases: ***HeadRoom Corporation v. Peter Comitini d/b/a Peter Comitini Design***, FA0111000102522 (Forum December 27, 2001) ("Since Complainant has not met its burden of proof for two (2) of the three (3) essential elements of a U.D.R.P. claim, this Arbitrator need not decide whether Respondent is entitled to the benefit of the defense of the Doctrine of Laches.")

237 ***Square Peg Interactive***, *supra.*

238 ***BeMusic, Inc. v. Music Trading On-Line (BVI) Ltd. c/o Music Trading On-Line (HK) Ltd.***, FA0309000193874 (Forum November 10, 2003) (<cdwow.com>, <cd-wow.com>, <cdwow.net>, <cd-wow.net>, <cdwow.org> and <cd-wow.org>, Complaint denied: "Respondent's business has grown during the years since it began using the domain names. Substantial hardship could result if it would be ordered to transfer those names.")

239 ***U.S. Fence, LLC v. U. S. Pool Fence***, D2001-1397 (WIPO April 13, 2002) (<usfence.com>. Respondent proved that it had been using the domain name in connection with the *bona fide* offering of pool fencing materials for two years before any notice. No need to analyze Complainant's allegations of bad faith or Respondent's defense of laches.)

In other examples where complainants have waited inordinate lengths of time to challenge respondents and there is no hard evidence of bad faith use, Panels are generally reluctant to find bad faith registration.[240] The complainant that owns the Economist trademark waited 11 years; YIT Corporation waited respectively on two domain names 11 and 6 years; and Interior Design Media waited 15 years before filing the complaint. Respondent in another case waited 9 years before commencing its challenge.[241] The Panel noted that

> Standing by and allowing Respondent to use the domain name in the allegedly improper manner during ... lengthy periods of time, without any explanation for how the delays came about, leaves Complainant open to the conclusion that it did not believe the claim and also that it had waived its complaint and induced or allowed Respondent to continue with its use of the domain name in that manner.

In all these representative cases complainants failed to satisfy the evidentiary burden. The longer the time between the registration of a disputed domain name and the assertion of complainant's rights the harder, in general, to sustain an inference of bad faith registration.[242] Lapse of time imposes on complainant a heavier burden. It must not only explain its delay but also overcome respondent's claim (or appearance) of good faith registration (for example, incorporating a trademark composed of generic or descriptive language and website free of any taint of infringing use). Neverless, complainants have prevailed against defaulting respondents.

5.01-F "First-Come First-Served" Doctrine 5.01-F

5.01-F.1 Parties with Equal Rights 5.01-F.1

The "first-come first-served doctrine" recognizes that priority of domain name registration may outweigh priority of use in commerce.[243] As a general rule, if a domain name is available the first to register it stakes a claim. Whether the stake

---

[240] ***YIT Corporation v. Future Media Architects Inc.***, D2007-0588 (WIPO July 27, 2007); ***The Economist Newspaper Limited v. TE Internet Services***, D2007-1652 (WIPO February 5, 2008) (<theeconomist.com>, complaint denied); ***Interior Design Media Group, LLC v. P. A. Gordon***, FA1210001467034 (Forum December 19, 2012) (<interiordesign.com>).

[241] ***Vanguard Trademark Holdings***, *supra.*

[242] Hard evidence of infringement supports forfeiture regardless of the length of holding. See ***Maurice Mizrahi / Mizco International, Inc. v. Chi Hyon***, FA1710001754962 (Forum November 20, 2017) (<digipower.com>. 23 years: "[T]he only use Respondent has made of the Disputed Domain Name is to link it to batteries, which is the exact same business Complainant is in.") However, failure to explain choices by defaulting in the proceedings has also proved fatal to respondents even with weak evidence. See ***Irving Materials, Inc. v. Black, Jeff / PartnerVision Ventures***, FA171000 753342 (Forum November 7, 2017) (transferred <imi.com>. 23 years. ACPA challenge pending); ***Commonwealth Bank of Australia v. Registration Private, Domains By Proxy, LLC / Ravindra Patel, gbe***, D2017-0807 (WIPO July 6, 2017) (transferred <bankwest.com>. 20 years).

is lawful depends on answers to a menu of questions such as strength or weakness of the mark, its reputation at the date of registration, the content of the resolving website, etc.

While the registration does not affect complainant's standing to maintain the proceeding (paragraph 4(a)(i) of the Policy), the weaker the mark and its reputation the greater complainant's paragraph 4(a)(ii) burden to anticipate respondent's rebuttal which if persuasive undercuts the claim that respondent lacks rights or legitimate interests in the domain name.[244] However, if priority of domain name registration (as opposed to priority in choosing a domain name that is neither identical nor confusingly similar to an existing mark) were the sole criterion "then all registrants would have such rights or interests, and no Complainant could succeed on a claim of abusive registration."[245]

The doctrine simply affirms that complainant's earlier acquired mark alone is insufficient against registrants in one of three classes: whose registrations are not infringing and lawful[246]; who own competing marks[247]; or who operate active businesses with recognized trade names.[248] Since the second and third classes of complainants have no actionable claims of cybersquatting against respondents who

---

[243] ***VRL International Ltd. and International Lifestyles, Inc. v. Relevansanalys***, D2009-0974 (WIPO September 3, 2009). This principle is subject to proof of timing, by complainant in acquiring its trademark right, discussed further in "Timing of Trademark Acquisition Not a Factor in Determining Standing" (Sec. 4.01-E) and by respondent in acquiring the domain name, discussed further in "Registering Domain Names Opportunistically" (Sec. 6.01-C).

[244] The Jurisprudential Overview, Paragraph 4.17 states: "Panels have widely recognized that mere delay between the registration of a domain name and the filing of a complaint neither bars a complainant from filing such case, nor from potentially prevailing on the merits." Discussed further in Laches vs. Lapse of Time.

[245] ***Educational Tertiary Service v. TOEFL***, D2000-0044 (WIPO March 16, 2000) ("Construing the Policy so as to avoid an illogical result, the Panel concludes that mere registration does not establish rights or legitimate interests in a domain name so as to avoid the application of Paragraph 4(a)(ii) of the Policy.") Death of registrant is not a sufficient basis for capturing the domain name. Société Du Figaro S.A. v. Cut Company, DTV2013-0007 (WIPO February 2, 2014) (<figaro.tv>).

[246] ***Gabs S.r.l. v. Domain Administrator – Name Administrator Inc. (BVI)***, CAC 101331 (ADReu February 26, 2017) (GABS Complainant has nothing to complain about because Respondent is using a dictionary word for its commonly understood meaning); ***Fabricators & Manufacturers Association, International v. NameFind***, FA 1728625 (Forum June 1, 2017) (THE FABRICATOR and <fabricator.com>. "[T]he Panel agrees with Respondent's contentions that Complainant does not have any right to monopolize the dictionary word 'fabricator' alone because the mark is indivisible: neither the article 'the' nor the noun 'fabricator' is distinctive in its own right.")

[247] ***Can I Do Better Internet Corp. v. Blastapplications***, D2011-0055 (WIPO March 8, 2011) (Respondent owned a trademark in CAN DO BETTER; Complainant claimed a common law trademark in CAN I DO BETTER.)

[248] See ***Petrofac Services Limited v. Petrofac Qatar WLL***, D2016-0388 (WIPO May 16, 2016) (PETROFAC and <petrofac-qatar.com>) (While similarity of name may be confusing in an abstract

prevail on the paragraph 4(c)(i) and 4(c)(ii) defenses they will not be further discussed in this section except to note that a competitor who by happenstance registers a domain name descriptive of its services and not intentionally to disrupt a rival that has also adopted the mark is entitled to retain the domain name.[249]

For the first class, the doctrine is applicable to respondents whose domain names are capable of having distinctive associations unrelated to corresponding marks.[250] Respondents who register domain names composed of common words and descriptive terms "legitimately subject to registration as domain names on a 'first-come first-served basis'" are not in violation of the Policy.[251] But, they are not absolved for registering domain names that take advantage of corresponding marks (even if on the weak end of the classification) or longivity of holding them.[252]

That a temporal priority is established because complainants have chosen not to register domain names corresponding to their marks is neither a bar to later claims[253] nor to asserting defenses to cybersquatting. This is so because "complainants have no obligation to register all possible domain names related to their marks, and they can initiate proceedings under the Policy at any time for any domain names that are confusingly similar to their marks."[254]

---

sense it cannot trump accrued rights to a trade name legitimately registered with a national registry even if the parties are engaged (although not as competitors) in servicing parties in the same industry); ***Wisconsin Emergency Medical Technicians Association, Inc. v. Marsha Everts, EMS Professionals, Inc.***, D2018-2841 (WIPO February 7, 2019) (("[T]he mark has a descriptive connotation and the parties' respective uses are in separate zones of interest.")

249 ***Kaleidoscope Imaging, Inc. v. V Entertainment a/k/a Slavik Viner***, FA0310000203207 (Forum January 5, 2004); ***One Creative Place, LLC v. Kevin Scott***, D2006-0518 (WIPO June 16, 2006) "Both parties had a potential interest in using the highly relevant, descriptive words 'Montrose Jet Center,' as a name, as a domain name, or in descriptive advertising."

250 Discussed further in "Trademarks Not Equally Protected" (Sec. 5.01-D.1.a).

251 ***Zero Int'l Holding v. Beyonet Servs.***, D2000-0161 (WIPO May 12, 2000) (<zero.com>. Respondent appeared; Complaint denied); ***John Fairfax Publ'n Pty Ltd v. Domain Names 4U & Fred Gray***, D2000-1403 (WIPO December 13, 2000) (<financialreview.com>) (finding legitimate interests and no bad faith registration where Respondent is a seller of generic domain names); ***Asphalt Research Technology, Inc. v. National Press & Publishing, Inc.***, D2000-1005 (WIPO November 13, 2000) (Default; Complaint denied) (<ezstreet.net>); ***GR8 Industries B.V v. Graffito /Active8 Partnership***, D2005-1341 (WIPO March 24, 2006) (<gr8.com>) (Default; Complaint denied).

252 ***CVS Pharmacy, Inc. and MinuteClinic, L.L.C v. Pham Dinh Nhut***, FA170300 1723633 (Forum April 30, 2017) (MINUTE CLINIC and <minuteclinics.com>. "Complainant fails to explain why it waited some 13 years to bring this complaint" but it proved abusive registration.)

253 The Jurisprudential Overview, Paragraph 4.17 states: "Panels have widely recognized that mere delay between the registration of a domain name and the filing of a complaint neither bars a complainant from filing such case, nor from potentially prevailing on the merits." Discussed further in "Laches vs. Lapse of Time" (Sec. 5.01-E.1).

Domain name registrants in different markets or geographic or territorial locations than trademark owners cannot be said to have acted in bad faith when the trademarks are not particularly well-known outside their areas of recognition, and complainants fail to show how respondents could have known about them and their marks at the time of registration. Respondent's evidence that it had researched the name on prominent search engines and found that complainant's company was "not featured until 13 pages and 134 sites into the search" can also be conclusive against the complainant.[255]

Moreover, respondent is entitled to the disputed domain name when it is being used in a descriptive sense to communicate some aspect of the services offered by it at its website.[256] In these circumstances, the "first to register a domain name containing a generic or descriptive mark should prevail absent bad faith and a lack of legitimate interest."[257] This principle applies even to famous brands if the addition to the trademark describes an activity with no relationship to complainant.[258] In the words of one Panel, "it would take an exceptional case to succeed where there was no malicious or exploitative intent directed at complainant [or its trademark] at time of registration of the domain name."[259]

Finally, where the mark is used by a "multitude" of businesses Panels have approached the issue in one of two ways. Either the mark is too weak to satisfy the bad faith registration requirement, as in <nature.com>, or too diluted for protection by any of the multitude, in which event the first to register is entitled to keep it–<firstamerican.com>.

---

[254] ***Airbnb, Inc. v. Norman King / Target Marketing Group***, FA1707001738345 (Forum July 27, 2017) (<air-bnb.org>. "[Complainants] can initiate proceedings under the Policy at any time for any domain names that are confusingly similar to their marks.")

[255] ***Seaway Bolt & Specials Corp. v. Digital Income Inc.***, FA 114672 (Forum August 5, 2002) (<seaway.com>. The Panel found that SEAWAY was a dictionary word and denied the complaint. The question of joined dictionary words is whether the combination is distinctive and well-known. Discussed further in "Dictionary Words and Descriptive Phrases" (Sec. 5.01-D.1).

[256] ***Sweeps Vacuum & Repair Center, Inc. v. Nett Corp.***, D2001-0031 (WIPO April 13, 2001) (<sweeps.com>); ***Target Brands, Inc. v. Eastwind Group***, FA267475 (Forum July 9, 2004) (<target.org>. Respondent appeared; Complaint denied).

[257] ***CRS Technology Corporation v. Condenet, Inc.***, FA93547 (Forum March 28, 2000).

[258] Discussed further above in "Nominative Fair Use as Applied" (Sec. 5.01-C.2.a).

[259] ***Velcro Industries B. V. and Velcro USA Inc. v. allinhosting.com/Andres Chavez***, D2008-0864 (WIPO July 28, 2008) (<velcroart.net>).

5.01-F.2 Earlier Registered Domain Names; Subsequently Acquired Trademarks 5.01-F.2

Although the Policy is clear in its jurisdiction that later acquired trademarks have no priority of right to earlier registered domain names[260] instances have already been noted of complainants succeeding with the right Panel.[261] The consensus view discussed in Chapter 4 is that trademark owners cannot use the Policy as a tool "to simply wrest . . . disputed domain name[s]" away from respondents. Even though complainants may have legitimate grievances against infringing websites[262] they have no actionable claim to corresponding domain names registered before their existence.[263] Their remedy (if any) lies under trademark law.

It would defy logic if the law were otherwise. Whether or not a respondent lacks rights or legitimate interests in the domain name,[264] there is no merit to arguments under paragraph 4(a)(iii) that keeping a domain name inactive (passively holding),[265] using it in bad faith,[266] pointing it to a parking page,[267] underutilizing

---

260 The effort in some cases to create priority by claiming respondent renewed the domain name with knowledge of complainant's trademark is not availing. The reason for this is that bad faith registration is measured from the original registration, not the renewal of registration. ***Patricks Universal Export Pty Ltd. v. David Greenblatt***, D2016-0653 (WIPO June 21, 2016) (<patricks.com>) (Renewal not considered as equivalent to a new registration). An owner's recourse (if the facts support infringement) is under the Lanham Act.

261 The construction supporting this view has been rejected by a consensus of panelists. Discussed further in "Justifying Forfeiture Despite Good Faith Registration" (Sec. 4.03-A.4.b).

262 ***Edward Smith v. Douglas Bates***, FA1302001483682 (Forum March 27, 2013) (<joopa.com>). The issue is discussed further in "Reverse Domain Name Hijacking" (Sec. 7.11-A). Respondent's lack of state, federal or common law trademarks for "beautiful people" is irrelevant, since the question to be decided is not whether Respondent has a valid trademark but whether Respondent has rights or legitimate interests in the domain names that contain that phrase, which it proved it had from an earlier date than Complainant's acquisition of its trademark. ***Beautiful People Magazine, Inc. v. Domain Manager / PeopleNetwork ApS / Kofod Nicolai / People Network Aps / Nicolai Kofod / People Network***, FA1502001606976 (Nat. Arb. Forum May 4, 2015).

263 WIPO Overview 2.0, Paragraph 3.1: "Consensus view: Generally speaking, although a trademark can form a basis for a UDRP action under the first element irrespective of its date . . . when a domain name is registered by the respondent before the complainant's relied upon trademark right is shown to have been first established (whether on a registered or unregistered basis), the registration of the domain name would not have been in bad faith because the registrant could not have contemplated the complainant's then non existent right.")

264 ***Interep Nat'l Radio Sales, Inc. v. Internet Domain Names, Inc.***, D2000-0174 (WIPO May 26, 2000) (Respondent prevails on precedence of registration regardless whether it has rights or legitimate interests.)

265 ***John Ode d/ba ODE and ODEBOptimum Digital Enterprises v. Intership Limited***, D2001-0074 (WIPO May 1, 2001).

266 ***Digital Vision, Ltd. v. Advanced Chemill Systems***, D2001-0827 (WIPO September 23, 2001).

267 ***Geopack v. Name Administration Inc. (BVI)***, D2006-1590 (WIPO March 15, 2007).

it,[268] or being deceased[269] are grounds for forfeiture. A "later business cannot just register a trademark and then subsequently use this procedure to remove a website from the Internet that uses the same name."[270] Complainant garners no reward for failing to research domain name ownership before it adopts a mark or rebrands its business.[271]

Neither can a complainant establish a better right on evidence that respondent has never been commonly known by the domain name, made any legitimate commercial or fair use of it,[272] or no longer has a need for it as Complainant alleged in ***NETime Solutions***. It proposed that a respondent can lose its right to a domain name if

> his company has been dormant for at least 10 years; that his use of the domain name has not been in connection with bona fide offering of goods and services; that the domain name has been crippled by its non use; [and] that by ceasing to trade Respondent has extinguished his rights in the name.

Respondent does not forfeit its right to a domain name because an after-acquiring trademark owner believes it has a better or superior right to it.[273] That

---

[268] ***NETtime Solutions LLC v. NetTime Inc. c/o Chad Wagner***, FA0810001230152 (Forum December 19, 2008) ("In 1995 when Respondent registered his company and domain name, Complainant was not even in business and indeed, according to the evidence, only began to trade some 10 years later. Therefore to say that Respondent had no legitimate rights to the disputed domain name in 1995 is clearly ridiculous.")

[269] ***Société Du Figaro S.A. v. Cut Company***, DTV2013-0007 (WIPO February 2, 2014) (<figaro.tv>).

[270] ***Rohl, LLC v. ROHL SA***, D2006-0645 (WIPO July 12, 2006); Respondent in ***Alessandro International GmbH v. Alessandro Gualandi***, D2014-2111 (WIPO February 16, 2015) proved right or legitimate interest in on proof that "Alessandro" was his personal name. Panel found the following contentions without merit: 1) Respondent is not using the domain name; 2) Respondent is making no demonstrable preparations to use domain name in connection with a bona fide offering of good or services; and 3) Respondent should forfeit domain name because trademark owner has a better right than a non-famous individual who just happens to have the same name as the company and its trademarks.

[271] ***Hitcents.com v. Bob Blackard***, D2012-0063 (WIPO March 11, 2012) (<omniprise.com>. "Complainant should have been aware that Respondent owned registration of the disputed domain name when Complainant adopted its trademark. Complainant is not now in a position to claim that Respondent is taking unfair advantage of it by refusing to relinquish the disputed domain name on Complainant's terms.") Rebranding: See ***SiTV, Inc. d/b/a NUVO TV v. Javier F. Rodriguez***, D2014-1143 (WIPO August 14, 2014) ("The Complainant rebranded under the NUVO TV mark in July 2011. There is no evidence in the record suggesting that the Complainant's intentions were publicly known until the latter half of 2010, and no plausible explanation has been offered as to how the Respondent when registering the disputed domain names in July 2008 could have foreseen this development.")

[272] ***San Diego Hydroponics & Organics v. Innovative Growing Solutions, Inc.***, D2009-1545 (WIPO March 3, 2010).

respondent acquired the disputed domain name after its abandonment by a prior holder in the same industry as complainant is irrelevant. In ***Success Bank***[274] Respondent registered <successbank.com> following its abandonment by a bank known before its merger with another financial institution as "Success National Bank." Complainant, unrelated to the former Success National Bank, changed its corporate name in 2007 and in January 2008 obtained a federal registration for SUCCESS BANK.

It stretches the "argument to the extreme" to assert that "once a complainant shows good title in a mark, the burden shifts to Respondent to defend use and bad faith."[275] Having a trademark does not support complainant's right to a corresponding domain name. If this were the law "one could peruse the lightly used or parked domains, initiate a trademark registration application years after the disputed domain name was registered and then claim UDRP rights in the domain under the first element of the UDRP."[276]

Although it has been suggested otherwise,[277] speculative registrations of generic words and/or letter combinations in good faith with the intention of using them for non-infringing websites or reselling them later at a profit to newly minted trademark owners were never intended to be prohibited by the Policy.[278] Complainant in one

---

273 ***Live Earth, LLC v. Designers for Change Ltd c/o Mustafa Sami***, FA0908001280449 (Forum October 15, 2009) (<liveearth.com>) ("Is Complainant asking the Panel to believe that Respondent is so prescient as to register dishonestly the disputed domain name with foresight of Complainant's formation nearly a decade in advance (and to cover its malignant intent by cleverly founding a 'phony' organization, Live Earth Trust, nearly another decade prior to such registration)?") Death of registrant is not a sufficient basis for capturing the domain name. ***Société Du Figaro S.A. v. Cut Company***, DTV2013-0007 (WIPO February 2, 2014) (<figaro.tv>). ***RPG Life Sciences Ltd. v. James Mathe***, D2013-2094 (WIPO December 30, 2013) ("UDRP proceedings are concerned with abusive registration of domain names and are not a test of who has the better rights to a disputed domain name nor who holds the most similar domain names.")

274 ***Success Bank v. ZootGraphics c/o Ira Zoot***, FA0904001259918 (Forum June 29, 2009).

275 Id.

276 Id.

277 The dissent in ***The American Automobile Association, Inc. v. QTK Internet c/o James M. van Johns***, FA1261364 (Nat. Arb. Forum, July 25, 2009) opined that speculative registrations of generic words and/or letter combinations with the intention of selling them at a profit "[o]nce someone wants to acquire the domain name . . . were intended to be prohibited by the policy. . . ." Speculation prohibited is not the law. In a subsequent ACPA action, QTK Internet consented to judgment transferring <aaa.net> to The American Automobile Association, *The American Automobile Association, Inc. v. James M. Van Johns* (1:09-CV-002)(DC Western District Pennsylvania, Oct. 14, 2009).

278 Too numerous to cite. For early case see ***Micron Technology, Inc. v. Null International Research Center***, D2001-0608 (WIPO June 20, 2001) (<crucialtechnology.com>). Later cases include ***UTILIBILL, Pty.Ltd. v. JOHN POWERS / 191 Chandler Rd.***, FA161100 1705087 (Forum January 9, 2017) (<utilibill.com>) ("[T]here is nothing in the Policy to negate the right or a registrant to

case claimed a superior right to <lincs.com> because respondent's "sole intent [in registering the domain name was] to warehouse and sell the domain for profit."[279]

Another Complainant took the argument a step further by alleging that Respondent is "waiting for the right number to come along, but as he waits, complainant, a bona fide owner and user of the RESIN trademark, cannot use his RESIN trademark as a domain name."[280] The complainant assumes that an owner of a later-acquired trademark has a superior right to the corresponding domain name because it is a trademark owner. However, speculation (or, foresight as it would be regarded by the respondent) is not condemned under the Policy.

It is not to the corresponding, earlier registered domain names that owners have superior rights, but to remedies for unlawful use of their trademarks. Unlawful use presupposes that marks had acquired (or from the start their marks had inherent) distinctiveness before their alleged misappropriation, but lacking priority they have no actionable claims for cybersquatting. Priority looks forward from the owner's first use of its mark in commerce, not backward to a time that it had no reputation to trump another's earlier right to the domain name.[281] Panels have made it clear that complainants misconceive the UDRP by urging panelists to recognize a right despite respondents having priority.[282]

---

register a domain name with the intention of selling it at a profit, especially when, as in the present case, there was no trademark in existence or contemplation when the domain name was registered. Complainant's first and principal argument therefore does not succeed.")

[279] ***Spinsix Strategic Marketing Design, LLC v. RareNames, WebReg***, FA0907001273907 (Forum September 3, 2009); ***Kosmos SAS v. Domain Hostmaster - Customer ID: 48322848242624 / Domain Admin, Ashantiplc Limited***, D2015-2198 (WIPO February 19, 2016) (<kosmos.com>) (Denied. Complainant alleges that "the only goal of the Respondent is to sell the Disputed Domain Name at a high price.")

[280] ***Paper Denim & Cloth, LLC v. VertMarkets, Inc.***, FA1011001356783 (Forum December 22, 2010).

[281] In ***PPTP.NET, LLC v. Hoa But***, FA1002001310141 (Forum April 12, 2010) complainant argued that respondent "has not established any corporation, trademark or service mark pertaining to or referencing the domain name [<pptp.com>]." Neither has it responded to "multiple attempts at communication regarding the domain name." From these facts complainant infers that the "current domain holder . . . has acted in bad faith by . . . renewing the domain name registration . . . despite not having a website present (sic) at all."

[282] Although complainants have standing to initiate proceedings, since their marks were not in existence when the domain name was registered they have no actionable claim, and the complaint must be dismissed. See ***Charles E. Runels, Jr. v. Domain Manager / Affordable Webhosting, Inc., Advertising***, FA1709001749824 (Forum October 23, 2017) ("Without prior rights, there is just no UDRP case since there was no abusive registration. As the Panelist stated in Riveron Consulting, L.P. v. Stanley Pace, FA1002001309793 (Forum April 14, 2010) ("While Complainant currently has trademark rights in the at-issue mark by virtue of its RIVERON trademark registration, ***such rights do not magically relate back*** to the time that Respondent first registered the <riveron.com> domain name, a time well prior to Complainant's first use of its mark" (Emphasis added by Panel);

5.02 PRIOR USE OR DEMONSTRABLE PREPARATIONS TO USE BEFORE NOTICE—PARAGRAPH 4(c)(i) OF THE POLICY 5.02

5.02-A Construing "Before Any Notice of the Dispute" 5.02-A

Under the first of the paragraph 4(c) defenses, respondent retains the domain name if 1) "before any notice . . . of the dispute," 2) it "has used or [has] made demonstrable preparations to use the domain name," 3) "in connection with a bona fide offering of goods or services." [283] Except under 2) which provides for an either/or possibility, the elements are cumulative; each must be proved by a preponderance of the evidence. Adverse possession for a prescribed period (as in real property law) is not a defense.[284]

The term "before notice of the dispute" implies unawareness of the existence of complainant's trademark coupled with a *bona fide* use of the domain name prior to actual notice of a dispute. Statutory constructive notice under the U.S. Trademark Act does not satisfy the requisite "notice" under the UDRP.[285]

To come within paragraph 4(c)(i) of the Policy, "such use must effectively predate the cognizance of the dispute by the Respondent."[286] The defense is phrased in the past tense, "has used," or for demonstrable preparations, has already taken the prerequisite steps to use the disputed domain name. The use that qualifies as

---

Centroamerica Comercial, Sociedad Anonima de Capital Variable (CAMCO) v. Michael Mann, D2016-1709 (WIPO October 3, 2016) (Complainant represented by counsel for <dollarcity.com>); ***GWG Holdings, Inc. v. Jeff Burgar, Alberta Hot Rods***, D2016-1420 (WIPO October 13, 2016) (Complainant represented "internally" for <gwg.com>); ***Whispering Smith Limited v. Domain Administrator, Tfourh, LLC***, D2016-1175 (WIPO September 27, 2016) (Complainant represented by counsel for <bravesoul.com>). The sole consequence of overreaching trademark rights is a declaration of Reverse Domain Name Hijacking, which carries a moral censure rather than a monetary award. Discussed further in "Complaint Filed in Bad Faith" (Sec. 7.11).

283 The term "services" under Paragraph 4(c)(i) is not limited to commercial services but may include noncommercial services to the public. ***Estate of Gary Jennings and Joyce O. Servis v. Submachine and Joe Ross***, D2001-1042 (WIPO October 25, 2001); 2001 ***White Castle Way, Inc. v. Glyn O. Jacobs***, D2004-0001 (WIPO March 26, 2004).

284 While evidence of demonstrable preparations supports good faith registration, lack of demonstrable preparations where there is extended passive holding of a disputed domain name without persuasive evidence of good faith supports abusive registration.

285 ***Phone N Phone Services (Bermuda) Ltd v. Shlomi (Salomon) Levi***, D2000-0040 (WIPO 2000).

286 ***Corinthians Licenciamentos LTDA v. David Sallen, Sallen Enterprises, and J. D. Sallen Enterprises***, D2000-0461 (WIPO July 17, 2000) ("The Panel notes that the posting of biblical quotes by the Respondents followed notice of the dispute (fifteen months after the domain name registration) and is most likely an excuse for camouflaging the purpose of trafficking with the domain name. Had the Respondents in this instant case not contacted the Complainant for selling the domain name the belief and findings of this Panel might have been different.") However, Respondent successfully challenged the transfer in an ACPA action, *Sallen v. Corinthians Licenciamentos LTDA*, 273 F.3d 14, 28 (1st Cir. 2001).

legitimate must be continuous from past to present. Intended future use unaccompanied by evidence of demonstrable preparations is not a good defense. A protected use "must subsist at the date of the commencement of the administrative proceeding."[287] Respondent cannot rest its defense on a discontinued legitimate use.[288] It is not to be dismissed that businesses operating commercial ventures may have a stronger case than investors reselling domain names acquired after a mark's first use in commerce.[289]

Paragraph 4(c)(i) should be read on two levels. The first level explicitly addresses the economic issue, namely respondent's right to continue using the disputed domain name *as long as it is "in connection with a bona fide offering of goods or services."* It is necessary to qualify "right" because under some readings of the policy a respondent can lose its legitimate interest by subsequently using the domain name in bad faith.[290] A respondent that satisfies the three elements of the defense—"Before any notice", "has used," and "in connection with a bona fide offering"—has a legitimate interest in the disputed domain name, even though it has no right to the incorporated mark. The second level is an implicit warning to complainant that failing to police its trademark or unreasonably delaying action to protect it has consequences.

"Notice" has been construed to mean actual notice brought to the respondent's attention by complainant commencing a UDRP proceeding if not by prior communications. According to one Panel a "complainant has an affirmative duty not only to object to a respondent's conduct but equally importantly to actually notify respondent of that objection."[291] It is not "notice" to have a registered mark on the Principal Register. "Notice of a mark is not necessarily notice of a dispute."[292] The statutory concept of constructive notice does not apply in UDRP proceedings

---

287 ***Grupo Costamex, SA de C.V. v. Stephen Smith and Oneandone Private Registration / 1&1 Internet Inc.***, D2009-0062 (WIPO March 25, 2009).

288 Id. (A "previously held right or legitimate interest which has been lost by that date will not avail the respondent.")

289 Approximately twenty percent of UDRP cases filed are terminated, including (although unknown as to number) voluntary transfers.

290 Subsequent bad faith use is further discussed in "Justifying Forfeiture Despite Good Faith Registration" (Sec. 4.03-A.4.b). That a second generation respondent can lose the domain name also emphasizes the distinction between two kinds of "right." Unless respondent proves a competing legal right in the mark, the respondent's "right" is a "legitimate interest." This distinction is discussed further in "Distinguishing Rights and Legitimate Interests" (Sec. 4.02-A).

291 ***CafePress.com v. Michael Fragomele***, FA0502000428848 (Forum April 27, 2005) ("While such notice need not be in writing—and paragraph 4(c)(i) is devoid of any such written requirement, due process requirements dictate that complainant's objections must be adequately communicated to respondent both in an appropriate manner and with sufficient content to properly place respondent on notice of its objectionable conduct.")

292 ***Leap Real Estate Systems, LLC. v. BytePlay Limited***, D2009-1290 (WIPO November 25, 2009).

and neither is notice of the dispute established by implication or inference and neither is notice of a dispute established by implication or inference.

"Imputing requisite notice on a respondent, simply by virtue of its own actions and prior to the receipt of actual notice from a complainant, would require respondent to speculate about complainant's perceptions and intentions, possibly erroneously so and hence to the ultimate detriment of the respondent."[293] The smaller presence in the marketplace or lower classification of the trademark the greater the need for prompt notice. Conversely, the greater complainant's presence in respondent's market the less credibility respondent would have in denying knowledge of complainant's rights.

Panels construe the "before any notice to you" element literally. It is "totally unavailing for complainant to argue that "Respondent registered the disputed names after Complainant commenced use of its marks in commerce."[294] This is because the "operative time point referenced in paragraph 4(c)(i) of the Policy is not the date on which a complainant commenced use of its mark but rather the date on which a respondent received notice of the dispute." In ***ETS***[295] the Panel found "Respondent has been conducting, since well before he received notice of this dispute, a legitimate business using the trademark nominatively" to sell test preparation materials, although post-notice sanitizing of the website is evidence of bad faith.[296]

---

293 Id. ***CafePress.com.***

294 ***Michael Machat v. Jaden Thompson a/k/a Vaden Vampes, a/k/a Vampes Domains by Proxy***, FA0508000542036 (Forum October 6, 2005).

295 ***Educational Testing Service (ETS) v. Morrison Media LLC***, D2006-1010 (WIPO December 5, 2006). For use of correspondence to rebut Complainant's contentions of bad faith and support reverse domain name hijacking see ***IMB Textil S.A. v. Domain Administrator, Name Administrator Inc. (BVI)***, D2014-1057 (WIPO September 5, 2014) ("the Complainant was warned before it filed the Complaint what the Respondent's defence would be. Having received that warning, the Complainant could have taken fairly rudimentary steps to investigate the Respondent's claims. At a minimum, it could have verified how the disputed domain name was in fact being used. A properly advised complainant should also have taken steps to investigate the claim that the Respondent had been using the disputed domain name in an unobjectionable way "for a very long time". For example, The Wayback Machine maintained at "www.archive.org" is a well-known resource which can often provide some indication about how a domain name has been used at points in time in the past.")

296 See *Shields v. Zuccarini*, 254 F.3d 476 (3rd Cir. 2001) ("[B]y his own admission, Zuccarini submits that his alleged 'fair use' of the offending domain names for 'political protest' began only after Shields brought this action alleging a violation of the ACPA. We are aware of no authority providing that a defendant's 'fair use' of a distinctive or famous mark only after the filing of a complaint alleging infringement can absolve that defendant of liability for his earlier unlawful activities. Indeed, were there such authority we think it would be contrary to the orderly enforcement of the trademark and copyright laws.)

5.02-B 5.02-B Construing "*Bona Fide* Use"

Respondent satisfies its burden of persuasion under paragraph 4(c)(i) of the Policy if "before any notice to you of the dispute, your use of, or demonstrable preparations to use, the domain name or a name corresponding to the domain name [is made] in connection with a bona fide offering of goods or services."[297] The intent of paragraph 4(c)(i) "is to allow business entities with a bona fide offering of goods and services the opportunity to register domain names related to their business."[298]

It is said that "consideration of good faith is a key issue in determining whether use is bona fide under the Policy."[299] Panelists quickly recognized that the concept of "bona fide" offering extended even to the commodification of domain names provided they were not "chosen with the intent to profit from or otherwise abuse Complainant's trademark rights."[300] If a domain name is lawfully adopted and used a respondent can have rights even to arbitrary or entirely fanciful marks,[301] but offering legitimate goods or services of the same type with a domain name identical or confusingly similar to complainant's mark is not a defense under paragraph 4(c)(i) of the Policy.[302]

Whether the operation of a business is *bona fide* depends upon a number of factors: its history, either of operation or preparation for it, the contents of its website and respondent's explanation for choosing a domain name identical or confusingly similar to complainant's trademark. A *bona fide* business operation presupposes respondent is using the disputed domain name to market goods or services

---

297 The term "services" includes noncommercial services to the public. See ***Estate of Gary Jennings and Joyce O. Servis v. Submachine and Joe Ross***, D2001-1042 (WIPO October 25, 2001).

298 ***William S. Russell v. Mr. John Paul Batrice d/b/a the Clock Doc.***, D2004-0906 (WIPO December 13, 2004). The defense can be effective for parties that incorporate a complainant's trademark legitimately. Discussed further in "Nominative Fair Use" (Sec. 6.01-D.3), "Non-Authorized But Lawful Use of Trademarks" (Sec. 5.01-C.2) and "Nominative Fair Use As Applied" (Sec. 5.01-C.2.a). Construction of the Policy that brings it into line with U.S. law is traceable to ***Oki Data Americas, Inc. v. ASD, Inc.***, D2001-0903 (WIPO November 6, 2001).

299 ***San Francisco Museum of Modern Art v. Joshua S. Drapiewski***, D2000-1751 (WIPO April 25, 2001).

300 ***Allocation Network GmbH v. Steve Gregory***, D2000-0016 (WIPO March 24, 2000) (<allocation.com>). Buying, using and selling domain names is a legitimate business model.

301 ***7(S) Personal GmbH v. Zhaohua Luo***, D2010-1953 (WIPO February 3, 2011). (Complaint denied. However, the dissent insisted that there be "some semantic relationship between the domain name and the website for that use to be bona fide." In a concurring opinion dismissing the complaint one of the panelists stated that he did not disagree except that in this particular case "we are presented with such use of the disputed domain name over a long period of time, together with the paucity of evidence that the use was pretextual or otherwise illegitimate.")

302 ***Option One Mortgage Corporation v. Option One Lending***, D2004-1052 (WIPO February 27, 2005) (OPTION ONE MORTGAGE and <optiononelending.com>).

unrelated to those offered by complainant. In one case respondent proved that the links on the resolving website <target.org> "relate[d] to target practice, hunting, archery, and other sports equipment."[303]

A business with a history is more likely to be *bona fide* than one without, but if respondent is a direct competitor it falls afoul of paragraph 4(b)(iii) of the Policy; if it provides links to competitive goods or services it falls afoul of paragraph 4(b)(iv). *Bona fide* extends to resellers of generic domain names potentially attractive to many businesses: Panels have recognized that resellers of domain names are not excluded from a 4(c)(i) defense: "Acquiring domain names simply in order to trade them at a profit or to exploit them for pay-per-click revenue is not, of itself, objectionable in the absence of any targeting of the complainant."[304]

Respondents can satisfy the defense by proffering evidence which excludes any inference they had complainants in mind when registering their domain names. In one case the Panel found "that Respondent has been conducting, since well before he received notice of this dispute, a legitimate business selling test preparation materials."[305] The kind of use employed before notice as evidenced by the website's content is one of several factors Panels take into account, although "not all use prior to notice of the dispute can qualify as bona fide use."[306]

The conclusion to this line of reasoning is that no use is *bona fide* that shows intention to take advantage of complainant's reputation in the marketplace.[307] "[U]se which intentionally trades on the fame of another cannot constitute a 'bona fide' offering of goods or service. . . . [T]o conclude otherwise would mean that a Respondent could rely on intentional infringement to demonstrate a legitimate interest, an interpretation which is obviously contrary to the intent of the Policy."[308] Indeed, it would be "unconscionable to find a bona fide offering of services in a respondent's operation of website using a domain name which is confusingly similar to complainant's mark and for the same business."[309] "The mere fact that

---

303 ***Target Brands, Inc. v. Eastwind Group***, FA 267475 (Forum May 25, 2004).

304 ***Airtango AG v. Privacydotlink Customer 2290723 / Gustavo Winchester***, D2017-2095 (WIPO December 11, 2017) (<airtango.com>. "The Complainant has produced evidence to demonstrate that the Respondent is a domainer (i.e.,someone whose business is to exploit domain names for their commercial value). Insofar as the Policy is concerned that area of business is unexceptionable provided that the domainer, when registering or acquiring the domain name in issue is not targeting a trade mark owner.")

305 ***Educational Testing Service (ETS)***, *supra*.

306 ***World Wrestling Federation Entertainment, Inc. v. Rift***, D2000-1499 (WIPO December 29, 2000).

307 Discussed earlier in "Targeting: Appropriating for Trademark Value" (Sec. 4.02-C.4).

308 ***Madonna Ciccone, p/k/a Madonna v. Dan Parisi and "Madonna.com,"*** D2000-0847 (WIPO October 12, 2000).

309 ***Am. Online, Inc. v. Fu***, D2000-1374 (WIPO December 2000).

Respondent has a plan to use the Domain Names [in the future] does not create a right or legitimate interest in [them]. The Policy requires a plan to make bona fide use."[310] Competitors cannot claim *bona fide* use since their motivation cannot be separated from the infringing act.[311]

The key to assessing whether a respondent's use constitutes a *bona fide* offering of goods or services lies in answers to the following questions: does "(i) [does] respondent regularly engage[ ] in the business of registering and reselling domain names and/or using them to display advertising links; (ii) [does] respondent make[ ] good faith efforts to avoid registering and using domain names that are identical or confusingly similar to marks held by others; (iii) [is] the domain name in question . . . a 'dictionary word' or a generic or descriptive phrase; (iv) [is] the domain name . . . identical or confusingly similar to a famous or distinctive trademark; and (v) . . . is [there any] evidence that respondent had actual knowledge of complainant's mark."[312] Proof of *bona fide* use is determinative of lawful registration.

In making its assessment on this issue it is improper for the Panel to import into the test "an element of confusion or bad faith,"[313] although "the facts will often be common to both requirements."[314]

5.02-C

5.02-C Cease-and-Desist Letter

There is no rule that requires service of cease-and-desist letters, but their timimg (or decision not to serve one[315]) can be a critical factor in determining parties' respective rights to the disputed domain name; equally so for respondents to respond or ignore notices. While it is in complainant's interest to act promptly on knowledge of a violation of its rights the form of notice (whether by cease-and-desist letter or initiation of a proceeding) will be strategic. Failing to respond to a cease-and-design letter may have consequences, but so too for complainants if they proceed with meritless claims.[316] However, not serving a demand that may have

---

310 ***Chanel, Inc. v. Cologne Zone***, D2000-1809 (WIPO February 22, 2001).

311 Competitors are judged under 4(b)(iii) of the Policy. See ***Ultimate Elecs., Inc. v. Nichols***, FA 195683 (Forum October 27, 2003) and earlier decisions cited therein.

312 ***Zerospam Security Inc. v. Internet Retail Billing Inc., Host Master***, D2009-1276 (WIPO December 18, 2009).

313 ***Modefine S.A. v. A.R. Mani***, D2001-0537 (WIPO July 20, 2001).

314 ***FabJob Inc. v. Compana LLC***, D2010-1144 (WIPO September 8, 2010).

315 See ***Souq.com FZ LLC v. Ruiling Wang, Comcom Communications LLC***, D2016-2085 (WIPO December 12, 2016) (<kingsouq.com>) (failure to send notice "has allowed the Respondent to solidify its rights to the Disputed Domain Name.")

316 See ***TOBAM v. M. Thestrup / Best Identity***, D2016-1990 (WIPO November 21, 2016) (<tobam.com>) (Respondent's warning in response to Complainant's cease and desist notice is a factor in determining reverse domain name hijacking: "This warning should have given the Complainant

elicited a response setting forth a meritorious defense has been interpreted unfavorably to complainant.[317]

There are benefits and detriments to serving a cease-and-desist letter. On the benefit side "replies and/or subsequent conduct by a Respondent can often help to prove or infer bad faith registration."[318] Correspondence can prove decisive in complainant's favor when respondent threatens complainant or registers another domain name incorporating its mark[319] and in respondent's favor when it responds promptly to a cease-and-desist notice by removing offending links[320] or complainant's demand for transfer lacks merit.[321]

---

serious pause for thought but it ploughed on regardless"); ***Emazing B.V. v. Joe Pierce***, D2015-1252 (WIPO August 25, 2015) (<emazing.com>) ("I just received your letter regarding the EMAZING. COM domain. We have operated an email newsletter publishing business @ EMAZING.COM since July 1998. Additionally, we hold a registered trademark on the term EMAZING in the United States. This mark (2316782) was granted by the United States Patent and Trademark Office on February 8, 2000.")

In ***Airpet Animal Transport, Inc. v. Marchex Sales, Inc / Brendhan Hight***, FA1211001470056 (Forum January 2, 2013) (alleged common law trademark) the three-member Panel was unanimous is finding RDNH: "Complainant applied for a trademark after knowing about Respondent's domain name and did not disclose that fact to . . . the Panel. Once again, the question is why not? Presumably, Complainant wanted to improve its chances in registering its mark and this proceeding." Discussed further in "Domain Name Hijacking" (Sec. 7.11).

317 Complaint denied: ***Hôpitaux Universitaires de Genève v. Aydin Karadeniz***, D2016-1620 (WIPO October 10, 2016) ("[O]n the one hand, the Complainant did not send any cease-and-desist letter or put any allegation of misconduct to the Respondent before filing the Complaint; and, on the other hand, it does not appear that the Complainant carried out any investigation itself before filing the Complaint that might have revealed whether the Respondent was acting in good or bad faith.") Complaint granted: ***Associated Newspapers Limited v. Makhdoom Babar, Mail Group***, D2019-0049 (WIPO February 25, 2019) (<dailymailnews.com>. "[In the] Panel's experience, someone using a domain name in a non-infringing manner and in furtherance of a legitimate enterprise would have responded to a cease-and-desist letter by asserting its bona fides. Respondent's failure to do so here undermines its claim of legitimacy."

318 ***"21" Club Inc. v. 21 Club***, D2000-1159 (WIPO November 22, 2000).

319 ***Carso S.A. de C.V. v. RusliCyber.com and Trisakti University, Mr. Ahmad Rusli***, D2008-1767 (WIPO January 5, 2009) (Complainant did not respond to Respondent's communication and in retaliation Respondent threatened to divert traffic from the domain name to an "unpredictable destination"; ***Thule Sweden AB v. Cameron David Jackson***, D2016-0414 (WIPO April 12, 2016) ("[A] fter the Respondent's receipt of the Complainant's cease-and-desist letter and hence with knowledge of the Complainant and its marks ... targeting is obvious from the record.")

320 ***Spiliadis v. Androulidakis***, FA 1072907 (Forum October 17, 2007) (The panel accepted respondent's explanation that it did not know until receiving a cease-and-desist notice from the complainant that, without instructions, its registrar "had posted unauthorized third party links on the website and that when it discovered this fact it was 'shocked,' demanded that they be removed and when they were not removed, [the] respondent changed its registrar.")

321 ***Epitec, Inc. v. EPITEC***, FA1209001463139 (Forum October 24, 2012).

A cease-and-desist notice is also important for establishing an outside date. It stops the clock on the paragraph 4(c)(i) defense, which puts the onus on respondent to prove continuous non-infringing use "before any notice to you of the dispute." Although a domain name registrant has no obligation to respond to complainant's cease-and-desist notice—non-response is merely one circumstance among others—silence can have consequences.[322] However, the twin failure to reply to complainant's cease-and-desist notice or respond to the complaint is conclusive against respondent on the issue of right or legitimate interest in the domain name and may support a finding of abusive registration.[323] The inference is that if respondent had a right or legitimate interest it would have responded.[324] No such inference can be drawn if respondent answers the complaint.[325]

Communications prior to filing the complaint are part of the record. They can reveal respondent's motivation and position.[326] The Respondent in ***Red Bull*** challenged Complainant rather than explain the legitimacy of the registration:

> "Please sue me!" and later "Try this I own 'www.redbullsucks.com' 'http://www.redbullsucks.com' and I will continue to promote my business! A.C.T. is the best an thats that! SEE YA!!! Carl B. Gamel III."

Although "red" and "bull" are common words the combination is distinctive, and in this case a well-known mark and brand. When the "sucks" addition is deceitful (as it is in this case) it is cumulative with other factors in confirming bad faith (that is, it is revealing of motivation in registering the domain name).

Responding to cease-and-desist letters by making changes to content or redirecting it to a non-infringing website is equally revealing[327]:

---

[322] ***Certamen Miss España, S.L. v. P1ESOFT.COM***, D2006-0679 (WIPO September 12, 2006) ("Respondent received two cease and desist notices from Complainant, and did not reply to them. Although generally considered Respondent's silence does not necessarily equal to bad faith, in the circumstances of the present case it certainly does not allow to infer the contrary.")

[323] ***America Online, Inc. v. Antonio R. Diaz***, D2000-1460 (WIPO January 19, 2001); ***Nike, Inc. v. Azumano Travel***, D2000-1598 (WIPO February 17, 2001) ("Failure to positively respond to a complainant's efforts to make contact provides strong support for a determination of 'bad faith' registration and use"); ***Associated Newspapers Limited,*** *supra.* Respondent failed to respond to two cease and desist ktters.

[324] ***Compagnie Géneralé Des Etablissements Michelin v. Vaclav Novotny***, D2009-1022 (WIPO September 16, 2009).

[325] Representative cases: ***Cupa Materiales S.A. v. Stonepanel.com c/o Whois Identity Shield/Vertical Axis, Inc.***, D2009-0216 (WIPO April 29, 2009); ***New England Greens, LLC v. Stephen Emond***, D2009-0362 (WIPO May 21, 2009).

[326] ***Red Bull GmbH v. Carl Gamel***, D2008-0253 (WIPO April 14, 2008) (<redbullsucks.com>).

[327] ***Julie & Jason, Inc. d/b/a The Mah Jongg Maven v. Faye Scher d/b/a Where the Winds Blow***, D2005-0073 (WIPO March 6, 2005).

> Respondent's belated effort to come within paragraph 4(c)(iii) of the Policy is easily answered. Respondent's modification of the disputed domain name, to resolve to an alternate site, not only occurred after this dispute arose but also did not cure the fatal taint in her earlier competing use of the disputed domain name.

Respondent's manner in responding establishes a baseline for determining lawful registration. To take the opposite example, a response putting complainant on notice of a right or legitimate interest acts as a warning that the registration is lawful, and that filing a complaint with that knowledge is *prima facie* abusive of the administrative proceeding (discussed further in Section 7.11).

No right or legitimate interest is created by respondent filing a trademark application after receipt of the cease-and-desist notice[328]; or changing the website to remove links and other evidence of infringement.[329] In these circumstances respondent very likely undermines its defense.[330] If notice is given by a cease-and-desist letter complainant should move promptly to challenge the registration. Lengthy and unexplained delay may support a defense of acquiescence or laches.[331]

5.02-D Construing "Demonstrable Preparations" 5.02-D

A respondent's right to a domain name purchased for future use must accrue not after but "before any notice" and optimally be secure as of the date it registered the disputed domain name; actions taken post-notice favor complainant.[332] The phrase "demonstrable preparations" connotes measurable activity to launch a website associated with an intent to make a *bona fide* offering of goods or services.

---

328 ***Grand Lodge Fraternal Order of Police v. Scott***, FA 798845 (Forum October 30, 2006).

329 ***State Farm Mutual Automobile Insurance Company v. Sean Dada***, FA 1521298 (Forum October 25, 2013) (Where Respondent changed the content of the resolving website after a cease and desist letter, the Panel found that "the Respondent's modification of the at-issue website after receiving a cease and desist letter tends to show that the current content of the website is merely a front to avoid an adverse UDRP decision"); ***University Athletic Association, Inc. v. Frank Apuzzo / FKLA, Inc.***, FA1504001613918 (Forum June 1, 2015) (<floridagators.com>. Respondent changed the website from appearing to be an official site for the University's sports teams to "This is a Website about Florida Alligators. Florida Alligators Are Also Called Gators or Gator For Short. FloridaGators.com – Info About Florida Alligators & Real Alligator Products.")

330 However, a respondent's right or legitimate interest established for an earlier confusingly similar domain name found to be lawfully registered is not undercut by its registering another confusingly similar domain name with a different extension after notice. ***Simple Truths, LLC v. Edward Slack, Simple Truth Publishing***, D2010-1349 (WIPO September 20, 2010) (<simpletruth publishing.com> and <simpletruthpublishing.net>).

331 ***Sun Studio Entertainment, Inc. v. Memphis Recording Service***, FA0805001189842 (Forum June 19, 2008) (domain name identical to the U.S. trademark in MEMPHIS RECORDING SERVICE). Discussed further in "Sleeping on One's Rights" (Sec. 5.01-E).

332 ***DigiPoll Ltd. v. Raj Kumar***, D2004-0939 (WIPO February 3, 2005).

"Time" is prescribed as a factor in the phrase "[b]efore any notice to you of the dispute. . . ." Prior activity that meets the requirements of a *bona fide* business is evidence that respondent registered the domain name for legitimate purposes and not to take advantage of complainant's trademark. Post-notice changes has the hallmarks of opportunism, which negates rights or legitimate interests.

It is easier to catalog what is not proof of demonstrable preparations than what is. Mere registration of a domain name is not such evidence.[333] Nor is it sufficient to arrange for the domain name to resolve to an "under construction" page.[334] Passive holding or parking merely reserves the web address for future infringing use.[335] The consensus is for a rigorous showing "before any to notice to you of the dispute."

Proof of demonstrable preparations is intensely fact driven. Respondent's plans have to be described with particularity supported by evidence they are not illusory. There has to be a showing of "demonstrable preparations to use" with the emphasis on *demonstrable*.[336] This can consist of business plans or other evidence reasonably related to preparations persuasive of respondent's intention. Anything less "discredits any argument that it is preparing to make a bona fide use of the Domain Names."[337] The Policy "specifies that the demonstrable preparations must be assessed before any notice of the dispute is given."[338]

The "threshold to demonstrate preparations to use the disputed domain name in connection with a bona fide offering of goods or services . . . has to be higher than submitting a single, unpublished, and undated page with almost no content."[339] "[V]ague and unsupported assertion of 'plans to sell household goods, supplies and appliances over the Internet,'" is insufficient to be considered proof of a legitimate business plan.[340] "The fact that respondent has not yet developed its website for the Domain Name is no bar to it demonstrating that it has a right or legitimate interest in respect of the Domain Name, but it must nonetheless produce to the Panel something more than a bare assertion."[341]

---

333 ***Vestel Elektronik Sanayi ve Ticaret AS v. Kahveci***, D2000-1244 (WIPO November 11, 2000).

334 ***Hewlett-Packard Co. v. Rayne***, FA 101465 (Forum December 17, 2001).

335 ***Kevin Garnett v. Trap Block Technologies***, FA 128073 (Forum November 21, 2002).

336 ***Telaxis Communications Corp. v. William E. Minkle***, D2000-0005 (WIPO March 5, 2000); ***Activeworlds, Inc. v. Carnatic Trade Links Pvt. Ltd.***, D2001-0249 (WIPO April 14, 2001) Respondent claimed it had a business in mind but failed to provide proof of demonstrable preparations. ACTIVE WORLD and <activeworld.com>, transferred.

337 ***Venetian Casino Resort LLC. v. International Services Incorporated***, D2001-0678 (WIPO September 14, 2001).

338 ***The Napoleon Hill Foundation v. VivaCorp SA***, FA0604000672115 (Forum May 18, 2006).

339 ***Interactive Systems Inc. v. NameBubble LLC***, FA0806001212590 (Forum August 13, 2008).

340 ***Household Int'l, Inc. v. Cyntom Enter.***, FA 95784 (Forum November 7, 2000).

In support of demonstrable preparations Panels have recognized that there may be excusable delays in starting a business,[342] although "delays must be quantifiable and limited; they cannot extend indefinitely."[343] The Panel in the last cited case held there must be some proof that the business is either active or "demonstrably" in the process of being formed:

> A respondent cannot simply do nothing and effectively 'sit on his rights' for an extended period of time when that respondent might be capable of doing otherwise. Now, rather than drawing a fixed, bright line as to the acceptable bounds of such action, the Panel recognizes that the bounds and quanta of such action will clearly need to vary from one situation to another and be assessed against the relevant facts at hand.

The fact that respondent's preparations have not resulted in an active website is not determinative against it as long as it can demonstrate steps toward that goal "before any notice . . . of the dispute."[344] Demonstrable preparations are for respondent what proof of common law rights is to complainant: neither can be satisfied by mere assertion. Respondent in ***California Farm Bureau*** proved that from the mid-1980s it styled its interior decorating business as "California Country," contemporaneous with the issuance to complainant of an identical trademark.

While demonstrable preparation to use a disputed domain name does not require showing "a fully operational business,"[345] merely alleging an intention to use or making unsupported claims of plans to do something in the future is insufficient. Respondent's defense

> falls down because there is no evidence of what, if any, preparations he has made. There is no evidence of a business plan or partners, the proposed technology or how it would function, how the business would be financed, a timetable or, indeed, evidence of a single fact about the business other than the intention to develop it at some indeterminate time in the future.

The defense is only satisfied by offering quantifiable evidence, otherwise[346]

---

341 ***Oxygen Media, LLC v. Primary Source and Melbourne IT Ltd. v. Stafford***, D2000-1167 (WIPO October 16, 2000); ***RAI Radiotelevisione Italiana S.p.A. v. The Netwizzy Company S.L.***, D2008 1862 (WIPO January 24, 2009).

342 ***Meredith Corp. vs. CityHome, Inc.***, D2000-0223 (WIPO May 18, 2000) ("the non use of the name for eight months is not an unduly long time for a new business in the planning stage of expansion.")

343 ***LFP, Inc. v. B & J Props.***, FA 109697 (Forum May 30, 2002).

344 ***California Farm Bureau Federation v. Steven A. Sokol***, FA0811001235897 (Forum February 2, 2009) (Domain name inactive but sufficient proof of demonstrable preparations.)

345 ***DigiPoll Ltd. v. Raj Kumar***, supra.

346 ***Freddy v. Frank Fushille***, D2004-0682 (WIPO October 27, 2004).

> [i]t would be all too easy for a cybersquatter to concoct a plausible excuse and swear to its veracity if subjectively honorable intentions alone overcame the bad faith requirement of Paragraph 4(a)(iii).

In this particular case, and to illustrate respondent's evidentiary hurdle, it "had made substantial investments, adopted the name 'ERESMAS' as its corporate name and as the name of one of its subsidiaries and filed numerous 'ERESMAS' trademarks prior to the notification of the Complaint."[347]

Although "perfunctory preparations have been held to suffice for this purpose,"[348] there must at least be a plausible explanation that such use is intended and has been prepared for.[349] The ***DigiPoll*** Panel (citing precedent) noted that no right is established by mere registration of the domain name. There must be some evidence to "prove the particular element contended for," even if those preparations were merely "superficial or mechanical." [350]

5.02-E 5.02-E Legitimate Activities

5.02-E.1 5.02-E.1 **Monetizing and Reselling Domain Names**

Panelists have affirmed that monetizing, licensing, offering to sell, passively holding, and reselling domain names directly or on the secondary market are legitimate business models under paragraph 4(c)(i) of the Policy.[351] The application of this policy is influenced by the manner in which respondents acquire domain names and conditioned on a finding that "the registration of the domain name was not undertaken with intent to profit from or otherwise abuse a complainant's trademark rights."[352]

---

[347] ***Televisa v. Retevision Interactiva S.A.***, D2000-0264 (WIPO June 28, 2000). In ***Safeguard Operations LLC v. Safeguard Storage***, FA672431 (Forum June 5, 2006), respondent had undertaken a number of activities in furtherance of its plan to open this business, including purchasing land on which to operate, engaging an architectural firm to design its facility, purchasing advertisements for its business, as well as registering with Michigan authorities for permission to operate its business under the assumed name "Safeguard Storage."

[348] ***Maureen A. Healy v. Andreas Kuhlen***, D2000-0698 (WIPO August 24, 2000).

[349] ***PT Cruiser Club LLC v. Thompson Six Star, Inc.***, FA0096452 (Forum February 28, 2001).

[350] ***DigiPoll Ltd.***, *supra,* citing ***Donvand Limited trading as Gullivers Travel Associates v. Gullivers Travel/Gulliver's Travel Services, Gullivers Travel Agency and Metin Altun/GTA, D2004-0741 (WIPO December 16, 2004).***

[351] ***X6D Limited v. Telepathy, Inc.***, D2010-1519 (WIPO November 16, 2010) (<xpand.com>. "Due to the commercial value of descriptive or generic domain names it has become a business model to register and sell such domain names to the highest potential bidder.") Reselling is discussed further in "Not All Offers to Sell Violate the Policy" (Sec. 6-02-B). See Australia (auDRP) which had considered, but rejected, a policy of prohibiting reselling, Appendix C.

[352] ***mVisible Technologies, Inc. v. Navigation Catalyst Systems, Inc.***, D2007-1141 (WIPO November 30, 2007) (Where the links on a portal website are based on the trademark value of the domain

Different subsets of legal principles apply depending on the level of care respondents exercise in acquiring and using challenged domain names. Against high-volume respondents who make wholesale acquisitions the determination is likely to turn on three points: first, whether they are the original registrants or successors; second, "patterns of conduct" (evidenced by holding domain names of well-known or famous marks, or prior adjudications stamping respondents as serial cybersquatters)[353]; and third, proof that the challenged domain name was acquired for its semantic value.[354]

Against respondents whose acquisitions are more discriminate a different subset of principles is applied since they are more likely to have considered trademark issues. It is not sufficient (and likely irrelevant) to allege that the challenged domain names have been registered without complainant's permission or respondents are not commonly known by the domain names if respondents' websites are populated with material or links rebutting complainants' contentions that they lack rights or legitimate interests.[355]

As a general rule, investors specializing in particular categories of names, such as 2 to 5 letter strings, place names, surnames, dictionary words, and descriptive terms that have independent market values unrelated to any association with complainants' marks and used for their common meanings[356] are less vulnerable

---

name, rather than any descriptive value, the trend in decisions under the Policy is to recognize that such practices generally do constitute abusive cybersquatting.) However, landing pages are legitimate if "the domain names have been registered because of their attraction as dictionary words, and not because of their value as trademarks." ***Landmark Group v. DigiMedia.com, L.P.***, FA 285459 (Forum August 6, 2004).

353 ***Fandango, LLC v. 21562719 Ont Ltd***, FA1209001464081 (Forum November 2, 2012) ("Respondent's past conduct and UDRP history establishes a pattern of registered domain names in bad faith under Policy ¶ 4(b)(ii)"); ***Hobbex AB v. Vertical Axis Inc., Domain Administrator / Whois Privacy Services Pty Ltd***, D2013-2111 (<hobbex.com>. "The Respondent does not claim to have made any attempt to ascertain whether its use of the disputed domain name would or could infringe another's trademark rights. Rather, it states that it believed no one could claim exclusive rights in the term 'hobbex' because of its descriptive nature.... Further ... the Panel does not accept that the disputed domain name is a purely descriptive term and notes further that, even on the Respondent's case, the disputed domain name is not in fact being used for its claimed descriptive significance.")

354 ***Dialoga Servicios Interactivos, S.A. v. Finlead AG***, D2018-2768 (WIPO February 8, 2019) (<dialoga.com>. "There is no doubt in the Panel's mind that the Respondent registered the disputed domain name ... [for its semantic] value because it consists of a common word in no less than three languages which are spoken by many millions of people.")

355 ***Storm Guard Franchise Systems, LLC v. Domain Hostmaster, Whois Privacy Services Pty Ltd., Customer ID: 50451538860866 / Kwangpyo Kim, Mediablue Inc.***, D2015-0241 (WIPO April 21, 2015) (<storng、guard.com>. "Respondent's legitimate interest is bolstered by the fact that it uses the Domain Name to display advertising links related to the descriptive terms "storm" and "guard.")

356 Dictionary words—***Fakir Elektrikli EV Aletleri Diş Ticaret Anonim Şirketi v. Development Services, Telepathy, Inc.***, D2016-0535 (WIPO May 21, 2016) (<fakir.com>); ***FPT Industrie S.p.a.***

to losing their domain names than high-volume registrants who must explain how their acquisition policies avoid sweeping in infringing domain names.[357]

Respondents operating businesses offering 1) vanity e-mail services,[358] 2) domain names for sale directly or on the secondary market,[359] and 3) online search portals[360] have been found to be making *bona fide* offerings of goods or services. However, the safe harbor that protects original registrants does not necessarily extend to transferees and successors whose attestations of good faith are measured from their registration dates.[361]

5.02-E.2 5.02-E.2 Personalized (Vanity) E-Mail Services

The prevalent use of domain names is for websites,[362] but use as an e-mail, FTP or hosting service can constitute a legitimate interest under the Policy.[363] Vanity e-mail services for surnames are legitimate as long as any associated websites are

---

and REM Industrie S.r.l. v. HugeDomains.Com, D2017-0842 (WIPO July 7 2017) (<fastmill.com>)—descriptive terms—***Nilson Group AB v. Domain Admin, Frontline Media***, D2016- 0334 (WIPO May 27, 2016) (<feetfirst.com>)—idioms—***Easton Corp Pty Ltd v. Privacydotlink Customer 951873/DNS Admin, Best Web Limited***, D2016-1975 (WIPO November 12, 2016) (<hottie.com>)—surnames—***Micah Hargress v. PARAMOUNT INTERNET***, FA1509001638609 (Forum November 13, 2015) (<hargress.com>)—and three or four letter strings—***SOG Specialty Knives and Tools, LLC v. Val Katayev / Poise Media Inc.***, FA170400 1726464 (Forum May 23, 2017) (<sog.com).

[357] For example, Texas International Property Associates was a frequent respondent between 2005 and 2011; of several hundred claims, it lost more than 95% of the time. For discussion of high volume registrants see "Enhanced Investigative Responsibilities for High-Volume Registrants" (Sec. 6.03-B).

[358] ***Stephen Wheatcraft v. Reison, Inc. c/o Domain Manager***, FA0811001232650 (Forum December 22, 2008) (<wheatcraft.com>).

[359] ***CeWe Color AG & Co. OHG v. Shenbun Limited***, D2008-0810 (WIPO July 10, 2008) ("The buying and selling of domain names is, of itself, a perfectly legitimate trading activity").

[360] ***Decal (Depositi Costieri Calliope) S.p.A. v. Gregory Ricks***, D2008-0585 (WIPO June 11, 2008) (<decal.com>. "If a respondent is using a generic word to describe his product/business or to profit from the generic value of the word without intending to take advantage of complainant's rights in that word, then it has a legitimate interest.")

[361] For first generation registrants whose registration was in good faith a change to bad faith use is not grounds for forfeiture, but a transferee is vulnerable. Discussed earlier in "Subsequent Bad Faith Use" (Sec. 4.03-A.4) and "Transfer/Subsequent Holder=New Registration" (Sec. 4.03-B.2).

[362] ***Innotek, Inc. v. Sierra Innotek***, D2002-0072 (WIPO April 22, 2002) ("[T]he lack of a formal web page does not detract from these real and viable commercial uses."); ***Thrive Networks, Inc. v. Thrive Ventures, Inc.***, D2003-0534 (WIPO August 26, 2003) ("Although it may not be easy to discern whether a domain name is being used for email, FTP services, or simply as a host, such uses are legitimate.")

[363] ***Zero International Holding GmbH & Co. Kommanditgesellschaft v. Beyonet Services and Stephen Urich***, D2000-0161 (WIPO May 12, 2000) (<zero.com>, "[w]e do not accept that complainant's

not adulterated with illegitimate content.[364] The model is allowable because (unlike websites) e-mails carry no commercial content linking the surname to the putative trademark owner. In this respect, trademarks and e-mails exist on mutually exclusive platforms. However, once the respondent strays from its alleged business model it exposes itself to a charge of cybersquatting.

To qualify for a paragraph 4(c)(i) defense the domain name "must be registered solely because it is a *bona fide* surname and **only** for use with vanity email services"[365] (emphasis in original). In the cited case the domain name was a generic first name, "Sallie," not the trademark SALLIE MAY. The Panel held

> As long as said domain names are actually generic or common, as long as Respondent does not harm third parties and as long as legitimate trademark owners do not hold rights to any of the names that Respondent owns, Respondent's activity is normally not classified as illegitimate under the Policy.

Registration of the surnames "Rael" and "Roche" were similarly found to be legitimate for vanity e-mail,[366] although the dissent in ROCHE was unpersuaded since Complainant owned an internationally famous trademark.[367]

Similarly, Respondents in ***Ancien Restaurant Chartier***[368] and ***Markel Corporation***[369] persuaded Panels they were using the disputed domain names as part of their business offering "vanity email addresses" to customers containing their

---

contention that registration of a domain name which is only to be used for [e-mail and file transfer operations] is in some way improper and constitutes bad faith.") This comes with the proviso that legitimacy depends on the use to which the registrant "may ultimately make of a domain name," ***Government of Canada v. David Bedford a.k.a. DomainBaron.com***, D2001-0470 (WIPO June 30, 2001) (three member Panel); ***Mechoshade Systems, LLC v. DNS Admin / Mecho Investments***, FA1805001784649 (Forum June 18, 2018) (<mecho.com>. "Complainant continued to pursue this case, including with the frivolous and demonstrably incorrect argument that use of a Domain Name for purposes of a family email address is not a legitimate interest.").

364 ***Buhl Optical Co v. Mailbank.com, Inc.***, D2000-1277 (WIPO March 1, 2001) (<buhl.com> legitimate for site that sells vanity e-mails to persons with the surname "Buhl"); ***Int'l Raelian Religion & Raelian Religion of France v. Mailbank.com Inc.***, D2000-1210 (WIPO April 4, 2001) (<rael.com> legitimate for site that sells vanity e mails to persons with surname "Rael").

365 ***Champagne Lanson v. Development Services/MailPlanet.com, Inc.***, D2006-0006 (WIPO March 20, 2006) (emphasis in the original); ***Sallie Mae, Inc. v. Michele Dinoia***, D2004-0648 (WIPO October 18, 2004) (<sallie.com>).

366 ***International Raelian Religion and Raelian Religion of France v. Mailbank.com Inc.***, D2000-1210 (WIPO April 4, 2001); ***F. Hoffmann La Roche AG v. Domain Admin Tucows.com Co.***, D2006-1488 (WIPO February 27, 2007) (<roche.org>. Complaint denied).

367 *Id.*, ***F. Hoffman-La Roche***. The majority relied heavily on *Avery Dennison Corp. v. Sumpton*, 189 F. 3d 868 (9th Cir. 1999), a pre-ACPA action. However, see ***Marker Völkl (International) GmbH v. Tucows.com Co.***, D2012-1461 (WIPO November 14, 2012) questioning the application of *Avery Dennison* to non-U.S. parties. "The decision in Avery Dennison was . . . made based on interpretation of the US Federal Trademark Dilution Act. However, in this case, the Complainant is a Swiss entity and the Respondent a Canadian entity."

first and last names, not for their value as trademarks.[370] The Panel in ***Artemides Holdings***[371] noted that the name "Bardot" is "a common French family name, often connected to the famous French actress Brigitte Bardot. . . . [However, the] Respondent may well have had reasons for registering the disputed domain name other than complainant's trademark rights." The legal issue is not the commonness of the name but confining the use to the model, which necessarily excludes resolving to a website.[372]

The reasoning in these cases complements decisions that find *mala fide* use of common word domain names registered for the purpose of taking advantage of trademarks with established market reputations. Protection for the personalized model dissolves when "a respondent . . . builds its domain around a surname that has acquired the protection of a trademark . . . and uses that domain merely to operate a click-through advertising scheme."[373] The ***Cargill*** respondent in the cited case argued that it had a legitimate interest in <cargills.com> because the "domain name is comprised of no more than the plural or possessive form of a common surname widely used by numerous parties."

However, the question in assessing bad faith is "whether the formation of a plural or possessive form of the mark," which under some circumstances could be legitimate becomes illegitimate when its use creates a likelihood of confusion with complainant's trademark. Applying the factor "the use to which the name is put" to the facts in ***Cargill*** revealed that respondent did not operate the domain name as a vanity e-mail service but used it "to display third-party click-through links, including advertisements for Complainant's business competitors."

In ***Pernod Ricard***[374] the "surname/domain name in question (Ricard) [is] a very famous trademark in France and abroad." According to the Panel it was

---

368 ***Ancien Restaurant Chartier v. Tucows.com Co.***, D2008-0272 (WIPO May 6, 2008) (<chartier.com>). The Panel made no finding in relation to paragraph 4(a)(ii) of the Policy but held absence of bad faith under paragraph 4(a)(iii).

369 ***Markel Corporation. v. Tucows.com Co.***, D2007-1750 (WIPO June 5, 2008) (<markel.com>).

370 In ***Markel*** the three member Panel found that complainant's complaint was abusive "contrary to Paragraph 15 (e) of the Rules" although it did not declare complainant guilty of Reverse Domain Name Hijacking. Discussed further in "Complaint Filed in Bad Faith" (Sec. 7.10).

371 ***Artemides Holdings Pty Ltd v. Gregory Ricks***, D2008-1254 (WIPO October 29, 2008) (French Complainant; U.S. Respondent).

372 *Id.*, ***F. Hoffman-La Roche*** ("If (as is incontrovertibly the case) Roche is a surname, the Panel does not think that a rule can be adopted which depends on how common the surname is or how successful the Respondent's efforts to find customers have been.")

373 ***Cargill, Incorporated v. RN WebReg c/o Rare Names, Inc.***, FA0904001260307 (Forum June 12, 2009). Cf.: ***Experience Hendrix, L.L.C. v. Denny Hammerton and The Jimi Hendrix Fan Club***, D2000-0364 (WIPO August 15, 2000) (Using the "Jimi Hendrix" mark for a like purpose or as a fan club was found to be exploitative).

> patently clear that respondent does not use the disputed domain name solely with a vanity email service.

Rather,

> The domain name is the address of a web portal which displays a list of sponsored links to third-party websites and through which respondent receives revenue. . .. Those links, coupled with the Panel's finding that the respondent was aware of complainant and its mark when the disputed domain name was registered, point inevitably to the conclusion that respondent appreciated that some Internet users looking for sites associated with complainant would mistakenly come to the Respondent's website.

This being the case, "it is but a short step to conclude that respondent must have intended that such mistakes would occur, and was to that extent seeking to profit from the trademark value of the word 'Ricard'" or as a charade for targeting complainant.[375]

The Panel found Respondent had

> no reason to doubt that the term "horbiger" is a surname. . . [but] [c]ontrary to the Respondent's contention . . . it is not being used just for a generic search portal. As noted above, it is being used for a website according to its own banner "For resources and information on Compressor and Automation."

As with ***Cargill***, right or legitimate interest ceases when the evidence shows that the website to which the disputed domain name resolves hosts (or at the commencement of the administrative proceeding hosted) commercial links to complainant's products. Purging a website of infringing content after service of a complaint does not cure but adds weight to the charge of abusive registration.[376]

---

[374] ***Pernod Ricard v Tucows.com Co.***, D2008-0789 (WIPO August 21, 2008).

[375] ***Hoerbiger Holding AG v. Texas International Property Associates***, D2007-0943 (WIPO October 19, 2007) involving the surname "Horbiger." Respondent alleged it was operating a vanity e-mail service but populated the website with links to complainant's competitors. It subsequently commenced an ACPA action, *Texas International Property Associates v. Hoerbiger Holding AG*, 624 F. Supp. 2d 582 (N.D. Tex. May 12, 2009), in which the court granted summary judgment to defendant on counterclaim of cybersquatting.

[376] ***Marker Völkl (International) GmbH v. Tucows.com Co.***, D2012-1461 (WIPO November 14, 2012) (Request to suspend UDRP proceeding in view of filing of a court action, denied. "As to use of the disputed domain name to generate click through revenue, the Respondent's case is that it has purged any such misuse by suspending the advertising complained of. . . . That does not, however, in the Panel's view alter the nature of the use current at the date of the Complaint in this administrative proceeding.")

5.02-E.3

5.02-E.3 Advertising

It is not illegitimate for a respondent to operate an online advertising portal from a domain name identical or confusingly similar to a trademark composed of a generic word or descriptive phrase that offers goods and services unrelated to complainant.[377] "Neither the current UDRP nor current ICANN registrar contracts preclude" the practice of registering domain names in connection with an advertising venture,[378] or pay-per-click websites,[379] or paid link-farm services.[380] It may also be legitimate to direct Internet traffic to websites that host pop-up advertising if the hyperlinking is done through domain names composed of common or generic words chosen for "their attraction as dictionary words, and not because of their value as trademarks."[381]

However, registration in good faith is suspect when the website to which the domain name resolves links to the complainant and competitors or contains direct reference to complainant's products or services. If it appears the site offers advertising and links to complainant's competitors, or if the registrant itself is a competitor, it can be inferred respondent registered the domain name in bad faith. This is so because content is evidence of intention and cannot be disclaimed.

In ***Aquascape Designs, Inc.*** the Panel explained that while there may be circumstances under which the use may be legitimate, it is infringing when[382]

> the links are apparently to competitive websites, especially when there is no indication that the links are not sponsored by or affiliated with the relevant trademark owner, such activity indicates bad faith under the Policy.

Legitimacy is lost equally when respondent misleads the Internet user into believing the website is associated with the trademark owner[383] as when it directs Internet users to complainant's competitors.

---

377 ***First Am. Funds, Inc. v. Ult.Search, Inc.***, D2000-1840 (WIPO May 1, 2001); Complainants in ***The American Automobile Association, Inc. v. QTK Internet c/o James M. van Johns***, FA090500 1261364 (Forum July 25, 2009) (<aaa.net>) contended that "pay per click advertising site[s] cannot give rise to a legitimate claim to a domain name," but Panels have declined the invitation "to find [them] per se illegitimate." Discussed further in "Attracting Internet Traffic" (Sec. 6.01-D).

378 ***Williams, Babbitt & Weisman, Inc. v. Ultimate Search***, FA98813 (Forum October 8, 2001).

379 ***Terana, S.A. v. RareNames, WebReg***, D2007-0489 (WIPO June 7, 2007); ***Fratelli Carli S.p.A. v. Linda Norcross***, D2006-0988 (WIPO October 4, 2006).

380 ***Aquascape Designs, Inc. v. Vertical Axis, Inc c/o Domain Adminstrator***, FA0601000629222 (Forum March 7, 2006) (<aquascape.com>) (Complaint dismissed).

381 ***The Landmark Group v. Digimedia L.P.***, FA 285459 (Forum August 6, 2004).

382 ***Aquascape Designs, citing Wal-Mart Stores, Inc. v. Whois Privacy, Inc.***, D2005-0850 (WIPO September 26, 2005).

383 ***Wells Fargo & Co. v. Party Night Inc. and Carrington***, FA 144647 (Forum March 18, 2003) (Respondent's use of confusingly similar derivatives of Complainant's WELLS FARGO mark to

5.03 COMMONLY KNOWN BY THE DOMAIN NAME— PARAGRAPH 4(c)(ii) OF THE POLICY 5.03

5.03-A What It Means to Be "Commonly Known By The Domain Name" 5.03-A

The Whois Directory is a first stop in determining respondent's rights or legitimate interests based on the individual, business or organization name declared in its registration of the disputed domain name. If respondent's name is different from the domain name it cannot have been commonly known by it[384]; if it is the same respondent must demonstrate the timing and genuineness of its adoption. "Mere ownership of a domain name is not sufficient to show that a respondent has been 'commonly known by the domain name'; if it were, every domain name registrant automatically could claim protection under paragraph 4(c)(ii) of the Policy."[385]

Paragraph 4(c)(ii) of the Policy is written in the past tense, "*have been* commonly known by the domain name" (emphasis added). Although the Policy does not specify when respondent is deemed to have become known by the domain name, panelists have construed the defense to "require a showing that [Respondent] has been commonly known by the domain name prior to registration of the domain name to prevail."[386]

Not being "commonly known by the domain name" is irrelevant if respondent demonstrates a paragraph 4(c)(i) or 4(c)(iii) defense. Because paragraph 4(c)(ii) has no qualifier other than "known by that name" it would be irrelevant also if the domain name corresponds to the trademark or respondent is holding it passively. Respondent's right is reinforced if it also has priority in a trademark sense

---

divert Internet users to websites featuring pop up advertisements was not a bona fide offering of goods or services); ***Bank of America Corp. v. Out Island Props., Inc.***, FA 154531 (Forum June 3, 2003).

384 The defense of "commonly known by the domain name" can be satisfied if there is "sufficient commonality" between the domain name and the name of the business." ***Adam Summers v. Georgina Nelson, CEO and Founder of truRating Limited***, D2015-0592 (WIPO May 24, 2015), giving as examples <vaughan.com> / "Vaughan Enterprises" and <kronopol.com> / "Kronopol Marketing."

385 ***Neiman Marcus Group, Inc. v. Neiman-Marcus***, FA 135048 (Forum January 13, 2003) (respondent called itself NEIMAN-MARCUS). Discussed further in "Pretending to Be Complainant" (Sec. 6.01-C.2).

386 ***Sony Kabushiki Kaisha aka Sony Corporation v. Sony Holland***, D2008-1025 (WIPO October 2, 2008) (<sonyholland.com>, Complaint denied. Respondent's nickname "Sony" derives from "Sonia." The problem for complainant is that Respondent's married name, "Holland," is also the name of a country in which Complainant does business). Earlier decisions include ***RMO, Inc. v. Burbidge***, FA 96949 (Forum May 16, 2001) (<rmo.com>. "A family information site is a legitimate non commercial use.") ***The California Milk Processor Board v. Center Ring Productions***, LLC, D2011-1689 (WIPO December 1, 2011) (<gotmilke.com>. Respondent's surname is "Milke.") See also discussion at "Faux Registrant" (Sec. 6.01-C.2.a).

and qualifies under paragraph 4(c)(i) as well as 4(c)(ii) as indicated in ***Digitronics Inventioneering***.[387]

5.03-B
5.03-B Qualifying for the Defense

5.03-B.1
5.03-B.1 Business Names

Priority of use is not a factor in qualifying for the defense under subparagraph 4(c)(ii) of the Policy. Close proximity of goods or services and location strengthens complainant's argument but cannot overcome proof that respondent's choice is the name by which it is "commonly known." Businesses in different classes[388] or the same class geographically separated may have a legal right to the domain name if they are known by it.[389]

This factor is illustrated in ***Verisign v. Venesign***, ***Avnet***, and the ***Carlyle Group***. In ***Verisign*** the Respondent did not appear, but the record contained an exchange of correspondence in which it asserted a right to the domain name: "Our certification service is for our country 'VENEzuela', the name VeneSign is derived by our country name."[390] In ***Avnet*** Respondent proved that it was known by the name AVNET for at least ten years prior to its domain name registration. In ***Carlyle Group***[391] Complainant offered no counter-evidence refuting respondent's proof it was a business entity duly formed in 2000 under the laws of Toronto with an associated company Carlyle Coutts Capital Corporation SA formed under the laws of Panama. The Panel noted that "although it might have assisted its case, respondent is not required to provide evidence as to why it selected its corporate name." For

---

[387] ***Digitronics Inventioneering Corporation v. @Six.Net Registered***, D2000-0008 (WIPO March 2, 2000) (SIXNET and <six.net> and <sixnet.com>). See also ***Triple Crown Nutrition, Inc. v. Walter De Ruysser***, FA1402001545525 (Forum April 3, 2014) (TRIPLE CROWN and <triplecrownhorsefeeds.com>. Respondent registered trademark prior to acquiring domain name. Same products but the parties operate in separate geographic markets). In ***Kelly v. Qsoft Consulting Ltd.***, D2003-0221 (WIPO April 30, 2003) Respondent obtained a trademark registration prior to commencement of the proceedings which the Panel found legitimate. However, see "No 'Right' Where Trademark Registration is to Bolster Domain Name Registration" (Sec. 4.02-A.1.c.i).

[388] ***Avnet, Inc. v. Aviation Network, Inc.***, D2000-0046 (WIPO March 24, 2000) (<avnet.net>).

[389] ***The Trustees of the Williamson Family Trust, comprised of William Williamson and Dawn Williamson, as Trustees v. Domain Administrator / Williamson Orchards & Vineyards***, FA170700 1740611 (Forum August 23, 2017) (<williamsonwine.com> and <williamson.wine>).

[390] ***VeriSign Inc. v. VeneSign C.A.***, D2000-0303 (WIPO June 28, 2000) ("Even though Respondent does (obviously) not have its own trademark and is not licensed by Complainant to use this trademark, Respondent can point to the fact that the domain name equals its company name 'VeneSign C.A.', which could give Respondent rights to the domain.") For conflict of rights arising from trademarks registered in different countries see "Rival Trademarks in Foreign Jurisdictions" (Sec. 4.02-A.1.c).

[391] ***Carlyle Group v. Carlyle Coutts Capital Corporation***, D2008-1960 (WIPO February 19, 2009) (<carlyle-coutts.com> and <carlylecoutts.com>).

choices of less well-known marks the evidence must be more persuasive, and for well-known the mark itself is persuasive of its distinctiveness.[392]

5.03-B.1.a *Redirecting, Liquidating, and Passively Holding* 5.03-B.1.a

Where respondents have rights or legitimate interests in domain names they are assets, to be used or not used to suit respondent's strategic and business interests. Redirecting them to other business websites, deciding to liquidate them,[393] or passively holding them (refusing to sell them[394]) is not evidence of bad faith.[395] The three-member Panel in ***Voys*** found it "extraordinary" (given the facts of the case) that Complainant should be arguing that Respondent lacked rights or legitimate interests because (for other reasons) the domain name was clearly registered "with a view to selling it at a profit."

---

392 ***K 2 Corporation v. HTM Sport GmbH,*** D2011-1709 (WIPO November 27, 2011) (RIDE and <ridehead.com>. Both RIDE and HEAD are well-known trademarks. However, "[i]n choosing as a trade mark a word that is commonly used in the English language as a verb in relation to snowboarding, complainant had to accept the fact that the scope of protection of its registration was likely to be limited, and would not extend to protect against the use of the word in expressions where it was used as a verb, for example in the expression 'ride HEAD' as incorporated into the Disputed Domain Name.") See *Nissan Motor Co., Ltd. v. Nissan Computer Corp.*, 89 F.Supp. 2d 154 (C.D.Cal. 2000) (clear trading off goodwill where individual with the surname "Nissan" operated a computer services website that derived 90% of its advertising revenue from automotive industry advertisements).

393 ***Hôpitaux Universitaires de Genève v. Aydin Karadeniz,*** D2016-1620 (WIPO October 10, 2016) (<hug.com>, <hug.net> and <hug.org>. "The Respondent states that his plans to develop a search engine proved unsustainable and that he decided to dissolve Hug.com and liquidate its assets, including the valuable Domain Names"); ***Aether, LLC v. Aether Domains / Aether Things, Inc.,*** FA1707001739957 (Forum August 24, 2017) (<aether.com>). Redirecting as evidence of bad faith is discussed in "Redirection by Competitor to Its Own Website" (Sec. 6.05-B.2).

394 ***Voys B.V., Voys United B.V. v. Thomas Zou,*** D2017-2136 (WIPO January 9, 2018) (<voys.com>. "This is an extraordinary statement. It incorrectly assumes that (1) non-use of a domain name of itself prevents the registrant from acquiring a right or legitimate interest and (2) registration of a domain name for no reason other than to sell it necessarily deprives the registrant of a right or legitimate interest.") See *Southern Grouts & Mortars, Inc. v. 3M Company*, 575 F.3d 1235 (11th Cir. 2009). 3M had come into possession of <diamondbrite.com> legally by acquiring the company that owned it years earlier. Its offense (as the plaintiff saw it) was not that it was using the domain name but was holding it inactive. Southern Grouts "accuse[d] 3M not of a design to sell a domain name for profit but of a refusal to sell one." The Court stated that "The Senate Report accompanying the Anticybersquatting Consumer Protection Act bolsters our understanding that a 'bad faith intent to profit' is the essence of the wrong that the Act seeks to combat....The report says nothing about those who [acquire a domain name in good faith and] hold onto [it through repeat renewals of registration] to prevent a competitor from using it."

395 ***Williamson Family Trust,*** *supra*. The Respondent supported its argument by offering the following as examples: <WINDOWSXP.COM> redirects to <MICROSOFT.COM>; <TIMES.COM> redirects to <NYTIMES.COM>; <POLO.COM> redirects to <RALPHLAUREN.COM>.

5.03-B.2

5.03-B.2 Personal Names[396]

Owners of trademarks composed of given names or surnames compete for space and attention with living persons who are known by those names as well as with companies offering services to them.[397] While there are certainly trademarks of personal names that are well-known or famous it is difficult to claim bad faith registration if the domain name is not being used in commerce and there is no evidence respondent registered his or her personal name to take advantage of complainant's trademark.[398]

It is settled that a respondent has a right to a "domain name [that] reflects [his] initials [and his] . . . first and middle name, combined with [his] entire last name."[399] This is subject of course to the proviso that respondent is making a *bona fide* use of the domain name. However, the right is contingent on the legitimacy of the use. Using the domain name in its trademark rather than generic sense remains illegitimate. A respondent has no right or legitimate interest in a domain name "buil[t] . . . around a surname that has acquired the protection of trademark status, and uses that domain merely to operate a click-through advertising scheme."[400]

Paragraph 4(c)(ii) of the Policy legitimizes registration where the second level domain is the name by which respondent is commonly known. In this respect fame confers no advantages. Thus, in ***Harrods***[401] respondent demonstrated she had been in the salon business under her surname for ten years prior to registering the domain name.[402] In ***Mattel***[403] complainant argued that "Mattel is not a proper surname and

---

[396] Persons whose names have been used in a domain name do not have standing to complain in a UDRP proceeding unless their names qualify for trademark status. See "Personal Names" (Sec. 4.01.E.1).

[397] Discussed earlier in "Personalized (Vanity) E-Mail Service" (Sec. 4.01.D.1).

[398] Although holder may retain the domain name under the UDRP—e.g. ***Harrods Limited v. HDU Inc.***, D2004-0093(WIPO April 27, 2004) (HARRODS and <harrodssalon>, Complaint denied, respondent's surname satisfies paragraph 4(c)(ii))—he or she may nevertheless be liable for trademark infringement if it is used for a business arguably within the ambit of goods or services offered by owner of a well-known or famous mark. See *Chanel, Inc. v. Chanel's Salon LLC*, 2:14-v-00304 (N.D. Indiana Dec. 16, 2014) (Consent judgment for permanent injunction, CHANEL and defendant's given name Chanel Jones).

[399] ***Japan Airlines Company Limited v. TransHost Associates, JAL Systems and John A Lettelleir***, D2000- 0573 (WIPO August 21, 2000) (JAPAN AIRLINES and <jal.com>. "John Andrew Lettelleir . . . chose his initials as they were easy to remember and simpler to spell than his own last name"); ***Modefine S.A. v. A.R. Mani***, D2001-0537 (WIPO July 20, 2001) (ARMANI and <armani.com>, initials of given and middle names plus surname).

[400] ***Cargill, Incorporated v. RN WebReg c/o Rare Names, Inc.***, FA0904001260307 (Forum June 12, 2009) (CARGILL and <cargills.com>. "[W]hether Respondent has rights in that name does not depend upon its status as a surname, but rather upon the use to which the name is put.").

[401] ***Harrods Limited v. HDU Inc.***, D2004-0093 (WIPO April 27, 2004) (HARRODS and <harrods salon.com>).

was likely adopted by Respondent for the purpose of asserting rights in the domain name." However, the Panel held that it was not for the "Complainant to deem what is a 'proper' surname simply because it owns a trademark on the same name in conjunction with the sale of certain wares." A similar conclusion was reached in ***Ken's Foods***[404]:

> Notwithstanding complainant's contention that the KEN'S mark is distinctive in relation to the particular category of goods and services for which the mark is used, it is nonetheless a personal name—"Ken"—which is also the Respondent's given name.

Complainant in ***Lodgeworks***[405] owned a trademark for SIERRA SUITES. Respondent whose surname is "Sierra" had been active as a consultant in the hotel and hospitality fields for ten years and registered <sierrahotelgroup.com> and <sierra hotels.net> for his own business. In all these cases use or use coupled with personal history determines legitimacy. In ***Mathiesen***, for example, respondent submitted his birth certificate to prove his right to <mathiesen.com>[406] and in ***Arnoldo Mondadori Editore*** respondent showed that as a "Grazia" she was entitled to her choice of <grazia.us> for prospective use as a food-related website.[407]

5.03-B.3 Nicknames, False Names, and Stage Names 5.03-B.3

Nicknames and stage names are protected equally with given names and surnames provided their use is legitimate. False names or faux nicknames are generally rejected. Respondents claiming to be commonly known as "Krylon,"[408] "Redbull,"[409]

---

[402] The result is different when respondent, though properly surnamed, diverts the domain name to another website, ***Harrods Limited v. Harrod Exclusive Realty Service***, D2006-1061 (WIPO November 6, 2006). Diverting is further discussed in "Commercial Gain Through Hyperlinking" (Sec. 6.05-B).

[403] ***Mattel, Inc. v. Gopi Mattel***, FA0411000372847 (Forum February 15, 2005) (MATTEL and <mattel.org>).

[404] ***Ken's Foods Inc. v. kens.com***, D2005-0721 (WIPO September 11, 2005) (KENS and <kens.com>).

[405] ***Lodgeworks L.P. v. Sierra Hospitality***, FA0802001152964 (Forum April 21, 2008).

[406] ***Mathiesen S.A.C. v. Allan Mathiesen***, D2009-0087 (WIPO March 23, 2009).

[407] ***Arnoldo Mondadori Editore S.p.A. v. Grazia Solazzi***, FA1005001323771 (Forum June 23, 2010). The case also raised another issue having to do with the ".us" TLD. The rules promulgated by the designated registrar for ".us" TLDs (Neustar, Inc.) require registrants for .usTLDs to have a substantial nexus with the United States. Complainant had no such "substantial nexus."

[408] ***DIMC, Inc. v. Phan***, D2000-1519 (WIPO February 20, 2001) (Respondent offered no evidence of when the alleged nickname "Krylon" was adopted and how it was used).

[409] ***Red Bull GmbH v. Gutch***, D2000-0766 (WIPO September 21, 2000)(<redbull.org>. Respondent alleged that he had been known by the nickname "Red Bull" since childhood).

"Bromo Seltzer,"[410] "Uncle Ben,"[411] and "Gambro"[412] were rejected. The Panel in ***Tower Laboratories Ltd.*** (Trademark BROMO SELTZER) held that:

> [It] does not follow that registration of a nickname that is based squarely on a widely known and perhaps famous trademark vitiates against infringement when the mark is reused in another context by the Respondent.

However, in this case "[n]otably the ultimate reason that Respondent registered the domain name was because of its commercial notoriety. . . ."

False names have been rejected, although the database includes anomalous decisions in favor of respondents alleged to be known in their families as "[Mr.] Penguin"[413] and "Jollibee."[414] Respondent in ***Breitling***[415] tried a new tack for his appropriation of complainant's trademark by assuming a false identify to match the domain name. He registered <bretling.com> and adopted the moniker "Mr. BRET LING" for a pay-per-click website. A variant is reported in ***Shaw Industries.***[416]

Respondent's alleged principal was said to be called "Ms. Thompson Shaw." It contended (in its own words) that it "registered the disputed domain name on behalf of Gretta Thompson Shaw, who has possessed the latter name, Shaw, for at least thirty years." Respondent urged the Panel to draw a favorable inference that Ms. Shaw had "a legitimate surname, [and should be] allowed to include it in a domain name registration [<shawbydesign.com>]." Respondent alleged Ms. Shaw was a fashion and accessories designer, although other than the *ipse dixit* allegation there was no evidence to prove her existence.

Failure to come forward with tangible evidence of the existence of Ms. Shaw and her work "leaves the Panel with no alternative but to dismiss the Respondent's contention." The Panel held

> Given the ease with which a respondent in a Policy proceeding might claim that someone with a name corresponding to the domain name in dispute is the intended beneficiary of its registration, a UDRP panel must demand the

---

[410] ***Tower Laboratories Ltd. v. Eric Seltzer***, FA0609000791325 (Forum October 16, 2007). The nickname was conferred allegedly in memory of his father's deceased dog, "Bromo."

[411] ***Mars, Incorporated v. Ben Chen***, FA1109001405770 (Forum October 17, 2011) (<uncleben.com>).

[412] ***Gambro AB v. Family Health & Wellness Center***, D2001-0447 (WIPO May 25, 2001).

[413] ***Penguin Books Ltd. v. The Katz Family and Anthony Katz***, D2000-0204 (WIPO May 20, 2000) (<penguin.org>. The Panel concluded that it was obliged to accept Respondent's evidence in the absence of any rebuttal evidence from complainant.)

[414] ***Jollibee Foods Corp. v. Chrystman***, FA 95561 (Forum October 31, 2000) (finding that respondent had rights or legitimate interests in the <jollibee.com> domain name because his wife's nickname was "Jollibee" and he was not using the disputed domain name for commercial purposes).

[415] ***Breitling SA, Breitling USA Inc. v. Acme Mail***, D2008-1000 (WIPO August 24, 2008).

[416] ***Shaw Industries Group, Inc. and Columbia Insurance Company v. The Visual Image Solution***, D2008-1102 (WIPO September 3, 2008).

> presentation of tangible evidence to support such a claim, otherwise the purpose of the Policy would be totally eviscerated.

On the other side of the ledger are respondents who legitimately use stage names that are identical or confusingly similar to trademarks. Thus, there is a "Johnny Blaze,"[417] a "Lexus Michaels"[418] and a "Kianna Dior."[419]

5.04 NONCOMMERCIAL OR FAIR USE, WITHOUT INTENT—PARAGRAPH 4(c)(iii) OF THE POLICY 5.04

5.04-A Appropriating Complainant's Trademark for Noncommercial or Fair Use and Free Speech 5.04-A

5.04-A.1 Structure of the Defense 5.04-A.1

In contrast to paragraph 4(c)(i), which has both a past[420]—"before any notice to you of the dispute"—and future orientation—proof of "demonstrable preparations"—and paragraph 4(c)(ii),[421] which has only a past—"commonly known by" orientation—paragraph 4(c)(iii)'s orientation excludes the future—"you are making"—implying a "now" and not a "will be" use. Paragraph 4(c)(iii) of the Policy is a two-part either/or test.[422] It applies to use that is either "noncommercial" or "fair" as long as the use is "*without intent* for commercial gain *to misleadingly divert consumers*" or "to tarnish"[423] the trademark or service mark at issue" (emphasis added). The disjunctive "noncommercial [use]" or "fair use" elements expand the possibilities of good faith registration.[424]

---

[417] ***AST Sportswear, Inc. v. Steven R. Hyken***, D2001-1324 (WIPO March 26, 2002) (JOHNNY BLAZE and <johnnyblaze.com>, "Respondent has satisfied [his] burden. He has submitted conclusive documentary evidence that he used the stage name Johnny Blaze as a professional stage name during his career.")

[418] ***Toyota Motor Sales U.S.A. Inc. v. J. Alexis Prods.***, D2003-0624 (WIPO October 16, 2003) (TOYOTA and <lexusmichaels.com>). Compare *Nissan Motor Co., Ltd. v. Nissan Computer Corp.*, supra.

[419] ***CHRISTIAN DIOR COUTURE v. Kianna Dior Productions***, D2009-0353 (WIPO May 24, 2009) (DIOR and <kiannadior.com>).

[420] Discussed further in "Defining the Burden" (Sec. 6.01-A.1.a).

[421] Discussed further in "Pointing to Adult Oriented Website" (Sec. 6.05-C.1).

[422] "[Y]ou are making a legitimate noncommercial or fair use of the domain name, without intent for commercial gain to misleadingly divert consumers or to tarnish the trademark or service mark at issue."

[423] The term "tarnish" has a specialized meaning in UDRP jurisprudence, as discussed further in "Intent to Tarnish" (Sec. 5.04-C).

[424] ***Google Inc. v. Java Den Web Solutions***, FA1010001355351 (Forum March 20, 2011) ("Policy ¶4(c)(iii) is not only broadly framed as noted above, it leaves open the question of whether 'non commercial or fair use' is a single or bifurcated concept.") The Anticybersquatting Consumer

The term "fair use" is typically associated with protected speech (criticism and commentary) and fan websites but is not limited to those uses. It may equally be the case that a domain name resolves to a website that is fair but commercial (nominative fair use[425]), that is, it does not "misleadingly divert consumers."[426] This formulation announces a flexible principle. It recognizes in trademark and cybersquatting disputes that there may be a likelihood of confusion but accepts this possibility in favor of opening the market to lawful registrations.[427] The defense is available only to respondents whose present use of the domain name is either noncommercial or fair, as qualified by the balance of the sentence that its use is legitimate.[428]

Protection Act has a similar test but also contains a separate provision implied but not expressly stated in the UDRP. 15 U.S.C. §1125(d)(1)(B)(ii) reads: "Bad faith intent described under subparagraph (A) shall not be found in any case in which the court determines that the person believed and had reasonable grounds to believe that the use of the domain name was a fair use or otherwise lawful."

425 See "Nominative Fair Use" (sec. 6.01-D.3) and "Nominative Fair Use As Applied" (5.01-D.3).

426 The prescribed use in paragraph 4(c)(iii) is matched with proscribed gain from commercial use set forth in paragraph 4(b)(iv) of the Policy: "[B]y using the domain name, you have intentionally attempted to attract, for commercial gain, Internet users to your web site or other online location, by creating a likelihood of confusion with complainant's mark as to the source, sponsorship, affiliation, or endorsement of your web site or location or of a product or service on your web site or location." See ***Xtralis Technologies Limited v. Secusense BV***, DNL2014-0055 (WIPO February 26, 2015) ("The fact that the Complainant in its email of July 12, 2013 has stated that the use of the Trademark is not permitted without the express written consent of the Complainant, does not alter this. If the Respondent has a legitimate right or interest in the Domain Name, the Complainant cannot prohibit the use thereof under the Regulations.")

427 Artists and hobbyists have been exonerated under this provision, *Velcro Industries B. V. and Velcro USA Inc. v. allinhosting.com/Andres Chavez*, D2008-0864 (WIPO July 28, 2008) (<velcroart.net>, and (same panelist) in *Etihad Airways v. Whoisguard Protected, Whoisguard, Inc / Hamza Ali*, D2016-0615 (WIPO July 3, 2016) a hobbyist who registered <vetihadairways.com> for a virtual airline website.

428 As the Panel points out in ***Landmark Lofts Limited v. Anonyousspeech Anonymous speech***, D2014-1748 (WIPO November 20, 2014) there are conflicting principles: "the owner of a criticism website may have legitimate reasons to withhold their identity, for example, to protect themselves against harassment by supporters of the organization that is the subject of their criticism"; but this decision runs afoul of the registration agreement and the Policy in that "providing false information to a registrar is a breach of ICANN's Domain Name Registrants' Responsibilities policy, which is incorporated into all registration agreements." However, in this particular case the Panel denied the complaint because Complainant failed the paragraph 4(a)(i) and 4(a)(ii) requirements but noted that anonymity "is relevant to a finding of registration and use in bad faith," suggesting Complainant would have succeeded in capturing the domain name even if the resolving website contained noncommercial and fair use content. The question of anonymity is not without ambivalence. The Panel denied the complaint in ***Dr. A. Scott Connelly v. AnonymousSpeech AnonymousSpeech***, FA1109001406376 (Forum October 26, 2011).

Both noncommercial and fair: Respondent in ***Snapchat, Inc. v. Private Registrant / a Happy Dreamhost Customer***, FA1412001593519 (Forum January 12, 2015) registered after Complainant had a security breach. "Respondent's web site allows users to see if their data was leaked as part of that security breach (taking the web site at face value)."

The defense is not available to respondents holding domain names inactively, although a carve-out has been justified for intended future use for an arguably fair purpose.[429] In any one of the several possibilities, "[t]here remains the more general question of whether the Respondent is otherwise making a legitimate use."[430] It would therefore follow that the defense can succeed if respondent's use is either noncommercial and fair or noncommercial or fair as long as the use is legitimate[431]

WIPO and ICANN "intended to limit the circumstances in which legitimate noncommercial or fair use could successfully be claimed."[432] For example, the "prospect of posting critical commentary at some future time is not appropriate for consideration by the Panel."[433] Non-use and alleged future plans for use do not qualify for the "making use" element[434] any more than do bare rather than demonstrable "preparations" under paragraph 4(c)(i) of the Policy. However, within the limits of the test respondents have more scope than some panelists suggest. "Noncommercial [use]" and "fair use" are both fair where there is no intent to deceive. The elements refer to any use that in a business[435] or personal[436] context demonstrates that respondent is not engaged in taking unfair advantage of complainant or its trademark.

---

[429] Pfizer Inc v. Van Robichaux, D2003-0399 (WIPO July 16, 2003) ((LIPITOR and <lipitor info.com>. "Respondent essentially argues that in order to provide the public with information concerning the Complainant's product, including advice concerning treatment or legal advice, it is necessary or appropriate to use the Complainant's mark in its domain name."), citing Playboy Enters. v. Welles, 279 F.3d 796 (9th Cir. 2002) and Horphag Research v. Mario Pellegrini, 328 F. 3d 1108 (9th Cir. 2003). The Pfizer panelist has also stated in an earlier case that "there are contexts in which the registrant of a domain name should not be expected to make immediate use of that name, including for legitimate noncommercial or fair use purposes." Helen Fielding v. Anthony Corbert aka Anthony Corbett, D2000-1000 (WIPO May 28, 2000). See also Amylin Pharmaceuticals, Inc. v. Watts Guerra Craft LLP, D2012-0486 (WIPO April 29, 2012) (<byettacancer.com>. "[T]he website purports to offer truthful information about the link between the Complainant's drug and cancer.")

[430] ***Bulmers Ltd. and Wm. Magner Ltd. v. (FAST 12785240) magnersessions.com 1,500 GB Space and 15,000 Monthly Bandwidth, Bluehost.Corn INC/Jason LaValla***, D2010-1885 (WIPO January 17, 2011).

[431] ***Pfizer***, supra. as an example, but also see "Non-Authorized But Lawful Use of Trademarks" (Sec. 5.01-C.2).

[432] ***Helen Fielding v. Anthony Corbert aka Anthony Corbett***, D2000-1000 (WIPO September 25, 2000).

[433] ***Wal-Mart Stores, Inc. v. Jeff Milchen***, D2005-0130 (WIPO April 10, 2005) (<walmartfacts.biz>).

[434] Although Panels have noted that "a delay in using a domain name for a legitimate noncommercial or fair use purpose in response to a cease and desist demand might be justified." ***Apple Computer, Inc. v. DomainHouse.com, Inc.***, D2000-0341 (WIPO July 5, 2000) (Not justified in that particular case, but same Panel found justification in ***Pfizer***, supra.)

[435] Nominative fair use as previously noted. The alternative is to place nominative fair use as a nonenumerated example of good faith.

When a respondent invokes fair use as a defense to commercial use it is either coupled with paragraph 4(c)(i), which expressly covers "legitimate commercial use" or it is a non-enumerated defense. In finding against respondent, the term "commercial gain" is construed to mean gain by any party with whom respondent is associated even if there is no direct gain to the respondent. This was explained earlier in discussing populating the website with infringing content. A respondent's *post hoc* offer to use the website for a noncommercial purpose provides no defense under the Policy. This is because promises to act in the future are not sufficient to cure present bad faith use.[437]

5.04-A.2

5.04-A.2 Ambivalent Application

Commentary and criticism as general categories of "free speech" rest on the proposition that speaking critically of a trademark owner and its goods or services is a protected right. Although free speech is not specifically listed as a circumstance supporting a right or legitimate interest in a domain name, in principle it is *prima facie* fair use and was early established as an implicit defense.[438] The right is expressly announced in the WIPO Final Report: "Domain name registrations that are justified by legitimate free speech rights or by legitimate non-commercial considerations would . . . not be considered to be abusive"[439] but any commercial use of the domain name would render its registration infringing.

However, as quickly as free speech was recognized as a protected right two lines of reasoning developed which led to the ambivalence referred to in the subheading. The first line is more protective of trademark owners; the second line more

---

[436] ***RMO, Inc. v. Burbidge***, FA 96949 (Forum May 16, 2001) ("A family information site is a legitimate non commercial use"); ***Modefine S.A. v. A.R. Mani***, D2001-0537 (WIPO July 20, 2001) (ARMANI and <armani.com>, where the Respondent's name is "A.R. Manni"); ***The California Milk Processor Board v. Ryan Archer***, D2011-1812 (WIPO December 9, 2011) ("The Respondent appears to operate this website and others simply as an outlet for his creative works and to support others who create webcomics and videos. The Domain Name is not used to generate advertising revenue, which would undermine the Respondent's claim of noncommercial purpose."); ***David Unangst v. Aimee Rancer***, FA1307001508778 (Forum August 28, 2013) ("Respondent[] use[s] . . . the domain name to host a blog of her personal experiences. . . .")

[437] ***Avon Products, Inc. v. Mary Ultes***, D2009-0471 (WIPO June 3, 2009).

[438] ***Wal-Mart Stores, Inc. v. Richard MacLeod d/b/a For Sale***, D2000-0662 (WIPO September 19, 2000) ("A genuine criticism site, undertaken by its proprietors with no intent other than to protest, ridicule and mock its targets, does not fall astray of the dictates of the Policy, regardless of the outrageousness of the allegations it contains or the vigorousness with which they are made"); ***Shell International Petroleum Company Limited v. Alfred Donovan***, D2005-0538 (WIPO August 8, 2005) (<royaldutchshellgroup.com>. "[T]o criticize a company is *prima facie* fair use." U.K. Complainant; U.S. Respondent).

[439] WIPO Final Report, paragraph 172. Whether respondent's website is actionable under any legal theory other than choice of domain name such as defamation is an issue for a court of law.

protective of speakers. It is a difference of focus between the choice of domain name and the content of the website to which it resolves.

When WIPO issued its Original Edition of the Overview in 2005 it announced consensus on most of the issues it identified but not for fair use commentary and criticism (paragraph 2.4, discussed here) and Fan Sites (paragraph 2.5, discussed further in the text). The split continues in the Second Edition, but the Third Edition dispenses with the classifications View 1 and View 2.[440] The question at paragraph 2.4 (Original Edition) is, "Can a criticism site generate rights or legitimate interests in the disputed domain name?" WIPO splits the answer into two views:

> View 1: The right to criticize does not extend to registering a domain name that is identical or confusingly similar to the owner's registered trademark or conveys an association with the mark.
>
> View 2: Irrespective of whether the domain name as such connotes criticism, the respondent has a legitimate interest in using the trademark as part of the domain name of a criticism site if the use is fair and non commercial.

View 1 panelists—the "Domain Name itself is misleading" approach—believe that application of the defense is contingent on the form of the domain name. View 2 panelists focus on the composition of the website, which is generally consistent with U.S. case law. Some View 1 panelists are firmer on domain names identical to trademarks but allow fair use for domain names composed of <trademark+qualifier [such as "sucks"]>.

Although the WIPO Final Report offers no assistance about the composition of the domain name in neither view is "commercial [use]" compatible with "fair use." There can be no meritorious defense if content is designed to generate revenue at complainant's expense, deceive consumers into believing there is an association with the trademark owner, or the expression exceeds respondent's right.[441] Under either view, even if speech is accepted it does not protect respondent from liability if in a court of law the speech is determined to be defamatory or otherwise actionable.

The split among panelists is generally based on their engendered views of the domiciles of the parties. While legitimate free speech rights may be considered an international norm its parameters are not universally accepted. As a result,

---

See for example, *Mayflower Transit, LLC v. Dr. Brett Prince* (CV 005354, D.NJ., March 30, 2004) (Defendant's use of plaintiff's service mark in domains of noncommercial websites critical of plaintiff does not violate the ACPA since this is a "bona fide noncommercial" use of the mark which defendant had reasonable grounds to believe was lawful. However, defendant may nevertheless be exposed to liability for defamation if his statements are actionable).

440 For this discussion, the reference will be to the Second Edition. The Third Edition discusses the issues in paragraphs 2.6 and 2.7.

441 · Discussed further in "Extreme Expression" (Sec. 5.04-D).

panelists' philosophy and parties' citizenship can make a difference to the outcome of a dispute.[442]

The tussle among panelists comes down to this: Should respondent be permitted to use or incorporate complainant's trademark to publish his criticism of complainant?[443] The present answer is, It depends whether the panelist appointed is a View 1 or View 2 panelist.[444] This split continues even though WIPO Overview 3.0 no longer expressly reflects it.

5.04-A.2.a 5.04-A.2.a *View 1—Limitations on Critical Speech*

Adherents of View 1 reject the argument that a respondent has a right or legitimate interest in a domain name that "impersonates"[445] a complainant's trademark. For the "domain name itself is misleading" approach, pure commentary or criticism on the website is not sufficient to sustain a paragraph 4(c)(iii) defense.[446] "What is being curtailed is not free speech, but impersonation."[447] To succeed on the fair use defense, it must be clear from the composition of the domain name that it is a

---

442 Compare for example ***White Ribbon Australia v. Whois Privacy Protection Service, Inc / Erin Pizzey***, D2016-1234 (WIPO September 5, 2016) (<whiteribbon.org> in which the parties are Australian and U.S. citizens: "Respondent has the right to freedom of speech, [but the Panel] is of the view that there is a clear distinction between a right to express critical views and freedom of speech, and a right or legitimate interest in respect of a domain name which is identical to a complainant's trademark") and in ***Fraternal Order of Moai, Inc v. Tim Glazneraim***, FA160700 1686147 (Forum August 30, 2016) (<fraternalorderofmoai.com> in which the parties are U.S. citizens, and having considered the "First Amendment of the United States Constitution" the Panel held the registration of the domain name was not abusive.)

443 See ***Lockheed Martin Corporation v. Dan Parisi***, D2000-1015 (WIPO January 26, 2001) (<lockheedsucks.com>. The Panel found in the Respondent's favor but the dissent (only on the majority's conclusion that the addition of "sucks" precludes a finding of confusing similarity) would have held that the domain name was confusingly similar to complainant's trademark. He was concerned that a per se rule would protect registrants who disguised their intentionally adding "sucks." The consensus is that a pejorative addition does not preclude a finding of confusing similarity.)

444 The strong dissent in ***The Cedarville University***, supra. noted that "the website is critical of Complainant, overlapping to some extent with the subject matter of pending litigation brought against Complainant by a former employee, represented by Respondent. It does not appear that this litigation and the other disputes reported on Respondent's website are mere pretexts calculated to conceal an improper attempt to exploit the trademark value of the disputed domain names. To the contrary, it appears (at least to this Panelist) that the grievances of Respondent and those on whose behalf he acts are sincere, and that the website and the domain name <cedarvillealumni.com> are merely instruments being used in support of those efforts."

445 "Essentially, any use which gives rise to a right or legitimate interest must be fair and impersonation is not fair," ***David Foox v. Kung Fox & Bill Hicks***, D2002-0472 (WIPO July 25, 2002).

446 ***E. & J. Gallo Winery v. Hanna Law Firm***, D2000-0615 (WIPO August 3, 2000); ***Compagnie de Saint Gobain. Com Union Corp.***, D2000-0020 (WIPO March 14, 2000); ***Bandon Dunes v. DefaultData.com***, D2000-0431 (WIPO July 13, 2000).

protest site, for example, by adding the word "sucks" or some other pejorative to a trademark.[448]

The right to criticize is not the same as the right to use another's name to carry comments to Internet users.[449] Domain names identical to complainant's trademark are denied the free speech defense entirely even though there is no evidence of commercial use. The theory is that domain names identical or confusingly similar to a trademark potentially mislead or deceive consumers into believing they are a click away from complainant's website only to be disabused when they reach respondent's landing page.

View 1 Panels hold that "it is not the address of the web site that is protected by free speech principles, but rather the content of the web site."[450] In ***Compagnie Generale*** the Panel held that while Respondent has a "right to free speech and a legitimate interest in criticizing the activities of organizations like complainant . . . [that] is a very different thing from having a right or legitimate interest in respect of [a domain name that is identical to Complainant's mark]." The right respondents concededly have as a matter of policy comes with significant qualification.[451]

Two rationales have been advanced. The first rationale for rejecting the paragraph 4(c)(iii) defense holds that "there is a world of difference between, on the one hand, a right to express (or a legitimate interest in expressing) critical views and, on the other hand, a right or legitimate interest in respect of a domain name. The two are completely different."[452] Further, the argument that use of the disputed domain name "enables respondent to transmit his view more effectively is neither here nor

---

447 ***1066 Housing Association Ltd. v. Mr. D. Morgan***, D2007-1461 (WIPO January 18, 2008) (1066 Housing and <1066ha.com>).

448 ***Lloyds TSB Bank PLC v. Paul Brittain***, D2000-0231 (WIPO June 6, 2000) (<lloydstsb-visa.com>); ***Aspis Liv Försäkrings AB***, supra., citing ***1066 Housing*** with approval: "the use of a domain name which essentially comprise[s] a trademark without any additional 'modifier' for a criticism site will not provide 'rights' or 'legitimate interests.'"

449 See, for example, ***Packet One Networks (Malaysia) SDN BHD v. Wartog ID.***, KL 1200009 (ADNDRC August 17, 2012) ("Complainant exhibited . . . screenshots of some pages in this domain that [it] also alleges to be offensive and calculated to disparage the Complainant's products and services"), citing ***1066 Housing*** with approval.

450 Examples are: ***Valero Energy Corporation v. American Distribution Systems, Inc.***, D2001-0581 (WIPO August 12, 2001) (<valeroenergy.com>) and ***Compagnie Générale des Matieres Nucleaires v. Greenpeace Int'l***, D2001-0376 (WIPO May 14, 2001) (<cogema.org>) ("In short, what the Respondent has done is to select for the Domain Name a name which is not its own, which it knew at the time of registration to be the name and trade mark of the Complainant and which it proposed at the time of registration to use in a campaign against the Complainant to cause the Complainant disruption and damage. The Domain Name would be particularly useful for that purpose because it would catch by surprise visitors intending to reach the Complainant's website.")

451 The Panel in ***Eastman Chem. Co. v. Patel***, FA 524752 (Forum Sept. 7, 2005) (<east man-chemical.com>) made an even more radical contribution by stating that "[f]ree speech cannot be used as a defense against the use of a confusingly similar mark as a domain name."

there."[453] Forfeiting the domain name "does not deprive him of his right of free speech." He can "readily use a domain name which telegraphs . . . precisely what his site contains and thereby obviate any risk of deception."

Adherents to this view insist that "it is not correct to conclude that free speech rights trump all other rights in all circumstances."[454] The Panel in ***Curt Manufacturing***[455] makes it clear that this intolerance of domain names identical to trademarks extends to any domain name even if the website is clearly devoted to criticism or another noncommercial use such as parody (which is a form of commentary long recognized as protected speech). In ***1066 Housing Association***[456] the Panel conceded that the criticism was genuine but cited ***Triodos Bank*** in support of forfeiture: "A respondent can always choose a domain name that does not carry with it the perception of being authorized by the trademark owner."

The second rationale rests on the theory of "initial interest confusion," which is explained in a split decision in ***Joseph Dello Russo***.[457] In denying safe harbor for <dellorusso.info>, the majority explained that

> Respondent's selection of Complainant's name for her criticism site allows her to make use of Complainant's service mark in a manner that would lead an ordinary Internet user initially to believe that Respondent was Complainant or that Respondent had Complainant's permission to distribute her message. Such use is not legitimate under paragraph 4(a)(ii) of the Policy, and the safe

---

[452] ***Triodos Bank NV v. Ashley Dobbs.***, D2002-0776 (WIPO October 3, 2002) (<triodos-bank.com>).

[453] *Id.* See also ***Justice for Children v. R neetso / Robert W. O'Steen***, D2004-0175 (WIPO June 4, 2004) ("Respondent is not entitled to use a soapbox . . . to lure Complainant's audience to his harangue.") Dissent in ***Challenger Limited and Challenger Group Holdings Limited v. Domain Privacy Service FBO Registrant / Sean Butler***, D2014-0852 (WIPO July 21, 2014) explains that View 2 is premised on a "principal flaw," namely that

> [i]n an ordinary criticism case, in which the respondent in fact criticizes the complainant, View 2 panels emphasize the non-commercial nature of legitimate criticism and the need to safeguard free expression. That's not the issue in a Policy proceeding. The Policy does not impair the Respondent's or any other person's free speech rights in any way. The UDRP exists solely to determine a party's entitlement or not to use the complainant's mark in the domain name at issue – to borrow a metaphor I have used in other cases, to use the complainant's soapbox without authority as the broadcast medium.

The "soapbox" metaphor comes from *Justice for Children*, supra. where the Panel was the sole panelist and ordered the domain name transferred.

[454] ***The Cedarville University v. Mark Miller***, FA0905001262209 (Forum July 10, 2009) (transferred over a strong dissent). The quote is from one member of the majority.

[455] ***Curt Manufacturing, Inc. v. George Sabin***, FA0808001220025 (Forum September 23, 2008) (U.S. parties, <curtmfg.com>).

[456] ***1066 Housing Association Ltd. v. Mr. D. Morgan***, D2007-1461 (WIPO January 18, 2008) (<1066ha.com>).

[457] ***Joseph Dello Russo M.D. v. Michelle Guillaumi***, D2006-1627 (WIPO April 27, 2007).

> harbor of paragraph 4(c)(iii) is not available because Respondent undeniably intended 'to misleadingly divert consumers.'

However, adding a pejorative to the trademark is sufficient to pass the test. The majority granted safe harbor for <dellorussosucks.com> with the dissent insistent on the application of View 1 for both domain names.

There is no clear equivalent to View 1 under federal case law. The U.S. Circuit Court for the 4th Circuit rejected the opinion of the district court as well as the ICANN Panel's reasoning in ***The Reverend Dr. Jerry L. Falwell.***[458] The disputed domain name, <fallwell.com>, is either a typographical error (typosquatting as the Panel held) or a parody on the name with its emphasis on "fall" and not sufficient under the ACPA to deprive registrant of the domain name.[459] The Ninth Circuit takes a similar view of a domain name that is identical to the trademark, <bosley-medical.com>: "the noncommercial use of a trademark as the domain name of the website—the subject of which is consumer commentary about the products and services represented by the mark—does not constitute infringement under the Lanham Act."[460] The ICANN Panel in ***Bosley Med. Group*** had held in favor of respondent on the "fair use defense" (a View 2 holding).[461] The district court decision which the Ninth Circuit affirmed held that "Bosley's claims for trademark infringement . . . [and] cybersquatting . . . each require Bosley to prove that Kremer made commercial use of Bosley's marks" but this was something it could not do.[462]

---

458 ***The Reverend Dr. Jerry L. Falwell and The Liberty Alliance v. Lamparello International.***, FA0310000198936 (Forum November 20, 2003).

459 *Lamparello v. Falwell*, 420 F.3d 309 (2005). The Panel in ***Falwell*** had no ambivalence. In ordering the domain name transferred the Panel held that respondent registered and was using the domain name in bad faith, citing typosquatting and commercial use. It failed to examine the website or address the Respondent's fair use or free speech claims. In a subsequent federal action for a declaratory judgment under the ACPA, respondent now the Plaintiff initially fared no better, *Lamparello v. Falwell*, Civil Action No. 03-1503-A (U.S. Dist. Court, Eastern Dist. of VA, August 5, 2004). On appeal, however, the Court of Appeals in reversing summary judgment was critical of the District Court's analysis in failing to address the Plaintiff's free speech rights, 420 F.3d 309 (4th Cir. 2005). It held that the "use of another firm's mark to capture the mark holder's customers and profits [] simply does not exist when the alleged infringer establishes a gripe site that criticizes the mark holder."

460 *Bosley v. Kremer*, 403 F.3d 672 (2005).

461 ***Bosley Med. Group and Bosley Medical Institute, Inc. v. Michael Kremer***, D2000-1647 (WIPO February 28, 2001) ("The Panel . . . reluctantly concludes that the purpose of this proceeding is less to protect the Complainants' trademark rights than to squelch Respondent's criticism of Complainants—a practice sometimes called 'cyber bullying'. . . .")

462 01-1752 (S.D. Calif. April 29, 2004).

5.04-A.2.b

5.04-A.2.b *View 2—Critical Speech Without Limitations*

View 2 takes a "complaints site" approach in which the focus is the content of the website and the composition of the domain name as identical or confusingly similar is irrelevant. If the content qualifies, the right follows.[463] For Panels subscribing to this view no bright line should be "drawn denying the existence of a non commercial free speech right under the UDRP simply based upon whether Respondent has or has not added words . . . to Complainant's alleged trademark."[464] Although there may be initial interest confusion it "is a price well worth paying to preserve the free exchange of ideas via the Internet."[465]

Some Panels require the commentary or criticism to be "pure," that is, the message is unalloyed with any suggestion of commerce or self-promotion.[466] If there is some commercial use, the answer lies in the percentage of the part to the whole and what the part is that is not commentary or criticism.[467] Sanitizing the website after commencement of the proceedings will not cure the violation.[468]

Paragraph 4(c)(iii) of the Policy is satisfied when the website is a genuine complaint site registered without intention for commercial gain. The "goals of the Policy are limited and do not extend to insulating trademark holders from contrary and critical views when such views are legitimately expressed without an intention for commercial gain,"[469] even if they may cause financial loss.[470]

---

[463] ***TMP Worldwide Inc. v. Jennifer L. Potter***, D2000-0536 (WIPO August 5, 2000) (TMP WORLDWIDE and <tmpworldwide.net>. "The principal, if not sole, purpose of Respondent's Web site, the Panel holds, appears not to be for commercial gain, but, rather, to exercise her First Amendment right to criticize Complainant and comment on her experiences in dealing with Complainant."); ***Bridgestone Firestone, Inc. v. Myers***, D2000-0190 (WIPO July 6, 2000) (<bridgestonefirestone.net>) and ***Britannia Building Society v. Britannia Fraud Prevention***, D2001-0505 (WIPO July 6, 2001) (<britanniabuildingsociety.org>) are examples.

[464] ***Equality Charter School, Inc. v. Mona Davids / A Happy DreamHost Customer***, D2011-1226 (WIPO September 2011) (<equalitycharterschool.com>).

[465] ***Action Instruments, Inc. v. Technology Associates***, D2003-0024 (WIPO March 6, 2003) (<buswaredirect.com>).

[466] ***Compagnie de Saint Gobain v. Com-Union Corp.***, D2000-0020 (WIPO March 14, 2000) (SAINT GOBAIN and <saintgobain.net>. "The issue at hand is however not as Respondent seems to contend, the freedom of speech and expression but the mere choice of the domain name used to exercise this inalienable freedom of speech and expression.")

[467] Discussed further in "Mixing Innocent and Infringing Elements" (Sec. 6.01-F).

[468] Discussed further in "Intentionally Attempting to Attract for Commercial Gain" (Sec. 6.05).

[469] ***Legal & General Group Plc v. Image Plus***, D2002-1019 (WIPO December 30, 2002) (Domain name identical, <legal-and-general.com>; "A Panel cannot and should not try to distinguish between a disgruntled former employee and a genuine whistle blower.")

[470] ***Bakers Delight Holdings Ltd v. Andrew Austin***, D2008-0006 (WIPO February 25, 2008) (BAKERS DELIGHT and <bakersdelightlies.com>. "The issues whether the Complainant is

Where the *raison d'être* for the website is criticizing complainant's products or services it should not be silenced.[471] Adherents to View 2 are loath to unnecessarily narrow the privilege.[472] The Panel in the last cited case accepted the argument that "malicious dissemination of deliberately misleading material would not constitute legitimate or fair use," which enforces the view that there is a limit. However

> it is not the function of a Panel under the Policy to evaluate the merits of rival contentions on matters of public controversy. Unless it is clearly shown that the content is deliberately false and malicious, the principle of free speech must prevail.

Ordinarily, deliberate falsehood and malice cannot be "clearly shown." The "distinction between constructive criticism and tarnishment can be a difficult one to draw."[473]

Adherents of View 2 recognize the legitimacy of domain names identical to the trademark if the content of the website is what it purports to be.[474] The WIPO Overview notes that the second view appears to have been primarily adopted by U.S. panelists in proceedings involving U.S. parties and that few non-U.S. panelists have adopted this second view. This is surely a misimpression for it incorrectly suggests there is no international norm or that free speech principles are solely a feature of U.S. law.[475] Such a parochial view is unacceptable and has been rejected.[476] In an extensive footnote, the Panel in ***Coast Hotels*** concludes that while the "practical application of [many declarations and covenants adopted around the world are] not relevant to the Panel's deliberations on whether these reflect a normative

---

suffering financial loss due to incorrect statements being made by the Respondent, or infringement of intellectual property, [are] outside the realm of the Panel's powers.")

[471] ***Action Instruments, Inc. v. Technology Associates***, D2003-0024 (WIPO March 6, 2003) (<buswaredirect.com>: "The minimal confusion suffered by Complainant's potential customers is a price well worth paying to preserve the free exchange of ideas via the Internet.") See also ***Brahma Kumaris World Spiritual Organization v. John Allan***, FA0709001075486 (Forum November 19, 2007) (<brahmakumaris.info>. "[T]he challenged domain name is being used primarily in connection with a site that includes both commentary and criticism of Complainant and that such use is protected under the Policy.")

[472] ***Meat and Livestock Commission v. David Pearce a.k.a. OTC / The Recipe for BE***, D2003-0645 (WIPO October 27, 2003).

[473] ***Shell International Petroleum Company Limited v. Alfred Donovan***, D2005-0538 (WIPO August 8, 2005).

[474] Id.

[475] ***WHIZZ Air Hungary Airlines Limited Liability Company v. Holden Thomas***, D2009-1105 (WIPO September 22, 2009) (The competing views are "sometimes said to reflect differences in national laws relating to freedom of speech.")

[476] ***Chelsea and Westminster Hospital N.S. Foundation Trust v. Frank Redmond***, D2007-1379 (WIPO November 14, 2007); ***Coast Hotels Ltd. v. Bill Lewis and UNITE HERE.***, D2009-1295 (WIPO November 23, 2009) (<coasthotelsbadforbc.info> and <coasthotelsbadforbc.org>).

international legal principle [because they do not have the force of law, they arguably] reflect the customary international legal norm."[477]

View 2 rejects any reduction of respondent's free speech rights with or without a pejorative affixation.[478] "Nowhere is it expressly anticipated by the Policy that this paragraph may not operate if the domain name at issue is found to be identical . . . to complainant's trade mark."[479] Respondent in ***Howard Jarvis Taxpayers***[480] registered complainant's acronym, <hjta.com>. The Panel points out that "under Section 43(c) of the Lanham Act, there is no cause of action for trademark dilution (which encompasses both blurring and tarnishment) if a party is making a '[n]oncommercial use of a mark'[481] which is the case if the site is a legitimate gripe site."[482] The Policy in the view of the ***Howard Jarvis*** Panel, is not designed to insulate

> trademark holders from contrary and critical views when such views are legitimately expressed without an intention for commercial gain. . . . Use of the Policy to provide such insulation may undermine freedom of discourse on the

---

[477] Which is the reason U.S. law was applied in ***Coast Hotels*** (Canadian Complainant, U.S. Respondent.) The Panel found "respondent has on the record in this present case established under paragraph 4(c)(iii) of the Policy that its registration and use of the disputed domain name in respect of a website critical of complainant amounts to a legitimate non commercial or fair use of the Disputed Domain Names."

[478] Respondent's legitimate interest was vigorously supported by the dissent in ***Aspis Liv Försäkrings AB v. Neon Network, LLC***, D2008-0387 (WIPO June 2, 2008) (<aspis.com>). The dissenting member believed that "respondent has been improperly deprived of the Domain Name, in violation of his or its U.S. Constitutional rights of free speech, and feels that if this case were brought in virtually any court in the U.S., the result would be different." Respondent was vindicated in a subsequent action for declaratory relief under the Lanham Act § 1114(D)(v) in which complainant (now defendant) defaulted in appearance, *Neon Network, LLC v. Aspis Liv Försäkrings*, No. CV-08-1188-PHX-DGC (USDC Arizona July 22, 2009). The Court granted a default judgment declaring the registration and use of the domain name was not unlawful.

Similarly vindicated was the defendant in *Lucas Nursery and Landscaping, Inc.*, 2004 WL 403213 (6th Cir. March 5, 2004). Defendant registered a domain name identical to the plaintiff's trademark, <lucasnursery.com>. The Court explained that "One of the ACPA's main objectives is the protection of consumers from slick internet peddlers who trade on the names and reputations of established brands. The practice of informing fellow consumers of one's experience with a particular service provider is surely not inconsistent with this ideal."

[479] ***Covance, Inc. and Covance Laboratories Ltd., v. The Covance Campaign***, D2004-0206 (WIPO April 30, 2004) (Criticizing vivisection with <covancecampaign.com>); ***Norton Peskett v. Domain Privacy / Tom Hampson***, D2009-0724 (WIPO July 21, 2009) ("[t]his Panelist prefers View 2.").

[480] ***Howard Jarvis Taxpayers Association v. Paul McCauley***, D2004-0014 (WIPO April 22, 2004) (U.S. parties). The sole Panel was the dissenting member in ***Joseph Dello Russo***, supra. for <dellorusso.info>.

[481] 15 U.S.C. §1125(c)(4)B).

[482] Citing among other cases *Northland Insurance Co. v. Blaylock*, 115 F. Supp. 2d 1108 (D.C. Minn. 2000) (criticism site at <www.northlandinsurance.com> is protected speech and, because the

Internet and undercut the free and orderly exchange of ideas that the First Amendment seeks to promote.

Irrespective of "whether the domain name as such connotes criticism, respondent has a legitimate interest in using the trademark as part of the domain name of a criticism site if the use is fair and non commercial."[483]

5.04-A.2.c *Rejecting Views 1 and 2 in Favor of "Totality of the Circumstances"* 5.04-A.2.c

A third approach to assessing whether respondent's use is fair steers a middle path between Views 1 and 2. In fact, Jurisprudential 3.0 dispenses with the two views of the earlier Overviews.[484] This middle path approach rejects the either/or reasoning in favor of a more nuanced examination of the evidence. It takes into account the "totality of the circumstances": "[it] is neither inherently incompatible with the UDRP, nor always permitted by the UDRP, and that its compatibility with the UDRP depends on the circumstances."[485]

Respondent is still expected to demonstrate the genuineness of its website content, but where the panel finds respondent is using the disputed domain name for noncommercial, free speech content and complainant offers no evidence respondent's postings are pretexts for proscribed conduct, it would be inconsistent to find abusive registration.

Drawing on the analysis in ***Fundación Calvin Ayre Foundation***[486] the Panel in ***Midland Heart*** identifies seven criteria for assessing whether respondent has a legitimate interest in the disputed domain name:

---

website was noncommercial commentary it could not generate initial interest confusion and did not constitute dilution). See also ***322 West 57th Owner LLC v. Administrator, Domain***, D2008-0736 (WIPO August 8, 2008) (<sheffield57resident.com>. The Panel held that "there [is a] total absence on the record of any evidence whatsoever showing that Respondent Jansson's purpose in registering and using the disputed domain name was anything other than to disseminate her criticism of the Complainant.")

483 ***Coast Hotels***, supra. See *Cintas Corporation v. UNITE HERE*, 601 F. Supp.2d 571 (SDNY 2009), affd. 355 Fed.Appx. 508 (2nd Cir. 2009) (<www.cintasexposed.com>. The Court held that defendants "are not using the 'CINTAS' mark as a 'source identifier', but rather solely to criticize Cintas's corporate practices. . .. While the materials available on Defendants' websites may disparage Cintas, the likelihood that Cintas's actual or potential customers would be confused about who provides CINTAS goods and services is remote.")

484 ***American Home Shield Corporation v. Domains By Proxy / Morris Chera***, D2017-1142 (WIPO September 3, 2017) (<americanhomeshield.reviews>. "[U]se of a domain name is not 'fair' in circumstances where the domain name falsely suggests affiliation with the trademark owner; nor can a use be 'fair' if it is pretextual." The Panel cites Jurisprudential Overview 3.0, Paragraph 2.5).

485 ***Midland Heart Limited v. Uton Black***, D2009-0076 (WIPO March 30, 2009).

486 ***Fundación Calvin Ayre Foundation v. Erik Deutsch***, D2007-1947 (WIPO February 25, 2008).

(a) Has the domain name been registered and is it being used genuinely for the purpose of criticising the owner of the mark?

(b) Does the registrant believe the criticism to be well founded?

(c) Does the registrant have intent for commercial gain?

(d) Is it immediately apparent to Internet users visiting the website at the domain name that it is not a website of the owner of the mark?

(e) Has respondent registered all or most of the obvious domain names suitable for the owner of the mark?

(f) Where the domain name is one of the obvious domain names suitable for the owner of the mark, is a prominent and appropriate link provided to the latter's website (if any)?

(g) Where there is a likelihood that email intended for complainant will be sent using the domain name in issue, are senders immediately alerted in an appropriate way that their emails have been misaddressed?

These criteria suggest panelists should take a harder look at the evidence. To overcome respondent's legitimate interest requires "something more than criticism."[487] The "more" that is required may include, for example, threatening to publish confidential client information, encouraging readers to harass complainant's suppliers or making statements so intemperate and provocative as to suggest the registration was made for the purpose of disrupting complainant's business.

However, where the respondent is an acknowledged competitor its insistence that it acquired the domain name to post "reviews" of complainant's product and services lacks the necessary level of credibility to support the safe harbor defense.[488]

5.04-A.3

5.04-A.3 Political and Social Speech: Parody and Satire

Parody and satire without "intent to profit" are protected expression under both U.S.[489] and domain name law.[490] Political and social speech run the gamut from the "no-holds barred" criticism (*Utah Lighthouse* and ***Sutherland***[491]) and "unwanted"[492] to the benign[493] and playful.[494] The only question is whether the protection extends

---

[487] ***Southern California Regional Rail Authority v. Robert Arkow***, D2008-0430 (WIPO May 12, 2008).

[488] ***American Home Shield Corporation***, *supra.*

[489] See *Utah Lighthouse Ministry v. Found. for Apologetic Info. & Research*, 527 F.3d 1045, 1058 (10th Cir. 2008) ("The Lanham Act regulates only economic, not ideological or political competition"); *Lucas Nursery & Landscaping, Inc. v. Grosse*, 359 F.3d 806, 809 (6th Cir. 2004) (consumer complaining about nursery's work was not liable under ACPA); *Mayflower Transit, L.L.C. v. Prince*, 314 F.Supp.2d 362 (D.N.J. 2004) (Registrant's motive was to express dissatisfaction in doing business with the mark's owner).

[490] See *Farah v. Esquire Magazine*, 736, F.3d 528–29 (D.C. Cir. 2013) (Alleged defamatory content, not trademark infringement), and cases cited therein.

to the vehicle—the domain name—as well or only to the content. In the cited cases the domain names were either "virtually identical" (*Utah Lighthouse*) or "identical" (***Sutherland***). "In the world of debate about public affairs, many things done with motives that are less than admirable are protected by the First Amendment."[495]

In the UDRP context the issue was first analyzed in a 2001 dispute. The Panel formulated a two-step process for determining whether respondent is entitled to protection.[496] The case involved parody, but satire is a close relative so that the analysis of one is equally applicable to the other. First, does "the domain name itself have the capacity to constitute parody"? If the question can be answered in the affirmative, then the examination proceeds to the second step: "is Respondent's use of that domain name, on its web site or otherwise . . . consistent with its claim of parody"?

The Panel concluded in ***A & F Trademark*** that <abercombieandfilth.com> did not meet the qualifications. It reasoned that

> A parody must convey two simultaneous—and contradictory—messages: that it is the original, but also that it is not the original and is instead a parody. ... In the second step, we look to the content of Respondent's web site to determine whether Respondent's use of the domain name and of Complainants' marks is consistent with its claim of parody. In order to constitute parody, the web site must poke fun at the goods or services associated with Complainants' marks:

---

[491] See ***Sutherland Institute v. Continuative LLC***, D2009-0693 (WIPO July 10, 2009) (Complaint dismissed. In this case the domain name is identical to Complainant's trademark, but the content is authentically political speech); ***The Reverend Dr. Jerry Falwell and The Liberty Alliance v. Gary Cohn, Prolife.net, and God.info***, D2002-0184 (WIPO June 3, 2002) (Complaint dismissed; no trademark). The Reverend filed an ACPA action and was successful in district court, but lost on appeal, *Lamparello v. Falwell*, 420 F.3d 309 (4th Cir. 2005).

[492] *Koch Industries, Inc. v. John Does*, 1-25, 10CV1275DAK (District of Utah, Central Div. 9 May 2011) (<koch-inc.com>. "Koch's complaint is not that Defendants obtained the information without authorization, but rather that they ultimately used the information in an unwanted manner." Political speech; complaint dismissed).

[493] ***The Honorable Ron Paul v. DN Capital Inc., Martha Roberts***, D2013-0371 (WIPO May 11, 2013) (Fan club, directed to a website engaged in political speech).

[494] ***Harry Winston Inc. and Harry Winston S.A. v. Jennifer Katherman***, D2008-1267 (WIPO October 18, 2008) (<hairywinston.com>; confusingly similar to trademark, but playful parody as a business name—a dog salon—semantically appropriate supports legitimate interest).

[495] ***Mercury Radio Arts, Inc. and Glenn Beck v. Isaac Eiland Hall***, D2009-1182 (WIPO October 29, 20009) (<glennbeckrapedandmurderedayounggirlin1990.com>. "This Panel is very reluctant to reject Respondent's claim of legitimate noncommercial and fair use on the distinction between viewing of the disputed domain name itself and clicking through to Respondent's website"), citing *Garrison v. Louisiana*, 379 U.S. 64, 85 S.Ct. 209, 13 L.Ed.2d 125 (1964) ("[E]ven when a speaker or writer is motivated by hatred or ill will his expression [is] protected by the First Amendment.")

[496] ***A & F Trademark, Inc. and Abercrombie & Fitch Stores, Inc. v. Justin Jorgensen***, D2001-0900 (WIPO September 19, 2001) (<abercombieandfilth.com>, parody rejected).

> *use of another's trademark to poke fun at something unrelated to Complainant's mark is not parody.* (Emphasis added.)

The Panel rejected Respondent's defense because there was "no content conceivably poking fun at Complainant."

Political and social speech is most effective when its message is delivered with complainant's mark as though spoken by the complainant. However, as with consumer commentary panelists are split on protection for domain names identical to trademarks.[497] "As for fair use . . . it is not the address of the web site that is protected by free speech principles, but rather the content of the web site."[498] Such a test would exclude from protection both raw satire (as in ***Sutherland***) and benign parody (as with <hairywinston.com>) even where the intent is not for commercial gain.

The parodist's point of view is that the domain name expresses only half its agenda, of which the other half is the content of the website. The determination should be made on the basis of the whole expression. "On the same basis by which the Panel has determined the disputed domain name is confusingly similar to Complainant's trademark—that is, Internet users viewing the disputed domain name will be curious and motivated to visit the website—the Panel also considers that Respondent's speech should be assessed as a whole, both by reference to the disputed domain name and the content of Respondent's website."[499]

Of course, parody needs an audience that recognizes respondent's intention. Indecipherable speech is not protected. In one case the Panel failed to recognize respondent's intention, but (curiously) Complainant did![500] The Panel found it was "hard put to decipher Respondent's critical message—it undoubtedly expresses a critical perspective on Respondent's business. . . . [But, in] any event, Complainant itself characterizes the website as 'mock[ing] Complainant's technology and business,' which constitutes a concession that the site is fairly characterized as a criticism site."

---

[497] See ***Monsanto Company v. Decepticons***, FA0110000101536 (Forum December 18, 2001) (<monsantos.com> where the content would appear to be consistent with parody but which the Panel rejected. Respondent posed as complainant in making critical statements about its products, such as "Monsanto cares about 'your' health and 'your' cancer, and we hear your concerns. That's why we've gotten rid of our EqualTM and NutrasweetTM divisions—these products have been thought to be carcinogens for several years, even by our own scientists.") Compare ***Monsanto*** with ***Sutherland Institute***, *supra*, which did the same thing, registering a second level domain identical with Complainant's trademark, but was held constitutionally protected.

[498] ***Valero Energy Corporation v. American Distribution Systems***, Inc., D2001-0581 (WIPO August 12, 2001) (<valeroenergy.com>).

[499] ***Mercury Radio Arts***, supra.

[500] ***Action Instruments, Inc. v. Technology Associates***, D2003-0024 (WIPO March 6, 2003).

5.04-A.4 Celebrity Names and Fan Sites 5.04-A.4

Fan sites generally come into existence without express permission and sometimes over the objection (albeit, frequently delayed[501]) of the honoree to celebrate his or her life's work and achievements. The WIPO Overview Original Edition asks the following question: "Can a fan site constitute a right or legitimate interest in the disputed domain name?"[502] There are two views, denominated View 1 (an active, noncommercial fan site may be a legitimate interest) and View 2 (a fan has no right or legitimate interest in a domain name that infringes a celebrity's trademark). Even fanatics—"the flip side of critics" as one panelist noted[503]—have the right to establish a fan site.

5.04-A.4.a *View 1* *5.04-A.4.a*

View 1 reads

> An active and clearly non-commercial fan site may have rights and legitimate interests in the domain name that includes complainant's trademark. The site should be non-commercial and clearly distinctive from any official site.

The first sentence establishes a standard no different than for a non-fan site, although with a fan site (as with a criticism site) respondent cannot argue lack of knowledge of the celebrity. The rationale of View 1 is defeated if the alleged fan site is neither genuine nor active.

The tolerance expressed in View 1 applies to a respondent who is able to demonstrate that the website to which the domain name resolves is both noncommercial and active and benefits the celebrity,[504] even if the respondent lacks rights or legitimate interests in the domain name.[505] It has particular relevance where the proof shows that complainant "made repeated use of the website to further [its]

---

[501] The "fan" in ***Richard Dawkins v. J. Gabriel***, FA1004001317157 (Forum May 21, 2010) argued that his celebrant "was ill-known or little known, particularly in the U.S. in 1999, when respondent established the domain name." Although a complainant's reputation is an important element it is not decisive.

[502] Paragraph 2.5. WIPO Overview 3.0 does not emphasize the split views.

[503] ***Richard Starkey v. Mr. Bradley***, FA0612000874575 (Forum February 12, 2007) (<ringostarr.mobi>).

[504] ***Estate of Gary Jennings v. Submarine***, D2001-1042 (WIPO October 25, 2001) (<garyjennings.com>. Providing reviews of the author Gary Jennings' works is fair use of the Domain Name).

[505] ***Nintendo of America Inc. v. Alex Jones***, D2000-0998 (WIPO November 17, 2000) (<legend-ofzelda.com>. Respondent lacks rights or legitimate interests—"A Complainant has the right to decide how its mark will be used in the context of the product or products associated with the mark. . . . Insofar as a domain name which is identical to a name or mark is used solely in the context of the product of the owner of the name or mark and the owner objects to the use, it is not legitimate. The Complainant has the right to decide how its mark will be used in the promotion of its product"—but no evidence of bad faith.)

interests and in effect encouraged Respondent's activities"[506] or there "is no evidence that Respondent is making a commercial gain from the website, or that he acted with the intention of such gain."[507] In ***Swissbike***[508] complainant offered no evidence to rebut respondent's contention that the website is a noncommercial forum targeting fans of Raleigh bikes.

However, the term "commercial gain" is construed broadly against respondent even where the celebrity may receive some incidental publicity benefit. As with criticism sites, a domain name passively held but claimed as a nascent fan site is a contradiction in terms. The disputed domain name may resolve to a noncommercial website, but if it has "never acted as a fan site . . . it therefore fails the second of the requirements for legitimacy" under View 1."[509] It is not a defense that respondent "has not had the time and the money to create the website but that it is still in the planning process"[510] or that it is attempting to cash in on the celebrity's success in the guise of a fan club.[511]

Bundling celebrities in a directory that contains advertising violates the Policy.[512] The Panel in ***Celine Dion and Sony Music Entertainment (Canada) Inc.*** noted that

> So long as the admitted bunch of celebrity domain names were all directed to the "www.celebrity1000.com" site, the Respondent's conduct must be

---

[506] ***Blind Melon v. KWI 186 a/k/a Mark Makoul***, FA0606000741833 (Forum August 21, 2006): citing ***Van Halen v. Morgan***, D2000-1313 (WIPO December 20, 2000) (finding that respondent did not register the <edwardvanhalen.com> domain name in bad faith where she had a desire to use the domain name for a fan site devoted to complainant); ***Stuart. v. Marty Stuart Fan Page***, FA 192600 (Forum October 22, 2003) (finding that the respondent's registration and use of a domain name to host a fan website was not bad faith because the domain name was registered in support of complainant).

[507] ***2001 White Castle Way, Inc. v. Glyn O. Jacobs***, D2004-0001 (WIPO March 26, 2004). See ***The Estate of Tupac Shakur, v. R.J. Barranco***, AF-0348 (eResolution October 23, 2000) ("The position asserted by the Claimaint, if accepted, would effectively prohibit any fan club from being established on the Internet if it mentioned in the site name an artist's name. . . . It would . . . permit persons in the position of this Claimaint to unjustly enrich themselves by confiscating the work of fans and admirers in establishing a web site supporting their favorite artists without any opportunity for compensation." Although it lost on the ***Barranco*** case, the ***Estate of Tupac Shakur*** successfully prosecuted four other proceedings.)

[508] ***Swissbike Vertriebs GmbH v. Executive Standard Limited***, D2008-0498 (WIPO June 19, 2008) (<raleighbikes.com>).

[509] ***Stevland Morris a/k/a Stevie Wonder v. Enrique Matta***, FA0805001189962 (Forum July 9, 2008).

[510] ***Eddy Merckx Rijwielen Cycles NV vs. Irfan Khalil***, D2009-0074 (WIPO March 12, 2009) (eddymerckx.com). Worse yet, the "factual circumstances in this matter are that the website attached to the Disputed Domain Name points to a parking site which largely . . . offer[s] goods and services that compete with those of complainant."

[511] ***Freddy Adu v. Frank Fushille***, D2004-0682 (WIPO October 27, 2004).

characterized as a stockpiling of leading artistes' names, their only substantial function then being to attract people to view advertising on the site.

The issue was revisited in ***Tom Cruise***. A violation based on the bundling model is not cured by changing the business plan[513]:

> Respondent's recent shift to linking the disputed domain name directly to a "Tom Cruise" website does not cure the problem of failure to establish legitimate noncommercial or fair use. This tactic already was rejected in the *Celine Dion* and *Kevin Spacey* decisions. In any event, because the "Tom Cruise" website was almost wholly devoted to third-party advertisement links, it is difficult to see how this would better qualify as fair use of Complainant's mark (even with an intended link to the "www.celebrity1000.com" website).

The fair use defense is without merit when the website also or primarily serves respondent's commercial or other interests.[514] Other interests include "holding complainant hostage by coercing [Complainant] to take a position of sponsoring the particular environmental movement he was espousing." In ***Harrison*** the Panel stated that

> the nexus between Respondent's domain name sales business and its environmental pursuits is close enough to satisfy the commercial gain provision of Paragraph 4(b)(iv) of the Policy. See Jews for Jesus v. Brodsky, 993 F.Supp 282, 309 (D.N.J. 1998) (holding that to be considered commercial, it is not necessary for a website to make a profit).

Further, a "mixture of links negates the argument of 'fair use.'"[515]

5.04-A.4.b *View 2* *5.04-A.4.b*

View 2 of paragraph 2.5 of the WIPO Overview (like View 1 in paragraph 2.4) is skeptical of, if not hostile to, a respondent's use of another's trademark even for praising the honoree. The WIPO Overview reads:

> Respondent does not have rights to express its view, even if positive, on an individual or entity by using a confusingly similar domain name, as respondent is misrepresenting itself as being that individual or entity. In particular, where the domain name is identical to the trademark, the respondent, in its

---

512 ***Celine Dion and Sony Music Entertainment (Canada) Inc. v. Jeff Burgar operating or carrying on business as Celine Dion Club***, D2000-1838 (WIPO February 13, 2001); ***Tom Cruise v. Network Operations Center / Alberta Hot Rods***, D2006-0560 (WIPO July 5, 2006) (<tomcruise.com>).

513 Using celebrities in this way is also a violation of the right of publicity. The Restatement of the Law (Third) of Unfair Competition, Sec. 46 (1995) states that the right is invaded by "one who appropriates the commercial value of a person's identity by using without consent the person's name, likeness, or other indicia of identity for purposes of trade."

514 ***Harrison v. LOVEARTH.net***, FA 97085 (Forum June 4, 2001) (5 domains).

515 ***Richard Dawkins***, supra.

actions, prevents the trademark holder from exercising the rights to its mark and managing its presence on the Internet.

View 2 is essentially an analogue of later cases in which celebrities with unregistered trademarks have become increasingly aggressive in suing for the misuse of their names.

The rationale under View 2 is that celebrities are entitled to control use of their own names.[516] Generally, "panels that have deemed fan sites legitimate dealt with sites that served as alternatives to sites authorized by the celebrity or team that owned the name, and provided current information and often the opportunity for fans to learn about and discuss various topics related to their subject."[517]

5.04-B 5.04-B Adding Terms of Opposition or Pejorative Prefixes/Suffixes to Trademarks

5.04-B.1 5.04-B.1 "Sucks" Cases

English speakers recognize "sucks" as a colloquial pejorative conveying sardonic or angry disapproval. Although it has been said that foreign speakers may not fully understand its cultural significance,[518] the attuned know that joining the verb to the trademark announces a negative comment.[519] Dissenters apart,[520] a pejorative added to a trademark is treated as a non-distinguishing descriptive term for purposes of comparing it with the trademark for standing.[521] However, a finding of right or legitimate interest is likely to rest on how the domain name is being used[522] and for

[516] ***David Gilmour, David Gilmour Music Limited and David Gilmour Music Overseas Limited v. Ermanno Cenicolla***, D2000-1459 (WIPO December 15, 2000) (<davidgilmour.com>); ***Jay Leno v. Guadalupe Zambrano***, D2009-0570 (WIPO June 25, 2009) (merely having a famous name is not sufficient, but JAY LENO "has come to be recognized by the public as identifying and distinguishing complainant's goods and services from those of others.")

[517] ***Ain Jeem, Inc. v. Barto Enterprises, Inc., Philip Barto***, D2007-1841 (WIPO January 31, 2008).

[518] ***Société Air France v. Virtual Dates, Inc.***, D2005-0168 (WIPO May 24, 2005) ("far from all international customers (being) familiar with the pejorative nature of the term 'sucks' . . . a large proportion of internet users . . . are likely to be confused by 'sucks' domain names.")

[519] The word "'sucks' has entered the vernacular as a word loaded with criticism." *Bally Total Fitness Holding Corp. v. Faber*, 29 F. Supp. 2d 1161, 1164 (C.D. Cal. 1998). To the consternation of trademark owners, ICANN has approved a new gTLD ".sucks" that has potential for mischief.

[520] The dissent in ***Société Air France*** noted that <airfrancesucks.com> is not confusingly similar to AIR FRANCE: "[t]he domain name and mark do not look or sound alike and certainly do not convey the same commercial impression," citing ***FMR Corp. v. Native American Warrior Society, Lamar Sneed***, D2004-0978 (WIPO January 20, 2005) (<fidelity brokerageinvestmentsfraud.com> and <fidelityinvestmenttheft.com> not confusingly similar to FIDELITY and FIDELITY INVESTMENTS marks).

[521] WIPO 2nd Edition, paragraph 1.3. "Is a domain name consisting of a trademark and a negative term confusingly similar to the complainant's trademark? ('sucks cases').

the bad faith element whether the domain name resolves to an active website that supports commentary or criticism, directly or through a literary convention such as satire or parody.[523] Adding a pejorative to the trademark does not insulate a domain name from forfeiture unless it does what it purports to be, otherwise the Telstra analysis applies.[524]

As noted above in discussing political speech and critical commentary of commercial enterprises (View 2), the addition of a pejorative truly aimed is a factor in determining the merit of a paragraph 4(c)(iii) defense. A second level domain to which an opprobrious or pejorative modifier has been added (where the website is what it purports to be and there is no question of "impersonation") qualifies for protection regardless of possible economic damage,[525] although "[s]imply having a domain name with '-sucks' in the name cannot, by itself, establish fair use."[526] The right must be earned. "[O]ne must look to the content of the website to determine if there is an exercise of free speech which allows respondent to rely on the fair use exception. To do otherwise would legitimize cybersquatters, who intentionally

---

Consensus view: Generally, a domain name consisting of a trademark and a negative or pejorative term (such as [trademark] sucks.com) would be considered confusingly similar to the complainant's trademark for the purpose of satisfying the standing requirement under the first element of the UDRP (with the merits of such cases typically falling to be decided under subsequent elements). Panels have recognized that inclusion of a subsidiary word to the dominant feature of a mark at issue typically does not serve to obviate confusion for purposes of the UDRP's first element threshold requirement, and/or that there may be a particular risk of confusion among Internet users whose first language is not the language of the domain name."

522 ***Dell Inc. v. Innervision Web Solutions c/o Domain Registrar***, FA0503000445601 (Forum May 23, 2005) (<dellcomputerssuck.com>; "This web site advertised computer systems for sale by Respondent. Under the facts and circumstances of this case the Panel rejects Respondent's contention that the addition of the word 'sucks' prevents a finding of confusing similarity.")

523 ***Société Air France v. Mark Allaye Chan***, D2009-0327 (WIPO May 14, 2009) ("While the Response states that the disputed domain name was registered for the purpose of a legitimate protest site, there is no evidence to support this proposition. Respondent has not provided evidence before the Panel of any demonstrable steps it has taken to launch a website at the disputed domain name, related to his grievance with complainant. At the time of writing this decision, the website was not operational.")

524 ***Telstra Corporation Limited v. Nuclear Marshmallows***, D2000-0003 (WIPO February 18, 2000) (an inference will be drawn from respondent's choice of name when "it is not possible to conceive of any plausible actual or contemplated active use of the Domain Name by respondent that would not be illegitimate").

525 See ***Howard Jarvis***, supra. See *Taubman v. Webfeats*, 319 F.3d 770 (6th Cir. 2003) (<taubman sucks.com>. "[A]lthough economic damage might be an intended effect of Mishkoff's expression, the First Amendment protects critical commentary when there is no confusion as to source, even when it involves the criticism of a business. Such use is not subject to scrutiny under the Lanham Act.")

526 ***Wal Mart Stores, Inc. v. Walsucks & Walmarket Puerto Rico***, D2000-0477 (WIPO July 20, 2000) (<walmartcanadasucks.com>).

redirect traffic from a famous mark simply through the use of a derogatory term."[527] The general principle "taught by precedents seems to be that, when a -SUCKS domain name has been registered for the main purpose of making money, it has been registered in bad faith."[528]

According to the Panel in another case,[529] criticism or cybergripe cases fall into two broad categories: "pure" gripe sites and "gripe-plus" sites.[530] "[P]ure gripe sites are those that present no indicia of bad faith beyond the fact that they are highly critical of the target."[531] Whereas, "[g]ripe-plus sites present other evidence of bad faith, either intrinsically (such as offering competing goods for sale) or extrinsically (such as the registrant's offering to sell the domain name to the trademark owner at a profit." It is not a defense that "Respondent's activities might have had no net impact on complainant's business.")[532]

---

527 ***Wachovia Corp. v. Flanders***, D2003-0596 (WIPO September 19, 2003) (<wachoviasucks.com>); ***TRS Quality, Inc. v. Gu Bei***, D2009-1077 (WIPO September 25, 2009) (<radioshacksucks.com>) (No attempt to disguise the commercial purpose of the website).

528 ***Caixa d' Estalvis y Pensions de Barcelona (La Caixa) v. Namezero.com***, D2001-0360 (WIPO May 3, 2001) (Spanish Complainant; U.S. Respondent).

529 ***FMR***, supra. The Panel found in favor of complainant for domain names confusingly similar to its trademarks, <fidelityretirements.com>, <fidelitybrokerageservices.com> and <fidelityinvestmentsloss.com> but denied "the Complaint insofar as it requests the transfer or cancellation of the domain names <fidelitybrokerageinvestmentsfraud.com> and <fidelityinvestmenttheft.com>."

530 A third category includes sites that "do[] not even seem to carry any genuine message at all," ***Medimmune, Inc. v. Jason Tate***, D2006-0159 (WIPO April 14, 2006). The Panel concluded that these "[s]o-called 'sham speech' domain names [are] selected not for any genuine purpose of providing critical commentary about a product or company but rather solely for the purpose of avoiding transfer under the Policy while accomplishing some unrelated business purpose (e.g. obtaining click-through revenue)." Nevertheless, because the phrases "bad for you" and "not safe" added to SYNAGIS are instantly clear about their purpose, there can be no confusing similarity. Discussed earlier in "Incorporating Part of Trademark" (Sec. 4.01-A.2.c.i).

531 Respondent in ***Bloomberg L. P. v. Secaucus Group***, FA0104000097077 (Forum June 7, 2001) submitted evidence that the disputed name, <michaelbloombergsucks.com>, was being used in connection with a free speech website. For this reason, the Panel held that "respondent has effectively foreclosed complainant's ability to prove bad faith." Where there are mixed domain names, only the one with the pejorative passes the test. See ***Paul DiCocco v. Curtis Lee Mickunas / Curtis L. Mickunas / Curtis Mickunas***, D2017-1982 (WIPO January 15, 2018) ("The Panel grants the requested remedy with respect to eight of the disputed domain names. Specifically, the eight disputed domain names [that are identical to Complainant's mark] ... However, the Complainant's request to transfer the ninth disputed domain name <gianpaolo-dicocco-failed-predictions.com> is denied [because it contains a pejorative]").

532 ***Red Bull GmbH v. Carl Gamel***, D2008-0253 (WIPO April 14, 2008). (<redbullsucks.com>).

5.04-B.2 Other Pejoratives Positioned in Front of and Following the Mark 5.04-B.2

The possibilities for previewing content in the second level domain include a full palette of expressive modifiers other than the default term "sucks." Respondents have exercised their rights in a variety of ways, by adding words in front of the mark, such as <stopcompusa.com> and <bancompusa.com> as well as after the mark, such as "campaign," "scam," and "lies." Commentary has been stretched to include commercial, disputatious, and sloganeering language in the domain name,[533] although if respondent's purpose is to express an opinion on an issue unrelated to a mark owner's business practices or the quality of its goods or services, then the rationale for dismissing the complaint on a noncommercial or fair use argument is significantly lessened.[534] Gripe domain names that telegraph respondents' messages by shorthand qualifiers are generally not abusive even if confusingly similar to the mark as long as the websites are what they purport to be.[535]

For a successful defense, the composition of the second level domain must alert the Internet user to what the website carries, otherwise it impugns respondent's claim for protected speech. "[W]ebsites critical of a trademark holder do not have the right to confuse Internet users by using a Complainant's mark in the domain name itself, as this conflicted with the public's right not to be deceived by confusingly similar domain names."[536] According to the Panel in ***Nestle Waters*** (although an argument could be mounted otherwise) the "phrase 'truth about' had no such connotations [of carrying critical commentary]."[537]

---

[533] ***Twentieth Century Fox Film Corporation v. DISH Network LLC***, FA1010001350483 (Forum November 22, 2010). The majority ruled that incorporating FOX into <foxshake downdish.com>, <weofferedfoxafairdeal.com>, <foxrefused.com>, and <jointhefightagainstfox.com> was not confusingly similar, so the Panel did not have to reach the issue of bad faith.

[534] ***Covanta Energy Corporation v. Anthony Mitchell***, D2007-0185 (WIPO April 3, 2007) (<covantasucks.com>. "According to the Respondent, he registered a domain name incorporating the Complainant's COVANTA mark to attract internet users to a website that would promote his own views of the incineration technology utilized by the Complainant, which he claims are favorable to the Complainant.") Whatever the Respondent's intentions he had not acted on them for 6 years, which further supported abusive registration under the principles laid down in ***Telstra Corporation Limited v. Nuclear Marshmallows***, D2000-0003 (WIPO February18, 2000).

[535] ***ECG European City Guide v. Jules Woodell***, FA0308000183897 (Forum October 14, 2003) (<stopecg.org>). Compare ***Wal Mart Stores, Inc. v. Traffic Yoon***, D2006-0812 (WIPO September 20, 2006) (<boycottwalmart.com>) (Panel suggested that if "boycott" were positioned after "walmart" it may have supported a contrary finding and forfeiture.)

[536] ***Nestle Waters No. Am. Inc. v. JAT***, FA 220027 (Forum February 2, 2004) (<truthabout polandsprings.com>).

[537] Domain name transferred on the theory of misleading Internet users, ***Rockstar, Inc. v. RSRESELLER LTD c/o Andrey Litovchenko***, FA0908001279865 (Forum September 29, 2009) (<thetruthaboutrockstarenergydrink.com>).

5.04-C

5.04-C Intent to Tarnish

Complainants frequently misapply the term "tarnish" to conduct that is not condemned under the UDRP. Nothing in the WIPO Final Report or in the ICANN Second Staff Report is intended to stifle criticism, which may only colloquially be said to tarnish complainant but is otherwise protected speech.[538] The term is found in the second part of the paragraph 4(c)(iii) defense, which reads that the "legitimate noncommercial or fair use . . . [must be] without intent . . . to tarnish the trademark or service mark at issue." Tarnishment is not simply blackening or disparaging[539] complainant, although some panelists have drawn a line in the sand when the tenor of the content becomes abusive, evidenced by an increase in the use of disparaging, denigrating, and vituperative language.[540]

"Classic tarnishment" of the kind intended to be actionable under the UDRP means "associating the mark with unwholesome concepts such as drugs, violence or sexual activity."[541] The ICANN Second Staff Report of October 24, 1999 glossed the term "tarnishment" by noting that it is not intended to cover legitimate activities permitted in paragraph 4(c)(iii). The Report at Note 2 states

> Several commentators indicated that the concept of "tarnishment" in paragraph 4(c)(iii) might be misunderstood by those not familiar with [U.S.] law or might otherwise be applied inappropriately to noncommercial uses of parody names and the like. Staff is not convinced this is the case, but in any event

---

538 ***Amylin Pharmaceuticals, Inc. v. Watts Guerra Craft LLP***, D2012-0486 (WIPO April 29, 2012) (<byettacancer.com>. "Although the Respondent may be critical of the Complainant and its drug, that is not the kind of 'tarnishment' to which the Policy refers.")

539 *Taubman v. Webfeats*, 319 F.3d 770 (6th Cir. 2003) (<taubmansucks.com>; the Court held that "[even if] economic damage might be an intended effect of Mishkoff's expression, the First Amendment protects critical commentary when there is no confusion as to source, even when it involves the criticism of a business. Such use is not subject to scrutiny under the Lanham Act.") But see *E. & J. Gallo Winery v. Spider Webs Ltd.*, 286 F.3d 270 (5th Cir. 2002) ("[T]he fact that [defendant] hosted a web site using Gallo's trademarked name, at which it disparaged the instant litigation and alcohol, is evidence of intent to harm Gallo's goodwill and to tarnish its mark.")

540 ***Adam Milstein v. Benjamin Doherty***, FA1511001647496 (Forum January 11, 2016); *Jody Kriss and East River Partners, LLC v. Felix Sater / Larissa Yudina*, FA160200 1660728 (Forum March 22, 2016).

541 ***Howard Jarvis Taxpayers Association v. Paul McCauley***, D2004-0014 (WIPO April 22, 2004). The Panel cites U.S. district court cases, *American Express Co. v. Vibra Approved Labs. Corp.*, 10 U.S.P.Q. 2d 2006 (S.D.N.Y. 1989) (mark DON'T LEAVE HOME WITHOUT IT tarnished by condoms sold under the slogan "Never Leave Home Without It"); ***Hasbro, Inc. v. Internet Entertainment Group, Ltd.***, 40 U.S.P.Q. 2d 1479 (W.D. Wash. 1996) (adult entertainment site at domain name <candyland.com> is tarnishment of CANDYLAND trademark for children's games). Cf. ***Kidman v. Zuccarini***, D2000-1415 (WIPO January 23, 2001) (Linking actress's name to website selling adult entertainment tarnished her name).

wishes to point out that "tarnishment" in paragraph 4(c)(iii) is limited to acts done with intent to commercially gain.

If the term were not reserved for more extreme conduct "every website critical of a brand owner could be branded a tarnishing use."[542] Indeed, it would be a "mistake to conclude that commentary that lessens a consumer's opinion of the trademark or service mark holder constitutes tarnishment of the mark."[543] The Panel in ***MLP Finanzdienstleistungen AG*** held:

> If (as WIPO's Final Report appears to acknowledge) the Policy contemplates criticism of the trademark owner as a valid defence to some extent, characterizing any effect of lost sales or negative opinion of potential customers as tarnishment would render paragraph 4(c)(iii) nugatory.

Complainant in another case alleged that "Respondent's use tarnishes Complainant's mark, and thus is not legitimate, because the criticism on the site is false, disparaging and highly inflammatory, and appears designed to harm Complainant and its reputation."[544] The Panel rejected this scattershot approach. "Fair-use criticism, even if libelous, does not constitute tarnishment and is not prohibited by the Policy; rather, claims sounding in commercial libel must be brought in other legal venues."[545]

5.04-D Extreme Expression 5.04-D

Panels are reluctant to grant a blanket right of speech in all its registers. Commentary and criticism are indisputably protected; tarnishment may be tolerated depending on how it is deployed; while disparagement, particularly disparagement

---

542 ***Ryanair Limited v. Michael Coulston***, D2006-1194 (WIPO December 12, 2006).

543 ***FMR Corp. v. Native American Warrior Society, Lamar Sneed, Lamar Sneede***, D2004-0978 (WIPO January 20, 2005). See ***MLP Finanzdienstleistungen AG v. WhoisGuard Protected***, D2008-0987 (WIPO September 1, 2008).

544 ***Sermo, Inc. v. CatalystMD, LLC***, D2008-0647 (WIPO July 2, 2008). Earlier cases include ***Jules I. Kendall v. Donald Mayer Re skipkendall.com***, D2000-0868 (WIPO October 26, 2000) ("[T]his case involves alleged defamation, not cybersquatting.") In *Adodis Technologies Private Limited v. Eric Reao*, KL-1400023 (ADNDRC September 19, 2014) and *MUFG Union Bank, N.A. v. William Bookout*, DME2014-0008 (WIPO December 3, 2014) Complainants contended that Respondents' websites did not reflect "legitimate" fair uses because of the nature of their contents. The Adodis Complainant alleged the content was "hampering its business." The *MUFG* Complainant also alleged defamation that was having a negative effect on its business, but a "UDRP proceeding ... is not an appropriate or practical forum for ascertaining the truthfulness of the allegations published on the Respondent's website, as would be necessary in a legal action for defamation." Questions of truth or falsehood of disparaging statements is better left to a court.

545 *Id.*, ***Sermo***. A reported defamation action is noted as pending in ***HBT Investments, LLC d/b/a Valley Goldmine v. Christopher D. Bussing***, D2010-1326 (WIPO September 24, 2010) (The UDRP case hinged on violation of 4(b)(iii) of the Policy, undermining reputation of a competitor.) Discussed further in "Commercial Gain from Tarnishment" (Sec. 6.05-C).

shading into extreme language, is justifiably actionable as cybersquatting. In order to pass the fair use test content must specifically target the trademark owner, its goods or services; fair use does not extend to trademarks appropriated for general, political, and cultural commentary[546] or used for calumny or vituperation.[547] Thus, Panels have drawn a line between non-actionable conduct and extreme expressions. The Panels in ***Howard Jarvis, Ryanair***[548] and ***Sermo*** previously referred to would leave the question of alleged abusive and defamatory speech to a court of law. The alternative view is exemplified in ***Dykema*** and other cases in which different Panels have held abusive speech unprotectable under the UDRP.[549]

In the first case the Panel held that to come within the paragraph 4(c)(iii) safe harbor Respondent's criticism

> must be balanced with some degree of control, manner and regulation to avoid the arising of abuses; limits must be set.

The Panel based its holding on the content of Respondent's website, which accused Complainant of "reprehensible behavior." This conduct (according to Respondent) resulted in "victims who have suffered and had their lives destroyed" and who "took their lives as a result. . . ." However, the Panel found that Respondent neither specified nor explained what was meant by "reprehensible behavior" and concluded that

> Without support, this innuendo serves no purpose other than to tarnish the reputations of Complainants and their trademarks.

---

546 ***Dykema Gossett PLLC v DefaultData.com and Brian Wick***, FA0104000097031 (Forum May 29, 2001) ("The Panel views this material on Respondent's web site not as parody type commentary, but rather as a collection of metaphors and symbols serving to bring contempt or disdain upon the name DYKEMA GOSSETT, which normally is associated with a law firm of long standing. If, as claimed by Respondent, the purpose of his/its web site is to provide parody like commentary on the legal system in general, but not specifically the services and activities of Complainant, this is not parody."); ***The Saul Zaentz Company v. Sam Solomon***, FA1306001505579 (July 16, 2013) ("[A]ll of the disputed domain names reroute the Internet users to the <answering christianity.com> domain name, wherein Respondent requests Internet users to donate money to his cause so that he may allegedly advertise for some undefined purpose.")

547 *Jody Kriss and East River Partners, LLC v. Felix Sater / Larissa Yudina*, FA160200 1660728 (Forum March 22, 2016) ("Freedom of speech must be balanced with some degree of control, manner and regulation to avoid the arising of abuses; limits must be set," citing *The Royal Bank of Scotland Group and National Westminster Bank v. Pedro Lopez and A&A System Solutions and Alberto Rodriguez*, D2002-0823 (WIPO December 3, 2002).

548 The Panel suggested that the split between these two lines of decisions may reflect a difference in approach between cases involving U.S. parties and cases involving non U.S. parties.

549 ***The Royal Bank of Scotland Group*** and ***National Westminster Bank v. Pedro Lopez and A&A System Solutions and Alberto Robriguez***, D2002-0823 (WIPO December 3, 2002) (<nationalwestministerbank.com>); ***The Royal Bank of Scotland Group plc, National Westminster Bank plc A/K/A NatWest Bank v. Personal and Pedro Lopez***, D2003-0166 (WIPO May 9, 2003)(<natwestbanksucks.com>). See *Atigeo LLC v. Offshore Ltd.*, No. 2:13 cv 01694 JLR, 2014 WL 239096 (W.D.

The Panel in the second ***Royal Bank*** case acknowledged the limitations of the Policy that it "is not a forum to decide defamation issues," although

> it must be highlighted that the instant defamation and damage to goodwill not supported by any evidence nor substantiated in the Response, is occurring via use of a sign confusingly similar to complainants' registered trademarks and is therefore likely to tarnish and damage those marks irreparably.

According to this view unsupported statements of disparagement can only be justified, if at all, if they are legitimate criticism rather than extreme expression masquerading as free speech. The distinction is difficult to parse, particularly where in the second case Respondent added "sucks."

The view expressed in ***The Royal Bank*** cases is not a U.K. phenomenon. The issue was also addressed in a case involving U.S. parties, ***Council of American Survey Research Organizations [CASRO]***.[550] The Panel with one member dissenting noted that there are

> differing views expressed in other domain name decisions . . . some of which consider it fair and appropriate to use a trademark proprietor's mark as the vehicle for collecting and distributing critical comments about the mark or its proprietor or his business practices, regardless of the inherent tarnishment of the mark that results.

Nevertheless, the majority of the ***CASRO*** Panel rejected the Respondent's argument. In its view a Respondent's use of the trademark to "disparage that mark, the mark's product, the mark owner, or his business practice" was unacceptable. The Panel held that not all so-called criticism is "legitimate" or "fair" within the terms of the Policy:

> The right to criticize is fully enjoyed when expressed on the author's own web site under a domain name unique to the author. Our decision of course does not denigrate that constitutional right. But the right to criticize does not carry with it the right to tarnish another's mark, as we find Respondent is here doing, by the use of that mark as the domain name for a web site to criticize and disparage the mark and its proprietor.

Forfeiture is thus posited on expression either in the domain name itself or on the website to which the domain name resolves with free speech rights rejected as a defense. In these and continuing decisions extreme expression, coupled or not with other indicia of bad faith such as hiding identity or providing misleading and incorrect contact information, is a sufficient basis for abusive registration.[551]

Wash. Jan. 22, 2014) (slip op.) (Former employee creating libelous website. Motion to dismiss ACPA complaint denied).

550 ***Council of American Survey Research Organizations [CASRO] v. The Consumer Information Organization, LLC, aka Pinelands Web Services.***, D2002-0377 (WIPO July 19, 2002) (<casro.com>).

5.04-E

5.04-E Affiliate Programs

Trademark owners outsource the marketing of goods or services to third parties through affiliate programs. Affiliates receive commissions based on the number of visitors or customers directed from their websites to owners that deliver goods or perform services based on the referrals. It works by encoding a message in a host website, which acts as a portal for the business that initiated the affiliate program. However, the program can be gamed to accrue illicit gain by registering domain names identical or confusingly similar to the complainant's trademark.[552]

There are a handful of cases in which complainant is shown to have acquiesced to respondent's use of a domain name incorporating its trademark.[553] Generally, however, affiliate programs expressly prohibit use of the trademark, although some respondents have attempted to circumvent the prohibition by registering minor variations of the trademark.[554] The consensus is that "[r]egistration and use of a confusingly similar domain name for the purpose of collecting affiliate fees has been held to satisfy the requirement of bad faith."[555]

Various stratems have been attempted to support lawful registration but without permissive use or absent compelling circumstances respondents can have no claim to good faith acquisition. Respondent in one proceeding registered

---

551 ***AlgaeCal Inc. v. AlgaeCal Fraud***, D2013-1248 (WIPO September 12, 2013) ("Respondent posted to its website highly prejudicial allegations against the Complainant and its products—information which the Respondent expressly indicated on its website was then unsupported. . . . These allegations—regardless of whether they are true or not, just by being expressed, will simply drive those customers away from the Complainant's products and thus decrease the Complainant's sales.")

552 Affiliate programs are distinguished from affiliation as a form of strategic partnership. They are also distinguished from lawful use of marks to describe a respondent's business, discussed in " (Sec. 5.01-C.2.b). See WordPress Foundation v. clive clint, FA1806001793887 (Forum August 2, 2018) (<wordpresssupport.online>. "Respondent's conduct has created confusion and other customer relations problems for Complainant, as evidenced by the letter to Complainant from a customer who apparently contracted with Respondent for Wordpress support services thinking he was dealing with an agent or affiliate of Complainant.")

553 ***Authorize.Net LLC v. Cardservice High Sierra***, D2008-0760 (WIPO June 30, 2008) (<authorized.net>), citing ***National Futures Association v. John L. Person***, D2005-0690 (WIPO August 15, 2005) (<nationalfutures.com>).

554 For example, ***The Sports Auth. Mich., Inc. v. Elias Skander***, FA135598 (Forum January 7, 2002) (typosquatting for profit under affiliate program not a legitimate interest in domain); ***The Paragon Gifts, Inc. v. GOVS***, D2003-0892 (WIPO December 27, 2003); ***Ross Simons of Warwick, Inc. v. Admin Billing***, D2004-0696 (WIPO October 21, 2004) in which respondent "registered not one but a plethora of domain names incorporating phrases confusingly similar to complainant's mark, many of which included the type of misspellings universally condemned as typosquatting."

555 ***Barnesandnoble.com LLC v. Your One Stop Web Shop***, FA0603000670175 (Forum May 3, 2006), citing ***Expedia, Inc. v. Webpagesa2z.com***, FA 610151 (Forum January 30, 2006) (garnering click-through fees in affiliate program is registration and use in bad faith).

<harrypottercollection.com> to link to other websites, joining the affiliate programs of sites that sell HARRY POTTER products.[556] However, the business model described by Respondent which "directs Internet users to pages unaffiliated with, unrelated to and unsponsored by Complainant has been [addressed and squarely rejected as a legitimate use.]" Respondent in another proceeding and operating under a different model registered <bookingbuddyhotels.com> to "host a website featuring click through links which further resolve[d] to websites of Complainant's competitors."[557] Neither of these stragems passes the paragraph 4(c)(i) test for a *bona fide* offering of goods or services.

---

[556] ***Warner Bros. Entertainment Inc. v. Vivek Rana***, FA0407000304696 (Forum September 21, 2004).

[557] ***Smarter Travel Media LLC v. James Jacobs***, FA0905001263860 (Forum June 29, 2009).

6 Evidence That Respondent Has Registered and is Using Domain Name in Bad Faith 4(a)(iii) of the Policy

6.01 TORTIOUS CONDUCT THAT SUPPORTS BAD FAITH—PARAGRAPH 4(b) OF THE POLICY 6.01

6.01-A Circumstances of Bad Faith 6.01-A

6.01-A.1 Examples of Proscribed Conduct 6.01-A.1

6.01-A.1.a *Defining the Burden* *6.01-A.1.a*

6.01-A.1.a.i *Nonexclusive Circumstances for Conjunctive Bad Faith* *6.01-A.1.a.i*

Bad faith rests on proof of past and present intentional or willful acts by respondent in violation of complainant's exclusive right to use its mark in commerce[1] but the limited jurisdiction of the UDRP does not extend to resolving disputes for alleged trademark infringement.[2] Defined most broadly a domain name registration is abusive when it incorporates a term identical or confusingly similar to a complainant's trademark and uses (or passively holds[3]) it to gain an economic advantage in one of the ways proscribed in paragraph 4(b) and subdivisions (i through iv) thereof of the Policy.[4]

As already explained in Chapter 5, lack of rigthts or legitimate interests alone is not sufficient to have the domain name registration cancelled or transferred. "Rather than Respondent's conduct [being] directed to a mark in the abstract [there must be affirmative proof of] a nexus between the mark and the Complainant, which is

---

[1] WIPO Final Report, paragraph 135 [ii], states that the "notion of an abusive domain name registration is defined solely by reference to violations of trademark rights and not by reference to violations of other intellectual property rights, such as personality rights." Issues within and outside the scope of the Policy are discussed in "The Scope of the UDRP" (Secs. 3.02 and 3.03).

[2] The issue is raised and explained in ***Regency Furniture of Laurel, Inc. v. David Lively***, D2018-0919 (WIPO June 14, 2018) (<regencyfurnituregalleries.com>. "Although Complainant may have an ordinary trademark infringement claim, Respondent's use of the disputed domain name is not cybersquatting. RFNC's business is real and not pre-textual." U.S. trademark law is cited for the proposition of concurrent uses of marks).

[3] Discussed further in "Respondent has Registered and is Using the Domain Name in Bad Faith" (Sec. 4.03).

[4] The UDRP lists bad faith factors in subparagraphs 4(b)(i-iv); good faith factors in subparagraphs 4(c)(i-iii). Good faith factors are discussed in Chapter 5. In contrast, the Anticybersquatting Consumer Protection Act list at 15 U.S.C. §1125 (d)(1)(B)(ii) combines the factors. The ACPA reads: "In determining whether a person has a bad faith intent . . . a court may consider the following factors such as, but not limited to" (emphasis added)

[Factors I through IV and IX are quoted in Sec. 5.01.A.1]

> (V) the person's intent to divert consumers from the mark owner's online location to a site accessible under the domain name that could harm the goodwill represented by the mark, either for commercial gain or with the intent to tarnish or disparage the mark, by creating a likelihood of confusion as to the source, sponsorship, affiliation, or endorsement of the site [**equivalent to paragraph 4(b)(iv) of the Policy**];

known to the Respondent, before a finding of intentional misappropriation of the rights of that brand owner can be made."[5] What degree of nexus is explored in this Chapter.

The relevant consideration in assessing registration in bad faith is respondent's actual knowledge of the complainant and its trademark and the reasons for its choice. This is determined (if not through direct evidence, then circumstantially) from the relative timings of domain name registration and trademark acquisition, the geographic/goods and services proximity of the parties, the trademark's strength or weakness as measured by its reputation in national and international marketplaces,[6] and the content of the website. These facts (admitted, denied, or explained) are the clues that determine respondent's good or bad faith.

The policymakers intended the meaning of abusive registration to emerge from the collective wisdom of panelists' decision making. Even if respondent were found to lack any right or legitimate interest in the disputed domain name, forfeiture would be justified only on proof respondent purposely registered it to take advantage of complainant's mark and by extension its owner. Any other purpose such as using a dictionary word or common expression in their ordinary senses and not for their trademark value falls short. That is why likelihood of confusion—one of several elements of proof in paragraph 4(b)(iv) of the Policy—by itself is not probative of abusive registration. Trademark owners have no preemptive right to

---

> (VI) the person's offer to transfer, sell, or otherwise assign the domain name to the mark owner or any third party for financial gain without having used, or having an intent to use, the domain name in the *bona fide* offering of any goods or services, or the person's prior conduct indicating a pattern of such conduct [**equivalent to paragraph 4(b)(i) of the Policy**];
>
> (VII) the person's provision of material and misleading false contact information when applying for the registration of the domain name, the person's intentional failure to maintain accurate contact information, or the person's prior conduct indicating a pattern of such conduct [**implicit in paragraph 4(b) of the Policy**];
>
> (VIII) the person's registration or acquisition of multiple domain names which the person knows are identical or confusingly similar to marks of others that are distinctive at the time of registration of such domain names, or dilutive of famous marks of others that are famous at the time of registration of such domain names, without regard to the goods or services of the parties [implicit in paragraph 4(b) of the Policy]; and
>
> (IX) the extent to which the mark incorporated in the person's domain name registration is or is not distinctive and famous within the meaning of subsection (c)(1) of this section [implicit in paragraphs 4(b) and 4(c) of the Policy].

[5] ***Investone Retirement Specialists, Inc. v. Motohisa Ohno***, D2005-0643 (WIPO August 2, 2005) (<investone.com>. Weak mark, complaint denied); ***Randy A. Leslein v. Domain Hostmaster, Customer ID: 69323121876872, WhoIs Privacy Services Pty Ltd / Lisa Katz, Domain Protection LLC***, D2017-1233 (WIPO August 14, 2017) ("[U]nder the stringent rules of the Policy, which was designed to combat abusive cybersquatting, bad faith use is not enough.")

[6] Representative examples. No reputation: ***Sven Beichler v. chocri GmbH***, D2011-1629 (WIPO November 17, 2011) (<myswisschoclate.com>); ***McMullen Argus Publishing Inc. v. Moniker***

corresponding domain names that convey through use distinctive unrelated associations or were registered before use of the trademark in commerce.[7]

The nonexclusive acts of proscribed conduct are listed in the four subdivisions of paragraph 4(b). Of the four acts, three concern registration—4(b)(i-iii) "you have registered. . . ." which denotes a past act for the then and present purpose of taking advantage of the trademark owner—and 4(b)(iv) concerns the use of the domain name—"by using the domain name." To have registered the domain name for ransom (a violation of paragraph 4(b)(i) of the Policy) satisfies the conjunctive requirement regardless whether the website is inactive. Paragraph 4(b)(ii) targets respondents who "have engaged [past tense, but construed as past and present progressive] in a pattern of such conduct." If a pattern is found, bad faith registration is implicit. Paragraph 4(b)(iii) proscribes registrations of domain names whose primary purpose as competitors is to disrupt complainants' businesses.

In contrast, the fourth example of bad faith [paragraph 4(b)(iv)] is written in the present tense. The term "*by using*" denotes current and past predatory conduct in violation of the trademark owner's rights.[8] Where a domain name postdates acquisition of the trademark and resolves to a website that confuses visitors by suggesting an association with the complainant "as to the source, sponsorship, affiliation, or endorsement of [the] web site," failure to rebut the inference of targeting is conclusive of bad faith registration. No such inference can be drawn where the respondent registered the domain name prior to complainant acquiring its mark.

The UDRP model has resisted attempts to construe it disjunctively,[9] but paragraph 4(b)(iv) stands apart. Depending on the timing of the domain name acquisition and the reputation of the trademark complainant may fail for sufficient proof on the conjunctive requirement.[10] Speculating on, offering to sell, and monetizing domain names *without more evidence* are not actionable under the Policy even if respondent fails the right or legitimate interest test.[11] The *more* is proof of tortious intent at the time of registration to appropriate complainant's mark.[12] Paragraph 4(b) of the Policy introduces the elements of proof for satisfying the requirement

---

Privacy Services / Traverito Traverito, D2007-0680 (WIPO August 30, 2007) (<streetchopper.com>). Discussed further in "Knowledge, Awareness, and Implausible Denial" (Sec. 4.02-C.1).

7 Discussed further in "'First-Come First-Served' Doctrine" (Sec. 5.01-F).

8 ***Admiral Insurance Services Ltd v. Mr. Adam Dicker***, D2005-0241 (WIPO June 4, 2005). Other circumstances may also prove bad faith. Discussed further in "Commercial Gain Through Hyperlinking" (Sec. 6.05-B).

9 Discussed further in "Justifying Forfeiture Despite Good Faith Registration" (Sec.4.03-A.4.b).

10 As a general rule a domain name registered prior to complainant's acquisition of a trademark right cannot have been registered in bad faith, regardless of whether respondent has rights or legitimate interests in the domain name. The consensus on this issue is explained in Jurisprudential Overview, Paragraph 1.1.3. Domain names registered in good faith but subsequently used in bad faith defeat forfeiture. Discussed further in "Subsequent Bad Faith Use" (Sec. 4.03-A.4).

of bad faith under paragraph 4(a)(iii). It reads: "For the purposes of Paragraph 4(a)(iii), the following circumstances [set forth in the subdivisions of the paragraph], in particular but *without limitation*, if found by the Panel to be present, shall be evidence of the registration and use of a domain name in bad faith" (emphasis added).[13]

The four listed examples of bad faith are discussed further below in subsections 6.02, 6.03, 6.04, and 6.05. "Evidence" is construed as "some evidence" rather than conclusive evidence,[14] although some panelists have read the imperative "shall" as authority that violation under paragraph 4(b)(iv) of the Policy is conclusive of "registration *and* use of a domain name in bad faith" (emphasis added).[15] However, the conjunctive requirement is compelled by the language in paragraph 4(a)(iii) of the Policy. Complainant prevails or fails by offering proof that respondent both registered (past tense) and is (present tense) using the domain name in bad faith, even if respondent has discontinued that use, for strategic or other reasons.

6.01-A.1.a.ii

6.01-A.1.a.ii *Totality of the Circumstances*

That respondent's conduct does not fall within the enumerated circumstances in paragraph 4(b) of the Policy is not conclusive on the issue of bad faith.[16] "Given the human capacity for mischief in all its forms the Policy sensibly takes an open ended approach to bad faith, listing some examples without attempting to exhaustively enumerate all its varieties."[17] Panelists early concluded that the four

---

11 ***Audiopoint, Inc. v. eCorp a/k/a Chad Folkening***, D2001-0509 (WIPO June 20, 2001) ("[S]peculation in domain names when done without any intent to profit from others' trade mark rights may itself constitute a *bona fide* activity under paragraph 4(c)(i).")

12 Discussed further in "Opportunistic Bad Faith" (Sec. 6.01-C.1) and "Knowledge and Targeting Are Prerequisites to Finding Bad Faith Registration" (Sec. 4.02-C).

13 Some panelists have queried whether the meaning of the phrase in this context expands the Panel's authority to find bad faith registration where the evidence is conclusive on bad faith use, "Justifying Forfeiture Despite Good Faith Registration" (Sec.4.03-A.4.b). However, it should be noted that the conjunctive phrasing is a holdover from the WIPO Final Report: Paragraph 171(1)(iii) and was thus a deliberative decision in reaching consensus.

14 ***A. Nattermann & Cie. GmbH and Sanofi aventis v. Watson Pharmaceuticals, Inc.***, D2010-0800 (WIPO August 31, 2010). The majority denied the complaint while the dissent provided a cogent analysis of the view expressed in the cases in the next footnote that evidence of bad faith use justifies a finding of abusive registration.

15 ***Octogen Pharmacal Company, Inc. v. Domains By Proxy, Inc. / Rich Sanders and Octogen e-Solutions***, D2009-0786 (WIPO August 19, 2009). In the line of cases stemming from ***Octogen*** bad faith use warrants a finding of abusive registration, but this construction has not found any significant support, ***BioClin B.V v. MG USA***. D2010-0046 (WIPO March 22, 2010) and ***Camon S.p.A. v. Intelli-Pet, LLC***, D2009-1716 (WIPO March 12, 2010). Discussed further in "Justifying Forfeiture Despite Good Faith Registration" (Sec. 4.03-A.4.b).

16 ***Mattel, Inc. v. Unknown c/o Dora Marks***, FA0506000490083 (Forum July 11, 2005) (It "is not a limitation.")

enumerated circumstances are "intended to be illustrative, rather than exclusive."[18] "[J]ust because Respondent's conduct does not fall within the 'particular' circumstances set out in [paragraph 4(b)], does not mean that the domain names at issue were not registered in and are not being used in bad faith."[19] Unidentified are other abusive practices covered under the catchall phrase "in particular *but without limitation*."[20] "It does not matter that the facts . . . may not fall within any of the circumstances described at paragraph 4(b) of the Policy."[21] If not on any one of the four examples the Panel can rule on the "totality of the circumstances."[22] Panels have identified a variety of circumstances beyond the enumerated acts.[23]

---

17 ***Worldcom Exchange, Inc v. Wei.com, Inc.***, D2004-0955 (WIPO January 5, 2005) (<wei.com>).

18 ***Do The Hustle, LLC v. Tropic Web***, D2000-0624 (WIPO Aug. 21, 2000). The list of nonexclusive bad faith examples does not include non use, but it was quickly recognized as a factor in making the assessment. The principal decision is ***Telstra Corporation Limited v. Nuclear Marshmallows,*** D2000-0003 (WIPO February 18, 2000) (<telsra.com>. The issue is discussed further below in "Inactive or Passive Use" (Sec. 5.01-B.2); ***Cellular One Group v. Brien***, D2000-0028 (WIPO March 10, 2000) ("The Panel believes that bad faith use can also exist in situations, such as the instant one, where (i) the Domain Name contains in its entirety, and is for all essential purposes only, Complainant's trademark, (ii) such trademark is a coined word, has been in use for a substantial time prior to the registration of the Domain Name and is a well-known mark, and (iii) Respondent has alleged no good faith basis for use by it of the Domain Name.")

19 ***Home Interiors & Gifts, Inc. v. Home Interiors***, D2000-0010 (WIPO March 7, 2000); ***Validas, LLC v. SMVS Consultancy Private***, D2009-1413 (WIPO January 29, 2010) ("The Panel may have regard to other evidence in determining whether the requirements of 4(a)(iii) have been proved," citing ***Passion Group Inc. v. USEARCH Inc.***, AF-0250 (eResolution undated 2000) (three member Panel which included the ***Validas*** Panelist: "[While] use of the kind described in 4(b)(iv) is to be taken as evidence of bad faith registration as well as evidence of bad faith use [it is] not necessarily conclusive. Furthermore, the panel is not required to assign substantial weight to evidence of constructive bad faith registration furnished by paragraph 4(b)(iv), and the panel may have regard to other evidence in determining whether the requirements of 4(a)(iii) have been proved.")

20 Paragraph 4(b) of the Policy.

21 ***Fox News Network, LLC v. Sam Solomon***, D2005-0022 (WIPO March 25, 2005).

22 ***CBS Broad., Inc. v. LA-Twilight-Zone***, D2000-0397 (WIPO June 19, 2000) ("[T]he Policy expressly recognizes that other circumstances can be evidence that a domain name was registered and is being used in bad faith"); ***Twentieth Century Fox Film Corp. v. Risser***, FA 93761 (Forum May 18, 2000) ("The requirement in the ICANN Policy that a complainant prove that domain names are being used in bad faith does not require that it prove in every instance that a respondent is taking positive action. Use in bad faith can be inferred from the totality of the circumstances even when the registrant has done nothing more than register the names."). The dissent in ***Deutsche Lufthansa AG v. Future Media Architects, Inc.***, FA0802001153492 (Forum April 17, 2008) (<lh.com>) had a different view. It concurred only to the extent of agreeing that the totality approach is not inappropriate in some circumstances.

23 Example: ***Wendy Ida v. Farid Azam***, FA0901001240643 (Forum February 27, 2009) (fraudulent transfer not included in the list). Among other practices not on the list are hijacking domain names by surreptitiously transferring them to new Registrars and Registrants and assuming the trademark owner's identity for Phishing expeditions. See below, "Spoofing and Phishing" (Sec. 6.01-C.2.c).

Prominent among the non-enumerated acts include threatening to point the disputed domain name to a website featuring "adult content" (extortion),[24] holding hostage a domain name fraudulently transferred (conversion), and collecting personal information from visitors who believe they have reached complainant's website, which is bait for spoofing and phishing (larceny). These acts are such that to have registered (or be the registered holder) supports a finding of bad faith *per se*. For other acts respondents are more likely to be called to account and registrations found abusive where the domain names are identical or confusingly similar to trademarks with well-established reputations,[25] and less likely to be abusive where the disputed domain names are composed of combinations of common words or descriptive phrases being used in non-infringing ways.[26]

6.01-A.1.b 6.01-A.1.b *Identifying the Right Theory of Predation*

Cybersquatters are defined as "people who register domain names knowing them to be the trademarks of others and with the intention of causing damage or disruption to the trademark owners and/or unfairly exploiting the trademarks to their own advantage."[27] While a respondent's conduct may be actionable under more than one theory, it is preferable to identify which theory best suits the circumstances. The elements for proving tortious interference with contract, for example, are entirely different from tortious interference with prospective advantage. A plaintiff in a court action cannot hope to win the first by offering as proof the elements of the second. It is no different in prosecuting a UDRP proceeding.

Paragraph 4(b)(i) of the Policy provides the most specific example of abusive conduct. It proscribes registering a domain name "primarily for the purpose of selling, renting, or otherwise transferring [it] to complainant who is the owner of the trademark or service mark or to a competitor of that Complainant, for valuable consideration in excess of your documented out of pocket costs directly related to the domain name."[28]

---

[24] Representative example: ***Gryphon Internet v. than you corp. / Jon Shakur***, FA1108001405610 (Forum, October 11, 2011), threatening to point the domain name to adult content.

[25] ***General Motors LLC v. Shenzhen Belding Golf Planning Co., ltd.***, D2009-1781(WIPO February 10, 2010) (<cadillacgolf.com>) in which the Chinese Respondent targeted an English language audience. It alleged that in China complainant had a registration only for automobiles and automobile manufacturing. However, the evidence was to the contrary: "[O]n the evidence filed by complainant, the Trade Mark is in fact registered and used by complainant in respect of golfing products and accessories and the sponsoring of golf exhibitions and tournaments."

[26] Discussed further in "Common Words, Common Phrases" (Sec. 5.01-D.1.c).

[27] ***Tomatis Developpement SA v. Jan Gerritsen*** D2006-0708 (WIPO August 1, 2006).

[28] It is not a violation of the Policy to respond to a complainant's interest in purchasing the disputed domain name. Discussed further in "Not All Offers to Sell Violate the Policy" (Sec. 5.01-D.3).

The proscription encompasses holding domain names for ransom and other forms of extortion to obtain from complainant benefits respondent may otherwise not be entitled to receive. These actors fall principally into two classes: respondents known to complainant—former employees, partners, consultants, agents, and service providers[29]; and respondents unknown to complainants who have acquired domain names "primarily for the [proscribed] purpose."[30] Domain names acquired for other purposes are actionable under subparagraphs 4(b)(iii) and 4(b)(iv) of the Policy or an unenumerated circumstance.[31]

Paragraph 4(b)(ii) focuses on respondents who "engage[ ] in a pattern of" registrations that "prevent the owner of the trademark or service mark from reflecting the mark in a corresponding domain name." Whether or not the domain name is active, complainant satisfies paragraph 4(a)(iii) if the evidence demonstrates respondent is engaged in a pattern of like conduct toward other trademark owners (horizontal infringement) or against the complainant (vertical infringement).[32] The specificity of proscribed conduct in the first two of the 4(b) examples of bad faith resists blurring. Each is a distinctive cause of action resting on specific elements of proof.

When it comes to paragraphs 4(b)(iii) and (iv) some parties and panelists tend to blur the different predatory factors. The two paragraphs have reference to

---

29 Parties known to each other discussed further in "Disputes Between Formerly Related Parties" (Sec. 3.03-C).

30 Discussed further in "Opportunistic Bad Faith" (Sec. 6.01-C.1).

31 Representative examples: ***Grace From Fire, LLC v. ConnectDomain.com Worldwide domains, Inc***, D2010-0143 (WIPO March 9, 2010) (<jackjackass.com>. "Respondent's rather frank admission that he intends to use the disputed domain name to leverage compensation for copyright materials allegedly taken from his website suggests that the motive was to use the domain name as a bargaining means for another dispute. This is improper and in the Panel's view is a clear illustration of bad faith," ***Coppertown Drive-Thru Systems, LLC v. R. Snowden***, FA0605000715089 (Forum July 17, 2006); also, ***Nexxt Development Corp. v. Richard Spence***, D2008-0530 (WIPO May 29, 2008): "passively holding the domain names for use in possible settlement negotiations of the dispute between the parties constitutes use of the domain names in bad faith." Ultimately, "non-payment of fees by complainant to respondent does not establish rights or legitimate interests in the disputed domain name in the Respondent," ***Ecoyoga Ltd. siteleader.com, Siteleader Hosting***, D2009-1327 (December 11, 2009); ***National Securities Corporation v. Registration Private, Domains By Proxy, LLC / Ridgeway Support, Richard (Rick) Garber***, D2018-0290 (WIPO March 23, 2018) (<nationalsecuritiescorp.com>. "[I]t appears likely that the Respondent registered the Domain Name and immediately used it as leverage in the Garbers' dispute with the Complainant, to add pressure for a settlement because of the potentially disruptive value of the Domain Name.")

32 ***Produits Nestlé S.A. v. Above.com Domain Privacy, Shu Lin, Shu Lin Enterprises Limited***, D2010- 1882 (WIPO January 11, 2011). Discussed further in "Acts Construed as a 'Pattern of Conduct'" (Sec. 6.03-A).

different acts and targets. The first specifically targets the business of a competitor, whereas the second targets consumers through pretense of association with complainant:

> Paragraph 4(b)(iii): "[Y]ou have registered the domain name primarily for the purpose of disrupting the business of a competitor"; and
>
> Paragraph 4(b)(iv): "[B]y using the domain name, you have intentionally attempted to attract, for commercial gain, Internet users to your web site or other on line location, by creating a likelihood of confusion with complainant's mark as to the source, sponsorship, affiliation, or endorsement of your web site or location or of a product or service on your web site or location."

The blurring results from generalizing the definition of "competitor" in paragraph 4(b)(iii) to include domain name holders whose websites contain links to competitive goods or services. The error can be traced to a case from the first year of the UDRP in which the Panel stated that "the natural meaning of the word 'competitor' is one who acts in opposition to another."[33]

This reading has been questioned by subsequent Panels,[34] but continues to have life.[35] In ***Sony Corporation*** the Panel first noted that it "may be argued that respondent is not a competitor of complainant" but concludes otherwise, citing an earlier case that reasoned that in "engaging in . . . commercial activity, Respondent did (if only indirectly, become a competitor of Complainant and attracted Internet users for commercial gain.")[36]

No doubt the extended definition of a competitor to include those who "indirectly become" one through hyperlinks is consistent with the element of disruption, but it nevertheless blurs the distinction between paragraphs 4(b)(iii) and (iv).[37] Rather, paragraph 4(b)(iii) should be reserved for competitors who are "person[s] or entit[ies] in competition with a complainant for the provision of goods or services, and not merely any person or entity with an interest oppositional to that of a mark holder."[38]

---

[33] ***Mission Kwa Sizabantu v. Rost***, D2000-0279 (WIPO June 7, 2000).

[34] The Panel in ***Vishwa Nirmala Dharma a.k.a. Sahaja Yoga v. Sahaja Yoga Ex Members Network and SD Montford***, D2001-0467 (WIPO June 16, 2001) among later panelists declined "to accept the contention of complainant that the broad definition of 'competitor' will include not only commercial or business competitors, but anyone acting in opposition to another."

[35] ***IGBnvestments, Inc. v. Donald Baker***, D2007-1320 (WIPO November 9, 2007). The Panel found that in drawing traffic to itself "it must have been apparent to respondent that this would have a disruptive effect on the business of complainant."

[36] ***Sony Corporation v. John Stewart Last, Dragon Domains Limited***, D2008-0812 (WIPO July 2, 2008).

[37] As well as supporting bad faith, displaying hyperlinks to competitors' businesses is not a bona fide offering of goods or services under paragraph 4(c)(i) of the Policy.

In ***Birinyi Associates***[39] (a representative case) the Panel rejected complainant's contention that respondent was a competitor even though it could possibly become one in the future. Competitor respondents have been found to violate both paragraph 4(b)(iii)—where they are in the same business and same location or region and truly compete for Internet visitors—and paragraph 4(b)(iv) where their domain name and websites also "creat[e] a likelihood of confusion with complainant's mark as to the source, sponsorship, affiliation, or endorsement."[40] A noncompetitor respondent populating its website with links to competing goods or services is liable under paragraph 4(b)(iv) of the Policy.

6.01-A.2 Parking for Revenue 6.01-A.2

6.01-A.2.a *Revenue Model Not Condemned* *6.01-A.2.a*

The Policy does not condemn the parking for revenue model.[41] Domain names can be identical or confusingly similar to trademarks without implying any association with or endorsement from their owners. In those cases in which respondents have priority they have protectable interests. Where complainants have priority the issue turns on motivation. The Policy condemns registering the disputed domain name "in the hope and expectation that . . . similarity [to complainant's trademark] would lead to confusion on the part of Internet users and result in an increased number of Internet users being drawn to that domain name parking page."[42]

---

[38] ***Britannia Building Society v. Britannia Fraud Prevention***, D2001-0505 (WIPO July 6, 2001).

[39] ***Birinyi Associates, Inc. v. Convert***, D2001-0395 (WIPO June 20, 2001).

[40] ***Identigene, Inc. v. Genetest Labs.***, D2000-1100 (WIPO November 30, 2000) (Respondent's use of the domain name at issue to resolve to a website where similar services are offered to Internet users is likely to confuse the user into believing that the complainant is the source of or is sponsoring the services offered at the site); ***DatingDirect.com Ltd. v. Aston***, FA 593977 (Forum December 28, 2005) (DATING DIRECT and <sexdatingdirect.com>); ***Toner Connect, L.L.C. v. Privacy Protect, LLC / Realogue Corporation,*** D2018-2829 (WIPO February 21, 2019) (<tonerconnect.com>. "Respondent's sole owner and president is a direct competitor of Complainant.")

[41] Too numerous to cite. See ***Micron Technology, Inc. v. Null International Research Center***, D2001-0608 (WIPO June 20, 2001) (<crucialtechnology.com>). "[However,] [t]his decision, like all UDRP decisions, is without prejudice to the filing of a new UDRP complaint should a subsequent purchaser acquire and use the domain name in bad faith, such as to divert consumers for commercial gain by creating a likelihood of confusion as to the source of its goods or services."). Passive use of domain names may result in a finding that respondent lacks rights or legitimate interests but is not conclusive on the issue of bad faith. "Inferring Bad Fait Registration from Passive Use" (Sec. 5.01-B.2.a) and "Non-Use No Evidence of Bad Faith Registration" (Sec. 5.01-B.2.b). Also see URS Procedure:

5.9.1: Trading in domain names for profit, and holding a large portfolio of domain names, are of themselves not indicia of bad faith ....

5.9.2: Sale of traffic (i.e. connecting domain names to parking pages and earning click-per-view revenue) does not in and of itself constitute bad faith under the URS.

The general rule is that where respondents use parking services to populate their websites with links that direct Internet users to goods or services competitive with complainants or create noncompetitive links having no semantic connection to the goods or services referenced it violates paragraph 4(b)(iv) of the Policy. Even though respondent may not control the content[43] "it is ultimately [the] respondent who is responsible for how its domain name is used."[44]

Without departing from this view of responsibility there are excusable circumstances. A respondent is "entitled to give an explanation as to how inappropriate advertisements and links came to appear on its website."[45] Ultimate responsibility is reserved for the egregious rather than the "temporary and inadvertent" display of hyperlinks.[46] Unintentional hyperlinking quickly removed upon receipt of notice (either a cease-and-desist notice or complaint) may reinforce a respondent's assertion of good faith registration.[47] "Modifying . . . a website also may attenuate the harm to a complainant whose trademark or commercial interests are allegedly compromised by the website prior to remediation."[48] A distinction has also been drawn between a holding page created by the registrar following registration of the domain name and a parking page intentionally created by respondent.[49] The former is not *ipso facto* bad faith; the latter more than likely is.

---

42 ***Fundação CPqD Centro de Pesquisa e Desenvolvimento em Telecomunicações v. Gary Lam***, D2009-1403 (WIPO November 27, 2009); also ***Slickdeals, Inc. v. Chad Wright a/k/a WebQuest.com Inc.***, FA0910001289878 (Forum January 29, 2010) (<slickdeals.com>).

43 Discussed further in "Commercial Gain Through Hyperlinking" (Sec. 6.05-B).

44 ***State Farm Mutual Auto. Insr. Co. v. Pompilio***, FA 1092410 (Forum November 20, 2007).

45 ***Costas Spiliadis v. Nicholas Androulidakis***, FA0708001072907 (Forum October 17, 2007).

46 ***Electronic Arts Inc. v. Abstract Holdings International LTD / Sherene Blackett***, FA1111001415905 (Forum January 4, 2012); See also ***Fireman's Fund Insurance Company v. Steve Schwartz***, FA1010001355350 (Forum December 15, 2010) ("Respondent contends that he only learned of the holding page upon notification from complainant, and was blocked from changing it because of the instant UDRP. Complainant does not disagree. So while Respondent may be responsible for the referred webpage in that he set the wheels in motion for the holding page to be displayed, there is no evidence that Respondent intended the particular webpage and its content ever be linked to the at issue domain name.")

47 ***Churchill Insurance Co., Ltd. v. Churchhill financial Services, Ltd.***, FA 0906001270466 (Forum September 1, 2009) ("Respondent's use of the Domain Name . . . occurred before Respondent received actual notice of the dispute from Complainant and after Respondent made bona fide use of the Domain Name. Further, Respondent promptly removed these links upon receipt of notice and substituted featured and grouped links not related to insurance.")

48 This explanation notwithstanding, the Panel in ***American Airlines v. James Manley d/b/a Webtoast Internet Services, Inc.***, FA1006001330044 (Forum July 27, 2010) concluded that respondent lacked rights or legitimate interests in the domain name and its registration of <americanway.com> was abusive.

49 ***Fireman's Fund Insurance Company***, supra. The Panel makes reference to the provision in the ACPA that "preclude[s] finding bad faith intent where the registrant reasonably believed that the

6.01-A.2.b *Mimicking Strong Marks*

6.01-A.2.b

Determining legitimacy lies in part with the classification of the trademark. On the taxonomic scale strong trademarks, those classified as suggestive, arbitrary and fanciful, have greater protection than weak marks. Dictionary words and common phrases on the lower end of the trademark scale are protectable only to the extent respondent acquired the domain name intentionally to take advantage of complainant's goodwill. Particularly with common word domain names registered many years prior to the proceedings, complainant's failure to address the longevity of bad faith use undermines its contention of bad faith registration. Since the Internet Archive is a ready resource, failure to marshal this evidence supports a negative inference in favor of a respondent whose website inadvertently and for a short period may have posted a link suggesting (although not proving) awareness of complainant and its trademark.[50]

The difficulty is illustrated in cases in which respondent removes links after receiving notification. One three-member Panel concluded that the existence of the link alone is not evidence of bad faith. It rejected complainant's argument that "the Respondent's removal of an 'OUTSIDE magazine' link from its home page, following correspondence from complainant, was an 'admission' of bad faith" and accepted respondent's contention that "it removed the link as a 'courtesy' to complainant," which it interpreted as a "rational effort to avoid a costly dispute."[51]

Liability attaches where respondent has "registered the domain name then placed it on a parking service, which redirect[s] the user to a website advertising [goods or] services competitive with Complainant."[52] By identifying complainant on the landing page together with its competitors respondent is indirectly acknowledging

---

domain name was a fair use of the relevant mark [15 U.S.C. §1125(d)(1)(B)(i) and (ii)]. There is no reason that the concept of domain name related 'bad faith' under federal law and under the UDRP should not be consistent."

50 ***Johnson & Johnson v. Chad Wright, WebQuest.com, Inc.***, D2012-0010 (WIPO April 5, 2012) (<tucks.com>. "That the Complaint does not address the earlier appearance of the website is a matter of some concern to the Panel. Moreover, the Complaint appears to mischaracterize the historical content on Respondent's website. The allegation 'upon information and belief' that Respondent's website was used only to display competitive links or as a 'non-functional holding website posted by the Registrar' is inconsistent with readily available archives at <archive.org>, showing substantial periods when the website displayed several links based on dictionary meanings of the 'tucks' term. This heightens the Panel's concerns in light of the obligation to certify accuracy of a Complaint under the Rules, paragraph 3(b)(xiv).")

51 ***Mariah Media Inc. v. First Place7 Internet Inc.***, D2006-1275 (WIPO December 6, 2006) (<outside.com>).

52 ***Cloer Elektrogeräte GmbH v. Motohisa Ohno***, D2006-0026 (WIPO March 29, 2006); ***Bayerische Motoren Werke AG v. bmwrider llc***, D2008-0610 (WIPO June 23, 2008), citing ***Villeroy & Boch AG v. Mario Pingerna***, D2007-1912 (WIPO February 14, 2008).

its awareness of complainant's goods or services. Respondents' attempts in these representative cases to rebut any negative inferences of knowledge or awareness by arguing they are not responsible for website content and should not be held accountable is undercut by the content and hyperlinks on the site.

Absent a plausible explanation for inappropriate hyperlinking, the no responsibility argument for content of parking pages has on the whole been rejected.[53] "[T]he fact that a third party is effectively operating the website on behalf of Respondent, and making payments to respondent on the basis of that use, does not insulate Respondent from the conduct of its authorized agent."[54] Under these circumstances knowledge of the use to which a parked domain is being put is attributed to respondent despite denial. The reasoning is that respondent or someone else derives a benefit from parking the domain. This does not exclude *bona fide* use of domain names resolving to websites that collect hyperlinks consistent with their semantic values even though they may coincidentally also link to complainants.

6.01-B 6.01-B Interfering with the Proceedings

Until ICANN amended the rules, there was an interval between respondent's notice of infringement and formal commencement of an administrative proceeding. This interval presented an opportunity for respondent to interfere with the proceedings by transferring the disputed domain name to an unrelated party before notice of claim is communicated to the registrar.[55]

ICANN was induced to amend the rule because although locking was informally recommended—it was "not something that is literally required by the UDRP

---

[53] Discussed further below, "Populating Web Pages: the 'Not Me' Defense" (Sec. 6.05-F).

[54] ***Park Place Entertainment Corporation v. Anything.com Ltd.***, D2002-0530 (WIPO September 16, 2002) (<flamingo.com>) (Majority held in favor of Complainant.)

[55] ***British Broadcasting Corporation v Data Art Corporation/Stoneybrook***, D2000-0683 (WIPO September 20, 2000) (<bbcnews.com>) ("where a registrant of a domain name, when named as Respondent in a domain name dispute case, systematically transfers the domain name to a different registrant to disrupt the proceeding.")

ICANN amended rule 3(b)(xii) effective July 1, 2015 to eliminate the requirement for serving respondent a copy of the complaint before filing with the provider, thereby avoiding an unnecessary interval. The amended rule also includes:

— "Lock" and "pendency" are now defined terms in the UDRP Rules;

— UDRP complainants no longer have to transmit a copy of the complaint to the respondent (rule 3(b)(xii));

— Rule 4(b) requires registrars to lock the disputed domain name(s) within two (2) business days of receiving a UDRP complaint from a UDRP provider;

— Rule 4(e) provides that when a UDRP provider informs the registrar that the UDRP proceeding has been withdrawn or dismissed, the registrar must remove the lock within one (1) business day of receiving notice;

as [a] written [requirement]"—the practice in the registrar industry was not uniform. Although cyberflight is now largely eliminated by the amended rules it does not prevent respondents from changing registrars and delaying proceedings after receiving communications earlier than a complaint (such as cease-and-desist letters, for example.[56])

Prior to an amendment to the rules in 2015 cyberflight was relatively rare but it received appropriate attention. Commenting on the interval between complaint (and any prior notice) the Panel in ***British Broadcasting*** stated:

> To interpret section 8(a) of the Policy in such a way as to permit transfers of registration after notice of the complaint to respondent but before official commencement of the proceedings by way of notification from the provider would not do justice to complainants who have initiated complaints in accordance with the Policy and the Rules. Moreover such an interpretation would appear to permit, if not encourage the phenomenon of cyberflying, where a registrant of a domain name dispute case, systematically transfers the domain name to a different registrant to disrupt the proceeding.

Change of registration on the same day the transferor received complainant's e-mail notification of the complaint is *prima facie* evidence of cyberflyte.[57] The conclusion

— Rule 5(b) provides that respondents may request an additional four (4) calendar days to respond to a complaint and UDRP providers will automatically grant the extension, if requested;

— Rule 16(a) provides that registrars must notify the parties, the provider and ICANN of the date for implementation of the decision within three (3) business days of receiving the decision from the provider;

— Rule 17 outlines a new procedure to be used in cases that are settled between parties outside the UDRP case.

[56] See Initial Report on the Locking of a Domain Name Subject to UDRP Proceedings Policy Development Process (prepared by ICANN staff for submission to the GNSO Council on March 15, 2013) at 11: "[But] there is no uniform approach, which has resulted in confusion and misunderstandings." The report and its recommendations were adopted unanimously by the GNSO Council on August 1, 2013. Prohibiting cyberflight is found in paragraph 8(a) of the Policy. It prohibits transfer to "another holder (i) during a pending administrative proceeding." Paragraph 8(b) prohibits "transfer[ring] your domain name registration to another registrar" during the same period. However, with locking in place cyberflight has been eliminated, although (as indicated) not for changing registrars or transferring following communications prior to filing the complaint). See ***BOSU Fitness, LLC v Kolombo Networks***, FA0906001266587 (Forum July 22, 2009) (finding that switching WHOIS information in anticipation of a UDRP complaint "constitutes 'cyberflying.'")

See also WIPO Overview 2.0, Paragraph 3.9, second sentence: "Identification by a registrar or privacy or proxy service of another such service as the purported registrant of the domain name may also constitute evidence of cyberflight and bad faith, as may failure in response to a UDRP provider's request to timely confirm the identity and contact information of the registrant of the domain name where the registrant listed in the WhoIs is a privacy or proxy service (although such failure would not prevent a panel from deciding such cases, with the privacy or proxy service typically being regarded as the relevant respondent of record)."

was bolstered in the cited case by evidence that the transferee company did not exist before the proceeding was commenced but incorporated after. If the transferor acts in concert or conspires to avoid the effect of the Policy by transferring the domain name, its conduct will be imputed to the transferee.[58]

Cyberflying describes a "quick-witted respondent seek[ing] to escape the jurisdiction of the panel by transferring the domain name to a new holder or to a new registrar after receipt of the copy of the complaint but before the formal commencement of the proceeding."[59] By its terms section 8(a) is limited to "a pending administrative proceeding," but cyberflight can also occur before service of a complaint, which, although not technically a violation is evidence of bad faith.[60]

Any notice that announces an intention to vindicate a right (a cease-and-desist notice or other communication) carries "the risk . . . that respondent might . . . dispose of the domain names . . . and put complainant to the cost and inconvenience of having to pursue individually the multiple new owners."[61] In ***Fifth Third Bancorp.*** the Respondent engaged in a "flurry of deregistration and re-registration immediately following Complainant's cease-and-desist email." A transferee is presumed to have knowledge of complainant's claim. The failure of the transferor to explain the transfer of domain name or the transferee to explain its acquisition of

---

[57] ***Pologne 4 S.P.A. v Carrent Bank-Promotuls, SA. Inc./ Esidro Fentis A/K/A Alex Bars***, D2004-0830 (WIPO December 2, 2004); ***Sutton Group Financial Services Ltd. and Sutton Group Realty Services, Inc. v. Bill Rodger***, 2005-0126 (WIPO June 27, 2005) (Respondent alleged that it had sold the domain name in dispute.)

[58] This applies also to prior transfers, but some caution must be exercised to "avoid any injustice to an innocent transferee of a domain name." ***Rovos Rail (Pty) Limited v. Innovative Technical Solutions***, D2001-1299 (WIPO February 10, 2002) ("In this case the Panel concludes (after much anxious consideration) that it would not be unjust to the Respondent for the Panel to accept the Complainant's submissions on this point. . . .The Respondent must be taken to have known that it was by then the registrant of the disputed domain name.") See also the discussions at "Renewal of Registration" (Sec. 4.03-A.4.c) and "Renewal of Registration vs. Registration by Transfer" (Sec. 4.03-B).

[59] ***Enterprises, Inc. v John Zuccarini, Cupcake City and Cupcake Patrol***, D2001-0489 (WIPO June 19, 2001), citing ***British Broadcasting Corporation***, supra.

[60] ***Fifth Third Bancorp v. Secure Whois Information Service***, D2006-0696 (WIPO September 14, 2006); ***Pandora Jewelry, LLC v. wutianhao***, D2010-0286 (WIPO April 19, 2010).

[61] ***The Cartoon Network LP, LLLP v. Mike Morgan***, D2005-1132 (WIPO January 5, 2006): "The Panel notes that complainant could have prevented the transfer of the Six Denied Domain Names by respondent by immediately commencing an administrative proceeding in order to lock the domain name registrations (paragraph 8 of the Policy). It is common practice for complainants to make a demand for transfer before commencing an administrative proceeding, but the risk in this course . . . is that respondent might, as here, dispose of the domain names on receipt of complainant's notice and put complainant to the cost and inconvenience of having to pursue individually the multiple new owners."

the domain name and its relationship, if any, with transferor are consistent with a pattern of evasion and non-responsiveness.

Even though "[n]either a change of registrar nor a change of registrant in these circumstances affects the proceedings"[62] a transfer raises an issue as to naming the proper party.[63] In ***AT & T Corp.*** the Panel included in its transfer order both the registrant at the time the complaint was received and the registrant to whom the name was transferred shortly thereafter. It is appropriate to name both.[64] A transferee being named as an interested party is properly named and implicitly "has consented to this course."[65] Complainant's offer of proof of cyberflying shifts the burden to respondent, whose silence is conclusive against it.[66] Manipulations of the Whois Directory, such as resorting to a privacy service after the filing of a complaint, are "strongly evocative of cyberflight [when they] appear to have been calculated to obstruct or delay this proceeding under the Policy."[67] However, merely making changes to the Whois Directory that have no effect on the proceedings is not evidence of bad faith.[68]

---

[62] ***Wm Satellite Radio Inc. v. Michael Backer***, FA0612000861120 (Forum February 27, 2007).

[63] ***AT & T Corp v. W.N.A. (with various aliases)***, D2001-1160 (WIPO November 16, 2001).

[64] A similar conclusion has been reached in dealing with proxy and privacy services. See "Use and Abuse of Proxy and Privacy Services" (Sec. 2.04).

[65] ***Gloria Werke H. Schulte Frankenfeld GmbH & Co v. Internet Development Corporation and Gloria MacKenzie***, D2002-0056 (WIPO April 26, 22) (<gloria.com>). However, the majority concluded that the transfer, although in violation of Paragraph 8, was benign. "Basically, this is another case of a trademark owner in country A expecting that a domain name registrant in country B would have heard of its mark at the date of registration. The majority of the Panel is unable to make that deduction." A lengthy dissent passionately disagreed "with the majority['s] . . . benign treatment of the 'cyberflying'. . . . The incidence of this invidious practice, which has been increasing exponentially of late, takes place almost always with the intention of illegally interfering with the due process of a dispute resolution mechanism which the Respondent had agreed to abide by when obtaining the right to use its domain name."

[66] ***Tomas Sziranyi v. RegisterFly.com***, D2006-0320 (WIPO May 29, 2006).

[67] The Panel in *The Jennifer Lopez Foundation v. Jeremiah Tieman, Jennifer Lopez Net, Jennifer Lopez, Vaca Systems LLC.*, D2009-0057 (WIPO March 24, 2009) (<jenniferlopez.net> and <jenniferlopez.org>).

[68] ***Les Développements Angelcare Inc. v. Radio plus, spol.s r.o.***, D2012-1210 (WIPO September 10, 2012) ("The Panel finds that this is no case of 'cyberflying,' as the Respondent did not change the WhoIs data in terms of changing ownership but only changed its registrar and took down the privacy protection. The Respondent's actions did not avoid or delay the present proceedings.")

6.01-C 6.01-C Registering Domain Names Opportunistically

6.01-C.1 6.01-C.1 Opportunistic Bad Faith

6.01-C.1.a 6.01-C.1.a *Well-Known and Famous Marks*

"Opportunistic bad faith" refers to registrations targeting well-known and famous trademarks.[69] Its principal feature is registering domain names with undeniable knowledge of complainant's preexisting rights. Absent justification (non-authorized but lawful use of trademarks), abusive registration is presumed.[70] A rarer form of opportunism noted in the following footnote concern registrants found to be acting abusively in registering domain names under the guise of lawful conduct. Because these disputes can test the jurisdiction of the UDRP they are *sui generis*.[71]

The phrase "opportunistic bad faith" was initially coined by early Panels to refer to disputed domain names so obviously connected with well-known and famous marks that their use by someone with no connection with them or complainant's products suggests respondents taking advantage to lure Internet users to alternative websites.[72] It has been extended to include registrations that immediately follow widely disseminated publicity of an imminent event.[73] The phrase is not found in the WIPO Final Report. The concept was among the earliest principles enunciated in domain name law and remains vital although it has been criticized. [74]

---

[69] A "famous" mark is defined under U.S. trademark law as one that is "widely recognized by the general consuming public ... as a designation of the source of the goods or services of the mark's owner." 15 U.S.C. § 1125(c). See *Avery Dennison Corp. v. Sumpton*, 189 F.3d 868, 875 (9th Cir.1999): "Dilution is a cause of action invented and reserved for a select class of marks — those marks with such powerful consumer associations that even non- competing uses can impinge on their value."

[70] See ***Parfums Christian Dior v. Javier Garcia Quintas***, D2000-0226 (WIPO May 17, 2000) (Where a domain name is "so obviously connected with such a well-known name and products," "its very use by someone with no connection with the products suggests opportunistic bad faith"); ***Time Inc. v. Max Martel***, D2004-0122 (WIPO May 4, 2004) (<sportsbookillustrated.com>. "[T]here is no circumstance under which the Respondent, unless authorized by the Complainant, could legitimately use the Domain Name under dispute incorporating the [Complainant's] mark without creating a false impression of an association with the Complainant").

[71] See ***Boxador, Inc. v. Ruben Botn-Joergensen***, D2017-2593 (WIPO February 27, 2018) (Three-member unanimous Panel rejected Respondent's USPTO trademark as evidence of lawful registration of <brandbucket.org> and <brandbucket.shop> and found its conduct as well as its domain name registrations abusive).

[72] ***Mariah Media Inc. v. First Place7 Internet, Inc.***, D2006-1275 (WIPO December 6, 2006) in which the Panel noted "[u]nless there is persuasive evidence that the Domain Name was selected opportunistically to create confusion and exploit complainant's marks, the Panel would conclude that respondent has a legitimate interest in using the Domain Name for a commercial purpose."

[73] Cybersquatting even though there is no registered mark. Discussed further below in "Acting on Media Coverage and Insider Information" (Sec. 6.01-C.1.b)

Analytically, bad faith requires the registrant to have actual knowledge of complainant and its trademark. For well-known and famous trademarks opportunistic bad faith is assumed or, if denied, likely to be rejected as unworthy of belief. Respondent in one case acknowledged the worldwide fame of Ringo Starr[75] but denied intention to take advantage of his name. The Panel found that the

> juxtaposition of the timing of the introduction of the .mobi suffix and the registration of a domain name of such an internationally famous person as Ringo Starr indicates a high degree of opportunism. . . . The fact that respondent has also registered .mobi names for other British musicians casts doubt on his statement that he is not in the business of cyber squatting.

Opportunistic bad faith includes registrations incorporating in whole or in part 1) well-known or famous brands that have deep market penetration [Veuve Clicquot[76]], [Google] [Hermes] [Home Depot] [Victoria's Secret]; 2) hotels, casinos, and brand-name resorts in multiple domestic and foreign locations [Fairmont Hotel Management]; and 3) famous personalities such as movie stars [Nicole Kidman] [Morgan Freeman], best-selling authors [Margaret Drabble], and sports personalities [Dan Marino] [Tiger Woods]. It also includes registrations of lapsed domain names of companies with marketplace recognition [Donna Karan Studio] [Walt Disney Studios[77]] and domain names incorporating trademarks of entities that have received bouts of publicity (discussed below).

In ***June Bug Enterprises***[78] Respondent stated that it registered <magicjohnsontravelgroup.com> "hoping perhaps in the future that there might be a need for it and maybe come in contact with Magic's Enterprise." The respondent in another case advanced an argument (rejected by the Panel) that "it should be complainant's responsibility to prove that [the respondent] has benefitted from directing the disputed domain name to his [that is, respondent's] website."[79]

In ordering domain names transferred to complainants panelists implicitly reject arguments that respondents' registrations are protected under the "first-come

---

[74] The concept implied by the term was rejected by the dissent in ***Ha'aretz Daily Newspaper Ltd. v. United Websites, Ltd.***, D2002-0272 (WIPO August 21, 2002): "As for 'opportunistic bad faith,' I must make it clear that I reject the validity of that poorly-conceived bad faith precedent." Nevertheless, the concept is well established and is frequently dusted off.

[75] ***Richard Starkey v. Mr. Bradley***, FA0612000874575 (Forum February 12, 2007) (<ringostarr.mobi>).

[76] ***Veuve Clicquot Ponsardin, Maison Fondée en 1772 v. The Polygenix Group Co.***, D2000-0163 (WIPO May 1, 2000). In ACPA actions, see *Harrods Limited v. Sixty Internet Domain Names*, 302 F.3d 214 (4th Cir. 2002).

[77] ***Disney Enterprises, Inc. v. Intec Solutions OU***, FA1305001500886 (Forum July 3, 2013) (<disneymusicals.com>. Registered three months after lapse).

[78] ***June Bug Enterprises, Inc. v. myspecialprice.com***, FA0611000833078 (Forum December 27, 2006).

first-served" doctrine. That doctrine applies only where respondent's proof supports priority of right and refutes bad faith registration regardless of whether it lacks legitimate use. Opportunism is intentionally targeting complainant's trademark for its revenue creating potential or commercial value. That a domain name identical[80] or confusingly similar[81] to a trademark is available is not a defense to abusive registration. An owner's failure to acquire a domain name corresponding to its trademark is not an abandonment of its right to challenge an infringing registrant. Registering a domain name under circumstances tantamount to opportunism such as offering counterfeit goods is *prima facie* predatory.[82]

6.01-C.1.b

6.01-C.1.b *Acting on Media Coverage and Insider Information*

In assessing conduct Panels have considered the time when a disputed domain name was registered as an indication of opportunistic bad faith. One aspect of this conduct is identified in the Jurisprudential Overview which describes respondents who act on publicity about parties' contemplated actions and register domain names in anticipation of their filing trademark registrations.[83] Several different circumstances are included in this class of abusive registration. The following have come before Panels: mergers and acquisitions, corporate name changes, hotel openings, and sporting events. "[P]recedents of WIPO make it clear that registrations made solely for the purposes of profiting from the merger or proposed merger of two or more trade mark holders fall squarely within the provisions of paragraph 4[b] of the Policy."[84]

The principle is illustrated in ***Pharmacia & Upjohn***[85] and ***The Chase Manhattan Corporation.***[86] In those cases the domain names were registered on the

---

[79] ***Jay Leno v. Guadalupe Zambrano***, D2009-0570 (WIPO June 25, 2009) (<thejaylenoshow.com>).

[80] ***Clicquot Ponsardin***, supra.; ***Parfums Christian Dior v. Javier García Quintas and Christiandior.net***, D2000-0226 (WIPO May 17. 2000) (<christiandior.com> and <christiandior.net>); ***Research In Motion Limited v. Dustin Picov, D2001-0492 (WIPO May 31, 2001)*** (<researchinmotion.com>); ***Orchard Supply Hardware LLC v. RareNames, Web Reg***, FA0804001178941 (Forum June 27, 2008) (<orchardsupply.com>. "Deletion can be the consequence of a deliberate abandonment but also of an unintentional mistake").

[81] ***Expedia, Inc. v. European Travel Network***, D2000-0137 (WIPO April 18, 2000) (<xpediatravel.com>).

[82] ***Car Freshner Corporation and Julius Sämann Ltd. v. li yongbo***, FA0901001244741 (Forum April 1, 2009) (default, <carfreshners.com>).

[83] Jurisprudential Overview 3.0, Paragraph 3.8.2. The consensus is referred to as an exception to the rule that an earlier registered domain name could not have been in bad faith if the trademark was not then in existence. Discussed further in "Earlier Registered Domain Names; Subsequently Acquired Trademarks" (Sec. 5.01.F.2).

[84] ***Clifford Chance LLP And Pünder GmbH v. CPIC Inc.***, D2000-1603 (WIPO January 28, 2001).

same day news was first published of merger talks. "[W]here a registrant [has] speculated on an impending merger between companies that would create a new name combining in whole or in part the names of the merger partners. . . [and] where a registrant based its registration of the domain name on its insider knowledge of the intentions of a (former) business partner or employer in relation to the latter's development [of] a new trademark" it will not be rewarded as having acted in good faith.[87]

Widespread media attention has the effect of establishing a putative trademark right that in some instances may precede the date of its application or registration by a national registry. Thus, Respondent in another case "took advantage of the public announcement that Tandy Corporation was changing its name to RadioShack by registering the domain names on the same day as a public announcement of a company's name change."[88]

Anticipating a corporate name does not elevate a respondent's right or legitimate interest:[89]

> It is eminently clear to this Panel that the Respondent's actions involving the contested domain names amount to nothing more than opportunistic exploitation for his own pecuniary benefit of inevitable Internet use confusion—which can never denote rights or legitimate interests in a domain name.

In ***Meloche Monnex***[90] the Panel found that respondent was well aware the two companies owning the trademarks had merged:

> This is even confirmed by Respondent himself when he observed in his Response that complainants "had ample opportunity to register the domain name in question since the two companies merged in March 1992."

---

85 ***Pharmacia & Upjohn v. Sol Meyer***, D2000-0785 (WIPO August 23, 2000).

86 ***The Chase Manhattan Corporation and Robert Fleming Holdings Limited v. Paul Jones***, D2000 0731 (WIPO October 23, 2000).

87 ***Ezcommerce Global Solutions, Inc. v. Alphabase Interactive***, D2002-0943 (WIPO November 21, 2002).

88 ***Tech. Props., Inc. v. Hussain***, FA 95411 (Forum September 14, 2000). See also, ***Thermo Electron Corp. v. Xu***, FA 713851 (Forum July 12, 2006) ("If there had been any doubt as to bad faith, the fact that registration was on the same day the news leaked about the merger, which was put in evidence, is a compelling indication of bad faith that [the] respondent has to refute and which he has failed to do. The panel finds a negative inference from this."); ***3M Co. v. Jeong***, FA 505494 (Forum August 11, 2005) ("Respondent's registration of the disputed domain name the same day that Complainant issued the press release regarding the acquisition constitutes opportunistic bad faith.")

89 ***Caesars World, Inc. and Park Place Entertainment Corporation v. Japan Nippon***, D2003-0615 (WIPO September 30, 2003) (communicated with Complainant to sell the domain name).

90 ***Meloche Monnex Inc., and The Toronto-Dominion Bank v. Konstantin Vydria***, D2004-1045 (WIPO February 22, 2005).

Receipt of confidential information and public knowledge acquired from media coverage of a complainant's plans followed by registration of a disputed domain name in anticipation of a trademark registration is evidence of bad faith. It "is clearly irrelevant whether a registrant intended to abuse an existing trademark right or one which that registrant specifically knew would arise."[91] The timing of registrations and in many cases the geographic and product/service proximity of the parties clearly spell out respondent's intentions.[92] In a case involving the opening of a hotel "notoriously advertised by Romanian media" the Panel awarded the disputed domain name to complainant.[93]

For sporting and cultural events held at regular intervals the consensus rejects[94] the first to register principle that would allow a respondent to anticipate a trademark filing.[95] As in ***UEFA***, Respondent in ***Madrid 2012*** anticipated complainant's own filing for <madrid2012.com> by registering the domain name two days before complainant filed the first application for MADRID2012 and before the company was renamed MADRID 2012, S.A. Although respondent

> probably did not know about the imminent filing. . . [nevertheless] as Madrid's bid for the 2012 Olympic Games had been published months before and as respondent provides information about Madrid under his website "www.madridman.com," he can be deemed to have been aware of this fact. Respondent was, to the Panel's belief, also aware of the fact, that the Olympic Games have always been identified by the name of the host city followed by the year of the games, such as Sydney 2000, Athens 2004 or Beijing 2008.

A similar assessment was made in ***OpBiz***,[96] where the domain name was registered in the same month that construction began on the first of the three towers to be part

---

[91] ***ExecuJet Holdings Ltd. v. Air Alpha America, Inc.***, D2002-0669 (WIPO October 7, 2002); ***Bragg v. Condon***, FA 92528 (Forum March 2, 2000).

[92] ***General Growth Properties, Inc., Provo Mall L.L.C. v. Steven Rasmussen/Provo Towne Centre Online***, D2003-0845 (WIPO January 15, 2004). Respondent subsequently commenced an ACPA action for declaratory judgment in which General Growth counterclaimed and was awarded the domain name (<provotownecentre.com>) by summary judgment. *Rasmussen v. General Growth Properties, Inc.*, 2005 WL 3334752 (D. Utah, December 7, 2005).

[93] ***Pro Confort SRL v. P IER56, Ion Robu***, D2008-0801 (WIPO August 8, 2008) (RIN GRAND HOTEL).

[94] The Panel in ***Union des associations europeennes de football (UEFA) v. Chris Hallam***, D2001-0717 (WIPO July 10, 2001) (<uefa2004.com>) denied the complaint because the domain name was "obviously not registered or otherwise protected at that time." Commenting on UEFA, the Panel in ***Pacific 10 Conference v. Kevin Lee***, D2011-0200 (WIPO May 17, 2011) noted that "[l]ater panels are not bound by the decisions of earlier panels [where they] consider[ ] that the approach set out [in later cases] more accurately reflect[s] the purpose and intent of this requirement under the Policy."

[95] ***MADRID 2012, S.A. v. Scott Martin-MadridMan Websites***, D2003-0598 (WIPO October 8, 2003).

of the PH Towers by Westgate, a partnership between Planet Hollywood Resort & Casino and Westgate Resorts.

6.01-C.2 Pretending to Be Complainant 6.01-C.2

6.01-C.2.a *Faux Registrant* *6.01-C.2.a*

A faux registrant is one that assumes an identity to camouflage its opportunistic conduct. What is meant by faux in this section are registrants who create registrations mimicking complainants' names both in the second level domains as well as on the Whois Directory.[97] They make no attempt to differentiate their choices or themselves except in obviously infringing ways, such as typosquatting[98], attaching prefixes to disguise their appropriations[99], or pretending to be complainants by mimicking page designs or purloining website contents.[100] None of these ploys qualifies for any of the paragraph 4(c) defenses.

Faux registrants are more likely cybersquatting to commit consumer fraud by confusing consumers as to their affiliation with complainants. The most noxious purpose is phishing for personal information or redirecting to pornography websites.[101] Intention in these factual circumstances to take advantage of marks or consumers is so obvious respondents rarely appear.

---

96 ***OpBiz, LLC d/b/a Planet Hollywood Resort & Casino v. Steven Davis***, FA0810001229112 (Forum December 8, 2008).

97 Examples of faux registrations include: ***Neiman Marcus Group, Inc. v. Neiman-Marcus***, FA 135048 (Forum January 13, 2003) (NEIMAN MARCUS and <neiman-marcus.net>. Default, transfer); ***City News & Video v. Citynewsandvideo***, FA 244789 (Forum May 5, 2004) (<citynewsandvideo.com>. Default, transfer); ***Club Monaco Corp. v. clubmonacoonline***, D2011-1186 (WIPO August 30, 2011) (CLUB MONACO and <clubmonaco online>. Default, transfer); ***Homer TLC, Inc. v. HomeDepo Inc.***, FA1109001408632 (Forum October 28, 2011) (HOME DEPOT and <homedepo.com>. Default, transfer); ***Nobel Learning Communities, Inc. v. Chesterbrookacademy***, D2005-0753 (WIPO September 20, 2005) (CHESTER BROOK ACADEMY and <chesterbrookacademy.com>. "Apart from the domain name having been registered in the name of 'chesterbrook academy', there is no evidence to suggest that the Respondent has been commonly known by the disputed domain name.")

98 ***Bodybuilding.com, LLC v. Richard Hergerton***, FA1306001506350 (Forum July 31, 2013) (Typosquatting. BODYBUILDING.COM and <bodvbuildinq.com>. Default, transfer. "[T]he resolving page features the BODYBUILDING.COM mark, logo, and webpage design.")

99 ***Yoga Works, Inc. v. Arpita***, FA 155461 (Forum June 17, 2003) (finding that respondent was not "commonly known by" the <shantiyogaworks.com> domain name despite listing its name as "Shanti Yoga Works" in its WHOIS contact information because there was "no affirmative evidence before the Panel that respondent was ever 'commonly known by' the disputed domain name prior to its registration of the disputed domain name.")

100 ***Jim Williams v. Louis Smith***, FA0904001257389 (Forum May 28, 2009) (HURRICANE CITY and <hurricancity.net>, <hurrycancity.org> and <hurricancity.info>.

Some deceptions are accepted as part and parcel of protected speech, as when, for example, respondent appropriates the whole or varies complainant's trademark to criticize, comment, or parody a mark owner or its goods and services, sometimes in the owner's name.[102]

6.01-C.2.b 6.01-C.2.b *Fraudulent Transfer of Domain Names*

There is a common theme in losing a domain name by hacking of the registrar and by inadvertent lapse of registration. In both, a domain name formerly registered in complainant's name is latterly found in another's, but the different factual circumstance demands a different approach to assessing respondent's intention. While respondent's post-lapse registration is not inconsistent with good faith, hacking is conclusive of bad faith.[103]

Hacking (and phishing discussed below) is one of three circumstances warranting a finding of abusive registration *per se*. (The third circumstance is extortion by threatening to point a domain name to a pornography website). Proof of transfer alone whether to a new registrar or a new registrant with the same registrar is sufficient to find respondent lacks rights or legitimate interests in the domain name. Claims of domain name hijacking by hacking a complainant's account or establishing a phishing website are within the scope of the Policy, but relief is based on abusive registration and not on theories of conversion, grand larceny, or fraudulent transfer.[104]

The means by which respondent came to be the registered holder of the domain name is not a controlling factor in deciding bad faith. *Characterization merely adds color to the claim.* Whether or not respondent is the party who caused

---

101 ***Target Brands, Inc. v. JK Internet Servs***, FA 349108 (Forum December 14, 2004) (<porn-target.com>. The panel found evidence of bad faith where the respondent not only registered Complainant's famous TARGET mark, but also "reproduced [on the resolving page] Complainant's TARGET mark . . . [and] added Complainant's distinctive red bull's eye [at the domain name] . . . to a point of being indistinguishable from the original.")

102 ***Sutherland Institute v. Continuative LLC***, D2009-0693 (WIPO July 10, 2009) ("[I]n the world of debate about public affairs, many things done with motives that are less than admirable are protected by the First Amendment.")

103 Combining Faux Registration with Fraudulent Transfer. See ***John Dilks v. Privacy Administrator / Anonymize, Inc.***, FA1506001623023 (Forum July 10, 2015) (<eht.com>) ("There is no credible explanation as to why one would purchase a domain name for the apparent purpose of resolving it to a website with which one has no association, but which is still the site of the Complainant from whom the domain name was stolen. Additionally, it is certainly the case that the Respondent could not have obtained good title from a thief through some chain of laundering transactions.")

104 Panelists have not hesitated to condemn fraudulent transfers and return domain names to complainants on the theory of abusive registration. "Abusive registration" is the highest level of actionable conduct; it subsumes cybersquatting. In addition to the cases cited in the text see ***Chiu Tsen Hu v. Andy Rose***, HK-1500719 (ADNDRC April 16, 2015), citing several other cases from

the transfer to occur it is the registrant of a domain name that corresponds to complainant's trademark and as a new registrant (even though it can remain silent) it will be called upon to explain its holding and use. "Although a fraudulent transfer raises potential contract or tort issues that are [technically] outside the scope of the Policy, the Panel may still decide to [order] the disputed domain name [transferred] if it finds that Complainant has established that all requirements of the Policy, aside from the fraudulent transfer issue, are met."[105] There is justification in this approach because "[i]f allegations [of] conversion were always to put a complaint outside of the scope of the Policy, the Policy would be ineffective."[106]

Complainants can invoke the Policy to remedy abusive conduct in the acquisition and use of domain names as long as they prove all the Policy requirements for relief. The Panel in ***Worldcom Exchange*** lists six acts that in the aggregate constitute bad faith registration and bad faith use, as follows:[107]

> (a) Respondent knew or ought to have known that the Domain Name was in use and had been used for many years in connection with an active website;
>
> (b) Respondent gained access to the NSI ownership database through improper (likely fraudulent) means;
>
> (c) Respondent changed the ownership records for the Domain Name covertly, without any notice to the rightful owner;
>
> (d) Respondent used misleading and false contact information when it changed the ownership records;
>
> (e) Respondent failed to respond to correspondence from complainant, and never offered any explanation or justification for its conduct;

ADNDRC including ***Dracco Company Ltd. v. NJ T Ech Solutions Inc.***, HK-1400577 (ADNDRC April 14, 2014).

See also ***GPZ Technology, Inc. v. Aleksandr Vedmidskiy / Private Person***, FA1504001612935 (Forum May 11, 2015). "[W]hile Complainant does not make any contentions that fall within the articulated provisions . . . , the Panel notes that these provisions are meant to be merely illustrative of bad faith, and that Respondent's bad faith may be demonstrated by ancillary allegations considered under the totality of the circumstances." Disputed domain name acauiredthrough hacking.

Victimized owners have also used the ACPA's in rem jurisdiction to return control of domain names fraudulently transferred to other registrars or registrants. Too many to cite but as an illustrative example see *European Performance Engineering, Inc. v. John Doe, et al.*, 16-cv-00982 (ED Va, Alexandria Division September 9, 2016). However, unresolved is whether plaintiff has standing as a trademark owner for the fraudulently transferred domain name other than the fiction that it does.

105 ***Bill Clark v. HiNet, Inc.***, FA0501000405057 (Forum March 4, 2005).

106 ***ITX sarl, and Ziad M. Mugraby v. Tom Steiner***, FA0809001222737 (Forum October 24, 2008) ("A panel appointed under the Policy cannot determine whether a fraud has been committed but in every case it must determine whether a domain name has been registered and used in bad faith.")

107 ***Worldcom Exchange, Inc v. Wei.com, Inc.***, D2004-0955 (WIPO January 5, 2005) (<wei.com>).

> (f) Respondent has disrupted the legitimate business activities of complainant, depriving it of access to the domain name and website it had created and maintained for more than [x number of] years.

"Complainant [the Panel continues] seeks to expand the territory of bad faith, presenting a new type of abusive conduct on the part of the Respondent, one that on its face cries out for relief: the hijacking of a domain name through the manipulation of password access."

Fraudulent transfers or hijackings of domain names reached such frequency in 2004 and 2005 that the abuse was noticed by ICANN.[108] In cases that raise these issues in which domain names are unlawfully transferred Panels have consistently ruled complainants are entitled to relief.[109] The question is whether the UDRP remedy is fast enough to prevent further transfers that could cause complications for recovery rather than taking emergency action under the ACPA.[110]

Whereas unauthorized transfers of infringing domain names are implicitly within the scope of the Policy, fraudulent transfers of non-infringing domain names—that is where complainants have no trademark right—are not.[111] Complainant in those circumstances may clearly be aggrieved "and, if his allegations are correct, rightfully so. However, the Policy is not designed to deal with allegations of fraud

---

108 Report entitled "Domain Name Hijacking: Incidents, Threats, Risks and Remedial Actions," dated July 12, 2005.

109 ***8x Entertainment, Inc., Gener8Xion Television, Inc., Gener8Xion Entertainment, Inc. v. EXC International AG***, D2005-1126 (WIPO December 28, 2005) (The Panel noted that "the fact is that someone unlawfully took control of Complainants' e mail account and used it to fraudulently represent to Network Solutions and OnlineNic, Inc. that Complainants had authorized a transfer of the domain name in dispute, when in fact Complainants had not"); ***Teenee Media Company Limited v. Linda C. Austin***, HK-1300566 (ADNDRC March 14, 2014) (<teenee.com>. "Not only is it clear from the evidence that this was and apparently still is the Respondent's plan, but she has brazenly admitted and asserted it in emails she wrote to the Complainant which are annexed to the Complaint and which are clear attempts at extortion.")

Compare ***Lawrence Gurreri v. To Thai Ninh***, FA1006001328554 (Forum July 12, 2010) (<internationalcircuit.com>) in which the Panel stated that "the alleged theft of a domain name falls outside the narrow scope of the UDRP policy"and cites two cases that address scope but not theft. While the conclusion is inconsistent with a number of other decisions that hold complainant is entitled to recapture the domain name, the better reason for denying the complaint in ***Gurreri*** followed well settled law, namely that Complainant although clearly victimized, was unable to prove a trademark right and thus lacked standing to maintain the UDRP proceeding.

110 The proper venue for such an emergency action (most likely under the in rem jurisdiction of the ACPA, §1125(d)(2)(A)) would be in the district in which the registry is located, which for dot com is Verisign, Inc. located within the jurisdiction of the District Court for the Eastern District of Virginia, Alexandria Division.

111 ***Lawrence Gurreri***, supra; ***Taeho Kim v. Skelton Logic***, FA1002001305934 (Forum March 22, 2010) (No trademark; no standing to complain. "Complainant says he purchased the domain names <recent.net>, <they.net> and <than.net> from escrow.com on June 30, 2009. His GoDaddy.com

and theft."[112] While this is true, complainants are not precluded from establishing ownership of unregistered trademarks to recapture fraudulently transferred domain names on proof they have been used in commerce for a sufficient period of time.[113]

6.01-C.2.c *Spoofing and Phishing*

6.01-C.2.c

The term "abusive registration" is sufficiently elastic to include use of domain names for fraudulent and malicious purposes.[114] Spoofing (payment instruction fraud), phishing, and other kinds of fraud (such as pretending to be a company offering career opportunities) are *per se* violations of the Policy.[115] Respondents are not just looking for visitors, they are using brands to target victims. Where there is evidence of spoofing and phishing actual knowledge is presumed.[116] No explanation can bring them into the ambit of paragraph 4(c) defenses. They are veritable

---

account was hacked into on December 18, 2009 and the domain names were sold to a third party and re-sold to Respondent. Thus, Complainant alleges that Respondent purchased stolen domain names.")

[112] ***Jimmy Alison v. Finland Property Services (Pty) Ltd.***, D2008-1141 (WIPO September 8, 2008) (<didyouknow.com>); also, ***Taeho Kim v. Skelton Logic***, FA1002001305934 (Forum March 22, 2010) ("Complainant concedes that he has no trademark or service mark rights and relies solely on his prior registration of the domain names and his stated intent to use marks corresponding to the domain names in the future. Given the generic nature of the second level domains, 'recent,' 'they' and 'that,' the mere acquisition by Complainant of the disputed domain names cannot possibly give rise to trademark rights in RECENT.NET, THEY.NET or THAT.NET. Nor can intent to use give rise to trademark rights.")

[113] *Traffic Names, Ltd. V. Zhenghui Yiming*, In Re: 224.com, 604.com; and 452.com, 1:14cv1607 (E.D. Va, Alexandria Division May 12, 2015). Magistrate's Report dated April 14, 2015 (In Rem action under the ACPA for fraudulent transfer of domain names. Magistrate Judge found: "Plaintiff's registration of the Subject Domain Names and use of them in business since that registration establishes his common law rights in the marks. Therefore, plaintiff is entitled to enforce the provisions of § 1125(d) against any domain name that violates its rights in the protected marks." The court entered default judgment ordering Verisign, Inc. to cancel defendant's registrations and transfer the names to plaintiff.)

[114] Examples of the various forms of malicious conduct include 1) soliciting private, sensitive information (***CommScope, Inc. of North Carolina v. Chris Lowe / comm-scope / Chris Lowe / comm-scopes / Chris Lowa / commmscope***, FA1707001742149 (Forum September 7, 2017); 2) targeting job seekers (***Novartis AG v. CHRIS TAITAGUE***, FA170800 1744264 (Forum September 11, 2017); 3) misdirecting funds in emails for illegal and fraudulent purposes (***Goodwin Procter LLP v. GAYLE FANDETTI***, FA170600 1738231 (Forum August 8, 2017); 4) distributing malware (***Shotgun Software Inc. v. Domain Admin / Hulmiho Ukolen, Poste restante***, D2017-1273 (WIPO August 23, 2017).

[115] The practice of impersonation through emails is described in ICANN Security and Stability Advisory Committee Report (May 2008). Actual findings of impersonation in domain names see ***Crayola Properties, Inc. v. Domain Contact, Protected WHOIS @INR***, D2018-2091 (WIPO December 2, 2018) (<crayolla.com>. "Complainant argues that Respondent's actions are not a bona fide offering of goods or services because Respondent's website redirects users to a rotating series

Trojan horses. By definition they are quintessentially abusive[117] in being created to "facilitate a scheme"[118] to deceive unwary Internet users by impersonating complainant and pretending to speak in its name, or deceiving third parties to belief they are receiving communications from employees or officers.[119]

They are designed to entrap them into disclosing credit card information, Social Security numbers and other personal information to steal identities, run up fraudulent bills, and create databases for spam e-mail.[120]

---

of third-party websites; Complainant refers to this as 'Automatic Rapid Reduction to Malware' (or 'ARRM') and that this practice has been also referred to as 'fast-flux DNS' (or 'FFDNS'". See ***Oracle International Corporation v. Above.com Domain Privacy / Protection Domain***, D2017-1987 (WIPO December 26, 2017) (<oraacle.com> citing Wikipedia "Fast flux is a DNS technique used by botnets to hide phishing and malware delivery sites behind an ever-changing network of compromised hosts acting as proxies.")

For spoofing and phishing see ***Arla Foods Amba v. ESMM EMPIRE staincollins***, CAC 101578 (ADR.eu August 14, 2017), ***optionsXpress Holdings, Inc. v. David A.***, FA1701001711999 (Forum February 15, 2017) (<optionexpress.net>); ***Goodwin Procter LLP v. GAYLE FANDETTI***, FA1706001738231 (Forum August 8, 2017) (Targeting law firm to "to misdirect funds in an e mail for an illegal and fraudulent purpose"); ***Intersystems Corporation v. Contact Privacy Inc. / Maree F Turner***, D2017-1383 (WIPO September 18, 2017) ("[O]n numerous occasions, Complainant's customers received notices to pay licensing fees for Complainant's products in an email that appeared, to a casual observer, to come from Complainant.... The confusion arises when recipients mistakenly believe they have received an email from Complainant. Recipients appear to be subjects of an effort to get them to send funds to Respondent believing they are sending the funds to Complainant.") For career fraud see ***Novartis AG v. CHRIS TAITAGUE***, FA170800 1744264 (Forum September 11, 2017) (<sandozcareers.com>. Targeting job seekers).

116 ***DaVita Inc. v. Cynthia Rochelo***, FA1706001738034 (Forum July 20, 2017) (<davita health.com>). ("Respondent uses the disputed domain name to fraudulently send emails to Complainant's customers in hopes of receiving personal or financial information).

117 ***Steelcase Inc. v. Cimpress Schweiz GmbH***, FA1706001737556 (Forum July 25, 2017) (<steelca-see.com>. " In light of the mark's notoriety and Respondent's overt use of the domain name to impersonate an employee and officer of Complainant, there can be no doubt that Respondent was well aware of Complainant's STEELCASE mark when it registered the confusingly similar <steelca-see.com> domain name.")

118 ***Grupo Financiero Inbursa, S.A. de C.V.v. Inbuirsa***, D2006-0614 (WIPO July 5, 2006), in which the Panel found that spoofing and phishing have become serious problems in the financial services industry worldwide. Adding words to popular marks has also been referred to as "combosquatting," a term unfamiliar in UDRP cases but the concept is well known and treated under the "confusingly similar" analysis See *Hiding in Plain Sight: A Longitudinal Study of Combosquatting Abuse*, Georgia Institute of Technology and Stony Brook University (August 17, 2017) ("Combosquatting is a type of domain name squatting in which website addresses confusingly similar to well-known brands are deliberately registered, often with a view to committing fraudulent activity. Specifically, it involves the registration of a popular trademark combined with another phrase – for example, 'brand-shop.com'." In another part of the paper the investigators find that "attackers are able to capitalize on a trademark's recognition to perform social engineering, phishing, affiliate abuse, trademark abuse, and even targeted attacks." The study is available at http://iisp.gatech.edu/sites/default/files/images/hiding_in_plain_sight-_a_longitudinal_study_of_combosquatting_abuse.pdf.)

Fake websites, often posing as brand names[121] and imitating their look and feel,[122] generally employ e-mails,[123] pop-ups[124] and other methods to create a false impression of genuineness.[125] Respondent's actions "may also well be a crime in the United States of America, but the Panel believes any possible criminal aspect of the Respondent's conduct [separate and apart from violation of ¶4(b)(iv)] lies beyond the bounds of the UDRP."[126] However, forfeitures in these cases do not rest on criminal liability but on using domain names for abusive or malicious purposes. Since the subterfuge resides in the content, panelists have exercised discretion for assessing the confusingly similar element for standing by examining the facts and evidence of bad faith.[127]

---

[119] ***Amazon Technologies, Inc. v. Gerek Tranmer***, FA1708001746278 (Forum September 22, 2017) (<payment-amazon-orders.com>); ***Google Inc. v. 1&1 Internet Limited***, FA1708001742725 (Forum August 31, 2017) (<web-account-google.com>. Respondent used the complainant's mark and logo on a resolving website containing offers for technical support and password recovery services, and soliciting Internet users' personal information).

[120] ***HOPE worldwide, Ltd. v. Jin***, FA 320379 (Forum November 11, 2004) (<hopeworldwide.org>) (finding that a domain name that "is confusingly similar to Complainant's mark, redirects Internet users to a website that imitates Complainant's website, and is used to acquire personal information from Complainant's potential associates fraudulently" is evidence of bad faith registration and use.)

[121] ***Am. Int'l Group, Inc. v. Busby***, FA 156251 (Forum May 30, 2003) (Respondent's website "duplicated Complainant's mark and logo, giving every appearance of being associated or affiliated with Complainant's business . . . to perpetrate a fraud upon individual shareholders who respected the goodwill surrounding the AIG mark.")

[122] ***Juno Online Servs, Inc. v. Nelson***, FA 241972 (Forum Mar. 29, 2004) (imitating Complainant's billing website).

[123] ***CareerBuilder, LLC v. Stephen Baker***, D2005-0251 (WIPO May 6, 2005). The Panel noted that respondent used "the disputed domain name to solicit credit card information from persons seeking complainant's services by imitating complainant's website at <careerbuilder.com> and sending e-mails that appear to be from complainant, 'spoofing'. . . . The Panel agrees with complainant that the Respondent's motive must be to somehow cash in on the personal data thus obtained."

[124] ***Twitter, Inc. v. Whois Agent, Whois Privacy Protection Service, Inc. / Domain Support***, D2015-1488 (WIPO October 6, 2015) (Respondent defaulted, but "[b]ased on the evidence provided by Complainant, Respondent only uses the Domain Name as part of a common phishing scheme known as 'tech support scam pop-up'; such tech support scam presents itself to the user while browsing the web in the form of a pop-up message saying that a virus or other suspicious activity has been detected, often providing a phone number which the user can call to get 'support' for the problem. Obviously, such phishing scam cannot be considered a bona fide offering of goods or services nor a legitimate noncommercial or fair use of the Domain Name. Respondent did not submit any response."

[125] ***The Royal Bank of Scotland Group plc v. Teddy Jackson***, FA0705000992134 (Forum July 2, 2007) (fraudulent lottery scheme); ***Sodexo v. Sodexo Consulting***, D2013-1126 (WIPO August 9, 2013) (Job scam).

[126] SIMILARLY DECIDED: ***Bank for International Settlements v. James Elliott***, D2003-0987 (WIPO March 3, 2004) (bad faith where e-mails emanating from the disputed domain name

6.01-C.2.d

6.01-C.2.d *Redacting Victims' Names*

Where the person disclosed by the registrar denies any ownership interest in the domain name and the record supports identity theft the Panel is authorized to redact his or her name from the decision. ***The Royal Bank of Scotland Group***[128] is illustrative. The Panel found that the unknown phisher registered <rbs-partners.com> in a third party's name for "a fraudulent scheme that seeks to obtain personal financial information from Internet users in the United States."

Paragraph 4(j) of the Policy reads, "[a]ll decisions under this Policy will be published in full over the Internet, except when an Administrative Panel determines in an exceptional case to redact portions of its decision." Identity theft is an "exceptional case" that justifies redacting of personal information.[129] Panels have adopted a procedure for communicating instructions to the registrar through an annex to the award.[130]

---

purported to represent that a large amount of money would be paid to the recipient upon provision by the recipient of personal information); ***Western Union Holdings, Inc. v. XYZ a/k/a Chahat Topiwala***, D2005-0945 (WIPO October 20, 2005) (bad faith where respondent used the domain name to masquerade as complainant as part of a fraudulent scheme to solicit monetary deposits to a sham banking institution); ***Kmart of Michigan, Inc. v. WhoisGuard Protected c/o WhoisGuard***, FA0509000569042 (Forum November 11, 2005) (Collecting personal information); ***Banca di Roma S.p.A. v. Overlord Designs Inc.***, D2006-0123 (March 13, 2006) ("Via other keystrokes they were led to a fake website masquerading as Banca di Roma, itself copied from the Luxembourg website 'www.bancaroma.lu' of Banca di Roma International, and then induced to divulge their confidential login details in the belief that these were being requested legitimately."); ***HPR Commodities LLC v. John Galledo***, D2007-0154 (WIPO May 26, 2007) (Respondent used the domain name in a scam targeted at persons in Australia, who may have been confused into believing that <hprglobal.com> was connected to an international division of HPR Commodities, which is based in New York.); ***National Westminster Bank plc v. Bryant Smith***, FA0806001209998 (WIPO July 28, 2008) (<natwestbusinessbanking.com>; the evidence established that Respondent's landing page imitated Complainant's official website in order "to fraudulently obtain Internet users' confidential financial information.")

[127] ***Kames Capital PLC v. Tom Harrison / Kames Capital Plc Limited***, FA1604001671583 (Forum May 20, 2016) ("Having regard to prior UDRP decisions the Panel finds that it has some, although limited, discretion in determining whether or not to consider the content of the resolving webpage in making a Policy ¶ 4(a)(i) decision. Having regard to all the circumstances of the instant case, including the evidence of the fraudulent activities for which the domain name has been used, the Panel finds that it may have regard to the contents of the website and having done so finds that the disputed domain name is confusingly similar to Complainant's trademark.")

[128] ***The Royal Bank of Scotland Group plc v. [Redacted]***, FA0908001282153 (Forum October 28, 2009). ***Beam Suntory Inc. v. Name Redacted***, D2018-2861(WIPO April 3, 2019).

[129] National Westminster Bank plc v. [Redacted], FA0606000724496 (Forum July 20, 2006), citing ***Wells Fargo & Co. v. John Doe as Holder of Domain Name***, FA 362108 (Forum December 30, 2004) and ***Wells Fargo & Co. v. John Doe as Holder of Domain Name***, FA 453727 (Forum May 19, 2005): "The panels omitted the respondent's personal information from the decision in an attempt to protect the respondents claiming to be victims of identity theft from any further injury";

6.01-D Initial Interest Confusion and Nominative Fair Use 6.01-D

6.01-D.1 Unauthorized Incorporation of Trademark 6.01-D.1

"Initial interest confusion" and "nominative fair use" are opposing propositions. The first is evidence of abusive registration and the second qualifies as a defense. There are clearly circumstances under which a trademark may be incorporated into a domain name without permission from the trademark owner. These lawful registrations are discussed in later sections.[131] Disclaimers are expected to be conspicuous on the landing page. Just as clearly there are domain names, allegedly being used with infringing intent conspicuously disclaimed, that exploit the trademark's value and infringe the owner's legal rights. Such acts are not excused by a disclaimer (discussed below in Sec. 6.01-D.4).

Differentiating initial interest confusion and nominative fair use hinges on the composition of the domain name and whether it is fulfilling the purpose for its registration. Is respondent conducting a business distinguishable from and noncompetitive with complainant's (nominative fair use)? Or, is it attracting Internet traffic based solely on the value of the trademark (initial interest confusion)? A nominative fair use website is allowable if dedicated to a business distinguishable from the trademark owner's and displaying an appropriate disclaimer. Initial interest confusion websites may also contain disclaimers, but here the disclaimers are used to support the fiction that the websites are not taking advantage of complainants' trademarks. Passive holdings of disputed domain names do not support claims for nominative fair use or excuse confusion under any defense of bad faith. When an Internet user arrives at an initial confusion website he or she will likely find that it offers goods or services competitive with those of complainant.

National Westminster Bank plc v. [REDACTED], FA0807001215821 (Forum August 21, 2008) ("Apparently, Respondent is a victim of identity theft and the Panel elects to redact Respondent's personal information from the decision to prevent the further victimization of Respondent.")

130 ***Urban Outfitters Inc. v. Name Redacted***, D2018-0070 (WIPO March 7, 2018) ("[T]he Panel has attached as Annex 1 to this Decision an instruction to the Registrar regarding transfer of the disputed domain name, which includes the name of Respondent. The Panel has authorized the Center to transmit Annex 1 to the Registrar as part of the order in this proceeding, and has indicated Annex 1 to this Decision shall not be published due to the exceptional circumstances of this case.")

131 Incorporating a trademark licitly principally occurs in two circumstances, namely bona fide offering of goods or services informed by the words that qualify the trademark (nominative fair use) and noncommercial fair use or free speech (First Amendment rights). The first is discussed in "Non-Authorized But Lawful Use of Trademarks" (Sec. 5.01-C.2). The second is discussed in "Appropriating Complainant's Trademark for Noncommercial or Fair Use and Free Speech" (Sec. 5.01-C.2).

6.01-D.2

6.01-D.2 Initial Interest Confusion

Panels use the phrase "initial interest confusion" in two contexts: "[1] confusion of authorship upon reading the content of a website and [2] confusion of an Internet user who is seeking the mark owner's website but is attracted to the alternative website by its similarity (in this case, identity) to a recognized mark."[132] The Panel in ***Justice for Children*** continued that the content of the website is "irrelevant to the harm to the mark owner and to the unwary consumer." What is relevant is that

> harm results from the confusion caused by the initial attraction to the site by means of borrowing complainant's mark. And that is exactly the harm the Policy was adopted to address.

However, confusion alone is not conclusive of bad faith. There must also be an element of deception, one that conveys an impression that the resolving website is sponsored by or affiliated with the mark owner.

Panels have identified three circumstances in which the doctrine of initial interest confusion is inapplicable, although not without qualification as to the third: where complainant's mark does not qualify as a right (e.g., it has disclaimed words used in the domain name[133]); respondent is found to have rights or legitimate interests in the domain name[134]; and the domain name is being used for legitimate, protected speech (although the decision may turn on the Panel's view of protected speech, whether made in <trademark.tld> or <trademark+derogatoryword.tld>).[135]

The harm occurs when the website to which the domain name resolves is "a web page advertising the products of a competitor, so that an Internet user opening that page would presumably realize that it was not affiliated with Complainant after all."[136] Misleading consumers is half the harm. The

---

[132] ***Justice for Children v. R neetso / Robert W. O'Steen***, D2004-0175 (WIPO June 4, 2004). The concept is traced to decisions in U.S. federal courts. See *Brookfield Communications, Inc. v. West Coast Entertainment Corp.*, 174 F.3d 1036 (9th Cir. 1999). "Initial interest confusion" is severely criticized by the dissent in ***Aspis Liv Försäkrings AB v. Neon Network, LLC***, D2008-0387 (WIPO June 2, 2008) (<aspis.com>). See *Lamparello v. Falwell*, 420 F.3d 309, 317 (4th Cir. 2004) (the "'critical element' of initial interest confusion—'use of another firm's mark to capture the markholder's customers and profits'—simply does not exist when the alleged infringer establishes a gripe site that criticizes the markholder.")

[133] ***668 North, LLC v. Junyun Bi***, FA1711001759137 (Forum December 27, 2017) (<phoenixchineseculturalcenter.com>, disclaimed in trademark application "Chinese Cultural Center").

[134] ***YETI Coolers, LLC v. Ryley Lyon / Ditec Solutions LLC***, FA1605001675141 (Forum July 11, 2016) (<yeti handles.net>, <yetihandle.net>, <yeticuphandles.com> and <yeticuphandle.com>).

[135] ***Yellowstone Mountain Club LLC v. Offshore Limited D and PCI***, D2013-0097 (WIPO April 12 2013) (Two domain names transferred, but complaint denied for <yellowstoneclubscandal.com>. Discussed further in "Ambivalence of Application" (Sec. 5.04-A.2).

[136] ***Converse Inc. v. Perkins Hosting***, D2005-0350 (WIPO May 17, 2005).

> question under Policy paragraph 4(a) [iii] is whether the Domain Name itself, without regard to the content of an associated website, creates confusion as to the sponsorship of the domain. This approach is necessary because cybersquatters—those who register and use domain names in bad faith—frequently achieve their purposes simply by creating "initial interest confusion" at the point where an Internet user types an address or selects one of the results of a search engine query in an effort to find a website related to the trademark owner.

The close connotative resemblance of domainn name and mark may be punctured upon the Internet user arriving at the landing page but by then respondent has achieved its goal. The harm lies in diverting business to another website and to advertising for competing or different products. "The fact that such confusion may be dispelled, and replaced by annoyance or disgust once the nature of the site is revealed, does not negate the fact of initial confusion."[137]

Initial interest confusion generally arises in circumstances where the products or services advertised are in close competitive proximity and used by domain name holders for substantially the same purpose. It can also be applied in certain noncommercial misuse of domain names.[138] It is inapplicable to criticism and commentary websites, although the distinction has not always been observed. In some cases, Panels have held that a second level domain identical to the trademark that resolves to a criticism website takes impermissible "advantage of Complainant's commercial interests in the mark."[139] Other Panels have pointed out that the term "initial interest confusion" applies where respondent has a commercial purpose, but not otherwise.[140] This view has been criticized as "frustrat[ing] rather than promot[ing] the purpose of the Policy."[141] The majority Panel in Yellowstone prefers the more nuanced approach of assessing abusive registration based on a balancing of rights and not determined by whether or not there is a commercial context.

---

137 ***Ticketmaster Corporation v. Iskra Service***, D2002-0165 (WIPO April 8, 2002); ***Ticketmaster Corporation v. Polanski***, D2002-0166 (WIPO April 8, 2002); ***Ticketmaster Corporation v. Dotsan***, D2002-0167 (WIPO April 8, 2002).

138 ***SEB and Grouped SEB UK Limited v. Dim soft Limited***, D2013-0252 (WIPO March 26,2013) (non-profit complainant; no commercial content); ***Countryside Alliance Limited v. David Pearce, Anti-Censorship Alliance***, D2001-0862 (WIPO August 20, 2001) (competing non-profits, no commerce).

139 ***Monty & Pat Roberts Inc. v. J.Bartell***, D2000-0300 (WIPO June 13, 2000) [U.S. parties] and ***Myer Stores Limited v. Mr. David John Singh***, D2001-0763 (WIPO July 10, 2001) [Australian parties]. Discussed further in "Ambivalence of Application" (Sec. 5.04-A.2).

140 ***BioCryst Pharmaceuticals, Inc. v. Kumar Patel***, D2005-0674 (WIPO August 4, 2005).

141 ***Yellowstone Mountain Club***, *supra*. The dissent would hold that "so long as a registrant and user of a domain name is not using that domain name to profit from or recognize commercial gain from the use of the trademark of another there is not bad faith registration and use."

6.01-D.3

6.01-D.3 Nominative Fair Use

Nominative fair use is the converse of initial interest confusion. A distinction has been made between proper and improper confusion.[142] Confusion results when a respondent knowingly incorporates complainant's mark for a prohibited purpose, but it is not unlawful to incorporate a mark where the domain name "seek[s] to communicate the nature of the service or product offered at [respondent's] sites [and] to consumers, who would be deprived of an increasingly important means of receiving such information."[143]

However, an argument for nominative fair use is misplaced where the parties are competitors.[144] Only if the facts support the theory is the use of the trademark within the string non-infringing.[145] Attempts to distinguish a domain name incorporating a trademark "within a website" as nominative fair use or within "domain names or banners" as non-infringing have been rejected.[146] Fair use is not satisfied unless the factual circumstances support a *bona fide* offering of goods or services.

---

[142] ***Minnesota Mining and Manufacturing Company v. Mark Overbey***, D2001-0727 (WIPO October 15, 2001) (<3mtapes.com>, <3mabrasives.com>, <3madhesives.com>. "Assuming [it is true that Respondent intended to associate the Domain Names with a website used in connection with the legitimate distribution of 3M products], it is possible that Respondent may well have a 'nominative fair use' defense to Complainant's claims. Several panels have held that the truthful, nominative use of a trademark in connection with the sale of the goods or services that are properly identified by that trademark does not constitute bad faith under the Policy.") See also "Nominative Fair Use As Applied" (Sec. 5.01-C.2.a).

[143] *Toyota Motor Sales USA Inc. v. Tabari*, 610 F.3d 1171(9th Cir. 2010) (<buy-a-lexus.com> and <buyorleaselexus.com>), cited favorably in a number of UDRP decisions and said to be applicable where both parties are from the U.S. An example is ***The California Milk Processor Board of San Clemente v. Ryan Leonard***, D2011-1665 (WIPO December 5, 2011) (<gotmilkads.com>). As this is an issue of permissive use it is discussed earlier in Chapter 5, "Non-Authorized But Lawful Use of Trademarks" (Sec. 5.01-C.2).

The concurring panelist in ***Statoil ASA v. Giovanni Laporta, Yoyo.Email Ltd.***, D2014-0637 (WIPO July 16, 2014) explains that the European Court of Justice has interpreted the Trade Marks Directive (Directive 2008/95/EC) in a manner similar to the Lanham Act 15 U.S.C. § 1115(b)(4). A third party may use a trademark "in accordance with honest practices in industrial or commercial matters" (article 6[1]). One has "a duty to act fairly in relation to the legitimate interests of the trade mark owner" (Case C-100/02 *Gerolsteiner Brunnen GmbH & Co. v. Putsch GmbH*, [2004] E.C.R. I-691 at [24]), and violates this duty if the use "may give the impression that there is a commercial connection between the [user] and the trade mark proprietor" (*Gillette Co. v. LA-Laboratories Ltd Oy* [2005] ECR I-2337 at [42]).

[144] ***Land Rover v. ABC Productions***, FA1208001458560 (Forum September 26, 2012) ("[T]he use of such a theory in a case, such as this, where the parties are competitors in the car repair business is misplaced. This theory, if given the broad effect advanced by the Respondent, would dilute the requirements set out in the UDRP.") But where the parties are not competitors the theory is not misplaced, see above and ***JAGUAR LAND ROVER LIMITED v. parvez ali***, FA1608001690453 (Forum October 1, 2016) (rangeroverchauffeur.com>) (Respondent uses the domain name to advertise its business of providing Ranger Rover chauffeured cars for hire.)

6.01-D.4 Disclaimer in Website 6.01-D.4

Disclaimers do not settle the question of good faith and in many cases are ineffective to legitimize a disputed domain name,[147] but a legitimate reason for a disclaimer cannot be ruled out.[148] In most instances they tend to bolster respondents' bad faith when their domain names resolve to websites whose content is inconsistent with their professions of good faith. However, two circumstances stand out: legitimate use of a trademark for a *bona fide* offering of goods or services[149] and noncommercial and fair use.[150] In commenting on the latter, the Panel in ***Covance*** found that the disclaimer in <covancecampaign.com>[151]

> makes it clear from the very outset that this site has no connection with complainant and is against the use of animal testing by complainant. In these circumstances it is extremely difficult to see how members of the public could be misled into thinking that the site is associated with, or has any connection with complainant.

---

[145] There is also a separate nominative fair use theory under UDRP jurisprudence. See discussion in "Non-Authorized But Lawful Use of Trademarks" (Sec. 6.01-C.2).

[146] ***Giddings & Lewis LLC v. Neal McKean d/b/a Machineworks, Inc. d/b/a Imachine Tools.com***, D2000-1150 (WIPO March 14, 2001) ("[The] distinction . . . may have some superficial appeal but upon scrutiny is one without a difference.")

[147] ***Thomas & Betts Int'l, Inc. v. Power Cabling Corp.***, AF 0274 (eResolution October 23, 2000) (finding bad faith based upon initial interest confusion despite disclaimer and link to complainant's website on the respondent's website). "[W]here the overall circumstances of a case point to the respondent's bad faith, the mere existence of a disclaimer cannot cure such bad faith. In such cases, panels may consider the respondent's use of a disclaimer as an admission by the respondent that users may be confused." Jurisprudential Overview, Paragraph 3.7.

[148] ***Realmark Cape Harbour L.L.C. v. Lewis***, D2000-1435 (WIPO December 11, 2000) ("Although a disclaimer of association generally may not be an adequate defense to trademark infringement, Respondent's use of a disclaimer in this case did serve to alert users of its services that it was not Complainant or its affiliate.")

[149] ***DaimlerChrysler A.G. v. Donnald Drummonds***, D2001-0160 (WIPO June 18, 2001) (Nominative fair use), was resolved on a split decision in favor of the Respondent. The majority found "the website (i) was 'descriptive of the business conducted there' because respondent was 'serving as a clearinghouse for information concerning Complainant's vehicles and is selling parts and accessories exclusively for Complainant's vehicles' and (ii) it contained 'a clear disclaimer.'"

However, on a refiling of the complaint after transfer to a new Respondent, the Panel found that the website had become commercial and was not limited to complainant's products, in which case the disclaimer had lost meaning. ***Daimler AG v. William Wood***, D2008-1712 (WIPO February 25, 2009). The subsequent use of the domain name by the new registrant violated the Oki Data proof elements. Discussed further in "Non-Authorized but Lawful Use of Trademarks" (Sec. 6.01-C.2).

[150] Fan sites: ***2001 White Castle Way, Inc. v. Glyn O. Jacobs***, D2004-0001 (WIPO March 26, 2004) a fan site for which the Panel found that there "is no evidence that Respondent is making a commercial gain from the website, or that he acted with the intention of such gain. Respondent's website clearly disclaims sponsorship or endorsement by Complainant and the recording artist";

However, the "presence of a disclaimer on a website does not remedy improper registration of the domain name."[152] Neither does the presence of numerous disclaimers "cure the initial and illegitimate diversion."[153] This would be an instance of initial interest confusion. Even if the disclaimer is properly positioned it would do nothing to correct the domain name being confusingly similar to complainant's trademark or "to mitigate the initial interest confusion the name creates."[154] It is not relevant in considering confusing similarity under the first limb of the Policy, but is when considering the second and third limbs of the Policy. For example, it has been held that a disclaimer is particularly ineffective where "the disclaimer appears only towards the bottom of the home page, after the customer's ordering option."[155] "[I] n fact, the disclaimer itself actually proves the knowledge of complainant's mark."[156] Since "the appropriate behavior to consider is Respondent's behavior prior to its receipt of notice from complainant"[157] a disclaimer added after notice suggests a conscious effort to bolster rights or legitimate interests in the domain name and avoid any implication of bad faith.

While a pre-notice disclaimer is not necessarily conclusive of bad faith[158] it is evidence that respondent had actual knowledge of complainant's mark. Having once "attracted Internet traffic to [a] site by trickery, respondent cannot resort to disclaimers at the web site, however explicit . . . [ ] to clothe the domain name

---

Ms. Stefani Germanotta v. oranges arecool XD, FA1108001403808 (Forum September 21, 2011) (<ladygaga.org>).

151 ***Covance, Inc. and Covance Laboratories Ltd. v. The Covance Campaign***, D2004-0206 (WIPO April 30, 2004).

152 ***Alpha Xi Delta, Inc. v. Befriend Internet Services***, FA 100681 (Forum November 28, 2001), citing *Paccar, Inc. v. Telescan Technologies LLC*, 115 F.Supp.2d 772 (E.D. Michigan 2000): "A disclaimer that purports to disavow association with the trademark owner after the consumer has reached the site comes too late; the consumer has already been misdirected."

153 ***Estée Lauder Inc. v. estelauder.com, estelauder.net and Jeff Hanna***, D2000-0869 (WIPO September 25, 2000).

154 ***Thomas & Betts Int'l***, supra.

155 ***Pliva Inc v. Eric Kaiser***, D2003-0316 (WIPO June 9, 2003); ***SENSIS Pty Ltd., Research Resources Pty Ltd. v. Kevin Goodall***, D2006-0793 (WIPO August 22, 2006).

156 ***Société pour l'œuvre et la mémoire d'Antoine de Saint Exupéry-Succession Saint Exupéry D'Agay v. The Holding Company***, D2005-0165 (WIPO June , 2005); ***Coolmath.com LLC v. PrivacyGuardian.org / Aamir Munir Butt, cool math games***, D2016-2203 (WIPO December 4, 2016) (<coolmath-mathgames.com>. "The Panel finds it inconceivable that the Respondent came up with the Domain Name and the content of the website to which the Domain Name is connected without knowledge of the Complainant. If there were any doubt on that score, it is resolved by the presence of the notice/disclaimer appearing on the Respondent's website (see section 4 above), which expressly recognizes the existence of the Complainant. Indeed, in the Response the Respondent asserts that the presence of the notice/disclaimer is "evidence of the Respondent's lack of intent to divert consumers/viewers.")

157 ***Vide Universal City Studios, Inc. v. G.A.B. Enters.***, D2000-0416 (WIPO June 29, 2000) .

with legitimacy."[159] The Panel in ***International Organization for Standardization ISO***[160] pointed out that "[t]he brand recognition in this case centers on complainant and not the Respondent." Of the two disclaimers, one was written at the

> very bottom of the first page of the sites in question: A visitor to these sites would only see it after going through all the language about ISO and how the respondent can help in this regard by providing various consultancy and other services. Giving such low profile to such a significant disclaimer only serves to belittle its importance in considering the third test of the Policy.

The settled rule is that respondent's failure to centrally position a disclaimer that should properly be made on a website to distinguish itself from the complainant undercuts its good faith intentions. To be accepted, the disclaimer must appear in an appropriate setting that at once explains respondent's legitimate interest in the domain name and justifies its use of complainant's trademark.[161] Where respondent incorporates complainant's trademark and copies its logo and images a disclaimer fails to be a renunciation of bad faith and directly impugns its conduct.[162]

If the website is being used for criminal purposes such as phishing a disclaimer furthers the deception; in fact its presence "fails to [but rather increases] consumer confusion [and assists the fraud]."[163] A website designed to confuse the Internet user into believing that it is genuine cannot be absolved of abusive registration by a disclaimer.[164] A disclaimer is nonsensical where a respondent attempts to disown responsibility for the contents on its website.[165]

6.01-E Rights to Domain Name After Termination of Permission 6.01-E

Contract terms that expressly permit a respondent to use an owner's trademark and provide for its return upon termination of services are conclusive against a respondent's claim of good faith registration.[166] The principle was underscored in

---

[158] *Brookfield Comm., Inc. v. West Coast Entertainment Corp.,* 174 F.3d 1036 (9th Cir. 1999), "[r]espondent's use of a disclaimer on its website is insufficient to avoid a finding of bad faith. First, the disclaimer may be ignored or misunderstood by Internet users. Second, a disclaimer does nothing to dispel interest confusion that is inevitable from Respondent's actions. Such confusion is a basis for finding a violation of Complainant's rights."

[159] ***Arthur Guinness Son & Co. (Dublin) Limited v. Dejan Macesic***, D2000-1698 (WIPO January 25, 2001).

[160] ***International Organization for Standardization ISO v. ISO Easy***, D2005-0984 (WIPO November 8, 2005) (<isoeasy.com>).

[161] ***USA DANCE, INC. v. Rhapsody Ballroom***, FA1102001372072 (Forum April 4, 2011) ("disclaimer . . . in a prominent, conspicuous place disclaiming any affiliation with Complainant to avoid confusion.")

[162] ***Ganz v. Schuessler Enterprises, Inc.***, FA0810001230809 (Forum December 10, 2008).

[163] ***Staples, Inc. and Staples the Office Superstore, LLC v. Cpn Now***, FA0904001257595 (Forum July 1, 2009).

an early case and has precedential authority: "registration of a domain name can lose its *bona fides* if the registrant subsequently breaches one of the terms upon which he was authorized to register it."[167] However, this assumes the terms are clearly expressed. Uncertainty of intent, oral termination, and rights terminable subject to arbitration are insufficient to support abusive registration of the domain name.[168]

Transfer of the disputed domain name to complainant is most likely where complainant's contract expressly prohibits a respondent "from using the trademark . . . in any domain name without Complainant's permission"[169] and less likely when the rights and obligations of the respondent are not expressly spelled out in an agreement.[170] Once an agreement is terminated, subsequent registration of a domain name incorporating a trademark without the complainant's permission or knowledge is a species of fraud.[171]

There are two lines of reasoning for domain names registered with permission whose use continues beyond termination. Generally, for a right that springs from a license certain in its terms, termination extinguishes any continuing use[172]; a reseller's interest is extinguished when its reseller status is terminated.[173] In one case,[174] the Panel found that since Respondent's retail contract was terminated its continued "use of the domain name . . . appears to be an intentional attempt[ ] to attract, for commercial gain, Internet users to Respondent's web site by creating

---

164 Discussed further below in "Populating Web Pages: The 'Not Me' Defense" (Sec. 6.05-F).

165 ***Frontline GmbH v. Gem Domains***, D2009-0991 (WIPO September 4, 2009).

166 This discussion focuses on contracts that expressly provide for post-termination surrender. Consent by acquiescence and lawful, non-consensual use of trademarks are discussed in "Rights or Legitimate Interests: Expressly, Impliedly, and Lawfully" (Sec. 5.01-C). ***TSM Pacific International Pty Ltd. v. Private Ranger Limited, Mustafa Filizkok, Blackwood Foodstuff Trading LLC, Dominic Sum, Cascadale Holdings Limited***, D2017-2279 (WIPO January 29, 2018) ("The fact that the disputed domain name was registered in good faith and subsequently used in bad faith does not, as numerous UDRP panels have noted, change the original registration into a bad faith registration.") Discussed further in "Subsequent Bad Faith Use" (Sec. 4.03-A.4).

167 ***UVA Solar GmbH & Co K.G. v. Mads Kragh***, D2001-0373 (WIPO May 7, 2001) (where "[t]he respondent's authority to register the disputed domain name had been . . . given subject to certain terms and conditions; breach of such conditions can alter what would otherwise have appeared to have been a bona fide registration.") See also ***Maree Gaye Miller v. Peter Horner***, D2008-1492 (WIPO December 29, 2008), citing ***R&M Italia SpA, Tycon Technoglass Srl v. EnQuip Technologies Group, Inc.***, D2007-1477 (WIPO December 7, 2007).

168 ***Salton, Inc. v. George Foreman Foods, Inc.***, D2004-0777 (WIPO December 3, 2004).

169 It is not excusable for respondent to infringe published guidelines. ***Herbalife International of America, Inc. v. Myherbalife.com***, D2002-0101 (WIPO April 13, 2002), in which the registration of the domain name "was contrary to Respondent's obligation as an independent distributor of Complainant's products."

170 ***Western Holdings***, supra.

a likelihood of confusion with complainant's mark as to the source, sponsorship, affiliation, or endorsement of the web site or the products offered at this site."[175]

Use in bad faith is reinforced by other conduct, such as offering to sell the domain name to complainant or using it in an unauthorized manner.[176] In effect, the termination of an agency or distributorship agreement under which the disputed domain names were registered leaves the agents/distributors without any "rights or legitimate interests" within the meaning of paragraph 4(a)(ii) of the Policy.[177] A stranger to a contract who is a transferee after termination of a right does not have standing to argue that the issue of termination is a contractual dispute for resolution by a court of competent jurisdiction.[178]

6.01-F Mixing Innocent and Infringing Elements 6.01-F

6.01-F.1 Transient Infringement 6.01-F.1

Mixing innocent and infringing elements in a website demands an explanation to rebut doubts about respondent's good faith registration if use appears to be infringing. Two distinct possibilities have emerged.[179] The first occurs when a website resolving from a newly acquired domain name is under construction and

---

[171] ***Senco Products, Inc. v. Camp Creek Co., Inc.***, D2000-0590 (WIPO September 11, 2000) (Respondent registered the disputed domain name after the license termination as a form of retaliation).

[172] ***UVA Solar***, supra. (distributorship agreement had expired).

[173] ***Geckodrive Inc. v. Jon Hollcvraft***, AF 1047 (eResolution, November 20, 2001). Extinguishment of interest, which answers the paragraph 4(a)(ii) question in complainant's favor, is not necessarily conclusive of bad faith under paragraph 4(a)(iii) of the Policy since respondent's argument that the domain name was registered in good faith is not easily overcome.

[174] ***C. & A. Veltins GmbH & Co. KG v. Heller Highwater Inc***, D2004-0466 (WIPO August 27, 2004).

[175] The Panel's view in ***C. & A. Veltins GmbH & Co. KG*** that there is a presumption that the right to continued exploitation of the domain name is "on the condition that the parties remain in a business relationship" is not shared by the Panel in ***Green Tyre Company Plc. v. Shannon Group***, D2005-0877 (WIPO October 5, 2005) who held that:

> Considering complainant's explicit permission for registration of the Domain Name by respondent in the present case, the Panel finds that respondent did not have the requisite bad faith when it registered the Domain Name. Furthermore, the Panel finds that the circumstances as mentioned by complainant which are of a later date than the registration of the Domain Name, cannot lead to the conclusion that the original registration in good faith in retrospective has become a registration in bad faith.

[176] Pornography: ***Motorola Inc. v. NewGate Internet, Inc.***, D2000-0079 (WIPO April 20, 2000) (Threat to offer pornography on the website. Over a vigorous dissent, the majority held that the "right to resell products does not create the right to use the mark more extensively than required to advertise and sell the product.")

[177] ***Lonely Planet Publications Pty Ltd v. Mike Tyler***, D2004-0670 (WIPO October 27, 2004).

temporarily populated with advertising links to complainant's competitors.[180] The second involves a metamorphosis that occurs incrementally over time.[181] Understandably, for complainants there is no such category as innocent infringement. However, transient infringement is excusable absent proof that respondent chose the domain name to take advantage of complainant or its trademark. In ***Karsten***, although Pingify's website posted some pay-per-click, competitive advertising while it was under construction, it proved its *bona fides* by demonstrating preparations for a proprietary website.

The test for actionable bad faith rests on an objective standard. For example, an innocent holder's offer to sell a domain name originally registered in good faith that becomes redundant to its business is not transformed into a violation of the Policy.[182] The "primary purpose" test of paragraph 4(b)(i) of the Policy discussed below exonerates respondent's alleged bad faith in rejecting complainant's offer in preference for a higher bidder. However, there are circumstances that warrant forfeiture for imputed bad faith registration under paragraph 4(b)(iv) of the Policy where subsequent use violates the terms under which respondent is legally permitted to hold the domain name. Authorized and unauthorized resellers of a complainant's goods or services for example have some leeway when incorporating the trademark in their domain names, but are prohibited from offering competing brands on their websites.[183] The principal case prohibits any mixing.[184]

---

[178] ***RE/MAX International Inc. v. NCR Northcoast Realty***, FA0906001266756 (Forum August 4, 2009).

[179] Note: This analysis only applies to resolving websites of domain names postdating marks; where they predate marks complainants have no actionable claim even though there may be bad faith use. The Panel in ***thinkThin, LLC v. Domain Administrator / Vertical Axis Inc.***, FA1401001540853 (Forum March 31, 2014) analyzed the contents as it would do for marks predating domain names and concluded there was no infringement for transient infringement: "[A]lhough the evidence undoubtedly reveals instances of conduct which, without more, might be seen as bad faith use, this should not negate or outweigh the Respondent's other bona fide actions and motivations."

[180] ***Karsten Manufacturing Corporation v. Pingify Networks Inc***, FA0811001232823 (Forum January 5, 2009) (<ping.me>. "[T]he better view is that this conduct should form part of the complete equation which measures whether there were in fact preparations to use the domain name, or a name corresponding to the domain name, in connection with a bona fide offering of goods or services.")

[181] ***Daimler AG v. William Wood***, D2008-1712 (WIPO February 25, 2009) ("***Daimler 2***"), and ***Aubert International SAS and Aubert France SA v. Tucows.com Co.***, D2008-1986 (WIPO March 17, 2009). That "the underlying use of a domain name may evolve over time (with the consequence that the use of a domain name may become infringing through, for example, the offering for sale of goods of a different sort to those previously offered on the website)" was raised in the Interim and Final WIPO Reports. See WIPO Final Report at paragraph 197.

[182] This issue was the centerpiece in a formative decision, ***Teradyne, Inc. v. 4Tel Technology***, D2000-0026 (WIPO May 9, 2000) in which the Panel was attempting to parse liability for bad faith registration. The Respondent offered to sell the disputed domain name because "any business it

6.01-F.2 Incremental Infringement Over Time 6.01-F.2

The website to which <daimlershop.com> resolved is an example of change over time. Whatever its beginnings the website evolved from making a *bona fide* offering of goods or services—a forum for Daimler enthusiasts—to one using the trademark for commercial gain. This has been analogized to a bait and switch tactic. When change occurs over time the infringement may become apparent only when illegal use finally dominates innocent use. Imperceptible change is a challenge until it crosses a threshold and becomes perceptible.[185] The original intention in ***Daimler 1*** is important mainly to gauge the distance traveled to respondent's new business model.

There are two issues. First, does innocent use excuse subsequent commercial exploitation? Second, does the change over time taint registration? The answer to the first depends on the factual circumstances "in the round." The answer to the second depends in part on whether the domain name continues to be owned by the original registrant. It has already been pointed out that an assignment or transfer of interest in the registration constitutes a new registration. It is from that date that bad faith is measured.[186] The ***Daimler*** and ***Aubert*** decisions both feature mixtures of use and transfers, but ***Aubert*** has the further distinction of being a personal name.

The ***Daimler 2*** finding of abusive registration was made on a refiled complaint.[187] ***Daimler 1*** was resolved on a split decision in favor of respondent. The majority held "the website (i) was 'descriptive of the business conducted there' because respondent was 'serving as a clearinghouse for information concerning Complainant's vehicles and is selling parts and accessories exclusively for Complainant's vehicles' and (ii) it contained 'a clear disclaimer.'" Subsequent to the decision in the earlier case the original registrant sold his interest in "MercedesShop.com LLC," which operated the website, to one of his partners and transferred the domain name to the new owner.

---

operated in connection with the domain name has now expired." A year prior to the commencement of the proceedings, respondent offered to sell the domain name to complainant, who counter-offered to buy it for $100; respondent then sold it to a foreign party in the same business as complainant. However, the evidence did not support bad faith registration and the Panel concluded that it was "not ready to extend the Policy to cover cases clearly intended to be outside its scope. That is a task for ICANN, or for the courts." Discussed further in "Not All Offers to Sell Violate the Policy" (Sec. 5.01-D.3).

[183] Discussed further in "Subsequent Bad Faith Use" (Sec. 4.03-A.4).

[184] ***Oki Data Americas, Inc. v. ASD, Inc.***, D2001-0903 (WIPO November 6, 2001) (<okidataparts.com>). Discussed further in "Non-Authorized But Lawful Use of Trademarks" (Sec. 5.01-C.2).

[185] ***DaimlerChrysler A.G. v. Donnald Drummonds***, D2001-0160 (WIPO June 18, 2001) ("***Daimler 1***").

[186] ***iFranchise Group v. Jay Bean / MDNH, Inc. / Moniker Privacy Services [2658]***, D2007-1435 (WIPO December 18, 2007).

In ***Daimler 2*** the new owner argued that the "real respondent" was not he but "MercedesShop.com LLC." The Panel accepted only that the business "enjoys the use of the disputed domain name registration," but since "the current registrant and legal owner is William Wood, the Respondent, while the registrant, legal owner and respondent in the prior proceedings was Donnald Drummond," the critical date for assessing good faith must be the date William Wood acquired the registration from his transferor. Neither party in ***Daimler 2*** analyzed changes over time, yet change was the crux of complainant's argument and also featured in respondent's declaration of his and his partners' original intention for the website. For this reason, the Panel researched the history of the website in the Internet Archive, the Wayback Machine.[188] "[R]ecognising the care required with this resource . . . [the result of the research] suggest[ed] that respondent has been selling or preparing to sell parts for other brands of automobile since around the time of the Prior Decision." The Panel continued:

> Further evidence would have been helpful, but in the final analysis the legitimate elements of the website (such as the forum, and the sale of MERCEDES parts, and perhaps afterparts for MERCEDES automobiles) cannot redeem the flagrant use of the MERCEDES trademark to sell parts for a wide range of competing automobiles and the other commercial activities that have no connection with Mercedes Benz. Respondent has chosen to use a successful website for an illegitimate purpose. He has chosen to increase the website traffic and his sales and revenue, by offering parts for a wide range of automobile brands, as well as other products.

While use of the domain name as a forum—the original intention—was an acceptable, non-infringing use, expanding the business out of a noncommercial niche was not. "In doing so, [the Respondent] has forfeited any rights or legitimate interest in the disputed domain name that may once have existed (as recognized in the Prior Decision) and may have continued to exist if the website had remained confined to spare parts for MERCEDES automobiles."

---

[187] The rule for refiling complaints is discussed further in "Refiling a Complaint: New Facts or Fresh Evidence" (Sec. 7.02-B).

[188] Independent research is permitted, but the emphasis is on "limited." See Jurisprudential Overview, Paragraph 4.8: "[I]t has been accepted that a panel may undertake limited factual research into matters of public record if it would consider such information useful to assessing the case merits and reaching a decision."

6.02 SELLING, RENTING, OR OTHERWISE TRANSFERRING—PARAGRAPH 4(b)(i) OF THE POLICY 6.02

6.02-A Elements to be Proved 6.02-A

Domain names acquired later than earlier corresponding marks that are passively held but offered for sale to the general public (which includes mark owners and competitors) are vulnerable to forfeiture regardless how long they have been held.[189] This should not be surprising for domain names composed of words that are not commonly found together except in a complainant's mark.[190] Forfeiture should also not be surprising if the content of the website or the passive holding of the domain name supports an inference that the domain name was registered for the goodwill associated with the mark rather than any semantic meaning conveyed by the domain name.[191]

Paragraph 4(b)(i) of the Policy reads:

> [C]ircumstances indicating that you have registered or you have acquired the domain name primarily for the purpose of selling, renting, or otherwise transferring the domain name registration to complainant who is the owner of the trademark or service mark or to a competitor of that Complainant, for valuable consideration in excess of your documented out-of-pocket costs directly related to the domain name."

Complainant must prove 1) respondent acquired the domain name primarily for the proscribed purpose; 2) is offering it for sale to complainant or competitor;

---

[189] Why this is so is discussed further in "Laches vs. Lapse of Time" (Sec. 5.01-E.1). See ***Maurice Mizrahi / Mizco International, Inc. v. Chi Hyon***, FA1710001754962 (Forum November 20, 2017) Respondent contended it "registered <digipower.com> on June 22, 2001 [23 years before complaint] because it is a combination of two English words 'digi' (abbreviation of digital) and 'power', to which Respondent believed no party could claim exclusive rights." However, the record shows that "the only use Respondent has made of the Disputed Domain Name is to link it to batteries, which is the exact same business Complainant is in.")

[190] ***American Society of Hematology v. Maneet Tikku***, D2018-1209 (WIPO July 16, 2018) (<ashmeeting.com>. Acronym plus dictionary word. "[I]t is clear that Respondent is using the Domain Name and the associated website for providing misleading and deceptive data entry forms to obtain personal data from Internet users who assume that they are providing such information to Complainant." "[W]hether or not [the respondent] had any intention of selling the domain names to [the trademark owner], he clearly had the intention to profit from the goodwill associated with the trademarks that comprised the domain names." *Webadviso v. Bank of Am. Corp.*, 448 F. App'x 95, 98 (2d Cir. 2011). "Intention to profit from the goodwill" is a Paragraph 4(b)(iv) violation (Respondent in ***Bank of America Corporation and Merrill Lynch & Co., Inc. v. Webadviso***, FA090300 1254121(Forum May 15, 2009)).

[191] See for example ***Pepperdine University v. BDC Partners, Inc.***, D2006-1003 (WIPO September 25, 2006) (<pepperdineuniversitywaves.com> and <pepperdineuniversitywaves.net>. "Respondent asserts that it has never attempted to sell the Domain Names to Complainant, which is literally true but begs the question of how one defines 'sale.' It is also true that Respondent has refused

and 3) at a price exceeding the documented out-of-pocket costs for acquiring it. However, proof of motivation is the controlling element.[192]

It is not necessarily the case that if element 3 is found that element 1 can be inferred, but if element 2 is also found it strengthens the inference that the domain name was acquired for its trademark value. The reverse is also true, namely that the more common the word (or combination of words) the heavier the burden,[193] which is the reason for the focus on the primary focus test. Respondents are less vulnerable to forfeiture if their domain names resolve to pay-per-click websites offering links to goods and services consistent with the semantic meaning of the words, which would render them defensible under paragraph 4(c)(i) of the Policy.

6.02-B 6.02-B The "Primary Purpose" Test

6.02-B.1 6.02-B.1 Violating the "Primary Purpose"

The Policy does not prohibit commerce in domain names[194] or condemn selling them for their market value to arm's-length purchasers. Domain names acquired in good faith, paragraph 4(c) and subsections, or for which complainants fail to prove bad faith, paragraph 4(b) and subsections, are disposable assets. Paragraph 4(b)(i) is violated when the respondent is found to have registered or acquired the domain name "*primarily for the purpose of*" extorting a benefit from the trademark owner.[195] The provision addresses situations in which a domain name purchased with knowledge of complainant's trademark is being held or ransomed for profit.

Complainant's requests to transfer the Domain Names to Complainant but has instead attempted to negotiate a business arrangement with Complainant to use the Domain Names to develop a commercial website. As Complainant notes, this places Complainant in the position of having to contract with a party with whom it does not wish to do business or effectively cede to Respondent a substantial measure of control over the use of its own trademarks and goodwill."

[192] "Purpose" as an element of proof is also found in paragraph 4(b)(iii) of the Policy.

[193] "Print" and "factory" for example in ***Aurelon B.V. v. AbdulBasit Makrani***, D2017-1679 (WIPO October 30, 2017) (<printfactory.com>).

[194] ***Teradyne, Inc.Teradyne, Inc.[sic] v. 4Tel Technology***, D2000-0026 (WIPO May 9, 2000). Were it otherwise "trade in domain names would of itself be objectionable, which it is not," ***The Monticello Group, Ltd. v. Teletravel, Inc.***, D2002-1157 (WIPO April 16, 2003). ACPA cases include *Virtual Works, Inc. v. Volkswagen of Am., Inc.*, 238 F.3d 264, 269 (4th Cir. 2001) ("mere offer to sell a domain name is not itself evidence of unlawful trafficking," citing H.R. Conf. Rep. No. 106 464, at 111 (1999)); *Interstellar Starship Serv. Ltd. v. Epix, Inc.*, 304 F.3d 936, 947 (9th Cir. 2002).

[195] The Policy reads: "[C]ircumstances indicating that you have registered or you have acquired the domain name primarily for the purpose of selling, renting, or otherwise transferring the domain name registration to complainant who is the owner of the trademark or service mark or to a competitor of that Complainant, for valuable consideration in excess of your documented out of pocket costs directly related to the domain name." Jurisprudential Overview focuses on whether the "claimed purpose" is supported by evidence. See *Webadviso v. Bank of Am. Corp., supra.* and Sec. 6.05 below.

That a domain name matches a complainant's mark is not by itself evidence of bad faith. Complainant must show that the registration is for the proscribed purpose, namely targeting complainant who is the owner of the mark or competitor of that complainant as a potential purchaser of the domain name.[196] The proscription excludes domain name registrations that predate trademark acquisition because the phrase "primarily for the purpose of" presupposes an existing mark.

Infringement may be inferred where respondent passively holds a domain name registered after complainant's acquisition of rights and (without explanation for its choice) offers it to complainant at a price in excess of its out-of-pocket costs.[197] This is not to imply that passive use or inactivity alone informs the inference, but suspicion of bad faith registration gains strength from the offer and is made conclusive by respondent's silence. The proscription has been construed to include all forms of solicitation,[198] ranging from "general offers to sell the domain name, even if no certain price is demanded"[199] to offers to the general public[200] or

---

"[W]hether or not [the respondent] had any intention of selling the domain names to [the trademark owner], he clearly had the intention to profit from the goodwill associated with the trademarks that comprised the domain names." *Webadviso v. Bank of Am. Corp.*, 448 F. App'x 95, 98 (2d Cir. 2011). "Intention to profit from the goodwill" is a Paragraph 4(b)(iv) violation (Sec. 6.05).

[196] The weaker the mark the greater complainant's burden. Three and four letter strings that to complainants are acronyms of their marks to respondents are merely strings of random letters. See ***Electronic Arts Inc. v. Abstract Holdings Int'l LTD / Sheren Blackett***, FA 1415905 (FORUM January 4, 2012) (<ssx.com>. "Respondent would certainly have sold the name to Complainant, as Respondent would have sold to any person interested in purchasing the name, but it did not intend to sell the disputed domain name to Complainant.") Further discussion in "Legitimate Use by Many Third Parties" (Sec. 4.01-C.1).

[197] ***Robert Ellenbogen v. Mike Pearson***, D2000-0001 (WIPO February 17, 2000) ("[I]ntent by the domain name registrant to sell a domain name constitutes a 'commercial use' under United States antidilution law (15 U.S.C. §1125(c))," citing *Intermatic Inc. v. Toeppen*, 947 F. Supp. 1227 (N.D. Ill. 1996) (The court characterized the defendant as a "spoiler" who prevented the trademark holder from doing business on the Internet under its trademark name unless it paid the Respondent's fee). If the purpose is primarily to obtain a benefit not covered by the examples then the violation must be matched with a different theory. Discussed further in "Identifying the Right Theory of Predation" (Sec. 6.01-A.1.b).

[198] ***Salomon Smith Barney Inc. v. Daniel Singer d/b/a Build Me A Website.com***, D2000-1722 (WIPO February 28, 2001).

[199] ***Am. Anti-Vivisection Soc'y v. AInfa dot Net" Web Serv.***, FA 95685 (Forum November 6, 2000) (<aavs.org>. Lapse of registration as a result of web designer going out of business); ***Mattel, Inc. v. Unknown c/o Dora Marks***, FA0506000490083 (Forum July 11, 2005) (<barbie.us>. Respondent alleged that it purchased the domain name as an "investment.")

[200] ***Parfums Christian Dior S.A. v. QTR Corp.***, D2000-0023 (WIPO October 3, 2000) (holding bad faith where Whois information included the phrase "this domain name is for sale"); ***Randstad General Partner (U.S.), LLC v. Domains For Sale For You,*** D2000-0051 (WIPO March 24, 2000)

to the "Internet universe . . . which necessarily includes both Complainant and its competitors."[201] Offering to sell the disputed domain name to "anyone" for "the right price" is circumstantial evidence of respondent's primary purpose in registering it and conclusive if the only party with a legal right to the name is the trademark owner.[202]

"Primarily for the purpose" also applies to extortionate attempts for business concessions,[203] threats as in the suggestion that the company "may wish to purchase these domains before I do something else with them,"[204] demands for concessions in pre-arbitration communications veiled as opportunities, "passively holding the domain names for use in possible settlement negotiations of the dispute between the parties,"[205] and "leveraging" for a settlement of a dispute.[206] It has been held that

> Respondent's rather frank admission that he intends to use the disputed domain name to leverage compensation for copyright materials allegedly taken from his website suggests that the motive was to use the domain name as a bargaining means for another dispute. This is improper and in the Panel's view is a clear illustration of bad faith.[207]

A respondent who tries "to force Complainant to use his independent web hosting service is a classic form of cybersquatting except that he sought work rather than cash."[208] Very often "it is . . . an opening gambit in an exercise of inducing the trademark owner to offer to buy the domain name without providing direct evidence to support a complaint under the Policy."[209] The Panel in ***Takaso Rubber*** held that

---

("At the web site linked to the officespecialists.com domain name, Respondent offers to sell the officespecialists.com domain name for $24,000, together with a description that states 'Temp Agencies, Office Supplies, or business only practices this is the name for you'"); ***Systea GmbH v. Marketpoints.com New Media Branding Services/DNS Administrator***, D2006-0324 (WIPO May 13, 2006) (Domain name "offered for sale on a publicly accessible website").

201 ***Cargill, Incorporated v. RN WebReg c/o Rare Names, Inc.***, FA0904001260307 (Forum June 12, 2009).

202 ***PRIMEDIA Magazine Finance, Inc. v. Richard Manzo***, D2001-1258 (WIPO December 13, 2001) (Respondent noted that "everyone knows that everything is for sale at the right price.")

203 ***Cello Holding, LLC v. Lawrence A. Storey, d.b.a. Lawrence-Dahl Co.***, AF-506 (eResolution December 21, 2000); ***Takaso Rubber Products Sdn Bhd v. Selim Tasci and Tasci Dis Tic. Ltd. STI***, D2006-1263 (WIPO December 16, 2006).

204 ***Atlantic Industries v. Insight Visual Communications***, D2009-0291 (WIPO May 4, 2009).

205 ***Nexxt Development Corp. v. Richard Spence***, D2008-0530 (WIPO May 29, 2008).

206 ***Bank of Alabama v. Sumith Rodrigo & Co.***, D2004-0912 (WIPO December 16, 2004).

207 ***Coppertown Drive-Thru Systems, LLC v. R. Snowden***, FA0605000715089 (Forum July 17, 2006).

208 ***Westfield Corp. v. Graeme Michael Hobbs***, D2000-0227 (WIPO May 18, 2000).

209 ***Google Inc. v. Jeltes Consulting/N. Tea Pty Ltd***, D2008-0994 (WIPO August 20, 2008).

> The demand by Respondent for such a business concession in exchange for transfer of the disputed domain name constitutes an offer to transfer the disputed domain name for valuable consideration in excess of its documented out of pocket costs directly related to the domain name.

Takaso Rubber and other cited decisions confirm the consensus view that the "consideration demanded in exchange for a domain name registration does not have to be monetary in nature to run afoul of UDRP paragraph 4(b)(i), but can be anything of value that exceeds the amount spent in registering and maintaining the domain name."[210]

Although a complainant's solicitation and respondent's interested response generally exonerate bad faith, as discussed earlier in "Not All Offers to Sell Violate the Policy" (Sec. 5.01-D.3) the fact that complainant initiates negotiation to transfer the domain name does not preclude the Panel from concluding that respondent registered and is using it in bad faith.[211] This finding may be based on prior communications or even statements against interest in the response to a cease-and-desist notice.

6.02-B.2 Proving "Primary Purpose" 6.02-B.2

Complainant has the burden of proving an infringing "primary purpose." This necessarily requires proof that the complainant's trademark predates respondent's acquisition of the domain name.[212] If it does the proof has to exclude other purposes, such as the attractiveness of the name unrelated to the significance of the trademark. To demand a price exceeding "documented out of pocket costs" is not *prima facie* bad faith where respondent 1) refuses "to amicably settle the [domain name] dispute or engage in negotiations"[213]; 2) registered the domain name many years before making an offer of sale and plausibly denies any knowledge of complainant at the time of registration[214]; 3) has a right in the domain name it is pricing

---

210 ***Gutterbolt, Inc. v. NYI Bldg. Prods. Inc.***, FA 96076 (Forum December 29, 2000); ***Takaso Rubber v. Selim Tasci***, D2006-1263 (WIPO December 16, 2006).

211 ***Treeforms, Inc. v. Cayne Industrial Sales, Corp.***, FA0010000095856 (Forum December 8, 2000) ("the Panel is unconcerned that the solicitation did not elicit a specific dollar offer inasmuch as it is eminently reasonable for the Panel to infer, particularly when the record fails to indicate otherwise, that respondent clearly sought a sum that exceeded its costs; otherwise, why would it solicit an offer in the first place.")

212 ***Ryan P. Boggs v. Name Administration Inc. (BVI)***, D2013-0583 (WIPO June 4, 2013) ("The Complainant contends that the Respondent's failure . . . to use the disputed domain name commercially [and its refusal] to sell the disputed domain name for less than USD 16,000, is 'evidence of cyber squatting with intent to resell' for an amount in excess of out of pocket expenses.")

213 ***EAuto, L.L.C. v. Triple S. Auto Parts d/b/a Kung Fu Yea Enterprises, Inc.*** D2000-0047 (WIPO March 24, 2000).

214 ***SOUTHBank v. Media Street***, D2001-0294 (WIPO April 11, 2001).

for its market value[215]; 4) is responding to complainant's solicitation to purchase the domain name[216]; or 5) registered and is legitimately holding and using a common word/descriptive phrase domain name for its semantic rather than its trademark value.[217]

A respondent's self-interest in demanding a price complainant thinks excessive is not for that reason alone evidence of bad faith.[218] Price is not a factor unless the domain name was registered after trademark acquisition and there is some evidence respondent had complainant in mind.[219] "[I]f the drafters . . . had intended to broadly cover offers to any and all potential purchasers as evidence of bad faith, it would have been a simple matter to refer to all offers to sell the domain name, and not offers to specific parties or classes of parties."[220] If respondent has a right or legitimate interest in the domain name willingness to sell it to a complainant for a substantial price in excess of its "documented out of pocket costs directly related to the domain name" does not justify dispossessing it of its property.[221] When a complainant "indicates a willingness to engage in a market transaction for the name

---

[215] ***Avnet, Inc. v. Aviation Network, Inc.***, D2000-0046 WIPO March 24, 2000); ***Lodgeworks L.P. v. Sierra Hospitality***, FA0802001152964 (Forum April 21, 2008).

[216] ***Container Research Corp. v. Markovic***, FA 328163 (Forum November 2, 2004) (Complainant cannot prod respondent into offering a transfer price and then invoke paragraph 4(b)(i) of the Policy to show respondent's bad faith registration and use.)

[217] ***Letstalk.com, Inc. v. Inofirma, Ltd c/o Domain Administrator***, FA1002001310279 (Forum April 21, 2010); ***Robert Norcross, Jr. Norcross Corporation v. Marchex Sales, Inc. / Brendhan Hight***, FA12032001437030 (Forum May 8, 2012) (Respondent asked $30,000 for <norcross.com>. "Norcross" is a geographic location outside of Atlanta, Georgia, and Respondent uses it in its descriptive sense.)

[218] Representative cases: ***Etam, plc v. Alberta Hot Rods***, D2000-1654 (WIPO January 31, 2001); ***General Machine Products Company, Inc. v. Prime Domains***, Case No. FA0001000092531 (Forum January 26, 2000); ***Cool Cat Fashion B.V. v. Cool Kat***. D2005-0385 (WIPO June 2, 2005); ***Barlow Lyde & Gilbert v. The Business Law Group***, D2005-0493 (WIPO June 24, 2005).

[219] ***Manufacturas Muñoz S.A. Colombia v. Choi Sungyeon***, D2010-0312 (WIPO April 26, 2010) (Even if the price is high, there is no evidence that Respondent registered the domain name in bad faith since at the time of registration Complainant's trademark did not then exist.)

[220] ***Educational Testing Service v. TOEFL***, D2000-0044 (WIPO March 16, 2000).

[221] ***Meredith Corp. vs. CityHome, Inc.***, D2000-0223 (WIPO May 18, 2000) (<country home.com>. "The fact that Respondent is seeking substantial money for what it believes to be a valuable asset is not tantamount to bad faith. Rather, it tends to show a reasonable business response to an inquiry about purchasing a business asset where Respondent had already expended time and money to develop a new part of its business, including the sums it spent on an outside law firm to search the possible trademark and in obtaining the domain name registration.") ***Personally Cool Inc. v. Name Administration Inc. (BVI)***, FA 1474325 (Forum January 17, 2013) (<coldfront.com>. "If the Respondent has legitimate interests in the domain name, it has the right to sell that domain name for whatever price it deems appropriate regardless of the value that appraisers may ascribe to the domain name.")

respondent is not penalized for putting a price on it."[222] Panels have consistently rejected the notion often advanced by complainants that respondents' demands of "outrageous prices" for domain names constitute abusive registration.[223]

Offering "to sell . . . descriptive, non-source identifying domain name[s] does not make [a respondent's] interest illegitimate."[224] Indeed, "[o]ffers to sell are not of themselves objectionable under the Policy."[225] "Were that the case, trade in domain names would of itself be objectionable, which it is not"[226] and "responding to an unsolicited offer to sell a domain name does not exhibit bad faith."[227]

Domain names plausibly registered without intent to infringe a trademark are not the intended targets of the Policy. Respondents are not condemned for offering to sell a domain name at a high price, particularly where the initial contact is made by complainant[228] and there is no evidence that respondent's acquisition of the domain name violated complainant's trademark rights. Buying low and selling high "is a very common business practice." [229] This extends to well-known trademarks that have generic meanings in other industries.[230] Respondents only run afoul of the Policy "when domain names are registered for resale with knowledge that the names consist of another's trademark."[231] Dissenting voices to this principle on the theory that domain names are a "scarce resource" have received no encouragement.[232]

---

[222] ***Pocatello Idaho Auditorium Dist. v. CES Marketing Group, Inc.***, FA 103186 (Forum February 21, 2002) (Geographical term, <pocatello.com>. "[W]hen a Complainant indicates a willingness to engage in a market transaction for the name, it does not violate the policy for a [Respondent] to offer to sell for a market price, rather than out of pocket expenses.")

[223] ***Meredith Corp.***, supra. ***Glory Ltd. v. MicroStrategy, Inc.***, D2017-1900 (WIPO January 3, 2018) (<glory.com>, "Unreasonable"); ***Well-Link Industry Co. Ltd. v. Jeff Park, Nexpert, Inc.***, D2017-0036 (WIPO March 1, 2017) (<welllink.com>, "Disproportionate"); ***Pet Life LLC v. ROBERT RIESS / blue streak marketing llc***, FA1810001810870 (Forum November 11, 2018) (<petlife.com>, "Unreasonable,").

[224] ***General Machine Products Company, Inc. v. Prime Domains (a/k/a Telepathy, Inc.)***, FA0001000092531 (Forum March 16, 2000) (<craftwork>).

[225] ***Teradyne, Inc.Teradyne, Inc.[sic] v. 4Tel Technology***, D2000-0026 (WIPO May 9, 2000) .

[226] ***The Monticello Group, Ltd. v. Teletravel, Inc.***, D2002-1157 (WIPO April 16, 2003).

[227] ***Mirama Enterprises Inc, d/b/a Aroma Housewares Company v. NJDomains, Abuse Contact: abuse@mail.com c/o Gerald Gorman***, FA0510000588486 (Forum January 16, 2006).

[228] ***Barlow Lyde & Gilbert v. The Business Law Group***, D2005-0493 (WIPO June 24, 2005).

[229] Id.

[230] The trademark SPRITE owned by The Coca-Cola Company is also used generically in the computer software industry, ***The Coca-Cola Co. v. Svensson***, FA0201000103933 (Forum February 27, 2002) (<sprite.nu>).

[231] ***Primal Quest, LLC v. Gabriel Salas***, D2005-1083 (WIPO December 15, 2005).

[232] ***Shoe Mart Factory Outlet, Inc. v. DomainHouse.com, Inc. c/o Domain Administrator***, FA0504000462916 (Forum June 10, 2005) (<shoemart.com>. "With all due respect to my brother

The value of domain names composed of generic elements is measured by the potential number of businesses interested in acquiring them. "Selling or leasing non source identifying combinations in widespread use in a descriptive sense"[233] is a *bona fide* offering of goods. Two or three letter domain names are "extremely prized."[234] The Policy is not "interpret[ed] . . . to mean that a mere offer for sale of the domain name for a large sum of money is, of itself, proof of cybersquatting."[235] Indeed,

> some of the largest sums of money paid for domain names have been for generic names and it is clear to anyone who follows reports of domain name sales that 2-letter.com registrations are extremely prized.

In these cases respondents gauge the market values of the domain names and complainants accept the prices, negotiate or move on.

A complainant who acquires a trademark after the domain name registration has no actionable claim to the domain name held by the original registrant.[236] Rather, the original registrant/respondent "has the right to value its assets by listing them for sale and the right to sell its assets if it chooses to do so."[237] In ***Teradyne***, respondent had registered a domain name to reflect its own business name but subsequently offered to sell the name for profit when its business dissolved. Under these circumstances the panel found that to decide the case on the theory that offering a redundant domain name for sale at a price exceeding respondent's out of pocket expenses would "extend the Policy to cover cases clearly intended to be outside its scope."

Panelists, I must dissent. As an overall matter, I believe the UDRP was designed to regulate a scarce resource (domain names) rather than to provide a mechanism to protect registered trademarks .") See ***Aurelon B.V. v. AbdulBasit Makrani***, D2017-1679 (WIPO October 30, 2017) (<printfactory.com>. "Speculating in domain names is a lawful business model regardless whether the domain names correspond to marks as long as the proof establishes either 1) respondents have rights or legitimate interests in the domain name; or 2) complainants are unable to prove bad faith registration and use. The three-member Panel in this case reminds us that "the domaining business was not an activity which was intended when the Domain Name System was created. Admittedly, the domaining business is less known in Europe than in other parts of the world, and trademark holders keep being surprised by speculative business models that are developed around the scarce resource that domain names are.")

[233] ***General Machine Products***, supra.

[234] ***Deutsch Welle v. Diamondware Capital Ltd***, D2000-1202 (WIPO January 2, 2001) (<dw.com>).

[235] Id.

[236] A qualification to this principle is discussed further in "Acting on Media Coverage and Insider Information" (Sec. 6.01-C.1.b). The trademark owner may have a claim against a subsequent holder, discussed further in "Transfer/Subsequent Holders=New Registration" (Sec. 4.03-B.2)

[237] ***Scholastic Inc. v. Master Games Int'l, Inc.***, D2001-1208 (WIPO January 3, 2002) (<scholastics.com>).

The Panel made a similar finding in ***Leineweber GmbH & Co.***[238] In response to Complainant's inquiry about the domain name Respondent stated that it "would not sell the domain name [<brax.com>] for less than USD $1 million." Complainant in ***Leineweber*** advanced two arguments, "lack of necessity" (respondent had other domain names for its business) and speculative registration—on the theory that Respondent registered the domain name ten years earlier "awaiting a convenient opportunity to sell the domain name to the real trademark owner." However,

> a mere lack of necessity (however defined) is no argument against respondent under paragraph 4(a)(ii) or otherwise. It is common for domain name registrants to register any number of domain names, including variations or abbreviations of a mark or name. The Respondent's lack of use of the disputed domain name for a number of years is not relevant in the circumstances of this case, where respondent has otherwise established a legitimate interest.

Respondent's shortening its trading name, "Braxton," to "Brax" does not deprive it of the paragraph 4(c)(ii) defense. "It is no requirement of the Policy that a domain name exactly correspond to a respondent's trading or legal name for a respondent to establish a right or legitimate interest [as reflecting the name by which it is commonly known]." For the second argument to have merit, speculating on registration requires proof rather than conjecture of a respondent's motive rising in degrees of difficulty as terms chosen either descend to the generic and descriptive end of the spectrum or, as in the case of Braxton Manufacturing, the first four letters of the SLD spell out its trading name.[239]

6.03 PATTERN OF CONDUCT—PARAGRAPH 4(b)(ii) OF THE POLICY 6.03

6.03-A Acts Construed as a "Pattern of Conduct" 6.03-A

Of the four examples of bad faith, paragraph 4(b)(ii) of the Policy refers to multiple current or past acts that together can be said to constitute a pattern of abusive registration. Where such a pattern exists that "prevent[s] the owner of the trademark or service mark from reflecting the mark in a corresponding domain name"[240] respondents are in violation of the Policy. If complainant is not prevented from

[238] ***Leineweber GmbH & Co. KG. v. Braxton Manufacturing Co., Inc.***, D2008-1057 (WIPO December 28, 2008). See also ***Togu gebruder Obermaier oHG v. Whois Privacy Protection Service, Inc. / PortMedia Domains***, D2013-0914 (WIPO August 8, 2013) (rejected Complainant's argument for bad faith on three bases not enumerated in paragraph 4(b)).

[239] Discussed further in "'First-Come First-Served' Doctrine" (Sec. 6.01-F).

[240] The Policy is violated if respondent "registered the domain name in order to prevent the owner of the trademark or service mark from reflecting the mark in a corresponding domain name, *provided that [it has] . . . engaged in a pattern of such conduct*" (emphasis added). The proscription is also applied in disputes in which complainant's have inadvertently lost their registrations by missing

reflecting its mark in a corresponding domain name—where, for example, disputed domain names are composed of misspellings or minor variations of trademarks that constitute classic examples of typosquatting—the violation is more properly actionable under paragraph 4(b)(iv) of the Policy. The rationale for the "pattern of conduct" theory is to protect innocent registrations: "[d]ue to the ease with which an innocent domain registrant can create an inadvertent collision with an existing trademark . . . the Policy requires a pattern of such conduct in order to establish bad faith."[241]

The term "pattern of conduct" has been construed to mean targeting trademarks of many owners as well as multiple trademarks of one owner. It applies to respondents currently infringing a single owner's rights with multiple registrations at one time[242] or having a history of multiple registrations involving a diversity of trademarks over a period of time.[243] Such a pattern of abusive registration can occur in two distinct dimensions:[244]

> "First, a domain registrant can operate 'horizontally', targeting multiple entities, perhaps in multiple industries.
>
> "Second, a domain registrant can operate 'vertically', targeting a single entity, but registering multiple domains which reflect either different aspects of the target's business, or different alphabetic variations of the target's trademark."

Proof of either dimension satisfies the "pattern of conduct" requirement and supports a finding of abusive registration.[245]

---

the renewal deadlines. As a representative case, see ***Armor Building Solutions, LLC v. Al Perkins***, FA1708001745973 (Forum November 2, 2017) (<armorbuildingsolutions.com>. "The Panel agrees that the foregoing constitutes evidence that the instant dispute is merely a piece of a larger pattern of Respondent's pattern of bad faith domain name registration and usage under Policy ¶ 4(b)(ii).")

241 ***Smokey Mountain Knife Works v. Deon Carpenter***, AF-230 (a, b) (eResolution July 3, 2000) (<www.smokymountainknife.net> and <www.smokymountainknifes.com>).

242 ***Caterpillar Inc. v. Miyar***, FA 95623 (Forum December 14, 2000) (registering multiple domain names in a short time frame indicates an intention to prevent the mark owner from using its mark and provides evidence of a pattern of conduct).

243 ***Siemens Aktiengesellschaft v. Telmex Management Services, Inc.***, D2003-0995 (WIPO February 14, 2004) ("[Respondent had against it]18 Panel decisions under the Policy, concerning instances of . . . domain names incorporating well known marks in which it was found not to have any rights or legitimate interests.") See *Pinterest, Inc. v. Qian Jin*, C12-04586 (N.D. CA SF Div. 9/30/13) (Serial cybersquatter; 100 domain names including plaintiff's).

244 ***Smokey Mountain***, supra: "In the instant case, not only does the Respondent presumably have a sophisticated understanding of the cutlery industry, but Respondent has actively targeted several of its most prominent direct competitors. We find this pattern of conduct, even without more, to be persuasive evidence of bad faith."

245 Horizontal: ***Australian Stock Exch. v. Cmty. Internet (Australia) Pty Ltd***, D2000-1384 (WIPO November 30, 2000) (registering multiple infringing domain names containing the trademarks or

"Pattern of conduct" cannot be satisfied by isolated examples of arguably proscribed conduct and should be "viewed with a high degree of scrutiny."[246] A respondent's history is probative of bad faith, but "each case has to be decided on its own merits."[247] In the case cited in the footnote Respondent had a mixed history. It had successfully defended itself in several disputes involving domain names composed of generic terms or strings of random letters. The probative value in such factual situations "may be one of weight . . . which can be taken into account in assessing the implications of all of the information that an administrative panel has at hand."[248] Where, for example, the facts "reveal a scheme or plan . . . a course of operations, is not irrelevant." It is irrelevant that there may be no monetary gain to the cybersquatter.[249] However, "a pattern of abusive conduct under the Policy can only succeed if the Panel is satisfied that when registering the Domain Name respondent was targeting complainant."[250]

The fact that a serial respondent may have successfully defended itself against one or more complaints in earlier proceedings does not make its conduct less a pattern in the current case if the disputed domain name is identical or confusingly similar to complainant's trademark and respondent is found to lack any right or

---

service marks of other widely known Australian businesses). Vertical: ***Harcourt, Inc. v. Fadness***, FA 95247 (Forum September 8, 2000) (registering more than one domain name [6 in this case] of complainant's various magazines, supporting the inference that Respondent knew of Complainant's marks upon registering the domain names.)

246 ***Foundation Fitness LLC v. Jiang Zhou***, D2015-1054 (WIPO September 3, 2015), citing ***Investone Retirement Specialists, Inc. v. Motohisa Ohno***, D2005-0643 (WIPO August 2, 2005).

247 ***Nursefinder, Inc. v. Vertical Axis, Inc.***, D2007-0417 (WIPO July 5, 2007). See also ***Airpet Animal Transport, Inc. v. Marchex Sales, Inc / Brendhan Hight***, FA1211001470056 (Forum January 2, 2013) (<petexpress.com>. "Respondent has prevailed in all but three instances of the nearly two dozen UDRP proceedings to which it has been a party. This Panel believes each case must be judged on its merits.")

248 ***Collections ETC., Inc. v. Cupcake Patrol***, D2001-0305 (WIPO May 10, 2001); ***Youi Pty Ltd. v. Xedoc Holding SA***, D2012-1329 (WIPO September 3, 2012) (Complaint denied with strong dissent: "The Respondent may not have had actual knowledge of the Complainant (and I even doubt this), but would clearly have been aware of the traffic that the disputed domain name was generating at the time it decided to acquire the disputed domain name.")

249 ***Sun Microsystems, Inc. v. Cyber Business Holdings Ltd.***, D2007-1439 (WIPO January 11, 2008) ("The Panel notes the Respondent's contention that the disputed domain names receive relatively few hits. Nevertheless, the Panel is satisfied that the Respondent is using these domain names with the intention of attracting internet users to its websites through confusion with the Complainant's mark and thereby obtaining click through commissions from sponsored links accessed by such internet users.")

250 When it is not abusive, ***eSnipe, Inc. Modern Empire Internet, Ltd.***, D2009-0719 (WIPO August 5, 2009) (<snipeit.com>). When it is abusive conduct, ***Little Acorns Fostering Ltd. v. W P, The Cloud Corp / Al Perkins***, D2017-1776 (WIPO October 18, 2017) (<littleacorn fostering.com>.

interest in it.[251] That respondent is shown to have a history of cybersquatting is not sufficient in itself[252] if the facts do not support a violation.[253]

6.03-B 6.03-B Enhanced Investigative Responsibilities for High-Volume Registrants

6.03-B.1 6.03-B.1 Imposing a Different Standard for High-Volume Registrants

Neither the WIPO Final Report nor the ICANN Second Report implementing the UDRP distinguishes among different classes of registrants. The Policy does not require any registrants to research trademark databases for infringement,[254] but the higher a trademark lies on the classification scale and the stronger its reputation the less plausible a respondent's plea of good faith registration. Complainants whose trademarks are composed of common words and descriptive terms have a greater burden to prove bad faith registration even where respondents are in the domain name business and there is proof of temporary infringing use of the domain name.

Respondents in the business of acquiring, monetizing, and selling domain names (popularly known as domainers[255]) and others experienced or knowledgeable in Internet technology and culture early came under additional scrutiny.[256] In time this view developed into a lower tolerance for high-volume registrants who

---

"[I]t is unfortunate that the business practices of Mr. Perkins appear to have carried on for the most part unchecked for many years, notwithstanding the multiple findings made against him in UDRP proceedings and the brazen nature of his conduct.")

[251] ***Société BIC v. Domain Deluxe***, D2005-0369 (WIPO June 2, 2005).

[252] Id., ***AirpetAnimal*** ("The fact Respondent is a frequent party to UDRP proceedings is immaterial.")

[253] ***Intesa Sanpaolo S.p.A. v. RareNames***, WebReg, D2007-0671 (WIPO July 30. 2007).

[254] All respondents are bound by the representations and warranties signed in connection with their domain name acquisition so that all registrants have some basic responsibility for avoiding infringing third party rights even if it stops short of researching databases. Discussed further in "Registrant's Responsibility for Determining Whether Domain Name Infringes Third Party Rights" (Sec. 2.02). Some panelists have extended the representations and warranties to renewals of registrations, discussed further in "Justifying Forfeiture Despite Good Faith Registration" (Sec. 4.03-A.4.b).

[255] Nominet UK, the ".uk" registry, defines "domainer" as "someone who buys and sells domain name registrations, often generating income through domain parking and/or website development, with the main purpose of generating revenue from advertising click through. Income is also generated through sales, advertising and affiliate commissions."

[256] ***Red Nacional De Los Ferrocarriles Espanoles v. Ox90***, D2001-0981 (WIPO November 21, 2001) Respondent who admitted to being a knowledgeable Internet analyst registered a recently lapsed, commonly searched domain name. The Panel held that "where there is an intentional registration of a domain name by one with obvious reason to believe that it might be the trademarked name of another, combined with an intentional or reckless failure to verify whether that is the case and without making even the most basic inquiry, constitutes registration of that domain name in

"through automated programs . . . snap up domain names as they become available, with no attention whatsoever to whether they may be identical to trademarks."[257] "Such practices" (the Panel continued) "may well support a finding that respondent is engaged in a pattern of conduct that deprives trademark owners of the ability to register domain names reflecting their marks."

Whether there are such "patterns of conduct" is answered by taking into account respondents' business histories. Panels have drawn distinctions among different commercial models. Registrants who specialize in particular kinds of domain names, generic words, idioms, surnames, and three or four-letter strings for example,[258] and include their histories are generally persuasive in arguing good faith, although there are exceptions.[259] With some degree of plasticity, the consensus is that high volume registrants must clear a higher evidentiary bar.

While not condemning trawling as a *per se* violation of the Policy panelists concluded that there should be some limit to the practice, which they formulated as an enhanced duty of care. This does not go so far as to impose an impossible burden to investigate every domain name in a bulk acquisition but it does establish an expectation of proof that high-volume registrants have exercised some degree of care. Panels have generally rejected respondents' assurances of good faith as a defense to bad faith in favor of a standard that provides transparency to their acquisition policies.

The standard that appears most acceptable is traceable to a 2006 dispute.[260] It applies to registrants who regularly engage in the business of registering and reselling

---

bad faith." See also ***Aspen Holdings Inc. v. Rick Natsch, Potrero Media Corporation***, D2009-0776 (WIPO August 20, 2009).

[257] ***Media General Communications, Inc. v. Rarenames, WebReg***, D2006-0964 (WIPO September 23, 2006) (<wcmh.com>).

[258] ***Creative NetVentures, Inc. v. Webheads***, D2000-1655 (WIPO March 14, 2000) (<anteup>. Idiom); ***Micah Hargress v. PARAMOUNT INTERNET***, FA1509001638609 (Forum November 13, 2015) (<hargress.com>. Respondent has "100s of similar registrations for generic terms and surnames"); ***Easton Corp Pty Ltd v. Privacydotlink Customer 951873/DNS Admin, Best Web Limited***, D2016-1975 (WIPO November 12, 2016) (<hottie.com>, Idiom); ***SOG Specialty Knives and Tools, LLC v. Val Katayev / Poise Media Inc.***, FA170400 1726464 (Forum May 23, 2017) (<sog.com>, specializing in three-letter domain names); ***FPT Industrie S.p.a. and REM Industrie S.r.l. v. HugeDomains.Com***, D2017-0842 (WIPO July 7, 2017) (<fast mill.com>. Respondent has registered over 1,000 other generic words incorporating the word "fast"); ***Commune de Versailles Collectivité Territoriale v. Kimberly Kubalek, Kubalek, LLC***, D2017-0985 (WIPO August 24, 2017) (<visitversailles.com>, operating tourism websites).

[259] ***Constellation Brands, Inc. and its wholly owned subsidiary Ruffino SRL v. Stanley Pace***, FA1706001735061 (Forum July 20, 2017) (RUFFINO and <rufino.com>. Although Respondent has accumulated over 10,000 surnames Complainant points out in its additional statement that "U.S. Census Bureau (2010 Census) shows only 795 individuals with the surname "Rufino" in the U.S. making its surname usage *de minimus*.")

domain names and/or using them to display advertising links. The Panel explained that high-volume registrants were acquiring "large swaths of domain names through the use of automated programs." To defeat the imputation of bad faith registration (as formulated by the Panel in ***Media General***), respondents must be able to show that

1. They made good faith efforts to avoid registering and using domain names that are identical or confusingly similar to marks held by others;

2. The domain name in question is a dictionary word or a generic or descriptive phrase;

3. The domain name is not identical or confusingly similar to a famous or distinctive trademark; and

4. There is no evidence that respondent had actual knowledge of complainant's mark.

A number of influential panelists have agreed with these requirements[261] but as noted in the next section the rationale for creating a separate class has been questioned. The Panel in ***Media General*** rejected respondent's defense on the ground it failed to "indicate that it explored the possibility of third-party rights in any way before registering the Domain Name and offering it for sale."[262] In that case Respondent registered a four letter domain name that began with the letter "w" [<wcmh.com>]. The Panel noted that "a four letter string beginning with 'W' should have triggered some further investigation" because such strings are "used as distinctive call signs for hundreds of licensed broadcast television and radio stations in the United States, many of which are trademarked."[263] According to the ***Mobile*** Panel "even a cursory search on search engines like Yahoo! and Google would have shown that MOBILCOM is a trademark."

---

[260] ***Mobile Communication Service Inc. v. WebReg, RN.***, D2005-1304 (WIPO February 24, 2006) (<mobilcom.com>). Respondent submitted an untimely answer, which the Panel rejected, although noting he would have reached the same conclusion if the answer had been timely.

[261] Among others, ***mVisible Technologies Inc v. Navigation Catalyst Systems Inc.***, D2007-1141 (WIPO November 30, 2007) ("a sophisticated domainer who regularly registers domain names for use as PPC landing pages cannot be willfully blind to whether a particular domain name may violate trademark rights," adding that "a failure to conduct adequate searching may give rise to an inference of knowledge [of complainant's mark]"); ***Ticketmaster Corporation v. Global Access***, D2007-1921 (WIPO February 13, 2008) (respondent acquired the domain name in a commercial acquisition of a domain name portfolio); ***BAWAG***, supra.; and ***The Carphone Warehouse Limited and The Phone House B.V. v. Navigation Catalyst Systems, Inc.***, D2008-0483 (WIPO June 20, 2008) (18 domain names).

[262] ***Media General***, supra.

[263] Two, three, and four letter strings are generally regarded as generic. See ***BAWAG P.S.K. Bank für Arbeit und Wirtschaft und Österreichische Postsparkasse Aktiengesellschaft v. Future Media Architects, Inc.***, D2006-0534 (WIPO July 28, 2006) (<psk.com>); ***Electronic Arts Inc. v. Abstract***

The three-member Panel in ***mVisible Technologies*** took this reasoning one step further. It concluded that "it is reasonable to infer, based upon the circumstantial evidence available, that Respondent, a sophisticated party in the PPC landing page business, must have been aware of the relevant trademark . . . [and that] a failure to conduct adequate searching may give rise to an inference of knowledge [of complainant's mark]." The Panel noted that "this case require[s it] to traverse largely uncharted waters in resolving issues of bad faith registration and use under the third element of the Policy." The Panel rejected "unwavering adherence to conventional wisdom" of putting domainers on the same footing as other registrants where doing so "may unduly and unnecessarily frustrate the fundamental purposes of the Policy."[264]

Automated registration programs used by professional traders to snap up expired domain names are not "a shield against bad faith" and should not be discounted as a factor in determining abusive registration.[265] Rather, "those who register domain names, and particularly those who register domain names in large numbers using automated programs and processes, are not allowed to simply turn a blind eye to the possibility that the names they are registering will infringe or violate the rights of trademark owners."[266] Some Panels have suggested that the failure to perform a Google search prior to acquiring the domain name is grounds for finding bad faith.[267] Other Panels have gone even further, holding that where a domainer has the technological means to prevent infringement of third party rights there is "no reason why Respondent, as a domain name company with filtering technology,

---

Holdings International LTD / Sherene Blackett, FA1111001415905 (Forum January 4, 2012) disputing over <ssx.com>. Further discussion in "Legitimate Use by Many Third Parties" (Sec. 4.01-C.1).

The dissent in ***Bewag*** suggested that registrants who use their vast accumulations to exploit a business opportunity have "a greater duty . . . to verify that the use of a domain name . . . is legitimate." The dissents in ***BAWAG*** and ***Banco do Brasil, S.A. v. The Universal Kingdom, LLC***, D2008-0389 (WIPO June 6, 2008) (<bb.com>) concluded: "a registrant must exercise a certain degree of diligence, clear from paragraph 2 of the Policy." The dissent's views are discussed further in "Justifying Forfeiture Despite Good Faith Registration" (Sec. 4.03-A.4.b).

264 ***Balglow Finance S.A., Fortuna Comércio e Franquias Ltda. v. Name Administration Inc. (BVI)***, D2008-1216 (WIPO November 10, 2008).

265 ***Geopack v. Name Administration Inc. (BVI)***, D2006-1590 (WIPO March 15, 2007).

266 ***Grundfos A/S v. Tex. Int'l Prop. Assocs.***, D2007-1448 (WIPO December 14, 2007). See also ***Traditional Medicinals Inc. v. Worldwide Media Inc. c/o Domain Administrator***, FA090200 1247728 (Forum April 7, 2009), citing U.S. Supreme Court in *Safeco Insurance Company of America v. Burr*, 551 U.S. 47, 127 S. Ct. 2201 (2007), "[w]here willfulness is a statutory condition of civil liability, we have generally taken it to cover not only knowing violations of a standard, but reckless ones as well[.]" 127 S. Ct. at 2208 09." The Panel notes that "[t]his standard is appropriate in the context of a UDRP proceeding." Further discussed in "Willful Blindness Standard" (Sec. 4.02-C.2).

267 ***CTV Inc. v. Murat Yikilmaz***, FA0804001177671 (Forum June 10, 2008) (<ctv.com>, transferred over dissent who stated that registering "a domain name without a prior Google search seems

could not have added code to its web page system in order to avoid furniture related PPC links."[268]

6.03-B.2 ### 6.03-B.2 Discomfort in Imposing a Higher Standard

The Mobile rationale discussed above for imposing an enhanced duty on the domainer class cannot extend to worldwide investigations into trademarks beyond the domainer's home country, particularly for domain names composed of common words or phrases.[269] Even a more limited enhanced duty "is not universally accepted."[270] The ***Aubert International*** Panel noted that

> If there is nothing *per se* inimical to the Policy in dealing in domain names or the creation of large domain name portfolios for the purposes of financial gain, it is difficult to see the logic or justification within the words of the Policy of applying a different investigatory burden on the wholesale dealer in domain names than that which applies to a person who has registered a single domain name.

It rested its position on an earlier case[271] that held that "[w]hile the Domain Name was acquired by respondent from a batch of lapsed domain names by way of an automated process, this Panel is uncomfortable with the concept of constructive bad faith." This discomfort is understandable but bad faith is not limited to that theory.

---

to me to be willful blindness.") The same conclusion was reached in another dissent in ***Vaga lume Midia Ltda v. Kevo Ouz d/b/a Online Marketing Realty***, FA0910001287151 (Forum December 7, 2009) (Transferred over a vigorous dissent. The majority held that a Google search would have disclosed that complainant headed the list of returns. The dissent noted that "imposing this [heightened] requirement on respondent is also requiring him to search in the Portuguese language. . . . Again, it is difficult to see where this requirement comes from and why it is not imposing an impossible burden on registrant. . . .")

[268] ***Carol House Furniture, Inc. v. Registrant [3458020]: Oversee Domain Management LLC***, D2010-2103 (WIPO March 21, 2011) ("Is it too much to expect that Respondent should prove that it was unaware of Complainant's mark, when this evidence is only within the zone of Respondent's own operations?") ***General Electric Company v. Marketing Total S.A***, D2007-1834 (WIPO February 1, 2008) ("The circumstances of this case suggest that it was the Respondent's intention to bulk-register domain names that had some value in directing Internet traffic to its portal websites. Domain names that include, or are confusingly similar to, trademarks naturally have more value for this purpose. There is no evidence in this case that the Respondent took any measures to avoid exploiting the value of others' trademarks.")

[269] See Dissent in ***Tecnologia Bancaria S.A. v. Marchex Sales Inc.***, D2014-0834 (WIPO September 24, 2014). In a subsequent federal action under the Anticybersquatting Consumer Protection Act, *Marchex Sales, Inc. v. Tecnologia Bancaria, S.A.* 14cv1306 (E.D. Va. Alexandria Division May 21, 2015) Complainant (now defendant) defaulted and the transfer was enjoined.

[270] ***Aubert International SAS and Aubert France SA v. Tucows.com Co.***, D2008-1986 (WIPO March 17, 2009).

[271] ***Promatic International Limited v. Name Administration Inc.***, D2006-0673 (WIPO July 19, 2006) (<promatic.com>. "[T]here is no evidence nor suggestion that the reason why the Domain

The Panel's discomfort in ***Promatic International***, however, rested on the absence of evidence that Respondent had registered the disputed domain name (automatically or otherwise) "as a result of any goodwill or reputation that complainant has built up in the name."[272] It also matters that the second level domain is composed (or not) of alphabetical elements without particular source information—<bioshock> (a term not unique to Complainant) as opposed to <mobilecom.com> (which is). Trademarks composed of common words and phrases which have a lower level of protection raise the level of difficulty in establishing registration and use with a complainant's mark as a target.[273] The question is whether the "PPC links genuinely relate[] to the generic meaning of the domain name at issue."[274]

The Panel in ***American Wealth Alliance***[275] suggested a middle ground that requires examining respondent's conduct more directly and applying objective criteria. The question is not respondent's status as a high-volume registrant but whether its denials and professions of good faith are plausible in view of the circumstances or simply a case of willful blindness to another's rights. The key concerns remain the same: "[e]ven [in] bulk registrations or acquisitions of domain names by professional domainers, the critical consideration seems to be whether or not it can be said that the disputed domain name has been acquired because of its generic value, or because of its identification and association with a third party's trade mark."[276]

Also in complainant's favor was the fact that it was already on the Internet as <breedersclub.net> and had "built valuable good will and a strong reputation" in its unregistered mark since 2001. The Panel was skeptical that for a respondent

---

Name was registered (whether automatically or otherwise) was as a result of any goodwill or reputation that the Complainant has built up in the name.") See also ***Take Two Interactive Software Inc. v. Name Administration Inc.*** D2010-0845 (WIPO August 6, 2010) (<bioshock.com>).

[272] Although the Panel in ***Aubert International*** rejected the approach of charging domainers with a heightened duty it found bad faith in respondent "allow[ing] the domain name to continue to be used to take advantage of the trade mark association of the term 'aubert'."

[273] Jurisprudential Overview, Paragraph 2.9 states that "Panels have recognized that the use of a domain name to host a page comprising PPC links would be permissible – and therefore consistent with respondent rights or legitimate interests under the UDRP – where the domain name consists of an actual dictionary word(s) or phrase and is used to host PPC links genuinely related to the dictionary meaning of the word(s) or phrase comprising the domain name, and not to trade off the complainant's (or its competitor's) trademark."

[274] ***BrightSign LLC v. Administrator, Domain / Vertical Axis, Inc.***, FA1103001379395 (Forum May 4, 2011). Discussed further in "Knowledge and Targeting are Prerequisites for Bad Faith Registration" (Sec. 4.02-C).

[275] ***American Wealth Alliance, Inc. v. KB a/k/a Katarzyna Bieniek***, FA0801001139762 (Forum March 17, 2008) (<breedersclub.com>).

[276] There must be proof that respondent knowingly appropriated the trademark to take advantage of complainant's reputation in the marketplace. Without knowledge and "in the absence of wilful

"admittedly steeped in the acquisition of domain names" it would be unaware of complainant's website. It stated

> It is beyond the pale to assert, as Respondent does, that Respondent was unaware, at the time of registration and at the creation of its website, that the owner of 'breedersclub.net' would likely claim trademark rights in the BREEDERSCLUB mark.

Only if "the links on a given landing page are truly based on the generic value of the domain name . . . may [such use] be bona fide because [then] there are no trademark rights implicated by the landing page." The Panel concluded that it was "more likely than not that the attraction of adding the particular domain name to Respondent's bank of domain names was because of its trademark value not because of any descriptive quality that the domain name might have." For this reason the Panel granted the complaint and ordered registration of the domain name transferred to complainant.

6.04 6.04 DISRUPTING BUSINESS OF COMPETITOR—PARAGRAPH 4(b)(iii) OF THE POLICY

6.04-A 6.04-A Proscribed Conduct Must be Disruptive to Business of a Competitor

Paragraph 4(b)(iii) of the Policy is directed at respondents who purchase domain names "primarily for the purpose" of disrupting the business of a competitor. The phrasing is identical to the element of proof found in paragraph 4(b)(i). The term "disruption" carries a meaning as complex as the purpose for the registration. The proscription applies to respondents acting intentionally against competitors in the same markets regardless of the strength of the mark. It does not apply to respondents who are competitors by happenstance in a distant market.

The consequence is not merely an interruption of a complainant's business but an interference designed to have a negative impact, whether by redirecting the domain name to respondent's own website or using the website for critical commentary.[277] If the latter, there is no protection under free speech principles.[278] The rule proscribes unfair competition and deception by a registrant appropriating another's sign for its own business as well as through pretense of association with complainant's business. Respondent is benefitted whether or not it has pecuniary gain and supports

---

or Nelsonian blindness" it would be "difficult to show that a respondent has the necessary intent for bad faith. But the existence (or otherwise) of knowledge does not of itself prove intent," ***Aubert International***, supra.

[277] ***Toner Connect, L.L.C. v. Privacy Protect, LLC / Realogue Corporation***, D2018-2829 (WIPO February 21, 2019) (<tonerconnect.com>. "Given that the evidence submitted shows that Respondent's sole owner and president is a direct competitor of Complainant, it is highly likely that Mr. Steffens knowingly registered or acquired the disputed domain name based on the TONER

an actionable claim without regard to the weakness of the mark.[279] In the footnote examples LETS DRIVE and DATING DIRECT are undoubtedly weak trademarks describing in literal terms complainants' services, but respondent in the first dispute registered a domain name identical to the trademark and in the second respondent added a prefix that implicitly associates the service with the trademark owner.

The term "disruption" is unique to this provision. It denotes an intentional act by a competitor who has "registered the domain name primarily" for that purpose. Strictly speaking, disruption applies only to respondents whose conduct is directed to the "business of a competitor." It does not apply to a registrant who merely holds a position "with an interest oppositional to that of a mark holder,"[280] because if that were the case many registrants would fit the description. The Panel in the cited case is responding to earlier decisions in which panelists mistakenly extended the term "competitor" to include any party acting in opposition to complainant, including respondents whose identical or confusingly similar domain names resolve to websites containing links to complainant's competitors.[281] It does not require the domain name to resolve to an active site. Disruption is associated with parties directly in competition in the same market, niche, or specialized field.[282]

CONNECT mark and then started using the disputed domain name to gain a competitive advantage over Complainant."

278 ***Deciso Group B.V. v. Registration Private, Domains By Proxy, LLC / Jamie Thompson, Rubicon Communications dba Netgate***, D2017-1828 (WIPO November 12, 2017) (<opnsense.com>. "The Respondent invokes the fair use defence, indicating that the disputed domain name has been used for a parody website . . . [but] [t]he circumstances of the case suggest that the Respondent used the disputed domain name to discredit the Complainant's competing products and, as such, disrupt the Complainant's business and derive an indirect illegitimate commercial advantage.")

279 ***Mentor ADI Recruitment Ltd (trading as Mentor Group) v. Teaching Driving Ltd.***, 2003-0654 (WIPO September 29, 2003) (LETS DRIVE and <letsdrive.com>. Both parties are residents of the U.K. "[P]ointing . . . the Domain Name to the Respondent's competing website is evidence that it was acquired and has been used to disrupt the Complainant's business. . . . Even if, as appears from the Respondent's evidence, the Respondent has not been very successful in attracting users to its site through the Domain Name, the Panel finds on the balance of probabilities that the Domain Name was acquired and has been used for this purpose"); ***Dating Direct.com Ltd. v. Aston***, FA 593977 (Forum December 28, 2005) (DATING DIRECT and <sexdatingdirect.com>. "Respondent is appropriating Complainant's mark to lead Internet users to Respondent's dating service"); ***Toner Connect, L.L.C.*** supra.

280 ***Howard Jarvis Taxpayers Ass'n v. Paul McCauley***, D2004-0014 (WIPO April 22, 2004).

281 Violation of the Policy, but not under this paragraph: ***ACCOR v. Vista Holdings, Inc.***, D2008-0291 (WIPO April 21, 2008) (<accorhoteels.com>, typosquatting, mistyping of "hotels" is proof of abusive registration).

282 In many cases there is an overlap between 4(b)(iii) and 4(b)(iv) where "[Respondent's] use of the confusingly similar domain name . . . creates [a likelihood of] confusion as to Complainant's affiliation with the disputed domain name, allowing Respondent to use this confusion for commercial

For example, Respondent in ***Spence-Chapin Services to Families and Children***[283] used the disputed domain names, <spencechapin.biz>, and <spencechapinllc.com> to offer information about the same services complainant had offered since 1948. Respondent's act of diverting Internet visitors to its own website is evidence conclusive of the proscribed purpose. Physical location and similarity of products and services alone or combined with other factors are *prima facie* knowledge of complainant and its mark.[284]

The Panel in ***Slep-Tone Entm't*** held that the "likelihood of confusion is further increased by the fact that Respondent and [Complainant] operate within the same industry." Increased likelihood of confusion is even more apparent where the parties operate in the same territory or geographic area. In ***Harbord Real Estate***[285] Respondent operated a business within 100 meters of Complainant:

> By using complainant's name in the disputed domain name and by constructing the relevant website as he has [with meta tags, keyword sections and source code], it is as if respondent built a second entrance to his office, over which he put the sign 'Harbord Real Estate', inviting customers into the office under the pretext that they would be entering the office of Harbord Real Estate, when he knew that they would in fact be entering the office of A & J Robinson First National Real Estate. On any test, that is conduct in bad faith.

It "is not necessary to show that complainant's business was actually disrupted—only that the Respondent's primary purpose is disruption."[286] Wrongful conduct concerns both a state of mind to the extent it can be inferred from the evidence and consequences substantially certain or threatened.[287] Where the parties belong to the same highly specialized field it is "obvious" that the domain name was registered for the primary purpose of disrupting the competitor's business.[288] Where "each party's services relate to assisting job-seekers to find employment, it is apparent that Respondent registered each of the disputed domain names in order

---

gain," ***Mid America Pool Renovations, Inc. v. Robert Perry***, FA1206001451212 (Forum August 20, 2012) (INTER-GLASS and <interglass4pools.com>). In this case, the Panel made its finding under paragraph 4(b)(iv). Although there is no difference in the result the correct theory is both 4(b)(iii) and 4(b)(iv) of the Policy. Discussed further in "Identifying the Right Theory of Predation" (Sec. 6.01-A.1.b).

283 ***Spence-Chapin Services to Families and Children v. Spence-Chapin, LLC a/k/a Stanley Wynman***, FA00105945 (Forum May 6, 2002).

284 ***Slep-Tone Entm>t Corp.v. Sound Choice Disc Jockeys, Inc.***, FA 93636 (Forum March 13, 2000).

285 ***Harbord Real Estate v. Austin Robinson***, D2006-0418 (WIPO May 15, 2006).

286 ***RuggedCom, Inc. v. LANstore, Inc.***, D2005-0760 (WIPO November 15, 2005). The dispute reemerged in ***RUGGEDCOM, Inc. v. James Krachenfels***, D2009-0119 (WIPO March 31, 2009) and ***RUGGEDCOM, Inc. v. James Krachenfels***, D2009-0130 (WIPO April 7, 2009). In the second case respondent is disclosed as a senior executive of LANStore, a competitor.

287 ***Reuters Ltd. v. Teletrust IPR Ltd.***, D2000-0471 (WIPO September 8, 2000) ("[T]hreatened use is equivalent to actual use.")

to gain more internet users and to disrupt Complainant's business of providing job placement related services."[289] Another respondent admitted that he had registered the disputed domain names with "gleeful malice aforethought."[290]

What is true of famous and well-known trademarks can be equally so for weak marks. "[I]ntentional use of a competitor's mark, even a 'weak' mark, to attract, divert, or mislead the competitor's customers is not legitimate use."[291] However, outside the geographic market, niche, or specialized field,[292] the probability respondent is a competitor is less certain, particularly so for less well-known or unknown trademarks in distant jurisdictions.

The disruption contemplated in paragraph 4(b)(iii) is demonstrated by showing respondent is using complainant's mark for a proscribed purpose, either redirecting it to its own website—which "only serves as a pass-through site to the Respondent's competing website"[293]; commenting unfavorably on complainant or its goods or services[294]; or holding the domain name passively. In ***Ethnic Grocer*** Respondent registered the disputed domain name shortly after Complainant had received nationwide press coverage. A weak mark, but proof established appropriation by a competitor.

6.04-B Weak Marks Registered for Their Commercial Values 6.04-B

Paragraph 4(b)(iii) does not exclude competitors from registering similar terms. Complainant carries the burden of proof, which is heavier for generic terms and descriptive phrases confusingly similar to the mark but appropriate for respondent's business, even though competitive.[295] A weak mark registered as a domain

---

288 ***SR Motorsports v. Rotary Performance***, FA 95859 (Forum January 4, 2001) (<srmotorsports.com> and <srmotorsports.com>).

289 ***Express Servs, Inc. v. Personnel Plus a/k/a Tony Mayer***, FA 112624 (Forum June 20, 2002).

290 ***Sunlane Media v. De Cassan***, D2002-0093 (WIPO March 27, 2002)

291 ***Memorydealers.com, Inc. v. Dave Talebi***, D2004-0409 (WIPO July 20, 2004) (<memorydealer.com>) ("Respondent's unauthorized use and alteration of Complainant's graphic serves both to emphasize the illegitimate nature of Respondent's use of the descriptive term and as an admission that he was aware of Complainant's trade name when he registered the Disputed Domain Name.")

292 ***Uovo Art LLC v. Mira Hold, Mira Holdings, Inc.***, D2016-0214 (WIPO April 18, 2016) (<uovo.com>. Transportation of art objects).

293 ***EthnicGrocer.com, Inc. v. Unlimited Latin Flavors, Inc.***, FA 94385 (Forum July 7, 2000).

294 ***Realm Entertainment Limited v. mark engels / PrivacyProtect.org***, D2013-0830 (WIPO July 15, 2013) (BETS 10 and <bets10.com>. "[T]he website associated with the disputed domain name holds itself out to be an objective guide to gaming sites and states that the services provided by the Complainant at <www.bets10.com> are no longer recommended and that they recommend another online betting site. These statements strongly suggest that the Respondent has registered the disputed domain name primarily for the purpose of disrupting the business of a competitor, namely the Complainant.")

name by a competitor who plausibly denies knowledge of complainant does not forfeit the domain name because its choice is identical or confusingly similar to complainant's mark.

There is no prohibition against businesses in another market targeting the same consumers without impinging on complainant's rights.[296] A "registration of a generic top-level domain name by an existing legitimate business in one jurisdiction that is also sought after by another existing legitimate business in another jurisdiction is not evidence of an intention to disrupt the other's business."[297] If the purpose is other than disruption of a competitor the provision does not apply.[298] Non-competitor respondents whose websites contain links to competitive goods are more properly chargeable under paragraph 4(b)(ii) or (iv) of the Policy.[299] A legitimate interest may be established where a respondent has registered a domain name consisting of a dictionary term and is using it for its semantic value.[300] What a respondent cannot do is register a dictionary term with the complainant's trademark in mind.[301]

---

[295] An example would be variation of a weak mark, AUSTIN AREA BIRTHING CENTER and <austinbirthcenter.com>, ***Austin Area Birthing Center, Inc. v. Centre Vida Birth and Wellness Center c/o Faith Beltz and Family Centered Midwifery c/o June Lamphier***, FA0911001295573 (Forum January 20, 2010).

[296] ***Gigglesworld Corporation v. Mrs Jello***, D2007-1189 (WIPO November 16, 2007) (Complaint denied. Complainant sells adult novelties and sex aids in a few stores and over the Internet; it has no registered mark for "giggles." Respondent determined that the most lucrative use of <giggles.com> was a link farm in the sex category.)

[297] ***Rogers Cable Inc v. Arran Lal***, D2001-0201 (WIPO March 30, 2001) (<rogersvideo.com>, Complainant domiciled in Canada; Respondent domiciled in the Netherlands). See also "Concurrent Use of Common Lexical Strings" (Sec. 4.02-A.1.d).

[298] ***InfoSpace.com, Inc. v. Tenenbaum Ofer***, D2000-0075 (WIPO April 27, 2000) (<infospace.com>). The Panel rejected complainant's theory of bad faith under subparagraph 4(b)(iii) because "[t]here is no evidence to show that Respondent is a competitor seeking to disrupt Complainant's business." Instead, it found bad faith under 4(b)(iv).

[299] A representative example is ***Intellectual Property Holdings AS v. Sunny Nathan***, D2012-1199 (WIPO July 27, 2012) ("The Respondent has used the disputed domain name, which contains the entirety of the Complainant's AKER mark, to advertise competing goods and services to those of the Complainant, and may have attempted to impersonate the Complainant's business. Thus, it is clear to the Panel that the Respondent was fully aware of the Complainant and its marks when it selected the disputed domain name.").

[300] See ***Zerospam Security Inc. v. Internet Retail Billing, Inc., Host Master***, D2009-1276 (WIPO December 18, 2009) ("Overall, it appears to this Panel to be more likely than not that the Respondent registered the disputed domain name due to its descriptive quality, and not its trademark quality.")

[301] Respondent in ***Aspect Capital Limited v. Fluder (aka Pierre Fluder)***, D2015-0475 (WIPO April 14, 2015) failed the semantic test by coupling the dictionary term "aspect" it with a new TLD

6.05 INTENTIONALLY ATTEMPTING TO ATTRACT FOR COMMERCIAL GAIN—PARAGRAPH 4(b)(iv) OF THE POLICY 6.05

6.05-A Violating Complainant's Right by Intentionally Attempting to Attract Internet Users for Commercial Gain 6.05-A

6.05-A.1 Conduct That Violates the Policy 6.05-A.1

While it is unlawful to exploit the Internet by infringing third party rights and deceiving consumers, it is not unlawful to acquire domain names identical or confusingly similar to marks for commercial gain. It has already been established that bad faith (as the ultimate test of lawfulness) rests on the timing of domain name registrations and mark acquisitions, location of the parties, strength and reputation of mark predating registration of domain name, and content of the resolving website.

In contrast to the other circumstances of bad faith, paragraph 4(b)(iv) focuses specifically on the use to which the domain name is put rather than its registration.[302] The first three subsections of paragraph 4(b) include the phrase "you have registered" whereas 4(b)(iv) begins with the phrase "by using the domain name." The key elements are: respondent has 1) "intentionally attempted to attract," for 2) "commercial gain" by 3) directing the Internet user to an online location, thus 4) "creating a likelihood of confusion with complainant's mark" 5) "as to the source, sponsorship, affiliation, or endorsement of [that online] location, or of a product or service [at that] web site or location."

There is a fundamental difference between "confusingly similar" (found in paragraph 4(a)(i)) and the more rigorous proof demands for "likelihood of confusion." The latter is not established simply by proving the former. Either by direct or circumstantial evidence respondent must be shown to have had complainant's trademark in mind when it registered the domain name. Where the domain name postdates the mark proof of bad faith use alone may support an inference of registration in bad faith, but domain names registered before complainant has acquired its trademark are subject to an entirely different set of considerations. This is so because if the mark did not exist when respondent chose the domain name, no inference of bad faith registration can be drawn.[303]

"capital" to form <aspect.capital> that is identical to the trademark. See also ***Riverbed Technology, Inc. v. Nicholas Bonner***, FA1503001608365 (Forum April 17, 2015) (<riverbed.technology>).

302 Compare Sec. 43(a) of the Trademark Act of 1946 (Lanham Act), as amended, 15 U.S.C. §1125(a), which prohibits "any word, term, name, symbol, or device, or any combination thereof" that is "likely to cause confusion, or to cause mistake, or to deceive as to the affiliation, connection, or association of such person with another person; or as to the origin, sponsorship, or approval of his or her goods, services, or commercial activities by another person."

303 The anomaly under UDRP jurisprudence is that trademark owners can have standing to maintain proceedings but no actionable claim for cybersquatting. In contrast, the Anticybersquatting Consumer Protection Act expressly denies standing to trademarks postdating registration of domain

Where the domain name postdates the mark proof of bad faith use alone may support an inference of registration in bad faith. Domain names registered before commercial use of a trademark are subject to an entirely different set of considerations because if the mark did not exist when respondent chose the domain name no inference of bad faith registration can be drawn.

All five elements must be found. It is not bad faith to register a domain name for the purpose of attracting Internet users for commercial gain, and there is no prohibition against websites offering hyperlinks to wide categories of goods or services or diverting Internet users to another website. The violation lies in registering a domain name incorporating or varying a trademark in whole or in part that either contains hyperlinks to businesses competitive with complainant[304] or redirects consumers to respondent controlled[305] or third-party websites.[306] In this manner respondent achieves commercial gain at complainant's expense.[307] The phrase "intentionally attempted to attract" refers to conduct from which respondent's motivation may be inferred.

"Commercial gain" has been construed to mean any use of a domain name by respondent or its agent that generates revenue or equivalent value in the open market, presently if active or in the future if inactive.[308] It is broadly construed to include gain not only by respondent but also by others in the chain of revenue from the website. Paragraph 4(b)(iv) does not require the holder of the domain name to be the entity that gains commercially from the conduct. The requirement is "simply . . . that it is intended that somebody does."[309]

---

names. 15 U.S.C. § 1125(d)(1)(A)(ii)(I): "mark [had to be] is distinctive [or famous] at the time of the registration of the domain name." See *Philbrick v. Enom*, 593 F.Supp.2d 352, 375 (D. New Hampshire, 2009) (<philbricksports.com>. "Because the plaintiffs' mark is not distinctive (or famous), it is simply not entitled to protection under the ACPA.")

304 ***Zions Bancorporation v. Randall Comstock***, D2010-1095 (WIPO September 8, 2010) (<zion mortgageline.com>).

305 ***DatingDirect.com Ltd. v. Aston***, FA 593977 (Forum December 28, 2005) (<sexdatingdirect.com>. "Respondent is appropriating Complainant's mark to lead Internet users to Respondent's dating service."), citing ***Yahoo! Inc. v. Web Master***, FA 127717 (Forum November 27, 2002) (<yahgo.com>).

306 ***Excelsior College v. Super Group, LLC / Jason Morecraft***, FA1308001513832 (Forum September 26, 2013) (CPNE and <cpneworkshop>). In redirecting Internet traffic competitors infringe both 4(b)(iii) and 4(b)(iv). Competing businesses and disrupting a complainant's business are discussed further in "Disrupting Business of Competitor" (Sec. 6.04).

307 The fact that respondent uses the disputed domain name to divert Internet users to a non-competing destination does not assist it. Discussed further in "Commercial Gain Through Hyperlinking" (Sec. 6.05-B).

308 Discussed further in "Inactive or Passive Use" (Sec. 5.01-B.2).

309 ***Associated Professional Sleep Societies v. l.c./Li Chow***, D2007-0695 (WIPO July 11, 2007); ***Kmart v. Khan***, FA 127708 (Forum November 22, 2002).

The fourth element, "likelihood of confusion"—meaning consumer confusion as to the source of goods or services—is a concept familiar from trademark disputes under the Lanham Act. Likelihood of confusion increases in proportion to the strength of the trademark, but owners of weaker trademarks are no less protected if the evidence establishes violation of the Policy.[310] A trademark measured in market strength has a wider zone of protection, which makes confusion more likely. The weaker the trademark the more proof necessary to support violation.

If the proof demonstrates that more likely than not a respondent has appropriated the trademark to capitalize on its goodwill to attract Internet users to a business unrelated to complainant's—that is, "[t]here is nothing in the domain name to suggest that it is not endorsed or affiliated with Complainant"[311]—then complainant is entitled to relief. Where the trademark is well-known and the domain name includes a descriptive addition that corresponds to the goods or services offered by complainant (as opposed to an addition that describes an entirely different business[312]) it is "inconceivable that respondent registered the domain names without knowledge of complainant. . . . This assumption is supported by the fact that the disputed domain names are identical with the SGAM Marks except for the addition of 'bank' and 'banque' describing complainant's business."[313] Actual confusion is not a required element.[314] Inference of intention is read into the respondent's use of the website or its passive holding of the domain name.

---

310 Under *Polaroid Corp. v. Polarad Elec. Corp.*, 287 F.2d 492 (2d Cir. 1961) a court must evaluate 8 factors prior to finding an entity has used a trademark in such a way that would result in a likelihood of confusion in the mind of a consumer regarding the source of a product. They are: 1) the strength of the plaintiff's mark; 2) the degree of similarity between plaintiff's mark and defendant's mark; 3) the proximity of the products or services; 4) the likelihood that the plaintiff will bridge the gap; 5) evidence of actual confusion; 6) defendant's good faith in adopting the mark; 7) the quality of defendant's product or service; and 8) the sophistication of the buyers. See also *AMF Inc. v. Sleekcraft Boats*, 599 F.2d 341, 348–49 (9th Cir. 1979).

311 ***Disney Enterprises, Inc. v. Janice McSherry d/b/a Florida Vacation Homes***, FA0304000 154589 (Forum June 13, 2003) (<disneyvacationvillas.com>. See also ***Deep Foods, Inc. v. Jamruke, LLC. c/o Manish Patel***, FA0602000648190 (Forum April 10, 2006) (DEEP and <deepfood.com>, where Complainant is a leading manufacturer of Indian foods in the United States. Diverted to website that promotes unrelated goods and services).

312 Discussed further in "Non-Authorized But Lawful Use of Trademarks" (Sec. 5.01-C.2).

313 ***Société Générale Asset Management v. Dulce de Sanogueira Fontes***, D2007-0059 (WIPO March 16, 2007). Registration in bad faith was evidenced by offering the domain names and "rival trademarks" for sale; use in bad faith was evidenced by diverting traffic for click-through fees. Trademarks obtained to justify registration of domain names are consistent with abusive conduct. See "Rival Trademarks in Foreign Jurisdictions" (Sec. 4.02-A.1.c).

314 ***SAP AG v. UniSAP, Inc.***, D2009-0297 (WIPO April 28, 2009) (<unisap.com>).

6.05-A.2 6.05-A.2 Intentional Act

Only paragraph 4(b)(iv) includes the word "intention" as an element of proof—"intentionally attempted to attract." Tort law instructs that a person is considered to intend the consequences of an act whether or not he or she had a particular consequence in mind. Use is instructive because it compels examination of content that can be manipulated to support an argument of good faith even in cases of blatant infringement. Panelists have found different ways of defining the requisite proof of bad faith registration. The Panel in ***Paule Ka v. Paula Korenek***[315] asked, How is the term "intentional" to be defined? It answered the question as follows:

> a subjective test of intent (thus considered more or less as a mens rea element) would be difficult if not impossible to apply given that credibility must be assessed only on the basis of documentary evidence. It is difficult to enter the minds of the parties to determine their subjective intent.

Therefore, the proper test

> is whether the objective consequence or effect of the Respondent's conduct is to free-ride on complainant's goodwill, whether or not that was the primary (subjective) intent of the Respondent.

It is clearly evident that determining "primary (subjective) intent" is only truly achievable when infringing conduct is admitted (which respondent is unlikely to offer) and that in its absence the most persuasive evidence is based on the actual and likely consequences of use. The phrase "primary (subjective) intent" is cognate with "primary purpose" found in paragraphs 4(b)(i) and 4(b)(ii) of the Policy where infringement is discoverable indirectly through circumstantial evidence of respondent's intention in acquiring the disputed domain name. The same reasoning is applied in assessing conduct under paragraph 4(b)(iv).

Since the issue is conduct, the respondent's tax status is not a defense against infringement. A charitable organization has no greater rights than any other entity to use complainant's mark for commercial gain, because "the charitable organization is still running a business to make money."[316] The Panel in ***The Professional Golfers' Association of America*** held:

> In fact, the Panel finds that previous UDRP decisions have not recognized commercial use of a trademark by a charitable organization to be a "fair use" under the Policy at paragraph 4(c)(iii). . . . What the charitable organization does with the money after it makes it does not concern the Policy, but

---

[315] D2003-0453 (WIPO July 23, 2003).

[316] ***The Professional Golfers' Association of America (PGA) v. Provisions, LLC.***, D2004-0576 (WIPO September 13, 2004); ***Share Our Gifts Foundation, Inc. v. Freedom Bands Inc., Fan Bandz Inc a/k/a fanbanz***, D2004-1070 (WIPO March 18, 2005) ("while Respondent claims that its business is charitable, it was not until after the Complaint was filed that Respondent incorporated the not for profit foundation that is allegedly in charge of the sale of its "FREEDOMBANDSJ.")

> using complainant's trademark and identity at the disputed domain to derive income is a commercial use under the Policy, not a fair use.

Even if a respondent appears not to benefit from its actions or cause any damage, a trademark owner is entitled to control the use of its own trademark on the Internet, "including choosing whether and how domain names incorporating those trademarks resolve to particular web pages."[317] The Panel found that "Respondent caused the domain name to resolve to a selected portion of Complainant's website pertaining to online loans." It held that this constituted bad faith registration and use because it

> prevented Complainant from choosing whether to have the domain name resolve to that particular portion of the site, or indeed to that particular site at all.

The bad faith in pointing a disputed domain name to an interior page on complainant's website rests on its uninvited intrusion. It is both a cyber trespass and an acknowledgment of respondent's knowledge of complainant's trademark.

6.05-B Commercial Gain Through Hyperlinking 6.05-B

6.05-B.1 Pay-Per-Click and Link-Farm Models 6.05-B.1

Pay-per-click and link-farm models containing hyperlinks to goods and services unrelated to those offered by complainant are not *per se* illegitimate.[318] A respondent's right or legitimate interest in its choice of domain name is ultimately measured by intentions inferred from intrinsic (website content) and extrinsic evidence (strength of trademark, timing of domain name registration, etc.). Bad faith use is established when marks well known to consumers are deployed as websites regardless whether the hyperlinks redirect visitors to competitive or noncompetitive goods and services. The higher the mark on the classification scale the more difficult for respondent to establish either good faith under paragraph 4(a)(ii) or lack of bad faith under paragraph 4(a)(iii) of the Policy.

Domain names that resolve to websites offering search engine services and sponsored links to third party websites that redirect visitors to complainant's competitors[319] or without persuasive explanation offer links to websites unrelated to

---

[317] ***Ameriquest Mortgage Co v. Jason Banks***, D2003-0293 (WIPO June 6, 2003).

[318] "[P]ay per click websites are not in and of themselves unlawful or illegitimate," ***McMullen Argus Publ'g Inc. v. Moniker Privacy Servs.***, D2007-0676 (WIPO July 24, 2007). According to the Jurisprudential Overview, Paragraph 2.9: "Panels have recognized that the use of a domain name to host a page comprising PPC links would be permissible – and therefore consistent with respondent rights or legitimate interests under the UDRP – where the domain name consists of an actual dictionary word(s) or phrase and is used to host PPC links genuinely related to the dictionary meaning of the word(s) or phrase comprising the domain name, and not to trade off the complainant's (or its competitor's) trademark."

complainant's business can be evidence of abusive registration.[320] In both cases, the conduct raises a rebuttable presumption of infringement,[321] although on the ultimate issue of abusive registration complainant's burden rests on the classification of the mark, as discussed below.[322]

For the complainant, the lower the mark on the classification scale and the closer the semantic relationship of the domain name to the content of the website—for example <groceryoutlet.com> offering groceries[323] or <downundertravel.com> for travel bookings in Australia[324]—the greater the complainant's burden of proving abusive registration. The Policy is violated if the proof demonstrates an unexplained coincidence, for example of links pointing to other websites that provide services or goods similar to those offered by complainant on its own website.[325]

Redirecting Internet users to target sites containing hyperlinks and banner advertisements for goods or services competing with complainant is illegitimate.[326] This principle holds true for weak as well as strong marks as long as the evidence establishes that complainant was the target. Examples include redirecting Internet users to websites of competing organizations[327] or to another website that "promotes travel and hotel services . . . identical to the services offered by complainant."[328]

---

319 ***Mudd, LLC v. Unasi, Inc.***, D2005-0591 (WIPO September 27, 2005) ("The use of the disputed domain name for a website that shows sponsored links with the name of products competing with those of Complainant, and is used to indirectly market products of complainant's competitors, constitutes an improper use of Complainant's mark and is evidence of the Respondent's bad faith [registration and use].")

320 ***WeddingChannel.com Inc. v. Vasiliev a/k/a NA & Free Domains Parking***, FA 156716 (Forum June 12, 2003) ("Respondent use[s] the disputed domain name to redirect Internet users to websites unrelated to the WEDDING CHANNEL mark, websites where Respondent presumably receives a referral fee for each misdirected Internet user. This diversionary and commercial use of Complainant's mark is not a bona fide offering of goods or services of the disputed domain name.")

321 ***Haas Automation, Inc. v. Rodney Baker***, FA1409001578667 (Forum October 2, 2014) citing ***Victoria's Secret Stores Brand Management, Inc. v. PabloPalermao***, FA0805001191651 (Forum July 6, 2008) for the proposition that absent explanation from Respondent Panel can presume that "revenue is generated every time an Internet user clicks on a sponsored link."

322 Discussed further in "Dictionary Words and Descriptive Phrases" (Sec. 5.01-D.1).

323 ***Canned Foods, Inc. v. Ult. Search Inc.***, FA 96320 (Forum February 13, 2001).

324 ***Goway Travel Limited v. Tourism Australia***, D2006-0344 (WIPO June 6, 2006).

325 Too many examples. All major brand owners have prosecuted claims for cybersquatting that are rarely defended, and when they are—as against Bloomberg or Trump, for example—respondents' indignation is palpable.

326 ***Tercent Inc. v. Lee Yi***, FA 139720 (Forum February 10, 2003).

327 ***Edmunds.com, Inc. v. Ult. Search, Inc.***, D2001-1319 (WIPO February 1, 2002); ***Marriott International, Inc. v. Vladimir Kyznetsov***, FA95648 (Forum October 24, 2000) (<marriottrewards.com>).

However, while directing Internet visitors with hyperlinks is some evidence of bad faith it is not conclusive.[329] Panelists must draw a calibrated distinction between respondents motivated to take advantage of a complainant's trademark and those who either have a right by priority or use their websites legitimately for commercial gain. The consensus view is that a respondent is responsible for hyperlinks to websites offering goods or services competitive with those of complainant even if it did not create them.[330] The trespass is weighed against proof of respondent's motivation in registering the domain name and its explanation for the links.

Intentional linking at complainant's expense is condemned under the Policy. Hyperlinks innocently placed or unauthorized by respondent, which are removed immediately upon notice, may rebut abusive registration.[331] Establishing intent for redirecting traffic to a noncompeting site is less clear because there may be a persuasive argument for good faith registration.[332] The Panel in ***Shirmax*** noted:

> use on the web merely for the purpose of redirecting visitors to a different site constitutes a legitimate fair use, as long as this use is not misleading to consumers and does not tarnish a trademark.

"Because the disputed domain name uses a common term, the fact that it redirects Internet users to other third party websites is not a *per se* illegitimate use by Respondent".[333] "Pay-per-click" advertising is perfectly legitimate if the registration is in good faith,[334] but "redirection occur[ing] as a result of a 'mistake' by 'a programmer' lacks credibility."[335]

---

328 *Id.* ***Marriott International.*** Also, ***Netwizards, Inc. v. Spectrum Enterprises***, D2000-1768 (WIPO April 4, 2001).

329 ***4355768 Canada Inc. v. PrivacyProtect.org / Jambo Silver***, D2013-1225 (WIPO October 2, 2013).

330 Discussed further in "Populating Web Pages: The 'Not Me' Defense" (Sec. 6.05-F).

331 Indeed, the proof may support a finding under paragraph 4(c)(I) of the Policy, in which case the hyperlinking is inconsequential. See ***Hershey Chocolate & Confectionery Corporation v. Raymond Mah***, D2010-1151 (WIPO August 31, 2010): "[Since] the for profit use made of the disputed domain name was clearly neither intended nor authorized by respondent [and since upon his being put] 'on notice' of such use [he] took effective steps to ensure [cessation] of that use" it is not evidence of bad faith. "Indeed, had complainant made contact with respondent before initiating the Complaint in this administrative proceeding, the Panel considers it highly unlikely that complainant would have proceeded with it provided respondent agreed to take the action (which he, in fact, did) to have the unauthorized website taken down."

332 ***Shirmax Retail Ltd / dataillants Shirmax Lted v. CES marketing group Inc.***, AF-0104 (March 20, 2000).

333 ***Ace Cash Express, Inc. v. R9 DomainGuard Proxy Service***, FA0710001095275 (Forum February 21, 2008) (<ace.net>).

334 ***Plan.Net Concept Specialagentur fur interactive Kommunikation GmbH v. Murat Yikilmaz***, D2006-0082 (WIPO March 24, 2006) (<plan.net>, "a very plain English word plus a gTLD").

Redirecting Internet users to an interior page of complainant's own website is an abusive act because it creates an impression of association. It also interferes with a complainant's control over its website: "Generally, such an owner of rights should be able to control how such trademarks, names and indicia are used in the course of trade and when so used to control who is directed to its website and by whom."[336] Moreover, (the same Panel holds):

> [in] the absence of explanation in this case, it is found that an unconnected party [that is, a party not connected to the trademark owner] has no right or legitimate interest to use an otherwise deceptive trademark, name or indicia to redirect Internet traffic, even if it is directed to the legitimate owner of the trademark, name or indicia and provider of the services.

Proof that paragraphs 4(b)(iv) and 4(a)(iii) of the Policy have been violated can be satisfied even where respondent claims to take no active part in redirecting traffic to advertising hyperlinks. The registrar's act in populating the website is imputed to the respondent.[337]

6.05-B.2

6.05-B.2 Redirection by Competitor to Its Own Website

There is a distinction between lawful hyperlinking models discussed above that use dictionary words and descriptive phrases to attract Internet users to their websites[338] and models based on appropriating complainants' marks that registrants use to redirect to their own or others' websites for competitive goods or services[339] or for goods or services unrelated to complainant's business[340] or register domain names in different extensions in pretense of the mark owner.[341] "Any intentional use of a

---

335 ***Miss Universe L.P., LLLP v. Andre Miron***, D2013-0628 (WIPO May 27, 2013) (Respondent appeared).

336 ***Altavista Company v. Brunosousa, aka Bruno Sousa***, D2002-0109 (WIPO April 3, 2002). ("This redirection [from <altavistasoftware.com> to Complainant's website] seems to be a seamless one and it is hard to see how the Respondent presently benefits from the situation. It is contended by the Complainant that such redirection will allow the Respondent to divert future users to competing web sites after having built up mistaken confidence in the source of the content at "www.altavista-software.com" on the part of consumers.")

337 Discussed further in "Populating Web Pages: The 'Not Me' Defense" (Sec. 6.05-F).

338 ***ETH Zürich (Eidgenössische Technische Hochschule Zürich) v. Andre Luiz Silva Rocha, Construtora Norberto Odebrecht S/A***, D2016-0444 (WIPO April 18, 2016) (<eth.com>. "The redirection of web traffic aimed at the Disputed Domain Name to another website is itself use – whether it is legitimate or not is a different issue. In the present case the redirection following a change of corporate name to a website relating to the new corporate name seems entirely legitimate.")

339 See ***VIA VAREJO S/A, v. Domain Admin***, D2015-1304 (WIPO October 17, 2015) (<casas ahia.com>. Transferred). Respondent's subsequent ACPA action determined in favor of mark owner. *Direct Niche, LLC v. Via Varejo S/A*, 15-cv-62344 (S.D. Fla., August 10, 2017) ("It is clear to the Court that Direct Niche intended to profit from prospective Via Varejo customers who are unaware that Via Varejo's Casas Bahia website is found, not at *casasbahia.com*, but at *casasbahia.com.br*.")

[complainant's] mark, even a 'weak' mark, to attract, divert, or mislead the [complainant's] customers is not legitimate use."[342]

It is not the act of redirecting that is actionable, but the purpose as established by the use. Respondent in ***Summit Group*** boosted traffic by redirecting consumers to its competing website. Respondent in ***Thrifty*** argued that the domain name registrations could not have been abusive because their use "generates business for Complainants' licensees." However, adding adverbial or adjectival qualifiers to complainants' marks to attract visitors heightens the "likelihood of confusion" that respondents are associated with complainants, thence acquired to injure them[343] or commit fraud on consumers and the public generally as earlier described in "Spoofing and Phishing" (Sec. 6.01-C.2.c).

6.05-C Commercial Gain from Tarnishment 6.05-C

6.05-C.1 Pointing to Adult Oriented Website 6.05-C.1

Pointing to adult oriented websites is actionable where use of the domain name targets complainant's trademark;[344] but the paragraph 4(c)(i) defense is available when supported by the evidence, for reasons described in the next section.[345]

---

340 ***T-Mobile USA, Inc. v. utahhealth***, FA 697821 (Forum June 7, 2006) (holding that "the registration and use of a domain name confusingly similar to a complainant's mark to direct Internet traffic to a commercial 'links page' in order to profit from click-through fees or other revenue sources constitutes bad faith under Policy ¶ 4(b)(iv) "); ***Dana Bissett v. Above.com Domain Privacy***, FA1609001693416 (Forum October 27, 2017) (<wonderforest.com>. Abusive registration can be found even where the hyperlinks are to goods or services unrelated to Complainant's business).

341 See for example, ***Thrifty, Inc. and Thrifty Rent-a-Car System, Inc. v. Airportparking lots. com***, FA0211000129123 (Forum January 2, 2003) (Diverting <thriftyairportparking.com> and <thriftyvaletairportparking.com> to <airportparkinglots.com>); ***Ashley Furniture Industries, Inc. v. domain admin / private registrations aktien gesellschaft***, FA1506001626253 (Forum July 29, 2015) ("Respondent is using the disputed domain name to resolve to a web page containing advertising links to products that compete with those of Complainant"); ***Mavenvista Technologies Pvt. Ltd. v. IT Comms, Ariba, Inc.***, D2017-1130 (WIPO July 19, 2017) (<futureofprocurement.com>. "The Complainant's evidence, uncontested, shows the disputed domain name to have resolved to the Respondent's website "www.ariba.com", which refers to business services similar to the Complainant's."). Discussed further in "Disrupting Business of Competitor."

342 ***Memorydealers.com, Inc. v. Dave Talebi***, D2004-0409 (WIPO July 20, 2004) (MEMORY DEALERS and <memorydealer.com>); ***Summit Group, LLC v. LSO, Ltd.***, FA 758981 (Forum September 14, 2006) (LIFESTYLE LOUNGE and <lifestylelounge-travel.com>; ***Life Extension Foundation, Inc. v. PHD Prime Health Direct Limited***, FA0910001289603 (Forum November 25, 2009) (LIFE EXTENSION FOUNDATION and <lifeextensionfoundation.com>).

343 ***PCM, Inc. v. Elio Nager / Domain Privacy Service***, D2013-0894 (WIPO August 2, 2013) (PC MALL and <pcmallonline.com>. "Respondent also lists Complainant's business address under the 'Terms and Conditions' on the Domain Name website, and provides a link to Complainant's privacy policy, without authorization."). See also ***Excelsior College v. Super Group, LLC / Jason Morecraft***, FA1308001513832 (Forum September 26, 2013) (CPNE and <cpneworkshop>).

Redirecting a domain name to pornography is said to tarnish complainant's mark by "associating it with things that dilute or damage its commercial value."[346] Although the term "tarnish" is found only in paragraph 4(c)(iii)[347] as an element that if present negates a claim of fair use, it is nevertheless implicit in paragraph 4(b)(iv) of the Policy, which (in contrast to the other three circumstances of bad faith) focuses on respondent's use of the domain name.[348]

Tarnish refers to uses that affect the reputation of the trademark owner by linking unsavory images or information[349] "to an otherwise wholesome mark."[350] Co-opting complainant's mark for a sexually explicit website, especially where complainant's mark has been associated with household marketing,[351] entertainment personalities,[352] or children's entertainment services[353] are instances of *per se* bad

---

344 ***Nokia Corporation v. Nokiagirls.com a.k.a IBCC***, D2000-0102 (WIPO April 18, 2000) (NOKIA and <nokiagirls.com>. "In the opinion of the Administrative Panel, [the average visitor would view the content as adult oriented and this] constitutes an aggravating element in the assessment of the bad faith.")

345 ***Instalaciones De Domótica, Electricidad y Telecomunicaciones, S.L. v. Shen Zhe***, D2017-2561 (WIPO February 19, 2018) (<ideltec.com>. "[W]hat the Policy condemns is not all pornography sites but misappropriation of another's trademark intentionally to attract unsuspecting Internet users to the site.")

346 ***Bulmers Ltd. and Wm. Magner Ltd. v. (FAST-12785240) magnersessions.com 1,500 GB Space and 15,000 Monthly Bandwidth, Bluehost.Corn INC/Jason LaValla***, D2010-1885 (WIPO January 17, 2011) (This particular case did not involve an adult oriented website and the Panel found Respondent registered the domain name in good faith.)

347 Paragraph 4(c)(iii) reads: "[Y]ou are making a legitimate noncommercial or fair use of the domain name, without intent for commercial gain to misleadingly divert consumers or to tarnish the trademark or service mark at issue."

348 *Nokia, supra.*; ***Mattel, Inc. v. domainsforsalenow@hotmail.com***, FA 187609 (Forum October 6, 2003) (<barbieporn.net>. "Respondent has merely added the descriptive word 'porn' to Complainant's registered BARBIE mark, and the addition of this word does not create a notable distinction between Complainant's mark and the domain name currently in dispute."); ***Arla Foods amba v. Cirtex Corp.***, D2011-1143 (WIPO September 27, 2011) (BUKO and <bukoporn.com>). See also ***Wells Fargo & Co. v. Party Night Inc.***, FA 144647 (Forum March 18, 2003) where Respondent registered several typosquatting domain names that did not include the word "porn" and redirected them to adult oriented websites.

349 See also ***Howard Jarvis Taxpayers Association v. Paul McCauley***, D2004-0014 (WIPO April 22, 2004). Tarnishment is discussed further in "Appropriating Complainant's Trademark for Noncommercial or Fair Use and Free Speech" (Sec. 5.04-A).

350 ***Britannia Building Society v. Britannia Fraud Prevention***, D2001-0505 (WIPO July 6, 2001) (distinguishing bad faith use and "fair use criticism [which] even if libelous, does not constitute tarnishment and is not prohibited by the Policy.")

351 ***Williams Sonoma, Inc. dba Pottery Barn Kids v. Ed Domains***, D2004-0640 (WIPO October 8, 2004) (<potterybarnkid.com>, redirecting users to "sites containing erotic or sexual material.")

352 ***Kidman v. Zuccarini***, D2000-1415 (WIPO January 23, 2001) (<nicolekidmannude.com>).

353 ***William H. Cosby, Jr. v. Sterling Davenport***, D2005-0756 (WIPO August 30, 2005).

faith. ICANN emphasized in its implementation report that tarnishment does not apply to instances of fair use, but is "limited to acts done with intent to commercially gain."[354]

Condemnation is directed at respondents who divert Internet users to offending websites by fostering the belief that the domain names belong to, are associated with or sponsored by complainants. "[I]t is well-known that pornographers rely on misleading domain names to attract users by confusion, in order to generate revenue from click-through advertising, mouse-trapping and other pernicious online marketing techniques"[355]; linking unsuspecting Internet traffic to an adult oriented website containing images of scantily clad women in provocative poses does not constitute a connection with a *bona fide* offering of goods or services or a noncommercial or fair use.[356] "Where a disputed domain name directs a user to a pornographic website, a UDRP panel may infer an intention that the domain name was registered and used in bad faith."[357] The same principles apply in relation to the promotion of "escort and 'erotic pleasure' services."[358]

The Panel in ***Sound Unseen*** held:

> [B]ad faith under the Policy may very well arise where a domain name, which infringes on the mark of another by virtue of being identical or confusingly similar to that mark, is used by a respondent as an instrumentality to intentionally link and direct unsuspecting users, who seek information on a good or service associated with that mark, to a pornographic site instead. In such instances, those users would not be exposed to a respondent's pornographic content but for that linkage.

"[W]hatever the motivation of Respondent, the diversion of the domain names to an adult oriented site is itself certainly consistent with the finding that the Domain Name was registered and is being used in bad faith."[359]

---

[354] Second Staff Report, October 24, 2009, footnote 2: "Several commentators indicated that the concept of 'tarnishment' in paragraph 4(c)(iii) might be misunderstood by those not familiar with [U.S.] law or might otherwise be applied inappropriately to noncommercial uses of parody names and the like. Staff is not convinced this is the case, but in any event wishes to point out that 'tarnishment' in paragraph 4(c)(iii) is limited to acts done with intent to commercially gain."

[355] ***National Association of Stock Car Auto Racing, Inc. v. RMG Inc.- BUY Lease by E-MAIL***, D2001-1387 (WIPO January 23, 2002).

[356] ***Isleworth Land Co. v. Lost In Space, SA***, FA 117330 (Forum September 27, 2002).

[357] ***Sound Unseen, Ltd.; Apple Bottoms, LLC; and Cornell Haynes p/k/a "Nelly" v. Patrick Vanderhorst***, D2005-0636 (WIPO August 18, 2005) (<missapplebottom.com>, <missapplebottoms.com>, <msapplebottom.com> and <msapplebottoms.com>).

[358] ***Sonja Junkers v. Domain Admin, Whois Privacy Corp.*** D2017-0836 (WIPO June 28, 2017) (<sonjajunkers.com>).

[359] ***Six Continents Hotels, Inc. v. Nowak***, D2003-0022 (WIPO Mar. 4, 2003) (<holidayinnakron.com> linked to an adult oriented website,); ***Alpha One Foundation, Inc. v. Alexander Morozov***, FA0608000766380 (Forum September 20, 2006).

The consensus is illustrated further in two cases involving the trademark CHRISTIAN DIOR.[360] The "essence of bad faith in cases such as this lies in the capacity of the confusingly similar domain name to tarnish the relevant mark" (***Farley***). Farley's defense in the "Anna Dior" case is that it is the name by which the dominatrix is commonly known. She "offers bondage, discipline and sado masochism services . . . to customers in the San Francisco Bay and Washington D.C. areas of the United States." However, "Anna Dior" is not the respondent and it is not her domain name or website. In fact there is a question as to whether "Anna Dior" or "Ms. Anna" (as Respondent Farley styles her) is invented to direct Internet users to adult sites on which she is featured.

The Respondent Zournas in the other case asserts in his answer that "Complainant has no greater right or legitimate interest in the name 'Chloe Dior' [an alleged stage name] than respondent himself [who admittedly is not 'Chloe Dior']." This is premised on the fact that "Dior" is a common surname. He claimed to have registered the domain name to operate a fan website, but Chloe Dior makes no appearance on the website that contains links going to "unrelated adult content."

The question in these cases is whether respondents had complainants or their trademarks in mind when they registered the domain names. Targeting increases in certainty where the dominant word is joined by a generic. It decreases where the dominant word is itself generic.[361] The intent to profit from the reputation of the trademark is manifest in the choice. The magnet in the domain name is "Dior," not "Anna" or "Chloe." Combining the two words increases the likelihood that respondent is using the famous mark to attract Internet traffic. "There is no suggestion anywhere in the evidence that the word 'Dior' would have meaning to the great majority of Internet users, other than as a reference to complainant's DIOR mark." Migration of adult content to the .xxx gTLD does not absolve respondent of bad faith where the evidence condemns the registration.

6.05-C.2 6.05-C.2 Adult Oriented Website, Legitimate Use

It is clear that where there is intention to trade on complainant's reputation respondent loses, but without intention pornographic content may constitute a *bona fide* offering of goods or services.[362] A domain name is not condemned for the

---

[360] ***CHRISTIAN DIOR COUTURE v. Paul Farley***, D2008-0008 (WIPO February 2, 2008) (<anna-dior.com>. Transferred); ***Christian Dior Couture & Chloé v. Konstantinos Zournas***, D2008-1440 (WIPO December 22, 2008) (<chloedior.com>. Transferred).

[361] ***SIX Group AG v. Xedoc Holding SA***, D2012-1548 (WIPO October 11, 2012) (<six.com>. "Complainant's offer [to purchase the domain name] was unsolicited and anonymous and made no reference to any trade mark rights.")

[362] See Jurisprudential Overview 3.0, Paragraph 3.12: "Noting that [while] noncommercial fair use without intent to tarnish a complainant's mark is a defense under the second element, using a

content it offers if the respondent has rights or legitimate interests in the domain name or its registration was not in bad faith.

The consensus is that "adult sex sites are perfectly legal and constitute *bona fide* offerings of goods or services."[363] Unless there is evidence of deliberate intention to take advantage of complainant's mark linking is not evidence of bad faith. "[T]he linking of the domain name to a pornographic site is no different to the use of the domain name in connection with any other service offering."[364] One test is whether respondent has a history of abusive registration, and another the likelihood of its having knowledge of complainant or its mark.[365]

The factual circumstances in ***Sound Unseen*** referred to earlier supported bad faith, but the Panel underlined the point that "display of pornographic imagery on a web page . . . no matter how offensive, repulsive or antithetical to contemporary society mores—and some of Respondent's imagery certainly falls within that rubric—does not as such constitute bad faith under the Policy." This view assumes respondent registered the domain name before complainant's acquisition of its trademark,[366] or that it is the name by which respondent was "commonly known,"[367] or the domain name is composed of common words suggestive of the use to which it is being put. This last possibility is illustrated by <porntrumps.com>: "porn + trumps" is not "Trump + porn."[368]

---

domain name to tarnish a complainant's mark (e.g., by posting false or defamatory content, including for commercial purposes) may constitute evidence of a respondent's bad faith." See ***Instalaciones De Domótica, Electricidad y Telecomunicaciones, S.L.*** *supra.* ("In the Respondent's favor, nothing in the record or a quick search by the Panel reveals any other circumstance that the Respondent has engaged in similar conduct.")

[363] ***Motorola, Inc. v. NewGate Internet, Inc.***, D2000-0079 (WIPO April 20, 2000).

[364] ***The Perfect Potion v. Domain Administrator***, D2004-0743 (WIPO November 6, 2004). (Panels are "consistent in calling for evidence of a deliberate intention on the part of the respondent to ride on the back of the complainant's goodwill/trademark and that on this point the linking of the domain name to a pornographic site is no different to the use of the domain name in connection with any other service offering"); ***Knud Jepsen A/S v. Rick Schwartz, Virtual Dates Inc.***, D2017-0679 (WIPO June 20, 2017) (<queen.com>. "Where a domain name registrant tries to obtain financial gain by registering and using a non-generic domain name in which it has no rights or legitimate interests, the offering of adult content may be evidence of bad faith use, However, as the Disputed Domain Name [in this case, 'queen'] has a dictionary meaning, those cases do not apply.")

[365] Paragraph 4(c)(iii) reads: "[Y]ou are making a legitimate noncommercial or fair use of the domain name, without intent for commercial gain to misleadingly divert consumers or to tarnish the trademark or service mark at issue."

[366] ***G.W.H.C.-Serviços Online Ltda., E Commerce Media Group Informação e Tecnologia Ltda. v. eRealEstate.com***, D2012-0498 (WIPO May 31, 2012) (14 years. <saveme.com>).

[367] ***CHRISTIAN DIOR COUTURE v. Kianna Dior Productions***, D2009-0353 (WIPO May 24, 2009). Respondent defended herself "as an individual, business, or other organization) [that] has been commonly known by the domain name." See "What it Means to Be 'Commonly Known By The Domain Name'" (Sec. 5.03-A).

6.05-D 6.05-D Forming a Domain Name by Incorporating Complainant's Trademark Plus an Additional Term

6.05-D.1 6.05-D.1 When the Additional Term Leads Back to the Trademark

Domain names composed of trademarks or close variants plus qualifying parts of speech that either personalize the brand—<**your**valium.com>, <**my**easyjet.com>—or suggest an association with the complainant—<sap-**cloud**.com>, <**us**weekend.com>, <tmobile**shops**.com>—are *prima facie* evidence of abusive registration. When marks are well-known or famous, appropriating them as dominant elements of domain names signals implicit knowledge of them,[369] therefore cannot be defended regardless of use. In fact, they are rarely defended unless there is persuasive proof for nominative fair use—<sap**userlist**.com>, <nascar**tours**.com> or fair use comment or criticism.

Additions which summon up complainant's rather than respondent's business "merely compound the confusion created by the incorporation of complainant's trademark."[370] If the underlying mark is one that would be recognized by consumers and Internet users as distinguishing the goods or services of one enterprise from another[371] any addition will be found confusingly similar to the trademark and support both elements of bad faith. A well-known or famous trademark incorporated into a domain name increases respondent's burden "to express himself . . . by responding to communications and/or indicating a good faith use of the domain name."[372]

---

368 ***Donald J. Trump and Trump Hotel & Casino Resorts, Inc. v. olegevtushenko a/k/a Oleg Evtushenko***, FA0110000101509 (Forum December 11, 2001).

369 ***Gateway, Inc. v. Bellgr, Inc.***, D2000-0129 (WIPO) ("lamps" added to trademark EAUTO); ***Kmart of Mich., Inc. v. Cone***, FA 655014 (Forum April 25, 2006) (<kmart-cameras.net>). See also ***De Beers Intangibles Limited v. Ivetta Mavrova***, D2016-1466 (WIPO August 30, 2016) ("[I]t has been held in many UDRP decisions and has become a consensus view among panelists that the addition of a generic or descriptive term or geographic wording to a trademark in a domain name is normally insufficient in itself to avoid the finding of confusing similarity under the first element of the UDRP.")

370 ***Fairmont Hotel Management L.P. v. Puts***, D2001-0431 (WIPO May 17, 2001), in which Respondent added the words "hotel" and "resort" (<fairmonthotels.com> and <fairmont-resort.com>).

371 ***General Electric Company v. FORDDIRECT.COM, INC.***, D2000-0394 (WIPO June 22, 2000) (<gecapitaldirect>).

372 The Panel makes this observation in ***Sanofi Aventis v. Davie Kearney***, D2006-0861 (WIPO August 21, 2006) with respect to famous marks in the pharmaceutical industry. It also suggests more generally that a respondent has a final opportunity to rebut the accusation of bad faith. For example, respondents in ***Pfizer Inc. v. Van Robichaux***, D2003-0399 (WIPO July 16, 2003) (U.S parties) (Complaint denied, LIPITOR and <lipitorinfo.com>); and ***Amylin Pharmaceuticals, Inc. v. Watts Guerra Craft LLP.***, D2012-0486 (WIPO April 29, 2012) in which Respondents offered sufficient

Domain names incorporating trademarks + common words,[373] geographic designations,[374] legal terms,[375] and associated concepts that "strongly lead [ ] an average Internet user back to a complainant's trademark"[376] have been found to violate paragraph 4(b)(iv) of the Policy. Registrant's choice of domain name is not legitimized by using a different gTLD from that which the trademark owner utilizes for its site, registering a ".net" where the trademark owner has a ".com" and ".org."[377] The Panel in ***MSNBC Cable*** held

> [T]o permit a party . . . unrelated to a trademark owner (or its licensee), to incorporate its trademark as a formative element of a[n] URL [but with a different gTLD] imposes a duty not only on this Panel, but also others like it, to remain ever vigilant against such intrusions on trademark rights—intrusions that, if not thwarted in their infancy, would only intensify as additional gTLDs become available, to the detriment of trademark holders and their licensees, and certainly to Internet users.

Simply adding "www"[378] or "e"[379] as prefix to the second level domain violates the Policy. Parts of speech added to the trademark run afoul of the Policy when specific to well-known trademarks,[380] but not in combination with common words where the name is consonant with use.[381]

---

evidence of their intentions to rebut complainants' claims they lacked rights or legitimate interests in the domain names.

[373] ***General Electric***, supra.

[374] ***BP p.l.c. v. Kang Sungkun Portraits Production***, D2001-1097 (WIPO November 14, 2001) (<bpjapan.com>); ***Red Bull GmbH v. Chai***, D2003-0709 (WIPO November 11, 2003) (<thairedbull.com>, "Thailand"); ***Apple Inc. v. David Shaban***, D2012-1176 (WIPO August 7, 2012) (<asiaapple.com>).

[375] ***American International Group, Inc. v. Bruce Levin***, FA0511000591254 (Forum December 21, 2005 (<aigcomplaints.com>, <aiglawsuits.com>, <aigcomplaint.com>, <aigclassaction.com>, <aigclassactionlawsuit.com>, <aiginvestigation.com>, <aigfrauds.com> and <aiglitigation.com>).

[376] ***Enterprise Rent-a-Car Co. v. Richard Lanoszka a/k/a Silent Register***, FA 1242244 (Forum February 25, 2009).

[377] ***Awesome Kids LLC and/or Awesome Kids L.L.C. v. Selavy Communications***, D2001-0210 (WIPO April 16, 2001) (<awesomekids.net>), citing ***MSNBC Cable, LLC v. Tysys.com***, D2000-1204 (WIPO December 8, 2000).

[378] ***Reuters Limited v. Global Net 2000, Inc.***, D2000-0441 (WIPO July 13, 2000) (<wwwreuters.com>).

[379] ***Canadian Tire Corp. v. 849075 Alberta Ltd.***, D2000-0985 (WIPO October 19, 2000) (<ecanadiantire.com> and <e-canadiantire.com>).

[380] ***ESPN, Inc. v. MySportCenter.com***, FA 95326 (Forum September 5, 2000) (SPORTSCENTER and <mysportscenter.com>). ***Air France v. Kitchkulture***, D2002-0158 (WIPO May 9, 2002) (AIR FRANCE and <my-airfrance.com>); ***Sony Kabushiki Kaisha also trading as Sony Corporation v. Sin, Eonmok***, D2000-1007 (WIPO November 16, 2000) (SONY and <mysony.com>); ***PC2Call Limited v. Bernard Ferrie***, FA 0112000103181 (Forum February 21, 2002) (PC2CALL and <mypc2call.com>).

6.05-D.2

6.05-D.2 When the Additional Term is Added to a Weak Trademark

When the additional term is added to a weak trademark complainant is put on the defensive, even where the right allegedly infringed passes the jurisdictional threshold and complainant is successful on its *prima facie* case (paragraph 4(a)(ii) of the Policy). The general rule is that a complainant has exclusive rights to the trademark, but they are unenforceable without proof respondent registered the domain name to "divert and redirect Internet users away from complainant."[382]

A generic term added to a trademark composed of common words which creates or suggests a new association distinct from complainant is neither similar nor confusing in a trademark sense.[383] Although DINERS is well-known for credit card services, it is "technically a weak trademark as it is wholly comprised of a common dictionary term having descriptive value apart from its trademark usage." The Panel also points out that "[t]here are many benign uses of the word DINERS that do not conflict with Complainant's trademark rights."

Complainant in ***Marriott International***[384] argued that "[t]he addition of a dictionary term to a trademark ['avalon' meaning an 'island'] does not make the disputed domain name [<avalon-courtyard.com>] substantially different to the mark." This is true as a general proposition, and while sufficient for jurisdiction in this case was not sufficient to overcome Respondent's right based on a registered trademark for AVALON in India for accommodation services under the name "Avalon Courtyard." This is because "Complainant's mark is comprised of a common dictionary term which might have any number of associations not connected with the Complainant."

---

381 ***Southwest Airlines Co. v. Cattitude a/k/a LJ Gehman***, D2005-0410 (WIPO June 12, 2005) (SOUTHWEST and <mysouthwest.com>); ***National Grid Electricity Transmission Plc, NGrid Intellectual Property Limited v. Re Tron Technologies***, D2013-0925 (WIPO July 11, 2013) (NATIONAL GRID and <mygridpower.com> and <mygridstore.com>. The domain names "incorporate only the 'grid' element of the Complainant's trade marks. . . . The term 'grid' (on its own) is a generic, non-distinctive term, which is not associated exclusively with the Complainant's business.")

382 "In a case where the proposed mark consists of a combination of highly descriptive terms, a party seeking to establish exclusive rights carries a heavy burden of proof in removing those terms from the public domain," ***Bar Code Discount Warehouse, Inc. v. Barcodes, Inc., dba Barcode Discount and Dan Reynolds***, D2001-0405 (WIPO July 27, 2001).

383 ***Diners Club International Ltd. v. Mark Jenkins***, FA0906001266752 (Forum July 27, 2009) (<contactdiners.com> complaint denied. Respondent stated that it "also owns the URLs <ContactShoppers.com>, ContactTourists, and ContactGolfers, to name a few, for which he is developing websites. Respondent also owns the URL <ContactArkansas.com>, among others, all of which I am developing to support an electronic newsletter service for merchants. There is nothing 'generic' about the term 'Contact' as it relates to my business.")

384 ***Marriott International Inc. and Marriott Worldwide Corporation v. Avalon Resorts Pvt. Ltd.***, D2010-0172 (WIPO March 22, 2010) (COURTYARD and <avaloncourtyard.com>).

Respondent in ***Atlantic Station***[385] added "condo" to form <atlanticstation-condo.com>. Complainant is in the real estate development and sales business. "As such, the addition of the word 'condo' does not create a meaningful distinction," and the domain name is confusingly similar to complainant's trademark. Complainant argued that respondent was a competitor motivated to divert and redirect Internet users to its own website. Ordinarily, this would be dispositive in complainant's favor except that its mark is generic as a geographic location.[386] In concluding that respondent had a legitimate interest in the disputed domain name the Panel stated it was "swayed by the absence of a reasonable alternative available to Respondent to accurately reflect in a domain name his connection to the physical place known as 'Atlantic Station.'"

A domain name composed of common terms violates a trademark owner's rights if it is used in a manner that suggests an association reserved to the owner, but it cannot preclude uses that create different associations. In ***Austin Area Birthing Center***[387] complainant owned AUSTIN AREA BIRTHING CENTER and alleged abusive registration of a domain name that incorporated "Austin Area" but substituted "midwife" for "birthing center." While "birthing" and "midwife" suggest similar services <austinareamidwife.com> does not create any unequivocal association with Complainant. "Birthing includes activities other than those provided by midwives."

This reasoning is equally applicable to famous designer initials. "LV" could stand for Louis Vuitton, as complainant alleges in ***Louis Vuitton***[388] but to others it could be the ISO country code for Latvia; or, as found in an earlier case by the same Complainant it could be Las Vegas.[389] Since there are multiple registrations for LV on the Principal Register it would be difficult for Complainant to prove that LV on its own is associated only with its goods.

Although not inconceivable that the incorporation of "lv" to form the domain name <lvmobile.com> may in fact be a trademark infringement, it is not an abusive registration because "the combination [lv and mobile] does not clearly and obviously associate to complainant." Whatever the truth may be, "an Internet user seeing the domain name <lvmobile.com> is more likely to expect to find information on

---

[385] ***Atlantic Station, LLC v. Dargan Burns III***, FA0903001250592 (Forum April 26, 2009).

[386] Respondent "provide[d] examples of newspaper articles that make reference to this place and . . . envelopes cancelled by the US Post Office exhibiting in the address 'Atlantic Station' in the spot reserved for the city identifier."

[387] ***Austin Area Birthing Center, Inc. v. CentreVida Birth and Wellness Center c/o Faith Beltz and Family Centered Midwifery c/o June Lamphier***, FA0911001295573 (Forum January 20, 2010).

[388] ***Louis Vuitton Malletier S.A. v. Demand Domains, Inc.***, FA1003001310816 (Forum April 14, 2010).

[389] ***Louis Vuitton Malletier S.A. v. Manifest Information Services c/o Manifest Hostmaster***, FA0609000796276 (Forum November 7, 2006) (<lv.com>).

Latvian mobile phones on the connecting site than the fashion goods/luxury accessories of complainant." While

> adding generic terms associated with a certain trademark will add to the risk of confusion . . . [a]dding a generic term that associate[s] with specific goods or services completely non related to the trademark, and especially when such trademark is not unique but having different generic meanings apart from being someone's registered mark, may on the other hand reduce the risk of confusion.

It is not that complainant's iterated "lv"design on its fashion products is not instantly recognizable to the public; the problem is that it has no plain LV registered in the Class that includes mobile phones. However, this does not foreclose an action for trademark infringement under trademark law if the evidence leads in that direction.

6.05-E 6.05-E Letter and Word Ordering and Reordering

6.05-E.1 6.05-E.1 Typosquatting

6.05-E.1.a 6.05-E.1.a *Implicit Knowledge of Mark*

Typosquatting is defined as the "intentional misspelling of words with intent to intercept and siphon off traffic from its intended destination, by preying on Internauts who make common typing errors."[390] Ordinarily, typosquatting domain names involves fractional changes to trademarks—examples are "leauge" as in <minorleaugebaseball.com> (reversal of letter) and "jounal" as in <wallstreetjounal.com> (omission of letter). Where intent to take advantage of the trademark is evident knowledge is implied. "Typosquatting" (the Panel continued) "is inherently parasitic." *De minimis* changes "immediately raise[ ] suspicions and call[ ] for an explanation."[391]

There is no legal support for the proposition that "I have just as much right to own the Domain Names as the person who owns the correct spelling of . . . wallstreet journal.com has."[392] Respondents of misspelled domain names are not excused on the theory that the words they misspell are common or generic terms. While it is true that not all that is similar is confusing—single letter differences can create distinguishable terms as illustrated below in "Small Differences Matter"—misspellings (that are not distinguishable terms) call attention to themselves,

---

[390] ***Nat'l Ass'n of Prof'l Baseball League, Inc. v. Zuccarini***, D2002-1011 (WIPO January 21, 2003). See WIPO Overview 2.0, Paragraph 1.10: "Consensus view: A domain name which contains a common or obvious misspelling of a trademark normally will be found to be confusingly similar to such trademark, where the misspelled trademark remains the dominant or principal component of the domain name." Jurisprudential Overview 3.0, Paragraph 1.9 revises this slightly to read: "A domain name which consists of a common, obvious, or intentional misspelling of a trademark is considered by panels to be confusingly similar to the relevant mark for purposes of the first element."

[391] ***CareerBuilderLC v, L. Azra Kha***, D2003-0493 (WIPO August 5, 2003).

although a persuasive case has been made for misspelling where the registration has an explainable purpose that is demonstrably without intention to take advantage of the trademark.[393]

Where the variation of spelling is within the word it "create[s] a difference without a distinction and indeed with the intention of creating confusion rather than removing it."[394] The proscribed practice encompasses cases in which alterations neither "change[ ] the meaning or colouration of the trademark [n]or change[ ] it in such a way that it sounds or looks like an entirely different concept." The slight variations that "[do not] change[ ] the meaning or coloration of the trademark" telegraph knowledge of complainant and its identity in the marketplace. They imply both knowledge of complainant's trademark[395] and intention to capitalize on the associated goodwill.[396]

Many trademarks are composed of lexical strings containing ampersands[397] and punctuation marks[398] that are not fully reproducible as domain names, and as

---

392 ***Dow Jones & Company, Inc. and Dow Jones LP v. John Zuccarini***, D2000-0578 (WIPO September 10, 2000) ("It is plain that [in registering the domain names] Zuccarini [was] taking advantage of the tendency of Internet users to misspell." Also, ***Eddie Bauer, Inc. v. John Zuccarini aka Cupcake Party***, D2001-0224 (WIPO April 26, 2001) (<eddiebaurer.com> and <eddiebaur.com>).

393 The respondent in ***Florim Ceramiche S.p.A. v. Domain Hostmaster, Customer ID: 24391572426632, Whois Privacy Services Pty LTD / Domain Administrato, Vertical Axis Inc.***, D2015-2085 (WIPO February 11, 2016) holds a domain name which it claims is a purposeful variant of "credit." It explained that it registered <cedit.com> "in good faith based on the inherent value of the common dictionary word 'credit'. This is not a case of a 'typosquatter' profiting from the typo of a trademark; the disputed domain name is rather a typo of a highly valuable and regularly searched dictionary word. Accordingly, the Respondent has used the disputed domain name in connection with a bona fide offering of goods and services in the form of pay-per-click ads related to the word 'credit.'"

394 ***NaturaLawn of America, Inc. v. Jeff Edwards***, FA1102001372111 (Forum March 16, 2011) (NATURALAWN and <naturallawns.com>) ("Panels have rightly given short shrift to such attempts to pretend that, because of such minor changes, there is no confusing similarity. But in cases where panels have taken that course the additions or subtractions of a letter or two have not changed the meaning or colouration of the trademark or changed it in such a way that it sounds or looks like an entirely different concept.")

395 ***Gannett Co., Inc. v. Henry Chan***, D2004-0117 (WIPO April 8, 2004) (ARIZONA REPUBLIC and <arizonarepblic.com>. "In order to make such modifications to Complainant's trademarks, respondent necessarily knew these trademarks prior to registering the contested domain names.")

396 ***Amazon.com, Inc. v. Victor Korotkov***, D2002-0516 (WIPO August 13, 2002) (<ammazon.com>) ("The ploy of 'typo-piracy' is well recognized, whereby a domain name is composed with the intention of trapping users who seek the web site of a known trademark but make a predictable spelling or typing mistake.") Other examples of typosquatting include converting one part of speech to another. The Respondent in ***Google Inc. v. Jan Jeltes***, DAU2008-0012 (WIPO October 20, 2008) and ***Google Inc. v. Jeltes Consulting/N. Tea Pty Ltd***, D2008-0994 (WIPO August 20, 2008) converted the verb "to google" into "googler"—<googler.com.au> and <adgoogler.com>—who is

such are commonly disregarded in assessing identity or confusing similarity. The composition of the second level domain designed to take advantage of a trademark typically involves (as will be shown more fully below) adding, omitting, reversing, and transposing letters. These refashionings plus the omission of spaces and unreproducible symbols, such as ampersands, do not create distinctive names. If they are not identical they are confusingly similar to complainant's trademark.

Typosquatting made its first appearance in the case of an omission of the hyphen in the trademark C-COM.[399] In ***Chernow Communications***, complainant alleged the domain name was "identical" rather than "confusingly similar." WIPO appointed a three-member Panel. The dissenting panelist took the position complainant should be limited to its pleadings. Since the domain name was not identical he would have dismissed the complaint. This uncharitable view failed to impress his colleagues, was tacitly rejected in contemporary cases, and has left no mark on the jurisprudence. Complainant's failure by inadvertence or design to state whether the disputed domain name is identical or confusingly similar—that is, in the particular case, whether <ccom.com> is identical or confusingly similar to C-COM—is of no account, for it is surely one or the other.

With some exceptions mere replacement of a single letter with another one lexically equivalent or in near proximity on the QWERTY keyboard, adding and omitting a letter, or rearranging them is too tenuous and insubstantial to qualify as creating a name distinctive from a trademark. Indeed, "a deviation in the form of a typographical error, namely, an additional letter 'e' appears in the non-distinctive part of the disputed domain name does not change this evaluation."[400] Where the "only apparent purpose would be to trade on mistakes by users seeking Complainant's web site" the registration is abusive.[401]

---

presumably someone who "googles." The country code .co has been implicated in typosquatting of mark in Complaints identical .com domain. See ***New Dream Network, LLC v. Yuanjin Wu***, DCO2010-0013 (WIPO October 25, 2010) (DREAM HOST and <dreamhost.co>).

[397] ***PG&E Corporation v. Samuel Anderson and PGE in the year 2000***, D2000-1264 (WIPO November 22, 2000) (PG&E and <pge2000.com>); ***McKinsey Holdings, Inc. v. Indidom***, D2000-1616 (WIPO January 31, 2001) (MCKINSEY & COMPANY and <mckinseycompany.com>); ***B&H Foto & Electronics Corp. v. Avi Lang***, D2016-0525 (WIPO May 19, 2016) (<bhphoto.video>); ***Fosbrooke, Inc. v. ravindra bala***, FA1608001689535 (Forum October 1, 2016) (T&N and <tnmattress.com>. Complainant is a direct seller of mattresses to consumers).

[398] ***Barney's Inc. v. BNY Bulletin Board***, D2000-0059 (WIPO April 2, 2000) (BARNEYS NEW YORK and <barneysnewyork.com>).

[399] ***Chernow Communications, Inc. v. Jonathan D. Kimball***, D2000-0119 (WIPO May 18, 2000) (C-COM and <ccom.com>).

[400] ***ACCOR v. Vista Holdings, Inc.***, D2008-0291 (WIPO April 21, 2008) (<accorhoteels.com>). Also, ***Telstra Corporation Limited v. Nuclear Marshmallows***, D2000-0003 (WIPO February 18, 2000) (TELSTRA and <telsra.com>).

The most common facets of typosquatting are: 1) omitting letters, [<reters.com>, <ruters.com> and <reuers.com> for REUTERS[402] and "<finshline.com> for FINISH LINE[403]]; 2) adding letters or terms [<xgoogle.com>]; 3) misspelling names [<macafee.com> for MCAFEE[404]]; 4) creating an aurally identical name [<phizer.com> for PFIZER[405]]; 5) reversing or transposing letters [<cableas.com>[406], <ceasars-palace.com>, <googel.com>]; 6) adding or omitting hyphens or dashes [<dream-works-llc.com>[407], <creditagricole.info>[408]]; and 7) changing "&" to "and"or lower for upper cases [<atandt.com>[409]]. Some Panelists have found that the QWERTY keyboard is an invitation to typosquatting. Selecting adjacent letters suggests deliberation: an "f" for "g" and "i" or "p" for "o"[410]; an "x" instead of a "c"[411]; a "q" for a "w"[412]; and a "y" for a "t."[413] The Panel in a non-qwerty case held that substituting a "c" for a "k" and "p' for an "f" did not save the domain name from being confusingly similar to complainant's trademark.[414]

---

401 ***Oxygen Media, LLC v. Primary Source***, D2000-1167 (WIPO October 16, 2000) in which the Panel held that "one struggles without success to think of any legitimate purpose for registering a domain name based on [a] typographically erroneous variation of Complainant's well-known mark."

402 ***Reuters Ltd. v. Global Net 2000, Inc.***, D2000-0441 (WIPO July 13, 2000).

403 ***The Finish Line, Inc. v. Privacy Ltd. Disclosed Agent for YOLAPT c/o Domain Admin.***, FA0904001260276 (Forum June 23, 2009) (<finshline.com>).

404 ***McAfee, Inc. v. QTK Internet/Name Proxy/Private Registration /Damian Macafee***, FA1010001351950 (Forum December 3, 2010).

405 ***Pfizer Inc. v. BargainName.com***, D2005-0299 (WIPO Apr. 28, 2005) (<pfzer.com>).

406 ***Cabela's, Inc. v. Elisa Browning***, FA1009001345984 (Forum November 7, 2010) (CABELA'S).

407 ***Dreamworks L.L.C. v. Carol Maleti***, D2003-0548 (WIPO September 10, 2003).

408 ***Crédit Agricole S.A. v. Dick Weisz***, D2010-1683 (WIPO December 1, 2010). Respondent added a hyphen between "Credit" and "Agricole"and omitted the accent from the letter "e" in "Credit."

409 ***AT&T Corp. v. ATandT.com***, D2002-1178 (WIPO February 17, 2003).

410 ***Go Daddy Software, Inc. v. Daniel Hadani***, D2002-0568 (WIPO August 1, 2002).

411 ***IndyMac Bank F.S.B. v. Ebeyer***, FA 175292 (Forum September 19, 2003) (<indymax.com>, <indymax.biz>, <indymax.info>).

412 ***Wachovia Corporation v. American Consumers First***, D2004-0150 (WIPO July 7, 2004) (<qachovia.com>, the letter "q" is on the left-hand side of "w"). Similarly, ***Amazon.com, Inc. v. Steven Newman a/k/a Jill Wasserstein a/k/a Pluto Newman***, D2006-0517 (WIPO June 28, 2006) (<amazoh.com>, <qmqzon.com>, and <smszon.com>); also, ***Apple Inc. v. Oakwood Services Inc. N/A N/A***, D2010-1917 (WIPO December 28, 2010) (<aplle.com>, on the qwerty keyboard, striking "l" instead of "p,"which is above it on the right).

413 ***Target Brands, Inc. v. Modern Empire Internet Ltd.***, FA1201001425387 (Forum February 22, 2012) (<yarget.com>). However, the Panel in ***Google Inc. v. Andrey Korotkov***, FA120900 1463221 (Forum October 31, 2012) declined to find <woogle.com> confusingly similar to GOOGLE. Since "w" is not adjacent to "g" on the qwerty keyboard "[t]his Panel does not believe Respondent's disputed domain name can be confused with Complainant's mark."

414 ***Korn/Ferry International v. The Careermosaic Cornperry, Inc***, FA0508000538465 (Forum October 7, 2005) (<cornperry.com> and <ecornperry.com>).

In those cases the aural similarity is controlling. The panelist inferred abusive registration from the fact respondent "operate[d] a website featuring employment recruiting services which directly competes with those offered by Complainant's business." These inferences are acceptable because, absent a plausible explanation,[415] one can infer from slight differences, changes, or variations that respondent 1) had knowledge of complainant's trademark; 2) made the changes intentionally; and 3) expected to obtain a benefit from registering and using the domain name.[416]

6.05-E.1.b

6.05-E.1.b *Small Differences Matter*

As there are lexical variations intended to target specific trademarks there are others that are distinctive in their own right. The made up trademark, NATURALAWN, is not infringed by the domain name, <naturallawns.com>, even if the word "natural" can be said to appear in both.[417] Single letter additions or substitutions incorporating the mark or allegedly confusingly similar but projecting different associations are not to be confused with typosquatting[418] Pluralizing or singularizing descriptive strings[419] and abbreviations[420] can be fair use where the name creates a distinctive impression from the trademark and there is no evidence of targeting.

---

415 ***NaturaLawn of America, Inc.***, supra, "invoking a generalized concept of natural lawns."

416 Introduction in 2010 of the country code for Colombia, ".co" creates an opportunity for confusion with the ".com" suffix where the domain name is identical to the trademark. The Panel in ***New Dream Network, LLC v. Yuanjin Wu***, DCO2010-0013 (WIPO October 25, 2010) found that the registration in the ccTLD space of <dreamhost.co> amounted to typosquatting. It explained that "While usually the domain name extension is disregarded for the purpose of comparison under paragraph 4(a)(i) of the Policy, that standard approach does not prevent a Panel finding, in relevant circumstances, that confusion might be created by a 'misspelling' of a gTLD. The difficulty is determining whether the circumstances indicate that there is, in fact, a deliberate misspelling, rather than a legitimate registration of a domain name in a particular ccTLD space. In this case, the Panel considers that the circumstances suggest a deliberate misspelling. There is no evidence of any connection between respondent and Colombia, to which the ccTLD relates."

An alternative analysis to typosquatting—which should be reserved to changes to the second level domain—would be to focus on the respondent's failure to explain its "connection . . . [with the country] to which the ccTLD relates."

417 ***NaturaLawn of America***, supra. ("Complainant has apparently either taken the invented word 'natura' and added to it the word 'lawn', to create a brand or trade name of Natura Lawn or compressed the two words 'natural' and 'lawn' into one word by omitting the letter 'l', thereby creating a brand or trade name Naturalawn.")

418 ***Tibolli, LLC v. Michael Schiavinato***, FA1807001796010 (Forum August 16, 2018) (GKHAIR and <igkhair.com>. "A difference of even a single letter between a Respondent's domain name and Complainant's mark is sufficient to render them non-identical under the Policy."). Earlier cases: ***Forest Laboratories, Inc. v. Natural Products Solutions LLC***, D2011-1032 (WIPO July 29, 2011) (LEXAPRO and "flexapro"); ***Namecheap, Inc. v. KY SONG***, FA1401001537272 (Forum March 12, 2014) (<namechap.com>).

Some differences genuinely spell other common words,[421] as is illustrated in a domain name omitting the letter "d" from "drug" to form "rug."[422] As there are limits to statutory monopoly of names and symbols there are limits to inferring bad faith. Under principles of trademark law[423] and UDRP jurisprudence it is well established that small differences matter.[424] The Panel in ***Caesars World***[425] was unwilling to find confusing similarity between "Caesars" and "teasers." "Teasers" is a common word that evokes a different "mental image[ ]" than CAESARS. It also does not "match . . . the gaming and associated services stated to be on offer by complainant." Moreover, "there can be little realistic expectation that a significant

---

419 ***Tire Discounters, Inc. v. TireDiscounter.com***, FA0604000679485 (Forum June 14, 2006) where respondent registered its domain name in the singular, TIRE DISCOUNTERS and <tire-discounter>; or pluralizing as in, ***Sears Brands, LLC v. Domain Asset Holdings***, FA091200 298052 (Forum January 22, 2010) (NORTHWEST TERRITORY and <northwestterritories.com>.)

420 ***LivingSocial, Inc. v. chris jensen***, FA1208001456244 (Forum September 10, 2012) (LIVING SOCIAL and <livingsocal.com>. Complainant charged that the omitted "i" following "c" was intentional to capture its customers. However, Respondent countered that "socal" was an abbreviation for "Southern California" and that it uses the domain name "to host a website describing the real estate market in Southern California and providing information regarding Respondent's real estate practice.")

421 Discussed further in "Similar, But Not Confusingly Similar" (Sec. 4.01-A.2.c).

422 ***5127173 Manitoba Ltd., carrying on as "Canada Drugs IT" v. Suucess Incorporated***, FA1001001302812 (Forum March 8, 2010) involving <canadarugs.com> and the trademark CANADA DRUGS. Rugs are not likely to be confused with drugs. The Panel in ***Forest Laboratories***, *supra.* observed in footnote 5 "Would <pride.com> or <bride.net> be confusingly similar to RIDE, a popular brand of snowboard? The English language has many words that when a single letter is added at the beginning yield words of an entirely different meaning: heat and cheat, race and grace, hew and phew, to name but a few. The point is that a difference of one letter does not automatically result in confusion."

423 *Entrepreneur Media, Inc. v. Smith*, 279 F.3d 1135, 1147 (9th Cir. 2002). ("Similarity of marks or lack thereof are context-specific concepts. In the Internet context, consumers are aware that domain names for different Web sites are quite often similar, because of the need for language economy, and that very small differences matter.") See also *Advertise.com, Inc. v. AOL Advert., Inc.*, 616 F.3d 974 (9th Cir. 2010) (<advertise.com> and ADVERTISING.COM).

424 ***In Tire Discounters***, *supra.* FA0604000679485 (Forum June 14, 2006) respondent omitted a single letter from the mark, "s" from TIRE DISCOUNTERS (Complaint denied); ***Webvisions Pte Ltd. v. WebVision***, D2010-1702 (WIPO November 26, 2010) (WEBVISIONS and <webvision.com>) (confusingly similar but no evidence of bad faith.); ***Sears Brands, LLC v. Domain Asset Holdings***, FA0912001298052 (Forum January 22, 2010) (NORTHWEST TERRITORY and <northwestterritories.com>. No evidence that in registering the domain name respondent had complainant in mind. The "'Northwest Territories' are a vast area of wilderness where outdoor activities are a predominant feature, which warrants the use of link[s] relating to this element on Respondent's website.")

425 ***Caesars World, Inc. v. Starnet Communications and Atlantic West Gaming Entertainment, Ltd.***, D2002-0066 (WIPO April 19, 2002) (<teaserspalance.com>).

number of users of would hit 't' [on the top alphabetic row] in mistake for 'c' [on the bottom alphabetic row]."

Confusing similarity of a misspelled word to a word that forms part of a trademark—"natiional" for example—is not conclusive that the registration is abusive even if the misspelling is intentional.[426] In the cited case the three-member Panel held that a variation of a common word prevents a finding for Complainant: the word "'national' is simply too common for the registration and use of the typosquatting variation 'natiional' to be considered 'bad faith.'" Although it has been said that typosquatting is "as close as it is possible to come to *per se* cybersquatting,"[427] complainant must still prove that it and no other trademark owner is respondent's target for the typographical variation.

6.05-E.2 6.05-E.2 Contractions and Abbreviations

Contractions such as "st" for "street"[428] and abbreviations such as "hufpost" for the full name of the publication[429] that conjure complainant's trademark cannot be defended under 4(c)(i) or 4(c)(iii) of the Policy.[430] Respondent in ***LSG Lufthansa***[431] abbreviating from LSG SKY CHEFS) omitted "chefs." The Panel held that the:

[426] ***Vanguard Trademark Holdings USA LLC v. Administrator, Domain / Vertical Axis, Inc.***, FA1104001383694 (Forum May 31, 2011) (<natiional.com>, Complaint denied even though the Panel found that "natiional" was "an intentional registration of a misspelling of a common word which happens to be part of or a common element of a large number of trademarks. However, some marks are stronger than others. This is not a misspelling of a relatively unique mark.")

The respondent in ***Florim Ceramiche S.p.A. v. Domain Hostmaster, Customer ID: 2439 1572426632, Whois Privacy Services Pty LTD / Domain Administrato, Vertical Axis Inc.***, D2015-2085 (WIPO February 11, 2016) holds a domain name which it claims is a purposeful variant of "credit", but Complainant charges that the omission of "r" infringes its trademark, CEDIT, which does not exist as an English word—complaint denied.

[427] ***Apple Inc. v. Andrew Sievright, Domain Source***, D2010-1916 (WIPO December 8, 2010) (omitting "e" from trademark <appl.com>)

[428] ***Dow Jones & Company, Inc. & Dow Jones LP v. T.S.E. Parts***, D2001-0381 (WIPO May 4, 2001) (<ewallstjournal.com>).

[429] ***AOL Inc. v. Above.com Domain Privacy***, FA1302001485082 (Forum April 23, 2013) (<hufpost.com>); ***Banque Saudi Fransi v. ABCIB***, D2003-0656 (WIPO October 14, 2003) (<alfransi.com> abbreviating from AL BANK AL SAUDI AL FRANSI).

[430] ***Smith Travel Research, Inc. v. Victor An***, FA0904001259999 (Forum June 15, 2009) (<str.com>. "Despite Respondent's protestations to the contrary, the Panel determines that the Complainant and the Respondent both compete in the travel business. The Panel finds that Respondent was clearly trying to associate its offerings with the goodwill of Complainant's well known mark, creating confusion as to whether Complainant was the source of, or had some affiliation with Respondent's website, and profiting from the confusion by receiving click through fees.")

[431] ***LSG Lufthansa Service Holding AG v. Syed Hussain***, D2009-0636 (WIPO July 2, 2009) (<lsgsky.com>).

> use in the Disputed Domain Name which partially incorporates the Trademarks to capture the more distinctive elements of those Trademarks (i.e. the terms "lsg sky") can be viewed as identifying complainant's Trademarks. Such partial incorporation of the Trademarks in the Disputed Domain Name does not prevent the finding of confusing similarity between the Disputed Domain Name and the Trademarks owned by complainant.

The distinctiveness of a trademark is not weakened by contracting it if the contraction (or, in the case of an abbreviation) suggests the trademark.

Where Respondent has registered a disputed domain name, <conap.com> for example (in which the second level domain sounds like a contraction), it is no defense for Respondent to assert it is developing a software product that will be a "connection application" (which it asserts is a recognized contraction for "conap").[432] This would have been a complete defense had Respondent in fact actually created the fantasy it alleged, rather than using the domain name as a link farm that included goods competing with Complainant. Confusing similarity supports standing; but "likelihood of confusion" calls for a different level of assessment.

In ***Modern Props***[433] the Panel agreed that the <modprops.com> was confusingly similar to MODERN PROPS—"'Mod' connotes 'modern' regardless of any other dictionary meanings, so the names are substantially similar in meaning"[434]—but the Panel rejected Complainant's assertion that Respondent's registration and use of the domain name were in bad faith. The Panel's point is that Complainant has standing, but no actionable claim. Respondent's proof in ***Modern Props*** established that "[e]ven though [it] may have been aware of Complainant's business, or Complainant's website (and there is nothing in the record to support this), such awareness does not establish that the use of a similar domain name violates the Policy."

6.05-F Populating Web Pages: The "Not Me" Defense 6.05-F

6.05-F.1 Responsibility for Content 6.05-F.1

The general rule for web pages is that respondents are responsible for content.[435] Transient infringement may be excusable if quickly removed after notice,[436] but where infringing content persists respondents cannot avoid imputation of bad faith

---

432 ***Cytec Industries Inc. v. Aybit GmbH / A. Bron***, FA1212001473883 (Forum January 22, 2013). Complainant inadvertently lost the domain name three years earlier by failing to renew registration.

433 ***Modern Props, Inc. v. Wallis***, FA 152458 (Forum June 2, 2003).

434 *Id.*

435 Examples too numerous to cite, but a representative example is ***StaffEx Corp. v. Lionheat Publ'g***, FA 1069901 (Forum October 18, 2007) (Third party placement of links "no excuse"). See Jurisprudential Overview 3.0, Paragraph 2.9, "Do "parked" pages comprising pay-per-click links support respondent rights or legitimate interests?" The answer is Yes, when they are not infringing; No when they are.

use by arguing they contracted operation of the website to third parties. Whether there may be factual circumstances absolving respondents of bad faith (a point discussed in the next section) marks composed of common words, descriptive phrases, and acronyms that could also be random letters acquired prior to domain name registration are more vulnerable to apparent infringement than are suggestive, arbitrary and fanciful marks.

With these various possibilities in mind "[t]he fact that a third party is effectively operating the website on behalf of Respondent, and making payments to Respondent on the basis of that use, does not insulate Respondent from the conduct of its authorized agent."[437] In practical terms an infringing website is deemed to benefit the holder whether or not it does and without regard to other beneficiaries. That the offending content occurred in the past, but the domain name is presently parked and inactive is not a defense regardless the length of time respondent has held it.[438]

Argument that outsourcing content and operation to third parties should immunize respondents has been rejected by both WIPO and Forum Panels. Even though the owner of a parked domain name may not control the content "it is ultimately [the] respondent who is responsible for how its domain name is used."[439] Under these circumstances knowledge of the use to which a parked domain is being put is imputed to respondent despite denial. The reasoning is that someone derives a benefit from the parked domain at complainant's expense even if not respondent directly. In ***Sanofi-Aventis***[440] the Panel found that respondent either passively condoned or was indifferent to the material posted to its domains by another party:

> The Panel believes that registrations made as part of such a scheme [to drive traffic through the website] are made and used in bad faith for the purposes of

---

436 See ***A. D. Banker & Company v. Domain Invest***, D2010-1044 (WIPO September 30, 2010) discussed more fully below. An example of transience is where respondent has not had time to propagate its own content.

437 ***Park Place Entertainment Corporation v. Anything.com Ltd.***, D2002-0530 (WIPO September 16, 2002) (<flamingo.com>).

438 ***Maurice Mizrahi / Mizco International, Inc. v. Chi Hyon***, FA1710001754962 (Forum November 20, 2017) (<digipower.com>. Held for 16 years).

439 ***State Farm Mutual Auto. Insr. Co. v. Pompilio***, FA 1092410 (Forum November 20, 2007); ***Oracle International Corporation v. Danny B / Admedia***, FA1605001674542 (Forum June 27, 2016) (Eighteen-year old registration of <oracl.com> used at times to distribute malware and other times directed to adult websites. Respondent's argument rejected that he "was not in control of the <oracl.com> domain name during the time in which it was being used for malware. Respondent uses the domain as a shopping portal which sells products to end consumers, which is a legitimate non-competing business.")

440 ***Sanofi-Aventis Aventis Pharma SA, Aventis Pharma Deutchland GmbH .v. IN4 Web Services***, D2005-0938 (WIPO November 24, 2005).

> this Policy if it is held that the domain name in point is confusingly similar to a mark in which a third-party complainant has rights.

By agreeing to its registrar's "parking policy" and not "un-park[ing]" Respondent violates the Policy.[441] Stated differently, the "relationship between a domain name registrant and the Registrar does not affect the rights of a complainant under the Policy."[442]

6.05-F.2 Factual Circumstances Absolving Respondent of Bad Faith 6.05-F.2

A less strict standard calibrated to take into account the context and factual circumstances of the website holds that registrar posting is not sufficient in itself for a finding of respondent bad faith.[443] This view excuses respondent where "deception of Internet users and commercial gain were [not] central to the Respondent's plans along the lines of paragraph 4(b)(iv) of the Policy."[444] Without proof of targeting, designing web pages to attract Internet users for commercial gain is not a violation of the Policy. There may be circumstances where, through inadvertence, accident, or otherwise a website's infringing content should not be charged to the domain name holder.[445]

Alleged infringing content either existed before notice and has been removed or it exists and has not been removed. In the former case, there must be a balancing of rights. Removing infringing matter on notice is not tantamount to an admission of liability.[446] In the latter case, there are two classes of respondent whose registrations have been found to be immune from presumptive bad faith use even though the websites to which the domain names resolve at the commencement of the proceeding contain links that would otherwise be considered a violation of the Policy.

---

[441] ***Diners Club International Ltd. v. O P Monga***, FA0603000670049 (Forum May 22, 2006).

[442] ***Villeroy & Boch AG v. Mario Pingerna***, D2007-1912 (WIPO February 14, 2008), citing ***Ogden Publications, Inc. v. MOTHEARTHNEWS.COM c/o Whois IDentity Shield/OGDEN PUBLICATIONS INC., Administrator, Domain***, D2007-1373 (WIPO November 26, 2007).

[443] Discussed further in "Parking for Revenue" (Sec. 6.01-A.2).

[444] ***Groupalia Compra Colectiva, S.L. v. Andrea Santini***, D2010-1979 (WIPO January 26, 2011) (Footnote 3: "While the Panel is aware that there have been decisions to the effect that it matters not whether the pay-per-click revenue goes to the respondent, it being enough that there is commercial gain, the Panel is not persuaded that those decisions are necessarily to be followed in cases such as the present.")

[445] Inadvertent hyperlinking may be excusable. Discussed further in "Making Changes to the Website After Notice and Filing of Complaint" (Sec. 7.04-E). The principle has also been applied to applicable disputes under the Uniform Rapid Suspension System (URS).

[446] See ***Rosefield Watches B.V. v. Bryan Wick, Cheapyellowpages.com***, D2016-2187 (WIPO December 15, 2016) in which Respondent upon notice that its parking site was targeting the Complainant's area of business "promptly gave instructions to adjust the algorithm being used in

These are newly acquired domain names populated either by 1) a prior registrant that has allowed its registration to lapse and the successor registrant (the respondent) has not had time to post its own content[447] or 2) the registrar for its own account before the registrant has launched its own website.[448]

The dispositive issue in determining bad faith use is whether respondent intended to profit[449] from the similarities with complainant's mark rather than any generic meaning of the domain name. If it did, the domain name is likely to have been registered and used in bad faith. In ***A.D. Banker***, the Panel resolved the key issue in Respondent's favor, not because it was persuaded by its arguments but because complainant failed to respond to respondent's "technical claims" in its supplemental submission. The "technical claims" related to the timing of web page changes, that there had not been time for the changes to be "reflected in the various cached servers throughout the world." According to respondent and reluctantly accepted by the Panel, "it would be unfair to draw any conclusions adverse to the Respondent's motivations and intentions from web pages that were dated the day after the Domain Name was transferred."[450]

---

order to remove the offending links from its website." The Panel concluded that "Respondent's modification of the content displayed on the website at the disputed domain name after receipt of the Complainant's cease and desist letter [did not] amount[ ] to bad faith as alleged by the Complainant."

447 ***A. D. Banker***, supra.

448 ***Fireman's Fund Insurance Company v. Steve Schwartz***, FA1010001355350 (Forum December 15, 2010).

449 The Panel in ***Amylin Pharmaceuticals, Inc. v. Watts Guerra Craft LLP***, D2012-0486 (WIPO April 29, 2012) points out in footnote 2 that "[t]he fact that Respondent may profit from use of the disputed domain name does not prevent him from establishing a nominative fair use defense," as the defense is not dependent on whether the Respondent profits," citing ***Pfizer Inc v. Van Robichaux***, D2003-0399 (WIPO July 16, 2003), citing *Playboy Enters. v. Welles*, 279 F.3d 796 (9th Cir. 2002) and *Horphag Research v. Mario Pellegrini*, 328 F. 3d 1108 (9th Cir. 2003).

450 The Panel's reluctance is noted in the final paragraph of the decision, inviting complainant to refile if subsequent use "would seriously undermine *the credibility of a number of the assertions that have been* made by respondent and which have been key to the Panel's findings in this case." The principle is equally applicable to URS disputes. See ***BancBilbao Vizcaya Argentaria, S.A. v. Gandiyork SL et al.***, FA1403001548656 (Forum March 28, 2014) (<bbva.land>. Respondent stated that "it was 'most surprised' to learn of the page, which differed from its own review of the website, and that its attempts to 'cancel' the monetized parking page were unsuccessful because 'the domain is blocked because of this dispute.'")

7 Selected Rules of the Policy

7.01 RULE 2—COMMENCING A PROCEEDING 7.01

7.01-A Service of Complaint and Notice 7.01-A

The UDRP hews to procedural due process in its own way, which is different from commencing an action in a court of competent jurisdiction. Personal jurisdiction is satisfied by a two-step postal- and electronic-mail process.[1] Filing a complaint precedes notice of complaint. "Written Notice" is defined in Rule 1 as "hardcopy notification by the Provider to the Respondent of the commencement of an administrative proceeding under the Policy which shall inform the respondent that a complaint has been filed against it."

The mechanism for serving the complaint and annexes is set forth in Rule 2.[2] Following the Provider's request to the registrar for confirmation of the identity of the beneficial holder of the challenged domain name[3] and the registrar's locking of the domain name, the Provider is charged with giving notice of the commencement of the administrative proceeding (Rule 2(a)(i)) and separately serving the complaint and annexes "in electronic form by e-mail> (Rule 2(a)(ii)).[4]

Under original Rule 3(xii) complainants were required to state "that a copy of the complaint . . . had been sent or transmitted to the Respondent (domain-name holder) [at the same time as filing it with the Provider]." The rule change was necessary because the original requirement opened up an opportunity for respondents to transfer the challenged domain name to another registrar before becoming locked—another feature of the amended rules—which the amended provision prevents.[5]

---

[1] ICANN amended the Rules effective July 15, 2015. The amendment included a new definition in Rule 1 for the term "Written Notice" and language revisions to Rule 2 affirming service by e-mail.

[2] Rule 2(a) reads: "When forwarding a complaint, including any annexes, electronically to the Respondent, it shall be the Provider's responsibility to employ reasonably available means calculated to achieve actual notice to Respondent. Achieving actual notice, or employing the following measures to do so, shall discharge this responsibility.

[3] Prior to May 25, 2018, personal contact information of beneficial holders of domain names was available in the Whois directory unless protected by proxy or privacy services. Under the EU's General Data Protection Regulation (GDPR) personal information of individuals is redacted. Complainants must now commence proceedings by filing a complaint against John Doe, to be amended once the information is disclosed by the registrar. See "Impact of the GDPR" (Sec. 2.05-B).

[4] Claims of non receipt of mailed notice and e-mail complaint are unlikely to be challenged except in the rare case of a valuable string. The registrant of <imi.com> alleged non receipt in a pending federal action under the ACPA, *Black v. Irving Materials, LLC*, 3:17-cv-06734(ND CA 2018). The arguments and proof on dueling motions to summary judgment put in issue both the generic nature of the three-letter string as well as its original acquisition 20 years earlier in connection with a new business.

[5] Paragraph 8 of the Policy prohibits transfers during a dispute. The amended Rules provide at Rule 4 that the "Registrar shall not notify the Respondent of the proceeding until the Lock status has been applied."

Notice is complete regardless whether the WhoIs information is correct, outdated, or intentionally false. The WIPO Overview 2.0 stated that "if the WhoIs information is not readily usable for communication purposes in such case the registrant must expect to bear any consequences. . . . [W]hat matters in terms of notification obligations under the UDRP Rules is not so much the name that may 'formally' appear on the complaint, but that the latter has been duly notified to the reasonably available contact information of the 'registrant', whatever its identity."[6]

7.01-B 7.01-B Certifying the Pleadings: Complaint and Response

Parties to a UDRP proceeding must include a certification similar in U.S. practice to Rule 11 of the Federal Rules of Civil Procedure (and undoubtedly a feature in procedural codes in other judicial jurisdictions) "that the information contained in this [Complaint or Response] is to the best of [Complainant's or Respondent's] knowledge complete and accurate, that this [Complaint or Response] is not being presented for any improper purpose, such as to harass, and that the assertions in this [Complaint or Response] are warranted under these Rules and under applicable law, as it now exists or as it may be extended by a good-faith and reasonable argument."[7]

The practical purpose of certification is to induce parties on pain of having their claims or defenses disregarded to offer clear evidence of provable facts[8] or sufficient proof from which positive or adverse inferences may be drawn. Lacking "this basic certification of accuracy is significant [because] it leaves little room for a panel to confer credibility on anything a respondent has asserted"[9] (discussed further in Section 7.05-C).

The consequences of failing to comply with the terms of the certification falls most heavily on complainants. Non-disclosure, withholding documents, mischaracterizing, perjurious representation, or reckless disregard of material facts are among the circumstances that undermine claims. Not only do they undermine the

---

6 Paragraph 4.9(e): "(i) there are limits to what can reasonably be done by parties and providers to identify an 'underlying registrant' in the context of the UDRP." Not in Jurisprudential Overview 3.0 but there is no change to the accepted view.

7 Rules 3(b)(xiv) (complainant) and 5(b)(viii) (respondent).

8 ***Anyclean Premium Limited v. Jethro Denahy, Any-Clean***, D2017-0581 (WIPO April 28, 2017) (<any-clean.com> "A Panel should be able to rely upon the certification that a Complainant gives that 'the information presented in this Complaint is to the best of the Complainant's knowledge complete and accurate'. The Panel considers this is a case where such certification could not properly have been given, for the following reasons.")

9 ***The American Automobile Association, Inc. v. 555 Metro Airport Transportation Service LLC.***, D2011-0588 (WIPO May 17, 2011) (<aaametrocars.com>. Respondent failed to submit a certification); ***Flying Dog Brewery, LLLP v. WhoIs Privacy Protection Services, Inc. / Phil Allen, Flying Dog Enterprises***, D2018-1683 (WIPO September 22, 2018) (<flyingdog.com>. "The Complainant submitted a bare bones complaint unsupported by any evidence, and blatantly misrepresented to the

veracity of the certification and raise issues of credibility (Section 7.04-C); they also alone or together support reverse domain name hijacking (Section 7.11).[10] For respondents, the consequences are cancellation or transfer of the domain names,[11] although respondents may be excused where the evidence in the record clearly disproves complainant's claim.[12]

7.02 RULE 3—CONCERNING COMPLAINANT 7.02

7.02-A Proper Party Complainant(s) 7.02-A

7.02-A.1 Single or Multiple Related Complainants 7.02-A.1

7.02-A.1.a *Trademark Owners* *7.02-A.1.a*

Rule 3(a) of the Rules provides that "[a]ny person or entity may initiate a complaint" by filing it with an ICANN certified provider who examines it for form and content as noted above in Section 7.01-A.[13] "Any person" can be the trademark owner, licensee, or trademark assignee.[14] Typically, complainant is a person or entity in the singular, although the "any" phrase has long been construed to include more

---

Panel that the Respondent had hired an undisclosed agent seeking to sell the disputed domain name to the Complainant at an exorbitant price." .

[10] ***Johnson & Johnson v. Chad Wright, WebQuest.com, Inc.***, D2012-0010 (WIPO April 5, 2012) (<tucks.com>. "That the Complaint does not address the earlier appearance of the website is a matter of some concern to the Panel. Moreover, the Complaint appears to mischaracterize the historical content on Respondent's website"); ***Whispering Smith Limited v. Domain Administrator, Tfourh, LLC***, D2016-1175 (WIPO September 27, 2016) (<bravesoul.com>. Panel found the "Complainant (or rather, its attorney) has tried to mislead the Panel by mischaracterizing its trademark rights along with having made unsupported arguments under the third element of the UDRP Policy"); ***Hôpitaux Universitaires de Genève v. Aydin Karadeniz***, D2016-1620 (WIPO October 10, 2016) (<hug.com>, <hug.net> and <hug.org>. "[I]t does not appear that the Complainant carried out any investigation itself before filing the Complaint that might have revealed whether the Respondent was acting in good or bad faith. This suggests at best a reckless disregard of the respondent's possible entitlement to retain the disputed domain name.")

[11] ***Express Scripts, Inc. v. Windgather Investments Ltd. / Mr. Cartwright***, D2007-0267 (WIPO April 26, 2007) (Respondent's failure to comply with the requirements of paragraph 5(b) "is something that the Panel has very much borne in mind when considering the evidential weight of the assertions of fact made by the Respondent in this document.")

[12] ***B-Boy TV Ltd v. bboytv.com c/o Whois Privacy Service / Chief Rocka LTD, formerly named BreakStation LTD.***, D2012-2006 (WIPO November 23, 2012) (Mark not in existence when respondent registered the domain name).

[13] Pleadings must comply with the Rules as to length and content and include a certification similar in U.S. practice to Rule 11 of the Federal Rules of Civil Procedure (and undoubtedly a feature in procedural codes of other jurisdictions). The certification reads "that the information contained in this [Complaint or Response] is to the best of [Complainant's or Respondent's] knowledge complete and accurate, that this [Complaint or Response] is not being presented for any improper purpose, such as to harass, and that the assertions in this [Complaint or Response] are warranted under these

than one and may be several persons or entities.[15] There is no express provision in either the Policy or Rules which answers the question of multiple complainants[16] and it is not addressed in WIPO's Supplemental Rules. The issue is addressed in the Forum's Supplemental Rules where the party initiating a complaint is defined as a "single person or entity claiming to have rights in the domain name, or *multiple persons or entities who have a sufficient nexus who can each claim to have rights to all domain names listed in the Complaint*" (emphasis added).[17]

The issue of one or more was framed in an early case in which respondent argued for dismissal of a complaint by two complainants.[18] In rejecting the argument the Panel held it is not only permissible to name both a parent and subsidiary as complainants but "preferable [in such a circumstance] that a dispute concerning the domain names be considered in a single proceeding than in a multiplicity of proceedings." It is no longer questioned that "members of the same group of companies may constitute an 'entity' for the purposes of this provision."[19]

Although there is no limitation on the number of related complainants each must demonstrate it has a right to vindicate.[20] There must be a familial or contractual link between or among the entities,[21] such as "a license, a partnership or an affiliation that would establish the reason for the parties bringing the complaint as

---

Rules and under applicable law, as it now exists or as it may be extended by a good-faith and reasonable argument," Rules 3(b)(xiii) and 5(viii). Further discussed in "False Certification of Merits" (Section 7.11-A.2).

[14] ***Remithome Corp v. Pupalla***, FA 1124302 (Forum February 21, 2008) (Assignee of federally registered mark).

[15] See Jurisprudential Overview 3.0, paragraph 1.4.1. The question "Can a trademark licensee or a related company to a trademark holder have rights in a trademark for the purpose of filing a UDRP case?" is answered in the affirmative.

[16] A trademark right is demonstrated by attaching a copy of the registration certificate or (if unregistered) documents proving reputation and use in the marketplace for a sufficient period of time to have acquired distinctiveness. Proof of a trademark right is discussed further in Chapter 4.

[17] Supplemental Rule 1(e).

[18] ***Société Générale and Fimat International Banque v. Lebanon Index/La France DN and Elie Khouri***, D2002-0760 (WIPO November 1, 2002).

[19] ***L'Oréal, Biotherm, Lancôme Parfums et Beauté & Cie v. Unasi, Inc.***, D2005-0623 (WIPO August 15, 2005), citing ***Société Générale and Compagnie Générale des Etablissements Michelin CGEM—Michelin & Cie, Michelin Recherche et Technique S.A. v. Horoshiy Inc.***, D2004-0752 (WIPO January 17, 2005).

[20] See ***Tasty Baking, Co. & Tastykake Investments, Inc. v. Quality Hosting***, FA0311000208584 (Forum December 28, 2003) (<tastycake.com>. One Complainant is the operating company of the other and between them they own all the marks). The Panel in ***PartyGaming Plc v. WHOis Privacy Protection Service, Inc./Henao Berenice***, D2006-0508 (WIPO June 26, 2006) prefers the view "that the parent company must have some right to use or otherwise deal with the mark itself, whether under an express or implied license from its subsidiary, or perhaps because the subsidiary holds the mark in trust for [others within the group including the parent company]."

one entity."[22] In addition, among themselves they must designate the complainant to whom the disputed domain name is to be transferred.[23] It is not the number that determines whether multiple complainants can act as a unity but the nature of their interests and their relationship to each other. This formulation does not require complainant to be the owner of the mark[24] or even have an exclusive right.[25]

Notwithstanding the above it is possible for two unrelated mark owners to join as complainants, as when the domain name incorporates both marks.[26] Where the challenged domain name is composed of two or more marks, only one of which is owned by complainant and the other owned by another entity the consensus supports granting relief to the complaining mark owner.[27] In the absence of the other mark owner any "such decision would be expressly without prejudice to any rights, which may be asserted by third party trademark holder."[28]

7.02-A.1.b *Licensees* *7.02-A.1.b*

A licensee (filing alone or with the trademark owner) may be a proper complainant if it is invested with the right to protect an owner's trademark from unauthorized third parties.[29] To establish its credentials, complainant must produce a copy of the license or owner's declaration that it has granted complainant rights to

---

[21] ***Vancouver Organizing Committee for the 2010 Olympic and Paralymic Games and International Olympic Committee v. Hardeep Malik***, FA 666119 (Forum May 12, 2006) ("It has been accepted that it is permissible for two complainants to submit a single complaint if they can demonstrate a link between the two entities such as a relationship involving a license, a partnership or an affiliation that would establish the reason for the parties bringing the complaint as one entity.")

[22] *Id.* See also ***Keane Construction, Inc. and Three Boys Enterprises, LLC v. Chris White,*** FA1606001680295 (Forum July 28, 2016).

[23] ***Grupo Televisa SA v. Party Night Inc***, D2003-0796 (WIPO December 2, 2003) (4 Complainants) ("It has been accepted in several decisions that a company related as subsidiary or parent to the registered holder of a mark may be considered to have rights in the mark.")

[24] ***Miele Inc v Absolute Air Cleaners and Purifiers***, D2000-0756 (WIPO September 11, 2000); ***DigiPoll Ltd. v. Raj Kumar***, D2004-0939 (WIPO February 3, 2005) ("Complainant need not be the only person or entity with rights in the trademark. This aspect is sometimes expressed by saying that the rights that must be established in complainant need not be exclusive rights.")

[25] ***Smart Design LLC v. Carolyn Hughes***, D2000-0993 (WIPO October 18, 2000) (Paragraph 4(a)(i) does not mention "exclusive right."); ***UEFA v. Fuzi Furniture***, D2000-0710 (WIPO October 25, 2000) ("the Policy does not talk of exclusive rights.")

[26] ***NIKE, Inc., Nike Innovate, C.V., and Google Inc. v. Mattia Lumini / Yykk Snc***, FA160800 1687597 (Forum September 20, 2016).

[27] Decisions to the contrary stray from precedent and create unpredictability. Discussed further below in "Domain Names Combining Complainant's Marks with Marks of Third Parties" (Sec. 7.02-A.4).

[28] ***Decathlon SAS v. Nadia Michalski***, D2014-1996 (WIPO January 27, 2015) (<decathlon-nke.com>>. "It is the consensus view among UDRP panelists that neither the Policy nor the Rules expressly

the mark.[30] Complainant cannot *sua sponte* nominate itself the owner's proxy[31] or claim a license from a party with a pending application for a trademark.[32] Having a naked commercial relationship with a trademark owner is not an actionable right.[33]

For some Panels, the dividing line on licenses is the exclusive versus the nonexclusive. One Panel has suggested "there can be discerned two main, yet conflicting, streams of thought."[34] These are as follows:

> (a) That a licence provides contractual rights in relation to a trademark and that these are sufficient to constitute rights in a trademark for the purposes of the Policy; and
>
> (b) A licence is sufficient but only if as a matter of the law of the territory of the relevant mark that licence provides rights in the trademark over and above the contractual rights granted in that licence.

The first approach focuses on complainant's contractual right to use the trademark; the second focuses on local law to determine "whether in a particular jurisdiction

---

require the consent of a third party and previous panels have accepted complaints request[ing] that a domain name may be transferred to the complainant, noting that such decision would be expressly without prejudice to any rights, which may be asserted by third party trademark holder").

[29] ***American Family Health Services Group, LLC v. Logan***, FA 220049 (Forum Feb. 6, 2004) (the panel found a sufficient link between the complainants where there was a license between the parties regarding use of the TOUGHLOVE mark).

[30] In ***DigiPoll Ltd. v. Raj Kumar***, supra, the registered trademark owner, who was also the founder of complainant company, issued a statement that complainant had been given "full authority and license" and that complainant was "the de facto owner of the trademark." In ***HQUK Limited v. Head Quarters***, D2003-0942 (WIPO February 5, 2004), complainant and the trademark owner were "sister companies" and the latter had consented to the UDRP proceeding. In ***Miele, Inc.***, supra, the Panel found that complainant had rights in and duties concerning the trademark "through its affiliation with its grandparent corporation which owns the trade mark registration."

[31] No proof: ***NBA Props., Inc. v. Adirondack Software Corp.***, D2000-1211 (WIPO December 8, 2000) (denying complaint because complainant was not the owner of the KNICKS trademarks) ("There may well be circumstances in which the contract rights possessed by an exclusive licensee vest in him substantially all the powers of an owner of the licensed property. However, such circumstances have not been shown to exist here.") Proved: ***Kimmel Center, Inc. v. Tech Support, Trade Out Investments Ltd.***, D2011-0293 (WIPO April 22, 2011). In ***Shopware AG v. Laurent Bernardin***, D2013-0536 (WIPO May 10, 2013) (<shopware.com>) the Panel disregarded a particular trademark because complainant failed to provide any evidence of a licensing agreement.

[32] ***FUNimation Entertainment v. mohamed chennani***, FA1311001529907 (Forum December 18, 2013) (Trademark applicant but not licensee may have an actionable claim for infringement of common law rights).

[33] ***Blue Mountain Coffee, Inc. v. Fundacion Private Whois / Domain Administrator***, FA 1204001439829 (Forum May 21, 2012) (<blue-mountain-coffee>: "The Panel finds no reason to doubt that Complainant has the right to import, market and sell products marked with the Coffee Marks Limited JAMAICA BLUE MOUNTAIN COFFEE trademark," but no "clear rights to represent" the mark owner).

[34] ***Evolution USA, Inc. v. Alexei Doicev***, D2006-0086 (WIPO March 24, 2006).

the licence in question grants rights in addition to contractual rights particularly vis à vis third parties."

A variant of the issue had earlier been raised by the Panel in ***HQUK Limited***, which offers some insight into the problem. The trademarks in that case were issued pursuant to Article 22(3) of the Community Trade Marks Regulation (40/94/EEC), which provides as follows:

> Without prejudice to the provisions of the licensing contract, the licensee may bring proceedings for infringement of a community trade mark only if its proprietor consents thereto. However, the holder of an exclusive licence may bring such proceedings if the proprietor of the trade mark, after formal notice, does not bring infringement proceedings within an appropriate period.

According to the Panel this raises a number of questions: "Does the grant of a licence either alone or in conjunction with the rights afforded by Article 22 grant the licensee sufficient rights for the Policy? If the rights under Article 22 are significant here, must the licensee also show that it has been granted the right to pursue infringement claims [that affect its rights] or alternatively that it is an exclusive licensee that has given 'formal notice' to the trade mark owner and that an 'appropriate period' has now passed?"

The second approach is "likely to add a significant complication for licensee complainants . . . [because it] may result in a different treatment of different licensees . . . dependent upon the geographical accident of where the licensee has rights."[35] The Panel "finds this inherently unattractive and is an outcome that should generally be avoided." Under U.S. law, "even a non-exclusive licensee has the right to assert trademark rights in a licensed mark and to take action to protect the licensed mark."[36]

7.02-A.2 Multiple Domain Names—Aliases for Controlling Entity 7.02-A.2

7.02-A.2.a *Multiple Registrants in One Dispute* 7.02-A.2.a

Rule 1 of the Rules of the Policy (definitions) defines "Respondent" as "the holder of a domain-name registration against which a complaint is initiated." Rule 3(c) states that the "complaint may relate to more than one domain name, provided that the domain names are registered by the same domain name holder." The domain name holder is typically the beneficial owner if disclosed or if not disclosed, a proxy.[37]

---

35 ***Evolution USA***, *supra*.

36 ***Toyota Motor Sales USA Inc. v J. Alexis Productions***, D2003-0624 (WIPO October 16, 2003) (Stage name Lexis Michaels, <lexusmichaels.com>. Both parties U.S. residents. Complainant satisfied the first element of the Policy, but the complaint was denied on other grounds.)

If it becomes apparent after disclosure of the beneficial owner, or a second level proxy is put forward as the owner,[38] and complainant discovers the putative holder is the registrant of other domain names infringing its rights, complainant is permitted to amend the complaint [39] and amend again[40] to include later discovered domain names as long as the requests are made prior to submission to a Panel. Additional domain names registered after submission to the Panel can only be added upon application to the Panel.[41]

7.02-A.2.b 7.02-A.2.b *Multiple Disputes Consolidated*

A single proceeding is appropriate "where the particular circumstances of a given case indicate that [a] common [ownership or] control is being exercised over the disputed domain names or the websites to which the domain names resolve."[42] The phrase "same domain name holder" has been construed liberally to include registrants who are not the same person but circumstances suggest the domain names are controlled by a single person or entity.[43]

Undisclosed beneficial or controlling ownership has been found by matching addresses, telephone numbers, and e-mail accounts across a spectrum of domain

---

[37] This is illustrated where the Whois Directory shows that the "holder" is a privacy or proxy registration service rather than the beneficial owner or controlling party of the domain name. Discussed further in "Use and Abuse of Proxy and Privacy Services" (Sec. 2.04).

[38] See ***WSFS Financial Corporation v. Private Registrations Aktien Gesellschaft 2***, D2012-0033 (WIPO March 5, 2012) ("the so called 'Russian doll' scenario.")

[39] ***PepsiCo, Inc. v. Whois Privacy Protection Service, Inc., Abdulah Shmre***, D2011-0016 (WIPO February 20, 2011). The ability to add new domain names is likely to be weakened by the redaction of contact information as a result of the General Data Protection Regulation. See "Impact of the GDPR" (Sec. 2.05-B).

[40] ***PepsiCo, Inc. v. Henry Chan***, D2004-0033 (WIPO April 20, 2004).

[41] ***De Beers Intangibles Limited v. Romano Mudano***, D2017-0323 (WIPO April 15, 2017) (<adiamondisforever.cloud> and <adiamondisforever.store>, registered after the commencement of the of the proceedinge>. "[I]t is expedient to hear and determine them together in order to avoid the potentially varying decisions resulting from separate proceedings and to incur supplemental unnecessary costs for the Complainant.")

[42] ***Speedo Holdings B.V. v. Programmer, Miss Kathy Beckerson, John Smitt, Matthew Simmons***, D2010-0281 (WIPO May 18, 2010).

[43] Jurisprudential Overview 3.0, Paragraph 4.11.2: "Complaint consolidated against multiple respondents." Criteria set forth include "[where] the domain names or the websites to which they resolve are subject to common control." See ***Dr. Ing. h.c. F. Porsche AG v. Kentech, Inc. a.k.a. Helois Lab a.k.a. Orion Web a.k.a. Titan Net a.k.a. Panda Ventures a.k.a. Spiral Matrix and Domain Purchase, NOLDC, Inc.***, D2005-0890 (WIPO September 25, 2005) (22 domain names found to be controlled by the same person, some of which were switched into different registrant names to obstruct complainant following service of a cease-and-desist e-mail); ***Kimberly Clark Corporation v. N/A, Po Ser and N/A, Hu Lim***, D2009-1345 (WIPO December 7, 2009). ("Holder" can either be the registrant or the person with practical control of the domain name.)

names, within voicemail directories of associated business entities and reverse e-mail look-up.[44] In ***General Electric Company v. Marketing Total S.A*** the disputed domain names were registered under seven different names traceable to a controlling party.[45] However, alleging multiple domain names are jointly controlled is not sufficient to satisfy the rule.[46]

If the registrants "were, in fact, separate legal entities the Policy would usually require complainant to initiate separate proceedings against each (absent a successful request for the consolidation of multiple disputes under paragraph 10(e) of the Rules)."[47] Some WIPO Panels partially dismiss complaints without prejudice to the extent they include additional unrelated respondents.[48]

Where the evidence establishes several respondents are aliases they will be treated as alter egos of the controlling entity and "a single complaint will be properly brought in respect of multiple domain names."[49] A common feature of the several permutations of holder is that "while the registrant of record has apparent control

---

[44] ***Asset Marketing Systems, LLC v. SmartBuy Corporation, Chan Organization, Mitchell de la Cruz, Gongju Jung et. al.***, D2004-0492 (WIPO September 17, 2004); ***Speedo Holdings B.V. v. Programmer, Miss Kathy Beckerson, John Smitt, Matthew Simmons***, D2010-0281 (WIPO May 18, 2010).

[45] D2007-1834 (WIPO February 1, 2008).

[46] ***Kimberly-Clark Corporation***, supra.; ***Valeant Pharmaceuticals International, Inc. / iNova Pharmaceuticals (Australia) Pty Limited v. Luca Radu / Fundacion Private WhoIs / Maxim Conovalov / Vasju Pere***, D2013-1918 (WIPO February 3, 2014) ("The Complaint does not sufficiently address the question of consolidation in respect of the four Respondents. The Complainants, which have the onus of doing so, have not advanced any significant and specific evidence that would link any two or more of the Respondents together convincingly.") See also ***O2 Worldwide Limited v. Dan Putnam / Rodolfo a. Barcenas / Rhonda Peterson / Bob Terry / Whois Privacy Service / Eric Chan / Cecil Morgan / Whois Privacy Service / Christopher Redding / Domain ID Shield Service / Mary Martin / Ella Gee / John White, Rebecca Graphics / Thomas Heard / Dotty Krause / Jess Brown / Whoisguard Protected Whoisguard, Inc. / Andrew Rollinson, LetUsClose***, D2017-0658 (WIPO June 29, 2017) (Originally 77 domains. "The Panel is satisfied that consolidation in this case is not appropriate, on at least two grounds: (i) it would not be procedurally efficient; and (ii) it would not be fair and equitable to all parties. In addition, the Panel strongly doubts that it can be said that all of the disputed domain names are subject to "common control", in the sense in which that concept has been used by previous UDRP panels to date to justify consolidation, although it makes no finding to that effect."

[47] General Electric, supra.

[48] ***Boehringer Ingelheim Pharma GmbH & Co. KG v. Domains by Proxy, Inc / Pradeep Dadha / Jonathan Valicenti***, D2006-0465 (WIPO June 14, 2006) (dismissed without prejudice).

[49] ***United Parcel Services of America, Inc. v. Sean Selvidge et. al.***, FA1709001748088 (Forum October 30, 2017) (122 domain names. "In support of that claim Complainant refers to the facts that (i) all 122 domain names were registered in October 2016, (ii) all 122 names have the same registrar, Wild West Domains, LLC, (iii) all 122 names were initially registered using the same privacy service, Domains By Proxy, (iv) the email addresses listed for each of the 122 infringing domain names follow the same general format—FirstNameLastName@FirstNameLastName.onmicrosoft.

over the domain name, some other person has practical control. . . . [In that event] both persons should be considered to be a 'holder' of the disputed domain name."[50] A later Panel accepted a list from Complainant of the various factors (in its view) that pointed to common control[51]:

> (1) The use of common registration information such as administrative contact details, technical contact details, postal addresses, email addresses, IP addresses, and telephone and fax numbers;
>
> (2) The use of the same or similar names in the registration information;
>
> (3) That the disputed domain names resolve to the same or similar websites;
>
> (4) The same domain name servers are used;
>
> (5) The same registrars are used; and that
>
> (6) There is a close similarity between the disputed domain names, each of which incorporates the trade mark in its entirety in conjunction with non-distinctive, generic or geographical terms.

"It is appropriate where the facts support an alias of a multiple of registrants holding a multiple of domain names to consolidate them into a single complaint,"[52] although the GDPR redactions (Sec. 2.05-B) negatively impact this.

The Forum's Supplemental Rules address directly the situation where complainant fails to prove control.[53] The Rule provides that "[i]f the Panel determines that insufficient evidence is presented to link the alleged aliases, the domain names held by the unrelated registrants will not be subject to further consideration by that Panel."[54]

The procedure is illustrated in ***Farouk Systems***.[55] The Panel found "Respondents [were shown to] share the same identical address, telephone number, fax number and e-mail address . . . notwithstanding the use of different initials

---

com, and (v) all resolve to the same website – an inactive website displaying the same error message, "The page cannot be displayed."

50 Id.

51 ***Guccio Gucci S.p.A v. Andrea Hubner, et al.***, D2012-2212 (WIPO February 8, 2013) (128 domain names). The test was adopted by the Panel in ***Seiko Holdings Kabushiki Kaisha (trading as Seiko Holdings Corporation) v. L. Collins Travis, et al.***, D2013-0994 (WIPO August 6, 2013) (138 domains names, 22 different primary IP addresses, all of which are closely related in five groups).

52 See ***Beachbody, LLC v. Ashoeclothe.Inc @ aka Focus Limited, et al***, D2014-0382 (WIPO June 30, 2014).

53 Rule 4(f)(ii). Not covered in the WIPO Supplemental Rules.

54 ***Deckers Outdoor Corporation v. Karen McDougall, Frances Kirwan, Richard Abbots, Nicola Hammill, Sadika Ekemen, Stephen Gould, Christina Papadaki, Felicity Poole, Wang Changgui and [redacted]***, FA0908001281082 (Forum November 30, 2009).

55 D2009 1658 (WIPO January 19, 2010) commenced 11 separate cases; petition for consolidation granted. For consolidation of multiple complaints paragraph 4(f) of the Policy the petition shall

in respect of the owner's registration details for the disputed domain names." Respondent defaulted, so there was no counter evidence to contradict complainant's proof. There was also a similarity of design and details on each of the websites to which the domain names resolved. The panel in ***Speedo Holdings*** (decided a few months later) extracted the following general principles:

> 1. Consolidation of multiple registrants as respondents in a single administrative proceeding may in certain circumstances be appropriate under paragraphs 3(c) or 10(e) of the Rules provided the complainant can demonstrate that the disputed domain names or the websites to which they resolve are subject to common control, and the panel having regard to all of the relevant circumstances, determines that consolidation would be procedurally efficient and fair and equitable to all parties.
>
> 2. The dispute resolution service provider should act as a preliminary gatekeeper in such cases by determining whether or not such complaints fulfill the requisite criteria. Once a case is admitted on a prima facie basis, the respondent has the opportunity to make its submissions on the validity of the consolidation together with its substantive arguments. In the event that the UDRP panel makes a finding that the complaint has not satisfied the requisite criteria, the complainant is not precluded from filing the complaint against the individual named respondents.

Where there are substantial commonalities among the respondents of record and similarities of websites it would be procedurally efficient to consolidate and inefficient not to do so.[56] However, where there is evident diversity of interests among respondents consolidating is both inefficient and unfair. It creates "a danger that separate Respondents in potentially different positions would be 'tarred with the same brush'. That would not be fair and equitable."[57]

7.02-A.3 Multiple Unrelated Complainants in Consolidated Proceeding 7.02-A.3

Société Générale and Fimat International Banque, discussed earlier, and similar cases concern related persons or entities with trademark rights. However, consolidation is also possible by unrelated parties having "common grievances."

be made "before ... the first Administrative Panel appointed to hear a pending dispute between the parties ... provided that the disputes being consolidated are governed by this Policy or a later version of this Policy adopted by ICANN."

56 ***Smart Voucher Ltd T/A UKASH v. Ukash Paysafe, Ukash Kart***, D2011-1843 (WIPO January 3, 2012) (71 domain names).

57 ***O2 Worldwide Limited v. Dan Putnam / Rodolfo a. Barcenas / Rhonda Peterson / Bob Terry / Whois Privacy Service / Eric Chan / Cecil Morgan / Whois Privacy Service / Christopher Redding / Domain ID Shield/ Dotty Krause / Jess Brown / Whoisguard Protected Whoisguard, Inc. / Andrew Rollinson, LetUsClose***, D2017-0658 (WIPO June 29, 2017) ("The Panel believes that, given the diversity of the Respondents and their relatively loose connection to each other (membership of a

There are also factual circumstances in which an unrelated group of Complainants have a common grievance. The issue first arose in 2008 in which an unrelated group of Complainants with no shared interest in a particular trademark initiated a consolidated complaint under the Australian Domain Resolution Policy (auDRP).[58]

The Panel divided the issue into two parts:

> First, the panel should answer the question: do these complainants have a truly common grievance against the respondent? If the answer to that question is 'no', consolidation should not be permitted. If the answer to that question is 'yes', it is necessary to answer the second question: would it be equitable and procedurally efficient to permit consolidation of complainants? If the answer to the second question is 'no', consolidation should not be permitted. If the answer to the second question is 'yes', consolidation should be permitted.

In the absence of any "overarching legal structure" or "overarching legal entity" persons and entities would have to qualify (if they could) by having a "truly common grievance." This requires proof of infringing conduct common to complainants, which in the case of ***National Dial A Word*** complainants were unable to provide.

It has been pointed out that in many salient respects the auDRP mirrors the UDRP. When consolidating unrelated complainants subsequently arose as an issue under the UDRP, Panels adopted the analysis in ***National Dial A Word.*** It was first applied to a group of complainant football clubs in the U.K.[59] Where multiple parties unrelated except for their "common grievance" do not have a common legal interest since each is protecting its own trademark their interest must be found in "common conduct" and involve readily identifiable commonalities.

As formulated in ***Fulham Football Club***, if there are readily identifiable commonalities and a clear pattern of registration and use of all the disputed domain names the Panel should turn to the following set of questions:

---

multi-level marketing scheme), the Complainant should have understood that consolidation of this Complaint would not be procedurally efficient and would not be fair and equitable to all parties.")

[58] ***National Dial A Word Registry Pty Ltd and others v. 1300 Directory Pty Ltd***, DAU2008-0021 (WIPO March 6, 2009). See Jurisprudential Overview 3.0 Paragraph 4.11.1 and 4.11.2: "In order for the filing of a single complaint brought by multiple complainants or against multiple respondents which meets the above criteria to be accepted, such complaint would typically need to be accompanied by a request for consolidation which establishes that the relevant criteria have been met. The onus of establishing this falls on the filing party/parties, and where the relevant criteria have not been met, the complaint in its filed form would not be accepted."

[59] ***Fulham Football Club (1987) Limited, Tottenham Hostpur Public Limited, West Ham United Football Club PLC, Manchester United Limited, The Liverpool Football Club And Athletic Grounds Limited v. Domains by Proxy, Inc./ Official Tickets Ltd.***, D2009-0331(WIPO May 12, 2009). Unrelated parties sharing a common interest had joined in an early UDRP dispute but there was no issue of consolidation because the lead Complainant was jointly owned by the thirty two Member

> (i) whether there is any apparent reason why it would not be equitable to permit consolidation of complainants;
>
> (ii) the extent to which complainants' substantive arguments made under each of the three elements of the Policy appear to be common to the disputed domain names;
>
> (iii) whether all complainants are represented by a single authorized representative for the purpose of the proceedings;
>
> (iv) whether complainants clearly stipulate each disputed domain name, the individual complainant making a claim thereto, the right or rights relied upon by that complainant, the remedy sought in respect of the disputed domain name, and the registrar with whom the disputed domain name is registered;
>
> (v) whether the case involves a relatively small number of domain names;
>
> (vi) that relevant filings, including any annexes, would not appear to be unreasonably voluminous;
>
> (vii) whether there is an applicable fee schedule covering the complaint as filed.

Judged by these criteria the Panel in ***Fulham Football Club*** found in favor of consolidation and ordered the domain names transferred, each corresponding name to the right Complainant.[60]

What particularly marks ***National Dial A Word*** and distinguishes ***Fulham Football Club*** and similar cases is disparateness among complainants. The existence of "potential[ly] . . . different outcomes of one or more domain name disputes based on the differing nature of the rights asserted by the individual Complainants" so undercuts procedural efficiency that "it would be equitabl[y] and procedurally [in]efficient to permit consolidation."[61] Where the disparate complainants do not

---

Clubs of the National Football League, ***NFL Properties, Inc. et al. v. Rusty Rahe***, D2000-0128 (WIPO April 26, 2000).

[60] The Panel in ***National Dial A Word*** approves an "appropriate and balanced [review]. . . in as efficient and cost effective a manner as is fairly possible" with one caution, that "the test must be applied judiciously and depending upon the circumstances of particular cases may require the exercise of a panel's discretion in adapting it as appropriate." See also ***London Court of International Arbitration (LCIA), International Chamber of Commerce (ICC), Singapore International Arbitration Centre (SIAC), Arbitration Institute of the Stockholm Chamber of Commerce (SCC), American Arbitration Association/ International Center for Dispute Resolution (AAA/ICDR) v. ICSID Lawyers, LLC***, D2013-0685 (WIPO June 21, 2013) ("The Respondent argues that its use is not in bad faith because it is part of modern search engine optimisation practice. While it may be legal to register descriptive domain names to build a business or to improve a business's rankings on Google (the Panel makes no findings on this point), it is not permitted under the UDRP to deliberately register a domain name that by its very nature will create a likelihood of confusion with a complainant's trademark for commercial purposes (unless a registrant itself has demonstrated rights or legitimate interests, which is not the case here.")

[61] ***Grupo Bimbo S.A.B. de C.V., Bimbo Hungria ZRT., Arnold Products, Inc., Orograin Bakeries Products, Inc., Bimbo Bakeries USA, Inc. v. John Paulsen***, D2010-1647 (WIPO December 3, 2010).

qualify for a consolidated hearing it is appropriate to dismiss the complaint without prejudice and allow each to commence its own administrative proceeding.[62]

7.02-A.4 7.02-A.4 Domain Names Combining Complainant's Marks with Marks of Third Parties

Where there are multiple, related complainants each will be entitled to the domain name in which it has a right and to the remedy it elects. However, where the challenged domain name is composed of trademarks owned by different parties, but only one is complaining the question turns on whether the proper remedy is cancellation or transfer absent joinder or consent from the other trademark owner. Consensus on this issue has been developing, although with more clarity from WIPO Panels than Forum's.

Some Panels (appointed by WIPO) have "reach[ed] the conclusion that cancellation [but not transfer] may be an apt remedy when there is no consent by the third-party trademark holder."[63] Other panelists are of the view that while "a complainant ideally should try to obtain the third party's consent before seeking transfer" it is not absolutely necessary.[64]

Forum appointed panelists have granted standing and transfer without the detailed analyses by WIPO panelists but other Forum panelists have dismissed complaints unless all mark owners join in the proceeding on the theory the "Complaint alleges no nexus between it and the owner of the [co-joined] mark." The Panel

---

[62] This should not fall afoul of any doctrine precluding refiling complaints. "[I]n these circumstances the individual complaints should not constitute re-filed complaints," ***Fulham Football Club***, supra.

[63] ***Dr. Ing. h.c. F. Porsche AG v. Automotive Parts Solutions***, D2003-0725 (WIPO November 17, 2003) (<911hyundai.com>), *cited in* ***Lilly ICOS LLC v. Tudor Burden, Burden Marketing***, D2004-0794 (WIPO December 20, 2004). Several UDRP panels have reached the opposite result, granting transfer in the absence of third-party consent but in doing so emphasize that "such decision would be expressly without prejudice to any rights, which may be asserted by third party trademark holder," *citing* ***Decathlon SAS v. Nadia Michalski***, *supra*. See, e.g., ***F. Hoffmann-La Roche AG v. Bob***, D2006-0751. (WIPO July 20, 2006).

[64] ***Kabbage, Inc. v. Oneandone Private Registration, 1&1 Internet Inc. - www.1and1.com / Robert Hanssen, Ridiculous File Sharing***, D2015-1507 (WIPO November 20, 2015) (<kabbage4amazon.com>. "[W]here Complainant has fulfilled all the elements of Policy paragraph 4(a), expressed a strong preference for transfer over cancellation, and demonstrated to the satisfaction of the Panel that it is cognizant of its obligations to respect the rights of third-party trademark holders, the Panel is willing" to grant the request. See also ***Incase Designs Corp. v. Rogenie LLC, Rogenie Cordero***, D2012-1491 (WIPO September 12, 2012) (<iponeincase.com>. "There is no indication in the record that Apple Inc. would consent to the remedy of transfer to Complainant, and indeed, Complainant appears to be disinclined to request Apple Inc.'s authorization. In these circumstances, therefore, the Panel has determined that it is most consistent with the Policy and its injunction of efficiency not to delay the proceedings by ordering Complainant to seek such authorization.").

[65] There is no precedent for the "nexus" theory; it appeared from nowhere in late 2016 in ***NIKE, Inc. and Nike Innovate, C.V. v. Mattia Lumini and Yykk Snc***, FA1606001679233 (Forum July 15,

continues, "[a]s such, Complainant essentially has standing to bring this claim regarding the NSK mark but not the SKF mark."[65]

As noted above in 7.02-A.1.a, the concept of a nexus requirement for multiple complainants is written into the Forum's Supplemental Rule 1(e) (WIPO has no corresponding rule), but its application to combined marks where there is no nexus is at once a departure from precedent and an attempt to expand the scope of the Policy to include such hybrids.[66]

7.02-B Refiling a Complaint: New Facts or Fresh Evidence 7.02-B

7.02-B.1 Standard for Reopening Closed Case 7.02-B.1

7.02-B.1.a *Eligibility for Refiling Complaint* *7.02-B.1.a*

Unlike some country code Policies UDRP Panels have no appellate authority to rehear a decided dispute.[67] "Once a party has been given a defended hearing . . . and a decision rendered, then a case cannot be re-litigated."[68] Grievances must be carried to a court of competent jurisdiction.[69] Although nowhere expressly provided in the UDRP or Rules there are circumstances under which a Panel will accept a refiled complaint. The grounds for examining a claim for cancellation or transfer of the same disputed domain name are narrow. Authority has been found to rest on the second clause of Rule 15(a), which grants Panels discretion to apply "any rules and principles of law that it deems applicable."

UDRP Panels have adopted as a test of eligibility for refiling a complaint rules commonly articulated in common law jurisdictions, namely proof of "a) serious misconduct by a judge, juror, witness or lawyer; [or] b) perjured evidence being offered to the Court; [or] c) the discovery of credible and material evidence which could not have been reasonably foreseen or known at trial; [or] d) a breach of natural

---

2016) (<nikegoogle.com>) and cited in ***NSK LTD. v. Li shuo***, FA1701001712449 (Forum February 16, 2017) (<skfnsk.com>) and ***Dell Inc. v. Ionel Adrian Nicolae***, FA 1683104 (FORUM August 22, 2016) ("Nvidia Corp. has not been joined as a Complainant in this matter and there is no nexus available through which Complainant can claim to have rights to the transfer of the <alienware-nvidia.xyz> domain name"); The "nikegoogle" dispute was refiled by both mark owners and the domain name transferred, ***NIKE, Inc., Nike Innovate, C.V., and Google Inc. v. Mattia Lumini / Yykk Snc***, FA160800 1687597 (Forum September 20, 2016).

[66] Consistency and predictability are discussed earlier in Section 1.05.

[67] Nominet (ukDRS) (Revised 2016, effective October 1, 2016).

[68] ***Grove Broadcasting Co. Ltd. v. Telesystems Commc'ns Ltd.***, D2000-0703 (WIPO November 10, 2000) ("In the present situation, there are no Rules relating to a 'reapplication', 'rehearing' or 'reconsideration' of a Complaint. It is therefore appropriate to consider by analogy well understood rules and principles of law relating to the re litigation of cases determined after a defended hearing," citing cases from the United Kingdom and New Zealand.)

[69] A stay procedure is set forth in Rule 4(k) of the Rules of the Policy. Discussed further in "Plenary Adjudication After an Adverse Decision" (Sec. 8.01-B).

justice/due process."[70] Tests b and c are the usual battlegrounds in a UDRP case. In neither a court of competent jurisdiction nor a UDRP proceeding is a complainant permitted to commence a new proceeding to supplement a prior deficient record.[71] The party offering proof has to get it right the first time.[72]

The ***Grove Broadcasting*** test was further refined in ***Creo Products***[73] and ***Jones Apparel Group***.[74] In ***Creo 2*** the Panel held that 1) the burden of establishing grounds for entertaining a refiled complaint rests on complainant; 2) the burden is "high"; and 3) complainant should clearly identify the grounds for entertaining the refiled complaint. A rehearing under the third ground would require 1) proof the evidence could not have been obtained with reasonable due diligence for use during the initial arbitration; 2) proof that, if the evidence had been presented at the initial arbitration, it would probably have had an important influence on the result of the arbitration (though not necessarily decisive); and 3) the evidence must be credible, although it need not be incontrovertible.

In ***Jones Apparel*** the Panel reaffirmed the value of upholding the principle of *res judicata* and deterring UDRP "forum shopping" by carefully scrutinizing refiled complaints. It noted the four conditions named in ***Grove*** for accepting a refiled complaint and argued sensibly for applying "common sense" to the circumstances

---

70 Grove, supra.: "The integrity of the ICANN Policy and procedure requires that if a reconsideration of the same Complaint is to be entertained, there should be proof that one of the strict grounds discussed in this decision has been made out." The law applied under the Canadian Internet Registration Authority (CIRA) is conceptually different. "There is nothing in the CDRP or its rules prohibits the resubmission of a complaint involving the same facts and the same parties." ***The Corporation of Scouts Canada v. Lima Morland***, CIRA Dispute # 00298 (2015), citing ***Bowring and Co., Inc. v. Eric Maddeaux***, CIRA Dispute #00166 (2008).

71 Id. Where "complainant initiated proceeding without proper documentation or proof . . . [it] has to take the consequences."

72 *Id*: The Panel citing U.K. law emphasized that complainant must show "the [new] evidence could not have been obtained with reasonable diligence for use at the trial; second, the evidence must be such that, if given, it would probably have an important influence on the result of the case, although it need not be decisive; third, the evidence must be such as is presumably to be believed, or in other words, it must be apparently credible, although it need not be incontrovertible." This warning has been applied to other circumstances where complainants have been remiss in providing proof. See ***Florida Weimaraner Rescue, Inc. d/b/a Weimaraner Rescue of Florida v. weimaraner rescue of florida a/k/a Lauren R Simmons and TechKraft Inc. c/o Jim Horn***, FA101100 1356030 (Forum December 28, 2010) ("If title in the Trademark had, in fact, been transferred to Complainant, then, evidence of that important fact should have been submitted in this proceeding."); ***CAM London Limited and Comgest Asset Management International Limited v. Cam LondonLtd***, D2013-2190 (WIPO February 4, 2014) (Certificate of incorporation, not proof of common law right). "Second bite at the apple" discussed further in "Procedural Orders" (Sec. 7.07-A).

73 ***Creo Products Limited v. Website in Development ("Creo 2")***, D2000-1490 (WIPO January 19, 2001).

74 ***Jones Apparel Group Inc. v. Jones Apparel Group.com***, D2001-1041 (WIPO October 16, 2001).

of each case.[75] Substantial injustice has also been found to support a refiling of the complaint, but exercised with care.[76] Complainant who is either unable to establish a present right or marshal sufficient evidence of bad faith belongs in a court of competent jurisdiction.[77]

The standard for proving new facts or fresh evidence can be illustrated in two cases in which Complainants were unsuccessful, ***Furrytails***[78] and ***Assurant***.[79] In the first case Respondent formerly owned Complainant, a U.K. company. The terms of the sale included a six-month noncompetition clause. After the stipulated period respondent set up a business in the United States marketing promotional resin collectibles of animals and characters and registered <furrytails.com>. The first Panel concluded Respondent had complied with the terms of the sale agreement and his registration of the domain name was not in bad faith.

The second Panel concluded Respondent's offer to sell the domain name and goodwill associated with his business in the United States "could not indicate an intention to sell a domain name for an amount greater than the Respondent's out of pocket costs directly related to the domain name (absent any evidence of an apportionment of the separate values of the business and the domain name) for the purposes of section 4(b)(i) of the Policy." The subsequent acts were "either a repetition of, or substantially the same as, the acts on which the previous complaint was based."

In the original proceeding in ***Assurant 1***[80] Respondent offered persuasive evidence it had made demonstrable preparations to use the domain name under paragraph 4(c)(i) of the Policy. The refiled complaint alleged respondent was a serial cybersquatter, a statement that was apparently true but irrelevant. Complainant

---

[75] Id. A separate basis for accepting the refiled complaint was that the first Panel did not exercise its discretion under Rule 12 to request further evidence of trademark rights in that proceeding. See also ***Sensis Pty Ltd, Telstra Corporation Limited v. Yellow Pages Marketing B.V.*** , D2011-0057 (WIPO March 15, 2011) ("Sensis 2") discussed below.

[76] ***High Speed Productions, Inc. d/b/a Thrasher Magazine v Thrasher Magazine, Ltd.***, FA0103000097008 (Forum June 20, 2001); ***Ascentive, LLC v. Jiang Lixin***, FA1202001428642 (Forum March 20, 2012) (failed second time for lack of evidence of unregistered rights predating domain name registration).

[77] Example, complainant with a pending trademark application, ***Ascentive, LLC v. Jiang Lixin***, FA1202001428642 (Forum March 20, 2012) (failed second time for lack of evidence of unregistered rights predating domain name registration). See also, ***Bulbs 4 East Side Inc., d/b/a Just Bulbs v. Fundacion Private Whois/Gregory Ricks***, D2013-1779 (WIPO January 13, 2014) (Complaint denied, but successful in ACPA action, *Bulbs 4 E. Side, Inc. v. Ricks*, (S.D. Tex., Houston Div. July 18, 2017) together with a damages award of $50,000 and attorney's fees.

[78] ***Furrytails Limited v. Andrew Mitchell d/b/a Oxford Die Cast***, D2001-0857 (WIPO September 5, 2001) (three-member Panel).

[79] ***Assurant, Inc. v. Tom Baert.***, FA0802001143728 (Forum June 25, 2008) (***Assurant 2***).

[80] FA 893437 (Forum March 5, 2007).

failed to "show . . . development of new, credible, material evidence *which was not foreseen at the time of the previous dispute*" (emphasis added).

Complainant has a threshold burden in filing a new complaint to reopen a closed case that is preclusive if unsatisfied. The refiling also exposes it to a declaration of abusive conduct.[81] However, once complainant shows there is "new, credible, material evidence" respondent's *res judicata* defense falls.[82] The filing of a new complaint against a successor registrant unrelated to respondent in an earlier proceeding is not barred by the doctrine of *res judicata*.[83]

7.02-B.1.b 7.02-B.1.b *New Acts by Respondent*

New acts by respondent include 1) pattern of conduct[84]; 2) changing its website to include new meta-tags incorporating complainant's trademarks[85]; and 3) change of content or business model over time.[86] Fresh evidence unavailable at the time of the first submission and changed circumstances include subsequent acquisition of a trademark registration.[87] In ***Alpine Entertainment*** the second Panel drew a distinction between the circumstances in ***Grove*** in which complainant chose to withhold evidence—"[t]he learned panel in [Grove] . . . also concluded by observing that while complainant should have presented all of its evidence the first time, it chose not to do so"—and the refiled case:

> while [complainant] may have chosen the original time of filing, [it] has nevertheless presented new and probative evidence which was not in existence at that point, and of which the previous panel did not have the benefit in rendering its earlier decision.

---

[81] ***Ficep v. Daniel Dimov***, CAC 100739 (ADR.eu February 13, 2014) ("Given the unequivocal nature of the First Decision, the Complainant must therefore have known that the Second Complaint had no reasonable chance of success.") Discussed further in "Reverse Domain Name Hijacking" (Sec. 7.11-A).

[82] ***Abt Electronics, Inc. v. Gregory Ricks***, FA0701000904239 (Forum March 27, 2007). See Circuit Court decision in *Storey v. Cello Holdings*, LLC., 347 F.3d 370, 385 387 (2nd Cir. 2003) (the district court "erred by treating a registrant's right to use a domain name as akin to a property interest, fixed by events that occurred at a specific point in the past, and shielded from subsequent attack by res judicata.")

[83] ***Pier Giorgio Andretta v. Corrado Giubertoni***, D2016-2496 (WIPO February 2017) (<giordana. com>).

[84] ***Gassan Diamonds B.V. v. Internet Dating.Com***, D2011-0774 (WIPO July 29, 2011) (transferred).

[85] ***Legal & General Group Plc v. Image Plus***, D2003-0603 (WIPO September 23, 2003). See *Network Automation, Inc. v. Advanced Systems Concepts, Inc.*, 638 F.3rd 1137, 1146 n.3 (9th Cir., 2011) ("Modern search engines such as Google no longer use metatags. Instead they rely on their own algorithms to find websites.")

[86] ***Daimler AG v. William Wood***, D2008-1712 (WIPO February 25, 2009).

[87] ***Alpine Entertainment Group, Inc. v. Walter Alvarez***, D2007-1082 (WIPO December 4, 2007).

Once a trademark issues the owner's right is retroactive to the date of the application, which may be earlier than registration of the domain name.[88]

New circumstances have also included a showing the first Panel was misled by respondent's inaccurate facts as well as its own "private investigations." This issue was examined by a three-member Panel in accepting a refiling of the disputed domain name.[89] While a consensus approves "private investigations" the results are extrinsic to the record and raise a fairness issue.[90] The ***Sensis 2*** Panel found "this also to be a sufficient reason for accepting the refiled Complaint, in the interests of achieving procedural fairness and a fully considered decision on this material issue."

According to the ***Sensis 2*** Panel "it often would be fair—and helpful in reaching a just and informed decision—for a UDRP panel to request information and comments from the parties concerning new or reasonably unanticipated facts or legal issues." It can do this under Rule 12. The Panel proposed applying a standard developed for accepting unsolicited supplemental filings to reply to unexpected issues raised in responses. "In our view, the same standard should apply when the panel is considering new or unanticipated factual or legal material on its own initiative, where that material could be dispositive and where it is reasonably subject to challenge or interpretation."

Panels have declined to rule on *res judicata* and issue preclusion defenses on cases that return to UDRP proceedings following unresolved civil court actions. They are uncertain as to whether the "intricacies of issue preclusion . . . can be used in a proceeding [of this kind]"[91] and that "strict application of principles of claim and issue preclusion could work an injustice."[92]

7.02-B.2 Dismissal as Outside the Scope of the Policy 7.02.B.2

Grove Broadcasting applies to proceedings in which the claim of abusive registration was within the scope of the Policy. Paragraph 4(k) of the Policy advises the parties that the "mandatory administrative proceeding requirements . . . shall not prevent either you or complainant from submitting the dispute to a court of competent jurisdiction for independent resolution before such mandatory administrative proceeding is commenced. . . ." A prior pending action in a court of law

---

88 Jurisprudential Overview 3.0, Paragraph 1.1.4. An application pending before the trademark authority does not support jurisdiction under paragraph 4(a)(i) of the Policy. Discussed further in "No Right Accrues to Pending Application for Trademark" (Sec. 4.01-A.3.c).

89 ***Sensis 2***, supra, D2011-0057 (Transferred). ***Sensis 1*** is found at D2006-0793 (WIPO August 22, 2006) (Complaint denied).

90 See "Researching on the Internet" (Sec. 7.06-B) and Jurisprudential Overview 3.0, Paragraph 4.8.

91 ***Marcus R. Schatte d/b/a Sex v. Pers.***, FA 124756 (Forum November 4, 2002).

92 ***High Speed Prod., Inc. v. Thrasher Magazine, Ltd.***, FA 97008 (Forum June 20, 2001). See also ***SAS Institute, Inc. v. ALU a/k/a J. Barein***, FA 126631 (Forum November 8, 2002).

or one commenced after service of the UDRP complaint in which the disputed domain name is in issue necessarily removes the case from the Panel. If a complaint is filed notwithstanding the prior pending action it will be dismissed.[93] The Panel in ***Automobile Atlanta*** stated that it "defers to a tribunal that will have the benefit of all the evidence and, in any case, a UDRP decision cannot be implemented during the pendency of a related civil action."[94]

However, if the related civil action is brought to an end without resolution of the substantive claims and the action is dismissed a new factual circumstance springs into existence that supports a refiling of the UDRP complaint. In this event there should be no impediment to proceeding anew to determine whether respondent is liable for abusive registration. In ***Automobile Atlanta 2*** respondent contended the complaint should be dismissed on the principle of claim or issue preclusion.[95] "Curiously, Respondent appears to labour under the delusion that . . . dismissal [of the civil action] is of no account, arguing that due to the mediated settlement and the panel's previous denial, the principles of *res judicata* should be enforced." Since the dismissal of the civil action clearly brings it "to an end . . . the Panel sees no reason why those proceedings should prevent it from rendering a Decision on the present Complaint."[96] In that event the decision rests upon the settled rules established in ***Grove Broadcasting***.

7.02.B.3 7.02-B.3 Complaint Dismissed With and Without Prejudice

The UDRP (as panelists consistently point out) is not a process designed to render decisions in which parties have competing rights. Such disputes belong in a court of competent jurisdiction. It may be appropriate to dismiss a complaint with prejudice where the Panel finds the domain name claim is inextricably bound up with other issues beyond the scope of the Policy,[97] but without prejudice and even

---

93 ***Automobile Atlanta, Inc. v. Treadway Solutions***, FA0905001264729 (Forum July 20, 2009).

94 ***Automobile Atlanta, Inc. v. Treadway Solutions***, FA0905001292305 (Forum December 18, 2009) (***Automobile Atlanta*** "2").

95 "[A]s to whether principles of claim or issue preclusion apply in proceedings under the Policy . . . common law principles should not be applied in this relatively new and developing area," ***Digital Logic AG v. Jordano Daemonti***, FA 273488 (Forum July 9, 2004), and "strict application of principles of claim and issue preclusion could work an injustice," ***High Speed Prod., Inc. v. Thrasher Magazine, Ltd.***, FA 97008 (Forum June 20, 2001).

96 The Panel invited complainant to refile in ***Jetfly Aviation SA v. Jens K. Styve / Domains by Proxy, Inc. and Happy Landings S.A.***, D2010-0244 (WIPO April 5, 2010) if the court established its right to the trademark without ruling on the corresponding domain name.

97 See ***Fuze Beverage, LLC v. CGEye, Inc. c/o Thomas Siedleczka***, FA844252 (Forum January 8, 2007) (finding dismissal with prejudice appropriate where "it is not the kind of controversy, grounded exclusively in abusive cyber-squatting, that the Policy was designed to address.")

invite complainant to return to a UDRP proceeding on proof of changed circumstances.[98] Sufficiency "would be a matter for a subsequent panel to determine."[99]

A number of panelists have expressly granted permission to complainants or paved their way to refiling complaints on grounds that stretch the test announced in ***Grove Broadcasting***.[100] In ***Cluett, Peabody*** the panel allowed a complaint to be refiled because the previous Panel had "expressly reserved the right of Complainant to recharge bad faith registration and use of the domain name in issue."[101] The Panel in ***Jones Apparel*** allowed refiling because the previous panelist gave the "green light in the clearest possible way to refiling the Complaint to correct [the previous Complaint's omissions]."[102]

"Dismissal without prejudice" appears to be more common among Forum panelists than WIPO's. For example, in ***Maple Donuts***[103] the Panel found that

---

[98] See ***Suspensions, LLC v. The LBC Group, Inc. d/b/a Creative Associates***, FA0701000 886217 (Forum March 27, 2007) (successful on a refiled complaint) and ***Suspensions, LLC v. The LBC Group, Inc. d/b/a Creative Associates***, FA0603000662305 (Forum May 5, 2006) (dismissed without prejudice). In *Newport News Holdings Corporation v. Virtual City Vision, Incorporated, d/b/a Van James Bond Tran*, 650 F3d 423 (4th Cir. 2011) the trademark owner (complaint dismissed in ***Newport News, Inc. v. Vcv Internet***, AF 0238 [eResolution July 18, 2000]) chose to commence an action under the Lanham Act rather than refile a UDRP proceeding when in 2008 the respondent/defendant "shifted its focus away from the legitimate service of providing information related to the City of Newport News" to competing with the plaintiff for Internet traffic. The court held a domain name holder "cannot escape the consequences of its deliberate metamorphosis." Plaintiff successfully moved for partial summary judgment on its ACPA claim and obtained in addition to the domain name substantial statutory damages.

[99] ***A. D. Banker & Company v. Domain Invest***, D2010-1044 (WIPO September 30, 2010).

[100] In ***Leah Kando v. Elms Web Services, Inc.***, FA0805001192082 (Forum July 2, 2008), the Panel dismissed the complaint "without prejudice" because complainant failed to submit any evidence on her alleged unregistered trademark. Also, ***Umpqua Investments, Inc. v. Private Registrations Aktien Gesellschaft***, FA1005001324718 (Forum June 15, 2010); ***Air Serbia a.d. Beograd Jurija v. Domains By Proxy, LLC / Meijun Lu***, D2017-1986 (WIPO December 18, 2017) (<jat.com>. "Should subsequent evidence come to light which would demonstrate a bad faith intent on the Respondent's part, it is possible that a future panel may entertain a refiling of this Complaint (on this topic, see section 4.18 of the WIPO Overview 3.0). However, if the Complainant chooses to refile the Complaint at some point in the future, this Panel would certainly expect the Complainant to provide a full and complete description of the history of the disputed domain name and the Complainant's part in that history along with relevant new evidence.")

[101] ***Cluett, Peabody & Co., Inc. v. Sanford Bus. Writing Serv.***, FA 95842 (Forum December 12, 2000).

[102] ***Jones Apparel Group Inc. v. Jones Apparel Group.com***, D2001-1041 (WIPO October 16, 2001). See also, ***Scottish Provident Limited v. Scottish Provident Ministry***, D2002-1059 (WIPO January 9, 2003) (The Panel concluded the decision with the words, "If it (the Complainant) were to discover new facts that were evidence of bad faith it could consider requesting another Administrative Panel to consider the matter, whether that Administrative Panel could or would do so is an issue to be resolved at the time.")

complainant had a trademark on its design for MAPLE DONUTS, but because it disclaimed both words apart from the design mark as shown, it had demonstrated no trademark right. It held "complainant is free to refile with more evidence of its common law rights in the MAPLE DONUTS mark."

In another case involving infringement claims to five domain names the Panel found for complainant on three of them and granted it a right to refile its complaint with respect to the other two:[104]

> The CRAFTSMAN and KMART marks are well known in the American culture; and Complainant probably is able to show that the CRAFTSMAN and KMART marks are protected by registrations with the USPTO dating from a period that is much earlier than the dates of Respondent's registrations of the disputed domain names. However, Complainant did not provide the Panel with either allegations or documents to permit the Panel to make a ruling in that regard.

A refiled complaint was thereafter submitted to the same panelist and decided in complainant's favor.[105]

At least one WIPO Panel, finding it "difficult . . . to resolve [the issue of bad faith] on the present record" adopted the procedure of inviting complainant to return "if, for example it was to come to light only after the issuing of the present decision that respondent had in fact been aware of and utilizing complainant's Terms of Service at or prior to the registration of the first disputed domain name, or other new evidence of actual knowledge of complainant's marks and business."[106] There is an implicit invitation in the Panel's coda in ***Hostess Brands***[107]:

> [I]f Respondent, in the future, would attempt to extract a significant sum from Complainant for purchase of this Domain Name identical to Complainant's HOSTESS trademark, these circumstances may provide support for application of the Policy's paragraph 4(b). . . .

"In the future" includes any successor holder acquiring the domain name for a proscribed purpose.

---

[103] ***Maple Donuts, Inc. v. Technology Investments Group, Inc.***, FA0703000930711 (Forum April 13, 2007).

[104] ***Sears Brands, LLC & Kmart of Michigan, Inc. v. Domain Administration Limited a/k/a David Halstead a/k/a DomainAdministrationLimited a/k/a William Vaughan***, FA0802001143502 (Forum April 3, 2008).

[105] FA0804001177524 (Forum June 12, 2008).

[106] ***UpsideOut, Inc. v. Lin Han***, D2009-0388 (WIPO July 7, 2009).

[107] ***Hostess Brands, Inc. f/k/a Interstate Bakeries Corporation v. Domain Capital***, D2009-1357 (WIPO December 1, 2009).

7.03 RULE 5—CONCERNING RESPONDENT 7.03

7.03-A Rule of Timely Submission or Lose Right to Defend 7.03-A

7.03-A.1 Timely Submission 7.03-A.1

> Rule 5(a): Within twenty (20) days of the date of commencement of the administrative proceeding respondent shall submit a response to the Provider.
>
> Rule 5(b): The Respondent may expressly request an additional four (4) days in which to respond to the complaint, and the Provider shall automatically grant the extension.

Except that Providers and Panels may on application extend due dates[108] there are different levels of tolerance for untimeliness.[109] Individual panelists notwithstanding, Panels in the formative cases generally showed flexibility in ruling on respondents' late submissions, particularly where facsimile responses were timely, but not receipt of hard copies. This problem is mitigated in the revision to the Rules effective March 1, 2010, by having pleadings and annexes served electronically as attachments to e-mails.[110] The revision did not address the issue of time zones.[111]

Panel approaches are uneven, but as a general rule late responses are accepted where they are not filed substantially late and before commencement of the decision making process; where failure to take the response into account would have led to a miscarriage of justice; and where the response is late by only one day and did not

---

[108] ***Telstra Corp. v. Chu***, D2000-0423 (WIPO June 21, 2000). Providers and Panels also have authority to suspend proceedings to accommodate the parties, but this is always a temporary cessation. By Provider: Requested in expectation that respondent will execute document to voluntarily transfer domain name, which generally does not happen. ***Efficient Networks, Inc. v. Speedstream***, D2000-1136 (WIPO December 10, 2000). By Panel: Disappointed expectation of settlement. ***Novartis AG v. Barry Shisgal***, D2012-0420 (WIPO May 9, 2012) (Complainant's representative filed application for suspension of the proceedings to enable the parties to discuss settlement. Reinstated after 32 days.)

[109] ***Talktalk Telecom Limited, CPW Brands Limited v. Hélio Bragança (a.k.a. N/A)***, D2010-0361 (WIPO April 22, 2010) ("The Panel does not accept the Respondent's assertion that he thought that the time limit was 20 working days from notification of the Complaint, since the Center's notification explicitly informed respondent that '[y]ou have 20 calendar days . . . within which to submit to us any Response . . .' Since respondent has not provided any other explanation for not complying with the time limit, the Panel does not accept that there are exceptional circumstances such that the time for the Response should be extended. On the contrary, to allow an extension in these circumstances would give out an undesirable message that parties can obtain relief from failure to observe procedural requirements by making submissions which lack candour.")

[110] Rule 2, Communications.

[111] See ***SPS Commerce, Inc. v. Pooranan Balasubramanian, and Singapore Post Limited***, FA1703001724584 (Forum May 24, 2017) ("Neither the UDRP Rules nor the FORUM Supplemental Rules specifies any particular time zone that applies for purposes of submission deadlines. Nor did the FORUM in its Notice of Complaint indicate that it interpreted deadlines in

prejudice the complainant.[112] In one such case the Panel stated it may consider a response that is one day late, and received before a panelist is appointed and any consideration made.[113] "[R]uling a Response inadmissible because of formal deficiencies would be an extreme remedy inconsistent with the basic principles of due process. . . ."[114]

This view is carried forward to later cases. One Panel stated it "holds the view that it is sufficient that Respondent has met the deadline in its time zone."[115] And, even "if it is assumed that the Response was filed one day late, the panels would agree with the views held in previous UDRP decisions that the lateness of Respondent's response is *de minimis* and has not prejudiced complainants nor has it delayed the Decision in this Administrative Proceeding."[116]

Another Panel carried tolerance one step further and accepted a response several days late even though respondent demonstrated no "exceptional hardship."[117] The Panel held "there is no indication of significant prejudice to complainant." Complainant had sent a cease-and-desist letter to respondent five years after the domain name was registered and "then waited another three years before initiating this proceedings. After years of tolerating respondent's ownership of the parked Domain Name [<juicydetails.com>], complainant could not credibly in this Panel's view object to a six-day delay for the Response." The Panel found Complainant's assertion that "Respondent [located in the U.K.] was aware of the commercial activities of Complainant," who was located in the Netherlands, "mystifying" since the phrase is "commonly used [in the English language] . . . to denote gossip or titillating information" and dismissed the complaint.

That some panelists are forgiving does not mean that untimely submission will be rewarded. "[I]t is important to apply the Rules as written, absent a good reason . . . [o]therwise, parties will feel free to disregard deadlines and Respondents will

---

accordance with a particular time zone. The Panel thus finds that the Response, submitted on May 1, 2017 according to Respondent's time zone, was timely.")

112 See ***bwin.party digital entertainment plc and ElectraWorks Limited v. B7win Ltd***, D2015-1709 (WIPO November 25, 2015. Requested extension "almost a month after the expiry of the deadline to do so.").

113 ***Bd. of Governors of the Univ. of Alberta v. Katz***, D2000-0378 (WIPO June 22, 2000).

114 ***Strum v. Nordic Net Exch. AB***, FA 102843 (Forum Feb. 21, 2002).

115 ***AIB-Vincotte Belgium ASBL, AIB-Vincotte USA Inc./Corporation Texas v. Guillermo Lozada***, D2005-0485 (WIPO August 29, 2005).

116 Respondent in ***Credit Europe Bank N.V. v. Peter Yu***, D2010-0737 (WIPO July 14, 2010) was timely in transmitting the response from the United States, but the response was received "by the Center in Geneva some five hours after midnight on the due date of its submission." This complies with the requirement of paragraph 2(f)(i) of the Rules.

117 ***Juicy Details B.V. v. Another.com***, D2010-0809 (WIPO July 15, 2010) (JUICY DETAILS and <juicydetails.com>).

regularly submit late responses. Thus, absent good cause, the majority of the Panel holds that late-filed responses should be disregarded."[118] Nevertheless, every effort is made to give respondent ample opportunity to appear and plead.

In ***Museum of Science***[119] respondent was given "ample warning that his registration and use of the Domain Name created a dispute that would likely lead to a proceeding such as this one." Furthermore,

> the Center provided Respondent with repeated notice and information about this proceeding including repeated notification about the deadline for filing a Response and the procedures for responding, yet Respondent failed to respond on time or show "good cause" why he was not able to respond timely. Accordingly, the Response will not be considered.

Similarly, in ***Stevland Morris a/k/a Stevie Wonder***,[120] the Panel gave Respondent further time to cure the deficiency by issuing a procedural order granting it leave to file a response by an extended date. It still failed to cure the deficiency.

The presiding panelist in ***1099 Pro*** revisited the issue of untimely submissions in a later decision, in which he enlarged on his approach for a more rigid application of the rule.[121] In order for a late response to be considered the circumstances must be "exceptional," hewing to the literal prescription in Paragraph 5(d) of the Rules of the Policy:

> As noted above, paragraphs 5(d) and 10(c) of the Rules contemplate extensions only in "exceptional" cases. An "exceptional" case, by its very nature, must be the exception, not the rule. This Panel is aware, though, of other cases in which Respondent's counsel has sought an extension or filed submissions late, allegedly for exceptional reasons.

Furthermore (the same Panel noted), the decision should not be influenced by the possibility the late response might have dictated a contrary result:

> A panel presented with a late or otherwise improper filing for which good cause has not been shown should not normally be swayed by the fact that the outcome might have been changed had the submission been accepted. Otherwise, if panels had to consider how a late or improper submission might affect their decision, it would render meaningless the inquiry into good cause. If the Rules are to be fairly applied, panels must be prepared to enforce them regardless of their potential effect on the outcome.

The severity of this view is counterbalanced by excusable circumstances. For example, where respondent submitted a timely Response electronically but failed to

---

118 ***1099 Pro, Inc. v. Convey Compliance Systems, Inc.***, D2003-0033 (WIPO April 1, 2003).

119 ***Museum of Science v. Jason Dare***, D2004-0614 (WIPO October 11, 2004).

120 ***Stevland Morris a/k/a Stevie Wonder v. Enrique Matta***, FA0805001189962 (Forum July 9, 2008).

121 ***Mobile Communication Service Inc. v. WebReg, RN***, D2005-1304 (WIPO February 24, 2006).

submit a hard copy of the Response on time, "[t]he Panel is of the view that given the technical nature of the breach and the need to resolve the real dispute between the parties that this submission should be allowed and given due weight."[122] Other Panels have held that ruling a Response inadmissible because of formal deficiencies would be an extreme remedy is inconsistent with the principles of due process.

While acceptance of an untimely response is within the discretion of the Panel the Panel has no authority to waive the certification requirement.[123] In ***Stevland Morris a/k/a Stevie Wonder*** the Panel held that "[e]ven had the required certification been included, Respondent's claims would not be entitled to significant weight, as they are unaccompanied by any supporting evidence." A Panel may choose not to consider any factual statements, even in the case of *pro se* parties.[124]

7.03-A.2

7.03-A.2 Extension of Time to Submit

> Rule 5(d):
> At the request of the Respondent, the Provider may, in exceptional cases, extend the period of time for the filing of the response. The period may also be extended by written stipulation between the Parties, provided the stipulation is approved by the Provider.

It has been suggested that it is "generally desirable for any respondent seeking an extension first to apply to complainant or its representative before approaching the Center for an extension."[125] A stipulation agreeing to an extension supports an application without the need to demonstrate "exceptional" circumstances. A request for an extension without proof of "exceptional" circumstances "appears to be yet another attempt by a respondent to keep its domain names a bit longer, for whatever reason."[126]

---

[122] ***J.W. Spear & Sons PLC v. Fun League Mgmt.***, FA 180628 (Forum October 17, 2003).

[123] ***Talk City, Inc. v. Robertson***, D2000-0009 (WIPO February 29, 2000) ("Although the Panel is granted discretion to consider late responses, it is not granted similar discretion to waive the Rule 5(b)(viii) certification requirement.") There is a mirror image requirement for complainants at Paragraph 3(b)(xiv) of the Rules. Paragraph 5(b)(viii) of the Rules of the Policy: "Respondent certifies that the information contained in this Response is to the best of Respondent's knowledge complete and accurate, that this Response is not being presented for any improper purpose, such as to harass, and that the assertions in this Response are warranted under these Rules and under applicable law, as it now exists or as it may be extended by a good faith and reasonable argument."

[124] ***Churchill Insurance Co., Ltd. v. Churchhill Financial Services, Ltd.***, FA 0906001270466 (Forum September 1, 2009).

[125] ***World Wrestling Entertainment Inc. v. Israel Joffe***, D2010-0860 (WIPO July 1, 2010).

[126] Id.

7.03-B Consequences of Default 7.03-B

A complainant does not prevail on its pleadings alone any more than a respondent forfeits the domain name for failing to answer the complaint.[127] The general rule in commercial arbitration is that default is treated as a denial of the substantive allegations rather than an admission of liability, as it would be in a court of competent jurisdiction.[128] There is no equivalent of a default judgment, but failing to respond to the complaint has consequences. Silence speaks.[129] It makes respondent "vulnerable to the inferences that flow naturally from a complainant's not unreasonable assertion of fact."[130]

A complaint typically alleges a mix of facts and inferences reasonably to be drawn from them and conclusory allegations supported by the evidence attached as annexes. Rule 5(e) of the Rules of the UDRP reads: "If a Respondent does not submit a response, in the absence of exceptional circumstances, the Panel shall decide the dispute based upon the complaint."

As a general rule where respondent fails to contest the contentions and submits no evidence, the Panel "is left to render its decision on the basis of the uncontroverted contentions made, and the evidence supplied, by complainant."[131] Some

---

127 ***Dean & Simmons, Sàrl and Heintz Van Landewyck S.à.r.l. v. Domain Capital / Moniker Privacy Services,*** D2015-0080 (WIPO March 27, 2015) (<fiesta.com>. "Few things are more settled, or more fundamental under the Policy and Rules, than the requirement that material factual allegations must be proven, not simply alleged"); ***Mister Auto SAS v. Wharton Lyon & Lyon***, D2018-1330 (WIPO August 3, 2018) (<mrauto.com>. "[T]he onus of proving [the three UDRP] elements remains on the Complainant even though the Respondent has not filed a Response."

128 ***DNA (Housemarks) Limited v. Tucows.com Co.***, D2009-0367 (WIPO May 5, 2009) ("One of [complainant's] arguments, that the failure to provide a response results in a default judgment (as would occur in civil litigation in the United States or Canada), is mistaken as a matter of Policy precedent. Failure to respond in a Policy proceeding does not of itself constitute an admission of any pleaded matter or result in the Policy equivalent of the default judgment.") See Fed. R. Civ. P. 8(b)(6) ("An allegation — other than one relating to the amount of damages — is admitted if a responsive pleading is required and the allegation is not denied.")

129 ***Solahart Industries Pty Ltd. v. Ciccarelli Luigi***, D2006-0051 (WIPO April 16, 2006) ("Respondent had an opportunity to contest that assertion of fact, but has chosen not to do so.") See also ***Nexans S.A. v. Mr. Edip Özdemir / MXN Kablo San. Tic. Ltd. Sti.***, D2015-1056 (WIPO September 28, 2015) ("The stance that the Respondent has taken in the Response on this issue also speaks volumes. A complainant bears the burden of proof under the Policy. However, it is striking that although the Respondent obviously knows its own motives for choosing the term [that was used in the Domain Name], it has failed to offer any explanation for that choice in this case. Where a respondent decides to participate in proceedings under the Policy but fails to address head on what is often the most important issue in proceedings under the Policy; i.e., why the domain name was registered, a panel is entitled to draw an inference adverse to the respondent from that failure.")

130 ***MC Enterprises v. Mark Segal (Namegiant.com)***, D2005-1270 (WIPO January 27, 2006). See further discussion on inferences at "Drawing Inferences" (Sec. 7.09-A).

131 ***Talk City***, supra.

panelists take the position that "[i]n the absence of a response, it is appropriate to accept as true all allegations of the Complaint.,[132] but this misreads the Policy and governing law by converting default into an admission of liability. Rather, acceptance presupposes that "the contended factual and legal conclusions [are] proven by [the submitted] evidence."[133] This is generally interpreted to mean the Panel will accept all *reasonable* allegations of fact, unless the evidence is clearly contradictory.

While respondent's failure to respond is not necessarily conclusive of abusive registration (when for example the complaint is "fatally defective"[134]) it gives a complainant an advantage if its allegations are facially plausible and supported by the record. It would be misleading, however, to suggest that "uncontroverted contentions" are sufficient in themselves. The evidence must be probative of the issues and preponderant in complainant's favor.[135] Otherwise complainant has failed to state its case and its request for relief must be denied and the complaint dismissed.

The Policy requires evidence, not just allegedly factual but unsupported contentions. One line of cases emphasizes that default permits Panels to draw "reasonable" inferences in favor of a complainant,[136] "unless the evidence is clearly contradictory."[137] The Panel in ***Honeywell*** qualified the "reasonable" by stating that Respondent's failure to respond to the complaint "functions both as an implicit admission that Respondent lacks rights to and legitimate interests in the domain names, as well as a presumption that Complainant's reasonable allegations are true."[138]

While lack of rights or legitimate interests may be conclusive for Paragraph 4(a)(ii) it is not for Paragraph 4(a)(iii)—example, domain names with priority over corresponding marks. However, as a general proposition it is nevertheless a harbinger of abusive registration for domain names acquired after a mark's first use in commerce.

---

[132] ***Tianrong Internet Products and Services, Inc. v. Josue da Silva,*** FA0208000123866 (Forum October 22, 2002 (<phonecalls.com>) citing ***Talk City***, supra.

[133] ***Viacom International Inc. v. Ir Suryani***, D2001-1443 (WIPO March 20, 2002).

[134] ***Yao Ming v. Evergreen Sports, Inc.***, FA 154140 (Forum May 29, 2003) ("The Panel assumes that Complainant is the well known basketball player for the Houston, Texas, Rockets Basketball team. However, Complainant's submission is fatally defective. Although the Panel will presume that the Yao Ming may have common law rights in the name YAO MING, Complainant submitted no evidence to support a finding of such rights with the Complaint.")

[135] ***Hagerty Insurance Agency, Inc. v. Whoisguard/Chris Hagerty***, D2008-1452 (WIPO December 11, 2008). The Panel noted that statements by counsel are not evidence.

[136] ***Wells Fargo & Co. v. Shing***, FA 205699 (Forum December 8, 2003).

[137] ***Vanguard Group, Inc. v. Collazo***, FA 349074 (Forum December 1, 2004); similarly, ***Advanta Corp. v. ADVANTACARD INTL. INC.***, FA0601000625997 (Forum March 1, 2006).

[138] ***Honeywell International Inc. v. Domain Deluxe***, FA 269166 (Forum June 29, 2004).

7.04 RULES 6(d) AND 6(e)—CONSTITUTION OF THE ARBITRAL PANEL 7.04

Sole member Panels are appointed by the provider.[139] For three-member Panels Rules 6(d) and 6(e) of the Rules of the Policy empower each party to nominate one panelist, but the presiding panelist is chosen from a list created by the provider.[140] There is no provision in the Policy or Rules to disqualify an appointee or a nominee. The "selection process for a three-member panel is deliberately designed to ensure that each party may make a significant contribution to the selection of one panel member and to the decision by the provider on the third member of the panel."[141] While neither party chooses the presiding panelist, both contribute to his or her appointment.

This procedure is designed to yield two party appointed panelists and a presiding neutral, which is a model familiar in commercial arbitration. Under the UDRP all three appointees are required to be independent and impartial and to submit a Declaration to that effect. However, a legitimate question has arisen on the issue of partiality and bias.[142] In ***Britannia Building Society*** the sole Panel concluded that it was

> appropriate for a party with concerns about a panelist's impartiality to communicate with the provider in order to raise any such concerns and to seek a prompt and fair resolution. [And, that in] the event the provider declines to disqualify the panelist, it is equally appropriate for the party to move for the panelist's recusal.

---

139 In contrast, commercial arbitration providers distribute a list of candidates from which parties are invited to make a selection. The provider then appoints a jointly selected candidate to hear and determine the dispute. For a three member panel, the presiding panelist is chosen by the provider.

140 Rule 6(d) reads: "Unless it has already elected a three member Panel, the Complainant shall submit to the Provider, within five (5) calendar days of communication of a response in which the Respondent elects a three member Panel, the names and contact details of three candidates to serve as one of the Panelists. These candidates may be drawn from any ICANN approved Provider's list of panelists."

Rule 6(e) reads: "In the event that either the Complainant or the Respondent elects a three member Panel, the Provider shall endeavor to appoint one Panelist from the list of candidates provided by each of the Complainant and the Respondent. . . . The third Panelist shall be appointed by the Provider from a list of five candidates submitted by the Provider to the Parties, the Provider's selection from among the five being made in a manner that reasonably balances the preferences of both Parties. . . ."

141 ***Two Way NV/SA v. Moniker Privacy Services, LLC / [4079779]: Domain Administrator***, D2012-2413 (WIPO June 7, 2013) (<yu.com>).

142 Id., citing ***Britannia Building Society v. Britannia Fraud Prevention***, D2001-0505 (WIPO July 6, 2001) (Sole Panel) and ***Kathleen Kennedy Townsend v. B. G. Birt***, D2002-0030 (WIPO April 2002) (Three member Panel).

The presiding Panelist in ***Kathleen Kennedy Townsend*** drew the opposite conclusion:

> [Since there was nothing in the Rules or Supplemental Rules] [t]he presiding Panelist therefore has no jurisdiction to deal with this request. Moreover, even if the Presiding Panelist had such jurisdiction, he would decline to exercise it, because such exercise would be inappropriate and unseemly. Accordingly, the Presiding Panelist declines to rule on the Request for Recusal or to consider it for any purpose.

The majority Panelists in ***Two Way NV/SA*** concurred that the Panel "has no jurisdiction to entertain Complainant's challenge to the appointment of [the challenged Panelist]." The Panel in ***Grupo Costamex*** found it "difficult to see how a panel could ensure fair and equal treatment in any sensible way if, notwithstanding each panelist's self certification of independence and impartiality, it was apparent that a panelist was, for example, determined to decide the case in favour of one of the parties because of a pre-existing bias, regardless of the facts."[143]

The Policy, Rules, and the WIPO Supplemental Rules are silent on the issue; the Forum Supplemental Rules provide for a mechanism for disqualifying a panelist "if circumstances exist that create a conflict of interest or cause the Panelist to be unfair and biased." The Panel in ***Grupo Costamex*** identified two approaches to the issue: that there be 1) justifiable doubt (***Britannia Building Society***); and 2) compelling evidence of improper bias (***Two Way NV/SA***). It was not enthusiastic about either approach but pointed out that "a standard that requires compelling evidence of improper bias sets a threshold that would bar nearly all challenges to panelists."[144]

As a touchstone, it is a common practice in commercial arbitration for a party to apply to the Provider to disqualify an appointee where the evidence shows (i) partiality or lack of independence; (ii) inability or refusal to perform his or her duties with diligence and in good faith; or (iii) any grounds for disqualification provided by applicable law.[145] As indicated in the Forum Supplemental Rules this practice

---

[143] ***Grupo Costamex, S.A. de C.V. (COSTAMEX), Operación y Supervisión de Hoteles, S.A. de C.V. (OPYSSA) v. Vertical Axis Inc.***, D2013-1829 (WIPO February 10, 2014).

[144] In ***Two Way NV/SA*** the provider saw "no evidence of material conflict as such and accordingly we will proceed to invite party nominated co-panelist candidates as provided under the Rules." Complainant's argument rested on the assertion that Respondent's counsel had previously nominated the same nominee in other UDRP cases; therefore he had "a financial interest in as much as possible finding in favor of 'counsel for Respondent and its clients.'" In ***Grupo Costamex*** the majority of the Panel (the challenged panelist did not participate) concluded that "whichever test applies, the Complainants have not made an adequate showing that [the challenged panelists] should be disqualified . . . [in that] the Complainants have not made an adequate showing for recusal. . . ."

[145] WIPO's Supplemental Rules, Rule 9 requires panelists to sign a Declaration of Independence and Impartiality using the form set out in Annex C. It does not specifically address the issue of disqualification. Forum's Supplemental Rules, Rule 10(c) specifically addresses the issue of disqualification:

should apply equally to a UDRP proceeding. Disqualification or recusal depends on evidence establishing a basis for the provider to rule on the application.

An application for disqualification must rest (as it does in commercial arbitration) on submission of evidence (not speculation) that establishes a *material* conflict. It is not a disqualifying bias for panelists to have dismissed complaints on the merits, or previously to have ruled in favor of complainants whose attorneys or law firms (objectionable to respondents) reappear before later Panels in which respondents are parties.[146]

7.05 RULE 10(d)—ADMISSIBILITY, RELEVANCE, MATERIALITY, AND WEIGHT OF THE EVIDENCE 7.05

7.05-A Prosecuting a UDRP Complaint and Defending Rights or Legitimate Interests in Disputed Domain Name 7.05-A

7.05-A.1 Standards 7.05-A.1

7.05-A.1.a *Burden of Creating a Record* *7.05-A.1.a*

UDRP may be "adjudication lite" in the words of a federal judge,[147] but it would be a mistake to disregard the very definite standards the parties are expected to meet. Neither party can hope to prevail who fails to submit a record that supports its contentions. It must also be recognized that UDRP proceedings have to be approached with an understanding of their evidentiary demands. It must also be recognized that UDRP proceedings have to be approached with an understanding of their evidentiary demands. In Barcelona.com the court held that Complainant had no preemptive right to a geographic term, in essence approving the view that the first to register a domain name comprising a generic term cannot be deprived of its rights.

Unlike litigation as practiced in common law jurisdictions in which claims are commenced by filing a summons and complaint, a UDRP proceeding is initiated

---

"[the request must include] the circumstances and specific reasons for the disqualification." See also American Arbitration Association, Commercial Arbitration Rules, Rule 17(a). Rule 17 (b) continues: "Upon objection of a party to the continued service of an arbitrator, or on its own initiative, the AAA shall determine whether the arbitrator should be disqualified under the grounds set out above, and shall inform the parties of its decision, which decision shall be conclusive."

146 Other cases on motions to disqualify include ***The Teaching Company, LLC, d/b/a The Great Courses v. Brendhan Hight, Marchex Sales, LLC***, D2014-0448 (WIPO June 4, 2014) and ***The Teaching Company, LLC d/b/a The Great Courses v. Worldwide Media Inc.***, D2014-0457 (WIPO June 4, 2014). Same Panel in both cases. Complainant's "only basis for its serious allegation of bias is that when in prior UDRP proceedings Mr. [Neil A.] Brown has been nominated by the Respondent's counsel, Mr. Brown has consistently voted in favor of the Respondent's counsel's client in 15 of 16 instances." Mr. Brown recused himself on this issue. Motion to disqualify denied.

147 *Barcelona.com, Inc. v. Excelentisimo Ayuntamiento De Barcelona*, 330 F.3d 617, 624-25 (4th Cir. 2003). (Holding in favor of domain name holder and vacating the UDRP award).

by filing a complaint which is more akin to a motion for summary judgment. While the parties may have a chance to supplement the record (Section 7.13) if either's submission is deficient the opposing party will prevail. This understanding should inform parties' submissions as indicated in the decisions cited in the footnotes

Claims of cybersquatting and denials of unlawful registration cannot succeed on assertions of belief or speculative theories[148] for which there are no evidentiary basis.[149] Panelists have construed from the Policy's language a palette of formal demands parties are expected to satisfy. Complainants have the burden of proof for each requirement[150]; respondents have a rebuttal burden if complainant succeeds with its *prima facie* case on the second requirement, but otherwise the onus rests on complainant to prove its case.[151]

The first two requirements of the Policy demand either/or evidence—a domain name is either identical or confusingly similar to a complainant's existing right (paragraph 4(a)(i) of the Policy); or respondent lacks rights or legitimate interests in the challenged domain name (paragraph 4(a)(ii)) (or the mirror image for respondent, to demonstrate it has either rights or legitimate interests in the challenged domain name). To satisfy the third requirement complainant must prove conjunctive bad faith. Any proof less than both elements is insufficient to establish

---

148 ***ACE Limited v. WebMagic Ventures, LLC c/o WebMagic Staff***, FA0802001144016 (Forum April 22, 2008) (<ace.us>. "Merely relying on unattested to statements by counsel for a party is not evidence, but conjecture, and we decline to make any rulings on conjecture, since we are constrained to rely on evidence.") ***Bloomberg Finance L.P. v. zhang guo jie***, FA1704001727926 (Forum June 8, 2017) (<Bloomberg.site>. "[E]ven taking account of the public use which has been made of the trademark, it is a common family name which might remain open to use in good faith by any number of traders.... This is not a case of an invented word with no connotation other than the goods or services of a single trader.")

149 ***Fender Musical Instruments Corporation v. Christopher Ruth***, FA1007001333857 (Forum August 9, 2010) (The Panel found that "Complainant's assertions, without any supporting evidence or analysis, do not sufficiently establish Respondent lacks rights or legitimate interests in the <fendercustomshop.com> domain name.")

150 See for example ***Insight Energy Ventures LLC v. Alois Muehlberger, L.M. Berger Co.Ltd.***, D2016-2010 (WIPO December 12, 2016) (<powerly.com>. "Complainant has provided no evidence to suggest that its brand 'Powerley' or either of its trade marks is famous, or that the Complainant was even operating in 2004, at the time the Disputed Domain Name was registered"); ***Richard Izzo Toughman Enterprises v. TJ Tryon***, FA1704001728347 (Forum May 30, 2017) (<toughmaninindiana.com>) ("[E]ven when a respondent does not submit a response in a proceeding, the complainant still must make a prima facie case ... [and it] fails to make a prima facie case when it fails to provide any evidence whatsoever of a respondent's use of a disputed domain name.")

151 ***Yumiko, LLC v. Domain Hostmaster, Customer ID: 44519875664713, Whois Privacy Services Pty Ltd / Stanley Pace***, D2015-1669 (WIPO December 9, 2015) (<yumiko.com> allegedly acquired for the surname but website links to competitive goods); ***Retail Royalty Company and AE Direct Co LLC v. Daniel Cormier***, FA1610001698852 (Forum November 23, 2016) (<aeried.com>. Respondent failed to demonstrate domain name was not typosquatting on AERIE).

infringement. However, bad faith use can be presumptive evidence (albeit, rebuttable) of bad faith registration.[152]

Lack of priority which under the ACPA is a bar to maintaining an action is shifted under the UDRP to the third requirement. While lack of priority is not a bar to standing, if the mark is not distinctive prior to the registration of the domain name complainant has no actionable claim under the UDRP[153] even if respondent is found to lack rights or legitimate interests in the domain name.[154]

Rule 10(d) provides "[t]he Panel shall determine the admissibility, relevance, materiality and weight of the evidence [comprising the record]." Since the determination is made entirely on paper submissions—there is no discovery, no cross-examination and no confrontation in open hearing[155]—it is imperative to pay close attention to the evidence offered in support and opposition to parties' contentions. Each requirement is self-contained. It is not enough for complainant to establish respondent's lack of right or legitimate interest in the disputed domain name if proof is lacking of bad faith registration. Respondents cannot succeed on assertions of good faith or alleged ignorance of complainant and its mark when inferences can be drawn to the contrary.[156] There must be additional layers of evidentiary facts sufficient to draw appropriate conclusions from them or by inference.[157]

Submissions in support of cancellation/transfer and good faith are comparable to what would be expected in a civil action motion for summary judgment. The greater the relevance and materiality of the supported factual allegations the greater their weight. Each party has a role in producing a written record which means that what is not produced and ought to have been is part of the record. The record is complete and closed either upon submission of the pleadings or 1) discretionary

---

152 ***Pixers Ltd. v. Whois Privacy Corp.***, D2015-1171 (WIPO April 8, 2016) ("In short, paragraph 4(b)(iv) provides an evidentiary presumption of bad faith registration where there is evidence of a certain kind of bad faith use. In many cases, it may be difficult for the Respondent to rebut this evidentiary presumption.")

153 ***Entertainment Technology Investments, Inc. d/b/a Gloo, LLC v. Contact Privacy Inc. Customer 011945202 / K Blacklock***, D2017-0606 (WIPO May31, 2017) (<gloo.com>. "[T]he date at which the Respondent acquired the Domain Name is a critical question.... The Complainant has referred to a number of cases, being the Octogen cases, where bad faith registration was found in circumstances where the Domain Name was registered prior to the establishment of trade mark rights [but the views in these cases of retroactive bad faith have been rejected].")

154 ***Bellhops, Inc. v. WhoisAgent, Whois Privacy Protection Services, Inc. / Domain Vault, Domain Vault LLC***, D2016-0756 (WIPO July 4, 2016) (<bellhops.com>).

155 See Rule 13 of the Rules of the Policy.

156 ***BML Group Limited v. Rikard Beach, Proxy My Whois AB***, D2015-1897 (WIPO November 21, 2015) ("[A]lthough the Respondent has filed a detailed Response in this case in which it alleged that it is engaged in a completely different business to the Complainant, no attempt is made to explain what that different business is.")

157 Further discussed in "No Record, No Case" (Sec. 7.04-B).

with the Panel or permitted by Providers' Supplemental Rules regarding acceptance of additional submissions; or 2) receipt of documents requested by the Panel pursuant to Rule 12.

Parties succeed or fail on their pleadings (discussed further below in Complaint[158] and Response[159]), supporting affidavits/declarations of facts made on personal knowledge, documentary submissions, and the quality of substantive evidence they marshal. Complainants carry the burden of proving their case; respondents carry the burden of defending their rights or legitimate interests in the domain names or refuting claims of bad faith registration. ***Ascendes*** in an earlier footnote and ***Randgold Resources*** cited below are apt illustrations. In the first, Complainant failed to marshal sufficient evidence to prove Respondent complicit in an alleged wrongful act; and, in the second, the Respondent denied relevance of an item of documentary evidence without explaining what it meant if it did not have the meaning ascribed to it by Complainant.

Panels have pointed out in response to parties requesting them to inquire and obtain proof that "[i]t is not for the Panel to undertake an inquisitional role"[160] or for a Panel "to complete the evidentiary record" of a party's case.[161] The inquisitional role, however, is not entirely missing from the UDRP. A Panel "may request, in its sole discretion, further statements or documents from either of the Parties."[162] The burden (which includes respondent's burden of production to defend its right or legitimate interest in the domain name under paragraph 4(a)(ii) of the Policy) is on the parties "to complete the evidentiary record."[163]

---

[158] ***Ascendes Corporation dba MarketTouch v. Market Touch Limited***, D2001-1186 (WIPO January 14, 2002) (<markettouch.net>. Complaint denied: "Complaints are determined on the basis of the evidence the parties themselves choose to put before the Panelist.")

[159] ***Shensmith Group Ltd v. Maureen Tarmey***, D2012-1086 (WIPO July 10, 2012) ("The Complainant asserts that the relationship, at least so far as the website is concerned, was based on a 'verbal MOU' and there is reference to an email sent by the Complainant to the Respondent on February 2, 2009, requesting that an 'MOU contract be finalized within 7 days.' The Respondent says in her response that there is nothing to suggest that the MOU has anything to do with this dispute *without explaining what it does have to do with.* The Respondent also says that the MOU is indicative of some relationship between the parties *but again fails to elucidate.* The Panel find it odd that the Respondent should decide not to deal with an issue that clearly may have some relevance, particularly as it is acknowledged that an MOU is indicative of a relationship and, importantly, most probably indicative of a relationship other than the one the Respondent contends for i.e., that of employee/employer" [emphasis added]).

[160] ***Randgold Resources Limited and Randgold & Exploration Co.Ltd. v. Pico Capital Corp.***, D2001-1108 (WIPO October 24, 2001) (addressing Respondent); ***Pleasure Cake SL v. TechTools***, D2009-0580 (WIPO July 14, 2009) (addressing Complainant).

[161] Id., ***Pleasure Cake.***

[162] Rule 12 is discussed further in "Procedural Orders" (Sec. 7.06-A).

It is pointless to initiate a proceeding (as it is in moving for summary judgment in a civil action) without understanding the scope of the Policy and its evidentiary expectations. A complainant cannot prevail unless evidence of its factual claims is conclusive in its favor.[164] This does not mean respondent is absolved from liability for trademark infringement, only (as the Panel in the case cited in the previous footnote explains) that there is insufficient evidence to convict respondent of cybersquatting under the UDRP.[165]

7.05-A.1.b *Evidentiary Expectations* 7.05-A.1.b

Parties to a UDRP proceeding are entitled to a full and fair opportunity to present their best cases.[166] Complainant has the burden of demonstrating respondent lacks rights or legitimate interests in the subject domain name and abusive registration. These expectations are not satisfied by respondent's default since under arbitration rules failing to respond is not an admission of liability, as it is in a civil lawsuit, rather the allegations are deemed denied. However, there are consequences to silence. Regardless whether respondent appears or defaults, if complainant's *prima facie* case is unrebutted it is likely (absent to succeed on the paragraph 4(a)(ii) limb of the Policy.[167] Respondent has the lesser burden of production which essentially consists in undermining complainant's proof.

Preponderance is defined as "rest[ing] with that evidence which, when fairly considered, produces the stronger impression, and has the greater weight, and is more convincing as to its truth when weighed against the evidence in opposition."[168] The term "burden of proof" is frequently said to have two distinct meanings: (1) the

---

163 ***Pleasure Cake***, *supra*. (addressing complainant). Nevertheless, panelists are authorized to research the public record; see Jurisprudential Overview, Paragraph 4.8, "May a panel perform independent research when reaching a decision?"

164 ***Adaptive Molecular Technologies, Inc. v. Priscilla Woodward & Charles R. Thorton, d/b/a Machines & More***, D2000-0006 (WIPO February 28, 2000) ("The decision is limited to the fact that, on this record, the existence of significant factual and legal issues makes this case inappropriate for resolution under the Policy.")

165 ***Diamond Resorts Holdings, LLC v. Walter P. Dolan, American Dream Connection***, D2012-2483 (WIPO March 7, 2013) ("[T]he UDRP is not always the most appropriate forum for finding the truth among competing factual claims.")

166 Rules of the Policy, Rule 10(b) "In all cases, the Panel shall ensure that the Parties are treated with equality and that each Party is given a fair opportunity to present its case."

167 See Jurisprudential Overview 3.0, Paragraph 4.2, which also uses the expression "balance of probabilities." In at least one early case, a dissenting Panel member argued for a higher standard, "clear and convincing," ***Bootie Brewing Company v. Deanna D. Ward and Grabebottie Inc.***, D2003-0185 (WIPO May 28, 2000) a standard, however, that has not been adopted; indeed it was rejected by her fellow panelists. A clear and convincing standard is applied in Uniform Rapid Suspension System (URS) cases, discussed earlier in Sec. 2.03-A.

168 *Black's Law Dictionary* (rev. 4th ed. 1968).

duty of producing evidence as the case progresses, and (2) the duty to establish the truth of the claim by a preponderance of the evidence.

Existence of the essential elements in each of the Policy limbs is not presumed. A complainant does not automatically prevail because it has a trademark. A respondent does not forfeit a domain name simply because it fails to respond to the complaint. A respondent will be permitted to keep its choice of domain name under one of two circumstances: either complainant fails to satisfy its paragraph 4(a)(ii) and 4(a)(iii) burdens or respondent satisfies one or more of the paragraph 4(c) defenses. In both trademark and domain name law "a weak mark weighs heavily against finding infringement."[169]

Proof by a preponderance of the evidence is typically expressed in such phrases as "more likely than not" and "balancing of probabilities" and sometimes metaphorically as weighing evidence on the "scales of justice." The preponderance standard requires complainant to offer sufficient evidence to tip the scale in its favor.[170] Complainant is entitled to cancellation or transfer of the domain name when "it appears more likely than not from the evidence offered by Complainant that Respondent has registered the Domain Name in a deliberate attempt to attract users to its planned website for commercial gain due to confusion with Complainant's mark."[171] The assessment involves a "balancing of probabilities."[172]

Thus, conclusory allegations of intent without corroboration, even if undisputed, are not proof of bad faith.[173] Supposition is not elevated to fact by assertion however passionately expressed.[174] The burden does not shift on the ultimate issue.

---

[169] *Entrepreneur Media, Inc. v. Smith*, 279 F.3d 1135, 1147 (9th Cir. 2002). Examples too numerous to cite. Discussed further in "Concurrent Use of Common Lexical Strings" (Sec. 4.02-A.1.d).

[170] See ***Yao Ming v. Evergreen Sports, Inc.***, FA 154140 (Forum May 29, 2003) ("Complainant has not alleged any facts related to Respondent's use of the disputed domain name. The Complaint merely asserts a legal conclusion."); ***O.C. Seacrets, Inc. v. S. TradeWINs, Inc.***, FA 328042 (Forum October 29, 2004) ("Complainant has provided no evidence as to the use of the <jamaicausa.com> domain name and has merely asserted that Respondent has no rights or legitimate interests, which is not sufficient to support a finding that Respondent lacks rights or legitimate interests."); ***Jireh Industries Ltd. v. DVLPMNT MARKETING, INC. / Domain Administrator***, FA1703001719671 (Forum April 14, 2017) (<jireh.com>) ("Complainant has failed to provide any evidence of the kind that would satisfy its burden of proving common law rights. Complainant's evidence is limited merely to the statements that it has been using its JIREH mark initially on food processing equipment and later on oilfield equipment since 1983 and on nondestructive testing equipment for industrial applications since 2002. Such assertions alone, without facts to support a claim of common law rights, are insufficient to satisfy the requirements of the Policy.")

[171] ***Infospace.com v. Tenenbaum Ofer***, D2000-0075 (WIPO April 4, 2000).

[172] ***AT & T Corp v. WNA***, D2001-1160 (WIPO November 16, 2001).

[173] ***Jana Partners LLC v Zhang Si***, FA1712001760820 (Forum January 2, 2018) (<janaparters.com>. The Panel (over severely?) held that while "Complainant asserts that Respondent uses the disputed domain name with the intent for commercial gain, to defraud Internet users, to obtain

The Panel in ***Bootie Brewing Company*** noted that "although . . . facts . . . hotly contested . . . create[] a challenge for the trier of fact given the expedited nature of these proceedings and the limited record presented to the Panel," it concluded that this

> does not mean . . . that the Panel should abdicate its responsibility to analyze the record as best it can to determine whether cybersquatting has occurred. . . . Similarly, just because the record is complex does not mean that the Panel should decline to review it. Rather, the Panel's obligation when faced with such disputed facts is to make the best findings it can, by a preponderance of the evidence, based on the record submitted.

If a party's record is long on speculation and short on specific facts it fails to satisfy its burden of proof or production. That a respondent is using the domain name in bad faith is not conclusive evidence it had that intention when it registered it. A conflict of evidence the Panel is unable to resolve favors respondent because complainant has the onus of proving each requirement. "In the context of an overall dispute which involves so many factual and legal issues, the Panel does not believe it to be either safe or sensible for the Panel to make such a determination."[175]

7.05-A.2 **Proof Requirements** 7.05-A.2

7.05-A.2.a *General Observations* *7.05-A.2.a*

The sufficiency demanded in asserting or defending a claim applies in equal measure to both parties. Giving a party the benefit of the doubt is shorthand for insufficiency of the other's evidence. "Just as a Panel should require a complainant to establish by means other than mere bald assertions that it is the owner of registered marks, so should the panel require that a respondent come forward with concrete evidence that the assertions made in the response are true."[176] Conjecture or speculation "is of no force or effect under the Policy"[177] but evidence based on

---

goods at Complainant's expense, or to tarnish Complainant's marks … it provides no evidence of these assertions and no evidence whatsoever of Respondent's use of the disputed domain name.")

[174] ***Martin Stevens d/b/a Forum Publishing v. forumpublishing.com / NULL NULL***, FA111200 1418982 (Forum January 25, 2012) ("Complainant asserts that the disputed domain name resolves to a website which is under construction but states that it will eventually offer copyrights and other CD based software publications. Additionally, the disputed domain name allegedly causes downloading of malicious software. However, Complainant fails to submit any evidence which corroborates this claim.")

[175] ***S.L.I. Société des Lubrifiants IPONE v. CLIX International, L.L.C., Carbon Development, Chad Boulton***, D2004-0334 (WIPO June 26, 2004).

[176] ***Do The Hustle, LLC v. Tropic Web***, D2000-0624 (WIPO August 21, 2000).

[177] ***Scandinavian Leadership AB, Mindo AB v. Internet Masters***, D2012-1273 (WIPO July 26, 2012). Since UDRP pleadings effectively act as a motion for summary judgment parties must be prepared to allege facts supported by documentary evidence, not mere conclusory statements.

inferences is acceptable (discussed further in section 7.09) as are conclusions based on the totality of the evidence. However, in drawing inferences and relying on the "totality" of evidence Panels have stepped into error, as later determined by courts of competent jurisdiction.[178]

Complainants must satisfy the express requirements in each of paragraphs 4(a)(i–iii). It becomes progressively harder for less well-known marks and marks composed of generic terms capable of having multiple associations without infringing third party rights to satisfy the evidentiary requirements.[179] If respondents affirmatively prove they have rights or legitimate interests in the domain names or complainants prove respondents lack either but fail to prove conjunctive bad faith the complaint must be denied. In making their determinations Panels have to avoid the Scylla of "elevat[ing] form over substance" and the Charybdis of making an award based on "benefit of the doubt."

In one early case, the dissent would have dismissed the complaint because the Complainant alleged the domain name was "identical" when it was really only "confusingly similar".[180] In his view Complainant lacked standing because it made an "elect[ion] not to pursue a claim of confusing similarity for strategic reasons or (perhaps more likely) due to oversight." Whichever it was, "I see no need to supplement the allegations that Complainant actually made with others that Complainant chose not to include, or to afford Complainant a second opportunity to allege what

---

The point is made by the Panel in ***Michael Jastremski v. Jaisen Mathai***, DME2014-0006 (WIPO November 10, 2014) ("The Complainant argues 'on information and belief' that the Respondent had prior knowledge of the Complainant's mark and so registered the Domain Name with the intent to disrupt and mislead. Assertions 'on information and belief' are not helpful in the context of a UDRP proceeding. 'Information and belief' is a formula that is common in 'notice pleading' at the commencement of legal actions in the United States. It is designed only to put opposing parties on notice of the claims and defenses to be asserted and tested in the course of the proceeding." See also ***ROAR, LLC v. Jonathan Shalit, ROAR Global Limited***, D2016-1574 (WIPO October 4, 2016) (<roarglobal.com>) ("It is the Complainant's responsibility to present a complete case to the Panel, and it made the decision to rely on bare allegations with no evidentiary backing.)

178 ***Bulbs 4 East Side Inc., d/b/a Just Bulbs v. Fundacion Private Whois/ Gregory Ricks***, D2013-1779 (WIPO January 13, 2014) (Complaint denied, but successful in ACPA action, *Bulbs 4 E. Side, Inc. v. Ricks*, (S.D. Tex., Houston Div. July 18, 2017 together with an award of damages for $50,000 and attorney's fees); ***Camilla Australia Pty Ltd v. Domain Admin, Mrs Jello, LLC.***, D2015-1593 (WIPO November 30, 2015) (<camilla.com>. Complaint granted, but in a subsequent ACPA action Camilla Australia (now defendant) stipulated to vacate the UDRP award in its entirety. *Mrs. Jello, LLC v. Camilla Australia Pty Ltd.* 15-cv-08753 (D. NJ 8/1/2016).

179 ***Darryl Davis Seminars, Inc. v. Privacydotlink Customer 656889 / Domain Admin, Abstract Holdings International Ltd.***, D2018-2238 (WIPO January 21, 2019) (<poweragent.com>. "Respondent has satisfied the Panel that it registered the disputed domain name for its inherent value as a domain name incorporating a common descriptive term, as part of its business as an investor in such domain names.

180 ***Chernow Communications, Inc. v. Jonathan D. Kimball***, D2000-0119 (WIPO May 18, 2000) (C-COM and <ccom.com>).

frankly is an obvious component of a prima facie case under the UDRP." As previously noted this uncharitable view failed to impress his colleagues, was tacitly rejected in contemporary cases, and has left no mark on the jurisprudence.

In a second case the majority justified its decision denying the complaint on the grounds that "just as we are procedurally strict with Respondent, so too must we be strict with Complainant."[181] Complainant's sin? It did not allege bad faith use of the disputed domain name, although its focus on paragraph 4(b)(iv) could not have been clearer that Respondent was in violation for precisely that reason. The concept of strict equality, however, is a reminder to the parties of what is expected of them, even if the application of this principle—the dissent in ***Chernow*** and the majority in ***Advance Magazine***—appears overly rigid.

Paragraphs 4(a)(ii) and 4(c)(i–iii) are designed to level the playing field. A Panel "must be careful"[182] because any acceptable showing by respondent of good faith under paragraphs 4(c)(i-iii) ends in respondent's favor under paragraph 4(a)(ii). If the facts are either not pleaded or pleaded and not proved there is no basis for a complainant award.[183] If the Panel is left to speculate on respondent's motive under paragraph 4(a)(iii) in registering the disputed domain name the complaint has to be denied.[184] Just as it is not sufficient for a complainant to succeed under paragraph 4(a)(i) if the domain name is not identical or confusingly similar to its trademark neither is it enough for respondent to merely assert a safe harbor defense

---

181 ***Advance Magazine Publishers Inc. v. Premier Models International Inc.***, D2013-0757 (WIPO July 5, 2013) (<voguefashionmodels.com>. Respondent did not appear, although it responded to a cease-and-desist notice which is in the record. The majority recognized that the case "present[ed] a difficult close question.")

182 ***Banco Espirito Santo S.A. v. Bancovic***, D2004-0890 (WIPO December 16, 2004) (<bancoespiritosanto.com>. "The mere assertion of the Respondent, without any evidence, is not sufficient to counter the Complainant's submissions. Accordingly, the Panel finds that the Respondent has failed to show that he is commonly known by the domain name at issue.")

183 Complainant failure: ***Mediaset S.p.A. v. Didier Madiba, Fenicius LLC***, D2011-1954 (WIPO February 4, 2012) ("It is well established that general allegations or mere assertions of bad faith without supporting facts or specific examples do not supply a sufficient basis upon which a panel may conclude that a respondent acted in bad faith" to which the Panel in ***CENECT Centro Integrado de Educação, Ciência e Tecnologia Ltda. v. Above.com Domain Privacy / Transure Enterprise Ltd.***, D2012-2516 (WIPO March 28, 2013) adds "even more so, a panel cannot conclude that a respondent registered a domain name in bad faith when the complainant totally omitted any indication or reference or argument about such a circumstance.")

184 ***JPI Commercial, LLP v. Alan Capalditallon***, FA1208001458587 (Forum September 12, 2012) ("With little or no evidence on either side, the Panel is left to speculate as to Respondent's motives upon registering the disputed domain name. The similarity to Complainant's mark is substantial, but the mark is not sufficiently famous or distinctive to lead the Panel to reject Respondent's explanation as entirely implausible, nor to support an inference that Respondent must have had Complainant's mark in mind upon registering the domain name. The Panel, therefore, is left to decide this issue

under paragraph 4(c). The requirement is satisfied only by offering concrete evidence of the alleged facts supporting the opposing contentions.

"'Concrete evidence' constitutes more than mere speculation, although it can be based on inferences drawn from the factual matrix. Just as a Panel should require a complainant to establish by means other than mere bald assertions that it is the owner of registered marks, so should the panel require that a respondent come forward with concrete evidence that the assertions made in the response are true."[185] The Panel in one case found that Respondent's explanation was "hopelessly deficient."[186]

7.05-A.2.b 7.05-A.2.b *Complaint*

Complainants fail to prove abusive registration in 12% to 15% of the filings. Over a five-year period, from 2008 through 2012, WIPO reports around 11,000 decisions, which translates into dismissal or denial of a significant number of complaints per year. A persuasive submission starts with the complaint, a template form provided by the chosen Provider. The form requires complainants to detail facts and circumstance as they relate to each of three requirements of the Policy with annexes supporting the truth or warranting inferences that complainant proposes can reasonably be drawn. Rule 3(b) requires a Complaint to:

> (ix) Describe, in accordance with the Policy, the grounds on which the complaint is made including, in particular;
>
> (1) the manner in which the domain name(s) is/are identical or confusingly similar to a trademark or service mark in which the Complainant has rights; and
>
> (2) why the Respondent (domain name holder) should be considered as having no rights or legitimate interests in respect of the domain name(s) that is/are the subject of the complaint; and
>
> (3) why the domain name(s) should be considered as having been registered and being used in bad faith.
>
> (The description should, for elements (2) and (3), discuss any aspects of Paragraphs 4(b) and 4(c) of the Policy that are applicable. . .).

Panels have noted evidentiary deficiencies ranging from inadequate preparation of the complaint (barely proving standing if at all for unregistered marks[187]) to

---

based upon the burden of proof, and finds that Complainant has failed to meet its burden of showing that Respondent registered and used the disputed domain name in bad faith.")

185 ***Do the Hustle***, supra.

186 ***Soda-Club (CO2) S.A. v. Percom Ltd. d/b/a WebBooster.com***, D2005-0465 (WIPO June 29, 2005).

failure to show how a respondent's choice of domain name could be an abusive registration. The following are representative examples of allegations that fail to prove unlawful registration: 1) domain names composed of a dictionary word—such as "Post" in <post.com>[188] or addition of an article to the phrase "local transplant"[189]—which can have independent associations distinct from that of the trademark; 2) offering a domain name for sale that respondent no longer has any use for[190]; or 3) confusing the trademark concept of confusion in the marketplace with "creating a likelihood of confusion with the complainant's mark as to the source, sponsorship, affiliation, or endorsement of the respondent's website," which is actionable under paragraph 4(b)(iv) of the Policy.[191]

7.05-A.2.c *Response*

7.05-A.2.c

Respondents appear in approximately 15% of the cases, and of those approximately 30% in sole member panels and approximately 50% in three-member Panels prevail on their paragraph 4(c) defenses. Of those who default a small percentage do not forfeit their registrations for one of two reasons: either the record establishes good faith or there is no proof of bad faith. Where respondent appears and its registration postdates complainant's mark its evidence is expected to establish an affirmative right or legitimate interest in the disputed domain name that *outweighs* any statutory right that complainant may have in its mark. Respondent has no burden to disprove bad faith but it may offer proof of lawful registration if it fails to rebut complainant's *prima facie* case, such as the generic quality of the domain name.

Rule 5(b) charges respondent to

---

187 ***PJS International SA v. Carl Johansson***, D2013-0807 (WIPO June 25, 2013) ("[I]t is not unreasonable to expect the Complainant to take the trouble to actually state the argument. . . . [T]he Panel is of the opinion that the Complainant's submission does not even qualify as one which merely repeats or paraphrases the UDRP . . .; it completely omits any discussion of the merits of a critical component, i.e., identity or confusing similarity between the Complainant's trademark and the disputed domain name, which it has to prove.")

188 ***Deutsche Post AG v. NJDomains***, D2006-0001 (WIPO March 1, 2006).

189 ***David Unangst v. Aimee Rancer***, FA1307001508778 (Forum August 28, 2013) (LOCAL TRANSPLANTS and <thelocaltransplant.com>).

190 ***Teradyne, Inc. v. 4Tel Technology***, D2000-0026 (WIPO May 9, 2000) (<4tel.com>. "Rather than the classic cybersquatting model of a Registrant who registers the trademark of another, hoping to profit from the trademark owner's desire to reflect its trademark in a corresponding domain name, we have here a company which registered a domain name to reflect the name of its own business, which seeks to sell that domain name to others for profit now that its business has dissolved.")

191 ***Credit Management Solutions, Inc. v. Collex Resource Management***, D2000-0029 (WIPO March 17, 2000).

(i) Respond specifically to the statements and allegations contained in the complaint and include any and all bases for the Respondent (domain name holder) to retain registration and use of the disputed domain name.

The instructions are pointedly simple and the should be followed: respondents are expected to focus on the the facts and circumstances that support their rights or legitimate interests or (if they cannot do that affirmatively in rebuttal) their lawful registrations in countering complainant's claim of bad faith. Providers have designed their template response forms in the same spirit, to elicit counter-contentions anchored to evidentiary proof exhibited in the annexes.

Where respondent contends it is using the mark for a *bona fide* offering of goods or services (paragraph 4(c)(i)) its assertion is bolstered or undermined by the evidence that proves it so.[192] For the 4(c)(ii) defense a respondent is not "commonly known" by merely having registered the domain name. It must establish it was known by that name prior to its registration if the registration postdates the trademark.[193] For paragraph 4(c)(iii) of the Policy respondent must explain, and the contents of its website confirm, its noncommercial or fair use of the domain name. Respondent cannot prove its good faith by arguing that "it should be complainant's responsibility to prove that [Respondent] has benefitted from directing the disputed domain name to his website."[194]

Respondents have prevailed where they have established the domain names were acquired and are being used (or passively held) for their values as Internet addresses rather than mark values. Two illustrations of this (additional to the examples cited in Chapters 4 and 5) are Net App[195] and Javier Narvaez Segura, Grupo Loading Systems.[196] Respondent in the first case contended for its good faith without proof and lost; and in the second case it contended lawful registration with proof and prevailed.

---

[192] ***Groupe Industriel Marcel Dassault v. Robaire Godbout,*** D2017-1401 (WIPO September 25, 2017) (<dassault.group>. Domain name forfeited for among other reason Respondent's admissions by letter and website contend: "After some text extolling the benefits for a company wishing to present itself as operating globally of registering in a Top Level Domain, the Respondent set up an extensive range of text and images about the Complainant and its business.... According to the Respondent, he did this to demonstrate to the Complainant how valuable the disputed domain name could be to it.")

[193] Respondent failure discussed further in 'Commonly Known By The Domain Name'" (Sec. 5.03-A).

[194] ***Jay Leno v. Guadalupe Zambrano***, D2009-0570 (WIPO June 25, 2009).

[195] ***NetApp, Inc. v. July Linett c/o Jolly Co.***, FA0812001238829 (Forum February 5, 2009) (<netapp.org>)..

[196] ***Javier Narvaez Segura, Grupo Loading Systems S.L. v. Domain Admin, Mrs. Jello, LLC***, D2016-1199 (WIPO August 31, 2016) (<loading.com> "Respondent's arguments are supported by the case

Respondent in ***NetApp*** did not deny <netapp.org> incorporated complainant's trademark NETAPP, but contended the term "has a dictionary definition, namely, an acronym for the phrase 'network application' and also is defined as 'a purpose built appliance that performs a specific limited function on a network.'" However, Respondent's sole evidence was "an extract from the Free Dictionary Online *where the acronym is also associated with complainant's trademark and name.* This was not sufficient to establish that NETAPP is a term commonly used" (emphasis added). Respondent's "proof" was further undercut by the fact that "the resolving website contains a prominent hyperlink to a commercial website in direct competition with complainant's business." Where respondent has failed to respond specifically "the Panel is entitled to prefer a specific allegation in the Complaint to a generalized denial in the Response."[197]

Terms that in the actual marketplace function as trademarks in cyberspace can just as easily (the facts not demonstrating otherwise) be used for their semantic value. In ***Javier Narvaez Segura, Grupo Loading Systems***, the Panel noted that "the dominant word element of the trademark is descriptive . . . [and] considers that a respondent has a right to register and use a domain name to attract Internet traffic based on the appeal of commonly used descriptive or dictionary terms, in the absence of circumstances indicating that the respondent's aim in registering the disputed domain name was to profit from and exploit the complainant's trademark."

Since respondent's ultimate purpose is only known to itself it is called upon to explain and justify its registration. For example, situations involving "passive holding,"[198] in which no present benefit can be discerned, an inference will be drawn from respondent's choice of name when "it is not possible to conceive of any plausible actual or contemplated active use of the Domain Name by respondent that would not be illegitimate."[199]

7.05-A.3 Varieties of Evidence 7.05-A.3

In addition to the pleadings properly certified,[200] parties are expected to support their contentions with documentary proof drawn from public and private sources and declarations or affidavits on personal knowledge.[201] Archival information about

---

file, and the Panel finds that there is no evidence showing that Respondent's conduct was aimed at creating confusion with Complainant's trademark at any point in time.")

197 ***eDreams, Inc. v. CK Ventures Inc.***, D2009-1508 (WIPO January 8, 2010).

198 Panels invented the oxymoron "passive use" for domain names that do not resolve to active websites. Discussed further in "Inactive or Passive Use" (Sec. 5.01.B.2).

199 ***Telstra Corporation Limited v. Nuclear Marshmallows***, D2000-0003 (WIPO February 18, 2000).

200 For complainant, Rule 3(b)(xiv) of the Rules of the Policy. For the Respondent, Paragraph 5(b)(viii).

websites (to the extent it exists) is available from several services, including <archive. org>. Trademark information affirming or countering allegations of priority is easily accessible on official national databases.

Evidence under the control of a party such as business or corporate records, official filings, proof of ownership or reputation, timing of entry into the marketplace, and first use in commerce (for proof of common law rights) if not submitted will support adverse inferences against the party whose burden or rebuttal it is to establish the truth of a contention material for the claim or defense.

7.05-A.3.a 7.05-A.3.a *Declaration or Affidavit*

A declaration or affidavit is a formal statement made on personal knowledge of the relevant and material facts in a case. Statements proffered for their truth are accorded great weight (even against skepticism in some cases) but are undermined if embellished with opinion based on incomplete evidence or presented in unattested form. The demands on the declarant or affiant are illustrated in two representative cases in which the proffers were rejected.[202]

The Complainant in ***CNRV*** "sells Recreational Vehicle parts, accessories and supplies under the name AdventureRV, in which it [claims to] ha[ve] common law trademark rights." Complainant's affidavit is essentially accusatory. The three-member Panel was in accord the complaint was an abuse of the process, but the affidavit elicited from one of its members a fuller explanation for rebuking Complainant. He found "Complainant's disparaging allegations against Respondent (such as that Respondent relied on affidavits of 'dubious credibility', that it conducted 'reckless, perfunctory searches and that, in effect, it concealed unfavourable evidence') were made without evidence or argument to justify them." The deficiency lies in the use of the affidavit to vilify the Respondent without offering any substantive evidence of Complainant's rights.

In ***Which?*** Complainant's "registered trademarks WHICH and WHICH? CAR are widely known trademarks in the UK." In an attempt to rebut complainant's *prima facie* case respondent filed a declaration of a manager who stated that "We registered the Disputed Domain on February 20, 2002 because it was a descriptive term to which we believed no party could claim exclusive rights." The deficiency lies in the declarant's claim of personal knowledge, whether 1) he was an officer of respondent having access to company records; and 2) (more significantly) whether he was even employed by respondent when it acquired the infringing domain name.

---

[201] Rule 3(b)(ix) for Complaint ("describe the grounds on which the complaint is made"; Rule 5(c)(i) for Response ("Respond specifically to the statements and allegations contained in the complaint").

[202] ***CNRV, Inc. v. Vertical Axis Inc.***, FA0912001300901 (Forum May 3, 2010) (<adventurerv. com>); ***Which? Limited v. Whichcar.com c/o Whois Identity Shield / Vertical Axis, Inc.***, D2008-1637 (WIPO January 27, 2009).

Consistency of factual claims supports credibility; inconsistency undermines it. In ***Ustream*** respondent submitted a declaration which stated it had registered the domain name years prior to complainant's first use in commerce, which, if true, would have negated registration in bad faith and required dismissing the complaint.[203] However, in a subsequent declaration it revised the date though failed to disclose when it actually acquired the domain name.

The majority found respondent's "shifting story . . . [to be] inherently incredible." Important in reaching this conclusion was respondent's "failure to provide a compelling explanation for why its first declaration was materially incorrect . . . [which] smacks of being a post hoc justification for a date just prior to the date complainant began public use of its mark." It could have been expected "to provide a compelling explanation" because it alone knows the true facts relating to the acquisition of the domain name.

7.05-A.3.b *Researching the Past: Historical Screenshots from the Wayback Machine* 7.05-A.3.b

The Wayback Machine is a searchable database created, maintained, and operated as a public service by the Internet Archive ("IA").[204] Upon a request for historical information it displays dates of archived screenshots thereby making available to researchers a window on the past use of domain names.[205] It has been likened to "a paper library . . . [that] provide[s] free access to researchers, historians, scholars, and the general public."[206] IA has particular benefit to parties in a UDRP proceeding as a major source of information about the adversary in preparing the complaint and opposing the claim of abusive registration. However, because respondents control what can be copied they can undermine the usefulness of the IA.

The unanimous three-member Panel in the last cited case observed that "[IA] respects robots.txt instructions [not to crawl a particular site], and even does so retroactively," thereby preventing the researcher from uncovering targeted pages. The antidote to such instructions is for complainant to argue and the Panel to draw an adverse inference in favor of complainant's "reasonable factual allegations . . . as to the historical use of the web site to which the domain name at issue resolves . . .

---

203 ***Ustream.TV, Inc. v. Vertical Axis, Inc.***, D2008-0598 (WIPO July 29, 2008) (<ustream.com>).

204 IA was founded in 1996. It started building a better-rounded collection in late 1999 by using Alexa to crawl the Web. A history of screenshots is accessible on the Internet at http://www.archive.org.

205 More extensive fee-based services are provided by DomainTools at http://www.domaintools.com though impacted by GDPR.

206 ***The iFranchise Group v. Jay Bean / MDNH, Inc. / Moniker Privacy Services [23658]***, D2007-1438 (WIPO December 18, 2007) (Complaint denied on the grounds that the alleged mark, which is registered on the Supplemental Register, is not distinctive, but the Panel was otherwise critical of the use of a Robot Exclusion Standard).

and that the use of robots.txt in the particular case may be considered as an indicia of bad faith."[207] This standard has come to be known as the "robots.txt doctrine."

Blocking is not *per se* illegitimate, although timing in denying access to the website may be a critical factor in deducing intention.[208] The question is whether blocking access to page content is undertaken for a legitimate business purpose or intended to mask infringement of complainant's statutory rights.[209] Respondent in ***Rba Edipresse*** employed robots.txt for years before Complainant filed its complaint. It explained why registrants may have legitimate reasons for blocking the collection of information on pay-per-click websites for inclusion in the Internet Archive and identified five such reasons, which the Panel sets forth in full "for the benefit of other panels in future cases."

The five reasons for disallowing access are 1) it imposes a cost in bandwidth by taxing respondent's server capacity for which it has to pay "without any return of revenue to the Respondent"; 2) and 3) promotes click fraud[210] and related scams associated with archiving (respondent explained that "[b]ecause of concerns of click fraud and related scams, the confidential contracts between PPC feed providers and publishers forbid archiving, reverse engineering, and copyright violation inherent in allowing third party content storage of current ads"[211]); 4) creates confusion with respect to parked pages; and 5) provides inaccurate information about the

---

[207] ***Id.*** See also Jurisprudential Overview 3.0, Paragraph 3.11: "Can the use of "robots.txt" or similar mechanisms to prevent website content being accessed in an online archive impact a panel's assessment of bad faith? Panels have found that, absent convincing justification in a given case for the employment of 'robots.txt' or other similar circumvention mechanisms to prevent access to historical website content on a repository such as the Internet Archive (at www.archive.org), the use of such device may be considered as an attempt by the domain name registrant to block access by the panel to relevant evidence (for example, if robots.txt is implemented only after the registrant is put on notice of third party rights)."

[208] ***Rba Edipresse, S.L. v. Brendhan Hight / MDNH Inc.***, D2009-1580 (WIPO March 2, 2010) ("[A]ccess was blocked before this dispute arose. Hence, whatever view one might take as to whether such a doctrine is appropriate, having regard to the justifications for archive blocking advanced by the Respondent (and the Panel finds it unnecessary to express a view), that doctrine cannot apply in this case.")

[209] ***SCOLA v. Brian Wick d/b/a CheapYellowPages.com***, FA0711001115109 (Forum February 1, 2008) (Transferred); ***Balglow Finance S.A., Fortuna Comércio e Franquias Ltda. v. Name Administration Inc.*** (BVI), D2008-1216 (WIPO November 10, 2008) (Transferred).

[210] Respondent explained that "[c]lick fraud is the subject of some controversy and increasing litigation because the advertising networks are a key beneficiary of the fraud. Use of a computer to commit this type of Internet fraud is a felony in many jurisdictions, for example, as covered by Penal code 502 in California, United States. It is illegal in the United Kingdom under the Computer Misuse Act 1990."

[211] Respondent explained that "[b]ecause of concerns of click fraud and related scams, the confidential contracts between PPC feed providers and publishers forbid archiving, reverse engineering, and copyright violation inherent in allowing third party content storage of current ads."

geographic distribution of use because the archived pages show only what was visible in one location.[212]

Archived pages from the IA have been accepted as reliable proof of web images in UDRP proceedings. ***The E.W. Scripps Company*** Panel held that "[o]n the balance of probabilities. . . they are accurate records of the home page accessed by the domain Name on those dates."[213] The usefulness of the Wayback Machine in laying a foundation for abusive registration has been demonstrated in many cases. Two representative examples illustrate the consensus view: ***Eidos Interactive***[214] and ***CytoSport.***[215]

In ***Eidos Interactive*** Complainant explained that while it acquired its trademark many years after the registration of the disputed domain name respondent was not the original registrant but a successor. It had purchased <justcause.com> one and a half to two years after complainant's first use of the trademark. This was established by examining the IA records. In some cases delay is fatal to complainant's claim. That was not the case in ***Eidos*** because respondent failed to explain the absence of IA records after it acquired the domain name. The historical record showed

> no use of the disputed domain name from 2004-2005. The first subsequent apparent use of disputed domain name as shown in the Internet Archive is on December 2, 2006, which screenshot shows the text: "justcom.com expired on 11/20/2006 and is pending renewal or deletion" (screenshots throughout all of 2006 reflect the same text). Then, according to the screenshot of January 1, 2007, the website at the disputed domain name was "under construction and coming soon". From January 6, 2007 to the present, screenshots of the website at the disputed domain name are not in the Internet Archive.

In ***CytoSport*** the results from the IA search were offered by respondent, which used the Wayback Machine to support its position. Complainant attempted to capture <monsterfood.com>, which was confusingly similar to its registered

---

212 Respondent also pointed out there is another service that captures "historical screenshots." In contrast to IA DomainTools.com stores images of the home pages without following links or storing text or site code. "In point of fact, if the archive.org agent did store the copies seen by it of the Respondent's web pages, only the history 'as seen in the US' would be available. The archive would thus conflict with what is actually seen elsewhere in the world, because the archive agent uses a US IP address. As evidence of what, for example, this Complainant may have seen at the page, the archive would not support it, if this domain name were tagged for geo targeting." IA is a free service; DomainTools.com is a subscription service.

213 ***The E.W. Scripps Company v. Sinologic Industries***, D2003-0447 (WIPO July 1, 2003).

214 ***Eidos Interactive Limited v. BWI Domains***, D2008-1818 (WIPO February 12, 2009); ***Heraeus Kulzer GmbH v. Whois Privacy Services Pty Ltd / Stanley Pace***, D2016-0245 (WIPO May 2, 2016) (<kulzer.com>).

215 ***CytoSport Inc. v. Personal***, D2008-0976 (WIPO August 18, 2008) (Complaint denied); ***Dreamlines GmbH v. Darshinee Naidu / World News Inc.***, D2016-0111 (WIPO March 8, 2016) (<dreamlines.com>).

design mark featuring a man with exaggerated muscles and the words "MONSTER FOOD" in stylized letters. Respondent alleged he acquired the domain name at an eBay auction for $71 and that he bid on it because it matched the services he was offering on the website to which it resolved. The Wayback Machine showed that "the website associated with the Domain Name [at the time of its acquisition] allowed Internet users to search for, and link to, restaurants that accepted online orders for meals." This was a business respondent alleged it was preparing to launch.

Historical screenshots from the Wayback Machine initially received a mixed reception in U.S. courts.[216] However, the trend appears to be in favor of judicial notice of the screenshots.[217] Use of historical screenshots collected as evidence in a legal proceeding is not a copyright infringement.[218]

7.05-B 7.05-B No Record, No Case

7.05-B.1 7.05-B.1 Satisfying the Burden of Proof or Production

Nothing is clearer in asserting claims of abusive registration or defending lawful registrations than that each party has a role in establishing the record, but complainant has the burden of establishing its claim. Complainants fail when they

[216] *Telewizja Polska USA, Inc. V. Echostar Satellite Corp.*, No. 02 C 3293, 2004 WL 2367740, at *5 (N.D. Ill. October 15, 2004); see also *Louis Vuitton Malletier v. Burlington Coat Factory Warehouse Corp.*, 426 F.3d 532, 535 (2nd Cir. 2005) (evidence of defendant's website advertisements presented through archive.org capture of the site content at a particular time).

[217] ***Id.***, *Telewizja Polska USA, Inc. V. Echostar Satellite Corp.*, No. 02 C 3293, 2004 WL 2367740, at *5 (N.D. Ill. October 15, 2004) (screenshots admissible as "an admission of a party-opponent and are not barred by the hearsay rule"); see also *Louis Vuitton Malletier v. Burlington Coat Factory Warehouse Corp.*, 426 F.3d 532, 535 (2nd Cir. 2005) (evidence of defendant's website advertisements presented through archive.org capture of the site content at a particular time).

Not self-authenticating: 2007 was a particularly fruitful year on this issue. For example, in a patent case, *Chamilia, LLC v. Pandora Jewelry, LLC.*, 04-cv-6017 (S.D.N.Y. September 24, 2007) plaintiff alleged Pandora failed to submit its patent application to the USPTO for more than a year after marketing its product. It offered a series of archived web pages from the Wayback Machine, which Pandora moved to strike. The Court held that this "putative evidence suffers from fatal problems of authentication under Fed.R.Evid. 901." In *Novak v. Tucows, Inc.*, No. 06-CV-1909, 2007 WL 922306, at *5 (E.D.N.Y. March 26, 2007) the Court struck Wayback Machine evidence for lack of authentication of Internet printouts "combined with the lack of any assertion that such printouts fall under a viable exception to the hearsay rule." Wayback Machine evidence has also been excluded in TTAB cases, *Hiraga v. Arena*, 90 U.S.P.Q.2d 1102, 1106 (TTAB 2009); *Paris Glove of Canada, Ltd. v. SBC/Sporto Corp.*, 84 USPQ2d 1856 (TTAB 2007) ("Wayback Machine" feature not self-authenticating and no reason to treat its existence as authenticating the pages in its historical record). In *My Health, Inc. v. General Electric Co.*, 15-cv-80 (W.D. Wis. December 28, 2015) "the court declined to take judicial notice of Wayback Machine documents on the basis that the Seventh Circuit had previously required authentication by an Archive employee."

[218] Also dating from 2007, *O'Toole v. Northrop Grumman Corp.*, 499 F.3d 1218 (10th Cir. 2007) in which the court held that "[i]t is not uncommon for courts to take judicial notice of factual

are only able to prove two of the three requirements; respondents prevail if they either establish rights or legitimate interests or rebut the contention that they registered and are using the domain names in bad faith. It has previously been noted that respondent can prevail without offering any evidence, but the party who controls the evidence (which may be a defaulting respondent on the issue of intention) is expected to create a record or suffer the consequences.[219]

Allegations based on facts supported by evidence in the record are favored; bare legal conclusions and implausible allegations are not. Unless a complainant submits evidence demonstrating abusive registration it merely asserts a legal conclusion, which is insufficient for the Panel to "make a finding of bad faith on the merits of the case."[220] Another Panel offers a useful guide to parties by marshaling discerning insights from a number of earlier cases to showcase the seriousness of the evidentiary burden:[221]

> "An Administrative Panel must not deal with propositions not asserted."
>
> "It is for complainant to plead the issues and to support them with some arguments and evidence."
>
> "Simply stating the reasons will not normally be sufficient to meet complainant's burden of proof."
>
> "Assertions that any use of the Domain Name by another party would likely mislead or deceive complainant's customers, without evidence, is not of much use."

Unsatisfied expectations for production of evidence are a significant factor in adverse rulings. A complainant does not meet its evidentiary burden when it fails to provide any factual proof of allegedly infringing conduct,[222] nor does a respondent that presents no evidence of good faith registration. It is not the Panel's job to make a party's case. Rather, a "party is under a duty to produce evidence in support of

---

information found on the world wide web." This was read by the court in *Marten Transport, Ltd v. PlattForm Advertising, Inc.* 14-2464 (D.C. District of Kansas April 29, 2016) as meaning that the 10th Circuit "expressly [does not] require authentication for Wayback Machine documents and sanctioned taking judicial notice of factual information on the Internet."

[219] Complainant in ***Credit Europe Bank N.V. v. Peter Yu***, D2010-0737 (WIPO July 14, 2010) failed to disclose a fact "crucial to the merits of [its] case" and was compelled to correct the record. In ***Wix.com v. Domain Admin, Privacy Protect, LLC (PrivacyProtect.org) / Luciana Gomes***, D2019-0264 (WIPO March 20, 2019) Complainant "allege[s] no facts (and provide[s] no evidentiary basis)" to support its claim.

[220] ***VeriSign Inc. v. VeneSign C.A.***, D2000-0303 (WIPO June 28, 2000).

[221] ***Nike, Inc. v. Crystal International***, D2002-0352 (WIPO August 2, 2002).

[222] ***Clark Associates, Inc. v. Belize Domain WHOIS Service Lt***, FA1010001353058 (Forum December 6, 2010) (Complainant provided "no detailed descriptions of the offending website or screen captures of the website . . .; the Complaint is merely composed of basic assertions. For this reason the Panel declines to find that Complainant made a prima facie showing.")

its case. It is not for the Panel to undertake an inquisitional role."[223] Moreover, the "UDRP is based on the adversary system and not on the inquisitorial system . . . and it is not for the Panel to complete the evidentiary record of complainant's case."[224] Failure to meet the minimal level of proof is fatal to a party's position. An example is a complainant's allegation that there is no conceivable non-infringing use of the disputed domain name,[225] which is persuasive only if proved; that is, more likely than not based on uncontradicted facts consistent with the respondent's narrative.[226]

Direct and tangible evidence in the form of declarations and affidavits is acceptable, but disregarded if not on personal knowledge.[227] Other proof includes communications between the parties exchanged prior to filing the complaint, results of independent investigations, current and historical content of websites,[228] allegations either not contested or admitted,[229] and conduct of the parties. Documents offered in evidence to prove a contention are intrinsically more trustworthy than a pleading alleging unsupported facts. "Evidence in the form of documents or third party declarations should be furnished in support of such assertions."[230]

Further, "[m]ere belief and indignation by Complainant that Respondents have registered and are using the Domain Name in bad faith are insufficient to warrant the making of such a finding in the absence of conclusive evidence."[231] If contested facts are unamenable to summary resolution or alleged "nefarious motive[s]" cannot be proved "complainants should consider whether a court, with

---

[223] ***Randgold Resources Limited and Randgold & Exploration Co.Ltd. v. Pico Capital Corp.***, D2001-1108;(WIPO October 24, 2001) (addressing Respondent).

[224] ***Pleasure Cake SL v. TechTools***, D2009-0580 (WIPO July 14, 2009) (addressing Complainant).

[225] ***Telstra Corporation Limited v. Nuclear Marshmallows***, D2000-0003 (WIPO February 18, 2000). Discussed further in "Inactive or Passive Use" (Sec. 5.01-B.2).

[226] ***Bulmers Limited and Wm. Magner Limited v. (FAST 12785240) magnersessions.com 1,500 GB Space and 15,000 Monthly Bandwidth, Bluehost.Corn INC/Jason LaValla***, D2010-1885 (WIPO January 17, 2010)(The "difficulty with this argument is that respondent has put forward a plausible reason for his registration and use of the disputed domain name." And, the "evidence of the Respondent's website also supports his story. . . . The website otherwise does not suggest to the Panel that there is an ulterior motive behind it.")

[227] ***Hagerty Insurance Agency, Inc. v. Whoisguard/Chris Hagerty***, D2008-1452 (WIPO December 11, 2008) ("[Complainant's general counsel stated only that he had] authority to act on behalf of the organization.")

[228] See below, "Researching the Past: Historical Screenshots from the Wayback Machine" (Sec. 7.04-A.3.b).

[229] ***General Motors LLC v. Flashcraft, Inc DBA Cad Company***, D2011-2117 (WIPO January 30, 2012) ("At the outset the Panel stresses that no one involved in this proceeding, including complainant, questions the legitimacy of the Respondent's business.")

[230] ***Radio Globo SA v. Diogo Pimentel***, D2000-1705 (WIPO, January 31, 2001). Uncertainty works against complainant.

[231] ***Loris Azzaro BV, SARL v. Asterix & De Vasconcellos***, D2000-0608 (WIPO September 4, 2000).

the prospect of discovery, would be a more appropriate forum for cybersquatting claims."[232]

The power of the Wayback Machine to test the truth of statements has not gone unnoticed. It applies to both complainants and respondents. In ***Ustream*** Respondent committed a number of errors compounded by falsely stating in a Declaration when it acquired the domain name.[233] The Wayback Machine revealed archived pages from 2003 through February 2005 with nothing further until March 2007, which, as the dissent acknowledged, was after the spate of publicity complainant received in February 2007. These facts supported the inference the disputed domain name was unregistered (or at least unused) during the period between February 2005 and March 2007 and was registered or activated to take advantage of complainant's trademark.

Complainants in the cases cited below were represented: one by an attorney and the other by an individual not identified as an attorney but nevertheless responsible for reviewing the complainant's submission.[234] Respondents did not appear in either case. In ***Unex***, complainant submitted insufficient proof to satisfy a *prima facie* case. ***Free Bridge Auto Sales*** is only slightly different. On the thinnest of records, based on respondent's default alone the Panel held complainant sustained its burden of proving respondent lacked rights or legitimate interests in the disputed domain name. There was some evidence in the record that the use of the domain name was in bad faith, which is sufficient for the *prima facie* case.

"It is true," the Panel noted "that Complainant registered its trademark prior to Respondent's registration of the Domain Name, that Respondent hails from the same state as Complainant, and that Respondent has a business in the same field." However, on bad faith registration the critical fact is that

> Complainant has submitted no evidence beyond those assertions to support a finding that Respondent likely knew of Complainant's mark at the time it registered the Domain Name. For example, Complainant claims that it advertised heavily using the mark, but it has not alleged when, where, or how it ran these advertisements, including whether it ran any of those advertisements prior to Respondent's registration of the Domain Name.

---

232 ***EAuto, L.L.C. v. Triple S. Auto Parts d/b/a Kung Fu Yea Enterprises, Inc***, D2000-0047 (WIPO March 24, 2000).

233 ***Ustream.TV, Inc. v. Vertical Axis, Inc.***, D2008-0598 (WIPO July 29, 2008) ("In light of the Respondent's shifting story [as to when it acquired the domain name], its failure to provide any documentary evidence to support its assertions, its failure to provide a compelling explanation for why its first declaration was materially incorrect, and the fact that the Respondent's latest story smacks of being a post hoc justification for a date just prior to the date that the Complainant began public use of its mark, the majority of the Panel finds the Respondent's declaration testimony to be inherently incredible and the majority of the Panel therefore disregards it.")

234 ***Unex Corporation v. Belize Domain Whois Service***, FA0903001250370 (Forum April 29, 2009) and ***Free Bridge Auto Sales Inc. v. Larry Ross***, FA0903001250951 (Forum April 28, 2009).

In addition complainant conceded that respondent "may not have known at the time of the registration [of the Domain Name] that he was registering a pre-dated trademark name and violating someone else's trademark." In the Panel's view "[t]hat concession is fatal to Complainant's claim."

7.05-B.2

7.05-B.2 Evidence Controlled by Party

The record from which inferences are drawn can be thought of as a combination of statements and silences. As discussed in the next section, credibility is a significant factor in weighing statements. What a party omits in its submission can be equally as important as what it includes. There are different kinds of silence. Failing to respond to a complaint is a silence that, although not an admission of liability, nevertheless has consequences.[235] In one case the respondent was present in the record through correspondence rather than appearance.

Withholding facts "uniquely within the knowledge and control of the respondent ... is tantamount to admitting the truth of complainant's assertions."[236] Silence supports an adverse inference.[237] For complainant, failure to disclose a fact undermining its claim to priority can be fatal. In ***inExile Entertainment*** Complainant alleged a date of first use in commerce that was contradicted by its trademark application (evidence offered by respondent).[238] On the other hand, in ***Lacoste Alligator*** respondent's default was compensated by its presence in the record through correspondence submitted by Complainant which proved it had rights.[239]

If a complainant fails to produce evidence of its reputation as it existed at the time respondent registered the domain name the inference must be that it

---

[235] Rule 5(e) of the Rules of the Policy reads: "If a Respondent does not submit a response, in the absence of exceptional circumstances, the Panel shall decide the dispute based upon the complaint." See also discussion in Rule 15(a), below.

[236] ***Do The Hustle, LLC v. Tropic Web***, D2000-0624 (WIPO August 21, 2000) (Respondent's failure to present information "uniquely within the knowledge and control of the respondent ... is tantamount to admitting the truth of complainant's assertions").

[237] ***Valeant International Bermuda v. DNS Administrator***, FA 1573544 (Forum September 15, 2014) (Allowing adverse inferences based upon the failure of a party to present evidence within its knowledge and control), citing, ***Do The Hustle, LLC v. Tropic Web***, D2000-0624 (WIPO August 21, 2000) ***Mondich v. Brown***, D2000-0004 (WIPO February 16, 2000) ("Respondent's failure to present any such evidence or to deny complainant's allegations allows an inference that the evidence would not have been favorable to respondent").

[238] ***inExile Entertainment, Inc. v. Telecom Tech Corp.***, D2009-0655 (WIPO July 3, 2009).

[239] ***Lacoste Alligator S.A. v. LaCoste Healing Jewelry***, D2009-0700 (WIPO July 16, 2009) (<lacostejewelers.com>. "The Panel concludes from the available facts that in practical terms Audrey LaCoste has reflected the name by which she is commonly known, and in which she would have certain rights, in a domain name related to her activities. Irrespective of the lack of a formal Response, the Panel is not satisfied that the Complainant has established on the balance of probabilities that the Respondent is without rights or legitimate interests in the disputed domain name.")

had none.[240] Similarly with geographic or temporal distance. Reputation does not necessarily travel to foreign or distant markets.[241] Current reputation is not proof complainant had one in the past.

If intent is to be found reputation must already have been earned before respondent registered the domain name. This is illustrated particularly in cases involving unregistered rights in which complainant fails to offer evidence of secondary meaning.[242] It also occurs in cases that can be proved only by offering evidence of historical facts under a party's control which it fails to produce. Neither of these claims supports forfeiture regardless of a respondent's use of the domain name in bad faith any more than it does if bad faith continues after renewal of registration.[243]

The point is illustrated in another representative case where the Panel had to determine whether evidence of bad faith use could be inferred from bad faith registration and held that it could not on the submitted deficient record involving the parties' relationship[244]:

> [I]t would have been an easy matter for Complainants to provide evidence (if it exists) of friction between the parties in 2007 or other facts from which the Panel might infer registration in bad faith. Even Complainants' allegations do not address any events prior to 2009. There is on the provided record no basis for an inference of bad faith in 2007.

The party with the burden either bares its hand or fails to persuade the Panel that it should prevail.

---

240 Reputation over time: ***Transportes AEROMAR S.A. SE C.V. v. Aeromar, Inc.***, D2010-0098 (WIPO March 19, 2010) (No proof of reputation when the domain name was registered).

241 Reputation over space: ***Rba Edipresse, S.L. v. Brendhan Hight / MDNH Inc.***, D2009-1580 (WIPO March 2, 2010) (Complainant argued that it had a Spanish trademark for CLARA that was "well known" but offered no proof for reputation beyond the borders of Spain.)

242 In the case of complainant in ***Brooke Bollea, a.k.a Brooke Hogan v. Robert McGowan***, D2004-0383 (WIPO June 29, 2004) evidence of her celebrity status postdated registration of the disputed domain name. The Panel noted that "Complainant offers no evidence to support her allegation . . . of her desired legal conclusion that 'It was not until complainant has gained notoriety that respondent registered the domain name <brookehogan.com> in bad faith.' While that allegation has no evidentiary value, it does serve as Complainant's recognition that some showing of celebrity (though not necessarily a registered mark) at the date the Disputed Domain Name was registered is required for her to prevail."

243 Until mid-2009 there was consensus that renewal of registration did not affect a registrant's right to a domain name registered in good faith. Several panelists have suggested a different construction of the Policy that would dictate retroactive bad faith. There has been no disturbance to consensus. Discussed further in "Justifying Forfeiture Despite Good Faith Registration" (Sec. 4.03-A.4.b).

244 ***Nectar International Limited and Desmo Enterprises Limited v. Arej Net, Arej***, D2009-0883 (WIPO August 19, 2009).

7.05-B.3

7.05-B.3 Curating Content

Domain names composed of generic terms carry no connotative accretions of brand awareness, unless and until the resolving websites accrue details that may support a likelihood of confusion "with complainant's mark as to the source, sponsorship, affiliation, or endorsement of [respondent's] web site" (paragraph 4(b)(iv) of the Policy). What is unlawful for domain names composed of generic terms is most often defined by content coupled with offers to sell them.

Content is either transiently infringing (and possibly excusable when plausibly explained (discussed earlier in 6.01-F.1) or "carelessly infringing" which is not excusable (extensively examined in earlier Chapters).[245] Of the latter, the antidote is in properly curating content. Where that is done successfully domain names must remain with respondent,[246] but failure to curate content will favor complainants.[247] Curation means controlling content to avoid suggesting any reference to or affiliation with complainant that would otherwise violate any of the subparagraphs of paragraph 4(b) of the Policy. This puts a premium on curated content, with particular focus on the timing of any transition to bad faith use.

Uncurated domain names identical or confusingly similar to marks predating their registration to generate income ("commercial gain" under 4(b)(4)(iv)) combined with offers to sell them for valuable consideration (paragraph 4(b)(i) of the Policy) will likely satisfy the requirements of the Policy for abusive registration. However, for curated domain names "precedents [that] might [mislead] the Complainant to believe that domaining is not admissible under any circumstances"[248] will learn that the "speculative business models" that have "developed around" the "scarce resources" of domain names[249] are, in fact, lawful registrations.[250]

---

[245] See Sections 4.03-A.3, Content as a Factor in Determining Bad Faith, and 4.03-A.4, Good Faith Registration, Subsequent Bad Faith Use. The principle articulated in ***Teradyne, Inc. v. 4tel Technology***, 2000-0026 (WIPO May 9, 2000)—that it "was not the intent . . . to extend the definition of 'abusive registration' to include domain names originally registered in good faith"—is the unquestioned consensus.

[246] ***Modz v. He Ming Huang***, D2017-2008 (WIPO December 21, 2017) (<modz.com>).

[247] ***Micro Electronics, Inc. v. Shawn Downey / Sensible.Domains***, FA1902001829812 (Forum April 11, 2019) (<micro.center>. "Respondent argues that it is entitled to register and hold a domain name for sale. The Panel generally agrees. However, while Respondent is offering the Disputed Domain Name for sale, the Disputed Domain Name (it being confusingly similar to Complainant's Mark) cannot be used to resolve to a website on which is presented active hyperlinks to Complainant's competitors."

[248] ***Aurelon B.V. v. AbdulBasit Makrani***, D2017-1679 (WIPO October 30, 2017) (<pco.com>. "A number of UDRP cases relating to three-letter domain names reflect the fact that such terms are generally in widespread use as acronyms or otherwise and it is entirely conceivable that a respondent registered such a domain name for bona fide purposes.

[249] *Id.* The buying and selling of domain name is a bona fide business under 4(c)(i) of the Policy.

7.05-C Role of Credibility in a UDRP Proceeding 7.05-C

Credibility should not be discounted in determining a party's rights even in a paper only proceeding such as the UDRP. A party's submission will be judged by its candor or lack of it,[251] the plausibility of its arguments,[252] its statements or silences and the evidence it produces, withholds or suppresses. The *persona* a party projects can be critical to the Panel's perception of its assertions and contentions and ultimately to its success or failure in the proceeding: "a party who makes an untrue statement, or offers an internally inconsistent set of allegations, or fails to corroborate with documentary evidence an assertion that can be easily corroborated if true, that party runs the risk of impairing its credibility in general.[253]

Evaluating parties' claims and defenses for credibility originally found expression in an early case in which the majority rejected the view that the panel should "put away [its] common sense before [it] open[s] a file."[254] "Common sense" in that dispute favored the Complainant, but Panels are neutral in their evaluations. Since complainants bear the burden of proof they must be particularly mindful of claims for exclusive use of marks composed of dictionary words, common expressions, and strings of random letters. A three-member Panel was particularly disapproving in one case in which Complainant "failed to disclose a number of material facts, including (1) its prior ownership and subsequent abandonment of the disputed domain name; (2) the eventual purchase of the domain name at auction by the

---

250 Investors specializing (for example) in registering dictionary words, misspellings of common words, or acronyms and accused of typosquatting or infringement are not ipso facto acting in bad faith. ***Florim Ceramiche S.p.A. v. Domain Hostmaster, Customer ID: 24391572426632, Whois Privacy Services Pty LTD / Domain Administrato, Vertical Axis Inc.***, D2015-2085 (WIPO February 11, 2016) holds <cedit.com> which it successfully argued is a purposeful variant of "credit." See also ***Inspectorate America Corporation v. Netcorp, LLC***, D2017-1930 (WIPO December 13, 2017) (LOAMS and <loams.com> where the domain name is an intentional misspelling of "loans." LOAMS appears to be an acronym of an analytical and measuring process for lubricants)

251 ***Pret A Manger (Europe) Limited v. Jack Tang***, D2018-2059 (WIPO November 5, 2018) (<pret.app>. Respondent offered proof of his entrepreneurship: "[N]o reason to doubt [his] credibility."

252 In ***Greyson International, Inc. v. William Loncar***, D2003-0805 (WIPO December 3, 2003), the Panel noted respondent "has presented a plausible explanation . . . and Complainant has offered no evidence to the contrary."

253 ***Associated Newspapers Limited v. Makhdoom Babar, Mail Group***, D2019-0049 (WIPO February 25, 2019) (<dailymailnews.com>. Transferred. Where a panel has nothing more than "the documentary evidence placed into the record ... [it] is often left with nothing more than ... the application of logic, experience, and common sense.")

254 ***Time Inc. v. Chip Cooper***, D2000-1342 (WIPO February 13, 2001) (<lifemagazine.com>. "The dissent spends much time in an attempt to explain Respondent's inaction, but none explaining his actions. The dissent believes that the panel should refrain from evaluating the credibility of the parties. The majority disagrees. As panelists, we are not obliged to put away our common sense before we open a file.")

Respondent; and (3) that [it] attempted to partially base its trademark rights on a cancelled registration."[255] For complainants, lack of candor is grounds for a reverse domain name hijacking sanction (below Sec.7.11).[256] For respondents, failure to explain their choices for domain names identical or confusingly similar to well-known and famous marks undercuts credibility of any claim of lawful registration.[257]

It is expected of parties in arguing their positions that their proof matches their allegations. Rhetorical overstatement (***The Chancellor, Masters and Scholars of the University of Cambridge***), failure to disclose material facts,[258] and facts offered and withheld[259] undercut credibility. Panelists "feel[] that it is [their] responsibility, wherever possible, to evaluate the evidence and to provide the parties with a speedy, cost effective resolution of their domain name dispute."[260] However, "[t]he Policy ... requires the Panel to act on the evidence, not suspicion or suggestion."[261] Where parties are involved in disputes in which neither side can be credited for the truth of

---

[255] ***iPayment, Inc. v. Domain Hostmaster, Customer ID: 83314393006017, Whois Privacy Services Pty Ltd / Kwangpyo Kim, Mediablue Inc.***, D2015-1014 (WIPO September 2, 2015).

[256] In ***The Chancellor, Masters and Scholars of the University of Cambridge v. Kirkland Holdings LLC.***, D2015-1278 (WIPO October 5, 2015) (<cambridge.com>) the three-member Panel criticized Complainant's counsel for "exceed[ing] the bounds of advocate's hyperbole."***Proeza, S.A. de C.V. v. Domain Admin***, D2018-0535 (WIPO June 12, 2018) (<proeza.com>. "The Panel finds it troubling that a Mexican Complainant could omit the fact that "proeza" is a dictionary word in the Spanish language – Mexico's official language. Arguably, if Respondent had not filed a response, the dictionary meaning of "proeza" would not have been brought to the Panel's attention, the Domain Name more likely would have been transferred, and an injustice would have been done.")

[257] Consider ***Telstra Corporation Limited v. Nuclear Marshmallows***, D2000-0003 (WIPO February 18, 2000) in which the Panel formulated the "inconceivability principle" that an inference will be drawn from respondent's choice of name when "it is not possible to conceive of any plausible actual or contemplated active use of the Domain Name by respondent that would not be illegitimate."

[258] ***Anyclean Premium Limited v. Jethro Denahy, Any-Clean***, D2017-0581 (WIPO April 28, 2017) (<any-clean.com>) ("The Panel considers that one situation where a finding of RDNH is appropriate is where a Complaint has been presented in a manner which is misleading and inaccurate.")

[259] Complainant lacking credibility: In ***Edward G. Linskey Jr. v. Brian Valentine***, D2006-0706 (WIPO September 18, 2006) there were two different problems: first, "Complainant's evidence in this proceeding . . . is not sufficient to demonstrate any use of <finances.com> as the source of his claimed consulting services or any public recognition of his mark or website." Second, the question of "perjury and manufactured evidence." Complaint denied with three concurring opinions. See also ***Libertad Servicios Financieros, S.A. de C.V. S.F.P. v. Telepathy, Inc.***, D2011-1635 (WIPO January10, 2012) (Panel was "very concerned by the apparent lack of candour on the part of complainant"); ***CEAT Limited v. DNS Administrator, Cykon Technology Limited***, D2018-2339 (WIPO January 14, 2019) (<ceate.org>. Complainant had put its business name into the search field. The Panel agreed that the proof had "been clearly fabricated in an attempt to create evidence of the Respondent's bad faith" and sanctioned it for reverse domain name hijacking (Sec. 7.11).

[260] Respondent lacking credibility: ***Share Our Gifts Foundation, Inc. v. Freedom Bands Inc., Fan Bandz Inc a/k/a fanbanz***, D2004-1070 (WIPO March 18, 2005) ("While there will certainly be cases in which a Panel cannot determine credibility, it would serve neither the interests of the parties

their statements the matter is outside the scope of the Policy. Although complexity is not reason for abdicating making a decision, it sometimes is. See "Complexity Is Not Reason for Abdicating Making a Decision" (Sec. 3.03-B).

As the footnotes indicate, credibility issues are not confined to respondents although their deficiencies are more frequently cited. One Panel cautioned that an indefensible position "necessarily harms [a party's] credibility. . . . Parties would be better advised to admit facts or conclusions that are not genuinely in dispute and instead focus their arguments on the true areas of disagreement."[262] The Panel in ***Interactive Television***[263] was "troubled by Complainant's apparent lack of candor in not disclosing the Trademark Office Actions issued prior to the filing of this Complaint."

In ***Starwood Hotels***[264] the Panel sustained Complainant's *prima facie case* on "this admittedly skimpy record" but on bad faith stated bluntly:

> Complainant's allegations in the Complaint are so conclusory, and so obviously unsupported by evidence, that it calls Complainant's other assertions into question. Parties in UDRP proceedings are well advised not to advance arguments that are so patently without merit that it undermines their credibility.

It is not enough merely to repeat the language of the Policy. Rather (the Panel continued) "to prove bad faith, Complainant must present facts showing how Respondent is competing or obtaining an unfair commercial advantage."

The Panel's advice in ***Starwood*** turns on both form and substance. Fortuity or "unfortunate coincidence"[265] in the choice of domain name cannot be ruled out, but plausibility bolsters credibility while improbability undermines it.[266] Some assertions are so highly dubious as to stretch credulity. Thus, "Respondent argues that its selection of the domain name <h-droadhouse.com> reflects the fact that his business is called 'Hagerty's Drivin Roadhouse.' However, Respondent failed to

---

nor the integrity of the process to dismiss any case in which one of the parties submits evidence which creates a colorable issue of credibility, leaving the parties to expensive and prolonged court proceedings.")

261 ***Coty Deutschland GmbH v. PrivacyProtect.org / Mr. Domain Admin / Peter Colman / Tom Marks***, D2013-1914 (WIPO January 20, 2014) ("The Panel is troubled by the possible cyberflight, concealed identity, unexplained ownership transfers, and incomplete information furnished to the Registrar. Such monkey business does, as the Complainant asserts, raise a suspicion that the Respondent has been less than candid with the Panel, and that the omissions are material to this dispute. The Policy, however, requires the Panel to act on the evidence, not suspicion or suggestion.")

262 ***R.T. Quaife Engineering, Ltd. v. Luton***, D2000-1201 (WIPO November 14, 2000).

263 ***Interactive Television Corporation v. Noname. Com.***, D2000-0358 (WIPO June 26, 2000).

264 ***Starwood Hotels & Resorts Worldwide, Inc. v. Samjo CellTech.Ltd.***, FA0501000406512 (Forum March 9, 2005) (<starwoods.com>).

265 ***Mowitania Wendt & Molitor GbR v. Eric Clermont***, D2011-0052 (WIPO February 22, 2011).

present any evidence supporting this contention, even after being given a second opportunity to do so by Interlocutory [Procedural] Order."[267]

In another case Complainant alleged it had rights to ELITE CRUISES and disclosed a USPTO serial number but failed to disclose its application had been denied.[268] Respondent's credibility in ***Hurriyet Gazetecilik***[269] was vouched for by his "track record." The three-member Panel listed four factors weighing in Respondent's favor, one of which was "[t]he fact that [he] has a track record of using his domain names in connection with his interests." He persuaded the Panel that his list of interests—he was a "distinguished scientist"—included the subject matter of the domain name.

In ***Scarlett Johansson***[270] and other celebrity name cases that find abusive registration, respondents' explanations fail to be persuasive even if superficially plausible.[271] In ***Fiji Rugby*** the majority stated that although the case was "finely balanced" it was able to "draw inferences from the manner in which respondent has argued its case, retreated from formal statements of fact and generally been less than forthcoming."[272] The Respondent's contemptuous attitude in ***Scarlett Johansson***—his disdain for "the entire concept of bad faith, a concept that he described in his Response as 'pragmatically speaking, beside the point, since bad faith is an arbitrary qualitative identifier that is neither culturally, neither structurally universally applicable'"—did "nothing to inspire confidence in the credibility of the Response."

Questionable candor—what a party chooses to leave out—as much as paucity of evidence offered, undermines a party's argument.[273] Further illustrations are declarations the Panel finds deficient because of selective information.[274] The majority in ***Ruggedcom*** stated:

---

266 Id., "The Respondent's explanation does not ring true for the Panel. It is presented by way of mere assertions which are unaccompanied by any form of supporting evidence."

267 ***H-D Michigan LLC v. Paul Hagerty***, FA0906001269352 (Forum August 24, 2009). The "interlocutory order" refers to the Paragraph 12 request for additional material. Discussed further in "Procedural Orders" (Sec. 7.07-A).

268 ***Jay S. Cohen d/b/a Elite Cruises v. Smoking Domains, LLC***, FA0803001155799 (Forum May 7, 2008).

269 ***Hurriyet Gazetecilik Ve Matbaacilik A.S. v. INFOMED***, D2008-0127 (WIPO March 30, 2008) (<hurriyet.net>, Turkish parties. The SLD is the name of a geographical district).

270 ***Scarlett Johansson v. Tristan Dare***, D2008-1650 (WIPO December 16, 2008).

271 ***Carol House Furniture, Inc. v. Registrant [3458020]: Oversee Domain Management LLC***, D2010-2103 (WIPO March 21, 2011) (<carrollhouse.com>. "Here, the Panel considers that, although Respondent's assertions of entitlement to register the combination of the terms 'Carroll' and 'house' as surname and generic word would appear to have superficial plausibility. . . [it fails to be persuasive].")

272 ***Fiji Rugby Union v. Webmasters Limited***, D2003-0643 (WIPO December 24, 2003).

273 ***Quaife Engineering and Starwood Hotels***, supra, same panelist.

> In the declaration, respondent took care to state that he did not register the Domain Name for the bad faith purpose which is described at paragraph 4(b)(i) of the Policy, and that he did not register the Domain Name in order to profit from any goodwill that complainant might claim in its claimed marks. *Conspicuously absent from the relevant paragraph of the Respondent's declaration, was any denial that he registered the Domain Name for the purpose of disrupting complainant's business* (emphasis added).

The same point about omissions in a declaration was made in an earlier case involving the same Complainant and the Respondent's employer.[275] The failure to deny a material fact can be read as an implicit admission of its truth.

Good faith and credibility are undermined when prior to the complaint being filed respondent demands an excessive price for the domain name and shortly thereafter changes content on the website.[276] In one case, the Panel dismissed respondent's contentions it "did not really" make such a demand and in any event "it was in response to approaches from complainant" as not meriting "any serious consideration."[277] On the issue of changing content the Panel noted that "[w]hilst respondent is at complete liberty to establish a website offering IPO related advice, it has failed to furnish any evidence to suggest it has the right to resolve the disputed domain name, comprising the Trade Marks, to such a website."

7.05-D Admissibility of Communications Relating to Settlement 7.05-D

As a general proposition, under rules of evidence in the United States parties are forbidden to disclose settlement discussions (if they fail) as antithetical to resolution of disputes, which courts encourage.[278] ICANN Panels with some exceptions[279] have taken a different approach.[280] Assertions and statements made in communications

---

274 ***RuggedCom, Inc. v. James Krachenfels***, D2009-0130 (WIPO April 7, 2009).

275 ***RuggedCom, Inc. v. LANstore, Inc.***, D2005-0760 (WIPO November 15, 2005).

276 This is to be distinguished from a circumstance in which mark owner makes first approach and respondent responds as in a negotiation. If a demand precedesmark owner's approach the demand violates Paragraph 4(b)(i) of the Policy. See "Not All Offers to Sell Violate the Policy" Sec. 5.01-D.3)

277 ***DigiPoS Store Solutions v. Hiname Inc.***, D2010-0297 (WIPO Apil16, 2010).

278 Federal Rules of Evidence at Rule 408.

279 Cf.: ***Nokia Corp. v. Just Phones Ltd., Nominet***, DRS0058 (Nominet January 7, 2002), citing dictum in *WHSmith Ltd. v. Peter Coleman*, [2001] FSR 9. The court held:

> It is desirable that any Dispute Resolution Service should be operated in a manner, which encourages the parties to settle between themselves if possible. In particular, in a case like this one, where complainant had the option of pursuing legal proceedings as an alternative to using the Nominet DRS, it cannot be equitable for a Respondent to be potentially subject to two distinct privilege regimes—on the one hand, if complainant opts for Court action, a Respondent can expect to have a settlement offer considered *"without prejudice"*, whereas on the other, if complainant opts to use the DRS, a Respondent can only be confident that a settlement offer will not be used against

prior to the initiation of a UDRP proceeding by or between the parties or their counsel are admissible regardless of notations of confidentiality.[281] Claiming privilege to exclude communications has been rejected by numerous Panels. In one case the Panel reasoned the history leading up to adoption of the Policy suggests that an offer to sell, absent a legitimate interest and evidence of good faith, is so likely to be evidence of bad faith and use that its exclusion is likely to result in injustice.[282] Furthermore:

> The Panel is of the opinion that the Policy's goal of preventing cybersquatting would not be furthered by excluding evidence of a registrant's offer to sell or otherwise transfer the domain name for consideration in excess of out-of-pocket costs, even if the offer is made after the registrant is on notice of the dispute.

Similar reasoning has been applied to letters marked "without prejudice." In ***McMullan Bros.***, Respondent's counsel marked two of his letters "without prejudice." The Panel concluded it was appropriate to take the letters into account in making its decision, although "that is not to say that the without prejudice doctrine, or something akin to it, might never be applicable to proceedings under the Policy."[283] For example, there "would exist a strong argument for excluding" communications

> where both parties have expressly or implicitly agreed that discussions between them with a view to settlement should not be brought before a panel. . . .

> him if he waits for proceedings to reach the "Informal Mediation" stage. Such inconsistency cannot assist in promoting early resolution of a dispute.

See also, ***The Vanguard Group, Inc. v. Emilio Sa***, D2001-1453 (WIPO April 7, 2002). The Panel, making reference to ***Nokia Corp.***, *supra*, stated:

> It would be incorrect to lay down a rule, which is absolute in its effect. The qualifying language in both Rule 408 ("This rule also does not require exclusion when the evidence is offered for another purpose") and the English Court of Appeal ("unambiguous impropriety") make it clear that under the common law, the principle applies only where the intent of the communication is to make a bona fide attempt to compromise a disputed claim and not where made to advance nefarious schemes.

280 The Jurisprudential Overview 3.0 asks and answers the following question, Paragraph 3.10: "Will panels consider statements made in settlement discussions?" "In the UDRP context, panels tend to view settlement discussions between the parties as 'admissible', particularly insofar as such discussions may be relevant to assessing the parties' respective motivations."

281 WIPO Overview 2.0 frames the question differently: "Can statements made in settlement discussions be relevant to showing bad faith?" The answer is equally on point.

"*Consensus view*: Evidence of offers to sell the domain name in settlement discussions is admissible under the UDRP, and is often used to show bad faith. This is because many cybersquatters often wait until a trademark owner launches a complaint before asking for payment and because panels are competent to decide whether settlement discussions represent a good faith effort to compromise or a bad faith effort to extort. Also the legal criteria for showing bad faith directly specify that an offer for sale can be evidence of bad faith."

Without agreement to exclude "a party might deliberately lure the other party into discussions, supposedly on a without prejudice basis, but in the hope that the other side might make a statement to its detriment during those discussions which could then be brought before a panel. This, the Panel believes, would be grossly unconscionable."

There is some authority for excluding statements made "without prejudice" but Panels that apply the doctrine base their determinations on other grounds. The Panel in ***Donna Karan Studio***[284] stated it did not take the without prejudice communications into account, but it rejected the notion their submission tainted the proceedings:

> Otherwise, in every case in which such documents were submitted there would be an automatic obligation to start anew. The issue is whether those documents have been taken into account in reaching the decision.

Similarly, the question was early raised as to whether an offer made in the context of settlement discussions should be barred from consideration as evidence on the basis of exclusionary rules.[285] The dissent in another case held such evidence was barred.[286] However, this view was immediately attacked as flawed: "An offer to sell the domain name for valuable consideration in excess of the documented out-of-pocket costs directly related to the domain name is not only evidence of, but conclusively establishes that, the domain name has been registered and is being used in bad faith. Policy, §4(b)(i)."[287]

7.05-E Making Changes to the Website After Notice and Filing of Complaint 7.05-E

Despite misgivings expressed by some panelists,[288] where there is no evidence of bad faith registration the Policy does not penalize a respondent for changing use before notice.[289] Changing a website after commencement of a proceeding may also be excusable if the complaint is the first notice of infringement. "Modifying such a website . . . may attenuate the harm to a complainant whose trademark or

282 ***Magnum Piering, Inc. v The Mudjackers and Garwood S. Wilson, Sr.***, D2000-1525 (WIPO January 21, 2001) (U.S. residents).

283 ***McMullan Bros. Limited, et al. v. Web Names Ltd.***, D2004-0078 (WIPO April 16, 2004) (Irish residents).

284 ***Donna Karan Studio v. Raymond Donn***, D2001-0587 (WIPO June 27, 2001).

285 ***Nokia Corp. v. Just Phones Ltd.***, supra.

286 ***Motorola, Inc. v. Newgate Internet, Inc.***, D2000-0079 (WIPO April 20, 2000).

287 ***CBS Broadcasting, Inc. v. Gaddoor Saidi***, D2000-0243 (WIPO June 2, 2000).

288 Discussed further in "Justifying Forfeiture Despite Good Faith Registration" (Sec. 4.03-A.4.b). Changing content after a cease-and-desist notice from owner of a well-known trademark is not excusable. See ***Wal Mart Stores, Inc. v. Walmarket Canada***, D2000-0150 (WIPO, May 2, 2000)

commercial interests are allegedly compromised by the website prior to remediation."[290] Some Panels have held that changing a website after being notified of a dispute cuts against or negates a finding of rights or interests in a disputed domain name.[291] Others see "such holdings as unwarranted departures from long standing evidentiary rules and rational[e] concerning subsequent remedial measures."[292]

Respondents should not be discouraged from "this positive behavior. . . . [T]he fact of a website's remediation should not create an evidentiary inference adverse to the respondent."[293] The Panel's reasoning is that such action "arguably reduces further harm from such website to the consuming public."[294] Other Panels take a different view. The consensus is that the paragraph 4(c)(i) defense is limited to actions taken "before any notice to you of the dispute," hewing strictly to the letter of the Policy. "To allow Respondent's claim that he has made post-filing changes to his website to alter the outcome of this dispute would open the door for all future respondents . . . to avoid the consequences of their actions."[295] Change implies sanitizing: "[i]f use following complaints were taken into account, the Policy could be rendered wholly ineffective by respondents rapidly posting websites which ostensibly constituted fair use of disputed domain names."[296]

(<walmartcanada.com>. "Respondent admits that it was only after receiving the 'cease and desist' letter that he turned his mind to developing the site for the sale of wall products etc.")

[289] Changes before notice and filing of complaint are discussed further in "Good Faith Not Vitiated by Change of Use" (Sec. 4.03-A.4.a).

[290] ***American Airlines v. James Manley d/b/a Webtoast Internet Services, Inc.***, FA1006001330044 (Forum July 27, 2010) (<americanway.com>. The change occurred after a cease-and-desist notice. Although the Panel observed that "[m]odifying such a website ... may attenuate the harm to a complainant" it did not find that was the case in this particular dispute.

[291] ***MB Fin. Bank v. MB Bank***, FA 644517 (Forum April 4, 2006); ***IslandAir, Inc. v. Flanders***, FA 96098 (Forum February 8, 2001).

[292] ***American Airlines,*** *supra.* (Although the Panel stated that "[c]ontrary to Complainant's urging, the Panel draws no adverse inference from the fact that Respondent made post complaint changes to its website," it found abusive registration.)

The rationale for this conclusion is the Federal Rules of Evidence §407 citing *GMC v. Keystone Auto. Indus.*, 453 F.3d 351, 359 (6th Cir. 2006) for the proposition that "finding that evidence of post litigation changes to the form of an allegedly infringing trademark device was prohibited pursuant to FRE 407." Since "Rule 407 is applied in trademark litigation . . . there is no reason why its rational[e] should not be consider[ed] and its principles applied to UDRP disputes where appropriate."

[293] ***American Airlines***, supra.

[294] *Id.* Respondent in ***Costas Spiliadis v. Nicholas Androulidakis***, FA0708001072907 (Forum October 17, 2007) alleged that it did not know until receiving a cease-and-desist letter from complainant that its registrar "had posted unauthorized third party links on the website and . . . demanded that they be removed and when they were not removed, [the] respondent changed its registrar.")

[295] ***Hewlett-Packard Company v. Alvaro Collazo***, FA0302000144628 (Forum March 5, 2003).

This view has a rational basis and is applied in most circumstances unless there is persuasive counter evidence. Respondent should not be rewarded for sanitizing its website upon notice of infringement. However, the determination is highly fact specific. There are certainly respondents who inadvertently transgress but where the evidence nevertheless supports a right or legitimate interest. Just as certainly, respondent in ***American Airlines*** being a good example, there are respondents who intentionally infringe a complainant's trademark right in an attempt to cover up their actionable conduct.

7.06 RULE 11(a)—LANGUAGE OF THE PROCEEDINGS 7.06

In whose language the proceedings are conducted is ultimately an issue of due process. For fairness, respondents are entitled to receive notification of the complaint. Rule 2(a) instructs Providers to communicate with respondents "in the language prescribed in Paragraph 11", that is the language of the registration agreement. Thus, if a complaint is filed in the English language the Provider will give notification to the foreign respondent in its language advising it that a complaint has been filed and complainant has requested the proceedings to go forward in English. Communications in this manner provide foreign respondents "a fair opportunity to present its case" as provided in Rule 10(b).[297]

Rule 11(a) contains two clauses. The first clause provides that "[u]nless otherwise agreed by the Parties, or specified otherwise in the Registration Agreement, the language of the administrative proceeding shall be the language of the Registration Agreement." The second clause dilutes the imperative of the first by providing that the decision is "subject to the authority of the Panel to determine otherwise, having regard to the circumstances of the administrative proceeding."

Holding the proceeding in complainant's language rather than the language of the Registration Agreement[298] is justified in one of two instances: 1) where the content of the website is created for Internet speakers in complainant's language (which demonstrates proficiency in it); and 2) extrinsic evidence of proficiency such

---

[296] ***Poker Host Inc. v. Russ "Dutch" Boyd***, D2008-1518 (WIPO December 1, 2008).

[297] The Provider is responsible for communications consistent with the Rule. See, for example, ***K & N Distributors LLC v. enjoymagic***, FA1701001712422 (Forum February 25, 2017) ("Pursuant to Rule 11(a), the Panel determines that the language requirement has been satisfied through the Japanese language Complaint and Commencement Notification, and, absent a Response, determines that the remainder of the proceedings may be conducted in English." Although Respondent defaulted the Complainant's complaint was dismissed because the mark postdated the registration of the domain name.)

[298] Where the Registration Agreement is in both languages, complainant can decide which language it will use. ***Warner Bros. Entertainment Inc. v. David Haddad / Warner Bros***, FA1706001736053 (Forum July 17, 2017) (<warnerbroscareers.com.co>).

as communications between the parties prior to commencement of the proceeding.[299] Whatever the reason, the decision "must be exercised in the spirit of fairness and justice to both parties taking into consideration matters such as command of the language, time and costs."[300]

Panelists take the following factors into account: a) the language or characters of the domain name; b) respondent's familiarity with complainant's language as evidenced by factor a) and the content of the website or any communications between the parties or with the provider; and c) respondent's response (if any) to complainant's request for its language to be the language of the proceeding. The analysis is illustrated in the following cited cases in which the registrations were in Korean.[301]

In the first, the complaint was submitted in English. Prior to its submission respondent answered complainant's cease-and-desist notice with an offer to sell the domain name in English, which was unsuccessful, and respondent defaulted in answering the complaint. The Panel decided to hold the proceedings in English on the theory respondent had shown proficiency in the language. In the second, respondent defaulted but objected in English in an initial response to the Center. The Panel found the "disputed domain name displays content entirely in English. . . [and] [t]he content is generated by a domain name parking service (smartnames.com) that operates entirely in English."[302]

The rule derived from the above cases is that if the website is set up to address an audience of native speakers, or other languages, and respondent demonstrates fluency in complainant's language it is appropriate to conduct the proceedings in complainant's language regardless of the language of the registration agreement. In ***UpsideOut***[303] respondent had two registrations, in English and Chinese. It

---

[299] Paragraph 11(b) provides that "The Panel may order that any documents submitted in languages other than the language of the administrative proceeding be accompanied by a translation in whole or in part into the language of the administrative proceeding." In ***Pearl Jam, LLC. f/k/a Pearl Jam, A General Partnership v. J.S.E. Janssen a/k/a Stijn Enzo Holding BV***, FA0905001262659 (Forum July 1, 2009) respondent submitted trademark application forms in Dutch and ignored a Procedural Order to translate them on the grounds that their meaning was easily understandable, which the Panel held was not the case since he did not understand Dutch.

[300] ***Transtrands Handelsaktiebolag v. Jack Terry***, D2005-0057 (WIPO March 21, 2005).

[301] ***Alstom, Bouygues v. Webmaster***, D2008-0281 (WIPO May 8, 2008) and ***Krizia S.p.A. v. Hong Hee Dong***, D2009-0141 (WIPO April 30, 2009).

[302] The evidence in ***Farouk Systems, Inc. v. QYM***, D2009-1658 (WIPO January 19, 2010) demonstrated that respondent 1) used English to "promote and sell its unauthorised and/or counterfeit products on the Websites"; 2) "advertise[d] and accept[ed] US dollars as the currency for payment"; and 3) stated in its "Conditions of Use" that "any activities or transactions occurring on the Websites will be resolved by arbitration in the State of Victoria, Australia." Cf. ***Jackson National Life Insurance Company v. guojianguang/LinYu***, D2013-1370 (October 1, 2013) (JACKSON NATIONAL LIFE and <jnlife.com>. Transfer denied.)

demanded Chinese translations, although it mostly used English on the websites. For this reason, the Panel "tends to believe"

> that respondent has the capability to understand the English language. On the other hand, complainant is a US entity and its authorized representative is a US citizen. They do not have the capability to understand the Chinese language. If complainant was required to submit all documents in Chinese, the administrative proceeding will be unduly delayed and complainant would have to incur substantial expenses for translation. Therefore, the Panel decides that English shall be the language of this administrative proceeding.

A third alternative is for the provider to take initial procedural steps to comply with the first clause of the Rule. In ***Too Faced Cosmetics***[304] the Forum sent a Chinese Language Notification of Complaint and Commencement of Administrative Proceeding to the Respondent, who defaulted in appearance. The Panel concluded the language requirement had been satisfied through the Chinese language Notice of Complaint and Commencement Notification and, absent a Response, conducted the remainder of the proceedings in English. Complainant's language trumps registration language when respondent's content establishes an intention to take advantage of the mark's reputation.

However, in the absence of any evidence that respondent is conversant in complainant's language the Panel has the discretion of terminating the administrative proceeding. Sympathy for complainant having to bear translation costs to the language of the registration "is outweighed by the requirement for the Respondent to have a fair opportunity to review the Complaint in a language it understands and to reply."[305]

7.07 RULES 12 AND 10(a): WHAT PANELS CAN AND CANNOT DO 7.07

> 7.07-A Procedural Orders (Rule 12).
>
> Rule 12 of the Rules of the Policy: "In addition to the complaint and the response, the Panel may request, in its sole discretion, further statements or documents from either of the Parties."
>
> 7.07-B Researching on the Internet (Rule 10[a]).
>
> Rule 10(a) of the Rules of the Policy: "The Panel shall conduct the administrative proceeding in such manner as it considers appropriate in accordance with the Policy and these Rules."

---

303 ***UpsideOut v. Lin Han***, D2009-388 (WIPO July 7, 2009).

304 ***Too Faced Cosmetics Inc. v. Sun Liang***, FA0807001216825 (Forum September 12, 2008).

305 ***Jimdo GmbH v. Dong Da Yang***, CAC 101940 (ADR.eu October 2, 2018) (<jimdo.top>. "The Panel finds that there is nothing in the case file to indicate that the Respondent has any understanding of the English language, and importantly nothing to show it has understood or is likely to understand any of the procedural aspects or submissions written in English in these proceedings.... There needs to be a fair balance between the interests of both parties in any UDRP proceedings."

7.07-A

7.07-A Procedural Orders

Rule 12 grants Panels "sole discretion" to request "further statements or documents from either of the parties." Sometimes they exercise this discretion circumspectly,[306] other times not at all, and at still other times they compel production to clarify facts and documents absent from the record.[307] However, exercising sole discretion raises questions of fairness and it should be exercised cautiously. Incautiously, it can be viewed as giving an unfair advantage to a party who has failed to marshal a full record.

In ***DigiPoll***[308] the Panel asked and complainant responded by clarifying its position with documentary proof sufficient to win transfer of the domain name. In contrast the three-member Panel in another case did not even consider requesting further "statements or documents" through a Procedural Order. It dismissed the complaint because it could not "tell from the record submitted if Complainant has any legitimate claim to these registrations or not."[309]

---

[306] Panel-requested Rule 12 is properly used to clarify issues, but is applied sparingly. ***Precyse Corporation v. Punta Barajas, SA***, D2002-0753 (WIPO October 2, 2002) (The Panel "considered using [his] discretion under Rule 12 to request additional submissions, but have determined not to do so for three reasons. First, the Policy and the Rules clearly impose on each party an obligation to come forward in the one pleading expressly allowed it with adequate evidence to sustain the legal conclusions it desires. Second, I believe that sua sponte requests for additional material should be used sparingly, and then only to permit a response to a matter a Complainant could not reasonably have anticipated or to provide evidence on a single discrete item. . . . Third, the parties here share, almost equally, the blame for [the] unsatisfactory state of the record. In that circumstance I do not believe the Panel should be seen as assisting either party to correct errors in its submission. It is not for a panel to save a party from its own mistakes or the consequences that flow from them.")

[307] See ***Viacom International Inc. and MTV Networks Europe v. Rattan Singh Mahon***, D2000-1440 (WIPO December 22, 2000) ("[I]t would, and should, be in exceptional cases only that supplementary submissions are requested by a Panel. If requesting supplementary submissions were to become unexceptional, the dispute resolution procedure under the Uniform Policy and Rules would most likely become significantly more resource-consuming to all the actors (i.e. the parties, the dispute resolution service provider, and the Administrative Panel) than is currently the case, as the unfolding scenario in this case demonstrates. Such an outcome seems contrary."

It should not be used to assist a party, ***VideoLink, Inc. v. Xantech Corporation***, FA150300 1608735 (Forum May 12, 2015) ("At the request of the Panel pursuant to Rule 12, Complainant provided an Additional Submission contending that the UDRP analysis should occur not when Respondent originally registered the domain name but when Respondent renewed the domain name in June 2010.") However, renewal of registration is not grounds for forfeiture under the UDRP. See 7.12-B.2 Provider Supplemental Rules, Forum for discussion on Rule 7 which provides for additional submissions.

[308] ***DigiPoll Ltd. v. Raj Kmar***, D2004-0939 (WIPO February 3, 2005).

[309] ***Helen of Troy Limited v. Mailadmin, Ltd. and Vitali Fed***, D2005-0371 (WIPO July 15, 2005) ("The registrations on which [Complainant] relies appear in the name of Bristol Myers, who is not a party to this proceeding. Complainant has not explained its relationship to these registrations or to Bristol Myers.")

Since complainant has the burden of proof on all issues its failure to respond to a Procedural Order can be fatal. The Panel in ***Fast-teks*** issued a Procedural Order "[i]n light of Respondent's questioning of whether Complainant had adequately established through evidence, the existence of its alleged license."[310] Complainant thereupon "provided a copy of the license agreement in question. In further compliance with the Procedural Order, Complainant [also] provided evidence that ML Capital's trademark has now been federally registered." In another case, however, the Panel found there was no explanation "why Complainant failed to respond to the Panel's express invitation to provide further information," with the result "the Panel on balance concludes that it has no choice but to decline to make a finding of bad faith in this matter."[311]

In yet another case, the Panel issued the Procedural Order because complainant "made assertions but omitted supporting evidence." It determined to give complainant an opportunity to provide evidence of its superior right to the domain name but it still failed.[312] Similarly in ***Fasthosts Internet***[313] the Panel issued the Procedural Order with some misgiving—"it is questionable whether it was appropriate for the Panel to have issued the procedural order that it did in this case"—because it "is for complainant to prove its case and it is not for a panel to do so on a complainant's behalf."

The Panel nevertheless decided to give complainant "an opportunity to address a number of gaps in its case. It did so because complainant was not legally represented "and because the gaps in question were ones that it seemed complainant might have been able to fill." On the other hand, it is not likely to extend tolerance to represented parties. Some panelists withhold discretion because complainants are expected to "get it right" the first time and should provide all the information

---

310 ***Fast-teks, Inc. v. Rescuecom Corporation***, D2005-0683 (WIPO September 29, 2005).

311 ***Motorola, Inc. v. R3 Media***, D2006-1393 (WIPO February 15, 2007). See also ***BinckBank N.V. v. Silue Tiessolikaabdoul***, D2011-1980 (WIPO December 29, 2011) ("The Complainant was given ample opportunity to provide such evidence, but did not use it; as a result, it has to bear the consequences of its own action (or inaction) in that regard.")

312 ***McMullen Argus Publishing Inc. v. Moniker Privacy Services / Traverito Traverito***, D2007-0680 (WIPO August 30, 2007) (<streetchopper.com>. In response to the Procedural Order the Complainant submitted a declaration, but it did not appear the declarant was "making these statements from personal knowledge, but from undisclosed sources. In support of this assertion, he provides a document filed in the United States Patent and Trademark Office which again makes an unsupported assertion of use since 1969."); ***Leonard Hardy v. Amrit Resort***, D2008-0698 (WIPO July 21, 2008) (three member Panel denied complaint because the submission of evidence in response to the Procedural Order did not support complainant's contention and the Panel denied the complaint.)

313 ***Fasthosts Internet Ltd v. Jamie Scott, Smudge It Solutions Ltd.***, D2008-0841 (WIPO July 24, 2008) (However, so far as the issue of bad faith registration was concerned "complainant chose not to avail itself of that additional opportunity.")

necessary to prove their case from the material contained in the complaint and its annexes alone.[314]

How far a Panel will reach to obtain further "statements or documents" is illustrated in ***Renalo Investments***. Respondent alleged complainant's facts were "fabricated" to "create confusion and deceipt [sic] to infringe on our patented invention . . . and should be ignored by this panel, and the complaint should be dismissed."[315] The question: Which party was fabricating evidence to confuse the Panel? In assessing the additional evidence, the Panel noted two different kinds of problems with respondent's submission. First, its alleged patent or patents applications to the USPTO for software were dated subsequent to the institution of the UDRP proceeding, thereby highlighting its misguided attempt to improve its position. Second, it refused to produce evidence requested by the Panel to supplement the Record, thereby undermining its credibility.

Setting aside the unusual scope of Procedural Orders in ***Renalo Investments***, the Panel simply wanted more evidence to supplement deficiencies in the record; to prompt complainant to establish priority of rights and respondent to demonstrate rights or legitimate interests. Complainant had to provide "relevant evidence of the registration and use of [its] domain name <sentimente.ro> in 2001 and/or prior to January 3, 2002 [the date of the registration of the infringing domain name]". Respondent was directed to "produce documentary evidence supporting or in connection to [its] statement of 'have been promoting and selling the software to numerous prestigious companies' such as copies of communication sent and also received from such companies before November 20, 2008."

The Panel gave each party an opportunity to produce documentary evidence under its custody and control. Complainant complied with the Procedural Order but Respondent did not. Rather, it "indicat[ed] that the communications pertaining to the software transactions were 'sealed under confidentiality agreement and thus could not be disclosed' to the Panel." Since Respondent refused to produce its evidence and Complainant did Respondent could not establish any rights or legitimate interests in the disputed domain name. And, since Respondent's composition of the website was "almost identical to complainant's official website"—raising the specter of copyright infringement in addition to a violation of paragraph 4(b)(iv) of the Policy by falsely implying an association with complainant—the Panel inferred the domain name had been registered and was being used in bad faith.

---

[314] ***CAM London Limited and Comgest Asset Management International Limited v. Cam LondonLtd***, D2013-2190 (WIPO February 4, 2014) ("[T]o give the Complainant 'a second bite at the apple' would not be in line with the spirit of expediency and efficiency suggested in the Policy.")

[315] ***Renalo Investments Limited v. Dot Coms, Inc. / Mr. Fulviu Fodoreanu***, D2008-1791 (WIPO February 28, 2009) (<sentimente.com>).

There are still other cases in which complainants have failed to submit full records and have not been given the opportunity to supplement their submissions even though the evidence appeared to point to abusive registration. This could be a costly deficiency. In ***Brent Redmond Transportation*** the Panel stated its decision was "not intended as slavish insistence on procedure or the final stroke in a game of 'gotcha,'"[316] but of course it was gotcha since the Panel also observed about respondent that if the facts pleaded in the complaint were true, it "make[s] out a garden variety case of cybersquatting: a newly-formed company registers a domain name incorporating a competitor's mark and re-directs Internet users seeking Complainant to the competitor's website." In an analogous situation, although involving insufficient evidence of trademark rights [paragraph 4(a)(i)], the Panels in ***Gable & Gotwals***[317] and ***Thomas D. Hathaway***[318] dismissed the complaints but ameliorated the decisions by dismissing them without prejudice.[319]

7.07-B Researching on the Internet 7.07-B

> Rule 10(a): "The Panel shall conduct the administrative proceeding in such manner as it considers appropriate in accordance with the Policy and these Rules."

In addition to supplemental materials requested and provided by the parties, panelists may "independently visit the Internet in order to obtain additional light" on a case[320] and perform "limited modest factual research." This could conceivably strain the Panel's neutrality if the party prejudiced by it is not given an opportunity to respond to the research. Paragraph 4.8 of the Jurisprudential Overview 3.0 reads:

> [Research] may include visiting the website linked to the disputed domain name in order to obtain more information about the respondent or its use of the domain name, consulting historical resources such as the Internet Archive (www.archive.org) in order to obtain an indication of how a domain name may have been used in the relevant past, reviewing dictionaries or encyclopedias (e.g., Wikipedia), or accessing trademark registration databases.

The editors continue: "In some circumstances, a panel may also rely on personal knowledge (e.g., to take "judicial notice" of the reputation of a well-known mark, or a corporate affiliation/structure)."[321]

---

316 ***Brent Redmond Transportation, Inc. v. SSI Express***, D2008-1765 (WIPO December 30, 2008); ***CAM London***, *supra*. and cases cited therein.

317 ***Gable & Gotwals, Inc. d/b/a GableGotwals v. Dave Jackson***, FA0806001212305 (Forum September 18, 2008).

318 ***Thomas D. Hathaway v. DJ Wimberly***, FA0807001216935 (Forum September 18, 2008).

319 Dismissal without prejudice is a curious procedure. Discussed further in "Complaint Dismissed With and Without Prejudice" (Sec. 7.01-B.3).

320 ***InfoSpace.com, Inc. v. Hari Prakash***, D2000-0076 (WIPO April 6, 2000).

Panels have drawn on the following resources for their research on the Internet[322]:

- published UDRP decisions and other official documents relating to the Policy, such as ICANN and WIPO reports;
- documents establishing relevant "rules and principles of law" pursuant to Rules, paragraph 15(a), such as constitutions, statutes and statutory instruments, legislative history, rules and regulations, international conventions, court decisions, administrative decisions, official guidance by trademark registration bodies, legal treatises, and scholarly articles;
- official trademark databases;
- official databases of registered companies and trade names;
- domain name registrars' WhoIs databases and historical WhoIs databases;
- websites associated with the domain names, and websites linked from those websites, to establish how and by whom the domain names are used;
- historical versions of websites associated with domain names, prominently those available through the Internet Archive's "Wayback Machine";
- other websites and social media pages operated by the parties or their associates, as well as advertising, press releases, and other public statements by the parties, especially where these tend either to corroborate or impeach the parties' statements in a UDRP proceeding, reveal an admission against interest, or furnish information about an absent respondent;
- standard reference works, such as dictionaries, encyclopedias, Wikipedia, and materials published by relevant industry associations.

However, it "is one thing for a panelist to view a web site to verify . . . parties' assertions and quite another to embark upon an independent investigation as to what a complainant's case may be."[323] The skepticism in ***Silvie Tomcalová*** is notable because the Overview's endorsement of factual research in order 'to reach the right decision' could be problematic in that it appears to give panelists the authority to shed their neutrality in favor of a higher cause. Although the right decision may theoretically deliver justice it nevertheless has the result of relieving the benefiting party from having to prove its case. This is particularly problematic with a defaulting respondent who benefits from the Panel's factual research.

To some extent this lapse of neutrality is mitigated by the Panel invoking a best practice in arbitration of disclosing what it did and providing an opportunity for the parties to respond.[324] The problem was identified in a 2001 case regarding

---

321 WIPO Overview 2.0 identified this as "consensus." It is not labeled as such in 3.0 but it remains the "consensus" view.

322 The list that follows was compiled by the three-member Panel in ***Sensis Pty Ltd, Telstra Corporation Limited v. Yellow Pages Marketing B.V.***, D2011-0057 (WIPO March 15, 2011).

323 ***Silvie Tomcalová a.k.a. Sylvia Saint v. Juan Campos***, D2006-0379 (WIPO May 5, 2006).

a refiled complaint.[325] The Panel "accepted a refiled complaint where the earlier panelist found the respondent's conduct abusive but also found inadequate evidence of the complainant's trademark rights, and yet did not exercise its discretion under paragraph 12 of the Rules to request further evidence of trademark rights in that proceeding." In other words, the earlier procedural error in not giving Complainant an opportunity to provide the missing evidence warranted accepting the complaint and ordering the domain name transferred.

Nevertheless, there are examples of panelists making the respondent's case.[326] In ***Pick 'N Pay Retailers***[327] the Panel issued a Procedural Order which respondent ignored, and the Panel proceeded "to conduct a search of the internet archive in relation to the Domain Name." In doing that the Panel marshaled the evidence that was properly respondent's burden. Based on his research and not on the record before him he was able to find in Respondent's favor. Paragraph 10(d) of the Rules of the Policy reads: "The Panel shall determine the admissibility, relevance, materiality and weight of the evidence," which means the evidence *submitted by the parties.* In ***Pick 'N Pay***, the Panel made Respondent's case, which respondent was either unwilling or unable to make for itself, and became Respondent's advocate, thereby exceeding the Panel's authority under the Policy.[328]

---

324 The WIPO Overview continues: "If a panel intends to rely on information from these or other sources outside the pleadings, especially where such information is not regarded as obvious, it will normally consider issuing a procedural order to the parties to give them an opportunity to comment. Alternatively, or additionally, if the panel feels that it requires supplemental information to make a decision in a proceeding, it can issue a procedural order to the parties requesting the submission of such information."

325 ***Jones Apparel Group Inc v. Jones Apparel Group.com***, D2001-1041 (WIPO October 16, 2001). Proper use of independent research and Procedural Orders is demonstrated in ***Wild PCS, Inc. and Tom Yang v. Perfect Privacy, LLC / Choi Lam***, D2016-0017 (WIPO February 17, 2016); and also (same Panel) ***Singapore Pools (Private) Limited v. Vietnam Domain Privacy Services / To Thi Thanh Tam***, D2016-0292 (WIPO March 26, 2016).

326 In ***Eneco BV v. Eneco***, D2010-0548 (WIPO July 7, 2010) the Panel searched for <eneco.com> on the Internet Archive's Wayback Machine and found that respondent had registered and used the disputed domain name in years prior to complainant's trademark.

327 ***Pick 'N Pay Retailers (Proprietary) Limited v. Dependable Internet LLC.***, D2009-0499 (WIPO May 28, 2009); ***MAGIX Software GmbH v. The Music Connection***, D2015-1216 (WIPO October 1, 2015) (<musicmaker.com>); ***Adam Summers v. Georgina Nelson, CEO and Founder of truRating Limited***, D2015-0592 (WIPO May 24, 2015) (Respondent defaulted but the Panel made the Respondent's case after researching both parties). Compare ***Wild PCS, Inc. and Tom Yang v. Perfect Privacy, LLC / Choi Lam***, D2016-0017 (WIPO February 17, 2016) in which "Complainants have produced very little in the way of evidence to support the existence of service mark rights," but "in the course of the Panel's DomainsTools.com searches . . . the Panel viewed screenshots of the website connected to the Domain Name dating from 2008 when the Domain Name was used by Wild PCS Inc.'s predecessor, Wild PCS Accessories, to the present day when the website relates to the business of Wild PCS Inc. as it has done since 2010. The Panel is satisfied that the name 'Wild PCS' has been in continuous use in trade for the last eight years by Wild PCS Inc. and its predecessor."

7.08 7.08 RULE 13—IN PERSON HEARING

> 13: There shall be no in person hearings (including hearings by teleconference, video conference, and web conference), unless the Panel determines, in its sole discretion and as an exceptional matter, that such a hearing is necessary for deciding the complaint.

Rule 13 allows the Panel to hold an in person hearing if it determines "in its sole discretion and as an exceptional matter, that such a hearing is necessary for deciding the complaint." There have been no recorded cases of in-person hearings, although it was threatened in one instance. In that case the Panel solomonically stated:[329]

> If the Forum has any doubt that respondent has filed his Response under a false identity or if it has any doubt that Respondent's allegations are completely false, the surest way to resolve those doubts is to require Respondent to appear in person at a hearing before the Forum. [Complainant] along with counsel, is willing to appear at a hearing.

Evidently in the cited case Respondent did not respond to Complainant's offer to appear physically for a hearing.

7.08 7.09 RULE 14—INFERENCES

> 14. Default.
>
> (a) In the event that a Party, in the absence of exceptional circumstances, does not comply with any of the time periods established by these Rules or the Panel, the Panel shall proceed to a decision on the complaint.
>
> (b) If a Party, in the absence of exceptional circumstances, does not comply with any provision of, or requirement under, these Rules or any request from the Panel, the Panel shall draw such inferences therefrom as it considers appropriate.

7.09-A 7.09-A Drawing Inferences

7.09-A.1 7.09-A.1 Creating a Proper Foundation

The sole mention of "inference" appears in Rule 14(b) where it authorizes the Panel to "draw such inferences . . . as it considers appropriate." Rules 14(a) and 14(b) are nominally applied to circumstances of default which may suggest limited authority but in fact Rule 14(b) is construed more broadly. In the absence of "exceptional circumstances" it authores drawing inferences for nomcompliance "with any provision of, or requirement under, these Rules." The only proviso is that drawn

---

[328] In ***General Electric Company v. Estephens Productions***, D2009-1438 (WIPO December 17, 2009) the Panel reviewed complainant's annual report, which was not in the record.

[329] ***ITX sarl, and Ziad M. Mugraby v. Tom Steiner***, FA0809001222737 (Forum October 28, 2008).

inferences should be appropriate or reasonable, not conjectural, and justified by the evidence.[330]

Except for paragraph 4(a)(i) which requires direct evidence of a registered or unregistered mark (the only evidence under the direct control of complainant), the evidentiary demands for the other elements of the Policy (which are under the direct control of respondent) are satisfied with a mix of direct evidence and inferences that are logically consistent with the facts of record. It is settled law that in "the absence of direct evidence, complainant and the panel must resort to reasonable inferences from whatever evidence is in the record."[331] Where there is either a paucity of direct evidence or (as discussed in the next section) the factual circumstances demand a response from either party which is not forthcoming, it is logical to apply the tools of reasoning to uncover either a respondent's intention for its choice and knowledge of the mark in registering a domain name or a complainant's motivation in challenging the registration.

The Rule applies where either party fails "to comply with any provision of, or requirement under, these Rules or any request from the Panel." Any "provision of or requirement under" includes Rule 3 (for complainant) and Rule 5 (for respondent) that provide checklists for the pleadings. Rule 5 directs respondent to "[r]espond specifically to the statements and allegations contained in the complaint and include any and all bases for the Respondent (domain-name holder) to retain registration and use of the disputed domain name."[332]

Regardless whether marks are inherently distinctive or have acquired distinctiveness, they are equally protected. There is no merit to the argument that Panels cannot "infer [that is, are not authorized to deduce] that respondent targeted complainant in adopting the disputed domain name unless there is evidence that complainant's mark is inherently distinctive or famous" has been consistently rejected.[333] The trademark may be neither but the domain name may still be infringing a complainant's right.

---

330 Inferences answer the "what" and "why" questions: "what is the purpose for registering the domain name" and "why is the domain name being challenged"? As marks ascend the classification scale inferences of abusive registration strengthen; and the reverse is true for weak marks, so that although default is not probative of bad faith the inference strengthens in complainants favor that respondent has no defense to cybersquatting. For further discussion on drawing inferences of intention on default see "Consequences of Default" (Sec. 7.03-B) and "Evidentiary Expectations" (Sec. 7.05-A.1.b).

331 The principle was formulated early in the jurisprudence. An example is ***Euromarket Designs, Inc. v. Domain For Sale VMI***, D2000-1195 (WIPO October 26, 2000). ("[I]n the absence of direct evidence, complainant and the panel must resort to reasonable inferences from whatever evidence is in the record." See also Rule 10(d).

332 The reference in Rule 14(b) to "any request from the Panel" parallels Rule 12 that the Panel may request "further statements or documents from either of the Parties."

This is highlighted in ***Health Studies Institute*** in which Complainant prevailed under paragraphs 4(a)(ii) and 4(a)(iii) and ***Public Service Electric & Gas Company*** in which Complainant failed under paragraph 4(a)(iii)[334]:

> For the Panel to make the necessary inferences Complainant must put forward evidence from which the Panel finds it more likely than not that Respondent registered and used the disputed domain name with knowledge of Complainant's mark and an intent ('targeting') to take advantage of the fame of the mark for its own commercial purposes."

A proper inference requires a foundation. It cannot be based on supposition or guesswork. Suspicion is not a substitute for proof.[335] Silence when explanation is expected or failure to offer evidence to rebut reasonable inferences can be persuasive evidence in favor of the other party's contentions.[336]

The Rule authorizing drawing inferences is intended to remove any constraint upon a Panel that may otherwise exist in the exercise of its power. Reasonable allegations of fact unopposed[337] may be accepted as true.[338] Unopposed in this context means either that respondent defaults in answering the complaint or answers but is either unresponsive to the allegations or fails to prove a paragraph 4(c) defense. This is so because failure to "deny the facts which complainant asserts" or "not deny the

---

[333] The Respondent in ***Health Studies Institute, Inc. v. Texas International Property Associates***, D2008-1012 (WIPO September 22, 2008) argued that <healthstudiesinstitute.com> was composed of dictionary words and available to the first to register. It cited ***Terana, S.A. v. RareNames, WebReg***, D2007-0489 (WIPO June 7, 2007) which it misread as "suggesting that the Panel cannot infer that the Respondent targeted the Complainant in adopting the disputed domain name unless there is evidence that the Complainant's mark is inherently distinctive or famous." The ***Terana*** three member Panel held that "An inference of targeting may be drawn from the inherent distinctiveness of the mark in question or from the circumstance that the mark is famous or well known." Complaint granted.

Public Service Electric & Gas Company v. Definitive Sports Management LLC, D2012-0617 (WIPO May 4, 2012) (<psegsolutions.com>. "[I]n a Policy proceeding, without provision for discovery and live testimony, a complainant has little or no opportunity to obtain evidence routinely available in civil litigation but ordinarily within the control of the respondent. For this reason bad faith may be proven inferentially." Complaint denied.)

[334] Id., ***Public Service Electric.***

[335] Discussed further in "No Record, No Case" (Sec. 7.05-B).

[336] ***inExile Entertainment, Inc. v. Telecom Tech Corp***, D2009-0655 (WIPO July 3, 2009) (Complainant's silence on discrepancy between statement of alleged first use in commerce in trademark application and statement in complaint); ***Lacoste Alligator S.A. v. LaCoste Healing Jewelry***, D2009-0700 (WIPO July 16, 2009) (Respondent silent by not appearing but its presence in the record through correspondence established that it lawfully registered <lacostejewelers>).

[337] A distinction is made between allegations of fact and allegations of contention. The latter are not accorded the same respect.

[338] Discussed further in "Prosecuting a UDRP Complaint and Defending Rights or Legitimate Interests in Disputed Domain Name" (Sec. 7.05-A) and "Satisfying the Burden of Proof or

conclusions which complainant asserts can be drawn from those facts"[339] is conclusive in complainant's favor. Panelists generally agree that all "reasonable inferences of fact in the allegations of the complaint are deemed true,"[340] irrespective of the mark's classification.[341]

Generally, no inference can be drawn to support bad faith for a domain name registered prior to complainant's acquisition of its trademark.[342] Conversely, an inference of bad faith is certain where the attraction of the domain name to Internet visitors lies in its trademark value.[343] Panels have emphasized that "[i]t is no excuse that Complainant may not be familiar with clear Policy precedent, the Policy, or the Rules."[344] If complainant possesses facts or in pre-proceeding communications learns that respondent's holding of the domain name is consistent with lawful registration, complainant will be faulted for commencing a UDRP proceeding.[345]

Parties who argue rights (or, in the case of respondents, rights or legitimate interests) they do not have, or where complainants accuse respondents of abusive registration and respondents accuse complainants of abuse of process, they confuse distinctions between "allegations of fact" and "allegations of inference." They are different concepts. Allegations of inference have no weight without facts from which it would be reasonable to deduce a conclusion.

Production" (Sec. 7.05-B.1). Creditworthiness cannot be discounted. See "Role of Credibility in a UDRP Proceeding" (Sec. 7.05-C).

339 ***Reuters Limited v. Global Net 2000, Inc.***, D2000-0441 (WIPO July 13, 2000).

340 ***Vertical Solutions Mgmt., Inc. v. webnet-marketing, inc.***, FA 95095 (Forum July 31, 2000).

341 ***Terana, S.A.***, supra.

342 To succeed on a 4(c) defense the respondent is expected to prove that there is "some semantic relationship between the domain name and the website for that use to be bona fide." In ***7(S) Personal GmbH v. Zhaohua Luo***, D2010-1953 (WIPO February 3, 2011) the majority found Respondent had a history of good faith use prior to the Complainant acquiring its trademark. The quotation is from the dissent. One of the majority panelists in a concurring decision agreed with the dissent's view "that an arbitrary use of a domain name normally does not create rights or legitimate interests. In this case, however, we are presented with such use of the disputed domain name [<7s.com>] over a long period of time, together with the paucity of evidence that the use was pretextual or otherwise illegitimate." Discussed further in "Dictionary Words and Descriptive Phrases" (Sec. 5.01-D.1).

343 ***Health Studies Institute***, *supra*. "[A]n inference of targeting may ... be drawn from other circumstances surrounding a respondent's adoption or use of a domain name." This could include fame, notoriety, or strength of the mark. See ***Google Inc. v. Ahmed Humood***, FA1411001591796 (Forum January 7, 2015).

344 ***Andrew Etemadi, Founder and Chief Technology Officer for Eyemagine Technology LLC v. Clough Construction and Deanne Clough***, D2012-2455 (WIPO February 14, 2013).

345 Discussed further in "Complaints Without Merit" (Sec. 7.11-B).

7.09-A.2 7.09-A.2 Inferring from Evidence Withheld

Panelists are authorized to rest conclusions both on what parties offer into evidence and what can be deduced from what should have been offered but was withheld from the record. When the burden shifts under Paragraph 4(a)(ii) of the Policy and respondents fail to respond, the Panel will assume that "the evidence would not have been favorable to respondent."[346] Rule 5(b) requires respondent to "respond specifically to the statements and allegations contained in the complaint."[347]

Drawing inferences is necessary because "matters involving a respondent's motive, intent, purpose and other subjective factors determinative under Paragraphs 4(a)(ii) and 4(a)(iii) will not always be susceptible of direct proof."[348] A respondent put to its proof cannot with impunity ignore what logically can be deduced from the facts. Failure to rebut supports an adverse inference. The reasoning is that if there were evidence in its favor, the party would have presented it. Thus, in ***AAA Employment***[349] the Panel stated that it

> draws the inference that there is in reality no evidence that Respondent was given permission to register the domain name in its own name for, if there were any such evidence, it would have been very easy to say what that evidence was. Accordingly, Respondent had no rights or interests in the domain name to justify its registration.

It is reasonable to conclude that where complainant's evidence is unpersuasive no amount of argument of respondent's motivation will suffice.[350] Any doubt favors the respondent. In moving to Paragraph 4(a)(iii) of the Policy, the more generic and descriptive the trademark the more concrete the evidence must be that respondent is targetting complainant; that it had complainant in mind.[351] Adverse inferences

---

[346] ***Mary-Lynn Mondich and American Vintage Wine Biscuits, Inc. v. Shane Brown, doing business as Big Daddy's Antiques***, D2000-0004 (WIPO February 16, 2000).

[347] Discussed further in "Consequences of Default" (Sec. 7.02-B).

[348] ***Brooke Bollea, a.k.a Brooke Hogan v. Robert McGowan***, D2004-0383 (WIPO June 29, 2004).

[349] ***AAA Employment, Inc. v. Ahearn and Associates***, FA0507000520670 (Forum September 6, 2005). The Panel in ***Commonwealth Bank of Australia v. Registration Private, Domains By Proxy, LLC / Ravindra Patel, gbe***, D2017-0807 (WIPO July 6, 2017) goes even further in drawing a negative inference: "Given that the Respondent is represented the Panel is left concluding that this silence on such critical issues is not simply inadvertent but represents a deliberate decision."

[350] ***Leyton & Associés (SAS), Thésée (SAS), Leyton Consulting UK and Ireland Limited, Leyton Maroc, Leyton Belgium, Leyton UK Limited v. Drela Mateusz, Elephant Orchestra***, D2009-1589 (WIPO January 20, 2010) ("It seems to this Panel at least as likely as not that the Respondent, who is doing online business in the United Kingdom, acquired the disputed domain name because of its generic meaning and not with a view to complainant's possible rights, and in that sense, the benefit of the doubt on the present record must be afforded to the Respondent.")

[351] ***Quester Group, Inc. v. DI S.A.***, D2010-1950 (WIPO February 14, 2011) ("[While the] descriptive use of common dictionary words to link to sites that deal in the described goods may not avoid

can also be drawn from complainant's submission as, for example, where it alleges it is well-known or respondent should have known, but fails to demonstrate secondary meaning or why respondent should have known. The ***Brooke Bollea***[352] Panel explains that just as there are subjective matters entirely within the knowledge of the respondent, so there are with complainant:

> [R]enown or goodwill of a mark is an objective matter entirely within the knowledge of and documentation available to a complainant. Every plaintiff in an infringement action must prove as an affirmative aspect of his case that his mark has commercial recognition at the date of infringement; a complainant under the Policy must do so to show that the domain name was registered in bad faith. In this proceeding such proof from 2002—if it exists—could have been found and submitted by Complainant without the need to obtain anything from Respondent.

Failure of proof giving rise to adverse inferences can occur when complainants fail to respond to Panels offering them the opportunity to correct the record (Section 7-07-A).[353] However, no inference can reasonably be drawn from complainant alleging that respondent has manufactured evidence for its defense.[354] This is so because allegations of inference cannot trump "[Respondent's] sworn statements . . . as ex post facto attempts to concoct a defense to this Complaint."[355] An offer of proof may appear true; or, given the limitations of discovery, may be beyond complainant's ability to refute or disprove, in which circumstance the dispute is inappropriate for UDRP resolution.

7.09-B Conflicting Inferences 7.09-B

Concern that proper inferences are drawn and established principles of law applied has been raised in a number of cases[356] Different assessments are particularly challenging in cases involving the same parties in which differently constituted three-member Panels contemporaneously reach opposite conclusions. The dissent

---

capitalizing on a similar trade mark using the same words . . . that is an exposure that owners of descriptive marks must accept when they select their brands using common product names. In fact, it is the very ability to draw consumers by the descriptiveness that leads mark owners to choose such terms in the first place. Absent some evidence that complainant was specifically targeted, it is the opinion of the majority of the Panel that the benefit of the doubt should favor the descriptive user.")

352 Discussed above in "Evidence Controlled by Party" (Sec. 7.05-B.2).

353 ***McMullen Argus Publishing Inc. v. Moniker Privacy Services / Traverito Traverito***, D2007-0680 (WIPO August 30, 2007).

354 ***Ringling Bros.B Barnum & Bailey Combined Shows. v. Kenneth Lima***, 49-413-000002-05 (AAA May 13, 2005) (<ringling.us>).

355 ***Metro Goldwyn Mayer Studios Inc. v. World Readable c/o R.L. Cadenhead***, FA0612000868828 (Forum January 31, 2007) ("Indeed, they explain the acquisition in 2004 of the sales and use tax permit and the subscription to the Drop Ship Source Directory as being related to Respondent's intended online wargames store.")

in ***Drugstore 1*** (complaint denied) observed that "[t]he cases are being administered by different Presiding Panelists, but the co-Panelists are the same."[357] The presiding panelist in ***Drugstore 1*** voted in the majority. The majority in ***Drugstore 2*** (including the presiding panelist) noted the different results "may in part simply reflect a differing assessment of facts and likely motive given the examined record in each case, rather than any underlying divergence of opinion as to applicable principles under the Policy." This may be correct but parties will find different rulings for essentially identical factual circumstances confusing.

While for the most part Panels adhere to established principles of UDRP jurisprudence,[358] the *Drugstore* cases expose a weakness in the lack of an appeal mechanism to harmonize differences in applying the law. The dissent's criticism in ***Drugstore 1*** was that his

> co-panelists made a subjective determination regarding the Respondent's intent without any analysis of the nonexclusive, objective criteria of bad faith set forth in paragraphs 4(b)(i)-(iv) of the Policy. Once this failure was called to their attention, they simply added language that they had considered paragraphs 4(b)(i)-(iv) without conducting any evidentiary analysis.

The dissent[359] concluded

> I do not believe that the arbitrators in a UDRP proceeding can ignore the objective criteria of paragraphs 4(b)(i)-(iv) and substitute their subjective determination or personal motivations that a claimed mark is generic or is weak as descriptive, then proceed to find a lack of bad faith and deny relief to complainant.

In ***Drugstore 2*** the co-panelist dissenter in ***Drugstore 1***—now in the majority—was joined by the different presiding panelist and held Complainant had established its case. The dissent's position in ***Drugstore 2*** was grounded on his "substantial doubt[ ] regarding the legitimacy of Respondent's online pharmacy

---

356 ***Drugstore.com, Inc. v. Nurhul Chee/ Robert Murry***, D2008-0230 (WIPO May 9, 2008) (<drugstoretm.com> "***Drugstore 1***," Complaint denied over dissent); ***Drugstore.com, Inc. v. Kevin Andrews***, D2008-0231 (W IPO May 9, 2008) (<mydrugstore1.com> "***Drugstore 2***," transferred over dissent.)

357 See also ***Park Place Entertainment Corporation v. Anything.com Ltd.***, D2002-0530 (WIPO September 16, 2002) (<flamingo.com>. However, the dissent disputes "the majority's conclusion that it is appropriate to hold Respondent vicariously responsible for activities undertaken by a third party to whom it has effectively delegated partial control over the domain name, but merely its willingness to use such third party conduct as the primary or sole basis for inferences regarding Respondent's prior state of mind.")

358 The reason for the qualification "for the most part" is that (to take one of several examples) there is a divergence of views in applying the Policy's requirement for conjunctive bad faith. Discussed further in "Justifying Forfeiture Despite Good Faith Registration" (Sec. 4.03-A.4.b).

359 The same panelist dissented for the same reasons in ***Super Supplements, Inc. v. Vertical Axis, Inc.***, D2008-0244 (WIPO May 13, 2008) (SUPER SUPPLEMENTS ["supplements" disclaimed] and <supersupplements.com>).

business." Assessments are particularly vulnerable to second-guessing when the second level choice is identical or confusingly similar to trademarks on the lower end of the classification scale such as "drugstore" and "super supplements."

However, it would be difficult for respondent to prove good faith (or the Panel to misdraw an inference) by registering a domain name identical or confusingly similar to complainant's trademark that by its terms falsely suggests an association with complainant. Thus, in ***Household Int'l*** complainant proved it had conducted its financial business under the names Household and Household Bank for many decades.[360] The Panel held it was

> inconceivable that the existence of this prominent firm was not present in the mind of the respondent when he chose his domain name [<householdbank.com>]. The only reasonable inference is that he knew perfectly well that he would create confusion, or was wilfully blind to this fact.

Where respondent links the disputed domain name to services competing with complainant's it is reasonable to infer that only someone familiar with the mark and what it stood for would have gone to the trouble of registering the domain name.[361] Similarly in ***Caesar World*** where respondent added the generic terms "grand" and "casino" to CAESAR. The additions indicate an awareness of the market in which the trademark owner operates. The Panel concluded respondent's intent was to "free-ride on complainant's goodwill." Moreover, it "would be unconscionable to find a bona fide offering of services in a respondent's operation of [a] web-site using a domain name which is confusingly similar to complainant's mark and for the same business."[362]

The Panel in ***The Vanguard Group*** held that "Respondent's knowledge and intention may be determined by common sense inferences from circumstantial evidence."[363] "Vanguard" is both a dictionary word in the English language and a trademark, but the only inference that can be drawn from "vanguar" (absent proof to the contrary the word has meaning in a foreign language) is that it is a misspelling for "Vanguard." When the registrant has done nothing more than register a name evidence of intention can be inferred from the totality of the circumstances, which most likely includes the marketplace in which complainant is active. In ***Vanguard*** the respondent was selling financial magazines, which suggested a relationship with

---

360 ***Household Int'l, Inc. v. Cyntom Enter***, FA 95784 (Forum November 7, 2000).

361 ***Caesar World, Inc. v. Contessa Marketing Services, Inc.***, D2003-0529 (WIPO September 15, 2003) (CAESAR and CAESARS PALACE and <caesargrandcasino.com>).

362 ***Am. Online, Inc. v. Fu***, D2000-1374 (WIPO December 11, 2000) (ICQ and <icq520.com>); ***Computerized Sec. Sys., Inc. v. Hu***, FA 157321 (Forum June 23, 2003).

363 ***The Vanguard Group, Inc. v. Lorna Kang***, D2002-1064 (WIPO January 20, 2003) (VANGUARD and <vanguar.com>).

Complainant and likelihood of confusion with its mark as to the source of the website.

Determinations based on weak inferences are liable to be reversed if challenged in legal proceedings as illustrated in two decisions under the ACPA. In ***Freebies Publishing***[364] the Court determined that as a generic term "freebies" could have multiple associations.[365] The UDRP majority in ***Nike, Inc.***[366] denied the complaint even though it was "suspicious of Respondent's claim that use of the domain name merely as a redirect to its website <crgq.com> is a bona fide offering of goods and services." It concluded that lapse of time made "Complainant's task in proving bad faith registration . . . more difficult" and that it had only "itself to blame." This is generally true, particularly as trademarks descend to the generic, but in *Nike v. Circle Group* the district court disagreed, as the trademark was too well-known to have been registered unintentionally and granted Nike summary judgment.[367]

7.10 7.10 RULE 15(a)— LOOKING OUTSIDE THE FOUR CORNERS OF THE POLICY

> A Panel shall decide a complaint on the basis of the statements and documents submitted and in accordance with the Policy, these Rules and any rules and principles of law that it deems applicable.

Rule 15(a) has two parts. In the first part the Panel is told how it "shall decide" the complaint, namely "on the basis of statements and documents submitted." In the second part, the Panel is granted flexibility that in addition to "these Rules" it may also apply "*any* principles of law that [the Panel] deems applicable" (emphasis added).

Generally, Panels focus on the first part. A party's failure to create a record containing "statements" and "documents" that either conclusively or inferentially establish its contentions will be read against the proponent of the claim or defense. It is for complainant to make its case; it is for the respondent to prove either that it

---

364 ***Freebies Publishing v. Retail Services, Inc.***, FA0204000112565 (Forum July 15, 2002) (use of a metatag to support opportunistic bad faith. Transfer denied in ACPA case, *Retail Services, Inc. v. Freebies Publishing*, 364 F.3d 535, 542 (4th Cir. 2004)).

365 *Freebies Publishing*, at 542. The Court noted that the "presumption of validity flowing from trademark registration . . . has a burden shifting effect, requiring the party challenging a registered mark to produce sufficient evidence to establish that the mark is generic by a preponderance of evidence." The plaintiff overcame the presumption of validity.

366 ***Nike, Inc. v. Circle Group Internet, Inc.***, D2002-0544 (WIPO September 10, 2002) (Transfer denied; UDRP award vacated in *Nike, Inc. v. Circle Group Internet, Inc.*, 318 F.Supp.2d 688 (N.D. IL, May 21, 2004).

367 The dissent in the UDRP proceeding pointed out that "[n]ot only has Respondent not given a plausible reason for registering Complainant's trademark as its domain name, but also Respondent has not given any reason for doing so; and none is self evident."

has a right or legitimate interest in the domain name (subsection 4(a)(ii)) or it did not register the domain name in bad faith (subsection 4(a)(iii) of the Policy).

In its original form in the WIPO Final Report the Rule did not include the tail, "any rules and principles of law that [the Panel] deems applicable."[368] The added authority is truly remarkable in not chaining panelists to the four corners of the Policy. Although the Rules do not expressly invite application of equitable principles[369] equity is not absent from the jurisprudence; it can be found in the safe harbor circumstances, particularly in subsections 4(c)(i) and 4(c)(iii) of the Policy.[370]

So, for example, while the bar of laches is generally denied untimeliness in challenging a domain name favors respondent.[371] The remedy for infringement under the UDRP is a mandatory-like injunction (an equitable remedy) cancelling the registration or transferring the domain name to complainant. Infringement of distinctive and famous trademarks under U.S. law triggers principles of equity—"[t]he owner of a famous mark shall be entitled, subject to the principles of equity and upon such terms as the court deems reasonable, to an injunction against another person's commercial use in commerce of a mark or trade name."[372] Similar reasoning and considerations are employed by UDRP Panels.

---

[368] The Ur-Rules are set forth in Annex V to the WIPO Final Report. Article 31 states only that "[t]he Panel shall determine the Complaint in accordance with the Policy."

[369] "[I]t would appear unlikely that when [those who drafted the Rules] . . . used the expression 'principles of law that it deems applicable,' [they] . . . meant 'principles of law but not equity,'" Concurring Opinion, ***Visual Systems, Inc. v. Development Services Telepathy, Inc.***, FA1004001318632 (Forum June 28, 2010).

[370] The majority in ***Board of Trustees of the University of Arkansas v. FanMail.com, LLC***, D2009-1139 (WIPO November 2, 2009) noted that "in many if not most jurisdictions in the United States and in countries such as the United Kingdom and Australia, the formerly sharp line between law and equity has been blurred if not effaced by the amalgamation of law and equity."

[371] Decisions too numerous to cite. See ***Harvard Lampoon, Inc. v. Reflex Publishing Inc.***, D2011-0716 (WIPO July 26, 2011) ("the Panel has taken Complainant's inaction into account in deciding certain of the issues above.") There is further discussion and cases in "Sleeping on One's Rights" (Sec. 5.01-E).

[372] 15 USCS § 1125(c): "In determining whether a mark is distinctive and famous, a court may consider factors such as, but not limited to (A) the degree of inherent or acquired distinctiveness of the mark; (B) the duration and extent of use of the mark in connection with the goods or services with which the mark is used; (C) the duration and extent of advertising and publicity of the mark; (D) the geographical extent of the trading area in which the mark is used; (E) the channels of trade for the goods or services with which the mark is used; (F) the degree of recognition of the mark in the trading areas and channels of trade used by the marks' owner and the person against whom the injunction is sought; [and] (G) the nature and extent of use of the same or similar marks by third parties. . . ."

7.11 7.11 RULE 15(e)—COMPLAINT FILED IN BAD FAITH

7.11-A 7.11-A Reverse Domain Name Hijacking

7.11-A.1 7.11-A.1 Intentional Act Directed at Domain Name Holder

Reverse domain name hijacking (RDNH) "means using the Policy in bad faith to attempt to deprive a registered domain name holder of a domain name."[373] Its application is said to be discretionary,[374] but this is not conceded by consensus and Panels have drawn highly nuanced lines to mark differences warranting or denying the sanction. Mere lack of success, offering weak arguments, or having misguided beliefs are not in themselves sufficient causes. There must be some evidence of bad faith.[375]

The controlling factor is abusive conduct, either of process as a means of achieving the proscribed end or "brought primarily to harass the domain-name holder." Rule 15(e) authorizes the Panel "to declare in its decision that the complaint was brought in bad faith and constitutes an abuse of the administrative proceeding . . . [i]f after considering the submissions the Panel finds that the complaint was brought in bad faith." The Rule implies a scaling of conduct; something beyond a simple failure of judgment and more in the nature of a deliberate act.[376]

Significantly the Rule does not define bad faith categorically. It gives two examples that may constitute "bad faith": either "an attempt at Reverse Domain

---

[373] Rule 1 of the Rules of the Policy, Definitions.

[374] ***The Chancellor, Masters and Scholars of the University of Cambridge v. Kirkland Holdings LLC.***, D2015-1278 (WIPO October 5, 2015) (<cambridge.com>. "[While] [s]ufficient grounds for a finding of abuse plainly exist ... [a] finding of abuse ... is always discretionary with the Panel.") However, the word "discretionary" is nowhere to be found in the Policy or Rules and is not accepted by consensus. Rather, other Panels have taken the view that Rule 15(e) is not "discretionary" but "peremptory." It instructs Panels to grant RDNH if "sufficient ground[s] for a finding of abuse plainly exist." (*The Chancellor*).

[375] The first application of RDNH appeared in ***Smart Design LLC v. Carolyn Hughes***, D2000-0993 (WIPO October 18, 2000) ("Had the Complainant sat back and reflected upon what it was proposing to argue, it would have seen that its claims could not conceivably succeed.")

[376] ***Compañía Logística de Hidrocarburos CLH, S.A. v. DropCatcher.Info / Badminton, Inc.***, D2018-0973 (WIPO June 25, 2018) (<clh.com>. "The Complaint was weak but a number of the *indicia* of a complainant's conduct which are sometimes associated with RDNH, such as untrue assertions of fact, inappropriate personal attacks on the integrity of a respondent or heavy-handed conduct are not present. It is certainly not essential that such factors are present, but the Panel is required to make an overall assessment as to whether a finding of RDNH is appropriate in these proceedings.")

The General Data Protection Regulation (GDPR) effective May 25, 2018 will influence Panels determining RDNH because they will recognize that in commencing the proceedings complainants will lack knowledge of respondent until disclosure of redacted personal information and receiving the response. See Van der Graaf Inc. v. Privacydotlink Customer 3564326 / DUBAI DOMAINS, D2018-2236 (WIPO January 25, 2019) (<vdg.com>. "[P]rior to the submission of the Complaint,

Name Hijacking" or "brought primarily to harass the domain-name holder." The two examples necessarily have a familial relationship. Even though they are generally merged into a finding of RDNH, each is a distinct category of abusive conduct.[377]

RDNH is ordinarily pleaded as a counterclaim although granting it is without the remedial penalty under the ACPA of damages and attorney's fees against overreaching trademark owners.[378] Formally, respondents have the initial burden of proof, but this raises a what-if question of whether there can be a declaration of RDNH if respondent does not request or defaults in responding to the complaint.

There is a mixed history on whether RDNH must be requested, as noted further below. Part of the answer to this conundrum lies in the nature of arbitral proceedings, that default is not an admission of liability as it is in a court of law; and in other part the answer lies in the application of Rule 3(b)(xiii), the certification rule: "this Complaint is not being presented for any improper purpose," which is discussed in the next section.

Abusive use of the proceedings presupposes complainant is acting in willful disregard of respondent's right, whatever its subjective belief of its right.[379] Rather than being a consensus in declaring RDNH there is a diversity of views about the conduct that would support it. Some panels refrain; are even reluctant to sanction first time offenders[380]; others are more severe.[381] Ordinarily, in an action at law

---

the Complainant did not have access to information about the identity of the Respondent, and prior to the submission of the Response, the Complainant could not have been aware of the December 22, 2017 acquisition of the disputed domain name by the Respondent or by the entity that controls the Respondent. In such situation, the Panel finds no evidence that the Complainant was acting in bad faith when it based its Complaint on the assumption that the Respondent had acquired the disputed domain name in April 2018.")

[377] Abusive conduct has been stretched to include unfounded representations of fraud. See ***Comercializadora de Lacteos y Derivados, S.A. de C.V. v. Apple Inc.***, D2017-1351 (WIPO October 23, 2017) (<lala.com>. "The majority of the Panel considers that rashly accusing anybody of bad faith is an abuse of the system.")

[378] See, Jurisprudential Overview 3.0, Paragraph 4.16: "NB, parties may be aware that unlike in the UDRP system, certain national courts may (where invoked) impose monetary penalties (including punitive damages) where the equivalent of RDNH is found." For the U.S., see 15 U.S.C. §§1117(a) and 1117(d). Discussed further in "No Deference to UDRP Award" (Sec. 8.01-B.1).

[379] Consider analogy with "good faith" under 15 U.S.C. §1125 (d)(1)(B)(ii) ("bad faith shall not be found in any case in which the court determines that the person believed and had reasonable grounds to believe that the use of the domain name was a fair use or otherwise lawful." See *Direct Niche, LLC v. Via Varejo S/A*, 15-cv-62344 (S.D. Fla., August 10, 2017) rejecting plaintiff's argument that it commenced the action in good faith (here, domain name holder but equally applicable to mark owner). The court held that "[a]lthough Knight may subjectively believe that Direct Niche's use of the Casas Bahia Domain was lawful, the Court concludes that his belief is not objectively reasonable."

[380] The Panel in ***Happy as Clams, Inc., a California Corp., DBA Date Like a Grownup v. Heather Dugan***, D2014-1655 (WIPO November 1, 2014) explained that it could have sanctioned

a party is expected to request relief to receive it. Panelists in UDRP proceedings generally follow this practice, although it has become more common to determine RDNH even if not requested.[382]

Declaring RDNH where it is not requested has a rational basis if the record contains sufficient evidence that filing the complaint "constitutes an abuse of the administrative proceedings." If it does, the burden to prove otherwise should shift to complainant (the same shift expected of respondent in rebutting complainant's *prima facie* case under paragraph4(a)(ii) of the Policy) to show that the declaration is not warranted for the reasons that it proceeds to express.[383]

There are essentially two streams of reasoning about respondent's burden. The WIPO Overview 2.0 in paragraph 4.17 records both views and an in-between without identifying a consensus. For panelists subscribing to the first view respondents must offer an "extraordinary level" of proof to justify RDNH.[384] They are "reluctant to make a finding of Reverse Domain Name Hijacking except in the clearest of cases."[385] It is understandable that where the facts are in balance there

---

Complainant but refrained: "A finding of abuse of the administrative proceeding is always discretionary with the Panel. . . [However], [i]n recognition that . . . this appears to be the first time this Complainant or its representative has brought a proceeding, the Panel will refrain from making one in this case."

381 ***Cyberbit Ltd. v. Mr. Kieran Ambrose, Cyberbit A/S***, D2016-0126 (WIPO February 26, 2016) (<cyberbit.com>) ("the deficiencies [of proof] must have been obvious to anyone remotely familiar with the Policy"). See further below "Appearing by Counsel" (Sec. 7.11-D.1).

382 Jurisprudential Overview 3.0, Paragraph 4.16 states that "following some early cases to the contrary, panels have more recently clarified that, for an RDNH finding to be made, it is not necessary for a respondent to seek an RDNH finding or prove the presence of conduct RDNH." ***Goway Travel Limited v. Tourism Australia***, D2006-0344 (WIPO June 6, 2006) ("The Rules specifically put the burden on the Panel to determine whether a complainant has tried to use 'the Policy in bad faith to attempt to deprive a registered domain name holder of a domain name.'"); ***Timbermate Products Pty Ltd v. Domains by Proxy, LLC/Barry Gork***, D2013-1603 (WIPO November 3, 2013) (Panel is "under an obligation to so declare.") See dissent in ***Quality Logo Products, Inc. v. Get On The Web, Ltd.***, D2013-1691 (WIPO December 4, 2013), citing ***Timbermate.***

383 See ***Georg Mez AG v. Mez Kalra***, D2016-1932 (WIPO January 6, 2017) (<mez.com>. "The Complainant in its supplemental filing expressly declined to respond to the Respondent's assertion of RDNH. The Complainant submitted simply that 'Statements in relation to Reverse Domain Name Hijacking are not required'. In the context of this proceeding, statements in relation to RDNH were certainly required and it is not unreasonable to expect that they would have been provided. If so, they would certainly have been admitted. When a panel finds that a party will not engage in debate on a particular issue, it is entitled to conclude that the party's case on the issue in question has some inherent deficiencies.")

384 See ***ACE Limited v. WebMagic Ventures, LLC***, FA0802001143448 (Forum April 8, 2000). Although the factual circumstances weighed heavily in Respondent's favor the three member Panel held that "Complainant's presentation and circumstances in this case *does not rise to anywhere near the extraordinary level* that is required for a finding of reverse domain name hijacking" (emphasis added). At least one member of that Panel is no longer a subscriber to that view.

is reason to step back from censure,[386] but View 1 Panels insist respondent has the onus of proving by more than simply a preponderance of evidence complainant acted in bad faith in commencing the proceeding.

The second stream of reasoning, which focuses more on the abusive use of the proceedings, holds that negligent initiation of a UDRP proceeding is grounds for RDNH. Complainant is not relieved of abuse by requesting cancellation rather than transfer.[387] Once the complaint is shown to be without merit the claim dissolves; it should either never have been brought or withdrawn once respondent's evidence is in the record. Where the complaint is not withdrawn RDNH is warranted.[388]

As a general proposition if the mark is weak or the claim without merit (as for example registration of the domain name before acquisition of trademark) the more likely complainant will be found culpable of abusive conduct.[389] Culpability is less likely for complainants with colorable common law rights predating domain name registration even though they may be unable to prove bad faith.

RDNH is also less likely where "Complainant had no reason to know of the factual background leading up to the Respondent's acquisition of the Domain

---

385 ***Libertad Servicios Financieros, S.A. de C.V. S.F.P. v. Telepathy, Inc.***, D2011-1635 (WIPO January10, 2012) (Concurring in denying complaint but expressing different view on RDNH).

386 ***Jazeera Space Channel TV Station v. AJ Publishing aka Aljazeera Publishing***, D2005-0309 (WIPO July 19, 2005) (Even though "Complainant probably did appreciate that its Complaint could not succeed if the Respondent chose to defend it," the majority denied RDNH. However, the Panel also noted that "Complainant does not emerge from this process with any credit, but it would be going too far to censure its conduct under paragraph 15(e) of the Rule.")

387 ***G.W.H.C. - Serviços Online Ltda., E-Commerce Media Group Informação e Tecnologia Ltda. v. eRealEstate.com***, D2012-0498 (WIPO May 31, 2012) (<saveme.com>. "The Complainant argued that RDNH cannot arise because the Complainant has merely sought cancellation of the disputed domain name, not transfer. The Panel disagrees.")

388 ***Avaya Inc. v. Avayo Electronics***, FA1302001487607 (Forum April 19, 2013) ("When it filed the Complaint, the Complainant could plausibly have been unaware of the fact that the disputed domain name corresponds to the Respondent's business name. However, the Complainant could not have ignored this after the Response was filed. . .. Not only did the Complainant fail to withdraw its Complaint when it was obvious that it could not succeed, it actually pressed its case by submitting Additional Submissions that did not address the pertinent facts, thus harassing the Respondent.")

389 But this conduct has also been excused by panelists who take the position that it is not bad faith if complainant's argument has merit "under applicable law, as it now exists or as it may be extended by a good-faith and reasonable argument." Rule 3(b)(xiv). As an example of this reasoning, see ***Sony Pictures Television Inc. v. Thomas, Jeff***, FA150600 1625643 (Forum August 6, 2015) (<shark-tank.com>). Although the three-member Panel rejected the proposition advocated by a minority of panelists that subsequent renewals of disputed domain name "with knowledge of Complainant's trademark suffice to establish bad faith registration" nevertheless denied RDNH on the rejected proposition citing several UDRP decisions to that effect, including ***Big 5 Corp. v EyeAim.com***, FA 1513704 (NAF, Oct. 11, 2013). In reaching this decision, the Panel inexplicably elevated the minority view into an official "minority position" (which it is not). See discussion at "Inappropriate Alignment with the ACPA" (Sec. 4.03-A.4.d).

Name"[390] or respondent only recently acquired the domain name.[391] This is because in these situations complainants may have no facts to inform themselves about respondents' histories, the circumstances of their registrations, and uses of the domain names, all of which argue against intentional abuse of the proceedings.

No inference can be drawn from complainant's failure to prove abusive registration, but failure to prove both the 4(a)(ii) and 4(a)(iii) requirements of the Policy strengthens the argument in respondent's favor.[392] Although it has been said a declaration of RDNH is "an empty gesture" (because the Policy does not authorize monetary sanctions[393]) it is "the only way for a panel to deter future abuse of the Policy and to remind parties and professionals who invoke the Policy of its limits, rules, and means of abuse."[394] It is not a deterrent, however, to determined complainants of later acquired trademarks from challenging respondents of earlier registered domain names, because there is no economic disincentive to proceeding abusively and they may be fortunate in the appointment of the Panel.[395]

7.11-A.2

7.11-A.2 **Falsely Asserting Superior Rights**

A claim of RDNH ultimately rests on complainant's false certification that "the information contained in th[e] Complaint is to the best of [its] knowledge complete and accurate [and] that th[e] Complaint is not being presented for any improper

---

[390] ***Brian Fera v. Media Options S.A.***, D2015-1470 (WIPO October 16, 2015).

[391] ***MSC Mediterranean Shipping Company Holding S.A, v. Registration Private / Sedo GmbH / Paul Kocher***, D2014-0694 (WIPO June 22, 2014).

[392] It is clear from the summary of views in WIPO Overview 4.17, conduct that View 1 Panels find "may be" grounds are the very grounds View 2 Panels find "are" grounds for RDNH.

[393] Under the Canadian Internet Registration Authority (CIRA) respondent may recover damages for reverse domain name hijacking:
"4.6 Bad Faith of Complainant. If the Registrant is successful, and the Registrant proves, on a balance of probabilities, that the Complaint was commenced by complainant for the purpose of attempting, unfairly and without colour of right, to cancel or obtain a transfer of any Registration which is the subject of the Proceeding, then the Panel may order complainant to pay to the Provider in trust for the Registrant an amount of up to five thousand dollars ($5000) to defray the costs incurred by the Registrant in preparing for, and filing material in the Proceeding."

[394] See ***Intelligentsia Coffee & Tea, Inc. v. Ashantiplc Ltd / NamingRights.Com, LLC***, D2012-2075 (WIPO January 7, 2013) (Concurring Panel in denying complaint, but would include a finding of RDNH. "As with any statement by any panel, it has no collateral estoppel or res judicata effect in any subsequent litigation or administrative proceeding, indeed even in any subsequent Policy proceeding brought by the same party or representative.")

The parallel provision (although not the phrase "reverse domain name hijacking" under the Anticybersquatting Consumer Protection Act is found in 15 U.S.C. §1114(2)(D)(v)) which reads: "a domain name registrant whose domain name has been suspended, disabled, or transferred under a policy . . . may, upon notice to the mark owner, file a civil action to establish that the registration or use of the domain name by such registrant is not unlawful under this Act."

purpose, such as to harass [the respondent]."[396] "Improper purpose" connotes an intentional act, whether taken willfully or from lack of knowledge.[397] It is applicable to circumstances in which complainant "knew or should have known" it could not "prove one of the essential elements required by the UDRP."[398] A finding is warranted when complainant initiates a UDRP proceeding with the should-have-known knowledge respondent has a superior claim to the domain name.[399]

For good reason RDNH is more likely to be found where respondent registers the domain name prior to complainant's right coming into existence,[400] it is composed of a generic term or descriptive phrase,[401] or complainant is caught making a material misrepresentation.[402] Material misrepresentation is not limited to asserting untruths or exaggerating facts supporting complainant's claim but extends to omitting or concealing material facts which if disclosed would undercut complainant's allegations.[403] In ***Procter & Gamble*** the Panel noted "[h]ad the Respondent failed to respond, there is a very real risk that the Panel, relying upon the 1993 International

---

[395] Discussed further in "Inappropriate Alignment with the ACPA" (Sec. 4.03-A.4.d).

[396] Discussed in Sec. 7.01-B. Paragraph 3(b)(xiv) of the Rules of the Policy: "Complainant certifies that the information contained in this Complaint is to the best of Complainant's knowledge complete and accurate, that this Complaint is not being presented for any improper purpose, such as to harass, and that the assertions in this Complaint are warranted under these Rules and under applicable law, as it now exists or as it may be extended by a good-faith and reasonable argument." Compare Rule 11 of the Federal Rules of Civil Procedure and the ABA Model Rules of Professional Conduct 3.3, which is essentially a certification and expansion of the duty of candor by legal counsel.

[397] ***Jazeera Space Channel***, *supra.*: "[T]he question for the Panel is whether the more likely explanation for those discrepancies is malice or mistake or muddle.... [T]his may not reflect well on the Complainant if the most likely explanation for the discrepancies is mistake or muddle...."

[398] Jurisprudential Overview 3.0, Paragraph 4.16. Where respondent provides plausible evidence of actual use and complainant is aware of that use, complainant will itself be chargeable with abusive conduct. ***JJGC Industria E Comercio de Materiais Dentarios S.A. v. Yun-Ki Kim***, D2013-1838 (WIPO December 20, 2013) (<neodent.com>. "No such inference can be made here as the Respondent appears to have used the mark to promote his own clinic, as likely a reason for selecting the disputed domain name as to take advantage of the Complainant's marks.")

[399] ***Aspen Grove, Inc. v. Aspen Grove***, D2001-0798 (WIPO October 17, 2001) ("The Panel finds the Complainant, even though apparently knowledgeable and assisted by reputable counsel, nonetheless chose to file a complaint without a colorable claim and thus abused the ICANN proceeding.")

[400] ***Urban Logic, Inc. v. Urban Logic, Peter Holland***, D2009-0862 (WIPO August 17, 2009).

[401] For example, there is no "constructive notice" under the UDRP as there is under the Lanham Act. As a result, use of a common word or generic phrase to position a business in cyberspace does not constitute an abusive registration unless complainant is able to show that respondent is a competitor for the same client base and registered the domain name to take advantage of complainant's trademark.

[402] ***The Procter & Gamble Company v. Marchex Sales, Inc.***, D2012-2179 (WIPO February 22, 2013) (Abuse of the process as well as maintaining the proceedings for an improper purpose); ***Jetgo Australia Holdings Pty Limited v. Name Administration Inc. (BVI)***, D2013-1339 (WIPO September 17, 2013) (Deliberate concealment of facts).

[trademark] registration [which Complainant acquired by assignment in 2008] and the substantial sales volumes claimed for the brand, would have found in favor of the Complainant."

Where the domain name registration precedes trademark rights complainants fall afoul of the ineluctable inference that a registration prior in time has superior rights.[404] Unless respondent has "psychic powers" to predict a future event it could not possibly have "contemplated complainant's then non-existent trademark."[405]

7.11-B 7.11-B Complaints Without Merit

7.11-B.1 7.11-B.1 Objectively Groundless Complaint

Ideally complainants should invoke the UDRP only when they have reasonable and credible belief they are entitled to succeed. Departure from this standard for *pro se* complainants by exempting them from incurring the ultimate penalty of reverse domain name hijacking is discussed below but the highest standard holds that an "objectively groundless" complaint should never have been brought, and for bringing it complainant deserves to be sanctioned.[406]

The Rule specifically addresses the issue of complainant's "improper conduct" toward respondent but it has also been extended to include abuse of process.[407] The classic improper conduct is using the Policy to increase leverage in negotiations

---

[403] ***DealerX Partners, LLC v. Domain Manager, Visionamics/Citytwist Inc. / Lyndon Griffin***, D2017-1680 (WIPO December 26, 2017) (<<conquestautomotive.com>. Complainant failed to disclose that "the word "conquest" has a special meaning within the argot of automotive marketing.")

[404] ***General Media Communications, Inc. v. Crazy Troll c/o CrazyTroll.com***, FA0602000 651676 (Forum May 26, 2006) (PENTHOUSE and <penthouseboutique.com>. Complainant alleged it had common law rights to "Penthouse boutique," but the Panel held that Complainant had only used the phrase for a short time as a trade name, which is non-actionable under the UDRP) ; in ***Airpet Animal Transport, Inc. v. Marchex Sales, Inc / Brendhan Hight***, FA121100 1470056 (Forum January 2, 2013) (alleged common law trademark) the three-member Panel was unanimous in finding RDNH: "Complainant applied for a trademark after knowing about Respondent's domain name and did not disclose that fact to . . . the Panel. Once again, the question is why not? Presumably, Complainant wanted to improve its chances in registering its mark and this proceeding."

[405] ***Success Bank v. ZootGraphics c/o Ira Zoot***, FA0904001259918 (Forum June 29, 2009), citing WIPO Overview 2.0, Paragraph 3.1: "the registration of the domain name would not have been in bad faith because the registrant could not have contemplated the complainant's then non existent right."

[406] ***Pick Enterprises, Inc. v. Domains by Proxy, LLC, DomainsByProxy.com / Woman to Woman Healthcare / Just Us Women Health Center f/k/a Woman to Woman Health Center***, D2012-1555 (WIPO September 22, 2012) (WOMEN TO WOMEN and <womantowomanhealthcenter.com>. "Regardless of actual intent, Respondent has been put to time and expense to address a Complaint that the Panel finds objectively groundless, one as to which this Panel believes 'the complainant in fact knew or clearly should have known at the time that it filed the complaint that it could not prove one of the essential elements required by the UDRP.'")

to purchase a domain name. This has evolved into a more abusive stratagem, the so-called "Plan B" ploy discussed further below by which trademark owners whose rights postdate the domain name attempt to obtain the domain name after failing to negotiate its purchase.[408]

It is unjustifiable to use the Policy "to pressure a domain name owner into releasing a legitimately held domain name predating any trademark rights held by the complainant"[409] or "as a tool to simply wrest the disputed domain name [from respondent] in spite of [complainant's] knowledge that [it] was not entitled to that name and hence had no colorable claim under the Policy"[410]; or "in the hope that the reviewing panel would overlook Complainant's lack of rights at the time the domain name was registered and erroneously rule in Complainant's favor."[411] Panels have pointedly stated some complaints "could never have succeeded" and should not have been brought.[412] One Panel "wishe[d] to place on record [its] firm view that a complainant should not commence UDRP proceedings unless believing on reasonable grounds that the Complaint is justified and that the allegations made against respondent are legitimate and based on fact."[413]

The most egregious examples of abusive use of the proceedings are by complainants whose trademark rights come into existence many years after domain name registration.[414] It is not an unimportant consideration that "complainant should have appreciated at the outset that its complaint could not succeed."[415] The Panel in ***Altru Health System*** held that while at "first sight" it may appear as though complainant "had fair reasons to file the Complaint," on second sight it did not.

---

407 ***The Procter & Gamble Company***, supra; ***Aspen Grove***, supra.

408 ***Patricks Universal Export Pty Ltd. v. David Greenblatt***, D2016-0653 (WIPO June 21, 2016) (<patricks.com>) ("Complainant's only real gripe is the price Respondent demanded for the Domain Name, making this a classic "Plan B" case).

409 ***Sustainable Forestry Management Limited v. SFM.com and James M. van Johns "Infa dot Net" Web Services***, D2002-0535 (WIPO September 13, 2002).

410 ***Labrada Bodybuilding Nutrition, Inc. v. Glisson***, FA 250232 (Forum May 28, 2004) (The Panel found that in spite of its knowledge Complainant "persisted and intentionally filed its Complaint. Accordingly, the Complainant's intentions are clear: use of the Policy as a tool to simply wrest the disputed domain name in spite of its knowledge that the Complainant was not entitled to that name and hence had no colorable claim under the Policy.")

411 ***Horizon Publishing, LLC v. Opulence Communications Ltd.***, FA1302001487500 (Forum April 2, 2013) ("[Or] to intimidate an unwitting domain name holder into making a favorable deal with Complainant, rather than risk an unfavorable decision where he or she would get nothing.").

412 ***David Robinson v. Brendan, Hight / MDNH Inc.***, D2008-1313 (WIPO October 27, 2008). See also ***Avaya Inc.***, supra.

413 ***Deutsche Post AG v. NJDomains***, D2006-0001 (WIPO March 1, 2006); ***Collective Media, Inc. v. CKV / COLLECTIVEMEDIA.COM***, D2008-0641 (WIPO July 31, 2008).

414 ***Success Bank v. ZootGraphics c/o Ira Zoot***, FA0904001259918 (Forum June 29, 2009) (To succeed on a claim of bad faith Respondent would have had to have had "psychic powers," which,

Complainant made false statements about its trademark which it compounded by making "deliberately false accusations of Respondent's commercial activities" at the website to which the domain name resolved.[416] What finally outraged the Panel was that

> Complainant's actions were made in an attempt to convince the Panel to decide in Complainant's favour in spite [of] the fact that the case had obvious flaws. It is this Panel's opinion that Complainant's behaviour constitutes an abuse of the administrative proceeding.

In another case complainant had the further opportunity to support its allegation of bad faith in response to a Procedural Order but failed to do so.[417] Complainant has to proffer some evidence "as to how respondent could possibly have been aware of complainant and complainant's mark when registering the disputed domain name, which occurred more than three years before complainant started using its [trademark]."[418] Failing to do so or proceeding with a complaint with knowledge respondent was operating a business under the domain name is "at least a reckless disregard of the likelihood that the Respondent had rights or legitimate interests in the name."[419]

---

for the record, it denied); ***Consuela, LLC v. Alberta Hot Rods***, FA1306001504547 (Forum August 3, 2013) (Domain name registered in 1999; Complainant first used its mark in commerce in 2006. "[N]ot only did the Complainant present its Complaint when it was obvious that it could not succeed, it actually pressed its case by submitting an Additional Submission which did not address the key issue raised by the Respondent. The Complainant thus harassed the Respondent by pursuing the Complaint after the Complainant knew it to be insupportable.").

[415] ***Yell Limited v. Ultimate Search***, D2005-0091 (WIPO April 6, 2005). This is particularly true because Complainant's own research "clearly demonstrate[s] that the Respondent (or its corporate predecessor) began to use the disputed domain name in the context of a business using the term 'Futuris' within a short period after registration of the disputed domain name and furthermore that this use continued over a period of many years." ***Futuris Automotive Interiors (Australia) Pty Ltd v. X9 Interactive LLC***, D2011-0596 (WIPO June 20, 2011).

[416] FA0805001195584 (Forum July 15, 2008).

[417] ***Genomatix Software GmbH v. Intrexon Corporation***, D2010-0778 (WIPO July 8, 2010); ***Tiny Prints, Inc. v. Oceanside Capital Corp. c/o Web Admin.***, FA1007001337650 (Forum October 8, 2010): "This Panel provided Complainant with a second chance, by interlocutory order, to provide evidence of its alleged trademark usage upon which it based its claim of common law rights. Even after this second chance, Complainant failed to provide any evidence of use of the mark whatsoever prior to Respondent's registration of the domain name." Procedural Orders are discussed further in Section 7.07.

[418] ***X6D Limited v. Telepathy, Inc.***, D2010-1519 (WIPO November 16, 2010).

[419] ***OnePhone Holding AB v. IndiGO Networks***, D2007-1576 (WIPO December 22, 2007) ("In the Panel's view, it was reckless for the Complainant to consider, if it did, that this was not a bona offering of services."). See also ***Coöperative Univé U.A. v. Ashantiplc Ltd/ c/o Domain Privacy LLC***, D2011-0636 (WIPO June 30, 2011) ("The Complainant failed to provide any argument or evidence

7.11-B.2 Alternative Purchase Strategy 7.11-B.2

A finding of RDNH is justified where complainant is "using the UDRP as an alternative purchase strategy after the acquisition of the disputed domain name failed,"[420] –the earlier referred to "Plan B" stratagem–or has no "reasonable and creditable belief it is entitled to succeed."[421] Where the "Complainant must have known it could not demonstrate bad faith registration and use," its commencement of the administrative proceeding was abusive.[422]

If on its face a complaint includes facts that demonstrate no likelihood of success[423] or in post-filing correspondence complainant admits that "filing the Complaint was 'to accelerate the process of coming to a settlement on how we can work together,'"[424] respondent is entitled to a finding of RDNH. Complainants undercut their claims by asserting positions which explicitly absolve respondent of bad faith registration.[425] Alleging abusive registration without any "plausible explanation as to the Respondent's use (and presumably choice) of the Disputed Domain

---

which could support its Complaint and its attempt to mislead the Panel and/or its willful recklessness in making incorrect factual allegations is a clear demonstration of bad faith.")

420 ***X6D Limited v. Telepathy, Inc.***, D2010-1519 (WIPO November 16, 2010).

421 ***Proto Software, Inc. v. Vertical Axis, Inc/PROTO.COM***, D2006-0905 (WIPO). ***Patricks Universal Export Pty Ltd.***, *infra.* ("Professional representatives of parties in UDRP proceedings are expected to be aware of or at least familiarize themselves with the Policy and Policy precedent, and to abide by the Policy and Rules.")

422 ***Mess Enterprises v. Scott Enterprises, Ltd.***, D2004-0964 (WIPO January 25, 2005) ("Complainant had no trademark rights at the time the Respondent registered the domain name, and knew it and, in spite of that knowledge, then proceeded to intentionally secure a trademark registration with an express purpose of fraudulently invoking the Policy as a means to wrest the disputed domain name from the Respondent. Compare ***Meeza QSTP-LLC v. Torsten Frank / medisite Systemhaus GmbH***, D2009-0943 (WIPO September 15, 2009) citing ***Smart Design*** for the proposition that "[c]learly, the launching of an unjustifiable Complaint with malice aforethought qualifies, as would the pursuit of a Complaint after the Complainant knew it to be insupportable"; ***News Group Newspapers Limited v. Privacydotlink Customer 2383026 / Blue Nova Inc.,*** D2019-0084 (WIPO April 10, 2019) (<thesun.com>. Complainant was anonymously bidding for the domain name which "alone demonstrates the Complainant's full awareness that the Respondent had a legitimate interest.")

423 ***Urban Logic, citing 1 Model Management, LLC. v. L.A.S. Inc., Latifa Aadess, 1 Models LLC***, D2008-1173 (WIPO October 24, 2008); ***Channel Intelligence, Inc. v. Ethan Lacey***, D2009-0551 (WIPO June 28, 2009).

424 ***Wall Street.com, LLC v. Marcus Kocak / Internet Opportunity Entertainment (Sports) Limited, Sportingbet PLC***, D2012-1193 (WIPO September 12, 2012).

425 ***Quality Logo Products***, supra. where concurring panelist points out that "[w]hile not acknowledging the 1999 registration date of the disputed domain name, the Complainant pleads that it was registered in 2005, more than one year before the Complainant's trademark rights accrued. The Complainant's own theory of the case thus precludes transfer under well established Policy precedent."

Name [is] itself . . . an act of bad faith."[426] The less credible the allegations the greater the likelihood complainant's conduct supports respondent's demand for RDNH.[427]

Complaining about a respondent whose surname is identical to complainant's trademark and arguing he lacks rights or legitimate interests in the disputed domain name because the "website is blank, idle, and has been unused" or he "has no trademarks or authorization to use his own given name" is unpersuasive absent any evidence of targeting.[428] In reviewing the record in the cited case the Panel concluded that neither contention had merit. Domain names genuinely intended for noncommercial use, particularly those registered by (or for) persons commonly known by that name [4(c)(ii)], do not require anyone's permission.

The ***Mathiesen*** Respondent offered his birth certificate among other documentary evidence. The Panel noted Complainant's attorney signed the complaint according to Paragraph 3(b)(xiv), but did not see how that certification properly could have been made:

> Before filing this proceeding, there was apparently no attempt to confirm whether Respondent possessed a legitimate interest in using his given name. Nonetheless, the Policy is clear that being commonly known by the disputed domain name is a clear ground establishing a respondent's right or legitimate interest. Complainant has therefore disregarded the mandatory rules governing this dispute, in particular, Policy paragraph 4(c)(ii).

There is little tolerance for a complainant whose counsel is ignorant of the Policy and its clear precedents and Rules.[429] On the other hand, complainants

---

[426] ***RPG Life Sciences Ltd. v. James Mathe***, D2013-2094 (WIPO December 30, 2013). See also ***S.C. ALTOM CONSULTING S.R.L. v. Domain Administrator, PortMedia and Moniker Privacy Services***, D2012-1326 (WIPO September 12, 2012) (Separate opinion, concurring on denying complaint, but argues for RDNH: "When it is then seen on such an examination that its own case, complete with accusations of bad faith and of other allegedly improper behaviour, is not only without merit but entirely baseless, a finding of Reverse Domain Name Hijacking is open and should be made in an appropriate case.")

[427] ***Wave59 Technologie Int'l Inc. v. VolumeDomains.com***, FA1110001413550 (Forum November 30, 2011) ("Complainant knew or should have known, based upon the facts known to it when it filed the Complaint in this proceeding, that it could not prove bad faith registration. Upon being called out for the obvious chronological deficiency in its case by the Response, Complainant attempted to change the facts, contradicting the evidence it had previously submitted. The Panel considers these circumstances sufficient to support a finding that the Complaint was brought in bad faith, in an attempt at reverse domain name hijacking.") See also ***The Procter & Gamble Company v. Marchex Sales, Inc.***, D2012-2179 (WIPO February 22, 2013) (Panel found that Complainant initiated and maintained the proceedings for an "improper purpose.")

[428] ***Mathiesen S.A.C. v. Allan Mathiesen***, D2009-0087 (WIPO March 23, 2009).

[429] ***Andrew Etemadi, Founder and Chief Technology Officer for Eyemagine Technology LLC v. Clough Construction and Deanne Clough***, D2012-2455 (WIPO February 14, 2013) ("It is no excuse that Complainant may not be familiar with clear Policy precedent, the Policy, or the Rules.")

appearing *pro se* are given the benefit of the doubt about evidentiary expectations and legal protocols and their ignorance is more likely than counsel's to be excused.

7.11-C Standards for Granting RDNH 7.11-C

Reverse Domain Name Hijacking is generally not warranted where respondent's rights are "not obvious from the outset"[430] or complainant has prevailed on two[431] or (for some panelists) even one[432] of the three elements required under the Policy. Since intention is predicated on knowledge of respondent's preexisting rights or legitimate interests, complainant cannot be charged with RDNH if the evidence is only disclosed in the response to the complaint.[433] This does not relieve complainant from investigating respondent's rights before accusing respondent of seeking to defraud complainant's customers.[434]

Respondent satisfies its burden by 1) offering proof from which no other inference can be drawn except that complainant intended "to deprive a registered domain name holder of a domain name"; or 2) pointing out and having the Panel accept that complainant's explanations are not credible. Panels are in accord that neither mere lack of success nor a weak case is sufficient in itself to constitute RDNH under either branch of the Rule,[435] but sufficiency is slippery and difficult to quantify. There is no cause for a declaration where complainant is doing no more than protecting its trademark.[436]

---

430 ***Game Truck Licensing, LLC v. Domains By Proxy, LLC / Chris Hampton***, D2012-1964 (WIPO January 12, 2013).

431 See for example, ***Globosat Programadora Ltda. v. J. Almeida***, D2005-0199 (WIPO May 26, 2000).

432 ***Upbeat, Inc. v. Scott Fabian***, D2006-0332 (WIPO May 15, 2006) Respondent was found to have legitimate interests in the domain name but was responsive to an offer from Complainant to sell the domain name, which Complainant used as a 4(b)(i) basis for the complaint.)

433 ***Houzz Inc. v. Hagop Doumanian / Netico, Inc.***, FA1707001739475 (Forum August 14, 2017) (Complainant had good faith believe there was no connection between Respondent and the original and current owner of the Domain Name); ***Groupement des cartes bancaires v. Domain Administrator, Coinbase, Inc.***, D2019-0263 (WIPO April 2, 2019) (Since domain name not used for a "public-facing service such as a website" Complainant would have no knowledge of good faith registration. It uses the domain name internally for backend infrastructure).

434 ***Comercializadora de Lacteos y Derivados, S.A. de C.V. v. Apple Inc.***, D2017-1351 (WIPO October 23, 2017) (<lala.com>. "The Complainant has put these assertions forward [its mark is well-known and that the Respondent has sought to defraud the Complainant's customer] without any supporting argumentation or evidence. Such a practice cannot be accepted.")

435 ***Jazeera Space Channel***, supra.

436 The Panel in ***Mirza Juddani v. CDN Properties Incorporated CDN Properties Incorporated***, D2014-1354 (WIPO October 24, 2014) held that RDNH is inappropriate where the Respondent may have registered the Domain Name innocently and without targeting Complainant and its trademarks but subsequently used the Domain Name in bad faith.

It is generally agreed that to prevail on a claim of RDNH the proof must be "utterly clear."[437] Ordinarily respondent is expected to offer some evidence of complainant's improper intention.[438] However, some panelists demand from respondent a greater certainty of complainant's intention: it should be "malice aforethought."[439] Others have suggested "reckless disregard," which is understood as meaning asserting untruthful allegations or even outright falsehoods of abusive registration.[440]

A still higher standard demands not only complainant's knowledge of respondent's right or legitimate interest in the disputed domain name but also "evidence of harassment or similar conduct by complainant in the face of such knowledge."[441]

---

437 ***Great American Insurance Company v. Ron Hamilton***, FA109753 (Forum October 14, 2002).

438 ***Goldline International, Inc. v. Gold Line***, D2000-1151 (WIPO January 4, 2001) (<goldline.com>. "Not only would a reasonable investigation have revealed these weaknesses in any potential ICANN complaint, but also, Respondent put Complainant on express notice of these facts and that any further attempt to prosecute this matter would be abusive and would constitute reverse domain name "hijack[ing].")

439 ***Smart Design LLC v. Carolyn Hughes***, D2000-0993 (WIPO October 18, 2000) ("Clearly, the launching of an unjustifiable Complaint with malice aforethought qualifies . . . [but so too] would the pursuit of a Complaint after complainant knew it to be insupportable.") See ***jazeera Space Channel TV Station v. AJ Publishing aka Aljazeera Publishing***, D2005-0309 (WIPO July 19, 2005) ("[T]he question for the Panel is whether the more likely explanation for those discrepancies is malice or mistake or muddle. . . . [T]his may not reflect well on the Complainant if the most likely explanation for the discrepancies is mistake or muddle. . . ." The Panel opted for "mistake or muddle" rather than malice, thus not RDNH).

440 RDNH granted: ***Fetish Factory, Inc. v. The Fetish Factory a/k/a Stanford Stuart a/k/a Pamela Hancock a/k/a Internetwork Partners***, FA0108000099610 (Forum November 8, 2001) ("[R]espondent must show that complainant knew of or was reckless in disregarding respondent's unassailable right or legitimate interest in the disputed domain name or the clear lack of bad faith registration and use, and nevertheless brought the complaint in bad faith.")

Except where complainant's claim is truly egregious for which there can be said to be a "settled policy" the standard for declaring reverse domain name hijacking is, at best, uncertain. The varying views starting with the settled policy are summarized in WIPO Overview 2.0, Paragraph 4.17.

The settled policy view is expressed in ***The American Association of the Order of St. Lazarus, Inc. v. Thierry Villejust***, D2014-0739 (WIPO August 11, 2014): "Complainant either knew or should have known, at the time of filing the Complaint, that it was not the 'only legitimate organization' to use the name 'The Military and Hospitaller Order of Saint Lazarus of Jerusalem' since the crusades." See also ***Clearwater Systems, Inc. v. Glenn Johnson/Clear Water Systems of Remington Inc.***, D2014-0878 (WIPO August 5, 2014) in which the Panel "on its own initiative ... finds the Complainant committed an abuse of process."

The settled policy can also be expressed to reject reverse domain name hijacking as in ***MD On-line, Inc. v. Yenta Marketing, Inc.***, D2014-1468 (WIPO November 8, 2014) where the Panel held that "although Respondent may have registered the Domain Name innocently and without targeting Complainant and its common law mark, it has since used the Domain Name in bad faith." The result is reached by applying an unclean hands theory. See also ***Happy as Clams, Inc., a California Corp., DBA Date Like a Grownup v. Heather Dugan***, D2014-1655 (WIPO November 1, 2014) in which the Panel adhered to the "settled policy" of sanctioning Complainant because it should have

The consensus takes a middle way: "[R]espondent must show that complainant knew of or was reckless in disregarding respondent's unassailable right or legitimate interest in the disputed domain name or the clear lack of bad faith registration and use, and nevertheless brought the complaint in bad faith."[442]

Where the parties have communicated with each other prior to commencement of the proceedings but respondent has withheld information it later submits in its defense, RDMH will be denied because "Complainant had no actual knowledge of Respondent's prior use" of the mark in its own business.[443] In effect respondent must show it disclosed evidence to complainant of such quality that *a fortiori* it was abusive to have commenced the administrative proceeding.[444] It is in this respect that failure to respond to cease-and-desist notices has consequences. "[T]he combination of failure to respond . . . [where] domain names . . . are relevant to a

---

known that it was unable to prove that the Respondent registered the disputed domain name in bad faith.

Divergence from the settled policy on the lenient side includes ***Bespoke Services Group S.A. v. Garth Piesse***, D2014-1533 (WIPO November 5, 2014) in which the Panel declined to find RDNH because it appeared "Complainant may have misunderstood the requirements of the Policy, rather than being motivated by bad faith."

Panels composed of members having different views can result in a schizophrenic decision expressing both views. In ***TV Sundram Iyengas and Sons Limited v. P.A. Gordon***, D2014-0814 (WIPO August 11, 2014) the Panel held that it was not making a formal finding of reverse domain name hijacking even though "Complainant's case has significant weaknesses and that its conduct in making numerous unsupported assertions of fraud and illegal behaviour" was not to be condoned, but nevertheless concluded that "making unsupported assertions of fraud and illegal behavior" is a sound basis for issuing the sanction.

441 Complaint dismissed; RDNH denied. ***Plan Express Inc. v. Plan Express***, D2000-0565 (WIPO July 17, 2000) ("To establish reverse domain name hijacking, the respondent must show knowledge on the part of the complainant of the respondent's right or legitimate interest in the disputed domain name and evidence of harassment or similar conduct by the complainant in the face of such knowledge."). RDNH denied (dictum, complaint granted): ***Sydney Opera House Trust v. Trilynx Pty. Limited***, D2000-1224 (WIPO October 31, 2000).

442 Jurisprudential Overview 3.0, Paragraph 4.16 (To establish Reverse Domain Name Hijacking, a respon-dent would typically need to show "clear knowledge of respondent rights or legitimate interests in, or clear knowledge of lack of respondent bad faith.") See ***Finell Co., LLC v. Domain Privacy Group***, FA1401001541303 (Forum March 13, 2014) ("In 2012, the Respondent wished to become anonymous with respect to the Disputed Domain Name so as to reduce the risk of internet piracy. To accomplish this goal, he engaged the services of the Domain Privacy Group to stand-in as the registrant of the Disputed Domain Name. If nothing else, this makes it difficult for someone in the Complainant's position to learn the relevant facts and make the decision whether or not to proceed with a complaint.")

443 ***Intellogy Solutions, LLC v. Craig Schmidt and IntelliGolf, Inc.***, D2009-1244 (WIPO November 24, 2009).

444 Complainant in ***Altametrics, Inc. v. Ryan Sveinsvoll***, FA1008001343628 (Forum November 11, 2010) argued and the Panel concurred that it is "unreasonable to expect Complainant, who

complainant's general field of activity, and the facilitation of pay-per-click advertising . . . is frequently present in cybersquatting situations (even if complainant has failed to prove that this is such a situation)."[445]

Undisclosed facts favor complainant because "it cannot be said that [it] should have been aware of Respondent's likely case before the Complaint was filed."[446] Plausible uncertainty about a respondent's right or legitimate interest in a domain name has also been found to justify lack of bad faith in maintaining the proceeding.[447] However, if the facts supporting RDNH are clear and complainant fails to rebut them its failure supports the sanction.[448]

7.11-D 7.11-D Different Standards: Appearing by Counsel and *Pro Se*

7.11-D.1 7.11-D.1 Appearing by Counsel

Panels are more tolerant of *pro se* complainants and less of those represented by counsel.[449] Where a "Complainant appears to be a substantial enterprise ... represented by competent legal counsel" it is not expected to "initiate[ ] a proceeding that is quite clearly devoid of merit."[450] Attorneys are expected to have an appreciation for the jurisprudence of the forums in which they practice.[451] Although ignorance is no defense to a finding of RDNH "[a] non lawyer party might be excused from

originally filed this proceeding against a 'Domains by Proxy' undisclosed registrant, to know the myriad individual and corporate identities he maintains."

445 ***Ville de Paris v. Salient Properties LLC***, D2009-1279 (WIPO December 3, 2009).

446 ***Affin Bank Berhad v. Affinity Partners***, D2009-1266 (WIPO March 19, 2010).

447 ***Dentaid S.L. v. Domains by Proxy, Inc., Yoon Jinsoo, Michael Grady***, D2011-1270 (WIPO October 7, 2011).

448 See ***Tupras Turkiye Petrol Rafinerileri A.S. v. See PrivacyGuardian.org / Wizarc Computing***, D2017- 0818 (WIPO June 6, 2017) (<hexmon.com>. "Although the Respondent does not make any allegation of Reverse Domain Name Hijacking (RDNH) against the Complainant, the Response by the Respondent acting in person makes it clear that he regards the Complaint as totally unjustified and oppressive. The Rules do not require the Respondent to have made an express allegation of RDNH. In the circumstances, the Panel considers it appropriate to consider the issue of RDNH of its own volition."

449 See Jurisprudential Overview 3.0, Paragraph 4.16: "Given the undertakings in paragraphs 3(b)(xiii) and (xiv) of the UDRP Rules, some panels have held that a represented complainant should be held to a higher standard." See ***Color Image Apparel, Inc. v. Whois Privacy Services by DOMAINCA / unitedeurope consulting***, D2017-0650 (WIPO June 19, 2017) (<alo.com>. "Complainant ought to have known that it could not succeed under any fair interpretation of facts reasonably available prior to the filing of the Complaint.")

450 ***Sustainable Forestry Management Limited v. SFM.com and James M. van Johns 'Infa dot Net' Web Services***, D2002-0535 (WIPO September 13, 2002) ("[F]rivolous complaints such as this risk diminishing the credibility of the entire UDRP process"); ***The Procter & Gamble Company v. Marchex Sales, Inc***, D2012-2179 (WIPO February 22, 2013) (<swash.com>. "Had the Respondent failed to respond, there is a very real risk that the Panel, relying upon the 1993 International

failing to distinguish registration in bad faith from use in bad faith, or not understanding that both must be proven (and proven with evidence not allegations), but counsel must further certify that 'the assertions in this Complaint are warranted under these Rules and under applicable law, as it now exists or as it may be extended by a good faith and reasonable argument' Rules, paragraph 3(b)(xiv)."[452]

While it is true a complainant's failure to prove its case does not necessarily rise to the level of bad faith—"[a] complainant with a weak claim may present his complaint in good faith"—the majority in ***David Robinson*** found the complaint was "not simply the phenomenon of a weak case that failed such as, for example, an inadequately proven claim for a common law trademark. The case could never have succeeded." The Panel made a point of noting complainant was "represented by well known United Kingdom solicitors [who] should have known at the time of filing the Complaint that he could not prove one of the essential elements of the Policy."[453]

Nevertheless, what appears sanctionable abuse to one panelist may have an entirely different complexion to another. In ***General Media Communications***[454] the Panel found that Complainant's or its counsel's conduct was so egregious that it

---

registration and the substantial sales volumes claimed for the brand, would have found in favor of the Complainant. This Complaint fell very far short of what the Panel was entitled to expect from a Complainant of this stature." Application of different standards between counsel and pro se arbitrants is also found in proffers of proof. It can affect issuance of a Procedural Order—for which see ***CAM London Limited and Comgest Asset Management International Limited v. Cam LondonLtd***, D2013-2190 (WIPO February 4, 2014) ("[T]o give the Complainant <a secondbite at the apple> would not be in line with the spirit of expediency and efficiency suggested in the Policy").

451 ***The California Milk Processor Board v. Center Ring Productions, LLC.***, D2011-1689 (WIPO December 1, 2011). Although the Panel noted that in his opinion the "Complaint would not pass muster under Rule 11 of the United States Federal Rules of Civil Procedure, which treats counsel's signature on a pleading as his certification" he rejected a request for RDNH. See also ***Timbermate Products Pty Ltd v. Domains by Proxy, LLC / Barry Gork***, D2013-1603 (WIPO November 3, 2013) in which the Panel identifies seven circumstances that warrant a declaration of RDNH and concluded that "Complainant (through its representative) was only too well aware of the conjunctive requirement and instead of citing any previous decisions on the topic under the Policy elected to cite an Irish decision [under the IE Domain Name Dispute Resolution Policy which was 'particularly inept' in that the IEDR is an either/or model].")

452 ***Urban Logic***, supra; ***Mathiesen S.A.C.***, supra.

453 The dissent in ***David Robinson*** (dissenting only on the issue of RDNH) believed there should be actual proof of "harassment or bad faith or similarly reprehensible conduct," thereby seemingly demanding a clear and convincing standard to prevail on RDNH. However, the term "reprehensible conduct" is not found in the WIPO Final Report and there is no jurisprudential basis for elevating the quantum of proof beyond preponderance.

454 ***General Media Communications, Inc. v. Crazy Troll c/o CrazyTroll.com***, FA0602000651676 (Forum May 12, 2006).

> would likely warrant sanctions and/or referral of the matter to the appropriate Bar Association for disciplinary action, were this case being handled in a federal or state court of record. Here it forms the basis for the required Finding, set out above, that Complainant has wrongfully attempted a Reverse Domain Name Hijacking by virtue of its abuse of the arbitration proceeding through its omission of material facts and its intentional or negligent misstatement of some of the most significant and material facts in its briefs and exhibits.

In a subsequent ACPA action whatever in the UDRP submission shocked and disturbed the Panel and ruffled his equanimity, failed utterly to impress the Magistrate Judge who concluded otherwise:[455]

> Obviously, if there was evidence that established—or even arguably established—all three elements of the UDRP test, GMCI could not have brought its proceeding in bad faith as the sole panelist found. There further was no basis for a finding that GMCI engaged in reverse domain name hijacking in violation of the UDRP by bringing the UDRP proceeding against Crazy Troll.

Panels have also rejected RDNH despite representation on the grounds that "on balance [it has found Complainant] was misguided rather than dishonest."[456] Complainant had initiated contact for <nutrihome.com> but the three-member Panel found it "commercially reasonable both that the Complainant should investigate the possibility of purchasing the disputed domain name before incurring the costs of proceedings under the UDRP and that it should avoid disclosing any existing connection with a name similar to the disputed domain name."

7.11-D.2 7.11-D.2 Appearing *Pro Se*

Appearing pro se has advantages in mitigating complainant's conduct. Respondent in ***BFS of the Americas***[457] alleged "the Complaint was superficially investigated and not done in a professional way." The Panel "accepted" this judgment:

> The Complaint was obviously prepared without the benefit of legal advice, and there was evident naiveté in complainant telling the Center that it had attempted to have the claimed trademark registered, but had been unable to do so because 'it is a generic naming nomenclature'.

Complainant's "frank acknowledgment" of what it could not do "does not seem to the Panel to be consistent with any dishonest intent."

---

[455] *General Media Communications, Inc. v. Crazy Troll LLC and Gene Heu*, 06-CV-40581 [Not for Publication] (S.D.N.Y. Jan. 16, 2007).

[456] ***Fresenius Kabi S.A. v. Domain Manager, EWEB Development, Inc.***, D2018-0491 (WIPO May 24, 2018) (<nutrihome.com>).

[457] ***BFS of the Americas LLC, dba Battery Filling Systems v. Matthias Pahlke, Fillwatch Landau GmbH***, D2008-1786 (WIPO January 29, 2009).

The analogy with malicious prosecution may be instructive. The victim has to prove the accused (1) intentionally (and maliciously) instituted and pursued or caused a legal action to be instituted or pursued and it (2) brought the action without probable cause.[458] In ***PJS International***, a three-member Panel absolved Complainant of RDNH because "the original Complaint has been filed directly by APE & Partners, the company that is licensed for the purpose of using the trademark, rather than by an independent counsel."[459]

7.12 RULE 17—CONSENT TO TRANSFER 7.12

7.12-A Terminating Proceeding: Respondent's Request 7.12-A

UDRP proceedings may be terminated in either one of two circumstances: 1) the parties agree on a settlement; or 2) some intervening contingency makes it either "unnecessary or impossible to continue the administrative proceeding for any reason." In either case "the Panel shall terminate the administrative proceeding, unless a Party raises justifiable grounds for objection within a period of time to be determined by the Panel."[460]

Although the rule ostensibly concerns "termination of proceedings" it does no violence to stretch it to include consents that shortcut the traditional UDRP analysis. It is clear under Rule 17(a) that no purpose is served by going forward with the proceedings where parties have settled their dispute; there is also no purpose served where the parties have mutually consented to one of the UDRP remedies. However, where there is no mutual consent or respondent's consent is equivocal

---

[458] See ***LaFrance Corp. v. David Zhang***, D2009-0415 (WIPO May 15, 2009), ("[h]ad Complainant been represented by counsel the Panel would not have hesitated to make an RDNH finding. . . . Nevertheless, in his discretion the Panel declines to enter a finding of RDNH, but does find, as provided in paragraph 15(e) of the Rules, that the Complaint "was brought primarily to harass the domain name holder.")

[459] ***PJS International SA v. Vertical Axis Inc. / Whois Privacy Services Pty Ltd.***, D2013-0805 (WIPO August 8, 2013) ("[T]he Panel is led to believe that no thorough examination of the facts of the case and of the rules applicable has been undertaken beforehand by an independent counsel on behalf of the Complainant.")

[460] Rule 17:

(a) If, before the Panel's decision, the Parties agree on a settlement, the Panel shall terminate the administrative proceeding.

(b) If, before the Panel's decision is made, it becomes unnecessary or impossible to continue the administrative proceeding for any reason, the Panel shall terminate the administrative proceeding, unless a Party raises justifiable grounds for objection within a period of time to be determined by the Panel.

In contrast the rules for the Uniform Rapid Suspension System (URS) do not empower the Examiner to transfer a registration to complainant. Rule 14(a) states that "the sole remedy available to Complainant . . . shall be limited to suspension of the domain name for the balance of the

and begrudging there is good reason to perform the traditional UDRP analysis. Rule 17(b) subsumes two circumstances: 1) where the parties consent to a result—that is, it is "unnecessary" to proceed (unless complainant otherwise objects)—or 2) a situation in which the matter is removed from the administrative proceedings following the commencement of an action in a court of competent jurisdiction—that is, it is "impossible" to proceed.

As a general rule, complainants would have little incentive to "agree on a settlement" once the dispute is submitted, since doing so rewards respondents for their strategic decisions to hold onto domain names until the last possible moment. Rather, the incentive is for a ruling on the merits. However, where both parties consent to the transfer it is inappropriate for the Panel to do otherwise than "simply make an order for the transfer of the domain name to Complainant." There are three possibilities where respondent initiates the request for termination: complainant stipulates to a formal settlement (which is rare),[461] objects (more likely),[462] or fails to object (common).[463]

Panels have generally adopted the fiction that failure to object to dismissal is equivalent to acquiescence because in that case the two parties desire the same result and it would be "expedient and judicial to forgo the traditional UDRP analysis and order the transfer of the domain names."[464] A Panel should not "issue a decision that would be either less than requested, or more than requested by the parties."[465] It "must recognize the common request of the two parties."[466]

Whether to accept respondent's unilateral request even in the face of complainant's refusal to stipulate may depend upon the genuineness of respondent's offer and the circumstances under which the domain name was registered. In ***The Cartoon Network*** the Panel concluded that respondent's offer was genuine and that such unilateral consent "provides a basis for an immediate order for transfer without consideration of the paragraph 4(a) elements."[467] The consent in fact may

---

registration period." See ***Michael Page Recruitment Group Limited v. Tassanee Atsawasakundee, KTI Recruitment Consultants Co. Ltd.***, HKS-1400001 (ADNDRC May 11, 2014).

461 ***Williams-Sonoma, Inc. d/b/a Pottery Barn v. EZ-Port***, D2000-0207 (WIPO May 5, 2000) (No formal stipulation of settlement, but "[b]ecause Respondent has consented to the relief requested by Complainant, it is not necessary to review the facts supporting the claim.")

462 ***Boehringer Ingelheim Int'l GmbH v. Modern Ltd. Cayman Web Dev.***, FA 133625 (Forum, January 9, 2003) (Panel disregarded Complainant's preference for a decision.)

463 ***Disney Enterprises, Inc. v. Elmer Morales***, FA0505000475191 (Forum June 24, 2005) ("the Panel felt it to be expedient and judicial to forego the traditional UDRP analysis and order the transfer of the domain names.").

464 Id., ***Disney Enterprises.***

465 ***Digg Inc. v. Damien Overeem***, FA 836770 (Forum December 20, 2006).

466 ***The Body Shop International plc v. Agri, Lacus, and Caelum LLC***, FA 679564 (Forum May 25, 2006).

be accompanied by a strong denial of any violation, "for example, where a domain name was registered in error."

Except where the offer is deemed genuine termination benefits respondent because it prevents a finding of bad faith. A decision to terminate would be questionable where there is a credible basis for concluding the consent is offered to avoid such a declaration, although for some respondents the purpose in consenting to transfer is to avoid a finding they have violated the Policy. Their stratagem is designed to maintain a clean slate which has elicited an adaptive response to perform a merits analysis.[468]

For example, in ***Messe Frankfurt GmbH***[469] the Complainant expressly did not consent and "request[ed] that [the Panel] look at the wider merits of the situation." The Panel in rejecting respondent's request to terminate the proceedings without a decision stated:

> [I]n cases of this type it would be contrary to the spirit and intent of the Policy for a party to use the expedient of offering to transfer the disputed domain name at the last minute, in order to avoid a decision on the merits and thereby minimize the risk of adverse findings/comments.

This conduct, the Panel stated, is particularly egregious where the party appears to have done the same previously[470] and the purpose of the step appears to be to circumvent the Policy.

The ***Messe Frankfurt*** Panel inferred that "the purpose of this strategy is not only to delay the inevitable (as found in [other cases]) but also effectively to thwart the Policy (where patterns of questionable conduct have always been relevant) and that this is an abuse of process and a further indication of bad faith conduct." This view, which honors the language of the Rule, is not followed by all panelists. Panels in subsequent cases have split on the issue. In ***Almaden Valley Athletic Club***[471] and ***Graebel Van Lines***[472] the Panels followed ***Messe***, while in ***Dryvit Systems***[473] the

---

[467] ***The Cartoon Network LP, LLLP v. Mike Morgan***, D2005-1132 (WIPO January 5, 2006).

[468] "As a matter of the Policy's procedural rules, as well as to minimize the risk that the "consent-to-transfer" approach might allow cybersquatters to avoid adverse rulings against them, several panels have held that a merits decision is required," ***MM Herman & Associates, LLC v. Black Knight Publishing c/o Black Knight***, FA1005001324437 (Forum June 16, 2010).

[469] ***Messe Frankfurt GmbH v. Texas International Property Associates***, D2008-0375 (April 29, 2008).

[470] The Panel noted that respondent had been found by prior Panels to be a serial cybersquatter in violation of paragraph 4(b) of the Policy with over a hundred claims against it.

[471] ***Almaden Valley Athletic Club v. Texas International Property Associates-NA NA***, D2008-0600 (WIPO June 11, 2008).

[472] ***Graebel Van Lines, Inc. v. Texas International Property Associates-NA NA.***, FA080500 1195954 (Forum July 17, 2008).

Panel did not and accepted respondent's unilateral consent to transfer the domain name to complainant.

7.12-B

7.12-B Terminating Proceeding: Complainant's Request

A request by a complainant to voluntarily terminate the administrative proceeding after submission to a Panel is most unusual. This contingency is foreseen in the Forum's Supplemental Rules (noted further below), but neither part of Rule 17 is applicable and it would be particularly inappropriate to terminate the proceedings when opposed by respondent seeking sanctions against complainant for instituting the proceedings.

The Panel in ***Comité Interprofessionnel du vin de Champagne***[474] explained that Rule 17(a) did not apply since respondent objected to termination and Rule 17(b) did not apply because "[c]learly it was not 'impossible' for the Panel to continue this proceeding, so the issues were whether it was 'unnecessary' for the Panel to do so, and whether respondent had raised any justifiable objection to the termination." Moreover, "the net effect of refusing an objection in these terms would be to allow any complainant to avoid the only form of sanction which the Policy provides for the making of a complaint in bad faith merely by applying for voluntary termination of proceeding once it becomes aware that a response has been filed."[475]

The ***Comité Interprofessionnel du vin de Champagne*** Panel reasoned that termination raised a fairness issue. Complainant requested permission to withdraw its complaint "at this stage" but failed to explain what "at this stage" meant. "Did that mean that complainant was reserving the right to refile the Complaint, perhaps with extensive additional evidence, or possibly merely in the hope that a different panel would be appointed? In the Panel's view, it would not be fair to the Respondent, which had been put to the expense and trouble of filing a substantial response, if it were obliged to go through that process again."[476]

---

[473] ***Dryvit Systems, Inc. v. Texas International Property Associates***, D2008-0599 (WIPO June 17, 2008).

[474] ***Comité Interprofessionnel du vin de Champagne v. Steven Vickers***, DCO2011-0026 (WIPO June 21, 2011); ***Tarheel Take Out, LLC v. Versimedia, Inc.***, D2012-1668 (WIPO October 18, 2012).

[475] ***Intellect Design Arena Limited v. Moniker Privacy Services/David Wieland, iEstates.com, LLC***, D2016-1349 (WIPO August 29, 2016) (<unmail.com>. "[T]he question of whether or not to allow voluntary termination does not turn exclusively upon whether a complainant qualifies such request as 'termination with prejudice' or 'termination without prejudice.' The issue is also bound up with the fact that, if a panel considers that a complaint may be opportunistic, unmeritorious or brought in bad faith, it will often be fairer to deal with the matter there and then in the context of the live administrative proceeding, in particular addressing any question of RDNH which arises, rather than simply to 'sweep the issue under the carpet' on the ground that this accords with the complainant's wishes.")

Withdrawal of a complaint filed with the Forum is expressly addressed by Paragraph 12 of its Supplemental Rules, which regulates the effects of a withdrawal request depending on the stage of the administrative proceeding when it is submitted.[477] If prior to or after commencement but before a response has been received, complainant may withdraw its complaint without prejudice and the administrative proceeding will be terminated. If after a response has been received but before a Panel decision is published, the complaint may be withdrawn if both parties agree to the withdrawal: "A Complaint dismissed by the Forum pursuant to Supplemental Rule 12(c) will be *dismissed with prejudice*" (emphasis added).[478] Under Supplemental Rule 12(d), the complaint cannot be withdrawn after a Panel decision is published."

7.13 SUPPLEMENTAL RULES ADOPTED BY PROVIDERS 7.13

7.13-A Supplementing the Record 7.13-A

ICANN's Rules of the Policy are silent on the issue of supplementing the record.[479] Rule 3 (governing the complaint) and Rule 5 (governing the response) limit each party to one pleading, which may be supplemented in either of two ways, by the parties submitting supplementary material requested by the Panel under Rule 12 or with the Panel's permission upon a party's request. Rule 15(a) discussed in Section

---

[476] Id. The Panel noted the possibility of forum shopping, citing ***Sensis Pty Ltd, Telstra Corporation Limited v. Yellow Pages Marketing B.V.***, D2011-0057 (WIPO March 15, 2011) ("It is conceivable that a well funded complainant could simply refile successive complaints until it found a panel willing to order the transfer of the disputed domain name. This would not be a fair burden to impose on respondents, it would not be an efficient use of the resources of the dispute resolution service provider, and it would not promote consistency and predictability in UDRP decisions.") See also ***Donald J. Trump v Point Pub Liquors***, D2010-1946 (WIPO January 27, 2012) ("Allowing Complainant to withdraw without prejudice at this point in the proceeding, after Respondent has invested significant time and money defending its position, would be unfair to Respondent, as nothing would prevent Complainant from reinitiating the proceedings at any time in the future.")

[477] Discussed further in "Forum Practice" (Sec. 7.12-B.2). There is no comparable rule in WIPO's Supplemental Rules. Discussion in ***David H. Pratt d/b/a Solar Mart v. Mushka***, FA1202001429169 (Forum March 28, 2012).

[478] The Rule contemplates that the Forum (prior to submitting file to Panel) will terminate the proceeding if both parties agree. If the withdrawal request is made to the Panel there is no need for a mutual agreement. ***H. Pratt d/b/a Solar Mart v. Mushka***, FA1202001429169 (Forum March 28, 2012) ("The Panel therefore, concludes that Respondent will not oppose said withdrawal. Even if the supplemental rules state a time and a manner in which said withdrawal request must have been submitted, the Panel cannot ignore the Complainant's will: Whereas his initial will to get the domain name <solarmart.com> transferred was this proceeding's raison d'etre, his ultimate disinterest in the disputed domain name justifies this proceeding's termination.")

[479] The Rules of the Policy allow providers to establish supplemental rules, although the definition does not specifically refer to replies and sur-replies. The term "Supplemental Rules means the rules

7.10 instructs the Panel to "decide a complaint on the basis of the statements and documents submitted" by the parties, which together constitute the record.

The two principal providers, WIPO and the Forum, interpret Rule 12 differently with respect to supplemental submissions. The Forum expressly authorizes supplemental submissions through its Rule 7 discussed further below. The WIPO Supplemental Rules are silent but adhere more literally to ICANN's Rule 12. In its Overview at Paragraph 4.2 WIPO records two views. The majority view is that panels "have discretion to accept an unsolicited supplemental filing from either party, bearing in mind the obligation to treat each party with equality and ensure that each party has a fair opportunity to present its case."

The minority view is that "[u]nless the panel specifically solicits a supplemental filing, it will not consider a supplemental filing in its decision." Panels have stated their reason for rejecting unsolicited supplemental filings is that they delay resolution, increase expenses and compromise the purposes of the Policy for an expeditious and relatively inexpensive procedure for resolving domain name disputes. However, being overly punctilious runs afoul of Rule 10(b), which states that "the Panel shall ensure that the Parties are treated with equality and that each Party is given a fair opportunity to present its case."[480]

7.13-B

7.13-B Provider Supplemental Rules

7.13-B.1

7.13-B.1 WIPO Practice

The WIPO Overview notwithstanding, panelists are ambivalent about supplemental submissions. The vocal minority insist that "[i]t is now well established from previous panel decisions that a supplemental [unsolicited] filing will rarely be considered."[481] They are acceptable where the complainant "could not reasonably have addressed issues in its initial complaint."[482] Supplemental submissions that simply reargue the same issues already submitted are unacceptable.[483]

---

adopted by the provider administering a proceeding to supplement these Rules. Supplemental Rules shall not be inconsistent with the Policy or these Rules and shall cover such topics as fees, word and page limits and guidelines, file size and format modalities, the means for communicating with the provider and the Panel, and the form of cover sheets."

[480] The Panel in *Ministre des Relations internationales, de la Francophonie et du Commerce extérieur (Minister of International Relations, La Francophonie and External Trade), acting in this proceeding for and on behalf of the Government of Québec v. Anything.com, Ltd.*, D2013-2181 (WIPO March 7, 2014) gave a pragmatic reading of the rule: "Whether it is appropriate to submit a supplemental submission will depend on its relevance to the issues in the case, whether the panel considers the content of the submission essential to reaching a fair decision on the facts, and whether the submission could have been made earlier and, if so, why it was not."

[481] ***Olymp Bezner GmbH & Co. KG v. Olympus Access Service***, D2003-0958 (WIPO February 17, 2003).

[482] ***Trade Me Limited v. Vertical Axis Inc***, D2009-0093 (WIPO April 7, 2009) (<trademe.com>).

Acceptance, if at all, has been limited to the following circumstances: 1) when offered to present new, pertinent evidence not reasonably available until after the party's initial submission[484]; 2) to bring new and highly relevant legal authority not previously available to the attention of the panel[485]; and 3) to rebut arguments of the opposing party that could not reasonably have been anticipated.[486] If for any of these reasons either party submits unsolicited statements or documents the "reasons why the Panel is invited to consider the further material should, so far as practicable, be set out separately from the material itself."[487]

One reason for strict enforcement of the submission rules is "to discourage the litigation tactic of always trying to secure the last word on any subject of dispute. Accordingly, the panel refuses to accept or to consider for any purpose the supplemental pleadings submitted in this matter."[488] The position is consistent with that of like-minded panelists in rejecting unsolicited supplemental pleadings.[489] In view of this uncertainty it is prudent for complainant to anticipate both the Panel's position on Rule 12 and the respondent's factual and legal argument should it choose to appear.[490]

Not all Panels are comfortable with such strict construction against supplemental filings and take the position that decisions on this issue should be guided by circumstances. For example, if a respondent raises matters the complainant could not have been expected to address in its complaint, acceptance of an uninvited reply may be warranted in the interests of fairness. "It would be an odd result if the panel may request a reply in such circumstances under Rule 12 but must refuse an

---

483 ***World Wrestling Federation Entertainment, Inc. V. Ringwide Collectibles***, D2000-1306 (WIPO January 24, 2001).

484 ***Top Driver, Inc. v. Benefits Benefits***, D2002-0972 (WIPO January 7, 2003).

485 ***Pet Warehouse v. Pets.Com, Inc.***, D2000-0105 (WIPO April 13, 2000) (<petwarehouse.com>).

486 ***Interactive Study Systems Inc. v. BFQ***, D2008-0205 (WIPO April 2, 2008); ***Afrisport Intellectual Property (PTY) Ltd. v. Domainsonoffer.com***, D2007-1449 (WIPO November 26, 2007) ("[b]ecause the supplemental filing does not address any new facts or legal precedents not available at the time of the Complaint, the Panel declines to consider Complainant's supplemental filing.")

487 ***The E.W. Scripps. Company v. Sinologic Industries***, D2003-0447 (WIPO July 1, 2003).

488 ***The Reverend Dr. Jerry Falwell and The Liberty Alliance v. Gary Cohn, Prolife.net, and God. info***, D2002-0184 (WIPO June 3, 2002).

489 However, in this particular case the Panel's decision to order the domain name transferred was ultimately rejected by the Fourth Circuit Court of Appeals. 420 F.3d 309 (4th Cir. 2005). The court held that the "use of another firm's mark to capture the markholder's customers and profits [ ] simply does not exist when the alleged infringer establishes a gripe site that criticizes the markholder." Further, "we can only conclude that Reverend Falwell cannot demonstrate that Lamparelo 'had a bad faith intent to profit from using the <www.fallwell.com> domain name.'"

490 See ***Trade Me Limited***, supra: "Ordinarily, a complainant will attempt, in anticipation of a response, to deny any factual basis for that provision to operate. Although there is no express requirement for a complainant to address itself to that provision, the absence of any automatic right of

uninvited reply on the same topic, simply because there is no express provision for such a reply in the Rules."[491]

The Panel explained that

> While the Rules clearly delineate a procedure for resolving disputes under the Policy, that, for the sake of expediency, relies on a single complaint and response, there is no prohibition—contrary to the Respondent's view—in either the Policy or the Rules which circumscribes a panel's authority to consider any additional material submitted by any party on its own initiative.

However,

> That being said, panels generally frown on receiving additional submissions—particularly after a panel has been fully appointed and the case provided to it for decision—for the simple reason that such submissions tend to complicate the process, delay decision of the underlying dispute and run counter to the goals, embodied in the Policy, of providing a dispute resolution mechanism that is relatively simple, expeditious and cost-effective to the parties.

Acceptance of unsolicited supplemental submissions depends on whether "a panel in assessing the underlying circumstances of a case . . . in its sole discretion and on a case-by-case basis [determines] to accept such a submission or not."

Sole discretion means the Panel can pick and choose whether to accept or reject a part or the whole supplemental submission. Complainant will be permitted to reply to matter it could not "reasonably" have foreseen but may not supplement what it could have. The Panel in another case decided to admit only some paragraphs of a Complainant's reply.[492] Its rationale was

> [w]hile complainant could not reasonably have anticipated all of the allegations which would be made by the Respondent, these further submissions of complainant are unnecessary and therefore do not comply with the requirement that any additional material should be limited so as to minimize prejudice to the procedure.

---

reply to a response under the Policy makes it prudent for a complainant to address that provision in anticipation"; ***Metinvest Holdings NV v. O. Bogatov***, DNL2008-0025 (WIPO September 19, 2008) ("The nature of this procedure in principle does not allow for extensive fact finding. . . . Hence, a complainant should in principle anticipate that the complaint will be its only possibility to present its arguments and to deliver evidence. For this reason a complainant should try to anticipate possible defenses of a respondent, given that there is fair chance that a respondent will defend itself and will challenge the contentions of complainant.")

491 ***Toyota Jidosha Kabushiki Kaisha d/b/a Toyota Motor Corporation v. S&S Enterprises Ltd.***, D2000-0802 (WIPO September 9, 2000).

492 ***General Electric Company v. Edison Electric Corp. a/k/a Edison Electric Corp. General Energy, Edison GE, Edison-GE and EEEGE.COM***, D2006-0334 (WIPO August 13, 2006).

In ***Interactive Study Systems Inc. v. BFQ***[493] the Panel granted Complainant leave to submit a Reply but all it "offered [was] its counsel's unsupported statement [that is had common law rights]."

7.13-B.2 Forum Practice 7.13-B.2

In contrast to the "minority" view recorded in the WIPO Overview, the Forum permits supplemental submissions as of right but discourages submissions that do not advance the case by establishing an absolute deadline. Supplemental Rule 7 provides in part that a "party may submit additional written statements and documents to NAF and the opposing party(s) within five (5) calendar days after the date the Response was submitted or the last date the Response was due to be submitted to NAF, whichever occurs first." The parties must act in a timely manner.

Additional submissions that comply with the rule are likely to be accepted as a general practice (with dissenting views discussed below) and some Panels tend to leniency in accepting even late submissions.[494] The Panel in ***Gaiam*** explained that

> In the interest of having claims decided on the merits and not by default and because Complainant has not been prejudiced in the presentation of its case by the late submission, Respondent's opposition documents are accepted as timely.

However, in general panelists insist that submissions must be timely to be acceptable.[495]

Other Panels take a more severe position in accord with the minority position recorded in the WIPO Overview. Additional submissions should be considered only in exceptional circumstances. The Panel in one case explicitly criticized Forum's Supplemental Rule 7.[496] It stated:

> To the extent Supplemental Rule 7 seeks to force a Panel to accept supplemental submissions, it is inconsistent with ICANN's Rules, and it creates a false expectation among parties that their supplemental materials, prepared on a tight five-day deadline, will be accepted by the Panel. This Panel has previously criticized the National Arbitration Forum's Supplemental Rule 7 as being inconsistent with the Rules, as promulgated by ICANN. Under Rule

---

[493] ***Interactive Study Systems Inc. v. BFQ***, D2008-0205 (WIPO April 2, 2008).

[494] ***Gaiam, Inc. v. Nielsen***, FA 112469 (Forum July 2, 2002).

[495] ***Glenwood Springs Chamber Resort Ass'n. v. College Transp. Inc. d/b/a Website For Sale***, FA 98825 (Forum October 31, 2001) (declined to consider Complainant's second additional submission because it was untimely and submitted without the required fee).

[496] ***Alain-Martin Pierret d/b/a Bordeaux West v. Sierra Technology Group***, LLC, FA 0505000472135 (Forum July 1, 2005), citing ***Elec. Commerce Media, Inc. v. Taos Mountain***, FA 95344 (Forum October 11, 2000). The same panelist repeated his criticism in ***Town of Easton Connecticut v. Lightning PC Inc.***, FA0808001220202 (Forum October 12, 2008).

12, only the Panel may decide whether to request or accept supplemental submissions.

While technically correct that Rule 7 is inconsistent with Paragraph 12 of the Rules of the Policy this position has not attracted general support from other Forum panelists, although it is not without adherents.[497] In the view of these panelists

> [T]he controlling provision is Paragraph 12 of ICANN's Rules for Uniform Domain Name Dispute Resolution Policy . . . under which discretion to request such supplementation rests with the Panel. In general, a Panel should consider additional submissions only in exceptional circumstances, such as where they reflect newly discovered evidence not reasonably available to the submitting party at the time of its original submission or rebut arguments by the opposing party that the submitting party could not reasonably have anticipated.

The purpose of a reply is to respond to evidence and factual assertions that would not have been reasonable for a complainant to have anticipated. The prudent course is to file a complete record and not withhold any evidence or factual assertion for strategic purposes to get the last word.

---

[497] ***Deep Foods, Inc. v. Jamruke, LLC***, FA 648190 (Forum April 10, 2006). Other decisions by the same Panel include ***Am. Online, Inc. v. Thricovil***, FA 638077 (Forum March 22, 2006) and ***HotCam, Ltd. RNIS Telecommunication Inc.***, FA0907001273417 (Forum August 24, 2009).

8

Before, During, and After UDRP Proceedings

8.01 PARAGRAPH 4(k) OF THE POLICY 8.01

8.01-A Submitting Dispute to a Court of Competent Jurisdiction 8.01-A

Paragraph 4(k) emphasizes that the Policy, although by its terms mandatory, is a nonexclusive, alternative dispute resolution regime. It provides that either party may challenge the Panel's award in a court of competent jurisdiction: "It shall not prevent either you or the complainant from submitting the dispute [before, during, or after] to a court of competent jurisdiction for independent resolution." This accords well with U.S. law in granting relief to "domain name registrant[s] whose domain names ha[ve] been suspended, disabled, or transferred."[1] However, in regard to other national laws the Policy may be aspirational. Where there is no subject matter jurisdiction, as there is not (for example) under U.K. law,[2] the UDRP is the exclusive remedy.

Paragraph 4(k) conveys these procedural possibilities in three sentences: the first sentence addresses respondent's right to submit "the dispute to a court of competent jurisdiction for independent resolution before such mandatory administrative

---

[1] In the U.S. a plenary action for cybersquatting or for a declaration that the registration of an accused domain name was registered in good faith is governed by the Trademark Act of 1946 (the "Lanham Act"). In particular, there are two sections of interest in the Lanham Act. The first section is the Anticybersquatting Consumer Protection Act (ACPA), §1125(d), which is the legal underpinning for adjudicating cybersquatting disputes that were either decided unfavorably under the UDRP or by a trademark owner's direct action in federal court. The second section of interest, §1114(2)(D), is the legal underpinning for resolving complaints by domain name holders who have lost their domain names (or are in immediate jeopardy of losing them) as a result of an award in a UDRP proceeding.

Section 1114(2)(D)(v) provides that "A domain name registrant whose domain name has been . . . transferred under a policy . . . may, upon notice to the mark owner, file a civil action to establish that the registration or use of the domain name by such registrant is not unlawful under this act."

Canada: Damages, costs and mandatory injunction for infringement pursuant to Trade Mark Law. *SOURCE MEDIA GROUP CORP. v. BLACK PRESS GROUP LTD. AND LISA FARQUHARSON*, 2014 FC 1014 (Oct. 24, 2014) ("Defendants, being publishing professionals, have infringed through publication of the Plaintiff's trade-mark for a little more than two years and have kept on using the trade-mark online via the website: www.newhomelivingbc.com until January 2014. By using and insisting in using the trade-mark, the Defendants demonstrated a reproachable attitude.")

See *Direct Niche, LLC v. Via Varejo S/A*, 15 cv 62344 (S.D. Fla., August 10, 2017). In finding in favor of defendant (who as Complainant prevailed in the UDRP, ***VIA VAREJO S/A, v. Domain Admin***, D2015 1304 (WIPO October 17, 2015) (<casasbahia.com>), the court held that "It is not necessary that the 'mark,' as described in the statute, be a trademark registered with the U.S. Patent and Trademark Office, nor need it be a trademark for which a party has ***applied*** for federal registration. Via Varejo (a Brazilian company) demonstrated that it had a common law trademark in the U.S. for CASAS BAHIA. Affirmed on appeal, 898 F.3d 1144 (11th Cir. 2018).

[2] See *Yoyo.email v. Royal Bank of Scotland Group PLC and Others*, [2015] EWHC 3509 (Ch): "[P]roper construction of the UDRP clause 4k does not give rise to a separate cause of action in favour of the claimant [aggrieved domain name registrant]."

proceeding is commenced or after such proceeding is concluded"[3]; the second sentence addresses the authority of the Administrative Panel appointed by a provider to decide whether "your domain name registration should be canceled or transferred"; and the third sentence addresses execution of the award by the service provider "who will . . . implement the decision unless we have received from you during that ten (10) business day period official documentation . . . that you have commenced a lawsuit."

If respondent commences a lawsuit after receiving the UDRP complaint or "during an administrative proceeding" the "Panel shall have the discretion to decide whether to suspend or terminate the administrative proceeding, or to proceed to a decision."[4] Whether a dispute is removed "before" or "during" the proceeding respondents have a choice of venue as provided in their registration agreements to file lawsuits in a "mutual jurisdiction," or, alternatively, in a court in which the complainant is amenable to personal jurisdiction.[5] For the losing domain name holder failure to commence a legal proceeding within the ten (10) day window provided in sentence 3 of paragraph 4(k) results in loss of registration but not its right to challenge the award (if in the U.S) in an ACPA declaratory judgment action.

Complainants' choices for direct action are dictated (in the case of U.S. jurisdiction) either where defendant can be made subject to personal jurisdiction,[6]

---

[3] A federal district court sitting in New York construed the Policy to mean that parties can commence an action in court "at any time," not limited as in Paragraph 4(k) "before [or] after such proceeding is concluded." *Broadbridge Media, LLC v. Hypercd.com*, 106 F.Supp.2d 505, 55 USPQ2d 1426 (S.D.N.Y. 2000). Since complainant establishes the mutual jurisdiction (Rules Definition and 3(b)(xii)) respondent cannot file an action in a district court of its address if complainant has elected the principal office of the Registrar. See *Green Jacket Auctions, Inc. v. Augusta Nat'l, Inc.* (S.D. Ga., April 26, 2018) (Action transferred to the United States District Court for the District of Arizona).

[4] Discussed below in "Suspending or Terminating, or Proceeding to a Decision" (Sec. 8.02-A).

[5] The Registrar Accreditation Agreement provides at 3.7.7.10: "For the adjudication of disputes concerning or arising from use of the Registered Name, the Registered Name Holder shall submit, *without prejudice to other potentially applicable jurisdictions*, to the jurisdiction of the courts (1) of the Registered Name Holder's domicile and (2) where Registrar is located" (emphasis added).

Rule 1 of the Rules of the Policy, Definitions: "Mutual Jurisdiction means a court jurisdiction at the location of *either* (a) the principal office of the Registrar (provided the domain name holder has submitted in its Registration Agreement to that jurisdiction for court adjudication of disputes concerning or arising from the use of the domain name) or (b) the domain name holder's address as shown for the registration of the domain name in Registrar's Whois database at the time the complaint is submitted to the Provider" (emphasis added).

There is a substantial body of case law on forum selection clauses: they are presumptively valid. "A party challenging a selection clause bears the heavy burden to show either that enforcement of the clause would be unjust, 'or that the clause was invalid.'" *Airfx.com v. Airfx LLC.* CV 11-01064 (D. Ariz. October 20, 2011).

[6] 28 U.S.C. §1391(b) Venue in General. A civil action may be brought in

or a jurisdiction authorized by the Anticybersquatting Consumer Protection Act (ACPA) for an *in rem* action, described further below.[7]

Paragraph 4(k) contemplates the direction of any challenge will be from the UDRP to courts of competent jurisdiction. However, there may be circumstances under which an adjudicated dispute will be arbitrated anew in a UDRP proceeding. The Panel in ***Gerolsteiner Brunnen GmbH*** concluded that "[o]n its face, the transfer of the disputed domain name to respondent (or an intermediate registrant) appears to have occurred contrary to [an] order [of the Regional Court of Koblenz, Germany]."[8] Respondent (transferee) denied he was the registrant of the domain name at the time judgment was entered and since his name corresponded to the domain name he had a right or legitimate interest in it.

The Panel rejected this contention and ordered the domain name transferred. It construed the term "dispute" as used in paragraph 4(k) "in the broad sense, of the dispute concerning the domain name . . . rather than the narrow sense, of the particular dispute as filed between complainant and Respondent." It explained that this "approach appears more consistent with the allowance in paragraph 4(k) of the dispute to be submitted to a court before there is a dispute filed under the Policy." This reasoning is also consistent with paragraph 8(a) of the Policy.[9]

---

(1) a judicial district in which any defendant resides, if all defendants are residents of the State in which the district is located;

(2) a judicial district in which a substantial part of the events or omissions giving rise to the claim occurred, or a substantial part of property that is the subject of the action is situated; or

(3) if there is no district in which an action may otherwise be brought as provided in this section, any judicial district in which any defendant is subject to the court's personal jurisdiction with respect to such action.

[7] 15 U.S.C. §1125(d)(2)(A). This provision has the effect of nullifying the mutual jurisdiction for foreign domain name holders who commence lawsuits in their domiciles. See *Mattel, Inc. v. Barbie-Club.com*, 310 F.3d 293, 303 (2nd Circ. 2002) ("[T]he ACPA's basic *in rem* jurisdictional grant … contemplates exclusively a judicial district within which the registrar or other domain-name authority is located. A plaintiff must initiate an in rem action by filing a complaint in that judicial district and no other." Although other circuits have not ruled on this question. See *Ezquest, Inc. V. Baorui*, 2:12-cv-730 (D. Utah, Central Division) (U.S. trademark owner, Chinese domain name holder. Injunction entered preventing registry from transferring domain names to a foreign registrar).

[8] ***Gerolsteiner Brunnen GmbH & Co., KG v. R4L Privacy Advocate / Gero Leon Steiner***, D2008-1450 (WIPO November 7, 2008) (<gerolsteiner.info>).

[9] "[Respondent] may not transfer your domain name registration to another holder.... We reserve the right to cancel any transfer of a domain name registration to another holder that is made in violation of this subparagraph." Cyberflight is discussed further in "Interfering with the Proceedings" (Sec. 5.01-B).

8.01-B

8.01-B Plenary Adjudication After an Adverse Decision

8.01-B.1

8.01-B.1 No Deference to UDRP Award

There is no provision under the UDRP for an administrative appeal,[10] but the aggrieved party has the express right (in contrast to typical commercial and consumer ADR proceedings in which awards are final and binding) to challenge an award *de novo* in a court of competent jurisdiction.[11]

Whichever party is the challenger, if the post-UDRP action is initiated under the ACPA, federal courts in the United States have held that 1) their "interpretation of [the ACPA] supplants a WIPO panel's interpretation of the UDRP"; 2) "because a UDRP decision is susceptible of being grounded on principles foreign or hostile to American law, the ACPA authorizes reversing a[n] [arbitration] panel decision if such a result is called for by application of the Lanham Act"[12]; 3) a UDRP hearing is not an "arbitration" as envisioned by the Federal Arbitration Act[13]; 4) the review

---

[10] The Nominet Dispute Resolution Service Policy, in contrast, has an appeal procedure for .uk domain names, but the U.K. has no statute comparable to the ACPA that provides a cause of action for a *de novo* challenge of the UDRP award. For losing parties under the .uk country code extension the "DRS and Procedure put in place a regime in which the question of abusive registration is one for, and only for, the Expert appointed under the DRS" (55). See *Toth v. Emirates and Nominet*, [2-12] EWHC 517 (Ch) (Mr. Justice Mann) in which the Court concluded that there is "[n]o room for parallel (or consecutive) court proceedings" (53).

In contrast to the UDRP Art.12 of the Uniform Rapid Suspension System (URS) provides for an administrative appeal. "Art. 12.6 The Providers' rules and procedures for appeals, other than those stated above, shall apply."

[11] In the United States, the Lanham Act of 1946, as amended, §1114 (Remedies), §1125(a) (false designation of origin), §1125(c) (Federal Trademark Dilution Act "FTDA") and §1125(d) ("ACPA").

For an action under the ACPA plaintiff does not have to be a citizen of the U.S. The parties in *The Heathmount A.E. Corp. v. Technodome.com*, 106 F.Supp.2d 860 (E.D. Virginia 2000) were both Canadian citizens. The defendant's only connection to the U.S. was that it had registered the domain name with Network Solutions, Inc., which is located in the Eastern District of Virginia.

There is no internal appeal under the self-administered country code policy for all French domain names (.FR, .RE, .WF, .PM and .YT) offered by Système de Résolution de Litiges (SYRELI) and administered by the French Association for Cooperative Internet Naming (AFNIC) but an aggrieved party can commence an action in a court of competent jurisdiction. See discussion on appeal to the Versailles Court of Appeal of three domain names from an AFNIC decision by Jane Seager at http://www.internationallawoffice.com/Newsletters/Intellectual-Property/France/Hogan-Lovells-International-LLP/Success-for-Saone-et-Loire.

[12] *Barcelona.com, supra.; Strong Coll. Students Moving, Inc. v. CHHJ Franchising*, CV-12-01156 (Ariz., May 15, 2013) ("[T]his Court will give no deference to the UDRP's ... findings.").

[13] *Parisi v. Netlearning, Inc.* 139 F. Supp. 2d 745 (E.D.Va. 2001) construing 9 U.S.C., §§ 1-14. Defendant, prevailing party in ***Netlearning, Inc. v. Dan Parisi***, FA 95471 (Forum October 16, 2000), moved to dismiss plaintiff's action on theory that the UDRP award was a final and binding

"must be de novo and independent of any WIPO panel conclusion"[14]; and 5) "the UDRP explicitly contemplates independent review in national courts."[15]

In electing a *de novo* review, the initiating party (particularly the respondent who is often the one less experienced in the legal culture) must be prepared for a burden vastly different from the UDRP.[16] U.S. federal courts and courts of other countries that have ruled on post-UDRP complaints have pointedly held they owe no deference to the UDRP decision.[17] The merits of parties' contentions are freshly weighed under national law. An argument initially made in Federal court for deference under the U.S. Federal Arbitration Act was rejected on the grounds that a UDRP decision is non-binding. Furthermore, as already discussed the circumstances that support a violation of the Policy and infringement under the ACPA are basically different in that the UDRP is a conjunctive model and the ACPA is a disjunctive model.

Good faith registration under a disjunctive model such as the ACPA is not a good defense against bad faith use.[18] Statistically, judicial challenges by losing

---

arbitration; motion denied. See also *Dluhos v. Strasberg*, 321 F.3d 365 (3rd Circ. 2003) (Respondent in ***CMG Worldwide, Inc. v. Eric Dluhos***, FA0005000094909 (Forum October 2, 2000) ("To shove Dluhos' square-peg UDRP proceeding into the round hole of the FAA would be to frustrate this aim, as judicial review of FAA-styled arbitration proceedings could be generously described only as extremely deferential.")

[14] *Parisi, Id.* at 752.

[15] *Sallen v. Corinthians Licenciamentos LTDA*, 273 F.3d 14, 20 (1st Cir. 2001), reversing the order in ***Corinthians Licenciamentos LTDA v. David Sallen, Sallen Enterprises, and J. D. Sallen Enterprises***, D2000-0461 (WIPO July 17, 2000) (<corinthians.com>).

[16] The financial consequences of cybersquatting under the ACPA can be substantial, up to $100,000—15 U.S.C. § 1117(d)— and significantly greater if the award includes damages for trademark infringement. Damages and attorney's fees have been assessed against both mark owners and domain name holders. In ***Nguyen v. Biondo***, 11-cv-81156 (S.D. Fla.) the District Court awarded damages in the amount of $850,000 plus another significant amount for attorney's fees and costs for trademark infringement and cybersquatting (aff'd 508 F. App'x 932 unpublished decision (11th Cir. 2013). The underlying premise of damages under the Lanham Act is the accused party's intentional and malicious acts of infringement. Section 1117(e) provides that "a violation . . . shall be a rebuttable presumption that the violation is willful for purposes of determining relief. . . ."

The ACPA does provide a safety net where "the court determines that the person believed and had reasonable grounds to believe that the use of the domain name was a fair use or otherwise lawful." 15 U.S.C. §1125 (d)(1)(B)(ii). However, "C]ourts should 'make use of this . . . defense very sparingly and only in the most unusual cases,'" *Lahoti v. VeriCheck, Inc.*, 586 F.3d 1190, 1203 (9th Cir. 2009) and 636 F.3rd 501 (9th Cir. 2011). See *Direct Niche, LLC v. Via Varejo S/A*, 15-cv-62344 (S.D. Fla., August 10, 2017) rejecting plaintiff's argument that it commenced the action in good faith. The court held that "[a]lthough Knight may subjectively believe that Direct Niche's use of the Casas Bahia Domain was lawful, the Court concludes that his belief is not objectively reasonable."

[17] *Barcelona.com, Inc., supra.* Summary judgment in favor of plaintiff, formerly Respondent in ***Excelentisimo Ayuntamiento de Barcelona v. Barcelona.com Inc.*** D2000-0505 (WIPO August 7, 2000).

complainants whose trademarks are well-known or famous are likely to succeed[19]; challenges by respondents domiciled in the U.S. against U.S. trademark owners are unlikely to succeed.[20] Challenges by domestic respondents against foreign complainants[21] have been successful where the disputed domain name is generic and use consistent with its semantic meaning.[22]

8.01-B.2 8.01-B.2 Award Contested by Complainant

A plaintiff/trademark owner able to satisfy venue requirements under the ACPA may contest an adverse award by commencing an *in personam* action if the domain name holder is amenable to service. However, there may be financial

---

Deference was also rejected by The Regional Court in Cologne in a case reversing the award in ***XM Satellite Radio Inc. v. Michael Bakker***, FA0612000861120 (Forum February 27, 2007): "In court proceedings under Paragraph 4(k) UDRP the national court shall only apply the relevant national law (e.g. trademark or unfair competition law). Whether the requirements stipulated by Paragraph 4(a) UDRP (on which the NAF Panel had based its decision) are satisfied or not is considered irrelevant." (Case no. 33 O 45/08, 16 June 2009, translation adr.eu.)

[18] 15 U.S.C. §1125(d)(1) "A person shall be liable in a civil action by the owner of a mark, including a personal name which is protected as a mark under this section, if, without regard to the goods or services of the parties, that person–

(i) has a bad faith intent to profit from that mark, including a personal name which is protected as a mark under this section; and

(ii) registers, traffics in, or uses a domain name [in proscribed ways]."

[19] ***Freebies Publishing v. Retail Services, Inc.***, FA0204000112565 (Forum July 15, 2002) (complaint granted). However, in the ACPA action judgment was entered in favor of Respondent, *Retail Services, INC. v. Freebies Publishing*, 364 F.3d 535, 542 (4th Cir. 2004): The "panelist's finding that the [use of a] meta-tag is evidence of plaintiff's opportunistic bad faith is directly contradicted by the evidence that the parties are not competitors"; *Volvo Trademark Holding AB v. Volvospares*, 1:09 cv 01247 (E.D. Va. Apr. 1, 2010) (unreported), summary judgment in favor of plaintiff, formerly Complainant, in ***Volvo Trademark Holding AB v. Volvospares / Keith White***, D2008-1860 (WIPO February 10, 2009).

[20] *Lahoti v. Vericheck*, 708 F.Supp.2d 1150 (W.D.WA, 2007), aff'd 586 F.3d 1190 (9th Cir. 2009) and 636 F.3rd 501 (9th Cir. 2011). UDRP decision reported at ***Vericheck, Inc. v. Admin Manager***, FA0606000734799 (Forum August 2, 2006) (website populated with links to Complainant's competitors); *Yung v. Bank of America Corp.* (S.D.N.Y. 2-16-2010), aff'd 448 F. App'x 95, 98 (2d Cir. 2011), contesting award in favor of Complainant in ***Bank of America Corporation and Merrill Lynch & Co., Inc. v. Webadviso,*** FA090300 1254121(Forum May 15, 2009) (District court awarded domain names to plaintiff, aff'd 448 F. App'x 95, 98 (2d Cir. 2011). See also ***Donald J. Trump v. Web adviso***, D2010- 2220 (WIPO March 5, 2011) and *Web-Adviso v. Trump*, 11-cv-1413 (E.D.N.Y March 7, 2013) for unsuccessful declaratory judgment action in which the district court rejected plaintiff's argument he had reasonable grounds to believe his conduct was lawful. The court awarded Trump damages in the amount of $32,000.); *Bulbs 4 E. Side, Inc. v. Ricks*, 199 F.Supp.3d 1151 (S.D. Tex., Houston Div. August 10, 2016). (Judgment included $50,000 and attorney's fees).

[21] *Sallen*, supra. and *Barcelona*, supra.

[22] *Sallen*, supra.

consequences if plaintiff is found liable for reverse domain name hijacking;[23] or, if plaintiff "is not able to obtain in personam jurisdiction over a person who would have been a defendant in a civil action under paragraph (1) [of the ACPA]"[24] it may contest the award in an *in rem* action against the domain name[25] in the location of the registry or domain name registrar.[26] A UDRP award dismissing the complaint and even finding reverse domain name hijacking does not prejudice a trademark owner's claim under the ACPA or other sections of the Lanham Act if the facts and law warrant a different result. A registrant is vulnerable to having its domain name forfeited if at any time it begins using the domain name in bad faith.[27]

---

[23] 15 U.S.C. §1117(d), "In a case involving a violation of section 1125 (d)(1) of this title, the plaintiff may elect, at any time before final judgment is rendered by the trial court, to recover, instead of actual damages and profits, an award of statutory damages in the amount of not less than $1,000 and not more than $100,000 per domain name, as the court considers just." In *Goforit Entertainment LLC v. Digimedia.com LP*, 750 F. Supp.2d 712 (N.D. Tex. October 25, 2010) the Court granted summary judgment in defendant's favor and awarded it statutory damages and attorney's fees in the combined amount of $103,717.66 (filed March 11, 2011).

[24] Id., at §1125(d) (2)(A)(ii)(i).

[25] *Id.* at §1125(d)(2)(A), "The owner of a mark may file an in rem civil action against a domain name in the judicial district in which the domain name registrar, domain name registry, or other domain name authority that registered or assigned the domain name is located. . . ."

An *in rem* action is authorized and service is complete when the plaintiff "(I) is not able to obtain in personam jurisdiction over a person who would have been a defendant in a civil action under paragraph (1); or (II) through due diligence was not able to find a person who would have been a defendant in a civil action under paragraph (1) by—(aa) sending a notice of the alleged violation and intent to proceed under this paragraph to the registrant of the domain name at the postal and e mail address provided by the registrant to the registrar; and (bb) publishing notice of the action as the court may direct promptly after filing the action."

[26] Id. The court has *in rem* jurisdiction regardless of respondent's and registrar's locations. In *Cable News Network v. Cnnews.com, Cable News Network v. CNNews.com*, 162 F.Supp.2d 484 (E.D.Va. September 18, 2001) the registrant and registrar were located in China, but the registry was located in Virginia (Domain name transferred by ordering Verisign to re-direct it to Plaintiff's account). The court in *Globalsantafe Corp. v. Globalsantafe.com*, 250 F.Supp.2d 610, 612 (E.D.Va. 2003) ruled that *in rem* jurisdiction was constitutionally proper when a court sits in the same district in which the registry is located. However, other district courts lack jurisdiction. *See Vizer v. Vizernews.com*, 11-00864 (District of Columbia, June 22, 2012) Plaintiff contended ICANN as a "domain name authority" satisfied the jurisdictional requirement. The court disagreed and dismissed the complaint. ICANN does not qualify because it is not a "domain name authority that registered or assigned the domain name."

[27] Award vacated under the Lanham Act for trademark infringement and cyberpiracy on default. *Dealerx v. Kahlon*, 2:17-cv-1444 (E.D. Cal., 2017) (previously ***DealerX v. Gurri Kahlon, RoiQ.com***, D2017-0488 (WIPO May 4, 2017) (<roiq.com>)). The Court held that "while the facts [Page 10] do not support a finding of bad faith in relation to defendant's initial acquisition of the 'roiq] domain name ... [however,] defendant did demonstrate bad faith upon learning of plaintiff's mark and attempting to improperly extract profit from plaintiff. Plaintiff has demonstrated defendant's

In ***General Media Communications***,[28] the UDRP Panel not only denied the complaint but also granted Respondent's application for a finding of reverse domain name hijacking. On challenge under the ACPA for partial summary judgment on the issue of reverse domain name hijacking the court held "GMCI did not initiate or pursue the UDRP proceeding or this action in bad faith and has not engaged in actual or attempted reverse domain name hijacking."[29] As a practical matter the order put an end to the lawsuit and any counterclaim to plaintiff's action.

8.01-B.3 8.01-B.3 Award Contested by Respondent

8.01-B.3.a 8.01-B.3.a *United States*

8.01-B.3.a.i 8.01-B.3.a.i ***Action Commenced for Relief under the ACPA***

As previously noted the ACPA is a symmetrical statute.[30] A losing domain name holder in a UDRP proceeding as a prevailing party in an ACPA action is entitled to injunctive relief and damages for establishing its right to the domain name as a mark owner would be if the situation were reversed.[31] The actionable claim in a challenge to a UDRP award in mark owner's favor is a species of fraud against the domain name holder. It is based on a "knowing and material misrepresentation" by a trademark owner that a domain name was registered in bad faith."[32] The court is not asked to decide whether the domain name infringes defendant's trademark

---

bad faith attempt to profit by submission of an e-mail chain between plaintiff and defendant showing defendant attempting to extract a high price from the plaintiff for purchase of the domain name.")

[28] ***General Media Communications, Inc. v. Crazy Troll c/o CrazyTroll.com.***, FA0602000651676 (Forum May 12, 2006, Order dated January 16, 2007).

[29] *General Media Communications, Inc. v. Crazy Troll c/o CrazyTroll.com*, 06 CIV 4051 (S.D.N.Y. 2006).

[30] 15 U.S.C. §1114(2)(D)(iv) and (v). Whichever party prevails registry and registrar have no liability to registrant "regardless of whether the domain name is finally determined to infringe or dilute the mark," §1114(2)(D)(iii).

[31] "[I]f a trademark owner 'overreaches' when exercising his ACPA rights, he 'reverse hijacks' the domain name from the person who registered it." *Barcelona.com*, supra.

[32] 15 U.S.C. §1114(D)(iv). "[T]he person making the knowing and material misrepresentation shall be liable for any damages, including costs and attorney's fees, incurred by the domain name registrant as a result of such action." See ***Beautiful People Magazine, Inc. v. Domain Manager / PeopleNetwork ApS / Kofod Nicolai / People Network Aps / Nicolai Kofod / People Network***, FA1502001606976 (Forum May 4, 2015) (<beautifulpeople.com>. Respondent had priority and prevailed; Complainant, now plaintiff commenced an ACPA, dismissed with an award of attorney's fees to defendant, *Joshua Domond and Harold Hunter, Jr v. PeopleNetwork APS d/b/a Beautifulpeople. Com, Beautiful People, LLC, Greg Hodge, and Genevieve Maylam*, 16-24026-civ (S.D. FL. Miami Div. 11/9/17). Also ***Corporacion Empresarial Altra S.L. v. Development Services, Telepathy, Inc.***, D2017-0178 (WIPO May 15, 2017) (<airzone.com>. The Panel denied the complaint but rejected

(assuming no counterclaim), but whether defendant materially misrepresented "that a domain name is identical to, confusingly similar to or dilutive of [its] mark."[33]

Arguing that trademark owner was "[m]erely defending [its] own trademark rights [in] bringing the successful UDRP action" does not shield it from an award of damages under the ACPA if the facts support a claim for reverse domain name hijacking.[34] However, where the trademark owner has prevailed on the facts and registrars located in foreign jurisdictions have "declined or ignored court orders to transfer registrations U.S. courts have ordered U.S. based registries to take possession of domain names, change the registrar of record and transfer them to prevailing trademark owners."[35]

If defendant (trademark owner or domain name holder residing in a foreign country) defaults in an ACPA action (and personal jurisdiction has not been obtained through The Hague Convention or other means) plaintiff's remedy is limited to declaratory and injunctive relief, but not damages or attorney's fees.[36] The

---

sanctioning Complainant. Respondent thereupon commenced an action under the ACPA for reverse domain name damages and defendant settled by stipulating to pay plaintiff $40,000 dollars.

[33] 15 U.S.C. §1114(D)(iv). See *iSystems v. Spark Network* (5th. Cir., 2011) ("The fact that [Plaintiff's] dating service was non-profit does not eliminate the possibility that ISystems earned revenue from the site due to its similarity to 'jdate.com.' ISystems' failure to allege any other facts showing lack of bad faith are fatal to its claim.")

[34] ACPA actions by losing respondents in UDRP proceedings: *Airfx.com v. Airfx LLC.* CV 11-01064 (D.Ariz. October 20, 2011) (An ACPA action by the domain name holder. The court held registration and renewal of the domain name was not unlawful. The issue of damages for reverse domain name hijacking was not before the court, but it invited an application.) In the earlier administrative proceeding in ***AirFX, LLC v. ATTN AIRFX.COM***, FA1104001384655 (Forum May 16, 2011) the Panel awarded <airfx.com> to the defendant.

Other ACPA actions commenced by Respondents that have been settled without any court decision include: *Hugedomains.com, LLC. v. Wills*, 14-cv-00946 (D. Colorado July 21, 2015) (***Austin Pain Associates v. Jeffrey Reberry***, FA1312001536356 (Forum March 18, 2014) (Defendant-trademark owner agreed to a consent judgment vacating the UDRP award and paying plaintiff $25,000); *Telepathy, Inc. v. SDT International SA-NV*, 14-cv-01912 (D. Columbia July 9, 2015) (***SDT International SA-NV v. Telepathy, Inc.***, D2014-1870 (WIPO January 13, 2015). Defendant-trademark owner agreed to a permanent injunction and $50,000).

[35] See *Virgin Enterprises Limited V. Enom, Inc.*, 08 Civ 0328 (S.D.N.Y. 7-17-2008) (referencing several other unreported cases in the Southern District of New York ordering change of registrars and transfers of VEL domain names), citing *AMERICA ONLINE, INC. v. AOL.ORG*, 259 F.Supp.2d 449, 457 (E.D.VA. 2003) ("In sum, the transfer order requested by plaintiff is clearly an authorized and available remedy under the ACPA. Furthermore, concerns of international comity do not counsel against issuing an order directing PIR to transfer the aol.org domain name to plaintiff as a remedy for the infringement of plaintiff's registered trademarks. To conclude otherwise would render the Lanham Act ineffective in an important commercial context, a result at odds with the Act's terms and purpose.")

[36] *Marchex Sales Inc. v. Tecnologia Bancaria S.A.*, 14-cv-01306 (E.D. VA, Alexandria Division June 15, 2015), challenging a UDRP award in favor of trademark owner, *Tecnologia Bancaria S.A. v.*

reason for this is that in agreeing to a mutual jurisdiction foreign trademark owners have not agreed to in personam jurisdiction. To construe the UDRP as "subject[ing] a party to anything more than a challenge to the panel's decision would be unfair and would be inconsistent with the due process clause of the U.S. Constitution."[37]

Proof of abusive conduct by the trademark owner in an ACPA action differs from that required under the UDRP. To state a claim for RDNH under UDRP a respondent must show complainant both knew of respondent's right or legitimate interest and commenced the proceeding with an intent to gain control of the domain name.

In contrast the ACPA requires plaintiff (or counterclaiming defendant) to prove four elements: (1) plaintiff is a domain name registrant; (2) plaintiff's domain name was "suspended, disabled, or transferred under a policy implemented by a registrar as defined in the Act"[38]; (3) the trademark owner who prompted the domain name to be transferred "has notice of the action"; and (4) plaintiff's use or registration of the domain name is not unlawful.[39]

8.01-B.3.a.ii

8.01-B.3.a.ii *Action Commenced in Foreign Jurisdictions to Frustrate Mark Owner's UDRP Remedy*

A losing respondent whose registrar and residence are in a national territory different from that of the trademark owner benefits by locating its challenge in a mutual jurisdiction which may be a foreign jurisdiction.[40] Such a move imposes a burden on the prevailing complainant. Unless a post-UDRP action challenging

---

Marchex Sales Inc., D2014-0834 (WIPO September 24, 2014) (<banco24 horas.com> and <banco-24horas.net>) (over a vigorous dissent).

[37] *Marchex*, Magistrate Judge's Proposed Findings of Fact and Recommendations, May 21, 2015.

[38] A UDRP decision to transfer the domain name "triggers the right to sue" for declaratory relief under the ACPA. *Mann v. AFN Invs., Ltd.* CV-07-0083 (S.D. Cal. July 27, 2007).

[39] A registrant must show its conduct was not unlawful under the ACPA, not under the whole of the Lanham Act. *Ricks v. BMEzine.com, LLC*, 727 F. Supp. 2d 936, 960 (D. Nev. 2010). Since courts pay no deference to a UDRP award, defendant (prevailing party in the UDRP proceeding) is unlikely to succeed in having the complaint dismissed on a pre-answer motion. See, for example, *Domain Name Vault LLC v. John C. Bush and EClinical Works LLC*, 14-cv-2621 (District of Colorado Apr. 15, 2015) (Domain Name Vault, Respondent in prior UDRP proceeding accused Defendant's lawyer, Bush of "falsely represent[ing] [to the UDRP Panel] that the eclinicalwork.com domain name was 'used to provide a mere parking page that links to Complainant's competitors.'") The court dismissed Bush out of the case but denied EClinical Works' Rule 12(b)(6) motion to dismiss the complaint as premature although in language that appears to forecast the ultimate result—"'a well-pleaded complaint may proceed even if it strikes a savvy judge that actual proof of those facts is improbable, and that a recovery is very remote and unlikely'" (citing *Bell Atl. Corp. v. Twombly*, 550 U.S. 544, 556 (2007).

[40] Policy, paragraph 3(b)(xii): "[Complainant must state that it] will submit, with respect to any challenges to a decision in the administrative proceeding canceling or transferring the domain

an award in a foreign jurisdiction is countered through legal procedures in complainant's home court[41] complainant can be put to substantial expense or lose the benefits it won in the administrative proceeding.

For U.S. parties challenging foreign domain name holders the ACPA can be a powerful tool to foil losing respondents' attempts to continue use of domain names where the registry is in the United States[42] regardless of the location of the registrar.[43] The ACPA gives a U.S. trademark owner some control over domain names that have been adjudicated in the UDRP proceeding without depriving respondent of its right to appear in opposition in a legal proceeding. In the cited cases respondents challenged the UDRP awards in courts in South Korea and China. In both cases the U.S. district courts entered orders that in effect nullified respondents' filed actions in their local courts by granting mandatory injunctions against the registries to prevent transfer or recapture transfers already made.

8.01-B.3.b *United Kingdom* *8.01-B.3.b*

There is no statutory mechanism in the United Kingdom comparable to the ACPA—which means, as already noted above in footnote 10, that paragraph 4(k) cannot be used to confer subject matter jurisdiction for a nonexistent cause of action. This preclusion applies equally to dot uk disputes as it does to UDRP disputes.[44] If respondent is ultimately found liable for bad faith registration or bad faith use following an appeal under the Nominet process (U.K. Domain Resolution Service)

---

name, to the jurisdiction of the courts in at least one specified Mutual Jurisdiction." The term "Mutual Jurisdiction" is defined in Rule 1 of the Rules of the Policy. See ***Draw Tite, Inc. v. Plattsburgh Spring Inc.***, D2000-0017 (WIPO March 14, 2000) for discussion of the Rule. The Panel states "Complainant's submission to a Mutual Jurisdiction benefits Respondent, not Complainant. . . . Complainant has provided Respondent with an additional forum where Respondent is amenable to suit. This additional forum is provided not by operation of law, but by contract between Complainant and the Center, and Respondent is a third party beneficiary of that contract."

[41] ***XM Satellite Radio***, supra.

[42] See *Continental Airlines, Inc. v. continentalairlines.com*, 390 F. Supp. 501 (E.D. Va. 2005) (Respondent commenced proceeding in South Korea; District Court ordered VeriSign, Inc., as registry of the domain names in issue to change the registrars of record for domain names <continentalairlines.com> and <continentalexpressairlines.com> to a registrar or registrars located in this country, so plaintiff may thereafter register the domain names in its own name.)

[43] *Ezquest, Inc. V. Baorui*, 2:12-cv-730 (D. Utah, Central Division) (***EZQUEST, INC. v. BAORUI***, FA1205001445631 (Forum July 12, 2012) (<ezq.com>).

[44] See *Toth v. Emirates*, supra, in which the court concluded that a ruling under the DRS is conclusive on the issue of abusive registration. The High Court extended this ruling in *Yoyo.email Limited v. Royal Bank of Scotland Group PLC and Others*, [2015] EWHC 3509 (Ch) to include UDRP awards. It held that "[P]roper construction of the UDRP clause 4k does not give rise to a separate cause of action in favour of the claimant [aggrieved domain name registrant]." The court further noted that

or award under the UDRP process, there is no further remedy it can pursue under UK law. This was made clear in the case cited in the footnote and others that for domain name holders the arbitration process is conclusive.[45]

In that earlier case the losing respondent (subsequently plaintiff in the civil action) claimed he intended to use the domain name as a criticism site. The WIPO Panel found the stated intention alone (that is, without evidence of "demonstrable preparations") could not lead to a finding respondent had a legitimate interest in the disputed domain name.[46] The landing page stated only the website would be used "in time" as "the focal point for people to share their bad experiences" in relation to complainant's services or products. Plaintiff offered no concrete evidence of his stated intention thereby failing to carry his burden under subsection 4(c)(iii) of the Policy.

The High Court reviewed plaintiff's causes of action including allegations that the UDRP award infringed his right to freedom of expression under Article 8 of the European Convention on Human Rights, defamation, malicious falsehood, and wrongful threats to sue for trademark infringement[47] and held that freedom of expression "is not an unqualified right." Rather, it "must be balanced against the rights of others, such as the rights of a minority not to suffer abuse or, as in this case, the rights of a trade mark owner freely to enjoy its own rights and property." The court concluded that plaintiff

> cannot accept that he is the aggressor, not the victim. He is not debarred from making legitimate criticisms of pharmaceutical companies nor from setting up proper criticism websites from which he and others might do so. Instead, he had chosen to usurp names and logos contrary to the UDRP policy.

The court dismissed plaintiff's complaint in its entirety as lacking merit.

"there is no practical utility in granting declaratory relief in this case because the UDRP scheme has dealt with the issue between the parties, because any declaration made by this Court could not alter the findings of the Panel and the effect of my conclusions on the application for summary judgment on the counterclaim render the claim otiose." "Otiose" most likely because the court held defendant prevailed on its trademark infringement counterclaim.

[45] *Patel v. Allos Therapeutics, Inc.*, [2008] EWHC 1730 (Ch) (Sonia Proudman QC).

[46] ***Allos Therapeutics, Inc. v. Kumar Patel***, D2007-0521 (WIPO June 11, 2007) (<allostherapeutics.com>). Patel has been an unsuccessful plaintiff in a prior court challenge in the U.K. as well as respondent in a number of WIPO and Forum cases. See ***Gilead Sciences, Inc. v. Kumar Patel***, D2005-0831 (WIPO November 17, 2005); ***Abbott Laboratories v. Kumar Patel***, FA 1740337 (Forum August 15, 2006).

[47] Compare *Oneida Tribe of Indians of Wisconsin v. Lester Harms d/b/aWorldShadow*, 05-c-0177 (E.D. Wisconsin 2005), dismissing counterclaim for defamation and retaliatory action in commencing a federal lawsuit following denial of its UDRP complaint, FA0408000318911 (Forum October 18, 2004). Filing a federal complaint to protect a trademark "cannot be said to be retaliatory or malicious; indeed, it is activity protected by the Noerr Pennington doctrine."

8.02 RULE 18 OF THE RULES OF THE POLICY 8.02

8.02-A Suspending or Terminating, or Proceeding to a Decision 8.02-A

Rule 18 has two parts.[48] If there is a pending court action or an action is commenced after a dispute has been submitted Panels have "the discretion to decide whether to suspend or terminate administrative proceedings."[49] In practice once a dispute is submitted to a UDRP Panel it will either be decided or terminated. Panels have ruled both ways; the consensus does not favor suspension. The dispute is more likely to proceed to a decision if the pending lawsuit does not touch on domain names.[50] It is less likely to proceed to a decision if the dispute raises issues outside the scope of the Policy.[51]

The decision to terminate or proceed to a decision should be carefully weighed.[52] One approach is to dismiss the proceedings without prejudice where there is a pending action likely to affect rights to the domain name.[53] Another approach

---

[48] The two subparagraphs of the Rule read in full:

(a) In the event of any legal proceedings initiated prior to or during an administrative proceeding in respect of a domain name dispute that is the subject of the complaint, the Panel shall have the discretion to decide whether to suspend or terminate the administrative proceeding, or to proceed to a decision.

(b) In the event that a Party initiates any legal proceedings during the pendency of an administrative proceeding in respect of a domain-name dispute that is the subject of the complaint, it shall promptly notify the Panel and the Provider.

[49] The Panel's decision may be influenced by parties' responses, if any, to any court proceedings. Rule 3(xi) (Complainant) and 5(vi)(Respondent) are mirror images of each other. Both Rules contain the following sentence: "identify any other legal proceedings that have been commenced or terminated in connection with or relating to any of the domain name(s) that are the subject of the complaint."

[50] ***W. Fla. Lighting v. Ramirez***, D2008-1122 (WIPO Oct. 2, 2008) (deciding to proceed under the UDRP despite concurrent court proceedings because "This administrative proceeding under the Policy concerns only control of the Domain Name, not any of the other remedies at issue in the federal litigation.")

[51] ***SDT International limited company v. Telepathy, Inc.***, D2014-1870 (WIPO January 13, 2015 ("While it is true that in circumstances where there are concurrent court proceedings, a panel has a discretion to terminate or suspend, in my view that discretion should only be exercised where for some reason there is a difficulty in the panel coming to a decision under the terms of the Policy, e.g., because there are conflicts of fact which cannot easily be resolved without the benefits of discovery, cross- examination etc. In my view the merits of the case are clear on the face of the Complaint.")

[52] ***DNA (Housemarks) Limited v. Tucows.com Co.***, D2009-0367 (WIPO May 5, 2009) ("Each Rule 18 application mandates a panel's scrutiny to detect, if possible, any such [gaming] activity. After careful examination of the facts and circumstances in this proceeding and the Declaratory Judgment Action filed by Respondent, this Panel believes that nothing untoward has been demonstrated on the record before it.")

[53] ***Lutton Invs., Inc. v. Darkhorse Distrib., Inc.***, FA 154142 (Forum June 4, 2003) ("[A] Panel decision on the merits (whether ordering transfer or denying the Complaint) will not advance final

is to proceed under the UDRP despite concurrent court proceedings because "the Panel does not find that it is necessary or advantageous to await a judicial determination of the issues raised in the federal litigation in order to reach a decision strictly under the Policy."[54] In the view of another Panel "Policy paragraph 4(k) requires that ICANN not implement an administrative panel's decision regarding a UDRP dispute until the court proceeding is resolved."[55] Removing a dispute to a court of law cannot be regarded as forum shopping since it is respondent's right to seek a judicial determination of the issue.[56]

A pattern has formed based on the nature of the civil action, the timing of its commencement, and the identity of the named parties.[57] An administrative proceeding is properly terminated and complaint dismissed when respondent has timely acted to bring the dispute to a court of competent jurisdiction.[58] When respondent is found to be manipulating the facts, its motion to terminate the proceedings will be denied.[59] The Panel will retain jurisdiction (further noted below) if it appears the dispute properly belongs in an administrative proceeding. The phrase "'in respect of a domain name dispute' . . . cannot be that mere reference to litigation on a website somehow makes the domain name at which the website is hosted the subject of the

---

resolution of that question by even one hour, assuming that Respondent continues to pursue its Declaratory Judgement Action, and the Registrar refuses to implement the Panel's decision on that basis.") See also ***Holley Performance Products, Inc. v. Tucows.com Co.***, FA1007001333239 (Forum August 19, 2010) (same Panel as ***Lutton Invs.***); ***Salba Corp. N.A., William A. Ralston and Richard L. Ralston v. X Factor Holdings, LLC***, FA1205001443427 (Forum June 25, 2012) (Dismissed without prejudice). Discussed further in "Refiling a Complaint: New Facts or Fresh Evidence" (Sec. 7.01-B).

54 ***W. Fla. Lighting v. Ramirez***, D2008-1122 (WIPO October 2, 2008).

55 ***AmeriPlan Corp. v. Gilbert***, FA105737 (Forum April 22, 2002) ("Rendering a decision on the merits when there is already a court action pending does violence to the one function of the UDRP—to reduce the cost and effort required to resolve domain name disputes issues by offering a simplified mechanism in lieu of litigation." To the same effect, ***The Grief Recovery Institute, LLC and The Grief Recovery Institute Educational Foundation, Inc. v. Grief Recovery Institute***, FA120900 1462781 (Forum January 8, 2013). Discussed further in "Complaint Dismissed With and Without Prejudice" (Sec. 7.01-B.3).

56 ***DNA (Housemarks)*** supra. See *Tucows.com Co. v. Lojas Renner, S.A.*, 106 O.R. (3d) 561, 211 ONCA 548 (Court of Appeal for Ontario, August 5, 2011) (Footnote 9: "[P]reemptive litigation limited to entitlement to the disputed domain name simply accelerates Respondent's right, granted under the Policy, to a judicial determination of the issue.")

57 ***BluMarble, LLC v. Steve Cherry / GENERAL DELIVERY***, FA1406001562590 (Forum July 8, 2014) ("Complainant makes no mention of the pending proceedings in its Complaint, but its Additional Submission contends it is not a party to that litigation. Respondent does not dispute that fact and no court document provided indicates that Complainant is a party to any such litigation.")

58 See ***The United States Olympic Committee (USOC) and Chicago 2016 v. Steve Frayne***, D2008-1079 (WIPO September 25, 2008) (<chicago2016.com>), terminated after commencement of *Frayne v. The United States Olympic Committee*, (N.D. IL, September 17, 2008). In ***E. Remy Martin & C° v. Whois Privacy Services Pty Ltd/ Emedia Development Ltd and Mr. Pepin***, D2013-1984

litigation."[60] However, allegations of tortious conduct and statutory infringement belong in a court of law.[61]

Cancellation proceedings before the Trademark Trial and Appeal Board of the United States Patent and Trademark Office have been found to constitute a legal action that supports termination of proceedings,[62] but not when respondent is a competitor.[63] Legal proceedings that do not qualify for UDRP termination include unsuccessful pre-arbitration applications in national courts to stay proceedings,[64] unsupported allegations referring to a pending action in a national court,[65] or lawsuits for copyright infringement and injunction that do not seek transfer of disputed domain names.[66] Subparagraph (b) requires the parties to give the Panel notice upon initiation of a legal proceeding.[67]

(WIPO February 3, 2014) Respondent refused to translate a German court document but the civil proceedings had been commenced timely. The Panel was also influenced by the fact the Registrar had confirmed to Respondent it would not transfer the domain name to the Complainant until the conclusion of the legal proceedings.

[59] ***Shandong Lingong Construction Machinery Co., Ltd. v. Stanley Pace and Whois Privacy Service Pty Ltd.***, D2012-1626 (WIPO November 12, 2012).

[60] ***Telstra Corporation Limited v. Sean Mullen, Network Administrator***, D2010-0724 (WIPO June 15, 2010).

[61] ***Proskauer Rose LLP v. Leslie Turner***, D2011-0675 (WIPO June 30, 2011) ("The Panel unanimously believes that this is not a clear case of cyber squatting which the Policy was designed to address. Rather, this looks like a protracted and contentious dispute among numerous parties, several of whom are not before the Panel in this proceeding that has spilled into the arena of Internet domain names. All parties are free to pursue their respective positions and interests in other fora better suited to consider evidence and grant appropriate relief.")

[62] ***Family Watchdog LLC v. Lester Schweiss***, D2008-0183 (WIPO April 23, 2008) (The Panel analogized the TTAB proceeding to a pending lawsuit and denied the complaint.) The reverse situation, Complainant's challenge to Respondent's application for a trademark, is not grounds for suspending a UDRP proceeding. ***Debbie Morgan Macao Commercial Offshore Limited, Missguided Limited v. Samir Voru***, D2013-0737 (WIPO June 14, 2013).

[63] ***Private Communities Registry, Inc. v. Himalaya Rankings LLC and John Sweeney***, FA0808001220432 (Forum October 23, 2008) (<usprivate communities.com> and PRIVATE COMMUNITIES. "Respondent has asserted the defense of genericness, which might have been persuasive if the parties were not competitors and if Respondent had demonstrated no knowledge of Complainant prior to registering the Domain Names. . . . Respondent could have chosen many different names for its website but, as Complainant has stated, Respondent was 'trying to ride on [Complainant's] coattails.'")

[64] ***Sonido, Inc. v. MU21C.COM Inc.***, D2006-0685 (WIPO September 6, 2006) (Respondent had applied for a stay, which the court denied, and in the UDRP proceeding requested that the complaint be dismissed, which the Panel rejected).

[65] ***Allstate Insurance Company v. Aardvark (a/k/a Joseph Bologna, John Day, Paul Day, Jay Arby, Jay Bologna), and d/b/a Aardvark Internet Services, Allstate Information Exchange, Inc., Allstate.org, Inc., and Professional Publications***, D2001-1346 (WIPO March 14, 2002) ("[T]he Panel believes that in the interest of efficiency it should proceed to a decision.")

The Rule presupposes that a motion to suspend or terminate the administrative proceeding will be filed by respondent. It would make no logical sense for a complainant to commence a legal proceeding on top of its UDRP complaint for the same relief. For complainant to take such a step calls into question its certification that the complaint "is not being presented for any improper purpose, such as to harass [respondent]."[68]

The Panel in the case cited in the footnote held "Complainant's conduct [was] deserving of public censure" for filing a "Complaint [to transfer <visibli.com> that] appears to be an unnecessary waste of legal resources, designed to put unnecessary pressure on the Respondent." When the issue is already before a national court it would be a waste of legal resources for the Panel to render a decision.[69] "No purpose is served by our rendering a decision on the merits to transfer the domain name, or have it remain, when as here, a decision regarding the domain name will have no practical consequence."[70]

8.02-B 8.02-B Retaining Jurisdiction over Dispute

The general rule is an arbitration should proceed if "the record is sufficiently developed to reach a conclusion under the Policy and [the decision will] not . . . interfere with either part[y's] claims in court."[71] It is not sufficient reason to terminate an administrative proceeding where a pending lawsuit concerns issues unrelated

---

66 ***Union Square Partnership, Inc., Union Square Partnership District Management Association, Inc. v. unionsquarepartnership.com Private Registrant and union squarepartnership.org Private Registrant***, D2008-1234 (WIPO October 22, 2008).

67 See also Rule 3(vi) [directed only to respondent]: "identify any other legal proceedings that have been commenced or terminated in connection with or relating to any of the domain name(s) that are the subject of the complaint."

68 ***Visible Technologies, Inc. v. Visibli Inc.***, D2012-0904 (WIPO June 15, 2012). See also ***Innovative Merchant Solutions, LLC v. S and S Bankcard Systems***, FA0204000109721 (Forum June 4, 2002) (Terminated, and Panel declared reverse domain name hijacking.)

69 ***Paul McMann v. J McEachern***, D2007-1597 (WIPO February 9, 2008) (Pending action in Massachusetts state court) and ***Jason Crouch and Virginia McNeill v. Clement Stein***, D2005-1201 (WIPO January 31, 2006) (Pending action in California state court) were dismissed at the Respondent's requests.

70 ***AmeriPlan Corp. id., v. Shane Gilbert d/b/a NewWave Solutions. Inc.***, FA 105737 (Forum April 22, 2002).

71 ***Western Holdings, LLC v. JPC Enterprise, LLC d/b/a Cutting Edge Fitness and d/b/a Strivectin SD Sales & Distribution***, D2004-0426 (WIPO August 5, 2004) ("doing so does not prevent either party, if dissatisfied with the result, from continuing to seek relief in court"), citing ***Weber-Stephen Products Co. v. Armitage Hardware***, D2000-0187 (WIPO May 11, 2000); ***Cognigen Networks, Inc. v. Pharmaceutical Outcomes Research a/k/a Cognigen Corporation***, D2001-1094 WIPO December 18 2001); ***AB SKF and SKF Beaings India Limited v. Vikas Pagaria***, D2001-0867 (WIPO October 11, 2001); and ***Fadesa Inmobiliaria, S.A. v. Flemming Madsen***, D2001-0570 (WIPO June 6, 2001).

to the disputed domain names,[72] and the UDRP claim is limited to control over the domain name.[73] The Panel in ***Donvand*** "decided to proceed to a decision because the Turkish court proceedings involve[d] complainant's Turkish registered trademarks, whereas the Panel is able to determine this proceeding without reference to those marks (which were registered after the disputed domain names) and because the issue of infringement does not arise in this proceeding."

It is also appropriate to retain jurisdiction where the Panel concludes that the filing is timed to delay determination of the dispute[74]; where complainant seeks to enforce a judgment from a court of law involving a different domain name against the same respondent[75]; where the issues raised in a legal proceeding do not directly touch on disposition of the disputed domain name[76]; where the complaint was filed in a court that did not commonly adjudicate intellectual property issues[77]; where the filing of the complaint is done in accordance with a court order that referred the matter to arbitration under the Policy despite pendency of the action[78]; where

---

[72] ***Donvand Limited trading as Gullivers Travel Associates v. Gullivers Travel/Gulliver's Travel Services, Gullivers Travel Agency and Metin Altun/GTA***, D2004-0741 (WIPO December 16, 2004) concerned trademark right and different domain names; ***Union Square Partnership, Inc., Union Square Partnership District Management Association, Inc. v. unionsquarepartnership.com Private Registrant and unionsquarepartnership.org Private Registrant***, D2008-1234 (WIPO October 22, 2008): "While this action is based upon the content of Respondent's website at the disputed domain names, Complainant asserts only claims for copyright infringement, seeking money damages and an injunction, among other things; it does not seek transfer of the disputed domain names."

[73] ***Marker Völkl (International) GmbH v. Tucows.com Co.***, D2012-1461 (WIPO November 14, 2012) (<marker.com>. "While the Respondent is clearly entitled to bring this dispute before the Ontario Court, in the Panel's opinion it is nevertheless appropriate for a decision to be made under the Policy." Vanity e-mail, but on filing date of the complaint the domain name was also being used for click-through revenue. "As to use of the disputed domain name to generate click through revenue, the Respondent's case is that it has purged any such misuse by suspending the advertising complained of. . . . That does not, however, in the Panel's view alter the nature of the use current at the date of the Complaint in this administrative proceeding.")

[74] ***Sanofi-aventis v. Milton R. Benjamin***, D2005-0544 (WIPO August 12, 2005). The Panel ordered the domain name transferred but the parties settled the federal action, *Medical Week News, Inc. and Milton R. Benjamin v. Sanofi-Aventis Group and Sanofi-Synthelab Inc.* (N.D. CA) by an agreement permitting Respondent to use the domain name.

[75] In ***MLP Finanzdienstleistungen AG v. WhoisGuard Protected***, D2008-0987 (WIPO September 10, 2008) (<mlpwatchblog.com>. Respondent denied it was defendant in the Oberlandesgericht Hamburg judgment, and, in any event, the case was concerned with a different, albeit similar, domain name and adjudicated a right of personality rather than a trademark right.)

[76] ***eProperty Direct LLC v. Miller***, FA 836419 (Forum January 3, 2007) (legal proceedings concluded); Western Florida Lighting v. Ramirez, D2008-1122 (WIPO October 2, 2008) (deciding to proceed under the UDRP despite concurrent court proceedings because "the Panel does not find that it is necessary or advantageous to await a judicial determination of the issues raised in the federal litigation in order to reach a decision strictly under the Policy.")

[77] ***Mary's Futons, Inc. v. Tex. Int'l Prop. Assocs.***, FA 1012059 (Forum August 13, 2007).

respondent, not a party to a prior lawsuit, argues estoppel[79]; where the complaint is filed in a court to which complainant has not submitted to jurisdiction[80]; and where there is persuasive evidence of bad faith registration and bad faith use.[81]

The Panel in ***Marker*** "believes that a failure by the Panel to address the merits of the case . . . would serve to frustrate the intended effect of the Policy, to which the Respondent as domain name registrant has submitted on its part." It based its decision on the documentary fact that as of the filing of the complaint Respondent was using the domain name "to generate click-through revenue."

---

[78] ***BD Real Hoteles, SA de C.V. v. Media Insights aka Media Insight***, D2009-0958 (WIPO September 15, 2009).

[79] ***The Carat Club Sdn. Bhd. v. Guangzhou Mickey Weinstock & Co. Diamonds Manufacturing Ltd.***, D2009-0052 (WIPO May 4, 2009).

[80] ***Shandong Lingong Construction Machinery Co., Ltd. v. Stanley Pace and Whois Privacy Service Pty Ltd.***, D2012-1626 (WIPO November 12, 2012).

[81] ***Vanity Shop of Grand Forks, Inc. V. Vanity.com, Inc.***, FA1205001443435 (Forum June 20, 2012); ***Marker Völkl (International) GmbH***, supra. ("While the Respondent is clearly entitled to bring this dispute before the Ontario Court, in the Panel's opinion it is nevertheless appropriate for a decision to be made under the Policy. The thrust of the Respondent's court case appears to be to obtain support under national law of the registrations it offers in its vanity email program. But, as noted, this Decision is based on what this Panel believes to be the Respondent's bad faith use of the disputed domain name to generate click through revenue.")

Appendices

APPENDIX A
BASIC DOCUMENTS ACCESSIBLE ON THE INTERNET

1. The Final Report of the WIPO Internet Domain Name Process, subtitled "The Management of Internet Names and Addresses: Intellectual Property Issues" (April 30, 1999) (http://www.wipo.int/amc/en/processes/process1/report/finalreport.html).
2. Report of the Second WIPO Internet Domain Name Process: Recognition of Rights and the Use of Names in the Internet Domain Name System, dated September 3, 2001 (http://www.wipo.int/amc/en/processes/process1/report/finalreport.html).
3. ICANN Second Staff Report (October 24, 1999) (Implementation document) (http://www.icann.org/udrp/udrp-second-staff-report-24oct99.htm).
4. The Uniform Domain Name Dispute Resolution Policy (http://www.icann.org/en/dndr/udrp/policy.htm).
5. The Rules of the Uniform Domain Name Dispute Resolution Policy (http://www.wipo.int/amc/en/domains/rules/supplemental/index.html).
6. Supplemental Rules, World Intellectual Property Organization (http://www.wipo.int /amc /en/domains/rules/supplemental/index.html).
7. Supplemental Rules, National Arbitration Forum (http://domains.adrforum.com /main.aspx?itemid'631&hideBar'False&navid'237&news=26).
8. ICANN Registrar Accreditation Agreement (http://www.icann.org/en/ registrars/ ra-agreement-21may09-en.htm).
9. WIPO Overview of WIPO Panel Views on Selected UDRP Questions, Third Edition (http://www.wipo.int/amc/en/domains/search/overview3.0/).

   WIPO Overview, Original Edition, http://www.wipo.int/amc/en/domains/search/ oldoverview/

   WIPO Overview, Second Edition, http://www.wipo.int/amc/en/domains/search/overview2.0.
10. WIPO Decisions (http://www.wipo.int/amc/en/domains/decisionsx/index.html).
11. WIPO Decisions by Year, http://www.wipo.int/amc/en/domains/decisionsx/index-gtld.html.
12. Forum (formerly known as the National Arbitration Forum) Decisions (http://domains.adrforum.com/decision. aspx).
13. eResolution Decisions (http://www.disputes.org/index.htm).
14. Arbitration Center for ".eu" disputes, 'http://www.arbcourt.cz/adreu/'Decisions (http://www.arbcourt.cz/adreu/).

15. Consolidated Search of all Providers, www.udrpsearch.com, UDRP.tools.
16. WIPO ccTLD Database (http://arbiter.wipo.int/domains/cctld_db/index.html).
17. WIPO Statistics, http://www.wipo.int/amc/en/domains/statistics/; see also DNDisputes.com for WIPO decisions.
18. Australia (.au Domain Authority, Ltd. (auDA)), http://www.auda.org.au/policies/current-policies/2010-05/
19. Canada Internet Registration Authority (CIRA), http://www.cira.ca/assets/Documents/Legal/Dispute/CDRPpolicy.pdf
20. New Zealand (nzDomain Name Commission), http://dnc.org.nz/story/policy
21. United Kingdom Domain Name Resolution Services (ukDRS), http://www.nominet.org.uk/disputes/when-use-drs/policy-and-procedure/drs-policy

A consolidated database of decisions from all service providers is available at <www.udrpsearch.com>.

HOT LINKS TO THESE DOCUMENTS ARE AVAILABLE AT <WWW.LEGALCORNERPRESS.COM/LINKS>

APPENDIX B
CHALLENGES TO UDRP AWARDS, DIRECT ACTION FOR CLAIMS OF CYBERSQUATTING, AND OTHER DISPUTES RELATING TO DOMAIN NAME CHALLENGES[1]

---

[1] Many of the decisions referred to below can be found on Google or Google Scholar. Selected list of court challenges and decisions to UDRP awards are also collected by WIPO in Select UDRP-related Court Cases, at http://www.wipo.int/amc/en/domains/challenged/

A. Domain Name Holder (as Plaintiff)

A(i) *UDRP Award Vacated*

Airfx.com v. Airfx LLC., CV 11-01064 (D.Ariz. October 20, 2011) (Respondent in ***Airfx, LLC v. Attn Airfx.com***, FA1104001384655 (Forum May 16, 2011) (Court held registration and renewal of the domain name was not unlawful and blocked defendant's appeal for failure to post a supersedeas bond to cover attorneys fees of $103,972.50).

Barcelona.com, Inc. v. Excelentisimo Ayuntamiento De Barcelona, 330 F.3d 617, 626 (4th Cir. 2003) (Respondent in ***Excelentisimo Ayuntamiento de Barcelona v. Barcelona.com Inc.***, D2000-0505 (WIPO August 7, 2000) (District Court Judgment reversed and remanded with instructions).

Mann v. AFN Invs., Ltd., CV-07-0083 (S.D. Cal. July 27, 2007) (Question whether Court has jurisdiction when the domain name has not been transferred. Answer: A UDRP decision to transfer the domain name "triggers the right to sue" for declaratory relief under the ACPA).

Marchex Sales Inc. v. Tecnologia Bancaria S.A., 14-cv-01306 (E.D. VA, Alexandria Division June 15, 2015) (Respondent in ***Tecnologia Bancaria S.A. v. Marchex Sales Inc.***, D2014-0834 (WIPO September 24, 2014) (UDRP award vacated on default. Since this was an *in rem* action, the ACPA remedy is limited to declaratory judgment. Magistrate Judge: "[To construe the UDRP as] subject[ing] a party to anything more than a challenge to the panel's decision would be unfair and would be inconsistent with the due process clause of the U.S. Constitution.")

Neon Network, LLC v. Aspis Liv Försäkrings, No. CV-08-1188-PHX-DGC (USDC Arizona July 22, 2009). The dissenting member inA***spis Liv Försäkrings AB v. Neon Network, LLC***, D2008-0387 (WIPO June 2, 2008) (<aspis.com>) believed that "respondent has been improperly deprived of the Domain Name, in violation of his or its U.S. Constitutional rights of free speech, and feels that if this case were brought in virtually any court in the U.S., the result would be different."

Defendant defaulted and the Court granted a default judgment declaring that the registration and use of the domain name was not unlawful.

Retail Services, INC. v. Freebies Publishing, 364 F.3d 535, 542 (4th Cir. 2004) (Respondent in ***Freebies Publishing v. Retail Services, Inc.***, FA0204000112565 (Forum July 15, 2002) (The "panelist's finding that the [use of a] meta-tag is evidence of plaintiff's opportunistic bad faith is directly contradicted by the evidence that the parties are not competitors"

Sallen v. Corinthians Licenciamentos LTDA, 273 F.3d 14, 20 (1st Cir. 2001) (Respondent in ***Corinthians Licenciamentos LTDA v. David Sallen, Sallen Enterprises, and J. D. Sallen Enterprises***, D2000-0461 (WIPO July 17, 2000) (Case of first impression; district court dismissed the action for lack of subject matter jurisdiction; reversed and remanded. District court does have jurisdiction under the ACPA).

Walter v. Ville de Paris, 4:2009cv03939 (S.D. Texas Houston Div.) (<parvi.org>. Respondent in ***Ville de Paris v. Jeff Walter***, D2009-1278 (WIPO November 19, 2009. UDRP award vacated on default; judgement included award of damages in the amount of $100,000).

A(ii) *UDRP Award Confirmed*

Int'l Bancorp, LLC v. Société des Bains de Mer et du Cercle des Étrangers à Monaco, 329 F.3d 359 (4th Cir., 2003) (Respondent in five UDRPs, D2000-1323, D2000-1326, D2000-1327, D2000-1328, and D2000-1315 (WIPO 2000) (Unregistered mark: "[T]he Lanham Act extends protection to marks that meet the statutory requirements for being 'used in commerce,' provided they also enjoy secondary meaning." Defendants satisfied that requirement).

iSystems v. Spark Network, 3:08-cv-1175-N (N.D. TX, Dallas Div. September 19, 2014) (Unreported) (Respondent in ***Spark Networks PLC v. J2DATE, Inc.***, FA0505000482640 (Forum June 28, 2005) (Unreported: "[T]he NAF arbitration award was not based on any misrepresentation that the JDate Domain was dilutive of the JDATE Mark, but rather on the true representation that the JDate Domain was identical to, or confusingly similar to, the JDATE Mark," Paragraph 10 Conclusions of Law).

Lahoti v. VeriCheck, Inc., 708 F.Supp.2d 1150 (WDWA, 2007), aff'd 586 F.3d 1190, 1203 (9th Cir. 2009) and 636 F.3rd 501 (9th Cir. 2011) (Respondent in ***Vericheck, Inc. v. Admin Manager***, FA0606000734799 (Forum August 2, 2006) (Affirmed, with damages and attorney's fees).

Ricks v. BMEzine.com, LLC, 727 F. Supp. 2d 936, 960 (D. Nev. 2010) (Respondent in ***BMEzine.com, LLC. v. Gregory Ricks / Gee Whiz Domains Privacy Service***, D2008-0882 (WIPO August 21, 2008) (Motion for partial summary judgment denied, but good faith registration of domain name that postdates first use of trademark in commerce under U.S. law does not protect a registrant who subsequently uses the domain name in bad faith.)

Scott Stephens v. Trump Organization LLC., 205 F.Supp.3d 305 (2016) (Respondent in ***Donald J. Trump v. Scott Stephens***, D2015-0478 (WIPO May 8, 2015) ("It is inconceivable that Stephens could, as the silence of his papers emphasizes, plead any facts that would entitle him to co-opt the Trump name.")

Texas International Property Associates v. Hoerbiger Holding AG, 624 F.Supp.2d 582 (N.D. Tex 2009) (Respondent in ***Hoerbiger Holding AG v. Texas International Property Associates***, D2007-0943 (WIPO October 19, 2007) ("[W]hen WIPO ruled that TIPA should transfer the domain name to Hoerbiger, TIPA refused to comply, instead protracting the issue by bringing this dispute. TIPA's claim on summary judgment that it intended to use horbiger.com as a surname belies the factual record herein.")

Virtual Point v. Hedera, 13-CV-5690 (N.D.Cal. 4-29-2014) (Respondent in ***Hedera AB v. Support Desk, Captive Media***, D2013-2102 (WIPO January 24, 2014) (UDRP complainant, a Swedish corporation whose U.S. attorney claimed she was not authorized to accept service. Plaintiff moved for an order to make alternative service but failed to comply with the form of service authorized by the Hague Convention: "Virtual cannot merely leapfrog over ... means authorized by the Hague Convention or other usual methods deemed to be 'reasonably calculated to give notice,' as stated in Rule [FRCP] 4(f)(1) and (2), without a sufficient reason to do so.")

Web-Adviso v. Trump, 927 F.Supp.2d 32 (E.D.N.Y., 2013) (Respondent in ***Donald J. Trump v. Web-adviso***, D2010-2220 (WIPO March 5, 2011) (Confirmed with damages in the amount of $32,000).

Yoyo.email Limited v. Royal Bank of Scotland Group PLC and Others, [2015] EWHC 3509 (Ch) (Respondent in ***Bank of Scotland Plc v. GYoyo Email / Yoyo. Email Limited***, D2015-1079 (WIPO August 25, 2015) (Chancery rejected for lack of subject matter jurisdiction).

Yung v. Bank of America Corp. 1:2009cv05769 (S.D.N.Y. 2-16-2010), aff'd 448 F. App'x 95, 98 (2d Cir. 2011) (Respondent in ***Bank of America Corporation and Merrill Lynch & Co., Inc. v. Webadviso***, FA090300 1254121(Forum May 15, 2009).

B. Domain Name Holders Defendant

B(i) *UDRP Award Vacated (in favor of Trademark Owner)*

Bulbs 4 E. Side, Inc. v. Ricks, 199 F.Supp.3d 1151 (S.D. Tex., Houston Div. August 10, 2016) (Complainant in ***Bulbs 4 East Side Inc., d/b/a Just Bulbs v. Fundacion Private Whois/ Gregory Ricks***, D2013-1779 (WIPO January 13, 2014) (Vacated with $50,000 and attorney's fees)).

Dealerx v. Kahlon, 2:17-cv-1444 (E.D. Cal., 2017) (Complainant in ***DealerX v. Gurri Kahlon, RoiQ.com***, D2017-0488 (WIPO May 4, 2017). Court held that "while the facts [Page 10] do not support a finding of bad faith in relation to defendant's initial acquisition of the 'roiq] domain name ... [however,] defendant did demonstrate bad faith upon learning of plaintiff's mark and attempting to improperly extract profit from plaintiff. Plaintiff has demonstrated defendant's bad faith attempt to profit by submission of an e-mail chain between plaintiff and defendant showing defendant attempting to extract a high price from the plaintiff for purchase of the domain name.")

Nike, Inc. v. Circle Group Internet, Inc., 318 F.Supp.2d 688 (N.D. Ill. May 21 2004) (Complainant in ***Nike, Inc. v. Circle Group Internet, Inc.***, D2002-0544 (WIPO September 10, 2002) (<justdoit.com>) ("Significantly, defendant has failed to produce any further evidence, documentary or testimonial, other than Mr. Halpern's self-serving testimony, that Halpern used the phrase 'just do it' prior to using it on its website. Without more, the court deems Halpern's representation insufficient to create a genuine issue of material fact regarding his use of, and defendant's connection to, the phrase 'just do it.'")

Volvo Trademark Holding AB v. Volvospares, 703 F.Supp.2d 563 (E.D. Va. Apr. 1, 2010) (unreported) (Complainant in ***Volvo Trademark Holding AB v. Volvospares / Keith White***, D2008-1860 (WIPO February 10, 2009).

B(ii) *UDRP Award Confirmed in favor of Trademark Owner*

Direct Niche, LLC v. Via Varejo S/A, 15-cv-62344 (S.D. Fla., August 10, 2017) ((UDRP award confirmed. Formerly Respondent in ***VIA VAREJO S/A, v. Domain Admin***, D2015-1304 (WIPO October 17, 2015) Affirmed on appeal (11th Circuit August 3, 2018).

Joseph L. Carpenter v. Domain Administrator / Original Web Ventures Inc., 15cv212 (E.D. Virginia Alexandria Div. October 26, 2015) Complainant in ***Joseph L. Carpenter v. Domain Administrator / Original Web Ventures Inc.***, FA1409001578228 (Forum September 14m 2914) (<myschool.com>) challenging UDRP award On summary judgment, the Court found "the evidence is clear in this case that the registrant has prior to the filing of this action used the domain name in connection with a bona fide offering of goods and services." However, the Court denied attorney's fees and damages in that the case was not "exceptional."

Joshua Domond and Harold Hunter, Jr v. PeopleNetwork APS d/b/a Beautifulpeople.Com, Beautiful People, LLC, Greg Hodge, and Genevieve Maylam, 16-24026-civ (S.D. FL. Miami Div. 11/9/17) (Unreported) (Complainant in ***Beautiful People Magazine, Inc. v. Domain Manager / PeopleNetwork ApS / Kofod Nicolai / People Network Aps / Nicolai Kofod / People Network***, FA1502001606976 (Forum May 4, 2015) (Complaint dismissed: "Plaintiffs' allegations in the Second Amended Complaint establish that Defendants have priority of use. The allegations simply cannot state claims for trademark infringement." Judgment includes attorney's fees in the amount of $62,434.25).

B(iii) *Interference with Transfer by Invoking Paragraph 4(k) (Transfer enjoined)*

Continental Airlines, Inc. v. continentalairlines.com, 390 F. Supp. 501 (E.D. Va. 2005) (Complainant in ***Continental Airlines, Inc. v. Mindal Park***, FA0403000250002 (Forum June 18, 2004) (Respondent commenced proceeding in South Korea under Paragraph 4(k) of the Policy to interfere with the transfer of the domain names. District Court ordered VeriSign, Inc., as registry of the domain names in issue to change the registrars of record for the domain names to a registrar or registrars located in this country, so plaintiff may thereafter register the domain names in its own name.)

Ezquest, Inc. V. Baorui, 2:12-cv-730 (D. Utah, Central Division) (Complainant in ***EZQUEST, INC. v. BAORUI***, FA1205001445631 (Forum July 12, 2012) (Chinese defendant attempting a Paragraph 4(k) filing in China to frustrate transfer. Injunction preventing registry from transferring domain names to a foreign registrar).

C. Trademark Owner as Plaintiff

C(i) *Personal Name (No UDRP)*

Wagner v. Lindawagner.com, 202 F. Supp. 3d 574 (E.D. VA, Alexandria Division, August 15, 2016) (Dismissed. Lack of jurisdiction. Plaintiff had no trademark).

Schmidheiny v. Weber, 319 F.3d 581 (3d Cir. 2003) (Person name, Transfer).

D. U.S. ACPA Decisions (Direct Statutory Actions) (See also below under U.S.)

D(i) *Trademark Owner Prevailed*

Coca-Cola Co. v. Purdy, 382 F.3d 774 (8th Cir., 2004) (Defendant contended First Amendment rights; enjoined from using the infringing domain names).

DSPT International v. Nahum, 624 F.3d 1213 (9th Cir. 2010) (The Court held that "[e]ven if a domain name was put up innocently and used properly for years, a person is liable under 15 U.S.C. §1125(d) if he subsequently uses the domain name with a bad faith intent to profit from the protected mark by holding the domain name for ransom.")

Heron Development Corp. V. Vacation Tours, Inc., et al., 16-20683 (S.D. Florida, Miami Div. 2/15/2019) (40 domain names, $10,000 per name statutory damages, plus attorneys fees based on finding the case is "exceptional.")

Newport News Holdings Corporation v. Virtual City Vision, Incorporated, d/b/a Van James Bond Tran, 650 F3d 423 (4th Cir. 2011), cert. denied,--- U.S. ----, 132 S.Ct. 575, 181 L.Ed.2d 425 (2011) (Complainant in ***Newport News, Inc. V. Vcv Internet***, AF-0238 (eResolution July 18, 2000 but this is a later action not a 4(k) contesting the earlier award) (Plaintiff's judgment together with damages in the amount of $80,000: "[T]he district court found that damages at the high end of the statutory range were proper because VCV's conduct was 'exceptional and egregious.'")

Nguyen v. Biondo, 11-cv-81156 (S.D. Fla.) (District Court awarded damages in the amount of $850,000 plus another significant amount for attorney's fees and costs for trademark infringement and cybersquatting (aff'd 508 F. App'x 932 unpublished decision (11th Cir. 2013).

Randazza v. Cox, 920 F.Supp.2d 1151 (D. Nevada, 2013) (granting temporary injunction and ordering the domain names transferred to plaintiff). See also Marc J. Randazza v. Reverend Crystal Cox, Eliot Bernstein, D2012-1525 (WIPO November 30, 2012).

Virtual Works, Inc. v. Volkswagen of Am., Inc., 238 F.3d 264, 267 (4th Cir. 2001) ("Virtual Works claims it is not similar because there is a distinction between the .net and .com TLD. According to Virtual Works, Volkswagen could not have registered vw.net in October of 1996 because it is an automaker and not an Internet service provider. This claim, however, is unavailing in light of the fact that NSI stopped enforcing the .com/.net distinction over a year before Virtual Works registered vw.net. The claim is also undermined by Virtual Works' admission that at the time of registration it was aware of the potential confusion with the VW mark, and by its statement to Volkswagen that users would instinctively use the vw.net address to link to Volkswagen's web site.")

D(ii) *Domain Name Holder Prevailed*

GOPETS Ltd. v. Hise, Digital Overture, Inc., 657 F.3d 1024, 1032 (9th Cir. 2011) (Complainant in ***GoPets Ltd. v. Edward Hise***, D2006- 0636 (WIPO July 26, 2006) (Court held that "Nothing in the text or structure of the statute indicates that Congress intended that rights in domain names should be inalienable.")

Koch Industries, Inc. v. John Does, 1-25, 10CV1275DAK (District of Utah, Central Div. 9 May 2011) (Political speech; complaint dismissed). Also, *Taubman v. Webfeats*, 319 F.3d 770 (6th Cir. 2003) (Dissolve injunction "Mishkoff's use was not 'in connection with the sale or advertising of goods or services,' and there is no likelihood of confusion among consumers.")

Kremen v. Cohen, 337 F.3d 1024, 1030 (9th Cir. 2003) ("Registering a domain name is like staking a claim to a plot of land at the title office.")

Lucas Nursery & Landscaping, Inc. v. Grosse, 359 F.3d 806, 809 (6th Cir. 2004) ((consumer complaining about nursery's work was not liable under ACPA).

Mayflower Transit, L.L.C. v. Prince, 314 F.Supp.2d 362 (D.N.J. 2004) (Registrant's motive was to express dissatisfaction in doing business with the mark's owner).

Mattel, Inc. v. Barbie-Club.com, 310 F.3d 293 (2nd Cir. 2002).

Philbrick v. Enom, 593 F.Supp.2d 352, 375 (D. New Hampshire, 2009) (<philbricksports.com>. "Because the plaintiffs' mark is not distinctive (or famous), it is simply not entitled to protection under the ACPA.")

Randazza v. Cox, 920 F.Supp.2d 1151 (D. Nevada, 2013) (granting temporary injunction and ordering the domain names transferred to plaintiff). See also ***Marc J. Randazza v. Reverend Crystal Cox, Eliot Bernstein***, D2012-1525 (WIPO November 30, 2012).

Tropic Ocean Airways, Inc. v. Floyd, 14-12424 (11th Cir., 2014) ("While using the name on the website may constitute advertising, Tropic failed to allege the nature and extent of advertising and promotion or its efforts to promote a conscious connection in the public's mind.")

Utah Lighthouse Ministry v. Fund. for Apologetic Info. & Research, 527 F.3d 1045, 1058 (10th Cir. 2008), citing decisions from different circuits but parody a complete defense to bad faith registration or bad faith use. U.S. courts have identified two "quintessential example[s]" of bad faith: 1) "purchas[ing] a domain name very similar to the trademark and then offer[ing] to sell the name to the trademark owner at an extortionate price; and 2) where a defendant] intend[s] to profit by diverting customers from the website of the trademark owner to the defendant's own website, where those consumers would purchase the defendant's products or services instead of the trademark owner's."

3700 Assocs., LLC v. Griffin, 2008 WL 4542000, at *6 (S.D. Fla. 2008) (<cosmopolitan resort.com> registered 16 months before trademark use).

E. Free Speech (Critical Commentary, Parody, etc.)

E(i) *UDRP Claims*

Lamparello v. Falwell, 420 F.3d 309, 319-320 (4th Cir.2005) (Respondent in ***The Reverend Dr. Jerry L. Falwell and The Liberty Alliance v. Lamparello International.***, FA0310000198936 (Forum November 20, 2003) ("[U]se of another firm's mark to capture the mark holder's customers and profits [ ] simply does not exist when the alleged infringer establishes a gripe site that criticizes the mark holder.")

E(ii) *Non-UDRP Claims*

Coca-Cola Co. v. Purdy, 382 F.3d 774 (8th Cir., 2004) (Defendant contended First Amendment rights; enjoined from using the infringing domain names).

Lucas Nursery & Landscaping, Inc. v. Grosse, 359 F.3d 806, 810 (6th Cir.2004).

TMI, Inc. v. Maxwell, 368 F.3d 433, 440 (5th Cir.2004) ([A]fter analyzing the statutory factors and ACPA's purpose, we are convinced that TMI failed to establish that Maxwell had a bad faith intent to profit from TMI's mark . . . the site's purpose as a method to inform potential customers about a negative experience with the company is key.")

Mayflower Transit, L.L.C. v. Prince, 314 F.Supp.2d 362 (D.N.J. 2004) (Registrant's motive was to express dissatisfaction in doing business with the mark's owner).

F. Garnishment (Domain Names as contract rights vs. intangible property)

Office Depot, Inc. v. Zuccarini, 621 F.Supp.2d 773, 778 (N.D. Cal. 2007), aff'd 596 F.3d 696 (9th Cir. 2010) ("[D]omain name[s] [are] subject to receivership in the district of domain name registrar.")

Sprinkler Warehouse, Inc. v. Systematic Rain, Inc., 859 N.W.2d 527 (Minn.App. 2-2-2015) (Garnishable).

Network Solutions v. Umbro International, Inc., 529 S.E. 80, 86-87 (Va. 2000), citing *Dorer v Arel*, 60 F. Supp. 2d 558 (E.D. Va 1999) (Pre-UDRP) (Not garnishable, 4th Circuit).

See also Canada, India, and UK below.

G. Settlements

Parties settle disputes for a variety of reasons including business decisions based on the cost, time, and effort litigating the merits of their claims and defenses. Although settlements in no way advance the jurisprudence of domain names they nevertheless have an instructive role of revealing the metes and bounds of parties' rights. This is particularly the case when settlements of record advertently reveal losers' recognition that they have no actionable claims of cybersquatting. The ACPA is crafted to encourage settlement or be exposed to statutory damages as explained in Chapter 8.

Domain Asset Holdings, LLC. v. Blue Ridge Fiberboard, Inc., 2:16-cv-00520 (W.D. Washington July 15, 2016) (Respondent in ***Blue Ridge Fiberboard, Inc. v. Domain Administrator / Domain Asset Holdings***, LLC, FA1602001661150 (Forum March 29, 2016) (<soundstop>. Stipulation for Dismissal of Action. Jurisdiction retained for the purpose of enforcing parties' settlement agreement).

Francois Carrillo v. AUTOBUSES DE ORIENTE ADO, S.A. DE C.V., 18-cv-00347-NYW (District of Colorado December 21, 2018) from a UDRP award in favor of Complainant inn Autobuses de Oriente ADO, S.A. de C.V. v. Private Registration / Francois Carrillo, D2017-1661 (WIPO February 1, 2018). In the settlement order the court "finds that the Motion is well taken and is GRANTED" for the reasons stipulated, namely "(i) Plaintiff's interests in respect of the ado.com domain name are legitimate; (ii) Plaintiff did not register or use the ado.com domain name in bad faith; (iii) Plaintiff's registration and current use of the ado.com domain name do not violate Defendant's rights under the Anticybersquatting Consumer Protection Act, 15 U.S.C. §§ 1114, 1125(a) and 1125(d)").

Hugedomains.com, LLC. v. Wills, 14-cv-00946 (D.Colorado July 21, 2015) (Respondent in ***Austin Pain Associates v. Jeffrey Reberry***, FA1312001536356 (Forum March 18, 2014) ("Plaintiff did not register or use <austinpain.com> domain name in bad faith and had no bad faith intent to profit from the domain name." Parties agreed to a consent judgment in which Defendant agreed to pay plaintiff $25,000).

Mrs. Jello, LLC v. Camilla Australia Pty Ltd., 15-cv-08753 (D. NJ 8/1/2016) (Respondent in ***Camilla Australia Pty Ltd v. Domain Admin, Mrs Jello, LLC.***, D2015-

1593 (WIPO November 30, 2015) (Discontinuance with prejudice; domain name remains with Plaintiff).

S.H., INC. v. The Law Society, United Kingdom, CV10-0248 (W.D. Washington, at Seattle July 15, 2010) (Respondent in ***The Law Society v. S.H. INC.***, D2009-1520 (WIPO January 22, 2010) ("Plaintiff and its principal Daniel Cox are hereby enjoined and restrained from filing for, acquiring, renewing, maintaining or using any other domain name or trademark that incorporates the LAW SOCIETY trademark or any phonetic or typographical variant thereof.")

Telepathy, Inc, Development Services v. Corporacion Empresarial Altra S.L., 1:17-cv-01030 (D. District of Columbia, November 28, 2017) (Respondent in ***Corporacion Empresarial Altra S.L. v. Development Services, Telepathy, Inc.***, D2017-0178 (WIPO May 15, 2017) (<airzone.com>. The Panel denied the complaint but rejected sanctioning Complainant. Respondent thereupon commenced an action under the ACPA for reverse domain name damages and defendant settled by stipulating to pay plaintiff $40,000 dollars).

Telepathy, Inc. v. SDT International SA-NV, 14-cv-01912 (D. Columbia July 9, 2015) (Respondent in ***SDT International SA-NV v. Telepathy, Inc.***, D2014-1870 (WIPO January 13, 2015) (Parties agreed to a Consent Judgment in which Defendant agreed to pay Plaintiff $50,000 together with a permanent injunction.)

H. Other Jurisdictions

1. Australia

Global Access c/o domain admin v. EducationDynamics, LLC, [2009] QSC 373 (Respondent in ***EducationDynamics, LLC v. Global Access c/o domain admin***, FA0905001265489 (Forum July 22, 2009) (Transferred. Court has subject matter jurisdiction but granted Defendant's motion to deposit security and Plaintiff discontinued the action).

2. Canada

Black v. Molson Canada (2002), 60 O.R. (3d) 457 (Ont. S.C.J.); Boaden Catering Limited v. Real Food for Real Kinds Inc., 2016 CarswellOnt 10560, 2016 ONSC 4098, 268 A.C.W.S. (3d) 688, aff'd 2017 CarswellOnt 4247, 2017 ONCA 248. (Canadian courts have subject matter jurisdiction; cf.: with India, U.K. and U.S.)

Tucows.com Co. v. Lojas Renner, S.A., 106 O.R. (3d) 561, 211 ONCA 548 (Court of Appeal for Ontario, August 5, 2011), leave to appeal to the Supreme Court of Canada denied, 2012 CanLII 28261 (SCC) ("A domain name is intangible personal property.")

Source Media Group Corp. V. Black Press Group Ltd. And Lisa Farquharson, 2014 FC 1014 (Oct. 24, 2014)

3. France

Muhsin E.Thiebaut, Walid Victor v. Teamreager AB, Paris Court of Appeal (November 8, 2016) Respondent in ***Teamreager AB contre Muhsin E.Thiebaut, Walid Victor***, D2013-0835 (WIPO July 29, 2013) (<moobittalk.com>. Declaration in favor of Respondent and domain name returned) (Discussion of the Paris Court of Appeal at https://www.lexology.com/library/detail.aspx?g=5899d5f9-3bbc-416e-a9a5-7233a147b62c.

4. Germany

Deference rejected by The Regional Court in Cologne in a case reversing the award in ***XM Satellite Radio Inc. v. Michael Bakker***, FA0612000861120 (Forum February 27, 2007): "In court proceedings under Paragraph 4(k) UDRP the national court shall only apply the relevant national law (e.g. trademark or unfair competition law). Whether the requirements stipulated by Paragraph 4(a) UDRP (on which the NAF Panel had based its decision) are satisfied or not is considered irrelevant." (Case no. 33 O 45/08, 16 June 2009, translation adr.eu.)

5. India

Satyam Infoway Ltd. vs Sifynet Solutions Pvt. Ltd., AIR 2004 SC 3540, 2004 (3) AWC 2366 SC (Supreme Ct of India, 6 May, 2004): "A domain name is easy to remember and use, and is chosen as an instrument of commercial enterprise not only because it facilitates the ability of consumers to navigate the Internet to find websites they are looking for, but also at the same time, serves to identify and distinguish the business itself, or its goods or services, and to specify its corresponding online Internet location. Consequently a domain name as an address must, of necessity, be peculiar and unique and where a domain name is used in connection with a business, the value of maintaining an exclusive identity becomes critical."

6. UK

O.G. Ltd. v. Allan, [2007] 1 A.C. 1 (H.L.) (Lord Hoffmann for the majority observed at para. 101: "I have no difficulty with the proposition that a domain name may be intangible property, like a copyright or trademark."

Patel v. Allos Therapeutics, Inc., [2008] EWHC 1730 (Ch) (Sonia Proudman QC) (Respondent in ***Allos Therapeutics, Inc. v. Kumar Patel***, D2007-0521 (WIPO June 11, 2007) (UDRP Award confirmed).

Toth v. Emirates and Nominet, [2-12] EWHC 517 (Ch) (Mr. Justice Mann) in which the Court concluded that there is "[n]o room for parallel (or consecutive) court proceedings [for Nominet arbitrated .uk disutes]" (53).

Yoyo.email v. Royal Bank of Scotland Group PLC and Others, [2015] EWHC 3509 (Ch) extended the Toth ruling *http://iplegalcorner.com/wp-content/uploads/2015/11/Yoyo-Final-judgment.pdfto* include UDRP awards. It held that "[P]roper construction of the UDRP clause 4k does not give rise to a separate cause of action in favour of the claimant [aggrieved domain name registrant]." The court further noted that "there is no practical utility in granting declaratory relief in this case because the UDRP scheme has dealt with the issue between the parties, because any declaration made by this Court could not alter the findings of the Panel and the effect of my conclusions on the application for summary judgment on the counterclaim render the claim otiose."

7. U.S. Anticybersquatting Consumer Protection Act (APCA)

(a) Judicial review *de novo* under ACPA)

Dluhos v. Strasberg, 321 F.3d 365 (3rd Circ. 2003) (Respondent in ***CMG Worldwide, Inc. v. Eric Dluhos***, FA0005000094909 (Forum October 2, 2000) ("Because the UDRP — a private covenant — cannot confer federal jurisdiction where none independently exists, the remaining question is whether the Congress has provided a cause of action to challenge its decisions. *In the Anticybersquatting Consumer Protection Act, we hold that it has*" (Emphasis added). See also *Parisi v. Netlearning, Inc.*, 139 F. Supp. 2d 745 (E.D.Va. 2001) construing 9 U.S.C., §§ 1-14. (Trademark Owner in Netlearning, Inc. v. Dan Parisi, FA 95471 (Forum October 16, 2000) moved to dismiss plaintiff's action on theory that the UDRP award was a final and binding arbitration; motion denied.)

(b) Preliminary Injunction

Super-Krete Int'l v. Sadleir, 712 F.Supp.2d 1023 (C.D. Cal. 2010) (Complainant in ***Super-Krete International, Inc. v. Concrete Solutions, Inc.***, D2008-1333 (WIPO October 14, 2008) (Court granted plaintiff preliminary injunction to prevent defendant's sale or transfer of the domain before the court decided the merits of plaintiff's claims).

(c) In Rem Jurisdiction

Mattel, Inc. v. Barbie-Club.com, 310 F.3d 293 (2nd Circ. 2002) ("[T]the ACPA's basic *in rem* jurisdictional grant, contained in subsection (d)(2)(A), contemplates exclusively a judicial district within which the registrar or other domain-name authority is located. A plaintiff must initiate an *in rem* action by filing a complaint in that judicial district and no other.

The Heathmount A.E. Corp. v. Technodome.com, 106 F.Supp.2d 860 (E.D. Virginia 2000) (In rem jurisdiction).

(d) Mutual Jurisdiction

Green Jacket Auctions, Inc. v. Augusta Nat'l, Inc. (S.D. Ga., April 26, 2018) (Action transferred to the United States District Court for the District of Arizona) (Complainant establishes the mutual jurisdiction, and if that is the principal office of the Registrar Respondent cannot file an action in a district court of its address).

(e) Secondary Meaning

Grand Gen. Accessories Mfg. v. United Pac. Indus.,Inc., 732 F. Supp. 2d 1014, 1028 (C. D. Cal. Aug. 9, 2010) (stating that"[p]laintiff has provided no evidence of the effectiveness of their advertising in creating secondary meaning other than providing the [$500,000] dollar figure of their advertising budget").

(f) U.S. Bankruptcy Court

LARRY KOENIG & ASSOC., LLC Debtor Martin A. SCHOTT, Trustee for Larry Koenig & Assoc., LLC and Larry and Nydia Koenig v. Andrea Lynn MCLEAR, Larry Koenig & Assoc., LLC and Larry and Nydia Koenig, 2004 WL 3244582 (Bkrtcy.M.D.La.) (If not disclosed petitioners risk losing unscheduled domain names in post-bankruptcy discharge proceedings to bidders for whom they have value.)

APPENDIX C
SOME DIFFERENCES BETWEEN DISPUTE RESOLUTION POLICIES
of Self-Administered Authorities in English Speaking Countries and the Uniform Domain Name Dispute Resolution Policy

- Country code dispute resolution policies for Australia, New Zealand and the U.K. differ from the UDRP principally in being disjunctive models; Canada differs in that it is a unitary (bad faith registration) model.
- Except for granting relief on a showing of an "either/or" violation (or in the case of Canada, registration in bad faith) all four country code resolution policies bear a close resemblance to the UDRP, which is their ur-model (the auDomain Authority explicitly acknowledges that its Policy and Rules are adaptations of the UDRP).
- Like the UDRP country code panelists are developing a common law of domain names within their jurisdictions. UDRP decisional law is cited where appropriate, and where inappropriate Panels have been quick to point that out.
- Two of the policies provide for informal mediation as the first in a two step process (United Kingdom and New Zealand).
- Three of the policies state the evidentiary standard "on a balance of probabilities" (Canada, New Zealand, and the U.K.).
- Three of the policies protect "names or trademarks" (Australia, New Zealand and the UK. The au.Domain Authority Policy defines "names" as "the complainant's company, business or other legal or trading name. It also includes personal names.)
- Two of the policies provide for an appeal process (the United Kingdom and New Zealand).
- One of the policies provides for a monetary award for reverse domain name hijacking (Canada).

A. Australia (.au Domain Authority, Ltd. [auDA])

1. ICANN recognized auDA as the suitable operator for .au under a Sponsorship Agreement in October 2001. The current auDRP is dated April 15, 2016.[2]
2. Paragraph 1.3 provides:

> The auDRP is an adaptation of the Uniform [Domain Name] Dispute Resolution Policy (UDRP) administered by the Internet Corporation for Assigned Names and Numbers (ICANN) with respect to the global Top Level Domains (gTLDs). The auDRP differs from the UDRP in two main respects:
>
> a) to take account of the policy rules that apply to .au domain names, that do not apply to gTLD domain names; and
>
> b) to address practical constraints that have become apparent since arbitrations under the UDRP began in 1999.

[2] WIPO is the principal dispute resolution provider for the dot au suffix.

3. Cautionary note, paragraph 1.4 states

> Please Note: Some parts of the auDRP are substantively different from the UDRP. Prospective complainants should not assume that principles derived from UDRP decisions will be applicable to auDRP disputes.

4. Note 1 to Paragraph 4(a)(i) provides

> For the purposes of this policy, auDA has determined that a "name … in which the complainant has rights" refers to:
>
> a) the complainant's company, business or other legal or trading name, as registered with the relevant Australian government authority; or
>
> b) the complainant's personal name.

5. Either/or model for determining bad faith. Paragraph 4(a)(iii) of Schedule A provides that "your domain name has been registered or subsequently used in bad faith."[3]
6. Paragraph 7.1: "There is no appeal process."

Note regarding reselling domain names. Policy 2012-04, Schedule A, paragraph 8: "A registrant may not register a domain name for the sole purpose of resale or transfer to another entity." The restriction has not been enforced. A Policy Review Board (2019) put forward a proposal to prohibit registrants from registering any open 2LD domain name for the primary purpose of (a) resale, (b) transfer to another entity, or (c) warehousing." The proposal was vigorously opposed and the proposal has been abandoned.

B. Canada Internet Registration Authority (CIRA)

1. The current CIRA Dispute Resolution Policy (CDRP) is dated August 22, 2011.
2. A complainant has standing only if its right predates registration of the domain name.[4] CDRP at paragraph 3.1 provides that

> A Registrant must submit to a Proceeding if a Complainant asserts in a Complaint submitted in compliance with the Policy and the Resolution Rules that:
>
> (a) the Registrant's dot ca domain name is Confusingly Similar to a Mark in which the Complainant had Rights prior to the date of registration of the domain name and continues to have such Rights. . . .[5]

---

[3] The adverbial modifier "subsequently" is unique to the auDRP. In contrast, under the UDRP bad faith use following good faith registration is not sufficient to cancel or transfer the domain name registration to complainant.

[4] Cf. Anticybersquatting Consumer Protection Act, §1125(d)(1)(A)(ii)(I) and (II), "at the time of the registration of the mark."

3. Paragraph 3.2(a) defines a mark as "a trade-mark, including the word elements of a design mark, or a trade name that has been used in Canada by a person, or the person's predecessor in title, for the purpose of distinguishing the wares, services or business of that person or predecessor or a licensor of that person or predecessor from the wares, services or business of another person."
4. The CDRP is ostensibly unitary—"registrant has registered the domain name in bad faith" (paragraph 3.1(c))—but use is evidence of abusive registration (paragraph 3.5).
5. Under paragraph 4.1 Complainant has "to prove [its claim of abusive registration] on a balance of probabilities."[6]
6. Respondent may recover damages for reverse domain name hijacking under CDRP paragraph 4.6, which reads:

> Bad Faith of Complainant. If the Registrant is successful, and the Registrant proves, on a balance of probabilities, that the Complaint was commenced by complainant for the purpose of attempting, unfairly and without colour of right, to cancel or obtain a transfer of any Registration which is the subject of the Proceeding, then the Panel may order complainant to pay to the Provider in trust for the Registrant an amount of up to five thousand dollars ($5000) to defray the costs incurred by the Registrant in preparing for, and filing material in the Proceeding. Complainant will be ineligible to file another Complaint in respect of any Registration with any Provider until the amount owing is paid in full to the Provider.

7. The CDRP recognizes noncommercial and fair use as defenses to abusive registration without using the phrase "fair use," but including such use as a "noncommercial activity":

> [3.4](d) the Registrant used the domain name in Canada in good faith in association with a noncommercial activity including, without limitation, criticism, review or news reporting.

C. New Zealand (nz Domain Name Commission)

1. The current New Zealand Domain Name Resolution Service Policy (nzDRS) is dated July 1, 2011.[7]
2. The nzDRS provides for a two step process: informal mediation under paragraph B6, followed by appointment of an Expert under B9 and B17 if the parties are unable to settle the dispute (modeled on the ukDRS, see below).

[5] Where UDRP has an either/or standing requirement, CDRP paragraph 3.1(a) omits "identical" and qualifies rights to "Rights prior to the date of registration." In contrast, UDRP decisional law has determined that standing is conferred regardless of the timing of mark acquisition.

[6] The phrase "on a balance of the probabilities" is not found in the UDRP or Rules but panelists have made it clear that it is the standard by rejecting "clear and convincing."

3. Paragraph 3, Definitions (as they reflect a difference with the UDRP):

   - Informal Mediation means impartial mediation, which is conducted under paragraph B6 to facilitate an acceptable resolution to the dispute;
   - Rights includes, but is not limited to, rights enforceable under New Zealand law. However, *a Complainant will be unable to rely on rights in a name or term which is wholly descriptive of the Complainant's business* (emphasis added);

4. "Unfair registration" (modeled on the ukDRS, see below) is defined as a domain name that

   i. Was registered or otherwise acquired in a manner which, at the time when the registration or acquisition took place, took unfair advantage of or was unfairly detrimental to the Complainant's Rights; OR

   ii. has been, or is likely to be, used in a manner which took unfair advantage of or was unfairly detrimental to the Complainant's Rights.

5. Paragraph 6.2. provides that "Fair use may include sites operated solely in tribute to or in criticism of a person or business."[8]
6. Paragraph 12.1 provides that

   either Party will have the right under paragraph B17 to appeal a Decision. The Appeal Panel will consider appeals on the basis of a full review of the matter and may review procedural matters.

D. United Kingdom Domain Name Resolution Services (ukDRS)

1. The UK domain name dispute resolution service is administered by Nominet UK, a UK internet registry company that manages the .uk domain space.[9]
2. A revised Policy substantially the same as the 2008 version but differing in some details including revising paragraph numbers, with additions and language similar to the UDRP becomes effective October 1, 2016.
3. Paragraph 1. The term "abusive registration" is defined as a domain name that

   i. Was registered or otherwise acquired in a manner which, at the time when the registration or acquisition took place, took unfair advantage of or was unfairly detrimental to the Complainant's Rights; OR

---

[7] Among several differences with the UDRP, the nzDRS provides for informal mediation and an appeal process.

[8] Both nzDRS and UDRP recognize a defense based on "noncommercial and fair use," but what satisfies the defense under the UDRP has been a development of decisional law.

[9] Among several differences with the UDRP the ukDRS provides for informal mediation and an appeal process.

ii. has been, or is likely to be, used in a manner which took unfair advantage of or was unfairly detrimental to the Complainant's Rights.

4. Paragraph 2: "A Respondent must submit to proceedings under the DRS if a Complainant asserts to us, according to the Procedure, that:

   i. The Complainant has Rights in respect of a name or mark which is identical or similar[10] to the Domain Name."

5. Like the nzDRP, the DRS provides for informal mediation (Paragraph 5):

   a. After we have received the Parties' submissions under the Procedure, we will initiate and conduct a period of Informal Mediation under paragraph 7 of the Procedure.

6. Paragraph 4(a)(i)(C).[11] Respondent may demonstrate that the domain name is not an abusive registration:

   [Respondent] made legitimate non commercial or fair use of the Domain Name; or

   [4(a)(ii)(C)]. The Domain Name is generic or descriptive and the Respondent is making fair use of it;

   iii. In relation to paragraph 3(a)(v); that the Respondent's holding of the Domain Name is consistent with an express term of a written agreement entered into by the Parties; or

   iv. In relation to paragraphs 3(a)(iii) and/or 3(c); that the Domain Name is not part of a wider pattern or series of registrations because the Domain Name is of a significantly different type or character to the other domain names registered by the Respondent.

   [4(b)]. Fair use may include sites operated solely in tribute to or in criticism of a person or business.

   [4(c)]. If paragraph 3(c) applies, to succeed the Respondent must rebut the presumption by proving in the Response that the registration of the Domain Name is not an Abusive Registration.

7. Appeal: Paragraph 10 provides that "a. Either Party will have the right to appeal a Decision under paragraph 18 of the Procedure. The appeal panel will consider appeals on the basis of a full review of the matter and may review procedural matters."

---

[10] The DRS uses "similar" with the qualifier "confusingly" probably because a domain name "similar" to the trademark carries the seed of confusion and is sufficient for the issue of standing even though it may not ultimately be found to have been an "abusive registration."

[11] The DRS expands on the UDRP's "rights or legitimate interests" defense. There are language variations throughout, but the quoted extract focuses solely on the "noncommercial or fair use" factors. Notice that the linguistic elaboration of the defense makes the provision prescriptive where the UDRP is more open to panelists' independently making those assessments.

Index

A

B

D

G

H

I

O

P

R

S

T

U

V

W

Gerald M. Levine is an attorney practicing in New York City. He began his career with a major New York law firm before founding his own firm in 1992. He has a litigation and counseling practice that includes protecting clients' intellectual property rights, representing them in UDRP and arbitration proceedings, registering trademark and copyright applications, advising and representing authors, and negotiating agent and publishing contracts. He serves as a neutral arbitrator for commercial and IP disputes for the American Arbitration Association and is on the panel of arbitrators for the Financial Industry Regulatory Authority (FINRA). He has published numerous articles on trademarks, domain names, cybersquatting, arbitration, copyright, and publishing issues. Mr. Levine has a J.D from Brooklyn Law School and also holds a Ph.D. in English from New York University.

Neil A. Brown is a prominent arbitrator and adviser in the domain name field. He has had a long and distinguished career in the Law and Government. He was a member of the Australian Parliament from 1969 and a Minister and Shadow Minister in the Federal Government of Australia. Since 1964 he has practiced in virtually every area of the law, mainly in commercial, construction and intellectual property matters and in 1980 he was appointed Queen's Counsel. After years of service in these fields he is now practicing in mediation, arbitration, the conduct of inquiries and consulting. His specialties are commercial contracts, trade and intellectual property. He is one of the leading international practitioners in the field of domain name arbitration.

CPSIA information can be obtained
at www.ICGtesting.com
Printed in the USA
BVHW010436030719
552379BV00030B/177/P

9 780991 582945